W9-DAB-772

CRIMINAL
PROCEDURE

NINTH EDITION

Joel Samaha

Horace T. Morse Distinguished Teaching Professor
University of Minnesota

CENGAGE
Learning

Australia • Brazil • Mexico • Singapore • United Kingdom • United States

CENGAGE
Learning®

Criminal Procedure, **Ninth Edition**
Joel Samaha

General Manager: Erin Joyner

Senior Product Manager: Carolyn Henderson Meier

Content Coordinator: Paige Leeds

Product Assistant: Audrey Espey

Media Developer: Ting Jian Yap

Senior Marketing Manager: Kara Kindstrom

Senior Content Project Manager: Christy A. Frame

Art Director: Brenda Carmichael, PreMedia Global

Senior Manufacturing Planner: Judy Inouye

Senior Rights Acquisitions Specialist: Dean Dauphinais

Production and Composition: Michelle Dellinger, Integra

Text Researcher: PreMedia Global

Text and Cover Designer: Brenda Carmichael, PreMedia Global

Cover Image: Bob Ingelhart/Getty Images

For product information and technology assistance, contact us at **Cengage Learning Customer & Sales Support, 1-800-354-9706.**

For permission to use material from this text or product, submit all requests online at **www.cengage.com/permissions.**
Further permissions questions can be e-mailed to **permissionrequest@cengage.com.**

Library of Congress Control Number: 2013944020

Student Edition:

ISBN-13: 978-1-285-45787-1

ISBN-10: 1-285-45787-0

Cengage Learning
200 First Stamford Place, 4th Floor
Stamford, CT 06902
USA

Cengage Learning is a leading provider of customized learning solutions with office locations around the globe, including Singapore, the United Kingdom, Australia, Mexico, Brazil, and Japan. Locate your local office at **www.cengage.com/global.**

Cengage Learning products are represented in Canada by Nelson Education, Ltd.

To learn more about Cengage Learning Solutions, visit **www.cengage.com.**

Purchase any of our products at your local college store or at our preferred online store **www.cengagebrain.com.**

Printed in the United States of America
1 2 3 4 5 6 7 17 16 15 14 13

ABOUT THE AUTHOR

Professor Joel Samaha teaches Criminal Law, Criminal Procedure, and Introduction to Criminal Justice at the University of Minnesota. He is both a lawyer and an historian whose primary interest is crime control in a constitutional democracy. He received his BA, JD, and PhD from Northwestern University. Professor Samaha also studied under the late Sir Geoffrey Elton at Clare Cambridge University, England. He was named the College of Liberal Arts Distinguished Teacher in 1974. In 2007 he was awarded the title of University of Minnesota Morse Alumni Distinguished Teaching Professor and inducted into the Academy of Distinguished Teachers.

Professor Samaha was admitted to the Illinois State Bar Association in 1962 and practiced law briefly in Chicago. He taught at UCLA before going to the University of Minnesota in 1971. At the University of Minnesota, he served as Chair of the Department of Criminal Justice Studies from 1974 to 1978. He now teaches and writes full time. He has taught both television and radio courses in criminal justice and has co-taught a National Endowment for the Humanities seminar in legal and constitutional history.

In addition to *Law and Order in Historical Perspective* (1974), an analysis of law enforcement in pre-industrial Essex County, England, Professor Samaha has transcribed and written a scholarly introduction to a set of local criminal justice records from the borough of Colchester during the reign of Elizabeth I. He has also written several articles on the history of criminal justice, published in the *Historical Journal*, *The American Journal of Legal History*, *Minnesota Law Review*, *William Mitchell Law Review*, and *Journal of Social History*. He has also written two other textbooks, *Criminal Law*, now in its eleventh edition, and *Criminal Justice*, now in its seventh edition.

DEDICATION

For my students: past, present, and future.

BRIEF CONTENTS

CONTENTS

12 Court Proceedings I: Before Trial 448

13 Court Proceedings II: Trial and Conviction 498

14 After Conviction: Sentencing, Appeals, and Habeas Corpus 532

15 Criminal Procedure in Times of Crisis 574

Criminal Procedure 9 is about the central promise of U.S. criminal justice: to balance the power of government to protect the safety and security of *all* persons against those who want to do them harm, while at the same time protecting their right to come and go as they please without government interference, *and* guaranteeing to all persons that the government will enforce the law equally: on the street, at the police station, in the courts, and in punishing wrongdoers. This promise is also its central problem—how close to social reality is the promise of *equal* rights and justice. This promise and this problem have fascinated my students for close to a half century. It stimulates them to think, discuss them in class and with their friends and family outside class.

I'm not surprised. The balance between government power and individual rights and equal justice has fascinated me since I had the great good fortune to study criminal procedure at Northwestern University Law School decades ago under the sparkling Claude R. Sowle and the legendary Fred E. Inbau. Professor Sowle, a brilliant advocate and a distinguished teacher, emphasized the philosophical underpinnings of the law of criminal procedure. Professor Inbau, a famous interrogator and a highly respected student of the law of interrogation, spoke from the 1930s right up to his death in the late 1990s with the authority of one who has actually applied abstract principles to everyday police practices.

In 1971, I taught criminal procedure for the first time. I've done so ever since. My students have included undergraduate, graduate, and law students. That many of these students are now police officers and administrators; corrections officers and administrators; criminal defense attorneys, prosecutors, and judges; legislators; and criminal justice scholars testifies to their enduring interest in the law and social reality of criminal procedure and to their commitment to the application of formal law to informal real-life decision making.

Criminal Procedure 9, like its predecessors, reflects my conviction that the best way to learn the law of criminal procedure is both to understand general principles and to critically examine the application of these principles to real problems. By "critically," I don't mean "negatively"; *Criminal Procedure* doesn't trash the system. Rather, it examines and weighs the principles that govern the balance between government power and individual life, liberty, privacy, and property. It tests the weight of strong, honest feelings about this balance in the bright light of reason, logic, and facts. *Criminal Procedure* proceeds on the assumptions that the general principles governing the balance between government power and individual rights have real meaning only in the context of a specific reality, and that reality makes sense only when seen in the light of general principles fitted to specific facts in particular circumstances.

TEXT AND CASES

Criminal Procedure 9 is a text-case book, meaning that it contains both text and excerpts of actual court opinions that apply the general principles discussed in the text to concrete cases. The text and case excerpts complement each other. The text enriches the understanding of the cases, while the cases enhance the understanding of the constitutional principles in the text. The cases aren't just examples, illustrations, or attention grabbers; they explain, clarify, elaborate, and apply the general principles and constitutional provisions to real-life situations. Moreover, the cases are excellent tools for developing students' critical thinking skills and applying them to everyday life.

The cases and the text are independent enough of each other that they can each stand alone. (Design differences clearly mark one from the other.) This separation of text from cases allows instructors who favor the case analysis approach to emphasize cases over text, leaving the text for students to read if they need to in order to understand the cases. Instructors who favor the text approach can focus on the text, allowing students to read the cases as enrichment or as examples of the principles, constitutional provisions, and rules discussed in the text.

The case excerpts are edited for nonlawyers. They supply students with a full statement of the facts of the case; key portions of the reasoning of the court; and the court's decision. Excerpts also contain portions of the dissenting opinions and, when appropriate, parts of the concurring opinions.

The question that opens each case focuses students on the main principle of the case. The case history gives a brief procedural history of the case. And the questions at the end of the case excerpts test whether students know the facts of the case, understand the law of the case, and comprehend the application of the law to the facts of the case. The questions also supply the basis for developing critical thinking skills, not to mention provoking class discussions on the legal, ethical, and policy issues raised by the case.

KEY CHANGES TO THE NINTH EDITION *New Cases* A total of 38 new cases, and many re-edited existing cases, appear in *Criminal Procedure 9*. I added, replaced, and re-edited cases for three reasons. First, I wanted to reflect new developments in the law since the last edition. Second, I included cases I've found since the last edition that explain the law better and apply the law to the facts in clearer and more interesting ways for students. Third, experiences through actual use in the classroom led me to re-edit some cases and sometimes cut excerpts from previous editions.

EMPIRICAL RESEARCH *Criminal Procedure 9* continues the practice of recent editions to include more of the growing, rich social science research that explains and evaluates criminal procedures.

CRIMINAL PROCEDURE IN TIMES OF CRISIS Chapter 15 reflects a major shift. In the immediate aftermath of the 9/11 attacks, the terrorism story primarily revolved around the issue of what to do with enemy combatants drawn from the ranks of Al-Qaeda who fought in Afghanistan and Iraq and were being detained at Guantanamo prison. That story has not ended. But increasingly, the story now is how to prevent another attack—namely counterterrorism and counterintelligence. That's a big and complicated story and it represents a crucial expansion of *Criminal Procedure 9*'s Chapter 15. In the new chapter, we focus on recalibrating the balance between the critical need for information to conduct counterterrorism and counterintelligence, and the First, Fourth, and Fifth Amendment rights you learn about in Chapters 2 through 7 (searches and seizures). And, of course, we'll update the immigration sections to reflect the U.S. Supreme Court's opinion in *Arizona v. U.S.* (2012) upholding key sections of the Arizona immigration law, a law emulated by a growing number of other states.

NEW REAL-WORLD EMPHASIS There are two new boxes incorporated into this new edition. First, at least one **CRIMINAL PROCEDURE IN ACTION** in each chapter adds a *practical application* of the law. A point of law introduces the box, such as "Fifteen minutes is not 'too long' to detain a stopped person." Second, each chapter also includes at least one **YOU DECIDE** feature that begins with a question to develop your critical thinking skills, such as "Are domestic drones Fourth Amendment searches?"

CHAPTER-BY-CHAPTER REVISIONS

Chapter 1

New

- Chapter title, to reflect the chronological decision points as cases progress (and diminish in numbers) through the major crime control agencies—police on the street and at the police station; prosecutors' offices; trial courts; and appellate courts
- Opener, to reflect the ultimate criminal procedure goal—accurately sorting out the criminals from innocents
- Section, "Criminal Procedure Road Map," to emphasize the chronological flow of cases through the criminal process, and the attrition of cases from police investigation through conviction
- Flowchart—Criminal Procedure Road Map, which redesigns and simplifies the universally used 1967 version
- YOU DECIDE (YD), "Brutality or Reasonable Force?"
- CRIMINAL PROCEDURE IN ACTION (CPIA), "Was 15 minutes 'too long' for a traffic stop?"

Revised

- Objective basis moved to Chapter 2, where it fits better with the purely constitutional issues

Chapter 2

New

- Section, "Criminal Procedure History: The Crime Control–Individual Autonomy Pendulum." Traces the history of the tension between crime control and individual rights from Ancient Rome to 2013
- Section, "The U.S. Supreme Court: Will of the People or Rule of Law?" The basic idea is to help students understand that the U.S. Supreme Court (SCOTUS) is a legal *and* a political institution. For that reason, it can't ever stray too far from popular opinion
- YD, "Did the Officer's Conduct 'Shock the Conscience'?"
- CPIA, "Equal protection of the law"

Chapter 3

New

- Opener on electronic communications in the age of social networking, e-mail, texting, and "pixting" and implications for Fourth Amendment protections
- Section, The Third Party Doctrine, on assumption of risk in the digital age of social networking, e-mail, and texting
- Section, "Essential Services Companies," to sharpen discussion of Fourth Amendment protections and the information we turn over to banks, telephone companies, and trash collection companies
- Section, "Electronic Surveillance in the 21st Century"
- Section, "GPS (Global Positioning System) Tracking"
- Figure, *U.S. v. Jones* (2012), a synopsis of this complicated case
- Table, "Some Questions SCOTUS Left Unanswered in *U.S. v. Jones* (2012)"
- Section, "E-Mail Content," on Fourth Amendment issues raised by electronic mail
- Figure, "Who Uses E-Mail?"
- Figure, "Yearly U.S. Texts in Trillions"
- Cases
  - o *U.S. v. Jones* (2012), on GPS tracking
  - o *U.S. v. Warshak* (2010), on e-mail content
  - o *State v. Patino* (2012), on text messaging
- YD, "Is Domestic Drone Surveillance a Fourth Amendment Search?"
- CPIA, "Reasonable expectation of privacy in text messages"

Chapter 4

New

- Section, "DWI Checkpoints"
- Section, "Drug Interdiction Checkpoints"
- Section, "Information-Seeking Checkpoints"
- Figure, "Workers Killed per 100,000, Year 2011"
- Table, "Danger Ratio for Officers during Traffic Stops"
- Cases
  - o *City of Indianapolis v. Edmond* (2000), on reasonableness of drug interdiction checkpoints
  - o *Illinois v. Lidster* (2004), on reasonableness of hit-and-run information-seeking checkpoint
- CPIA, "Driving in a circular fashion late at night in an area of high vehicle break-ins and home invasions is reasonable suspicion to stop a vehicle"
- YD, "Are Suspicionless DWI Stops Better?"
- YD, "Is It Reasonable to Stop and Frisk More Innocent Black and Hispanic Men than White Men?"

Expanded/Rewritten

- Section, "Roadblocks and Checkpoints"

Chapter 5

New

- Case, *Commonwealth v. Dunlap* (2007), on probable cause
- YD, "Was the Officer's Experience and Knowledge of the Neighborhood Probable Cause to Arrest?"
- CPIA, "Full custodial arrest for eating one French fry on the subway is not an unreasonable Fourth Amendment seizure"

Chapter 6

New

- Section on pretext searches and traffic stops
- Section, "Two Theories of Consent," on waiver test of consent to search and voluntariness test of consent to search
- Section rewrite, "Consent Searches," to clarify, update, and enrich introduction to consent searches
- Section rewrite, "Empirical Research and Consent Searches," to update
- Major section rewrite, "Third-Party Consent Searches, to elaborate on and critique "actual authority" and "apparent authority" theories of third-party consent
- Figure, "Drivers Searched during Traffic Stops, 2008," to show stops according to race—White, Black, or Hispanic
- Figure, Results of empirical research findings and Ohio traffic stops
- CPIA, "Consent after state trooper asked to search a stopped car was voluntary"
- CPIA, "A husband can overrule his estranged wife's consent"
- YD, "Did He Consent to the Search of His Crotch?"

Chapter 7

New

- Section, "Public School Student Searches"; major addition to include strip-searching public school students
- Table, "Definitions of 'Strip Search'"
- Cases
  - *Florence v. Board of Chosen Freeholders of the County of Burlington et al.* (2012), on strip searches of jail inmates without reasonable suspicion
  - *Safford Unified School District No. 1 v. Redding* (2009), on the strip search of a middle-school girl
- YD, "Should Hospitals Test Maternity Patients Suspected of Using Cocaine?"
- CPIA, "Requiring political candidates to pass a drug test is not a permissible suspicionless 'special needs' search"

Chapter 8

New

- Under "The Public Safety Exception," two new subsections: (1) "*New York v. Quarles* (1984)" and (2) "The Public Safety Exception in Action" examining empirical research on the number and reasons courts give for accepting or rejecting incriminating statements obtained in public safety cases
- Cases
  - *Miranda v. Arizona* (1966), re-edited to sharpen the focus on the prophylactic nature of the famous warnings—namely, that federal and state governments can use alternatives to the specific warnings
  - *New York v. Quarles* (1984), on the public safety exception, a "hot button" issue in reading terrorist suspects their rights (discussion of the Tsarnaev trial is included in Chapter 15, but it's relevant here too)
- Table, "The Public Safety Exception in Action"
- Figure, "Cases Admitting Unwarned Incriminating Testimony"
- CPIA, "Coercive conduct of basketball coach rendered player's confession inadmissible"
- YD, "Do the Police Have an 'Ethical' Responsibility to Video Record Interrogations?"

Chapter 9

New

- Section, "Forensic Science and Identification Evidence," with expanded DNA text to include other forensic evidence—fingerprints, blood type, bite marks, drug analysis; includes a subsection, "Flawed Forensic Evidence," discussing features of current forensic science that reduce the quality of forensic practitioners' work
- Text, on courts and "accidental show-ups," the problem of identification procedures police didn't arrange
- Figure, "Eyewitness Misidentification as the Leading Cause of Wrongful Conviction Compared to Other Causes"
- Cases
  - *Perry v. New Hampshire* (2012), SCOTUS on accidental show-ups
  - *Melendez-Diaz v. Massachusetts* (2009), on forensic lab technicians and the Sixth Amendment confrontation clause
- Table, on elements of state statutes allowing forensic certificates to replace testimony
- CPIA, "Evidence obtained from show-up is inherently suggestive and will not be admissible"
- CPIA, "Prisoners convicted by false forensic evidence can sue for their release"
- YD, "Should Police Departments Be Required to Adopt Lineup Procedure Reforms?"

Chapter 10

- Section rewrite, "History of the Exclusionary Rule" and leading cases: W*eeks v. U.S.* (1914), *Mapp v. Ohio* (1961), *U.S. v. Leon* (1984)
- Section rewrite, "Justifications for the Exclusionary Rule," to clarify and emphasize that
    - o for all the rhetoric about "judicial integrity," SCOTUS has always relied on deterrence as the only "real" justification
    - o SCOTUS ruled in *Leon* that the exclusionary rule is *not* a constitutional right
- Section rewrite, "Exceptions to the Exclusionary Rule"
- Section, "Exceptions to the 'Fruit of the Poisonous Tree' Doctrine," to define and explain "fruit of the poisonous tree" doctrine clearly to make sure students know this is an *expansion* of the exclusionary rule; and to show how the complicated, complex, important "attenuation," "independent source," and "inevitable discovery" doctrines are really exceptions to the "poisonous tree" expansion
- Section, "The 'Knock and Announce' Exception," to stress the possible far-reaching consequences of *Hudson v. Michigan* for the exclusionary rule
- Section, "The Exclusionary Rule after *Herring v. U.S.*," to examine the debate over whether the Roberts Court will abolish the exclusionary rule or at least revise it so it doesn't apply to ordinary police negligence, but only to intentional police misconduct in the most serious cases
- Cases
    - o *Hudson v. Michigan* (2006), on the exception to the "knock-and-announce" rule
    - o *Herring v. U.S.* (2009); re-edited to home in on key elements of the decision and streamline the excerpt
- Table, "Possible Negative Effects of the Exclusionary Rule"
- Table, "U.S. Supreme Court Opinions Expanding Good-Faith Exception"
- CPIA, "Affidavit containing false statements in 'reckless disregard' of the truth, requires suppression of DNA evidence"
- YD, "Should *Herring v. U.S.* Control the N.J. Court's Suppression of the Drugs?"
- YD, "Should Criminals Go Free Because Police Officers Violated the Fourth Amendment to Obtain Evidence?"

Chapter 11

New

- Major section rewrite, "Law Enforcement Duty to Protect"
    - o "The 'Special-Relationship Exception' to the 'No-Duty-to-Protect' Rule"
    - o "The 'State-Created-Danger' Exception to the 'No-Duty-to-Protect' Rule"
    - o " 'State-Created Danger' after *DeShaney* (1989)"
    - o " 'State-Created Danger' and Domestic Violence," on police duty to enforce restraining orders against abusing husbands and parents

- Cases
  - *Dwares v. City of New York* (1993), on the duty of police to protect protesters from a skinheads attack
- *Town of Castle Rock v. Gonzalez* (2005), in which SCOTUS rules that police have no constitutional duty to enforce restraining orders after a husband shot and killed his three children following police failure to enforce a restraining order
- CPIA, "A '911' operator had no affirmative duty to protect a mother and her daughter from their husband/father who murdered them"
- YD, "Did the Officers of the Public Mental Health Employees Have a Duty to Protect a State Resident from Being Murdered by a Released Mentally Ill Patient?"
- YD, "Is It Time to End Absolute Immunity for Prosecutors?"

Chapter 12

New

- Figure on inmates confined in local jails, 2000–2012
- YD, "Should Prosecutors Appoint Defendants' Public Defenders?"

Chapter 13

New

- CPIA, "The 'fast track' plea bargain was voluntary"
- YD, "Did He Prove That Being Jewish Infected the Peremptory Challenge?"

Chapter 14

New

Figure, "Minnesota Sentencing Guidelines Grid"
Case

- *McQuiggin (Warden) v. Perkins* (2013): "Did He Wait Too Long to File His Actual Innocence Claim?" This case illustrates SCOTUS's bitter division on habeas corpus review after AEDPA.

CPIA, "Fleeing from a law enforcement officer is a 'violent' felony"
YD, "Was His Sentence to Life without Parole 'Cruel and Unusual Punishment' because He Was a Juvenile?"

Chapter 15

This is a major revision. It reflects the shift away from the emphasis on dealing with the *reaction* to the 9/11 terrorist attacks to *proactive* prevention of future attacks, namely counterterrorism and counterintelligence. Most of the new material focuses on surveillance, but there's other new stuff too.

New

- Section, Renamed "War Powers" as "Counterterrorism and the War Powers" to reflect the shift to counterterrorism
- Section, "Counterterrorism, Counterintelligence, and the FBI"

- Section, "Foreign Intelligence Surveillance Act (FISA)," FISA history and Patriot Act revisions
- Section, "FISA Court (FISC)"
- Major section rewrite to reflect Patriot Act revisions of 2006 and 2011 involving surveillance provisions, plus First and Fourth Amendment implications
- Section, "Roving Wiretaps"
- Section, "'Lone Wolf' Terrorists"
- Section, "Business Records," on counterterrorism and counterintelligence aspects of business records
- Section, "National Security Letters (NSLs)," on the hot topic of government orders to Internet service providers to hand over subscriber information and the gag orders that accompany them
- Section, "FBI NSLs before the Patriot Act"
- Section, "FBI NSLs after the Patriot Act 2005 Amendments"
- Section, "NSL Targets and Data"
- Section, "NSLs and the Inspector General's Report"
- Section, "NSLs in Court"
- Section, "FBI Proactive Intelligence Gathering," on the "Capone approach" and counterintelligence/terrorism "sting" operations
- "*Miranda v. Arizona* and Terrorism Suspects," on the hot topic of the Boston Marathon bombing and the Dzhokhar Tsarnaev interrogation *before* and his silence *after* he was *Mirandized*
- "National Security Agency (NSA) Surveillance," on the Snowden leak/whistleblowing controversy
- Case
  - *Doe v. Holder* (2009) First Amendment challenge to NSL gag order

Figure, "Department of Justice Attorneys Working on FISA Applications"

- Table, "Sneak-and-Peek Warrants and Extensions, 2010"
- Figure on Patriot Act business records safeguards
- Table on financial institutions subject to Patriot Act business records FISC orders
- Table on grand jury subpoenas in nonnational security cases
- Figure on telephone billing records and subscriber information obtained by NSLs
- Figure on use of financial records obtained by NSLs
- Figure on use of consumer credit information obtained by NSLs
- Table on FISC orders in 2012
- Figure, "Custodial Interrogation for Public Safety and Intelligence-Gathering"
- Figure, the FISC secret order to Verizon
- Figure, U.S. District Court Judge Coughener's letter (2011) to the House of Representatives Subcommittee on Crime, Terrorism and Homeland Security, strongly arguing for trying terrorism cases in Article III courts
- CPIA, "NSLs are unreasonable searches and seizures"

- YD, "Should the NSL 'Gag' Order Remain in Effect?"
- CPIA, "Officers have a duty to determine the immigration status of any person lawfully stopped" (Supreme Court 2012 ruling on Arizona's immigration law)

SUPPLEMENTS

To access additional course materials, please visit www.cengagebrain.com. At the CengageBrain.com home page, search for the ISBN of your title (from the back cover of your book) using the search box at the top of the page. This will take you to the product page where these resources can be found.

Cengage Learning provides a number of supplements to help instructors use *Criminal Procedure*, ninth edition, in their courses and to aid students in preparing for exams. Supplements are available to qualified adopters. Please consult your local sales representative for details.

For the Instructor

INSTRUCTOR'S RESOURCE MANUAL WITH TEST BANK. An improved and completely updated Instructor's Resource Manual has been developed by Tosha Wilson-Davis of Bainbridge State College.

The manual includes learning objectives, key terms, a detailed chapter outline, a chapter summary, lesson plans, discussion topics, student activities, "What If" scenarios, media tools, a sample syllabus, and an expanded test bank with 30 percent more questions than the prior edition. The learning objectives are correlated with the discussion topics, student activities, and media tools. Each chapter's test bank contains questions in multiple-choice, true/false, completion, essay, and new critical thinking formats, with a full answer key. The test bank is coded to the learning objectives that appear in the main text, and includes the section in the main text where the answers can be found. Finally, each question in the test bank has been carefully reviewed by experienced criminal justice instructors for quality, accuracy, and content coverage. Our Instructor Approved seal, which appears on the front cover, is our assurance that you are working with an assessment and grading resource of the highest caliber.

POWERPOINT® SLIDES Helping you make your lectures more engaging while effectively reaching your visually oriented students, these handy Microsoft PowerPoint® slides outline the chapters of the main text in a classroom-ready presentation. The PowerPoint® slides have been updated by Tosha Wilson-Davis of Bainbridge State College to reflect the content and organization of the new edition of the text and feature some additional examples and real-world cases for application and discussion. Available for download on the password-protected instructor book companion website, the presentations and can also be obtained by e-mailing your local Cengage Learning representative.

CENGAGE LEARNING TESTING Powered by Cognero, the accompanying assessment tool is a flexible, online system that allows you to:

- import, edit, and manipulate test bank content from the Samaha test bank or elsewhere, including your own favorite test questions

- create ideal assessments with your choice of 15 question types (including true/false, multiple choice, opinion scale/Likert, and essay)
- create multiple test versions in an instant using drop-down menus and familiar, intuitive tools that take you through content creation and management with ease
- deliver tests from your LMS, your classroom, or wherever you want—plus, import and export content into other systems as needed

CENGAGE LEARNING VIDEO PROGRAM (COURTESY BBC, CNN, AND MORE) CNN videos feature short, high-interest clips from current news events as well as historic raw footage going back 30 years. CBS and BBC clips feature footage from nightly news broadcasts and specials to *CBS News Special Reports, CBS Sunday Morning, 60 Minutes*, and more. Taken together, the brief videos offer the perfect discussion-starters for your classes, enriching lectures and providing students with a new lens through which to view the past and present, one that will greatly enhance their knowledge and understanding of significant events and open up to them new dimensions in learning.

For the Student

COURSEMATE COMPANION WEBSITE Cengage Learning's Criminal Justice CourseMate brings course concepts to life with interactive learning, study, and exam preparation tools that support the printed textbook. CourseMate includes an integrated eBook as well as critical chapter review tools including pre-tests students can use to quiz themselves in advance of reading the assignment so they are focused on issues that present a particular challenge to them personally. Also included are quizzes mapped to chapter Learning Objectives, flashcards, and videos, plus EngagementTracker, a first-of-its-kind tool that monitors student engagement in the course. The accompanying instructor website offers access to password-protected resources such as an electronic version of the instructor's manual and PowerPoint® slides.

CAREERS IN CRIMINAL JUSTICE WEBSITE (available bundled with this text at no additional charge) Featuring plenty of self-exploration and profiling activities, the interactive Careers in Criminal Justice website helps students investigate and focus on the criminal justice career choices that are right for them. It includes interest assessment, video testimonials from career professionals, resume and interview tips, and links for reference.

CURRENT PERSPECTIVES: READINGS FROM INFOTRAC® COLLEGE EDITION These readings, designed to give students a closer look at special topics in criminal justice, include free access to InfoTrac College Edition. The timely articles are selected by experts in each topic from within InfoTrac College Edition. They're available free when bundled with the text and include the following titles:

Cyber Crime

Victimology

Juvenile Justice

Racial Profiling

White-Collar Crime

Terrorism and Homeland Security

Public Policy and Criminal Justice

Technology and Criminal Justice

Ethics in Criminal Justice

Forensics and Criminal Investigation

Corrections

Law and Courts

Policy in Criminal Justice

ACKNOWLEDGMENTS

Criminal Procedure 9 didn't get here by my efforts alone; I had a lot of help. I'm grateful for all those who have provided feedback over the years and, as always, I'm particularly indebted to the reviewers of this edition:

Andrew Kozal, Northwest State Community College

G. Anthony Wolusky, Everest College Online

William Pizio, Guilford College

Donna Nicholson, Manchester Community College

Thanks to the people at Cengage. One more time, my editor, Carolyn Henderson Meier, supported what I wanted to change in this edition and cajoled me to make changes I didn't want to make, while through it all putting up with my exasperating "mercurial temperament." *Criminal Procedure 9* is so much better because of her. Special thanks to Bob Kauser, Rights Acquisitions Director, and Raemi Wood, Intellectual Property Counsel ("Legal"). They led me through the ever more tangled thickets of "public domain" and "fair use." But more than that, they did it "right now," and even more, they put a human face on this most unpleasant business and definitely made it less unpleasant. I didn't think that was possible.

Thanks to Michelle Dellinger, Senior Project Manager at *Integra*, who was always available—even by telephone with no exasperating "Your call is very important to us" waits—to answer my questions about production, even giving me a live tutorial on how to use the editing functions of *Acrobat*. I don't know anything about production editing, but I don't think tutoring ignorant authors is in her job description. Thanks to my copy editor, Jo Ann Learman, who found too many of my errors and omissions in every chapter.

Then there's Derek Volk who has thrice blessed me. First, he was my student in all three courses I teach at the University of Minnesota—Introduction to Criminal Justice, Criminal Law, and Criminal Procedure. Second, he was my TA in Criminal Procedure and in Intro to CJ once. (Students respected and loved him in both courses.) Third, he was my indispensable assistant in preparing *Criminal Procedure 9* for publication. The revised **Learning Objectives, Chapter Summaries,** and **Review Questions** are utterly and invaluably his. His strong performance as a student (he was near the top of the class in Criminal Procedure) and twice as a TA Criminal Procedure uniquely qualified him to assist me. Countless times throughout the manuscript, I encountered comments like "I think students might understand this better if you worded it this way" or "I think this should be a *key term*; otherwise students might miss its significance" or "I'm glad you changed this; I think it'll be easier for students to understand now." I accepted *all* of Derek's suggestions. The result: For the first time, a student who used the book, and dealt with students' problems when he was a TA, actively participated in preparing an edition of *Criminal Procedure*. Don't take this to mean we "dumbed it down" and "spoon-fed" students. We just made a serious effort to write difficult matter in clear, straightforward prose.

Thanks to my son Luke, Meadowbrook Software, LLC, who redesigned the Criminal Justice Flowchart in Chapter 1 and the "Police-Citizen Contacts" graphic in Chapter 4. The flowchart appeared in President Lyndon Johnson's Crime Commission's final report, *The Challenge of Crime in a Free Society* way back in 1967!. Ever since, it's appeared in identical form in law school criminal procedure casebooks and criminal justice textbooks. It's time to make it more student-friendly and comprehensible. My own efforts to depict the concept of greater police intrusions and deprivations in their street encounters require greater objective basis to back them up were feeble. In both, we struggled and argued over the details. (Pitting my mercurial temperament against his stubbornness wasn't always a pretty picture. We even tested our efforts on our friends, with his backing him up and mine backing me.) In the end, the adversarial process produced a result that's both a pretty and effective tool to portray the concepts we were trying to depict.

What would I do without Steve and Doug? Doug takes me there and gets me here and everywhere, day in and day out, days that now have stretched into years. And my dear friend Steve, whom I've known from the days when he watched over my kids; over the decades when he kept the Irish Wolfhounds; to now, when he manages to keep our old, blind, beloved Siamese cat, the Standard Poodle, me, and a lot more around here in order. And they do it all while putting up with what my adored mentor at Cambridge, the late Sir Geoffrey Elton, called "Joel's mercurial temperament." Only those who really know me can understand how I can try the patience of Job!

I dedicate the book to my students, who say that I've challenged them, but who for more than 40 years have challenged me to explain and defend what *I* say and what *I* write. They, more than anyone or anything else, have made me a better teacher, and continue to inspire me to be the best teacher and write the best book I can. But, should I ever think I've done well enough, I've got what my long-departed German mother said when I brought my report card home with grades of 100 in all but one of my subjects. It was a 99. She asked, "What's this 99?" I asked, "What about the 100s?" Her answer lives with me still: "The 100s will take care of themselves. Get to work on that 99!"

Students, friends, families, and associates like these are behind whatever success *Criminal Procedure 9*, enjoys. As for its faults, I own them all. Are you listening, Mom?

Joel Samaha
Minneapolis
July 30, 2013

1

U.S. Criminal Procedure

A Road Map and Travel Guide

LEARNING OBJECTIVES

1 Appreciate the complexities of the "criminal justice road map"; know what role the various actors (judges, police, suspects, etc.) play in the various settings throughout the criminal process.

2 Appreciate that at the heart of our constitutional democracy is the idea of balancing the values of community safety and individual autonomy, and that the "ideal" balance between these two is not a fixed point but a range flexible enough to deal with many individual situations.

3 Know, understand, and appreciate that where the balance is struck between public safety and individual autonomy is often contested, and never satisfies everyone.

4 Appreciate that the deep commitment to equality in U.S. society reflects our deep commitment to equal justice for all in both criminal procedure law and practice.

5 Know, understand, and appreciate the significant role that discretionary decision making plays in fairly and impartially balancing community safety and individual liberty, privacy, and dignity.

6 Understand the importance, prevalence, and shortcomings of empirical and social scientific research regarding how often the criminal justice process accurately convicts criminals and frees innocents.

7 Understand and differentiate the two components of case facts: (a) the government official acts that the defendant claims violated the Constitution and (b) the objective basis or facts and circumstances that back up the official acts.

8 Know the importance of prior case decisions (precedent) and the obligation to follow prior decisions (stare decisis) in judicial reasoning and decision making.

Our criminal process is not punishing enough of the guilty, exonerating enough of the innocent, or doing equal justice under law. How could this be, thirty years after the Warren Court's criminal procedure revolution?

—Dripps (2003), xiv

It ended with the motorbike,
A search for evidence,
Poring over old photographs,
To make it all fake sense

—"Requiem in Denim and Leopard Skin"
Pet Shop Boys (2012)

Once we begin to believe something, we unconsciously begin seeking out information to reinforce that belief, often in the absence of facts. In fact, our biases can grow to be so strong that facts to the contrary will actually strengthen our own beliefs .... Once we grow biased enough, we lose our capacity to change our minds .... Talk to a Red Sox fan about whether or not the Yankees are the best team in baseball's history and you'll see this strong bias come out. Talk to MacBook owners about the latest version of Windows and you may see this same phenomenon.

—Clay A. Johnson (2012), 46–47

C*riminal Procedure 9* takes you on a chronological journey through the criminal process, stopping at the main points of interest along the way. It includes a road map and travelers' guide (Figure 1.1) The road map lays out our destinations. The journey begins with police investigation on the street and other public places, and later in police departments. Then the action shifts to lawyers—prosecutors, defense lawyers, and trial judges—and finally, to appeals courts that review trial court proceedings. The travelers' guide describes and explains three aspects of police, prosecutor, defense lawyer, and judicial decisions:

1. The commands of the U.S. Constitution
2. Professional discretionary judgments
3. Social science research

You won't be fully ready to begin your journey until you understand *Criminal Procedure 9*'s method. It's what I call the **text-case method**, which means that it's part text and part excerpts from real criminal procedure cases, edited for nonlawyers. The text part of the book explains the general principles, practices, and issues related to the law of criminal procedure. The excerpts let you see how the general principles apply to the specifics of real situations, allowing you to think critically about the principles and the issues they raise.

FIGURE 1.1 Criminal Procedure as a Journey

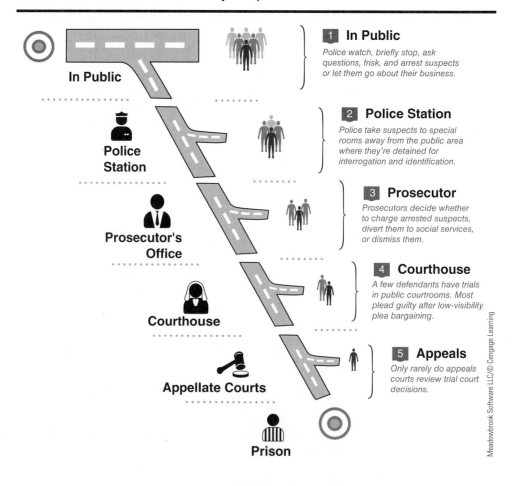

In Public

1 **In Public**
Police watch, briefly stop, ask questions, frisk, and arrest suspects or let them go about their business.

Police Station

2 **Police Station**
Police take suspects to special rooms away from the public area where they're detained for interrogation and identification.

Prosecutor's Office

3 **Prosecutor**
Prosecutors decide whether to charge arrested suspects, divert them to social services, or dismiss them.

Courthouse

4 **Courthouse**
A few defendants have trials in public courtrooms. Most plead guilty after low-visibility plea bargaining.

Appellate Courts

5 **Appeals**
Only rarely do appeals courts review trial court decisions.

Prison

Meadowbrook Software LLC/© Cengage Learning

CRIMINAL PROCEDURE ROAD MAP

 Criminal Procedure 9 takes you on a chronological journey through the day-to-day decision points in the law of criminal procedure (Figure 1.1).

Hey! Notice that hardly anyone ever goes further than the first leg on this journey. And the vast majority of minor offenders (say, those arrested for possession of a small amount of marijuana) won't go past the second leg. Only serious offenders (murderers, robbers, rapists, burglars) go much further.

Public Places

Our journey begins with police officers who investigate suspicious behavior in public places (Chapters 4–6). These include

1. Public streets, roads, and highways
2. Public parks and sports stadiums
3. Semipublic shopping malls
4. Privately owned businesses open to the public, such as restaurants, bars, and movie theaters

In public places, police officers can watch, approach, briefly stop, ask suspects a few questions, sometimes frisk them, and then let them go on about their business. Officers arrest some, and take them on the second leg of their journey—the police station.

Police Stations

The second destination, not-so-public police stations (Chapters 5–6), are nevertheless open to the public. Most suspects don't go to the police station willingly—the police *take* them there. When they arrive, they're usually taken to special rooms away from the public area. Here, they're detained for hours, sometimes days, for intense investigation, such as interrogation, and identification procedures.

Prosecutors' Offices

If the police believe arrested suspects should be charged with crimes, they refer them to prosecutors. While arrested suspects wait in jail or while they're free on bail, the action moves to prosecutors' officers. After reviewing the evidence and other criteria, prosecutors decide whether to charge suspects; divert them to other social services, such as drug or domestic abuse treatment; or dismiss them. If they decide to charge suspects with serious crimes, the case continues to the next destination, the courthouse.

Trial Courts

All suspects charged with serious crimes (now defendants) will appear briefly in court *before* trial to

1. Hear a judge read the charges against them and explain their constitutional rights to them

2. Ask how they plead to the charges

3. Determine whether they'll be released on bail, and decide if they can afford a lawyer; if they can't, the judge will appoint a lawyer to represent them

A few defendants (about five to ten out of a hundred) will have a public trial in one of the public courtrooms. The remaining vast majority will plead guilty in open court *after* low-visibility plea bargaining in prosecutors' offices, nooks and crannies of the courthouse, or restaurants and bars nearby.

After conviction, the action focuses on judges' sentencing of convicted defendants (now offenders).

Appellate Courts

Finally, in some cases (far fewer than most people believe), the action moves to appeals courts that review trial court decisions. Almost all of the excerpts that you'll read in this book derive from the official printed reports of these **appellate courts**.

Criminal Procedure 9 also provides you with a travel guide to help you get the most out of your journey. This travel guide focuses on three parts of the criminal procedure landscape:

1. *Crime control in the U.S. constitutional democracy* (the **law in the books**). The U.S. Constitution commands public officials to make sure that (a) communities are safe, *and* (b) they protect the rights and privacy of individuals from unjustified government interference, *and* (c) they do (a) and (b) both fairly and impartially.

2. *Discretionary professional judgments* (the **law in action**). The Constitution allows plenty of "play in the joints" for criminal justice professionals in their day-to-day operations. This allows them to rely on their professional training and experience to carry out the Constitution's commands.

3. *Empirical evidence.* Social science research sheds light on how effectively, fairly, and impartially these professionals and their lay helpers carry out the Constitution's commands. At the core, it tries to tell us how close the real world of criminal justice approaches its highest ideal—*always* convicting the guilty and *never* the innocent.

Let's look briefly at these guideposts. In the remaining chapters we'll enrich them with the details appropriate to each of the legs on our journey.

CRIME CONTROL IN U.S. CONSTITUTIONAL DEMOCRACY

LO **2, 3, 4**

If we lived in a police state, officials could break into our houses in the dead of night and shoot us in our beds based on nothing more than the whim of the current dictator. If we lived in a pure democracy, the majority who won the last election could authorize the police to shoot anyone whom they had a hunch was a street gang member. But we live in a **constitutional democracy**, where neither a single dictator nor an overwhelming majority of the people has total power over us as individuals.

Our constitutional democracy balances the need to provide for the public's safety and security against other values, including

1. Individual liberty, privacy, and dignity
2. Fairness
3. Impartiality

Let's look at the main guideposts on our journey.

LO 2   Balancing Community Safety and Individual Autonomy

In almost all conflicts, especially those that make their way into a legal system, there is something to be said in favor of two or more outcomes. Whatever result is chosen, someone will be advantaged and someone will be disadvantaged; some policy will be promoted at the expense of some other. Hence, it is often said that a "balancing operation" must be undertaken, with the "correct" decision as the one yielding the greatest net benefit. (Aleinikoff 1987, 943)

At the heart of our constitutional democracy is the idea of balancing two conflicting values, both of which we believe are essential to the quality of our lives. On one side of the balance is **community security**. Who can doubt the value of living in a community where we're safe (or at least where we *feel* safe)? Where our lives are safe from murder; our bodies are safe from rape and other assaults; our homes are safe from burglars, arsonists, and trespassers; our secrets are safe from exposure; and our "stuff" is safe from thieves and vandals.

On the other side of the balance is **individual autonomy**. *Autonomy* means individuals are free to control their own lives without government interference. They can come and go as they please; develop their body and mind as they wish to do; believe whatever or whomever they want to believe; worship any god they like; associate with anybody they choose to be with; and do whatever else they wish to do in the privacy of their own homes (assuming that they're competent adults and what they want to do doesn't include committing crimes that violate the community's or other persons' safety against their will). In other words, they can't tip the balance between community security and individual autonomy in their favor whenever and however they want.

Weighed on the community safety side of the balance is the amount of government power needed to control crime for everybody's safety and security. Weighed on the individual autonomy side is the amount of control individuals have over their own lives. Those who wrote and adopted the U.S. Constitution in the 1700s were realists. They accepted human nature for what it is: People aren't angels. Left to do as they please, ordinary individuals will break the law. And, because they're people, too, government officials left to do as they please will abuse their power. In James Madison's words,

> If men were angels, no government would be necessary. If angels were to govern men, neither external nor internal controls on government would be necessary. In framing a government which is to be administered by men over men, the great difficulty lies in this: You must first enable the government to control the governed; and in the next place, oblige it to control itself. (James Madison [1787], 1961, 349)

So the Founders expected excesses from both ordinary people and government officials who live in a real world inhabited by imperfect people. Let me be clear right at the beginning of our journey through the criminal process: I subscribe to Madison's view of human nature and the world.

Because both community security and individual autonomy are highly valued "goods," striking the balance between them is difficult, and where it's struck never satisfies anyone completely.

The balance between crime control and individual rights is flexible. Where exactly the balance is struck shifts, depending on the circumstances. Put another way, the right balance falls within a zone; it's not a fixed point on the spectrum between total control and total freedom (*Llaguno v. Mingey* 1985, 1565). The most extreme examples are emergencies, especially wartime. As one lawyer prosecuting suspected disloyalists during the Civil War put it (I'm paraphrasing here), "During wartime the Bill of Rights

YOU DECIDE
Brutality or Reasonable Force?

LO 2 The Department of Homeland Security is reviewing guidelines for use of force by border agencies amid a sharp increase in agent-involved killings along the U.S.-Mexico border. Under the agency's guidelines, agents are permitted to use lethal force in such situations because rocks and other projectiles have caused serious injuries. Most agents involved in fatal incidents in recent years have been cleared of wrongdoing. "CBP law enforcement personnel are trained to use deadly force in circumstances that pose a threat to their lives, the lives of their fellow law enforcement partners and innocent third parties," U.S. Customs and Border Protection said in a recent statement.

The scrutiny of U.S. Customs and Border Protection enforcement practices comes in response to a request by 16 members of Congress who expressed concern over the death of a Mexican man who suffered a fatal heart attack after being Tasered by a customs officer in 2010. Since 2010, at least 16 civilians have been killed by agents, many during rock-throwing confrontations involving suspected smugglers. Critics have grown increasingly vocal about rocks being met by bullets, which they consider disproportionate force.

[Between the middle of September 2012 and October 2012] . . . three people [were] . . . killed in confrontations involving Border Patrol officers, including a mother of five from the San Diego suburb of Chula Vista and a 16-year-old

suspected rock thrower from Nogales. During the boy's funeral [which was held in October, 2012] mourners carried his coffin along the border fence and shouted epithets at border officials, who bolstered security along the fence dividing Arizona from Sonora.

Critics question the self-defense claims by agents. Some of the suspects have been shot in the back, or from such long distances that their rock throwing wouldn't have posed a serious threat, they say. Mexican government officials said one man shot on the banks of the Rio Grande in Nuevo Laredo was picnicking with his family.

U.S. officials said the man, who had methamphetamine in his system, was resisting his deportation to Tijuana. Advocates say he was handcuffed and pleading for his life when the agent used the weapon, which is supposed to deliver a nonlethal jolt of electricity.

In the letter, the lawmakers urged the inspector general to determine whether the Hernandez incident is "emblematic of a broader cultural problem within CBP." They also questioned whether other fatal confrontations have been fully investigated.

Source: "U.S. reviewing guidelines for use of force by border agencies," Richard Marosi, *Los Angeles Times,* October 17, 2012, http://articles .latimes.com/2012/oct/17/local/la-me-border-patrol-20121018 (accessed January 15, 2013).

is put to sleep. We'll wake it up when the emergency passes" (Gayarré 1903, 601). But it's not just during war emergencies that we'll see the balance struck in various places in the zone. We'll see other examples where courts move around in the zone between order and liberty.

Balancing community safety and individual autonomy isn't the only constitutional command. Two others are at the core of our U.S. constitutional democracy: fairness and equal justice.

LO 3   Fairness

In the U.S. constitutional democracy, we don't believe in catching, convicting, and punishing criminals at any price. According to one court, "Truth, like all other good things, may be loved unwisely, may be pursued too keenly, may cost too much" (*Pearce v. Pearce* 1846, 950). The U.S. Constitution and provisions in every state constitution limit public officials' power to control crime (see Chapter 2, "Due Process of Law" and "Equal Protection of the Law").

How precisely to define fair procedures for everybody who gets embroiled in the criminal process, procedures that might interfere with the government's power to keep communities safe, never satisfies everyone. Throughout U.S. history, the tension between providing fair procedures for all individuals in the criminal process, and at the same time controlling crime for the sake of community safety has from time to time caused great frustration, even anger. Those who fear criminals more than they fear government abuses of power complain of rules or "technicalities" that "handcuff the police" and allow criminals to go free. Those who fear government abuses of power more than they fear criminals complain that we haven't obliged the government to "control itself," as Madison warned us to do.

Highly respected U.S. Court of Appeals Judge Learned Hand clearly took the side of government power in this debate. According to Judge Hand (1922), accused persons have all the advantages.

> Our dangers do not lie in too little tenderness to the accused. Our procedure has been always haunted by the ghost of the innocent man convicted. It is an unreal dream. What we need to fear is the archaic formalism and the watery sentiment that obstructs, delays, and defeats the prosecution of crime. (659)

Distinguished Professor Joseph Goldstein (1960), weighing in on the side of controlling government, strongly disagrees with Judge Hand's position. Goldstein believes that modern criminal procedure "gives overwhelming advantage to the prosecution." The result is "rejection of the presumption of innocence in favor of a presumption of guilt" (1152).

LO 4   Equal Justice

Most of the history of criminal procedure, especially state criminal procedure since the Civil War, developed in response to racial discrimination (see Chapter 2). You can't understand the law of criminal procedure unless you put it into this sociohistorical context. Racial discrimination has definitely lessened, but it hasn't disappeared. At all stages in the criminal process, race can infect decision making, especially at the early stages of the process, such as street stops and frisks (Chapter 4).

Racial discrimination is only one threat to our deep commitment to the ideal of equal justice for all. Others include discrimination based on class, sex, ethnicity, religion, or sexual orientation. Sex can affect who's excused from jury duty or excluded from jury service (Chapter 13). Ethnicity affects the same types of decisions as race (noted earlier; see also Chapter 4, "Race and Ethnicity"). Religion combined with ethnicity affects decisions involving terrorist crimes (Chapter 15).

Money can determine who gets the best lawyer, how early in the criminal process she gets one, and who can pay for expensive appeals. Despite the U.S. Supreme Court's command that the Sixth Amendment's right to counsel guarantees the right to "effective" counsel, even when you're too poor to afford a lawyer, the reality falls far short of the constitutional command (Chapter 12, "Right to Counsel").

DISCRETION

LO 5 The "real world" of criminal justice demonstrates that the Constitution has left plenty of "play in its joints." What does this mean? When criminal justice professionals are out there doing the day-to-day work of criminal investigation, prosecution, and conviction, they rely heavily on their professional training and experience to carry out the Constitution's commands. Hopefully, your journey will help you to understand and appreciate the role of discretion in fairly and impartially balancing community safety and individual liberty, privacy, and dignity. This is true not just for the police leg of the journey, but throughout the rest of the journey too.

Think of each leg in the journey, from investigation to appeals from convictions, as a decision point. Each point presents a criminal justice professional with the opportunity to decide whether to start, continue, or end the criminal process. Both the Constitution's rules (as courts create and interpret them) and discretionary judgment contribute to these decisions.

The police can investigate suspects, or not, and arrest them, or not—initiating the formal criminal process, or stopping it. Prosecutors can charge suspects and continue the criminal process, divert suspects to some social service agency, or take no further action—effectively terminating the criminal process.

Defendants can plead guilty (almost always on their lawyers' advice) and avoid trial. Judges can suspend sentences or sentence convicted offenders to the maximum allowable penalty—hence, either minimizing or maximizing the punishment the criminal law prescribes.

Justice, fairness, and impartiality depend on predictability; namely, the certainty and the protection against abuses that only written rules can provide. But, these same goals also require discretion to soften the rigidity of written rules. The tension between law and discretion—a recurring theme in criminal procedure—is as old as law. Arguments raged over it in Western civilization as early as the Middle Ages.

In the end, the criminal process in practice is a blend of the formal law of criminal procedure and informal influences that enter the process by way of discretion. Discretion and law complement each other in promoting and balancing the interests that the Constitution commands the government to uphold.

CRIMINAL PROCEDURE IN ACTION

Fifteen minutes wasn't "too long" for a traffic stop

On the night of March 28, 2009, David Marsh was a passenger in Julius Johnson's car when Officer Frederick Nelson of the Nashville Police Department pulled them over for running a stop sign. Officer Nelson approached Marsh and Johnson and asked for their identification and Johnson's vehicle registration. Officer Nelson observed Marsh holding a "blunt" cigar, and asked if there was anything illegal in the car. Officer Nelson radioed for a K-9 team and returned to his cruiser to check Johnson's vehicle records as well as write a citation.

After 5 to 10 minutes, Officer Alex Moore, who was not part of a K-9 team, arrived on the scene while Officer Nelson was still writing the citation in his cruiser. According to Officer Moore, Officer Nelson said he thought there "might be marijuana in the car." Officer Moore walked to the car to speak to Johnson and Marsh, shined a flashlight inside the car, and saw a green material on Marsh's shirt that Officer Moore believed to be marijuana. Officer Moore made this observation no more than 15 minutes after the beginning of the traffic stop and while Officer Nelson was still writing the citation in his cruiser. Officer Moore asked Marsh to step out of the car and placed him under arrest. He then searched the passenger-seat area, where he found marijuana. He arrested Marsh.

Marsh argued that "police do not need 15 minutes to conduct a traffic stop and write a citation."

DECISION

Even though 15 minutes might have been atypically long for a traffic stop, the record does not show that it was longer than necessary to complete the tasks related to the stop. The proper inquiry is not whether [Marsh] was detained longer than the *average* speeder, but whether he was detained longer than reasonably necessary for the officers to complete the purpose of the stop in this case.

During those 15 minutes, Officer Nelson spoke to Johnson and Marsh, checked Johnson's record, and wrote a citation, which are permissible actions during a traffic stop. In a traffic stop, an officer can lawfully detain the driver of a vehicle until after the officer has finished making record radio checks and issuing a citation.

Marsh presents no evidence that Officer Nelson was stalling. He relies only on a subjective belief that this stop was just too long. However, the stop was not impermissibly long because the police did not detain Marsh any longer than was reasonably necessary to issue the traffic citation.

Source: *U.S. v. Marsh*, U.S. Court of Appeals, 6th Circuit (Tennessee) No. 10-6473 (October 26, 2011); 443 F.Appx.94 (CA6 Tenn 2011).

EMPIRICAL EVIDENCE

 LO 6

To get the most out of your journey, you need to know at least a sampling of the rapidly growing empirical findings of social science researchers that evaluate the effectiveness of policies and decisions. We'll look at two examples of research: the effectiveness of the balancing approach to police decision making, and the accuracy of sorting guilty and innocents throughout the criminal process.

In 2000, two law professors (Meares and Harcourt 2000), one (Tracey Meares) who calls herself "conservative," the other (Bernard Harcourt) who calls himself "liberal," disagreed on most policy issues. But, in this article, they put aside their differences and link[ed] arms to call for "a **new generation of criminal procedure**. We are calling for . . . judicial decision making and academic debate that treats social scientific and empirical assessment as a crucial element in constitutional decision-making" (735).

Assessing the Constitutional Balancing Approach

The new procedure applies to all legs of our journey, as you'll discover in the remaining chapters. Conveniently for us, Meares and Harcourt discuss the first legs on our journey, the law enforcement legs, "where modern constitutional criminal procedure emerged" in the 1960s. The U.S. Supreme Court homed in on the "realities of street policing, custodial interrogations, investigations, and the impact of these activities on individual freedoms."

These "realities" were the real-world concerns about police investigative practices, especially police encounters with individuals on the streets and other public places, and police interrogations and identification procedures at the police station and the impact of these practices on individual civil liberties. These concerns later extended to the entire criminal process, from investigation, to pretrial, trial, sentencing, and post-conviction review of lower court decisions. And it's now a widespread practice to describe and think about criminal procedure constitutional rights as "guaranteeing a reasonable balance between liberty and order" (737).

The balancing approach stimulated judicial decision making and academic writing to focus on two empirical questions:

1. How effective are these practices in controlling crime?
2. What is their effect on individual liberty and privacy (736–37)?

The answers to these questions call for accurate, reliable, impartial empirical and social scientific evidence. This won't "guarantee the right answers in criminal procedure. But use of empirical evidence will produce a clearer picture of the existing constitutional landscape and spotlight the normative judgments at the heart of criminal procedure" (735).

By the 1970s, the balancing approach was taken for granted. The landmark consent search case *Schneckcloth v. Bustamonte* (1973) demonstrates how "pervasive" it had become (Meares and Harcourt 2000, 737–38). You'll read a fuller excerpt in Chapter 6 but we'll include a shorter version of it here to help you get ready to begin your journey.

CASE

Was the Consent Voluntary?

Schneckcloth v. Bustamonte
412 U.S. 218 (1973)

HISTORY

Clyde Bustamonte was tried in a California state court for possessing a check with intent to defraud. The trial judge denied his motion to suppress and Bustamonte was convicted. The California Court of Appeals affirmed. The California Supreme Court denied review. Bustamonte brought a petition for habeas corpus in the U.S. District Court for the Northern District of California. The District Court denied the petition. The U.S. Court of Appeals for the Ninth Circuit vacated the District Court's order, and remanded. The U.S. Supreme Court reversed.

—STEWART, J.

FACTS

While on routine patrol in Sunnyvale, California, at approximately 2:40 in the morning, Police Officer James Rand stopped an automobile when he observed that one headlight and its license plate light were burned out. Six men were in the vehicle. Joe Alcala and Robert Clyde Bustamonte were in the front seat with Joe Gonzales, the driver. Three older men were seated in the rear. After the six occupants had stepped out of the car at the officer's request and after two additional policemen had arrived, Officer Rand asked Alcala if he could search the car. Alcala replied, "Sure, go ahead." Prior to the search no one was threatened with arrest and, according to Officer Rand's uncontradicted testimony, it "was all very congenial at this time." Gonzales testified that Alcala actually helped in the search of the car, by opening the trunk and glove compartment. In Gonzales's words: "[T]he police officer asked Joe (Alcala), he goes, 'Does the trunk open?' And Joe said, 'Yes.' He went to the car and got the keys and opened up the trunk." Wadded up under the left rear seat, the police officers found three checks that had previously been stolen from a car wash.

OPINION

. . . The question whether a consent to a search was in fact "voluntary" or was the product of duress or coercion is a question of fact to be determined from the totality of all the circumstances. . . . Two competing concerns must be accommodated in determining the meaning of a voluntary consent—the legitimate need for such searches and the equally important requirement of assuring the absence of coercion. In situations where the police have some evidence of illicit activity, but lack probable cause to arrest or search, a search authorized by a valid consent may be the only means of obtaining important and reliable evidence. In the present case for example, while the police had reason to stop the car for traffic violations, the State does not contend that there was probable cause to search the vehicle or that the search was incident to a valid arrest of any of the occupants. Yet, the search yielded tangible evidence that served as a basis for a prosecution, and provided some assurance that others, wholly innocent of the crime, were not mistakenly brought to trial. In short, a search pursuant to consent may result in considerably less inconvenience for the subject of the search, and, properly conducted, is a constitutionally permissible and wholly legitimate aspect of effective police activity.

But the Fourth Amendment requires that a consent not be coerced.

In this case, there is no evidence of any inherently coercive tactics—either from the nature of the police questioning or the environment in which it took place.

Our decision today is a narrow one. We hold only that when the subject of a search is not in custody and the State attempts to justify a search on the basis of his consent, the Fourth Amendment requires that it demonstrate that the consent was in fact voluntarily given, and not the result of coercion. Voluntariness is a question of fact to be determined from all the circumstances.

Judgment of Court of Appeals REVERSED.

DISSENT

MARSHALL, J.

I find nothing in the opinion of the Court to dispel my belief that under many circumstances a reasonable person might read an officer's "May I" as the courteous expression of a demand backed by force of law. In most cases, in my view consent is ordinarily given as acquiescence in an implicit claim of authority to search. Permitting searches in such circumstances, without any assurance at all that the subject of the search knew that, by his consent, he was relinquishing his constitutional rights, is something that I cannot believe is sanctioned by the Constitution.

The holding today confines the protection of the Fourth Amendment against searches conducted without probable cause to the sophisticated, the knowledgeable, and, I might add, the few. In the final analysis, the Court now sanctions a game of blindman's buff, in which the police always have the upper hand, for the sake of nothing more than the convenience of the police.

But the guarantees of the Fourth Amendment were never intended to shrink before such an ephemeral and changeable interest. The Framers of the Fourth Amendment struck the balance against this sort of convenience and in favor of certain basic civil rights. It is not for this Court to restrike that balance because of its own views of the needs of law enforcement officers. I fear that that is the effect of the Court's decision today.

Questions

1. State the elements of the voluntariness test created by the U.S. Supreme Court.

2. List all the facts and circumstances relevant to deciding whether Clyde Bustamonte consented to the search of the car.

3. Describe the Court's application of the voluntariness test to consent in the case.

4. According to Justice Marshall, do individuals ever voluntarily consent to police requests, or are all police requests polite orders? Do you agree with Justice Marshall? Defend your answer.

You'll encounter empirical evidence throughout the book whenever it's available to elaborate on, correct, and modify the courts' rulings. This evidence happily exists for several important topics in the book, especially for searches and seizures (Chapters 3–7); the right against self-incrimination and confessions (Chapter 8); witness identification procedures (Chapter 9); the exclusionary rule (Chapter 10); pretrial proceedings (Chapter 12); guilty pleas (Chapter 13); and sentencing (Chapter 14). So even though courts are unaware of it, or consciously ignore it, or take pains to reject it outright, we'll include it.

Assessing the Accuracy of Sorting Guilty and Innocents

"Remember the innocent," I remind my students before and during our discussion of every case in this book. I've been saying this for a long time. But not until DNA demonstrated conclusively that our criminal process convicted innocent people, did I insist on it so urgently. And I'm pleased that by the end of the semester, at least some of my students tell me it's the most important takeaway from the course. It's even more satisfying when former students who are now criminal justice professionals tell me that they think about it in the course of their work in real-world criminal justice.

The most dramatic examples—and the ones getting most attention—are innocent people sentenced to death, and rape cases, like that of Ronald Cotton, who spent 11 years on death row for a rape he didn't commit. But the problem is bigger than that. According to Professor Brian Forst, former director of research at the Police Foundation and author of *Errors of Justice* (2004), errors that "harass" and "punish" innocent people and fail to punish the "real" criminals undermine our confidence in government institutions. In fact, "news of serious lapses in the workings of our formal system of justice can accelerate the drive for people to seek private remedies for protection and justice" (Forst 2004, 2).

Causes of inaccurate sorting

In *About Guilt and Innocence* (2003), Professor Donald Dripps surveys convincing social science research demonstrating that "half of all arrests don't lead to convictions," that "25 percent of all DNA tests performed at the request of the police exonerate the suspect," and that police decisions to stop, search, and arrest and prosecutorial decisions to charge clearly have a "massively disproportionate impact on Black Americans" (xiii–xiv). Professor Dripps wonders, "How could this be, 30 years after the Warren Court's criminal procedure revolution?" He concludes that the "revolution" failed "in large measure" because of legal rules that expanded suspects' and defendants' rights (xv; see also Chapter 2, pp. 45–46).

Dan Simon, professor of Law and Society, in his thought-provoking *In Doubt* (2012), focuses on the psychological causes of convicting the innocent and freeing the guilty. His case for psychological causes rests on several arguments. First, people operate the criminal justice system, namely "witnesses, detectives, suspects, lawyers, judges, and jurors" (2). These people's "memories, recognitions, assessments, inferences, social influence, and decisions, all tied in with moral judgments, and emotions, and motivations . . . turn the wheels of the system." Summing up decades of psychological research, he concludes that

The criminal justice process falls short of meeting the certitude that befits its solemn nature. This shortfall is generally overlooked or denied by the people entrusted with designing and governing the system—notably, police personnel, prosecutors, judges, and lawmakers—and it is not adequately recognized in scholarly and public debates. (3)

Professor Simon acknowledges that psychology alone doesn't explain the faulty system for sorting out the innocent from the guilty. (See Table 1.1 for more explanations why the system is faulty.)

Determining the numbers of convicted innocents and free guilty

We are not a modest nation. We frequently insist that the American criminal justice system . . . is "the best in the world." . . . We never (well, hardly ever) convict the innocent—prominent Americans forcefully assert with no evidence in support. (Gross 2008, 174)

To be sure, no reasonable person doubts that the American criminal justice system is more accurate than not. (Gould 2008, 1)

How often the criminal process frees the guilty and convicts the innocent is hotly contested. Dividing the number of exonerations by the number of felony convictions in the United States, Clapsop County, Oregon District Attorney Joshua Marquis calculated an error rate of 0.027 percent, which translates into a success rate of 99.973 percent (2006).

Others maintain that the known number of cases of innocents—mainly convicted innocents exonerated by DNA in murder and rape cases—is only the tip of an innocents' iceberg.

Unfortunately, we don't and can't know how big the iceberg is. Why? Professor Brandon Garrett (2011, 263–64) points out that instead of comparing the number of known exonerations to the number of known felony convictions, we should ask how high the exoneration rate is for the typical DNA exoneration cases—murders and rape-murders. They comprise only a fraction of a percent of felony convictions, "much, much lower than the 15 million felonies cited by Justice Scalia, most likely in the low tens of thousands, making the number of exonerations quite troubling" (264). (Professor Garrett is referring to U.S. Supreme Court Justice Scalia's reliance on

TABLE 1.1 Faulty system explanations

• Prosecutors' discretion
• Inconsistent policing
• Infrequent jury trials
• Too much plea bargaining
• Not enough access to legal representation
• Inadequate training and lack of law enforcement officers
• Improper forensic procedures
• Frequent reliance on unreliable evidence, such as informants

Source: Dan Simon, *In Doubt*, page 11.

Joshua Marquis's finding to support the justice's claim in *Kansas v. Marsh* (2006) that innocents are hardly ever convicted.)

Even if we can't know how big the iceberg of innocents is, Professor Garrett suggests that "error rates may be far higher" (264). This is especially true if we include the

> vast numbers of cases involving other types of crimes that cannot be examined using DNA and where we just do not know how many are wrongly convicted. As powerful as DNA testing is, it is limited to a small set of mostly rape convictions from the 1980s, in which the evidence just happened to be preserved. (264)

THE TEXT-CASE METHOD

There's one last and indispensable aid you'll need to prepare for your criminal procedure journey—*Criminal Procedure 9*'s method. *Criminal Procedure 9* is what I call a **text-case book**; it's part text and part excerpts from real criminal procedure cases, especially edited for nonlawyers. The text part of the book explains the general principles, practices, and issues related to the law of criminal procedure.

The case excerpts provide you with real-world encounters between criminal suspects, defendants, and offenders on one side and law enforcement officers, prosecutors, defense lawyers, and judges on the other. The excerpts show you how the general principles apply to the details of actual situations, stimulating you to think critically about how the general principles and practices apply to day-to-day criminal justice administration.

I believe the best way to test whether you understand the principles and issues is to apply them to real cases. So, although you can learn a lot from the text alone, you won't get the full benefit of what you've learned without applying and thinking about it by reading the case excerpts.

Most of the case excerpts are U.S. Supreme Court cases because, as pointed out earlier, Supreme Court justices are the "primary generators of rules for regulating the behavior of police, prosecutors, and the other actors who administer the criminal process" (page 12).

Occasionally, you'll also read U.S. Courts of Appeals cases (see Figure 1.2). These cases are included when they deal with issues not yet decided by the U.S. Supreme Court, or when they interpret rules already established by the Supreme Court. Occasionally, you'll also read cases from state courts. State cases are important for at least two reasons. First, every state has a bill of rights that contains provisions similar or identical to those in the U.S. Bill of Rights. Second, state courts decide for themselves how to interpret and apply their own state constitutional provisions.

Let's take a closer look at what you'll be reading in the case excerpts. We'll begin with a look at the parts of the case excerpts, which will help you to write your own case summary. Then, we'll examine the importance of three key concepts: precedent, stare decisis, and appellate cases.

Parts of the Case Summary

Don't worry if reading cases intimidates you at first. Like students before you, you'll get the hang of it before long. The instructions that follow should guide your reading and analysis, and help you get the most out of the case excerpts. I've also included instructions for finding the full case report. This way you can read the whole case if your instructor assigns it, or if you'd like to read it unedited.

FIGURE 1.2 The Structure of the U.S. Federal Court System

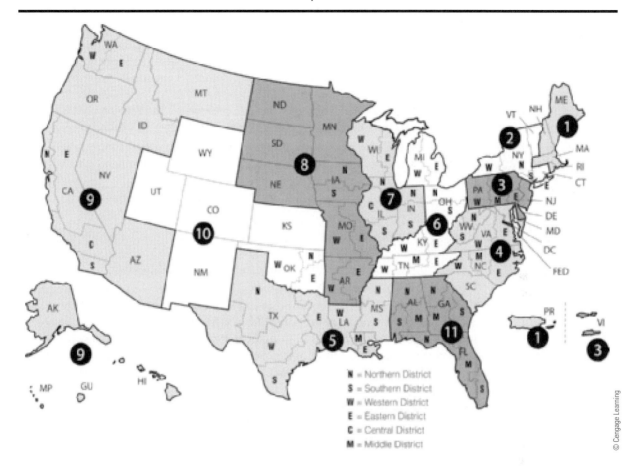

N = Northern District
S = Southern District
W = Western District
E = Eastern District
C = Central District
M = Middle District

© Cengage Learning

Here's an outline of the eight sections of every excerpt. If you get familiar with them right at the beginning, I'm sure you'll catch on to how to read and understand cases sooner. You should also write out summaries of these parts, or perform what lawyers call "briefing a case." I recommend using a separate document for each case. At the top, put the name and the citation of the case. Then, summarize briefly and accurately the parts of the case.

Title

The title in criminal cases consists of two names, one on either side of "*v.*" (the abbreviation for "versus" or "against"). The government (U.S. or the state, called variously "State," "People," or "Commonwealth," depending on what the state calls itself) is always the first party in the trial court because the government starts all criminal cases. The name on the right in the trial court is always the defendant's.

There are no trial court cases in this book because, unfortunately, trial records aren't usually published. We enter the case after the trial court has decided an issue in the case, a higher court has reviewed the trial court's decision, and it has decided to publish its opinion. (Reviewing courts don't have to publish their opinions; the decision to publish is discretionary.)

The placement of names to the left or right of the "*v.*" in cases of appeal varies. In federal cases, the party appealing the decision of the court below is placed to the left of the *"v."* Some states follow the federal practice. The others keep the order of the original case; that is, the name of the state is always to the left, and the defendant's is always to its right.

Notice that the government can't appeal a verdict of "not guilty." Why? Because the double jeopardy clause of the U.S. Constitution forbids it (Chapter 12). The government can appeal some trial court decisions (which, occasionally, we'll encounter) but never an acquittal.

Citation

After the title of the case, you'll see a string of letters and numbers. These are called the **case citation**. The case citation (like a footnote, endnote, or other reference in articles and books) tells you the source of the material quoted or relied upon. The citation tells you where you can find the published report of the case. The information in the citation tells you:

(a) the name of the court that's reporting the case,
(b) the date the court decided the case, and
(c) the book, volume, and page where the case report begins.

For example, in *Schneckloth v. Bustamonte* (excerpted on p. 12), the case citation is "412 U.S. 218 (1973)." This means that you'll find the case reported in Volume 412 of the *United States Reports* (abbreviated "U.S."), beginning on page 218; the volume includes cases decided by the Court in the year 1973. **United States Reports** is the official U.S. government publication of U.S. Supreme Court cases. Two other widely used nongovernment publications, *Supreme Court Reporter* (S.Ct.) and the *Lawyer's Edition* (L.Ed.), also report U.S. Supreme Court cases. The U.S. Court of Appeals decisions are reported in **The Federal Reporter** (F., F.2d, and F.3d).

Procedural history of the case

The **procedural history of the case** refers to the formal procedural steps the case has taken, and the actions taken at each of these steps, beginning usually with the indictment and moving through the trial court and appellate courts to the court whose excerpt you're briefing. This part of your brief puts the excerpt in its correct procedural place so that you'll know where the case has been, what decisions were made before it got to the appellate court, and the decision of the appellate court in the case whose excerpted facts and opinion you're about to read.

Judge

"Judge" refers to the name of the judge who wrote the opinion and issued the court's judgment in the case. U.S. Supreme Court judges and most state supreme court judges have the title "Justice"; intermediate appeals court judges have the title "Judge."

LO 7 Facts

The facts ("story") of the case are the critical starting point in reading and analyzing cases. Way back in 1959, one of my favorite law professors told us almost every day: "Remember, cases are stories, stories with a point. You can't get the point if you don't know the story." He also told us something else I think will help you: "Forget you're lawyers. Tell me the story as if you were telling it to your grandmother who doesn't know anything about the law." Take Professor Hill's advice. I do, because it's still pretty good after all these years.

There are two types of relevant facts in criminal procedure cases: acts by government officials and the objective basis for the actions. The **government officials' acts** are the actions that defendants claim violated the Constitution. List each act by the government accurately and in chronological order. Also, include circumstances surrounding the acts. I recommend that you put each act and circumstance on a separate line of your brief. Think of them as notes for a story that you're going to tell someone who doesn't know anything about what government officials did and the circumstances surrounding the acts.

The **objective basis** (also called the **quantum of proof**) refers to the facts and circumstances that back up the government officials' action. As you'll learn over and over in your study of criminal procedure, government officials can't restrict your freedom of movement or your privacy on a **hunch** (also known as **mere suspicion**); they have to justify their actions by facts and circumstances that back up their actions. For example, a law enforcement officer can't back up patting you down by claiming she had a "hunch" you were carrying a gun. But she can back it up by saying there was a bulge at your waist inside your shirt that resembled the shape of a gun.

Constitutional (legal) question

The point of the case stories is the constitutional question they raise. For example, "Was ordering the passenger Jimmy Lee Wilson out of the car stopped for speeding a 'reasonable' Fourth Amendment seizure?" (*Maryland v. Wilson*, Chapter 4).

Judgment (disposition) of the case

The **court's judgment (disposition)** is the most important *legal* action of the court; it's the court's official decision in the case. In the trial court, the judgments are almost always guilty or not guilty. In appeals courts, the judgments are that the lower court's decision/judgment is "affirmed," "reversed," or "reversed and remanded." (See below for definitions.)

Court opinion

Court opinions explain the court's judgment, namely, why the court decided and disposed of the case the way it did. The opinion contains two essential ingredients:

1. Holding of the court. The **court holding** refers to the legal rule the court applied to the facts of the case.

2. Reasoning of the court. The **court reasoning** refers to the reasons and arguments the court gives to support its holding.

Appellate courts, whether federal or state, can issue four types of opinions:

1. **Majority opinion.** The U.S. Supreme Court consists of nine justices, each of whom has a vote and the right to submit an opinion. The majority opinion is the law. In most cases, five justices make up the majority. Sometimes, fewer than nine justices participate; in these cases, the majority can be less than five.

2. **Concurring opinion.** Concurring opinions occur when judges agree with the conclusions of other judges in the case but rely on different reasons to reach the same conclusion.

3. **Plurality opinions.** If a majority of the justices agree with the decision in a case but they can't agree on the reasons, the opinion with the reasoning agreed to by

the largest number of justices is called the plurality opinion. For example, suppose that seven justices agree with the result and four give one set of reasons, three give another set of reasons, and two dissent. The opinion to which the four subscribe is the plurality opinion. A plurality opinion is a weak precedent.

4. **Dissenting opinion**. If justices don't agree with the court's decision and/or its reasoning, they can write their own dissenting opinions explaining why they don't agree with the majority's or plurality's reasoning, their decision, or both. Often, the dissenting opinions point to the future; many majority opinions of today are based on dissents from the past. The late Chief Justice Charles Evans Hughes once said a dissent should be "an appeal to the brooding spirit of the law, to the intelligence of a future day" (Lewis 1994, A13).

Courts don't have to write opinions. Many times (and in trial courts in almost every case) they don't. As students and teachers this is our loss (or maybe to you it's a blessing). The judgment of the case is the only binding action of the court. It states what's going to happen to the judgment of the court below and, ultimately, to the defendant or convicted offender. Common judgments in criminal cases include affirmed, reversed, or reversed and remanded.

1. Affirmed. **Affirmed** means the appellate court upheld a lower court's judgment.
2. Reversed and/or remanded. **Reversed** means the appellate court set aside, or nullified, the lower court's judgment. **Remanded** means that the appellate court sent the case back to the lower court for further action.

Notice that neither *reversed* nor *remanded* means that the defendant "walks" automatically. Fewer than half the defendants who win their cases in the U.S. Supreme Court ultimately triumph when their cases are reversed and/or remanded to lower courts, particularly to state courts. For example, in the famous *Miranda v. Arizona* case (Chapter 8), the prison gates didn't open for Ernesto Miranda. He was detained in jail while he was retried without the confession he made, promptly convicted, and sent from jail to prison.

The conflicting arguments and reasoning in the majority, plurality, concurring, and dissenting opinions challenge you to think about the issues in the cases, because, most of the time, all the justices argue their views of the case convincingly. First the majority opinion, then the concurring opinion(s), and finally the dissenting opinion(s) present arguments that will sway your opinion one way and then another. This is good. It teaches you that there's more than one reasonable position on all the important issues in the law of criminal procedure. Reasonable people do disagree!

LO 8   Precedent and Stare Decisis

You'll notice that court opinions refer to past cases to back up their reasons and their decision in the present case. These prior decisions are called **precedent**. They're part of the way lawyers think. The ancient and firmly entrenched doctrine called **stare decisis** commands judges to follow their precedents.

But stare decisis only binds judges to the prior decisions of either their own court or of courts superior to theirs in their own jurisdiction. **Jurisdiction** refers to the power to hear and decide cases in a specific geographical area (such as a county, a state, or a federal district) *or* dealing with a specific subject (for example, criminal appeals) that the court controls.

U.S. Supreme Court Justice and eloquent judicial philosopher Benjamin Cardozo (1921) once said this about precedent and the doctrine of stare decisis:

> It is easier to follow the beaten track than it is to clear another. In doing this, I shall be treading in the footsteps of my predecessors, and illustrating the process that I am seeking to describe, since the power of precedent, when analyzed, is the power of the beaten path. (62)

The idea of precedent isn't special to the law of criminal procedure, nor is it the basis only of legal reasoning (Schauer 1987, 571). We're accustomed to the basic notion of precedent in ordinary life. We like to do things the way we've done them in the past. For example, if a professor asks multiple-choice questions covering only material in the text on three exams, you expect multiple-choice questions on the fourth exam. If you get an essay exam instead, you won't like it. Not only won't you like it; you'll probably think it's unfair. Why? Because precedent—the way we've done things before—makes life stable and predictable.

Knowing what to expect, and counting on it, guides our actions in the future so we can plan for and meet challenges and solve problems. Changing this without warning is unfair. In ordinary life, then, as in criminal procedure, following past practice gives stability, predictability, and a sense of fairness and justice to decisions.

Of course, doing things the way we've always done them isn't always right or good. When we need to, we change (admittedly often reluctantly) and do things differently. These changes themselves become guides to future action—so, too, with legal precedent. Courts occasionally change precedent but not often, and then only reluctantly.

Courts, like individuals in ordinary life, don't like to change, particularly when they have to admit they were wrong. That's why, as you read the case excerpts, you'll rarely find a court that comes right out and says, "We were wrong, so we overrule our prior decision." Instead, when courts decide to get off the beaten path, they do it by **distinguishing cases**, meaning that a court decides that a prior decision doesn't apply to the current case because the facts are different. For example, the rule that controls the right to a lawyer in death penalty cases doesn't have to apply to a case punishable by a fine. As the Court has noted, "Death is different" (Schauer 1987, 571).

Appellate Court Cases

Most of the cases in this textbook are appellate court cases. In **appellate court cases**, a lower court has already taken some action in the case and one of the parties has asked a higher court to review the lower court's action. Parties seek appellate review of what they claim were errors by the trial court or unlawful actions by police, judges, prosecutors, or defense lawyers.

Only defendants can appeal convictions; the government can never appeal acquittals. However, many appellate reviews arise out of proceedings before trial and convictions. Both the government and the defendant can appeal **pretrial proceedings**. Most appellate cases in this book arise out of defendants' motions to throw out evidence obtained by law enforcement officers during searches and seizures, interrogation, and identification procedures, such as lineups. These motions are heard in a proceeding called a **suppression hearing**.

Courts call parties in appellate courts by different names. The most common parties in the appellate courts are the **appellant** (the party appealing) and the **appellee** (the party appealed against). Both of these terms originate from the word *appeal*.

In the excerpts of older cases, you'll find other names for the parties. The older cases refer to the "plaintiff in error," the party that claims the lower courts erred in their rulings, and to the "defendant in error," the party who won in the lower court. These names stem from an old and no longer used writ called the "writ of error."

Review by Petition

A **petitioner** is a defendant in a noncriminal case. The petitioner asks the higher court to review a decision made by either a lower court or some other official. The two main petitions you'll encounter in case excerpts are habeas corpus, Latin for "you have the body," and certiorari, Latin for "to be certified." Let's look at each.

Habeas corpus

Called a **collateral attack** because it's a separate proceeding from the criminal case, **habeas corpus** is a **civil action** (a noncriminal proceeding) that reviews the constitutionality of the petitioner's detention or imprisonment. You can recognize these proceedings by their title. Instead of the name of a state or the United States, you'll see two individuals' names, such as in *Adams v. Williams* (excerpted in Chapter 4). Williams, a state prisoner, sued Adams, the warden of the prison where Williams was held. Williams petitioned the court to order Adams to prove that Williams was being imprisoned lawfully.

Certiorari

Most appeals to the U.S. Supreme Court are based on **certiorari**. Certiorari is a proceeding in the U.S. Supreme Court to review decisions of lower courts. These proceedings begin when petitioners ask for reviews of court decisions.

The Court doesn't grant certiorari to prevent the punishment of innocent defendants. Petitioners would get nowhere if their petitions read, "I'm innocent; they convicted the wrong person." As a legal matter, the Court isn't interested in whether individual defendants are innocent or guilty; that's the job of the lower courts. The Supreme Court grants certiorari because a case raises an important constitutional issue that affects large numbers of individuals; in a sense, the defendant in the case reviewed represents these other individuals.

Granting certiorari is wholly discretionary, and the Court grants it—that is, it issues a **writ of certiorari** (an order to the court that decided the case to send up the record of its proceedings to the U.S. Supreme Court for review)—in only a tiny percentage of petitions. Four of the nine Supreme Court justices have to vote to review a case, a requirement known as the **rule of four**, before the Court will hear an appeal by issuing a writ of certiorari.

CHAPTER SUMMARY

LO 1 The criminal procedure road map is intricate, but the journey begins at the same spot: public spaces, such as streets, malls, restaurants, bars, and other businesses open to the public, where police officers investigate individuals' suspicious behavior. Although most individuals will end their journey here, some will be arrested, interrogated, and detained against their will. Very few will be convicted of a serious crime.

LO 1, 5 A citizen progresses through the criminal justice system via discretionary decision making from criminal justice professionals. Think of each leg of the journey as a decision point at which a criminal justice professional has the choice to start, continue, or end the criminal process. Discretion and law complement each other in promoting and balancing constitutional interests and demands.

LO 2 At the heart of our constitutional democracy is the idea of balancing values essential to the quality of life. One balance is between the value of the safety and security of the whole community and the value of individual autonomy, consisting of life, liberty, property, privacy, and dignity. The balance between crime control and individual rights is not fixed, however; exactly where the balance is struck shifts to accommodate current circumstances and public demands. Where it's struck is contested—sometimes hotly—and never satisfies everyone.

LO 3, 4 Fairness and equality are also highly valued principles in U.S. society that the criminal justice system has to balance accordingly. As a constitutional democracy, we don't believe in punishing criminals at any costs. We support the need to balance fair and impartial procedures for individuals against the government's power to control crime. Historically rooted in racial discrimination still apparent today, equality in criminal procedure is influenced by a plethora of external factors, such as race, sex, and socioeconomic status.

LO 6 The new generation of criminal procedure calls for accurate, reliable, impartial empirical and social scientific evidence primarily aimed at answering two questions: How effective are crime-controlling practices and what is their effect on individual liberty and privacy? As a compelling example, DNA exonerations conclusively demonstrate that our criminal justice system has wrongfully convicted innocent citizens. The exonerations we know about may be only the "tip of the iceberg," so we must not only remember the innocents, but also be aware of any possible shortcomings in the data presented to us.

LO 7 Two types of facts are relevant to criminal procedure cases: (1) acts by government officials and (2) the objective basis for the actions. The officials' acts refer to any action(s) that defendants claim violated their constitutional rights, as well as any relevant circumstances surrounding those acts. The objective basis (quantum of proof) refers to the facts and circumstances that back up the government officials' action; a "hunch" or "mere suspicion" alone is never justification for government officials to restrict your freedom of locomotion or privacy.

LO 8 Throughout the book, you'll notice that court opinions refer to past cases to support their reasoning and their decisions. This reliance on prior cases (precedent) is part of how lawyers think. Related to reliance on precedent is the doctrine of stare decisis, which requires courts to follow precedent in their decisions. Distinguishing cases can be thought of as outliers because a court has decided that a prior decision does not apply to the distinguishing case because the facts are different.

REVIEW QUESTIONS

1. Identify and describe the "highest ideal" of criminal procedure in the United States.
2. Identify and describe the difference between crime control for a police state, a pure democracy, and a constitutional democracy.

3. Identify the stages of the day-to-day operations of criminal procedure, which crime control agencies and officials control these operations, and the kind of law that controls their monopoly.

4. What does it mean to say that the Constitution leaves plenty of "play in the joints" in the criminal procedure process?

5. Describe how each leg of the criminal procedure journey is a "decision point" and identify the choices that criminal justice officials have at these decision points.

6. Who makes most constitutional law in the United States?

7. Describe the two elements of balancing community security and individual autonomy. Describe an argument supporting each side of the balance.

8. What does it mean to say that the proper balance between community safety and individual autonomy is a "spectrum"? Describe the extreme example of wartime as it relates to this balance.

9. To whom do the rules we make to control crime apply? Why is it important to remind yourself of the answer to this question?

10. Describe the two values balanced in the goal of fairness in the U.S. criminal justice system. Summarize the positions of Judge Learned Hand and Professor Joseph Goldstein to illustrate these values.

11. Explain the significance of racial discrimination in the history of U.S. criminal procedure as it relates to the principle of equal justice.

12. What does "Hunches are never enough" mean?

13. What does "a new generation of criminal procedure" mean? Identify and describe the two empirical questions used to assess the constitutional balancing approach.

14. Describe the empirical research surrounding wrongful convictions and innocence. Explain what is meant by the phrase, "the tip of the innocents iceberg" as it relates to criminal procedure.

15. Describe the significance of precedent as it relates to criminal procedure and everyday life.

KEY TERMS

text-case method, p. 4
appellate courts, p. 6
law in the books, p. 6
law in action, p. 6
constitutional democracy, p. 6
community security, p. 7
individual autonomy, p. 7
new generation of criminal
   procedure, p. 11
text-case book, p. 16
case citation, p. 18
United States Reports, p. 18
The Federal Reporter, p. 18
procedural history of the case, p. 18
government officials' acts, p. 19

objective basis (quantum of proof),
   p. 19
hunch (mere suspicion), p. 19
court's judgment (disposition), p. 19
court opinions, p. 19
court holding, p. 19
court reasoning, p. 19
majority opinion, p. 19
concurring opinion, p. 19
plurality opinion, p. 19
dissenting opinion, p. 20
affirmed, p. 20
reversed, p. 20
remanded, p. 20
precedent, p. 20

stare decisis, p. 20
jurisdiction, p. 20
distinguishing cases, p. 21
appellate court cases, p. 21
pretrial proceedings, p. 21
suppression hearing, p. 21
appellant, p. 21
appellee, p. 21
petitioner, p. 22
collateral attack, p. 22
habeas corpus, p. 22
civil action, p. 22
certiorari, p. 22
writ of certiorari, p. 22
rule of four, p. 22

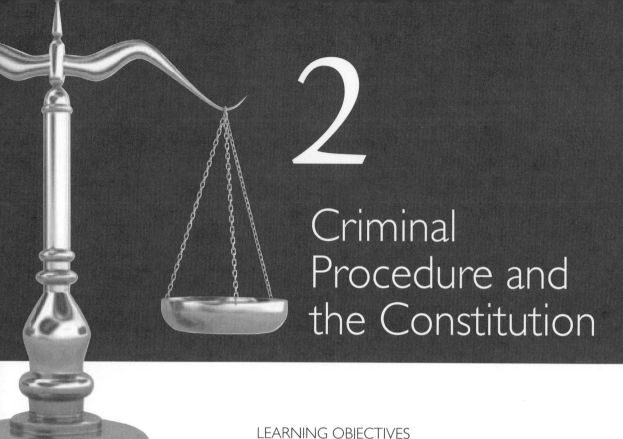

2

Criminal Procedure and the Constitution

CASE COVERED

Rochin v. California
342 U.S. 165 (1952)

LEARNING OBJECTIVES

1 Know and appreciate that in our constitutional democracy, constitutions adopted by the whole people are the highest form of law; the final authority of criminal procedure lies in the U.S. Constitution, especially in the Bill of Rights.

2 Know and appreciate that, although all criminal procedures have to answer to the U.S. Constitution, it's up to the courts to interpret the Constitution. Ultimately, the U.S. Supreme Court's interpretation trumps the interpretation of all other courts.

3 Know that every state constitution guarantees its citizens parallel criminal procedure rights. Understand that state constitutions can increase criminal procedure rights, but can't reduce them below the federal minimum standard defined by the U.S. Supreme Court.

4 Understand and appreciate that the struggle to define due process is historically rooted in the controversial issues of states' rights and equal rights for all citizens. Gradually, the U.S. Supreme Court expanded the meaning of criminal procedure rights within the federal system, and ruled that most of these rights apply to state and local criminal justice, too.

5 Know, understand, and appreciate that after a decades-long struggle, a Supreme Court majority came to agree that "due process" requires the incorporation of the specific criminal procedure provisions in the U.S. Bill of Rights; and that incorporation changed day-to-day criminal procedure by expanding its intervention from the courtroom to public space and not-so-public police stations.

6 Understand that although equality is a fundamental principle and a constitutional command in our constitutional democracy, the heavy burden of proving claims that government officials denied equal protection falls on the individual.

7 Understand and appreciate that the tension between crime control and individual liberty is an ancient controversy. The history of this tension has swung like a pendulum back and forth, between more emphasis on providing the government with enough power to enforce criminal law and guaranteeing individual autonomy and privacy.

8 Know and appreciate that the dualistic, political nature of the U.S. Supreme Court reflects U.S. society, committed at the same time to two opposing principles—fundamental law and popular sovereignty.

The Supreme Court has failed to hold true the balance between the right of society to convict the guilty and the obligation of society to safeguard the accused." A Commission [should be appointed "to determine whether the overriding public interest in law enforcement . . . requires a constitutional amendment."

—Assistant Attorney General William Rehnquist (1969)

LO 1

"We must never forget that it is a constitution we are expounding," Chief Justice John Marshall wrote in the great case of *McCulloch v. Maryland* (1819). The chief justice was referring to a deeply embedded idea in our constitutional democracy—the idea of **constitutionalism**. The core of the idea is that constitutions adopted by the whole people are a higher form of law than ordinary laws passed by legislatures. Constitutions are forever; ordinary laws are for now. Laws are detailed, constantly changing rules passed by legislatures; constitutions are a set of permanent (or at least very hard to change), general principles. We can boil down the difference between laws and constitutions into six contrasting characteristics (Gardner 1991, 814):

1. Constitutions are a higher form of law that speak with a political authority that no ordinary law or other government action can ever match.
2. Constitutions express the will of the whole people.
3. Constitutions always bind the government.
4. Constitutions can't be changed by the government.
5. Only the direct action of the whole people can change constitutions.
6. Constitutions embody the fundamental values of the people.

The **law of criminal procedure** consists of the principles and rules that government has to follow to detect and investigate crimes; apprehend suspects; prosecute and convict defendants; and punish criminals. The ultimate source, and the one you'll most often encounter throughout this book, is the U.S. Constitution, particularly the criminal procedure clauses in the Bill of Rights. Equally important are the rules generated by U.S. Supreme Court cases that interpret the Constitution's criminal procedure rights.

Occasionally, you'll also learn about criminal procedure law from other sources, including

1. Other federal sources
   a. U.S. courts of appeals and the U.S. district courts
   b. Federal statutes
   c. Rules of federal law enforcement agencies (the FBI, for example)
   d. Rules of procedure formulated by the U.S. Supreme Court
2. State sources
   a. State constitutions
   b. State courts
   c. State statutes
   d. Rules of state and local law enforcement agencies
3. The American Law Institute (hereafter ALI) **Model Code of Pre-Arraignment Procedure** (1975). ALI is a group of distinguished judges, lawyers, criminal justice professionals, law enforcement professionals, and scholars. As its title makes clear, the Model Code is not law, it's a *model* of pretrial procedures for law enforcement and courts.

The U.S. Constitution is the highest authority in criminal procedure; it's what we call a **court of last resort**, meaning its decisions trump the authority of all other sources of criminal procedure. The body of the Constitution guarantees two criminal procedure rights:

1. **Habeas corpus** (Article I, § 9) the right of individuals to challenge any government detention.
2. Trial by jury in the community where crimes were committed.

The criminal procedure rights are set out in the amendments to the U.S. Constitution known as the Bill of Rights. The Fourth, Fifth, Sixth, Eighth, and Fourteenth Amendments contain 20 guarantees to persons suspected of, charged with, and convicted of crimes (Table 2.1). For

TABLE 2.1 Criminal procedure rights in the U.S. Constitution

Fourth Amendment
1. The right to be free from unreasonable searches
2. The right to be free from unreasonable seizures
3. The right to probable cause to back up searches and seizures

Fifth Amendment
4. The right to grand jury indictment* (federal cases only)
5. The right against double jeopardy
6. The right to due process* (federal cases only, but see 19)
7. The right against self-incrimination

Sixth Amendment
8. The right to a speedy trial
9. The right to a public trial
10. The right to an impartial jury
11. The right to have a jury made up of persons from the state and district where the crime was committed* (federal cases only)
12. The right to be informed of the charges against the accused
13. The right to confront witnesses against the accused
14. The right to a compulsory process to obtain witnesses in favor of the accused
15. The right of the accused to defense counsel

Eighth Amendment
16. The right against excessive bail
17. The right against excessive fines* (federal cases and probably states)
18. The right against cruel and unusual punishment

Fourteenth Amendment
19. The right to due process of law in state criminal proceedings
20. The right to equal protection of the law in state criminal proceedings

rights definitely or probably applied to the states by incorporation under the Fourteenth Amendment due process clause (See the Appendix for the full text of these amendments.)

© Cengage Learning

most of U.S. history, the guarantees listed in Table 2.1 applied only to the federal government's power and actions. But in a series of U.S. Supreme Court cases in the 1960s, the Court decided that most of the criminal procedure rights apply to state and local governments, too.

In this chapter, we'll look at the U.S. Constitution and the principle of judicial review; state constitutions and the authority of state courts; the meaning of due process of law; and equal protection of the law.

THE U.S. CONSTITUTION AND THE COURTS

LO 2

Article VI of the U.S Constitution commands that:

This Constitution, and the laws of the United States which shall be made in pursuance thereof; and all treaties made, or which shall be made, under the authority of the United States, shall be the supreme law of the land; and the judges in every state shall be bound thereby, anything in the Constitution or laws of any State to the contrary notwithstanding.

Sounds simple enough, but there's a huge problem: The meanings of some of the Constitution's most important criminal procedure provisions are vague and ambiguous. Also, unfortunately, the drafters didn't leave us a "User's Guide." How then, do legislators, judges, and law enforcement officers (and you and me) know what they mean? Finally, in this and the remaining chapters you'll learn that the meanings were, and still are, hotly contested.

Let's look at the answer to the necessary preliminary question, Who gets the last word in these contests? Chief Justice John Marshall answered the question in *Marbury v. Madison* (1803). Writing for the Court, Marshall established what courts later called the **principle of judicial review**. According to that principle, the U.S. Supreme Court's interpretation trumps the interpretation of all other courts, federal and local, and of Congress and all state and local legislatures. (As you'll soon learn, on page 31, states have the last word in interpreting their state constitution.)

To recap, the **Supremacy Clause** in Article VI together with judicial review establish that all criminal procedures have to answer to the U.S. Constitution, and courts determine which procedures are in line with the Constitution. All courts can interpret the Constitution, but the U.S. Supreme Court has the last word. Its decisions bind all other courts, legislatures, executives, and criminal justice officials.

Despite this enormous power, you need to know two important limits on the Supreme Court's power. First, the U.S. Constitution and Supreme Court are at the top of a pyramid with a very wide state and local base of criminal justice administration. So, in the vast real world where most of the action is—law enforcement officers' contacts with individuals on the street and at the police station; and to a lesser extent, prosecutors' and defense counsel's negotiations—the Supreme Court has to rely on professionals far removed from its high chambers to carry out its decisions. In other words, the Court can command (judge) but has no power to enforce its commands because there's no Supreme Court Police Department. President Jackson allegedly put it this way when he refused to enforce one of the Court's decisions he disagreed with. "Chief Justice Marshall has made his decision, now let him enforce it" (Greeley 1864, I, 106).

Second, in the real world of criminal justice, lower federal courts (and more frequently *state trial courts*) have the final word. According to Professor Anthony Amsterdam, who represented countless criminal defendants and argued numerous cases before the Supreme Court,

> When and if the Supreme Court ventures to announce some constitutional right of a suspect, that "right" filters down to the level of flesh and blood suspects only through the refracting layers of lower courts, trial judges, magistrates and police officials. All pronouncements of the Supreme Court undergo this filtering process, but in few other areas of the law are the filters as opaque as in the area of suspects' rights. (1970, 791–92)

One final point: The U.S. Supreme Court has more power over criminal procedure in lower federal courts than it does over state courts. Why? Because it has **supervisory power** over them—that is, the power to make rules to manage how lower federal courts conduct their business. The Court can only control the law of criminal procedure in state courts if the states' rules violate the U.S. Constitution. Many procedures (some of them very important for defendants and the state) don't violate the U.S. Constitution.

STATE CONSTITUTIONS AND STATE COURTS

LO 2, 3

Every state constitution guarantees its citizens **parallel rights**—rights identical or similar to those in the U.S. Constitution and the Bill of Rights. For example, every state constitution guarantees rights against self-incrimination and unreasonable searches and seizures, as well as the right to counsel and to jury trial. In addition to parallel rights, some state constitutions provide additional rights not specifically mentioned in the U.S. Constitution, such as the right to privacy.

State courts are a source of criminal procedure law in two types of cases: (1) those that involve the U.S. Constitution that the U.S. Supreme Court hasn't decided yet and (2) those involving their own state constitutions. In cases that involve the U.S. Constitution, state court decisions aren't final, so they can be appealed to federal courts. Many cases excerpted in this book started in state courts and ended in the U.S. Supreme Court. But remember that in the real world of criminal procedure, most cases never get past state courts.

State courts are the final authority in cases based on their own state constitutions and statutes. The federal courts—even the U.S. Supreme Court—can't interpret state constitutions and statutes unless the state provisions and state courts interpreting them fail to meet the *minimum* standards set by the U.S. Constitution. In referring to this federal rights floor, a Supreme Court justice once said, "It doesn't pay a law much of a compliment to declare it constitutional." In other words, individual states are free to raise the minimum, and sometimes they do, but they're banned from lowering the floor.

DUE PROCESS OF LAW

LO 4

From colonial times until the Civil War, criminal justice was solely the responsibility of local governments. As early as 1833, Chief Justice John Marshall wrote that the question of whether the Bill of Rights extended to the states was "of great importance, but not of much difficulty" (*Barron v. Baltimore* 1833, 247).

> Had Congress [which proposed the Bill of Rights] engaged in the extraordinary occupation of improving the constitutions of the several states by affording the people additional protection from the exercise of power by their own governments in matters which concerned themselves alone, they would have declared this purpose "in plain and intelligible language" (250).

The Civil War changed all that. A main goal of the war was to establish federal supremacy over states' rights. The Union army's crushing defeat of the Confederate army on the battlefield vindicated the supremacy on the battlefield. The three Civil War amendments to the U.S. Constitution codified this supremacy, placing them beyond the power of ordinary laws. Two guarantees in the Fourteenth Amendment are our concern here.

> No state shall . . . deprive any citizen of life, liberty, or property without due process of law; nor deny to any person within its jurisdiction the equal protection of the laws.

The drafters of the amendment left the definitions of due process and equal protection vague. They left them vague, not by accident or negligence, but on purpose. You should already know why: They were writing *constitutional* provisions, not ordinary laws. The other reason is rooted in the history of the time: States' rights and equality were enormously controversial issues. No matter how decisive the Union *military* victory and the Confederate defeat, military force couldn't guarantee the triumph of the great principles for which millions had fought and died (Nelson 1988, Chapter 2). Don't forget this early history. It will help you to appreciate the struggle to define the due process and equal protection guarantees from the Civil War until today, when we're still struggling to define and apply them.

LO 5 The Meaning of Due Process

How do the courts, particularly the U.S. Supreme Court, define **due process**? Some courts lean on the "process" part, contending that due process guarantees fair procedures for deciding cases. (Tip: When you see "due process," think "fair procedures.")

What fair procedures does due process guarantee? The Bill of Rights lists several. Are these the specific ones due process guarantees? Yes, say some experts. According to these experts, the authors of the Bill of Rights were codifying a specific list of hard-fought and proudly won procedures to protect private persons against government excesses.

Other experts disagree. They maintain that if due process is just shorthand for "Bill of Rights," then the Fourteenth Amendment due process clause is wasted language, because the Fifth Amendment already includes a due process clause, "No person shall be denied life, liberty, or property without due process of law" (*Adamson v. California* 1947).

Besides, they say, the framers wouldn't have frozen criminal procedure at a particular 18th-century moment. According to Justice Matthews, in *Hurtado v. California* 1884, adhering only to provisions in the Bill of Rights would freeze the law in 1789 when it was written. But the authors of the Constitution and the due process clause wrote them for an unknown and growing future, full of "new and various experiences" that will mold it into new and "useful forms" (530).

But Justice John Marshall Harlan, the lone dissenter in *Hurtado*, argued that the Fourteenth Amendment due process clause "imposed upon the states the same restrictions, in respect of proceedings involving life, liberty, and property, which had been imposed upon the general government" (541).

Lawyers tried more than once to get the Court to see things the way Justice Harlan did. But the Court stuck steadfastly (some say stubbornly) to its position that state criminal procedure was a local matter and none of the U.S. government's business.

LO 4, 5 Early Application of Due Process to State Cases

Then came the German war machine of World War I, and the rise of fascism and other totalitarian governments that followed in its wake during the 1920s and 1930s. These developments revived old American suspicions of arbitrary government. It was probably no coincidence that the U.S. Supreme Court first applied the Fourteenth Amendment due process clause to state criminal procedures in a case it decided just as Hitler was rising to power in Nazi Germany (Allen 1978, 157–58). Let's look in some detail at the two landmark cases that began the federal government's gradual entry into state criminal justice.

The "Scottsboro boys," due process, and the right to counsel

That first case began in northern Alabama on a March morning in 1931 when seven scruffy White boys came into a railway station in northern Alabama and told the stationmaster that a "bunch of Negroes" had picked a fight with them and thrown them off a freight train. The stationmaster phoned ahead to Scottsboro, where a deputy sheriff deputized every man who owned a gun to form a posse. When the train got to Scottsboro, the posse rounded up nine Black boys and two White girls. The girls were dressed in men's caps and overalls. Five of the boys were from Georgia and four from Tennessee. They ranged in age from 12 to 20. One was blind in one eye and had only 10 percent vision in the other; one walked with a cane; all were poor and illiterate.

After the deputy sheriff had tied the boys together and was loading them into his truck, Ruby Bates told the sheriff that the boys had raped her and her friend, Victoria Price. By nightfall, a mob of several hundred people had surrounded the tiny Scottsboro jail, vowing to lynch the boys to avenge the rape.

When the trial began on Monday morning, April 6, 1931, 102 National Guardsmen struggled to keep several thousand people at least 100 feet away from the courthouse. Inside the courtroom, Judge Alfred E. Hawkins offered the job of defense attorney to anyone who would take it. Only Chattanooga lawyer Stephen Roddy—an alcoholic already drunk at 9:00 a.m.—who admitted he didn't know anything about Alabama law, accepted. Judge Hawkins then appointed as defense counsel "all members" of the local bar present in the courtroom.

By Thursday, eight of the boys had been tried, convicted, and sentenced to death. Only 12-year-old Roy Wright remained because the jury hung, with seven demanding death and five holding out for life imprisonment. Judge Hawkins declared a mistrial in Roy Wright's trial and sentenced the others to death by electrocution.

Liberals, radicals, and communists around the country rallied to the defense of the "Scottsboro boys," as the defendants became popularly known. In March 1932, the Alabama Supreme Court upheld all of the convictions except for that of Eugene Williams, who was granted a new trial as a juvenile. In November, the U.S. Supreme Court ruled in *Powell v. Alabama* (1932) that Alabama had denied the boys due process of law.

According to Justice Sutherland, there are exceptions to the sweeping rule in *Hurtado* that the criminal procedure amendments in the Bill of Rights don't apply to states. If ,under "compelling considerations," denying a right in the Bill of Rights violates "fundamental principles of liberty and justice which lie at the base of all our civil and political institutions," then it's "embraced within the due process clause of the Fourteenth Amendment." Under the facts of this case, the right to a lawyer is "of this fundamental character."

What facts? The Court focused on these six:

1. The ignorance and illiteracy of the defendants

2. Their youth

3. The public hostility

4. The imprisonment and the close surveillance of the defendants by the military forces

5. That the defendants' friends and families were all in other states, making communication with them difficult

6. Above all, that they stood in deadly peril of their lives (64–71)

Two members of the Court dissented. Justices James McReynolds and Pierce Butler argued that the record in the case failed to show that the proceedings denied the "Scottsboro boys" any *federal* constitutional right (76–77).

Brown v. Mississippi, *due process, and coerced confessions*

With monsters like Hitler, Stalin, Mussolini, and Franco in the background cowing, torturing, and mass murdering their own people, the Court soon revisited oversight of state criminal justice in the United States. In 1936, the Court inched ahead the process of applying the due process clause to state criminal proceedings in *Brown v. Mississippi* (1936).

On the night of March 30, 1934, a deputy sheriff named Dial and several other White men came to Yank Ellington's house and took him to a dead White man's house. There, they accused Ellington, a Black man, of murdering Raymond Stewart, the dead White man. When he denied it, they grabbed him, and with the deputy's help, they hanged him by a rope to the limb of a tree, let him down, hanged him again, and let him down a second time. He still protested his innocence, so they tied him to a tree and whipped him. Still, he refused to confess. Finally, they released him. With difficulty, he got home, "suffering intense pain and agony" (281).

The next day, the deputy and another man returned to Ellington's house and arrested him. On the way to jail, the deputy stopped and severely whipped him, telling Ellington that "he would continue the whipping until he confessed." Ellington agreed to whatever statement "the deputy would dictate." He signed, and they locked him up (281–82).

Two other "ignorant negroes," Ed Brown and Henry Shields, were also arrested and locked up in the same jail. On Sunday night, April 1, 1934, Deputy Dial, another officer, the jailer, and other White men forced Brown and Shields to strip, laid them over chairs, and "their backs were cut to pieces with a leather strap with buckles on it." Deputy Dial made clear to them that the whipping would continue "unless and until they confessed in every matter of detail" that the men demanded. They confessed, and, as the whipping continued, they "changed or adjusted their confession in all particulars of detail so as to conform to the demands of their torturers" (281–82).

When the "mob" got the confessions in "the exact form and contents" they wanted, they left, warning that if the defendants changed their story they'd be back to "administer the same or equally effective treatment" (281–82).

The next day, eight men, including the sheriff and other deputies, came to the jail to "hear the free and voluntary confession of these miserable and abject defendants" (282).

On April 5, the fake trial began. It ended the next day with a "pretended conviction with death sentences." The Mississippi Supreme Court affirmed the convictions.

The U.S. Supreme Court (7–2) reversed their convictions. In his majority opinion Chief Justice Charles Evans Hughes noted that the trial "transcript reads more like pages torn from some medieval account than a record made within the confines of a modern civilization which aspires to an enlightened constitutional government" (283). But when asked how severely they beat Ellington, Deputy Dial replied, "Not too much for a negro; not as much as I would have done if it were left to me" (284–85). During the trial, the sheriff admitted that one defendant was limping as he came to confess, and he didn't sit down. According to the defendant, he was "strapped so severely that he could not sit down." The sheriff also admitted that the "signs of the rope on the neck of another of the defendants were plainly visible to all" (282). Chief Justice Hughes wrote:

> The state is free to regulate the procedure of its courts in accordance with its own conceptions of policy, unless in so doing it "offends some principle of justice so rooted in the traditions and conscience of our people as to be ranked as fundamental." . . . The rack and torture chamber may not be substituted for the witness stand. The state may not permit an accused to be hurried to conviction under mob domination—where the whole proceeding is but a mask—without supplying corrective process.
>
> It would be difficult to conceive of methods more revolting to the sense of justice than those taken to procure the confessions of these petitioners, and the use of the confessions thus obtained as the basis for conviction and sentence was a clear denial of due process. (285–86)

LO 5 The Fundamental Fairness Doctrine

Powell v. Alabama and *Brown v. Mississippi* established what came to be called the **fundamental fairness doctrine of due process**. According to the doctrine, due process is a command to the states to provide two basics of a fair trial:

1. Notice to defendants of the charges against them
2. A hearing on the facts before convicting and punishing defendants

The doctrine leaves it up to the individual states to determine the specifics of notice and hearing. From the 1930s through the 1950s, except for cases of extreme physical brutality like *Brown* and *Powell*, where Mississippi and Alabama provided no real hearing at all, a majority of the Court continued to reject the claim that the specific rights guaranteed by the Bill of Rights applied to state criminal justice.

In *Palko v. Connecticut* (1937), "one of the most influential [opinions] in the history of the court," Justice Cardozo conceded that the Bill of Rights *might* include *some* of these fundamental rights. *Palko* asked whether double jeopardy was one of them. Justice Cardozo asked the question in two parts:

1. Did exposing Frank Palko to double jeopardy subject him to a hardship so shocking that our polity will not endure it?
2. Does it violate those "fundamental principles of liberty and justice which lie at the base of all our civil and political institutions"?

The justice answered no to both questions (328).

Justice Felix Frankfurter, the strongest defender of fundamental fairness, tried to capture its essence in two phrases:

1. Procedures that "offend the community's sense of fair play and decency" [*Rochin v. California* 1952, 173 (excerpt p. 37)], and the more evocative
2. "Conduct that shocks the conscience" (172).

LO 5 The Incorporation Doctrine

During the 1940s and 1950s, all the justices came to accept the idea that the Bill of Rights imposes limits on state criminal procedure. But they disagreed hotly over exactly what those limits are. A growing minority on the Court came to reject the fundamental fairness doctrine as a means to determine which criminal procedure rights applied to state criminal justice. In its place, they argued for the **incorporation doctrine**, which defined Fourteenth Amendment due process as applying the specific provisions of the Bill of Rights to state criminal procedure.

By the 1960s, incorporation had claimed a majority of the Court as advocates. Part of the explanation was that the Court's membership changed. The leaders of fundamental fairness, Justices Felix Frankfurter and Charles Whittaker, a Frankfurter ally, retired in 1962. President John F. Kennedy replaced them with two incorporationists, Justices Byron R. White and Arthur J. Goldberg.

The fundamental fairness doctrine and the incorporation doctrine differed significantly (see Table 2.2). First, the fundamental fairness doctrine focuses on general fairness, whereas the incorporation doctrine focuses on specific procedures. The proponents of fundamental fairness rely on commentators who traced its origins to the Magna Carta, which they believed had established a flexible standard of justice "less rigid and more fluid" than the rights named in the Bill of Rights (Israel 1982, 274). According to proponents of the fundamental fairness doctrine, due process *might* include *some* specific procedural rights in the Bill of Rights, but, if it does, it's only by chance.

Incorporationists maintain that due process is shorthand for the criminal procedure provisions in the Bill of Rights. According to Justice Hugo L. Black, the doctrine's strongest and most persistent advocate, that due process absorbs every specific right listed in the Bill of Rights (*Duncan v. Louisiana* 1968, 145, 169).

Second, fundamental fairness and incorporation differ in how much uniformity in state and local procedures due process requires. According to the fundamental fairness doctrine, states can define most of their own criminal procedure law. The incorporation doctrine says that the states have to apply the procedures outlined in the Bill of Rights.

When the Court finally adopted the incorporation doctrine, justices continued to disagree strongly over which provisions the Fourteenth Amendment incorporated. A few justices, such as Justice Black, called for **total incorporation**, meaning that all the provisions were incorporated under the due process clause. Most supported the more moderate **selective incorporation doctrine**, meaning that some rights were incorporated and others weren't (Table 2.2).

The conflict over the fundamental fairness and incorporation doctrines was clear in *Rochin v. California* (1952). Although the case was decided before the Court's shift to selective incorporation, it's an excellent example of the two doctrines and how they apply to police actions. Writing for the Court majority, Justice Frankfurter applied the fundamental fairness doctrine but not without spirited dissenting opinions from Justices Black and Douglas, who favored the incorporation doctrine.

TABLE 2.2 Fundamental fairness and total and selective incorporation

Fundamental Fairness	Total Incorporation	Selective Incorporation
General fairness	Entire Bill of Rights incorporated	Some of Bill of Rights incorporated
States define their own provisions	States have to follow procedures exactly as defined by U.S. Supreme Court	States have to follow those procedures defined by U.S. Supreme Court

The conflict over the fundamental fairness and incorporation doctrines is clear in our first

case excerpt, *Rochin v. California* (1952).

CASE

Did the Police Actions "Shock the Conscience"?

Rochin v. California
342 U.S. 165 (1952)

HISTORY

Antonin Rochin was brought to trial before a California superior court, sitting without a jury, on the charge of possessing "a preparation of morphine" in violation of the California Health and Safety Code. Rochin was convicted and sentenced to 60 days' imprisonment. The chief evidence against him were the two capsules. They were admitted over the petitioner's objection.

On appeal, the district court of appeal affirmed the conviction, despite the finding that the officers "were guilty of unlawfully breaking into and entering defendant's room and were guilty of unlawfully assaulting and battering defendant while in the room," and "were guilty of unlawfully assaulting, battering, torturing and falsely imprisoning the defendant at the alleged hospital."

One of the three judges, while finding that "the record in this case reveals a shocking series of violations of constitutional rights," concurred only because he felt bound by decisions of his supreme court. These, he asserted, "have been looked upon by law enforcement officers as an encouragement, if not an invitation, to the commission of such lawless acts." The California Supreme Court denied without opinion Rochin's petition for a hearing. This court granted certiorari, because a serious question was raised as to the limitations which the due process clause of the Fourteenth Amendment imposes on the conduct of criminal proceedings by the states.

—FRANKFURTER, J.

FACTS

Having "some information that Rochin was selling narcotics," three deputy sheriffs of the county of Los Angeles, on the morning of July 1, 1949, made for the two-story house in which Rochin lived with his mother, common-law wife, brothers, and sisters. Finding the outside door open, they entered and then forced open the door to Rochin's room on the second floor. Inside they found petitioner sitting partly dressed on the side of his bed, upon which his wife was lying. On a "night stand" beside the bed the deputies

spied two capsules. When asked, "Whose stuff is this?" Rochin seized the capsules and put them in his mouth. A struggle ensued, in the course of which the three officers "jumped upon him" and attempted to extract the capsules. The force they applied proved unavailing against Rochin's resistance.

He was handcuffed and taken to a hospital. At the direction of one of the officers a doctor forced an emetic solution through a tube into Rochin's stomach against his will. This "stomach pumping" produced vomiting. In the vomited matter were found two capsules which proved to contain morphine.

OPINION

In our federal system the administration of criminal justice is predominantly committed to the care of the States. . . . Broadly speaking, crimes in the United States are what the laws of the individual States make them. . . . Accordingly, in reviewing a State criminal conviction under a claim of right guaranteed by the Due Process Clause of the Fourteenth Amendment . . . we must be deeply mindful of the responsibilities of the States for the enforcement of criminal laws, and exercise with due humility our merely negative function in subjecting convictions from state courts to the very narrow scrutiny which the Due Process Clause of the Fourteenth Amendment authorizes. Due process of law, itself a historical product, is not to be turned into a destructive dogma against the States in the administration of their systems of criminal justice.

However, this Court too has its responsibility. Regard for the requirements of the Due Process Clause inescapably imposes upon this court an exercise of judgment upon the whole course of the proceedings . . . in order to ascertain whether they offend those canons of decency and fairness which express the notions of justice of English speaking peoples even toward those charged with the most heinous offenses. These standards of justice are not authoritatively formulated anywhere as though they

(*continued*)

were specifics. Due process of law is a summarized constitutional guarantee of respect for those personal immunities which are "so rooted in the traditions and conscience of our people as to be ranked as fundamental," or are "implicit in the concept of ordered liberty."

The vague contours of the Due Process Clause do not leave judges at large. We may not draw on our merely personal and private notions and disregard the limits that bind judges in their judicial function. Even though the concept of due process of law is not final and fixed, these limits are derived from considerations that are fused in the whole nature of our judicial process. These are considerations deeply rooted in reason and in the compelling traditions of the legal profession.

The Due Process Clause places upon this Court the duty of exercising a judgment upon interests of society pushing in opposite directions. In each case "due process of law" requires an evaluation based on a detached consideration of conflicting claims, on a judgment duly mindful of reconciling the needs both of continuity and of change in a progressive society.

Applying these general considerations to the circumstances of the present case, we are compelled to conclude that the proceedings by which this conviction was obtained do more than offend some fastidious squeamishness or private sentimentalism about combating crime too energetically. This is conduct that shocks the conscience. Illegally breaking into the privacy of Rochin, the struggle to open his mouth and remove what was there, the forcible extraction of his stomach's contents—this course of proceeding by agents of government to obtain evidence is bound to offend even hardened sensibilities. They are methods too close to the rack and the screw to permit of constitutional differentiation.

On the facts of this case the conviction of Rochin has been obtained by methods that offend the Due Process Clause. The judgment below must be REVERSED.

CONCURRING OPINION

BLACK, J.

. . . I believe that faithful adherence to the specific guarantees in the Bill of Rights insures a more permanent protection of individual liberty than that which can be afforded by the nebulous standards stated by the majority. What the majority hold is that the Due Process Clause empowers this Court to nullify any state law if its application "shocks the conscience," offends "a sense of justice" or runs counter to the "decencies of civilized conduct."

Of even graver concern, however, is the use of philosophy [of natural law] to nullify the Bill of Rights. I long ago concluded that the accordion-like qualities of this philosophy must inevitably imperil all the individual liberty safeguards specifically enumerated in the Bill of Rights.

Questions

1. Why did the police actions violate Rochin's due process?

2. Does the police conduct in this case "shock your conscience"? Why or why not?

3. Are "shocks the conscience," offending the "community's sense of fair play and decency," "traditions and conscience of our people," and "those canons of decency and fairness which express the notions of justice of English speaking peoples" purely a matter of personal opinion, or are they objective tests? Explain.

4. Summarize how Justice Frankfurter defines and defends the fundamental fairness doctrine.

5. Summarize how Justice Black defines and defends the incorporation doctrine.

6. Which doctrine is better? Back up your answer with the facts of the case and the arguments of the majority and concurring opinions.

YOU DECIDE
Did the Officer's Conduct "Shock *Your* Conscience"?

 LO 5 Did the officer engage in outrageous government conduct in violation of the right to due process?

FACTS

After receiving a tip that prostitution was occurring at Peaceful Image Tanning and Bodyworks, the Minneapolis Police Department conducted an undercover investigation in which an officer, in plain clothes and with a recording device hidden in his clothing, posed as a customer. Upon entering the establishment, the undercover officer was greeted by appellant Betsy Lou Burkland, with whom he arranged a one-hour massage for $70. Burkland took the officer to a room, asked him to disrobe, and left the room while he did so. After she returned and began the massage, Burkland offered to perform the massage topless for an additional $30. The officer accepted the offer.

The massage lasted for approximately one hour, during which Burkland and the officer engaged in small talk. Burkland then discussed the benefits of massage and the stigma attached to it, stating that "it's actually a . . . thing with a happy ending, it does release, release endorphins in your brain." After discussing the establishment's hours, the collapse of the Interstate 35W bridge, and the weather, Burkland directed the officer to turn onto his back and continued the massage.

Shortly thereafter, the officer asked, "Do you think I can touch your breasts now?" Burkland replied, "Um hmm." The officer massaged Burkland's bare breasts as she put oil on her hand and rubbed the officer's penis. The officer then asked, "Do you include the release with the 100 dollars?" Burkland responded, "Yeah." The officer then asked for additional sexual services if he put on a condom, which Burkland declined to perform. The officer testified that the word "condom" was the signal for other officers to enter and make the arrest. The officer also testified that "manual release" is a term used during massage to indicate that the masseuse will "give you a hand job until you have an orgasm."

Burkland was charged with misdemeanor prostitution. Burkland moved to dismiss the charges, arguing that the officer's outrageous conduct violated the right to due process. The district court denied the motion, and the case proceeded to trial. The jury found Burkland guilty of misdemeanor prostitution. This appeal followed.

ANALYSIS

The concept of fundamental fairness inherent in the due process requirement will prevent conviction . . . when police conduct violates fundamental fairness, shocking to the universal sense of justice. To determine whether the officer's conduct was justified by the need to gather sufficient evidence, we consider the elements of the offense. Prostitution is defined as "engaging or offering or agreeing to engage for hire in . . . sexual contact." Thus, the evidence needed to prove this offense is that Burkland "agree[d] to engage for hire" in sexual contact.

Police investigation is important in prosecuting and reducing the incidence of prostitution. But the officer could have successfully sought the necessary agreement to engage in sexual contact for hire by inquiring about the charge for the "release" at almost any point throughout the almost hour-long massage without ever initiating sexual contact by touching Burkland's breast.

We conclude that when a police officer's conduct in a prostitution investigation involves the initiation of sexual contact that is not required for the collection of evidence to establish the elements of the offense, this conduct, initiated by the investigating officer, is sufficiently outrageous to violate the "concept of fundamental fairness inherent" in the guarantee of due process.

Reversed.

Source: *State v. Burkland*, 775 N.W.2d 372 (Minn App. 2009) Permissions. *State v. Burkland*. http://caselaw.findlaw.com/mn-court-of-appeals/1501242.html.

STATE OF MINNESOTA BRIEF

Sergeant Pleoger's Conduct Is Not "Outrageous" Enough to "Shock the Conscience"

Sergeant David Pleoger's intent in requesting that he touch Burkland's bare breasts and in allowing her to touch his penis was to gather evidence of her intent to engage in prostitution, and to maintain his cover as someone interested in an exchange of a sexual act for money.

By act of the Minnesota Legislature, prostitution is a crime in this state. Citizens in neighborhoods in which prostitution is common frequently plead with police to assist their communities in combating this crime. It is not a negligible, "low-level" offense without consequences. The public interest in deterring prostitution is grounded in concerns for public health, welfare, and morals. Fighting prostitution requires the use of some level of deception by police. Prostitutes generally do not make offers of sex for money to individuals known by them to be police officers. The officers must often take actions to convince the alleged prostitute that they are not police in order to be effective.

Source: WestLaw, Brief for the City of Minneapolis.

By the 1970s, Justice William Brennan (1977) wrote, the incorporation doctrine had changed the "face of the law" (493). Cases decided in the 1960s specifically incorporated all but four of the Bill of Rights guarantees relating to criminal justice: public trial, notice of charges, prohibition of excessive bail, and prosecution by indictment (Table 2.3).

TABLE 2.3 Bill of rights provisions incorporated (as of 2010)

Bill of Rights Provision	Case
Unreasonable searches and seizures	*Wolf v. Colorado* (1949)
Exclusionary rule applied to state searches and seizures	*Mapp v. Ohio* (1961)
Self-incrimination	*Malloy v. Hogan* (1964)
Assistance of counsel	*Gideon v. Wainwright* (1963)
Right to confront witnesses against the accused	*Pointer v. Texas* (1965)
Compulsory process to obtain witnesses	*Washington v. Texas* (1967)
Speedy trial	*Klopfer v. North Carolina* (1967)
Cruel and unusual punishment	*Robinson v. California* (1962)

© Cengage Learning

In cases decided since the 1960s, the Court has implied that the Fourteenth Amendment due process absorbs all but indictment by grand jury.

Incorporated rights apply to the states exactly as the U.S. Supreme Court mandates the federal courts to practice them. States have to apply the rights "jot for jot and case for case," as one of the doctrine's severest critics, Justice John Harlan, put it (*Duncan v. Louisiana* 1968, 181). Justice Brennan defended the jot-for-jot standard: "Only impermissible subjective judgments can explain stopping short of the incorporation of the full sweep of the specific being absorbed" (Friendly 1965, 936).

The Court didn't just shift its reason for intervening in state criminal procedure, it did something far more consequential and controversial for day-to-day criminal procedure. It expanded its intervention from the courtroom to the police station in interrogation and right to counsel (Chapter 8); search and seizure (Chapters 3, 5–7); identification procedures (Chapter 9); and even onto the street and other public places (stop and frisk, Chapter 4).

The labels used to describe this expansion of federal intervention in local law enforcement ("handcuffing the police," "constitutionalizing criminal procedure," "policing the police," "judicial lawmaking") only hint at the firestorm of controversy the highest court in the land (and the least democratic branch of the government) set off when the U.S. Supreme Court got involved in reviewing the day-to-day activities of police officers in every city, town, and village in the country (Graham 1970).

The critics of incorporation—it had and still has many—charged that incorporation destroys federalism, interferes with local criminal justice, and guts the need for both local variety and experiments with different solutions to problems in criminal justice administration. They maintain that the great differences among the states and among federal, state, and local systems of criminal justice demand local control and variation.

Critics rightly observe that federal criminal justice consists mainly of cases involving fraud, tax evasion, and other highly complex crimes. Federal investigation takes place largely in offices, not in the field. Local law enforcement deals mainly with the hurly-burly street crimes that bring local police into contact with violent individuals and strangers who are difficult to identify, apprehend, and bring to trial. As a result, the critics say, the Bill of Rights works well for federal but not state and local criminal justice. Furthermore, most local police aren't highly trained college graduates, as are the federal police agents. So, according to the critics, the incorporation doctrine works effectively for the 0.6 percent of criminal cases that are federal cases but not for the remaining 99.4 percent that are state cases (Graham 1970).

The criticisms target all criminal justice agencies, but perhaps nothing generates more controversy than whether uniform standards ought to apply to local police departments. Cries that the U.S. Supreme Court was "running local police departments" from Washington and "handcuffing" local police by doing so were common during the late 1960s, following the decision in the *Miranda* case (Chapter 8). So damaging to the Court's prestige was *Miranda v. Arizona* (1966) that the decision was labeled one of three times in its history that the Court struck a "self-inflicted wound" (Graham 1970).

The Court may have wounded itself, but, by most accounts, contrary to its opponents' fears, the incorporation doctrine hasn't wounded criminal justice. The Supreme Court's flexible interpretations of the constitutional protections permit plenty of local diversity and experimentation. A good example is *Chandler v. Florida* (1981).

Noel Chandler argued that Florida's practice of televising trials violated his right to a fair trial. The Court rejected Chandler's claim. Chief Justice Warren Burger, no fan of television in the courts, supported the right of local jurisdictions to follow their own practices. He wrote that the Constitution didn't give the Court power to "oversee or harness" the states' efforts to experiment with procedures. The Court has to trust state courts to look out for procedures that "impair the fundamental rights of the accused." Unless the procedures are shown to establish a "prejudice of constitutional dimensions to these defendants, there is no reason for this Court either to endorse or to invalidate Florida's experiment" (582).

EQUAL PROTECTION OF THE LAW

LO **4, 6**

Constitutional democracy couldn't survive without protecting our right to fair procedures guaranteed by due process of law. But neither could it survive without securing equal protection of those procedures for everybody. Equality is embedded deeply in the concept of U.S. constitutionalism. In the years just prior to the Revolution, one commentator wrote, "The least considerable man among us has an interest equal to the proudest nobleman, in the laws and constitution of his country" (Inbau and others 1984, 209). I remember a blunter expression of the value of equality from the 1960s: "If the rich can beat the rap, then everyone should get to beat the rap."

Equality before the law is more than a slogan in criminal justice; since 1868, it's been a constitutional command. Recall the Fourteenth Amendment command that "No state shall . . . deny to any person within its jurisdiction the equal protection of the laws." Equal protection claims can arise out of actions by officers throughout the criminal process, including police investigation, pretrial bail, appointment of counsel, charging by the prosecutor, jury selection, and in right-to-trial transcripts.

However, you need to know that equal protection of the law doesn't mean state officials have to treat everybody exactly alike. It means they can't investigate, apprehend, convict, and punish people *unreasonably*. Courts look suspiciously at the reasonableness of certain classifications, particularly those based on race or ethnicity.

In practice, it's difficult to prove claims that officials denied equal protection because of two facts claimants have to prove. First, they have to prove that the official action had a **discriminatory effect**—that race or some other illegal group characteristic (not a legitimate criterion, such as seriousness of the offense or criminal record) accounts for the official decision.

Second, and far more difficult, claimants have to prove **discriminatory purpose**—that, in the case at hand, the specific officer intended to discriminate against the complainant because of her race or other illegal criteria. For example, proving an official said (and meant) "I hate Hispanics" isn't good enough to win an equal protection case. The claimant has to prove, for example, that a police officer decided to arrest a specific Hispanic because of her Hispanic ethnicity. So proving the officer said (and meant), "I arrested her because she was Hispanic" would be good enough. Of course, in this day and age of political correctness, it's unlikely that any officer would say that openly. But without such an admission, it's next to impossible for a claimant to prove discriminatory intent.

In addition to the difficulty of proving discriminatory effect and discriminatory purpose, there's another hurdle: the **presumption of regularity**. Government actions are presumed lawful unless there's "clear evidence to the contrary." Equal protection claimants have the heavy burden of proving that they were denied equal protection. Many equal protection claims have reached federal and state courts, but few claimants have overcome the heavy burden of overcoming the presumption of regularity (LaFave and others 2009, 720).

Many, if not most, of the equal protection cases that reach the courts aren't there because of the fact of discrimination. Instead, claimants want information from the government that can help them carry their heavy burden to overcome the presumption of regularity. This is called **discovery**, a legal action asking a court order to compel one side in a case to turn over information that might help the other side.

CRIMINAL PROCEDURE IN ACTION

Defendants have to prove people of other races were not prosecuted for similar crimes

LO 6   Christopher Lee Armstrong and others were indicted on federal charges of "conspiring to possess with intent to distribute more than 50 grams of cocaine base (crack) and conspiring to distribute the same." The Federal Bureau of Alcohol, Tobacco, and Firearms had monitored Armstrong and others prior to their indictment and arrest. Armstrong filed a motion for discovery or dismissal, alleging that he was selected for prosecution because he was Black. The district court granted the discovery order. It ordered the government to provide statistics on similar cases from the last three years. The government indicated it would not comply. Subsequently, the district court dismissed the case. The government appealed. The court of appeals affirmed the dismissal. It held that the proof requirements for a selective-prosecution claim do not require a defendant to demonstrate that the government has failed to prosecute others who are similarly situated.

The U.S. appealed to the U.S. Supreme Court. The question before the Court was: "Must criminal defendants who pursue selective-prosecution claims demonstrate that people of other races were not prosecuted for similar crimes?"

Yes (8–1) SCOTUS ruled. Writing for the majority, Justice William H. Rehnquist, held that in order to file selective-prosecution claims, defendants have to show that the government failed to prosecute similarly situated suspects of other races. "If the claim . . . were well founded," wrote Rehnquist, "it should not have been an insuperable task to prove that persons of a different race were not prosecuted."

It's time to turn to two final topics before we begin our journey through the criminal process. First, we'll trace the pendulum swing between crime control and due process that runs through Western European, English, and U.S. history. Then, we'll look at the political nature of the U.S. Supreme Court.

CRIMINAL PROCEDURE HISTORY: THE CRIME CONTROL–INDIVIDUAL AUTONOMY PENDULUM

LO **7**

The tension between crime control and individual liberty and privacy that we discussed in Chapter 1, has a long history. Roscoe Pound (the immensely influential legal scholar and early champion of the sociology of law), traced the Western history of what he maintained is a pendulum swing between them. Throughout that history, according to Pound, societies have swung back and forth between first a predominant concern for crime control and punishing the guilty, and second, in reaction to an excess of crime control and punishment, a turn to the values of protecting the innocent against a too-powerful government.

Ancient Roman History

The early Roman republic established strong safeguards for individuals against government power in its law of criminal procedure. And it created a criminal law "that in spite of abundant threats of capital punishment, became in practice the mildest ever known in the history of mankind" (Strachan-Davidson 1912, 168). One example comes from around 50 BC. Damio, a freed slave of the notorious Roman politician Clodius, "had committed every sort of violent crime" (Pound 1921, 9). The praetor (a Roman judicial officer with wide powers) seized Damio. Tribune Novius released him, saying, "Although I have been wounded by this hanger-on of Clodius, and driven from my official duties by armed men . . . , when appeal is made to me, I will quash this sentence" (Strachan-Davidson, 168). (Praetors were elected officials whose duty was to protect the people from oppression.)

In reaction to this mildness and its emphasis on process, the government of the Roman Empire went to the other extreme. In the era of Imperial Rome, the provincial governors came to act as both public prosecutors, and the "rise of imperial exercise of the whole magisterial [judicial] power" (Pound 1921, 9).

English History

Fast-forward 1,200 years to 11th-century England, to a similar conflict. In the Magna Carta, King John's barons got King John to agree to a number of checks on his royal power. These checks emphasized procedural protection at the expense of crime control. Excess in the exercise of these procedural checks led to a reaction expressed in the aggrandizement of royal power during the 16th and 17th centuries. By the reign of King Charles I in the early 1600s, the royal Court of the Star Chamber had abandoned the common law courts' procedural safeguards for the accused, and created new royal courts that made it easy for the monarchs to convict criminal defendants of a vast number of religious and political crimes. This expansion of royal power didn't stop with new royal courts; it extended to the kings' political domination of the common-law judges. Through intimidation, favor, and other influence, the 17th-century English kings were able to secure decisions favorable to their own and the aristocracy's interests.

Although interference in the business of the courts was by no means new, a rising "middle class," increasingly restive for greater political influence, regarded royal interference in judicial proceedings as intolerable. The English revolution—and the founding of the American colonies—was, at least in part, a reaction by the middle classes to this expansion of royal power and its restrictions on middle-class rights.

U.S. History

We'll divide our discussion of early U.S. history into the years of individual liberty in reaction to British tyranny through 1900 and the early 1900s return to crime control. Then, in the final two sections, we'll home in on where the rest of the book focuses—the 1960s "due process revolution" in individual rights and the return to crime control since 1970.

The early years, 1781–1900

The Articles of Confederation, written by the former British colonists in response to British tyranny, went to the other extreme, creating a government too weak to govern. The United States Constitution represented an effort to balance government power, particularly national government power, and individual liberty. Alexander Hamilton wrote of this balance:

> In the commencement of a revolution, which received its birth from the usurpations of tyranny, nothing was more natural than that the public mind should be influenced by an extreme spirit of jealousy. To resist these encroachments, and to nourish this spirit, was the great object of all our public and private institutions. The zeal for liberty became predominant and excessive.
>
> In forming our Confederation, this passion alone seemed to actuate us, and we appear to have had no other view than to secure ourselves from despotism. The object certainly was a valuable one, and deserves our utmost attention; but, sir, there is another object, equally important, and which our enthusiasm rendered us little capable of regarding: I mean a principle of strength and stability in the organization of our government, and vigor in its operations. (quoted in Storing 1981, 71) [Google Books, http://books.google.com/books?id=8MO_vGOmQOIC&q=alexander+hamilton#v=onepage&q=spirit%20of%20jealousy&f=false]

Even this balance didn't satisfy Anti-Federalists, who still feared government power. The Bill of Rights, added as amendments to the Constitution, reflects deep suspicion, even hostility, to government power among some of the middle classes who had experienced firsthand a royal government and a judiciary impatient with individual rights. The Bill of Rights demonstrates the determination of the Anti-Federalists to protect individuals against unwarranted government power.

Throughout the 19th century, concern for individual rights dominated the *law* of criminal procedure, if not its daily practices. A largely rural, widely scattered, sparse population that lived in villages and on farms and shared common values, dominated political life. A weak government that allowed individual autonomy to flourish worked in that society (Rutland 1955; McDonald 1985).

A new era of crime control, 1900–1960

> I submit . . . that the first and greatest evil in the administration of the criminal law, and one that should be corrected, is the undue protection still afforded to persons charged with crime by [the Fourth and Fifth Amendment in] the Constitution and like provisions in the State Constitutions. (Untermeyer 1910, 150)

By the early 20th century, the United States had changed enormously. It was increasingly urban, industrial, and inhabited by people with values different from those of the dominant 19th-century Anglo-Saxon Protestant culture. More people looked to government to solve the problems that arose in transportation, health, business regulation, employment conditions, consumer protection, and maintenance of public order and morals. Deficiencies in criminal justice led to calls for both more criminal law to regulate behavior and more government to enforce it. All of this was happening during what the public widely *perceived* as one more of endlessly recurring "crime waves." This wave, contemporaries imagined, had brought the incidence of crime to epidemic proportions.

Complaints spread that "technicalities" set criminals free and that constitutional safeguards made it difficult to convict known criminals. The newspapers, the new middle-class magazines, national conventions of criminal justice officials, professors, and lawyers loudly complained about how the criminal justice system favored criminals over innocent citizens. In other words, they believed that crime control trumped individual autonomy.

These complaints even provoked open demands to amend the Constitution, sometimes drastically. At the 1910 annual meeting of the American Academy of Political and Social Science, a prestigious New York criminal lawyer, Samuel Untermeyer, told the conference that the Fourth Amendment protection against unreasonable searches and seizures and the Fifth Amendment protection against self-incrimination gave too much protection to criminals. His solution—"at the risk of being charged with treason against this fetish which all lawyers are expected to worship"—*abolish* the Fourth and Fifth Amendments because

> I submit . . . that the first and greatest evil in the administration of the criminal law, and one what should be corrected, is the undue protection still afforded to persons charged with crime by these provisions of the Constitution and like provisions in the State Constitutions. (Untermeyer 1910, 150) [article, 6,270 words]

Others demanded similar treatment for the jury trial. This "palladium of liberty" and democracy ought to be abolished because it allowed sentimental jurors to set wanton criminals free to prey on innocent people (American Academy of Political and Social Science 1910, 46).

Complaints about the ideal balance between crime control and individual rights haven't subsided appreciably since 1900. The complaints about a "crime wave" in the early 20th century fostered what you should now recognize as a familiar reaction—a tough law-and-order atmosphere and an accompanying enhanced police power that continued from the 1920s through the 1950s.

LO 5, 7   The "due process revolution," 1960–1969

During the 1960s, this enhanced police power spawned a familiar reaction; this time it came to be called the **"due process revolution."** Led by the United States

Supreme Court (termed the "Warren Court" after its chief justice, Earl Warren), this revolution tilted the balance of power toward individuals' procedural rights. Its critics complained—sometimes loudly—that it handcuffed the police and unleashed the criminals to prey on law-abiding people the police could no longer protect.

(In the Chicago public high school where I was teaching at the time, one of my very senior colleagues expressed what many distraught teachers in our school felt. Frequently wringing her hands, she lamented "these times of violence and upheaval." And who wouldn't? Riots, gang violence, and violent crime were part of our life in those turbulent times.)

Reaction to the "due process revolution," 1969–2013

The due process revolution produced another pendulum swing that led to calls for more crime control. In 1969, William Rehnquist, one of President Nixon's assistant attorney generals, sent a memo to Associate Attorney General John Dean. In it, he contended that "the Supreme Court has failed to hold true the balance between the right of society to convict the guilty and the obligation of society to safeguard the accused." He recommended a commission "to determine whether the overriding public interest in law enforcement . . . requires a constitutional amendment." By 1985, now Associate Justice William Rehnquist was pleased that the Court had "called a halt to a number of the sweeping rulings of the Warren Court" in "the area of constitutional rights of accused criminal defendants" (Bradley 2010, 2). But by 2005, when Chief Justice Rehnquist died, he had not convinced enough justices to undo *all* of the Warren Court's criminal procedure work. Nevertheless, Craig Bradley, a former Rehnquist clerk and leading Rehnquist scholar, wrote that Chief Justice Rehnquist "enjoyed perhaps his greatest success after thirty-three years on the Court in trimming back Warren Court initiatives in virtually every area of criminal procedure and habeas corpus" (2010, 3). The Roberts Court from 2005 to the present has maintained the Rehnquist legacy, although admittedly with some exceptions, and frequently by 5–4 opinions. Most of these you'll read in the remaining chapters.

As we close this history of the pendulum swing between crime control and individual autonomy, let's not forget that both are essential to the quality of life in a free society. Individual freedom and privacy aren't worth much if we're not safe and secure from criminal attacks. On the other hand, a government that interferes too much with our right to be left alone, and to come and go as we please, impairs the core of life in a free society. In short, the law of criminal procedure attempts to provide the government with enough power to enforce the criminal law, but not with so much power that the government itself threatens individual autonomy and privacy (Packer 1968).

THE U.S. SUPREME COURT: WILL OF THE PEOPLE OR RULE OF LAW?

LO 8

"Courts are the mere instruments of the law, and can will nothing."
Chief Justice John Marshall, *Osborne v. Bank of U.S.* (1824, 866)

*

"Five votes can do anything around here."

Associate Justice William J. Brennan (Tushet 1997, 763, n.8)

*

"The mandates of the Supreme Court must be shaped with an eye not only to legal right and wrong, but with an eye to what popular opinion would tolerate."

Robert G. McCloskey
The American Supreme Court (1960), xvii

The idea of **fundamental law**, a law above the ordinary law created by legislatures, is ancient. Most Europeans, at the time of the Revolution, believed that fundamental law placed moral—but not legally enforceable—limits on governments. But not so to the colonial revolutionaries who later wrote the U.S. Constitution. They assumed that the higher law *was* legally enforceable. "The struggle with England turned assumption into fiery conviction as the colonists argued that Parliament was forbidden, not only morally, but literally to transgress the rights of Americans claimed under their charters and the British Constitution" (McCloskey, 6).

At the same time that they committed to the idea of a fundamental law above the government, the revolutionaries also committed to the idea of government by the **will of the people** (or **popular sovereignty**). Government by "consent of the governed," Thomas Jefferson wrote in the Declaration of Independence; "We, the people . . ." proclaimed the first three words in the Preamble to the U.S fundamental law—the U.S. Constitution.

These are contradictory ideas. "Will" of the people denotes the power of the people to create law; fundamental law places limits on that power. Most people hold these ideas side by side. "This propensity to hold contradictory ideas simultaneously is one of the most significant qualities of the American political mind at all stages in our national history" (McCloskey, 7).

This dualism in our political minds can help you understand the political nature of the Supreme Court. ("Political" here is a positive. It means public policy formation with the public good in mind, not manipulation of political power for personal or partisan gain.) According to Professor Robert G. McCloskey, the revered constitutional scholar,

> The fundamental law could be enforced only within delicately defined boundaries, . . . The mandates of the Supreme Court must be shaped with an eye not only to legal right and wrong, but with an eye to what popular opinion would tolerate (9). This is not to say that the Court should consult the latest bulletins on the popular climate and shape its judgments accordingly. But it is to say that public concurrence sets an outer boundary for judicial policy making; that judicial ideas of the good society can never be too far removed from popular ideas (13).
> [Robert McCloskey, *The American Supreme Court*, Fifth Edition]

CHAPTER SUMMARY

LO **1, 2** Constitutionalism, the idea that constitutions adopted by the whole people are a higher form of law than ordinary laws passed by legislatures, is deeply embedded in our constitutional democracy. The final authority on criminal procedure lies in the

U.S. Constitution, especially in the Bill of Rights, and the U.S. Supreme Court's interpretation of the Constitution trumps the interpretations of all other courts. Applying the Court's decisions in day-to-day operations, however, depends on both federal and state courts, prosecutors, and law enforcement officers. In practice, most cases never get to court, and the few that do usually end in the local trial court without a trial.

LO **3**   Every state constitution guarantees its citizens rights parallel to those in the U.S. Constitution, such as the rights against self-incrimination and unreasonable searches and seizures. State constitutions can increase criminal procedure rights but can't reduce them below the federal minimum defined by the U.S. Supreme Court. State courts are the final authority in cases based on their own constitutions and statutes, but cases involving the U.S. Constitution that the Supreme Court hasn't decided yet can be appealed to federal courts.

LO **4, 5**   Deeply rooted in the struggle to define "due process" are the historically controversial issues of states' rights and individual equality. Since the Civil War, the Supreme Court has gradually expanded the meaning of criminal procedure rights within the federal system and ruled that these expansions apply to state and local criminal justice as well. After a decades-long struggle within the Court, a majority agreed that "due process" requires the incorporation of the specific criminal procedure provisions codified in the U.S. Bill of Rights. These hotly contested Supreme Court rulings changed day-to-day criminal procedure by extending its intervention from the courtroom to the police station.

LO **6**   Equality is embedded in the concept of constitutionalism; our constitutional democracy couldn't survive without protecting our right to fair procedures *and* securing equal protection of those procedures for everybody. Although equality before the law is a constitutional command, it does not guarantee *identical* treatment for all individuals. Equal protection of the law means state officials can't investigate, apprehend, convict, and punish people *unreasonably* and the heavy burden of proving claims that officials have denied equal protection falls upon the individual.

LO **7, 8**   The tension between crime control and individual liberty extends throughout Western and U.S. history, from ancient Roman civilization to present-day U.S. society. Like a pendulum, societies have swung back and forth between a predominant concern for crime control and for the value of individual autonomy, free from government intrusion. In a series of decisions in the 1960s called the "due process revolution," the pendulum swung in favor of individuals' procedural rights. Since then, the pendulum has swung back in reaction to calls for more crime control. This dualistic, political nature of the U.S. Supreme Court, founded by the contradictory principles of fundamental law and popular sovereignty held side by side in our society, helps the Court adequately address society's ever-changing needs.

REVIEW QUESTIONS

1. Describe the differences between constitutions and laws.
2. Identify the five amendments to the U.S. Constitution that apply to criminal procedure and list the specific rights guaranteed by each amendment.
3. Identify and describe the two criminal procedure rights guaranteed by the body of the U.S. Constitution.

4. Describe two limits imposed on the U.S. Supreme Court's powers.

5. Explain the significance of the phrase, "It doesn't pay a law much of a compliment to declare it constitutional."

6. Trace the development of the application of the Bill of Rights to criminal procedure from colonial times to the present and describe the two historical issues surrounding the controversy.

7. Describe how the expansion of the Bill of Rights to state proceedings changed day-to-day criminal procedure.

8. Identify the significance of *Hurtado v. California* to the Fourteenth Amendment.

9. Summarize the ruling in *Powell v. Alabama*. Describe the six facts of the case that most influenced the Court's decision.

10. Describe the significance of *Brown v. Mississippi* for the Fourteenth Amendment. Explain how political movements in Europe and the social reality in the United States probably affected the decision.

11. Explain the differences between the fundamental fairness doctrine and the incorporation doctrine. Describe the arguments for and against each doctrine.

12. Explain the meaning of equality before the law and describe the two elements claimants have to prove violated their right to equal protection of the law.

13. Trace the history of the pendulum swing between crime control and individual autonomy from ancient Roman society to present-day U.S. criminal procedure.

14. Identify the major aspects and criticisms of the "due process revolution." Describe the Court's reaction to this revolution.

15. Identify and describe the two contradictory values inherent in the U.S. political mind. Describe how this dualism affects the political nature of the Supreme Court.

KEY TERMS

constitutionalism, p. 28
law of criminal procedure, p. 28
Model Code of Pre-Arraignment
    Procedure, p. 28
court of last resort, p. 28
habeas corpus, p. 28
principle of judicial review, p. 30
Supremacy Clause, p. 30

supervisory power, p. 30
parallel rights, p. 31
due process, p. 32
fundamental fairness doctrine
    of due process, p. 35
incorporation doctrine, p. 36
total incorporation, p. 36
selective incorporation doctrine, p. 36

discriminatory effect, p. 41
discriminatory purpose, p. 42
presumption of regularity, p. 42
discovery, p. 42
due process revolution, p. 45
fundamental law, p. 47
will of the people (popular
    sovereignty), p. 47

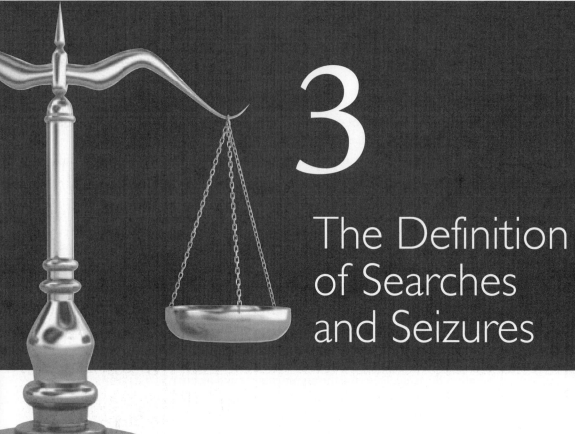

3

The Definition of Searches and Seizures

LEARNING OBJECTIVES

1 Understand that crime control depends on information that usually comes from reluctant sources. Know and appreciate that searches and seizures by government officials are important and controversial ways to obtain this information.

2 Know that Fourth Amendment analyses follow a three-stop process based on the answers to three questions in the following order: (1) Was the law enforcement action a "search" or "seizure"? (2) If the action was a search or seizure, was it reasonable? (3) If the search/seizure was unreasonable, does the Fourth Amendment ban its use as evidence?

3 Know that the original purposes for searches and seizures were to enforce sedition and customs laws, not the ordinary crimes that concern law enforcement today.

4 Understand that the Fourth Amendment bans only "unreasonable" searches and seizures made by law enforcement in order to balance the government's power to control crime and the liberty and privacy rights of individuals.

5 Know that if government actions don't invade an expectation of privacy that society is prepared to recognize, it's not a search, and the Fourth Amendment doesn't apply. In other words, the actions are left to the discretion of individual officers.

6 Understand and appreciate that the Fourth Amendment doesn't protect information voluntarily conveyed to a third party, even though some of these third parties provide services essential to our quality of life.

7 Appreciate the Supreme Court's difficult job of balancing government power to control crime with individual liberty and privacy in an age of increasingly rapid technological integration and advancement. Know that SCOTUS has yet to decide if there is a reasonable expectation of privacy in some common forms of communication, such as text messages and e-mails.

8 Know that discoveries of evidence in plain view, public places, open fields, or on abandoned property aren't searches, so the Fourth Amendment doesn't apply to them.

9 Understand that people aren't "seized" whenever officers approach them and ask questions; they're seized only when they're either physically detained or when they submit to an officer's display of authority. Know that SCOTUS has taken the position that police encounters with individuals aren't inherently coercive, but that empirical research doesn't support this position.

There is an electronic record of where I buy my coffee each morning. If anyone cared to, they could determine with a simple Internet search all of the places I have lived in the last decade; whether I rented or owned; how much I paid for each house I bought; and how much I made when I sold it. My local library keeps an electronic file of all the books I have ever borrowed, and my school keeps a similar database. The online vendor where I occasionally order clothing for my children keeps track of my buying preferences (and my children's sizes) to "assist" me in making future purchases. My local grocery store is kind enough to offer the same service, registering and indexing a list of every item I have ever purchased as part of the store's frequent shopper program. Consequently, my grocer knows that I have pets; that my kids are no longer in diapers; and that someone in the house is eating a lot of chicken nuggets. Along certain parts of my daily route, surveillance cameras silently record my passing image, presumptively for my own safety. Indeed, even communications with colleagues, family, and friends are subject to review by any adequately motivated member of my Internet provider's tech staff. The degree of monitoring I am subject to is staggering, and this is all without (as far as I know) being suspected of any wrongdoing.

—Renee McDonald Hutchins (2007, 410–11)

LO **I**

Crime control in our constitutional democracy depends on information. Almost all information the police need comes from what they see and hear. As long as what they see and hear by watching and listening is available to the general public, they're "free to use that tactic [surveillance] when and on whom they wish, free of legal constraint". (Stuntz 2002, 1387)

Unfortunately, information isn't always accessible to the naked eye and ear (or nose or fingers) in public. It comes from reluctant, sometimes stubborn, fearful, and even hostile sources—criminals, suspects, victims, and witnesses. Criminals don't want to incriminate themselves. Potential criminals don't want to give away their criminal schemes. Victims and other witnesses often are afraid to talk, or they don't want to give up their friends and family. So law enforcement officers, sometimes, have to rely on four involuntary methods to get information— searches and seizures (Chapters 3–7), interrogation (Chapter 8), and identification procedures (Chapter 9).

All four of these methods of obtaining evidence, which aren't available to the general public, are limited by the Fourth Amendment ban on "unreasonable searches and seizure" (discussed in this and the next four chapters); the Fifth Amendment ban on self-incrimination; and the right to due process (discussed in Chapters 8 and 9). In practice, when law enforcement officers use these methods, they have to follow rules generated by the U.S. Supreme Court in cases, many excerpts from which you'll read in this chapter and in Chapters 4 through 9. Incidentally, all the federal and state courts, the U.S. Congress and state legislatures, and city councils and all other governing and administrative bodies are also bound by the Supreme Court's rules.

Getting information to control crime is the main purpose of searches and seizures, but there are searches and seizures that go beyond law enforcement purposes to satisfy special needs. These special-needs searches include searches and seizures to:

- Protect officers from armed suspects (Chapters 4, 6)
- Prevent drunk driving (Chapter 4)
- Protect the property of detained suspects from loss or damage (Chapter 7)
- Protect officials from lawsuits (Chapter 7)
- Detect drug use among students and public employees (Chapter 7)

LO **2**

In this chapter, we'll first examine the history and purposes of the Fourth Amendment. Then we'll turn to the three main steps in Fourth Amendment analyses, phrased here in the form of three questions:

1. *Was the law enforcement action a "search" or a "seizure"?* (the subject of this chapter). If it wasn't, the Fourth Amendment isn't involved at all, and the analysis ends.

2. *If the action was a search or a seizure, was it reasonable?* (Chapters 4–7). If it was, the inquiry ends because the Fourth Amendment bans only unreasonable searches and seizures.

3. *If the action was an unreasonable search, does the Fourth Amendment ban its use as evidence?* (Chapter 10). If it does, the case isn't necessarily over because there may be enough other evidence to convict the defendant, either now or sometime in the future.

The first question may be the most important of the three. Why? Because if a law enforcement action isn't a search or a seizure, then it's beyond the reach of the limits mandated by the Fourth Amendment. Taking the action outside the Fourth Amendment means that appropriate law enforcement action depends on the good judgment (discretion) of individual officers. In Judge Charles E. Moylan's blunt language, if there's no search, "the law does not give a constitutional damn about noncompliance" (1977, 76).

Be careful that you don't carry the "constitutional damn" idea too far. Judge Moylan is referring specifically to the Fourth Amendment. Other constitutional provisions, such as the due process and equal protection clauses (Chapter 2), may apply. Also, officers' actions might be federal and/or state crimes (Chapter 11). Furthermore, the actions might give rise to private lawsuits in which plaintiffs can recover monetary awards for wrongdoing by law enforcement officials (Chapter 11). Finally, the actions might violate law enforcement agency rules that can result in agency disciplinary actions, such as demotions or termination (Chapter 11).

THE HISTORY AND PURPOSES OF THE FOURTH AMENDMENT

LO 3   The Fourth Amendment was created to make sure the government doesn't use illegal methods to get evidence. To understand why, let's look at a little history. Search and seizure law began long before the adoption of the Fourth Amendment. It started with the invention of the printing press and had nothing to do with the crimes law enforcement is concerned with today—murder, rape, robbery, burglary, theft, and crimes against public order and morals, such as prostitution, pornography, and especially illegal drug crimes.

Let's enter the story in the 1700s, when English monarchs had for two centuries been sending out their agents to conduct search and destroy missions against seditious libels (printed criticism of the government) and libelers. The practice reached a high point in the 1700s. The low level of respect the English had for their imported German kings (the four Georges of the House of Hanover) raised the number of seditious libels to epidemic proportions.

To fight this epidemic, the Crown relied on **writs of assistance** granting royal agents two enormous powers. The first part, called the "**general warrant**," empowered royal agents to search anyone, anywhere, anytime. The second part, the writ of assistance, empowered the agents to order anyone who happened to be nearby to help execute the warrant. Writs of assistance were issued at the beginning of a new monarch's reign and were good for the life of the monarch. Like the holder of a blank check who can fill in the amount, the writ permitted the officer to fill in names of persons, homes, shops, offices, private papers, and other items the officer wanted to search. So for the life of the monarch, officers of the Crown had total discretion as to whom, where, and what to search and seize. In the case of George III, that meant the authority was good for 60 years! (George III was king from 1760 to 1820.)

Writs of assistance weren't used just to search for and destroy seditious libels. They were also used to collect taxes on a long list of the most widely used commodities, including cider, beer, and paper. The British hated paying these taxes, and the American colonists hated paying customs duties on them; both were notorious for not paying any of them.

Smuggling goods into and out of the American colonies was rampant. Writs of assistance became the main weapon used to collect the hated customs in the American colonies. Notice what these original searches and seizures were *not* directed at: looking for and gathering evidence of felonies against individuals and their property or arresting suspects involved in these activities. So their purposes were very different from what they're used for today (Taylor 1969, Part I).

It was the use of the hated writs of assistance in these political and tax collection cases that prompted William Pitt to speak in the House of Commons the most famous words ever uttered against the power of government to search:

> The poorest man may in his cottage bid defiance to all the forces of the Crown. It may be frail—its roof may shake—the wind may blow through it—the storm may enter—but the King of England cannot enter—all his force dares not cross the threshold of the ruined tenement. (quoted in Hall 1993, 2:4)

In the United States, it was in a customs case that the young lawyer and future president John Adams watched the great colonial trial lawyer James Otis attack the writs of assistance in a Boston courtroom. Otis argued that writs of assistance were illegal because they were general warrants. According to Otis, only searches with specific dates, naming the places or persons to be searched and seized, were lawful where free people lived. Otis's argument moved John Adams to write years later: "There was the Child Independence born" (quoted in Smith 1962, 56). But the powerful oratory hurled against the writs of assistance didn't stop either the English Crown or American governors from using them.

 The authors of the Bill of Rights didn't forget their hatred for the general warrant, and they wrote their opposition to it into the Fourth Amendment to the U.S. Constitution. But the Fourth Amendment wasn't aimed at crippling law enforcement's power to protect the value of property and personal security. It was aimed only at limiting that power enough so as not to infringe "unreasonably" on two other values at the heart of a free society:

1. **liberty**, the right to come and go as we please, sometimes called the "right of locomotion," and
2. **privacy**, the right to be let alone by the government.

The Fourth Amendment is supposed to provide the government with enough power to make us safe and secure by looking for, getting, and using the evidence it needs to control crime, protect officers, seize suspects, and meet special needs beyond criminal law enforcement. It just can't do any of these by *unreasonable* searches and seizures.

In all of what follows in this chapter, and in Chapters 4 through 7, keep in mind that the Fourth Amendment protects us only from invasions by law enforcement officers; it doesn't protect us from invasions by private persons. Protection against invasion of our property, liberty, and privacy by other private persons depends on federal and state laws against trespass, false imprisonment, and invasions of privacy (Chapter 11).

Now let's turn to the question of what law enforcement actions are searches and seizures.

SEARCHES

 Until 1967, the U.S. Supreme Court defined searches mainly according to property law. According to the **trespass doctrine**, to qualify as a search, officers had to invade *physically* a "constitutionally protected area." **Constitutionally protected areas**

included only persons and places named in the Fourth Amendment—houses, papers, and *effects* (personal stuff). According to the Court, searching *persons* included touching their bodies, rummaging through their pockets, taking blood tests, and performing surgery to remove bullets. On the other hand, the Court ruled that orders for individuals to give handwriting samples, voice samples, and hair specimens aren't searches of their person because they're less invasive.

Houses include apartments, hotel rooms, garages, business offices, stores, and even warehouses. *Papers* include a broad range of personal writings, including diaries and letters. *Effects* include many items of personal property: cars, purses, briefcases, and packages.

In our study of searches, we'll look first at the U.S. Supreme Court's creation of the reasonable expectation of privacy doctrine, and its application to bank records, telephone numbers, and trash. Next, we'll look at how the Court defines plain view and the open fields searches; clarifies the distinctions between them; and assesses their effect on our privacy. Finally, we'll home in on the Court's electronic surveillance decisions. We'll assess the impact of the huge, and ever more rapid, increase and availability of electronic devices, especially GPS tracking devices.

LO 4, 5   The Privacy Doctrine

The privacy doctrine was suggested in a famous dissent in a Prohibition era case, *Olmstead v. U.S.* (1928). U.S. Prohibition agents tapped Roy Olmstead's telephones (the head of a massive Prohibition era conspiracy) and his coconspirators', hoping to find evidence of alcohol law violations. The government collected more than 775 pages of notes from the wiretaps. Based on this information, it indicted more than 70 people. Olmstead and several of the coconspirators were convicted.

The case eventually reached the Supreme Court, which held (5–4) that the government wiretaps were not Fourth Amendment searches because the agents didn't physically enter (trespass on) defendants' buildings. This holding became the trespass doctrine that defined a search as a physical trespass on the protected areas of the Fourth Amendment, namely persons, houses, papers, and effects. Justice Louis Brandeis disagreed in one of the most famous dissents in the history of the Court. He conceded that wiretaps were not physical trespasses. He argued that, nevertheless,

> The makers of the Constitution undertook to secure conditions favorable to the pursuit of happiness. They recognized the significance of man's spiritual nature of his feelings and of his intellect. They knew that only a part of the pain, pleasure and satisfactions of life are to be found in material things. They sought to protect Americans in their beliefs, their thoughts, their emotions and their sensations. They conferred, as against the Government, the right to be let alone—the most comprehensive of rights and the right most valued by civilized men. (478)

In 1967, Justice Brandeis's dissent became the law of the land when, in the landmark case *Katz v. U.S.* (1967), the Supreme Court replaced the trespass doctrine with the **reasonable expectation of privacy doctrine**.

Charlie Katz went into a public telephone booth on Sunset Boulevard in Los Angeles, closed the door, put his money in the slot, and took bets on the upcoming week's college basketball games. Katz was a bookie and his customers were from around the country. It was from these very unremarkable facts that the privacy test was created and that the majority of the Court decided that Katz had a reasonable expectation of privacy in his end of the betting conversations.

FBI agents suspected that Katz was using the booth to conduct his betting business—a federal crime. The agents attached a recorder to the outside of the booth that Katz used. With a microphone attached to the recorder, they recorded Katz's end of the conversations. Katz was convicted, based on transcriptions of the recordings. Katz appealed, arguing that the phone booth was "a constitutionally protected area so that the evidence obtained by attaching an electronic listening recording device to the top of the booth" violated his "right to privacy" (*Katz v. U.S.* 1967, 349). The court of appeals rejected Katz's argument, because there was no physical intrusion into the booth's interior (*Katz v. U.S.* 1966, 130).

The U.S. Supreme Court (7–1) reversed. According to Justice Potter Stewart, writing for the majority, physical trespass does not define a Fourth Amendment search.

> For the Fourth Amendment protects people, not places. What a person knowingly exposes to the public, even in his own home or office, is not a subject of Fourth Amendment protection. But what he seeks to preserve as private, even in an area accessible to the public, may be constitutionally protected . . . . What [Katz] sought to exclude when he entered the booth was not the intruding eye—it was the uninvited ear. He did not shed his right to do so simply because he made his calls from a place where he might be seen.
>
> No less than an individual in a business office, in a friend's apartment, or in a taxicab, a person in a telephone booth may rely upon the protection of the Fourth Amendment. One who occupies it, shuts the door behind him, and pays the toll that permits him to place a call is surely entitled to assume that the words he utters into the mouthpiece will not be broadcast to the world. To read the Constitution more narrowly is to ignore the vital role that the public telephone has come to play in private communication. (351–52)

Justice Stewart was a leading expert on Fourth Amendment law. He was not only an expert on the law, he was one of the Court's masters at turning phrases. One of his most memorable was, "The Fourth Amendment protects people, not places" (351).

Before we go on, let's clarify an important point about Justice Stewart's wonderful phrase. The Court's Fourth Amendment opinions almost always emphasize *where* people expect privacy. So places are still important and frequently the only basis for applying the privacy doctrine. (See examples in Table 3.1.)

TABLE 3.1 The expectation of privacy and places where we expect it

Search	No Search
Eavesdropping on telephone conversations	Overhearing a conversation on the street
Climbing over a backyard fence	Observing a backyard from the window of an airplane
Hiding in the bushes outside a house, looking inside	Standing on the street and looking into the living room through open curtains
Opening a briefcase and looking inside	Observing someone carrying a briefcase

Source: Based on Stuntz 2002, 1387.

LO 5   Furthermore, it isn't Justice Stewart's phrase, but Justice John Marshall Harlan's concurring opinion in *Katz* that defined the two-pronged **reasonable expectation of privacy test**, which the Court still follows:

1. **Subjective privacy.** Whether the "person exhibited an actual [personal] expectation of privacy"

2. **Objective privacy.** Whether the subjective expectation of privacy is reasonable—that is, an expectation "that society is prepared to recognize as 'reasonable'"

Also, keep in mind that when courts apply the reasonable expectation of privacy test, they "ask whether, at the moment the police officer observed the illegal behavior," he was where you or I might lawfully be. "The duration and intensity of the police observation does not matter." For example, police officers can stake out a private home, move in across the street, and watch who and what comes and goes for weeks. That's not a search because you and I could do it if we wanted to. Officers can follow someone down the street, into shops, bars, restaurants, and coffee shops. We could too, so it's not a search either (Stuntz 2002, 1387).

In theory, the privacy doctrine is a fine example of balancing the government's power to control crime and the individual's right to be let alone by the government. In practice, as you learned in the last paragraph, it allows the police a lot of leeway. A reasonable expectation of privacy is the kind of expectation any citizen might have with respect to any other citizen.

According to Professor Stuntz, one of the leading Fourth Amendment scholars, a "fair translation" of that standard might go as follows:

> Police can see and hear the things that any member of the public might see and hear, without fear of Fourth Amendment regulation. Only when they . . . see and hear things that members of the public would not be allowed to see and hear, has a 'search' taken place. (Stuntz 2002, 1387)

This narrow conception of the privacy doctrine led Professor William Heffernan (2001–2002) to conclude that we have a reasonable expectation of privacy only when we can demonstrate "eternal vigilance." In Professor Heffernan's words, "Even the slightest exposure of an item to the public can defeat a privacy claim" (38).

LO 6 ## The Third Party Doctrine

> We have held repeatedly that the Fourth Amendment does not prohibit obtaining information revealed to a third party and conveyed by [the third party] to Government authorities, even if the information is revealed on the assumption that it will be used only for a limited purpose and the confidence placed in the third party will not be betrayed. (*U.S. v. Miller* 1976, 443)

In *Katz*, law enforcement officers electronically eavesdropped on conversations, and neither Charlie Katz nor the person at the other end of the line was aware of being monitored—and most certainly didn't consent to it. In such cases, the Court ruled, the speaker has a reasonable expectation of privacy. But what if you tell your secrets to someone else? And what if that someone else—unbeknownst to you—is a law enforcement officer who *pretends* to be your friend and gains your confidence so you'll tell him incriminating secrets? And, you *do*. According to the Supreme Court **assumption of risk theory**, whenever we knowingly reveal our incriminating secrets, we assume the risk that our **false friends** will use them against us in criminal cases. In other words, if we tell secrets to someone we trust and they turn out to be government agents, it's our fault. "We have only ourselves to blame, and the Constitution provides no relief" (Ohm 2012, 1326). As one of my great law professors told us, "The Constitution doesn't protect gullible people."

Let's look at three kinds of third parties:

1. False friends
2. Companies we pay to provide essential services—banks, telephone companies, and trash collectors
3. Internet social networks

Just before the U.S. Supreme Court decided *Katz*, it decided the leading assumption of risk case, *Hoffa v. U.S.* (1967). The case began after labor boss Jimmy Hoffa's trial for labor law violations ended in a hung jury. The government then indicted Hoffa for attempting to bribe a member of the hung jury. Informant Edward Partin gained Hoffa's confidence, and in Hoffa's hotel, got Hoffa to admit that he tried to bribe a juror. The jury convicted Hoffa. Hoffa appealed. When the case reached the U.S. Supreme Court, the Court held that the Fourth Amendment doesn't protect evidence that the government obtains because of "a wrongdoer's misplaced belief that a person to whom he voluntarily confided his wrongdoing would not reveal it" (302). Notice that Partin didn't record or electronically transmit the information to government backup agents.

But what if the informant is carrying a hidden radio transmitter, sending his conversations with the target to backup agents? Does the target of the conversation (who doesn't know the "false friend" is wired to the police) have a reasonable expectation of privacy in the transmitted conversations?

In *U.S. v. White*, the U.S. Supreme Court decided whether a suspect's incriminating statements to a "false friend" wired for sound to law enforcement officers hiding outside are Fourth Amendment searches.

CASE

Were Statements Made to an Informant Wired for Sound to the Police, Searches?

U.S. v. White
401 U.S. 745 (1971)

HISTORY

James A. White was convicted in the U.S. District Court for the Northern District of Illinois, Eastern Division, of two narcotics violations. He was fined, and sentenced as a second offender to 25-year concurrent sentences. He appealed. The U.S. Court of Appeals for the Seventh Circuit reversed and remanded. The U.S. Supreme Court granted certiorari and reversed the judgment of the Court of Appeals.

—WHITE, J. (Plurality of 4)

FACTS

The issue before us is whether the Fourth Amendment bars from evidence the testimony of governmental agents who related certain conversations which had occurred between defendant White and a government informant, Harvey Jackson, and which the agents overheard by monitoring the frequency of a radio transmitter carried by Jackson and concealed on his person.

On four occasions the conversations took place in Jackson's home; each of these conversations was overheard by an agent concealed in a kitchen closet with Jackson's consent and by a second agent outside the house using a radio receiver. Four other conversations—one in White's home, one in a restaurant, and two in Jackson's car—were overheard by the use of radio equipment. The prosecution was unable to locate and produce Jackson at the trial and the trial court overruled objections to the testimony of the agents who conducted the electronic surveillance. The jury returned a guilty verdict and defendant appealed.

OPINION

The Fourth Amendment affords no protection to a wrongdoer's misplaced belief that a person to whom he voluntarily confides his wrongdoing will not reveal it. A police agent who conceals his police connections may write down for official use his conversations with a defendant and testify concerning them, without a warrant authorizing his encounters with the defendant and without otherwise violating the latter's Fourth Amendment rights.

For constitutional purposes, no different result is required if the agent instead of immediately reporting and transcribing his conversations with defendant, either simultaneously records them with electronic equipment which he is carrying on his person, or carries radio equipment which simultaneously transmits the conversations either to recording equipment located elsewhere or to other agents monitoring the transmitting frequency.

Our problem is not what the privacy expectations of particular defendants in particular situations may be or the extent to which they may in fact have relied on the discretion of their companions. Very probably, individual defendants neither know nor suspect that their colleagues have gone or will go to the police or are carrying recorders or transmitters. Otherwise, conversation would cease and our problem with these encounters would be nonexistent or far different from those now before us.

Our problem, in terms of the principles announced in *Katz*, is what expectations of privacy are constitutionally "justifiable"—what expectations the Fourth Amendment will protect in the absence of a warrant. So far, the law permits the frustration of actual expectations of privacy by permitting authorities to use the testimony of those associates who for one reason or another have determined to turn to the police, as well as by authorizing the use of informants. If the law gives no protection to the wrongdoer whose trusted accomplice is or becomes a police agent, neither should it protect him when that same agent has recorded or transmitted the conversations which are later offered in evidence to prove the State's case.

Inescapably, one contemplating illegal activities must realize and risk that his companions may be reporting to the police. If he sufficiently doubts their trustworthiness, the association will very probably end or never materialize. But if he has no doubts, or allays them, or risks what doubt he has, the risk is his. In terms of what his course will be, what he will or will not do or say, we are unpersuaded that he would distinguish between probable informers on the one hand and probable informers with transmitters on the other.

Given the possibility or probability that one of his colleagues is cooperating with the police, it is only speculation to assert that the defendant's utterances would be substantially different or his sense of security any less if he also thought it possible that the suspected colleague is wired for sound. At least there is no persuasive evidence that the difference in this respect between the electronically equipped and the unequipped agent is substantial enough to require discrete constitutional recognition, particularly under the Fourth Amendment which is ruled by fluid concepts of "reasonableness."

Nor should we be too ready to erect constitutional barriers to relevant and probative evidence which is also accurate and reliable. An electronic recording will many times produce a more reliable rendition of what a defendant has said than will the unaided memory of a police agent. It may also be that with the recording in existence it is less likely that the informant will change his mind, less chance that threat or injury will suppress unfavorable evidence and less chance that cross-examination will confound the testimony. Considerations like these obviously do not favor the defendant, but we are not prepared to hold that a defendant who has no constitutional right to exclude the informer's unaided testimony nevertheless has a Fourth Amendment privilege against a more accurate version of the events in question.

The judgment of the Court of Appeals is REVERSED. It is so ordered.

DISSENT

DOUGLAS, J.

The issue in this case is clouded and concealed by the very discussion of it in legalistic terms. What the ancients knew as "eavesdropping," we now call "electronic surveillance"; but to equate the two is to treat man's first gunpowder on the same level as the nuclear bomb.

(continued)

Electronic surveillance is the greatest leveler of human privacy ever known. How most forms of it can be held "reasonable" within the meaning of the Fourth Amendment is a mystery.

To be sure, the Constitution and Bill of Rights are not to be read as covering only the technology known in the 18th century. At the same time the concepts of privacy which the Founders enshrined in the Fourth Amendment vanish completely when we slavishly allow an all-powerful government, proclaiming law and order, efficiency, and other benign purposes, to penetrate all the walls and doors which men need to shield them from the pressures of a turbulent life around them and give them the health and strength to carry on.

We have become a fearful people. There was a time when we feared only our enemies abroad. Now we seem to be as fearful of our enemies at home, and depending on whom you talk to, those enemies can include people under thirty, people with foreign names, people of different races, people in the big cities. We have become a suspicious nation, as afraid of being destroyed from within as from without. Unfortunately, the manifestations of that kind of fear and suspicion are police state measures.

Must everyone live in fear that every word he speaks may be transmitted or recorded and later repeated to the entire world? I can imagine nothing that has a more chilling effect on people speaking their minds and expressing their views on important matters. The advocates of that regime should spend some time in totalitarian countries and learn firsthand the kind of regime they are creating here.

A technological breakthrough in techniques of physical surveillance now makes it possible for government agents and private persons to penetrate the privacy of homes, offices, and vehicles; to survey individuals moving about in public places; and to monitor the basic channels of communication by telephone, telegraph, radio, television, and data line. Most of the "hardware" for this physical surveillance is cheap, readily available to the general public, relatively easy to install, and not presently illegal to own.

As of the 1960s, the new surveillance technology is being used widely by government agencies of all types and at every level of government, as well as by private agents for a rapidly growing number of businesses, unions, private organizations, and individuals in every section of the United States. The scientific prospects for the next decade indicate a continuing increase in the range and versatility of the listening and watching devices, as well as the possibility of computer processing of recordings to identify automatically the speakers or topics under surveillance. These advances will come just at the time when personal contacts, business affairs, and government operations are being channeled more and more into electronic systems such as data-phone lines and computer communications.

DISSENT

HARLAN, J.

The impact of . . . third-party bugging . . . I think . . . undermines that confidence and sense of security in dealing with one another that is characteristic of individual relationships between citizens in a free society . . . . Authority is hardly required to support the proposition that words would be measured a good deal more carefully and communication inhibited if one suspected his conversations were being transmitted and transcribed. Were third-party bugging a prevalent practice, it might well smother that spontaneity—reflected in frivolous, impetuous, sacrilegious, and defiant discourse—that liberates daily life.

Much offhand exchange is easily forgotten and one may count on the obscurity of his remarks, protected by the very fact of a limited audience, and the likelihood that the listener will either overlook or forget what is said, as well as the listener's inability to reformulate a conversation without having to contend with a documented record. All these values are sacrificed by a rule of law that permits official monitoring of private discourse limited only by the need to locate a willing assistant.

Finally, it is too easy to forget—and, hence, too often forgotten—that the issue here is whether to interpose a search warrant procedure between law enforcement agencies engaging in electronic eavesdropping and the public generally. By casting its "risk analysis" solely in terms of the expectations and risks that "wrongdoers" or "one contemplating illegal activities" ought to bear, the plurality opinion, I think, misses the mark entirely. [It] . . . does not simply mandate that criminals must daily run the risk of unknown eavesdroppers prying into their private affairs; it subjects each and every law-abiding member of society to that risk. The very purpose of interposing the Fourth Amendment warrant requirement is to redistribute the privacy risks throughout society.

The interest that [the assumption of risk rule] fails to protect is the expectation of the ordinary citizen, who has never engaged in illegal conduct in his life, that he may carry on his private discourse freely, openly, and spontaneously without measuring his every word against the connotations it might carry when instantaneously heard by others unknown to him and unfamiliar with his situation or analyzed in a cold, formal record played days, months, or years after the conversation.

Interposition of a warrant requirement is designed not to shield "wrongdoers," but to secure a measure of privacy and a sense of personal security throughout our society. The Fourth Amendment does, of course, leave room for the employment of modern technology in criminal law enforcement, but in the stream of current developments in Fourth Amendment law I think it must be held that third-party electronic monitoring, subject only to the self-restraint of law enforcement officials, has no place in our society.

Questions

1. Is the plurality saying it's reasonable to expect people we confide in might be wired for sound to the police? Do you expect this?

2. Which is most intrusive: listening to James White in his home, in Harvey Jackson's home, in a restaurant, on the street, or in a car? Or are they all about the same? Why? Why not?

3. Does Justice Douglas in his dissent have a point when he says that everyone will live in fear that what she or he says will be reported, or transmitted by radio, to the police? Explain.

4. Should the police have been required to get a warrant here? Explain your answer.

LO 6 Essential Services Companies

Let's turn now to three third parties (commercial, paid businesses) whose services most of us depend on, and to whom we hand over our information (banks and telephone companies) and our stuff (trash). The U.S. Supreme Court has applied the third party rule to all three. This is not to say the cases were decided without dissents or criticism from the outside. One defender of the rule maintains that "The third-party doctrine is the Fourth Amendment rule scholars love to hate." In a footnote listing some of the critics' writing, Professor Owen Kerr quips, "A list of every article or book that has criticized the doctrine would make this the world's longest law review footnote" (2009, 563; footnote 5). Our next excerpt, *U.S. v. Miller* asks the question, "When you open a checking account and write checks; borrow money to pay back your student loan or buy a car; or charge items to your credit card, do you give up your Fourth Amendment rights in providing all the information these acts require?"

Mitch Miller appealed his conviction for illegal whiskey-related crimes. He claimed that federal agents violated the Fourth Amendment to obtain the bank records the U.S. attorneys used to convict him.

CASE Did He Give Up His Fourth Amendment Right in His Bank Records?

U.S. v. Miller
425 U.S. 435 (1976)

HISTORY

Mitch Miller was convicted before the United States District Court for the Middle District of Georgia, of possessing an unregistered still, carrying on the business of a distiller without giving bond and with intent to defraud the Government of whiskey tax, possessing whiskey upon which no taxes had been paid and conspiring to defraud the United States of tax revenues, and he appealed. The Court of Appeals for the Fifth Circuit reversed, and the U.S. Supreme Court granted certiorari, and reversed (7–2)

—Powell, J.

(continued)

Mitch Miller (Respondent) was convicted of possessing an unregistered still, carrying on the business of a distiller without giving bond and with intent to defraud the Government of whiskey tax, possessing 175 gallons of whiskey upon which no taxes had been paid, and conspiring to defraud the United States of tax revenues. Prior to trial, Miller moved to suppress copies of checks and other bank records. The District Court overruled Miller's motion to suppress, and the evidence was admitted. The Court of Appeals for the Fifth Circuit reversed on the ground that a depositor's Fourth Amendment rights were violated. It held that any evidence so obtained must be suppressed. Since we find that Miller had no protectable Fourth Amendment interest in the subpoenaed documents, we reverse the decision below.

FACTS

On December 18, 1972, in response to an informant's tip, a deputy sheriff from Houston County, Ga., stopped a van-type truck occupied by two of Mitch Miller's alleged co-conspirators. The truck contained distillery apparatus and raw material. On January 9, 1973, a fire broke out in a Kathleen, Ga., warehouse rented to Miller. During the blaze, firemen and sheriff department officials discovered a 7,500-gallon-capacity distillery, 175 gallons of nontax-paid whiskey, and related paraphernalia.

Two weeks later, agents from the Treasury Department's Alcohol, Tobacco and Firearms Bureau presented grand jury subpoenas issued in blank by the clerk of the District Court, and completed by the United States Attorney's office, to the presidents of the Citizens & Southern National Bank of Warner Robins and the Bank of Byron, where Miller maintained accounts. The subpoenas required the two presidents to appear on January 24, 1973, and to produce

> "all records of accounts, i.e., savings, checking, loan or otherwise, in the name of Mr. Mitch Miller (respondent), 3859 Mathis Street, Macon, Ga. and/or Mitch Miller Associates, 100 Executive Terrace, Warner Robins, Ga., from October, 1972, through the present date (January 22, 1973, in the case of the Bank of Byron, and January 23, 1973, in the case of the Citizens & Southern National Bank of Warner Robins)."

The banks did not advise Miller that the subpoenas had been served but ordered their employees to make the records available and to provide copies of any documents the agents desired. At the Bank of Byron, an agent was shown microfilm records of the relevant account and provided with copies of one deposit slip and one or two checks. At the Citizens & Southern National Bank microfilm records also were shown to the agent, and he was given copies of the records of Miller's account during the applicable period. These included all checks, deposit slips, two financial statements, and three monthly statements.

OPINION

We find that there was no intrusion into any area in which Miller had a protected Fourth Amendment interest and that the District Court therefore correctly denied Miller's motion to suppress. In Hoffa v. United States, 385 U.S. 293 (1966), the Court said that "no interest legitimately protected by the Fourth Amendment" is implicated by governmental investigative activities unless there is an intrusion into a zone of privacy, into "the security a man relies upon when he places himself or his property within a constitutionally protected area."

The documents here are not Miller's "private papers." He can assert neither ownership nor possession. He urges that he has a Fourth Amendment interest in the records kept by the banks because they are merely copies of personal records that were made available to the banks for a limited purpose and in which he has a reasonable expectation of privacy. He relies on Katz v. U.S. But in Katz the Court stressed that "what a person knowingly exposes to the public . . . is not a subject of Fourth Amendment protection."

We perceive no legitimate "expectation of privacy" in the documents' contents. All of the documents obtained, including financial statements and deposit slips, contain only information voluntarily conveyed to the banks and exposed to their employees in the ordinary course of business. The depositor takes the risk, in revealing his affairs to another, that the information will be conveyed by that person to the Government. United States v. White, 401 U.S. 745 (1971, case excerpt p. 58).

This Court has held repeatedly that the Fourth Amendment does not prohibit obtaining information revealed to a third party and conveyed by him to Government authorities, even if the information is revealed on the assumption that it will be used only for a limited purpose and the confidence placed in the third party will not be betrayed.

The judgment of the Court of Appeals is reversed. So ordered.

Mr. Justice BRENNAN, dissenting.

The customer of a bank expects that the documents, such as checks, which he transmits to the bank in the course of his business operations, will remain private, and that such an expectation is reasonable. The prosecution concedes as much, although it asserts that this expectation is not constitutionally cognizable. Representatives of several banks testified at the suppression hearing that information in their possession regarding a customer's account is deemed by them to be confidential.

Cases are legion that condemn violent searches and invasions of an individual's right to the privacy of his dwelling. The imposition upon privacy, although perhaps not so dramatic, may be equally devastating when other methods are employed. Development of photocopying machines, electronic computers and other sophisticated instruments have accelerated the ability of government to intrude into areas which a person normally chooses to exclude from prying eyes and inquisitive minds. Consequently judicial interpretations of the reach of the constitutional protection of individual privacy must keep pace with the perils created by these new devices.

Questions

1. List all facts relevant to deciding whether Mitch Miller gave up his Fourth Amendment rights in his bank records.

2. Summarize the majority opinion's reasons for deciding that Miller did give up his Fourth Amendment rights by turning over the records.

3. Summarize the dissent's argument that Miller didn't give up his Fourth Amendment right.

4. Do we "voluntarily" deal with banks? Is it desirable or even possible to live in 2014 without your checking account, car loan, student loan, or credit card?

Exploring The Third Party Rule Further

TELEPHONE NUMBERS

1. Did He Have a Reasonable Expectation of Privacy in Numbers Dialed from His Home Telephone?

Smith v. Maryland, 442 U.S. 745 (1979)

FACTS In Baltimore, Maryland, Patricia McDonough was robbed. She gave the police a description of the robber and of a 1975 Monte Carlo automobile she had observed near the scene of the crime. After the robbery, McDonough began receiving threatening and obscene phone calls from a man identifying himself as the robber. On one occasion, the caller asked that she step out on her front porch; she did so, and saw the 1975 Monte Carlo she had earlier described to police moving slowly past her home. On March 16, police spotted a man who met McDonough's description driving a 1975 Monte Carlo in her neighborhood. By tracing the license plate number, police learned that the car was registered in the name of Michael Lee Smith.

The next day, the telephone company, at police request, installed a pen register at its central offices to record the numbers dialed from the telephone at Smith's home. The police didn't get a warrant or court order before having the pen register installed. The register revealed that

on March 17 a call was placed from Smith's [the defendant's] home to McDonough's phone.

On the basis of this and other evidence, the police obtained a warrant to search the petitioner's residence. The search revealed that a page in Smith's phone book was turned down to the name and number of Patricia McDonough; the phone book was seized. Smith was arrested, and a six-man lineup was held on March 19. McDonough identified the petitioner as the man who had robbed her.

Smith was indicted in the Criminal Court of Baltimore for robbery. He moved to suppress "all fruits derived from the pen register" on the ground that the police had failed to secure a warrant prior to its installation. Did he have a reasonable expectation of privacy in the numbers he dialed from his home telephone?

DECISION No, said the U.S. Supreme Court. According to the majority:

We doubt that people in general entertain any actual expectation of privacy in the numbers they dial. Smith can claim no legitimate expectation of privacy here. When he used his phone, Smith voluntarily conveyed numerical information to the telephone company and "exposed" that information to its equipment in the ordinary course of business. In so doing, he assumed the risk that the company would reveal to police the numbers he dialed. The switching equipment that processed those numbers is merely the modern counterpart of the operator who, in an earlier day, personally completed calls for the subscriber.

DISSENT Justice Stewart disagreed. (Recall that Justice Stewart wrote the opinion in *Katz v. U.S.*) According to his dissent:

I think that the numbers dialed from a private telephone—like the conversations that occur during a call—are within the constitutional protection recognized in *Katz.* It seems clear to me that information obtained by pen register surveillance of a private telephone is information in which the telephone subscriber has a legitimate expectation of privacy. The information captured by such surveillance emanates from private conduct within a person's home or office—locations that without question are entitled to Fourth and Fourteenth Amendment protection.

The numbers dialed from a private telephone—although certainly more prosaic than the conversation itself—are not without "content." Most private telephone subscribers may have their own numbers listed in a publicly

(continued)

distributed directory, but I doubt there are any who would be happy to have broadcast to the world a list of the local or long distance numbers they have called. This is not because such a list might in some sense be incriminating, but because it easily could reveal the identities of the persons and the places called, and thus reveal the most intimate details of a person's life.

Justice Marshall also dissented:

Just as one who enters a public telephone booth is "entitled to assume that the words he utters into the mouthpiece will not be broadcast to the world," so too, he should be entitled to assume that the numbers he dials in the privacy of his home will be recorded, if at all, solely for the phone company's business purposes. Accordingly, I would require law enforcement officials to obtain a warrant before they enlist telephone companies to secure information otherwise beyond the government's reach.

TRASH

2. Did They Have a Reasonable Expectation of Privacy in Their Trash?

California v. Greenwood, 486 U.S. 35 (1988)

FACTS   Investigator Jenny Stracner of the Laguna Beach Police Department received information indicating that Billy Greenwood might be engaged in narcotics trafficking. Stracner asked the neighborhood's regular trash collector to pick up the plastic garbage bags that Greenwood had left on the curb in front of his house and to turn the bags over to her without mixing their contents with garbage from other houses. The trash collector cleaned his truck bin of other refuse, collected the garbage bags from the street in front of Greenwood's house, and turned the bags over to Stracner. The officer searched through the rubbish and found items indicative of narcotics use.

Stracner recited the information that she had gleaned from the trash search in an affidavit in support of a warrant to search Greenwood's home. Police officers encountered both Greenwood and Dyanne Van Houten at the house later that day when they arrived to execute the warrant. The police discovered quantities of cocaine and hashish during their search of the house. Did Greenwood and Van Houten have a reasonable expectation of privacy in the trash?

DECISION   No, said the U.S. Supreme Court. According to Justice White, writing for the majority:

It may well be that Greenwood and Van Houten did not expect that the contents of their garbage bags would become known to the police or other members of the public. An expectation of privacy does not give rise to Fourth Amendment

protection, however, unless society is prepared to accept that expectation as objectively reasonable. Here, we conclude that respondents exposed their garbage to the public sufficiently to defeat their claim to Fourth Amendment protection.

It is common knowledge that plastic garbage bags left on or at the side of a public street are readily accessible to animals, children, scavengers, snoops, and other members of the public. Moreover, respondents placed their refuse at the curb for the express purpose of conveying it to a third party, the trash collector, who might himself have sorted through respondents' trash or permitted others, such as the police, to do so. Accordingly, having deposited their garbage "in an area particularly suited for public inspection and, in a manner of speaking, public consumption, for the express purpose of having strangers take it," respondents could have had no reasonable expectation of privacy in the inculpatory items that they discarded.

Furthermore, as we have held, the police cannot reasonably be expected to avert their eyes from evidence of criminal activity that could have been observed by any member of the public. Hence, "what a person knowingly exposes to the public, even in his own home or office, is not a subject of Fourth Amendment protection."

DISSENT   Justices Brennan and Marshall disagreed. Justice Brennan wrote in his dissent:

Every week for two months, and at least once more a month later, the Laguna Beach police clawed through the trash that Greenwood left in opaque, sealed bags on the curb outside his home. Complete strangers minutely scrutinized their bounty, undoubtedly dredging up intimate details of Greenwood's private life and habits.

A trash bag is a common repository for one's personal effects and is therefore inevitably associated with the expectation of privacy. Almost every human activity ultimately manifests itself in waste products. If you want to know what is really going on in a community, look at its garbage. A single bag of trash testifies eloquently to the eating, reading, and recreational habits of the person who produced it. A search of trash, like a search of the bedroom, can relate intimate details about sexual practices, health, and personal hygiene.

Beyond a generalized expectation of privacy, many municipalities, whether for reasons of privacy, sanitation, or both, reinforce confidence in the integrity of sealed trash containers by prohibiting anyone, except authorized employees of the

Town to rummage into, pick up, collect, move or otherwise interfere with articles or materials placed on any public street for collection.

Had Greenwood flaunted his intimate activity by strewing his trash all over the curb for all to see, or had some nongovernmental intruder invaded his privacy and done the same, I could accept the Court's conclusion that an expectation of privacy would have been unreasonable. But all that Greenwood "exposed to the public" were the exteriors of several opaque, sealed containers. Until the bags were opened by police, they hid their contents from the public's view.

In holding that the warrantless search of Greenwood's trash was consistent with the Fourth Amendment, the Court paints a grim picture of our society. It depicts a society in which

local authorities may command their citizens to dispose of their personal effects in the manner least protective of the sanctity of the home and the privacies of life, and then monitor them arbitrarily and without judicial oversight—a society that is not prepared to recognize as reasonable an individual's expectation of privacy in the most private of personal effects sealed in an opaque container and disposed of in a manner designed to commingle it imminently and inextricably with the trash of others.

The American society with which I am familiar chooses to dwell in reasonable security and freedom from surveillance, and is more dedicated to individuals' liberty and more sensitive to intrusions on the sanctity of the home than the Court is willing to acknowledge.

LO 6 Electronic Surveillance

The subject of "false friend" undercover government agents and informants is sensitive and controversial, whether or not they use electronic surveillance. The year before *Katz v. U.S.*, the Supreme Court decided two cases on the same day in 1966 that did *not* depend on electronic surveillance. In *Hoffa v. U.S.* (1966), labor union boss Jimmy Hoffa was charged with violating the Taft-Hartley labor law. He was tried by a jury in a trial that lasted several weeks in a Nashville, Tennessee, federal court. The trial ended in a hung jury in 1962. In 1964, Hoffa and others were convicted of trying to bribe members of the 1962 hung trial jury.

The government's proof came largely from Edward Partin. Partin testified to several incriminating statements that he said Hoffa had made to him in Hoffa's hotel room during the 1962 trial. The Supreme Court upheld the convictions. It held that the informant Edward Partin's success in gaining Hoffa's confidence to get an incriminating statement from him didn't invoke Fourth Amendment issues because it involved only "a wrongdoer's misplaced belief that a person to whom he voluntarily confided his wrongdoing would not reveal it" (302).

In the same year as *Hoffa*, the Court decided *Lewis v. U.S.* On December 3, 1964, Edward Cass, an undercover federal narcotics agent, posing as a bar and grill owner, telephoned Duke Lewis's home to inquire about buying marijuana. Cass, who previously had not met or dealt with Lewis, falsely identified himself as "Jimmy the Polack." He said a mutual friend had told him Lewis might be able to get marijuana for him. "Yes," Lewis replied, "I believe, Jimmy, I can take care of you." Lewis told Cass to come to his home to buy the marijuana. The sale took place; two weeks later a second sale took place.

Lewis was charged with selling marijuana, in violation of the Federal Narcotics Act. He was convicted in the U.S. District Court for the District of Massachusetts, and sentenced to five years in prison for each of the two sales, to be served concurrently. He appealed to the U.S. Court of Appeals, where he contended that "any official intrusion upon the privacy of a home" without a warrant violated the Fourth Amendment (208). The court of appeals affirmed his conviction. The U.S. Supreme Court (8–1) affirmed.

Chief Justice Warren noted that Lewis had invited undercover agent Cass to his home for the specific purpose of selling marijuana to Cass, a federal felony. Lewis's only concern was whether Cass was a "willing purchaser who could pay the agreed price. Indeed, to convince the agent that his patronage at Lewis's home was desired, Lewis told him that, if he became a regular customer there, he would in the future receive an extra bag of marijuana at no additional cost; and in fact petitioner did hand over an extra bag at a second sale which was consummated at the same place and in precisely the same manner" (208).

Were we to hold the deceptions of the agent in this case constitutionally prohibited, we would come near to a rule that the use of undercover agents in any manner is virtually unconstitutional per se. Such a rule would, for example, severely hamper the Government in ferreting out those organized criminal activities that are characterized by covert dealings with victims who either cannot or do not protest. A prime example is provided by the narcotics traffic. (208)

LO 7 Electronic Surveillance in the 21st Century

Picture the communications technology in use when FBI agents attached a microphone to a recorder on top of the public telephone booth on Sunset Boulevard to eavesdrop on Charlie Katz taking small bets on Saturday college football games in the early 1960s. Or imagine the radio transmitter Harvey Jackson hid in his pocket to wire

YOU DECIDE
Should the Government Use Snitches?

Yes, say supporters like Bill McCollum:

I have no problems with informants because while they may not always be reliable, they give us leads and you go on and find other proof and when you go to try somebody in court, you have to prove they're guilty to a jury beyond a reasonable doubt, and if you can gain information from informants or snitches, that's fine. That's not what necessarily convicts somebody. That would be just one piece of evidence. But it does give you a lead. And you need that lead. How else are we going to find the bad guy? If you don't have informants and you can't eavesdrop, law enforcement would never be able to protect society from these major criminal enterprises.

—*Bill McCollum, former U.S. congressman*

No, says defense attorney Bob Clark:

Snitches are used by the government because it makes their life a lot easier. You put everybody in prison, and then you cut deals with those that are willing to rat on everybody else. And people generally tell the government what they want to hear. In fact, when they try people here in the southern district of Alabama, they put all the rats and the snitches together in one cell. And after they testify, they go back to the snitch cell and compare stories and compare notes. Do I feel that snitches lie? Only when their mouth is moving. You know, if they're asleep, most of the time they don't—oh, they'll say anything. They're prostitutes. I mean it is—I don't know how you could run a criminal justice system without the use of informants, but at the same time, it allows itself for such abuse. I mean absolutely unbelievable abuse.

—*Bob Clark, defense attorney*

INSTRUCTIONS

In your opinion, is the use of "snitches" ethical in prosecuting crime?

Source: *Frontline*, "Snitch" transcript. 1999. http://www.pbs.org/wgbh/pages/frontline/shows/snitch/etc/script.html.

his conversations with James White to nearby federal narcotics agents hiding close by in the late 1960s.

Now, contrast the technology of that world with this description of the world you live in. How many of these online communications systems do you use? How many have you never heard of?

> Moira wakes up in the one-bedroom apartment she shares with a roommate. She makes up the sofa bed she sleeps on in the living room and says good morning to her roommate, who is heading out the door. It is not quite time to leave for work, so she reads a novel on her Kindle for a few minutes before going online to check the weather, to look at her web-based calendar, and to check her e-mail.
>
> On her way to work, she listens to her iPod and stops at a favorite coffee shop, using her smartphone to check Foursquare just in case any of her friends are in the vicinity and want to join her for a latte.
>
> At work, Moira uses a cloud computing service to collaborate with colleagues in another state on drafting a report.
>
> During lunchtime, she orders food delivered to the office and spends some time catching up with family and friends on Facebook. She responds to her sister's wall post about Thanksgiving plans, joins a political debate with some acquaintances, posts the latest pictures from her vacation, and sends a private message to her boyfriend, who lives in another city, suggesting that they stream the same movie from Netflix that evening while simultaneously video-chatting via Skype.
>
> She also posts a link to a review of a play she is interested in seeing, customizes the post so that it is visible to a friend list she has made called "Going Out Friends," and asks whether any of those friends wants to attend it the following evening. While she is online, she sees that she has two friend requests—one from a high school friend she has not seen in 10 years and one from a guy she met briefly at a party last week. She accepts the request from the high school friend and ignores the request from the party guy.
>
> Meanwhile, a couple of people have responded to her post about the play. They make plans to meet after work for dinner and to go to the play. Moira posts that she will go on Yelp to find a restaurant close to the theater and will text everyone the location after work the following day. When Moira leaves a couple of days later to spend the weekend with her boyfriend, she takes her laptop, her smartphone, her iPod, and her Kindle with her.
>
> The Fourth Amendment protects Moira's sleeping space in the living room from warrantless government intrusions. But what of the rest of her life? (Strandburg 2011, 614–15)

Yes, think about "what of the rest of her life" the Fourth Amendment will protect in this age where advanced technology has become part of the "real world." The Internet is now a place where more and more of life takes place—our social and professional lives, our entertainment, business, health, and education. And it will almost certainly continue to grow in variety and complexity (Strandburg 2011, 616–19). The title of Professor Katherine Strandburg's article with the Moira vignette captures this changing world beautifully—"Home, Home, on the Web and Other Fourth Amendment Implications of the Technosocial Change" (2011).

Can the "reasonable expectation of privacy" test and the third party doctrine do the Fourth Amendment's job of protecting the people against government abuse of its power in this new age of social change brought on by new technology? Professor Strandburg warns that "a future is nearly upon us that will make it impossible to preserve the privacy of even the traditional Fourth Amendment bastions, such as the home, without considering the intertwined effects of technological and social change" (619). She argues for courts to adopt a **principle of technosocial continuity** in this time of rapid technological advance. "Technosocial continuity requires that courts consider both the ways in which technology facilitates intrusive surveillance and the ways in which technology spurs social change that makes citizens more vulnerable to existing surveillance technologies" (619).

We'll take a closer look at how the courts have applied the Fourth Amendment to four of these advanced technologies. The U.S. Supreme Court has ruled on two of them—thermal imaging (2001) and GPS tracking (2012). The third, e-mail surveillance, has not reached the Supreme Court, but the Sixth Circuit Court of Appeals has decided a claim that individuals have a reasonable expectation of privacy in the content of e-mail (2011). And regarding the fourth, several state courts have decided whether cell phone customers have a reasonable expectation of privacy in the content of their text messages.

LO 7 *Thermal Imaging*

Thermal imagers detect, measure, and record infrared radiation invisible to the naked eye. The imagers convert radiation into images based on the amount of heat (black is cool, white is hot, shades of gray are in between). What if police officers parked on the street outside your house, aimed a thermal imager at your house, and measured and recorded the amount of heat coming out of various parts of your house? Do you have an expectation of privacy in these heat waves? If you do, is it an expectation society is prepared to recognize? In our next case excerpt, the U.S. Supreme Court (5–4) held that the discovery and measurement of heat—something invisible to the naked eye—escaping from your home is a Fourth Amendment search in *Kyllo v. U.S.* (2001).

The U.S. Supreme Court ruled that the discovery and measurement of heat from a home by law enforcement is a Fourth Amendment search.

CASE
Was Measuring the "Heat" from Outside the House a Search?

Kyllo v. U.S.
533 U.S. 27 (2001)

HISTORY

After unsuccessfully moving to suppress evidence, Danny Kyllo entered a conditional guilty plea to manufacturing marijuana, and then appealed. Following remand, the U.S. District Court for the District of Oregon again denied Kyllo's suppression motion; Kyllo appealed again. The Ninth Circuit Court of Appeals affirmed. Certiorari was granted. The U.S. Supreme Court (5-4) reversed and remanded.

—SCALIA, J.

FACTS

In 1991 Agent William Elliott of the United States Department of the Interior came to suspect that marijuana was being grown in the home belonging to petitioner Danny Kyllo, part of a triplex on Rhododendron Drive in Florence, Oregon. Indoor marijuana growth typically requires high-intensity lamps. In order to determine whether an amount of heat was emanating from Kyllo's home consistent with the use of such lamps, at 3:20 a.m. on January 16, 1992, Agent Elliott and Dan Haas used an Agema Thermovision 210 thermal imager to scan the triplex. Thermal imagers detect infrared radiation, which virtually all objects emit but which is not visible to the naked eye. The imager converts radiation into images based on relative warmth—black is cool, white is hot, shades of gray connote relative differences; in that respect, it operates somewhat like a video camera showing heat images.

The scan of Kyllo's home took only a few minutes and was performed from the passenger seat of Agent Elliott's vehicle across the street from the front of the house and also from the street in back of the house. The scan showed that the roof over the garage and a side wall of Kyllo's home were relatively hot compared to the rest of the home and substantially warmer than neighboring homes in the triplex. Agent Elliott concluded that Kyllo was using halide lights to grow marijuana in his house, which indeed he was.

Based on tips from informants, utility bills, and the thermal imaging, a Federal Magistrate Judge issued a warrant authorizing a search of Kyllo's home, and the agents found an indoor growing operation involving more than 100 plants. Kyllo was indicted on one count of manufacturing marijuana, in violation of 21 U.S.C. § 841(a)(1). He unsuccessfully moved to suppress the evidence seized from his home and then entered a conditional guilty plea.

The Court of Appeals for the Ninth Circuit remanded the case for an evidentiary hearing regarding the intrusiveness of thermal imaging. On remand the District Court found that the Agema 210 "is a non-intrusive device which emits no rays or beams and shows a crude visual image of the heat being radiated from the outside of the house"; it "did not show any people or activity within the walls of the structure"; "the device used cannot penetrate walls or windows to reveal conversations or human activities"; and "no intimate details of the home were observed."

Based on these findings, the District Court upheld the validity of the warrant that relied in part upon the thermal imaging, and reaffirmed its denial of the motion to suppress. A divided Court of Appeals initially reversed, but that opinion was withdrawn and the panel (after a change in composition) affirmed, with Judge Noonan dissenting. The court held that Kyllo had shown no subjective expectation of privacy because he had made no attempt to conceal the heat escaping from his home, and even if he had, there was no objectively reasonable expectation of privacy because the imager "did not expose any intimate details of Kyllo's life," only "amorphous 'hot spots' on the roof and exterior wall." We granted certiorari.

OPINION

At the very core of the Fourth Amendment stands the right of a man to retreat into his own home and there be free from unreasonable governmental intrusion. The present case involves officers on a public street engaged in more than naked-eye surveillance of a home. We have previously reserved judgment as to how much technological enhancement of ordinary perception from such a vantage point, if any, is too much.

It would be foolish to contend that the degree of privacy secured to citizens by the Fourth Amendment has been entirely unaffected by the advance of technology. The question we confront today is what limits there are upon this power of technology to shrink the realm of guaranteed privacy. While it may be difficult to refine *Katz* when the search of areas such as telephone booths, automobiles, or even the curtilage and uncovered portions of residences is at issue, in the case of the search of the interior of homes there is a ready criterion, with roots deep in the common law, of the minimal expectation of privacy that exists, and that is acknowledged to be reasonable.

To withdraw protection of this minimum expectation would be to permit police technology to erode the privacy guaranteed by the Fourth Amendment. We think that obtaining by sense-enhancing technology any information regarding the interior of the home that could not otherwise have been obtained without physical "intrusion into a constitutionally protected area," constitutes a search—at least where (as here) the technology in question is not in general public use. This assures preservation of that degree of privacy against government that existed when the Fourth Amendment was adopted. On the basis of this criterion, the information obtained by the thermal imager in this case was the product of a search.

The Government maintains, however, that the thermal imaging must be upheld because it detected "only heat radiating from the external surface of the house." While the technology used in the present case was relatively crude, the rule we adopt must take account of more sophisticated systems that are already in use or in development.

The Government also contends that the thermal imaging was constitutional because it did not "detect private activities occurring in private areas." The Fourth Amendment's protection of the home has never been tied to measurement of the quality or quantity of information obtained. In Silverman, for example, we made clear that any physical invasion of the structure of the home, "by even a fraction of an inch," was too much, and there is certainly no exception to the warrant requirement for the officer who barely cracks open the front door and sees nothing but the nonintimate rug on the vestibule floor.

(continued)

In the home, our cases show, all details are intimate details, because the entire area is held safe from prying government eyes.

We have said that the Fourth Amendment draws "a firm line at the entrance to the house." That line, we think, must be not only firm but also bright—which requires clear specification of those methods of surveillance that require a warrant. While it is certainly possible to conclude from the videotape of the thermal imaging that occurred in this case that no "significant" compromise of the homeowner's privacy has occurred, we must take the long view, from the original meaning of the Fourth Amendment forward.

Where, as here, the Government uses a device that is not in general public use, to explore details of the home that would previously have been unknowable without physical intrusion, the surveillance is a "search" and is presumptively unreasonable without a warrant.

Since we hold the Thermovision imaging to have been an unlawful search, it will remain for the District Court to determine whether, without the evidence it provided, the search warrant issued in this case was supported by probable cause—and if not, whether there is any other basis for supporting admission of the evidence that the search pursuant to the warrant produced.

The judgment of the Court of Appeals is REVERSED; the case is REMANDED for further proceedings consistent with this opinion.

DISSENT

STEVENS, J.

There is, in my judgment, a distinction of constitutional magnitude between "through-the-wall" surveillance that gives the observer or listener direct access to information in a private area, on the one hand, and the thought processes used to draw inferences from information in the public domain, on the other hand. The Court has crafted a rule that purports to deal with direct observations of the inside of the home, but the case before us merely involves indirect deductions from "off-the-wall" surveillance, that is, observations of the exterior of the home. Those observations were made with a fairly primitive thermal imager that gathered data exposed on the outside of Kyllo's home but did not invade any constitutionally protected interest in privacy.

The notion that heat emissions from the outside of a dwelling are a private matter implicating the protections of the Fourth Amendment is quite difficult to take seriously. Heat waves, like aromas that are generated in a kitchen, or in a laboratory or opium den, enter the public domain if and when they leave a building. A subjective expectation that they would remain private is not only implausible but also surely not "one that society is prepared to recognize as 'reasonable.'"

There is a strong public interest in avoiding constitutional litigation over the monitoring of emissions from homes, and over the inferences drawn from such monitoring. Just as "the police cannot reasonably be expected to avert their eyes from evidence of criminal activity that could have been observed by any member of the public," so too public officials should not have to avert their senses or their equipment from detecting emissions in the public domain such as excessive heat, traces of smoke, suspicious odors, odorless gases, airborne particulates, or radioactive emissions, any of which could identify hazards to the community. In my judgment, monitoring such emissions with "sense-enhancing technology," and drawing useful conclusions from such monitoring, is an entirely reasonable public service.

On the other hand, the countervailing privacy interest is at best trivial. After all, homes generally are insulated to keep heat in, rather than to prevent the detection of heat going out, and it does not seem to me that society will suffer from a rule requiring the rare homeowner who both intends to engage in uncommon activities that produce extraordinary amounts of heat, and wishes to conceal that production from outsiders, to make sure that the surrounding area is well insulated. The interest in concealing the heat escaping from one's house pales in significance to "the chief evil against which the wording of the Fourth Amendment is directed," the "physical entry of the home," and it is hard to believe that it is an interest the Framers sought to protect in our Constitution.

Since what was involved in this case was nothing more than drawing inferences from off-the-wall surveillance, rather than any "through-the-wall" surveillance, the officers' conduct did not amount to a search and was perfectly reasonable.

I respectfully DISSENT.

Questions

1. Describe specifically the information agents Elliott and Haas got from Kyllo's house.

2. Describe exactly how the officers got the information.

3. Summarize the arguments the majority makes to support its conclusion that getting and recording thermal images constitute searches and seizures.

4. Summarize the arguments the dissent makes to support its conclusions that they aren't searches and seizures.

5. Justice Stevens distinguishes **"through-the-wall"** from **"off-the-wall"** surveillance. What does he mean by this, and does he have a point? Do you agree that it should make a difference?

LO **7**   *GPS (Global Positioning System) Tracking*

Equipped with a **GPS surveillance receiver**, a law enforcement officer can pinpoint exactly where someone is at any moment, 24/7, and can continue this "tracking" indefinitely. "GPS provides 24 hour per day global coverage. It is an all-weather system and is not affected by rain, snow, fog, or sand storms" (Langley 2008). It's fast and easy to convert GPS receivers into tracking devices by equipping them with a transmitter that sends location information to a tracking center. "GPS technology allows law enforcement officers to monitor suspects more successfully than with ordinary visual surveillance." LAPD cruiser air guns can "launch GPS-enabled 'darts' at suspects' cars. They're small (2.5 by 1.7 by 1 inch) and weigh only 3 ounces. They also work indoors (Hutchins 2007, 418).

Is installing and monitoring a GPS receiver a Fourth Amendment search? Yes, said all nine of the U.S. Supreme Court justices in *U.S. v. Jones* (2012). The story behind the Court's decision began with a major FBI/District of Columbia Police Department task force joint operation. The operation collected over 2,000 pages of data during 28 days by installing a GPS receiver in suspected drug kingpin Antoine Jones's wife's Jeep Grand Cherokee, and tracking his movements in the Jeep. Jones argued that the installation and tracking were Fourth Amendment searches. The Supreme Court agreed with Jones. Our next case excerpt explains why.

The U.S. Supreme Court (9–0) decided that attaching a GPS receiver and monitoring Antoine Jones's movements in his wife's Jeep Grand Cherokee was a Fourth Amendment search.

CASE

U.S. v. Jones Excerpt

U.S. v. Jones
565 U.S. (2012) *didn't know page yet*

HISTORY

A federal grand jury indicted Jones and others on drug trafficking conspiracy charges. The District Court suppressed the GPS data obtained while the vehicle was parked at Jones's residence, but held the remaining data admissible because Jones had no reasonable expectation of privacy when the vehicle was on public streets. Jones was convicted. The D.C. Circuit reversed, concluding that admission of the evidence obtained by warrantless use of the GPS device violated the Fourth Amendment. The U.S. Supreme Court granted certiorari, and reversed.

SCALIA, J., joined by ROBERTS, C.J., and KENNEDY, THOMAS, and SOTOMAYOR, JJ. SOTOMAYOR, J., filed a concurring opinion. ALITO, J., filed an opinion concurring in the judgment, in which GINSBURG, BREYER, and KAGAN, JJ., joined.

We decide whether the attachment of a global–positioning–system (GPS) tracking device to an individual's vehicle, and subsequent use of that device to monitor the vehicle's movements on public streets, constitutes a search or seizure within the meaning of the Fourth Amendment.

FACTS

In 2004, Antoine Jones (respondent), owner and operator of a nightclub in the District of Columbia, came under suspicion of trafficking in narcotics and was made the target of an investigation by a joint FBI and Metropolitan Police Department task force. Officers employed various investigative techniques, including visual surveillance of the nightclub, installation of a camera focused on the front door of the club, and a pen register and wiretap covering Jones's cellular phone.

Based in part on information gathered from these sources, agents installed a GPS tracking device on the undercarriage of the Jeep while it was parked in a public parking lot. Over the next 28 days, the Government used the device to track the vehicle's movements, and once had to replace

(*continued*)

the device's battery when the vehicle was parked in a different public lot in Maryland. By means of signals from multiple satellites, the device established the vehicle's location within 50 to 100 feet, and communicated that location by cellular phone to a Government computer. It relayed more than 2,000 pages of data over the 4-week period.

The Government ultimately obtained a multiple-count indictment charging Jones and several alleged co-conspirators with, as relevant here, conspiracy to distribute and possess with intent to distribute five kilograms or more of cocaine and 50 grams or more of cocaine base, in violation of 21 U.S.C. §§ 841 and 846. Before trial, Jones filed a motion to suppress evidence obtained through the GPS device. The District Court granted the motion only in part, suppressing the data obtained while the vehicle was parked in the garage adjoining Jones's residence. It held the remaining data admissible, because "a person traveling in an automobile on public thoroughfares has no reasonable expectation of privacy in his movements from one place to another." Jones's trial in October 2006 produced a hung jury on the conspiracy count.

In March 2007, a grand jury returned another indictment, charging Jones and others with the same conspiracy. The Government introduced at trial the same GPS-derived locational data admitted in the first trial, which connected Jones to the alleged conspirators' stash house that contained $850,000 in cash, 97 kilograms of cocaine, and 1 kilogram of cocaine base. The jury returned a guilty verdict, and the District Court sentenced Jones to life imprisonment.

The United States Court of Appeals for the District of Columbia Circuit reversed the conviction because of admission of the evidence obtained by warrantless use of the GPS device which, it said, violated the Fourth Amendment. The D.C. Circuit denied the Government's petition for rehearing en banc, with four judges dissenting. We granted certiorari.

OPINION

It is important to be clear about what occurred in this case: The Government physically occupied private property for the purpose of obtaining information. We have no doubt that such a physical intrusion would have been considered a "search" within the meaning of the Fourth Amendment when it was adopted. In *Entick v. Carrington*, undoubtedly familiar to every American statesman at the time the Constitution was adopted, Lord Camden expressed in plain terms the significance of property rights in search-and-seizure analysis:

> Our law holds the property of every man so sacred, that no man can set his foot upon his neighbour's close without his leave; if he does he is a trespasser, though he does no damage at all; if he will tread upon his neighbour's ground, he must justify it by law.

The text of the Fourth Amendment reflects its close connection to property, since otherwise it would have referred simply to "the right of the people to be secure against unreasonable searches and seizures;" the phrase "in their persons, houses, papers, and effects" would have been superfluous.

Our later cases, of course, have deviated from that exclusively property-based approach. In *Katz v. United States*, (1967) [p. 66], we said that "the Fourth Amendment protects people, not places." Our later cases have applied the analysis of Justice Harlan's concurrence in that case, which said that a violation occurs when government officers violate a person's "reasonable expectation of privacy," *Smith v. Maryland*, (1979), [p. 63].

At bottom, we must assure preservation of that degree of privacy against government that existed when the Fourth Amendment was adopted. For most of our history the Fourth Amendment was understood to embody a particular concern for government trespass upon the areas ("persons, houses, papers, and effects") it enumerates.

Katz established that property rights are not the sole measure of Fourth Amendment violations, but did not snuff out the previously recognized protection for property. *Katz* did not erode the principle that, when the Government does engage in physical intrusion of a constitutionally protected area in order to obtain information, that intrusion may constitute a violation of the Fourth Amendment. The *Katz* reasonable-expectation-of-privacy test has been added to, not substituted for, the common-law trespassory test.

The judgment of the Court of Appeals for the D.C. Circuit is affirmed. It is so ordered.

JUSTICE SOTOMAYOR, CONCURRING

I join the Court's opinion because I agree that a search within the meaning of the Fourth Amendment occurs, at a minimum, "where, as here, the Government obtains information by physically intruding on a constitutionally protected area." Of course, the Fourth Amendment is not concerned only with trespassory intrusions on property. Rather, even in the absence of a trespass, a Fourth Amendment search occurs when the government violates a subjective expectation of privacy that society recognizes as reasonable.

Physical intrusion is now unnecessary to many forms of surveillance. With increasing regularity, the Government will be capable of duplicating the monitoring undertaken in this case by enlisting factory—or owner—installed vehicle tracking devices or GPS-enabled smartphones. In cases of electronic or other novel modes of surveillance that do not depend upon a physical invasion on property, the majority opinion's trespassory test may provide little guidance. Situations involving merely the transmission of electronic signals without trespass would remain subject to *Katz* analysis. The same technological advances that have made possible nontrespassory surveillance techniques will also affect the *Katz* test by shaping the evolution of societal privacy expectations. At the very least, longer term GPS monitoring in investigations of most offenses impinges on expectations of privacy.

In cases involving even short-term monitoring, some unique attributes of GPS surveillance relevant to the *Katz* analysis will require particular attention. GPS monitoring generates a precise, comprehensive record of a person's public movements that reflects a wealth of detail about her familial, political, professional, religious, and sexual associations: trips to the psychiatrist, the plastic surgeon, the abortion clinic, the AIDS treatment center, the strip club, the criminal defense attorney, the by-the-hour motel, the union meeting, the mosque, synagogue or church, the gay bar and on and on.

The Government can store such records and efficiently mine them for information years into the future. And because GPS monitoring is cheap in comparison to conventional surveillance techniques and, by design, proceeds surreptitiously, it evades the ordinary checks that constrain abusive law enforcement practices: limited police resources and community hostility.

Awareness that the Government may be watching chills associational and expressive freedoms. And the Government's unrestrained power to assemble data that reveal private aspects of identity is susceptible to abuse. The net result is that GPS monitoring—by making available at a relatively low cost such a substantial quantum of intimate information about any person whom the Government, in its unfettered discretion, chooses to track—may "alter the relationship between citizen and government in a way that is inimical to democratic society."

I would take these attributes of GPS monitoring into account when considering the existence of a reasonable societal expectation of privacy in the sum of one's public movements. I would ask whether people reasonably expect that their movements will be recorded and aggregated in a manner that enables the Government to ascertain, more or less at will, their political and religious beliefs, sexual habits, and so on. I do not regard as dispositive the fact that the Government might obtain the fruits of GPS monitoring through lawful conventional surveillance techniques.

More fundamentally, it may be necessary to reconsider the premise that an individual has no reasonable expectation of privacy in information voluntarily disclosed to third parties. *United States v. Miller* (1976) [case excerpt on p. 61]. This approach is ill suited to the digital age, in which people reveal a great deal of information about themselves to third parties in the course of carrying out mundane tasks. People disclose the phone numbers that they dial or text to their cellular providers; the URLs that they visit and the e-mail addresses with which they correspond to their Internet service providers; and the books, groceries, and medications they purchase to online retailers.

Perhaps, some people may find the "tradeoff" of privacy for convenience "worthwhile," or come to accept this "diminution of privacy" as "inevitable," and perhaps not. I for one doubt that people would accept without complaint the warrantless disclosure to the Government of a list of every Web site they had visited in the last week, or month, or year. But whatever the societal expectations, they can attain constitutionally protected status only if our Fourth Amendment jurisprudence ceases to treat secrecy as a prerequisite for privacy. I would not assume that all information voluntarily disclosed to some member of the public for a limited purpose is, for that reason alone, disentitled to Fourth Amendment protection.

Justice ALITO, with whom Justice GINSBURG, Justice BREYER, and Justice KAGAN join, concurring in the judgment.

Recent years have seen the emergence of many new devices that permit the monitoring of a person's movements. In some locales, closed-circuit television video monitoring is becoming ubiquitous. On toll roads, automatic toll collection systems create a precise record of the movements of motorists who choose to make use of that convenience. Many motorists purchase cars that are equipped with devices that permit a central station to ascertain the car's location at any time so that roadside assistance may be provided if needed and the car may be found if it is stolen.

Perhaps most significant, cell phones and other wireless devices now permit wireless carriers to track and record the location of users—and as of June 2011, it has been reported, there were more than 322 million wireless devices in use in the United States. For older phones, the accuracy of the location information depends on the density of the tower network, but new "smart phones," which are equipped with a GPS device, permit more precise tracking. For example, when a user activates the GPS on such a phone, a provider is able to monitor the phone's location and speed of movement and can then report back real-time traffic conditions after combining ("crowdsourcing") the speed of all such phones on any particular road.

Similarly, phone-location-tracking services are offered as "social" tools, allowing consumers to find (or to avoid) others who enroll in these services. The availability and use of these and other new devices will continue to shape the average person's expectations about the privacy of his or her daily movements.

In the pre-computer age, the greatest protections of privacy were neither constitutional nor statutory, but practical. Traditional surveillance for any extended period of time was difficult and costly and therefore rarely undertaken. The surveillance at issue in this case—constant monitoring of the location of a vehicle for four

(*continued*)

weeks—would have required a large team of agents, multiple vehicles, and perhaps aerial assistance. Only an investigation of unusual importance could have justified such an expenditure of law enforcement resources. Devices like the one used in the present case, however, make long-term monitoring relatively easy and cheap.

In circumstances involving dramatic technological change, the best solution to privacy concerns may be legislative. A legislative body is well situated to gauge changing public attitudes, to draw detailed lines, and to balance privacy and public safety in a comprehensive way. To date, however, Congress and most States have not enacted statutes regulating the use of GPS tracking technology for law enforcement purposes. The best that we can do in this case is to apply existing Fourth Amendment doctrine and to ask whether the use of GPS tracking in a particular case involved a degree of intrusion that a reasonable person would not have anticipated.

Under this approach, relatively short-term monitoring of a person's movements on public streets accords with expectations of privacy that our society has recognized as reasonable. But the use of longer term GPS monitoring in investigations of most offenses impinges on expectations of privacy. For such offenses, society's expectation has been that law enforcement agents and others would not—and indeed, in the main, simply could not—secretly monitor and catalogue every single movement of an individual's car for a very long period.

In this case, for four weeks, law enforcement agents tracked every movement that respondent made in the vehicle he was driving. We need not identify with precision the point at which the tracking of this vehicle became a search, for the line was surely crossed before the four-week mark. Other cases may present more difficult questions. But where uncertainty exists with respect to whether a certain period of GPS surveillance is long enough to constitute a Fourth Amendment search, the police may always seek a warrant.

For these reasons, I conclude that the lengthy monitoring that occurred in this case constituted a search under the Fourth Amendment. I therefore agree with the majority that the decision of the Court of Appeals must be affirmed.

Questions

1. Identify the government interest and the intrusions on Jones's property and privacy.

2. Summarize how the majority applied the property theory to come to the conclusion that installing the GPS receiver and monitoring Jones's Jeep's movements was a search.

3. Summarize how the concurring opinion concluded that Jones had a reasonable expectation in the information gotten from the tracking.

4. How important is the "trespass" on Jones's Jeep?

5. How important is the location where the Jeep parks?

6. How important is the length of time involved and amount of information collected?

7. Is it time to dump the third party doctrine?

Note: The opinions in *Jones* may be complex; the synopsis below should help make them a little less so. But this we know for sure: All nine U.S. Supreme Court justices agreed that installing a GPS receiver and monitoring a vehicle for a month is a Fourth Amendment search. In addition to its complexity, the decision left several questions unanswered. (Table 3.2 lists some of them.)

SYNOPSIS

- A joint FBI and Washington, DC, Police Department task force suspected Antoine Jones of being the head of a large illegal drug operation.

- The task force secretly installed a GPS receiver on Jones's Jeep Grand Cherokee while it was parked in a public parking lot.

- For 28 days, the receiver broadcast all the Jeep's movements to a government computer. This generated more than 2,000 pages of location data, which led the agents to a stash house containing $850,000 and powder and crack cocaine worth about the same amount.

- Jones moved to suppress the drugs and cash on the ground that the installation and tracking were unreasonable searches.

PROPERTY THEORY (5 VOTES)

- The Fourth Amendment protects constitutionally protected physical areas, namely "persons, houses, papers, and effects."

- Jones's Jeep Cherokee is an "effect."

- Placing the GPS receiver on his Jeep was a trespass, and therefore a "search."

- Tracking the Jeep's movements was the result of the physical trespass and so it was part of the search.

REASONABLE EXPECTATION OF PRIVACY
THEORY (4 VOTES)

- The Fourth Amendment protects reasonable expectations of privacy.

- So the question is, Does GPS tracking in the totality of the circumstances of each individual case involve "a degree of intrusion that a reasonable person would not have anticipated?"

- Yes, if it lasts long enough in all but the most serious offenses.

- In this case, 28 days was long enough to satisfy the reasonable expectation of privacy.

- So, the installation and 28-day monitoring was a search.

SOTOMAYOR (SOLO)

- Justice Sotomayor joined four justices who applied the trespass doctrine.
- A Fourth Amendment search "occurs at a *minimum* where, as here, the Government obtains information by physically intruding on a constitutional area" for 28 days.
- But, she also agrees that "at the very least, longer GPS monitoring in investigations of most offenses impinges on expectations of privacy."
- Even short-term GPS monitoring potentially implicates the Fourth Amendment because it gathers so much information, is secret, has no limits, and it chills First Amendment freedoms of association and expression.
- She would ask "whether people reasonably expect their movements will be recorded and aggregated in a manner that enables the Government to ascertain, more or less at will, their political and religious beliefs, sexual habits and so on."
- And she criticizes the third party rule, claiming that *Miller* and *Smith* may not be enough in the digital age.
- "I would not assume that all information voluntarily disclosed to some member of the public for a limited purpose is, for that reason alone, disentitled to Fourth Amendment protection."

TABLE 3.2 Some questions SCOTUS left unanswered in *U.S. v. Jones* (2012)

1. Does *Jones* allow cell phone tracking?

"Under a new system set up by Sprint, law enforcement agencies have gotten GPS data from the company about its wireless customers 8 million times in about a year, raising a host of questions about consumer privacy, transparency, and oversight of how police obtain location data. What this means—and what many wireless customers no doubt do not realize—is that with a few keystrokes, police can determine in real time the location of a cell phone user through automated systems set up by the phone companies" (Elliott 2009).

2. Does *Jones* allow city surveillance cameras?

"Chicago, like a growing number of other cities, has dramatically extended its crime camera network by forging agreements with businesses and other private organizations. Perhaps half of the video feeds available to Chicago police now come from private cameras that can be accessed by law enforcement personnel, although the city won't release an exact breakdown. 'I think this is just another example of how we need to work together with our partners, and no government entity can do it all on its own,'" Lewin said.

"In all, police have access to 20,000 video feeds from public and private sources, according to Ruben Madrigal, deputy director of Chicago's Office of Emergency Management and Communications (OEMC). Crime surveillance experts access external feeds directly over the Internet through a public IP address. They tap into these feeds only during emergencies after owners are notified, according to the city. Police don't record feeds they don't own. In addition to private-sector cameras, Chicago's network includes thousands of cameras that are operated by agencies outside of public safety. For instance, Chicago Public Schools has more than 4,500 cameras; the Chicago Housing Authority has about 3,000 cameras; and O'Hare International Airport has at least 1,000 cameras. Private-sector cameras include units located on at least 11 buildings like Willis Tower and the Boeing and John Hancock buildings. Businesses and non–public safety agencies sign a memorandum of understanding to link their video feeds into the unified video surveillance network operated by the OEMC. The relationship is voluntary" (Collins 2012).

3. Does *Jones* allow domestic drone surveillance?

"The prospect of drone use inside the United States raises far-reaching issues concerning the extent of government surveillance authority, the value of privacy in the digital age, and the role of Congress in reconciling these issues. Although relatively few drones are currently flown over U.S. soil, the Federal Aviation Administration (FAA) predicts that 30,000 drones will fill the nation's skies in less than 20 years. Congress has played a large role in this expansion. In February 2012, Congress enacted the FAA Modernization and Reform Act (P.L. 112–95), which calls for the FAA to accelerate the integration of unmanned aircraft into the national airspace system by 2015.

4. Does *Jones* allow law enforcement to access text messages?

No, said the Rhode Island Superior Court. (See case excerpt.)

5. Does *Jones* allow law enforcement access to the content of e-mail messages?

No, said the U.S. Sixth Circuit Court of Appeals. (See case excerpt.)

YOU DECIDE
Is Domestic Drone Surveillance a Fourth Amendment Search?

LO 7

Drones, or unmanned aerial vehicles (UAVs), are aircraft that can fly without an onboard human operator. An unmanned aircraft system (UAS) is the entire system, including the aircraft, digital network, and personnel on the ground. Drones can fly either by remote control or on a predetermined flight path; can be as small as an insect and as large as a traditional jet; can be produced more cheaply than traditional aircraft; and can keep operators out of harm's way. These unmanned aircraft are most commonly known for their operations overseas in tracking down and killing suspected members of Al-Qaeda and related organizations. In addition to these missions abroad, drones are being considered for use in domestic surveillance operations, which might include in furtherance of homeland security, crime fighting, disaster relief, immigration control, and environmental monitoring.

Although relatively few drones are currently flown over U.S. soil, the Federal Aviation Administration (FAA) predicts that 30,000 drones will fill the nation's skies in less than 20 years. Congress has played a large role in this expansion.

In February 2012, Congress enacted the FAA Modernization and Reform Act (P.L. 112–95), which calls for the FAA to accelerate the integration of unmanned aircraft into the national airspace system by 2015. However, some Members of Congress and the public fear there are insufficient safeguards in place to ensure that drones are not used to spy on American citizens and unduly infringe upon their fundamental privacy. These observers caution that the "FAA is primarily charged with ensuring air traffic safety, and is not adequately prepared to handle the issues of privacy and civil liberties raised by drone use" (Thompson 2012).

This report* assesses the use of drones under the Fourth Amendment right to be free from unreasonable searches and seizures. The touchstone of the Fourth Amendment is reasonableness. A reviewing court's determination of the reasonableness of drone surveillance would likely be informed by location of the search, the sophistication of the technology used, and society's conception of privacy in an age of rapid technological advancement. While individuals can expect substantial protections against warrantless government intrusions into their homes, the Fourth Amendment offers less robust restrictions upon government surveillance occurring in public places and perhaps even less in areas immediately outside the home, such as in driveways or backyards. Concomitantly, as technology advances, the contours of what is reasonable under the Fourth Amendment may adjust as people's expectations of privacy evolve.

*Full report available at http://www.cfr.org/counterterrorism/crs-drones-domestic-surveillance-operations-fourth-amendment-implications-legislative-responses/p28960 (March 4, 2013)

LO 7   *E-Mail Content*

Ninety-two percent of all adults in the United States send or receive e-mail daily (Pew Research Center 2011, 1). According to the latest Pew Research Center's *Internet & American Life Project* tracking survey, for a decade—2001 to 2010, e-mail messages and Internet searches "form the core of online communication and online information gathering." And this is true despite new "platforms, broadband and mobile devices" that are changing the way we in the United States use the Internet and web. "Perhaps the most significant change over that time is that both activities have become more habitual. Today, roughly six in ten online adults engage in each of these activities on a typical day; in 2002, 49 percent of online adults used email each day, while just 29 percent used a search engine daily" (3). Also important is that this usage is not distributed evenly across all demographic groups (see Table 3.3).

How does all this e-mail implicate the Fourth Amendment? Do you have a "reasonable expectation of privacy" in what you send and receive, no matter how intimate the details? Do you give up that expectation when you hand over the e-mail

TABLE 3.3 Who uses e-mail?

Percent of online adults in each group who send or read e-mail

	Percent of each group who ever send or read e-mail	**Percent of each group who send and receive e-mail on a typical day**
All online adults	**92 Percent**	**61 Percent**
Gender		
Male	90	59
Female	93	64
Race/Ethnicity		
White	93	63
African American	87	48
Hispanic	88	53
Age		
18–29	94	64
30–49	91	63
50–64	91	61
65+	87	46
Education		
Some high school	90	39
High school	84	46
Some college	94	64
College graduate	96	77
Household income		
<$30,000	86	47
$30,000–$49,999	89	59
$50,000–$74,999	94	67
$75,000+	97	78

Source: The Pew Research Center's Internet & American Life Project, November 3–24, 2010 tracking survey. N = 2,257 adults ages 18 and older. Interviews conducted in English and Spanish.

to your ISP? Clearly, you can't send or receive Hotmail, Yahoo!, Gmail, or AOL mail without handing your messages over to Microsoft, Yahoo!, Google, or AOL, whichever offers you the service.

According to the U.S. Department of Justice (DOJ), your ISPs have to turn over all e-mail content that federal law enforcement agents ask for—even though the agents have no warrant, no probable cause, and no judge's approval to do so (Bellia and Freiwald 2008, 122). The government argued, in our next case excerpt, that e-mail content is "an important, widely used tool in criminal investigations involving fraud, terrorism, child pornography, drug trafficking, and other crimes." The case involved Steven Warshak and his mother Harriet Warshak, who were tried for fraud of more than $500 million connected with Berkeley Premium Nutraceuticals, Inc., an "incredibly profitable company" that distributed Enzyte, an herbal supplement purported to enhance male sexual performance.

Steven Warshak and his mother were indicted and convicted on the basis of incriminating e-mails. They appealed, arguing that they had a reasonable expectation of privacy in the e-mail messages they sent to each other.

CASE

Did They Have a Reasonable Expectation of Privacy in Their Email Messages?
U.S. v. Warshak
631 F.3d 266 (rehearing and rehearing en banc denied)

HISTORY

In September 2006, a grand jury indicted Steven Warshak and his mother Harriet Warshak for crimes related to Berkeley Premium Nutraceuticals, Inc (Berkeley). At the time, Berkeley was an incredibly profitable company that distributed Enzyte, an herbal supplement purported to enhance male sexual performance. Warshak was CEO and his mother was in charge of the credit card division. Before trial, Warshak moved to exclude thousands of emails that the government obtained from his Internet Service Providers (ISPs). That motion was denied. The case proceeded to trial. A jury convicted both defendants of multiple counts of fraud and money-laundering. Steven Warshak was sentenced to 25 years in prison, and forfeiture of $500 million in assets; Harriet was sentenced to 24 months in prison and jointly and individually liable for the forfeiture. Warshak appealed, but the Court of Appeals affirmed the conviction and sentence.

BOGGS, J.

To sell its products, Berkeley took orders over the phone, the mail, and over the Internet. Customers purchased products with their credit cards, and their credit-card numbers were entered into a database along with other information. In the latter half of 2001, Berkeley launched Enzyte, its flagship product. At the time of its launch, Enzyte was purported to increase the size of a man's erection. The product proved tremendously popular, and business rose sharply. By 2004, demand for Berkeley's products had grown so dramatically that the company employed 1,500 people, and the call center remained open throughout the night, taking orders at breakneck speed. Berkeley's line of supplements also expanded, ballooning from approximately four products to around thirteen. By year's end, Berkeley's annual sales topped out at around $250 million, largely on the strength of Enzyte.

THE AUTO-SHIP PROGRAM

The "life blood" of the business was its auto-ship program, which was instituted in 2001, shortly before Enzyte hit the market. The auto-ship program was a continuity or negative-option program, in which a customer would order a free trial of a product and then continue to receive additional shipments of that product until he opted out. Before each new continuity shipment arrived on the customer's doorstep, a corresponding charge would appear on his credit-card statement. The shipments and charges would continue until the customer decided to withdraw from the program, which required the customer to notify the company.

From August 2001 to at least the end of December 2002, customers were simply added to the program at the time of the initial sale without any indication that they would be on the hook for additional charges. Warshak explained that the auto-ship program was never mentioned because "nobody would sign up." If nobody signed up, "you couldn't make revenue."

This policy resulted in a substantial volume of complaints, both to Berkeley and to outside organizations. In October 2002, the Better Business Bureau ("BBB") contacted Berkeley and indicated that more than 1,500 customers had called to voice their consternation. Because of the complaints, Berkeley's sales scripts and website began to include some language disclosing the auto-ship program. A number of internal e-mails indicate that sales representatives were required to read the disclosure language and faced punishment if they failed to do so. To monitor the interactions between representatives and customers, Berkeley installed a recording system for all incoming calls.

However, as a number of Berkeley insiders testified, the compulsory disclosure language was not always read, and it was designed not to work. Shelley Kinmon testified that the disclosure of the continuity shipments was only made after the customer had placed his order. In other words, the sales representative had already taken the customer's credit-card information when auto-ship was mentioned. Also, the disclosures were deliberately made with haste, and they were placed after unrelated language that was intended to divert or deaden the customer's attention.

By July 2004, the complaints arising from Berkeley's auto-ship program had not slowed, so the President of the BBB reached out to Berkeley, sending a letter directly to Warshak. The purpose of the letter was to express "serious concerns about the number of complaints that [the BBB] had received." The complaints "related to a single issue, which was the [auto-ship] program." According to the President of the BBB, the organization "had asked on numerous occasions that [Berkeley] consider dropping [the program], and got no positive response."

In order for Berkeley's business to operate, it was essential that the company be able to accept credit cards as a form of payment. In the words of Greg Cossman, "without credit cards and the ability to charge them, there was no business." In early 2002, Warshak's merchant account at the Bank of Kentucky was terminated for excessive "chargebacks." A chargeback occurs when a customer calls the credit card company directly and contests or disputes a charge. Merchant banks—and credit-card processors—will generally not do business with merchants that experience high volumes of chargebacks, as those merchants present a greater financial risk.

Following the termination of the merchant account at the Bank of Kentucky, the company applied for merchant accounts with a number of other banks. In some instances, the applications, which often bore Harriet's signature, falsely listed her as the CEO and 100% owner of the company. In other instances, Warshak would complete the applications in his own name but falsely claim that he had never had a merchant account terminated. These prevarications were included in the applications because the prior termination would likely diminish Berkeley's chances of securing the services of other processors.

OPINION

Warshak argues that the government's warrantless, ex parte seizure of approximately 27,000 of his private emails constituted a violation of the Fourth Amendment's prohibition on unreasonable searches and seizures. Email was a critical form of communication among Berkeley personnel. As a consequence, Warshak had a number of email accounts with various ISPs, including an account with NuVox Communications. In October 2004, the government formally requested that NuVox prospectively preserve the contents of any emails to and from Warshak's email account. The request was made pursuant to 18 U.S.C. § 2703(f) and it instructed NuVox to preserve all future messages. NuVox acceded to the government's request and began preserving copies of Warshak's incoming and outgoing e-mails—copies that would not have existed absent the prospective preservation request. Per the government's instructions, Warshak was not informed that his messages were being archived.

Not all government actions are invasive enough to implicate the Fourth Amendment. The Fourth Amendment's protections hinge on the occurrence of a "search," a legal term of art whose history is riddled with complexity. A "search" occurs when the government infringes upon an expectation of privacy that society is prepared to consider reasonable. This standard breaks down into two discrete inquiries: first, has the target of the investigation manifested a subjective expectation of privacy in the object of the challenged search? Second, is society willing to recognize that expectation as reasonable?

Turning first to the subjective component of the test, we find that Warshak plainly manifested an expectation that his emails would be shielded from outside scrutiny. As he notes in his brief, his "entire business and personal life was contained within the . . . emails seized." Given the often sensitive and sometimes damning substance of his emails, we think it highly unlikely that Warshak expected them to be made public, for people seldom unfurl their dirty laundry in plain view. Therefore, we conclude that Warshak had a subjective expectation of privacy in the contents of his emails.

The next question is whether society is prepared to recognize that expectation as reasonable. This question is one of grave import and enduring consequence, given the prominent role that email has assumed in modern communication. Since the advent of email, the telephone call and the letter have waned in importance, and an explosion of Internet-based communication has taken place. People are now able to send sensitive and intimate information, instantaneously, to friends, family, and colleagues half a world away. Lovers exchange sweet nothings, and businessmen swap ambitious plans, all with the click of a mouse button. Commerce has also taken hold in email. Online purchases are often documented in email accounts, and email is frequently used to remind patients and clients of imminent appointments. Much hinges, therefore, on whether the government is permitted to request that a commercial ISP turn over the contents of a subscriber's emails without triggering the machinery of the Fourth Amendment.

In *Katz*, the Supreme Court held that Katz was "surely entitled to assume that the words he uttered into the mouthpiece would not be broadcast to the world." Since *Katz*, it has been abundantly clear that telephone conversations are fully protected by the Fourth and Fourteenth Amendments.

Letters receive similar protection. While a letter is in the mail, the police may not intercept it and examine its contents unless they first obtain a warrant based on probable cause. This is true despite the fact that sealed letters are handed over to perhaps dozens of mail carriers, any one of whom could tear open the thin paper envelopes that separate the private words from the world outside. Put another way, trusting a letter to an intermediary does not necessarily defeat a reasonable expectation that the letter will remain private.

Given the fundamental similarities between email and traditional forms of communication, it would defy

(continued)

common sense to afford emails lesser Fourth Amendment protection. Email plays an indispensable part in the Information Age. As some forms of communication begin to diminish, the Fourth Amendment must recognize and protect nascent ones that arise. Like the telephone earlier in our history, email is an ever-increasing mode of private communication, and protecting shared communications through this medium is as important to Fourth Amendment principles today as protecting telephone conversations has been in the past.

If we accept that an email is analogous to a letter or a phone call, it is manifest that agents of the government cannot compel a commercial ISP to turn over the contents of an email without triggering the Fourth Amendment. An ISP is the intermediary that makes email communication possible. Emails must pass through an ISP's servers to reach their intended recipient. Thus, the ISP is the functional equivalent of a post office or a telephone company. As we have discussed above, the police may not storm the post office and intercept a letter, and they are likewise forbidden from using the phone system to make a clandestine recording of a telephone call—unless they get a warrant, that is. It only stands to reason that, if government agents compel an ISP to surrender the contents of a subscriber's emails, those agents have thereby conducted a Fourth Amendment search, which necessitates compliance with the warrant requirement absent some exception.

While we acknowledge that a subscriber agreement might, in some cases, be sweeping enough to defeat a reasonable expectation of privacy in the contents of an email account, we doubt that will be the case in most situations, and it is certainly not the case here. The mere ability of a third-party intermediary to access the contents of a communication cannot be sufficient to extinguish a reasonable expectation of privacy. In *Katz*, the Supreme Court found it reasonable to expect privacy during a telephone call despite the ability of an operator to listen in. Similarly, the ability of a rogue mail handler to rip open a letter does not make it unreasonable to assume that sealed mail will remain private on its journey across the country. Therefore, the threat or possibility of access is not decisive when it comes to the reasonableness of an expectation of privacy.

Nor is the right of access. As the Electronic Frontier Foundation points out in its amicus brief, at the time *Katz* was decided, telephone companies had a right to monitor calls in certain situations. Specifically, telephone companies could listen in when reasonably necessary to "protect themselves and their properties against the improper and illegal use of their facilities." In this case, the NuVox subscriber agreement tracks that language, indicating that "NuVox may access and use individual Subscriber information in the operation of the Service and as necessary to protect the Service." Thus, under *Katz*, the degree of access granted to NuVox does not diminish the reasonableness of Warshak's trust in the privacy of his emails.

Our conclusion finds additional support in the application of Fourth Amendment doctrine to rented space. Hotel guests, for example, have a reasonable expectation of privacy in their rooms. This is so even though maids routinely enter hotel rooms to replace the towels and tidy the furniture. Similarly, tenants have a legitimate expectation of privacy in their apartments. That expectation persists, regardless of the incursions of handymen to fix leaky faucets. Consequently, we are convinced that some degree of routine access is hardly dispositive with respect to the privacy question.

We recognize that our conclusion may be attacked in light of the Supreme Court's decision in *United States v. Miller*, 425 U.S. 435, (1976). But *Miller* is distinguishable. First, *Miller* involved simple business records, as opposed to the potentially unlimited variety of "confidential communications" at issue here. Second, the bank depositor in *Miller* conveyed information to the bank so that the bank could put the information to use "in the ordinary course of business." By contrast, Warshak received his emails through NuVox. Thus, *Miller* is not controlling. [meaning *Miller* is not binding precedent in this case]

Accordingly, we hold that a subscriber enjoys a reasonable expectation of privacy in the contents of emails that are stored with, or sent or received through, a commercial ISP. The government may not compel a commercial ISP to turn over the contents of a subscriber's emails without first obtaining a warrant based on probable cause. Therefore, because they did not obtain a warrant, the government agents violated the Fourth Amendment when they obtained the contents of Warshak's emails.

LO 7   *Texting*

As Americans have turned to their cell phones to communicate (Figure 3.1), law enforcement has taken notice. Cell phones now represent a "powerful tool . . . to cull information on a wide range of crimes." Accordingly, law enforcement agencies made 1.3 million requests for consumer phone information—including text messages—from the nine largest cellular carriers in 2011. In doing so, law enforcement has taken advantage of information that these companies

FIGURE 3.1 Yearly U.S. Texts in Trillions

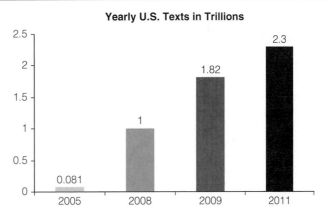

Yearly U.S. Texts in Trillions

Source: The Wireless Association, 2013.

have preserved, often without the knowledge or consent of their customers, knowing that the legislature or the courts may some day close their window of opportunity to access this data.

State v. Patino (2012)

In our next case excerpt, *State v. Patino* (2012), we'll look at the suppression hearing to exclude incriminating text messages that Cranston, Rhode Island, police officers pixted (picture message) from the defendant, Michael Patino's cell phone, without a warrant or any other judicial oversight. Patino argues that these were unreasonable searches.

Judge Savage granted the motion to suppress incriminating text messages because "it is objectively reasonable for people to expect the contents of their electronic text messages to remain private, especially vis-à-vis law enforcement."

CASE

State v. Patino
Providence, Rhode Island, Superior Court (2012)
http://www.courts.ri.gov/Courts/SuperiorCourt/DecisionsOrders/decisions/
10-1155.pdf

HISTORY

The State indicted Michael Patino for the alleged murder of Marco Nieves, the six-year-old son of Patino's girlfriend, Trisha Oliver. The case against Patino is built largely on cell phone text messages that the State claims were sent by Patino to his girlfriend and that he claims were illegally obtained by the Cranston Police Department, without a warrant, in violation of his privacy rights. He protests not only the way in which the police have attempted to build a case against him, but the charge of murder itself;

he contends that he at no time intended to hurt, much less kill, Marco, and that the text messages at issue do not prove otherwise.

The case is before this Court principally for decision with respect to a panoply of pre-trial motions to suppress filed by the Defendant by which he seeks to bar the State from introducing certain evidence at trial, including the text messages found on Trisha Oliver's cell phone, numerous cell phones and their contents, and his videotaped and written statements that were a product of his

(continued)

police interrogation. Defendant argues that the collection of evidence by the Cranston Police Department repeatedly violated his rights against unreasonable searches and seizures . . . as guaranteed by the Fourth Amendment to the United States Constitution and Article I, section 6 of the Rhode Island Constitution. This Court convened an unprecedented month-long series of evidentiary hearings to address the volume of issues presented by these and other pre-trial motions.

For the reasons set forth in this Decision, this Court holds that the Defendant has a reasonable expectation of privacy in his text messages and in the apartment where the subject cell phones were searched and seized, and that he has a right, under the Fourth Amendment, to challenge the legality of the searches and seizures of those phones and their contents by the police. Based on the tsunami of illegal evidence collected by the Cranston Police Department, this Court grants Patino a suppression motion and excludes the State's core evidence from being used at trial, including the text messages, all cell phones and their contents, all cell phone records, and critical portions of the Defendant's videotaped statement and his written statement given to the police. [Only the text messages part of the court's opinion are included in this excerpt.]

FACTS

On the morning of October 4, 2009, at approximately 6:08 a.m., Trisha Oliver placed a frantic 911 call from her Cranston apartment. According to the recording of the call, Trisha Oliver indicated that her six-year-old son, Marco Nieves, was unresponsive and not breathing. At approximately 6:11 a.m., Cranston Rescue and Fire Department responded to her apartment. Within minutes, rescue personnel transported Marco to Hasbro Children's Hospital. The dispatcher called ahead to alert emergency staff at the hospital that Marco was in full cardiac arrest.

While these events transpired at the hospital, the Cranston Police Department began its investigation at the scene. Sergeant Matthew Kite responded to the apartment at approximately 6:20 a.m. Trisha Oliver escorted Sgt. Kite into the apartment. Upon entering the apartment, Sgt. Kite observed a male, later identified as Trisha Oliver's boyfriend, Defendant Michael Patino. Defendant was sitting on the couch with a young child, later identified as his and Trisha Oliver's 14-month-old daughter, Jazlyn Oliver. Trisha Oliver showed Sgt. Kite into Marco's bedroom, where he observed a stripped bed and linens on the floor; she showed him into the master bedroom, where Sgt. Kite saw another stripped bed and a trash can that had been used as a vomit receptacle by Marco; and she showed him the bathroom, where Sgt. Kite observed dark brown vomit that looked like coffee grounds in the toilet.

Sgt. Kite's tour of the apartment, of necessity, took him through the dining and the living rooms that one must pass through upon entering the apartment to get to the bedrooms. The only room Sgt. Kite claims that Trisha Oliver did not specifically show him was the kitchen, although he may have accessed that area of the apartment on his own.

After the quick tour of the apartment, Sgt. Kite returned with Trisha Oliver to the entrance of the apartment. Officer Carroll transported her to the hospital soon thereafter. Upon their departure at approximately 6:30 a.m., Sgt. Kite requested that Officer Lee start a Crime Scene Roster. Though no officers yet considered the apartment a crime scene, Sgt. Kite testified that he believed it was prudent to record who entered and exited the apartment. Sgt. Kite remained on the scene looking for potentially hazardous materials that could have caused Marco's illness. In the process, he observed four cell phones: an LG Verizon cell phone on the kitchen counter; a Metro PCS Kyocera cell phone on the dining room table; a black T-Mobile Sidekick cell phone on the back headrest of the couch, near where Mr. Patino was sitting; and an iPhone on the far armrest of the couch.

During this time, Sgt. Kite asked Defendant what happened the night before, to which Defendant responded that he did not know because he had not spent the night there. Sgt. Kite subsequently asked Defendant when Trisha Oliver had called him and asked him to come over, to which Defendant responded that she had not called him because he did not own a cell phone. According to Sgt. Kite, Defendant asserted that he had arrived at the apartment in the early hours of the morning only by chance.

Afterwards, at some time before 7:15 a.m., Sgt. Kite picked up and manipulated the cell phone on the kitchen counter, later identified as an LG Verizon cell phone with phone number (401) 486-5573, which he claimed he did in response to a "beeping" sound that it had made. Because Defendant made no move to acknowledge or respond to the sound, Sgt. Kite felt that it was necessary to investigate the phone, in the event that it was a family member calling with respect to Marco's situation. In his testimony, Sgt. Kite maintained that he was most concerned about getting in touch with Marco's birth father, who had been unreachable up to that point.

Upon picking up the phone, Sgt. Kite said he viewed an alert on the front, exterior screen of the device that said there was one new message. He then opened the phone, allowing him to view the interior screen. That screen said there was one new message, but that it could not be received due to a lack of credit on the account. Sgt. Kite testified that he "manipulated a button" to "acknowledge receipt of the message to avoid repeat notifications." This manipulation led him to a list of text messages, with the most recent appearing at the top. As he saw the word "hospital" in the message at the top of the list, he clicked on this message. Subsequently, Sgt. Kite viewed the following message in the "SENT" folder, addressed to "DaMaster" at phone number (401) 699-7580: "Wat if I got 2 take him 2 da hospital wat do I say and dos marks on his neck omg."

Though this message was located in the "SENT" folder, it indicates that it was "Saved," implying that the attempt to send it failed and it never reached its intended recipient.

Though Sgt. Kite stated in his testimony that he was disturbed by this message and found it suspicious, he claimed that he did not scroll through the rest of the messages on the phone. Sgt. Kite testified that, after reading this one message, he closed and replaced the phone on the counter and called Lieutenant Sacoccia at headquarters to inform him of the suspicious text message.

[After officers arrived to escort Patino to Cranston Police Department headquarters for an interview,] Sgt. Kite noticed that the cell phone, which had previously been on the back headrest of the couch near where Defendant was sitting, was no longer there. He immediately called headquarters to alert officers of this fact and to suggest, "there's possibly some information that needs preservation and you might want to take [the cell phone] off [Defendant] upon arrival." He also relayed the contents of the text message that he had seen on the LG cell phone to Lt. Sacoccia.

Back at headquarters, Officer Machado testified that he confiscated the black T-Mobile cell phone that Defendant had on his person. Instead of placing the phone in a secure "trap" at the station, Officer Machado secured the phone on his person. Officer Machado subsequently gave Sgt. Walsh the cell phone taken from Defendant's person. Sgt. Walsh placed the cell phone in his pocket and did not turn it over to the Department of the Bureau of Criminal Investigation ("B.C.I.") until later that evening. At this point, this Court briefly notes that all the evidence which the Cranston Police Department seized and took into custody was not secured until much later in the day on October 4, 2009.

At 8:09 a.m., it appears that an officer at the apartment used the LG cell phone, phone number (401) 486-5573, to call the phone's voicemail account, though the officer hung up after 15 seconds. Sgt. Kite remained on scene in a supervisory capacity until 10:15 a.m., during which time Detectives Wayne Cushman and Peter Souza of B.C.I. arrived at 7:15 a.m. and 8:32 a.m., respectively. All detectives remained on standby at the scene until Lt. Sacoccia called them and confirmed that a search warrant for the apartment had been signed. At this point, B.C.I. detectives began photographing and videotaping the scene. Det. Cushman took still photographs, while Det. Souza videotaped the scene. Following the filming and photographing, both detectives gathered and bagged items for evidence.

Notably, the critical cell phones seized by the B.C.I. detectives were placed in little brown paper bags that were not securely sealed. Photographs of the apartment reveal that the officers picked up and moved the Metro PCS cell phone that morning. After Sgt. Walsh arrived at the apartment with a hard copy of the search warrant, he and Sgt. Kite decided to have B.C.I. photograph the contents of the LG cell phone ostensibly to protect the integrity of the investigation against the possibility of the relevant text messages being remotely deleted. The photographs taken at this point reveal incriminating text messages on the LG cell phone with profane language and references to punching Marco "three times," the hardest of which was in the stomach. Sgt. Kite was given the LG cell phone in an unsealed paper bag by B.C.I. detectives at approximately 10:15 a.m. Sgt. Kite turned the bag over to Det. Cushman at headquarters later that afternoon.

OPINION

Defendant argues, in support of his suppression motions, that he has standing to challenge the search of the LG cell phone and the seizure of the cell phones from the apartment because he has a reasonable expectation of privacy in the apartment, as a frequent overnight guest, and in the LG cell phone, because he purchased it and used it.

MOTION TO SUPPRESS TEXT MESSAGES AND OTHER EVIDENCE FROM CELL PHONES

The issues raised by Defendant's motions to suppress cell phone text messages and related evidence are issues of first impression in Rhode Island. These issues involve thoroughly contemporary problems of the relationship between rapidly evolving technology and the law. Not only have our own courts just begun to wade into these waters, but other courts around the country have just begun to put a proverbial toe in the water.

In treading into these unchartered waters, this Court is mindful that the Fourth Amendment concerns implicated by law enforcement's use of the contents of cell phones have become more urgent with the increasing ubiquity of cell phones and text messages.

For context, 83% of American adults—4 of 5 people— own a cell phone. The cell phone has, in effect, moved beyond a "fashionable accessory and into the realm of life necessity." Text messages, defined as short electronically-transmitted written communications between mobile devices, are closely intertwined with the popularity and adoption of cell phones. The typical adult sends or receives an average of 41.5 messages per day. Nationwide, an average of 4.1 billion text messages are exchanged daily. Moreover, text messaging stands to become an increasingly prominent aspect of society. Ninety-five percent of young adults, ages 18–29, use text messaging. This emerging group sends or receives an average of 87.7 daily text messages. American teenagers, perhaps more importantly, send an average of 3,146 text messages monthly. According to one media analyst, "texting is the form of communication for the next generation."

Texting has largely replaced calling as the preferred form of communication by many young adults, particularly because many service providers offer plans that make it less expensive to text than to call.

As Americans have turned to their cell phones to communicate, law enforcement has taken notice. Cell phones

(continued)

now represent a "powerful tool . . . to cull information on a wide range of crimes" (Eric Lichtblau, "More Demands on Cell Carriers in Surveillance," *New York Times*, July 8, 2012). Accordingly, law enforcement agencies made 1.3 million requests for consumer phone information—including text messages—from the nine largest cellular carriers in 2011. In doing so, law enforcement has taken advantage of information that these companies have preserved, often without the knowledge or consent of their customers, knowing that the legislature or the courts may some day close their window of opportunity to access this data. Indeed, this Court, though not unfamiliar with cell phones and text messaging, was stunned to learn during the evidentiary hearing in this matter that one cellular carrier that figures prominently in this case—Verizon—retains a record of the actual text messages sent and received by its customers, while another cellular carrier involved here—T-Mobile—does not.

Attempting to reconcile the difficult dichotomy between protecting the privacy of cell phone data and enabling law enforcement, the Rhode Island legislature recently approved a bill mandating a warrant in order to search the contents of a cell phone incident to an arrest. Governor Lincoln D. Chafee vetoed the bill, stating that the courts, not the legislature, were better suited to resolve the question of Fourth Amendment privacy rights in electronic communications.

Mindful of these unsettled waters, this Court begins its analysis and, as this case presents issues of first impression, looks to the jurisprudence of its sister states and federal courts for guidance.

DEFENDANT'S EXPECTATION OF PRIVACY IN THE CONTENTS OF HIS COMMUNICATIONS

This Court must determine if Defendant has a reasonable expectation of privacy in the contents of his text communications. At the outset, this Court notes that the question of whether people have an expectation of privacy in the contents of their text messages has not yet been settled.

With the issue not yet definitively resolved, however, this Court will apply the seminal *Katz* test to determine Defendant's expectation of privacy in his alleged text messages. Specifically, the Court will explore the extent to which Defendant has indicated a subjective expectation of privacy in the text messages on the LG cell phone and whether such expectation of privacy is one society accepts as objectively reasonable. *Smith v. Maryland*, 442 U.S. 735, 740 (1979) [excerpt p. 63].

Upon review, the Court is satisfied that Defendant has shown a subjective expectation of privacy in the contents of his alleged text messages on the LG cell phone. It appears that text messaging was the Defendant's primary means of communication with others, given the frequency and number of text messages sent to and received by Defendant. Indeed, the Court notes that Angie Patino

testified that Defendant's own cell phone did not even have the capability to make actual phone calls. Similar to many young adults today, Defendant did not call others, he texted them. Defendant's reliance on text messages as the primary means of communicating with his girlfriend, his sister, and other friends, therefore, supports a finding of a subjective expectation of privacy in their contents. This Court cannot justifiably find that Defendant did not have an expectation of privacy in the contents of his interpersonal communications, simply as a function of the means used to make those communications, especially where there is no danger that Defendant's alleged text messages were seen or overheard by parties other than the police.

Moreover, the Court is satisfied that both the tenor and the contents of Defendant's alleged text messages on the LG cell phone are indicative of his subjective expectation of privacy in them. Indeed, the very incriminating nature of the contents of the text messages supports this finding of a subjective expectation that the text messages would remain private between Defendant and Trisha Oliver. The State, in oral argument, effectively conceded Defendant's subjective expectation of privacy in his alleged text messages. It characterized those texts as revealing "the unfettered Michael Patino." It argued that "the text messages document how Defendant speaks and acts when he thinks no one is watching." This Court can conceive of no better definition of a subjective expectation of privacy than what the State offered.

Transitioning to the objective tier of the *Katz* test, this Court is satisfied that Defendant's expectation of privacy in his alleged text messages was also objectively reasonable. Cell phones have replaced telephones. People send and receive billions of text messages to and from their cell phones daily. Text messaging, especially among young adults, has become an oft-employed substitute for face-to-face conversations, cell phone conversations, or email. These text messages are often raw, unvarnished and immediate, revealing the most intimate of thoughts and emotions to those who are expected to guard them from publication. The text messages may be true or untrue. In addition, most individuals now keep their cell phones in their possession at all times. Individuals are closely associated with, if not identified by, their cell phone numbers.

Accordingly, this Court finds that it is objectively reasonable for people to expect the contents of their electronic text messages to remain private, especially vis-à-vis law enforcement. Moreover, this Court finds that the possibility that someone other than the intended recipient of a text message will be in possession of the receiving cell phone at any given time is unreflective of contemporary cell phone usage. Most cell phone owners are in immediate possession of their phones at all times; indeed, the primary convenience of cell—"mobile"—phones is largely predicated on the fact that they stay with a person at all times.

This Court, therefore, does not find that the remote possibility that an unintended party will receive a text message due to his or her possession of another person's cell phone is sufficient to destroy an objective expectation of privacy in such a message. Even if a cell phone were to be separated from its owner, the majority of cell phones now feature some type of locking or password system that prevents easy access to or reading of a text message. The risk that a text message will be viewed by someone other than the intended recipient is simply too remote to eliminate a person's objectively reasonable belief that his or her text message will, in fact, be viewed only by the intended recipient.

ELECTRONIC COMMUNICATIONS AND THE THIRD-PARTY DOCTRINE

In such an unsettled area of the law, however, it behooves this Court to make a thorough review of the preceding relevant jurisprudence before reaching a final determination. Accordingly, this Court will address the well-settled third-party doctrine to determine if it stands as an obstacle to finding an expectation of privacy in the contents of text messages and/or other electronic communications.

The third-party doctrine, succinctly stated, holds that a person does not have a reasonable expectation of privacy in information that he or she has voluntarily exposed or communicated to a third party. See *Smith v. Maryland*, 442 U.S. at 743-44 [excerpt p. 63] holding that where a person conveyed numerical information to the phone company and its equipment in the normal course of business, he assumed the risk that the company would reveal the information to the police.

If applied absolutely, the third-party doctrine would effectively defeat any expectation of privacy in text messages and, potentially, all electronic communications. This result is untenable, however, in our modern world where electronic communication is omnipresent and a cultural necessity. This Court, consequently, will further examine the doctrine in light of today's technological realities.

Historically, the third-party doctrine has been invoked to find that a person does not have a reasonable expectation of privacy in the address on an envelope, telephone numbers dialed, or certain financial information provided to a bank. Nevertheless, this Court reasons that the simple technological reality of how text messages are transmitted should not be allowed to entirely negate an individual's right to privacy. In an era before the advent of cell phones, the content of the text messages that Defendant allegedly sent to Trisha Oliver and that appeared on the LG cell phone would never have been public. The messages would have been exchanged by Defendant and Trisha Oliver in person or via landline phone outside the view of law enforcement. Surveillance of the Defendant and Trisha Oliver by law enforcement would have revealed the fact that Defendant and Trisha Oliver may

have spoken—via the exchange of text messages—but not the content of their communication.

This Court thus follows the ostensible logic of *Smith v. Maryland* and, consequently, holds that the third-party doctrine is not applicable with respect to the content of the text messages that were allegedly exchanged between Defendant and Trisha Oliver. The third-party doctrine, in this Court's view, defeats an expectation of privacy, at most, as to the fact that the two parties actually exchanged text messages.

Moreover, the third-party doctrine is impliedly based on a theory of assumption of risk—i.e., the theory that a sender of a text message assumes the risk that the recipient of that message will disclose its substance to a third party. Yet, this theory of assumption of risk does not match today's realities of electronic communications. In light of the widespread use of text messaging, to not partake in the medium is tantamount to actively choosing not to communicate.

This is particularly true for rising generations that have almost universally adopted the technology. It is even more true for young persons with limited financial resources, like Defendant and Trisha Oliver, who may feel compelled by the cost structure of the service plans offered by their cell phone service providers to text rather than call. While it is certainly possible to forgo text messaging, the choice is unpalatable, rather untenable, and disadvantageous relative to participating within our technologically dependent culture. Thus, unless an individual is ready to relinquish his or her ability to effectively communicate in today's technological climate, the risk of surveillance is not a choice, but an undeniable reality.

Further, cell phone service providers, like Internet Service Providers for emails, retain text messages, both sent and received, for varying periods of time. Again, were the third-party doctrine absolutely applied, an individual's expectation of privacy in text messages would be made dependent upon his or her service provider's text message retention policy. This result is fundamentally unfair because: (1) many people are unaware of their respective service provider's policies; (2) service providers maintain the right to change their text message retention policies without notice; and (3) many people may not have a choice in service providers depending on their location. Any discussion of the privacy rights in text messages, therefore, must go beyond consideration of the third-party doctrine.

All together, this Court finds that the usual tropes—such as letters and emails— through which courts have viewed the limits of a reasonable expectation of privacy in text messages are of only limited use as they are largely predicated on a misconception regarding the technology's nature and use in contemporary society. Text messages are not letters, email, or even an oral communication alone—they are a technological and functional hybrid. It follows that any consideration of people's subjective expectation of privacy in their text messages must reflect this reality.

(continued)

This Court will not strain, therefore, to apply existing law based on imperfect analogies.

Accordingly, this Court finds that the *Katz* test for determining whether a person has a reasonable expectation of privacy is the appropriate one to apply. In applying the *Katz* test, this Court finds further that the Defendant does have a reasonable expectation of privacy in the content of his alleged text messages. In so holding, the Court emphasizes that in viewing the contents of people's text messages, just as with GPS monitoring, law enforcement is able to obtain "a wealth of detail about [a person's] familial, political, professional, religious, and sexual associations." *U.S. v. Jones* (Sotomayor, J., concurring). It is hard to imagine information that could be any more private or worthy of protection from unfettered examination by law enforcement. Any other result would be untenable and out of keeping with the general goal of the Fourth Amendment to prevent a too-permeating police surveillance. This concern for protecting the security of one's privacy against arbitrary intrusion by the police, should be all the more salient when it comes to the contents of a person's communications because awareness that the Government may be watching chills associational and expressive freedoms.

Of all the rights of the citizen, few are of greater importance or more essential to his [or her] peace and happiness than the right of personal security, and that involves, not merely protection of his [or her] person from assault, but exemption of his [or her] private affairs, books, and papers [and this Court would add the content of his or her text messages] from the inspection and scrutiny of others. Without the enjoyment of this right,

all other rights would lose half their value. *In re Pacific Railway Comm'n*, 32 F. 241, 250 (C.C.N.D. Cal. 1887).

In light of the reviewed analogies and discussed considerations, this Court offers a series of interconnected holdings. This Court finds that the third-party doctrine is untenable for today's technological climate and thus should not be applied absolutely. It also finds that text messages should not be considered solely as the contents of a single individual's cell phone for purposes of analyzing an expectation of privacy in those messages under the Fourth Amendment. For this analysis, this Court finds that text messages sent and received should be viewed as a single entity due to their interdependent nature and form. Finally, in applying the *Katz* test for standing, this Court finds that a person has a reasonable expectation of privacy in the contents of his or her text messages.

Questions

1. List the reasons why the court finds that Michael Patino had a subjective expectation of privacy in his texts.

2. List the reasons why the court finds that Michael Patino's subjective expectation of privacy was reasonable.

3. According to the court, why doesn't the third party doctrine apply to Patino's texts?

4. According to the court, why doesn't the assumption of risk theory apply to Patino's texts?

5. According to the court, why do Michael Patino's text messages pass the *Katz* test?

CRIMINAL PROCEDURE IN ACTION

There is a reasonable expectation of privacy in text messages

LO 7   FACTS

On July 30, 2010, the State charged James Clampitt with first-degree involuntary manslaughter, and leaving the scene of a motor vehicle accident. The charges arose out of an automobile accident that occurred on June 13, 2010, in Audrain County, Missouri. On February 9, 2011, Clampitt filed a motion to suppress "all evidence obtained through or from the search and seizure of [his] cell phone and cell phone records." The State had obtained such information from U.S. Cellular through the use of four investigative subpoenas issued in June and July of 2010, requesting U.S. Cellular to provide the State with tower location information as well as

"text message content and detail for incoming and outgoing text messages."

At a hearing conducted on the motion, the Special Prosecutor testified that she requested Clampitt's incoming and outgoing text messages beyond the twenty-four-hour period surrounding the accident in hopes of obtaining an admission from Clampitt that either he or a member of his family was driving the vehicle at the time of the accident. The Special Prosecutor also testified that she did not seek a warrant because she believed the text messages "were records that were in possession of a third party" and that the investigative subpoenas were a sufficient means for obtaining such information from third parties.

On May 18, 2011, the trial court granted Clampitt's motion to suppress, finding Clampitt had a reasonable expectation of privacy in the text messages.

OPINION

In its appeal, the State claims that Clampitt had no reasonable expectation of privacy in the contents of his text messages because the text messages were in the possession of a third party. The State points out that generally, "a person has no legitimate expectation of privacy in information he voluntarily turns over to third parties." *Smith v. Maryland*, 442 U.S. 735 (1979). While this is true, courts have held that "the mere *ability* of a third-party intermediary to access the contents of a communication cannot be sufficient to extinguish a reasonable expectation of privacy."

Cell phone providers have the ability to access their subscribers' text messages; however, the providers' ability to access those messages does not diminish subscribers' expectation of privacy in their text message communications.

Rather, subscribers assume that the contents of their text messages will remain private despite the necessity of a third party to complete the correspondence. Callers have long enjoyed Fourth Amendment protection of the information they communicate over the phone. We see no reason why the same information communicated textually from that same device should receive any less protection under the Fourth Amendment.

Furthermore, society's continued expectation of privacy in communications made by letter or phone call demonstrates its willingness to recognize a legitimate expectation of privacy in the contents of text messages. What individuals once communicated through phone calls and letters can now be sent in a text message. Thus, as text messaging becomes an ever-increasing substitute for the more traditional forms of communication, it follows that society expects the contents of text messages to receive the same Fourth Amendment protections afforded to letters and phone calls.

We therefore find that the trial court did not err in concluding that Clampitt had a reasonable expectation of privacy in the contents of his text messages.

The Plain View Doctrine

According to the **plain view doctrine**, individuals have no reasonable expectation of privacy in what officers discover by their ordinary senses. Although the doctrine takes its name from the sense of sight, it applies to discovery by the other senses, too—namely, hearing, smell, and sometimes even touch. (Unless otherwise noted, we'll use "plain view" to include all the ordinary senses.)

There are two kinds of plain view. In both kinds, the issue is rarely whether there's a search; it's whether officers can *seize* the items in plain view. The first type is **search-related plain view**. It refers to items in plain view that officers discover while they're searching for items they're specifically authorized to search for. For example, in one leading Supreme Court case, an officer had a warrant to search for jewelry taken during a robbery. During the search, he saw an Uzi machine gun and other weapons in plain view (*Horton v. California* 1990). This kind of plain view we'll discuss in relation to seizures during frisks in Chapter 4; during arrests in Chapter 5; during searches for evidence in Chapter 6; and during inventory searches in Chapter 7.

The second type, **nonsearch-related plain view**, refers to plain view that doesn't involve a Fourth Amendment intrusion at all. This can occur in several settings. Here are a few examples: An officer sees a diner in a restaurant take a "joint" out of her pocket; an officer sees a passenger in a car stopped at a stoplight hand a joint to the driver; or an officer walking down the street sees a resident smoking pot in her living room in front of her ground-level apartment window that is clearly visible from the public sidewalk.

All three of our examples satisfy the two conditions of the plain view doctrine, which says that discoveries made under two conditions aren't searches:

1. Officers are where they have a legal right to be—namely, any place where you or I could lawfully be.

2. Officers haven't beefed up their ordinary senses with advanced technology that's not readily available to you or me.

Condition 2 requires that courts distinguish between technological enhancements that many people use and anyone can get easily—flashlights, bifocals, and magnifying glasses—and high-powered devices that only a few people have or can get easily. So eyesight enhanced by a flashlight is treated like ordinary eyesight; eyesight enhanced by X-ray isn't.

In *U.S. v. Kim* (1976), for example, FBI agents used an 800-millimeter telescope with a 60-millimeter opening to observe activities in Earl "The Old Man" Kim's apartment. The surveillance took place nearly a quarter mile from the apartment. The telescope was so powerful the agents could even see what Kim was reading. According to the U.S. District Court for the District of Hawaii, "It is inconceivable that the government can intrude so far into an individual's home that it can detect the material he is reading and still not have engaged in a search" (1255).

The U.S. Supreme Court came to a different result when it applied the plain view doctrine in *California v. Ciraolo* (1986). The police saw marijuana growing in Dante Ciraolo's yard from a plane 1,000 feet in the air. The police had hired the plane because two privacy fences blocked their view from the ground. According to the Court, the use of the plane didn't enhance the officers' naked eye such that it turned the observation into a Fourth Amendment search.

In a similar case, *Dow Chemical Corporation v. U.S.* (1986), Dow maintained elaborate security around a 2,000-acre chemical plant that bars ground-level observation. When Dow refused the Environmental Protection Agency's (EPA's) request for an on-site inspection, the EPA employed a commercial air photographer to fly over the plant and take photographs to determine whether Dow was complying with EPA standards. The U.S. Supreme Court ruled that such aerial observation and photography weren't Fourth Amendment searches.

So far, we've discussed the application of the doctrine only to what officers see (1) when they're where they have a legal right to be and (2) without the aid of technology not available to the general public. But, as we mentioned earlier, the doctrine also applies to what officers hear, smell, and even, sometimes, what they feel.

In *Illinois v. Caballes* (2005), the U.S. Supreme Court held that the Fourth Amendment didn't apply to a drug-sniffing dog that alerted officers at the trunk of Roy Caballes's car to what turned out to be marijuana inside.

CASE

Was the Dog Sniff a Search?

Illinois v. Caballes
543 U.S. 405 (2005)

HISTORY

Roy I. Caballes, Defendant, was convicted of cannabis trafficking, following a bench trial in the Circuit Court, La Salle County, and sentenced to 12 years' imprisonment and a $256,136 fine. He appealed. The Illinois Appellate Court affirmed. Granting petition for leave to appeal, the Illinois Supreme Court, reversed. The U.S. Supreme Court granted certiorari, vacated the judgment and remanded the case.

—STEVENS, J.

FACTS

Illinois State Trooper Daniel Gillette stopped Roy Caballes for speeding on an interstate highway. When Gillette radioed the police dispatcher to report the stop, a second trooper, Craig Graham, a member of the Illinois State Police Drug Interdiction Team, overheard the transmission and immediately headed for the scene with his narcotics-detection dog. When they arrived, Caballes's car was on the shoulder of the road and Caballes was in Gillette's vehicle. While Gillette was in the process of writing a warning ticket, Graham walked his dog around Caballes's car. The dog alerted at the trunk. Based on that alert, the officers searched the trunk, found marijuana, and arrested Caballes. The entire incident lasted less than 10 minutes.

OPINION

Official conduct that does not "compromise any legitimate interest in privacy" is not a search subject to the Fourth Amendment. Any interest in possessing contraband cannot be deemed "legitimate," and thus, governmental conduct that only reveals the possession of contraband compromises no legitimate privacy interest. This is because the expectation "that certain facts will not come to the attention of the authorities" is not the same as an interest in "privacy that society is prepared to consider reasonable."

In *U.S. v. Place* (1983), we treated a canine sniff by a well-trained narcotics-detection dog as unique because it discloses only the presence or absence of narcotics, a contraband item. Caballes likewise concedes that drug sniffs are designed, and if properly conducted are generally likely, to reveal only the presence of contraband. Although Caballes argues that the error rates, particularly the existence of false positives, call into question the premise that drug-detection dogs alert only to contraband, the record contains no evidence or findings that support his argument. Moreover, Caballes does not suggest that an erroneous alert, in and of itself, reveals any legitimate private information, and, in this case, the trial judge found that the dog sniff was sufficiently reliable to establish probable cause to conduct a full-blown search of the trunk.

Accordingly, the use of a well-trained narcotics-detection dog—one that does not expose noncontraband items that otherwise would remain hidden from public view during a lawful traffic stop, generally does not implicate legitimate privacy interests. In this case, the dog sniff was performed on the exterior of Caballes's car while he was lawfully seized for a traffic violation. Any intrusion on Caballes's privacy expectations does not rise to the level of a constitutionally cognizable infringement.

This conclusion is entirely consistent with our recent decision that the use of a thermal-imaging device to detect the growth of marijuana in a home constituted an unlawful search, *Kyllo v. U.S.* (2001) [excerpted on p. 68]. Critical to that decision was the fact that the device was capable of detecting lawful activity—in that case, intimate details in a home, such as "at what hour each night the lady of the house takes her daily sauna and bath."

The legitimate expectation that information about perfectly lawful activity will remain private is categorically distinguishable from Caballes's hopes or expectations concerning the nondetection of contraband in the trunk of his car. A dog sniff conducted during a concededly lawful traffic stop that reveals no information other than the location of a substance that no individual has any right to possess does not violate the Fourth Amendment.

The judgment of the Illinois Supreme Court is vacated, and the case is REMANDED for further proceedings not inconsistent with this opinion.

It is so ordered.

DISSENT

SOUTER, J.

The infallible dog is a creature of legal fiction. Although the Supreme Court of Illinois did not get into the sniffing averages of drug dogs, their supposed infallibility is belied by judicial opinions describing well-trained animals sniffing and alerting with less than perfect accuracy, whether owing to errors by their handlers, the limitations of the dogs themselves, or even the pervasive contamination of currency by cocaine. See, e.g., *U.S. v. Kennedy* (C.A.10 1997) (describing a dog that had a 71% accuracy rate); *U.S. v. Scarborough* (C.A.10 1997) (describing a dog that erroneously alerted 4 times out of 19 while working for the postal service and 8% of the time over its entire career); *U.S. v. Limares* (C.A.7 2001) (accepting as reliable a dog that gave false positives between 7% and 38% of the time); *Laime v. State* (Ark 2001) (speaking of a dog that made between 10 and 50 errors); *U.S. v. $242, 484.00* (C.A.11 2003) (noting that because as much as 80% of all currency in circulation contains drug residue, a dog alert "is of little value"); *U.S. v. Carr* (C.A.3 1994) ("[A] substantial portion of United States currency . . . is tainted with sufficient traces of controlled substances to cause a trained canine to alert to their presence"). Indeed, a study cited by Illinois in this case for the proposition that dog sniffs are "generally reliable" shows that dogs in artificial testing situations return false positives anywhere from 12.5% to 60% of the time, depending on the length of the search. K. Garner et al., Duty Cycle of the Detector Dog: A Baseline Study 12 (Apr. 2001) (prepared by Auburn U. Inst. for Biological Detection Systems). In practical terms, the evidence is clear that the dog that alerts hundreds of times will be wrong dozens of times.

Once the dog's fallibility is recognized, however, that ends the justification for treating the sniff as sui generis under the Fourth Amendment: the sniff alert does not necessarily signal hidden contraband, and opening the container or enclosed space whose emanations the dog has sensed will not necessarily reveal contraband or any other evidence of crime.

(continued)

d alert cannot claim the certainty that both in treating the deliberate use of sui generis and then taking that characterization as a reason to say they are not searches subject to Fourth Amendment scrutiny. And when that aura of uniqueness disappears, there is no good reason to ignore the actual function that dog sniffs perform. They are conducted to obtain information about the contents of private spaces beyond anything that human senses could perceive, even when conventionally enhanced.

Thus, in practice the government's use of a trained narcotics dog functions as a limited search to reveal undisclosed facts about private enclosures, to be used to justify a further and complete search of the enclosed area. And given the fallibility of the dog, the sniff is the first step in a process that may disclose "intimate details" without revealing contraband, just as a thermal-imaging device might do, as described in *Kyllo v. U.S.* (2001).

GINSBURG, J., JOINED BY SOUTER, J.

In my view, the Court diminishes the Fourth Amendment's force. A drug-detection dog is an intimidating animal. Injecting such an animal into a routine traffic stop changes the character of the encounter between the police and the motorist. The stop becomes broader, more adversarial, and (in at least some cases) longer. Caballes—who, as far as Troopers Gillette and Graham knew, was guilty solely of driving six miles per hour over the speed limit—was exposed to the embarrassment and intimidation of being investigated, on a public thoroughfare, for drugs. Even if the drug sniff is not characterized as a Fourth Amendment "search," the sniff surely broadened the scope of the traffic-violation-related seizure.

The Court has never removed police action from Fourth Amendment control on the ground that the action is well calculated to apprehend the guilty. Under today's decision, every traffic stop could become an occasion to call in the dogs, to the distress and embarrassment of the law-abiding population . . . .

Questions

1. List all the officers' acts that might qualify as ones in which there's a reasonable expectation of privacy.

2. Summarize the arguments in the majority and dissenting opinions regarding whether the dog sniff was (or wasn't) a search.

3. In your opinion, was the drug-sniffing dog circling Roy Caballes's car an enhancement of Officer Graham's sense of smell? Explain your answer.

4. In your opinion, what's the significance of the numbers Justice Souter cites in support of his argument?

LO 8 Public Places

The Fourth Amendment doesn't protect what officers can discover through their ordinary senses in public places, including streets, parks, and other publicly owned areas. Public places also include privately owned businesses that are open to the public. But "employees only" areas, such as offices, restrooms, basements, and other places not open to the public, aren't public places. Public restrooms are public places, too, even enclosed stalls—at least as much as officers can see over and under partitions or through cracks or other gaps in partitions (Hall 1993, 543–48).

LO 8 The Open Fields Doctrine

The Fourth Amendment protects our right to be secure in our persons, houses, papers, and effects, but through its decisions, the Supreme Court has made it clear that this protection doesn't extend to all places—namely, to open fields, public places, and abandoned property.

According to the **open fields doctrine**, "the special protection accorded by the Fourth Amendment to the people in their 'persons, houses, papers, and effects' is not extended to the open fields" (*Hester v. U.S.* 1924, 28). In *Oliver v. U.S.* (1984), the U.S. Supreme Court concluded that society isn't prepared to recognize any reasonable expectation of privacy in open fields, because open fields don't "provide the setting for those intimate activities that the Amendment is intended to shelter from government interference or surveillance. There is no societal interest in protecting the privacy of those activities, such as the cultivation of crops, that occur in open fields" (178).

What if owners give notice they expect privacy—for example, by building fences or putting up "No Trespassing" signs? Does the doctrine still apply? Yes, says the Supreme Court. Why? Because of the practical difficulties police officers would face in administering the policy with those kinds of exceptions. They'd have to "guess before every search" whether owners had erected fences high enough, or posted enough warning signs, or put contraband in an area secluded enough to "establish a right of privacy" (181).

On the other hand, the ground and buildings immediately surrounding a home (the **curtilage**), such as garages, patios, and pools, aren't open fields. Why? Because this is where family and other private activities take place. The Supreme Court has identified the following criteria to determine whether an area falls within the curtilage:

- The distance from the house
- The presence or absence of a fence around the area
- The use or purpose of the area
- The measures taken to prevent public view

In applying these criteria in *U.S. v. Dunn* (1987), the Court concluded that Ronald Dunn's barn wasn't part of the curtilage because it was 60 yards from the house; it was 50 yards beyond a fence surrounding the house; it wasn't used for family purposes; and Dunn took no measures to hide it from public view. So the crystal meth lab the officers discovered by shining a flashlight through a window in the barn wasn't a search.

SEIZURES

 LO 9 When are individuals "seized" in the Fourth Amendment sense? According to the U.S. Supreme Court in the landmark "stop and frisk" case, *Terry v. Ohio* (1968), which we'll discuss in Chapter 4: "Only when the officer, by means of physical force or show of authority, has in some way restrained the liberty of a citizen may we conclude that a 'seizure' has occurred" (21).

Terry was the first case in which the Court took up the question of when contacts between individuals and law enforcement officers trigger the Fourth Amendment's protection against an officer's interference with our right to come and go as we please. We learned very little about when a contact becomes a seizure.

TABLE 3.4 Show-of-authority seizures

Show of Authority	No Show of Authority
Setting up a roadblock	Approaching an individual on the sidewalk
Flashing an emergency light	Identifying oneself as a law enforcement officer
Ordering a person to leave a vehicle	Asking questions
Surrounding a car	Requesting to search
Drawing a weapon	Following a pedestrian in a police car
Several officers present	
Using a commanding tone of voice	

© Cengage Learning

What we didn't learn until later cases fleshed it out, is that there are two kinds of Fourth Amendment seizures (also known as "stops")—actual seizures and show-of-authority seizures. **Actual seizures** occur when officers physically grab individuals with the intent to keep them from leaving. **Show-of-authority seizures** take place when officers display their authority by ordering suspects to stop, drawing their weapons, or otherwise acting such that a reasonable person wouldn't feel free to leave or "otherwise terminate the encounter, and individuals submit to the authority." (See Table 3.4 for examples.)

The Court revisited the problem of defining seizure 12 years later in *U.S. v. Mendenhall* (1980). Federal DEA agents approached Sylvia Mendenhall as she was walking through a concourse in the Detroit airport, identified themselves, and asked to see her ID and ticket, which she handed to them. Justice Potter Stewart, in a part of his opinion joined only by Justice William Rehnquist, concluded the agents hadn't seized Mendenhall.

Here's how Justice Stewart defined a Fourth Amendment seizure: "A person has been 'seized' within the meaning of the Fourth Amendment only if, in view of all of the circumstances surrounding the incident, a reasonable person would have believed that he was not free to leave" (555). Justice Stewart explained why:

> On the facts of this case, no "seizure" of the respondent occurred. The events took place in the public concourse. The agents wore no uniforms and displayed no weapons. They did not summon the respondent to their presence, but instead approached her and identified themselves as federal agents. They requested, but did not demand to see the respondent's identification and ticket. Such conduct without more, did not amount to an intrusion upon any constitutionally protected interest. The respondent was not seized simply by reason of the fact that the agents approached her, asked her if she would show them her ticket and identification, and posed to her a few questions. Nor was it enough to establish a seizure that the person asking the questions was a law enforcement official. In short, nothing in the record suggests that the respondent had any objective reason to believe that she was not free to end the conversation in the concourse and proceed on her way, and for that reason we conclude that the agents' initial approach to her was not a seizure. (555)

A majority of the Court adopted Justice Stewart's "reasonable person would not feel free to leave" definition of seizure in *Florida v. Royer* (1983). Justice Byron White added this important passage to his opinion regarding officers who approach individuals and ask them questions:

> Law enforcement officers do not violate the Fourth Amendment by merely approaching an individual on the street or in another public place, by asking him if he is willing to answer some questions, [or] by putting questions to him if the person is willing to listen. Nor would the fact that the officer identifies himself as a police officer without more, convert the encounter into a seizure. (*Florida v. Royer* 1983, 497)

Because they're not "seized," individuals approached can walk away and ignore the officer's request. And walking away doesn't by itself provide the objective basis required to "seize" persons. Again, in Justice White's words:

> The person approached, however, need not answer any question put to him; indeed, he may decline to listen to the questions at all and may go on his way.

He may not be detained, even momentarily without reasonable, objective grounds for doing so; and his refusal to listen or answer does not, without more, furnish such grounds. (497–98)

The U.S. Supreme Court modified the "free to leave" definition when officers approach passengers in a bus who aren't physically able to leave, distinguishing it from when officers approach individuals in airports. In *Florida v. Bostick* (1991), two officers boarded a Greyhound bus during a brief stop at Fort Lauderdale on its 19-hour trip from Miami to Atlanta. Most of the passengers couldn't afford to fly. One of the passengers, Terrence Bostick, a 28-year-old Black man, was asleep on the backseat (Cole 1999, 16) when two officers woke him up. They were wearing their bright green "raid" jackets with the Broward County Sheriff's Office insignia and displaying their badges; one carried a gun in a plastic gun pouch. They were "working the bus," looking for passengers who might be carrying illegal drugs.

The officers asked for Bostick's identification; he gave it to them. Then, they asked him if they could search his bag; he said yes. They found a pound of cocaine. The officers admitted that until they found the cocaine they had no basis for suspecting Bostick was guilty of any crime. "Working" buses is a common tactic in drug law investigation. And it works. One officer testified that he had searched 3,000 bags without once being refused consent (Cole 1999, 16); one 13-month period produced 300 pounds of cocaine, 800 pounds of marijuana, 24 handguns, and 75 suspected drug "mules" (16).

The Court in *Bostick* acknowledged that a reasonable person wouldn't feel free to leave the bus. Nonetheless, the Court concluded that no Fourth Amendment seizure took place. According to the Court:

> Bostick's freedom of movement was restricted by a factor independent of police conduct, i.e., by his being a passenger on a bus. Accordingly, the "free to leave" analysis on which Bostick relies is inapplicable. In such a situation, the appropriate inquiry is whether a reasonable person would feel free to decline the officers' requests or otherwise terminate the encounter. (436)

The Court applied this **_Bostick_ standard** in *U.S. v. Drayton* (2002). During a bus stop, the driver left the bus, leaving three police officers in charge of the bus. One stood guard at the front of the bus, another at the rear, while the third questioned every passenger without telling them their right not to cooperate. The Court held that there was no seizure because reasonable people would have felt free to get up and leave the bus. But would they? Let's look at the answer provided by the empirical evidence.

LO 9   Empirical Findings

It's clear from the discussion of *Mendenhall*, *Royer*, *Bostick*, and *Drayton* that the Supreme Court has firmly, and repeatedly, taken the position that police encounters with citizens are not usually coercive. Scientific findings, as you'll also learn in consent searches (Chapter 6), police interrogation (Chapter 8), and identification procedures (Chapter 9), don't support the Court's position.

Professor Janice Nadler (2002), in her survey of Fourth Amendment empirical research on encounters with law enforcement, has demonstrated an "ever-widening gap" between Fourth Amendment court decisions and scientific findings regarding the psychology of compliance. Whether an individual "feels free to terminate a police encounter" can't "reliably be answered solely from the comforts of one's armchair, while reflecting only on one's own experience."

An examination of the existing empirical evidence on the psychology of coercion suggests that in many situations where citizens find themselves in an encounter with the police, the encounter is not consensual because a reasonable person would not feel free to terminate the encounter. Even worse, the existing empirical evidence also suggests that observers outside of the situation systematically overestimate the extent to which citizens in police encounters feel free to refuse. Members of the Court are themselves such outside observers, and this partly explains why the Court has repeatedly held that citizen encounters are consensual. (155–56)

LO 9   Fleeing Suspects

When are you seized when you run away from the police? According to the U.S. Supreme Court in our next excerpt, *California v. Hodari D.* (1991), you're seized when you're either grabbed by the chasing officer or when you submit to a display of police authority.

Officers Brian McColgin and Jerry Pertoso were on patrol in a high-crime area of Oakland, California. When Hodari D., a juvenile, saw the officers, he ran. Just as Officer Pertoso was about to catch up to him, Hodari tossed a "rock" of crack cocaine away, and was later charged with possession of cocaine. The juvenile court denied his motion to suppress and found that he was in possession of cocaine. The California Court of Appeal reversed; the California Supreme Court denied the state's application for review; the U.S. Supreme Court reversed and remanded.

According to the U.S. Supreme Court in *California v. Hodari D.* (1991), you're seized when you're either grabbed by the chasing officer or when you submit to a display of police authority.

CASE   When Did the Police Seize Him?

California v. Hodari D.
499 U.S. 621 (1991)

HISTORY

Hodari D., a juvenile, appealed from an order of the Superior Court, Alameda County, denying his motion to suppress and finding that he was in possession of cocaine. The California Court of Appeal reversed. The California Supreme Court denied the state's application for review. Certiorari was granted. The Supreme Court reversed and remanded.

—SCALIA, J., joined by REHNQUIST, C.J., and BLACKMUN, O'CONNOR, KENNEDY, and SOUTER, JJ.

FACTS

Late one evening in April 1988, Officers Brian McColgin and Jerry Pertoso were on patrol in a high-crime area of Oakland, California. They were dressed in street clothes but wearing jackets with "Police" embossed on both front and back. Their unmarked car proceeded west on Foothill Boulevard, and turned south onto 63rd Avenue. As they rounded the corner, they saw four or five youths huddled around a small red car parked at the curb. When the youths saw the officers' car approaching they apparently panicked, and took flight. The respondent here, Hodari D., and one companion ran west through an alley; the others fled south. The red car also headed south, at a high rate of speed.

The officers were suspicious and gave chase. McColgin remained in the car and continued south on 63rd Avenue. Pertoso left the car, ran back north along 63rd, then west on Foothill Boulevard, and turned south on 62nd Avenue. Hodari, meanwhile, emerged from the alley onto 62nd and ran north. Looking behind as he ran, he did not turn and see Pertoso until the officer was almost upon him, whereupon he tossed away what appeared to be a small rock. A moment later, Pertoso tackled Hodari, handcuffed him, and radioed for assistance. Hodari was found to be carrying $130 in cash and a pager; and the rock he had discarded was found to be crack cocaine. In the juvenile proceeding brought against him, Hodari moved to suppress the evidence relating to the cocaine. The court denied the motion without opinion. The California Court of Appeal reversed, holding that Hodari had been "seized" when he saw Officer Pertoso running toward him, that this seizure was unreasonable under the Fourth Amendment, and that the evidence of cocaine had to be suppressed as the fruit of that illegal seizure. The California Supreme Court denied the state's application for review. We granted certiorari.

OPINION

We have long understood that the Fourth Amendment's protection against "unreasonable seizures" includes seizure of the person. From the time of the founding to the present, the word "seizure" has meant a "taking possession." Hodari contends (and we accept as true for purposes of this decision) that Pertoso's pursuit qualified as a "show of authority" calling upon Hodari to halt. The narrow question before us is whether, with respect to a show of authority as with respect to application of physical force, a seizure occurs even though the subject does not yield. We hold that it does not.

Hodari contends that his position is sustained by the so-called *Mendenhall* test, formulated by Justice Stewart's opinion in *U.S. v. Mendenhall* (1980): A person has been "seized" within the meaning of the Fourth Amendment only if, in view of all the circumstances surrounding the incident, a reasonable person would have believed that he was not free to leave. In seeking to rely upon that test here, Hodari fails to read it carefully. It says that a person has been seized "only if," not that he has been seized "whenever"; it states a necessary, but not a sufficient, condition for seizure—or, more precisely, for seizure effected through a "show of authority."

Mendenhall establishes that the test for existence of a "show of authority" is an objective one: not whether the citizen perceived that he was being ordered to restrict his movement, but whether the officer's words and actions would have conveyed that to a reasonable person. Application of this objective test was the basis for our decision in the other case (*Michigan v. Chesternut*) principally relied upon by respondent, where we concluded that the police cruiser's slow following of the defendant did not convey the message that he was not free to disregard the police and go about his business. We did not address in *Michigan v. Chesternut*, however, the question whether, if the *Mendenhall* test was met—if the message that the

defendant was not free to leave had been conveyed—a Fourth Amendment seizure would have occurred.

Quite relevant to the present case, however, was our decision in *Brower v. Inyo County* (1989). In that case, police cars with flashing lights had chased the decedent for 20 miles—surely an adequate "show of authority"—but he did not stop until his fatal crash into a police-erected blockade. The issue was whether his death could be held to be the consequence of an unreasonable seizure in violation of the Fourth Amendment. We did not even consider the possibility that a seizure could have occurred during the course of the chase because, as we explained, that "show of authority" did not produce his stop.

In sum, assuming that Pertoso's pursuit in the present case constituted a "show of authority" enjoining Hodari to halt, since Hodari did not comply with that injunction he was not seized until he was tackled. The cocaine abandoned while he was running was in this case not the fruit of a seizure, and his motion to exclude evidence of it was properly denied.

We REVERSE the decision of the California Court of Appeal, and REMAND for further proceedings not inconsistent with this opinion.

It is so ordered.

DISSENT

STEVENS, J., joined by MARSHALL, J.

The court's narrow construction of the word "seizure" represents a significant, and in my view, unfortunate, departure from prior case law construing the Fourth Amendment. Almost a quarter of a century ago, in two landmark cases—one broadening the protection of individual privacy [*Katz v. U.S.* excerpt p. 66] and the other broadening the powers of law enforcement officers [*Terry v. Ohio*, excerpt p. 112]—we rejected the method of Fourth Amendment analysis that today's majority endorses. In particular, the Court now adopts a definition of "seizure" that is unfaithful to a long line of Fourth Amendment cases.

Even if the Court were defining seizure for the first time, which it is not, the definition that it chooses today is profoundly unwise. In its decision, the Court assumes, without acknowledging, that a police officer may now fire his weapon at an innocent citizen and not implicate the Fourth Amendment—as long as he misses his target.

Whatever else one may think of today's decision, it unquestionably represents a departure from earlier Fourth Amendment case law. The notion that our prior cases contemplated a distinction between seizures effected by a touching on the one hand, and those effected by a show of force on the other hand, and that all of our repeated descriptions of the *Mendenhall* test stated only a necessary, but not a sufficient, condition for finding seizures in the latter category, is nothing if not creative lawmaking. Moreover, by narrowing the definition of the term seizure,

(continued)

instead of enlarging the scope of reasonable justifications for seizures, the Court has significantly limited the protection provided to the ordinary citizen by the Fourth Amendment.

In this case the officer's show of force—taking the form of a head-on chase—adequately conveyed the message that respondent was not free to leave. There was an interval of time between the moment that respondent saw the officer fast approaching and the moment when he was tackled, and thus brought under the control of the officer.

The question is whether the Fourth Amendment was implicated at the earlier or the later moment. Because the facts of this case are somewhat unusual, it is appropriate to note that the same issue would arise if the show of force took the form of a command to "freeze," a warning shot, or the sound of sirens accompanied by a patrol car's flashing lights. In any of these situations, there may be a significant time interval between the initiation of the officer's show of force and the complete submission by the citizen.

At least on the facts of this case, the Court concludes that the timing of the seizure is governed by the citizen's reaction, rather than by the officer's conduct. One consequence of this conclusion is that the point at which the interaction between citizen and police officer becomes a seizure occurs, not when a reasonable citizen believes he or she is no longer free to go, but rather, only after the officer exercises control over the citizen.

It is too early to know the consequences of the Court's holding. If carried to its logical conclusion, it will encourage unlawful displays of force that will frighten countless innocent citizens into surrendering whatever privacy rights they may still have. The Court today defines a seizure as commencing, not with egregious police conduct, but rather, with submission by the citizen. Thus, it both delays the point at which "the Fourth Amendment becomes relevant" to an encounter and limits the range of encounters that will come under the heading of "seizure." Today's qualification of the Fourth Amendment means that innocent citizens may remain "secure in their persons against unreasonable searches and seizures" only at the discretion of the police.

Some sacrifice of freedom always accompanies an expansion in the executive's unreviewable law enforcement powers. A court more sensitive to the purposes of the Fourth Amendment would insist on greater rewards to society before decreeing the sacrifice it makes today. Alexander Bickel presciently wrote that "many actions of government have two aspects: their immediate, necessarily intended, practical effects, and their perhaps unintended or unappreciated bearing on values we hold to have more general and permanent interest." The Court's immediate concern with containing criminal activity poses a substantial, though unintended, threat to values that are fundamental and enduring.

I respectfully DISSENT.

Questions

1. What are the relevant facts in determining when the officer seized Hodari D.?

2. What criteria does the Court use in determining when seizures occur?

3. Why does the dissent see a danger in distinguishing between show-of-authority stops and actual-seizure stops? Do you agree that this poses a danger?

4. When do you think the officer stopped Hodari D.? Why is it important in this case?

5. Why is it important generally?

Consider the following remarks of Professor Richard Uviller, who observed the police in New York City for a period of a year:

[T]he manifest confidence [exuded by the police] begets submission. And the cops learn the firm tone and hand that informs even the normally aggressive customer of the futility of resistance. It's effective. In virtually every encounter I have witnessed, the response of the person approached was docile, compliant, and respectful.

6. Do you think Professor Uviller's observations support the argument that no reasonable person feels free to leave the presence of a police officer? Do you believe that they support the argument that a request by a police officer is really a command that citizens aren't free to deny? Defend your answer.

LO 9 Restraints on Movement That Are Not "Seizures"

It's important to note two kinds of restraints on freedom of movement that have no Fourth Amendment significance: psychological pressure and a sense of moral duty. You may feel a psychological pressure—and, as responsible members of your community, you should also feel a moral duty—to cooperate with police officers. But neither psychological pressure nor your sense of moral duty, by themselves, can turn a police encounter into a Fourth Amendment seizure (*INS v. Delgado* 1984). Why? Because these are self-imposed restraints; law enforcement officers didn't impose them on you.

The American Law Institute (ALI) (1975) also takes the position that simple questioning by law enforcement officers isn't a seizure. According to its respected Model Code of Pre-Arraignment Procedure:

§110.1 Requests for Cooperation by Law Enforcement Officers

(1) Authority to Request Cooperation.

A law enforcement officer may request any person to furnish information or otherwise cooperate in the investigation or prevention of crime. The officer may request the person to respond to questions, to appear at a police station, or to comply with any other reasonable request. In making requests no officer shall indicate that a person is legally obliged to furnish information or otherwise to cooperate if no such legal obligation exists.

Compliance with a request for information or other cooperation shall not be regarded as involuntary or coerced solely on the ground that such request was made by one known to be a law enforcement officer. (3)

CHAPTER SUMMARY

LO 1, 8 Crime control depends on information that usually comes from reluctant sources. Fourth Amendment searches and seizures are an important and controversial source of this information. As long as the information that officers can see or hear is also available to the general public, they may use it without violating the Fourth Amendment.

LO 2 Fourth Amendment analyses follow a three-step process based on answering three questions in the following order: (1) *Was the law enforcement action a "search" or "seizure"?* If not, the analysis ends because the Fourth Amendment only protects actions that *are* searches or seizures. (2) *If the action was a search or seizure, was it reasonable?* If it was, the inquiry ends because the Fourth Amendment bans only *unreasonable* searches and seizures. (3) *If the action was an unreasonable search or seizure, does the Fourth Amendment ban its use as evidence?* If it does, the case isn't necessarily over because there may be enough evidence to convict the defendant, either now or sometime in the future.

LO 3 Searches and seizures were originally intended to combat two kinds of crime prominent in British and American colonial history: sedition and customs violations. With their hatred for the broad powers of the general warrant in mind, the authors of the Bill of Rights wrote the Fourth Amendment to make sure the government doesn't use illegal methods to obtain evidence. The Fourth Amendment was aimed at the same ideological and economic offenses, not the types of crimes law enforcement is concerned with today.

LO 4, 5 The Fourth Amendment balances government power to control crime and individual rights of liberty and privacy. To achieve this balance, the Fourth Amendment bans only "unreasonable" searches and seizures made by government officials, not actions of private individuals. If government actions don't infringe upon a reasonable expectation of privacy, the Fourth Amendment doesn't apply and those actions are left largely up to officer discretion.

LO **6, 8**   According to the Supreme Court, there is no reasonable expectation of privacy for information voluntarily conveyed to third parties, even those whose services are essential to our quality of life. The Fourth Amendment also doesn't apply to discoveries of evidence in plain view, public places, open fields, or on abandoned property.

LO **7**   In a time of rapid technological advancement, the Supreme Court has the difficult duty of deciding which types of electronic surveillance violate the Fourth Amendment. To balance the government's power to control crime and individual rights of liberty and privacy, SCOTUS has decided that thermal imagers and GPS tracking are Fourth Amendment searches while other common technologies, such as texting and e-mail communications, have yet to reach the Supreme Court. Some lower federal courts and state courts have decided that the third party doctrine and the assumption of risk theory don't apply to e-mail and text messages.

LO **9**   People aren't "seized" any time they have an encounter with police officers. According to the Supreme Court, individuals are seized only when they're physically detained or submit to an officer's display of authority. Although SCOTUS does not deem police encounters as inherently coercive, empirical research refutes this claim.

REVIEW QUESTIONS

1. Identify four sources law enforcement officers depend on to obtain information necessary to control crime. Why is each one hesitant to share this information?

2. List four involuntary methods law enforcement officials use to obtain information. Identify the constitutional amendments limiting these powers.

3. Identify five special needs for searches and seizures beyond the main purpose of crime control.

4. Identify and describe each of the three steps in Fourth Amendment analyses. Why is the first step the most important?

5. Explain the significance of Judge Moylan's statement "the law does not give a constitutional damn about noncompliance" regarding the Fourth Amendment. Why should you not carry this "constitutional damn" idea too far?

6. Describe the original purposes of searches and seizures. Contrast these purposes with the types of crimes searches and seizures are aimed at today.

7. Describe the two components of the historical writs of assistance. Explain their relation to the Fourth Amendment.

8. Identify and describe the balance of interests the Fourth Amendment is designed to protect.

9. Describe the trespass doctrine and give four examples of constitutionally protected areas.

10. Identify and describe the two prongs of the reasonable expectation of privacy test adopted by the Supreme Court in *Katz v. U.S.* List two examples that fall within a reasonable expectation of privacy and two that do not.

11. Compare the privacy doctrine in theory and in practice. According to Professor Heffernan, what defeats claims to a reasonable expectation of privacy?

12. Describe the third party doctrine as it relates to the Fourth Amendment. Identify three types of third parties to which we convey information in the course of our everyday lives.

13. Summarize the facts of *Lewis v. U.S.* What reason did Chief Justice Warren cite for ruling that Lewis's conversations were not protected by the Fourth Amendment?

14. Identify the two requirements courts are supposed to consider according to the principle of technosocial continuity. Why does Professor Strandburg argue that courts should adopt this principle?

15. Describe the types of information gathered by thermal imagers and GPS tracking devices. According to the Supreme Court, are the uses of these advanced technologies considered Fourth Amendment searches?

16. Identify and provide an example of the two types of plain view. State the two conditions that define when discoveries made by law enforcement aren't searches according to the plain view doctrine. Explain how courts distinguish between technologies that qualify under the second condition and those that don't.

17. Explain why discoveries made in open fields aren't protected by the Fourth Amendment. List the four criteria courts use to determine if an area qualifies as curtilage.

18. Identify and provide an example of the two types of seizures.

19. Summarize the facts of *U.S. v. Mendenhall* and describe Justice Stewart's definition of a Fourth Amendment seizure in his opinion of the case. Explain Justice White's expansion of this definition in *Florida v. Royer.*

20. Summarize the facts of *Florida v. Bostick* and explain the Court's decision that no Fourth Amendment search took place. Compare this decision with the application of the *Bostick* standard in *U.S. v. Drayton.*

21. Summarize the empirical findings regarding the coerciveness of police-citizen encounters.

22. Identify the two restraints on your freedom of movement that do not implicate the Fourth Amendment at all.

KEY TERMS

4

Stop and Frisk

Cases Covered

LEARNING OBJECTIVES

1 Understand that Fourth Amendment stops are seizures of persons that allow officers to briefly freeze suspicious people and situations to investigate possible criminal activity. Fourth Amendment frisks are searches of persons that allow officers to pat down the outer clothing of a suspect to protect the officer from the use of concealed weapons during stops.

2 Understand and appreciate that warrantless searches and seizures, including Fourth Amendment stops and frisks, must satisfy the two requirements of the reasonableness test: (1) the need to search/seize must outweigh the invasion of individual liberty and privacy and (2) there must be enough facts and circumstances to back up the search/seizure.

3 Know that reasonable suspicion is the objective basis required to back up Fourth Amendment stops and frisks. More than a hunch but less than probable cause, reasonable suspicion can be built upon articulable facts from individualized and categorical suspicion, random procedures, and even race and ethnicity. With the exception of individuals suspected of violent crimes, the facts and circumstances that justify the stop do not automatically justify a frisk.

4 Understand that empirical and social scientific research doesn't always support the factual assertions made in balancing the government's ability to control crime against individual rights of liberty and privacy. Appreciate that many innocent people will be stopped and frisked, most of whom are Black or Hispanic.

5 Know that the Supreme Court views police work, especially during traffic stops, as very dangerous and has created bright-line rules expanding police powers during traffic stops in order to balance the increased need of officer safety against individual Fourth Amendment rights.

6 Know and appreciate that law enforcement officers do not need individualized suspicion to stop individuals at roadblocks and checkpoints to serve special public interests. Understand the three prongs of the balancing test SCOTUS uses to determine the reasonableness of these seizures: (1) the gravity of the public interest being served; (2) the effectiveness of the seizure in advancing the public interest; and (3) the degree of intrusion upon individual liberty and privacy.

7 Know and appreciate that routine detentions at international borders do not require reasonable suspicion to back up lengthy detentions and frisks. The Supreme Court has determined that the strong government interest in controlling who and what enters the country outweighs the significant reductions of individual liberty and privacy.

Suppose you belatedly realize, during your child's birthday party, that you forgot to get candles for the cake. Or, perhaps, you wish to buy some chips and dip before your favorite show or a big ball game on television. Maybe you simply wish to pop out just before your spouse comes home to surprise him or her with a thoughtful gift after a hard day at work. Such small errands typically present little trouble. Indeed, entire businesses have evolved to profit from such needs. Some offer "convenience" stores where people, on a whim, can quickly buy a snack or lottery ticket. The major grocery chains all offer "express lanes" to help rushed shoppers. Some restaurants, cleaners, even pharmacies, have drive-through windows. All of these efforts, however, in light of the United States Supreme Court's ruling in Illinois v. Lidster, *may be for naught. Now, any spontaneity will be limited by having to factor in a random interruption—a government checkpoint.*

—Dery and Meehan 2004, 106

The power to stop and question suspicious persons is ancient. From at least the Middle Ages, English constables were bound by their office to detain suspicious people, especially the dreaded "nightwalkers." Anybody walking around between dusk and dawn was automatically suspected of being up to no good (Stern 1967, 532). The English brought "stop and frisk" to their American colonies, and nobody challenged it until the 1960s.

Then, during the due process revolution of that decade (Chapter 2), civil libertarians *did* challenge the power of police to detain suspicious people on a hunch that they were up to no good. On what basis? Private individuals, they argued, especially "outsiders," need the courts to protect their rights whenever they're out on the streets and other public places.

Not surprisingly, law enforcement officers didn't see it that way. They argued that until they made an **arrest** (Chapter 5)—took suspects to the police station and kept them there against their will—their good judgment, based on their professional expertise gained from training and experience, was enough to justify their actions. Formal rules written by judges who had no knowledge and experience of the "street" and "street people" wouldn't protect innocent law-abiding people; they would protect guilty criminals (Remington 1960, 390).

LO **1, 2**

Fourth Amendment stops are brief detentions that allow law enforcement officers to freeze suspicious people and situations briefly, so they can investigate them. They're the least intrusive Fourth Amendment **seizure** of persons (Figure 4.1). **Fourth Amendment frisks** are once-over-lightly pat downs of outer clothing by officers to protect themselves by taking away suspects' weapons. (We don't expect officers to risk their lives when they approach a person to check out possible danger.)

Fourth Amendment **searches** of persons include everything from these once-over-lightly protective pat downs for weapons all the way to highly invasive strip and body-cavity searches. Chapters 5 and 6 analyze the greater invasions of arrests and full-blown searches in the unfamiliar and isolated surroundings of police stations and jails. Here, we look at the less invasive stops and frisks of persons in familiar and more comfortable public places, mostly streets (but also parks, restaurants, bars, and malls), and in their more private (also more comfortable) vehicles.

You know that the U.S. Constitution requires police officers to have an **objective basis** (suspicious facts and circumstances), not just hunches ("gut feelings"), to back up unwanted interferences with individuals' rights to liberty and privacy (Chapters 2 and 3). Equally important, the greater the invasion, the greater the objective basis the Constitution requires to back it up (Figure 4.1). So, in Fourth Amendment terms, officers need to prove fewer suspicious facts and circumstances to back up stops and frisks than they do for arrests (Chapter 5) and full-blown searches (Chapter 6).

Stops and frisks are the first leg of our chronological journey through the investigative process, beginning with the more frequent and more-visible (but less-intrusive) searches and seizures in public and continuing to the more-intrusive (but less-visible) searches and seizures out of sight in police stations.

Stops and frisks aren't just fine points for constitutional lawyers and courts to debate. They also reflect broad public policies aimed at balancing the values of crime control and individual liberty and privacy. Although they may take place in the less-intimidating atmosphere of public places, stops and frisks affect a lot more people. The ratio of stops to arrests is about one arrest to every nine stops (Spitzer 1999, Table I.B.1). In fact, for most people, stops and frisks are the only uninvited (and unwanted) contact with the police they'll ever have.

Just as important, because stops and frisks take place in public, the display of police power is there for everybody to see. This visibility of stops and frisks probably shapes public opinion of police power more than the greater invasions of arrest and searches that we never see. Deciding which is more important—crime control by means of less-intrusive public stops and frisks affecting more people, or invisible arrests and searches affecting fewer people—is both a constitutional and public policy question of great importance.

FIGURE 4.1 Police–Citizen Contacts

1 Voluntary Contacts

Citizens approach police or police approach citizens to ask questions. It's not a seizure—and officers need no reasonable suspicion—to approach citizens and ask questions. So, the Fourth Amendment does not apply.

2 Stops

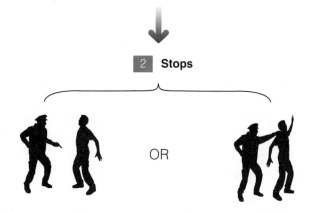

OR

2a Show of Authority

Police have reasonable suspicion that crime may be afoot, and a citizen submits to an officer's "show of authority."

2b Actual Seizure

Police have reasonable suspicion that crime may be afoot and the suspect is physically grabbed.

3 Arrest

Officers that have established "probable cause" to arrest may take suspects into custody.

The importance of the constitutional and policy dimensions of stops and frisks isn't due solely to their numbers but also to where and whom they affect. Black and Hispanic young men living in poor urban neighborhoods, or who happen to be in White neighborhoods, experience stops and frisks far more frequently than Whites. Even poor Whites living in the same poor neighborhoods as Blacks and Hispanics experience fewer stops and frisks (Spitzer 1999).

As we examine the social realities of stop and frisk, keep in mind these four facts:

1. Officers are going to stop many people who haven't done anything wrong, and they'll frisk lots of people who aren't armed.

2. Most of these same people want police protection and (at least in high-crime neighborhoods) need it more than people who live in safe neighborhoods.

3. Both lawbreakers and law abiders in high-street-crime neighborhoods form lasting opinions about the police from street encounters they've either watched or experienced.

4. Stops and frisks aren't distributed evenly; they fall most heavily on Black and Latino young men in poor urban neighborhoods.

STOP-AND-FRISK LAW

LO 1

Stop-and-frisk law follows the three-step analysis we used to decide whether an officer's action was a search or a seizure at all in Chapter 3:

1. Was the officer's action a stop or a frisk?

2. If the officer's action was a stop or a frisk, was it unreasonable?

3. If the stop or frisk was unreasonable, should evidence obtained during the stop and/or frisk be excluded from legal proceedings against the defendants (Chapter 10)?

Recall that if the action wasn't a stop or a frisk, then the Fourth Amendment doesn't apply at all and the analysis ends (Chapter 3). In other words, courts don't have the authority to review what officers do in such situations; it's left to officers' discretion. If the action is a stop or a frisk, then the analysis proceeds to the next step—namely, whether it was reasonable (step 2, this chapter). If it was reasonable, the analysis is over. If it was unreasonable, the analysis proceeds to decide whether the evidence has to be excluded (step 3, Chapter 10).

LO 2 ## Two Approaches to Fourth Amendment Analysis

Before we analyze stops and frisks, we need to break down the two parts of the Fourth Amendment:

1. **Reasonableness clause.** "The right of the people to be secure in their persons, houses, papers, and effects against unreasonable searches and seizures shall not be violated."

2. **Warrant clause.** ". . . and no warrants shall issue but upon probable cause, supported by oath or affirmation, and particularly describing the place to be searched, and the persons or things to be seized."

Until the 1960s, the U.S. Supreme Court followed the **conventional Fourth Amendment approach**, which says the warrant and reasonableness clauses are firmly connected. Specifically, the reasonableness clause is a stirring introduction to the heart of the people's right against unreasonable searches and seizures—the warrant clause. So, the warrant clause guarantees that only searches and seizures based on warrants and probable cause are reasonable.

LO 2

In the 1960s, the Supreme Court shifted away from the conventional approach to the **reasonableness Fourth Amendment approach**. According to the *reasonableness approach*, the two clauses are separate, and they address separate problems. The warrant clause tells us what the Fourth Amendment requires only when law enforcement officers obtain warrants (Chapter 6). In practice, only a tiny fraction of searches and seizures are made with warrants, and some searches and seizures don't require probable cause either. That means the searches with warrants are rare.

According to the Court, the Fourth Amendment can't mean that searches and seizures without warrants and probable cause are *always* unreasonable. Since the 1960s, the Court has spent a lot of its time reviewing, case by case, the circumstances that make a search or seizure unreasonable. By now it should be obvious to you that the Court's decisions aren't always clear. But don't blame the Court; after all, "unreasonable" is probably the vaguest, and therefore also one of the toughest words to define, in the Constitution.

Reasonableness is a broad—and some say too subjective—standard. According to Professor John M. Copacino (1994), in balancing the interests of the government in crime control and special needs against the invasions of individual liberty and privacy, the Court has adopted a broad definition of the government's interest, usually without "any hard evidence" to justify it. At the same time, the Court has "proclaimed its subjective judgment" of the harm the government's intrusions cause to individuals without citing "any empirical evidence, expert testimony, or individual testimony from those who have been affected by the search or seizure" (236).

When the U.S. Supreme Court decided there were more reasonable searches and seizures without than with warrants, it created two major challenges:

1. When does the Fourth Amendment require warrants?

2. What does "unreasonable" mean?

LO 2

The Court has a formula for meeting these challenges. One type of reasonable search and seizure is based on warrants and probable cause. The other type—which, in practice, includes the vast majority of searches and seizures—has to pass the **reasonableness test**. The reasonableness test consists of two elements that are the government's burden to prove:

Balancing element. The need to search and/or seize outweighs the invasion of liberty and privacy rights of the individuals.
Objective basis. There are enough facts and circumstances to back up the search and/or seizure.

According to the U.S. Supreme Court, courts have to decide whether searches and seizures are reasonable on a **case-by-case basis**. How do they do it? The Court has repeatedly said the lower courts have to look at the totality of circumstances surrounding the specific searches and seizures in individual cases. Officers make a preliminary (usually on the spur of the moment, under pressure) reasonableness decision on the street and in police stations.

In making their decision, officers are allowed to view the totality of circumstances through the lens of their professional training and experience. But officers' decisions aren't final. Judges review the totality of the circumstances the officers acted on and decide whether they're *constitutionally* reasonable. But, as you'll learn later in this chapter (*Maryland v. Wilson*), and most of the others in the book, the Court has increasingly created (some critics say "legislated") **"bright-line"** (specific) **rules** to tell officers, courts, and the rest of us what's reasonable.

The test of reasonableness also requires a case-by-case evaluation of whether there was enough objective basis to back up the searches and seizures. The objective basis ranges from the probable cause required to back up full-blown searches (Chapter 6) and seizures (arrests, Chapter 5) to the lesser reasonable suspicion required to back up stops and frisks. Both probable cause (always) and reasonable suspicion (usually) require **individualized suspicion**, meaning suspicion that points to specific individuals. However, DWI roadblocks (discussed later in this chapter) and some noncriminal law enforcement searches (Chapter 7) don't require individualized suspicion. In these cases, the objective basis consists of standard procedures such as random stops.

Today's stop-and-frisk law grew out of the Supreme Court's ruling in one case. Let's look at the Fourth Amendment issues surrounding that case, *Terry v. Ohio*, and at stop-and-frisk law after *Terry*.

Terry v. Ohio and Stop and Frisk

Today's stop-and-frisk law grew out of the practical problems police officers face in preventing and investigating crime on the streets and other public places in our largest cities. In these investigations, officers are usually dealing with people they don't know and probably won't ever see again. Usually, these strangers' suspicious behavior doesn't add up to the probable cause needed to arrest them (Chapter 5).

For example, suppose an officer doesn't have enough facts and circumstances viewed through the lens of her professional experience and training to arrest two men who peer into a store window, look around as if to see if anyone is watching them, and pace up and down the street, repeating this pattern for several minutes. What should the officer do? Nothing? Keep watching them? Briefly detain them and pat them down for weapons? Take them to the police station? These were the issues raised in *Terry v. Ohio*.

The answer depends on three possible interpretations of the Fourth Amendment (Dix 1985, 853–55):

1. The Fourth Amendment applies only to full searches and arrests; so short of full arrests and searches, officers' discretion controls their contacts with individuals in public places.

2. Even brief street detentions are arrests, and pat downs are searches, so the police can't do anything unless they've got probable cause.

3. Stops and frisks are searches and seizures, so officers have to back them up with suspicious facts and circumstances. But, they're "minor" ones, so they require fewer facts and circumstances than arrests and searches to back them up.

If officers can't take any action until they've got probable cause (alternative 2), crime control suffers because they'll probably never see the suspects again. But if the Fourth Amendment doesn't apply at all to these street encounters (alternative 1), then people on the street are subject to the whims of every officer. So both alternatives 1 and 2 are unacceptable; the U.S. Supreme Court chose alternative 3.

LO **1, 2**

According to the Court, the Fourth Amendment gives the police enough power to "freeze" suspicious events and people briefly to find out if criminal activity "may be afoot." The Fourth Amendment also gives officers the power to protect themselves by frisking the people they stop. (We can't expect officers to risk life and limb to fulfill their constitutional duties.) But officers can't freeze all the events and lay hands on all the people they've got a hunch may be up to no good; their stops and frisks have to be "reasonable." In the real world, judges will review only a tiny share of officers' stops and frisks to make sure they're reasonable (Chapter 2, p. 48). But they *can,* and officers know their stops and frisks might be among the few the judges review.

What's "reasonable"? First, in the balance between crime control and individual freedom and privacy, in each case, the need to control crime has to outweigh the invasions against the individuals' rights. Second, officers can't stop and frisk people on a hunch, whim, or "mere suspicion." They need facts—not as many as would add up to probable cause (Chapters 5 and 6) but enough so that a neutral judge can decide later if there was enough objective basis to back up both the stop and the frisk.

In *Terry v. Ohio* (1968), our next case excerpt, the U.S. Supreme Court applied alternative 3, holding that the stop and frisk of John Terry satisfied the reasonableness requirement of the Fourth Amendment.

CASE

Was He Seized and Searched?

Terry v. Ohio
392 U.S. 1 (1968)

HISTORY

John W. Terry was prosecuted for carrying a concealed weapon. The Court of Common Pleas of Cuyahoga County, Ohio, overruled a pretrial motion to suppress. Terry was convicted and sentenced to one to three years in the Ohio Penitentiary. Terry appealed. The Court of Appeals for the Eighth Judicial District of Ohio affirmed. The Ohio Supreme Court dismissed an appeal on the ground that no substantial constitutional question was involved. The U.S. Supreme Court granted certiorari, and affirmed.

—WARREN, J.

This case presents serious questions concerning the role of the Fourth Amendment in the confrontation on the street between the citizen and the policeman investigating suspicious circumstances.

FACTS

Officer Martin McFadden testified that while he was patrolling in plain clothes in downtown Cleveland at approximately 2:30 in the afternoon of October 31, 1963, his attention was attracted by two men, Chilton and Terry, standing on the corner of Huron Road and Euclid Avenue.

He had never seen the two men before, and he was unable to say precisely what first drew his eye to them. However, he testified that he had been a policeman for 39 years and a detective for 35 and that he had been assigned to patrol this vicinity of downtown Cleveland for shoplifters and pickpockets for 30 years. He explained that he had developed routine habits of observation over the years and that he would "stand and watch people or walk and watch people at many intervals of the day." He added: "Now, in this case when I looked over they didn't look right to me at the time."

His interest aroused, Officer McFadden took up a post of observation in the entrance to a store 300 to 400 feet away from the two men. "I get more purpose to watch them when I seen their movements," he testified.

He saw one of the men leave the other one and walk southwest on Huron Road, past some stores. The man paused for a moment and looked in a store window, then walked on a short distance, turned around, and walked back toward the corner, pausing once again to look in the same store window. He rejoined his companion at the corner, and the two conferred briefly.

Then the second man went through the same series of motions, strolling down Huron Road, looking in the

(*continued*)

same window, walking on a short distance, turning back, peering in the store window again, and returning to confer with the first man at the corner.

The two men repeated this ritual alternately between five and six times apiece—in all, roughly a dozen trips. At one point, while the two were standing together on the corner, a third man approached them and engaged them briefly in conversation. This man then left the two others and walked west on Euclid Avenue.

Chilton and Terry resumed their measured pacing, peering, and conferring. After this had gone on for 10 to 12 minutes, the two men walked off together, heading west on Euclid Avenue, following the path taken earlier by the third man.

By this time Officer McFadden had become thoroughly suspicious. He testified that after observing their elaborately casual and oft-repeated reconnaissance of the store window on Huron Road, he suspected the two men of "casing a job, a stick-up," and that he considered it his duty as a police officer to investigate further. He added that he feared "they may have a gun."

Thus, Officer McFadden followed Chilton and Terry and saw them stop in front of Zucker's store to talk to the same man who had conferred with them earlier on the street corner. Deciding that the situation was ripe for direct action, Officer McFadden approached the three men, identified himself as a police officer, and asked for their names. At this point his knowledge was confined to what he had observed. He was not acquainted with any of the three men by name or by sight, and he had received no information concerning them from any other source.

When the men "mumbled something" in response to his inquiries, Officer McFadden grabbed petitioner Terry, spun him around so that they were facing the other two, with Terry between McFadden and the others, and patted down the outside of his clothing. In the left breast pocket of Terry's overcoat, Officer McFadden felt a pistol. He reached inside the overcoat pocket, but was unable to remove the gun.

At this point, keeping Terry between himself and the others, the officer ordered all three men to enter Zucker's store. As they went in, he removed Terry's overcoat completely, removed a .38-caliber revolver from the pocket, and ordered all three men to face the wall with their hands raised. Officer McFadden proceeded to pat down the outer clothing of Chilton and the third man, Katz. He discovered another revolver in the outer pocket of Chilton's overcoat, but no weapons were found on Katz.

The officer testified that he only patted the men down to see whether they had weapons, and that he did not put his hands beneath the outer garments of either Terry or Chilton until he felt their guns. So far as appears from the record, he never placed his hands beneath Katz's outer garments. Officer McFadden seized Chilton's gun, asked the proprietor of the store to call a police wagon, and took all three men to the station, where Chilton and Terry were formally charged with carrying concealed weapons.

OPINION

The Fourth Amendment right against unreasonable searches and seizures belongs as much to the citizen on the streets of our cities as to the homeowner closeted in his study to dispose of his secret affairs. Unquestionably Terry was entitled to the protection of the Fourth Amendment as he walked down the street in Cleveland. The question is whether in all the circumstances of this on-the-street encounter, his right to personal security was violated by an unreasonable search and seizure.

We would be less than candid if we did not acknowledge that this question thrusts to the fore difficult and troublesome issues regarding a sensitive area of police activity. In this context we approach the issues in this case mindful of the limitations of the judicial function in controlling the myriad daily situations in which policemen and citizens confront each other on the street.

The rule excluding evidence seized in violation of the Fourth Amendment has been recognized as a principal mode of discouraging lawless police conduct. But a stern refusal by this Court to condone such activity does not necessarily render it responsive to the exclusionary rule. Regardless of how effective the rule may be where obtaining convictions is an important objective of the police, it is powerless to deter invasions of constitutionally guaranteed rights where the police either have no interest in prosecuting or are willing to forgo successful prosecution in the interest of serving some other goal.

Proper adjudication of cases in which the exclusionary rule is invoked demands a constant awareness of these limitations. The wholesale harassment by certain elements of the police community, of which minority groups, particularly Negroes, frequently complain, will not be stopped by the exclusion of any evidence from any criminal trial. Yet a rigid and unthinking application of the exclusionary rule, in futile protest against practices which it can never be used effectively to control, may exact a high toll in human injury and frustration of efforts to prevent crime.

We turn our attention to the quite narrow question posed by the facts before us: whether it is always unreasonable for a policeman to seize a person and subject him to a limited search for weapons unless there is probable cause for an arrest.

Our first task is to establish at what point in this encounter Officer McFadden "seized" Terry and whether and when he conducted a "search." There is some suggestion in the use of such terms as "stop" and "frisk" that such police conduct is outside the purview of the Fourth Amendment because neither action rises to the level of a "search" or "seizure" within the meaning of the Constitution.

We emphatically reject this notion. Whenever a police officer accosts an individual and restrains his freedom to walk away, he has "seized" that person. And it is nothing less than sheer torture of the English language to suggest that a careful exploration of the outer surfaces of a person's clothing all over his or her body in an attempt to find weapons is not a "search." Moreover, it is simply fantastic to urge that such a procedure performed in public by a policeman while the citizen stands helpless, perhaps facing a wall with his hands raised, is a "petty indignity." It is a serious intrusion upon the sanctity of the person, which may inflict great indignity and arouse strong resentment, and it is not to be undertaken lightly.

The central inquiry under the Fourth Amendment is the reasonableness in all the circumstances of the particular governmental invasion of a citizen's personal security. In this case there can be no question that Officer McFadden "seized" Terry and subjected him to a "search" when he took hold of him and patted down the outer surfaces of his clothing. We must decide whether at that point it was reasonable for Officer McFadden to have interfered with petitioner's personal security as he did.

In determining whether the seizure and search were "unreasonable" our inquiry is a dual one—whether the officer's action was justified at its inception, and whether it was reasonably related in scope to the circumstances which justified the interference in the first place.

In justifying the particular intrusion the police officer must be able to point to specific and articulable facts which, taken together with rational inferences from those facts, reasonably warrant that intrusion. The Fourth Amendment is meaningful only if at some point the conduct of those charged with enforcing the laws can be subjected to the more detached, neutral scrutiny of a judge who must evaluate the reasonableness of a particular search or seizure. In making that assessment it is imperative that the facts be judged against an objective standard: would the facts available to the officer at the moment of the seizure or the search "warrant a man of reasonable caution in the belief" that the action taken was appropriate?

Anything less would invite intrusions upon constitutionally guaranteed rights based on nothing more substantial than inarticulate hunches. And simple "good faith on the part of the arresting officer is not enough." If subjective good faith alone were the test, the protections of the Fourth Amendment would evaporate, and the people would be "secure in their persons, houses, papers, and effects" only in the discretion of the police.

Applying these principles to this case, we consider first the nature and extent of the government interests involved. One general interest is of course that of effective crime prevention and detection; it is this interest which underlies the recognition that a police officer may in appropriate circumstances and in an appropriate manner approach a person for purposes of investigating possibly criminal behavior even though there is no probable cause to make an arrest. It was this legitimate investigative function Officer McFadden was discharging when he decided to approach Terry and his companions. He had observed Terry, Chilton, and Katz go through a series of acts, each of them perhaps innocent in itself, but which taken together warranted further investigation.

There is nothing unusual in two men standing together on a street corner, perhaps waiting for someone. Nor is there anything suspicious about people in such circumstances strolling up and down the street, singly or in pairs. Store windows, moreover, are made to be looked in.

But the story is quite different where, as here, two men hover about a street corner for an extended period of time, at the end of which it becomes apparent that they are not waiting for anyone or anything; where these men pace alternately along an identical route, pausing to stare in the same store window roughly 24 times; where each completion of this route is followed immediately by a conference between the two men on the corner; where they are joined in one of these conferences by a third man who leaves swiftly; and where the two men finally follow the third and rejoin him a couple of blocks away. It would have been poor police work indeed for an officer of 30 years' experience in the detection of thievery from stores in this same neighborhood to have failed to investigate this behavior further.

The crux of this case, however, is not the propriety of Officer McFadden's taking steps to investigate Terry's suspicious behavior, but rather, whether there was justification for McFadden's invasion of Terry's personal security by searching him for weapons in the course of that investigation. We are now concerned with more than the governmental interest in investigating crime; in addition, there is the more immediate interest of the police officer in taking steps to assure himself that the person with whom he is dealing is not armed with a weapon that could unexpectedly and fatally be used against him. Certainly it would be unreasonable to require that police officers take unnecessary risks in the performance of their duties.

We must still consider, however, the nature and quality of the intrusion on individual rights which must be accepted if police officers are to be conceded the right to search for weapons in situations where probable cause to arrest for crime is lacking. Even a limited search of the outer clothing for weapons constitutes a severe, though brief, intrusion upon cherished personal security, and it must surely be an annoying, frightening, and perhaps humiliating experience.

Our evaluation of the proper balance that has to be struck leads us to conclude that there must be a narrowly drawn authority to permit a reasonable search for weapons for the protection of the police officer, where he has reason to believe that he is dealing with an armed and

(continued)

dangerous individual. In determining whether the officer acted reasonably in such circumstances, due weight must be given, not to his inchoate and unparticularized suspicion or "hunch," but to the specific reasonable inferences which he is entitled to draw from the facts in light of his experience.

We must now examine the conduct of Officer McFadden in this case to determine whether his search and seizure of petitioner were reasonable, both at their inception and as conducted. He had observed Terry, together with Chilton and another man, acting in a manner he took to be preface to a "stick-up." We think on the facts and circumstances Officer McFadden detailed before the trial judge a reasonably prudent man would have been warranted in believing petitioner was armed and thus presented a threat to the officer's safety while he was investigating his suspicious behavior.

The actions of Terry and Chilton were consistent with McFadden's hypothesis that these men were contemplating a daylight robbery—which, it is reasonable to assume, would be likely to involve the use of weapons—and nothing in their conduct from the time he first noticed them until the time he confronted them and identified himself as a police officer gave him sufficient reason to negate that hypothesis. Although the trio had departed the original scene, there was nothing to indicate abandonment of an intent to commit a robbery at some point.

The manner in which the seizure and search were conducted is, of course, as vital a part of the inquiry as whether they were warranted at all. The Fourth Amendment proceeds as much by limitations upon the scope of governmental action as by imposing preconditions upon its initiation. Such a search is not justified by any need to prevent the disappearance or destruction of evidence of crime. The sole justification of the search in the present situation is the protection of the police officer and others nearby, and it must therefore be confined in scope to an intrusion reasonably designed to discover guns, knives, clubs, or other hidden instruments for the assault of the police officer.

The scope of the search in this case presents no serious problem in light of these standards. Officer McFadden patted down the outer clothing of petitioner and his two companions. He did not place his hands in their pockets or under the outer surface of their garments until he had felt weapons, and then he merely reached for and removed the guns. Officer McFadden confined his search strictly to what was minimally necessary to learn whether the men were armed and to disarm them once he discovered the weapons. He did not conduct a general exploratory search for whatever evidence of criminal activity he might find.

We conclude that the revolver seized from Terry was properly admitted in evidence against him. Each case of this sort will, of course, have to be decided on its own facts.

We merely hold today that where a police officer observes unusual conduct which leads him reasonably to conclude in light of his experience that criminal activity may be afoot and that the persons with whom he is dealing may be armed and presently dangerous, where in the course of investigating this behavior he identifies himself as a policeman and makes reasonable inquiries, and where nothing in the initial stages of the encounter serves to dispel his reasonable fear for his own or others' safety, he is entitled for the protection of himself and others in the area to conduct a carefully limited search of the outer clothing of such persons in an attempt to discover weapons which might be used to assault him. Such a search is a reasonable search under the Fourth Amendment, and any weapons seized may properly be introduced in evidence against the person from whom they were taken.

AFFIRMED.

CONCURRING OPINIONS

HARLAN, J.

I would make it perfectly clear that the right to frisk in this case depends upon the reasonableness of a forcible stop to investigate a suspected crime. Where such a stop is reasonable, however, the right to frisk must be immediate and automatic if the reason for the stop is, as here, an articulable suspicion of a crime of violence. A limited frisk incident to a lawful stop must often be rapid and routine. There is no reason why an officer, rightfully but forcibly confronting a person suspected of a serious crime, should have to ask one question and take the risk that the answer might be a bullet.

I would affirm this conviction for what I believe to be the same reasons the Court relies on. I would, however, make explicit what I think is implicit in affirmance on the present facts. Officer McFadden's right to interrupt Terry's freedom of movement and invade his privacy arose only because circumstances warranted forcing an encounter with Terry in an effort to prevent or investigate a crime. Once that forced encounter was justified, however, the officer's right to take suitable measures for his own safety followed automatically. Upon the foregoing premises, I join the opinion of the Court.

WHITE, J.

I think an additional word is in order concerning the matter of interrogation during an investigative stop. There is nothing in the Constitution which prevents a policeman from addressing questions to anyone on the streets. Absent special circumstances, the person approached may not be detained or frisked but may refuse to cooperate and go on his way.

However, given the proper circumstances, such as those in this case, it seems to me the person may be briefly detained against his will while pertinent questions are directed to him. Of course, the person stopped is not obliged to answer, answers may not be compelled, and refusal to answer furnishes no basis for an arrest, although it may alert the officer to the need for continued observation.

In my view, it is temporary detention, warranted by the circumstances, which chiefly justifies the protective frisk for weapons. Perhaps the frisk itself, where proper, will have beneficial results whether questions are asked or not. If weapons are found, an arrest will follow. If none are found, the frisk may nevertheless serve preventive ends because of its unmistakable message that suspicion has been aroused. But if the investigative stop is sustainable at all, constitutional rights are not necessarily violated if pertinent questions are asked and the person is restrained briefly in the process.

DISSENT

DOUGLAS, J.

The requirement of probable cause has roots that are deep in our history. The general warrant, in which the name of the person to be arrested was left blank, and the writs of assistance, against which James Otis inveighed, both perpetuated the oppressive practice of allowing the police to arrest and search on suspicion. Police control took the place of judicial control, since no showing of "probable cause" before a magistrate was required.

The infringement on personal liberty of any "seizure" of a person can only be "reasonable" under the Fourth Amendment if we require the police to possess "probable cause" before they seize him. Only that line draws a meaningful distinction between an officer's mere inkling and the presence of facts within the officer's personal knowledge which would convince a reasonable man that the person seized has committed, is committing, or is about to commit a particular crime.

To give the police greater power than a magistrate is to take a long step down the totalitarian path. Perhaps such a step is desirable to cope with modern forms of lawlessness. But if it is taken, it should be the deliberate choice of the people through a constitutional amendment. Until the Fourth Amendment is rewritten, the person and the effects of the individual are beyond the reach of all government agencies until there are reasonable grounds to believe (probable cause) that a criminal venture has been launched or is about to be launched.

There have been powerful hydraulic pressures throughout our history that bear heavily on the Court to water down constitutional guarantees and give the police the upper hand. That hydraulic pressure has probably never been greater than it is today. Yet if the individual is no longer to be sovereign, if the police can pick him up whenever they do not like the cut of his jib, if they can "seize" and "search" him in their discretion, we enter a new regime. The decision to enter it should be made only after a full debate by the people of this country.

Questions

1. List in chronological order all of McFadden's actions from the time he started watching Terry until he arrested him.

2. According to Professor Lewis Katz (2004), who worked on one of the briefs in the case:

   The Court played fast and loose with the most important fact in the case: the number of trips Terry and Chilton made up the street and how many times they looked into the store window. [Chief Justice] Warren reported that the two men looked into the window twenty-four times. That figure is reported with a certainty that the evidence does not support. McFadden was confused about how many times this occurred; a fair reading of the many times he stated what happened leads to the conclusion that they looked into the window between four and twenty-four times. His police report written immediately after the arrests stated that each man made three trips. This fact is critical because it is unclear as to whether the seizure would have been reasonable based on fewer observations of the store window. (454)

3. Do you agree that Chief Justice Warren "played fast and loose with the most important fact in the case"? Does this added information affect your opinion? Does it bother you that the chief justice isn't clear on the facts? Explain your answers.

4. According to the Court, at what point did McFadden seize Terry? Summarize the Court's reasons for picking that point.

5. According to the Court, at what point did McFadden search Terry? Summarize the Court's reasons for picking that point.

6. What was the objective basis (facts and circumstances) for McFadden's "stop" of Terry?

7. What was the objective basis (facts and circumstances) for McFadden's "frisk" of Terry?

8. Summarize the main points of Justice Harlan's concurring opinion. What do they add to your understanding of Chief Justice Warren's opinion?

9. During the oral argument before the Supreme Court, it came out that in all of Officer McFadden's experience, he'd never investigated a robbery; his experience was limited to spotting and investigating shoplifters and pickpockets. Does this matter? Explain your answer.

10. It was also learned during the oral argument that Terry, Chilton, and Katz were a lot bigger than Officer McFadden. Does this matter? Why? Why not?

(continued)

11. Consider the following excerpt from an amicus curiae brief filed in *Terry v. Ohio*:

> In the litigation now before the Court—as is usual in cases where police practices are challenged—two parties essentially are represented. Law enforcement officers, legal representatives of their respective States, ask the Court to broaden police powers, and thereby to sustain what has proved to be a "good pinch."
>
> Criminal defendants caught with the goods through what in retrospect appears to be at least shrewd and successful (albeit constitutionally questionable) police work ask the Court to declare that work illegal and to reverse their convictions.
>
> Other parties intimately affected by the issues before the Court are not represented. The many thousands of our citizens who have been or may be stopped and frisked yearly, only to be released when the police find them innocent of any crime, are not represented. The records of their cases are not before the Court and cannot be brought here. Yet it is they, far more than those charged with crime, who will bear the consequences of the rules of constitutional law which this Court establishes.
>
> The determination of the quantum of "belief" or "suspicion" required to justify the exercise of intrusive police authority is precisely the determination of how far afield from instances of obvious guilt the authority stretches. To lower that quantum is to broaden the police net and, concomitantly, to increase the number (and probably the proportion) of innocent people caught up in it.
>
> The innocent are those this Court will never see.

What's the point the brief makes? What's the importance of the point?

12. During oral arguments of the case before the Supreme Court, Louis Stokes, Terry's lawyer, revealed some of what happened at the suppression hearing. Stokes said, among other things, that Officer McFadden testified that he didn't know the men, that they walked normally, that they were standing in front of a store talking normally, and that they were facing away from the store windows. When asked why he approached Terry, Chilton, and Katz, Officer McFadden replied, "Because I didn't like them." Is this testimony important? Also, McFadden was White and Terry and Chilton were Black. Is this important?

LO 2 Stop-and-Frisk Law after *Terry v. Ohio*

Judge Michael R. Juviler (1998) was a prosecutor in 1968. On the same day that *Terry v. Ohio* was argued, he argued in favor of the power to stop and frisk in a New York case before the U.S. Supreme Court. On the 30th anniversary of the decision, he recalled:

> After the *Terry* opinions were filed, we felt perhaps like the makers of the hydrogen bomb. What had we created? What had we contributed to? Would this lead to further racial divisions, police abuse, police "testilying [police perjury]"? (743–44)

At the time *Terry* was decided, many commentators, and some judges, interpreted the decision as a grudging watering down of the protections of the right against unreasonable search and seizure. This watering down seemed necessary in the climate of the times. The case was decided at a time when race riots, mass antiwar protests that sometimes turned violent, and skyrocketing crime rates (including murder) plagued our largest cities. Law enforcement had to have tools to respond to this violence, crime, and disorder. The decision was praised for balancing the need for safety and the rights of individuals.

As you read the remaining sections in the chapter, think about Judge Juviler's comment, and ask yourself whether his worries have come to pass. Certainly, it's true that the cases that followed *Terry* (some of which you'll read in the sections that follow) expanded the power of the police in several ways. First, they expanded the scope of the power beyond violent crimes against the person, such as armed robbery, to possessory crimes, especially illegal drug possession. Second, the cases expanded the time and location where the powers can be exercised. Third, the decisions expanded the objective basis for stops and frisks from firsthand observation by officers to include informants, anonymous tips, and even profiles.

Four years after the Court decided *Terry v. Ohio*, it began to flesh out what the balancing element and objective basis of the reasonableness approach to Fourth Amendment stops meant. That fleshing out signaled a trend (broken only rarely) that the Court has followed up to 2013—tipping reasonableness in favor of law enforcement. The case in which the Court fleshed out the reasonableness approach elements was our next excerpt, *Adams v. Williams* (1971). It decided that *Terry v. Ohio* wasn't limited to violent crimes against persons, backed up by individualized suspicion obtained by the direct observation of officers who stopped and frisked a suspect.

Adams v. Williams upheld a stop and frisk on informant information that Adams was armed with a handgun in his waistband.

CASE

Was the Stop and Frisk Reasonable?

Adams v. Williams
407 U.S. 143 (1972)

HISTORY

Robert Williams (Respondent) was convicted in a Connecticut state court of illegal possession of a handgun found during a "stop and frisk," as well as of possession of heroin that was found during a full search incident to his weapons arrest. After respondent's conviction was affirmed by the Supreme Court of Connecticut, the U.S. Supreme Court denied certiorari. Williams's petition for federal habeas corpus relief was denied by the District Court and by a divided panel of the Second Circuit, but on rehearing en banc the Court of Appeals granted relief. That court held that evidence introduced at Williams's trial had been obtained by an unlawful search of his person and car, and thus the state court judgments of conviction should be set aside. Since we conclude that the policeman's actions here conformed to the standards this Court laid down in *Terry v. Ohio*, we reverse.

—REHNQUIST, J.

FACTS

Police Sgt. John Connolly was alone early in the morning on car patrol duty in a high-crime area of Bridgeport, Connecticut. At approximately 2:15 a.m. a person known to Sgt. Connolly approached his cruiser and informed him that an individual seated in a nearby vehicle was carrying narcotics and had a gun at his waist.

After calling for assistance on his car radio, Sgt. Connolly approached the vehicle to investigate the informant's report. Connolly tapped on the car window and asked the occupant, Robert Williams, to open the door. When Williams rolled down the window instead, the sergeant reached into the car and removed a fully loaded revolver from Williams's waistband. The gun had not been visible to Connolly from outside the car, but it was in precisely the place indicated by the informant.

> Williams was then arrested by Connolly for unlawful possession of the pistol. A search incident to that arrest was conducted after other officers arrived. They found substantial quantities of heroin on Williams's person and in the car, and they found a machete and a second revolver hidden in the automobile. [The dissent points out that "Connecticut allows its citizens to carry weapons, concealed or otherwise, at will, provided only they have a permit, and gives its police officers no special authority to stop for the purpose of determining whether the citizen has one."]

OPINION

Williams contends that the initial seizure of his pistol, upon which rested the later search and seizure of other weapons and narcotics, was not justified by the informant's tip to Sgt. Connolly. He claims that absent a more reliable informant, or some corroboration of the tip, the policeman's actions were unreasonable under the standards set forth in *Terry v. Ohio*.

In *Terry* this Court recognized that "a police officer may in appropriate circumstances and in an appropriate

(continued)

manner approach a person for purposes of investigating possibly criminal behavior even though there is no probable cause to make an arrest." The Fourth Amendment does not require a policeman who lacks the precise level of information necessary for probable cause to arrest to simply shrug his shoulders and allow a crime to occur or a criminal to escape.

On the contrary, *Terry* recognizes that it may be the essence of good police work to adopt an intermediate response. A brief stop of a suspicious individual, in order to determine his identity or to maintain the status quo momentarily while obtaining more information, may be most reasonable in light of the facts known to the officer at the time.

The Court recognized in *Terry* that the policeman making a reasonable investigatory stop should not be denied the opportunity to protect himself from attack by a hostile suspect. "When an officer is justified in believing that the individual whose suspicious behavior he is investigating at close range is armed and presently dangerous to the officer or to others," he may conduct a limited protective search for concealed weapons. The purpose of this limited search is not to discover evidence of crime, but to allow the officer to pursue his investigation without fear of violence, and thus the frisk for weapons might be equally necessary and reasonable, whether or not carrying a concealed weapon violated any applicable state law. So long as the officer is entitled to make a forcible stop, and has reason to believe that the suspect is armed and dangerous, he may conduct a weapons search limited in scope to this protective purpose.

Applying these principles to the present case, we believe that Sgt. Connolly acted justifiably in responding to his informant's tip. The informant was known to him personally and had provided him with information in the past. This is a stronger case than obtains in the case of an anonymous telephone tip. The informant here came forward personally to give information that was immediately verifiable at the scene. Indeed, under Connecticut law, the informant might have been subject to immediate arrest for making a false complaint had Sgt. Connolly's investigation proved the tip incorrect.

Thus, while the Court's decisions indicate that this informant's unverified tip may have been insufficient for a narcotics arrest or search warrant, the information carried enough indicia of reliability to justify the officer's forcible stop of Williams.

In reaching this conclusion, we reject respondent's argument that reasonable cause for a stop and frisk can only be based on the officer's personal observation, rather than on information supplied by another person. Informants' tips, like all other clues and evidence coming to a policeman on the scene, may vary greatly in their value and reliability. One simple rule will not cover every situation. Some tips, completely lacking in indicia of reliability, would either warrant no police response or require further investigation before a forcible stop of a suspect would be authorized. But in some situations—for example, when the victim of a street crime seeks immediate police aid and gives a description of his assailant, or when a credible informant warns of a specific impending crime—the subtleties of the hearsay rule should not thwart an appropriate police response.

While properly investigating the activity of a person who was reported to be carrying narcotics and a concealed weapon and who was sitting alone in a car in a high-crime area at 2:15 in the morning, Sgt. Connolly had ample reason to fear for his safety. When Williams rolled down his window, rather than complying with the policeman's request to step out of the car so that his movements could more easily be seen, the revolver allegedly at Williams's waist became an even greater threat. Under these circumstances the policeman's action in reaching to the spot where the gun was thought to be hidden constituted a limited intrusion designed to ensure his safety, and we conclude that it was reasonable. The loaded gun seized as a result of this intrusion was therefore admissible at Williams's trial.

Under the circumstances surrounding Williams's possession of the gun seized by Sgt. Connolly, the arrest on the weapons charge was supported by probable cause, and the search of his person and of the car incident to that arrest was lawful [Chapter 5]. The fruits of the search were therefore properly admitted at Williams's trial, and the Court of Appeals erred in reaching a contrary conclusion.

REVERSED.

DISSENT

DOUGLAS, J., joined by MARSHALL, J.

The easy extension of *Terry v. Ohio*, to "possessory offenses" is a serious intrusion on Fourth Amendment safeguards. If it is to be extended to the latter at all, this should be only where observation by the officer himself or well authenticated information shows that criminal activity may be afoot.

BRENNAN, J.

The crucial question, as the Court concedes, is whether, there being no contention that Williams acted voluntarily in rolling down the window of his car, the State had shown sufficient cause to justify Sgt. Connolly's "forcible" stop. I would affirm, for the following reasons stated by Judge, now Chief Judge, Friendly, dissenting, that the State did not make that showing:

To begin, I have the gravest hesitancy in extending *Terry v. Ohio*, to crimes like the possession of narcotics. There is too much danger that, instead of the stop being the object and the protective frisk an incident thereto, the reverse will be true. Against that we have here the added fact of the report that Williams had a gun on his person. But Connecticut allows its citizens to carry weapons, concealed or otherwise, at will, provided only they have a permit, and gives its police officers no special authority to stop for the purpose of determining whether the citizen has one.

If I am wrong in thinking that *Terry* should not be applied at all to mere possessory offenses, I would not find the combination of Officer Connolly's almost meaningless observation and the tip in this case to be sufficient justification for the intrusion. The tip suffered from a threefold defect, with each fold compounding the others. The informer was unnamed, he was not shown to have been reliable with respect to guns or narcotics, and he gave no information which demonstrated personal knowledge or—what is worse—could not readily have been manufactured by the officer after the event.

Terry v. Ohio was intended to free a police officer from the rigidity of a rule that would prevent his doing anything to a man reasonably suspected of being about to commit or having just committed a crime of violence, no matter how grave the problem or impelling the need for swift action, unless the officer had what a court would later determine to be probable cause for arrest. It was meant for the serious cases of imminent danger or of harm recently perpetrated to persons or property, not the conventional ones of possessory offenses.

If it is to be extended to the latter at all, this should be only where observation by the officer himself or well authenticated information shows that criminal activity may be afoot. I greatly fear that if the (contrary view) should be followed, Terry will have opened the sluicegates for serious and unintended erosion of the protection of the Fourth Amendment."

MARSHALL, J., joined by DOUGLAS, J.

Four years have passed since we decided *Terry v. Ohio*, and its companion cases, *Sibron v. New York* and *Peters v. New York*. This case marks our first opportunity to give some flesh to the bones of *Terry*. Unfortunately, the flesh provided by today's decision cannot possibly be made to fit on *Terry*'s skeletal framework.

We upheld the stop and frisk in *Terry* because we recognized that the realities of on-the-street law enforcement require an officer to act at times on the basis of strong evidence, short of probable cause, that criminal activity is taking place and that the criminal is armed and dangerous. Hence, *Terry* stands only for the proposition that police officers have a "narrowly drawn authority to search for weapons" without a warrant.

In today's decision the Court ignores the fact that *Terry* begrudgingly accepted the necessity for creating an exception from the warrant requirement of the Fourth Amendment and treats this case as if warrantless searches were the rule rather than the "narrowly drawn" exception. This decision betrays the careful balance that *Terry* sought to strike between a citizen's right to privacy and his government's responsibility for effective law enforcement and expands the concept of warrantless searches far beyond anything heretofore recognized as legitimate. I dissent.

Mr. Justice Douglas was the sole dissenter in *Terry*. He warned of the "powerful hydraulic pressures throughout our history that bear heavily on the Court to water down constitutional guarantees." While I took the position then that we were not watering down rights, but were hesitantly and cautiously striking a necessary balance between the rights of American citizens to be free from government intrusion into their privacy and their government's urgent need for a narrow exception to the warrant requirement of the Fourth Amendment, today's decision demonstrates just how prescient Mr. Justice Douglas was.

It seems that the delicate balance that *Terry* struck was simply too delicate, too susceptible to the "hydraulic pressures" of the day. As a result of today's decision, the balance struck in *Terry* is now heavily weighted in favor of the government. And the Fourth Amendment, which was included in the Bill of Rights to prevent the kind of arbitrary and oppressive police action involved herein, is dealt a serious blow. Today's decision invokes the specter of a society in which innocent citizens may be stopped, searched, and arrested at the whim of police officers who have only the slightest suspicion of improper conduct.

Questions

1. List all of Officer Connolly's actions that infringed on Robert Williams's privacy and/or liberty.

2. List the facts that Connolly relied on to back up his actions.

3. Compare the facts in *Williams* with those in *Terry* in three respects: the crimes involved, the degree of the intrusions involved, and the objective basis for the officers' actions.

4. Summarize the majority opinion's reasons for ruling that the stop and frisk of Williams was reasonable.

5. Summarize the dissent's arguments for disagreeing with the majority opinion.

6. Do you agree more with the majority or the dissent? Explain your answer.

Now that you've got an overview of stops and frisks from the early cases, let's turn to a closer examination of each of these law enforcement actions. First, we'll look at stops, then at frisks, and finally at some special situations involving one or both—namely, vehicles, borders, and roadblocks.

STOPS AND THE FOURTH AMENDMENT

LO **1, 2** Beginning with *Terry v. Ohio*, we can divide the framework for analyzing police encounters with individuals into the three categories shown in Table 4.1. We've already examined the difference between voluntary encounters with the police (which are left to police discretion) and the two kinds of stops to investigate suspicious persons and circumstances that qualify as Fourth Amendment seizures (see Chapter 3, actual-seizure and show-of-authority stops).

Remember, the first question in the three-step analysis of Fourth Amendment seizures is, "Was the police action a stop?" If it wasn't, then the Fourth Amendment doesn't apply at all, and the analysis stops. But if the action was a stop, then the analysis proceeds to answering the question in step 2, "Was the stop reasonable?" What's a "reasonable" stop? Reasonableness depends on two elements:

1. Does the objective basis for the stop add up to reasonable suspicion? Reasonable suspicion (discussed later) consists of something more than a hunch but less than probable cause, the objective basis required to arrest a suspect (Chapter 5).
2. Are the requirements of the "scope of the stop" met?
   a. The duration is short.
   b. The location of the investigation is at or near the scene of the stop.

According to *Terry*, as long as officers can point to facts and circumstances amounting to reasonable suspicion, officers can "freeze" suspicious people and situations in time and space. But the freeze can last only long enough (duration) to let officers get enough information to arrest suspects; if they don't, they have to let them go. And the freeze has to take place (location) on the spot or very near the place where the stop took place.

TABLE 4.1 Three kinds of police-individual contacts

Voluntary encounters	Willing contacts without physical force or intimidation	Fourth Amendment doesn't apply
Stops	Brief (usually minutes), on-the-spot detentions that require reasonable suspicion to back them up	Fourth Amendment applies
Arrests	Longer detentions (hours or a few days) in police stations that require probable cause to back them up (Chapter 5)	Fourth Amendment applies

© Cengage Learning

How many facts are enough to add up to reasonable suspicion? How long is "only long enough," or, in Fourth Amendment terms, how long is reasonable? And exactly what is "on the spot"? How far, if any distance at all, is it reasonable for officers to move suspects from the spot? Let's try to answer these questions. First, we'll look at the objective basis for reasonable suspicion and then examine the scope of the stop allowed under the reasonableness test.

LO 3 Reasonable Suspicion to Backup Stops

According to the U.S. Supreme Court in *Terry v. Ohio*, hunches aren't enough to back up even brief stops on the street or other public places. Officers have to point to **articulable facts** that show "criminal activity may be afoot." Simply put, articulable facts are facts that officers can name to back up their stops of private persons, and, by definition, "hunches" aren't enough. In *Terry*, the nameable facts included Officer McFadden's direct observation of Terry and Chilton pacing up and down and peering into a store window in downtown Cleveland. Seeing this aroused his suspicion that the three men were "casing" the store and were about to rob it.

Chief Justice Warren never used the words "reasonable suspicion," but Justice Harlan did. In his concurring opinion, Justice Harlan defined the standard the Court has followed right up to 2013

> Officer McFadden had no probable cause to arrest Terry for anything, but he had observed circumstances that would reasonably lead an experienced, prudent policeman to suspect that Terry was about to engage in burglary or robbery. His justifiable suspicion afforded a proper constitutional basis for accosting Terry, restraining his liberty of movement briefly, and addressing questions to him, and Officer McFadden did so. (*Terry v. Ohio* 1968, 32)

In this book, we'll refer to **reasonable suspicion** as the totality of articulable facts and circumstances that would lead an officer, in the light of her training and experience, to suspect that crime may be afoot. (Notice the emphasis on "suspect" and "may" in contrast to the definition of arrest, which requires enough facts and circumstances to justify officers' *belief* that crime *is* afoot [Chapter 5].) The totality-of-facts-and-circumstances test—usually called just the "**totality-of-circumstances test**"—is a favorite standard the Court applies to decide whether official actions are constitutional. (You'll notice this as we work our way through the rest of the book.)

It might help you to call the test the whole picture test, an idea of Chief Justice Warren Burger. He wrote that the "essence" of reasonable suspicion is "that the totality of circumstances—the whole picture—must be taken into account." Based upon that whole picture, "the detaining officers must have a particularized and objective basis for suspecting the particular person stopped of criminal activity" (*U.S. v. Cortez* 1981, 417–18). According to the chief justice:

> When used by trained law enforcement officers, objective facts, meaningless to the untrained, can be combined with permissible deductions from such facts to form a legitimate basis for suspicion of a particular person and for action on that suspicion. (419)

CRIMINAL PROCEDURE IN ACTION

Driving in a circular fashion late at night in an area of high vehicle break-ins and home invasions is reasonable suspicion to stop a vehicle

LO 2, 3 At approximately 1:20 a.m. on October 19, 2007, Corporal Timothy Walsh and Officer Michael Gondek, riding together in a single police vehicle, of the Dearborn Heights, Michigan, Police Department responded to a report of a suspicious vehicle near the intersection of Beech Daly Road and Eton Street, a "regularly patrolled" area with a "high incidence of vehicle break-ins and home invasions." When they arrived at the intersection of Currier Street and Fellrath Avenue, the officers observed a white Dodge Neon, which they later learned was being driven by Alan Hoover. The officers were stopped at the intersection when the Dodge Neon approached, but they flashed their lights to indicate that it should enter the intersection before them.

Mr. Hoover then turned east on Currier Street, and the officers turned to follow. From behind the Dodge Neon, they could see that the car was "full of" clothing and household items that blocked the driver's view out of the rear windshield and side windows. As the officers followed the Dodge Neon, it drove east on Currier Street, took the first right to head south on South Beech Daly Road, took the third left to head east on Van Born Road, and then made a left onto the first through-street to head north on South Gulley Road. The car then went several blocks north, crossing the intersection with Currier Street.

This route aroused the officers' suspicions because it was not the most direct path the Dodge Neon could have taken to get from Beech Daly Road to that section of Gulley Road. The officers initiated a traffic stop on Gulley Road near Eton Street, approximately three blocks east and three blocks north of where they first began following Mr. Hoover. The traffic stop was recorded by a video camera in the officers' vehicle.

After stopping the Dodge Neon, Corporal Walsh approached the vehicle and requested that the driver—Mr. Hoover—produce his license and the car's registration. Mr. Hoover did not have his license with him and instead gave Corporal Walsh his military identification card. He did not provide his registration or any other documents. At the time, Mr. Hoover appeared "very nervous"; he was chain-smoking and refused to make eye contact with officers.

OPINION

As the Supreme Court held in *Terry v. Ohio*, (1968), an officer may seize an individual without offending the Fourth Amendment if the officer has reasonable suspicion that criminal activity may be afoot. We have explained that a *Terry* stop requires a particularized and objective basis for suspecting the particular person of criminal activity based on specific and articulable facts. We determine whether an officer has the requisite quantum of proof by looking at the totality of the circumstances. Pertinent circumstances include the officer's own direct observations, dispatch information, directions from other officers, and the nature of the area and time of day during which the suspicious activity occurred. We must consider these circumstances as a unified whole rather than as a series of disconnected facts; the lawfulness of an investigatory stop is judged by the totality of the circumstances to determine whether the individual factors, taken as a whole, give rise to reasonable suspicion, even if each individual factor is entirely consistent with innocent behavior when examined separately. Reasonable suspicion requires more than a mere hunch, but less than probable cause, and falls considerably short of satisfying a preponderance of the evidence standard.

In this case, officers responded to a suspicious vehicle complaint at 1:20 in the morning. When they arrived in the area described by the officers as "regularly patrolled ... [with] a high incidence of vehicle break[-]ins and home invasions," they encountered a white Dodge Neon that was packed with loose clothing and household items. They followed the car as it traveled east, south, east, and then north on main streets and neighborhood side streets, stopping it approximately three blocks east and three blocks north of where they first began following it. These circumstances, they contend, are sufficient to establish reasonable suspicion of criminality.

It is well settled that, standing alone, mere presence in a high-crime area is insufficient to support a reasonable, particularized suspicion that the person is committing a crime. However, the fact that the stop occurred in a high-crime area is among the relevant contextual considerations in a *Terry* analysis. The same is true with regard to the time of day: It is relevant without being independently dispositive. Similarly, nervous, evasive behavior is a pertinent factor in determining reasonable suspicion. Although headlong flight is the consummate act of evasion, it is clear that frantic flight from officers is not the only evasive act which will arouse an officer's reasonable suspicion.

We do not, and indeed must not, consider these factors in isolation. We do not consider, standing alone, the route that Mr. Hoover traveled—a route that involved main streets and side streets and included driving three blocks south only to drive north for six blocks on a nearby road. Nor may we dwell exclusively on whether a vehicle, loosely packed almost to the ceiling with personal items, was

suspicious. Such an occurrence might be entirely unremarkable if it took place at midday in a neighborhood with no particular reputation for burglaries or thefts. Here, however, officers observed a vehicle filled to the brim with piles of clothing and personal items and traveling, at least when police officers were behind it, apparently at random through a neighborhood known for theft and property crimes at 1:20 in the morning.

Although there may have been an innocent explanation for all this activity, courts and law enforcement officers must look beyond the possibility of innocent behavior to determine whether the facts support a reasonable suspicion of criminality. We conclude that, under the facts of this case, the officers' suspicion of criminality was reasonable, justifying an investigative detention.

Source: *Hoover v. Walsh*, 682 F.3d 481 (CA6 2012).

LO 3 Information that officers can rely on to build reasonable suspicion comprises two types:

1. *Direct information.* Facts and circumstances officers learn firsthand from what they themselves see, hear, smell, and touch

2. *Hearsay information.* Facts and circumstances officers learn secondhand from victims, witnesses, other police officers, and anonymous, professional, or paid informants

Table 4.2 elaborates on direct and hearsay bases for reasonable suspicion.

Recall that in 1968, when *Terry v. Ohio* was decided, reasonable suspicion was based on Officer McFadden's firsthand observations. Recall also, that four years later, in *Adams v. Williams*, the Court decided that an informant's tip plus the time (2:00 a.m.) and the location (a high-crime neighborhood) added up to reasonable suspicion to stop Williams. So, officers can rely on secondhand information, or hearsay, either partly or completely.

TABLE 4.2 Direct and hearsay bases for reasonable suspicion

Direct information	Hearsay information
Flight	Victim statement
Furtive movement	Eyewitness statement
Hiding	Statements by fellow officers
Resisting an officer	Statements by informants
Attempting to destroy evidence	Anonymous tip
Evasive answers	
Contradictory answers	
Weapons or contraband in plain view	

Officers usually get information secondhand through victims, witnesses, other police officers, and professional informants. In *Williams*, Officer Connolly knew the informant (even though he never named him). But what about anonymous tips? Are they enough to add up to reasonable suspicion? In *Alabama v. White* (1990), the police received an anonymous telephone tip

> stating that Vanessa White would be leaving 235-C Lynwood Terrace Apartments at a particular time in a brown Plymouth station wagon with the right taillight lens broken, that she would be going to Dobey's Motel, and that she would be in possession of about an ounce of cocaine inside a brown attaché case. (327)

By itself, the Court ruled, the tip wouldn't have justified a *Terry* stop. But when the officer's later direct observation confirmed the informant's prediction about White's movements, it was reasonable to suspect that the tipster had inside knowledge about the suspect and to credit his assertion about the cocaine. The Court called *White* a "close case." Then, in *Florida v. J. L.* (2000), the Court held unanimously that an anonymous tip that a "young Black male standing at a particular bus stop and wearing a plaid shirt was carrying a gun" did not amount to reasonable suspicion (268).

LO 3

In addition to anonymous tips, Table 4.3 lists other reasons that, according to the courts, are insufficient to cross the reasonable suspicion threshold unless they're backed up by other evidence. The examples in Table 4.3 point to two other kinds of information officers use to back up reasonable stops: individualized suspicion and categorical suspicion (Harris 1998).

TABLE 4.3 Reasons insufficient by themselves for reasonable suspicion

General suspicion that drug dealing went on in a tavern (*Ybarra v. Illinois*, 444 U.S. 85 [1979])
Driver double-parked within 10 feet of a pedestrian in a drug-trafficking location (*Rivera v. Murphy*, 979 F.2d 259 [1st Cir. 1992])
Other bar patrons, not the one detained, possessed weapons and contraband (*U.S. v. Jaramillo*, 25 F.3d 1146 [2nd Cir. 1994])
Passenger leaving airplane appeared nervous in the presence of officers (*U.S. v. Caicedo*, 85 F.3d 1184 [6th Cir. 1996])
Driver of a car with out-of-state license plates and no noticeable luggage avoided eye contact with a police car (*U.S. v. Halls*, 40 F.3d 275 [8th Cir. 1995])
"Hispanic-looking" males in a heavy truck near the border looked nervous, did not acknowledge police presence, and drove faster than the flow of traffic (*U.S. v. Garcia-Camacho*, 53 F.3d 244 [9th Cir. 1995])
Generalized suspicion of criminal activity in a high-crime neighborhood (*Brown v. Texas*, 443 U.S. 47 [1979])
Nervous man traveling alone who left an airline terminal quickly after picking up one suitcase and had a one-way ticket that he had bought with cash from a drug-source city (*U.S. v. Lambert*, 46 F.3d 1064 [10th Cir. 1995])
Driver failed to look at patrol car late at night (*U.S. v. Smith*, 799 F.2d 704 [11th Cir. 1986])
"Mexican-appearing" person, driving a car with out-of-state license plates and no suitcases, appeared nervous in talking with officers during discussion of a speeding ticket (*U.S. v. Tapia*, 912 F.2d 1367 [11th Cir. 1990])

Individualized suspicion consists of facts and circumstances that point to specific individuals. Terry and Chilton's casing Zucker's clothing store before Officer McFadden approached them is an excellent example of individualized suspicion.

Categorical suspicion can also help to cross that threshold. Categorical suspicion refers to suspicion that falls on suspects because they fit into a broad category of people, such as being in a particular location, being members of a particular race or ethnicity, or fitting a profile. Categorical suspicion is never enough by itself to amount to reasonable suspicion. But taken together with individualized suspicion, it can be one of the building blocks in the whole picture of reasonable suspicion.

The next three sections examine how the categories of location (with an in-depth look at flight from police officers in "high-crime areas"), race and ethnicity, and profiles can support individualized suspicion when it's not enough by itself to amount to reasonable suspicion.

LO 4 *"High-crime area"*

Whether you're stopped can depend on where you're stopped. The character of a neighborhood is a frequently used building block for establishing reasonable suspicion. Whether a neighborhood is considered a "**high-crime area**" (or a variation of the phrase, such as "known for drug trafficking") is often the basis for successfully arguing that highly ambiguous conduct amounts to reasonable suspicion that justified a Fourth Amendment stop (Raymond 1999, 100).

However courts define "high-crime area," the overwhelming majority of courts rely on law enforcement officers' testimony to prove that it's a "high-crime area." Also, most have taken the officers at their word, allowing officer reports of their arrests—even statements as weak as "several arrests"—to qualify as proof of a high-crime area. But some courts demand something more than officers' unsupported testimony, such as police department findings, citizen complaints, or the number of prior arrests the testifying officer has made. As a result, "high-crime area" differs from case to case, and from court to court, "because no court has required a threshold level of arrests, or complaints" (Ferguson and Bernache 2008, 1608–09).

A few courts have recognized the need for improved methods of proof. The U.S. Court of Appeals for the Ninth Circuit did so in *U.S. v. Montero-Camargo* (2000). The majority expressed concern that use of the term "high-crime area" . . . "may well be an 'invitation to trouble'" (1139, note 32) and "can serve as a proxy for race or ethnicity" (1138). It held that it takes more than "mere war stories" to prove a location is a high-crime area (1139).

But, according to the distinguished Judge Alex Kozinski, who concurred in the court's opinion, the majority accepted "nothing more than the personal experiences of two arresting agents" to prove the location was a high-crime area:

> Both agents testified only that they had detected criminal violations after stopping people in the area. How often? One agent said he'd been involved in 15–20 stops over eight and a half years, and "couldn't recall anywhere we didn't have a violation of some sort." The other agent testified to "about a dozen" stops in the same period, all but one of which led to an arrest.
>
> Does an arrest every four months or so make for a high-crime area? Can we rely on the vague and undocumented recollections of the officers here? Do the two officers' figures of "15–20" and "about a dozen" reflect separate pools of

incidents, or do they include some where, as here, both officers were involved? Are such estimates sufficiently precise to tell us anything useful about the area? I wouldn't have thought so, although I could be persuaded otherwise. But my colleagues don't even pause to ask the questions. To them, it's a high-crime area, because the officers say it's a high-crime area.

Just as a man with a hammer sees every problem as a nail, so a man with a badge may see every corner of his beat as a high-crime area. Police are trained to detect criminal activity and they look at the world with suspicious eyes. This is a good thing, because we rely on this suspicion to keep us safe from those who would harm us. But to rely on every cop's repertoire of war stories to determine what is a "high-crime area"—and on that basis to treat otherwise innocuous behavior as grounds for reasonable suspicion—strikes me as an invitation to trouble.

If the testimony of two officers that they made, at most, 32 arrests during the course of a decade is sufficient to turn the road here into a high-crime area, then what area under police surveillance wouldn't qualify as one? There are street corners in our inner cities that see as much crime within a month—even a week. I would be most reluctant to give police the power to turn any area into a high-crime area based on their unadorned personal experiences. I certainly would not reach out to decide the issue. (1143)

Andrew Guthrie Ferguson, a staff attorney for the Washington, D.C., Public Defender's Office, and Damien Bernache, a staff attorney for the Nassau/Suffolk Law Services Committee (2008), have proposed an "objective, quantifiable approach" to the "high-crime area" designation. It consists of three elements that the government has the burden of proving "to the appropriate standard":

1. *Crime and criminal activity.* The area has a high incidence of specific criminal activity compared to neighboring areas as measured by objective and verifiable data. As a practical matter, government lawyers would have to introduce objective and verifiable evidence to support the claim. It could include certified arrest or conviction statistics from such areas as official crime "hot spots" or "drug free zones." It might also include crime-mapping data, expert testimony, police logs, and citizen complaints. The key is "empirical data or documentation that could be verified and compared by the trial court" (1629–30). It might be difficult to draw the line as to how much higher than the neighboring areas would qualify as high. Ten to 20 percent higher? Probably. Five to 10 percent? Probably not.

2. *Geography and timing.* The area is defined narrowly to a certain location (for example, including specific blocks, parks, housing complexes, and intersections) and limited to recent criminal activity. Here, statistics have to relate to an area within specific boundaries, and they have to be recent.

   In practice, this will depend on how crime statistics are collected. It could be police districts, as it is in Chicago (see Wardlow, below), or it could be smaller. In Washington, D.C., the D.C. Police Department has a crime-mapping website where anyone can find out the number of crimes in the past two years for any block or intersection in the city (1631–32).

3. *Criminal activity/officer observation link.* There is a demonstrated connection between the specific criminal activity and the officer's observation. Why is this important?

Because the only reason the criminal activity is relevant is because it makes the suspicion more reasonable. For example, if an area is verifiably high in burglaries, it's more reasonable to suspect that a person loitering with a bag over his or her shoulder might have just committed a burglary than it would be to suspect a person seen transferring money to someone might be dealing drugs. The crime/officer observation link prevents including too much within the "high-crime area" designation (1635).

Of course, the officer has to know that it's a "high-crime area" before she observed the criminal activity; otherwise, the location is not a basis for suspicion.

The objective of these empirical elements is to guide litigants and courts in Fourth Amendment suppression hearings whenever the government raises the "high-crime area" issue (1628).

In *Illinois v. Wardlow* (5–4), the U.S. Supreme Court found that Sam Wardlow's unprovoked flight from Chicago police officers in "an area known for heavy narcotics trafficking" added up to reasonable suspicion to stop him.

CASE

Does Sudden Unprovoked Flight in a "Heavy Narcotics Trafficking" Area Amount to Reasonable Suspicion?

Illinois v. Wardlow
528 U.S. 119 (2000)

HISTORY

William "Sam" Wardlow (respondent) was arrested and charged with unlawful use of a weapon by a felon. The Illinois trial court denied his motion to suppress and convicted Wardlow of unlawful use of a weapon by a felon. The Illinois Appellate Court reversed Wardlow's conviction. The Illinois Supreme Court affirmed the Appellate Court's decision. Illinois petitioned for certiorari. The U.S. Supreme Court granted the petition and reversed (5–4).

—REHNQUIST, C.J.

FACTS

On September 9, 1995, Officers Nolan and Harvey and six others were working as uniformed officers in the special operations section of the Chicago Police Department. These two officers were driving the last car of a four-car caravan converging on an area known for heavy narcotics trafficking in order to investigate drug transactions.

The officers were traveling together because they expected to find a crowd of people in the area, including lookouts and customers.

As the caravan passed 4035 West Van Buren, Officer Nolan observed Wardlow standing next to the building holding an opaque bag. Wardlow looked in the direction of the officers and fled. Nolan and Harvey turned their car southbound, watched him as he ran through the gangway and an alley, and eventually cornered him on the street. Nolan then exited his car and stopped Wardlow. He immediately conducted a protective pat-down search for weapons because in his experience it was common for there to be weapons in the near vicinity of narcotics transactions.

During the frisk, Officer Nolan squeezed the bag Wardlow was carrying and felt a heavy, hard object similar to the shape of a gun. The officer then opened the bag and discovered a .38-caliber handgun with five live rounds of ammunition. The officers arrested Wardlow.

(continued)

OPINION

An individual's presence in an area of expected criminal activity, standing alone, is not enough to support a reasonable, particularized suspicion that the person is committing a crime. But officers are not required to ignore the relevant characteristics of a location in determining whether the circumstances are sufficiently suspicious to warrant further investigation. Accordingly, we have previously noted that a stop in a "high-crime area" can be among the relevant contextual considerations in a *Terry* analysis [see *Adams v. Williams* (1972), excerpted on p. 113].

In this case, it was not merely Wardlow's presence in an area of heavy narcotics trafficking that aroused the officers' suspicion but his unprovoked flight upon noticing the police. Our cases have also recognized that nervous, evasive behavior is a pertinent factor in determining reasonable suspicion. Headlong flight—wherever it occurs—is the consummate act of evasion: It is not necessarily indicative of wrongdoing, but it is certainly suggestive of such.

In reviewing the propriety of an officer's conduct, courts do not have available empirical studies dealing with inferences drawn from suspicious behavior, and we cannot reasonably demand scientific certainty from judges or law enforcement officers where none exists. Thus, the determination of reasonable suspicion must be based on commonsense judgments and inferences about human behavior. We conclude Officer Nolan was justified in suspecting that Wardlow was involved in criminal activity, and, therefore, in investigating further.

When an officer, without reasonable suspicion or probable cause, approaches an individual, the individual has a right to ignore the police and go about his business. And any "refusal to cooperate, without more, does not furnish the minimal level of objective justification needed for a detention or seizure." But unprovoked flight is simply not a mere refusal to cooperate. Flight, by its very nature, is not "going about one's business"; in fact, it is just the opposite. Allowing officers confronted with such flight to stop the fugitive and investigate further is quite consistent with the individual's right to go about his business or to stay put and remain silent in the face of police questioning.

Wardlow also argues that there are innocent reasons for flight from police and that, therefore, flight is not necessarily indicative of ongoing criminal activity. This fact is undoubtedly true, but does not establish a violation of the Fourth Amendment. *Terry* recognized that the officers could detain the individuals to resolve the ambiguity. In allowing such detentions, *Terry* accepts the risk that officers may stop innocent people. If the officer does not learn facts rising to the level of probable cause, the individual must be allowed to go on his way. But in this case the officers found Wardlow in possession of a handgun, and arrested him for violation of an Illinois firearms statute.

The judgment of the Supreme Court of Illinois is REVERSED, and the case is REMANDED for further proceedings not inconsistent with this opinion. It is so ordered.

CONCURRING AND DISSENTING OPINIONS

STEVENS, J., joined by SOUTER, GINSBURG, and BREYER, JJ., concurring in part and dissenting in part.

The State of Illinois asks this Court to announce a "bright-line rule" authorizing the temporary detention of anyone who flees at the mere sight of a police officer. Wardlow counters by asking us to adopt the opposite per se rule—that the fact that a person flees upon seeing the police can never, by itself, be sufficient to justify a temporary investigative stop. The Court today wisely endorses neither per se rule. Instead, it adheres to the view that the concept of reasonable suspicion is not readily reduced to a neat set of legal rules, but must be determined by looking to the totality of the circumstances—the whole picture.

The question in this case concerns "the degree of suspicion that attaches to" a person's flight—or, more precisely, what "commonsense conclusions" can be drawn respecting the motives behind that flight.*

Given the diversity and frequency of possible motivations for flight, it would be profoundly unwise to endorse either per se rule. The inference we can reasonably draw about the motivation for a person's flight, rather, will depend on a number of different circumstances. Factors such as the time of day, the number of people in the area, the character of the neighborhood, whether the officer was in uniform, the way the runner was dressed, the direction and speed of the flight, and whether the person's behavior was otherwise unusual might be relevant in specific cases.

This number of variables is surely sufficient to preclude either a bright-line rule that always justifies, or that never justifies, an investigative stop based on the sole fact that flight began after a police officer appeared

---

* "Compare, Proverbs 28:1: 'The wicked flee when no man pursueth: but the righteous are as bold as a lion' with Proverbs 22:3: 'A shrewd man sees trouble coming and lies low; the simple walk into it and pay the penalty.' I have rejected reliance on the former proverb in the past, because its 'ivory-towered analysis of the real world' fails to account for the experiences of many citizens in this country, particularly those who are minorities. That this pithy expression fails to capture the total reality of our world, however, does not mean it is inaccurate in all instances."

nearby. Still, Illinois presses for a per se rule regarding "unprovoked flight upon seeing a clearly identifiable police officer." The phrase "upon seeing," as used by Illinois, apparently assumes that the flight is motivated by the presence of the police officer.*

Even assuming we know that a person runs because he sees the police, the inference to be drawn may still vary from case to case. Flight to escape police detection may have an entirely innocent motivation:

> It is a matter of common knowledge that men who are entirely innocent do sometimes fly from the scene of a crime through fear of being apprehended as the guilty parties, or from an unwillingness to appear as witnesses. Nor is it true as an accepted axiom of criminal law that "the wicked flee when no man pursueth, but the righteous are as bold as a lion." Innocent men sometimes hesitate to confront a jury—not necessarily because they fear that the jury will not protect them, but because they do not wish their names to appear in connection with criminal acts, are humiliated at being obliged to incur the popular odium of an arrest and trial, or because they do not wish to be put to the annoyance or expense of defending themselves. *Alberty v. U.S.*, 162 U.S. 499, 511 (1896).

In addition to these concerns, a reasonable person may conclude that an officer's sudden appearance indicates nearby criminal activity. And where there is criminal activity there is also a substantial element of danger—either from the criminal or from a confrontation between the criminal and the police. These considerations can lead to an innocent and understandable desire to quit the vicinity with all speed.

Among some citizens, particularly minorities and those residing in high-crime areas, there is also the possibility that the fleeing person is entirely innocent, but, with or without justification, believes that contact with the police can itself be dangerous, apart from any criminal activity associated with the officer's sudden presence.**

For such a person, unprovoked flight is neither "aberrant" nor "abnormal." . . .*

Many stops never lead to an arrest, which further exacerbates the perceptions of discrimination felt by racial minorities and people living in high-crime areas. . . .[†]

Even if these data were race neutral, they would still indicate that society as a whole is paying a significant cost in infringement on liberty by these virtually random stops. Moreover, these concerns and fears are known to the police officers themselves, and are validated by law enforcement investigations into their own practices. The Massachusetts attorney general investigated allegations of egregious police conduct toward minorities. The report stated:

> Perhaps the most disturbing evidence was that the scope of a number of *Terry* searches went far beyond anything authorized by that case and indeed, beyond anything that we believe would be acceptable under the federal and state constitutions even where probable cause existed to conduct a full search incident to an arrest.
>
> Forcing young men to lower their trousers, or otherwise searching inside their underwear, on public streets or in public hallways, is so demeaning and invasive of fundamental precepts of privacy that it can only be condemned in the strongest terms. The fact that not only the young men themselves, but independent witnesses complained of strip searches, should be deeply alarming to all members of this community.

**See Casimir, "Minority Men: We Are Frisk Targets," *N.Y. Daily News*, Mar. 26, 1999, p. 34 (informal survey of 100 young Black and Hispanic men living in New York City; 81 reported having been stopped and frisked by police at least once; none of the 81 stops resulted in arrests); Brief for NAACP Legal Defense & Educational Fund as Amicus Curiae 17–19 (reporting figures on disproportionate street stops of minority residents in Pittsburgh and Philadelphia, Pennsylvania, and St. Petersburg, Florida); U.S. Dept. of Justice, Bureau of Justice Statistics, S. Smith, "Criminal Victimization and Perceptions of Community Safety in 12 Cities" (25 June 1998) (African American residents in 12 cities are more than twice as likely to be dissatisfied with police practices than White residents in same community.)

*See e.g., Kotlowitz, "Hidden Casualties: Drug War's Emphasis on Law Enforcement Takes a Toll on Police," *Wall Street Journal*, Jan. 11, 1991 ("Black leaders complained that innocent people were picked up in the drug sweeps. . . . Some teenagers were so scared of the task force they ran even if they weren't selling drugs.")

†See Goldberg, "The Color of Suspicion," *N.Y. Times Magazine*, June 20, 1999 (reporting that in a 2-year period, New York City Police Department Street Crimes Unit made 45,000 stops, only 9,500, or 20%, of which resulted in arrest); Casimir (reporting that in 1997, New York City's Street Crimes Unit conducted 27,061 stop-and-frisks, only 4,647 of which, 17 percent, resulted in arrest).

Note: Nowhere in Illinois's briefs does it specify what it means by "unprovoked." At oral argument, Illinois explained that if officers precipitate a flight by threats of violence, that flight is "provoked." But if police officers in a patrol car—with lights flashing and siren sounding—descend upon an individual for the sole purpose of seeing if he or she will run, the ensuing flight is "unprovoked." Illinois contends that unprovoked flight is "an extreme reaction," because innocent people simply do not "flee at the mere sight of the police." To be sure, Illinois concedes, an innocent person—even one distrustful of the police—might "avoid eye contact or even sneer at the sight of an officer," and that would not justify a *Terry* stop or any sort of per se inference. But, Illinois insists, unprovoked flight is altogether different.

Such behavior is so "aberrant" and "abnormal" that a per se inference is justified

(*continued*)

Accordingly, the evidence supporting the reasonableness of these beliefs is too pervasive to be dismissed as random or rare, and too persuasive to be disparaged as inconclusive or insufficient. In any event, just as we do not require "scientific certainty" for our commonsense conclusion that unprovoked flight can sometimes indicate suspicious motives, neither do we require scientific certainty to conclude that unprovoked flight can occur for other, innocent reasons.

"Unprovoked flight," in short, describes a category of activity too broad and varied to permit a per se reasonable inference regarding the motivation for the activity. While the innocent explanations surely do not establish that the Fourth Amendment is always violated whenever someone is stopped solely on the basis of an unprovoked flight, neither do the suspicious motivations establish that the Fourth Amendment is never violated when a *Terry* stop is predicated on that fact alone.

Guided by that totality-of-the-circumstances test, the Court concludes that Officer Nolan had reasonable suspicion to stop respondent. In this respect, my view differs from the Court's. The entire justification for the stop is articulated in the brief testimony of Officer Nolan. Some facts are perfectly clear; others are not. This factual insufficiency leads me to conclude that the Court's judgment is mistaken.

Wardlow was arrested a few minutes after noon on September 9, 1995. Nolan was part of an eight-officer, four-car caravan patrol team. The officers were headed for "one of the areas in the 11th District [of Chicago] that's high [in] narcotics traffic." The reason why four cars were in the caravan was that "normally in these different areas there's an enormous amount of people, sometimes lookouts, customers." Officer Nolan testified that he was in uniform on that day, but he did not recall whether he was driving a marked or an unmarked car.

Officer Nolan and his partner were in the last of the four patrol cars that "were all caravaning eastbound down Van Buren." Nolan first observed respondent "in front of 4035 West Van Buren." Wardlow "looked in our direction and began fleeing." Nolan then "began driving southbound down the street observing [respondent] running through the gangway and the alley southbound," and observed that Wardlow was carrying a white, opaque bag under his arm.

After the car turned south and intercepted respondent as he "ran right towards us," Officer Nolan stopped him and conducted a "protective search," which revealed that the bag under respondent's arm contained a loaded handgun.

This terse testimony is most noticeable for what it fails to reveal. Though asked whether he was in a marked or unmarked car, Officer Nolan could not recall the answer. He was not asked whether any of the other three cars in the caravan were marked, or whether any of the other seven officers were in uniform. Though he explained that the size of the caravan was because "normally in these different areas there's an enormous amount of people, sometimes lookouts, customers," Officer Nolan did not testify as to whether anyone besides Wardlow was nearby 4035 West Van Buren. Nor is it clear that that address was the intended destination of the caravan.

As the Appellate Court of Illinois interpreted the record, "it appears that the officers were simply driving by, on their way to some unidentified location, when they noticed defendant standing at 4035 West Van Buren." Officer Nolan's testimony also does not reveal how fast the officers were driving. It does not indicate whether he saw respondent notice the other patrol cars. And it does not say whether the caravan, or any part of it, had already passed Wardlow by before he began to run. Indeed, the Appellate Court thought the record was even "too vague to support the inference that . . . defendant's flight was related to his expectation of police focus on him."

Presumably, respondent did not react to the first three cars, and we cannot even be sure that he recognized the occupants of the fourth as police officers. The adverse inference is based entirely on the officer's statement: "He looked in our direction and began fleeing." No other factors sufficiently support a finding of reasonable suspicion.

Though respondent was carrying a white, opaque bag under his arm, there is nothing at all suspicious about that. Certainly the time of day—shortly after noon—does not support Illinois's argument. Nor were the officers "responding to any call or report of suspicious activity in the area."

Officer Nolan did testify that he expected to find "an enormous amount of people," including drug customers or lookouts, and the Court points out that "it was in this context that Officer Nolan decided to investigate Wardlow after observing him flee." This observation, in my view, lends insufficient weight to the reasonable suspicion analysis; indeed, in light of the absence of testimony that anyone else was nearby when respondent began to run, this observation points in the opposite direction.

The State, along with the majority of the Court, relies as well on the assumption that this flight occurred in a high-crime area. Even if that assumption is accurate, it is insufficient because even in a high-crime neighborhood unprovoked flight does not invariably lead to reasonable suspicion.

On the contrary, because many factors providing innocent motivations for unprovoked flight are concentrated in high-crime areas, the character of the neighborhood arguably makes an inference of guilt less appropriate, rather than more so. Like unprovoked flight itself, presence in a high-crime neighborhood is a fact too generic and susceptible to innocent explanation to satisfy the reasonable suspicion inquiry.

It is the State's burden to articulate facts sufficient to support reasonable suspicion. In my judgment, Illinois has failed to discharge that burden. I am not persuaded that the mere fact that someone standing on a sidewalk looked in the direction of a passing car before starting to run is sufficient to justify a forcible stop and frisk.

FIGURE 4.2 Stops and Arrests, NYPD

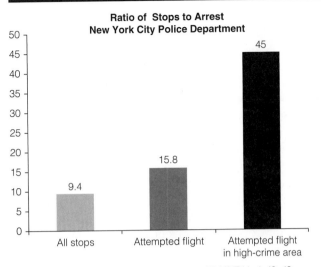

Source: Based on Harcourt and Meares (August 2010), Table 1, 62–63.

FIGURE 4.3 Facts Supporting Reasonable Suspicion (NYPD)

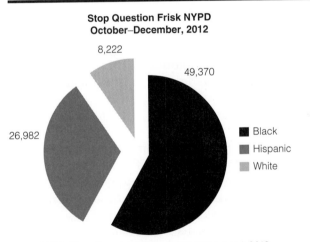

Source: NYPD, "Stop Question & Frisk Activity," October 1, 2012
through December 31, 2012

I therefore respectfully DISSENT from the Court's judgment to reverse the court below.

Questions

1. Identify the "articulable" facts Officer Nolan relied on to stop Wardlow.

2. List the Court's reasons for concluding these facts added up to reasonable suspicion.

3. Compare the facts Nolan possessed with those possessed by Officer McFadden in *Terry v. Ohio.* In your opinion, which officer had more articulable facts?

4. Even if one had more than the other, did they both have reasonable suspicion? Defend your answer.

5. Is reasonable suspicion enough of a safeguard to the right of all people, innocent and guilty, to come and go as they please? Defend your answer.

6. List and summarize the empirical evidence Justice Stevens includes in his dissenting opinion. Is the evidence reliable? Assuming the evidence is reliable, does it have anything to do with whether Nolan's stop and frisk of Wardlow was reasonable? Defend your answer.

7. Consider Figures 4.2 and 4.3. "Stops and Arrests, NYPD" and "Facts Supporting Reasonable Suspicion (NYPD)," respectively. What, if any, policies would you recommend on the basis of these numbers? Is there anything else you'd want to know before you recommended anything? Explain your answers.

LO **4** Should officers be allowed to view race and ethnicity through the lens of their training and experience as part of the totality of circumstances adding up to reasonable suspicion? Or must reasonable suspicion be color and ethnicity blind? Even asking this question generates explosive controversy (Kennedy 1997, Chapter 4).

The U.S. Supreme Court has made it clear that race and ethnicity by themselves can never amount to reasonable suspicion. But the Supreme Court and almost all lower courts have made it equally clear that when it comes to reasonable suspicion, color and ethnicity are part of reality, however uncomfortable that reality may be. "Facts are not to be ignored simply because they may be unpleasant," wrote U.S. Eighth Circuit Court of Appeals Judge Wollman in *U.S. v. Weaver* (1992, 394).

We need to distinguish between two uses of race and ethnicity as building blocks in reasonable suspicion. First, and usually not problematic, race or ethnicity is a building block when it's part of individualized suspicion, as when a witness identifies her attacker as White, or Black, or Hispanic. Second, race and ethnicity can be a building block when it's a categorical circumstance, such as it was in *U.S. v. Weaver*. The U.S. Eighth Circuit Court of Appeals held that law enforcement officers could use Weaver's race as part of reasonable suspicion.

Arthur Weaver caught the attention of Drug Enforcement Administration (DEA) agents and Kansas City detectives when he got off an early morning direct flight from Los Angeles. The DEA agent testified that several factors caused him to suspect that Weaver might be carrying drugs:

> Number one, we have intelligence information and also past arrest history on two Black—all-Black street gangs from Los Angeles called the Crips and the Bloods. They are notorious for transporting cocaine into the Kansas City area from Los Angeles for sale. Most of them are young, roughly dressed male Blacks. (394, n. 2)

According to Judge Wollman:

> We agree with the dissent that large groups of our citizens should not be regarded by law enforcement officers as presumptively criminal based upon their race. We would not hesitate to hold that a solely race-based suspicion of drug courier status would not pass constitutional muster. As it is, however, facts are not to be ignored simply because they may be unpleasant—and the unpleasant fact in this case is that Hicks had knowledge, based upon his own experience and upon the intelligence reports he had received from the Los Angeles authorities, that young male members of Black Los Angeles gangs were flooding the Kansas City area with cocaine. To that extent, then, race, when coupled with the other factors Hicks relied upon, was a factor in the decision to approach and ultimately detain Weaver. We wish it were otherwise, but we take the facts as they are presented to us, not as we would like them to be. (394)

Chief Judge Arnold dissented:

> When public officials begin to regard large groups of citizens as presumptively criminal, this country is in a perilous situation indeed. Airports are on the verge of becoming war zones, where anyone is liable to be stopped, questioned, and even searched merely on the basis of the on-the-spot exercise of discretion by police officers.

It's hard to work up much sympathy for Weaver. He's getting what he deserves, in a sense. What is missing here, though, is an awareness that law

YOU DECIDE
Is It Reasonable to Stop and Frisk More Innocent Black and Hispanic Men than White Men?

Just Take Away Their Guns?

The most effective way to reduce illegal gun carrying is to encourage the police to take guns away from people who carry them without a permit. This means encouraging the police to make street frisks . . . . Innocent people will be stopped. Young Black and Hispanic men will probably be stopped more often than older White Anglo males of any race. But we must get illegal guns off the street.

—*Wilson 1994, 46*

You've learned that "stops and frisks" are reasonable under the Fourth Amendment. And we can all agree that guns can be dangerous when not owned and operated properly. But what about the ethics of what the distinguished political scientist James Q. Wilson proposes?

---

enforcement is a broad concept. It includes enforcement of the Bill of Rights, as well as enforcement of criminal statutes. Cases in which innocent travelers are stopped and impeded in their lawful activities don't come to court. They go on their way, too busy to bring a lawsuit against the officious agents who have detained them. (397)

LO 3   *Profiles*

Profiles consist of lists of circumstances that might, or might not, be linked to particular kinds of behavior. Profiles have been popular law enforcement tools since the 1970s when the government introduced an airline hijacker profile.

In this section, we'll focus on drug courier profiles, lists of characteristics that drug traffickers are supposed to possess. Drug Enforcement Administration (DEA) Agent Paul Markonni developed the drug courier profile in 1974 while he was assigned to the Detroit DEA office and trained other agents in its use. Since then, it's become a "nationwide law enforcement tool." Officers stationed at airports observe travelers, looking for seven primary and four secondary characteristics (Table 4.4; *U.S. v. Elmore* 1979, 1039, n. 3).

If their suspicions are aroused, agents approach travelers, identify themselves, seek their consent to be questioned, and ask to see their identification and ticket. If this doesn't remove their suspicion, the agents ask travelers to come with them to another location, usually a room used by law enforcement officers. Once inside the room, agents ask travelers to consent to searches of their persons and luggage. If travelers refuse, agents either have to let them go or "seize" them (Cloud 1985, 848–49).

Since the introduction of the airport drug courier profile, law enforcement has introduced a number of other profiles: for illegal aliens entering the United States, international drug smugglers, customers of suspected domestic drug dealers, and highway drug couriers.

The Supreme Court, in *Reid v. Georgia* (1980), ruled that the drug courier profile by itself can't amount to reasonable suspicion. In *Reid*, a DEA agent suspected that Tommy Reid, Jr., possessed cocaine based on the DEA drug courier profile,

TABLE 4.4 Primary and secondary characteristics of drug couriers

Primary characteristics	Secondary characteristics
Arriving or departing from "source" cities	Using public transportation when leaving airports
Carrying little or no luggage, or empty suitcases	Making telephone calls immediately after getting off the plane
Traveling by an unusual itinerary	Leaving false or fictitious callback numbers when leaving the plane
Using an alias	Making excessively frequent trips to source or distribution cities
Carrying unusually large amounts of cash	
Purchasing tickets with large numbers of small bills	
Appearing unusually nervous	

© Cengage Learning

"a somewhat informal compilation of characteristics typical of persons unlawfully carrying narcotics" (440).

The Georgia Court of Appeals held that the following elements of the profile were enough to satisfy the reasonable suspicion requirement.

1. Reid had arrived from Fort Lauderdale, a principal place of origin of cocaine sold elsewhere in the country;

2. Reid arrived in the early morning, when law enforcement activity is diminished;

3. Reid and his companion appeared to the agent to be trying to conceal the fact that they were traveling together, and

4. Reid and his companion apparently had no luggage other than their shoulder bags. (441–42)

The U.S. Supreme Court disagreed. The Court conceded that the agent's observing Reid looking back occasionally at his companion as they walked through the concourse "relates to their particular conduct." Nevertheless, the four elements in this profile listed "describe a very large category of presumably innocent travelers, who would be subject to virtually random seizures were the Court to conclude that as little foundation as there was in this case could justify a seizure." Therefore, the Court held, the profile by itself didn't add up to reasonable suspicion, and the possibility that Reid and his companion were trying to conceal that they were traveling together "is simply too slender a reed to support" Reid's stop (442).

What about the characteristics in the profiles that fit the individual defendant? Can officers use them as part of the totality-of-circumstances test amounting to reasonable suspicion? Yes, ruled the Supreme Court in the frequently cited *U.S. v. Sokolow* (1989).

DEA agents stopped Andrew Sokolow in Honolulu International Airport after his behavior indicated he might be a drug trafficker. The behavior included:

- He'd paid $2,100 in cash for airline tickets.
- He wasn't traveling under his own name.
- His original destination was Miami.
- He appeared nervous during the trip.
- He checked none of his luggage. (3)

DEA agents arrested Sokolow and searched his luggage without a warrant. Later, at the DEA office, agents obtained warrants allowing more extensive searches, and they discovered 1,063 grams of cocaine. According to the Court, the agents had a reasonable suspicion that Sokolow "was engaged in wrongdoing." Just because some of that information is also part of a profile (probabilistic evidence) doesn't bar its use to build reasonable suspicion, as long as the "totality of the circumstances" adds up to reasonable suspicion (7–9).

LO 1   The Scope of Reasonable Stops

A brief freeze in time and in space—the scope of a reasonable stop has to include these two things. So there are two elements to the scope of a reasonable stop: short duration and on-the-spot location of the investigation. Let's look at each.

Short duration

According to the American Law Institute's (a group of distinguished prosecutors, defense lawyers, law enforcement officers, and academics) Model Code of Pre-Arraignment Procedure (1975), there ought to be a bright-line rule controlling the length of stops. Section 110.2 provides that law enforcement officers can stop a person "for such period as is reasonably necessary, but in no case for more than twenty minutes" to "obtain or verify" the stopped person's identification; to "obtain or verify an account of such person's presence or conduct"; or to determine whether to arrest the person.

The U.S. Supreme Court has so far declined to adopt this rule (*U.S. v. Sharpe and Savage* 1985). Why? Because the Court prefers to keep its options open and to give officers plenty of room for discretionary decision making. That way neither the Court nor officers are confined to a bright-line rule that may hamper crime control.

"On-the-spot" investigation

Before *Terry v. Ohio* (1968), whenever a law enforcement officer moved a suspect to another place, it was an "arrest," requiring probable cause to back it up. For example, a court in one case ruled that taking the suspect to a police call box less than a block away was an arrest (*U.S. v. Mitchell* 1959). But today officers are allowed some leeway. According to search and seizure expert Professor Wayne R. LaFave (2004), often quoted in criminal procedure cases, "some movement of the suspect in the vicinity of the stop is permissible without converting what would otherwise be a . . . [stop] into an arrest" (4:348). Recall that Officer McFadden moved Terry, Chilton, and Katz into the nearest store, and the Court didn't question this move.

Questioning stopped suspects

During the brief, on-the-spot freeze, what can officers do to find further information that will lead either to arrest or release? Most often, officers ask the suspect questions. Lies, or statements "that are incriminating, implausible, conflicting, evasive or unresponsive," can lead to a longer, more invasive arrest (LaFave and others 2009, 179). Knowing a suspect's identity can clear suspects and allow both officers and suspects to get back to their business by leading to their quick release. This is the purpose of the "stop-and-identify" statutes in 21 states that allow officers to ask for suspects' names and identification.

Refusal to answer can lead to arrest and prosecution for failure to produce identification when a law enforcement officer asks for it. That's what happened to Larry Hiibel when he refused to identify himself to Humboldt County, Nevada, Deputy Sheriff Lee Dove in our next case excerpt, *Hiibel v. Sixth Judicial District Court of Nevada, Humboldt County et al.* (2004).

In *Hiibel v. Sixth Judicial District Court of Nevada, Humboldt County et al.* (2004), the U.S. Supreme Court affirmed the Nevada Supreme Court's decision, supporting that state's "stop and identify" statute.

CASE

Is the "Stop and Identify" Law Reasonable?

Hiibel v. Sixth Judicial Court of Nevada, Humboldt County et al.
542 U.S. 177 (2004)

KENNEDY, J., delivered the opinion of the Court, in which REHNQUIST, C.J., and O'CONNOR, SCALIA, and THOMAS, JJ., joined. STEVENS, J., filed a dissenting opinion. BREYER, J., filed a dissenting opinion, in which SOUTER and GINSBURG, JJ., joined.

FACTS

The sheriff's department in Humboldt County, Nevada, received an afternoon telephone call reporting an assault. The caller reported seeing a man assault a woman in a red and silver GMC truck on Grass Valley Road. Deputy Sheriff Lee Dove was dispatched to investigate. When the officer arrived at the scene, he found the truck parked on the side of the road. A man was standing by the truck, and a young woman was sitting inside it. The officer observed skid marks in the gravel behind the vehicle, leading him to believe it had come to a sudden stop.

The officer approached the man and explained that he was investigating a report of a fight. The man appeared to be intoxicated. The officer asked him if he had "any identification on him," which we understand as a request to produce a driver's license or some other form of written identification. The man refused and asked why the officer wanted to see identification. The officer responded that he was conducting an investigation and needed to see some identification. The unidentified man became agitated and insisted he had done nothing wrong. The officer explained that he wanted to find out who the man was and what he was doing there.

After continued refusals to comply with the officer's request for identification, the man began to taunt the officer by placing his hands behind his back and telling the officer to arrest him and take him to jail. This routine kept up for several minutes: The officer asked for identification 11 times and was refused each time. After warning the man that he would be arrested if he continued to refuse to comply, the officer placed him under arrest.

We now know that the man arrested on Grass Valley Road is Larry Dudley Hiibel. Hiibel was charged with "willfully resisting, delaying or obstructing a public officer in discharging or attempting to discharge any legal duty of his office" in violation of Nev. Rev. Stat. (NRS) § 199.280 (2003). The government reasoned that Hiibel had obstructed the officer in carrying out his duties under § 171.123, a Nevada statute that defines the legal rights and duties of a police officer in the context of an investigative stop. Section 171.123 provides in relevant part:

> "1. Any peace officer may detain any person whom the officer encounters under circumstances which reasonably indicate that the person has committed, is committing or is about to commit a crime. . . .
>
> 3. The officer may detain the person pursuant to this section only to ascertain his identity and the suspicious circumstances surrounding his presence abroad. Any person so detained shall identify himself, but may not be compelled to answer any other inquiry of any peace officer." Hiibel was tried in the Justice Court of Union Township. Hiibel was convicted and fined $250.

OPINION

NRS § 171.123(3) is an enactment sometimes referred to as a "stop and identify" statute. The statutes vary from State to State, but all permit an officer to ask or require a suspect to disclose his identity. Stop and identify statutes have their roots in early English vagrancy laws that required suspected vagrants to face arrest unless they gave "a good account of themselves," a power that itself reflected common-law rights of private persons to "arrest any suspicious night-walker, and detain him till he give a good account of himself." In recent decades, the Court has found constitutional infirmity in traditional vagrancy laws.

The Court has recognized similar constitutional limitations on the scope and operation of stop and identify statutes. In *Brown v. Texas* (1979), the Court invalidated a conviction for violating a Texas stop and identify statute on Fourth Amendment grounds. The Court ruled that the initial stop was not based on specific, objective facts establishing reasonable suspicion to believe the suspect was involved in criminal activity. Absent that factual basis for detaining the defendant, the Court held, the risk of "arbitrary and abusive police practices" was too great and the stop was impermissible.

Here there is no question that the initial stop was based on reasonable suspicion, satisfying the Fourth Amendment requirements noted in *Brown*. Furthermore, the Nevada Supreme Court has interpreted NRS § 171.123(3) to require only that a suspect disclose his name. "The suspect is not required to provide private details about his background, but merely to state his name to an officer when reasonable suspicion exists." As we understand it, the statute does not require a suspect to give the officer a driver's license or any other document. Provided that the suspect either states his name or communicates it to the officer by other means—a choice, we assume, that the suspect may make—the statute is satisfied and no violation occurs.

Hiibel argues that his conviction cannot stand because the officer's conduct violated his Fourth Amendment rights. We disagree. Our decisions make clear that questions concerning a suspect's identity are a routine and accepted part of many *Terry* stops. Obtaining a suspect's name in the course of a *Terry* stop serves important government interests. Knowledge of identity may inform an officer that a suspect is wanted for another offense, or has a record of violence or mental disorder. On the other hand, knowing identity may help clear a suspect and allow the police to concentrate their efforts elsewhere. Identity may prove particularly important in cases such as this, where the police are investigating what appears to be a domestic assault. Officers called to investigate domestic disputes need to know whom they are dealing with in order to assess the situation, the threat to their own safety, and possible danger to the potential victim.

Although it is well established that an officer may ask a suspect to identify himself in the course of a *Terry* stop, it has been an open question whether the suspect can be arrested and prosecuted for refusal to answer. The principles of *Terry* permit a State to require a suspect to disclose his name in the course of a *Terry* stop. The reasonableness of a seizure under the Fourth Amendment is determined "by balancing its intrusion on the individual's Fourth Amendment interests against its promotion of legitimate government interests." The Nevada statute satisfies that standard. The request for identity has an immediate relation to the purpose, rationale, and practical demands of a *Terry* stop.

The threat of criminal sanction helps ensure that the request for identity does not become a legal nullity. On the other hand, the Nevada statute does not alter the nature of the stop itself: It does not change its duration, or its location. A state law requiring a suspect to disclose his name in the course of a valid *Terry* stop is consistent with Fourth Amendment prohibitions against unreasonable searches and seizures.

The judgment of the Nevada Supreme Court is AFFIRMED.

DISSENT

Justice BREYER, with whom Justice SOUTER and Justice GINSBURG join, dissenting.

This Court's Fourth Amendment precedents make clear that police may conduct a *Terry* stop only within circumscribed limits. And one of those limits invalidates laws that compel responses to police questioning. In *Terry v. Ohio* (1968), Justice White, in a concurring opinion, wrote: "Of course, the person stopped is not obliged to answer, answers may not be compelled, and refusal to answer furnishes no basis for an arrest, although it may alert the officer to the need for continued observation."

There is no good reason now to reject this generation-old statement of the law. There are sound reasons rooted in Fifth Amendment considerations for adhering to this Fourth Amendment legal condition circumscribing police authority to stop an individual against his will. Administrative considerations also militate against change. Can a State, in addition to requiring a stopped individual to answer "What's your name?" also require an answer to "What's your license number?" or "Where do you live?" Can a police officer, who must know how to make a *Terry* stop, keep track of the constitutional answers? After all, answers to any of these questions may, or may not, incriminate, depending upon the circumstances.

Indeed, as the Court points out, a name itself—even if it is not "Killer Bill" or "Rough 'em up Harry"—will sometimes provide the police with "a link in the chain of

(continued)

evidence needed to convict the individual of a separate offense." The majority reserves judgment about whether compulsion is permissible in such instances. How then is a police officer in the midst of a *Terry* stop to distinguish between the majority's ordinary case and this special case where the majority reserves judgment?

The majority presents no evidence that the rule enunciated by Justice White, which for nearly a generation has set forth a settled *Terry* stop condition, has significantly interfered with law enforcement. Nor has the majority presented any other convincing justification for change. I would not begin to erode a clear rule with special exceptions. I consequently dissent.

Questions

1. State the elements of the Nevada "stop and identify" statute.

2. List all the facts relevant to deciding whether the stop and identify law is "reasonable."

3. Summarize the majority opinion's argument supporting its holding that the statute meets the constitutional requirement of reasonableness.

4. Summarize the dissent's arguments that the statute doesn't meet the constitutional requirement of reasonableness.

FRISKS AND THE FOURTH AMENDMENT

LO 2

You learned in *Terry v. Ohio* (1968, p. 89) that there are three elements that make a frisk a reasonable Fourth Amendment search:

1. The officer has made a lawful Fourth Amendment stop *before* she frisks a suspect.

2. The officer reasonably suspects that the stopped suspect is armed and dangerous.

3. The search is limited to a once-over-lightly pat down to detect weapons only (not contraband or evidence).

Frisks are the least invasive searches; body-cavity searches stand at the other extreme (Chapter 7). However, to say that frisks are the least invasive doesn't mean they're not invasions of privacy at all. After all, even a slight touch, when it's not wanted, can be highly offensive, not to mention the crime of battery. So it's not surprising that, since *Terry*, the U.S. Supreme Court has never wavered from calling frisks Fourth Amendment searches.

Whether a frisk is reasonable depends on balancing the government's interest in protecting law enforcement officers against the individual's privacy right not to be touched by an officer. The basic idea is that we shouldn't expect police officers to risk their lives unnecessarily to investigate suspicious persons and circumstances. At the same time, we have to obey the Fourth Amendment command to keep people "secure in their persons" against unreasonable searches.

Let's turn from the important question of balancing to the answers to two other critical questions regarding frisks: (1) What's reasonable suspicion to frisk? and (2) What's the scope of lawful frisks? (See Table 4.5 for the elements of lawful frisks.)

LO 3

Reasonable Suspicion to Backup Frisks

Terry v. Ohio established that facts that back up a stop don't automatically also back up a frisk—with one major exception, when suspects are stopped for crimes of violence. The facts of *Terry* are an excellent example of the **violent crime–automatic-frisk exception**. Officer McFadden reasonably suspected that Terry and Chilton might be about to commit armed robbery. If it was reasonable to suspect that they might be about to commit armed robbery, it was also reasonable to suspect they might use weapons to commit it. So it was reasonable to frisk Terry and his companions for weapons.

In nonviolent crimes, the rule is that the circumstances must add up to a reasonable suspicion that stopped suspects may be armed. In practice, however, police frequently are told to assume that "every person encountered may be armed" (LaFave 2004, 624). Lower courts take the position that the power to frisk in a wide variety of situations and circumstances is automatic, including robbery, burglary, rape, assault with weapons, and dealing in large quantities of illegal drugs (625–26). Other offenses require specific facts suggesting suspects are armed. Table 4.5 lists some of the offenses courts have held don't justify automatic frisks.

Table 4.6 lists some of the many circumstances that courts have ruled justify frisks.

Some critics claim that the lower courts have weakened the reasonable suspicion requirement so much that, in practice, the power to frisk is left almost entirely to law enforcement officers' discretion. In other words, the power to frisk, in practice, requires no separate reasonable suspicion that suspects may be armed and dangerous. Instead, it follows automatically from the lawful stop.

According to Professor David Harris (1998), one of the leading critics of the automatic power to frisk, the lower courts have "consistently expanded" the number of "dangerous" offenses that justify a frisk.

When confronted with these offenses, police may automatically frisk, whether or not any individualized circumstances point to danger. Soon, anyone stopped by police may have to undergo a physical search at the officer's discretion, however benign the circumstances of the encounter or the conduct of the "suspect." (5)

TABLE 4.5 Examples of circumstances that don't justify automatic frisks

Trafficking in small amounts of illegal drugs	Passing bad checks
Possession of marijuana	Underage drinking
Illegal possession of alcohol	Driving under the influence
Prostitution	Minor assault without a weapon
Bookmaking	Curfew violation
Shoplifting	Vagrancy

Source: LaFave 2004, 626–27.

TABLE 4.6 Circumstances that justify frisks

Sudden inexplicable movement toward a pocket	Awareness of suspect's previous serious criminal conduct
Inexplicable failure to remove a hand from a pocket	Awareness suspect had been armed previously
Awkward movement in an apparent effort to conceal something	Awareness of suspect's recent aggressive behavior
Backing away from an officer	Discovery suspect possessed another weapon
Bulge in clothing	Discovery suspect is wearing a bulletproof vest

Source: LaFave 2004, 628–30.

TABLE 4.7 Examples that justify a frisk beyond an outer-clothing pat down

- Feeling a hard object inside a coat pocket that could be a weapon authorizes reaching inside the coat.
- Encountering unusually bulky winter clothing may require feeling underneath the outer clothing.
- Suspecting the contents of a closed handbag might be illegal can justify opening the handbag.

© Cengage Learning

LO 1 The Scope of Reasonable Frisks

The same day the Supreme Court decided *Terry v. Ohio*, it decided *Sibron v. New York* (1968), another important but less publicized case. In *Sibron*, the Court emphatically rejected New York's argument that after a lawful stop an automatic frisk for evidence and contraband was lawful. Why? Because, according to the Court, frisks are so intrusive that only the enormous interest in saving officers from "armed and dangerous" suspects who might wound or kill them justifies the invasion of a frisk during the brief "freeze" of a stop to investigate suspicious people and circumstances.

No matter how compelling the government's interest in protecting officers from armed and dangerous suspects is, they're allowed to use only the amount of bodily contact necessary to detect weapons. In most cases, this means officers may lightly touch suspects' outer clothing to locate and seize concealed weapons. Courts are vague about how much further police officers may lawfully go. Table 4.7 cites examples of when it may be permissible for officers to go further than pat downs of outer clothing.

In *Minnesota v. Dickerson*, the U.S. Supreme Court held that a Minneapolis police officer went too far when during a lawful frisk for weapons he rolled around a lump between his fingers to determine whether it was a rock of crack cocaine. But the Court made it clear that it's not always unreasonable to seize evidence and contraband during a frisk. Suppose an officer is patting down a suspect who was stopped lawfully and is reasonably suspected of being armed. She pats down the suspect and comes upon marijuana. Can she seize it? Yes, as long as the frisk for weapons isn't a pretext for looking for marijuana.

STOPS AND FRISKS AT ROADSIDE

A multi-volume legal tome could be written on the topic, "The Constitution at Roadside." Few Terms of the Supreme Court pass without at least one case testing how the Constitution—usually, the Fourth Amendment—applies when police officers pull over a car or truck for a traffic stop. (Denniston 2008)

LO 4, 5

Police work is very dangerous work, even (some say especially) when officers stop people in their vehicles. The idea of danger in policing runs deep in U.S. culture (Lichtenberg and Smith 2001, 419). So it's not surprising that every year my students are skeptical about—and many stubbornly resist—the results from the U.S. Bureau of Labor Statistics and the FBI depicted in Figure 4.4. What's your reaction? How do you explain the numbers

Whatever the "real" danger, courts are extremely reluctant to limit or second-guess officers' decisions during vehicle stops. This extends even to "judicially legislating" that power by means of creating "bright-line" rules that attempt to limit or remove

FIGURE 4.4 Occupational Danger

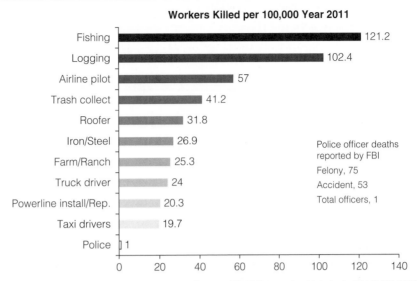

Workers Killed per 100,000 Year 2011

Fishing — 121.2
Logging — 102.4
Airline pilot — 57
Trash collect — 41.2
Roofer — 31.8
Iron/Steel — 26.9
Farm/Ranch — 25.3
Truck driver — 24
Powerline install/Rep. — 20.3
Taxi drivers — 19.7
Police — 1

Police officer deaths
reported by FBI
Felony, 75
Accident, 53
Total officers, 1

Sources: U.S. Bureau of Labor Statistics, 2012. "National Census of Fatal Occupational Injuries in 2011"; FBI, 2012, Press Release November 19, 2012.

second-guessing. So what happens if an officer lawfully stops a vehicle but lacks reason to suspect the people in the stopped vehicle are armed? Is she banned from taking any action to protect herself? No.

We'll look at two situations where the U.S. Supreme Court has created bright-line rules to protect officers during vehicle stops: (1) ordering people in stopped vehicles to get out of the vehicles and (2) frisking people in stopped vehicles.

LO 5

Ordering Occupants Out of Lawfully Stopped Vehicles

In *Pennsylvania v. Mimms* (1977), the Supreme Court created the bright-line rule that when an officer lawfully stops a vehicle, without any reason to suspect the driver is armed, the officer can always demand that the driver get out of the car to reduce "the possibility, otherwise substantial that the driver can make unobserved movements" (111). The Court concluded that removing the driver from the car is a "trivial invasion" because the driver is stopped already. The possible danger to the officer clearly outweighs the trivial invasion of removing the driver from the car.

But is it a trivial invasion to order passengers (whom officers don't suspect of any wrongdoing) out of the car while officers sort out their suspicions of the driver? And is it lawful to frisk passengers in lawfully stopped vehicles? Yes, the U.S. Supreme Court answered to both questions, and both decisions were influenced heavily by the concern for officer safety.

This isn't surprising when we consider that in the cases the Court reviews, guns and/or drugs were found and seized, especially when frisks follow the stops (Allen and others 2005, 577). The Court doesn't hear, and we don't often read about, innocent people stopped in vehicles. Still, both the majority and dissents rely on numbers to support, or challenge, the true level of danger vehicle stops present to officers. This was true in our next case excerpt, *Maryland v. Wilson* (1997).

In *Maryland v. Wilson*, the U.S. Supreme Court held that *Pennsylvania v. Mimms* applies to passengers in stopped vehicles, too. Therefore, officers making a traffic stop may order passengers to get out of the car pending completion of the stop.

CASE

Was the Order to Get Out of the Car Reasonable?

Maryland v. Wilson
519 U.S. 408 (1997)

HISTORY

Jerry Lee Wilson, Respondent, moved to suppress crack cocaine seized by a police officer during a traffic stop. The trial court granted the motion. The State appealed. The Maryland Court of Special Appeals affirmed, ruling that *Pennsylvania v. Mimms* does not apply to passengers. The Maryland Court of Appeals denied certiorari. The U.S. Supreme Court granted certiorari and reversed and remanded the case.

> —REHNQUIST, C.J., joined by O'CONNOR, SCALIA, SOUTER, THOMAS, GINSBURG, and BREYER, JJ.

FACTS

At about 7:30 p.m. on a June evening, Maryland state trooper David Hughes observed a passenger car driving southbound on I-95 in Baltimore County at a speed of 64 miles per hour. The posted speed limit was 55 miles per hour, and the car had no regular license tag; there was a torn piece of paper reading "Enterprise Rent-A-Car" dangling from its rear. Hughes activated his lights and sirens, signaling the car to pull over, but it continued driving for another mile and a half until it finally did so.

During the pursuit, Hughes noticed there were three occupants in the car and that the two passengers turned to look at him several times, repeatedly ducking below sight level and then reappearing. As Hughes approached the car on foot, the driver alighted and met him halfway. The driver was trembling and appeared extremely nervous, but nonetheless produced a valid Connecticut driver's license.

Hughes instructed him to return to the car and retrieve the rental documents, and he complied. During this encounter, Hughes noticed that the front-seat passenger, Jerry Lee Wilson (the respondent), was sweating and also appeared extremely nervous. While the driver was sitting in the driver's seat looking for the rental papers, Hughes ordered Wilson out of the car. When Wilson exited the car, a quantity of crack cocaine fell to the ground.

OPINION

In *Mimms*, we considered a traffic stop much like the one before us today. There, Mimms had been stopped for driving with an expired license plate, and the officer asked him to step out of his car. When Mimms did so, the officer noticed a bulge in his jacket that proved to be a .38-caliber revolver, whereupon Mimms was arrested for carrying a concealed deadly weapon.

Mimms, like Wilson, urged the suppression of the evidence on the ground that the officer's ordering him out of the car was an unreasonable seizure, and the Pennsylvania Supreme Court, like the Court of Special Appeals of Maryland, agreed. We reversed, explaining that the touchstone of our analysis under the Fourth Amendment is always the reasonableness in all the circumstances of the particular governmental invasion of a citizen's personal security, and that reasonableness depends on a balance between the public interest and the individual's right to personal security free from arbitrary interference by law officers.

On the public interest side of the balance, we noted that the State "freely conceded" that there had been nothing unusual or suspicious to justify ordering Mimms out of the car, but that it was the officer's practice to order all drivers [stopped in traffic stops] out of their vehicles as a matter of course as a precautionary measure to protect the officer's safety. We thought it too plain for argument that this justification—officer safety—was both legitimate and weighty. In addition, we observed that the danger to the officer of standing by the driver's door and in the path of oncoming traffic might also be "appreciable."

On the other side of the balance, we considered the intrusion into the driver's liberty occasioned by the officer's ordering him out of the car. Noting that the driver's car was already validly stopped for a traffic infraction, we deemed the additional intrusion of asking him to step outside his car "de minimis" [trivial]. Accordingly, we concluded that once a motor vehicle has been lawfully detained for a traffic violation, the police officers may order the driver to get out of the vehicle without violating the Fourth Amendment's proscription of unreasonable seizures.

Wilson urges, and the lower courts agreed, that this per se rule does not apply to Wilson because he was a passenger, not the driver. We must therefore now decide whether the rule of *Mimms* applies to passengers as well as to drivers. On the public interest side of the balance, the same weighty interest in officer safety is present regardless of whether the occupant of the stopped car is a driver or passenger. Regrettably, traffic stops may be dangerous encounters. In 1994 alone, there were 5,762 officer assaults and 11 officers killed during traffic pursuits and stops. Federal Bureau of Investigation, Uniform Crime Reports: Law Enforcement Officers Killed and Assaulted 71, 33 (1994).

In the case of passengers, the danger of the officer's standing in the path of oncoming traffic would not be present except in the case of a passenger in the left rear seat, but the fact that there is more than one occupant of the vehicle increases the possible sources of harm to the officer.

On the personal liberty side of the balance, the case for the passengers is in one sense stronger than that for the driver. There is probable cause to believe that the driver has committed a minor vehicular offense, but there is no such reason to stop or detain the passengers. But as a practical matter, the passengers are already stopped by virtue of the stop of the vehicle. The only change in their circumstances which will result from ordering them out of the car is that they will be outside of, rather than inside of, the stopped car.

Outside the car, the passengers will be denied access to any possible weapon that might be concealed in the interior of the passenger compartment. It would seem that the possibility of a violent encounter stems not from the ordinary reaction of a motorist stopped for a speeding violation, but from the fact that evidence of a more serious crime might be uncovered during the stop. And the motivation of a passenger to employ violence to prevent apprehension of such a crime is every bit as great as that of the driver.

In summary, danger to an officer from a traffic stop is likely to be greater when there are passengers in addition to the driver in the stopped car. While there is not the same basis for ordering the passengers out of the car as there is for ordering the driver out, the additional intrusion on the passenger is minimal. We therefore hold that an officer making a traffic stop may order passengers to get out of the car pending completion of the stop.

The judgment of the Court of Special Appeals of Maryland is REVERSED, and the case is REMANDED for proceedings not inconsistent with this opinion. It is so ordered.

DISSENT

STEVENS, J., joined by KENNEDY, J.

My concern is not with the ultimate disposition of this particular case, but rather with the literally millions of other cases that will be affected by the rule the Court announces. Though the question is not before us, I am satisfied that—under the rationale of *Terry v. Ohio*—if a police officer conducting a traffic stop has an articulable suspicion of possible danger, the officer may order passengers to exit the vehicle as a defensive tactic without running afoul of the Fourth Amendment.

Accordingly, I assume that the facts recited in the majority's opinion provided a valid justification for this officer's order commanding the passengers to get out of this vehicle. But the Court's ruling goes much farther. It applies equally to traffic stops in which there is not even a scintilla of evidence of any potential risk to the police officer. In those cases, I firmly believe that the Fourth Amendment prohibits routine and arbitrary seizures of obviously innocent citizens.

The majority suggests that the personal liberty interest at stake here is outweighed by the need to ensure officer safety. The Court correctly observes that "traffic stops may be dangerous encounters." The magnitude of the danger to police officers is reflected in the statistic that, in 1994 alone, "there were 5,762 officer assaults and 11 officers killed during traffic pursuits and stops." There is, unquestionably, a strong public interest in minimizing the number of such assaults and fatalities. The Court's statistics, however, provide no support for the conclusion that its ruling will have any such effect.

Those statistics do not tell us how many of the incidents involved passengers. Assuming that many of the assaults were committed by passengers, we do not know how many occurred after the passenger got out of the vehicle, how many took place while the passenger remained in the vehicle, or indeed, whether any of them could have been prevented by an order commanding the passengers to exit.

There is no indication that the number of assaults was smaller in jurisdictions where officers may order passengers to exit the vehicle without any suspicion than in jurisdictions where they were then prohibited from doing so.

Indeed, there is no indication that any of the assaults occurred when there was a complete absence of any articulable basis for concern about the officer's safety—the only condition under which I would hold that the Fourth Amendment prohibits an order commanding passengers to exit a vehicle. In short, the statistics are as consistent with the hypothesis that ordering passengers to get out of a vehicle increases the danger of assault as with the hypothesis that it reduces that risk.

Furthermore, any limited additional risk to police officers must be weighed against the unnecessary invasion

(continued)

that will be imposed on innocent citizens under the majority's rule in the tremendous number of routine stops that occur each day. We have long recognized that because of the extensive regulation of motor vehicles and traffic the extent of police–citizen contact involving automobiles will be substantially greater than police–citizen contact in a home or office.

Most traffic stops involve otherwise law abiding citizens who have committed minor traffic offenses. A strong interest in arriving at a destination—to deliver a patient to a hospital, to witness a kick-off, or to get to work on time—will often explain a traffic violation without justifying it. In the aggregate, these stops amount to significant law enforcement activity.

Indeed, the number of stops in which an officer is actually at risk is dwarfed by the far greater number of routine stops. If Maryland's share of the national total is about average, the State probably experiences about 100 officer assaults each year during traffic stops and pursuits. Making the unlikely assumption that passengers are responsible for one-fourth of the total assaults, it appears that the Court's new rule would provide a potential benefit to Maryland officers in only roughly 25 stops a year. These stops represent a minuscule portion of the total.

In Maryland alone, there are something on the order of one million traffic stops each year. Assuming that there are passengers in about half of the cars stopped, the majority's rule is of some possible advantage to police in only about one out of every twenty thousand traffic stops in which there is a passenger in the car. And, any benefit is extremely marginal. In the overwhelming majority of cases posing a real threat, the officer would almost certainly have some ground to suspect danger that would justify ordering passengers out of the car.

In contrast, the potential daily burden on thousands of innocent citizens is obvious. That burden may well be "minimal" in individual cases. But countless citizens who cherish individual liberty and are offended, embarrassed, and sometimes provoked by arbitrary official commands may well consider the burden to be significant. In all events, the aggregation of thousands upon thousands of petty indignities has an impact on freedom that I would characterize as substantial, and which in my view clearly outweighs the evanescent safety concerns pressed by the majority.

To order passengers about during the course of a traffic stop, insisting that they exit and remain outside the car, can hardly be classified as a trivial intrusion. The traffic violation sufficiently justifies subjecting the driver to detention and some police control for the time necessary to conclude the business of the stop. The restraint on the liberty of blameless passengers that the majority permits is, in contrast, entirely arbitrary.

In my view, wholly innocent passengers in a taxi, bus, or private car have a constitutionally protected right to decide whether to remain comfortably seated within the vehicle rather than exposing themselves to the elements and the observation of curious bystanders. The Constitution should not be read to permit law enforcement officers to order innocent passengers about simply because they have the misfortune to be seated in a car whose driver has committed a minor traffic offense.

Unfortunately, the effect of the Court's new rule on the law may turn out to be far more significant than its immediate impact on individual liberty. Throughout most of our history the Fourth Amendment embodied a general rule requiring that official searches and seizures be authorized by a warrant, issued "upon probable cause, supported by Oath or affirmation, and particularly describing the place to be searched, and the persons or things to be seized." During the prohibition era, the exceptions for warrantless searches supported by probable cause started to replace the general rule.

In 1968, in the landmark "stop and frisk" case *Terry v. Ohio*, the Court placed its stamp of approval on seizures supported by specific and articulable facts that did not establish probable cause. The Court crafted *Terry* as a narrow exception to the general rule that the police must, whenever practicable, obtain advance judicial approval of searches and seizures through the warrant procedure. The intended scope of the Court's major departure from prior practice was reflected in its statement that the "demand for specificity in the information upon which police action is predicated is the central teaching of this Court's Fourth Amendment jurisprudence."

In the 1970s, the Court twice rejected attempts to justify suspicionless seizures that caused only "modest" intrusions on the liberty of passengers in automobiles. Today, however, the Court takes the unprecedented step of authorizing seizures that are unsupported by any individualized suspicion whatsoever.

The Court's conclusion seems to rest on the assumption that the constitutional protection against "unreasonable" seizures requires nothing more than a hypothetically rational basis for intrusions on individual liberty. How far this ground-breaking decision will take us, I do not venture to predict. I fear, however, that it may pose a more serious threat to individual liberty than the Court realizes.

I respectfully DISSENT.

KENNEDY, J.

Traffic stops, even for minor violations, can take upwards of 30 minutes. When an officer commands passengers innocent of any violation to leave the vehicle and stand by the side of the road in full view of the public, the seizure is serious, not trivial. As Justice Stevens concludes, the command to exit ought not to be given unless there are objective circumstances making it reasonable for the officer to issue the order. (We do not have before us the separate question whether passengers, who, after all are in the car by choice, can be ordered to remain there for a reasonable time while the police conduct their business.)

Coupled with *Whren v. U.S.* [excerpted in Chapter 6] the Court puts tens of millions of passengers at risk of arbitrary control by the police. If the command to exit were to become commonplace, the Constitution would be diminished in a most public way. As the standards suggested in dissent are adequate to protect the safety of the police, we ought not to suffer so great a loss.

Most officers, it might be said, will exercise their new power with discretion and restraint; and no doubt this often will be the case. It might also be said that if some jurisdictions use today's ruling to require passengers to exit as a matter of routine in every stop, citizen complaints and political intervention will call for an end to the practice.

These arguments, however, would miss the point. Liberty comes not from officials by grace but from the Constitution by right. For these reasons, and with all respect for the opinion of the Court, I DISSENT.

Questions

1. List the specific invasions Jerry Lee Wilson experienced after the vehicle he was a passenger in was stopped.

2. Identify the government's interest that was furthered by ordering Wilson out of the car.

3. In your opinion, did the government's interest outweigh the degree of invasion against Wilson? In your answer, consider both the majority and dissenting opinions.

4. State specifically the objective basis for ordering Wilson out of the car.

5. State the Court's bright-line rule governing officers' power to order passengers out of cars they've stopped.

6. Summarize the arguments the majority gave to back up its bright-line rule.

7. Describe the empirical evidence the majority's opinion was based on. In view of the dissenting justices' criticism of the statistics, how much weight do they carry in your opinion?

8. How do the dissenting justices answer the majority's arguments in (7)? Which side has the better arguments? Defend your answer.

How dangerous to officers *are* traffic stops? Does the bright-line rule increase officer safety? During the oral argument in *Maryland v. Wilson*, Justice Scalia asked the Maryland attorney general:

> . . . I resent being put in the position of deciding this case on speculation. . . . You're telling us that it will increase police safety if we adopt this automatic rule. None of the briefs—and there's a brief here by 20 States or so—make any attempt to compare the assaults on police in the States that have the rule you're urging us to adopt and the States that don't have that rule, and that's the crucial question. We know we're going to inconvenience citizens to some extent. We don't know whether we're going to increase police safety. Why—aren't those statistics available? Why doesn't somebody come and say, this is the proof of what we're saying?

Illya Lichtenberg and Alisa Smith set out to find out just how dangerous routine traffic stops are (Table 4.8). They estimated the ratio of officers assaulted and killed over a 10-year period and the number of traffic stops over the same period. They found

TABLE 4.8 Danger ratio for officers during traffic stops

Average stops, 1988–1997	1 Homicide	1 Assault*
Low range, 60 million	6.7 million stops	10,256 stops
Mid range, 120 million	13.4 million stops	20,512 stops
High range, 180 million	20.1 million stops	30,768 stops

Source: Adapted from Lichtenburg and Smith (2001), 423–25.

*Assault includes everything from a mild threat or *suspected* threat all the way up to attempted murder.

Note: We don't know which or how many stops involved passengers outside or inside the car.

© Cengage Learning

the ratio could be as "high" as one officer killed for every 10 million stops or as "low" as one officer killed for every 30 million. They also found that the stop-to-assault ratio ranged from a "high" of one police officer for every 8,274 stops to a low of one for every 13,847 stops (424–25). Furthermore, they found that "no data exist to support the proposition that greater intrusions of citizen privacy rights will ensure greater safety to police officers" (420).

LO 5   Frisking Occupants of Lawfully Stopped Vehicles

What can officers do to protect themselves once they've got the drivers and/or passengers outside vehicles stopped for traffic violations? Can they order them to raise their hands above their heads until the summons is completed? Question them about possible weapons possession? Can they frisk them?

The Court demonstrated its deference to officers' decisions in vehicle stops in *Arizona v. Johnson* (2009), our next case excerpt. The Court struck the balance in favor of officer safety when it ruled that Officer Maria Trevizo and two detectives lawfully frisked Lemon Montrea Johnson, a passenger in a lawfully stopped vehicle. Note that the officers didn't suspect Johnson of any crime, but they did suspect that he might be armed and dangerous.

In *Arizona v. Johnson*, the U.S. Supreme Court held that it's lawful to frisk a passenger in a lawfully stopped vehicle, even if he wasn't suspected of committing a crime.

CASE   Was the Frisk of a Passenger after He Received a Traffic Citation "Reasonable"?

Arizona v. Johnson
129 S.Ct. 781 (2009)

HISTORY

Lemon Montrea Johnson was charged in state court with possession of a weapon by a prohibited possessor. He moved to suppress the evidence as the fruit of an unlawful search. The trial court denied the motion, concluding that the stop was lawful and that Trevizo had cause to suspect Johnson was armed and dangerous. A jury convicted Johnson of the gun-possession charge, and sentenced him to eight years in prison. A divided panel of the Arizona Court of Appeals reversed Johnson's conviction. The Arizona Supreme Court denied review. We granted certiorari, and now reverse the judgment of the Arizona Court of Appeals.

—GINSBURG, J., delivered the opinion for a unanimous Court.

FACTS

On April 19, 2002, Officer Maria Trevizo and Detectives Machado and Gittings, all members of Arizona's gang task force, were on patrol in Tucson near a neighborhood associated with the Crips gang. At approximately 9 p.m., the officers pulled over an automobile after a license plate check revealed that the vehicle's registration had been suspended for an insurance-related violation. Under Arizona law, the violation for which the vehicle was stopped constituted a civil infraction warranting a citation. At the time of the stop, the vehicle had three occupants—the driver, a front-seat passenger, and a passenger in the back seat, Lemon Montrea Johnson, the respondent here. In making the stop the officers had no reason to suspect anyone in the vehicle of criminal activity.

The three officers left their patrol car and approached the stopped vehicle. Machado instructed all of the occupants to keep their hands visible. He asked whether there were any weapons in the vehicle; all responded no. Machado then directed the driver to get out of the car. Gittings dealt with the front-seat passenger, who stayed in the vehicle throughout the stop. While Machado was getting the driver's license and information about the vehicle's registration and insurance, Trevizo attended to Johnson.

Trevizo noticed that, as the police approached, Johnson looked back and kept his eyes on the officers. When she drew near, she observed that Johnson was wearing clothing, including a blue bandana, that she considered consistent with Crips membership. She also noticed a scanner in Johnson's jacket pocket, which "struck [her] as highly unusual and cause [for] concern," because "most people" would not carry around a scanner that way "unless they're going to be involved in some kind of criminal activity or [are] going to try to evade the police by listening to the scanner." In response to Trevizo's questions, Johnson provided his name and date of birth but said he had no identification with him. He volunteered that he was from Eloy, Arizona, a place Trevizo knew was home to a Crips gang. Johnson further told Trevizo that he had served time in prison for burglary and had been out for about a year.

Trevizo wanted to question Johnson away from the front-seat passenger to gain "intelligence about the gang [Johnson] might be in." For that reason, she asked him to get out of the car. Johnson complied. Based on Trevizo's observations and Johnson's answers to her questions while he was still seated in the car, Trevizo suspected that "he might have a weapon on him." When he exited the vehicle, she therefore "patted him down for officer safety." During the pat down, Trevizo felt the butt of a gun near Johnson's waist. At that point Johnson began to struggle, and Trevizo placed him in handcuffs.

OPINION

Terry v. Ohio established that when a stop is justified by suspicion that criminal activity is afoot, the police officer must be positioned to act instantly on reasonable suspicion that the persons temporarily detained are armed and dangerous. Recognizing that a limited search of outer clothing for weapons serves to protect both the officer and the public, the Court held the pat down reasonable under the Fourth Amendment. This Court has recognized that traffic stops are especially fraught with danger to police officers. The risk of harm to both the police and the occupants of a stopped vehicle is minimized, we have stressed, if the officers routinely exercise unquestioned command of the situation (*Maryland v. Wilson*, 1997). *Wilson* held that an officer making a traffic stop may order passengers to get out of the car pending completion of the stop.

The same weighty interest in officer safety, the Court observed, is present regardless of whether the occupant of the stopped car is a driver or passenger. The Court emphasized, the risk of a violent encounter in a traffic-stop setting stems not from the ordinary reaction of a motorist stopped for a speeding violation, but from the fact that evidence of a more serious crime might be uncovered during the stop. The motivation of a passenger to employ violence to prevent apprehension of such a crime, the Court stated, is every bit as great as that of the driver. Moreover, the Court noted, as a practical matter, the passengers are already stopped by virtue of the stop of the vehicle, so the additional intrusion on the passenger is minimal.

Completing the picture, officers who conduct routine traffic stops may perform a pat down of a driver and any passengers upon reasonable suspicion that they may be armed and dangerous.

A lawful roadside stop begins when a vehicle is pulled over for investigation of a traffic violation. The temporary seizure of driver and passengers ordinarily continues, and remains reasonable, for the duration of the stop. Normally, the stop ends when the police have no further need to control the scene, and inform the driver and passengers they are free to leave. An officer's inquiries into matters unrelated to the justification for the traffic stop, this Court has made plain, do not convert the encounter into something other than a lawful seizure, so long as those inquiries do not measurably extend the duration of the stop.

In sum, a traffic stop of a car communicates to a reasonable passenger that he or she is not free to terminate the encounter with the police and move about at will. Nothing occurred in this case that would have conveyed to Johnson that, prior to the frisk, the traffic stop had ended or that he was otherwise free "to depart without police permission." Officer Trevizo surely was not constitutionally required to give Johnson an opportunity to depart the scene after he exited the vehicle without first ensuring that, in so doing, she was not permitting a dangerous person to get behind her.

For the reasons stated, the judgment of the Arizona Court of Appeals is REVERSED, and the case is REMANDED for further proceedings not inconsistent with this opinion.

It is so ordered.

Questions

1. List all the facts and circumstances relevant to deciding whether the frisk was reasonable.

2. Summarize the Court's arguments for deciding that Officer Maria Trevizo's frisk of Lemon Johnson was reasonable.

3. The Arizona Court of Appeals recognized that, initially, Johnson was lawfully detained incident to the legitimate stop of the vehicle in which he was a passenger. But, that court concluded, once Officer Trevizo undertook to question Johnson on a matter unrelated to the traffic stop (i.e., Johnson's gang affiliation), pat-down authority ceased to exist, absent reasonable suspicion that Johnson had engaged, or was about to engage, in criminal activity. Why would all justices disagree with the Arizona court's ruling? Does the Arizona court have a point?

Roadblocks and Checkpoints

Certain government searches are likely to get anyone's adrenaline pumping: political leaders using government agents to ferret out dissidents and silence their criticisms; the police battering down an innocent citizen's door based upon only the flimsiest of tips; officers indiscriminately rounding up citizens for questioning merely because their race matches a victim's vague description. . . . [They] raise our Fourth Amendment ire because they touch a deep republican chord in the [U.S.] American conscience and harken back to the colonists' struggles against oppression and overreaching government officials. (Sundby 2004, 501)

LO 6

James Otis's adrenaline was surely pumping during his five-hour speech against the writs of assistance in 1761. Recall (Chapter 3) that these hated writs were like blank checks good for the life of the king that allowed officers to enter and ransack homes and shops without warrants or individualized suspicion. In his stirring words, "One of the most essential branches of English liberty is the freedom of one's house. A man's house is his castle, and whilst he is quiet, he is as well guarded as a prince in his castle" (Otis, 1761).

Notice that Otis was railing against unbridled discretionary invasions of homes without judicial supervision or even individualized suspicion. But what about those who "whilst they are quiet" come up to a **roadblock** (police barricade with no "escape route") where everyone has to wait to pass through? Here, it's not an overreaching government invasion that makes the adrenaline pump; it's the fear and anger against the object of the roadblock, say to trap a serial killer who's just committed his latest murder. Those types of suspicionless stops (not based on *individualized* suspicion) we leave aside. But **checkpoints** (which allow all who don't want to pass through them to simply turn off and avoid them) hardly cause more than a "ho-hum" reaction against government among individuals. They're *usually* brief and they're *supposed* to apply to everybody (Sundby 2004, 502).

So roadblocks and checkpoints have little to nothing in common with the general warrants except that they're suspicionless. But they create a special Fourth Amendment problem: Can law enforcement officers stop groups of drivers and passengers without individualized suspicion that any one of them might be up to criminal activity? A few years after *Terry v. Ohio*, the U.S. Supreme Court upheld a permanent roadblock in southern California to check for illegal Mexican immigrants. Why? It cited balancing interests—namely, "the need to make routine checkpoint stops is great and the consequent intrusion on Fourth Amendment rights is quite limited" (*U.S. v. Martinez-Fuerte* 1976; excerpted in Chapter 15).

The Court has adopted a **three-prong balancing test** to determine whether roadblocks and checkpoints are reasonable.

1. The gravity of the public interest served by the seizure
2. The effectiveness of the seizure in advancing the public interest
3. The degree of interference with the stopped individual's liberty (*Michigan v. Sitz* 1990, 447)

Let's look at how SCOTUS applied the balancing test to three checkpoints: DWI, drug interdiction, and hit-and-run information-gathering checkpoints.

LO 6

DWI checkpoints

Some states have also created checkpoints to prevent drunk driving and apprehend and prosecute drunk drivers. Are DWI (driving while intoxicated) suspicionless checkpoints unreasonable stops? As you might expect by this point in reading the book, in *Michigan v. Sitz* (1990), our next case excerpt, the U.S. Supreme Court answered, "It all depends."

In *Michigan v. Sitz* (1990), the U.S. Supreme Court found that highway sobriety checkpoint programs are reasonable stops of citizens even when there's no individualized suspicion.

CASE

Was the DWI Roadblock an Unreasonable Seizure?

Michigan v. Sitz
496 U.S. 444 (1990)

HISTORY

Rick Sitz and other drivers (respondents) brought an action to challenge the constitutionality of a highway sobriety checkpoint program. The Circuit Court of Wayne County, Michigan, invalidated the program, and the Michigan Department of State Police (petitioners) appealed. The Court of Appeals of Michigan affirmed. The U.S. Supreme Court granted certiorari. The Supreme Court reversed and remanded the case.

—REHNQUIST, C.J., joined by WHITE, O'CONNOR, SCALIA, and KENNEDY, JJ.

FACTS

The Michigan Department of State Police and its Director (petitioners) established a sobriety checkpoint pilot program in early 1986. Under the plan, checkpoints would be set up at selected sites along state roads. All vehicles passing through a checkpoint would be stopped and their drivers briefly examined for signs of intoxication. In cases where a checkpoint officer detected signs of intoxication, the motorist would be directed to a location out of the traffic flow where an officer would check the motorist's driver's license and car registration and, if warranted, conduct further sobriety tests. Should the field tests and the officer's observations suggest that the driver was intoxicated, an arrest would be made. All other drivers would be permitted to resume their journey immediately.

The first—and to date the only—sobriety checkpoint operated under the program was conducted in Saginaw County with the assistance of the Saginaw County Sheriff's Department. During the hour-and-fifteen-minute duration of the checkpoint's operation, 126 vehicles passed through the checkpoint. The average delay for each vehicle was approximately 25 seconds. Two drivers were detained for field sobriety testing, and one of the two was arrested

for driving under the influence of alcohol. A third driver who drove through without stopping was pulled over by an officer in an observation vehicle and arrested for driving under the influence.

On the day before the operation of the Saginaw County checkpoint, Sitz and the other drivers (respondents) filed a complaint in the Circuit Court of Wayne County seeking declaratory and injunctive relief from potential subjection to the checkpoints. Sitz and each of the other drivers "is a licensed driver in the State of Michigan who regularly travels throughout the State in his automobile." During pretrial proceedings, the Michigan Department of State Police (petitioners) agreed to delay further implementation of the checkpoint program pending the outcome of this litigation.

After the trial, at which the court heard extensive testimony concerning the "effectiveness" of highway sobriety checkpoint programs, the court ruled that the Michigan program violated the Fourth Amendment and Art. 1, § 11, of the Michigan Constitution. On appeal, the Michigan Court of Appeals affirmed the holding that the program violated the Fourth Amendment and, for that reason, did not consider whether the program violated the Michigan Constitution. After the Michigan Supreme Court denied Department of State Police's application for leave to appeal, we granted certiorari.

To decide this case the trial court performed a balancing test derived from our opinion in *Brown v. Texas* (1979). As described by the Court of Appeals, the test involved "balancing the state's interest in preventing accidents caused by drunk drivers, the effectiveness of sobriety checkpoints in achieving that goal, and the level of intrusion on an individual's privacy caused by the checkpoints."

The Court of Appeals agreed that the *Brown* three-prong balancing test was the correct test to be used to

(*continued*)

determine the constitutionality of the sobriety checkpoint plan. As characterized by the Court of Appeals, the trial court's findings with respect to the balancing factors were that the State has a "grave and legitimate" interest in curbing drunken driving; that sobriety checkpoint programs are generally "ineffective" and, therefore, do not significantly further that interest; and that the checkpoints' "subjective intrusion" on individual liberties is substantial. According to the court, the record disclosed no basis for disturbing the trial court's findings, which were made within the context of an analytical framework prescribed by this Court for determining the constitutionality of seizures less intrusive than traditional arrests.

OPINION

The Department of State police (petitioners) concede, correctly in our view, that a Fourth Amendment "seizure" occurs when a vehicle is stopped at a checkpoint. The question thus becomes whether such seizures are "reasonable" under the Fourth Amendment. We address only the initial stop of each motorist passing through a checkpoint and the associated preliminary questioning and observation by checkpoint officers.

Detention of particular motorists for more extensive field sobriety testing may require satisfaction of an individualized suspicion standard. No one can seriously dispute the magnitude of the drunken driving problem or the States' interest in eradicating it. Drunk drivers cause an annual death toll of over 25,000 and in the same time span cause nearly one million personal injuries and more than five billion dollars in property damage. For decades, this Court has repeatedly lamented the tragedy. Conversely, the weight bearing on the other scale—the measure of the intrusion on motorists stopped briefly at sobriety checkpoints—is slight. The trial court and the Court of Appeals, thus, accurately gauged the "objective" intrusion, measured by the duration of the seizure and the intensity of the investigation, as minimal.

With respect to what it perceived to be the "subjective" intrusion on motorists, however, the Court of Appeals found such intrusion substantial. The court first affirmed the trial court's finding that the guidelines governing checkpoint operation minimize the discretion of the officers on the scene. But the court also agreed with the trial court's conclusion that the checkpoints have the potential to generate fear and surprise in motorists. This was so because the record failed to demonstrate that approaching motorists would be aware of their option to make U-turns or turnoffs to avoid the checkpoints. On that basis, the court deemed the subjective intrusion from the checkpoints unreasonable.

We believe the Michigan courts misread our cases concerning the degree of "subjective intrusion" and the potential for generating fear and surprise. The "fear and surprise" to be considered are not the natural fear of one who has been drinking over the prospect of being stopped at a sobriety checkpoint but, rather, the fear and surprise engendered in law-abiding motorists by the nature of the stop.

The Court of Appeals went on to consider as part of the balancing analysis the "effectiveness" of the proposed checkpoint program. Based on extensive testimony in the trial record, the court concluded that the checkpoint program failed the "effectiveness" part of the test, and that this failure materially discounted petitioners' strong interest in implementing the program.

We think the Court of Appeals was wrong on this point as well. Experts in police science might disagree over which of several methods of apprehending drunken drivers is preferable as an ideal. But for purposes of Fourth Amendment analysis, the choice among such reasonable alternatives remains with the governmental officials who have a unique understanding of, and a responsibility for, limited public resources, including a finite number of police officers.

This case involves neither a complete absence of empirical data nor a challenge of random highway stops. During the operation of the Saginaw County checkpoint, the detention of each of the 126 vehicles that entered the checkpoint resulted in the arrest of two drunken drivers. Stated as a percentage, approximately 1.5 percent of the drivers passing through the checkpoint were arrested for alcohol impairment. In addition, an expert witness testified at the trial that experience in other states demonstrated that, on the whole, sobriety checkpoints resulted in drunken driving arrests of around 1 percent of all motorists stopped.

In sum, the balance of the state's interest in preventing drunken driving, the extent to which this system can reasonably be said to advance that interest, and the degree of intrusion upon individual motorists who are briefly stopped, weighs in favor of the state program. We therefore hold that it is consistent with the Fourth Amendment. The judgment of the Michigan Court of Appeals is accordingly reversed, and the case is remanded for further proceedings not inconsistent with this opinion.

REVERSED.

DISSENT

BRENNAN, J., joined by MARSHALL, J.

Some level of individualized suspicion is a core component of the protection the Fourth Amendment provides against arbitrary government action. By holding that no level of suspicion is necessary before the police may stop a car for the purpose of preventing drunken driving, the Court potentially subjects the general public to arbitrary or harassing conduct by the police.

I do not dispute the immense social cost caused by drunken drivers, nor do I slight the government's efforts to prevent such tragic losses. Indeed, I would hazard a guess that today's opinion will be received favorably by a majority of our society, who would willingly suffer the minimal intrusion of a sobriety checkpoint stop in order to prevent drunken driving. But consensus that a particular law enforcement technique serves a laudable purpose has never been the touchstone of constitutional analysis.

The Fourth Amendment was designed not merely to protect against official intrusions whose social utility was less as measured by some "balancing test" than its intrusion on individual privacy; it was designed in addition to grant the individual a zone of privacy whose protections could be breached only where the "reasonable" requirements of the probable cause standard were met. Moved by whatever momentary evil has aroused their fears, officials—perhaps even supported by a majority of citizens—may be tempted to conduct searches that sacrifice the liberty of each citizen to assuage the perceived evil. But the Fourth Amendment rests on the principle that a true balance between the individual and society depends on the recognition of "the right to be let alone"—the most comprehensive of rights and the right most valued by civilized men.

In the face of the "momentary evil" of drunken driving, the Court today abdicates its role as the protector of that fundamental right. I respectfully DISSENT.

STEVENS, J., joined by BRENNAN and MARSHALL, JJ.

The record in this case makes clear that a decision holding these suspicionless seizures unconstitutional would not impede the law enforcement community's remarkable progress in reducing the death toll on our highways. Because the Michigan program was patterned after an older program in Maryland, the trial judge gave special attention to that state's experience. Over a period of several years, Maryland operated 125 checkpoints; of the 41,000 motorists passing through those checkpoints, only 143 persons (0.3%) were arrested. The number of man-hours devoted to these operations is not in the record, but it seems inconceivable that a higher arrest rate could not have been achieved by more conventional means.

Any relationship between sobriety checkpoints and an actual reduction in highway fatalities is even less substantial than the minimal impact on arrest rates. As the Michigan Court of Appeals pointed out, Maryland had conducted a study comparing traffic statistics between a county using checkpoints and a control county. The results of the study showed that alcohol-related accidents in the checkpoint county decreased by 10 percent, whereas the control county saw an 11 percent decrease; and while fatal accidents in the control county fell from sixteen to three, fatal accidents in the checkpoint county actually doubled from the prior year.

In light of these considerations, it seems evident that the Court today . . . overvalues the law enforcement interest in using sobriety checkpoints [and] undervalues the

citizen's interest in freedom from random, unannounced investigatory seizures.

A Michigan officer who questions a motorist at a sobriety checkpoint has virtually unlimited discretion to detain the driver on the basis of the slightest suspicion. A ruddy complexion, an unbuttoned shirt, bloodshot eyes, or a speech impediment may suffice to prolong the detention. Any driver who had just consumed a glass of beer, or even a sip of wine, would almost certainly have the burden of demonstrating to the officer that her driving ability was not impaired.

These fears are not, as the Court would have it, solely the lot of the guilty. To be law abiding is not necessarily to be spotless, and even the most virtuous can be unlucky. Unwanted attention from the local police need not be less discomforting simply because one's secrets are not the stuff of criminal prosecutions. Moreover, those who have found—by reason of prejudice or misfortune—that encounters with the police may become adversarial or unpleasant without good cause will have grounds for worrying at any stop designed to elicit signs of suspicious behavior. Being stopped by the police is distressing even when it should not be terrifying, and what begins mildly may by happenstance turn severe.

In my opinion, unannounced investigatory seizures are, particularly when they take place at night, the hallmark of regimes far different from ours; the surprise intrusion upon individual liberty is not minimal. On that issue, my difference with the Court may amount to nothing less than a difference in our respective evaluations of the importance of individual liberty, a serious albeit inevitable source of constitutional disagreement. On the degree to which the sobriety checkpoint seizures advance the public interest, however, the Court's position is wholly indefensible.

The evidence in this case indicates that sobriety checkpoints result in the arrest of a fraction of 1 percent of the drivers who are stopped, but there is absolutely no evidence that this figure represents an increase over the number of arrests that would have been made by using the same law enforcement resources in conventional patrols. Thus, although the gross number of arrests is more than zero, there is a complete failure of proof on the question whether the wholesale seizures have produced any net advance in the public interest in arresting intoxicated drivers.

The most disturbing aspect of the Court's decision today is that it appears to give no weight to the citizen's interest in freedom from suspicionless unannounced investigatory seizures. On the other hand, the Court places a heavy thumb on the law enforcement. Perhaps this tampering with the scales of justice can be explained by the Court's obvious concern about the slaughter on our highways, and a resultant tolerance for policies designed to alleviate the problem by "setting an example" of a few motorists. . . .

(continued)

This is a case that is driven by nothing more than symbolic state action—an insufficient justification for an otherwise unreasonable program of random seizures. Unfortunately, the Court is transfixed by the wrong symbol—the illusory prospect of punishing countless intoxicated motorists—when it should keep its eyes on the road plainly marked by the Constitution.

I respectfully DISSENT.

Questions

1. According to the Court, why are DWI checkpoints Fourth Amendment seizures?

2. Why, according to the Court, are they reasonable seizures?

3. What interests does the Court balance in reaching its result?

4. What does Justice Stevens mean when he says that he and the majority disagree over the meaning of freedom?

5. What does he have to say about the need for and effectiveness of DWI checkpoints?

6. What does Justice Brennan mean when he says that the degree of the intrusion begins, not ends, the inquiry about whether DWI checkpoints are reasonable seizures?

7. How would you identify and balance the interests at stake in the DWI checkpoints? Are the checkpoints effective? Explain.

8. According to the American Civil Liberties Union (ACLU), "highly publicized local law enforcement efforts such as random roadblocks" are "Orwellian intrusions into individual privacy." What does the ACLU mean? Do you agree? Explain.

YOU DECIDE
Are Suspicionless DWI Stops Better?

Sitz v. State
506 NW2d 209 (1993)

After SCOTUS decided *Michigan v. Sitz*, the Michigan supreme court decided that the Michigan search and seizure provision banned the type of suspicionless search created for DWI checkpoints in Michigan. The Michigan constitution search and seizure provision, art. 1, § 11, revised in 1963 closely parallels the Fourth Amendment. Here are excerpts from the Michigan supreme court's opinon.

The intent of the framers as expressed to the people of Michigan was that the Constitution of 1963 represented "no change" from the Constitution of 1908. Thus, to understand what art. 1, § 11 means regarding suspicionless seizures of automobiles, and, thus, what level of protection is required under the Michigan Constitution, we look to interpretation of the previous, nearly identical, constitutional provision. A review of the cases construing Const.1908, art. 2, § 10 discloses no support for the proposition that the police may engage in warrantless, suspicionless seizures of automobiles....

As long ago as 1889, the justices of this Court stated:

Personal liberty, which is guaranteed to every citizen under our Constitution and laws, consists of the right of locomotion,—to go where one pleases, and when,

and to do that which may lead to one's business or pleasure, only so far restrained as the rights of others may make it necessary for the welfare of all other citizens. One may travel along the public highways or in public places; and while conducting themselves in a decent and orderly manner, disturbing no other, and interfering with the rights of no other citizens, there, they will be protected under the law, not only in their persons, but in their safe conduct. The Constitution and the laws are framed for the public good, and the protection of all citizens, from the highest to the lowest; and no one may be restrained of his liberty, unless he has transgressed some law. [*Pinkerton v. Verberg*, 78 Mich. 573, 584, 44 N.W. 579 (1889).]

. . .

The Michigan Constitution has historically treated searches and seizures for criminal investigatory purposes differently than those for regulatory or administrative purposes. These administrative or regulatory searches and seizures have traditionally been regarded as "reasonable" in a constitutional sense. However, seizures with the primary goal of enforcing the criminal law have generally required some level of suspicion, even if that level has fluctuated over the years.

We do not suggest that in a different context we might not reach a similar result under the balancing test of reasonableness employed in *Sitz*. Indeed, our precedent regarding automobiles implicitly incorporates a balancing test that is inherent in assessing the reasonableness of warrantless searches and seizures. We hold only that the protection afforded to the seizures of vehicles for criminal investigatory purposes has both an historical foundation and a contemporary justification that is not outweighed by the necessity advanced. Suspicionless criminal investigatory seizures, and extreme deference to the judgments of politically accountable officials is, in this context, contrary to Michigan constitutional precedent.

LO 6   *Drug interdiction checkpoints*

The primary purpose of the DWI roadblock was highway safety—getting drunk drivers off the road so they won't kill and maim innocent people. Apprehending and prosecuting drunk drivers was clearly secondary or incidental to saving lives on the highway. What if the primary purpose of the checkpoint is to catch drug offenders? Can police officers stop all cars in a drug-infested neighborhood, without any suspicion against specific drivers or passengers, and look for signs of their illegal drug use while a drug-detecting dog walks around the car? That's the question the U.S. Supreme Court answered in our next case excerpt, *City of Indianapolis v. Edmond*.

James Edmond and others sued the city of Indianapolis, the mayor, and members of the IPD, seeking a court order to stop the drug interdiction checkpoint in Indianapolis.

CASE

Was the Drug Interdiction Checkpoint Objectively Unreasonable?

City of Indianapolis v. Edmond
531 U.S. 32 (2000)

6-3

HISTORY

James Edmond and other motorists brought an action seeking a preliminary injunction against the City of Indianapolis, the mayor, and members of Indianapolis PD, alleging that drug interdiction checkpoints violated the Fourth Amendment. The United States District Court for the Southern District of Indiana denied motorists' motion for preliminary injunction, and motorists appealed. The United States Court of Appeals for the Seventh Circuit reversed, the U.S. Supreme Court granted certiorari, and held that the Indianapolis drug interdiction checkpoints violated the Fourth Amendment.

— O'CONNOR, J., joined by STEVENS, KENNEDY, SOUTER, GINSBURG, and BREYER, JJ., joined.

In *Michigan Dept. of State Police v. Sitz*, (1990), and *United States v. Martinez—Fuerte*, we held that brief, suspicionless seizures at highway checkpoints for the purposes of combating drunk driving and intercepting illegal immigrants were constitutional. We now consider the constitutionality of a highway checkpoint program whose primary purpose is the discovery and interdiction of illegal narcotics.

FACTS

In August 1998, the city of Indianapolis began to operate vehicle checkpoints on Indianapolis roads in an effort to interdict unlawful drugs. The city conducted six such roadblocks between August and November that year, stopping 1,161 vehicles and arresting 104 motorists. Fifty-five arrests were for drug-related crimes, while 49 were for offenses unrelated to drugs. The overall "hit rate" of the program was thus approximately 9 percent.

At each checkpoint location, the police stop a predetermined number of vehicles. Approximately 30 officers are stationed at the checkpoint. Pursuant to written directives issued by the chief of police, at least one officer approaches the vehicle, advises the driver that he or she is being stopped briefly at a drug checkpoint, and asks the driver to produce a license and registration. The officer

(continued)

also looks for signs of impairment and conducts an open-view examination of the vehicle from the outside. A narcotics-detection dog walks around the outside of each stopped vehicle.

The directives instruct the officers that they may conduct a search only by consent or based on the appropriate quantum of particularized suspicion. The officers must conduct each stop in the same manner until particularized suspicion develops, and the officers have no discretion to stop any vehicle out of sequence. The city agreed to operate the checkpoints in such a way as to ensure that the total duration of each stop, absent reasonable suspicion or probable cause, would be five minutes or less.

According to Sergeant DePew, checkpoint locations are selected weeks in advance based on such considerations as area crime statistics and traffic flow. The checkpoints are generally operated during daylight hours and are identified with lighted signs reading, "'NARCOTICS CHECKPOINT ___ MILE AHEAD, NARCOTICS K–9 IN USE, BE PREPARED TO STOP.'" Once a group of cars has been stopped, other traffic proceeds without interruption until all the stopped cars have been processed or diverted for further processing. Sergeant DePew also stated that the average stop for a vehicle not subject to further processing lasts two to three minutes or less.

OPINION

The Fourth Amendment requires that searches and seizures be reasonable. A search or seizure is ordinarily unreasonable in the absence of individualized suspicion of wrongdoing. We have recognized only limited circumstances in which the usual rule does not apply. For example, we have upheld certain regimes of suspicionless searches where the program was designed to serve "special needs, beyond the normal need for law enforcement" [Chapter 7]. We have also upheld brief, suspicionless seizures of motorists at a fixed Border Patrol checkpoint designed to intercept illegal aliens, *Martinez–Fuerte* [excerpt pp. 625–628] and at a sobriety checkpoint aimed at removing drunk drivers from the road, *Michigan Dept. of State Police v. Sitz,* (1990) [excerpt p. 145]. In addition, we suggested that a similar type of roadblock with the purpose of verifying drivers' licenses and vehicle registrations would be permissible. In none of these cases, however, did we indicate approval of a checkpoint program whose primary purpose was to detect evidence of ordinary criminal wrongdoing.

It is well established that a vehicle stop at a highway checkpoint effectuates a seizure within the meaning of the Fourth Amendment. What principally distinguishes these checkpoints from those we have previously approved is their primary purpose. The Indianapolis checkpoint program unquestionably has the primary purpose of interdicting illegal narcotics. The IPD has made it clear that the purpose for its checkpoints is "to interdict narcotics traffic" and "the City concedes that its proximate goal is to catch drug offenders."

We have never approved a checkpoint program whose primary purpose was to detect evidence of ordinary criminal wrongdoing. Rather, our checkpoint cases have recognized only limited exceptions to the general rule that a seizure must be accompanied by some measure of individualized suspicion. Each of the checkpoint programs that we have approved was designed primarily to serve purposes closely related to the problems of policing the border or the necessity of ensuring roadway safety. Because the primary purpose of the Indianapolis narcotics checkpoint program is to uncover evidence of ordinary criminal wrongdoing, the program contravenes the Fourth Amendment.

The City emphasizes the severe and intractable nature of the drug problem as justification for the checkpoint program. There is no doubt that traffic in illegal narcotics creates social harms of the first magnitude. The law enforcement problems that the drug trade creates likewise remain daunting and complex, particularly in light of the myriad forms of spin-off crime that it spawns (*Montoya de Hernandez* [excerpt on p. 154]). But the gravity of the threat alone cannot be dispositive of questions concerning what means law enforcement officers may employ to pursue a given purpose. Rather, in determining whether individualized suspicion is required, we must consider the nature of the interests threatened and their connection to the particular law enforcement practices at issue. We are particularly reluctant to recognize exceptions to the general rule of individualized suspicion where governmental authorities primarily pursue their general crime control ends. We decline to suspend the usual requirement of individualized suspicion where the police seek to employ a checkpoint primarily for the ordinary enterprise of investigating crimes. We cannot sanction stops justified only by the generalized and ever-present possibility that interrogation and inspection may reveal that any given motorist has committed some crime.

Of course, there are circumstances that may justify a law enforcement checkpoint where the primary purpose would otherwise, but for some emergency, relate to ordinary crime control. For example, the Fourth Amendment would almost certainly permit an appropriately tailored roadblock set up to thwart an imminent terrorist attack or to catch a dangerous criminal who is likely to flee by way of a particular route. The exigencies created by these scenarios are far removed from the circumstances under which authorities might simply stop cars as a matter of course to see if there just happens to be a felon leaving the jurisdiction. While we do not limit the purposes that may justify a checkpoint program to any rigid set of categories, we decline to approve a program whose primary purpose is ultimately indistinguishable from the general interest in crime control.

Because the primary purpose of the Indianapolis checkpoint program is ultimately indistinguishable from the general interest in crime control, the checkpoints violate the Fourth Amendment. The judgment of the Court of Appeals is, accordingly, affirmed.

It is so ordered.

DISSENT

REHNQUIST, CJ., joined by THOMAS
and SCALIA, JJ

The State's use of a drug-sniffing dog, according to the Court's holding, annuls what is otherwise plainly constitutional under our Fourth Amendment jurisprudence: brief, standardized, discretionless, roadblock seizures of automobiles, seizures which effectively serve a weighty state interest with only minimal intrusion on the privacy of their occupants. Because these seizures serve the State's accepted and significant interests of preventing drunken driving and checking for driver's licenses and vehicle registrations, and because there is nothing in the record to indicate that the addition of the dog sniff lengthens these otherwise legitimate seizures, I dissent.

Roadblock seizures are consistent with the Fourth Amendment if they are carried out pursuant to a plan embodying explicit, neutral limitations on the conduct of individual officers. Specifically, the constitutionality of a seizure turns upon weighing the gravity of the public concerns served by the seizure, the degree to which the seizure advances the public interest, and the severity of the interference with individual liberty.

In *Michigan Dept. of State Police v. Sitz*, (1990), we upheld the State's use of a highway sobriety checkpoint after applying the framework set out [in the last paragraph]. There, we recognized the gravity of the State's interest in curbing drunken driving and found the objective intrusion of the approximately 25-second seizure to be "slight." Turning to the subjective intrusion, we noted that the checkpoint was selected pursuant to guidelines and was operated by uniformed officers. Finally, we concluded that the program effectively furthered the State's interest because the checkpoint resulted in the arrest of two drunk drivers, or 1.6 percent of the 126 drivers stopped.

This case follows naturally from *Sitz*. Petitioners acknowledge that the "primary purpose" of these roadblocks is to interdict illegal drugs, but this fact should not be controlling. Even accepting the Court's conclusion that the checkpoint at issue in *Sitz* was not primarily related to criminal law enforcement, the question whether a law enforcement purpose could support a roadblock seizure is not presented in this case. The District Court found that another "purpose of the checkpoints is to check driver's licenses and vehicle registrations," and the written directives state that the police officers are to "[l]ook for signs of impairment." The use of roadblocks to look for signs of impairment was validated by *Sitz*. That the roadblocks serve these legitimate state interests cannot be seriously disputed, as the 49 people arrested for offenses unrelated to drugs can attest.

Once the constitutional requirements for a particular seizure are satisfied, the subjective expectations of those responsible for it, be it police officers or members of a city council, are irrelevant. Subjective intent alone does not make otherwise lawful conduct illegal or unconstitutional. It is the objective effect of the State's actions on the privacy of the individual that animates the Fourth Amendment. Because the objective intrusion of a valid seizure does not turn upon anyone's subjective thoughts, neither should our constitutional analysis.

With these checkpoints serving two important state interests, the remaining prongs of the *Brown v. Texas* balancing test are easily met. The seizure is objectively reasonable as it lasts, on average, two to three minutes and does not involve a search. The subjective intrusion is likewise limited as the checkpoints are clearly marked and operated by uniformed officers who are directed to stop every vehicle in the same manner. The only difference between this case and *Sitz* is the presence of the dog. We have already held, however, that a "sniff test" by a trained narcotics dog is not a "search" within the meaning of the Fourth Amendment because it does not require physical intrusion of the object being sniffed and it does not expose anything other than the contraband items. And there is nothing in the record to indicate that the dog sniff lengthens the stop. Finally, the checkpoints' success rate—49 arrests for offenses unrelated to drugs—only confirms the State's legitimate interests in preventing drunken driving and ensuring the proper licensing of drivers and registration of their vehicles. These stops effectively serve the State's legitimate interests; they are executed in a regularized and neutral manner; and they only minimally intrude upon the privacy of the motorists. They should therefore be constitutional.

Questions

1. List the details of the drug interdiction checkpoint.
2. State the primary and secondary purpose of the checkpoints.
3. Summarize the majority's arguments for ruling why the checkpoint did not satisfy the three elements of a reasonable checkpoint.
4. Summarize the dissent's arguments why checkpoint did satisfy the three elements of a reasonable checkpoint.
5. In your opinion, was the checkpoint reasonable? Defend your answer.

LO 6 *Information-seeking checkpoints*

What if the *primary* purpose of the checkpoint is not to "catch criminals" in the stopped vehicles, but to collect information from the general public about a crime committed by someone else? That's the question that our next case excerpt, *Illinois v. Lidster,* answers. The purpose of the checkpoint was to gather information about a hit-and-run that killed 70-year-old postal worker Joseph Pytel, who was riding his bicycle home from work (Pytel road the bike the 15 miles to and from work for exercise.) (Nickelsberg 2005, 848).

Here's how the information checkpoint operated. Police cars with flashing lights partially blocked the eastbound lanes of the highway. The blockage forced traffic to slow down, leading to lines of up to 15 cars in each lane. As each vehicle drew up to the checkpoint, an officer would stop it for 10 to 15 seconds, ask the occupants whether they had seen anything happen there the previous weekend, and hand each driver a flyer. The flyer read "ALERT . . . FATAL HIT & RUN ACCIDENT" and requested "ASSISTANCE IN IDENTIFYING THE VEHICLE AND DRIVER INVOLVED IN THIS ACCIDENT WHICH KILLED A 70 YEAR OLD BICYCLIST."

Robert Lidster, convicted of driving while intoxicated, was discovered when he was stopped at the hit-and-run information checkpoint.

CASE

Was the Hit-and-Run Information Checkpoint Reasonable?

Illinois v. Lidster
540 U.S. 419 (2004) 6-3

FACTS

On Saturday, August 23, 1997, just after midnight, an unknown motorist traveling eastbound on a highway in Lombard, Illinois, struck and killed a 70-year-old bicyclist. The motorist drove off without identifying himself. About one week later at about the same time of night and at about the same place, local police set up a highway checkpoint designed to obtain more information about the accident from the motoring public.

Police cars with flashing lights partially blocked the eastbound lanes of the highway. The blockage forced traffic to slow down, leading to lines of up to 15 cars in each lane. As each vehicle drew up to the checkpoint, an officer would stop it for 10 to 15 seconds, ask the occupants whether they had seen anything happen there the previous weekend, and hand each driver a flyer. The flyer said "ALERT . . . FATAL HIT & RUN ACCIDENT" and requested "ASSISTANCE IN IDENTIFYING THE VEHICLE AND DRIVER INVOLVED IN THIS ACCIDENT WHICH KILLED A 70 YEAR OLD BICYCLIST."

Robert Lidster (respondent) drove a minivan toward the checkpoint. As he approached the checkpoint, his van swerved, nearly hitting one of the officers. The officer smelled alcohol on Lidster's breath. He directed Lidster to a side street where another officer administered a sobriety test and then arrested Lidster. Lidster was tried and convicted in Illinois state court of driving under the influence of alcohol.

OPINION

The Illinois Supreme Court basically held that our decision in *Edmond* governs the outcome of this case. We do not agree. *Edmond* involved a checkpoint at which police stopped vehicles to look for evidence of drug crimes committed by occupants of those vehicles. . . . We found that police had set up this checkpoint primarily for general "crime control" purposes, *i.e.,* "to detect evidence of ordinary criminal wrongdoing." We noted that the stop was made without individualized suspicion. And we held that the Fourth Amendment forbids such a stop, in the absence of special circumstances.

The checkpoint stop here differs significantly from that in *Edmond.* The stop's primary law enforcement purpose was *not* to determine whether a vehicle's occupants were committing a crime, but to ask vehicle occupants, as members of the public, for their help in providing information about a crime in all likelihood committed by others. The police expected the information elicited to help them apprehend, not the vehicle's occupants, but other individuals.

. . . We hold that the stop was constitutional. The relevant public concern was grave. Police were investigating a crime that had resulted in a human death. No one denies the police's need to obtain more information at that time. And the stop's objective was to help find the perpetrator of a specific and known crime, not of unknown crimes of a general sort.

The stop advanced this grave public concern to a significant degree. The police appropriately tailored their checkpoint stops to fit important criminal investigatory needs. The stops took place about one week after the hit-and-run accident, on the same highway near the location of the accident, and at about the same time of night. And police used the stops to obtain information from drivers, some of whom might well have been in the vicinity of the crime at the time it occurred.

Most importantly, the stops interfered only minimally with liberty of the sort the Fourth Amendment seeks to protect. Viewed objectively, each stop required only a brief wait in line—a very few minutes at most. Contact with the police lasted only a few seconds. Police contact consisted simply of a request for information and the distribution of a flyer. Viewed subjectively, the contact provided little reason for anxiety or alarm. The police stopped all vehicles systematically. And there is no allegation here that the police acted in a discriminatory or otherwise unlawful manner while questioning motorists during stops.

For these reasons we conclude that the checkpoint stop was constitutional. The judgment of the Illinois Supreme Court is *Reversed.*

DISSENT

STEVENS, J., joined by SOUTER and GINSBURG, JJ.

. . . In contrast to pedestrians, who are free to keep walking when they encounter police officers handing out flyers or seeking information, motorists who confront a roadblock are required to stop, and to remain stopped for as long as the officers choose to detain them. Such a seizure may seem relatively innocuous to some, but annoying to others who are forced to wait for several minutes when the line of cars is lengthened—for example, by a surge of vehicles leaving a factory at the end of a shift. Still other drivers may find an unpublicized roadblock at midnight on a Saturday somewhat alarming.

On the other side of the equation, the likelihood that questioning a random sample of drivers will yield useful information about a hit-and-run accident that occurred a week earlier is speculative at best. To be sure, the sample in this case was not entirely random: The record reveals that the police knew that the victim had finished work at the Post Office shortly before the fatal accident, and hoped that other employees of the Post Office or the nearby industrial park might work on similar schedules and, thus, have been driving the same route at the same time the previous week. That is a plausible theory, but there is no evidence in the record that the police did anything to confirm that the nearby businesses in fact had shift changes at or near midnight on Saturdays, or that they had reason to believe that a roadblock would be more effective than, say, placing flyers on the employees' cars.

In short, the outcome of the multifactor test prescribed in *Brown v. Texas* (1979), is by no means clear on the facts of this case. Because the Illinois Appellate Court and the State Supreme Court held that the Lombard roadblock was *per se* unconstitutional under *Indianapolis v. Edmond,* neither court attempted to apply the *Brown* test. We ordinarily do not decide in the first instance issues not resolved below. We should be especially reluctant to abandon our role as a court of review in a case in which the constitutional inquiry requires analysis of local conditions and practices more familiar to judges closer to the scene. I would therefore remand the case to the Illinois courts to undertake the initial analysis of the issue. To that extent, I respectfully dissent.

Questions

1. Describe the details of the checkpoint.
2. Summarize the majority's arguments that the checkpoint satisfied the three-prong balancing test.
3. Summarize the dissent's arguments that the checkpoint did not satisfy the balancing test.
4. Which argument do you support? Defend your answer.

DETENTIONS AT INTERNATIONAL BORDERS

LO 7   The strong government interest in controlling who and what comes into the United States substantially reduces the liberty and privacy rights of individuals at the Mexican and Canadian land boundaries, at the seaports along the East and West Coasts, and at all airports on flights coming from foreign countries. Routine detentions don't require reasonable suspicion to back up lengthy detentions or frisks. This includes examining purses, wallets, and pockets (*Henderson v. U.S.* 1967) and up-close dog sniffs (*U.S. v. Kelly* 2002).

The strong government interest extends to many kinds of people and to many things that demand preventive measures, but here we'll use as our example preventing illegal drug smuggling. Specifically, we'll look at the difficulty that balloon swallowers create for law enforcement. (We'll take up preventing terrorist attacks and apprehending terrorist suspects in Chapter 15.) These are smugglers who bring illegal drugs into the country hidden in their alimentary canals or vaginas.

The U.S. Supreme Court upheld a 16-hour detention of Rosa Elvira Montoya de Hernandez, a suspected "balloon swallower," in close confinement under constant surveillance and a strip search at Los Angeles International Airport in *U.S. v. Montoya de Hernandez* (1985).

In *U.S. vs. Montoya de Hernandez* (1985), our next case excerpt, the U.S. Supreme Court found that an extended detention of Colombian national Rosa Elvira Montoya de Hernandez to determine whether she was a balloon swallower was a reasonable stop.

CASE

Is the 16-Hour Detention of a Suspected "Balloon Swallower" a Reasonable Stop?

U.S. v. Montoya de Hernandez
473 U.S. 531 (1985)

HISTORY

Rosa Elvira Montoya de Hernandez was charged with narcotics violations. She moved to suppress the narcotics. The U.S. District Court denied the motion and admitted the cocaine in evidence. Montoya de Hernandez was convicted of possessing cocaine with intent to distribute and unlawful importation of cocaine. A divided U.S. Court of Appeals for the 9th Circuit reversed the conviction. The government appealed to the U.S. Supreme Court. The Supreme Court reversed.

—REHNQUIST, J., joined by BURGER, C.J., and WHITE, BLACKMUN, POWELL, and O'CONNOR, JJ.

FACTS

Montoya de Hernandez arrived at Los Angeles International Airport shortly after midnight, March 5, 1983, on Avianca Flight 080, a direct 10-hour flight from Bogotá, Colombia. Her visa was in order so she was passed through Immigration and proceeded to the customs desk. At the customs desk she encountered Customs Inspector Talamantes, who reviewed her documents and noticed from her passport that she had made at least eight recent trips to either Miami or Los Angeles.

Talamantes referred respondent to a secondary customs desk for further questioning. At this desk Talamantes and another inspector asked Montoya de Hernandez general questions concerning herself and the purpose of her trip. Montoya de Hernandez revealed that she spoke no English and had no family or friends in the United States. She explained in Spanish that she had come to the United States to purchase goods for her husband's store in Bogotá.

The customs inspectors recognized Bogotá as a "source city" for narcotics. Montoya de Hernandez possessed $5,000 in cash, mostly $50 bills, but had no billfold. She indicated to the inspectors that she had no appointments with merchandise vendors, but planned to ride around Los Angeles in taxicabs visiting retail stores such as J.C. Penney and K-Mart in order to buy goods for her husband's store with the $5,000.

Montoya de Hernandez admitted she had no hotel reservations, but said she planned to stay at a Holiday Inn. Montoya de Hernandez could not recall how her airline ticket was purchased. When the inspectors opened Montoya de Hernandez's one small valise they found about four changes of "cold weather" clothing. Montoya de Hernandez had no shoes other than the high-heeled pair she was wearing. Although Montoya de Hernandez possessed no checks, waybills, credit cards, or letters of credit, she did produce a Colombian business card and a number of old receipts, waybills, and fabric swatches displayed in a photo album. At this point Talamantes and the other inspector suspected that Montoya de Hernandez was a "balloon swallower," one who attempts to smuggle narcotics into this country hidden in her alimentary canal. Over the years Inspector Talamantes had apprehended dozens of alimentary canal smugglers arriving on Avianca Flight 080.

The inspectors requested a female customs inspector to take Montoya de Hernandez to a private area and conduct a pat down and strip search. During the search the female inspector felt Montoya de Hernandez's abdomen area and noticed a firm fullness, as if Montoya de Hernandez were wearing a girdle. The search revealed no contraband, but the inspector noticed that Montoya de Hernandez was wearing two pairs of elastic underpants with a paper towel lining the crotch area.

When Montoya de Hernandez returned to the customs area and the female inspector reported her discoveries, the inspector in charge told Montoya de Hernandez that he suspected she was smuggling drugs in her alimentary canal. . . . The inspector then gave Montoya de Hernandez the options of returning to Colombia on the next available flight, agreeing to an X-ray, or remaining in detention until she produced a monitored bowel movement that would confirm or rebut the inspectors' suspicions.

Montoya de Hernandez chose the first option and was placed in a customs office under observation. She was told that if she went to the toilet she would have to use a wastebasket in the women's restroom, in order that female inspectors could inspect her stool for balloons or capsules carrying narcotics. The inspectors refused Montoya de Hernandez's request to place a telephone call.

Montoya de Hernandez sat in the customs office, under observation, for the remainder of the night. She remained detained in the customs office under observation, for most of the time curled up in a chair leaning to one side. She refused all offers of food and drink, and refused to use the toilet facilities. The Court of Appeals noted that she exhibited symptoms of discomfort with "heroic efforts to resist the usual calls of nature."

At the shift change at 4:00 the next afternoon, almost 16 hours after her flight had landed, Montoya de Hernandez still had not defecated or urinated or partaken of food or drink. At that time customs officials sought a court order authorizing an X-ray, and a rectal examination. The Federal Magistrate issued an order just before midnight that evening, which authorized a rectal examination and involuntary X-ray. A physician conducted a rectal examination and removed from Montoya de Hernandez's rectum a balloon containing a foreign substance. Montoya de Hernandez was then placed formally under arrest. By 4:10 a.m. Montoya de Hernandez had passed 6 similar balloons; over the next four days she passed 88 balloons containing a total of 528 grams of 80 percent pure cocaine hydrochloride.

After a suppression hearing, the District Court admitted the cocaine in evidence against Montoya de Hernandez. She was convicted of possession of cocaine with intent to distribute and unlawful importation of cocaine. A divided panel of the United States Court of Appeals for the Ninth Circuit reversed Montoya de Hernandez's convictions.

OPINION

The Fourth Amendment commands that searches and seizures be reasonable. What is reasonable depends upon all of the circumstances surrounding the search or seizure itself. The permissibility of a particular law enforcement practice is judged by "balancing its intrusion on the individual's Fourth Amendment interest against its promotion of legitimate governmental interests."

Here the seizure of Montoya de Hernandez took place at the international border. Since the founding of our Republic, Congress has granted the Executive plenary authority to conduct routine searches and seizures at the border, without probable cause or a warrant, in order to regulate the collection of duties and to prevent the introduction of contraband into this country. The Fourth Amendment's balance of reasonableness is qualitatively different at the international border than in the interior. Routine searches of the persons and effects of entrants are not subject to any requirement of reasonable suspicion, probable cause, or warrant, and first-class mail may be opened without a warrant on less than probable cause.

These cases reflect long-standing concern for the protection of the integrity of the border. This concern is, if anything, heightened by the veritable national crisis in law enforcement caused by smuggling of illicit narcotics and in particular by the increasing utilization of alimentary canal smuggling. This desperate practice appears to be a relatively recent addition to the smugglers' repertoire of deceptive practices, and it also appears to be exceedingly difficult to detect.

(continued)

Balanced against the sovereign's interests at the border are the Fourth Amendment rights of Montoya de Hernandez. Having presented herself at the border for admission, and having subjected herself to the criminal enforcement powers of the Federal Government, she was entitled to be free from unreasonable search and seizure.

But not only is this expectation of privacy less at the border than in the interior, the Fourth Amendment balance between the interests of the Government and the privacy right of the individual is also struck much more favorably to the Government at the border.

We have not previously decided what level of suspicion would justify a seizure of an incoming traveler for purposes other than a routine border search. The Court of Appeals viewed "clear indication" as an intermediate standard between "reasonable suspicion" and "probable cause." No other court, including this one, has ever adopted "clear indication" language as a Fourth Amendment standard. We do not think that the Fourth Amendment's emphasis upon reasonableness is consistent with the creation of a third verbal standard in addition to "reasonable suspicion" and "probable cause."

We hold that detention of a traveler at the border, beyond the scope of a routine customs search and inspection, is justified at its inception if customs agents, considering all the facts surrounding the traveler and her trip, reasonably suspect that the traveler is smuggling contraband in her alimentary canal. The facts, and their rational inferences, known to customs inspectors in this case clearly supported a reasonable suspicion that Montoya de Hernandez was an alimentary canal smuggler.

The trained customs inspectors had encountered many alimentary canal smugglers and certainly had more than an inchoate and unparticularized suspicion or hunch, that Montoya de Hernandez was smuggling narcotics in her alimentary canal. The inspectors' suspicion was a common-sense conclusion about human behavior upon which practical people, including government officials, are entitled to rely.

The final issue in this case is whether the detention of Montoya de Hernandez was reasonably related in scope to the circumstances which justified it initially. In this regard we have cautioned that courts should not indulge in unrealistic second-guessing, and we have noted that creative judges, engaged in after the fact evaluations of police conduct can almost always imagine some alternative means by which the objectives of the police might have been accomplished.

The rudimentary knowledge of the human body which judges possess in common with the rest of humankind tells us that alimentary canal smuggling cannot be detected in the amount of time in which other illegal activity may be investigated through brief *Terry*-type stops. It presents few, if any external signs; a quick frisk will not do, nor will even a strip search.

In the case of Montoya de Hernandez, the inspectors had available, as an alternative to simply awaiting her bowel movement, an X-ray. They offered her the alternative of submitting herself to that procedure. But when she refused that alternative, the customs inspectors were left with only two practical alternatives: detain her for such a time as necessary to confirm their suspicions, a detention which would last much longer than the typical *Terry* stop, or turn her loose into the interior carrying the reasonably suspected contraband drugs.

The inspectors in this case followed this former procedure. They no doubt expected that Montoya de Hernandez, having recently disembarked from a 10-hour direct flight with a full and stiff abdomen, would produce a bowel movement without extended delay. But her visible efforts to resist the call of nature, which the court below labeled "heroic," disappointed this expectation and in turn caused her humiliation and discomfort.

Our prior cases have refused to charge police with delays in investigatory detention attributable to the suspect's evasive actions. Montoya de Hernandez alone was responsible for much of the duration and discomfort of the seizure. Under these circumstances, we conclude that the detention was not unreasonably long. It occurred at the international border, where the Fourth Amendment balance of interests leans heavily to the Government. Montoya de Hernandez's detention was long, uncomfortable indeed, humiliating; but both its length and its discomfort resulted solely from the method by which she chose to smuggle illicit drugs into this country.

REVERSED.

CONCURRING OPINION

STEVENS, J.

If a seizure and search of the person of the kind disclosed by this record may be made on the basis of reasonable suspicion, we must assume that a significant number of innocent persons will be required to undergo similar procedures. The rule announced in this case cannot, therefore, be supported on the ground that Montoya de Hernandez's prolonged and humiliating detention "resulted solely from the method by which she chose to smuggle illicit drugs into this country."

The prolonged detention of Montoya de Hernandez was, however, justified by a different choice that Montoya de Hernandez made; she withdrew her consent to an X-ray examination that would have easily determined whether the reasonable suspicion that she was concealing contraband was justified.

DISSENT

BRENNAN, J., joined by MARSHALL, J.

We confront a "disgusting and saddening episode" at our Nation's border. "That Montoya de Hernandez so degraded herself as to offend the sensibilities of any decent citizen is not questioned." That is not what we face. For "it is a fair summary of history to say that the safeguards of liberty have frequently been forged in controversies involving not very nice people." . . .

The standards we fashion to govern the ferreting out of the guilty apply equally to the detention of the innocent, and "may be exercised by the most unfit and ruthless officers as well as by the fit and reasonable." Nor is the issue whether there is a "veritable national crisis in law enforcement caused by smuggling illicit narcotics." In our democracy such enforcement presupposes a moral atmosphere and a reliance upon intelligence whereby the effective administration of justice can be achieved with due regard for those civilized standards in the use of the criminal law which are formulated in our Bill of Rights.

The issue, instead, is simply this: Does the Fourth Amendment permit an international traveler, citizen or alien, to be subjected to the sort of treatment that occurred in this case without the sanction of a judicial officer and based on nothing more than the "reasonable suspicion" of low ranking investigative officers that something might be amiss? The Court today concludes that the Fourth Amendment grants such sweeping and unmonitored authority to customs officials. I dissent.

Indefinite involuntary incommunicado detentions "for investigation" are the hallmark of a police state, not a free society. In my opinion, Government officials may no more confine a person at the border under such circumstances for purposes of criminal investigation than they may within the interior of the country. The nature and duration of the detention here may well have been tolerable for spoiled meat or diseased animals, but not for human beings held on simple suspicion of criminal activity.

Finally, I believe that the warrant and probable cause safeguards equally govern Justice STEVENS' proffered alternative of exposure to X-irradiation for criminal investigative purposes. The available evidence suggests that the number of highly intrusive border searches of suspicious-looking but ultimately innocent travelers may be very high. One physician who at the request of customs officials conducted many "internal searches"—rectal and vaginal examinations and stomach pumping—estimated that he had found contraband in 15 to 20 percent of the persons he had examined. It has similarly been estimated that only 16 percent of women subjected to body cavity searches at the border were in fact found to be carrying contraband. It is precisely to minimize the risk of harassing so many innocent people that the Fourth Amendment requires the intervention of a judicial officer.

The Court argues, however, that the length and "discomfort" of de Hernandez's detention "resulted solely from the method by which she chose to smuggle illicit drugs into this country," and it speculates that only her "heroic" efforts prevented the detention from being brief and to the point. Although we now know that de Hernandez was indeed guilty of smuggling drugs internally, such after the fact rationalizations have no place in our Fourth Amendment jurisprudence, which demands that we prevent hindsight from coloring the evaluation of the reasonableness of a search or seizure. At the time the authorities simply had, at most, a reasonable suspicion that de Hernandez might be engaged in such smuggling.

Neither the law of the land nor the law of nature supports the notion that petty government officials can require people to excrete on command; indeed, the Court relies elsewhere on "the rudimentary knowledge of the human body" in sanctioning the "much longer than typical" duration of detentions such as this. And, with all respect to the Court, it is not "unrealistic second-guessing" to predict that an innocent traveler, locked away in incommunicado detention in unfamiliar surroundings in a foreign land, might well be frightened and exhausted as to be unable so to "cooperate" with the authorities.

It is tempting, of course, to look the other way in a case that so graphically illustrates the "veritable national crisis" caused by narcotics trafficking. But if there is one enduring lesson to be learned in the long struggle to balance individual rights against society's need to defend itself against lawlessness, it is that it is easy to make light of insistence on scrupulous regard for the safeguards of civil liberties when invoked on behalf of the unworthy. It is too easy. History bears testimony that by such disregard are the rights of liberty extinguished, heedlessly at first, then stealthily, and brazenly in the end.

Questions

1. Identify the government interests the invasions of Montoya de Hernandez's liberty and privacy were intended to protect.

2. Compare the duration, location, and subjective invasiveness of Montoya de Hernandez's detention with that of John Terry in *Terry v. Ohio*.

3. Assume, first, you're a prosecutor and, then, a defense lawyer. Relying on the facts and opinion in *Terry v. Ohio*, argue, first, that the detention and searches of Montoya de Hernandez pass the reasonableness test and, then, that they fail the reasonableness test. Make sure you include all of the elements of reasonableness we've discussed in this chapter.

4. Now, assume you're a judge. Based on your view of the law, write an opinion supporting your decision whether the government actions in this case were reasonable under the Fourth Amendment.

CHAPTER SUMMARY

LO 1 Fourth Amendment stops are the least invasive seizures of persons; these short, on-the-spot detentions allow officers to briefly freeze suspicious people and situations to investigate possible criminal activity. Fourth Amendment frisks are light, once-over pat downs of outer clothing to protect officers from the use of concealed weapons during stops.

LO 2 Fourth Amendment stops and frisks are warrantless searches and seizures that must satisfy the two conditions of the reasonableness test: (1) the need to control crime must outweigh the intrusion on individual liberty and privacy and (2) the officer must have enough articulable facts and circumstances that amount to reasonable suspicion to justify stops and frisks.

LO 1, 2 The Fourth Amendment consists of two parts: (1) the reasonableness clause that applies to all searches and seizures and (2) the warrant clause that applies only to searches and arrests based on warrants. In practice, the majority of searches and seizures are performed without warrants.

LO 3 Reasonable suspicion requires articulable facts amounting to more than a hunch but less than probable cause that lead an officer, under the totality of circumstances, to suspect that crime may be afoot. Individualized and categorical suspicion, direct and hearsay information, and even random procedures may be used to build reasonable suspicion. Race, ethnicity, and profiles can be part of, but not by themselves, the "whole picture" in establishing reasonable suspicion.

LO 4, 5 Empirical research has challenged the accuracy and weight of some Supreme Court decisions regarding the definition of "high-crime areas" and the danger to police during traffic stops. Further, the majority of individuals stopped and frisked are innocent and Black or Latino.

LO 1, 2, 3 The scope of reasonable stops requires them to be brief, on-the-spot detentions during which officers may question stopped individuals to quickly decide whether to arrest or free them. The elements of a reasonable frisk include: (1) the officer lawfully stops an individual *before* the frisk; (2) the officer reasonably suspects that the person is armed; and (3) the officer limits her action to a once-over, light pat down of the outer clothing to detect concealed weapons only. With the exception of individuals stopped for violent crimes, the facts and circumstances that justify the stop do not automatically justify a frisk.

LO 4, 5 The Supreme Court views police work as especially dangerous during traffic stops. To accommodate the increased need for officer safety at the roadside, SCOTUS has created bright-line rules expanding police powers to ask occupants out of lawfully stopped vehicles and frisk them. Empirical research, however, does not support that these expansions of police power increase officer safety during routine traffic stops.

LO 6 Roadblocks and checkpoints stop drivers without individualized suspicion that crime may be afoot to meet special societal needs, such as preventing drunk driving and checking for illegal immigrants. The reasonableness of these roadblocks and checkpoints is determined by the following three-prong balancing test: (1) the gravity of the public interest being served by the seizure; (2) the effectiveness of the seizure in advancing the public interest; and (3) the degree of intrusion upon individual liberty.

LO 7 The strong government interest in controlling who and what enters the United States is balanced against the significant reductions of individual Fourth Amendment rights at international borders. Routine detentions at international airports, seaports, and the Canadian and Mexican land borders do not require reasonable suspicion to back up lengthy detentions and frisks, including examining purses, wallets, pockets, and even up-close dog sniffs.

REVIEW QUESTIONS

1. Trace the history behind police power to stop and question suspicious persons from colonial times to the present.
2. Explain the difference between Fourth Amendment stops and arrests. Explain the difference between Fourth Amendment frisks and other searches.
3. Describe four realities of stops and frisks. What's the ratio of all stops to arrests?
4. Identify the three steps of the Fourth Amendment analysis used to determine whether stops and frisks are reasonable searches and seizures.
5. Identify and describe the two parts of the Fourth Amendment. Explain the three possible interpretations of the Fourth Amendment and identify which interpretation the Supreme Court has deemed acceptable.
6. Identify and describe the two parts of the Fourth Amendment reasonableness test for warrantless searches and seizures.
7. Explain Judge Juviler's statement that, since the Supreme Court decided *Terry v. Ohio*, he and other lawyers feel "like the makers of the hydrogen bomb."
8. Describe three kinds of police-individual encounters.
9. Identify and describe the two elements of a reasonable stop.
10. Identify two types of information officers can rely on to build reasonable suspicion. Give two examples of each.
11. Explain the difference between individualized and categorical suspicion and give an example of each. Describe how categorical suspicion can be used in building reasonable suspicion.
12. Describe the empirical research regarding the designation of a location as a "high-crime area." Compare these findings to the decision in *Illinois v. Wardlow*.
13. Explain how race and ethnicity can be used to build reasonable suspicion. What groups of people are stopped and frisked most often?
14. Describe profiles as they relate to reasonable suspicion to stop and frisk. Identify four primary and secondary characteristics of drug courier profiles.
15. Describe the two necessary elements that define the scope of a reasonable stop.
16. Describe the extent to which officers may question stopped suspects. What are the repercussions for suspects who refuse to answer law enforcement inquiries?
17. Describe the three elements of a lawful frisk. What's the scope of a lawful frisk?
18. What amounts to reasonable suspicion to justify a frisk? When do the facts that justify a stop automatically justify a frisk?

19. Describe the Court's view on the dangerousness of police work. How does this relate to data from the U.S. Bureau of Labor Statistics and FBI data (Figure 4.4)?

20. According to the Supreme Court, why is it reasonable to remove occupants from a stopped vehicle and frisk them without suspicion that they might be involved in a crime? Compare the Court's reasoning with the empirical data regarding the danger to officers during traffic stops (Table 4.8).

21. According to SCOTUS, why are checkpoints and roadblocks reasonable stops even though they lack individualized suspicion that crime may be afoot?

22. Describe the three-prong balancing test courts use to determine whether roadblocks and checkpoints are reasonable. Provide two examples of societal interests that SCOTUS has ruled outweigh the invasions of individual liberty at checkpoints.

23. How are individual Fourth Amendment rights severely restricted at international borders?

24. Describe the government interest balanced against the limited rights of individual liberty and privacy at international borders. What areas do "international borders" include?

KEY TERMS

arrest, p. 102
Fourth Amendment
stops, p. 102
seizures, p. 102
Fourth Amendment frisks, p. 102
searches, p. 102
objective basis, p. 102
reasonableness clause, p. 104
warrant clause, p. 104
conventional Fourth Amendment
approach, p. 105

reasonableness Fourth Amendment
approach, p. 105
reasonableness test, p. 105
balancing element, p. 105
objective basis, p. 105
case-by-case basis, p. 105
"bright-line" rules, p. 106
individualized suspicion, p. 106
articulable facts, p. 117
reasonable suspicion, p. 117
totality-of-circumstances test, p. 117

direct information, p. 119
hearsay information, p. 119
individualized suspicion, p. 121
categorical suspicion, p. 121
"high-crime area," p. 121
profiles, p. 129
violent crime–automatic frisk
exception, p. 134
roadblock, p. 144
checkpoints, p. 144
three-prong balancing test, p. 144

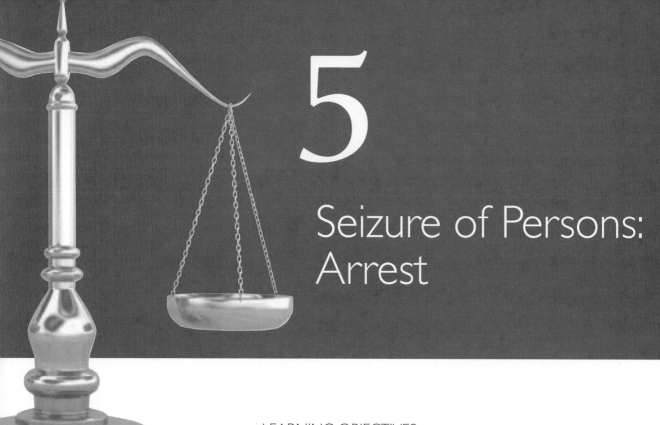

5

Seizure of Persons: Arrest

LEARNING OBJECTIVES

1 Know that arrests are a vital tool that can help law enforcement officers catch the guilty and free the innocent. Understand that arrests are Fourth Amendments seizures that are more invasive than stops but less invasive than imprisonment.

2 Know that lawful arrests must satisfy the following two elements of the Fourth Amendment's reasonableness requirement: (1) the arrest was based on probable cause and (2) the manner of the arrest was reasonable.

3 Appreciate that the probable cause requirement balances the societal interest of crime control against the individual right of locomotion. Know that probable cause depends on the totality of circumstances and can be built from both direct and hearsay information.

4 Know that arrest warrants are required to arrest suspects in their homes except when the need to act immediately exists at the time of the arrest.

5 Understand that officers can use only the amount of force necessary to get and maintain control of suspects they have probable cause to arrest.

6 Know that after an arrest, felony suspects are usually taken to the police station for official booking, photographing, and possible interrogation and identification procedures; misdemeanor suspects are typically issued a citation instead of arrested.

It was the start of another school year and the Washington Metropolitan Area Transit Authority (WMATA) was once again getting complaints about bad behavior by students using the Tenleytown/American University Metro rail station. In response, WMATA embarked on a weeklong undercover operation to enforce a "zero-tolerance" policy with respect to violations of certain ordinances, including one that makes it unlawful for any person to eat or drink in a Metro rail station.

The undercover operation was in effect on October 23, 2000, when 12-year-old Ansche Hedgepeth and a classmate entered the Tenleytown/AU station on their way home from school. Ansche had stopped at a fast-food restaurant on the way and ordered a bag of french fries—to go. While waiting for her companion to purchase a fare card, Ansche removed and ate a single french fry from the take-out bag she was holding. After proceeding through the fare gate, Ansche was stopped by a plain-clothed Metro Transit Police officer, who identified himself and informed her that he was arresting her for eating in the Metro rail station. The officer then handcuffed Ansche behind her back while another officer searched her and her backpack. Pursuant to established procedure, her shoelaces were removed. Upset and crying, Ansche was transported to the District of Columbia's Juvenile Processing Center some distance away, where she was fingerprinted and processed before being released into the custody of her mother three hours later.

The zero-tolerance policy was not, it turned out, carved in stone. The negative publicity surrounding Ansche's arrest prompted WMATA to adopt a new policy effective January 31, 2001, allowing WMATA officers to issue citations to juveniles violating § 35–251(b). WMATA went even further. Effective May 8, 2001, it adopted a new Written Warning Notice Program, under which juveniles eating in the Metro would be neither arrested nor issued citations, but instead given written warnings, with a letter notifying their parents and school. Only after the third infraction over the course of a year could a juvenile be formally prosecuted.

On April 9, 2001, Ansche's mother, Tracey Hedgepeth, brought this action as Ansche's *next friend* (representing a minor) in the United States District Court for the District of Columbia.

LO I   Arrests are a vital tool that can help law enforcement officers catch the guilty and free the innocent, but they also have to meet the requirements of the U.S. Constitution. The noble end of crime control doesn't justify unreasonable arrests to attain that end. Arrests, like the stops you learned about in Chapter 4, are Fourth Amendment seizures. But they're more invasive than stops, and they require a higher objective basis to make them reasonable.

Arrests are more invasive than stops in several ways. First, they last longer. Stops are measured in minutes; arrests often last hours, sometimes even days. Second, the location differs. Stops begin and end on the same spot on streets and in other public places in the presence of other people. Typically, arrests begin on the street but officers put arrested people in squad cars and take them to the isolated and intimidating surroundings of the local police department and jail, where they're held against their will for hours, sometimes even days.

Third, officers don't "write up" the vast majority of stops. The written police report that officers write up for most arrests becomes part of a person's record, or "rap sheet." Fourth, stops (unless accompanied by frisks) don't involve body searches. Full-body searches (usually) and strip and body-cavity searches (sometimes) accompany arrests (Chapter 6). Interrogations (Chapter 8) and lineups (Chapter 9) can also accompany arrests (Table 5.1).

Last, arrests can produce fear, anxiety, and loss of liberty. They can also cause loss of income and even the loss of a job. Furthermore, these losses don't just affect arrested suspects who turn out to be guilty; they also affect millions of innocent arrested people. And arrests embarrass and cause economic hardship to the families of both the innocent and the guilty people arrested. These embarrassments and hardships rarely accompany a Fourth Amendment stop.

These are the characteristics of **custodial arrests**, defined as an officer taking a person into custody and holding her to answer criminal charges. But considerably less-invasive seizures can also be arrests. Think of arrest as a zone, not a point, within a spectrum of invasions between investigatory stops at one end and imprisonment at the other end (see Table 5.2). That zone begins with detentions after stops end and continues through full custodial arrests that involve all the invasions listed in Table 5.1.

Within that zone, arrests may contain only some of the characteristics in Table 5.1. The duration and location also may vary significantly from the characteristics in the tables. How long does a seizure have to last to turn a stop into an arrest? How far do officers have to move an individual to turn a stop into an arrest? No "bright line" separates stops from arrests. But where we draw the line matters because of one element common to all arrests within the zone: The Fourth Amendment requires probable cause to make them reasonable.

TABLE 5.1 Characteristics of a custodial arrest

1. The police officer says to the suspect, "You're under arrest."
2. The suspect is put into a squad car.
3. The suspect is taken to the police station.
4. The suspect is photographed, booked, and fingerprinted.
5. The suspect is searched.
6. The suspect is locked up either at the police station or in a jail cell.
7. The suspect is interrogated.
8. The suspect may be put into a lineup.

TABLE 5.2 Deprivations of liberty, from stops to imprisonment

Deprivation	Objective basis	Duration	Location	Degree of invasion
Voluntary contact	None	Brief	On the spot	Moral and psychological pressure
Stop	Reasonable suspicion	Minutes	At or near the stop on the street or in another public place	Requirement to reveal identification and explain whereabouts
Arrest	Probable cause	Hours to a few days	Usually removal to a police station	Fingerprints, booking, photograph, interrogation, identification procedures
Detention	Probable cause	Days to months	Jail	Inventory, full-body, strip, and body-cavity searches; restricted contact with the outside
Imprisonment	Proof beyond a reasonable doubt	Years to life	Prison	Same as detention with heightened invasions of privacy, liberty, and property

© Cengage Learning

LO 2 The remainder of this chapter describes and analyzes the reasonableness requirement in a lawful arrest. Reasonable arrests consist of two elements:

1. *Objective basis.* The arrest was backed up by probable cause.
2. *Manner of arrest.* The way the arrest was made was reasonable.

First, we'll look at probable cause to arrest. Then, we'll examine how courts decide whether the following officers' actions before, during, and after arrests are reasonable:

1. Entering homes to arrest suspects
2. Using force to get control of suspects
3. Maintaining control of suspects after arrest

PROBABLE CAUSE TO ARREST

LO 2, 3 **Probable cause to arrest** requires that an officer, in the light of her training and experience, knows enough facts and circumstances to reasonably believe that:

1. A crime has been, is being, or is about to be committed, *and*
2. The person arrested has committed, is committing, or is about to commit the crime

(Contrast this definition with the reasonable-grounds-to-suspect standard for stops discussed in Chapter 4.) Probable cause lies on a continuum between reasonable suspicion on one end and proof beyond a reasonable doubt on the other. Table 5.2 shows how the requirement for an objective basis increases as the level of invasiveness increases in criminal procedure.

The probable cause requirement balances the societal interest in crime control and the individual **right of locomotion**—the freedom to come and go as we please. According to the frequently cited *Brinegar v. U.S.* (1949), probable cause balances the interest in safeguarding individuals from "from rash and unreasonable interferences with privacy and from unfounded charges of crime," with the need to give law enforcement officers "fair leeway for enforcing the law in the community's protection." Because officers have to confront many ambiguous situations, we have to leave room for officers to make "some mistakes." But they have to be the mistakes of "reasonable men, acting on facts leading sensibly to their conclusions of probability" (176).

The day-to-day application of finding probable cause rests mainly with officers on the street, who have to make quick decisions. They don't have the luxury that professors in their studies, judges in their chambers, and you wherever you're reading this chapter have to think deeply about technical matters. According to the Court in *Brinegar* (1949), "In dealing with probable cause, as the very name implies, we deal with probabilities. These are not technical; they are the factual and practical considerations of everyday life on which reasonable and prudent men, not legal technicians, act" (176).

So, although officers can't arrest on a hunch, a whim, or mere suspicion, and judges have the final say on whether the officers had probable cause, courts tend to accept the facts as police see them. According to one judge: Police officers don't "prearrange the setting" they work in and can't

> schedule their steps in the calm reflective atmosphere of some remote law library. Events occur without warning and policemen are required as a matter of duty to act as a reasonably prudent policeman would under the circumstances as those circumstances unfold before him. (*People v. Brown* 1969, 869)

The basis for reasonable belief can be either direct information or hearsay. Let's look at these two kinds of information.

LO 3 Direct Information

Direct information in probable cause to arrest is firsthand information, namely information arresting officers know from what they see, hear, feel, taste, and smell at the time of arrest. Direct information doesn't automatically make the case for probable cause. The courts look for patterns, or a totality of circumstances, that build the case for probable cause. Table 5.3 lists some of the facts and circumstances that officers usually know firsthand and which, either alone or in combination, form a pattern that a judge can decide adds up to probable cause.

TABLE 5.3 Probable cause information officers know firsthand

• Fleeing ("flight")	• Attempting to destroy evidence
• Resisting officers	• Matching fingerprints
• Making furtive movements	• Matching hair samples
• Hiding	• Matching blood samples
• Giving evasive answers	• Matching
• Giving contradictory explanations	• DNA profile

© Cengage Learning

LO 3   Hearsay

Officers don't have to rely on direct information alone to make their case for probable cause. They can (and often do) rely on hearsay in probable cause to arrest, namely information they get secondhand from victims, witnesses, other police officers, and professional informants. According to the **hearsay rule**, courts can't admit secondhand evidence to convict defendants in a trial. But, they can rely on it to prove probable cause to arrest.

Of course, even though arrests aren't convictions, they can still cost suspects their liberty—but only long enough to decide whether there's enough evidence to charge them with a crime (Chapter 12) and put them on trial (Chapter 13). At trial, there are legal experts in the courtroom to testify and time to weigh the evidence. However, police officers on the street—and at the station—aren't lawyers, and they're not supposed to be. They don't have the leisure to sort out the evidence they've acquired. As you learned earlier, officers either have to act immediately or forever lose their chance to arrest suspects. Allowing hearsay to show probable cause reflects the deference that courts concede to the realities of police work.

Whether built from direct information or hearsay, probable cause, like reasonable suspicion, depends on the totality of the circumstances in each case. The **totality of the circumstances test** requires courts to determine whether what officers knew *at the time of the arrest* is enough to back up the officers' belief that the suspect has committed or is committing a crime. What's reasonable to an officer isn't the same as what's reasonable to those of us who don't have the officers' training and experience. Our next case excerpt, *Commonwealth v. Dunlap* (2007) considers the totality of circumstances. Two of them, high-crime neighborhood and flight, you learned about in Chapter 3. But it also considers the role of officer training and experience.

The court considered whether Officer Sean Devlin's experience in narcotics arrests and familiarity with the neighborhood qualify as "totality of circumstances" in the probable cause to arrest.

CASE   Did He Have Probable Cause to Arrest?

Commonwealth v. Dunlap
941 A2d 671 (PA 2007)

HISTORY

Nathan Dunlap was convicted in the Philadelphia Municipal Court of possession of illegal drugs. On petition for writ of certiorari, the Court of Common Pleas, Philadelphia County, Criminal Division, affirmed the conviction and sentence. Dunlap appealed. The Superior Court affirmed. Dunlap appealed. The Pennsylvania Supreme Court reversed.

—CAPPY, C.J., and CASTILLE, SAYLOR, EAKIN, BAER, BALDWIN and FITZGERALD, JJ.

BALDWIN, J.

FACTS

On May 4, 2001, Officer Sean Devlin of the Philadelphia Police Department and his partner were conducting plainclothes surveillance at 2700 North Warnock Street in North Philadelphia, which is at the corner of Warnock and Somerset Streets. Officer Devlin watched as Nathan Dunlap (Dunlap) approached another individual standing on that same corner. After approaching, Dunlap engaged in a brief conversation with the other man, handed him money, and was, in return, handed "small objects." After Dunlap walked away, Officer Devlin broadcasted Dunlap's

(continued)

description over police radio. Officer Richard Stein apprehended Dunlap a short distance from the Warnock and Somerset corner. A search of Dunlap revealed three packets that contained crack cocaine.

Officer Devlin testified that, at the time of the encounter, he had been a police officer for almost five years. Further, he had been a member of the drug strike force for nine months. Officer Devlin testified that he had conducted "about 15 to 20" narcotics arrests in the general geographic area. According to him, North Warnock is a residential area that suffers from a high rate of nefarious activity, including drug crimes. Based on his experience and his characterization of the neighborhood, Officer Devlin believed that the transaction he witnessed involved illegal drugs.

Prior to trial, Dunlap filed a motion to suppress the evidence, alleging that the police lacked probable cause to conduct the warrantless arrest and subsequent search. The trial court heard Officer Devlin's testimony. The court denied the motion. Immediately thereafter, Dunlap was convicted of possession of a controlled substance in the Philadelphia Municipal Court. Dunlap then petitioned for a writ of certiorari in the Court of Common Pleas of Philadelphia County, arguing that the Municipal Court erred in denying his motion to suppress. The Court of Common Pleas rejected Dunlap's argument and affirmed the verdict and judgment of sentence. Dunlap timely appealed to the Superior Court. In a published opinion, the Superior Court, sitting en banc, affirmed in a five to four decision, finding that probable cause existed to support the warrantless arrest and subsequent search.

OPINION

We begin our discussion with the relevance of police training and experience to the probable cause determination. To be constitutionally valid, an arrest must be based on probable cause. The existence or non-existence of probable cause is determined by the totality of the circumstances. The totality of the circumstances test requires a Court to determine whether the facts and circumstances which are within the knowledge of the officer at the time of the arrest, and of which he has reasonably trustworthy information, are sufficient to warrant a man of reasonable caution in the belief that the suspect has committed or is committing a crime.

Our decision in *Commonwealth v. Lawson* (1973) is particularly important here as it set forth the relevant factors to be considered in situations such as the one presented in this case. In that case, police officers observed Mr. Lawson and his wife standing on a street corner at 11:50 p.m. They watched using binoculars, and at least one officer used high-powered day and night binoculars. The officers observed three separate transactions occur. In each transaction, a third person approached and handed money to Lawson. Lawson would then walk to his wife, who would retrieve a small sack from her bosom.

Lawson's wife would then take a small item from the sack and hand it to Lawson, who would in turn hand it to the third person. After observing the third transaction conducted in this manner, the police approached the Lawsons, who fled into a local bar where they were soon apprehended. In determining that probable cause existed to arrest the Lawsons, we indicated:

> All the detailed facts and circumstances must be considered. The time is important; the street location is important; the use of a street for commercial transactions is important; the number of such transactions is important; the place where small items were kept by one of the sellers is important; the movements and manners of the parties are important.

This list is not, nor did this Court ever intend it to be, exhaustive. Rather, it offers an illustration of the types of factors properly considered in assessing the existence of probable cause. Nonetheless, the absence of police training and experience from this list is notable.

Since *Lawson*, we have never formally recognized an officer's training and experience, *without more*, as a factor for purposes of the totality of the circumstances test. Instead, we have utilized officer training and experience as an aid in assessing the *Lawson* factors. We review probable cause pursuant to the totality of the circumstances test. In conjunction, we have long held that in applying this test to warrantless arrests, probable cause is to be *viewed* from the vantage point of a prudent, reasonable, cautious police officer on the scene at the time of the arrest *guided by his training and experience*. Thus, we hold that police training and experience, *without more*, is not a fact to be added to the quantum of evidence to determine if probable cause exists, but rather a "lens" through which courts view the quantum of evidence observed at the scene.

We do not seek to minimize the experience gained through years serving on the police force. Quite to the contrary, we recognize that many officers, particularly those with specialized training, are able to recognize trends and methods in the commission of various crimes. He or she may recognize criminal activity where a non-police citizen may not. However, a court cannot simply conclude that probable cause existed based upon nothing more than the number of years an officer has spent on the force. Rather, the officer must demonstrate a nexus between his experience and the search, arrest, or seizure of evidence. By doing so, a court aware of, informed by, and viewing the evidence as the officer in question, aided in assessing his observations by his experience, may properly conclude that probable cause existed. This is true even where the court may have been unable to perceive the existence of probable cause had the court viewed the same evidence through the eyes of a reasonable citizen untrained in law enforcement.

To be clear, we hold that, in reviewing probable cause, a police officer's training and experience is not a probable cause factor. If that were the case, the concept of probable cause as a constitutional barrier between the privacy of the citizen and unwarranted governmental intrusions would be undermined by an officer's ability to bootstrap a hunch based on constitutionally insufficient objective evidence simply by adverting to his experience as the foundation of his suspicion. While probable cause is a fluid concept, and requires only a showing that criminal activity *may* be reasonably inferred from a set of circumstances and need not be shown to, in fact, exist, we must nonetheless remain true to its purposes, one of which is protecting citizens from arbitrary police intrusions. If we were to conclude that a police officer's experience was a factor to be added to *every* probable cause determination, rather than serve as a lens through which to view the facts, then every time an experienced officer begins a shift, probable cause begins to be assessed against all citizens every time they fall under the watchful eye of a suspicious officer who has been on the job for a meaningful period of time. The danger of this, of course, is the potential for innocent citizens being unlawfully seized and/or searched, i.e., being searched or seized with less than probable cause.

For these reasons, we conclude that the Superior Court erred in this case by adding Officer Devlin's training and experience, as though it were a stand-alone factor, to the tally prescribed by *Lawson*. For the reasons that follow, and in light of our cases in this area, we are compelled to conclude that probable cause did not exist to support the warrantless arrest here, even viewing the facts and circumstances through the eyes of a trained officer. Thus, we find that the arrest and subsequent search of Dunlap was unconstitutional.

We begin by reaffirming the premise that every commercial transaction between citizens on a street corner when unidentified property is involved does not give rise to probable cause. First, we find that this case is immediately distinguishable from *Lawson*. In that case, officers observed three separate transactions. After observing the multiple transactions, the officers became suspicious and approached the Lawsons. They, undoubtedly fearing apprehension, fled into a local bar. In the case at bar, Officer Devlin observed only a single transaction, not multiple, complex transactions. Additionally, Dunlap made no attempt to flee upon police intervention as Lawson and his wife did.

This case is more analogous to *Commonwealth v. Banks* than it is to *Lawson*. In *Banks*, a marked police unit observed Banks standing on a Philadelphia street corner. As an unknown female approached, Banks reached into his pocket and retrieved an unknown object and handed it to the female. She, in turn, handed cash to Banks. As the police car approached, Banks fled but was apprehended very shortly thereafter. Banks was searched, resulting in the recovery of cocaine. After acknowledging that flight alone was insufficient to constitute probable cause, we nonetheless recognized that flight coupled with additional facts may establish sufficient probable cause. However, we held that *Banks* was not such a case: "We find that mere

police observation of an exchange of an unidentified item or items on a public street corner for cash (which alone does not establish probable cause) cannot be added to, or melded with the fact that flight occurred (which alone does not establish probable cause to arrest) to constitute probable cause to arrest. Such facts, even when considered together, *fall narrowly short* of establishing probable cause."

The evidence must be suppressed and the conviction reversed. Officer Devlin observed a single, isolated transaction. The transaction occurred in what Officer Devlin claimed was a high-crime area, a *Lawson* factor, which in and of itself does not give rise to probable cause. Based on this limited information, the officer's actions were based only on mere suspicion, not probable cause. It is well settled that mere suspicion alone will not support a finding of probable cause. This is not a case where the officer had prior reason to expect that Dunlap was involved in drug activity or was tipped off by an informant that a drug transaction was set to occur. The officer observed nothing that he could identify as narcotics, or even narcotics paraphernalia. Moreover, in *Banks*, we found that a similar transaction fell narrowly short of probable cause, even coupled with flight. In this case, Dunlap did not even attempt to flee. Accordingly, if probable cause was absent in *Banks* with flight, it must certainly be absent here as well. Even as we view the circumstances from the perspective of a reasonable, experienced police officer, probable cause remains absent. Because there was no probable cause to arrest and search Dunlap, we reverse.

DISSENT

CASTILLE, J.

Banks did not exhaust the variety of circumstances that attend street drug sales. This case is identical to *Banks* in that it involves the common, surreptitious exchange paradigm, but it is different in other material respects. Weighing against probable cause is the absence of flight. The factors weighing in favor of probable cause here, which were absent in *Banks*, include the fact of the officer's training in narcotics investigation, his hands-on experience, which included his experience in this very neighborhood, and the high volume of drug dealing in this particular neighborhood. In my view, these factors justified the suppression judge in concluding that the experienced police officer here acted upon probable cause.

The Majority, adopting the Superior Court dissent below, recharacterizes the additional factors of the specific police officer training and experience as a mere "lens" through which to view other factors, rather than as factors in the analysis in and of themselves. I confess that I do not understand the distinction. Indeed, the value of importing concepts from optometry escapes me. The U.S. Supreme Court—the final word on Fourth Amendment matters—has never embraced the "lens" theory of probable cause review. I would squarely reject it.

(continued)

To declare that the Majority feels practical police experience is only a "lens" through which to view probable cause factors provides no useful guidance to reviewing courts or police officers. How, and to what extent, the courts are to consider the "lens of experience" in reviewing an officer's conduct remains open to infinite permutations. The Commonwealth entrusts the protection of the public to police officers, and to ensure that they discharge their duty effectively, and fairly, provides them with specialized training, which is further enhanced by their on-the-job experience.

What should be preeminent is that the U.S. Supreme Court does not share the Majority's view on the relevance of high-crime locations and an officer's experience in the probable cause equation. That Court has long recognized that crime problems common in the location at issue, and of which police are aware, are an important factor in determining whether probable cause exists. Further, the High Court has recognized that police may rely on their training and experience to draw "inferences and make deductions that might well elude an untrained person." These precedents are the equivalent of the large "E" on the diagnostic eye chart. The Majority's preference for optometric metaphor leads to probable cause blindness. The Majority fails to cite or discuss a single case from the U.S. Supreme Court respecting probable cause, notwithstanding the centrality of such precedent to the Commonwealth's presentation.

Today's decision provides no useful standard for the courts. It provides even less to the police officers who witness surreptitious transactions in high-crime areas. In the wake of today's decision, officers on the street will now be left to guess the magic number of drug arrests before their observations will be deemed sufficiently supported by experience to allow the relevant factors to give rise to probable cause. And, in the interim, the criminally oppressed good citizens living in these neighborhoods will be consigned to a Court-ordered state of helplessness.

A further difficulty in the Majority's approach is its failure to appreciate just how reasonable and non-arbitrary the limited police response is in a case such as this. Because the central command of the Fourth Amendment is reasonableness, the restraints that courts impose on police should account for the practical realities of law enforcement. *Atwater v. City of Lago Vista,* (2001) [excerpt on p. 188] "Often enough, the Fourth Amendment has to be applied on the spur (and in the heat) of the moment, and the object in implementing its command of reasonableness is to draw standards sufficiently clear and simple to be applied with a fair prospect of surviving judicial second-guessing months and years after an arrest or search is made." The police officer here did nothing unreasonable. An apprehension following a street drug sale does not lend itself to the traditional "intermediate response" of a stop and frisk for weapons. A weapons frisk is of no avail when the object being sought is not a weapon, but a tiny vial or packet of drugs, or drug transaction proceeds. To conclusively confirm or dispel a reasonable belief that a suspect was dealing illegal narcotics, police need to see the goods. That is all the officer did in this case. The search was targeted and minimally intrusive. Such a limited search immediately confirms or dispels suspicion. The Fourth Amendment admits a more flexible analysis.

Questions

1. List all the facts and circumstances supporting the majority's conclusion that Officer Devlin lacked probable cause to arrest Nathan Dunlap.

2. Summarize the dissent's arguments that Officer Devlin had probable cause to believe that a crime was being committed and that Dunlap committed it.

3. Does the Court give clear guidelines in regard to what constitutes probable cause to arrest? Explain.

YOU DECIDE
Was the Officer's Experience and Knowledge of the Neighborhood Probable Cause to Arrest?

LO 3 SCOTUS denied the petition for certiorari in *Dunlap.* Chief Justice Roberts dissented from the denial. (Recall the "Rule of 4," p. 22.) Dissenters don't always write their reasons for opposing the denial. But, lucky for us, Chief Roberts wrote one for this case, giving us useful insights into the probable cause to arrest requirement. After reading the chief justice's opinion, would you grant "cert"?

North Philly, May 4, 2001. Officer Sean Devlin, Narcotics Strike Force, was working the morning shift. Undercover surveillance. The neighborhood? Tough as a three-dollar steak. Devlin knew. Five years on the beat, nine months with the Strike Force. He'd made fifteen, twenty drug busts in the neighborhood. Devlin spotted him: a lone man on the corner. Another approached. Quick exchange of words. Cash handed over; small objects handed back. Each man then quickly on his own way. Devlin knew the guy wasn't buying bus tokens. He radioed a description and Officer Stein picked up the buyer. Sure enough: three bags of crack in the guy's pocket. Head downtown and book him. Just another day at the office.

That was not good enough for the Pennsylvania Supreme Court, which held in a divided decision that the police lacked probable cause to arrest the defendant. The court concluded that a "single, isolated transaction" in a high-crime area was insufficient to justify the arrest, given that the officer did not actually see the drugs, there was no tip from an informant, and the defendant did not attempt to flee. I disagree with that conclusion, and dissent from the denial of certiorari. A drug purchase was not the only possible explanation for the defendant's conduct, but it was certainly likely enough to give rise to probable cause.

The probable-cause standard is a nontechnical conception that deals with the factual and practical considerations of everyday life on which reasonable and prudent men, not legal technicians, act. What is required is simply a reasonable ground for belief of guilt, a probability, and not a prima facie showing, of criminal activity. A police officer may draw inferences based on his own experience in deciding whether probable cause exists, including inferences that might well elude an untrained person.

On the facts of this case, I think the police clearly had probable cause to arrest the defendant. An officer with drug interdiction experience in the neighborhood saw two men on a street corner—with no apparent familiarity or prior interaction—make a quick hand-to-hand exchange of cash for small objects. This exchange took place in a high-crime neighborhood known for drug activity, far from any legitimate businesses. Perhaps it is possible to imagine innocent explanations for this conduct, but I cannot come up with any remotely as likely as the drug transaction Devlin believed he had witnessed. In any event, an officer is not required to eliminate all innocent explanations for a suspicious set of facts to have probable cause to make an arrest. In making a determination of probable cause the relevant inquiry is not whether particular conduct is innocent or guilty, but the degree of suspicion that attaches to particular types of noncriminal acts.

The Pennsylvania Supreme Court emphasized that the police did not actually see any drugs. But Officer Devlin and

his partner were conducting undercover surveillance. From a distance, it would be difficult to have a clear view of the small objects that changed hands. As the Commonwealth explains in its petition for certiorari, the "classic" drug transaction is a hand-to-hand exchange, on the street, of cash for small objects. The Pennsylvania Supreme Court's decision will make it more difficult for the police to conduct drug interdiction in high-crime areas, unless they employ the riskier practice of having undercover officers actually make a purchase or sale of drugs.

The Pennsylvania court also noted that the defendant did not flee. Flight is hardly a prerequisite to a finding of probable cause. A defendant may well decide that the odds of escape do not justify adding another charge to that of drug possession. And of course there is no suggestion in the record that the defendant had any chance to flee—he was caught redhanded.

Aside from its importance for law enforcement, this question has divided state courts, a traditional ground warranting review on certiorari. The New Jersey Supreme Court has held that an "experienced narcotics officer" had probable cause to make an arrest when—in a vacant lot in a high-drug neighborhood—he "saw defendant and his companion give money to [a] third person in exchange for small unknown objects." The Rhode Island Supreme Court reached the same conclusion in a case where the defendants—through their car windows—exchanged cash for a small "bag of suspected narcotics." In contrast, the Colorado Supreme Court held that a hand-to-hand exchange of unknown objects did not give the police probable cause to make an arrest, even where one of the men was a known drug dealer. All these cases have unique factual wrinkles, as any probable-cause case would, but the core fact pattern is the same: experienced police officers observing hand-to-hand exchanges of cash for small, unknown objects in high-crime neighborhoods.

The Pennsylvania Supreme Court speculated that such an exchange could have been perfectly innocent. But as Judge Friendly has pointed out, "judges are not required to exhibit a naivete from which ordinary citizens are free." Based not only on common sense but also his experience as a narcotics officer and his previous work in the neighborhood, Officer Devlin concluded that what happened on that street corner was probably a drug transaction. That is by far the most reasonable conclusion, even though our cases only require it to be a reasonable conclusion.

I would grant certiorari and reverse the judgment of the Pennsylvania Supreme Court.

The petition for a writ of certiorari is denied.
Pennsylvania v. Dunlap 555 U.S. 964 (2008)

THE ARREST WARRANT REQUIREMENT

In most situations, probable cause without an arrest warrant is enough to make an arrest a reasonable Fourth Amendment seizure. But, if officers want to arrest someone in her home, they have to get an arrest warrant. For centuries before the Fourth Amendment was adopted, felony arrests outside the home were lawful without warrants; probable cause was enough. (Note that warrants were required for misdemeanor arrests, unless the offense took place in the officer's presence.)

Let's turn to the three elements of obtaining a warrant to arrest suspects in their homes:

1. *A neutral magistrate.* A disinterested judge has to decide whether there is probable cause before officers arrest suspects.

2. *An affidavit (sworn statement).* This is made by someone (nearly always a law enforcement officer) who swears under oath to the facts and circumstances amounting to probable cause.

3. *The name of the person to be arrested.* The warrant has to identify specifically the person(s) the officers are going to arrest.

A Neutral Magistrate

The requirement that officers get approval from a **neutral magistrate** (one who will fairly and adequately review the warrant) before they arrest assumes that magistrates carefully review the information officers provide. However, both the outcomes of cases and social science research suggest otherwise. According to Professor Abraham S. Goldstein (1987):

> There is little reason to be reassured by what we know about magistrates in operation. The magistrate can know there are factual issues to be explored only if he looks behind the particulars presented. Yet it is rare for such initiatives to be taken. Most magistrates devote very little time to appraising the affidavit's sufficiency. They assume that the affiant is being honest.
>
> They tend to ask no questions and to issue warrants in routine fashion. Over the years the police have adapted their practice not only to the law's requirements but also to the opportunities presented by the manner in which the law is administered. They have often relied on the magistrate's passivity to insulate from review affidavits that are only apparently sufficient—sometimes purposely presenting them through officers who are "ignorant of the circumstances" and, therefore, less likely to provide awkward details in the unlikely event that questions are asked. . . . (1182)

Summarizing the results of a study of probable cause determination, Professor Goldstein found:

> Proceedings before magistrates generally lasted only two to three minutes and the magistrate rarely asked any questions to penetrate the boilerplate language or the hearsay in the warrant. Witnesses other than the police applicant were never called. And the police often engaged in "magistrate shopping" for judges who would give only minimal scrutiny to the application. (1183)

An Affidavit

The Fourth Amendment requires that magistrates base their probable cause determination on written information sworn to under oath (**affidavit**). The pain of perjury (the crime of lying under oath) charges encourages truthfulness. If the affidavit establishes probable cause, the magistrate issues the warrant.

The written statement isn't always enough to establish probable cause; sometimes it's purposely vague. For example, police officers who want to preserve the anonymity of undercover agents may make only vague references to the circumstances surrounding the information (*Fraizer v. Roberts* 1971). In these cases, supplemental oral information can satisfy the requirement in some jurisdictions. However, other courts require that all information be in writing (*Orr v. State* 1980).

Officers can appear before magistrates in person with their affidavits. Or, in many jurisdictions, they can do so electronically. According to the Federal Rules of Criminal Procedure, "A magistrate judge may consider information communicated by telephone or other reliable electronic means when reviewing a complaint or deciding whether to issue a warrant or summons" (Rule 4.1(a))

Some argue that modern electronic advances should eliminate the need for most warrantless arrests. According to Professor Craig Bradley (1985), a former clerk to Chief Justice Rehnquist, if courts adopted this practice:

> The Supreme Court could actually enforce the warrant doctrine to which it has paid lip service for so many years. That is, a warrant is always required for every search and seizure when it is practicable to obtain one. However, in order that this requirement be workable and not be swallowed by its exception, the warrant need not be in writing but rather may be phoned or radioed into a magistrate (where it will be tape recorded and the recording preserved) who will authorize or forbid the search orally. By making the procedure for obtaining a warrant less difficult (while only marginally reducing the safeguards it provides), the number of cases where "emergencies" justify an exception to the warrant requirement should be very small. (1471)

The Name of the Person to Be Arrested

The Fourth Amendment requires that the warrant identify the person officers intend to arrest. To satisfy this **particularity requirement**, the Federal Rules of Criminal Procedure provide that an arrest warrant "must contain the defendant's name or, if it is unknown, a name or description by which the defendant can be identified with reasonable certainty" (4[b][1][A]).

ARRESTS IN HOMES

Probable cause without a warrant is enough to satisfy the Fourth Amendment reasonableness requirement when officers want to make felony arrests outside the home. But they have to get a warrant to enter a home to arrest—except in emergencies. Let's look first at entering a home to arrest with an arrest warrant. Then, we'll look at exigent circumstances (emergencies) that make reasonable entering homes to arrest without warrants.

Entering Homes to Arrest

Why does the Fourth Amendment require a warrant to arrest in a home? Because officials entering homes "is the chief evil" the Fourth Amendment was intended to protect against (*U.S. v. U.S. District Court* 1972, 313). The Fourth Amendment has "drawn a firm line at the entrance to a home." Violating the sanctity of the home "is simply too substantial an invasion to allow without a warrant" (*Payton v. New York* 1980, 589; *Kirk v. Louisiana* 2002, 637). According to the Court in *Payton v. New York*, if it's a "routine case," and officers have "ample" time to get a warrant, the Fourth Amendment commands them to get one.

> Police officers had probable cause to believe that Theodore Payton had committed a robbery and a murder. At about 7:30 in the morning, six officers went to Payton's apartment without an arrest warrant, intending to arrest him. They heard music inside, and the lights were on. They knocked, but no one answered the door. After waiting for about a half hour, they broke open the metal door with crowbars, and entered. No one was there, but they seized an empty shell in plain view, which was later used as evidence in Payton's murder trial.

> Justice Stevens wrote, "we have no occasion to consider the sort of emergency or dangerous situation, described in our cases as 'exigent circumstances,' that would justify a warrantless entry into a home for the purpose of either arrest or search" (583).

Exigent Circumstances

In **exigent circumstances**, (emergency) situations where officers have to take immediate action to make an arrest, officers don't need to get an arrest warrant before they enter a home to arrest. The most common exigency is "hot pursuit," first recognized by the U.S. Supreme Court in *Warden v. Hayden* (1967).

In *Hayden*, police were informed that an armed robbery had taken place, and that Bennie Joe Hayden had entered 2111 Cocoa Lane less than five minutes before the officers had arrived. According to the Court, the officers acted "reasonably when they entered the house and began to search for a man of the description they had been given and for weapons which he had used in the robbery or might use against them." The Fourth Amendment doesn't mandate that officers put off their investigation if the delay would "gravely endanger their lives or the lives of others. Speed here was essential, and only a thorough search of the house for persons and weapons could have insured that Hayden was the only man present and that the police had control of all weapons which could be used against them or to effect an escape (298–99)."

Table 5.4 lists the major exigent circumstances that allow officers to enter homes to arrest without a warrant.

In our next case excerpt, *Brigham City, Utah v. Charles Stuart, Shayne Taylor, and Sandra Taylor* (2006), the U.S. Supreme Court defined imminent danger as an exigent circumstance that can eliminate the need for an arrest warrant to enter homes.

TABLE 5.4 Exigent circumstances that may make entering homes to arrest without arrest warrants reasonable

"Hot pursuit." *Warden v. Hayden*, 387 U.S. 294 (1967)	Police were informed that an armed robbery had taken place and that Bennie Joe Hayden had entered 2111 Cocoa Lane less than five minutes before the officers had arrived.
Imminent destruction of evidence. *Colorado v. Mendez*, 986 P.2d 285 (Colo. 1999)	Two officers smelled the strong odor of burning marijuana coming from a hotel room. They instructed the manager to open the door with the master key, entered, and found Edgar Mendez flushing the marijuana down the toilet.
Imminent escape of suspect. *Warden v. Hayden*, 387 U.S. 294 (1967)	The police were informed that an armed robbery had taken place, and that the suspect had entered 2111 Cocoa Lane less than five minutes before they reached it. They acted reasonably when they entered the house and began to search for a man of the description they had been given and for weapons which he had used in the robbery or might use against them. Speed here was essential, and only a thorough search of the house for persons and weapons could have ensured that Hayden was the only man present and that the police had control of all weapons which could be used against them or to effect an escape.

© Cengage Learning

In *Brigham City, Utah v. Charles Stuart, Shayne Taylor, and Sandra Taylor* **(2006)**, the U.S. Supreme Court defined imminent danger as an exigent circumstance that can eliminate the need for an arrest warrant to enter homes.

CASE

Did an Emergency Justify the Entry to Arrest without a Warrant?

Brigham City, Utah v. Charles Stuart, Shayne Taylor, and Sandra Taylor
547 U.S. 398 (2006)

HISTORY

Defendants Charles W. Stuart, Sandra Taylor, and Shayne T. Taylor were charged in state court with contributing to the delinquency of a minor, disorderly conduct, and intoxication. They filed a motion to suppress. The First District Court, Brigham City Department, granted the motion. The City appealed. The Utah Court of Appeals affirmed. The City again appealed. The Utah Supreme Court affirmed. The U.S. Supreme Court reversed.

ROBERTS, C.J., delivered the opinion for a unanimous Court. STEVENS, J., filed a concurring opinion.

—ROBERTS, CJ. for a unanimous Court.

In this case we consider whether police may enter a home without a warrant when they have an objectively reasonable basis for believing that an occupant is seriously injured or imminently threatened with such injury. We conclude that they may.

FACTS

This case arises out of a melee that occurred in a Brigham City, Utah, home in the early morning hours of July 23, 2000. At about 3 a.m., four police officers responded to a call regarding a loud party at a residence. Upon arriving at the house, they heard shouting from inside, and

(continued)

proceeded down the driveway to investigate. There, they observed two juveniles drinking beer in the backyard. They entered the backyard, and saw—through a screen door and windows—an altercation taking place in the kitchen of the home.

According to the testimony of one of the officers, four adults were attempting, with some difficulty, to restrain a juvenile. The juvenile eventually "broke free, swung a fist and struck one of the adults in the face." The officer testified that he observed the victim of the blow spitting blood into a nearby sink. The other adults continued to try to restrain the juvenile, pressing him up against a refrigerator with such force that the refrigerator began moving across the floor. At this point, an officer opened the screen door and announced the officers' presence. Amid the tumult, nobody noticed. The officer entered the kitchen and again cried out, and as the occupants slowly became aware that the police were on the scene, the altercation ceased.

The officers subsequently arrested Charles Stuart, Shayne Taylor, and Sandra Taylor (respondents), and charged them with contributing to the delinquency of a minor, disorderly conduct, and intoxication. In the trial court, respondents filed a motion to suppress all evidence obtained after the officers entered the home, arguing that the warrantless entry violated the Fourth Amendment. The court granted the motion, and the Utah Court of Appeals affirmed.

Before the Supreme Court of Utah, Brigham City argued that although the officers lacked a warrant, their entry was nevertheless reasonable on either of two grounds. The court rejected both contentions and, over two dissenters, affirmed. First, the court held that the injury caused by the juvenile's punch was insufficient to trigger the so-called "emergency aid doctrine" because it did not give rise to an "objectively reasonable belief that an unconscious, semi-conscious, or missing person feared injured or dead [was] in the home." Furthermore, the court suggested that the doctrine was inapplicable because the officers had not sought to assist the injured adult, but instead had acted "exclusively in their law enforcement capacity."

The court also held that the entry did not fall within the exigent circumstances exception to the warrant requirement. This exception applies, the court explained, where police have probable cause and where "a reasonable person [would] believe that the entry was necessary to prevent physical harm to the officers or other persons." Under this standard, the court stated, the potential harm need not be as serious as that required to invoke the emergency aid exception. Although it found the case "a close and difficult call," the court nevertheless concluded that the officers' entry was not justified by exigent circumstances.

We granted certiorari, in light of differences among state courts and the Courts of Appeals concerning the appropriate Fourth Amendment standard governing warrantless entry by law enforcement in an emergency situation.

OPINION

It is a basic principle of Fourth Amendment law that searches and seizures inside a home without a warrant are presumptively unreasonable. Nevertheless, because the ultimate touchstone of the Fourth Amendment is "reasonableness," the warrant requirement is subject to certain exceptions. We have held, for example, that law enforcement officers may make a warrantless entry onto private property to fight a fire and investigate its cause, to prevent the imminent destruction of evidence, or to engage in "hot pursuit" of a fleeing suspect. Warrants are generally required to search a person's home or his person unless the exigencies of the situation make the needs of law enforcement so compelling that the warrantless search is objectively reasonable under the Fourth Amendment.

One exigency obviating the requirement of a warrant is the need to assist persons who are seriously injured or threatened with such injury. The need to protect or preserve life or avoid serious injury is justification for what would be otherwise illegal absent an exigency or emergency. Accordingly, law enforcement officers may enter a home without a warrant to render emergency assistance to an injured occupant or to protect an occupant from imminent injury.

We think the officers' entry here was plainly reasonable under the circumstances. The officers were responding, at 3 o'clock in the morning, to complaints about a loud party. As they approached the house, they could hear from within "an altercation occurring, some kind of a fight." "It was loud and it was tumultuous." The officers heard "thumping and crashing" and people yelling "stop, stop" and "get off me." As the trial court found, "it was obvious that knocking on the front door" would have been futile.

The noise seemed to be coming from the back of the house; after looking in the front window and seeing nothing, the officers proceeded around back to investigate further. They found two juveniles drinking beer in the backyard. From there, they could see that a fracas was taking place inside the kitchen. A juvenile, fists clenched, was being held back by several adults. As the officers watch, he breaks free and strikes one of the adults in the face, sending the adult to the sink spitting blood.

In these circumstances, the officers had an objectively reasonable basis for believing both that the injured adult might need help and that the violence in the kitchen was just beginning. Nothing in the Fourth Amendment required them to wait until another blow rendered someone "unconscious" or "semi-conscious" or worse before entering. The role of a peace officer includes preventing violence and restoring order, not simply rendering first aid to casualties; an officer is not like a boxing (or hockey) referee, poised to stop a bout only if it becomes too one-sided.

The manner of the officers' entry was also reasonable. After witnessing the punch, one of the officers opened the screen door and yelled in "police." When nobody heard him, he stepped into the kitchen and announced himself again. Only then did the tumult subside. The officer's announcement of his presence was at least equivalent to a knock on the screen door. Indeed, it was probably the only option that had even a chance of rising above the din.

Under these circumstances, there was no violation of the Fourth Amendment's knock-and-announce rule. Furthermore, once the announcement was made, the officers were free to enter; it would serve no purpose to require them to stand dumbly at the door awaiting a response while those within brawled on, oblivious to their presence.

Accordingly, we REVERSE the judgment of the Supreme Court of Utah, and REMAND the case for further proceedings not inconsistent with this opinion.

It is so ordered.

CONCURRENCE

STEVENS, J.

This is an odd flyspeck of a case. The charges that have been pending against respondents for the past six years are minor offenses—intoxication, contributing to the delinquency of a minor, and disorderly conduct—two of which could have been proved by evidence that was gathered by the responding officers before they entered the home. The maximum punishment for these crimes ranges between 90 days and six months in jail. And the Court's unanimous opinion restating well-settled rules of federal law is so clearly persuasive that it is hard to imagine the outcome was ever in doubt.

Under these circumstances, the only difficult question is which of the following is the most peculiar: (1) that the Utah trial judge, the intermediate state appellate court, and the Utah Supreme Court all found a Fourth Amendment violation on these facts; (2) that the prosecution chose to pursue this matter all the way to the United States Supreme Court; or (3) that this Court voted to grant the petition for a writ of certiorari.

A possible explanation for the first is that the suppression ruling was correct as a matter of Utah law, and neither trial counsel nor the trial judge bothered to identify the Utah Constitution as an independent basis for the decision because they did not expect the prosecution to appeal. The most plausible explanation for the latter two decisions is that they were made so police officers in Utah may enter a home without a warrant when they see ongoing violence—we are, of course, reversing the Utah Supreme Court's conclusion to the contrary. But that purpose, laudable though it may be, cannot be achieved in this case. Our holding today addresses only the limitations placed by the Federal Constitution on the search at

issue; we have no authority to decide whether the police in this case violated the Utah Constitution.

The Utah Supreme Court, however, has made clear that the Utah Constitution provides greater protection to the privacy of the home than does the Fourth Amendment. And it complained in this case of respondents' failure to raise or adequately brief a state constitutional challenge, thus preventing the state courts from deciding the case on anything other than Fourth Amendment grounds. "Surprised" by "the reluctance of litigants to take up and develop a state constitutional analysis," the court expressly invited future litigants to bring challenges under the Utah Constitution to enable it to fulfill its "responsibility as guardians of the individual liberty of our citizens" and "undertake a principled exploration of the interplay between federal and state protections of individual rights."

The fact that this admonishment and request came from the Utah Supreme Court in this very case not only demonstrates that the prosecution selected the wrong case for establishing the rule it wants, but also indicates that the Utah Supreme Court would probably adopt the same rule as a matter of state constitutional law that we reject today under the Federal Constitution.

Whether or not that forecast is accurate, I can see no reason for this Court to cause the Utah courts to redecide the question as a matter of state law. Federal interests are not offended when a single State elects to provide greater protection for its citizens than the Federal Constitution requires. Indeed, I continue to believe that a policy of judicial restraint—one that allows other decisional bodies to have the last word in legal interpretation until it is truly necessary for this Court to intervene—enables this Court to make its most effective contribution to our federal system of government. Thus, while I join the Court's opinion, I remain persuaded that my vote to deny the State's petition for certiorari was correct.

Questions

1. Summarize the details of the arrest of Charles Stuart, Shayne Taylor, and Sandra Taylor.

2. List the "exigent circumstances" that the U.S. Supreme Court found were present in the case.

3. Summarize the Court's arguments for finding that exigent circumstances were present.

4. List the reasons why Justice Stevens wrote a concurring opinion. Should the U.S. Supreme Court not have taken what Justice Stevens called this "odd flyspeck" of a case?

5. Why should anyone object to the officers' entering the house? Why did the officers enter the house? To arrest the adults or to help people in trouble?

ARREST BY FORCE

Whether the manner of an arrest was reasonable is affected by whether the amount of force, if any, was reasonably necessary. Usually, when we hear about the use of force to make an arrest, it's when the officers have killed a suspect. This distorts the public's view of the frequency of the use of **deadly force**—restraint capable of producing death. In reality, there are far more forcible arrests using nondeadly force than deadly force. And the vast majority of all arrests are made without the use of any force at all. Keeping these facts in mind, let's look at the use of deadly and nondeadly force to arrest suspects.

Deadly Force

Throughout most of our history, states have followed the ancient common-law rule that allowed officers to use deadly force when it was necessary to apprehend fleeing felons. By the 1960s, many police departments had adopted rules that restricted this common-law rule. The gist of these rules is that officers can use deadly force only under two conditions: (1) it's necessary to apprehend "dangerous" suspects, *and* (2) it doesn't put innocent people in danger. In *Tennessee v. Garner* (1985), the U.S. Supreme Court adopted these two rules as Fourth Amendment requirements in using deadly force to make arrests.

In *Tennessee v. Garner* (1985), the U.S. Supreme Court adopted two Fourth Amendment requirements for the test of whether deadly force by an officer is reasonable.

CASE

Is Shooting a Fleeing Suspected Felon in the Back an Unreasonable Seizure?

Tennessee v. Garner
471 U.S. 1 (1985)

HISTORY

Memphis Police Department Officer Elton Hymon shot and killed fifteen-year-old Edward Garner when Garner fled the scene of a suspected burglary. His father, Cleamtree Garner, sued the Department under U.S.C.A. § 1983 [discussed in Chapter 11] for violating his son's Fourth Amendment right against unreasonable seizures. The U.S. District Court ruled that the shooting was not an unreasonable seizure. The U.S. Court of Appeals reversed. The U.S. Supreme Court affirmed.

—WHITE, J., joined by BRENNAN, MARSHALL, BLACKMUN, POWELL, and STEVENS, JJ.

FACTS

At about 10:45 p.m. on October 3, 1974, Memphis Police Officers Elton Hymon and Leslie Wright were dispatched to

answer a "prowler inside call." Upon arriving at the scene they saw a woman standing on her porch gesturing toward the adjacent house. She told them she had heard glass breaking and that "they" or "someone" was breaking in next door. While Wright radioed the dispatcher to say that they were on the scene, Hymon went behind the house. He heard a door slam and saw someone run across the backyard.

The fleeing suspect, Edward Garner, stopped at a six-feet-high chain link fence at the edge of the yard. With the aid of a flashlight, Hymon was able to see Garner's face and hands. He saw no sign of a weapon, and though not certain, was "reasonably sure" and "figured" that Garner was unarmed. He thought Garner was 17 or 18 years old and about 5'5" or 5'7" tall. While Garner was crouched at the base of the fence, Hymon called out "police, halt" and took a few steps toward him.

Garner began to climb over the fence. Convinced that if Garner made it over the fence he would elude capture, Hymon shot him. The bullet hit Garner in the back of the head. Garner was taken by ambulance to a hospital, where he died on the operating table. Ten dollars and a purse taken from the house were found on his body.

In using deadly force to prevent escape, Hymon was acting under the authority of a Tennessee statute, and pursuant to Police Department policy. The statute provides that "if, after notice of the intention to arrest the defendant, he either flee or forcibly resist, the officer may use all the necessary means to effect the arrest." Tenn. Code Ann. § 40–7–108 (1982). The Department policy was slightly more restrictive than the statute, but still allowed the use of deadly force in cases of burglary. The incident was reviewed by the Memphis Police Firearm's Review Board and presented to a grand jury. Neither took any action.

Cleamtree Garner, Edward's father, then brought this action in the Federal District Court for the Western District of Tennessee, seeking damages under 42 U.S.C. § 1983 for asserted violations of Garner's constitutional rights. The complaint alleged that the shooting violated the Fourth, Fifth, Sixth, Eighth, and Fourteenth Amendments of the United States Constitution. It named as defendants Officer Hymon, the Police Department, its Director, and the Mayor and City of Memphis.

After a three-day bench trial, the District Court entered judgment for all defendants. It dismissed the claims against the Mayor and the Director for lack of evidence. It then concluded that Hymon's actions were authorized by the Tennessee statute. Hymon had employed the only reasonable and practicable means of preventing Garner's escape. Garner had "recklessly and heedlessly attempted to vault over the fence to escape, thereby assuming the risk of being fired upon." The District Court found that the statute, and Hymon's actions, were constitutional. The Court of Appeals reversed and remanded.

OPINION

Whenever an officer restrains the freedom of a person to walk away, he has seized that person. There can be no question that apprehension by the use of deadly force is a seizure subject to the reasonableness requirement of the Fourth Amendment. A police officer may arrest a person if he has probable cause to believe that person committed a crime. Tennessee and the City of Memphis argue that if this requirement is satisfied the Fourth Amendment has nothing to say about how that seizure is made. The submission ignores the many cases in which this Court, by balancing the extent of the intrusion against the need for it, has examined the reasonableness of the manner in which a search or seizure is conducted.

The use of deadly force to prevent the escape of *all* felony suspects, whatever the circumstances, is constitutionally unreasonable. It is not better that *all* felony suspects die than that they escape. [Emphasis added] Where the suspect poses no immediate threat to the officer and no threat to others, the harm resulting from failing to apprehend him does not justify the use of deadly force to do so. It is no doubt unfortunate when a suspect who is in sight escapes, but the fact the police arrive a little late or are a little slower afoot does not always justify killing the suspect. A police officer may not seize an unarmed, nondangerous suspect by shooting him dead. The Tennessee statute is unconstitutional insofar as it authorizes the use of deadly force against such fleeing suspects.

Officer Hymon could not reasonably have believed that Garner—young, slight, and unarmed—posed any threat. Indeed, Hymon never attempted to justify his actions on any basis other than the need to prevent escape. The fact that Garner was a suspected burglar could not, without regard to the other circumstances, automatically justify the use of deadly force. Hymon did not have probable cause to believe that Garner, whom he correctly believed to be unarmed, posed any physical danger to himself or to others.

AFFIRMED.

DISSENT

O'CONNOR, J., joined by BURGER, C.J., and REHNQUIST, J.

The public interest involved in the use of deadly force as a last resort to apprehend a fleeing burglary suspect relates primarily to the serious nature of the crime. Household burglaries represent not only the illegal entry into a person's home, but also "pose a real risk of serious harm to others." According to recent Department of Justice statistics, "Three-fifths of all rapes in the home, three-fifths of all home robberies, and about a third of home aggravated and simple assaults are committed by burglars."

Against the strong public interests justifying the conduct at issue here must be weighed the individual interests implicated in the use of deadly force by police officers. The majority declares that "the suspect's fundamental interest in his own life need not be elaborated upon." This blithe assertion hardly provides an adequate substitute for the majority's failure to acknowledge the distinctive manner in which the suspect's interest in his life is even exposed to risk. For purposes of this case, we must recall that the police officer, in the course of investigating a nighttime burglary, had reasonable cause to arrest the suspect and ordered him to halt. The officer's use of force resulted because the suspected burglar refused to heed this command and the officer reasonably believed that there was no means short of firing his weapon to apprehend the suspect.

The policeman's hands should not be tied merely because of the possibility that the suspect will fail to cooperate with legitimate actions by law enforcement personnel.

(continued)

Questions

1. Should the Fourth Amendment apply to the manner of arrest? Defend your answer.

2. Professor H. Richard Uviller (1986), a longtime student of police power and the Constitution, commented on the decision in *Tennessee v. Garner*:

   It is embarrassing for a law professor to be blindsided in his own territory. But the truth is, I didn't see it coming. It had never occurred to me that a police officer shooting to kill a fleeing felon might be engaging in an unconstitutional search and seizure. Of course, I can see the connection now that it has been explained to me, but I did not spontaneously equate a deadly shot with an arrest. And I have had some prior acquaintance not only with the Fourth Amendment, but specifically with the issue of the bullet aimed at the back of a retreating felon. (706)

   Should shooting a suspect be considered a Fourth Amendment "seizure"?

3. Professor Uviller asks the following questions: Would the rule in this case permit an officer to shoot a drunk driver swerving erratically down the road headed toward a town? A person wanted for a series of violent crimes but not presently armed who flees from the police? How would you answer Professor Uviller's questions? Defend your answers.

4. Will this rule embolden criminals? Did the Court tilt the balance too far toward protecting criminal defendants and away from protecting society? Defend your answer.

LO 5   Nondeadly Force

Shooting is the most dramatic and publicized use of force to arrest suspects, but, in practice, officers are far more likely to use nondeadly force. The U.S. Supreme Court applied the objective standard in the nondeadly force case, *Graham v. Connor* (1989), our next case excerpt. According to the **objective standard of reasonable force**, the Fourth Amendment permits officers to use the amount of force necessary to apprehend and bring suspects under control. It's objective because it doesn't depend on the officer's intent or motives. The Court put it this way: "An officer's evil intentions will not make a Fourth Amendment violation out of an objectively reasonable use of force; nor will an officer's good intentions make an objectively unreasonable use of force constitutional" (398).

In *Graham v. Connor* (1989), the U.S. Supreme Court established the criteria that lower courts have to use to decide whether police use of force is "objectively reasonable."

CASE   Was the Police Use of Force Excessive?

Graham v. Connor
490 U.S. 386 (1989)

HISTORY

Dethorne Graham, a diabetic, sued several police officers to recover damages for injuries he suffered when the officers used physical force against him during an investigatory stop. The U.S. District Court directed a verdict for the defendant police officers. The court of appeals affirmed. The U.S. Supreme Court granted certiorari and reversed.

—REHNQUIST, C.J., joined by WHITE, STEVENS, O'CONNOR, SCALIA, and KENNEDY, JJ.

FACTS

On November 12, 1984, Dethorne Graham, a diabetic, felt the onset of an insulin reaction. He asked a friend, William Berry, to drive him to a nearby convenience store so he could purchase some orange juice to counteract the reaction. Berry agreed, but when Graham entered the store, he saw a number of people ahead of him in the checkout line. Concerned about the delay, he hurried out of the store and asked Berry to drive him to a friend's house instead.

Respondent Connor, an officer of the Charlotte, North Carolina, Police Department, saw Graham hastily enter and leave the store. The officer became suspicious that something was amiss and followed Berry's car. About one-half mile from the store, he made an investigative stop. Although Berry told Connor that Graham was simply suffering from a "sugar reaction," the officer ordered Berry and Graham to wait while he found out what, if anything, had happened at the convenience store. When Officer Connor returned to his patrol car to call for backup assistance, Graham got out of the car, ran around it twice, and finally sat down on the curb, where he passed out briefly.

In the ensuing confusion, a number of other Charlotte police officers arrived on the scene in response to Officer Connor's request for backup. One of the officers rolled Graham over on the sidewalk and cuffed his hands tightly behind his back, ignoring Berry's pleas to get him some sugar. Another officer said: "I've seen a lot of people with sugar diabetes that never acted like this. Ain't nothing wrong with the M. F. but drunk. Lock the S. B. up." Several officers then lifted Graham up from behind, carried him over to Berry's car, and placed him face down on its hood.

Regaining consciousness, Graham asked the officers to check in his wallet for a diabetic decal that he carried. In response, one of the officers told him to "shut up" and shoved his face down against the hood of the car. Four officers grabbed Graham and threw him headfirst into the police car. A friend of Graham's brought some orange juice to the car, but the officers refused to let him have it. Finally, Officer Connor received a report that Graham had done nothing wrong at the convenience store, and the officers drove him home and released him.

At some point during his encounter with the police, Graham sustained a broken foot, cuts on his wrists, a bruised forehead, and an injured shoulder; he also claims to have developed a loud ringing in his right ear that continues to this day. He commenced this action under 42 U.S.C.§ 1983 against the individual officers involved in the incident, all of whom are respondents here, alleging that they had used excessive force in making the investigatory stop, in violation of "rights secured to him under the Fourteenth Amendment to the United States Constitution and 42 U.S.C. § 1983."

[Civil Rights Act actions (called § 1983 actions because they're brought under Title 42, Section 1983, of the Civil Rights Act of 1871, passed just after the Civil War) allow plaintiffs to go into federal courts to sue state police officers and their agency heads; county sheriffs and their deputies; and municipal police officers and their chiefs for violating plaintiffs' federal constitutional rights.]

The case was tried before a jury. At the close of petitioner's evidence, respondents moved for a directed verdict. In ruling on that motion, the District Court considered the following four factors, which it identified as "the factors to be considered in determining when the excessive use of force gives rise to a cause of action under § 1983":

1. the need for the application of force;
2. the relationship between that need and the amount of force that was used;
3. the extent of the injury inflicted; and
4. whether the force was applied in a good faith effort to maintain and restore discipline or maliciously and sadistically for the very purpose of causing harm.

Finding that the amount of force used by the officers was "appropriate under the circumstances," that "there was no discernable injury inflicted," and that the force used "was not applied maliciously or sadistically for the very purpose of causing harm," but in "a good faith effort to maintain or restore order in the face of a potentially explosive situation," the District Court granted respondents' motion for a directed verdict. A divided panel of the Court of Appeals for the Fourth Circuit affirmed. We granted certiorari, and now REVERSE.

OPINION

Many courts have seemed to assume, as did the courts in this case, that there is a generic "right" to be free from excessive force, grounded not in any particular constitutional provision but rather in basic principles of § 1983 jurisprudence. We reject this notion that all excessive force claims brought under § 1983 are governed by a single generic standard.

As we have said many times, § 1983 is not itself a source of substantive rights, but merely provides a method for vindicating federal rights elsewhere conferred. In addressing an excessive force claim brought under § 1983, analysis begins by identifying the specific constitutional right allegedly infringed by the challenged application of force. In most instances, that will be either the Fourth Amendment's prohibition against unreasonable seizures of the person, or the Eighth Amendment's ban on cruel and unusual punishments, which are the two primary sources of constitutional protection against physically abusive governmental conduct. The validity of the claim must then be judged by reference to the specific

(continued)

constitutional standard, which governs that right, rather than to some generalized "excessive force" standard.

Where, as here, the excessive force claim arises in the context of an arrest or investigatory stop of a free citizen, it is most properly characterized as one invoking the protections of the Fourth Amendment, which guarantees citizens the right "to be secure in their persons . . . against unreasonable . . . seizures" of the person.

Today we hold that all claims that law enforcement officers have used excessive force—deadly or not—in the course of an arrest, investigatory stop, or other "seizure" of a free citizen should be analyzed under the Fourth Amendment and its "reasonableness" standard, rather than under a "substantive due process" [general right against excessive force] approach. Because the Fourth Amendment provides an explicit textual source of constitutional protection against this sort of physically intrusive governmental conduct, that Amendment, not the more generalized notion of "substantive due process," must be the guide for analyzing these claims.

Determining whether the force used to effect a particular seizure is "reasonable" under the Fourth Amendment requires a careful balancing of "the nature and quality of the intrusion on the individual's Fourth Amendment interests" against the countervailing governmental interests at stake. Our Fourth Amendment jurisprudence has long recognized that the right to make an arrest or investigatory stop necessarily carries with it the right to use some degree of physical coercion or threat thereof to effect it.

With respect to a claim of excessive force, the standard of reasonableness at the moment applies: Not every push or shove, even if it may later seem unnecessary in the peace of a judge's chambers, violates the Fourth Amendment. The calculus of reasonableness must embody allowance for the fact that police officers are often forced to make split-second judgments—in circumstances that are tense, uncertain, and rapidly evolving—about the amount of force that is necessary in a particular situation.

As in other Fourth Amendment contexts, however, the "reasonableness" inquiry in an excessive force case is an objective one: the question is whether the officers' actions are "objectively reasonable" in light of the facts and circumstances confronting them, without regard to their underlying intent or motivation. An officer's evil intentions will not make a Fourth Amendment violation out of an objectively reasonable use of force; nor will an officer's good intentions make an objectively unreasonable use of force constitutional.

Because petitioner's excessive force claim is one arising under the Fourth Amendment, the Court of Appeals erred in analyzing it under the four-part *Johnson v. Glick* test. That test, which requires consideration of whether the individual officers acted in "good faith" or "maliciously and sadistically for the very purpose of causing harm," is incompatible with a proper Fourth Amendment analysis.

We do not agree with the Court of Appeals' suggestion, that the "malicious and sadistic" inquiry is merely another way of describing conduct that is objectively unreasonable under the circumstances. Whatever the empirical correlations between "malicious and sadistic" behavior and objective unreasonableness may be, the fact remains that the "malicious and sadistic" factor puts in issue the subjective motivations of the individual officers, which our prior cases make clear has no bearing on whether a particular seizure is "unreasonable" under the Fourth Amendment.

Nor do we agree with the Court of Appeals' conclusion, that because the subjective motivations of the individual officers are of central importance in deciding whether force used against a convicted prisoner violates the Eighth Amendment, it cannot be reversible error to inquire into them in deciding whether force used against a suspect or arrestee violates the Fourth Amendment. Differing standards under the Fourth and Eighth Amendments are hardly surprising: the terms "cruel" and "punishment" clearly suggest some inquiry into subjective state of mind, whereas the term "unreasonable" does not. Moreover, the less protective Eighth Amendment standard applies only after the State has complied with the constitutional guarantees traditionally associated with criminal prosecutions.

The Fourth Amendment inquiry is one of "objective reasonableness" under the circumstances, and subjective concepts like "malice" and "sadism" have no proper place in that inquiry.

Because the Court of Appeals reviewed the District Court's ruling on the motion for directed verdict under an erroneous view of the governing substantive law, its judgment must be vacated and the case REMANDED to that court for reconsideration of that issue under the proper Fourth Amendment standard.

Questions

1. List all the specific uses of force by the officers.

2. State the standard that the Court adopted for determining whether the use of force violated the Fourth Amendment.

3. How does the Court's standard differ from the test that the Court of Appeals applied in the case?

4. Why did the Court change the standard? Which test do you favor? Explain your answer.

5. If you were applying the tests to the facts of this case, what decision would you reach? Defend your answer.

6. As noted in the text introducing *Graham v. Connor*, the Supreme Court left it to lower courts to apply the criteria of the objective-standard-of-reasonable-force test to a variety of types of force officers use to take and maintain control over arrested suspects. The major ones are listed in Table 5.5.

TABLE 5.5 Lower courts' applications of objective-standard-of-reasonable-force test

Type of force	Case
Directing police dog to bite and hold	*Kuha v. City of Minnetonka* (see excerpt on p. 184)
	Miller v. Clark County, 340 F.3d 959 (CA9 2003). A deputy's use of a police dog to bite and hold a plaintiff's arm until backup arrived a minute later was objectively reasonable.
Pepper spraying	*Isom v. Town of Warren*, 360 F.3d 7 (CA1 2004). An officer's use of pepper spray to disarm a suspect armed with an axe was objectively reasonable.
	McCormick v. City of Fort Lauderdale, 333 F.3d 1234 (CA11 2003). It was objectively reasonable to use pepper spray against a suspect who had recently assaulted another person; "pepper spray ordinarily causes only temporary discomfort."
	Vinyard v. Wilson, 311 F.3d 1340 (CA11 2002). Using pepper spray in a minor crime when the suspect is secured, is not acting violently, and "there is no threat to officers or anyone else," is objectively unreasonable. But it is objectively reasonable when the "plaintiff was either resisting arrest or refusing police requests, such as requests to enter a patrol car or go to the hospital."
Firing lead-filled bean bag rounds from shotgun	*Bell v. Irwin*, 321 F.3d 637 (CA7 2003). Firing a bean from shotgun bag rounds when a suspect threatened to blow up a home with propane and kerosene and then "leaned toward a tank with what appeared to be a cigarette lighter" was objectively reasonable.
	Deorle v. Rutherford, 272 F.3d 1272 (CA9 2001). Use of lead-filled bean bag rounds is objectively reasonable only when a strong government interest compels its use, because it can cause serious injury.
Hog tying	*Cruz v. City of Laramie*, 239 F.3d 1183 (CA10 2001). Binding the ankles to the wrists behind a suspect's back is "forbidden when an individual's diminished capacity is apparent" because of the high risk of suffocation. When permissible "such restraint should be used with great care and continual observation of the well-being of the subject."
Tight handcuffing	*Payne v. Pauley*, 337 F.3d 767 (CA7 2003). Handcuffing a suspect tightly was objectively reasonable when the suspect "resisted arrest, failed to obey orders, [and] was accused of a more serious or violent crime."
	Kopec v. Tate, 361 F.3d 772 (CA3 2004). Placing excessively tight handcuffs on a suspect and needlessly failing to respond for 10 minutes to pleas to loosen them, causing permanent damage, was objectively unreasonable.
Tasering (stun gun)	*Draper v. Reynolds*, 369 F.3d 1270 (CA11 2004). A deputy's use of a Taser to bring a motorist under control in a difficult, tense situation where a "single use of the Taser gun may well have prevented a physical struggle and serious harm to either" the driver or the officer was objectively reasonable.

© Cengage Learning

Our next excerpt, *Kuha v. Minnetonka* (2003), shows how one court applied the test, holding that the use of a dog trained only in the **bite-and-hold technique** met the requirements of the test. According to the technique used in the excerpt, "if given a 'find' command, Arco [the dog] will find, 'bite' and 'hold' a suspect until commanded to release." This technique was used instead of the **find-and-bark technique**, in which dogs are trained to find suspects and then bark until officers can get control of the suspect.

In *Kuha v. Minnetonka* (2003), a federal appeals court found that the city's dog bite-and-hold policy was objectively reasonable when officers used it to apprehend Jeff Kuha after he ran away during a traffic stop.

CASE

Was Bite and Hold Excessive Force?

Kuha v. City of Minnetonka
365 F.3d 590 (CA8 Minn., 2003)

HISTORY

Jeff Kuha, who was bitten by a police dog, brought an action against the city of Minnetonka, Minnesota, and police officers William Roth, Dennis Warosh, and K-9 team member Kevin Anderson in charge of "Arco," alleging the use of excessive force in violation of his civil rights under § 1983, and asserting state law claims of assault and battery and negligence. The U.S. District Court for the District of Minnesota granted summary judgment in favor of the defendants. Kuha appealed. The Court of Appeals affirmed in part and reversed in part, and rehearing was granted.

—MELLOY, J.

FACTS

On the evening of September 22, 1999, Jeff Kuha went to a bar with friends. He had four or five beers at the bar and then drove to a friend's house. Kuha claims he left his friend's home at approximately 1:00 a.m., intending to drive home. Shortly after leaving, he drove his car into a roadside curb, damaging the car and flattening the tire. Kuha walked back to his friend's house to get help. He and his friend changed the tire and placed the damaged tire on the front seat of the car. Kuha then continued on his way home.

At approximately 5:30 a.m., Kuha encountered Officer Roth, a Minnetonka police officer, who was driving in the opposite direction. Kuha failed to dim his lights when he approached the oncoming police car. Officer Roth made a U-turn and pulled Kuha over. Officer Roth called in the vehicle's license plate information and started to get out of the car for what appeared to be a routine traffic stop.

At this point, Kuha opened his door, got out, looked at the officer, and ran from his car, heading for a ditch and swamp abutting the road. Officer Roth attempted to follow Kuha but Kuha disappeared into the swamp. Beyond the swamp was a hilly area with high grass and dense brush and foliage. Beyond that were apartment and office buildings. Officer Roth returned to his police car

and called for back-up. While waiting for back-up, Officer Roth inspected Kuha's car, noting its damage and the flat tire on the front seat. He also found Kuha's wallet and concluded that the picture on the license matched that of the person who had fled from the scene.

Within minutes, Officers Warosh and Anderson arrived. They were accompanied by Officer Anderson's K-9 partner, "Arco." Arco is trained under a "bite-and-hold" method; thus, if given a "find" command, Arco will find, "bite" and "hold" a suspect until commanded to release. While tracking Kuha, Officer Anderson held Arco's leash in one hand and a flashlight in the other. Officer Warosh provided cover for the K-9 team. Arco remained on his leash as they tracked plaintiff up a steep, woody hill and toward a grassy field.

Approximately thirty minutes after the initial stop, and as the K-9 team reached the top of a hill, Arco alerted, indicating that Kuha was relatively nearby. At this point, Arco was around ten feet out on his lead. Arco bounded into the three-foot-high grass and "seized" Kuha. Arco is trained to bite and hold the first body part that he reaches. In this instance, Arco bit Kuha's upper leg. Kuha was naked except for his boxer shorts. He claims that he took off his clothes after swimming through the swamp because they were wet and cold.

Kuha states that he held his hands up to surrender as the officers approached and before Arco bit him, but concedes that the officers may not have seen him because of the high grass. The officers aver that they did not see the seizure but instead heard Kuha scream and arrived on the scene immediately thereafter. Prior to calling off Arco, Officers Anderson and Warosh inspected the area around and under Kuha to ensure he was unarmed. During this time, Kuha gripped Arco's head, trying to free his hold. Officer Anderson repeatedly told Kuha he would not call off the dog until Kuha let go of the dog and put his hands up. Kuha eventually complied and Officer Anderson called off the dog. It is undisputed that the entire apprehension, from bite to release, took no more than ten to fifteen seconds.

The officers then handcuffed Kuha and noticed that Kuha was bleeding from the site where Arco bit him. They applied pressure to the wound and called for an ambulance. A subsequent medical examination revealed that Arco's bite had pierced plaintiff's femoral artery, causing substantial blood loss.

On May 25, 2000, Kuha pled guilty to the charge of disobeying a police officer. According to Kuha, he ran from Officer Roth because he feared he may have been over the legal alcohol consumption limit. Kuha claims he was afraid of being convicted for driving under the influence which would have severely hindered his prospects for a career as a commercial pilot. A sample of Kuha's blood was taken at the hospital when he was treated for the dog bite. The sample placed Kuha's blood alcohol level above the legal limit. He was not charged with driving under the influence, however, because of concerns that his blood loss may have altered the results of the test. [Within minutes, one or two squad cars from nearby Hopkins, Minnesota, and a helicopter responded.]

OPINION

Kuha asserts that Officers Anderson and Warosh used excessive force in violation of the Fourth and Fourteenth Amendments in:

1. using a dog trained in the "bite-and-hold" method under the circumstances of the case—where Kuha had fled from a minor traffic violation and there was no legitimate concern that he was armed or dangerous;
2. allowing the dog to attack Kuha without warning; and
3. refusing to call off the dog when it was clear that Kuha was unarmed and not dangerous.

Kuha alleges municipal liability based on the City's failure to properly formulate a police dog policy that contemplates less dangerous methods—e.g., the "find-and-bark" method.

Kuha's excessive force claim is analyzed under the Fourth Amendment's "objective reasonableness" standard. The test of reasonableness under the Fourth Amendment is not capable of precise definition or mechanical application. However, its proper application requires careful attention to the facts and circumstances of each particular case, including the severity of the crime at issue, whether the suspect poses an immediate threat to the safety of the officers or others, and whether he is actively resisting arrest or attempting to evade arrest by flight. In sum, the nature and quality of the intrusion on the individual's Fourth Amendment interests must be balanced against the importance of the governmental interests alleged to justify the intrusion.

The reasonableness of a particular use of force must be judged from the perspective of a reasonable officer on the scene, rather than with the 20/20 vision of hindsight. The calculus of reasonableness must embody allowance for the fact that police officers are often forced to make split-second judgments—in circumstances that are tense, uncertain, and rapidly evolving—about the amount of force that is necessary in a particular situation. The question is whether the officers' actions are "objectively reasonable" in light of the facts and circumstances confronting them, without regard to their underlying intent or motivation. An officer's evil intentions will not make a Fourth Amendment violation out of an objectively reasonable use of force; nor will an officer's good intentions make an objectively unreasonable use of force constitutional.

In reviewing Kuha's claims, the relevant inquiry is whether Kuha presented enough proof in support of his claim that a jury could properly find that the degree of force used against him was not objectively reasonable. We conclude that he did. We conclude that a jury could properly find it objectively unreasonable to use a police dog trained in the bite-and-hold method without first giving the suspect a warning and opportunity for peaceful surrender.

The presence or absence of a warning is a critical fact in virtually every excessive force case involving a police dog. The district court held that the officers were not required to put themselves in danger by giving away their location to a hiding suspect whom they did not know for certain was unarmed. We agree that officer safety is paramount but disagree that the district court properly decided as a matter of law that requiring a verbal warning will put officers at increased risk. To the contrary, such a practice would likely diminish the risk of confrontation by increasing the likelihood that a suspect will surrender.

While there may be exceptional cases where a warning is not feasible, we see no reason why, in this case, a rational jury would be precluded from finding that the officers could have placed themselves out of harm's way—e.g., at the top of the hill where they had a good vantage point, or behind one of the nearby apartment buildings—and given a loud verbal warning that a police dog was present and trained to seize by force. Although a verbal warning will not always result in a peaceful surrender, it may be, as argued by plaintiff, that, without such a warning, seizure by force is a nearly foregone conclusion.

Kuha contends that the use of a police dog trained only in the bite-and-hold method was objectively unreasonable. In essence, Kuha argues that the governmental interest in apprehending a fleeing misdemeanant will never outweigh the potential harm inherent in

(continued)

canine-assisted apprehensions. We disagree. Police dogs serve important law enforcement functions, and their use is not inherently dangerous.

There are innumerable situations where the use of a properly trained and utilized police dog, even one trained only in the bite-and-hold technique, will not result in physical interaction with the suspect, most obviously because the dog remains on a leash until his handler releases him. Police are trained, and constitutionally obligated, to use only that amount of force reasonably necessary to effect a seizure. We will not presume that officers will abuse their discretion in this respect. And, as discussed above, we believe it will be the rare case where a verbal warning prior to releasing the dog would not facilitate a peaceful resolution of the situation.

In sum, the mere use of a police dog trained to bite and hold does not rise to the level of a constitutional violation. And in this particular case, we agree that, given the odd turn of events initiated by Kuha, the initial decision to use Arco to assist in Kuha's apprehension was objectively reasonable as a matter of law.

Kuha's claim of excessive force by the officers in the moments following his apprehension by Arco is a closer question. We must decide whether, construing the facts in the light most favorable to Kuha, a jury could properly conclude that it was objectively unreasonable for the officers to require Kuha to release Arco prior to calling off the dog. As Arco was biting Kuha's upper leg, Kuha's hands gripped the dog's head in an attempt to minimize the damage and pain. Officer Anderson repeatedly told Kuha that he would not call off the dog until Kuha raised his hands in the air. Kuha states that he tried to comply but his hands would instinctively return to the dog's head. Eventually Kuha did comply with Officer Anderson's order and the dog was called off. Kuha emphasizes that he was nearly naked during the attack, that he was clearly unarmed, and that the officers had no indication that he was dangerous.

Kuha's argument is compelling. It does not, however, end our analysis. *Graham* [*Graham v. Connor*, excerpted p. 180] requires "careful attention to the facts and circumstances of each particular case," and cautions against hindsight. Here, the officers were confronted with an inexplicable flight from a minor traffic stop in the early hours of the morning. They knew the suspect had chosen to swim through a swamp rather than encounter a police officer. The area they were searching was difficult to traverse. The officers knew there were inhabited apartment buildings nearby and that residents would soon be leaving for work. They knew that Officer Roth had not seen a gun in the brief moments before Kuha fled, but, given the totality of the circumstances, they were reasonably wary of what they might encounter when they found Kuha, and reasonably concerned for their safety.

Turning to the actual seizure, it is undisputed that the entire incident lasted only ten to fifteen seconds. Moreover, we note that this is not a case where the officers are accused of siccing a police dog on a manifestly unarmed and compliant suspect. It appears uncontested that the officers did not see the initial seizure since Arco was ten feet ahead on his lead. They heard the scream and arrived immediately thereafter. On arrival, the officers were confronted with Arco "holding" a nearly naked suspect who had been hiding in three-feet-high grass. During the ten seconds or so that ensued, the officers were searching the area under and around Kuha to ensure that he was not hiding a weapon which could be used against the officers or the dog. At the same time, Officer Anderson was ordering Kuha to release the dog's head.

In light of the short time frame at issue and the conditions under which Kuha fled and was found, we conclude that as a matter of law the officers' actions after Kuha was bitten were not objectively unreasonable. We are mindful that we must construe the facts in the light most favorable to Kuha, and we do so. But we cannot ignore the undisputed facts that are equally relevant to our analysis. To do otherwise would vitiate *Graham's* explicit recognition of, and allowance for, a measure of deference to officer judgment given the "tense, uncertain, and rapidly evolving" circumstances that officers often confront. . . .

With respect to Kuha's § 1983 claim, we REVERSE the district court's judgment in favor of the City and REMAND for further proceedings consistent with this opinion.

Questions

1. List in chronological order all the actions taken by Officers William Roth, Dennis Warosh, and K-9 team member Kevin Anderson, in charge of "Arco."

2. List the objective basis for each of the actions.

3. Summarize the court's arguments to support its decision.

4. Label each of the actions as either "objectively reasonable" or "objectively unreasonable." Defend your answer.

5. The Los Angeles Police Department changed from a "bite-and-hold" to "find-and-bark" policy in 1992. Researchers (Hutson and others 1997) reported the effects of the change of policy by collecting information about dog-bite patients in police custody from 1988 to 1995. Consider the results of their study in Figures 5.1 and 5.2. In view of these findings, is "bite and hold" instead of "find and bark" a reasonable use of force?

FIGURE 5.1 Number of K-9 Dog-Bite Patients in Police Custody

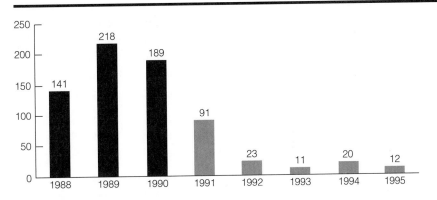

Source: Hutson and others. 1997. p. 639.

FIGURE 5.2 Some Characteristics of Dog-Bite Patients by Percent

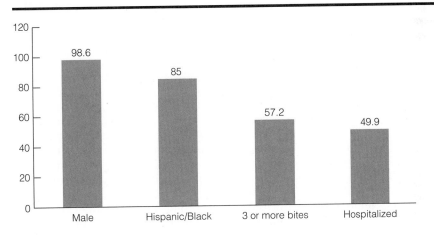

Source: Hutson and others. 1997. p. 637.

AFTER ARREST

 Immediately after an arrest, police officers may use force to subdue unruly suspects; to prevent their escape; and to protect suspects, officers, other people, or property. When they arrest suspects for *felonies*, officers almost always take the following actions:

1. Search suspects (see Chapter 6)
2. Take suspects to the police station and then "book" them, by putting their name and address, the time the crime was committed, and other information into the police blotter
3. Photograph and fingerprint them
4. Interrogate them (Chapter 8)
5. Put them into lineups (Chapter 9)
6. Turn the results of the initial investigations over to prosecutors (Chapter 12)
7. Present prisoners to a magistrate (Chapter 12)

Misdemeanor suspects are not usually arrested; they're issued a **citation** (an order to appear before a judge on a certain date to defend against a charge, often a traffic violation). But not always. Sometimes, officers make a custodial arrest and take some or all of the seven actions in the preceding list. Are these full custodial arrests reasonable Fourth Amendment seizures? A sharply divided U.S. Supreme Court (5–4) answered yes in the next excerpted case, *Atwater v. City of Lago Vista*.

In *Atwater v. City of Lago Vista* (2001), the U.S. Supreme Court held that the Fourth Amendment authorized a police officer to make a full custodial arrest for committing a fine-only criminal offense in his presence.

CASE

Was the Custodial Arrest Reasonable?

Atwater v. City of Lago Vista
532 U.S. 318 (2001)

HISTORY

Gail Atwater was charged with driving without her seat belt fastened, failing to secure her children in seat belts, driving without a license, and failing to provide proof of insurance. She pleaded no contest to the misdemeanor seat belt offenses and paid a $50 fine; the other charges were dismissed. Atwater and her husband, Michael Haas, sued Officer Bart Turek, the City of Lago Vista, and the Lago Vista Chief of Police Frank Miller. The City removed the suit to the U.S. District Court for the Western District of Texas. The District Court granted the City's summary judgment motion. A panel of the U.S. Court of Appeals for the Fifth Circuit reversed. Sitting en banc, the Court of Appeals vacated the panel's decision and affirmed the District Court's summary judgment for the City. The U.S. Supreme Court affirmed.

—SOUTER, J., joined by REHNQUIST, C.J., and SCALIA, KENNEDY, THOMAS, JJ.

FACTS

[The facts are taken from 165 F.3d 380, 382–383 (1999).] Gail Atwater and her family are long-term residents of Lago Vista, Texas, a suburb of Austin. She is a full-time mother and her husband is an emergency room physician at a local hospital. On the pleasant spring afternoon of March 26, 1997, as Gail Atwater was driving her children home after their soccer practice at 15 miles per hour through her residential neighborhood, she violated Section 545.413 of the Texas Transportation Code. Neither Gail Atwater, her four-year-old son Mac, nor her six-year-old daughter Anya were wearing their seat belts.

Detecting this breach of the peace and dignity of the state, Lago Vista police officer, Bart Turek, set about to protect the community from the perpetration of such a crime. In doing so, he brought to bear the full panoply of means available to accomplish his goal—verbal abuse, handcuffs, placing Gail Atwater under custodial arrest, and hauling her to the local police station. It was not a proud moment for the City of Lago Vista.

When Officer Turek pulled over Atwater's pickup, she and her children remained in the vehicle. Officer Turek approached the driver's side window and aggressively jabbed his finger toward her face. Turek screamed either that they had met before or had this conversation before. Turek's conduct frightened her children, so Atwater calmly and in a normal tone requested that Turek lower his voice. According to Atwater, the request that Turek lower his voice further triggered his wrath. Turek responded immediately by telling Atwater that she was going to jail. Atwater remained calm. Atwater was not acting suspiciously, she did not pose any threat to Turek, and she was not engaged in any illegal conduct other than failing to wear a seat belt when Turek told her she was going to jail.

Turek continued to speak to Atwater in a verbally abusive manner, accusing her of not caring for her children. Atwater's children and bystanders including friends and other Lago Vista residents who drove or walked by witnessed Turek's tirade. Turek stated that he recently stopped Atwater for not having her children in seat belts, but such was not the case. Turek had in fact stopped her several months before for allowing her son to ride on the front seat arm rest, but the seat belt was securely fastened. No citation was issued.

After telling Atwater that she would be taken to jail, Turek demanded her driver's license and proof of insurance. When Atwater informed Turek that her license and insurance card were in her purse that had been stolen a couple of days before, Turek ridiculed her and implied she was a liar, even though, assuming he followed standard procedures during the previous stop, he knew she had a valid driver's license and was an insured driver. Atwater eventually provided her driver's license number and address from her checkbook. Atwater then asked Turek to allow her to take her children to a friend's home just two houses down before taking her to jail, but he refused her request. Turek stated that her children could accompany her to the police station. Fortunately, a friend of Atwater's who came to the scene took the children into her care.

Although under Texas law Turek could have issued Atwater a traffic citation if she signed a promise to appear, (1) he instead chose to handcuff Atwater with her hands behind her back, load her into his squad car, and take her to the police station. Once at the police station, Atwater was required to remove her shoes and glasses, empty her pockets and have her picture taken. She was then placed in a jail cell for approximately one hour before being taken before a magistrate.

Atwater pleaded no contest to not wearing a seat belt and allowing her children to not wear seat belts. Charges of driving without a license or proof of insurance were dismissed. This incident caused Atwater and her children extreme emotional distress and anxiety. Her youngest child has required counseling, and Atwater has been prescribed medication for nightmares, insomnia, and depression resulting from this incident.

Frank Miller, the chief of police for Lago Vista, was the ultimate authority in the police department in the areas of management of department personnel. Lago Vista's policy for enforcement of traffic violations allows for the use of custodial arrests to promote its goals of increased traffic ordinance compliance. The policy specifically leaves to the officer's judgment whether to take a motorist into custody for violations of a traffic ordinance, and according to Appellants, encourages the very conduct engaged in by Officer Turek.

OPINION

The question is whether the Fourth Amendment forbids a warrantless arrest for a minor criminal offense, such as a misdemeanor seat belt violation punishable only by a fine. We hold that it does not.

If we were to derive a rule exclusively to address the uncontested facts of this case, Atwater might well prevail. She was a known and established resident of Lago Vista with no place to hide and no incentive to flee, and common sense says she would almost certainly have buckled up as a condition of driving off with a citation. In her case, the physical incidents of arrest were merely gratuitous humiliations imposed by a police officer who was (at best) exercising extremely poor judgment. Atwater's claim to live free of pointless indignity and confinement clearly outweighs anything the City can raise against it specific to her case.

[Atwater argues for a new] arrest rule forbidding custodial arrest, even upon probable cause, when conviction could not ultimately carry any jail time and when the government shows no compelling need for immediate detention. But we have traditionally recognized that a responsible Fourth Amendment balance is not well served by standards requiring sensitive, case-by-case determinations of government need, lest every discretionary judgment in the field be converted into an occasion for constitutional review. Often enough, the Fourth Amendment has to be applied on the spur (and in the heat) of the moment, and the object in implementing its command of reasonableness is to draw standards sufficiently clear and simple to be applied with a fair prospect of surviving judicial second-guessing months and years after an arrest or search is made.

Courts attempting to strike a reasonable Fourth Amendment balance thus credit the government's side with an essential interest in readily administrable rules. Fourth Amendment rules ought to be expressed in terms that are readily applicable by the police in the context of the law enforcement activities in which they are necessarily engaged and not qualified by all sorts of ifs, ands, and buts (*New York v. Belton*, 1981).

Atwater's rule promises very little in the way of administrability. It is no answer that the police routinely make judgments on grounds like risk of immediate repetition; they surely do and should. But there is a world of difference between making that judgment in choosing between the discretionary leniency of a summons in place of a clearly lawful arrest, and making the same judgment when the question is the lawfulness of the warrantless arrest itself. It is the difference between no basis for legal action challenging the discretionary judgment, on the one hand, and the prospect of evidentiary exclusion or (as here) personal § 1983 liability for the misapplication of a constitutional standard, on the other.

Atwater's rule therefore would not only place police in an almost impossible spot but would guarantee increased litigation over many of the arrests that would occur. For all these reasons, Atwater's various distinctions between permissible and impermissible arrests for minor crimes strike us as "very unsatisfactory lines" to require police officers to draw on a moment's notice.

One may ask, of course, why these difficulties may not be answered by a simple tie breaker for the police to follow in the field: if in doubt, do not arrest. Whatever help the tie breaker might give would come at the price of a systematic disincentive to arrest in situations where arresting would serve an important societal interest. [For example,] an officer not quite sure that drugs weighed enough to warrant jail time or not quite certain about a suspect's risk of flight would not arrest, even though

(continued)

it could perfectly well turn out that, in fact, the offense called for incarceration and the defendant was long gone on the day of trial. Multiplied many times over, the costs to society of such underenforcement could easily outweigh the costs to defendants of being needlessly arrested and booked, as Atwater herself acknowledges.

Just how easily the costs could outweigh the benefits may be shown by asking, as one Member of this Court did at oral argument, "how bad the problem is out there." The very fact that the law has never jelled the way Atwater would have it leads one to wonder whether warrantless misdemeanor arrests need constitutional attention, and there is cause to think the answer is no. So far as such arrests might be thought to pose a threat to the probable cause requirement, anyone arrested for a crime without formal process, whether for felony or misdemeanor, is entitled to a magistrate's review of probable cause within 48 hours, and there is no reason to think the procedure in this case atypical in giving the suspect a prompt opportunity to request release, see Tex. Tran. Code Ann. §543.002 (1999) (persons arrested for traffic offenses to be taken "immediately" before a magistrate).

Many jurisdictions, moreover, have chosen to impose more restrictive safeguards through statutes limiting warrantless arrests for minor offenses. It is, in fact, only natural that States should resort to this sort of legislative regulation, for it is in the interest of the police to limit petty-offense arrests, which carry costs that are simply too great to incur without good reason.

Finally, the preference for categorical treatment of Fourth Amendment claims gives way to individualized review when a defendant makes a colorable argument that an arrest, with or without a warrant, was "conducted in an extraordinary manner, unusually harmful to [her] privacy or even physical interests."

The upshot of all these influences, combined with the good sense (and, failing that, the political accountability) of most local lawmakers and law-enforcement officials, is a dearth of horribles demanding redress. Indeed, when Atwater's counsel was asked at oral argument for any indications of comparably foolish, warrantless misdemeanor arrests, he could offer only one. We are sure that there are others, but just as surely the country is not confronting anything like an epidemic of unnecessary minor-offense arrests. That fact caps the reasons for rejecting Atwater's request for the development of a new and distinct body of constitutional law.

Accordingly, we confirm today what our prior cases have intimated: the standard of probable cause "applies to all arrests, without the need to 'balance' the interests and circumstances involved in particular situations." If an officer has probable cause to believe that an individual has committed even a very minor criminal offense in his presence, he may, without violating the Fourth Amendment, arrest the offender.

Atwater's arrest satisfied constitutional requirements. There is no dispute that Officer Turek had probable cause to believe that Atwater had committed a crime in his presence. She admits that neither she nor her children were wearing seat belts, as required by Tex. Tran. Code Ann. §545.413 (1999). Turek was accordingly *authorized* (not *required*, but authorized) to make a *custodial* [italics added] arrest without balancing costs and benefits or determining whether or not Atwater's arrest was in some sense necessary. Nor was the arrest made in an "extraordinary manner, unusually harmful to her privacy or physical interests."

The question whether a search or seizure is "extraordinary" turns, above all else, on the manner in which the search or seizure is executed: *Tennessee v. Garner* (1985) ("seizure by means of deadly force") [excerpted earlier on p. 178], *Wilson v. Arkansas* (1995) ("unannounced entry into a home") [excerpted in Chapter 6], and *Winston v. Lee* (1985) ("physical penetration of the body").

Atwater's arrest was surely "humiliating," as she says in her brief, but it was no more "harmful to privacy or physical interests" than the normal custodial arrest. She was handcuffed, placed in a squad car, and taken to the local police station, where officers asked her to remove her shoes, jewelry, and glasses, and to empty her pockets. They then took her photograph and placed her in a cell, alone, for about an hour, after which she was taken before a magistrate, and released on $310 bond. The arrest and booking were inconvenient and embarrassing to Atwater, but not so extraordinary as to violate the Fourth Amendment.

The Court of Appeals' en banc judgment is AFFIRMED.

DISSENT

O'CONNOR, J., joined by STEVENS, GINSBURG, and BREYER, JJ.

A full custodial arrest, such as the one to which Ms. Atwater was subjected, is the quintessential seizure. When a full custodial arrest is effected without a warrant, the plain language of the Fourth Amendment requires that the arrest be reasonable. We evaluate the search or seizure by assessing, on the one hand, the degree to which it intrudes upon an individual's privacy and, on the other, the degree to which it is needed for the promotion of legitimate governmental interests. In determining reasonableness, each case is to be decided on its own facts and circumstances.

A custodial arrest exacts an obvious toll on an individual's liberty and privacy, even when the period of custody is relatively brief. The arrestee is subject to a full search of her person and confiscation of her possessions. If the arrestee is the occupant of a car, the entire passenger compartment of the car, including packages therein, is subject to search as well. The arrestee may be detained for up to 48 hours without having a magistrate determine whether there in fact was probable cause for the arrest. Because people arrested for all types of violent and nonviolent offenses may be housed together awaiting such review, this detention period is potentially dangerous. And once the period of custody is over, the fact of the arrest is a permanent part of the public record.

The record in this case makes it abundantly clear that Ms. Atwater's arrest was constitutionally unreasonable. Atwater readily admits—as she did when Officer Turek pulled her over—that she violated Texas's seat belt law. While Turek was justified in stopping Atwater, neither law nor reason supports his decision to arrest her instead of simply giving her a citation. The officer's actions cannot sensibly be viewed as a permissible means of balancing Atwater's Fourth Amendment interests with the State's own legitimate interests.

There is no question that Officer Turek's actions severely infringed Atwater's liberty and privacy. Turek was loud and accusatory from the moment he approached Atwater's car. Atwater's young children were terrified and hysterical. Yet when Atwater asked Turek to lower his voice because he was scaring the children, he responded by jabbing his finger in Atwater's face and saying, "You're going to jail." Having made the decision to arrest, Turek did not inform Atwater of her right to remain silent. He instead asked for her license and insurance information.

Atwater asked if she could at least take her children to a friend's house down the street before going to the police station. But Turek—who had just castigated Atwater for not caring for her children—refused and said he would take the children into custody as well. Only the intervention of neighborhood children who had witnessed the scene and summoned one of Atwater's friends saved the children from being hauled to jail with their mother.

With the children gone, Officer Turek handcuffed Ms. Atwater with her hands behind her back, placed her in the police car, and drove her to the police station. Ironically, Turek did not secure Atwater in a seat belt for the drive. At the station, Atwater was forced to remove her shoes, relinquish her possessions, and wait in a holding cell for about an hour. A judge finally informed Atwater of her rights and the charges against her, and released her when she posted bond. Atwater returned to the scene of the arrest, only to find that her car had been towed.

Ms. Atwater ultimately pleaded no contest to violating the seat belt law and was fined $50. Even though that fine was the maximum penalty for her crime, and even though Officer Turek has never articulated any justification for his actions, the city contends that arresting Atwater was constitutionally reasonable because it advanced two legitimate interests: "the enforcement of child safety laws and encouraging [Atwater] to appear for trial." It is difficult to see how arresting Atwater served either of these goals any more effectively than the issuance of a citation. With respect to the goal of law enforcement generally, Atwater did not pose a great danger to the community.

She had been driving very slowly—approximately 15 miles per hour—in broad daylight on a residential street that had no other traffic. Nor was she a repeat offender; until that day, she had received one traffic citation in her life—a ticket, more than 10 years earlier, for failure to signal a lane change. Although Officer Turek had stopped Atwater approximately three months earlier because he thought that Atwater's son was not wearing a seat belt, Turek had been mistaken. Moreover, Atwater immediately accepted responsibility and apologized for her conduct. Thus, there was every indication that Atwater would have buckled herself and her children in had she been cited and allowed to leave. With respect to the related goal of child welfare, the decision to arrest Atwater was nothing short of counterproductive.

Atwater's children witnessed Officer Turek yell at their mother and threaten to take them all into custody. Ultimately, they were forced to leave her behind with Turek, knowing that she was being taken to jail. Understandably, the three-year-old boy was "very, very, very traumatized." After the incident, he had to see a child psychologist regularly, who reported that the boy "felt very guilty that he couldn't stop this horrible thing . . . he was powerless to help his mother or sister." Both of Atwater's children are now terrified at the sight of any police car. According to Atwater, the arrest "just never leaves us. It's a conversation we have every other day, once a week, and it's—it raises its head constantly in our lives."

Citing Atwater surely would have served the children's interests well. It would have taught Atwater to ensure that her children were buckled up in the future. It also would have taught the children an important lesson in accepting responsibility and obeying the law. Arresting Atwater, though, taught the children an entirely different lesson: that "the bad person could just as easily be the policeman as it could be the most horrible person they could imagine."

The City also contends that the arrest was necessary to ensure Atwater's appearance in court. Atwater, however, was far from a flight risk. A 16-year resident of Lago Vista, population 2,486, Atwater was not likely to abscond. Although she was unable to produce her driver's license because it had been stolen, she gave Officer Turek her license number and address. In addition, Officer Turek knew from their previous encounter that Atwater was a local resident.

The city's justifications fall far short of rationalizing the extraordinary intrusion on Gail Atwater and her children. Measuring "the degree to which [Atwater's custodial arrest was] needed for the promotion of legitimate governmental interests," against "the degree to which it intruded upon her privacy," it can hardly be doubted that Turek's actions were disproportionate to Atwater's crime. The majority's assessment that "Atwater's claim to live free of pointless indignity and confinement clearly outweighs

(continued)

anything the City can raise against it specific to her case," is quite correct. In my view, the Fourth Amendment inquiry ends there.

The Court's error, however, does not merely affect the disposition of this case. The per se rule that the Court creates has potentially serious consequences for the everyday lives of Americans. A broad range of conduct falls into the category of fine-only misdemeanors. In Texas alone, for example, disobeying any sort of traffic warning sign is a misdemeanor punishable only by fine, as is failing to pay a highway toll, and driving with expired license plates. Nor are fine-only crimes limited to the traffic context. In several States, for example, littering is a criminal offense punishable only by fine.

To be sure, such laws are valid and wise exercises of the States' power to protect the public health and welfare. My concern lies not with the decision to enact or enforce these laws, but rather with the manner in which they may be enforced. Under today's holding, when a police officer has probable cause to believe that a fine-only misdemeanor offense has occurred, that officer may stop the suspect, issue a citation, and let the person continue on her way. Or, if a traffic violation, the officer may stop the car, arrest the driver, search the driver, search the entire passenger compartment of the car including any purse or package inside, and impound the car and inventory all of its contents. Although the Fourth Amendment expressly requires that the latter course be a reasonable and proportional response to the circumstances of the offense, the majority gives officers unfettered discretion to choose that course without articulating a single reason why such action is appropriate.

Such unbounded discretion carries with it grave potential for abuse. The majority takes comfort in the lack of evidence of "an epidemic of unnecessary minor-offense arrests." But the relatively small number of published cases dealing with such arrests proves little and should provide little solace. Indeed, as the recent debate over racial profiling demonstrates all too clearly, a relatively minor traffic infraction may often serve as an excuse for stopping and harassing an individual. After today, the arsenal available to any officer extends to a full arrest and the searches permissible concomitant to that arrest. An officer's subjective motivations for making a traffic stop are not relevant considerations in determining the reasonableness of the stop. But it is precisely because these motivations are beyond our purview that we must vigilantly ensure that officers' poststop actions—which are properly within our reach—comport with the Fourth Amendment's guarantee of reasonableness.

The Court neglects the Fourth Amendment's express command in the name of administrative ease. In so doing, it cloaks the pointless indignity that Gail Atwater suffered with the mantle of reasonableness. I respectfully dissent.

Questions

1. List all of Officer Turek's actions leading up to, during, and following Gail Atwater's arrest.
2. List all the actions taken by booking officers after Officer Turek turned her over to them.
3. According to the majority opinion, what is the bright-line rule regarding arrests for fine-only offenses?
4. Summarize the majority's arguments supporting the bright-line rule.
5. According to the majority, what are the exceptions to the bright-line rule?
6. Summarize the dissent's arguments against the bright-line rule.
7. State the rule the dissent recommends for fine-only offenses.
8. Summarize the dissent's arguments in favor of the rule it recommends.
9. List the exceptions the dissent recommends should apply to its rule.

CRIMINAL PROCEDURE IN ACTION

Full custodial arrest for eating one french fry on the subway is not an unreasonable fourth amendment seizure.

LO 6   FACTS

On October 23, 2000, 12-year-old Ansche Hedgepeth and a classmate entered the Tenleytown/AU station on their way home from school. Ansche had stopped at a fast-food restaurant on the way and ordered a bag of french fries—to go. While waiting for her companion to purchase a fare card, Ansche removed and ate a french fry from the take-out bag she was holding. After proceeding through the fare gate,

Ansche was stopped by a plain-clothed Metro Transit Police officer, who identified himself and informed her that he was arresting her for eating in the Metro rail station. The officer then handcuffed Ansche behind her back while another officer searched her and her backpack. Pursuant to established procedure, her shoelaces were removed. Upset and crying, Ansche was transported to the District of Columbia's Juvenile Processing Center some distance away, where she was fingerprinted and processed before being released into the custody of her mother three hours later.

It was the start of another school year and the Washington Metropolitan Area Transit Authority (WMATA) was once again getting complaints about bad behavior by students using the Tenleytown/American University Metro rail station. In response WMATA embarked on a weeklong undercover operation to enforce a "zero-tolerance" policy with respect to violations of certain ordinances, including one that makes it unlawful for any person to eat or drink in a Metro rail station.

"Zero tolerance" had more fateful consequences for children than for adults. Adults who violate § 35–251(b) typically receive a citation subjecting them to a fine of $10 to $50. District of Columbia law, however, does not provide for the issuance of citations for nontraffic offenses to those under 18 years of age. Instead, a minor who has committed what an officer has reasonable grounds to believe is a "delinquent act" "may be taken into custody."

Committing an offense under District of Columbia law, such as eating in a Metro rail station, constitutes a "delinquent act." The upshot of all this is that zero-tolerance enforcement of § 35–251(b) entailed the arrest of every offending minor but not every offending adult.

The no-citation policy was not, it turned out, carved in stone. The negative publicity surrounding Ansche's arrest prompted WMATA to adopt a new policy effective January 31, 2001, allowing WMATA officers to issue citations to juveniles violating § 35–251(b). Zero tolerance was also not a policy for the ages. Effective May 8, 2001, WMATA adopted a new Written Warning Notice Program, under which juveniles eating in the Metro were neither arrested nor issued citations, but instead given written warnings, with a letter notifying their parents and school. Only after the third infraction over the course of a year could a juvenile be formally prosecuted.

On April 9, 2001, Ansche's mother Tracey Hedgepeth brought this action as Ansche's next friend (representing her minor child) in the United States District Court for the District of Columbia. The complaint was filed under 42 U.S.C. § 1983 and named WMATA, its General Manager, the arresting officer, and the District of Columbia as defendants. It alleged that Ansche's arrest was an unreasonable seizure under the Fourth Amendment. The complaint sought declaratory and injunctive relief against the enforcement policies leading to Ansche's arrest, and expungement of Ansche's arrest record.

OPINION

Ansche Hedgepeth challenges her arrest on the ground that it was an unreasonable seizure in violation of the Fourth Amendment. This claim quickly runs into the Supreme Court's recent holding in *Atwater v. City of Lago Vista*. The Court in *Atwater* undertook a two-step inquiry in addressing the plaintiff's argument that a warrantless arrest for a fine-only offense was unreasonable under the Fourth Amendment. It first concluded that Atwater's argument that such arrests were not supported by the common law at the Founding, "while by no means insubstantial," ultimately failed. Reasoning that "the standard of probable cause 'applies to all arrests, without the need to balance the interests and circumstances involved in particular situations,'" the Court concluded that "if an officer has probable cause to believe that an individual has committed even a very minor criminal offense in his presence, he may, without violating the Fourth Amendment, arrest the offender."

While we can inquire into the reasonableness of the manner in which an arrest is conducted, the only cases in which we have found it necessary actually to perform the balancing analysis involved searches and seizures conducted in an extraordinary manner, unusually harmful to an individual's privacy or even physical interests: *Graham v. Connor* [excerpted earlier on p. 180]; *Tennessee v. Garner* [excerpted earlier on p. 178]. The most natural reading of *Atwater* is that we cannot inquire further into the reasonableness of a decision to arrest when it is supported by probable cause.

Source: *Hedgepeth v. Washington Metro Area Transit and others*, 284 F. Supp.2d 145 (D.D.C. 2003).

CHAPTER SUMMARY

LO 1 Arrests are Fourth Amendment seizures that can help law enforcement catch the guilty and free the innocent. Arrests are more invasive than Fourth Amendment stops because they can last longer, result in the suspect being taken to the police station, and are officially recorded.

LO 2 To satisfy the Fourth Amendment's reasonableness requirement, arrests require both probable cause before and a reasonable execution during and after the arrest. The noble end of crime control doesn't justify unreasonable arrests to attain that end.

LO 3 The probable cause requirement balances the societal interest in crime control against the individual right to locomotion. To account for the totality of circumstances in each case, officers can rely on both direct and hearsay evidence to build probable cause.

LO 4   Most arrests based on probable cause are reasonably executed without warrants. Warrants are required, however, to arrest suspects in their home unless exigent circumstances exist that would require the immediate law enforcement action. The most common exigent circumstances include hot pursuit, imminent danger to officers, preventing the destruction of evidence, and preventing the escape of suspects.

LO 5 During and after arrests, officers can only use the amount of force that is objectively reasonable to apprehend and maintain control of suspects they have probable cause to arrest. Under this standard, "An officer's evil intentions will not make a Fourth Amendment violation out of an objectively reasonable use of force; nor will an officer's good intentions make an objectively unreasonable use of force constitutional." Furthermore, reasonableness is determined at the moment of the use of force. "Not every push or shove, even if it may later seem unnecessary in the peace of a judge's chambers, violates the Fourth Amendment."

LO 6 After an arrest, felony suspects are usually taken to the police station for official booking, photographing, and possible interrogation and identification procedures; misdemeanor suspects are usually issued a citation. It's constitutionally reasonable, but not necessarily wise, for officers to make full custodial arrests for fine-only offenses.

REVIEW QUESTIONS

1. Compare and contrast Fourth Amendment stops with full custodial arrests. Explain four ways arrests are more invasive than stops.
2. Identify the characteristics of a full custodial arrest.
3. Describe the two elements of a reasonable arrest.
4. What two societal interests are balanced by the probable cause requirement?
5. Identify and define the two sources of information officers can use to build probable cause to arrest.
6. Describe the two elements of the Fourth Amendment reasonableness requirement.
7. Identify and describe the three elements of an arrest warrant.
8. Summarize the empirical research regarding the neutral magistrate requirement.
9. Why are some arrest warrant affidavits purposefully vague?

10. Summarize Professor Craig Bradley's views about the process of obtaining a warrant.

11. Why do officers need to obtain warrants to arrest a suspect in a home?

12. Define and give an example of the exceptions to the arrest warrant requirement to enter homes.

13. Contrast deadly force with nondeadly force. Which is used more often to subdue suspects?

14. What two conditions must be satisfied to justify the use of deadly force?

15. Describe the role of law enforcement intentions in the use of reasonable force.

16. Summarize the empirical research regarding police dog techniques of bite and hold and find and bark. Compare these findings to the decision in *Kuha v. Minnetonka*.

17. Identify the actions taken after an arrest for a felony.

18. Why is it reasonable for officers to arrest suspects for a misdemeanor offense?

KEY TERMS

custodial arrests, p. 164
probable cause to arrest, p. 165
right of locomotion, p. 166
direct information in probable
    cause, p. 166
hearsay rule, p. 167

totality of the circumstances
    test, p. 167
neutral magistrate, p. 172
affidavit, p. 173
particularity requirement, p. 173
exigent circumstances, p. 174

deadly force, p. 178
objective standard of reasonable
    force, p. 180
bite-and-hold technique, p. 183
find-and-bark technique, p. 183
citation, p. 188

6

Searches for Evidence

LEARNING OBJECTIVES

1 Understand that crime control couldn't survive without searches. Appreciate that the need to search is balanced against the invasion of individual privacy rights.

2 Know that there are many exceptions to the warrant requirement and warrantless searches far outnumber searches performed with warrants.

3 Know that search warrants require both particularity and probable cause. Appreciate that, with some exceptions, officers must knock, announce their presence, and give occupants an opportunity to open the door before forcefully entering a home.

4 Understand that searches incident to lawful arrests are reasonable because they help: (1) protect officers from potentially dangerous suspects; (2) prevent the escape of arrested suspects; and (3) prevent the destruction of evidence.

5 Know that consent searches are performed without warrants or probable cause, allowing officers to conduct searches that would otherwise be unlawful.

6 Understand that the voluntariness of consent is determined by the totality of circumstances in each case. Appreciate the empirical research regarding the voluntariness of consent searches.

7 Know how to determine the scope of consent; when consent can be withdrawn; and when one person can consent for another.

8 Know that third-party consent searches allow an individual to consent to the search for another. Understand that the Supreme Court has ruled that apparent authority is the minimum required by the Fourth Amendment.

9 Understand that the searches of vehicles without warrants are reasonable because of their mobility and the reduced expectation of privacy of vehicles. Know that searches of containers and persons within vehicles must be based on probable cause.

10 Understand that emergency searches are based on the idea that it's sometimes impractical or dangerous to require officers to obtain warrants before they search.

Police were summoned to the residence of Dorothy Jackson on South Wolcott in Chicago. They were met by Ms. Jackson's daughter, Gail Fischer, who showed signs of a severe beating. She told the officers that she had been assaulted by Edward Rodriguez earlier that day in an apartment on South California. Fischer stated that Rodriguez was then asleep in the apartment, and she consented to travel there with the police in order to unlock the door with her key so that the officers could enter and arrest him. During this conversation, Fischer several times referred to the apartment on South California as "our" apartment, and said that she had clothes and furniture there. It is unclear whether she indicated that she currently lived at the apartment, or only that she used to live there.

The police officers drove to the apartment on South California, accompanied by Fischer. They did not obtain an arrest warrant for Rodriguez, nor did they seek a search warrant for the apartment. At the apartment, Fischer unlocked the door with her key and gave the officers permission to enter. They moved through the door into the living room, where they observed in plain view drug paraphernalia and containers filled with white powder that they believed (correctly, as later analysis showed) to be cocaine. They proceeded to the bedroom, where they found Rodriguez asleep and discovered additional containers of white powder in two open attaché cases. The officers arrested Rodriguez and seized the drugs and related paraphernalia.

Rodriguez was charged with possession of a controlled substance with intent to deliver. He moved to suppress all evidence seized at the time of his arrest, claiming that Fischer had vacated the apartment several weeks earlier and had no authority to consent to the entry.

LO I

Crime control couldn't survive without searches, but, like all good things, the power to search comes at a price. Searches invade the privacy of individuals' bodies, their homes, their private papers, and their property. Like all power, the power to search tempts those who hold it to abuse it.

No one appreciated the price and the temptation to abuse the power to search more than U.S. Supreme Court Justice Robert H. Jackson. At the end of World War II, President Truman appointed Justice Jackson chief prosecutor at the Nazi war crimes trials in Nuremberg, Germany. There, Justice Jackson learned details of the Nazis' atrocities against the German people's "persons, houses, papers and effects" (Hockett 1991, 257–99).

These discoveries were a defining moment for Justice Jackson, and when he returned to the Supreme Court, he spoke eloquently of the right against unreasonable searches and seizures. Worried that Americans didn't fully appreciate the importance of the Fourth Amendment, Justice Jackson disapproved of what he believed was the Supreme Court's tendency to treat the rights against unreasonable searches and seizures as "second-class rights."

He wrote that the rights against unreasonable searches and seizures

> are not mere second-class rights but belong in the catalog of indispensable freedoms. Among deprivations of rights, none is so effective in cowing a population, crushing the spirit of the individual and putting terror in every heart. Uncontrolled search and seizure is one of the first and most effective weapons in the arsenal of every arbitrary government. And one need only briefly to have dwelt and worked among a people possessed of many admirable qualities but deprived of these rights to know that the human personality deteriorates and dignity and self-reliance disappear where homes, persons and possessions are subject at any hour to unheralded search and seizure by the police. But the right against searches and seizures is one of the most difficult to protect. Since the officers are themselves the chief invaders, there is no enforcement outside of court. (*Brinegar v. U.S.* 1949, 180–81)

Notice that Justice Jackson didn't condemn *all* searches, only "unreasonable" searches. That's because he knew how important searches are in controlling crime. (Jackson had been an aggressive prosecutor.) But he also knew that the Fourth Amendment doesn't just confer power on good officers searching guilty people, their homes, and stuff; it bestows the same power on bad officers searching innocent people. So, Jackson urged, courts had to balance the need for searches against the privacies they invade.

The three-step analysis we used to examine government actions in Chapter 3, stops and frisks in Chapter 4, and arrests in Chapter 5 also applies to the searches we'll examine in this chapter:

1. Was the government action a search? (Chapter 3)
2. If it was a search, was it reasonable?
3. If it was unreasonable, then should the evidence be excluded? (Chapter 10)

We won't repeat the first step in the analysis (the definition of search) because we already examined it in Chapter 3. We'll begin with the issues affecting the reasonableness of searches. We'll divide our discussion into searches for evidence of crime (this chapter) and special-needs searches that go beyond crime control (Chapter 7). In this chapter, we'll examine searches with warrants, and then the searches that are reasonable without warrants—searches incident to lawful arrest; consent searches; vehicle searches; and emergency searches.

SEARCHES WITH WARRANTS

LO 2 The Fourth Amendment commands that "no warrants shall issue, but upon probable cause, supported by oath or affirmation, and particularly describing the place to be searched, and the persons or things to be seized." According to the distinguished U.S. Supreme Court Justice Felix Frankfurter, "With minor and severely confined exceptions every search is unreasonable when made without a magistrate's authority expressed through a validly issued warrant" (*Harris v. U.S.* 1947, 162; see "A Neutral Magistrate" in Chapter 5).

Despite Justice Frankfurter's frequently repeated words, there are so many exceptions to the warrant requirement (up to 30, depending on how you count them) that the searches without warrants far outnumber searches with warrants. With that in mind, let's look at each of the three elements required to satisfy the Fourth Amendment's warrant requirement:

1. The particularity requirement
2. An affidavit supporting probable cause
3. The "knock-and-announce" rule

LO 3 The Particularity Requirement

To comply with the Fourth Amendment, search warrants have to "particularly describe the place to be searched"; this is known as the **particularity requirement**. The address of a single-dwelling house, "404 Blake Road," particularly describes the place to be searched; a warrant to search "1135 Stone Street," a 16-floor apartment complex, doesn't.

Warrants also have to "particularly describe the things to be seized." A warrant to search for and seize "one book entitled *Criminal Procedure*, 9th edition, by Joel Samaha" is good enough. So are warrants naming whole classes of items, such as "address books, diaries, business records, documents, receipts, warranty books, guns, stereo equipment, and a color television" in a list of stolen property.

Catchall categories might also meet the requirement. For example, a search warrant that named "records, notes, and documents indicating involvement in and control of prostitution activity" was particular enough in one case, because the officers were directed to seize only items related to prostitution.

LO 3 Probable Cause Affidavit

This is the same as the requirement for arrest warrants (Chapter 5), so we won't repeat the details here. One notable difference: The probable cause in search warrant affidavits has to include evidence to support the claim that the items or classes of items named in the warrant will be found in the place to be searched.

LO 3 Knock-and-Announce Rule

Most states and the U.S. government have many specific requirements for how search warrants are supposed to be executed. One of these rules, the **knock-and-announce rule**, has 700 years of English and U.S. history behind it; it also has centuries of controversy surrounding it. According to the rule, officers have to knock and announce that they're officers with a search warrant before they enter the places they're about to search.

Does the Fourth Amendment demand this knock-and-announce rule, or is a no-knock entry reasonable, too? Oddly enough, for all the history behind the rule, and the controversy surrounding it, the U.S. Supreme Court didn't answer this important question until 1995, when a unanimous opinion decided that the Fourth Amendment commands officers to knock and announce before they enter (*Wilson v. Arkansas* 1995).

Announcing their presence doesn't automatically authorize officers to break and enter. They have to "wait a reasonable amount of time" before they break and enter, unless occupants refuse to allow them to come in (LaFave 2004, 2:672–73; *U.S. v. Spikes* 1998, 925). How long is reasonable? The Sixth Circuit U.S. Court of Appeals put it this way: "The Fourth Amendment's 'knock and announce' cannot be distilled into a constitutional stop-watch where a fraction of a second assumes controlling significance" (*U.S. v. Spikes* 1998, 926). The test is reasonableness based on the totality of circumstances in an individual case. Very brief waits, say 2 to 4 seconds, probably aren't reasonable; 10 to 20 seconds usually are (LaFave 2004, 673–74).

The U.S. Supreme Court ruled unanimously in *U.S. v. Banks* (2003) that the totality of circumstances made it reasonable for officers to use the "ultimate 'master key,' a battering ram," to break down Lashawn Banks's front door after calling out "police search warrant" and waiting 10 seconds (33). North Las Vegas Police Department officers had a warrant to search Banks's two-bedroom apartment, based on information that Lashawn Banks was selling cocaine at home. As soon as they got to the apartment at two o'clock in the afternoon, the officers called out "police search warrant" and rapped hard enough on the door to be heard by officers at the back door. After waiting for 15 to 20 seconds with no answer, the officers broke open the front door with the battering ram. They searched and found weapons, crack cocaine, and other evidence of drug dealing.

Banks was charged with drug and firearms offenses. Banks moved to suppress the evidence, arguing that the officers executing the search warrant waited an unreasonably short time before forcing entry and so violated the Fourth Amendment. The U.S. District Court for the District of Nevada denied the motion. Banks pleaded guilty, reserving his right to challenge the search on appeal. A divided panel of the U.S. Court of Appeals for the Ninth Circuit reversed the conviction. The U.S. Supreme Court reversed the Court of Appeals.

Writing for the unanimous Court, Justice Souter noted that the details of reasonable execution of search warrants have to be "fleshed out case by case," according to the totality of "facts of cases so various that no template is likely to produce sounder results than examining the totality of circumstances in a given case" (35–36). Although the Court found this case "a close one," it held that it was reasonable to "suspect imminent loss" of the cocaine after the 15 to 20 seconds the officers waited before they battered the door down:

> One point in making an officer knock and announce is to give a person inside the chance to save his door. That is why, in the case with no reason to suspect an immediate risk, the reasonable wait time may well be longer. The need to damage property in the course of getting in is a good reason to require more patience than it would be reasonable to expect if the door were open. Police seeking a stolen piano may be able to spend more time to make sure they really need the battering ram. (41)
>
> Attention to cocaine rocks and pianos tells a lot about the chances of their respective disposal and its bearing on reasonable time. Instructions couched in terms like "significant amount of time," and "an even more substantial amount of time," tell very little. (42)

The Fourth Amendment "knock-and-announce" command, like all constitutional commands, is not absolute. The U.S. Supreme Court has recognized several situations that justify entry without call for immediate attention ("exigencies," to use the Court's language).

And it's not surprising that we expected more to come because of Justice Thomas's not-too-subtle invitation to lower courts:

> . . . We leave to the lower courts the task of determining the circumstances under which an unannounced entry is reasonable under the Fourth Amendment. We simply hold that although a search or seizure of a dwelling might be constitutionally defective if police officers enter without prior announcement, law enforcement interests may also establish the reasonableness of an unannounced entry. (936)

The Wisconsin Supreme Court wasted no time in accepting Justice Thomas's invitation in *State v. Richards* (1996). It approved a blanket "drug house" exception to the knock-and-announce rule. Steiney Richards, the defendant, argued "The blanket 'drug house' exception to the 'knock and announce' rule violates the Fourth Amendment's reasonableness requirement" (219).

The Wisconsin Supreme Court disagreed, holding that "police are not required to adhere to the rule of announcement when executing a search warrant involving felonious drug delivery." According to the court:

> Exigent circumstances are always present in the execution of search warrants involving felonious drug delivery: an extremely high risk of serious if not deadly injury to the police as well as the potential for the disposal of drugs by the occupants prior to entry by the police. The public interests inherent in these circumstances far outweigh the minimal privacy interests of the occupants of the dwelling for which a search warrant has already been issued. (219)

Richards appealed to the U.S. Supreme Court (*Richards v. Wisconsin* 1997). Justice Stevens, writing for a unanimous Court, acknowledged that "flexible requirement of reasonableness should not be read to mandate a rigid rule of announcement that ignores countervailing law enforcement interests," and left "to the lower courts the task of determining the circumstances under which an unannounced entry is reasonable under the Fourth Amendment." But, he continued, "We disagree with the court's conclusion that the Fourth Amendment permits a *blanket* exception to the knock-and-announce requirement for this entire category of criminal activity" (387–88, emphasis added).

Nevertheless, the Court upheld the Wisconsin Supreme Court's decision "because the evidence presented to support the officers' actions in this case establishes that the decision not to knock and announce was a reasonable one under the circumstances" (388).

SEARCHES WITHOUT WARRANTS

LO 2   The U.S. Supreme Court has repeatedly said that the Fourth Amendment expresses a strong preference for search warrants with only a few well-defined exceptions. That's the *law*, but what's the *practice*? The vast majority of searches are made without warrants, because the exceptions are interpreted broadly to satisfy the strong preference of law enforcement officers and the clear practical need for searches without warrants (Haddad 1977, 198–225; Sutton 1986, 411). According to one former Washington, D.C., assistant U.S. attorney, "As anyone who has worked in the criminal justice system knows, searches conducted pursuant to these exceptions, particularly searches incident to arrest, automobile and 'stop and frisk' searches, far exceed searches performed pursuant to warrants" (Bradley 1985, 1475). Why is this so? According to the same attorney, the reason "is simple: the clear rule that warrants are required is unworkable and to enforce it would lead to exclusion of evidence in many cases where the police activity was essentially reasonable" (1475).

Law enforcement officers frequently express frustration with how long it takes to get search warrants. One police officer said it takes four hours from the time he decides he wants a warrant until the time he has one in his hand:

> And that's if everything goes right. You find people and get 'em typed and you can find the judges when they are sitting at the bench—because a lot of judges won't see people in their offices. If you miss them there, they leave and go to lunch and you have to wait until they come back for the afternoon dockets, and if they are already into the afternoon dockets, they are not going to interrupt the procedures for a warrant. So you sit and wait through three or four docket sessions. It can take all day. (Sutton 1986, 411)

Frustration tempts officers to "get around" the Fourth Amendment. One way around is by "shamming" consent. One detective put it this way:

> You tell the guy, "Let me come in and take a look at your house." And he says, "No, I don't want to." And then you tell him, "Then I'm going to leave Sam here, and he's going to live with you until we come back. Now we can do it either way." And very rarely do the people say, "Go get your search warrant, then." (Sutton 1986, 415)

Let's look at the five major exceptions to the warrant requirement approved by the U.S. Supreme Court:

- Searches incident to (at the time of) arrest
- Consent searches
- Vehicle searches
- Container searches
- Emergency searches (also called "exigent circumstances searches")

LO 4 Searches Incident to Arrest

The brilliant constitutional lawyer and historian Telford Taylor (1969) concluded from his research into the history of search and seizure "that search of an arrested person and premises without warrants or probable cause is as old as the institution of arrest itself" (28). **Searches incident to (at the time of) arrest**—searches of lawfully arrested suspects without either warrants or probable cause—are old. But are they reasonable Fourth Amendment searches? Yes, says the U.S. Supreme Court. Why? Three reasons:

1. They protect officers from suspects who might injure or kill them.
2. They prevent arrested suspects from escaping.
3. They preserve evidence that suspects might destroy or damage.

There's some debate about Professor Taylor's history (Davies 1999), but as for searches of arrested persons without warrants, there's no doubt about their constitutionality. The same certainty doesn't extend to searching the place where arrests take place. In fact, decisions by the U.S. Supreme Court, the lower federal courts, and the state courts and commentators couldn't seem to reach anything close to agreement about just how extensive "incident" was. Some courts held that spending hours searching every nook and cranny of a house was "incident"; others, at the other extreme, held that "incident" means only searching the arrested person and as far as s/he could reach. And even the U.S. Supreme Court seemed to zig and zag between the extremes. All of this created great confusion, which the Supreme Court tried to clear up in 1969, when it decided *Chimel v. California* (1969), our next case excerpt. The Court decided that officers who arrested Ted Chimel in his home could search only as far as Chimel could reach either to grab a weapon or to destroy evidence.

Before we get to the case, you should be aware of one critical fact the cases hardly ever mention about what officers do in practice when they arrest suspects. According to available evidence, after officers arrest suspects, they immediately handcuff them. That's what department rules prescribe; it's what police cadets are trained to do; it's what most officers do (Moskovitz 2002). Keep this in mind as you read Chimel and all the materials in this section on searches incident to arrest.

The U.S. Supreme Court reversed Ted Chimel's conviction for the burglary of a coin shop, because his home was searched without a warrant or his permission.

CASE

Was the Search "Incident" to the Arrest?

Chimel v. California
395 U.S. 752 (1969)

HISTORY

Ted Chimel was prosecuted for the burglary of a coin shop. He was convicted in the Superior Court, Orange County, California, and appealed. The California Supreme Court affirmed, and Chimel petitioned the U.S. Supreme Court for a writ of certiorari. The Supreme Court granted the writ and reversed the California Supreme Court's judgment.

—STEWART, J.

FACTS

Late in the afternoon of September 13, 1965, three police officers arrived at the Santa Ana, California, home of Ted Chimel with a warrant authorizing his arrest for the burglary of a coin shop. The officers knocked on the door, identified themselves to Chimel's wife, and asked if they might come inside. She ushered them into the house, where they waited 10 or 15 minutes until Chimel returned home from work. When Chimel entered the house, one of

the officers handed him the arrest warrant and asked for permission to "look around." Chimel objected, but was advised that "on the basis of the lawful arrest," the officers would nonetheless conduct a search. No search warrant had been issued.

Accompanied by Chimel's wife, the officers then looked through the entire three-bedroom house, including the attic, the garage, and a small workshop. In some rooms the search was relatively cursory. In the master bedroom and sewing room, however, the officers directed Mrs. Chimel to open drawers and "to physically move contents of the drawers from side to side so that (they) might view any items that would have come from (the) burglary." After completing the search, they seized numerous items—primarily coins, but also several medals, tokens, and a few other objects. The entire search took between 45 minutes and an hour.

At Chimel's subsequent state trial on two charges of burglary, the items taken from his house were admitted

(continued)

into evidence against him, over his objection that they had been unconstitutionally seized. He was convicted, and the judgments of conviction were affirmed by both the California Court of Appeal, and the California Supreme Court. We granted certiorari in order to consider Chimel's substantial constitutional claims.

OPINION

When an arrest is made, it is reasonable for the arresting officer to search the person arrested in order to remove any weapons that the latter might seek to use in order to resist arrest or effect his escape. Otherwise, the officer's safety might well be endangered, and the arrest itself frustrated. In addition, it is entirely reasonable for the arresting officer to search for and seize any evidence on the arrestee's person in order to prevent its concealment or destruction. And the area into which an arrestee might reach in order to grab a weapon or evidentiary items must, of course, be governed by a like rule. A gun on a table or in a drawer in front of one who is arrested can be as dangerous to the arresting officer as one concealed in the clothing of the person arrested.

There is ample justification, therefore, for a search of the arrestee's person and the area "within his immediate control"—construing that phrase to mean the area from within which he might gain possession of a weapon or destructible evidence. There is no comparable justification, however, for routinely searching any room other than that in which an arrest occurs—or, for that matter, for searching through all the desk drawers or other closed or concealed areas in that room itself. Such searches, in the absence of well-recognized exceptions, may be made only under the authority of a search warrant. The "adherence to judicial processes" mandated by the Fourth Amendment requires no less.

It is argued in the present case that it is "reasonable" to search a man's house when he is arrested in it. But that argument is founded on little more than a subjective view regarding the acceptability of certain sorts of police conduct, and not on consideration relevant to Fourth Amendment interests. Under such an unconfined analysis, Fourth Amendment protection in this area would approach the evaporation point. After arresting a man in his house, to rummage at will among his papers in search of whatever will convict him, appears to us to be indistinguishable from what might be done under a general warrant; indeed, the warrant would give more protection, for presumably it must be issued by a magistrate.

Application of sound Fourth Amendment principles to the facts of this case produces a clear result. The search here went far beyond the petitioner's person and the area from within which he might have obtained either a weapon or something that could have been used as evidence against him. There was no constitutional justification, in the absence of a search warrant, for extending the search beyond that area. The scope of the search was, therefore, "unreasonable" under the Fourth and Fourteenth Amendments and the petitioner's conviction cannot stand.

REVERSED.

DISSENT

WHITE, J., joined by BLACK, J.

The Fourth Amendment does not proscribe "warrantless searches" but instead it proscribes "unreasonable searches" and this Court has never held nor does the majority today assert that warrantless searches are necessarily unreasonable. This case provides a good illustration that it is unreasonable to require police to leave the scene of an arrest in order to obtain a search warrant when they already have probable cause to search and there is a clear danger that the items for which they may reasonably search will be removed before they return with a warrant.

Chimel was arrested in his home. There was doubtless probable cause not only to arrest Chimel, but also to search his house. He had obliquely admitted, both to a neighbor and to the owner of the burglarized store, that he had committed the burglary. In light of this, and the fact that the neighbor had seen other admittedly stolen property in petitioner's house, there was surely probable cause on which a warrant could have issued to search the house for the stolen coins.

Moreover, had the police simply arrested Chimel, taken him off to the station house, and later returned with a warrant, it seems very likely that Chimel's wife, who in view of Chimel's generally garrulous nature must have known of the burglary, would have removed the coins. For the police to search the house while the evidence they had probable cause to search out and seize was still there cannot be considered unreasonable.

Questions

1. Describe the search that followed Chimel's arrest.
2. How does the Court define the area "within [a suspect's] immediate control"?
3. If you were defining the phrase, would you have included the whole house within the scope of the rule? Explain your answer, including what interests you consider paramount in formulating your definition.
4. Does Justice White, in his dissent, have the better argument in the case? Summarize his argument and then evaluate it.

Now, let's look at other issues raised by searches incident to arrests, including how the courts define the "**grabbable**"—or **searchable**—**area** and whether it extends to vehicles; the time frame officers have to conduct a search before it's no longer considered incident to the arrest; and searches incident to misdemeanors and pretext arrests.

LO 4 *The "grabbable" area*

According to *Chimel v. California*, law enforcement officers can only search the "grabbable" area—namely, the arrested person and the area under her immediate physical control. The rule seems clear enough, but confusion arose when police were faced with applying the rule to arrests of suspects in vehicles. The courts were divided over whether the grabbable area rule even applied to searches of vehicles. Some courts quickly said it did; others were reluctant.

New York v. Belton (1981) is a good example of this division. The trial court said the grabbable-area rule applied even when the arrested person was outside the car and under the control of the police and so highly unlikely to escape, grab a weapon, or destroy evidence *inside* the vehicle. The intermediate appeals court agreed, but a divided Court of Appeals, New York's highest court, said the rule didn't include a search of the car when the arrested suspects were outside the car. The U.S. Supreme Court *supposedly* resolved the problem, not only for New York but for the country, when it upheld the car search incident to Roger Belton's arrest by a vote of 5–4 in *New York v. Belton* (1981). (Also, see Table 6.1.)

In *Belton*, New York State Trooper Douglas Nicot chased and pulled over a speeding car occupied by four college students. Trooper Nicot smelled burned marijuana, ordered the four young men out of the car, and arrested them for unlawful possession of marijuana. Then, he returned to the car. During a search of the passenger compartment, he found Roger Belton's black leather jacket on the backseat. He unzipped the pocket and removed the cocaine he found in it. Belton was convicted of attempted criminal possession of a small amount of cocaine, and he appealed. The New York Supreme Court, Appellate Division, affirmed. The New York Court of Appeals reversed. The U.S. Supreme Court granted certiorari and reversed (Table 6.1).

TABLE 6.1 *New York v. Belton* (1981) majority's argument

1. Fourth Amendment protections can only be realized if the police are acting under a set of rules which, in most instances, make it possible to reach a correct determination beforehand as to whether an invasion of privacy is justified in the interest of law enforcement.
2. No straightforward rule has emerged from the decided cases respecting the question involved here.
3. This has caused the trial courts difficulty and has put the appeals courts in disarray.
4. The cases suggest that articles inside the passenger compartment of cars are, generally, if not inevitably, in an area that suspects can reach and grab a weapon or evidence.
5. So the workable rule in this category of cases is best achieved by holding that when a policeman has made a lawful custodial arrest of the occupant of an automobile, he may, as a contemporaneous incident of that arrest, search the passenger compartment of that automobile.
6. And it follows that the police may also examine the contents of any containers found within the passenger compartment, for if the passenger compartment is within reach of the arrestee, so also will containers in it be within his reach.

Source: New York v. Belton (1981)

After *Belton*, lower courts and police officers treated searches incident to traffic arrests as "a police entitlement rather than as an exception to the warrant requirement justified by the twin rationales" of officer protection and evidence preservation (*Thornton v. U.S.* 2004, 624). As interpreted by those courts, officers could *always* search the passenger compartment and all the containers in it, as long as they had probable cause to arrest an occupant.

Also since *Belton*, officers can use searches incident to minor traffic offenses as a "powerful investigative tool" (Amacost 2010, 276). In these pretext arrests, officers can stop and arrest motorists for minor traffic offenses, not to enforce the traffic laws but so they can search for evidence of more serious crimes that they don't have probable cause to arrest them for (see Chapter 5, "Probable Cause to Arrest"). According to Jeffrey Fisher, in an amicus brief (2008) supporting Rodney Gant's side in *Arizona v. Gant* (2009), our next case excerpt, "The upshot of all this is that the current search-incident-to-arrest doctrine encourages officers to arrest people whom they would not otherwise arrest, in order to conduct exploratory searches they would not otherwise be allowed to conduct" (10).

In addition to the broad reading given to *Belton*, and the pretext traffic arrest problem, there's empirical research (Moskovitz (2002) that challenges at least two of the *Belton* Court's generalizations listed in Table 6.1. This research was cited in *Arizona v. Gant*:

1. "The cases suggest that articles inside the passenger compartment of cars are, generally, if not inevitably, in an area which suspects can reach and grab a weapon or evidence."

2. It follows from the generalization in 1, "that the police may also examine the contents of any containers found within the passenger compartment, for if the passenger compartment is within reach of the arrestee, so also will containers in it be within his reach."

Before we look at these challenges raised by Moskovitz's (2002) research, you should note the limits of his sources and methods. Moskovitz wrote to police departments in California's 30 largest cities and about 50 California sheriff's departments; about a dozen federal law enforcement agencies; and about 30 state and municipal police agencies around the country (664). Although his hit rate was "small," he "received enough information to challenge both generalizations."

As for the first challenge, he found wide support for it. In his inquiries to various police departments, "Not a single respondent said or even suggested that a police officer should search a vehicle while the arrestee is in the vehicle or unsecured" (675–76). According to Moskovitz, "No sensible police officer will allow an arrestee to remain in reach of any such area—he'll get the arrestee out of the car immediately" (674).

What about the second claim? Moskovitz found this generalization was even further from officers' actual procedures in the field:

Because they are instructed to remove and secure the arrestee before searching the vehicle, it is highly unlikely (if not impossible) that an arrestee would be able to remove his handcuffs, escape from a police car and/or surveillance by a cover officer, run to the vehicle, enter it or reach into it, open a container, and remove a weapon or item of evidence—all before an officer could intervene and stop him. And yet this strange scenario would have to be the norm for *Belton* to mesh with *Chimel's* rationales for a search incident to arrest. (677)

With the empirical reality of police work, lower court approval of its broad reading of the *Belton* bright-line rule, and a growing "chorus" of criticism of *Belton* by academic lawyers in the background, the U.S. Supreme Court decided *Arizona v. Gant* (2009), our next excerpted case.

In *Arizona v. Gant* (2009), the U.S. Supreme Court upheld a Fourth Amendment challenge to a car search conducted after the driver Rodney Gant was arrested for a traffic offense, handcuffed, and locked in the backseat of the police car.

CASE

Was the Car Search "Incident" to the Driver's Arrest?

Arizona v. Gant

129 S.Ct. 1710 (2009)

HISTORY

Rodney Joseph Gant (Defendant) was convicted in the Superior Court, Pima County, Arizona, Clark W. Munger, J., of possession of a narcotic drug for sale and possession of drug paraphernalia. Defendant appealed. The Court of Appeals of Arizona, Brammer, J., reversed. The Supreme Court of Arizona, Berch, Vice Chief Justice, affirmed. The U.S. Supreme Court affirmed.

—STEVENS, J., joined by SCALIA, SOUTER, THOMAS, and GINSBURG, JJ.

FACTS

On August 25, 1999, acting on an anonymous tip that the residence at 2524 North Walnut Avenue was being used to sell drugs, Tucson police officers Griffith and Reed knocked on the front door and asked to speak to the owner. Gant answered the door and, after identifying himself, stated that he expected the owner to return later. The officers left the residence and conducted a records check, which revealed that Gant's driver's license had been suspended and there was an outstanding warrant for his arrest for driving with a suspended license.

When the officers returned to the house that evening, they found a man near the back of the house and a woman in a car parked in front of it. After a third officer arrived, they arrested the man for providing a false name and the woman for possessing drug paraphernalia. Both arrestees were handcuffed and secured in separate patrol cars when Gant arrived. The officers recognized his car as it entered the driveway, and Officer Griffith confirmed that Gant was the driver by shining a flashlight into the car as it drove by him. Gant parked at the end of the driveway, got out of his car, and shut the door. Griffith, who was about 30 feet away, called to Gant, and they approached each other, meeting 10 to 12 feet from Gant's car. Griffith immediately arrested Gant and handcuffed him.

Because the other arrestees were secured in the only patrol cars at the scene, Griffith called for backup. When two more officers arrived, they locked Gant in the backseat of their vehicle. After Gant had been handcuffed and placed in the back of a patrol car, two officers searched his car: One of them found a gun, and the other discovered a bag of cocaine in the pocket of a jacket on the backseat.

Gant was charged with two offenses—possession of a narcotic drug for sale and possession of drug paraphernalia (i.e., the plastic bag in which the cocaine was found). He moved to suppress the evidence seized from his car on the ground that the warrantless search violated the Fourth Amendment. Among other things, Gant argued that *Belton* did not authorize the search of his vehicle because he posed no threat to the officers after he was handcuffed in the patrol car and because he was arrested for a traffic offense for which no evidence could be found in his vehicle. When asked at the suppression hearing why the search was conducted, Officer Griffith responded: "Because the law says we can do it."

The trial court rejected the State's contention that the officers had probable cause to search Gant's car for contraband when the search began, but it denied the motion to suppress. Relying on the fact that the police saw Gant commit the crime of driving without a license and apprehended him only shortly after he exited his car, the court held that the search was permissible as a search incident to arrest. A jury found Gant guilty on both drug counts, and he was sentenced to a three-year term of imprisonment.

OPINION

In *Chimel v. California* (excerpted on p. 203), we held that a search incident to arrest may only include "the arrestee's person and the area 'within his immediate control'" ("the area from within which he might gain possession of a weapon or destructible evidence"). In *New York v. Belton* (1981), we considered Chimel's application to the automobile context. We held that when an officer lawfully arrests "the occupant of an automobile, he may, as a contemporaneous incident of that arrest, search the passenger compartment of the automobile" and any containers therein. That holding was based in large part on our

(*continued*)

assumption that articles inside the relatively narrow compass of the passenger compartment of an automobile are in fact generally, even if not inevitably, "within 'the area into which an arrestee might reach.'"

The Arizona Supreme Court read our decision in *Belton* as merely delineating "the proper scope of a search of the interior of an automobile" incident to an arrest. That is, when the passenger compartment is within an arrestee's reaching distance, *Belton* supplies the generalization that the entire compartment and any containers therein may be reached. On that view of *Belton*, the state court concluded that the search of Gant's car was unreasonable because Gant clearly could not have accessed his car at the time of the search. It also found that no other exception to the warrant requirement applied in this case. Gant now urges us to adopt the reading of *Belton* followed by the Arizona Supreme Court.

Despite the support for the Arizona Supreme Court's reading of *Belton*, our opinion has been widely understood to allow a vehicle search incident to the arrest of a recent occupant even if there is no possibility the arrestee could gain access to the vehicle at the time of the search. Since we decided *Belton*, Courts of Appeals have given different answers to the question whether a vehicle must be within an arrestee's reach to justify a vehicle search incident to arrest. As Justice O'Connor observed, "lower court decisions seem now to treat the ability to search a vehicle incident to the arrest of a recent occupant as a police entitlement rather than as an exception justified by the twin rationales of *Chimel*." Justice Scalia has similarly noted that, although it is improbable that an arrestee could gain access to weapons stored in his vehicle after he has been handcuffed and secured in the backseat of a patrol car, cases allowing a search in "this precise factual scenario are legion." Indeed, some courts have upheld searches under *Belton* even when the handcuffed arrestee has already left the scene.

Under this broad reading of *Belton*, a vehicle search would be authorized incident to every arrest of a recent occupant notwithstanding that in most cases the vehicle's passenger compartment will not be within the arrestee's reach at the time of the search. Accordingly, we reject this reading of *Belton* and hold that the *Chimel* rationale authorizes police to search a vehicle incident to a recent occupant's arrest only when the arrestee is unsecured and within reaching distance of the passenger compartment at the time of the search.

We also conclude that circumstances unique to the vehicle context justify a search incident to a lawful arrest when it is reasonable to believe evidence relevant to the crime of arrest might be found in the vehicle. In many cases, as when a recent occupant is arrested for a traffic violation, there will be no reasonable basis to believe the vehicle contains relevant evidence. But in others, including *Belton*, the offense of arrest will supply a basis for

searching the passenger compartment of an arrestee's vehicle and any containers therein.

Neither the possibility of access nor the likelihood of discovering offense-related evidence authorized the search in this case. Unlike in *Belton*, which involved a single officer confronted with four unsecured arrestees, the five officers in this case outnumbered the three arrestees, all of whom had been handcuffed and secured in separate patrol cars before the officers searched Gant's car. Under those circumstances, Gant clearly was not within reaching distance of his car at the time of the search. An evidentiary basis for the search was also lacking in this case. Whereas Belton was arrested for drug offenses, Gant was arrested for driving with a suspended license—an offense for which police could not expect to find evidence in the passenger compartment of Gant's car. Because police could not reasonably have believed either that Gant could have accessed his car at the time of the search or that evidence of the offense for which he was arrested might have been found therein, the search in this case was unreasonable.

The State argues that *Belton* searches are reasonable regardless of the possibility of access in a given case because that expansive rule correctly balances law enforcement interests, including the interest in a bright-line rule, with an arrestee's limited privacy interest in his vehicle. We reject the State's argument. The State seriously undervalues the privacy interests at stake. It is particularly significant that *Belton* searches authorize police officers to search not just the passenger compartment but every purse, briefcase, or other container within that space. A rule that gives police the power to conduct such a search whenever an individual is caught committing a traffic offense, when there is no basis for believing evidence of the offense might be found in the vehicle, creates a serious and recurring threat to the privacy of countless individuals.

Construing *Belton* broadly to allow vehicle searches incident to any arrest would serve no purpose except to provide a police entitlement, and it is anathema to the Fourth Amendment to permit a warrantless search on that basis. For these reasons, we are unpersuaded by the State's arguments that a broad reading of *Belton* would meaningfully further law enforcement interests and justify a substantial intrusion on individuals' privacy.

The experience of the 28 years since we decided *Belton* has shown that the generalization underpinning the broad reading of that decision is unfounded. We now know that articles inside the passenger compartment are rarely within the area into which an arrestee might reach, and blind adherence to *Belton*'s faulty assumption would authorize myriad unconstitutional searches.

Police may search a vehicle incident to a recent occupant's arrest only if the arrestee is within reaching distance of the passenger compartment at the time of the search or it is reasonable to believe the vehicle contains evidence of the offense of arrest. When these justifications are absent, a search of an arrestee's vehicle will be unreasonable unless police obtain a warrant or show that another exception to the warrant requirement applies. The Arizona Supreme Court correctly held that this case involved an unreasonable search.

Accordingly, the judgment of the State Supreme Court is AFFIRMED. It is so ordered.

CONCURRING OPINION

SCALIA, J.

It is abundantly clear that traditional standards of reasonableness do not justify what I take to be the rule set forth in *New York v. Belton* (1981): that arresting officers may always search an arrestee's vehicle in order to protect themselves from hidden weapons. When an arrest is made in connection with a roadside stop, police virtually always have a less intrusive and more effective means of ensuring their safety—and a means that is virtually always employed: ordering the arrestee away from the vehicle, patting him down in the open, handcuffing him, and placing him in the squad car.

Law enforcement officers face a risk of being shot whenever they pull a car over. But that risk is at its height at the time of the initial confrontation; and it is not at all reduced by allowing a search of the stopped vehicle after the driver has been arrested and placed in the squad car. I observed in *Thornton v. U.S.* (2004) that the government had failed to provide a single instance in which a formerly restrained arrestee escaped to retrieve a weapon from his own vehicle. Arizona and its amici have not remedied that significant deficiency in the present case.

In my view we should simply abandon the *Belton-Thornton* charade of officer safety and overrule those cases. I would hold that a vehicle search incident to arrest is ipso facto "reasonable" only when the object of the search is evidence of the crime for which the arrest was made, or of another crime that the officer has probable cause to believe occurred. Because respondent was arrested for driving without a license (a crime for which no evidence could be expected to be found in the vehicle), I would hold in the present case that the search was unlawful.

DISSENT

ALITO, J., joined by ROBERTS, CJ., and KENNEDY, BREYER, JJ.

The precise holding in *Belton* could not be clearer. The Court stated unequivocally: "We hold that when a policeman has made a lawful custodial arrest of the occupant of an automobile, he may, as a contemporaneous incident of that arrest, search the passenger compartment of that automobile."

The *Chimel* Court concluded that there are only two justifications for a warrantless search incident to arrest— officer safety and the preservation of evidence. The Court stated that such a search must be confined to "the arrestee's person" and "the area from within which he might gain possession of a weapon or destructible evidence." Unfortunately, *Chimel* did not say whether "the area from within which [an arrestee] might gain possession of a weapon or destructible evidence" is to be measured at the time of the arrest or at the time of the search, but unless the *Chimel* rule was meant to be a specialty rule, applicable to only a few unusual cases, the Court must have intended for this area to be measured at the time of arrest.

This is so because the Court can hardly have failed to appreciate the following two facts. First, in the great majority of cases, an officer making an arrest is able to handcuff the arrestee and remove him to a secure place before conducting a search incident to the arrest. Second, because it is safer for an arresting officer to secure an arrestee before searching, it is likely that this is what arresting officers do in the great majority of cases. (And it appears, not surprisingly, that this is in fact the prevailing practice.) Thus, if the area within an arrestee's reach were assessed, not at the time of arrest, but at the time of the search, the *Chimel* rule would rarely come into play. Moreover, if the applicability of the *Chimel* rule turned on whether an arresting officer chooses to secure an arrestee prior to conducting a search, rather than searching first and securing the arrestee later, the rule would create a perverse incentive for an arresting officer to prolong the period during which the arrestee is kept in an area where he could pose a danger to the officer. If this is the law, the D.C. Circuit observed, "the law would truly be, as Mr. Bumble said, 'a ass.'"

Questions

1. List the facts relevant to deciding whether the search of Rodney Gant's car was a lawful search "incident" to Gant's arrest.

2. What does Justice O'Connor mean when she writes that "lower court decisions seem now to treat the ability to search a vehicle incident to the arrest of a recent occupant as a police entitlement rather than as an exception justified by the twin rationales of *Chimel*"?

3. According to Justice Scalia, when is a vehicle search incident to arrest reasonable?

4. According to Justice Alito, what interpretation of *Chimel* would make the law "a ass"?

LO 4   *The time frame of "incident to"*

According to the U.S. Supreme Court, "**incident to arrest**" (or as it's sometimes called, "**contemporaneous with arrest**") includes the time before, during, and after arrest. For example, in *Cupp v. Murphy* (1973), immediately before Portland, Oregon, police officers arrested Daniel Murphy, they scraped his fingernails for blood residue to see if it matched his strangled wife's. The U.S. Supreme Court held that because the officers could have arrested Murphy before they searched him (they had probable cause), the search was incident to the arrest.

In *U.S. v. Edwards* (1974), Eugene Edwards was arrested shortly after 11:00 p.m. and put in jail. The next morning, officers took his clothing and searched it for paint chips that would link Edwards to a burglary. Despite the 10-hour gap between the arrest and the search, and over a strong dissent arguing the officers had plenty of time to present their evidence to a neutral magistrate to get a search warrant, the Supreme Court ruled that the search was incident to the arrest.

Searches incident to misdemeanor arrests

Until now, we've looked at the reasonableness of searches incident to felony arrests, but what about searches incident to arrests for misdemeanors? The U.S. Supreme Court answered the question in *U.S. v. Robinson* (1973). Officer Richard Jenks, a 15-year veteran of the Washington, D.C., Police Department, arrested Willie Robinson for driving without a license (a misdemeanor). Jenks then searched Robinson. During the search, Jenks felt a lump in Robinson's coat pocket. Reaching inside, he found a crumpled-up cigarette package. Jenks took the package out of Robinson's pocket, opened it, and found heroin inside.

Robinson was charged with illegally possessing narcotics. He moved to suppress the evidence, but the court denied his motion and admitted the heroin. The heroin was the main evidence that convicted Robinson. The Supreme Court upheld the conviction and formulated a bright-line *Robinson* rule: Officers can always search anyone they're authorized to take into custody. (Be clear that officers don't *have* to search; many times they don't, but whether they do is a matter of individual officer discretion.)

According to Justice Rehnquist, writing for the majority:

> A police officer's determination as to how and where to search the person of a suspect whom he has arrested is necessarily a quick ad hoc judgment which the Fourth Amendment does not require to be broken down in each instance into an analysis of each step in the search. A custodial arrest of a suspect based on probable cause is a reasonable intrusion under the Fourth Amendment; that intrusion being lawful, a search incident to the arrest requires no additional justification. It is the fact of the lawful arrest which establishes the authority to search, and we hold that in the case of a lawful custodial arrest a full search of the person is not only an exception to the warrant requirement of the Fourth Amendment, but is also a "reasonable" search under that Amendment. (234–35)

What's the justification for the bright-line *Robinson* rule? Two reasons, according to the Court:

1. The possible danger to police officers taking suspects into custody

2. The logical impossibility of the Court's reviewing every police decision

The rule highlights the Court's continuing reluctance to second-guess law enforcement decisions. But six state courts haven't shown the same reluctance. Alaska, California, Hawaii, New York, Oregon, and West Virginia rejected the rule. Another five have specifically adopted it—Illinois, Michigan, Montana, New Hampshire, and Texas (Latzer 1991, 64).

Is a bright-line rule authorizing law enforcement officers to *always* search incident to traffic **citations** reasonable under the *Robinson* rule? (Citations are substitutes for arrests.) A unanimous U.S. Supreme Court struck down an Iowa statute creating such a rule in *Knowles v. Iowa* (1998). In *Knowles*, an Iowa police officer stopped Patrick Knowles for going 43 miles an hour in a 25-m.p.h. zone. The police officer issued a citation to Knowles. (Under Iowa law, he *could* have arrested him.) The officer then conducted a full search of the car, including under the driver's seat. Under the driver's seat he found a bag of marijuana and a "pot pipe." He arrested Knowles, and Knowles was charged with possessing a controlled substance.

Before trial, Knowles moved to suppress the marijuana evidence. At the suppression hearing, the police officer conceded that Knowles didn't consent to the search, and that he didn't have probable cause to arrest him. He relied on Iowa Code Ann. § 321.485(1)(a):

> Iowa peace officers having cause to believe that a person has violated any traffic or motor vehicle equipment law *may* arrest the person and immediately take the person before a magistrate. (emphasis added)

Section 805.1(4) "also authorizes the far more usual practice of issuing a citation in lieu of arrest." The Iowa Supreme Court "interpreted this provision as providing authority to officers to conduct a full-blown search of an automobile and driver in those cases where police elect not to make a custodial arrest and instead issue a citation—that is, a search incident to citation" (*Knowles v. Iowa* 1998).

According to the U.S. Supreme Court, searches incident to citation can't be justified by comparing them to searches incident to arrests, namely to protect either officer safety or preservation of evidence.

> A routine traffic stop . . . is a relatively brief encounter and is more analogous to a *Terry* stop than to a formal arrest. Where there is no formal arrest a person might well be less hostile to the police and less likely to take conspicuous, immediate steps to destroy incriminating evidence. This is not to say that the concern for officer safety is absent in the case of a routine traffic stop. It plainly is not. But while the concern for officer safety in this context may justify the "minimal" additional intrusion of ordering a driver and passengers out of the car, it does not by itself justify the often considerably greater intrusion attending a full field-type search.
>
> Nor has Iowa shown the second justification for the authority to search incident to arrest—the need to discover and preserve evidence. Once Knowles was stopped for speeding and issued a citation, all the evidence necessary to prosecute that offense had been obtained. No further evidence of excessive speed was going to be found either on the person of the offender or in the passenger compartment of the car. (117–18)

LO 4 | *Searches incident to pretext arrests*

Suppose an officer has only a hunch that a college student has marijuana in her car. The officer sees her make a left turn without signaling. "What luck," he thinks,

"Now, I've got my chance." He stops her for turning without signaling so that he can search the car for marijuana—the arrest is simply a pretext for the search. **Pretext arrests** (arrests for one offense where officers have probable cause because officers want to search for evidence of another unrelated offense where they don't have probable cause) are powerful investigative tools in the "drug war." Most people commit traffic offenses, so officers can use this fact of life to act on their hunches that drivers are committing drug crimes. In our next case, *Whren v. U.S.* (1996), a unanimous U.S. Supreme Court decided that police officers' search of Michael Whren's Nissan Pathfinder incident to Whren's arrest for traffic violations was a reasonable Fourth Amendment search.

In *Whren v. U.S.* (1999), the U.S. Supreme Court held that officers' search of Michael Whren's Nissan Pathfinder incident to his pretext arrest for a traffic violation did not violate the Fourth Amendment.

CASE

Was the Search Incident to a Pretext Arrest Reasonable?

Whren v. U.S.
517 U.S. 806 (1996)

HISTORY

Michael A. Whren and James L. Brown were convicted in the U.S. District Court for the District of Columbia of drug offenses, and they appealed. The Court of Appeals affirmed. The U.S. Supreme Court granted certiorari. The U.S. Supreme Court affirmed.

—SCALIA, J.

FACTS

On the evening of June 10, 1993, plainclothes vice-squad officers of the District of Columbia Metropolitan Police Department were patrolling a "high drug area" of the city in an unmarked car. Their suspicions were aroused when they passed a dark Nissan Pathfinder with temporary license plates and youthful occupants waiting at a stop sign, the driver looking down into the lap of the passenger at his right. The Pathfinder remained stopped at the intersection for what seemed an unusually long time—more than 20 seconds.

When the police car executed a U-turn in order to head back toward the truck, the Pathfinder turned suddenly to its right, without signaling, and sped off at an "unreasonable" speed. The policemen followed, and in a short while overtook the Pathfinder when it stopped behind other traffic at a red light. They pulled up alongside, and Officer Ephraim Soto stepped out and approached the driver's door, identifying himself as a police officer and directing the driver, James Brown, to put the vehicle in park. When Soto drew up to the driver's window, he immediately observed two large plastic bags of what appeared to be crack cocaine in Michael Whren's hands. Brown and Whren were arrested, and quantities of several types of illegal drugs were retrieved from the vehicle.

Brown and Whren were charged with violating various federal drug laws, including 21 U.S.C. §§ 844(a) and 860(a). At a pretrial suppression hearing, they challenged the legality of the stop and the resulting seizure of the drugs. They argued that the stop had not been justified by probable cause to believe, or even reasonable suspicion, that they were engaged in illegal drug-dealing activity; and that Officer Soto's asserted ground for approaching the vehicle—to give the driver a warning concerning traffic violations—was pretextual.

The District Court denied the suppression motion. Whren and Brown were convicted. The Court of Appeals affirmed the convictions.

OPINION

The decision to stop an automobile is reasonable where the police have probable cause to believe that a traffic violation has occurred. Brown and Whren accept that

Officer Soto had probable cause to believe that various provisions of the District of Columbia traffic code had been violated:

1. 18 D.C. Mun. Regs. §§ 2213.4 (1995) An operator shall . . . give full time and attention to the operation of the vehicle;
2. 2204.3 No person shall turn any vehicle . . . without giving an appropriate signal;
3. 2200.3 No person shall drive a vehicle . . . at a speed greater than is reasonable and prudent under the conditions.

They argue, however, that "in the unique context of civil traffic regulations" probable cause is not enough. Since, they contend, the use of automobiles is so heavily and minutely regulated that total compliance with traffic and safety rules is nearly impossible, a police officer will almost invariably be able to catch any given motorist in a technical violation. This creates the temptation to use traffic stops as a means of investigating other law violations, as to which no probable cause or even articulable suspicion exists.

Whren and Brown, who are both Black, further contend that police officers might decide which motorists to stop based on decidedly impermissible factors, such as the race of the car's occupants. To avoid this danger, they say, the Fourth Amendment test for traffic stops should be, not the normal one (applied by the Court of Appeals) of whether probable cause existed to justify the stop; but rather, whether a police officer, acting reasonably, *would* [emphasis added] have made the stop for the reason given.

Whren and Brown contend that the standard they propose is consistent with our past cases' disapproval of police attempts to use valid bases of action against citizens as pretexts for pursuing other investigatory agendas.

Not only have we never held, outside the context of inventory search [discussed in Chapter 7] or administrative inspection, that an officer's motive invalidates objectively justifiable behavior under the Fourth Amendment, but we have repeatedly held and asserted the contrary. [The Court discussed several cases omitted here.] We think these cases foreclose any argument that the constitutional reasonableness of traffic stops depends on the actual motivations of the individual officers involved.

We of course agree with Whren and Brown that the Constitution prohibits selective enforcement of the law based on considerations such as race. But the constitutional basis for objecting to intentionally discriminatory application of laws is the Equal Protection Clause, not the Fourth Amendment. Subjective intentions play no role in ordinary, probable-cause Fourth Amendment analysis.

Whren and Brown's claim that a reasonable officer *would* not [emphasis added] have made this stop is based largely on District of Columbia police regulations which permit plainclothes officers in unmarked vehicles to enforce traffic laws "only in the case of a violation that is so grave as to pose an immediate threat to the safety of others." This basis of invalidation would not apply in jurisdictions that had a different practice. And it would not have applied even in the District of Columbia, if Officer Soto had been wearing a uniform or patrolling in a marked police cruiser.

Whren and Brown argue that the balancing inherent in any Fourth Amendment inquiry requires us to weigh the governmental and individual interests implicated in a traffic stop such as we have here. That balancing, they claim, does not support investigation of minor traffic infractions by plainclothes police in unmarked vehicles; such investigation only minimally advances the government's interest in traffic safety, and may indeed retard it by producing motorist confusion and alarm—a view said to be supported by the Metropolitan Police Department's own regulations generally prohibiting this practice.

It is of course true that in principle every Fourth Amendment case, since it turns upon a "reasonableness" determination, involves a balancing of all relevant factors. With rare exceptions not applicable here, however, the result of that balancing is not in doubt where the search or seizure is based upon probable cause. Where probable cause has existed, the only cases in which we have found it necessary actually to perform the "balancing" analysis involved searches or seizures conducted in an extraordinary manner, unusually harmful to an individual's privacy or even physical interests—such as, for example, seizure by means of deadly force, see *Tennessee v. Garner* (1985) [Chapter 5, p. 178], unannounced entry into a home, see *Wilson v. Arkansas* (1995), *Richards v. Wisconsin* (1984), or physical penetration of the body, see *Winston v. Lee* (1985).

The making of a traffic stop out-of-uniform does not remotely qualify as such an extreme practice, and so is governed by the usual rule that probable cause to believe the law has been broken "outbalances" private interest in avoiding police contact.

Whren and Brown urge as an extraordinary factor in this case that the "multitude of applicable traffic and equipment regulations" is so large and so difficult to obey perfectly that virtually everyone is guilty of violation, permitting the police to single out almost whomever they wish for a stop. But we are aware of no principle that would allow us to decide at what point a code of law becomes so expansive and so commonly violated that infraction itself can no longer be the ordinary measure of the lawfulness of enforcement. And even if we could identify such exorbitant codes, we do not know by what standard (or what right) we would decide, as Whren and Brown would have us do, which particular provisions are sufficiently important to merit enforcement.

(continued)

For the run of the mine case, which this surely is, we think there is no realistic alternative to the traditional common-law rule that probable cause justifies a search and seizure. Here the District Court found that the officers had probable cause to believe that petitioners had violated the traffic code. That rendered the stop reasonable under the Fourth Amendment, the evidence thereby discovered admissible, and the upholding of the convictions by the Court of Appeals for the District of Columbia Circuit correct.

—Judgment AFFIRMED.

Questions

1. List all the actions Officer Soto and his partner took that affected Whren and Brown's liberty and privacy.

2. What's the evidence that Officer Soto and his partner conducted a pretext search?

3. Did Officer Soto and his partner have probable cause to arrest Whren and Brown? List the relevant facts and circumstances relevant to deciding whether they had probable cause.

4. For what "crimes" did the officers have probable cause to arrest Brown and Whren?

5. Explain the "could have" and "would have" tests to determine the reasonableness of the pretext search. What test did the Court adopt? Why?

6. Consider this quote from Professor Daniel Jonas (1989):

The conflict between liberty and law enforcement is particularly sharp in the area of pretextual police conduct. Police would have a powerful investigative tool if it were constitutional, for example, to arrest a felony suspect on the basis of a parking ticket that had not been paid, when the facts relating to the felony did not provide probable cause. Precisely because its investigative potential is so great, pretextual police conduct poses an alarming threat to individual freedom from government intrusion. (1792)

Do you agree that pretext searches threaten individual rights too much? That they give the government too much power? Or do you believe that the government needs this power to fight the "war on drugs"?

Critics maintain that illegitimate criteria infect pretext arrest searches. Professor David Cole (1999) tells this story to illustrate how race infected one Black family's traffic arrest. Robert Wilkins, a young Black Harvard-educated lawyer working as a public defender in Washington, D.C., his aunt, uncle, and cousin were driving home from a family funeral in Chicago. Maryland State Trooper Bryn Hughes stopped their rented car for driving 60 miles an hour in a 45-mile zone. Trooper Hughes asked Wilkins's cousin, who was driving the car, if he would sign a consent form to search his car. With Wilkins by his side, his cousin said no. Hughes held them for 30 minutes while he called for a drug-sniffing dog.

When the dog arrived, Hughes ordered the family out of the car, where they stood in the rain while the German shepherd sniffed all around the car. The dog didn't alert, so Trooper Hughes wrote out a speeding ticket. (Earlier, he had told Wilkins's cousin he would issue only a warning.) (Cole 1999, 34–35)

How many traffic arrest searches does discrimination infect? The most recent Bureau of Justice Statistics household survey, *Contacts between Police and the Public 2008* (2011), provides empirical support for the discrimination infection argument. Although officers arrest Black (8.8 percent), Hispanic (9.1 percent), and White (8.4 percent) drivers for traffic offenses at about the same rate, they *search* Black drivers at much higher rates (Figure 6.1).

CONSENT SEARCHES

 LO 5

In **consent searches,** individuals give officers permission to search them, their houses, private papers, and personal belongings without either warrants or probable cause. We don't know how many searches without warrants are consent searches, and estimates vary widely. In one sample of seven cities selected for their regional and procedural

FIGURE 6.1 Drivers Searched during Traffic Stops, 2008

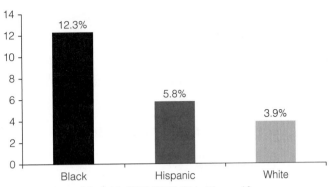

Source: BJS, *Contacts between Police and the Public 2008* (2011), Table 14, page 10.

diversity, estimates ranged from a low of 10 percent in "Plains City," to a high of 98 percent in "Mountain City" (Van Duizen, Sutton, and Carter 1985, 68).

We do know that "the vast majority of people" who do consent to full body searches or pat downs are innocent (Nadler 2002, 209–10), and that most of the people who consent are young, poor, and not White (Cole 1999, 28).

We also know that police officers "highly favor consent searches" (Maclin 2008, 31). The reasons why they prefer them include:

1. They make officers' job easier, because they don't have to go through the hassle of either getting warrants before they search, or proving probable cause to a judge later.

2. They're the safest way to minimize the risk of judges throwing out the evidence in a suppression hearing.

3. They provide officers the authority and discretion to "conduct an open-ended search with virtually no limits" (Maclin 2008, 31).

4. They allow police "to exercise their discretion and power in contexts that affect literally hundreds of thousands of persons where the target is unlikely to say 'no' to a request to a consent search (Maclin 2008, 31).

We see some mix of these reasons in the endless "war on drugs," where convenience and necessity drive officers to ask for consent. For example, drug dealers often travel by bus or plane, but officers rarely have probable cause to search most passengers. So they approach travelers, ask if they can talk to them, explain the seriousness of the drug problem, and ask them if they mind having officers search them and their belongings. According to the anecdotal evidence supplied by officers, most travelers give their consent, especially when officers are polite and respectful.

In *U.S. v. Blake* (1988), Detective Perry Kendrick, who worked the Fort Lauderdale Airport, testified that people willingly consent even to searches of their crotches in the public part of airports (*U.S. v. Rodney*, excerpted later in this chapter). In just one day,

> [H]e talked with 16 to 20 people and most consented, but one or two did not. He testified further that initially some complain after the search, but that after the deputies explain their mission in interdicting narcotics moving from airport to airport within the United States, that the persons understand and many "thank us for the job we're doing." (927)

With this general background to consent searches, let's turn to four legal questions connected with consent searches.

1. Did the suspect consent?
2. What's the scope of consent?
3. When can suspects withdraw consent after they give it?
4. When can one person consent for someone else?

LO 6   Two Theories of Consent

Suppose a police officer knocks on your door. You open the door and ask, "What can I do for you, officer?" She replies, "We've had lots of complaints of marijuana smoking in the building. Do you mind if I come in and look around?" "Sure, C'mon in. You won't find any weed in here."

Courts view consent searches in two different ways. One way is to look at the state of mind of the person giving up the right, namely whether she intended to give up (waive) her right against unreasonable searches. This test, often called the **waiver test of consent to search**, asks (1) whether the person knew she had a right to refuse consent, (2) intended to give up (waive) the right, and (3) gave it up voluntarily. The other, called the **voluntariness test of consent to search** (also called the **totality-of-circumstances test of consent to search**), looks at the police officer's state of mind. Here, the test is whether under all of the circumstances, the officer reasonably believed that you consented voluntarily to the search.

Table 6.2 lists the most common of these circumstances (Thomas 2009, 1).

A signed consent form can prove that a suspect voluntarily consented to a search. The New Jersey "Consent to Search" form adopted by the New Jersey State Police authorizes a trooper to conduct a "complete search" of a motor vehicle or other premises as described by the officer on the face of the form.

The form also requires that the person sign off on the following:

1. I also authorize the above member of the New Jersey State Police to remove and search any letters, documents, papers, materials, or other property which is considered pertinent to the investigation, provided that I am subsequently given a receipt for anything which is removed.
2. I have knowingly and voluntarily given my consent to the search described above.

TABLE 6.2 Circumstances that may form part of voluntary consent

• Knowledge of constitutional rights in general
• Knowledge of the right to refuse consent
• Sufficient age and maturity to make an independent decision
• Intelligence to understand the significance of consent
• Education in or experience with the workings of the criminal justice system
• Cooperation with officers, such as saying, "Sure, go ahead and search"
• Attitude toward the likelihood that officers will discover contraband
• Length of detention and nature of questioning regarding consent
• Coercive police behavior surrounding the consent

3. I have been advised by [the investigating officer] and fully understand that I have the right to refuse giving my consent to search.

4. I have been further advised that I may withdraw my consent at any time during the search.

The form is filled out by the officer and includes, among other things, the officer's name and a description of the vehicle or premises the officer wants to search. Then, the officer presents the form to the consenting person for her to sign (*State v. Carty* 2002, 907).

The U.S. Supreme Court adopted the voluntariness (totality-of-circumstances) test in our next case excerpt, *Schneckcloth v. Bustamonte* (1973) by a 6–3 majority.

In *Schneckloth v. Bustamonte* (1973), the U.S. Supreme Court upheld the search of the car

Clyde Bustamonte was a passenger in because it passed the totality-of-circumstances test

for consent searches.

CASE

Was the Consent Voluntary?

Schneckcloth v. Bustamonte
412 U.S. 218 (1973)   6-3

HISTORY

Clyde Bustamonte was tried in a California state court for possessing a check with intent to defraud. The trial judge denied his motion to suppress and Bustamonte was convicted. The California Court of Appeals affirmed. The California Supreme Court denied review. Bustamonte brought a petition for habeas corpus in the U.S. District Court for the Northern District of California. The District Court denied the petition. The U.S. Court of Appeals for the Ninth Circuit vacated the District Court's order, and remanded. The U.S. Supreme Court reversed.

—STEWART, J.

FACTS

While on routine patrol in Sunnyvale, California, at approximately 2:40 in the morning, Police Officer James Rand stopped an automobile when he observed that one headlight and its license plate light were burned out. Six men were in the vehicle. Joe Alcala and Robert Clyde Bustamonte were in the front seat with Joe Gonzales, the driver. Three older men were seated in the rear. When, in response to the policeman's question, Gonzales could not produce a driver's license, Officer Rand asked if any of the other five had any evidence of identification. Only Alcala produced a license, and he explained that the car was his brother's.

After the six occupants had stepped out of the car at the officer's request and after two additional policemen had arrived, Officer Rand asked Alcala if he could search the car. Alcala replied, "Sure, go ahead." Prior to the search no one was threatened with arrest and, according to Officer Rand's uncontradicted testimony, it "was all very congenial at this time." Gonzales testified that Alcala actually helped in the search of the car, by opening the trunk and glove compartment. In Gonzales's words: "[T]he police officer asked Joe (Alcala), he goes, 'Does the trunk open?' And Joe said, 'Yes.' He went to the car and got the keys and opened up the trunk." Wadded up under the left rear seat, the police officers found three checks that had previously been stolen from a car wash.

OPINION

It is well settled under the Fourth Amendment that one of the exceptions to the requirements of both a warrant and probable cause is a search that is conducted pursuant to consent. The precise question in this case is what must the prosecution prove to demonstrate that a consent was "voluntarily" given. And upon that question there is a square conflict of views between the state and federal courts that have reviewed the search involved in the case before us.

The Court of Appeals for the Ninth Circuit concluded that it is an essential part of the State's initial

(*continued*)

burden to prove that a person knows he has a right to refuse consent. The California courts have followed the rule that voluntariness is a question of fact to be determined from the totality of all the circumstances, and that the state of a defendant's knowledge is only one factor to be taken into account in assessing the voluntariness of a consent.

The most extensive judicial exposition of the meaning of "voluntariness" has been developed in those cases in which the Court has had to determine the "voluntariness" of a defendant's confession [Chapter 8]. The ultimate test has remained the same in Anglo-American courts for two hundred years: the test of voluntariness. Is the confession the product of an essentially free and unconstrained choice by its maker? If it is, if he has willed to confess, it may be used against him. If it is not, if his will has been overborne and his capacity for self-determination critically impaired, the use of his confession offends due process.

The significant fact about all of these decisions is that none of them turned on the presence or absence of a single controlling criterion; each reflected a careful scrutiny of all the surrounding circumstances. In none of them did the Court rule that the Due Process Clause required the prosecution to prove as part of its initial burden that the defendant knew he had a right to refuse to answer the questions that were put. While the state of the accused's mind, and the failure of the police to advise the accused of his rights, were certainly factors to be evaluated in assessing the "voluntariness" of an accused's responses, they were not in and of themselves determinative.

The question whether a consent to a search was in fact "voluntary" or was the product of duress or coercion is a question of fact to be determined from the totality of all the circumstances. While knowledge of the right to refuse consent is one factor to be taken into account, the government need not establish such knowledge as indispensable to an effective consent. As with police questioning, two competing concerns must be accommodated in determining the meaning of a voluntary consent—the legitimate need for such searches and the equally important requirement of assuring the absence of coercion.

In situations where the police have some evidence of illicit activity, but lack probable cause to arrest or search, a search authorized by a valid consent may be the only means of obtaining important and reliable evidence. In the present case for example, while the police had reason to stop the car for traffic violations, the State does not contend that there was probable cause to search the vehicle or that the search was incident to a valid arrest of any of the occupants. Yet, the search yielded tangible evidence that served as a basis for a prosecution, and provided some assurance that others, wholly innocent of the crime, were not mistakenly brought to trial. In short, a search pursuant to consent may result in considerably less inconvenience for the subject of the search, and, properly conducted, is a constitutionally permissible and wholly legitimate aspect of effective police activity.

But the Fourth Amendment requires that a consent not be coerced. In examining all the surrounding circumstances to determine if in fact the consent to search was coerced, account must be taken of subtly coercive police questions, as well as the possibly vulnerable subjective state of the person who consents. Those searches that are the product of police coercion can thus be filtered out without undermining the continuing validity of consent searches.

The approach of the Court of Appeals for the Ninth Circuit that the State must affirmatively prove that the subject of the search knew that he had a right to refuse consent, would, in practice, create serious doubt whether consent searches could continue to be conducted. There might be rare cases where it could be proved from the record that a person in fact affirmatively knew of his right to refuse—such as a case where he announced to the police that if he didn't sign the consent form, "you (police) are going to get a search warrant." But more commonly where there was no evidence of any coercion, the prosecution would nevertheless be unable to demonstrate that the subject of the search in fact had known of his right to refuse consent.

[Bustamonte also argues] that the Court's decision in the *Miranda* case [excerpted in Chapter 8] requires the conclusion that knowledge of a right to refuse is an indispensable element of a valid consent. In *Miranda*, the Court found that the techniques of police questioning and the nature of custodial surroundings produce an inherently coercive situation. The Court noted that "without proper safeguards the process of in-custody interrogation of persons suspected or accused of crime contains inherently compelling pressures which work to undermine the individual's will to resist and to compel him to speak where he would not otherwise do so freely."

In this case, there is no evidence of any inherently coercive tactics—either from the nature of the police questioning or the environment in which it took place. Indeed, since consent searches will normally occur on a person's own familiar territory, the specter of incommunicado police interrogation in some remote station house is simply inapposite. There is no reason to believe, under circumstances such as are present here, that the response to a policeman's question is presumptively coerced; and there is, therefore, no reason to reject the traditional test for determining the voluntariness of a person's response.

It is also argued that the failure to require the Government to establish knowledge as a prerequisite to a valid consent, will relegate the Fourth Amendment to the special province of "the sophisticated, the knowledgeable and the privileged." We cannot agree. The traditional definition of voluntariness we accept today has always taken into account evidence of minimal schooling, low intelligence, and the lack of any effective warnings to a person of his rights; and the voluntariness of any statement taken under those conditions has been carefully scrutinized to determine whether it was in fact voluntarily given.

Our decision today is a narrow one. We hold only that when the subject of a search is not in custody and the State attempts to justify a search on the basis of his consent, the Fourth Amendment requires that it demonstrate that the consent was in fact voluntarily given, and not the result of coercion. Voluntariness is a question of fact to be determined from all the circumstances, and while the subject's knowledge of a right to refuse is a factor to be taken into account, the prosecution is not required to demonstrate such knowledge as a prerequisite to establishing a voluntary consent.

—Judgment of Court of Appeals REVERSED.

DISSENT

MARSHALL, J.

I would have thought that the capacity to choose necessarily depends upon knowledge that there is a choice to be made. But today the Court reaches the curious result that one can choose to relinquish a constitutional right—the right to be free of unreasonable searches—without knowing that he has the alternative of refusing to accede to a police request to search. I am at a loss to understand why consent cannot be taken literally to mean a "knowing choice." In fact, I have difficulty in comprehending how a decision made without knowledge of available alternatives can be treated as a choice at all. I can think of no other situation in which we would say that a person agreed to some course of action if he convinced us that he did not know that there was some other course he might have pursued.

The Court contends that if an officer paused to inform the subject of his rights, the informality of the exchange would be destroyed. I doubt that a simple statement by an officer of an individual's right to refuse consent would do much to alter the informality of the exchange, except to alert the subject to a fact that he surely is entitled to know. It is not without significance that for many years the agents of the Federal Bureau of Investigation have routinely informed subjects of their right to refuse consent, when they request consent to search.

I must conclude with some reluctance that when the Court speaks of practicality, what it really is talking of is the continued ability of the police to capitalize on the ignorance of citizens so as to accomplish by subterfuge what they could not achieve by relying only on the knowing relinquishment of constitutional rights. Of course it would be "practical" for the police to ignore the commands of the Fourth Amendment, if by practicality we mean that more criminals will be apprehended, even though the constitutional rights of innocent people also go by the board. But such a practical advantage is achieved only at the cost of permitting the police to disregard the limitations that the Constitution places on their behavior, a cost that a constitutional democracy cannot long absorb.

I find nothing in the opinion of the Court to dispel my belief that under many circumstances a reasonable person might read an officer's "May I" as the courteous expression of a demand backed by force of law. In most cases, in my view, consent is ordinarily given as acquiescence in an implicit claim of authority to search. Permitting searches in such circumstances, without any assurance at all that the subject of the search knew that, by his consent, he was relinquishing his constitutional rights, is something that I cannot believe is sanctioned by the Constitution.

The proper resolution of this case turns, I believe, on a realistic assessment of the nature of the interchange between citizens and the police. Although the Court says it "cannot agree," the holding today confines the protection of the Fourth Amendment against searches conducted without probable cause to the sophisticated, the knowledgeable, and, I might add, the few.

The Court's half-hearted defense, that lack of knowledge is to be "taken into account," rings rather hollow, in light of the apparent import of the opinion that even a subject who proves his lack of knowledge may nonetheless have consented "voluntarily," under the Court's peculiar definition of voluntariness. In the final analysis, the Court now sanctions a game of blind man's buff, in which the police always have the upper hand, for the sake of nothing more than the convenience of the police.

But the guarantees of the Fourth Amendment were never intended to shrink before such an ephemeral and changeable interest. The Framers of the Fourth Amendment struck the balance against this sort of convenience and in favor of certain basic civil rights. It is not for this Court to restrike that balance because of its own views of the needs of law enforcement officers. I fear that that is the effect of the Court's decision today.

Questions

1. State the elements of the voluntariness test created by the U.S. Supreme Court.

2. List all the facts and circumstances relevant to deciding whether Clyde Bustamonte consented to the search of the car.

3. Describe the Court's application of the voluntariness test to consent in the case.

(*continued*)

4. Explain why the Court says there's a fundamental difference between rights guaranteeing a fair trial and the rights against searches and seizures.

5. According to Justice Marshall, do individuals ever voluntarily consent to police requests, or are all police requests polite orders? Do you agree with Justice Marshall? Defend your answer.

6. State the elements of the waiver test favored by Justice Marshall.

7. Apply the majority's voluntariness test and the dissent's waiver test to the facts of the consent in the case.

8. Consider the consent form used in New Jersey (page 216–217). If Bustamonte had signed this form, would his consent have been voluntary? Would it matter if the officer just handed the form to him without explaining its importance? Explain your answer.

CRIMINAL PROCEDURE IN ACTION

LO 6   Consent after state trooper asked to search a stopped car was voluntary

Ohio v. Robinette, 117 S.Ct. 417 (1996)

FACTS

This case arose on a stretch of Interstate 70 north of Dayton, Ohio, where the posted speed limit was 45 miles per hour because of construction. Robert D. Robinette was clocked at 69 miles per hour as he drove his car along this stretch of road, and he was stopped by Deputy Roger Newsome of the Montgomery County Sheriff's office. Newsome asked for and was handed Robinette's driver's license, and he ran a computer check, which indicated that Robinette had no previous violations. Newsome then asked Robinette to step out of his car, turned on his mounted video camera, issued a verbal warning to Robinette, and returned his license.

At this point, Newsome asked, "One question before you get gone: Are you carrying any illegal contraband in your car? Any weapons of any kind, drugs, anything like that?" Robinette answered "no" to these questions, after which Deputy Newsome asked if he could search the car. Robinette consented. In the car, Deputy Newsome discovered a small amount of marijuana and, in a film container, a pill that was later determined to be Ecstasy (MDMA). Robinette was then arrested and charged with knowing possession of a controlled substance (Ohio Rev.Code Ann. § 2925.11(A) (1993)).

OPINION

Robinette voluntarily consented to the search, the U.S. Supreme Court decided. According to the Court,

> We have long held that the "touchstone of the Fourth Amendment is reasonableness." Reasonableness, in turn, is measured in objective terms by examining the totality of the circumstances. In applying this test we have consistently eschewed bright-line rules, instead emphasizing the fact-specific nature of the reasonableness inquiry.
>
> In *Schneckloth v. Bustamonte*, (1973) [excerpted p. 217], it was argued that such a consent could not be valid unless the defendant knew that he had a right to refuse the request. We rejected this argument: "While knowledge of the right to refuse consent is one factor to be taken into account, the government need not establish such knowledge as the sine qua non of an effective consent." And just as it "would be thoroughly impractical to impose on the normal consent search the detailed requirements of an effective warning," so too would it be unrealistic to require police officers to always inform detainees that they are free to go before a consent to search may be deemed voluntary.

LO 6 Empirical Research and Consent Searches

Now that you've learned something about the waiver and voluntariness theories of consent searches, and how the U.S. Supreme Court has applied the voluntariness doctrine, let's look at what social scientists' empirical research tells us about how voluntary people's consent to search was. The Court expressed great confidence that lower courts would carefully scrutinize the "totality of circumstances" in each case to make sure consent searches were *in fact* voluntary. In practice, the available empirical evidence shows that the lower courts find that consent was voluntary in all but the most extreme cases.

One unpublished study conducted by a Georgetown University Law Center student (cited in Cole 1999) examined all consent cases decided by the U.S. D.C. Court of Appeals from January 1989 to April 15, 1995. In every case, the court found the consent was voluntary. In most of the cases, the court didn't even discuss the circumstances the Supreme Court said in *Schneckloth* were important in determining voluntariness. "When they did mention them, the courts turned a blind eye to factors strongly suggesting a less than voluntary encounter." For example, in one case, the lower court found that 24-year-old Dylan Rodney four times voluntarily consented to a request to search him. Rodney had a 10th-grade education, previously had refused to consent four times, and was searched anyway (Cole 1999, 32).

The majority of justices in *Schneckloth v. Bustamonte* (1973) also claimed that if suspects know they have a right to refuse consent, it "would, in practice, create serious doubt whether consent searches could continue to be conducted" (229–30). Available empirical evidence suggests otherwise. Professor Illya Lichtenberg (2001) examined Ohio State Police data on all highway stops between 1995 and 1997. These years included the year before and after the Ohio Supreme Court ruled that Ohio officers had to warn drivers stopped for traffic violations that they had the right to refuse officers' requests to search. He found no decrease in consent rates after police had to give the warning.

Lichtenberg interviewed a random sample of a group of drivers from the Ohio data. Of the 54 in the sample, 49 consented, 5 refused (251). Of the 49 who consented, 47 said they consented because they were afraid of what would happen to them if they refused. Here are a few answers:

> #15373. I knew legally I didn't have to, but I kind of felt I had to. (264)

> #3371. It would be very, very inconvenient to be locked up for the night. I didn't know if that was an option, and I didn't want to find out. (261)

> #4337 . . . I realized that if I didn't [consent to the search,] they would do it anyway. (261)

> #16633. To this day I do not know what would have happened if I had said, "No, absolutely not." (263)

Finally, the Supreme Court interprets a consent search as an act of good citizenship; it reinforces the rule of law and should, in the words of Justice Kennedy for the majority in *U.S. v. Drayton* (2002), be "given a weight and dignity of its own" (207). Did Lichtenberg's sample drivers see their experience as a

> wholesome picture of a citizen and a police officer engaging in polite conversation, in which the officer and citizen amicably agree that the officer is free to search her person or possessions, after which the citizen bids the officer good day and goes on her way? (Nadler 2012, 339)

At the end of Lichtenberg's survey, he asked the drivers, "When you think about the search, what feelings come to mind?" Their answers to this open-ended question varied, with 1 positive; 13 indifferent; 39 negative:

Positive

#01568. I wish they would do it more. (283)

Indifferent

#14735. I'm just glad I had nothing to hide. (284)

#07267. I guess they were just doing their job. (284)

#01126. Laugh about it I guess. (284)

Negative

#12731. I'm mad. Upset that they can continue to do this and it doesn't matter that they get taken into court and the courts say they're not allowed to do it and they continue to do it. That they don't abide by the law that they're sworn out there to uphold. I get frustrated that they get away with whatever they wanna do. (285)

#14735. It was embarrassing. It pissed me off. . . . They just treat you like you're nothing. . . . I think about it every time I see a cop. (283)

#14735. It just scares me. Ya know, they just search your possessions and stuff and it's none of their business. (285)

#12731. I don't trust the police anymore. I've lost all trust in them. (288)

Professor Janice Nadler (2012) summed up Lichtenberg's findings in her survey of empirical studies of Fourth Amendment consent searches this way:

When police question citizens or rummage through their possessions and find nothing, they leave in their wake, a flood of shaken people. Those feelings of . . . personal insecurity frustrate well-being. At best, subjecting citizens to suspicion-less searches amounts to loss of liberty. At worst, it threatens the legitimacy of the police and the legal system more broadly. People who feel the legal system is worthy of respect are more likely to comply with legal rules regulating their everyday experiences. (339)

LO 7 The Scope of Consent

How far can officers go in searching after they get permission to search? Only as far as the person who gave it consented to. But how far is that? As far as the person who gave it intended the search to be? Or as far as the officer believes the consent goes? According to the U.S. Supreme Court, the consent is as broad as the *officers* reasonably believe it to be.

In *Florida v. Jimeno* (1991), officers asked for permission to search Jimeno's "car." He agreed. The police searched not only the car itself but also a brown paper bag found in the trunk of the car. (The officer found drugs in the paper bag.) The U.S. Supreme Court upheld the reasonableness of the search. According to the Court, "The Fourth Amendment is satisfied when, under the circumstances, it is objectively reasonable for the officer to believe that the scope of the suspect's consent permitted him to open a particular container within the automobile" (248–49).

The scope of consent searches is a major issue in crotch searches, a tactic used in drug law enforcement. Specially trained officers who patrol bus stations, airports, and railway stations approach persons with no reasonable suspicion. They get into some light conversation and then ask, "Do you mind if I search you?" If the persons agree, the officers immediately pat down their crotch area.

The U.S. Supreme Court hasn't decided whether consent to search "you" includes searching the genital area, especially if the consent to search occurs on a public street or in the public areas of busy airports, bus stations, and railway stations. The U.S. Circuit Courts are divided. Some say consent to search "you" includes the groin area. Others say officers have to ask specifically, "Can I search your genital area?" In the next excerpt, *U.S. v. Rodney* (1992), the D.C. Circuit Court decided that Dylan Rodney's consent to search his person included his groin area.

The U.S. District Court for the District of Columbia upheld Dylan Rodney's conviction after finding that he had consented to a crotch search, which revealed hidden drugs.

CASE

Did Dylan Rodney Consent to a Search of His Crotch?

U.S. v. Rodney
956 F.2d 295 (CADC 1992)

HISTORY

Dylan Rodney (Defendant) was convicted upon his guilty plea to possession with intent to distribute crack cocaine before the United States District Court for the District of Columbia, after the court denied his motion to suppress. Rodney appealed. The Court of Appeals panel affirmed (2–1), and held that: (1) the district court committed no clear error in finding consent to the search voluntary; (2) defendant's general consent to a body search for drugs, without more, authorized a *Terry* frisk which included defendant's crotch area; and (3) the officer had probable cause to make warrantless arrest of defendant. Before WALD, GINSBURG, and THOMAS, JJ.

—THOMAS, Circuit Justice

FACTS

Dylan Rodney stepped off a bus that had arrived in Washington, D.C., from New York City. As Rodney left the bus station, Detective Vance Beard, dressed in plain clothes and carrying a concealed weapon, approached him from behind. A second officer waited nearby. Beard displayed identification and asked if Rodney would talk to him. Rodney agreed. Beard asked Rodney whether he lived in either Washington or New York. Rodney replied that he lived in Florida, but had come to Washington to try to find his wife. She lived on Georgia Avenue, Rodney said,

although he was unable to identify any more precise location. Beard asked Rodney whether he was carrying drugs in his travel bag. After Rodney said no, Beard obtained permission to search the bag. As he did so, the other officer advanced to within about five feet of Rodney. The search failed to turn up any contraband.

Beard then asked Rodney whether he was carrying drugs on his person. After Rodney again said no, Beard requested permission to conduct a body search. Rodney said "sure" and raised his arms above his head. Beard placed his hands on Rodney's ankles and, in one sweeping motion, ran them up the inside of Rodney's legs. As he passed over the crotch area, Beard felt small, rock-like objects. Rodney exclaimed: "That's me!" Detecting otherwise, Beard placed Rodney under arrest. At the police station, Beard unzipped Rodney's pants and retrieved a plastic bag containing a rock-like substance that was identified as cocaine base. Rodney was charged with possession and intent to distribute.

OPINION

Rodney contends that the district court erred in finding that his consent to the body search was voluntary, and therefore not prohibited by the Fourth Amendment. In determining the voluntariness of a consent, a district court must examine the totality of all the surrounding circumstances—both

(continued)

the characteristics of the accused and the details of the interrogation *Schneckloth v. Bustamonte* (1973). Relevant factors include: the youth of the accused; his lack of education; or his low intelligence; the lack of any advice to the accused of his constitutional rights; the length of detention; the repeated and prolonged nature of the questioning; and the use of physical punishment such as the deprivation of food or sleep.

On this record, we find no clear error. On the one hand, some evidence suggests an involuntary consent. Rodney testified that he thought three, rather than two, officers were covering him; that the officers were much bigger than he; and that he was young (24) and relatively uneducated (to the 10th grade) at the time. He also testified that before the events leading to his arrest, he had had four unpleasant encounters with the police: each time he had refused their request to search him, but each time they had searched him anyway.

On the other hand, Beard's testimony indicates that the police conduct here bore no resemblance to the sort of aggressive questioning, intimidating actions, or prolonged police presence, that might invalidate a consent. During the encounter, according to Beard, his gun was concealed; he wore plain clothes and spoke in a conversational tone; and no other officer came within five feet of Rodney. The district court could have weighed Beard's evidence more heavily than Rodney's. Thus, even assuming that the court credited Rodney's testimony in addition to Beard's, the court committed no clear error in finding the consent voluntary.

Rodney next argues that even if he consented voluntarily to the body search, he did not consent to the search of his crotch area. A consensual search cannot exceed the scope of the consent. The scope of the consent is measured by a test of "objective reasonableness": it depends on how broadly a reasonable observer would have interpreted the consent under the circumstances. Here, Rodney clearly consented to a search of his body for drugs. We conclude that a reasonable person would have understood that consent to encompass the search undertaken here. In this case, Rodney authorized a search for drugs. Dealers frequently hide drugs near their genitals. Indeed, Beard testified that his colleagues make up to 75 percent of their drug recoveries from around the crotch area. For these reasons, we conclude that a request to conduct a body search for drugs reasonably includes a request to conduct some search of that area.

Although the scope of a search is generally defined by its expressed object, we doubt that the Supreme Court would have us apply that test unflinchingly in the context of body searches. At some point, we suspect, a body search would become so intrusive that we would not infer consent to it from a generalized consent, regardless of the stated object of the search. For example, although drugs can be hidden virtually anywhere on or in one's person, a generalized consent to a body search for drugs surely does not validate everything up to and including a search of body cavities.

The search undertaken here, however, was not unusually intrusive, at least relative to body searches generally. It involved a continuous sweeping motion over Rodney's outer garments, including the trousers covering his crotch area. At the suppression hearing, Rodney mimicked the search. Without objection, the prosecutor asked for the record to reflect that Rodney "ran both his hands from the base of his feet or ankle area up through the interior of his legs and including the crotch area with one motion." In this respect, the search was no more invasive than the typical pat-down frisk for weapons described by the Supreme Court in *Terry v. Ohio*.

We conclude that Rodney voluntarily consented to a search of his body for drugs, which encompassed the frisk undertaken here. As a result of that frisk, we conclude further, Beard had probable cause to arrest Rodney. Accordingly, the judgment of conviction is
AFFIRMED.

DISSENT

WALD, J.

The issue before us is whether a person against whom there is no articulable suspicion of wrongdoing who is asked to submit to a body search on a public street expects that search to include manual touching of the genital area. I do not believe any such expectation exists at the time a cooperative citizen consents to an on-the-street search. Rather, that citizen anticipates only those kinds of searches that unfortunately have become a part of our urban living, searches ranging from airport security personnel passing a hand-held magnometer over a person's body, to having a person empty his pockets, and subject himself to a patting-down of sides, shoulders, and back. Any search that includes touching genital areas or breasts would not normally be expected to occur in public.

In all aspects of our society, different parts of the body are subject to very different levels of privacy and expectations about intrusions. We readily bare our heads, arms, legs, backs, even midriffs, in public, but, except in the most unusual circumstances, certainly not our breasts or genitals. On the streets, in elevators, and on public transportation, we often touch, inadvertently or even casually, each others' hands, arms, shoulders, and backs, but it is a serious affront, and sometimes even a crime, to intentionally touch another's intimate body parts without explicit permission; and while we feel free to discuss other people's hair, facial features, weight, height, noses or ears, similar discussions about genitals or breasts are not acceptable. Thus in any consensual encounter, it is not "objectively reasonable" for a citizen desiring to cooperate with the police in a public place to expect that permission to search her body includes feeling, even "fully clothed," the most private areas of her body. Under our social norms that requires "special permission," given with notice of the areas to be searched.

Nor can the mere fact that drug couriers often hide their stash in the crotch area justify the search of such area without some elementary form of notice to the citizen that such an offensive procedure is about to take place. The ordinary citizen's expectation of privacy in intimate parts of her body is certainly well enough established to merit a particularized request for consent to such an intimate search in public.

Minimally, in my view, Fourth Amendment protection of a nonsuspect citizen's reasonable expectations of privacy requires that the police indicate that the search will entail a touching of private areas. A general consent to a search of a citizen's "person" in a public place does not include consent to touch the genital or breast areas. The majority today upholds a practice that allows police under the rubric of a general consent to conduct intimate body searches, and in so doing defeats the legitimate expectations of privacy that ordinary citizens should retain during cooperative exchanges with the police on the street.

I believe the search was impermissible under the Fourth Amendment, and the drugs seized should have been suppressed.

Questions

1. State the specific rule the majority adopted to cover the scope of consent searches of a person.

2. State exactly what the officers asked Rodney to consent to.

3. Assume you're Rodney's lawyer. Relying on the facts as they're outlined in the case, argue that Rodney didn't consent to a search of his crotch.

4. Now assume you're the prosecutor, and argue that Rodney voluntarily consented to the search of his crotch.

5. Now assume you are the judge. Rule on the consent and its scope.

YOU DECIDE

LO 7 Did He Consent to the Search of His Crotch?

U.S. v. Blake 888 F.2d 795 (CA11, 1989)

FACTS

On December 11, 1987, three Broward County Sheriff's Deputies were working at the South Terminal in the Fort Lauderdale/Hollywood International Airport. As defendants Blake and Eason were leaving the Piedmont Airlines ticket counter and entering into the middle of an airport corridor, they were approached by two of the deputies. One of the officers testified that he had no reason for choosing the defendants, but that his actions were simply part of a random, voluntary drug interdiction policy. He admitted that he saw nothing suspicious about the defendants and that he was not relying upon a "drug courier" profile.

The officers, dressed in plain-clothes, identified themselves as deputy sheriffs to Blake and Eason by showing their badges and asked Blake and Eason if they would consent to speak with them. After Blake and Eason gave their consent, the officers asked them for their plane tickets and identification. Blake responded that he had a driver's license; Eason said that he had no identification. One of the officers, Detective Hendrick, renewed the request to see their tickets.

When Blake responded that the tickets were in his carry-on bag, Hendrick suggested that they move over to

a bench approximately five feet away. At the bench, Blake opened his bag and gave Hendrick the airline tickets. The tickets were one-way tickets to Baltimore in the names of "Omar Blake" and "Williams." After examining the tickets, Hendrick immediately returned them to Blake and again asked to see their identification. Blake gave Hendrick his driver's license, and Eason again responded that he did not have any identification. Hendrick noted that Blake's driver's license was in his name and returned the license to him immediately.

Detective Hendrick then asked defendants for permission to search their baggage and their persons for drugs. He explained to Blake and Eason that they had the right to refuse consent to the search. Both defendants agreed to a search of their luggage and their persons. Within seconds of Blake's having given his consent, Hendrick reached into Blake's groin region where he did a "frontal touching" of the "outside of [Blake's] trousers" in "the area between the legs where the penis would normally be positioned." Upon reaching into Blake's crotch, Hendrick felt an object and heard a crinkling sound.

Hendrick repeated this procedure upon receiving Eason's consent and, as with Blake, felt a foreign object in

(continued)

Eason's crotch and heard a crinkling sound. Hendrick and the other officers then handcuffed Blake and Eason and advised them of their Miranda rights. Blake and Eason were then taken to the airport's drug interdiction office outside the public concourse where Hendrick removed a package of suspected crack cocaine from each of their crotches. A narcotics-sniffing dog was employed to search the defendants' bags. A subsequent search of the bag revealed drug paraphernalia in the form of numerous glassine envelopes and little zip-lock bags typically used for packaging crack cocaine among the contents of the luggage.

DECISION

The search was not consensual, both the U.S. District Court and the U.S. 11th (now 5th) Circuit Court of Appeals held.

Although defendants did consent to a brief, noncoercive encounter with the officers, defendants could not have possibly foreseen the course that the arresting officers would choose to pursue in their search of defendants. Defendants clearly did not consent to the intimate search of their persons that was conducted in the public area of the Fort Lauderdale Airport. The request by the officers to search defendants' "person" was ambiguous at best and it is not clear whether the defendants understood exactly what was entailed by the phrase "body search."

The consent given by the defendants allowing the officers to search their "persons" could not, under the circumstances, be construed as authorization for the officers to touch their genitals in the middle of a public area in the Fort Lauderdale Airport. The search constituted such a serious intrusion into the defendants' privacy that, under the circumstances, it could not be said that the defendants had knowingly and voluntarily consented to the search in question.

It must be remembered that the request for the search took place in a public airport terminal—a setting in which particular care needs to be exercised to ensure that police officers do not intrude upon the privacy interests of individuals. Given this public location, it cannot be said that a reasonable individual would understand that a search of one's person would entail an officer touching his or her genitals.

Judge Schoob, in his concurring opinion, wrote:

> I share the district court's "amazement that there have apparently been no complaints lodged or fists thrown by indignant travelers" subjected to these searches. A layperson consenting to a search in the public area of an airport might expect a search of his or her pockets, sides and shoulders or use of a hand-held magnometer. It is a different matter entirely when the search begins with the law enforcement officer's reaching for and touching the individual's genital area.
>
> Airport terminals are settings where particular care must be exercised to protect the privacy rights of individuals. I would prefer a holding establishing that crotch searches during random airport stops must be preceded by a specific request and voluntary consent. In all other respects, I concur in the majority opinion.

LO 7 Withdrawing Consent

The U.S. Supreme Court hasn't decided if someone who has voluntarily consented to a search may later withdraw the consent. Some lower federal courts and state courts have ruled unanimously that people can withdraw their consent but with a major qualification: "any such withdrawal must be supported by unambiguous acts or unequivocal statements" (*U.S. v. Sanders* 2005, 774).

In *U.S. v. Miner* (1973), two airline employees at Los Angeles International Airport asked Gary Miner to walk through a magnetometer, a gadget designed to detect the presence of metal on boarding passengers. Miner complied, but the machine did not register. Miner was then asked to open a small suitcase that he was carrying but refused, saying, "No, it's personal." According to the court, "No, it's personal" signaled withdrawal of his consent, fulfilling the **unequivocal acts or statements withdrawal of consent rule**:

> At that point, the airline employees would have been justified in refusing to permit him to fly, but they could not compel him to submit to further search.

Asking Miner to open his suitcase could be justified only if he continued to manifest an intention to board the plane, or if he otherwise consented to the search. (1077)

The court in *U.S. v. Gray* (2004) reached the opposite conclusion. Arkansas State Trooper Kyle Drown stopped a car and issued the driver a warning citation for following a truck too closely and weaving in her lane. At 11:09 a.m., after Drown issued the warning citation, Denise Lawrence, the driver, and her companion, Darnell Gray, allowed Drown to search the vehicle. Not finding any contraband, he turned to Rudy, his drug detection dog, who alerted to narcotics.

Drown searched the vehicle and its contents for about 20 minutes without finding anything. Shortly after 11:30 a.m., Gray and Lawrence got impatient. Gray testified that he said, "This is ridiculous" and asked how long the search was going to take. A few minutes later, Gray and Drown had a second conversation, which they recall differently. Drown testified that Gray merely asked him to speed up the search but didn't withdraw consent. Gray testified that he attempted to withdraw consent by again saying the length of the search was "ridiculous" and told Drown twice that he and Lawrence were "ready to go now."

According to the court, withdrawing consent doesn't require "magic words," but those who give consent have to communicate their intent to withdraw by an "unequivocal act or statement" (Table 6.3). At most, Gray's conversations with Drown were only "an expression of impatience, which is not sufficient to terminate consent."

LO **7, 8** Third-Party Consent Searches

Third-party consent searches (consenting to search for someone else) comprise two types of consent.

1. **Actual authority consent**, adopted by the U.S. Supreme Court in 1964, is when someone *in fact* has the legal authority to consent to a search of your home and stuff.

2. **Apparent authority consent,** adopted by the Court in 1984, is when someone who officers *reasonably believe* (but who in fact doesn't) have the authority to consent to a search of your home and stuff.

TABLE 6.3 "Unequivocal" withdrawal of consent

Defendant exclaimed, "The search is over. I am calling off the search." (*U.S. v. Dichiarinte* 1971)
Prospective airline passenger balked at search of luggage, saying, "No, it's personal." (*U.S. v. Miner* 1973)
Defendant's statement: "That's enough. I want you to stop." (*U.S. v. Bily* 1975)
Motorist's act of closing and locking trunk of his car after a police officer's consensual warrantless search of trunk. (*U.S. v. Ibarra* 1990; noting motorist's actions constituted withdrawal of that consent and barred further search)
After freely giving consent to search his airplane, the defendant locked the plane after he taxied it to a hangar area and before being driven by police to a nearby motel. (*Cooper v. State* 1985)

LO **8**   *Actual authority to consent*

In *Stoner v. California* (1964), two Pomona, California, Police Department officers without either an arrest or search warrant went to the Mayfair Hotel in Pomona, and asked the night clerk if they could search Joey Stoner's room, telling the clerk they suspected Stoner had a weapon. The clerk answered, "I'll be more than happy to give you permission and I'll take you directly to the room." The night clerk opened the door, and said, "Be my guest." (487).

The state of California argued that the search was constitutional because the clerk had either the actual or apparent authority to consent for Stoner. First, the Court rejected the claim that the clerk had the actual authority to consent to search Stoner's room. The Court (8–1) also rejected the state's apparent authority claim. According to Justice Stewart,

> The rights protected by the Fourth Amendment are not to be eroded by strained applications of the . . . unrealistic doctrines of "apparent authority" (488). It is important to bear in mind that it was petitioner's constitutional right which was at stake here, and not the night clerk's or the hotel's. It was a right, therefore, that only the petitioner could waive by word or deed, either directly or through an agent. (489)

Five years later, in *Frazier v. Cupp* (1969), the Court introduced the **assumption of risk source of third-party consent authority** (the consenting party takes the chance that someone else might consent for her). During a search of Jerry Lee Rawls's house, police officers asked if they could search Rawls's duffle bag, which he shared with his cousin Martin Frazier, and which was in the house. Rawls agreed. They found items of Frazier's clothing that they later used in court against Frazier. Frazier argued that Rawls couldn't consent for him.

The Supreme Court concluded that Frazier's claim "could be dismissed rather quickly. Frazier, in allowing Rawls to use the bag and in leaving it in his house, must be taken to have assumed the risk that Rawls would allow someone else to look inside" (740).

Next came *U.S. v. Matlock* (1974). In *Matlock*, William Earl Matlock was arrested in the yard in front of the house where he lived with William Marshall, his wife, several of his children, including their 21-year-old daughter, Matlock's common-law wife, Gayle Graff, and her three-year-old son. Three of the arresting officers went to the door. Graff, dressed in a robe and holding her son in her arms, let the officers in. They told her they were looking for money and a gun and asked if they could search the house. She consented. They searched the house, including the east bedroom on the second floor, which Graff said she and Matlock shared. In a diaper bag in the only closet in the room, they found $4,995 in cash (179).

In his majority opinion, Justice White didn't rely on the doctrine of apparent authority; in fact, he made clear that Graff wasn't giving up Matlock's right. She was exercising *her* authority as Matlock's cohabitant to consent to the search of *their* room. Furthermore, Matlock couldn't claim that Graff's consent violated his right to privacy in the room they shared. Why? Because, when he moved in with Graff, he assumed the risk that Graff might expose their privacy to the world. So, it was *his* action in becoming Graff's cohabitant that diluted his Fourth Amendment right (Davies 1991, 33).

LO **8**   *Apparent authority consent*

In 1990, the U.S. Supreme Court expanded third-party consent searches to include an **apparent authority test of third-party consent**. In apparent authority, someone whom officers reasonably believe has the authority to consent for someone else (but who, in fact, doesn't) makes the search reasonable. The case that expanded third-party consent to include apparent authority was our next case excerpt, *Illinois v. Rodriguez* (1990). Gail Fischer consented to using a key she had in her possession to open Ed Rodriguez's apartment door. Fischer didn't actually have the authority to consent, but the officers reasonably believed she did.

Illinois v. Rodriquez (1990) expanded third-party consent to include apparent authority to consent.

CASE

Did She Have the Authority to Consent?

Illinois v. Rodriguez
497 U.S. 177 (1990)

HISTORY

Edward Rodriguez, who was charged with possession of a controlled substance with intent to deliver, moved to suppress seized evidence. The Circuit Court, Cook County, Illinois, granted the motion, and the People appealed. The Appellate Court affirmed. The People petitioned for leave to appeal. The Supreme Court denied the petition without published opinion. The People petitioned for a writ of certiorari. The Supreme Court granted the writ and reversed and remanded.

  —SCALIA, J., joined by REHNQUIST, C.J., and WHITE, BLACKMUN, O'CONNOR, and KENNEDY, JJ.

FACTS

On July 26, 1985, police were summoned to the residence of Dorothy Jackson on South Wolcott in Chicago. They were met by Ms. Jackson's daughter, Gail Fischer, who showed signs of a severe beating. She told the officers that she had been assaulted by Edward Rodriguez earlier that day in an apartment on South California. Fischer stated that Rodriguez was then asleep in the apartment, and she consented to travel there with the police in order to unlock the door with her key so that the officers could enter and arrest him. During this conversation, Fischer several times referred to the apartment on South California as "our" apartment, and said that she had clothes and furniture there. It is unclear whether she indicated that she currently lived at the apartment, or only that she used to live there.

The police officers drove to the apartment on South California, accompanied by Fischer. They did not obtain an arrest warrant for Rodriguez, nor did they seek a search warrant for the apartment. At the apartment, Fischer unlocked the door with her key and gave the officers permission to enter. They moved through the door into the living room, where they observed in plain view drug paraphernalia and containers filled with white powder that they believed (correctly, as later analysis showed) to be cocaine. They proceeded to the bedroom, where they found Rodriguez asleep and discovered additional containers of white powder in two open attaché cases. The officers arrested Rodriguez and seized the drugs and related paraphernalia.

Rodriguez was charged with possession of a controlled substance with intent to deliver. He moved to suppress all evidence seized at the time of his arrest, claiming that Fischer had vacated the apartment several weeks earlier and had no authority to consent to the entry. The Cook County Circuit Court granted the motion, holding that at the time she consented to the entry Fischer did not have common authority over the apartment.

The Court concluded that Fischer was not a "usual resident" but rather an "infrequent visitor" at the apartment on South California, based upon its findings that Fischer's name was not on the lease, that she did not contribute to the rent, that she was not allowed to invite others to the apartment on her own, that she did not have access to the apartment when Rodriguez was away,

(continued)

and that she had moved some of her possessions from the apartment.

The Circuit Court also rejected the State's contention that, even if Fischer did not possess common authority over the premises, there was no Fourth Amendment violation if the police reasonably believed at the time of their entry that Fischer possessed the authority to consent. The Appellate Court of Illinois affirmed the Circuit Court in all respects. The Illinois Supreme Court denied the State's petition for leave to appeal, and we granted certiorari.

OPINION

The Fourth Amendment prohibits the warrantless entry of a person's home, whether to make an arrest or to search for specific objects. The prohibition does not apply, however, to situations in which voluntary consent has been obtained, either from the individual whose property is searched, *Schneckloth v. Bustamonte* (1973) [excerpt on p. 217], or from a third party who possesses common authority over the premises, *U.S. v. Matlock* (1974). The State of Illinois contends that that exception applies in the present case.

As we stated in *Matlock*, "common authority" rests "on mutual use of the property by persons having joint access or control." The burden of establishing that common authority rests upon the State. On the basis of this record, it is clear that burden was not sustained. The evidence showed that although Fischer, with her two small children, had lived with Rodriguez beginning in December 1984, she had moved out on July 1, 1985, almost a month before the search at issue here, and had gone to live with her mother. She took her and her children's clothing with her, though leaving behind some furniture and household effects. During the period after July 1 she sometimes spent the night at Rodriguez's apartment, but never invited her friends there, and never went there herself when he was not home. Her name was not on the lease nor did she contribute to the rent. She had a key to the apartment, which she said at trial she had taken without Rodriguez's knowledge (though she testified at the preliminary hearing that Rodriguez had given her the key). On these facts the State has not established that, with respect to the South California apartment, Fischer had "joint access or control for most purposes." To the contrary, the Appellate Court's determination of no common authority over the apartment was obviously correct.

The State contends that, even if Fischer did not in fact have authority to give consent, it suffices to validate the entry that the law enforcement officers reasonably believed she did. Rodriguez asserts that permitting a reasonable belief of common authority to validate an entry would cause a defendant's Fourth Amendment rights to be "vicariously waived." We disagree.

What Rodriguez is assured by the Fourth Amendment is not that no government search of his house will occur unless he consents; but that no such search will occur that is unreasonable. Reasonableness does not demand that the government be factually correct. What is demanded is not that officers always be correct, but that they always be reasonable. As we put it in *Brinegar v. U.S.* (1949):

> Because many situations which confront officers in the course of executing their duties are more or less ambiguous, room must be allowed for some mistakes on their part. But the mistakes must be those of reasonable men, acting on facts leading sensibly to their conclusions of probability.

We see no reason to depart from this general rule with respect to facts bearing upon the authority to consent to a search. Whether the basis for such authority exists is the sort of recurring factual question to which law enforcement officials must be expected to apply their judgment; and all the Fourth Amendment requires is that they answer it reasonably.

The Constitution is no more violated when officers enter without a warrant because they reasonably (though erroneously) believe that the person who has consented to their entry is a resident of the premises, than it is violated when they enter without a warrant because they reasonably (though erroneously) believe they are in pursuit of a violent felon who is about to escape.

What we hold today does not suggest that law enforcement officers may always accept a person's invitation to enter premises. Even when the invitation is accompanied by an explicit assertion that the person lives there, the surrounding circumstances could conceivably be such that a reasonable person would doubt its truth and not act upon it without further inquiry. As with other factual determinations bearing upon search and seizure, determination of consent to enter must be judged against an objective standard: would the facts available to the officer at the moment, warrant a man of reasonable caution in the belief that the consenting party had authority over the premises? *Terry v. Ohio* (1968) [excerpted in Chapter 4]. If not, then warrantless entry without further inquiry is unlawful unless authority actually exists. But if so, the search is valid.

In the present case, the Appellate Court found it unnecessary to determine whether the officers reasonably believed that Fischer had the authority to consent, because it ruled as a matter of law that a reasonable belief could not validate the entry. Since we find that ruling to be in error, we remand for consideration of that question.

The judgment of the Illinois Appellate Court is REVERSED, and the case is REMANDED for further proceedings not inconsistent with this opinion.

DISSENT

MARSHALL, J., joined by BRENNAN and STEVENS, JJ.

Dorothy Jackson summoned police officers to her house to report that her daughter Gail Fischer had been beaten. Fischer told police that Ed Rodriguez, her boyfriend, was her assaulter. During an interview with Fischer, one of the officers asked if Rodriguez dealt in narcotics. Fischer did not respond. Fischer did agree, however, to the officers' request to let them into Rodriguez's apartment so that they could arrest him for battery. The police, without a warrant and despite the absence of an exigency, entered Rodriguez's home to arrest him. As a result of their entry, the police discovered narcotics that the State subsequently sought to introduce in a drug prosecution against Rodriguez.

The Court holds that the warrantless entry into Rodriguez's home was nonetheless valid if the officers reasonably believed that Fischer had authority to consent. The majority's defense of this position rests on a misconception of the basis for third-party consent searches. That such searches do not give rise to claims of constitutional violations rests not on the premise that they are "reasonable" under the Fourth Amendment, but on the premise that a person may voluntarily limit his expectation of privacy by allowing others to exercise authority over his possessions.

Thus, an individual's decision to permit another joint access to or control over the property for most purposes, limits that individual's reasonable expectation of privacy and to that extent limits his Fourth Amendment protections. If an individual has not so limited his expectation of privacy, the police may not dispense with the safeguards established by the Fourth Amendment.

We have recognized that the physical entry of the home is the chief evil against which the wording of the Fourth Amendment is directed. We have further held that a search or seizure carried out on a suspect's premises without a warrant is per se unreasonable, unless the police can show that it falls within one of a carefully defined set of exceptions. The Court has often heard, and steadfastly rejected, the invitation to carve out further exceptions to the warrant requirement for searches of the home because of the burdens on police investigation and prosecution of crime.

Our rejection of such claims is not due to a lack of appreciation of the difficulty and importance of effective law enforcement, but rather to our firm commitment to the view of those who wrote the Bill of Rights that the privacy of a person's home and property may not be totally sacrificed in the name of maximum simplicity in enforcement of the criminal law. The concerns of expediting police work and avoiding paperwork are never very convincing reasons and, in these circumstances, certainly are not enough to bypass the constitutional requirement. In this case, no suspect was fleeing or likely to take flight.

The search was of permanent premises, not of a movable vehicle. No evidence or contraband was threatened with removal or destruction.

Unlike searches conducted pursuant to these recognized exceptions to the warrant requirement, third-party consent searches are not based on an exigency and therefore serve no compelling social goal. Police officers, when faced with the choice of relying on consent by a third party or securing a warrant, should secure a warrant and must therefore accept the risk of error should they instead choose to rely on consent.

A search conducted pursuant to an officer's reasonable but mistaken belief that a third party had authority to consent is on an entirely different constitutional footing from one based on the consent of a third party who in fact has such authority. Even if the officers reasonably believed that Fischer had authority to consent, she did not, and Rodriguez's expectation of privacy was therefore undiminished.

Our cases demonstrate that third-party consent searches are free from constitutional challenge only to the extent that they rest on consent by a party empowered to do so. The majority's conclusion to the contrary ignores the legitimate expectations of privacy on which individuals are entitled to rely. That a person who allows another joint access to his property thereby limits his expectation of privacy does not justify trampling the rights of a person who has not similarly relinquished any of his privacy expectation.

Questions

1. List all the facts relevant to determining whether the search in this case was a lawful search.

2. How does the majority define third-party consent? How does the dissent define it?

3. Why did the Supreme Court hold that Fischer's consent made the search of Rodriguez's apartment a lawful search?

4. Do you agree that someone can consent for another even when the person giving consent doesn't have the authority to do so?

5. Do you agree that if you share your property with someone else you "assume the risk" that the other person may give the police permission to search the property?

6. What arguments does the dissent make to reject the validity of Fischer's consent to search Rodriguez's apartment?

7. How do the majority and the dissent balance differently Rodriguez's rights and law enforcement's needs for consent searches? How would you balance the interests in the case?

CRIMINAL PROCEDURE IN ACTION

LO **7,8** A husband can overrule his estranged wife's consent

Georgia v. Randolph, 126 S.Ct. 1515 (2006)
SOUTER, J.

FACTS

Scott Randolph and his wife, Janet, separated in late May 2001, when she left the marital residence in Americus, Georgia, and went to stay with her parents in Canada, taking their son and some belongings. In July, she returned to the Americus house with the child, though the record does not reveal whether her object was reconciliation or retrieval of remaining possessions.

On the morning of July 6, she complained to the police that after a domestic dispute her husband took their son away, and when officers reached the house she told them that her husband was a cocaine user whose habit had caused financial troubles. Shortly after the police arrived, Scott Randolph returned and explained that he had removed the child to a neighbor's house out of concern that his wife might take the boy out of the country again.

One of the officers, Sergeant Murray, went with Janet Randolph to reclaim the child, and when they returned she not only renewed her complaints about her husband's drug use, but also volunteered that there were "items of drug evidence" in the house. Sergeant Murray asked Scott Randolph for permission to search the house, which he unequivocally refused. The sergeant turned to Janet Randolph for consent to search, which she readily gave. She led the officer upstairs to a bedroom that she identified as Scott's, where the sergeant noticed a section of a drinking straw with a powdery residue he suspected was cocaine.

DECISION

We have lived our whole national history with an understanding of the ancient adage that a man's home is his castle to the point that the "poorest man may in his cottage bid defiance to all the forces of the Crown." Disputed permission is thus no match for this central value of the Fourth Amendment, and the State's other countervailing claims do not add up to outweigh it. Yes, we recognize the consenting tenant's interest as a citizen in bringing criminal activity to light. And we understand a co-tenant's legitimate self-interest

in siding with the police to deflect suspicion raised by sharing quarters with a criminal.

This case invites a straightforward application of the rule that a physically present inhabitant's express refusal of consent to a police search is dispositive as to him, regardless of the consent of a fellow occupant. Scott Randolph's refusal is clear, and nothing in the record justifies the search on grounds independent of Janet Randolph's consent.

The State does not argue that she gave any indication to the police of a need for protection inside the house that might have justified entry into the portion of the premises where the police found the powdery straw (which, if lawfully seized, could have been used when attempting to establish probable cause for the warrant issued later). Nor does the State claim that the entry and search should be upheld under the rubric of exigent circumstances, owing to some apprehension by the police officers that Scott Randolph would destroy evidence of drug use before any warrant could be obtained.

The judgment of the Supreme Court of Georgia is therefore AFFIRMED.

DISSENT

The dissent concluded otherwise. Chief Justice Roberts, joined by Justice Scalia, wrote:

The rule the majority fashions does not implement the high office of the Fourth Amendment to protect privacy, but instead provides protection on a random and happenstance basis, protecting, for example, a co-occupant who happens to be at the front door when the other occupant consents to a search, but not one napping or watching television in the next room. And the cost of affording such random protection is great, as demonstrated by the recurring cases in which abused spouses seek to authorize police entry into a home they share with a nonconsenting abuser.

The correct approach is clearly mapped out in our precedents: The Fourth Amendment protects privacy. If an individual shares information, papers, or places with another, he assumes the risk that the other person will in turn share access to that information or those papers or places with the government. Just because the individual happens to be present at the time, so too someone who shares a place with another cannot interpose an objection when that person decides to grant access to the police, simply because the objecting individual happens to be present.

A warrantless search is reasonable if police obtain the voluntary consent of a person authorized to give it. Co-occupants have assumed the risk that one of their number might permit a common area to be searched. Just as Mrs. Randolph could walk upstairs, come down, and turn her husband's cocaine straw over to the police, she can consent to police entry and search of what is, after all, her home, too.

THOMAS, J.

The Court has long recognized that it is an act of responsible citizenship for individuals to give whatever information they may have to aid in law enforcement. No Fourth Amendment search occurs where, as here, the spouse of an accused voluntarily leads the police to potential evidence of wrongdoing by the accused.

LO 9 Vehicle Searches

Searching vehicles without warrants began with a 1789 act of Congress. This was the same Congress that had adopted the Fourth Amendment, so the hated British general warrants were fresh in Congress's mind. Despite these bitter memories, the 1789 statute authorized law enforcement officers without a warrant "to enter any ship or vessel, in which they shall have reason to suspect any goods, wares or merchandise subject to duty shall be concealed; and therein to search for, seize, and secure any such goods, wares or merchandise."

Ships were one thing; homes were quite another. Officers who suspected people were hiding taxable stuff in their houses had to get a warrant based on probable cause before they searched. Why the difference between boats and houses? Necessity: "Goods in course of transportation and concealed in a movable vessel readily could be put out of reach of a search warrant."

In 1815, Congress authorized officers "not only to board and search vessels within their own and adjoining districts, but also to stop, search, and examine any vehicle, beast, or person on which or whom they should suspect there was merchandise which was subject to duty." In the Indian Appropriation Act of 1917, Congress authorized officers without warrants to seize and forfeit "automobiles used in introducing or attempting to introduce intoxicants into the Indian territory" (*Carroll v. U.S.* 1925, 152–53).

Not a single U.S. Supreme Court case ever challenged this exception until 1925 during Prohibition when the modern history of the vehicle exception began. You saw the impact of technology on the Fourth Amendment in several cases in Chapter 3 (eavesdropping microphones in *Katz v. U.S.*, radio transmitters in *U.S. v. White*, and thermal imaging in *Kyllo v. U.S.*). Their impact, however, can't compare with the single greatest technological advance of the 20th century that affected the Fourth Amendment—the car, and now SUVs and trucks.

As car ownership spread throughout all classes in society, its use as a crime tool advanced and so did Fourth Amendment law. The U.S. Supreme Court added another rationale for the vehicle exception—a reduced expectation of privacy in vehicles. Prohibition, the fear of alcohol-related crimes, and the ubiquity of the car were behind the landmark vehicle exception case, *Carroll v. U.S.* (1925), in the 1920s. (The fear of illegal drugs still drives the interpretation of the Fourth Amendment that so many cases in Chapters 3 through 6 clearly demonstrate.)

In *Carroll*, federal Prohibition agents Cronenwett, Scully, and Thayer and Michigan state trooper Peterson had probable cause to believe bootleggers George Carroll and John Kiro were illegally carrying liquor from Detroit to Grand Rapids in their Oldsmobile convertible. While on regular duty patrolling the road looking for Prohibition law violations, they stopped the car and searched it without a warrant. They found 68 bottles of blended Scotch whiskey and Gordon gin stuffed in hollowed-out upholstery, which they had to rip open to find.

The U.S. Supreme Court upheld the search without a warrant based on the rationale that it was "not practicable to secure a warrant, because the vehicle can be quickly moved out of the locality or jurisdiction in which the warrant must be sought" (153).

The decision was immediately controversial. We were fighting an earlier war on drugs; alcohol was the drug. Cars were a new technological weapon used by the enemy and the government. As in our own drug wars, critics complained that we were sacrificing our rights to fight the war. The dissent joined the critics. Justice McReynolds wrote:

> The damnable character of the "bootlegger's" business should not close our eyes to the mischief which will surely follow any attempt to destroy it by unwarranted methods. To press forward to a great principle by breaking through every other great principle that stands in the way of its establishment; in short, to procure an eminent good by means that are unlawful, is as little consonant to private morality as to public justice. (163)

Following *Carroll*, the Court began a slow, although not steady, expansion of what was soon called the **vehicle exception to the warrant requirement**. One expansion was to add to the mobility of vehicles the rationale that there's a reduced expectation of privacy in vehicles. In a series of other decisions, the exception came to include all searches of vehicles without warrants, as long as they're based on probable cause to believe they contain contraband or evidence. The exception extended to the passenger compartment, the glove compartment, and the trunk. Then, the Court turned its attention to two other very important related searches: of containers inside vehicles and to occupants and their belongings. Let's look at each of these searches.

LO 9 *Searches of containers in vehicles*

Until 1991, Supreme Court cases upheld searches of containers in vehicles without warrants only if officers had separate probable cause to search both the vehicle and the container. If they had probable cause to search the container but not the vehicle, they had to get a warrant. Then, in *California v. Acevedo* (1991), the Court ruled that officers with probable cause but without warrants can search containers inside vehicles, if the container isn't an essential part of the vehicle.

In *Acevedo*, officers observed Charles Acevedo leave an apartment where officers knew there was marijuana. Acevedo was carrying a brown paper bag the size of marijuana packages the officers had seen earlier. Acevedo put the bag into the trunk of his car. As he drove away, the police stopped his car, opened the trunk, opened the bag, and found marijuana in it. The Court held that it was reasonable to search the container without a warrant because they had probable cause to believe the bag contained marijuana. The Court acknowledged Acevedo's expectation of privacy in the brown bag, but concluded that the risks the car might drive off and the marijuana might disappear trumped Acevedo's expectation of privacy.

LO 9 *Searches of vehicle passengers*

Before *Acevedo*, car searches focused on containers (luggage, purses, and paper bags) and a debate about if and when the Fourth Amendment allowed officers to open them to see what was inside them. *Acevedo* seemed to settle the debate: As long as officers have probable cause to believe they contain contraband, they can search containers in the vehicle. But it didn't. It didn't answer a very important question: Can officers search containers attached to people in the car, such as the wallet in your jacket pocket, or the purse hanging over your shoulder, or lying on the seat beside you?

Recall that one of the reasons for the vehicle exception to the warrant requirement is a reduced expectation of privacy in vehicles. Do passengers as well as drivers have a reduced expectation of privacy? And, if they do, can officers search a passenger's purse when they have no probable cause to suspect her of the crime they arrested the driver for? In our next case excerpt, *Wyoming v. Houghton* (1999), a divided U.S. Supreme Court (6–3) answered yes.

In *Wyoming v. Houghton* (1999), a divided (6–3) U.S. Supreme Court found that the vehicle exception included the search of passenger Sandra Houghton's purse.

CASE

Was Her Purse within the Vehicle Exception?

Wyoming v. Houghton
526 U.S. 295 (1999)

HISTORY

Sandra Houghton was convicted in the District Court, Natrona County, Wyoming, of felony possession of methamphetamine, and she appealed. The Wyoming Supreme Court reversed and remanded. The U.S. Supreme Court granted certiorari and reversed.

—SCALIA, J., joined by REHNQUIST, C.J., and O'CONNOR, KENNEDY, THOMAS, and BREYER, JJ.

FACTS

In the early morning hours of July 23, 1995, a Wyoming Highway Patrol officer (Officer Baldwin) stopped an automobile for speeding and driving with a faulty brake light. There were three passengers in the front seat of the car: David Young (the driver), his girlfriend, and Diane Houghton. While questioning Young, the officer noticed a hypodermic syringe in Young's shirt pocket. He left the occupants under the supervision of two backup officers as he went to get gloves from his patrol car. Upon his return, he instructed Young to step out of the car and place the syringe on the hood. The officer then asked Young why he had a syringe; with refreshing candor, Young replied that he used it to take drugs.

At this point, the backup officers ordered the two female passengers out of the car and asked them for identification. Houghton falsely identified herself as "Sandra James" and stated that she did not have any identification. Meanwhile, in light of Young's admission, the officer searched the passenger compartment of the car for contraband. On the backseat, he found a purse, which Houghton claimed as hers. He removed from the purse a wallet containing Houghton's driver's license, identifying her properly as Sandra K. Houghton. When the officer asked her why she had lied about her name, she replied: "In case things went bad."

Continuing his search of the purse, the officer found a brown pouch and a black wallet-type container. Houghton denied that the former was hers, and claimed ignorance of how it came to be there; it was found to contain drug paraphernalia and a syringe with 60 cc's of methamphetamine.

Houghton admitted ownership of the black container, which was also found to contain drug paraphernalia, and a syringe (which Houghton acknowledged was hers) with 10 cc's of methamphetamine—an amount insufficient to support the felony conviction at issue in this case. The officer also found fresh needle-track marks on Houghton's arms. He placed her under arrest.

The State of Wyoming charged Houghton with felony possession of methamphetamine in a liquid amount greater than three-tenths of a gram. After a hearing, the trial court denied her motion to suppress all evidence obtained from the purse as the fruit of a violation of the

(*continued*)

Fourth and Fourteenth Amendments. The court held that the officer had probable cause to search the car for contraband, and, by extension, any containers therein that could hold such contraband. A jury convicted Houghton as charged.

The Wyoming Supreme Court, by divided vote, reversed the conviction and announced the following rule:

> Once probable cause is established to search a vehicle, an officer is entitled to search all containers therein which may contain the object of the search. However, if the officer knows or should know that a container is the personal effect of a passenger who is not suspected of criminal activity, then the container is outside the scope of the search unless someone had the opportunity to conceal the contraband within the personal effect to avoid detection.

The court held that the search of Houghton's purse violated the Fourth and Fourteenth Amendments because the officer "knew or should have known that the purse did not belong to the driver, but to one of the passengers," and because "there was no probable cause to search the passengers' personal effects and no reason to believe that contraband had been placed within the purse."

OPINION

We have read the historical evidence to show that the Framers would have regarded as reasonable (if there was probable cause) the warrantless search of containers within an automobile. In *U.S. v. Ross* (1982), we upheld as reasonable the warrantless search of a paper bag and leather pouch found in the trunk of Ross's car by officers who had probable cause to believe that the trunk contained drugs.

To be sure, there was no passenger in *Ross*, and it was not claimed that the package in the trunk belonged to anyone other than the driver. Even so, a passenger's personal belongings, just like the driver's belongings or containers attached to the car like a glove compartment, are "in" the car, and the officer has probable cause to search for contraband in the car. Passengers, no less than drivers, possess a reduced expectation of privacy with regard to the property that they transport in cars.

Whereas the passenger's privacy expectations are considerably diminished, the governmental interests at stake are substantial. Effective law enforcement would be appreciably impaired without the ability to search a passenger's personal belongings when there is reason to believe contraband or evidence of criminal wrongdoing is hidden in the car. As in all car-search cases, the "ready mobility" of an automobile creates a risk that the evidence or contraband will be permanently lost while a warrant is obtained. In addition, a car passenger will often be engaged in a common enterprise with the driver, and have the same interest in concealing the fruits or the evidence of their wrongdoing.

To be sure, these factors favoring a search will not always be present, but the balancing of interests must be conducted with an eye to the generality of cases. To require that the investigating officer have positive reason to believe that the passenger and driver were engaged in a common enterprise, or positive reason to believe that the driver had time and occasion to conceal the item in the passenger's belongings, surreptitiously or with friendly permission, is to impose requirements so seldom met that a "passenger's property" rule would dramatically reduce the ability to find and seize contraband and evidence of crime.

Of course these requirements would not attach (under the Wyoming Supreme Court's rule) until the police officer knows or has reason to know that the container belongs to a passenger. But once a "passenger's property" exception to car searches became widely known, one would expect passenger-confederates to claim everything as their own. And one would anticipate a bog of litigation—in the form of both civil lawsuits and motions to suppress in criminal trials—involving such questions as whether the officer should have believed a passenger's claim of ownership, whether he should have inferred ownership from various objective factors, whether he had probable cause to believe that the passenger was a confederate, or to believe that the driver might have introduced the contraband into the package with or without the passenger's knowledge.

When balancing the competing interests, our determinations of "reasonableness" under the Fourth Amendment must take account of these practical realities. We think they militate in favor of the needs of law enforcement, and against a personal-privacy interest that is ordinarily weak.

We hold that police officers with probable cause to search a car may inspect passengers' belongings found in the car that are capable of concealing the object of the search.

The judgment of the Wyoming Supreme Court is REVERSED.

CONCURRING OPINION

BREYER, J.

I point out certain limitations upon the scope of the bright-line rule that the Court describes. Obviously, the rule applies only to automobile searches. Equally obviously, the rule applies only to containers found within automobiles. And it does not extend to the search of a person found in that automobile. As the Court notes, the search of a person, including even "a limited search of the outer clothing," is a very different matter in respect to which the law provides "significantly heightened protection."

Less obviously, but in my view also important, is the fact that the container here at issue, a woman's purse, was found at a considerable distance from its owner, who did not claim ownership until the officer discovered her identification while looking through it. Purses are special containers. They are repositories of especially personal items that people generally like to keep with them at all times. So I am tempted to say that a search of a purse involves an intrusion so similar to a search of one's person that the same rule should govern both. However, given this Court's prior cases, I cannot argue that the fact that the container was a purse automatically makes a legal difference, for the Court has warned against trying to make that kind of distinction.

But I can say that it would matter if a woman's purse, like a man's billfold, were attached to her person. It might then amount to a kind of "outer clothing." In this case, the purse was separate from the person, and no one has claimed that, under those circumstances, the type of container makes a difference. For that reason, I join the Court's opinion.

DISSENT

STEVENS, J., joined by SOUTER and GINSBURG, JJ.

In all of our prior cases applying the automobile exception to the Fourth Amendment's warrant requirement, either the defendant was the operator of the vehicle and in custody of the object of the search, or no question was raised as to the defendant's ownership or custody. In the only automobile case confronting the search of a passenger defendant—*U.S. v. Di Re* (addressing searches of the passenger's pockets and the space between his shirt and underwear, both of which uncovered counterfeit fuel rations)—the Court held that the exception to the warrant requirement did not apply.

In *Di Re*, as here, the information prompting the search directly implicated the driver, not the passenger. Today, instead of adhering to the settled distinction between drivers and passengers, the Court fashions a new rule that is based on a distinction between property contained in clothing worn by a passenger and property contained in a passenger's briefcase or purse. In cases on both sides of the Court's newly minted test, the property is in a "container" (whether a pocket or a pouch) located in the vehicle.

Moreover, unlike the Court, I think it quite plain that the search of a passenger's purse or briefcase involves an intrusion on privacy that may be just as serious as was the intrusion in *Di Re*. I am not persuaded that the mere spatial association between a passenger and a driver provides an acceptable basis for presuming that they are partners in crime or for ignoring privacy interests in a purse. Whether or not the Fourth Amendment required a warrant to search Houghton's purse, at the very least the trooper in this case had to have probable cause to believe that her purse contained contraband. The Wyoming Supreme Court concluded that he did not.

Finally, in my view, the State's legitimate interest in effective law enforcement does not outweigh the privacy concerns at issue. I am as confident in a police officer's ability to apply a rule requiring a warrant or individualized probable cause to search belongings that are—as in this case—obviously owned by and in the custody of a passenger as is the Court in a "passenger-confederate's" ability to circumvent the rule. Certainly the ostensible clarity of the Court's rule is attractive. But that virtue is insufficient justification for its adoption. Moreover, a rule requiring a warrant or individualized probable cause to search passenger belongings is every bit as simple as the Court's rule; it simply protects more privacy.

Instead of applying ordinary Fourth Amendment principles to this case, the majority extends the automobile warrant exception to allow searches of passenger belongings based on the driver's misconduct. Thankfully, the Court's automobile-centered analysis limits the scope of its holding. But it does not justify the outcome in this case.

I respectfully dissent.

Questions

1. State the rule the majority of the Court adopted for searching passengers' "containers."

2. Explain how the majority applied the rule to the search of Sandra Houghton's purse.

3. Summarize the dissent's arguments for concluding the purse search was unreasonable.

4. Summarize Justice Breyer's hesitation about supporting the majority decision.

5. Consider your summaries. Which opinion do you think is the most convincing? Defend your answer.

LO 10 Emergency Searches

Emergency searches (also called **exigent circumstance searches**) are based on the idea that it's sometimes impractical (even dangerous) to require officers to obtain warrants before they search. The danger might be (1) to officers' safety, justifying frisks or pat downs for weapons (Chapter 4); (2) that suspects or others might destroy evidence during the time it takes to get a search warrant; (3) that fleeing felons might escape while officers are trying to obtain search warrants; or (4) that individuals in the community are in immediate danger. Because we've already examined frisks, in which officers' reasonable suspicion that a lawfully stopped suspect is armed justifies a pat down for weapons (Chapter 4), we won't repeat that discussion here. Let's look at the other three types of emergencies.

Destruction of evidence

If police officers have probable cause to search, and they reasonably believe evidence is about to be destroyed right now, they can search without a warrant. For example, in *Cupp v. Murphy* (1973), the U.S. Supreme Court held that police officers who had probable cause to believe Daniel Murphy had strangled his wife didn't need a warrant to take scrapings of what looked like blood under his fingernails. Why? Because Murphy knew the officers suspected he was the strangler, so he had a motive to destroy the short-lived bloodstain evidence.

In *Schmerber v. California* (1966, Chapter 8), the Supreme Court held that rapidly declining blood alcohol levels justified giving a blood alcohol test to Schmerber without a warrant. And in *Ker v. California* (1963), the Court held that a warrantless entry into a home was justified by the reasonable fear that Ker was about to destroy or hide marijuana.

Hot pursuit

Hot pursuit is another emergency created by the need to apprehend a fleeing suspect. If officers are chasing a suspect whom they have probable cause to arrest, they can follow the suspect into a house without getting a warrant (*U.S. v. Santana* 1976). So officers wouldn't need a warrant to enter a home to search for a fleeing armed robbery suspect and weapons.

But how extensive can the search be? Only as extensive as is necessary to prevent the suspect from escaping or resisting. So officers can't search every nook and cranny of a house just because they got in lawfully during a hot pursuit (*Warden v. Hayden* 1967). For example, they can't search dresser drawers for contraband. Nor can they search every room of a hotel because a robber entered the hotel (*U.S. v. Winsor* 1988).

Danger to the community

Police officers can also sidestep the warrant requirement if they have probable cause to believe either that a suspect has committed a violent crime or that they or others in the community are in immediate danger. So officers could enter and search a house in a residential area because they reasonably believed guns and bombs were in the house (*U.S. v. Lindsey* 1989). It was also reasonable to enter a house without a warrant to search for a weapon when police found a dead body on the front porch (*U.S. v. Doe* 1985).

Other dangers to the public include fires and explosions. Police officers at the scene of a fire don't need a warrant to stay inside a burned building long enough to look for possible injured victims and to investigate the cause of the fire or explosion. But once they determine the cause of the fire, officers have to get a warrant if they want to search for evidence of a crime (*Michigan v. Clifford* 1984). Furthermore, they can't enter just because a fire or explosion might be in the offing. For example, a court ruled that it wasn't reasonable for officers to enter a house where they knew a man had kept dangerous chemicals in his house for two weeks and wasn't at home (*U.S. v. Warner* 1988).

CHAPTER SUMMARY

LO 1 Crime control couldn't survive without searches, but the power to search tempts those who hold it to abuse it. To balance the need to search against the invasion of individual privacy rights, the Fourth Amendment bans only "unreasonable" searches. But the Fourth Amendment doesn't just bestow the power to search upon "good" officers searching "bad" people, their homes, and their belongings; bad officers have the same power to search good people.

LO 3 Searches of homes require warrants to be "reasonable." To comply with the Fourth Amendment, search warrants must include a detailed description of the place to be searched, the specific things to be seized, and an affidavit supporting probable cause. With important exceptions, when executing warrants to search homes, officers must "knock and announce" their presence before forcefully entering.

LO 2, 4 There are many exceptions to the warrant requirement and these exceptions are interpreted broadly so that most searches don't require warrants to be reasonable. Millions of searches incident to lawful arrests based on probable cause are reasonable without warrants because they protect officers, prevent escape, and preserve evidence. They include searches of arrested persons and the "grabbable area" around them and to the passenger compartment of vehicles they occupied when they were arrested. Despite these compelling reasons to search incident to arrest, empirical research has shown that officers immediately handcuff suspects after arresting them.

LO 5, 6, 7 Consent searches require neither warrants nor probable cause, allowing officers to search in places that it would be otherwise unlawful to do so. Consenting persons can withdraw their consent at any time if they demonstrate clear intent to stop the search. The scope of the consent search depends on what the officer reasonably believes the person consented to at the time of the search. Although the government has to prove that, under the totality of circumstances, consent was voluntary, empirical research has shown that few people refuse consent searches and lower courts almost always find consent to be voluntary.

LO 8 Third-party consent searches are when one individual consents to the search for another. Apparent authority is the minimum required by the Fourth Amendment and relies upon an officer's reasonable belief that the third party has the authority to consent to the search when, in fact, he does not.

LO 9 According to the Supreme Court, searches of vehicles without warrants are reasonable because of vehicle mobility and the reduced expectation of privacy within vehicles. Searches of containers and passengers within vehicles are reasonable without warrants as long as they are based on probable cause.

LO 10 Emergency searches are based on the idea that it's sometimes impractical or dangerous for officers to obtain warrants before executing a search. The most common exigent circumstances include the immediate destruction of evidence, hot pursuit, and an immediate danger to the community.

REVIEW QUESTIONS

1. Describe Supreme Court Justice Jackson's experience in dealing with search and seizure law. What does he mean by "second-class rights"?

2. Identify and describe each of the elements required to meet the Fourth Amendment's warrant requirement.

3. According to the "knock-and-announce" rule, what's a reasonable amount of time to wait before breaking and entering into a home to execute a search warrant?

4. Identify and describe the main exceptions to the knock-and-announce rule.

5. Compare and contrast the constitutional preference and practice regarding searches with warrants and without.

6. Identify five major exceptions to the warrant requirement approved by the U.S. Supreme Court.

7. List three reasons why searches incident to arrest are reasonable.

8. Identify the scope and time frame of "incident" to arrest.

9. Summarize Moskovitz's empirical research regarding searches incident to traffic arrests and describe the *Belton* Court's generalizations it challenges. Describe the limitations of Moskovitz's sources and methods.

10. Describe the *Robinson* rule and the justification for it.

11. Summarize the decision in *Knowles v. Iowa*. According to the U.S. Supreme Court, why can't officers always search incident to traffic citations?

12. Describe why pretext arrests are a powerful investigative tool.

13. What does it mean to say that racial discrimination has infected traffic arrest searches? Summarize the Bureau of Justice Statistics' survey results regarding race and searches incident to traffic arrests.

14. According to the Supreme Court, how broad is the scope of a consent search?

15. Identify some characteristics the courts use to determine the voluntariness of consent.

16. Summarize the main empirical research findings regarding consent searches.

17. Describe the elements of scope of consent and the withdrawal of consent.

18. Give an example of a third-party consent search.

19. Compare and contrast actual and apparent authority to consent. Which is the higher standard? According to the Supreme Court, which is the minimum required by the Fourth Amendment?

20. Identify the two reasons why vehicle searches are reasonable without warrants.

21. According to *Wyoming v. Houghton*, what's the rule regarding searches of containers in passenger vehicles?

22. Identify three emergency searches, and tell why the Supreme Court finds them reasonable searches without warrants.

KEY TERMS

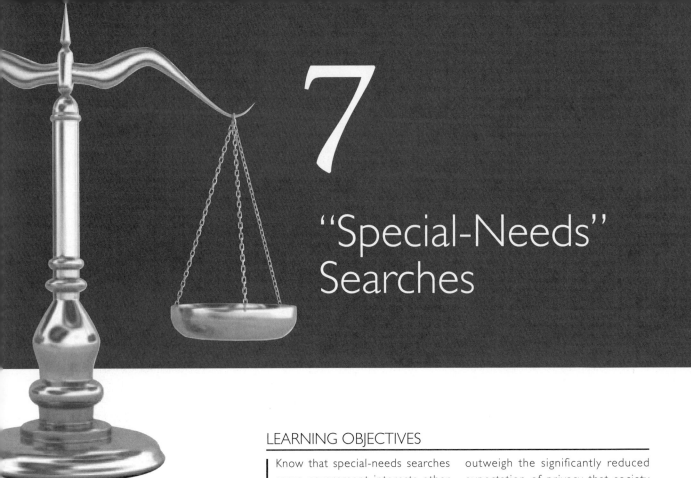

7

"Special-Needs" Searches

CASES COVERED

South Dakota v. Opperman
428 U.S. 364 (1976)

Florence v. Board of Chosen
Freeholders of the County
of Burlington et al. (2012)

Samson v. California
126 S.Ct. 2193 (2006)

Safford Unified School District
No. 1 v. Redding (2009)

State v. Ellis
2006 WL 82736
(OhioApp. 2006)

Ferguson and others v. City
of Charleston and others
532 U.S. 67 (2001)

LEARNING OBJECTIVES

1 Know that special-needs searches serve government interests other than the ability to control crime. Understand that special-needs searches are aimed at people generally, can result in criminal prosecution, and don't require warrants or probable cause to make them reasonable.

2 Know that following routine, department-approved procedures allows law enforcement to conduct inventory searches without probable cause or warrants to protect the owners' property, to prevent lawsuits against law enforcement departments, and to protect law enforcement agents.

3 Know that the special need to control who and what enters the United States makes international border searches reasonable without warrants or probable cause.

4 Understand that the special needs to maintain safety, security, and discipline over people locked up in jails and prisons, probationers and parolees outweigh the significantly reduced expectation of privacy that society grants people in custody.

5 Appreciate that probationers and parolees have significantly limited Fourth Amendment rights, even though they're not physically locked up.

6 Know that students' constitutional rights are balanced against school officials' ability to discipline, maintain order, and prevent violence and drug use within public schools.

7 Understand that the reasonableness of a public college's or university's entry and inspection of dormitory rooms requires balancing the institution's ability to maintain a suitable learning environment against the students' right against unreasonable searches of their "home."

8 Understand that searches for drug use through drug testing are directed at the special need to reduce danger to public safety, not to collect evidence of crime.

242

A resident assistant in the university dormitory where Sherman Ellis lived entered Ellis's room to conduct an unannounced safety inspection. These inspections were done on a regular basis by resident assistants and were not performed for obtaining evidence for criminal prosecution. These searches were conducted consistent with the policies and procedures set forth by the university.

Upon entering the room, the resident assistant, joined shortly thereafter by another resident assistant, discovered a beer can on a desktop. Possession of alcoholic beverages is a violation of the university policies and procedures. During the course of obtaining the beer, the resident assistant observed an open drawer in the desk and could smell, as well as see, bags of what he referred to as "weed," which he identified as marijuana.

University police officers were notified and watched while the resident assistants completed their safety search and inspection. The police officers did not participate in the search. The resident assistants turned over several items obtained from their search, which were later used to prosecute Sherman Ellis.

—*State v. Ellis* (2006)

243

LO 1

Until now, we've only discussed searches and seizures conducted to gather evidence of crime. But crime control isn't the only reason for searches. The U.S. Supreme Court has applied the Fourth Amendment to a wide range of **special-needs searches** that go beyond criminal law enforcement. They include the following searches that we'll discuss in this chapter:

- *Inventory searches.* Documenting inventory searches of persons and containers in government custody to protect the owners from theft and damage, government agencies from lawsuits, and jails from danger

- *International border searches.* Conducting international border checks to control who and what comes into and goes out of the country

- *Airport searches.* Examining airport passengers and their baggage to protect the safety of travelers

- *Custody-related searches.* Searching prisoners, probationers, parolees, and visitors and employees of prisons and jails to control contraband

- *Public college and university dormitory inspections.* Conducting health, safety, and drug and alcohol inspections to provide a healthy school environment

- *Employee workplace drug testing.* Testing employees for drug use to increase workplace safety

- *Prenatal patient drug testing.* Testing pregnant public hospital clinic patients suspected of illegal drug use

- *Public middle and high school student drug testing.* Testing students to maintain a thriving learning environment

- *Other special-needs searches.* "Inspecting" businesses, such as restaurants and bars, to make sure they're complying with health and safety codes, and conducting vehicle safety checks to make the roads safer

"Special needs" doesn't mean that these searches are totally unrelated to law enforcement. Take the best example, the frisks you learned about in Chapter 4. Their sole purpose is to protect officers, *but* if evidence of a crime inadvertently turns up during the frisk, officers can seize it, prosecutors can use it to charge and prosecute defendants, and courts can introduce it to convict defendants in criminal cases. The same is true of all the special-needs searches that you'll learn about in this chapter; in fact, many of the cases discussed in the chapter involve evidence of crimes discovered during the special need beyond law enforcement that justified the search in the first place.

Despite their variety, special-needs searches have four common characteristics:

1. They're directed at people generally, not criminal suspects and defendants specifically.
2. They can result in criminal prosecution and conviction.
3. They don't require warrants or probable cause.
4. Their reasonableness depends on balancing special government needs against invasions of individual privacy.

Let's turn to each of the special-needs searches in the bulleted list so you can understand how it serves the aims of protecting the public.

INVENTORY SEARCHES

LO **2**

Inventory searches take place when persons and/or their property is in police custody. **Inventory searches** consist of making a list of people's personal property and containers that the government holds in custody. Containers include vehicles, purses, clothing, or anything else where people in custody might put their belongings. After looking through ("searching") the containers, officials make a list of the items and put them away ("seize") for safekeeping.

The reasonableness of inventory searches depends on satisfying two elements (Chapter 4):

1. *Balancing interests.* Searches have to balance the government's special need to inspect against the invasion of individuals' privacy caused by the search. If the government's special need outweighs the individual's right to privacy (courts almost always find that it does), the search is reasonable.

2. *Objective basis.* Routine procedures, not probable cause or even reasonable suspicion, are required in special-needs searches.

Let's look at each element.

Law enforcement officers take inventories to satisfy three government interests that aren't directly connected to searching for evidence of a crime:

1. To protect owners' personal property while they, or their vehicles and other containers, are in police custody

2. To protect law enforcement agencies against lawsuits for the loss, destruction, or theft of owners' property

3. To protect law enforcement officers, detained suspects, and offenders from the danger of bombs, weapons, and illegal drugs that might be hidden in owners' property

According to the U.S. Supreme Court, inventories made by law enforcement officers are Fourth Amendment searches, but they're reasonable without either probable cause or warrants. Why? Because they're not conducted to collect evidence to prosecute crimes. This doesn't mean inventory special-needs searches are left entirely to officers' discretion. The objective basis that satisfies the reasonableness requirement is following **routine procedures** that police departments draw up and approve, and that their officers follow, when they conduct the inventory. Following routine, department-approved, written procedures substitutes for probable cause and reasonable suspicion in inventory searches.

Inventory searches of vehicles were firm and long-established practices throughout U.S. history, but they received no attention in their most common "special-needs" form until the 1970s. In 1976, the U.S. Supreme Court agreed to hear *South Dakota v. Opperman,* our next case excerpt. The Court held that the Vermillion, South Dakota, police department's inventory search procedures were reasonable Fourth Amendment searches.

In *South Dakota v. Opperman* (1976), the U.S. Supreme Court held that the Vermillion,

South Dakota, police department's inventory search procedures were reasonable

Fourth Amendment searches.

CASE

Was the Inventory a Reasonable Search?

South Dakota v. Opperman

428 U.S. 364 (1976)

HISTORY

Donald Opperman was convicted before the District County Court, Second Judicial District, Clay County, South Dakota, of possession of less than one ounce of marijuana, and he appealed. The South Dakota Supreme Court reversed, and certiorari was granted. The U.S. Supreme Court reversed the South Dakota Supreme Court and remanded.

—BURGER, C.J.

FACTS

Local ordinances prohibit parking in certain areas of downtown Vermillion, S. D., between the hours of 2 a.m. and 6 a.m. During the early morning hours of December 10, 1973, a Vermillion police officer observed respondent's (Donald Opperman's) unoccupied vehicle illegally parked in the restricted zone. At approximately 3 a.m., the officer issued an overtime parking ticket and placed it on the car's windshield. The citation warned: "Vehicles in violation of any parking ordinance may be towed from the area."

At approximately 10 o'clock on the same morning, another officer issued a second ticket for an overtime parking violation. These circumstances were routinely reported to police headquarters, and after the vehicle was inspected, the car was towed to the city impound lot. From outside the car at the impound lot, a police officer observed a watch on the dashboard and other items of personal property located on the backseat and back floorboard. At the officer's direction, the car door was then unlocked and, using a standard inventory form pursuant to standard police procedures, the officer inventoried the contents of the car, including the contents of the glove compartment, which was unlocked. There he found marijuana contained in a plastic bag. All items, including the contraband, were removed to the police department for safekeeping.

During the late afternoon of December 10, Opperman appeared at the police department to claim his property. The marijuana was retained by police. At Opperman's trial, the officer who conducted the inventory testified as follows:

Q: And why did you inventory this car?
A: Mainly for safekeeping, because we have had a lot of trouble in the past of people getting into the impound lot and breaking into cars and stealing stuff out of them.

Q: Do you know whether the vehicles that were broken into . . . were locked or unlocked?
A: Both of them were locked, they would be locked.

In describing the impound lot, the officer stated:

A: It's the old county highway yard. It has a wooden fence partially around part of it, and kind of a dilapidated wire fence, a makeshift fence.

Opperman was subsequently arrested on charges of possession of marijuana. His motion to suppress the evidence yielded by the inventory search was denied; he was convicted after a jury trial and sentenced to a fine of $100 and 14 days' incarceration in the county jail. On appeal, the Supreme Court of South Dakota reversed the conviction. The court concluded that the evidence had been obtained in violation of the Fourth Amendment prohibition against unreasonable searches and seizures. We granted certiorari, and we reverse.

OPINION

In the interests of public safety and as part of community caretaking functions, automobiles are frequently taken into police custody. When vehicles are impounded, local police departments generally follow a routine practice of securing and inventorying the automobiles' contents. These procedures developed in response to three distinct needs: the protection of the owner's property while it remains in police custody; the protection of the police against claims or disputes over lost or stolen property; and the protection of the police from potential danger. The practice has been viewed as essential to respond to incidents of theft or vandalism. In addition, police frequently attempt to determine whether a vehicle has been stolen and thereafter abandoned.

The Vermillion police were indisputably engaged in a caretaking search of a lawfully impounded automobile. The inventory was conducted only after the car had been impounded for multiple parking violations. The owner, having left his car illegally parked for an extended period, and thus subject to impoundment, was not present to make other arrangements for the safekeeping of his belongings. The inventory itself was prompted by the presence in plain view of a number of valuables inside the car. There is no suggestion whatever that this standard procedure, essentially like that followed throughout the country, was a pretext concealing an investigatory police motive. The inventory was not unreasonable in scope. Opperman's motion to suppress in state court challenged the inventory only as to items inside the car not in plain view. But once the policeman was lawfully inside the car to secure the personal property in plain view, it was not unreasonable to open the unlocked glove compartment, to which vandals would have had ready and unobstructed access once inside the car.

On this record we conclude that in following standard police procedures, prevailing throughout the country and approved by the overwhelming majority of courts, the conduct of the police was not "unreasonable" under the Fourth Amendment. The judgment of the South Dakota Supreme Court is therefore reversed, and the case is remanded for further proceedings not inconsistent with this opinion.

REVERSED and REMANDED.

DISSENT

MARSHALL, J., joined by BRENNAN and STEWART, JJ.

The Court's opinion appears to suggest that its result may be justified because the inventory search procedure is a "reasonable" response to "three distinct needs: the protection of the owner's property while it remains in police custody; the protection of the police against claims or disputes over lost or stolen property; and the protection of the police from potential danger." It is my view that none of these "needs," separately or together, can suffice to justify the inventory search procedure approved by the Court.

First, this search cannot be justified in any way as a safety measure, for though the Court ignores it, the sole purpose given by the State for the Vermillion police's inventory procedure was to secure valuables. Nor is there any indication that the officer's search in this case was tailored in any way to safety concerns, or that ordinarily it is so circumscribed. I do not believe that any blanket safety argument could justify a program of routine searches of the scope permitted here. Ordinarily there is little danger

associated with impounding unsearched automobiles. Thus, while the safety rationale may not be entirely discounted when it is actually relied upon, it surely cannot justify the search of every car upon the basis of undifferentiated possibility of harm; on the contrary, such an intrusion could ordinarily be justified only in those individual cases where the officer's inspection was prompted by specific circumstances indicating the possibility of a particular danger. The very premise of the State's chief argument, that the cars must be searched in order to protect valuables because no guard is posted around the vehicles, itself belies the argument that they must be searched at the city lot in order to protect the police there.

The Court suggests a further "crucial" justification for the search in this case: protection of the public from vandals who might find a firearm, or contraband drugs. There is simply no indication the police were looking for dangerous items. Indeed, even though the police found shotgun shells in the interior of the car, they never opened the trunk to determine whether it might contain a shotgun. Aside from this, the suggestion is simply untenable as a matter of law. If this asserted rationale justifies search of all impounded automobiles, it must logically also justify the search of all automobiles, whether impounded or not, located in a similar area, for the argument is not based upon the custodial role of the police. But this Court has never permitted the search of any car or home on the mere undifferentiated assumption that it might be vandalized and the vandals might find dangerous weapons or substances.

Second, the Court suggests that the search for valuables in the closed glove compartment might be justified as a measure to protect the police against lost property claims. Again, this suggestion is belied by the record, since although the Court declines to discuss it, the South Dakota Supreme Court's interpretation of state law explicitly absolves the police from any obligation beyond inventorying objects in plain view and locking the car. Moreover, it may well be doubted that an inventory procedure would in any event work significantly to minimize the frustrations of false claims. Even were the State to impose a higher standard of custodial responsibility upon the police, however, it is equally clear that such a requirement must be read in light of the Fourth Amendment's pre-eminence to require protective measures other than interior examination of closed areas. Indeed, if such claims can be deterred at all, they might more effectively be deterred by sealing the doors and trunk of the car so that an unbroken seal would certify that the car had not been opened during custody.

Finally, the Court suggests that the public interest in protecting valuables that may be found inside a closed compartment of an impounded car may justify the inventory procedure. I recognize the genuineness of this governmental interest in protecting property from pilferage.

(continued)

But even if I assume that the posting of a guard would be fiscally impossible as an alternative means to the same protective end, I cannot agree with the Court's conclusion.

In my view, if the owner of the vehicle is in police custody or otherwise in communication with the police, his consent to the inventory is prerequisite to an inventory search. The Constitution does not permit such searches as a matter of routine; absent specific consent, such a search is permissible only in exceptional circumstances of particular necessity.

The Court's result in this case elevates the conservation of property interests, indeed mere possibilities of property interests, above the privacy and security interests, protected by the Fourth Amendment. For this reason I dissent. On the remand it should be clear in any event that this Court's holding does not preclude a contrary resolution of this case or others involving the same issues under any applicable state law.

WHITE, J.

Although I do not subscribe to all of my Brother MARSHALL's dissenting opinion, particularly some aspects of his discussion concerning the necessity for obtaining the consent of the car owner, I agree with most of his analysis and conclusions and consequently dissent from the judgment of the Court.

Questions

1. List all the actions taken by the Vermillion police department related to the inventory of Donald Opperman's impounded car.

2. List all of Opperman's personal belongings the police inventoried, and state where they were found.

3. Summarize the majority opinion's arguments for finding the inventory search was reasonable.

4. Summarize the dissent's arguments for concluding that the inventory search was unreasonable.

5. Do you agree with the dissent that "The Constitution does not permit such searches as a matter of routine; absent specific consent, such a search is permissible only in exceptional circumstances of particular necessity"? Defend your answer.

Most courts have adopted the majority rule in *Opperman* that "following standard police procedures" is enough to satisfy the minimum standard of Fourth Amendment reasonableness. But some courts have adopted a narrower rule that officers conducting inventory searches of vehicles without warrants can't exceed what they can see in plain view (LaFave and others 2009, 235). And the U.S. Supreme Court has rejected the dissenters' call for "reasonable efforts under the circumstances to identify and reach the owner of the property to facilitate alternative means of security or to obtain his consent to the search." In *Colorado v. Bertine* (1987), the Court held that the Fourth Amendment doesn't require police officers to use the least intrusive means to secure property of seized vehicles. But they have to follow "standardized criteria" spelled out in police regulations.

INTERNATIONAL BORDER SEARCHES

LO **3**   According to the U.S. Supreme Court in *U.S. v. Ramsey* (1977), searches at international borders are reasonable even without warrants or probable cause. This is known as the **border search exception**. The special need of border searches is the right to control who and what comes into and goes out of the country.

In *Ramsey*, a batch of incoming, letter-sized airmail envelopes from Thailand (a known source of narcotics) was bulky and much heavier than normal airmail letters. So a customs inspector opened the envelopes for inspection at the General Post Office in New York City (considered a "border") and found heroin in them. The inspector seized the heroin and used it to convict the recipient. The customs inspector didn't obtain a warrant to search the envelopes, even though he had time to get one.

Still, according to the U.S. Supreme Court, it wasn't an illegal search and seizure. Border searches are reasonable simply because they're conducted at international borders. The Court turned to history to support this holding:

> The Congress which proposed the Bill of Rights, including the Fourth Amendment, to the state legislatures on September 25, 1789 had, some two months prior to that proposal, enacted the first customs statute. Section 24 of this statute granted customs officials "full power and authority" to enter and search "any ship or vessel, in which they shall have reason to suspect any goods, wares or merchandise subject to duty shall be concealed. . . ." This acknowledgement of plenary customs power was differentiated from the more limited power to enter and search "any particular dwelling-house, store, building, or other place where a warrant was required." The historical importance of the enactment of this customs statute by the same Congress which proposed the Fourth Amendment is, we think, manifest. (616)

Applying the balancing test to border searches, the U.S. Supreme Court found that the national interest in controlling our international borders outweighs the invasions of individual privacy caused by border searches. So border checks require neither warrants nor individualized suspicion. However, reasonable suspicion is required to back up strip searches for contraband and weapons, because people coming into the country are "forced to disrobe to a state which would be offensive to the average person." Body-cavity searches at the border are reasonable only if they're backed up by probable cause (LaFave and others 2009, 265).

AIRPORT SEARCHES

LO 3

Ever since a series of airline hijackings and terrorist bombings in the 1970s, travelers have had to pass through metal detectors before they can board airplanes. Passengers also must pass their luggage through X-ray machines for examination. Additionally, inspectors sometimes open and look through baggage. If they discover suspicious items, they investigate further.

Applying the balancing test of Fourth Amendment reasonableness, the U.S. Supreme Court has held that airport searches are reasonable even without warrants or probable cause. According to the Court, airport searches serve two extremely important special needs—the security and the safety of air travelers. These special needs clearly outweigh the minimal invasion of privacy caused by having passengers pass through metal detectors and allowing their luggage to be observed by X-ray. Furthermore, these invasions apply equally to all passengers, who are notified in advance that they're subject to them. So passengers are free not to board the airplane if they don't want to subject their person and their luggage to these intrusions (LaFave and Israel 1984, 1:332–33).

Since September 11, 2001, the searches have become more frequent and more intrusive, but so has the sense of urgency about security. To date, there have been no court challenges to these security changes. But if a court challenge arises, it's not likely that the balance will be struck against the current practice. Of course, if passengers are singled out for more-frequent and more-invasive measures because of their Middle Eastern background and/or their Muslim religion, that's a different matter.

CUSTODY-RELATED SEARCHES

 All of the following can be searched without warrants or probable cause—or in some cases without any objective basis at all:

- Prisoners and their cells
- Prison visitors and employees
- Prisoners released on parole
- Probationers who could be but aren't locked up
- Defendants detained before they're convicted

Why don't these searches require warrants, probable cause or reasonable suspicion, or possibly any individualized suspicion at all? Because the special need to maintain safety, security, and discipline over people locked up in jails and prisons, and probationers and parolees under state supervision in the community, outweighs the significantly reduced expectation of privacy that society grants to people in the custody of the criminal justice system.

Let's look at how the U.S. Supreme Court has balanced the special need and individual privacy as it applies to prisoners, probationers and parolees, and prison visitors and employees.

LO 4 Searches of Prisoners

Historically, prisoners had no Fourth Amendment rights; the Constitution stopped at the prison gate. Referring to convicted prisoners, the Virginia court in *Ruffin v. Commonwealth* (1871) said, "The bill of rights is a declaration of general principles to govern a society of freemen." Prisoners "are the slaves of the State" (1025). As for people detained in jails *before* they're convicted, in *Lanza v. New York* (1962), the U.S. Supreme Court ruled that "a jail shares none of the attributes of privacy of a home, automobile, an office or hotel room, and official surveillance has traditionally been the order of the day in prisons" (139).

In the 1980s, the Court conceded that prisoners have an expectation of privacy that society recognizes. According to the Court, in *Hudson v. Palmer* (1984), "We have repeatedly held that prisons are not beyond the reach of the Constitution. No 'iron curtain' separates one from the other." But, the Court continued, "*imprisonment carries with it the circumscription or loss of many significant rights*" (emphasis added) (523).

The reasonableness of prisoner searches depends on balancing the need to maintain prison and jail security, safety, and discipline against the invasion of prisoners' substantially reduced reasonable expectation of privacy. The Court applied the balancing approach in *Hudson v. Palmer* (1984). According to the prisoner Russell Thomas Palmer,

> Officer Hudson shook down my locker and destroyed a lot of my property, i.e.: legal materials, letters, and other personal property only as a means of harassment. Officer Hudson has violated my constitutional rights. The shakedown was no routine shakedown. It was planned and carried out only as harassment. Hudson stated the next time he would really mess my stuff up. I have plenty of witnesses to these facts. (541)

The Court accepted Palmer's version of the facts. Still, Chief Justice Burger, writing for the majority, held that the "shakedown routine"—unannounced searches of prisoners and their cells for weapons and contraband—was not a search at all. "Society is not prepared to recognize as legitimate any expectation of privacy that a prisoner might have in his prison cell," so "the Fourth Amendment proscription against unreasonable searches does not apply within the confines of the prison cell." Privacy for prisoners in their cells "cannot be reconciled with the concept of incarceration and the needs and objectives of penal institutions" (525–26).

The Court went further, holding that the Fourth Amendment doesn't apply even if the motive behind the shakedown was harassment. Four justices disagreed. According to Justice Stevens, writing for the dissenters:

> Measured by the conditions that prevail in a free society, neither the possessions nor the slight residuum of privacy that a prison inmate can retain in his cell, can have more than the most minimal value. From the standpoint of the prisoner, however, that trivial residuum may mark the difference between slavery and humanity.
>
> Personal letters, snapshots of family members, a souvenir, a deck of cards, a hobby kit, perhaps a diary or a training manual for an apprentice in a new trade, or even a Bible—a variety of inexpensive items may enable a prisoner to maintain contact with some part of his past and an eye to the possibility of a better future. Are all of these items subject to unrestrained perusal, confiscation, or mutilation at the hands of a possibly hostile guard? Is the Court correct in its perception that "society" is not prepared to recognize any privacy or possessory interest of the prison inmate—no matter how remote the threat to prison security may be? . . . (542–43)
>
> The restraints and the punishment which a criminal conviction entails do not place the citizen beyond the ethical tradition that accords respect to the dignity and intrinsic worth of every individual. By telling prisoners that no aspect of their individuality, from a photo of a child to a letter from a wife, is entitled to constitutional protection, the Court breaks with the ethical tradition that I had thought was enshrined forever in our jurisprudence. (557–58)

Now let's look at two other Fourth Amendment issues that prisoners have raised: strip and body-cavity searches and the testing and storing of their DNA.

LO 4 Strip Searches of Jail Inmates

Police officers arrested about 12.5 million people in 2011 (FBI Persons Arrested 2012, Table 29). When any of these arrested individuals is detained in jail, the U.S. Supreme Court concedes that strip-searching them is a Fourth Amendment search. Definitions of *strip search* vary, as the Court acknowledged in its latest strip-search case (Table 7.1).

But, whatever the definition, the Court has also held that strip searches are reasonable without either warrants or probable cause *if*, in the particular situation, the need for security, safety, or discipline outweighs prisoners' reasonable expectation of privacy in the particular circumstances of the case. For example, in *Bell v. Wolfish* (1979; Chapter 12), (until 2012 the only U.S. Supreme Court strip-search case) the Court held that it was reasonable to require jail inmates awaiting trial to expose their body cavities for visual inspection after every contact visit with a person from outside the jail. They could be searched even when there was no probable cause to believe visitors were carrying hidden contraband. The searches were reasonable because they helped to maintain safety and order in the jail.

TABLE 7.1 Definitions of "strip search"

Florence v. Board of Chosen Freeholders

The opinions in earlier proceedings, the briefs on file, and some cases of this Court refer to a "strip search." The term is imprecise.

- It may refer simply to the instruction to remove clothing while an officer observes from a distance of, say, five feet or more.
- It may mean a visual inspection from a closer, more uncomfortable distance.
- It may include directing detainees to shake their heads or to run their hands through their hair to dislodge what might be hidden there.
- It may involve instructions to
    - Raise arms
    - Display foot insteps
    - Expose the back of the ears
    - Move or spread the buttocks or genital areas
    - Cough in a squatting position.

Source: Florence v. Chosen Freeholders, page 1515.

In *Florence v. Board of Chosen Freeholders* (2012), our next case excerpt, the Court returned to strip searches in jails. This time, the jail officers strip-searched individuals arrested for minor offenses (like Gail Atwater, arrested and jailed for the fine-only offense of violating the Texas seat belt law, excerpted in Chapter 5, page 188). Furthermore, the Court had to resolve a conflict growing among the circuits in the years since they decided *Bell.* Some circuits held that jail officers couldn't strip-search individuals arrested for minor offenses without reasonable suspicion. Other circuits, including *Florence,* held that they *could.*

The specific question the Court agreed to hear was:

> Whether the Fourth Amendment permits a jail to conduct a suspicionless strip search of every individual arrested for any minor offense no matter what the circumstances. (Petition for writ of Certiorari, quoted in Shapiro 2012, 132)

In *Florence v. Board of Chosen Freeholders,* the U.S. Supreme Court (5–4) decided that strip-searching Albert Florence before he entered the general jail population was reasonable.

CASE

Were the Searches Reasonable to Further "Special Needs"?

Florence v. Board of Chosen Freeholders of the County of Burlington et al. (2012)
132 S.Ct. 1510 (2012)

HISTORY

Albert W. Florence (Samson), arrested on an outstanding bench warrant after traffic stop, brought a § 1983 class action against Burlington and Essex counties, alleging that invasive searches conducted before he entered the jails' general population violated his Fourth and Fourteenth Amendment rights. The United States District Court for the District of New Jersey granted Florence summary judgment. The Counties appealed. A three-member panel of the U.S. Court of Appeals for the Third Circuit reversed (2-1). The U.S. Supreme Court granted certiorari, holding that the strip searches were not unreasonable.

FACTS

In 1998, seven years before the incidents at issue, Albert Florence (Samson) was arrested after fleeing from police officers in Essex County, New Jersey. He was charged with obstruction of justice and use of a deadly weapon. Samson entered a plea of guilty to two lesser offenses and was sentenced to pay a fine in monthly installments. In 2003, after he fell behind on his payments and failed to appear at an enforcement hearing, a bench warrant was issued for his arrest. He paid the outstanding balance less than a week later; but, for some unexplained reason, the warrant remained in a statewide computer database.

Two years later, in Burlington County, New Jersey, Samson and his wife were stopped in their automobile by a state trooper. Based on the outstanding warrant in the computer system, the officer arrested Samson and took him to the Burlington County Detention Center. He was held there for six days and then was transferred to the Essex County Correctional Facility. It is not the arrest or confinement but the search process at each jail that gives rise to the claims before the Court.

Burlington County jail procedures required every arrestee to shower with a delousing agent. Officers would check arrestees for scars, marks, gang tattoos, and contraband as they disrobed. Samson claims he was also instructed to open his mouth, lift his tongue, hold out his arms, turn around, and lift his genitals. (It is not clear whether this last step was part of the normal practice.) Samson shared a cell with at least one other person and interacted with other inmates following his admission to the jail.

The Essex County Correctional Facility, where Samson was taken after six days, is the largest county jail in New Jersey. It admits more than 25,000 inmates each year and houses about 1,000 gang members at any given time. When Samson was transferred there, all arriving detainees passed through a metal detector and waited in a group holding cell for a more thorough search. When they left the holding cell, they were instructed to remove their clothing while an officer looked for body markings, wounds, and contraband.

Apparently without touching the detainees, an officer looked at their ears, nose, mouth, hair, scalp, fingers, hands, arms, armpits, and other body openings. This policy applied regardless of the circumstances of the arrest, the suspected offense, or the detainee's behavior, demeanor, or criminal history. Samson alleges he was required to lift his genitals, turn around, and cough in a squatting position as part of the process. After a mandatory shower, during which his clothes were inspected,

Samson was admitted to the facility. He was released the next day, when the charges against him were dismissed.

OPINION

The Federal Courts of Appeals have come to differing conclusions as to whether the Fourth Amendment requires correctional officials to exempt some detainees who will be admitted to a jail's general population from the searches here at issue. This Court granted certiorari to address the question.

The difficulties of operating a detention center must not be underestimated by the courts. Jails (in the stricter sense of the term, excluding prison facilities) admit more than 13 million inmates a year. The largest facilities process hundreds of people every day; smaller jails may be crowded on weekend nights, after a large police operation, or because of detainees arriving from other jurisdictions. Maintaining safety and order at these institutions requires the expertise of correctional officials, who must have substantial discretion to devise reasonable solutions to the problems they face. The Court has confirmed the importance of deference to correctional officials and explained that a regulation impinging on an inmate's constitutional rights must be upheld "if it is reasonably related to legitimate penological interests."

The Court's opinion in *Bell v. Wolfish*, 441 U.S. 520, (1979), is the starting point for understanding how this framework applies to Fourth Amendment challenges. That case addressed a rule requiring pretrial detainees in any correctional facility run by the Federal Bureau of Prisons "to expose their body cavities for visual inspection as a part of a strip search conducted after every contact visit with a person from outside the institution." Inmates at the federal Metropolitan Correctional Center in New York City argued there was no security justification for these searches. Officers searched guests before they entered the visiting room, and the inmates were under constant surveillance during the visit. There had been but one instance in which an inmate attempted to sneak contraband back into the facility.

The Court nonetheless upheld the search policy. It deferred to the judgment of correctional officials that the inspections served not only to discover but also to deter the smuggling of weapons, drugs, and other prohibited items inside. The Court explained that there is no mechanical way to determine whether intrusions on an inmate's privacy are reasonable. The need for a particular search must be balanced against the resulting invasion of personal rights.

The Court has also recognized that deterring the possession of contraband depends in part on the ability to conduct searches without predictable exceptions. In *Hudson v. Palmer*, 468 U.S. 517 (1984), it addressed the question of whether prison officials could perform random searches of inmate lockers and cells even without

(continued)

reason to suspect a particular individual of concealing a prohibited item. The Court upheld the constitutionality of the practice, recognizing that "for one to advocate that prison searches must be conducted only pursuant to an enunciated general policy or when suspicion is directed at a particular inmate is to ignore the realities of prison operation" (1981). Inmates would adapt to any pattern or loopholes they discovered in the search protocol and then undermine the security of the institution.

These cases establish that correctional officials must be permitted to devise reasonable search policies to detect and deter the possession of contraband in their facilities. Maintaining institutional security and preserving internal order and discipline are essential goals that may require limitation or retraction of retained constitutional rights of both convicted prisoners and pretrial detainees. The task of determining whether a policy is reasonably related to legitimate security interests is peculiarly within the province and professional expertise of corrections officials. This Court has repeated the admonition that, in the absence of substantial evidence in the record to indicate that the officials have exaggerated their response to these considerations courts should ordinarily defer to their expert judgment in such matters.

Persons arrested for minor offenses may be among the detainees processed at these facilities. This is, in part, a consequence of the exercise of state authority that was the subject of *Atwater v. Lago Vista*, 532 U.S. 318, (2001). *Atwater* addressed the perhaps more fundamental question of who may be deprived of liberty and taken to jail in the first place. [Excerpted, Chapter 5, pp. 188] *Atwater* did not address whether the Constitution imposes special restrictions on the searches of offenders suspected of committing minor offenses once they are taken to jail. Some Federal Courts of Appeals have held that corrections officials may not conduct a strip search of these detainees, even if no touching is involved, absent reasonable suspicion of concealed contraband. The Courts of Appeals to address this issue in the last decade, however, have come to the opposite conclusion.

Correctional officials have a significant interest in conducting a thorough search as a standard part of the intake process. The admission of inmates creates numerous risks for facility staff, for the existing detainee population, and for a new detainee himself or herself. The danger of introducing lice or contagious infections, for example, is well documented. Persons just arrested may have wounds or other injuries requiring immediate medical attention. It may be difficult to identify and treat these problems until detainees remove their clothes for a visual inspection.

Jails and prisons also face grave threats posed by the increasing number of gang members who go through the intake process. The groups recruit new members by force, engage in assaults against staff, and give other inmates a reason to arm themselves. Fights among feuding gangs

can be deadly, and the officers who must maintain order are put in harm's way. These considerations provide a reasonable basis to justify a visual inspection for certain tattoos and other signs of gang affiliation as part of the intake process. The identification and isolation of gang members before they are admitted protects everyone in the facility.

Detecting contraband concealed by new detainees, furthermore, is a most serious responsibility. Weapons, drugs, and alcohol all disrupt the safe operation of a jail. Correctional officers have had to confront arrestees concealing knives, scissors, razor blades, glass shards, and other prohibited items on their person, including in their body cavities. They have also found crack, heroin, and marijuana. The use of drugs can embolden inmates in aggression toward officers or each other; and, even apart from their use, the trade in these substances can lead to violent confrontations.

There are many other kinds of contraband. The textbook definition of the term covers any unauthorized item. Contraband obviously includes drugs or weapons, but it can also be money, cigarettes, or even some types of clothing. Something as simple as an overlooked pen can pose a significant danger. Inmates commit more than 10,000 assaults on correctional staff every year and many more among themselves. Contraband creates additional problems because scarce items, including currency, have value in a jail's culture and underground economy. Correctional officials inform us "the competition . . . for such goods begets violence, extortion, and disorder." Gangs exacerbate the problem. They "orchestrate thefts, commit assaults, and approach inmates in packs to take the contraband from the weak." This puts the entire facility, including detainees being held for a brief term for a minor offense, at risk.

It is not surprising that correctional officials have sought to perform thorough searches at intake for disease, gang affiliation, and contraband. Jails are often crowded, unsanitary, and dangerous places. There is a substantial interest in preventing any new inmate, either of his own will or as a result of coercion, from putting all who live or work at these institutions at even greater risk when he is admitted to the general population.

Samson acknowledges that correctional officials must be allowed to conduct an effective search during the intake process and that this will require at least some detainees to lift their genitals or cough in a squatting position. These procedures, similar to the ones upheld in *Bell*, are designed to uncover contraband that can go undetected by a pat down, metal detector, and other less invasive searches. Samson maintains there is little benefit to conducting these more invasive steps on a new detainee who has not been arrested for a serious crime or for any offense involving a weapon or drugs. In his view these detainees should be exempt from this process unless they give officers a particular reason to suspect them of hiding contraband. It is reasonable, however, for correctional officials to conclude this standard would be unworkable. The record provides evidence that the seriousness of an offense is a poor predictor of who has contraband and that it would be difficult in practice to determine whether individual detainees fall within the proposed exemption.

People detained for minor offenses can turn out to be the most devious and dangerous criminals. Hours after the Oklahoma City bombing, Timothy McVeigh was stopped by a state trooper who noticed he was driving without a license plate. Officers at the Atlantic County Correctional Facility discovered that a man arrested for driving under the influence had "2 dime bags of weed, 1 pack of rolling papers, 20 matches, and 5 sleeping pills" taped under his scrotum. A person booked on a misdemeanor charge of disorderly conduct in Washington State managed to hide a lighter, tobacco, tattoo needles, and other prohibited items in his rectal cavity. San Francisco officials have discovered contraband hidden in body cavities of people arrested for trespassing, public nuisance, and shoplifting. There have been similar incidents at jails throughout the country.

Even if people arrested for a minor offense do not themselves wish to introduce contraband into a jail, they may be coerced into doing so by others. This could happen any time detainees are held in the same area, including in a van on the way to the station or in the holding cell of the jail. If, for example, a person arrested and detained for unpaid traffic citations is not subject to the same search as others, this will be well known to other detainees with jail experience. A hardened criminal or gang member can, in just a few minutes, approach the person and coerce him into hiding the fruits of a crime, a weapon, or some other contraband. As an expert in this case explained, "the interaction and mingling between misdemeanants and felons will only increase the amount of contraband in the facility if the jail can only conduct admission searches on felons."

It also may be difficult, as a practical matter, to classify inmates by their current and prior offenses before the intake search. Jails can be even more dangerous than prisons because officials there know so little about the people they admit at the outset. The laborious administration of prisons would become less effective, and likely less fair and evenhanded, were the practical problems inevitable from the rules suggested by Samson to be imposed as a constitutional mandate. Even if they had accurate information about a detainee's current and prior arrests, officers, under Samson's proposed regime, would encounter serious implementation difficulties. They would be required, in a few minutes, to determine whether any of the underlying offenses were serious enough to authorize the more invasive search protocol. Other possible classifications based on characteristics of individual detainees also might prove to be unworkable or even give rise to charges of discriminatory application. Most officers would not be well equipped to make any of these legal determinations during the pressures of the intake process. To avoid liability, officers might be inclined not to conduct a thorough search in any close case, thus creating unnecessary risk for the entire jail population. The restrictions suggested by Samson would limit the intrusion on the privacy of some detainees but at the risk of increased danger to everyone in the facility, including the less serious offenders themselves.

Samson's *amici* raise concerns about instances of officers engaging in intentional humiliation and other abusive practices. There also may be legitimate concerns about the invasiveness of searches that involve the touching of detainees. These issues are not implicated on the facts of this case, however, and it is unnecessary to consider them here.

Even assuming all the facts in favor of Samson, the search procedures at the Burlington County Detention Center and the Essex County Correctional Facility struck a reasonable balance between inmate privacy and the needs of the institutions. The Fourth and Fourteenth Amendments do not require adoption of the framework of rules Samson proposes. The judgment of the Court of Appeals for the Third Circuit is affirmed.

It is so ordered.

DISSENT

BREYER, J., joined by GINSBURG, SOTOMAYOR, KAGAN, JJ.

A strip search that involves a stranger peering without consent at a naked individual, and in particular at the most private portions of that person's body, is a serious invasion of privacy. The Courts of Appeals have more directly described the privacy interests at stake, writing, for example, that practices similar to those at issue here are "demeaning, dehumanizing, undignified, humiliating, terrifying, unpleasant, embarrassing, [and] repulsive, signifying degradation and submission" (*Mary Beth G. v. Chicago*, 723 F.2d 1263, 1984). The harm to privacy interests would seem particularly acute where the person searched may well have no expectation of being subject to such a search, say, because she had simply received a traffic ticket for failing to buckle a seatbelt, because he had not previously paid a civil fine, or because she had been arrested for a minor trespass.

Albert Florence states that his present arrest grew out of an (erroneous) report that he had failed to pay a minor civil fine previously assessed because he had hindered a prosecution (by fleeing police officers in his automobile). *Amicus* briefs present other instances in which individuals arrested for minor offenses have been subjected to the humiliations of a visual strip search. They include a nun, a Sister of Divine Providence for 50 years, who was arrested for trespassing during an antiwar demonstration. They include women who were strip-searched during periods

(continued)

of lactation or menstruation. They include victims of sexual violence. They include individuals detained for such infractions as driving with a noisy muffler, driving with an inoperable headlight, failing to use a turn signal, or riding a bicycle without an audible bell.

I need not go on. I doubt that we seriously disagree about the nature of the strip search or about the serious affront to human dignity and to individual privacy that it presents. The basic question before us is whether such a search is nonetheless justified when an individual arrested for a minor offense is involuntarily placed in the general jail or prison population.

The majority, like the Counties, argues that strip searches are needed. I, like the majority, recognize: that managing a jail or prison is an inordinately difficult undertaking; that prison regulations that interfere with important constitutional interests are generally valid as long as they are "reasonably related to legitimate penological interests;" that finding injuries and preventing the spread of disease, minimizing the threat of gang violence, and detecting contraband are legitimate penological interests; and that we normally defer to the expertise of jail and prison administrators in such matters.

Nonetheless, the "particular" invasion of interests must be "reasonably related" to the justifying "penological interest" and the need must not be "exaggerated." It is at this point that I must part company with the majority. I have found no convincing reason indicating that, in the absence of reasonable suspicion, involuntary strip searches of those arrested for minor offenses are necessary in order to further the penal interests mentioned. And there are strong reasons to believe they are not justified.

The lack of justification is fairly obvious with respect to the first two penological interests advanced. The searches already employed at Essex and Burlington include: (a) pat-frisking all inmates; (b) making inmates go through metal detectors (including the Body Orifice Screening System (BOSS) chair used at Essex County Correctional Facility that identifies metal hidden within the body); (c) making inmates shower and use particular delousing agents or bathing supplies; and (d) searching inmates' clothing.

In addition, Samson concedes that detainees could be lawfully subject to being viewed in their undergarments by jail officers or during showering (for security purposes). No one here has offered any reason, example, or empirical evidence suggesting the inadequacy of such practices for detecting injuries, diseases, or tattoos. In particular, there is no connection between the genital lift and the "squat and cough" that Florence was allegedly subjected to and health or gang concerns.

The lack of justification for such a strip search is less obvious but no less real in respect to the third interest, namely that of detecting contraband. The information demonstrating the lack of justification is of three kinds. First, there are empirically based conclusions reached

in specific cases. In *Dodge v. County of Orange,* 282 F. Supp.2d 41 (S.D.N.Y.2003), the New York Federal District Court conducted a study of 23,000 persons admitted to the Orange County correctional facility between 1999 and 2003. These 23,000 persons underwent a strip search. Of these 23,000 persons, the court wrote, "the County encountered three incidents of drugs recovered from an inmate's anal cavity and two incidents of drugs falling from an inmate's underwear during the course of a strip search." The court added that in four of these five instances there may have been "reasonable suspicion" to search, leaving only one instance in 23,000 in which the strip search policy "arguably" detected additional contraband. The study is imperfect, for search standards changed during the time it was conducted. But the large number of inmates, the small number of "incidents," and the District Court's own conclusions make the study probative though not conclusive.

Similarly, in *Shain v. Ellison,* 273 F.3d 56, 60 (C.A.2 2001), the court received data produced by the county jail showing that authorities conducted body-cavity strip searches, similar to those at issue here, of 75,000 new inmates over a period of five years. In 16 instances the searches led to the discovery of contraband. The record further showed that 13 of these 16 pieces of contraband would have been detected in a pat down or a search of shoes and outer-clothing. In the three instances in which contraband was found on the detainee's body or in a body cavity, there was a drug or felony history that would have justified a strip search on individualized reasonable suspicion.

Second, there is the plethora of recommendations of professional bodies, such as correctional associations, that have studied and thoughtfully considered the matter. The American Correctional Association (ACA)—an association that informs our view of "what is obtainable and what is acceptable in corrections philosophy," has promulgated a standard that forbids suspicionless strip searches. And it has done so after consultation with the American Jail Association, National Sheriff's Association, National Institute of Corrections of the Department of Justice, and Federal Bureau of Prisons.

Moreover, many correctional facilities apply a reasonable suspicion standard before strip-searching inmates entering the general jail population, including the U.S. Marshals Service, the Immigration and Customs Service, and the Bureau of Indian Affairs. The Federal Bureau of Prisons (BOP) itself forbids suspicionless strip searches for minor offenders, though it houses separately (and does not admit to the general jail population) a person who does not consent to such a search.

Third, there is general experience in areas where the law has forbidden here-relevant suspicionless searches. Laws in at least 10 States prohibit suspicionless strip searches [Colorado, Florida, Illinois, Iowa, Kansas, Kentucky, Michigan, Missouri, Tennessee, Washington].

At the same time at least seven Courts of Appeals have considered the question and have required reasonable suspicion that an arrestee is concealing weapons or contraband before a strip search of one arrested for a minor offense can take place. Respondents have not presented convincing grounds to believe that administration of these legal standards has increased the smuggling of contraband into prison.

Indeed, neither the majority's opinion nor the briefs set forth any clear example of an instance in which contraband was smuggled into the general jail population during intake that could not have been discovered if the jail was employing a reasonable suspicion standard. The majority does cite general examples from Atlantic County and Washington State where contraband has been recovered in correctional facilities from inmates arrested for driving under the influence and disorderly conduct. Similarly, the majority refers to information, provided by San Francisco jail authorities, stating that they have found handcuff keys, syringes, crack pipes, drugs, and knives during body-cavity searches, including during searches of minor offenders, including a man arrested for illegally lodging (drugs), and a woman arrested for prostitution and public nuisance ("bindles of crack cocaine"). And associated statistics indicate that the policy of conducting visual cavity searches of *all* those admitted to the general population in San Francisco may account for the discovery of contraband in approximately 15 instances per year.

But neither San Francisco nor the respondents tell us *whether reasonable suspicion was present or absent* in *any* of the 15 instances. Nor is there any showing by the majority that the few unclear examples of contraband recovered in Atlantic County, Washington State, or anywhere else could not have been discovered through a policy that required reasonable suspicion for strip searches. And without some such indication, I am left without an example of any instance in which contraband was found on an individual through an inspection of their private parts or body cavities which could not have been found under a policy requiring reasonable suspicion. Hence, at a minimum these examples, including San Francisco's statistics, do not provide a significant counterweight to those presented in *Dodge* and *Shain*.

Nor do I find the majority's lack of examples surprising. After all, those arrested for minor offenses are often stopped and arrested unexpectedly. And they consequently will have had little opportunity to hide things in their body cavities. Thus, the widespread advocacy by prison experts and the widespread application in many States and federal circuits of "reasonable suspicion" requirements indicates an ability to apply such standards in practice without unduly interfering with the legitimate penal interest in preventing the smuggling of contraband.

The majority is left with the word of prison officials in support of its contrary proposition. And though that word is important, it cannot be sufficient.

For the reasons set forth, I cannot find justification for the strip-search policy at issue here—a policy that would subject those arrested for minor offenses to serious invasions of their personal privacy. I consequently dissent.

Questions

1. Identify the "special needs" that the searches were designed to further.

2. List the facts relevant to determining whether the two searches were reasonable to further the "special needs" they were designed to further.

3. Summarize the majority's reasons for concluding the searches were reasonable.

4. Summarize the dissent's reasons for concluding the searches were not reasonable.

5. Justice Alito voted with the majority, but he wrote a concurring opinion. Does the passage from it, quoted here, weaken the majority opinion's holding?

   It is important to note . . . that the Court does not hold that it is *always* reasonable to conduct a full strip search of an arrestee whose detention has not been reviewed by a judicial officer and who could be held in available facilities apart from the general population. Most of those arrested for minor offenses are not dangerous, and most are released from custody prior to or at the time of their initial appearance before a magistrate. In some cases, the charges are dropped. In others, arrestees are released either on their own recognizance or on minimal bail. In the end, few are sentenced to incarceration. For these persons, admission to the general jail population, with the concomitant humiliation of a strip search, may not be reasonable, particularly if an alternative procedure is feasible. The Court does not address whether it is always reasonable, without regard to the offense or the reason for detention, to strip-search an arrestee before the arrestee's detention has been reviewed by a judicial officer. The lead opinion explicitly reserves judgment on that question. In light of that limitation, I join the opinion of the Court in full.

6. Do you agree with the majority or the dissent? Defend your answer. Assume Albert Florence had prevailed. What should he get? Lots of money? Some money? Something in addition to, or instead of, money? If so, what should the "addition to" or "instead of" be?

7. Summarize the statistics relied on by the dissent to support its position. How important should these statistics be in deciding the reasonableness of the strip searches? Explain your answer.

LO 4   Testing and Storing Prisoners' DNA

Every state and the federal government now have statutes that mandate DNA testing of all incarcerated felons (*State v. Raines* 2004). Courts have defined the testing and storing of DNA as Fourth Amendment searches and seizures. The U.S. Supreme Court hasn't ruled on the reasonableness of the testing, but the U.S. Eleventh Circuit Court of Appeals upheld Georgia's statute (*Padgett v. Donald* 2005). The statute requires convicted, incarcerated felons to provide a sample of their DNA to the Georgia Department of Corrections for analysis and storage in a data bank maintained by the Georgia Bureau of Investigation (1275).

The DNA profiles can be released from the data bank "to federal, state, and local law enforcement officers upon a request made in furtherance of an official investigation of any criminal offense." The statute applies to all persons convicted of a felony and incarcerated on or after July 1, 2000, and all felons incarcerated as of that date (1275):

> In implementing the statute, the Georgia Department of Corrections (DOC) formulated policy dictating that members of the prison staff obtain the samples by swabbing the inside of felons' mouths for saliva. The GDOC then sends the swabs to the GBI for typing and placement in the DNA database. Inmates that refuse to submit to the procedure are subjected to disciplinary reports followed by hearings and possible disciplinary action. If any inmate still refuses to cooperate, the prison staff takes the sample by force. (1275–76)

Roy Padgett and several other imprisoned convicted felons brought a civil suit asking for an injunction against testing them on the ground that it was an illegal search and seizure of their saliva. The U.S. Court of Appeals affirmed the U.S. District Court's rejection of the prisoners' claim. The court found that the statute was "reasonable under a totality of the circumstances analysis":

> We employ a balancing test, weighing the degree to which the search intrudes on an individual's privacy against the degree to which it promotes a legitimate governmental interest. Because we believe that Georgia's legitimate interest in creating a permanent identification record of convicted felons for law enforcement purposes outweighs the minor intrusion involved in taking prisoners' saliva samples and storing their DNA profiles, given prisoners' reduced expectation of privacy in their identities, we . . . hold that the statute does not violate the Fourth Amendment. (1280)

LO 4, 5   Searching Probationers and Parolees

Probationers and parolees also have diminished Fourth Amendment rights, even though they're not locked up (LaFave and others 2009, 272–74). **Probationers** are convicted offenders who are sentenced to supervised release in the community *instead of* serving time in jails or prison. **Parolees** are prisoners who have served time in prison and who remain under supervision *after* their release from prison. Both have a reduced expectation of privacy that subjects them to arrest and searches of their persons, their vehicles, and their houses without warrants, probable cause, reasonable suspicion, or even without any objective basis at all. Three theories support these reduced expectations of privacy:

1. *Custody.* Some courts say it's because they're still in state custody, and conditional release is a privilege, not a right. After all, they could still be locked up; it's only by

the grace of the state they're conditionally released, and one of the conditions for release is to be searched at the discretion of the state.

2. *Consent.* Other courts say they're consent searches and seizures, signed and agreed to in their "contract" of release.

3. *Balancing.* Still other courts adopt a balancing approach to the searches of probationers and parolees. On the "special-need" side of the balance is the government's interest in protecting society and reducing recidivism; on the other side is privacy and the right against unreasonable searches and seizures.

Let's look at searching probationers and parolees.

LO 5   *Searching probationers*

The U.S. Supreme Court applied the balancing approach in *Griffin v. Wisconsin* (1987), the first and still the most frequently cited case involving the Fourth Amendment rights of probationers. Wisconsin law puts probationers in the custody of the Wisconsin Department of Health and Social Services. One of the department's regulations permits probation officers to search probationers' homes without a warrant as long as the searches are backed up by reasonable suspicion that contraband is in the house (870–71).

Michael Lew, Joseph Griffin's probation officer's supervisor, had reasonable suspicion that "there might be guns in Griffin's house." Lew went to the house without a warrant and searched the house. He found a handgun, a violation of Griffin's probation. Griffin was charged with possession of a firearm by a convicted felon, a felony in Wisconsin. The trial court denied Griffin's motion to suppress the gun, a jury convicted him, and the court sentenced him to two years in prison. The Wisconsin Court of Appeals and the Wisconsin Supreme Court affirmed his conviction (871–72).

The U.S. Supreme Court also affirmed. According to the Court, the Fourth Amendment protects probationers' homes from "unreasonable searches." Probationers and parolees don't enjoy "the absolute liberty to which every citizen is entitled, but only conditional liberty properly dependent on observance of special [probation] restrictions." The "special need" of supervision allows the relaxing of the probable cause and warrant requirements that apply to ordinary people's houses (873–74):

> These restrictions are meant to assure that the probation serves as a period of genuine rehabilitation and that the community is not harmed by the probationer's being at large. These same goals require and justify the exercise of supervision to assure that the restrictions are in fact observed. Supervision, then, is a "special need" of the State permitting a degree of impingement upon privacy that would not be constitutional if applied to the public at large. (875)

The matter of balancing *seemed* settled: Probation officers can search probationers' homes without warrants as long as they're backed up by reasonable suspicion. Then, 13 years later, *U.S. v. Knights* (2001) expanded the relaxed standard of reasonableness to searches by law enforcement officers.

Mark James Knights was convicted of a drug offense and was placed on probation, subject to the condition that he "submit his person, property, place of residence, vehicle, personal effects, to search at anytime, with or without a search warrant, warrant of arrest or reasonable cause by any probation officer or law enforcement officer." Knights signed the probation order, which stated immediately above his signature that "I HAVE RECEIVED A COPY, READ AND UNDERSTAND THE ABOVE TERMS AND CONDITIONS OF PROBATION AND AGREE TO ABIDE BY SAME" (114).

Three days later, Todd Hancock, a sheriff's detective, without Knights's knowledge or participation, searched his apartment without a warrant but with enough information to suspect, reasonably, that there might be "incendiary materials" in the apartment (115–16).

A unanimous U.S. Supreme Court ruled that the search passed the balancing test. Conceding that the search condition "significantly diminished Knights's reasonable expectation of privacy" (120), the Court turned to the special-needs side of the balance:

> The State has a dual concern with a probationer. On the one hand is the hope that he will successfully complete probation and be integrated back into the community. On the other is the concern, quite justified, that he will be more likely to engage in criminal conduct than an ordinary member of the community. We hold that when an officer has reasonable suspicion that a probationer subject to a search condition is engaged in criminal activity, there is enough likelihood that criminal conduct is occurring that an intrusion on the probationer's significantly diminished privacy interests is reasonable. (120–21)

LO 5   *Searching parolees*

According to the U.S. Supreme Court, parolees have less Fourth Amendment expectation of privacy than probationers because

> parole is an established variation of imprisonment of convicted criminals. The essence of parole is release from prison, before the completion of the sentence, on the condition that the prisoner abides by certain rules during the balance of the sentence. (*Samson v. California* 2006, 2198)

Not all members of the Court subscribe to this view, and there's a lot of controversy over whether the empirical data support the majority view. You'll learn more about the majority's and the dissent's views of parole and the empirical data in our next case excerpt, *Samson v. California* (2006).

In *Samson v. California* (2006), the Court expanded the rule in *Knights*, holding that law enforcement officers can search parolees' homes without either warrants or individualized reasonable suspicion.

CASE

Was the Suspicionless Search of Parolee Reasonable?

Samson v. California
126 S.Ct. 2193 (2006)

HISTORY

Donald Curtis Samson, Defendant, was convicted by a jury in the California Appellate Division of the Superior Court of possession of methamphetamine, and sentenced to seven years in prison. The California Court of Appeal affirmed. The U.S. Supreme Court granted certiorari and affirmed.

—THOMAS, J., joined by ROBERTS, C.J., and SCALIA, KENNEDY, GINSBURG, and ALITO, JJ.

HISTORY

California law provides that every prisoner eligible for release on state parole "shall agree in writing to be subject to search or seizure by a parole officer or other peace officer at any time of the day or night, with or without a search warrant and with or without cause." Cal. Penal Code Ann. § 3067(a). We granted certiorari to decide whether a suspicionless search, conducted under the authority of this statute, violates the Constitution. We hold that it does not.

FACTS

In September 2002, Samson Donald Curtis Samson (petitioner) was on state parole in California, following a conviction for being a felon in possession of a firearm. On September 6, 2002, Officer Alex Rohleder of the San Bruno Police Department observed Samson walking down a street with a woman and a child. Based on a prior contact with Samson, Officer Rohleder was aware that Samson was on parole and believed that he was facing an at large warrant. Accordingly, Officer Rohleder stopped Samson and asked him whether he had an outstanding parole warrant. Samson responded that there was no outstanding warrant and that he "was in good standing with his parole agent." Officer Rohleder confirmed, by radio dispatch, that Samson was on parole and that he did not have an outstanding warrant.

Nevertheless, pursuant to Cal.Penal Code Ann. § 3067(a) and based solely on Samson's status as a parolee, Officer Rohleder searched Samson. During the search, Officer Rohleder found a cigarette box in Samson's left breast pocket. Inside the box he found a plastic baggie containing methamphetamine.

We granted certiorari, to answer a variation of the question this Court left open in *U.S. v. Knights* (2001)— whether a condition of release can so diminish or eliminate a released prisoner's reasonable expectation of privacy that a suspicionless search by a law enforcement officer would not offend the Fourth Amendment. Answering that question in the affirmative today, we affirm the judgment of the California Court of Appeal.

OPINION

An inmate-turned-parolee remains in the legal custody of the California Department of Corrections through the remainder of his term, and must comply with all of the terms and conditions of parole, including mandatory drug tests, restrictions on association with felons or gang members, and mandatory meetings with parole officers. Parolees may also be subject to special conditions, including psychiatric treatment programs, mandatory abstinence from alcohol, residence approval, and "any other condition deemed necessary." The extent and reach of these conditions clearly demonstrate that parolees have severely diminished expectations of privacy by virtue of their status alone.

Additionally, the parole search condition under California law—requiring inmates who opt for parole to submit to suspicionless searches by a parole officer or other peace officer "at any time" was "clearly expressed" to Samson. He signed an order submitting to the condition and thus was "unambiguously" aware of it. Examining the totality of the circumstances pertaining to Samson's status as a parolee, an established variation on imprisonment, including the plain terms of the parole search condition, we conclude that Samson did not have an expectation of privacy that society would recognize as legitimate.

The State's interests, by contrast, are substantial. This Court has repeatedly acknowledged that a State has an "overwhelming interest" in supervising parolees because "parolees are more likely to commit future criminal offenses." Similarly, this Court has repeatedly acknowledged that a State's interests in reducing recidivism and thereby promoting reintegration and positive citizenship among probationers and parolees warrant privacy intrusions that would not otherwise be tolerated under the Fourth Amendment.

The empirical evidence presented in this case clearly demonstrates the significance of these interests to the State of California. As of November 30, 2005, California had over 130,000 released parolees. California's parolee population has a 68-to-70 percent recidivism rate. This Court has acknowledged the grave safety concerns that attend recidivism. The Fourth Amendment does not render the States powerless to address these concerns effectively. California's ability to conduct suspicionless searches of parolees serves its interest in reducing recidivism, in a manner that aids, rather than hinders, the reintegration of parolees into productive society.

The California Legislature has concluded that, given the number of inmates the State paroles and its high recidivism rate, a requirement that searches be based on individualized suspicion would undermine the State's ability to effectively supervise parolees and protect the public from criminal acts by reoffenders. This conclusion makes eminent sense. Imposing a reasonable suspicion requirement, as urged by Samson, would give parolees greater opportunity to anticipate searches and conceal criminality. This Court concluded that the incentive-to-conceal concern justified an "intensive" system for supervising probationers in *Griffin*. That concern applies with even greater force to a system of supervising parolees.

Thus, we conclude that the Fourth Amendment does not prohibit a police officer from conducting a suspicionless search of a parolee. Accordingly, we AFFIRM the judgment of the California Court of Appeal. It is so ordered.

DISSENT

STEVENS, J., joined by SOUTER and BREYER, JJ.

Our Fourth Amendment jurisprudence does not permit the conclusion, reached by the Court here for the first time,

(continued)

that a search supported by neither individualized suspicion nor "special needs" is nonetheless "reasonable." The suspicionless search is the very evil the Fourth Amendment was intended to stamp out. While individualized suspicion is not an irreducible component of reasonableness under the Fourth Amendment, the requirement has been dispensed with only when programmatic searches were required to meet a "'special need' divorced from the State's general interest in law enforcement."

None of our special needs precedents has sanctioned the routine inclusion of law enforcement, both in the design of the policy and in using arrests, either threatened or real, to implement the system designed for the special-needs objectives. Ignoring just how closely guarded is that category of constitutionally permissible suspicionless searches, the Court for the first time upholds an entirely suspicionless search unsupported by any special need.

And it goes further: In special-needs cases we have at least insisted upon programmatic safeguards designed to ensure evenhandedness in application; if individualized suspicion is to be jettisoned, it must be replaced with measures to protect against the state actor's unfettered discretion. Here, by contrast, there are no policies in place—no standards, guidelines, or procedures, to rein in officers and furnish a bulwark against the arbitrary exercise of discretion that is the height of unreasonableness.

The Court is able to make this unprecedented move only by making another. Prisoners have no legitimate expectation of privacy; parolees are like prisoners; therefore, parolees have no legitimate expectation of privacy. The conclusion is remarkable not least because we have long embraced its opposite.

Threaded through the Court's reasoning is the suggestion that deprivation of Fourth Amendment rights is part and parcel of any convict's punishment. If a person may be subject to random and suspicionless searches in prison, the Court seems to assume, then he cannot complain when he is subject to the same invasion outside of prison, so long as the State still can imprison him. Punishment, though, is not the basis [for depriving prisoners of their Fourth Amendment rights].

Had the State imposed as a condition of parole a requirement that Samson submit to random searches by his parole officer, who is supposed to have in mind the welfare of the parolee and guide the parolee's transition back into society, the condition might have been justified either under the special-needs doctrine or because

at least part of the requisite "reasonable suspicion" is supplied in this context by the individual-specific knowledge gained through the supervisory relationship. Likewise, this might have been a different case had a court or parole board imposed the condition at issue based on specific knowledge of the individual's criminal history and projected likelihood of reoffending, or if the State had had in place programmatic safeguards to ensure evenhandedness.

Under either of those scenarios, the State would at least have gone some way toward averting the greatest mischief wrought by officials' unfettered discretion. But the search condition here is imposed on all parolees—whatever the nature of their crimes, whatever their likelihood of recidivism, and whatever their supervisory needs—without any programmatic procedural protections.

The Court seems to acknowledge that unreasonable searches "inflict dignitary harms that arouse strong resentment in parolees and undermine their ability to reintegrate into productive society." It is satisfied, however, that the California courts' prohibition against "arbitrary, capricious or harassing" searches suffices to avert those harms—which are of course counterproductive to the State's purported aim of rehabilitating former prisoners and reintegrating them into society.

I am unpersuaded. The requirement of individualized suspicion, in all its iterations, is the shield the Framers selected to guard against the evils of arbitrary action, caprice, and harassment. To say that those evils may be averted without that shield is, I fear, to pay lip service to the end while withdrawing the means.

Respectfully, I dissent.

Questions

1. Identify the government's "special needs" and Donald Curtis Samson's diminished expectations of privacy. How would you balance the needs and this reduction of privacy? Explain your answer.

2. Summarize the arguments of the majority supporting its decision that searching of parolees without either warrants or reasonable suspicion is reasonable.

3. Summarize the dissent's argument that searching parolees without either warrants or reasonable suspicion is unreasonable.

4. Which side has the better arguments? Explain your answer without just repeating the arguments.

PUBLIC SCHOOL STUDENT SEARCHES

LO 6

In the earliest public schools, teachers taught and students listened. Teachers commanded and students obeyed. Teachers did not rely solely on the power of ideas to persuade; they relied on discipline to maintain order (Justice Clarence Thomas, *Morse v. Frederick* 2007, 412).

The courts upheld the school regime captured so neatly in Justice Thomas's description of the power of schools to maintain order by enforcing rules intended to discipline students under the legal doctrine known as *in loco parentis* [Latin for "in the place of the parents"]. According to this doctrine, principals, teachers, and other school officials substitute for parents while children are in school. The great English common law commentator, Sir William Blackstone (1765, I, 44), put it this way: "A parent may delegate part of his parental authority . . . to the tutor or schoolmaster of his child; who is then *in loco parentis*, and has such a portion of the power of the parent committed to his charge, viz. that of restraint and correction, as may be necessary to answer the purposes for which he is employed."

The autonomy of schools to discipline students remained largely intact until the 1960s civil rights movement, which added youth rights to the list of empowered groups. Parents, with the help of (critics said pressure from) public interest lawyers, challenged school discipline practices in court. From the late 1960s until the mid-1970s, the U.S. Supreme Court upheld public students' free speech and due process rights. In the leading case, *Goss v. Lopez* (1975), the Court heard the case of dozens of Central High School students in Columbus, Ohio, suspended for up to 10 days without a formal hearing, and without notifying them of the charges against them. During a "patriotic assembly," students protested the lack of the Black American curricula.

The Court (5–4) sided with the students:

> Students facing temporary suspension have interests qualifying for protection of the Due Process Clause, and due process requires, in connection with a suspension of 10 days or less, that the student be given oral or written notice of the charges against him and, if he denies them, an explanation of the evidence the authorities have and an opportunity to present his side of the story. The Clause requires at least these rudimentary precautions against unfair or mistaken findings of misconduct and arbitrary exclusion from school. (581)

After 1975, the Supreme Court has shifted from students' rights to responding to public concern over violence and drugs in schools. Justices appointed by Presidents Nixon, Reagan, and both President Bushes, revealed a friendlier attitude toward school discipline. The quotes from Justice Thomas reflect this shift. So does our next case excerpt, *Safford United School District v. Redding* (2009). Even though the Court ruled (5–4) that a partial strip search of Savana Redding was unreasonable, it granted the assistant principal, an administrative assistant, and school nurse qualified immunity from paying damages for participating in the search.

The U.S. Supreme Court in *Safford Unified School District No. 1 v. Redding* (2009) held that partially strip-searching an eighth grader was unreasonable, but granted individual school officials qualified immunity from civil liability for the illegal search.

CASE

Was the Strip Search Reasonable?
Safford Unified School Dist. No. 1 v. Redding
557 U.S. 364 (2009)

HISTORY

Savana Redding, an eighth grader at Safford Middle School, was strip-searched by school officials on the basis of a tip by another student that Redding might have ibuprofen on her person in violation of school policy. April Redding, Savana's mother, later sued the school district and the assistant principal, an administrative assistant, and the school nurse responsible for the search in the District Court for the District of Arizona. She alleged her Fourth Amendment right to be free of unreasonable search and seizure was violated. The district court granted the defendants' motion for summary judgment and dismissed the case. On the initial appeal, the U.S. Court of Appeals for the Ninth Circuit affirmed. However, on rehearing before the entire court, the court of appeals held that Savana Redding's Fourth Amendment right to be free of unreasonable search and seizure was violated. The U.S. Supreme Court affirmed, but also held that the law regarding strip searches of students was not clearly established, and therefore the officials were entitled to qualified immunity.

—Souter, J., joined by Roberts, C.J., and Scalia, Kennedy, Breyer and Alito, J.J.

FACTS

The events immediately prior to the search in question began in 13-year-old Savana Redding's math class at Safford Middle School one October day in 2003. The assistant principal of the school, Kerry Wilson, came into the room and asked Savana to go to his office. There, he showed her a day planner, unzipped and open flat on his desk, in which there were several knives, lighters, a permanent marker, and a cigarette. Wilson asked Savana whether the planner was hers; she said it was, but that a few days before she had lent it to her friend, Marissa Glines. Savana stated that none of the items in the planner belonged to her.

Wilson then showed Savana four white prescription-strength ibuprofen 400-mg pills, and one over-the-counter blue naproxen 200-mg pill, all used for pain and inflammation but banned under school rules without advance permission. He asked Savana if she knew anything about the pills. Savana answered that she did not. Wilson then told Savana that he had received a report that she was giving these pills to fellow students; Savana denied it and agreed to let Wilson search her belongings. Helen Romero, an administrative assistant, came into the office, and together with Wilson they searched Savana's backpack, finding nothing.

At that point, Wilson instructed Romero to take Savana to the school nurse's office to search her clothes for pills. Romero and the nurse, Peggy Schwallier, asked Savana to remove her jacket, socks, and shoes, leaving her in stretch pants and a T-shirt (both without pockets), which she was then asked to remove. Finally, Savana was told to pull her bra out and to the side and shake it, and to pull out the elastic on her underpants, thus exposing her breasts and pelvic area to some degree. No pills were found.

The school's policies strictly prohibit the nonmedical use, possession, or sale of any drug on school grounds, including "any prescription or over-the-counter drug, except those for which permission to use in school has been granted pursuant to Board policy." A week before Savana was searched, another student, Jordan Romero (no relation of the school's administrative assistant), told the principal and Assistant Principal Wilson that "certain students were bringing drugs and weapons on campus," and that he had been sick after taking some pills that "he got from a classmate." On the morning of October 8, the same boy handed Wilson a white pill that he said Marissa Glines had given him. He told Wilson that students were planning to take the pills at lunch.

Wilson learned from Peggy Schwallier, the school nurse, that the pill was ibuprofen 400 mg, available only by prescription. Wilson then called Marissa out of class. Outside the classroom, Marissa's teacher handed Wilson the day planner, found within Marissa's reach, containing various contraband items. Wilson escorted Marissa back to his office.

In the presence of Helen Romero, Wilson requested Marissa to turn out her pockets and open her wallet.

Marissa produced a blue pill, several white ones, and a razor blade. Wilson asked where the blue pill came from, and Marissa answered, "I guess it slipped in when *she* gave me the IBU 400s." When Wilson asked whom she meant, Marissa replied, "Savana Redding." Wilson then enquired about the day planner and its contents; Marissa denied knowing anything about them. Wilson did not ask Marissa any follow-up questions to determine whether there was any likelihood that Savana presently had pills, neither asking when Marissa received the pills from Savana nor where Savana might be hiding them.

Schwallier did not immediately recognize the blue pill, but information provided through a poison control hotline indicated that the pill was a 200-mg dose of an anti-inflammatory drug, generically called naproxen, available over the counter. At Wilson's direction, Marissa was then subjected to a search of her bra and underpants by Romero and Schwallier, as Savana was later on. The search revealed no additional pills.

It was at this juncture that Wilson called Savana into his office and showed her the day planner. Their conversation established that Savana and Marissa were on friendly terms: while she denied knowledge of the contraband, Savana admitted that the day planner was hers and that she had lent it to Marissa. Wilson had other reports of their friendship from staff members, who had identified Savana and Marissa as part of an unusually rowdy group at the school's opening dance in August, during which alcohol and cigarettes were found in the girls' bathroom.

OPINION

Wilson had reason to connect the girls with this contraband, for Wilson knew that Jordan Romero had told the principal that before the dance, he had been at a party at Savana's house where alcohol was served. Marissa's statement that the pills came from Savana was thus sufficiently plausible to warrant suspicion that Savana was involved in pill distribution. This suspicion of Wilson's was enough to justify a search of Savana's backpack and outer clothing. If a student is reasonably suspected of giving out contraband pills, she is reasonably suspected of carrying them on her person and in the carryall that has become an item of student uniform in most places today. If Wilson's reasonable suspicion of pill distribution were not understood to support searches of outer clothes and backpack, it would not justify any search worth making. And the look into Savana's bag, in her presence and in the relative privacy of Wilson's office, was not excessively intrusive, any more than Romero's subsequent search of her outer clothing.

Here it is that the parties part company, with Savana's claim that extending the search at Wilson's behest to the point of making her pull out her underwear was constitutionally unreasonable. The exact label for this final step in the intrusion is not important, though strip search is a fair way to speak of it. Romero and Schwallier directed Savana

to remove her clothes down to her underwear, and then "pull out" her bra and the elastic band on her underpants. Although Romero and Schwallier stated that they did not see anything when Savana followed their instructions, we would not define strip search and its Fourth Amendment consequences in a way that would guarantee litigation about who was looking and how much was seen. The very fact of Savana's pulling her underwear away from her body in the presence of the two officials who were able to see her necessarily exposed breasts and pelvic area to some degree, and both subjective and reasonable societal expectations of personal privacy support the treatment of such a search as categorically distinct, requiring distinct elements of justification on the part of school authorities for going beyond a search of outer clothing and belongings.

Savana's subjective expectation of privacy against such a search is inherent in her account of it as embarrassing, frightening, and humiliating. The reasonableness of her expectation (required by the Fourth Amendment standard) is indicated by the consistent experiences of other young people similarly searched, whose adolescent vulnerability intensifies the patent intrusiveness of the exposure. The common reaction of these adolescents simply registers the obviously different meaning of a search exposing the body from the experience of nakedness or near undress in other school circumstances. Changing for gym is getting ready for play; exposing for a search is responding to an accusation reserved for suspected wrongdoers and fairly understood as so degrading that a number of communities have decided that strip searches in schools are never reasonable and have banned them no matter what the facts may be.

The indignity of the search does not, of course, outlaw it, but it does implicate the rule of reasonableness as stated in *T.L.O.*, that "the search as actually conducted [be] reasonably related in scope to the circumstances which justified the interference in the first place." The scope will be permissible, that is, when it is "not excessively intrusive in light of the age and sex of the student and the nature of the infraction."

Here, the content of the suspicion failed to match the degree of intrusion. Wilson knew beforehand that the pills were prescription-strength ibuprofen and over-the-counter naproxen, common pain relievers equivalent to two Advil, or one Aleve. He must have been aware of the nature and limited threat of the specific drugs he was searching for, and while just about anything can be taken in quantities that will do real harm, Wilson had no reason to suspect that large amounts of the drugs were being passed around, or that individual students were receiving great numbers of pills.

Nor could Wilson have suspected that Savana was hiding common painkillers in her underwear. Petitioners suggest, as a truth universally acknowledged, that "students hide contraband in or under their clothing," and cite a

(continued)

smattering of cases of students with contraband in their underwear. But when the categorically extreme intrusiveness of a search down to the body of an adolescent requires some justification in suspected facts, general background possibilities fall short; a reasonable search that extensive calls for suspicion that it will pay off. But nondangerous school contraband does not raise the specter of stashes in intimate places, and there is no evidence in the record of any general practice among Safford Middle School students of hiding that sort of thing in underwear; neither Jordan nor Marissa suggested to Wilson that Savana was doing that, and the preceding search of Marissa that Wilson ordered yielded nothing. Wilson never even determined when Marissa had received the pills from Savana; if it had been a few days before, that would weigh heavily against any reasonable conclusion that Savana presently had the pills on her person, much less in her underwear.

In sum, what was missing from the suspected facts that pointed to Savana was any indication of danger to the students from the power of the drugs or their quantity, and any reason to suppose that Savana was carrying pills in her underwear. We think that the combination of these deficiencies was fatal to finding the search reasonable.

In so holding, we mean to cast no ill reflection on the assistant principal, for the record raises no doubt that his motive throughout was to eliminate drugs from his school and protect students from what Jordan Romero had gone through. Parents are known to overreact to protect their children from danger, and a school official with responsibility for safety may tend to do the same. The difference is that the Fourth Amendment places limits on the official, even with the high degree of deference that courts must pay to the educator's professional judgment.

We do mean, though, to make it clear that the *T.L.O.* concern to limit a school search to reasonable scope requires the support of reasonable suspicion of danger or of resort to underwear for hiding evidence of wrongdoing before a search can reasonably make the quantum leap from outer clothes and backpacks to exposure of intimate parts. The meaning of such a search, and the degradation its subject may reasonably feel, place a search that intrusive in a category of its own demanding its own specific suspicions.

A school official searching a student is "entitled to qualified immunity where clearly established law does not show that the search violated the Fourth Amendment." To be established clearly, however, there is no need that "the very action in question [have] previously been held unlawful." *T.L.O.* directed school officials to limit the intrusiveness of a search, "in light of the age and sex of the student and the nature of the infraction," and as we have just said at some length, the intrusiveness of the strip search here cannot be seen as justifiably related to the circumstances. But we realize that the lower courts have reached divergent conclusions regarding how the *T.L.O.* standard applies to such searches. We think these differences of opinion from

our own are substantial enough to require immunity for the school officials in this case.

The strip search of Savana Redding was unreasonable and a violation of the Fourth Amendment, but petitioners Wilson, Romero, and Schwallier are nevertheless protected from liability through qualified immunity. Our conclusions here do not resolve, however, the question of the liability of petitioner Safford Unified School District No. 1. [See Chapter 11 on civil liability of government units.] The judgment of the Ninth Circuit is therefore affirmed in part and reversed in part, and this case is remanded for consideration of the *Monell* claim.

It is so ordered.

CONCURRING AND DISSENTING

Stevens, J., joined by Ginsburg, J.

This case applies *T.L.O.* to declare unconstitutional a strip search of a 13-year-old honors student that was based on a groundless suspicion that she might be hiding medicine in her underwear. This is, in essence, a case in which clearly established law meets clearly outrageous conduct. I have long believed that it does not require a constitutional scholar to conclude that a nude search of a 13-year-old child is an invasion of constitutional rights of some magnitude. The strip search of Savana Redding in this case was both more intrusive and less justified than the search of the student's purse in *T.L.O.*

Therefore, while I join the Court's opinion, [holding that the search was unreasonable], I disagree with its decision to extend qualified immunity to the school official who authorized this unconstitutional search.

DISSENT

Thomas, J.

For nearly 25 years this Court has understood that maintaining order in the classroom has never been easy, but in more recent years, school disorder has often taken particularly ugly forms: drug use and violent crime in the schools have become major social problems. In schools, events calling for discipline are frequent occurrences and sometimes require immediate, effective action. For this reason, school officials retain broad authority to protect students and preserve order and a proper educational environment under the Fourth Amendment. This authority requires that school officials be able to engage in the close supervision of schoolchildren, as well as enforce rules against conduct that would be perfectly permissible if undertaken by an adult.

School officials have a specialized understanding of the school environment, the habits of the students, and the concerns of the community, which enables them to formulate certain common-sense conclusions about human behavior. And like police officers, school officials are entitled to make an assessment of the situation in light of their specialized training and familiarity with the customs of the school.

Here, petitioners had reasonable grounds to suspect that Redding was in possession of prescription and nonprescription drugs in violation of the school's prohibition of the "non-medical use, possession, or sale of a drug" on school property or at school events. School officials were aware that a few years earlier, a student had become seriously ill and spent several days in intensive care after ingesting prescription medication obtained from a classmate. Fourth Amendment searches do not occur in a vacuum; rather, context must inform the judicial inquiry. In this instance, the suspicion of drug possession arose at a middle school that had a history of problems with students using and distributing prohibited and illegal substances on campus.

The school's substance-abuse problems had not abated by the 2003–2004 school year, which is when the challenged search of Redding took place. School officials had found alcohol and cigarettes in the girls' bathroom during the first school dance of the year and noticed that a group of students including Redding and Marissa Glines smelled of alcohol. Several weeks later, another student, Jordan Romero, reported that Redding had hosted a party before the dance where she served whiskey, vodka, and tequila. Romero had provided this report to school officials as a result of a meeting his mother scheduled with the officials after Romero became violent and sick to his stomach one night and admitted that "he had taken some pills that he had got[ten] from a classmate." At that meeting, Romero admitted that "certain students were bringing drugs and weapons on campus." One week later, Romero handed the assistant principal a white pill that he said he had received from Glines. He reported "that a group of students [were] planning on taking the pills at lunch."

Moreover, school districts have valid reasons for punishing the unauthorized possession of prescription drugs on school property as severely as the possession of street drugs; teenage abuse of over-the-counter and prescription drugs poses an increasingly alarming national crisis. As one study noted, "more young people ages 12–17 abuse prescription drugs than any illicit drug except marijuana—more than cocaine, heroin, and methamphetamine combined. And according to a 2005 survey of teens, nearly one in five (19 percent or 4.5 million) admit abusing prescription drugs in their lifetime.

By declaring the search unreasonable in this case, the majority has surrendered control of the American public school system to public school students by invalidating school policies that treat all drugs equally and by second-guessing swift disciplinary decisions made by school officials. The Court's interference in these matters of great concern to teachers, parents, and students illustrates why the most constitutionally sound approach to the question of applying the Fourth Amendment in local public schools would in fact be the complete restoration of the common-law doctrine of *in loco parentis*.

This principle is based on the societal understanding of superior and inferior with respect to the parent and child relationship. In light of this relationship, the Court has indicated that a parent can authorize a third-party search of a child by consenting to such a search, even if the child denies his consent. A father, as the head of the household with the responsibility and the authority for the discipline, training and control of his children, has a superior interest in the family residence to that of his minor son, so that the father's consent to search would be effective notwithstanding the son's contemporaneous on-the-scene objection. Certainly, a search by the parent himself is no different, regardless of whether or not a child would prefer to be left alone. Even if a minor child may think of a room as his, the overall dominance will be in his parents.

Restoring the common-law doctrine of *in loco parentis* would not, however, leave public schools entirely free to impose any rule they choose. If parents do not like the rules imposed by those schools, they can seek redress in school boards or legislatures; they can send their children to private schools or home school them; or they can simply move. Indeed, parents and local government officials have proved themselves quite capable of challenging overly harsh school rules or the enforcement of sensible rules in insensible ways.

In the end, the task of implementing and amending public school policies is beyond this Court's function. Parents, teachers, school administrators, local politicians, and state officials are all better suited than judges to determine the appropriate limits on searches conducted by school officials. Preservation of order, discipline, and safety in public schools is simply not the domain of the Constitution. And, common sense is not a judicial monopoly or a constitutional imperative.

The nationwide drug epidemic makes the war against drugs a pressing concern in every school. And yet the Court has limited the authority of school officials to conduct searches for the drugs that the officials believe pose a serious safety risk to their students. By doing so, the majority has confirmed that a return to the doctrine of *in loco parentis* is required to keep the judiciary from essentially seizing control of public schools. Only then will teachers again be able to govern their pupils, quicken the slothful, spur the indolent, restrain the impetuous, and control the stubborn by making rules, giving commands, and punishing disobedience without interference from judges. By deciding that it is better equipped to decide what behavior should be permitted in schools, the Court has undercut student safety and undermined the authority of school administrators and local officials. Even more troubling, it has done so in a case in which the underlying response by school administrators was reasonable and justified. I cannot join this regrettable decision. I, therefore, respectfully dissent from the Court's determination that this search violated the Fourth Amendment.

(continued)

Questions

1. List the facts relevant to deciding whether the school officials had reason to suspect Savana Redding had banned drugs in her backpack.

2. Explain the Court's reasons for ruling that the scope of the search was unreasonable.

3. Why did the Court grant the school officials immunity from liability for the illegal search?

4. Summarize Justice Thomas's reasons for dissenting from the majority opinion.

5. Which opinion do you agree with more? The majority of 5? Or the dissent of 4? Defend your position.

COLLEGE DORMITORY ROOM CHECKS

LO 7

The U.S. Supreme Court hasn't answered the question of how much protection the Fourth Amendment guarantees to college students in their dormitory rooms, and surprisingly few lower federal and state courts have done so either. As of 2006, there were only 29 reported appellate court cases involving college and university dormitory room searches (*People v. Superior Court of Santa Clara County* 2006, 844).

Before we go further into these few cases, it's important to recall that the Fourth Amendment's ban covers only government officers' or their agents' actions (Chapter 3). Why is this important? Because public college officials are state agents and, therefore, restricted by the Fourth Amendment; private school officials aren't. So the Fourth Amendment protections against unreasonable searches and seizures are wholly inapplicable to a search or seizure, even an unreasonable one, effected by a private individual not acting as an agent of the Government or with the participation or knowledge of any governmental official (*Duarte v. Commonwealth* 1991, 42, quoting *U.S. v. Jacobsen* 1984, 113).

Public college dormitory room search cases fall into two subdivisions—(1) searches conducted by college officials and (2) those conducted by local government law enforcement officers. Although the Fourth Amendment binds public college officials, the cases suggest that they have more leeway to conduct nonconsensual searches than local law enforcement (Jones 2007, 603). According to an Alabama U.S. District Court, public colleges have an "obligation to promulgate and to enforce reasonable regulations designed to protect campus order and discipline and to promote an environment consistent with the educational process" (*Moore v. Student Affairs Committee of Troy State University* [1968, 729–30]).

All the cases acknowledge the college's or university's claim to "preserve a healthy, structured, and safe learning environment." But courts vary as to the value they place on students' right against unreasonable searches. As a result, individual dormitory room searches boil down to "an undefined balancing test weighing the student's right to privacy against the college's or university's right to maintain a desired campus environment" (Jones 2007, 606).

The cases have variously adopted and blended three justifications to analyze and support their balancing responsibilities:

1. Emergency or exigent circumstances that require immediate action

2. The "special relationship" between the college or university and students

3. The college's or university's duty to provide the appropriate environment for learning (Table 7.2).

TABLE 7.2 Justifications for reduced privacy in college and university dorm rooms

Justification	Example
Emergency	University administrator permitted police officers to enter and search the room of a student suspected of burglary, because the administrator might "reasonably have concluded that any delay in ascertaining facts regarding the use of the room would indicate condonation of wrongful acts and would reflect discredit on the school, and therefore the circumstances called for immediate action." *People v. Kelly*, 195 Cal. App. 2d 669 (1961)
Special relationship between student and college or university	The dean of men allowed local police officers to search a student's room, where they found a small matchbox containing marijuana. The search was reasonable because "College students who reside in dormitories have a special relationship with the college involved. The relationship grows out of the peculiar and sometimes the seemingly competing interests of college and student. A student naturally has the right to be free of unreasonable search and seizures, and a tax-supported public college may not compel a 'waiver' of that right as a condition precedent to admission. The college, on the other hand, has an 'affirmative obligation' to promulgate and to enforce reasonable regulations designed to protect campus order and discipline and to promote an environment consistent with the educational process." *Moore v. Student Affairs Committee of Troy State University*, 284 F. Supp. 725, D.C. Ala. (1968)
Duty to maintain a "clean, safe, and well-disciplined environment"	Officials discovered marijuana while searching dormitory rooms following multiple reports of vandalism to the director of Housing and Food Services. The search was reasonable because students "require and are entitled to an atmosphere that is conducive to educational pursuits. In a dormitory situation, it is the university that accepts the responsibility of providing this atmosphere. Thus, it is incumbent upon the university to take whatever reasonable measures are necessary to provide a clean, safe, well-disciplined environment." *State v. Hunter*, 831 P.2d 1033 (Utah App. 1992)

Source: State v. Hunter, 831 P.2d 1033 (Utah App. 1992)

The Ohio Court of Appeals reversed and remanded Sherman Ellis's conviction and five-year sentence for trafficking in marijuana, because the evidence was seized during an unreasonable search by the campus police.

CASE

Was the Dormitory Room Search Reasonable?

State v. Ellis

2006 WL 82736 (OhioApp. 2006)

HISTORY

Sherman Ellis (Defendant) was indicted on one count of trafficking in marijuana, R.C. 2925.03(A)(2), and one count of possession of criminal tools, R.C. 2923.24(A), following a seizure by campus police of drugs that were found in Ellis's dormitory room at Central State University. Ellis filed a motion to suppress the evidence that was seized. The trial court overruled Ellis's motion to suppress

(continued)

following a hearing. Ellis then entered a plea of no contest to the trafficking in marijuana charge. In exchange, the State dismissed the criminal tools charge. The trial court found Ellis guilty of the marijuana charge and on his conviction sentenced Ellis to five years of community control sanctions and a two hundred fifty dollar fine. Ellis appealed to this court from his conviction and sentence, challenging the trial court's decision overruling his motion to suppress evidence. The Appeals court reversed and remanded.

—Grady, J.

FACTS

Sherman Ellis (Defendant), on October 7, 2004, was a student attending Central State University. Ellis was residing on campus in a dormitory room located on the campus of Central State University, Wilberforce, Ohio. As a student at Central State University, Ellis was subject to the safety and security policies and procedures set forth by the University. Ellis had agreed to recognize and be subject to the safety and security policies and procedures while a resident on the campus at Central State University. Ellis is not contesting the applicability of the safety and security policies and procedures.

Pursuant to these safety policies and procedures, a Resident Assistant in the dormitory in which Ellis resided was acting in accordance with the Resident's Hall Health and Safety checks portion of the policy and procedure by entering the room of Ellis to conduct an unannounced safety inspection. These inspections were done on a regular basis by Resident Assistants and were not performed for the purpose of obtaining evidence solely for the purpose of criminal prosecution. These searches were conducted consistent with the policies and procedures set forth by the University.

Upon entering the room, and joined shortly thereafter by another Resident Assistant, a beer can was discovered on a desktop. Possession of alcoholic beverages is a violation of the University policies and procedures. During the course of obtaining the beer, the Resident Assistant observed an open drawer in the desk and could smell, as well as see, bags of what he referred to as "weed," which he identified as marijuana.

Central State University police officers were then notified, who upon their later arrival, observed while the Resident Assistants completed their safety search and inspection. As a result of the inspection and search, the Resident Assistants turned over several items obtained from the dormitory to the Central State Police Department. While the police officers were at the dormitory after being notified, they did not participate in the search, which was conducted by the Resident Assistants. The Resident Assistants conducted the administrative search pursuant to the Resident's Hall Health and Safety checks pursuant to the University residence policies and the code of student conduct.

OPINION

A college student's dormitory room is entitled to the same protection against unreasonable search and seizure that is afforded to a private home for purposes of the Fourth Amendment. The state cannot condition attendance at a state college on a waiver of constitutional rights, nor can it require students to waive their right to be free from unreasonable searches and seizures as a condition of occupancy of a college dormitory room.

The Fourth Amendment limits only official government behavior or state action: it does not regulate searches by private persons. The mere fact that evidence found and obtained during a search by a private person is ultimately turned over to the police does not destroy the private nature of the search and render it official government action subject to the exclusionary rule.

If a private person acts as the agent of the police, however, the result is different. Official participation in the planning or implementation of a private person's efforts to secure evidence may taint the operation sufficiently as to require suppression of the evidence. The test of government participation is whether under all the circumstances the private individual must be regarded as an agent or instrument of the state.

The evidence presented in this case demonstrates that the University's Resident Assistants entered Ellis's dormitory room and the rooms of other students to determine whether students were bringing prohibited items such as alcohol or drugs to their rooms, a common occurrence during the school's homecoming celebrations. The search was conducted in accordance with Central State University's policies and procedures governing residence halls, which authorizes the Residence staff to inspect student rooms at any time to determine compliance with the University's safety and hygiene policies governing residence halls. Therefore, as the trial court found, the search the Resident Life staff performed, which yielded the marijuana that campus police seized, was an administrative search by private persons, and therefore not a search subject to the Fourth Amendment's warrant requirement.

Ellis argues that because campus police were in the room while the Resident Assistants conducted their search, and the police officers told the staff members to place the evidence they found on a desk or table in the room, that the Resident Assistants acted as agents of police in performing their search. While the question is a close one, we believe that more is required to show agency. There must be some evidence that police directed private persons where and how to search and what to look for. That's lacking here because the officers merely stood by in Ellis's room while the Resident Assistants searched it.

However, that does not resolve the Fourth Amendment issue that Ellis's motion to suppress presented. The problem arises in this case because, after the resident advisors initially discovered marijuana in Ellis's room and notified campus police, the campus police then came to the scene and entered Ellis's room. Police remained inside Ellis's room and observed while the Resident Assistants continued their search. After the Resident Assistants had completed their search and placed the contraband they discovered in a central location in the room, as the officers had directed, the police then seized and removed that contraband from Ellis's room.

By entering Ellis's dormitory room, campus police infringed upon the reasonable expectation of privacy that Ellis had in that place which, as we previously mentioned, is entitled to the same level of protection against unreasonable search and seizure as a private home. In order to lawfully enter Ellis's room, police needed either a warrant, which they did not have, or an established exception to the warrant requirement. None applies in this case, and the State argued none in opposition to Ellis's motion to suppress.

There was no consent given by Ellis for police to enter his room. He was not even present during the search. The plain view exception does not apply because police did not observe the contraband until after they had unlawfully entered Ellis's room, and any intrusion affording the plain view observation must otherwise be lawful. Neither does the exigent or emergency circumstances exception justify the entry, for instance to prevent the concealment or destruction of evidence. The Resident Assistants were in the room, Defendant was not, and Defendant could have easily been kept out of the room by police and the evidence preserved until police had secured a warrant.

We conclude that by entering Ellis's dormitory room without a warrant or an applicable recognized exception to the warrant requirement, and by further seizing and removing from that room contraband discovered by the Resident Assistants during their private search of that room, campus police violated Ellis's Fourth Amendment rights. Accordingly, the trial court erred when it denied Ellis's motion to suppress evidence.

The judgment of the trial court will be REVERSED and this case REMANDED for further proceedings consistent with this opinion.

Questions

1. List all the actions taken by the resident assistants and the Central State Police Department officers that invaded Ellis's reasonable expectation of privacy.

2. Explain why the court concluded that the resident assistants' actions were reasonable Fourth Amendment searches but the police officers' actions were unreasonable. Do you agree? Defend your answer.

3. Assume you're Ellis's lawyer. Argue that the search by resident assistants was unreasonable. Back up your answer with facts and arguments made by the state in the case.

4. Do you think that Ellis's privacy outweighs the college's special needs? Back up your answer.

5. Does it matter whether the resident assistants, campus police, or city police conducted the search? Defend your answer.

DRUG TESTING

LO 8   Courts, willingly, have relaxed Fourth Amendment warrant and probable cause requirements when it comes to upholding government alcohol and other drug testing that aims at the special need to protect the public health and safety. The Fourth Amendment requires courts to balance the legitimate government need to protect public health and safety against the privacy of individuals subject to the testing. According to U.S. Supreme Court Justice Sandra Day O'Connor, dissenting in *Vernonia School District v. Acton* (1995, 672): "State-compelled, state-monitored collecting of urine, while perhaps not the most intrusive of searches (visual body cavity searches) is still particularly destructive of privacy and offensive to personal dignity."

We'll examine the application of the balancing test in the leading U.S. Supreme Court cases in three settings: (1) testing employees in the workplace; (2) testing pregnant patients in hospitals; and (3) testing students in high schools and colleges.

LO 8   Employee Drug Testing in the Workplace

The Court dealt with the problem of balancing the government's special need and employees' privacy in the companion cases of *Skinner v. Railway Labor Executive*

Association (1989) and *National Treasury Employees Union v. Von Raab* (1989). The Court ruled in both cases that testing the blood, breath, and urine of some public employees, in accordance with administrative regulations, without either warrants or individualized suspicion, is reasonable.

In *Skinner* (7–2), the Court upheld Federal Railroad Administration (FRA) regulations mandating alcohol and other drug testing of employees following their involvement in major accidents and breath and urine tests for employees who violated safety rules. The Court stressed the need to "prevent and deter that hazardous conduct" (633) by "those engaged in safety-sensitive tasks" (620). It also stressed "the limited discretion exercised" by the employers during the testing (633).

In a closer call, *Von Raab* (5–4) approved Treasury regulations that required testing U.S. Customs Service employees whenever they were transferred or promoted to positions directly related to drug interdiction or to positions requiring them to carry firearms. According to the majority, the testing regulations passed the balancing test because although tests invade privacy, the "Government's compelling interest in preventing the promotion of drug users to positions where they might endanger the integrity of our Nation's borders or the life of the citizenry" outweighs the privacy interests of individual employees (672).

Justices Marshall and Brennan, the two dissenters in *Skinner*, reiterated their opposition to all "special-needs" exceptions to the probable cause requirement. They further protested the expansion of the exception to include body searches (breath, urine, and blood tests) without even reasonable suspicion, and challenged the majority's tipping the balance in favor of the government.

Justices Stevens and Scalia, who voted with the majority in *Skinner*, voted, with Justices Brennan and Marshall, to dissent in *Von Raab*. They argued that the result in *Skinner* was supported by "the demonstrated frequency of drug and alcohol use by the targeted class of employees, and the demonstrated connection between such use and grave harm." In *Von Raab*, on the other hand, the government didn't cite a single instance "in which the cause of bribe-taking, or of poor aim, or of unsympathetic law enforcement, or of compromise of classified information was drug use" (683).

According to Justice Scalia:

> I do not believe for a minute that the driving force behind these drug-testing rules was any of the feeble justifications put forward by counsel here and accepted by the Court. The only plausible explanation, in my view, is what the Commissioner himself offered in the concluding sentence of his memorandum to Customs Service employees announcing the program: "Implementation of the drug screening program would set an important example in our country's struggle with this most serious threat to our national health and security." . . . (686)
>
> What better way to show that the Government is serious about its "war on drugs" than to subject its employees on the front line of that war to this invasion of their privacy and affront to their dignity? To be sure, there is only a slight chance that it will prevent some serious public harm resulting from Service employee drug use, but it will show to the world that the Service is "clean," and—most important of all—will demonstrate the determination of the Government to eliminate this scourge of our society! I think it obvious that this justification is unacceptable; that the impairment of individual liberties cannot be the means of making a point; that symbolism, even symbolism for so

worthy a cause as the abolition of unlawful drugs, cannot validate an otherwise unreasonable search. (686–87)

Those who lose because of the lack of understanding that begot the present exercise in symbolism are not just the Customs Service employees, whose dignity is thus offended, but all of us—who suffer a coarsening of our national manners that ultimately give the Fourth Amendment its content, and who become subject to the administration of federal officials whose respect for our privacy can hardly be greater than the small respect they have been taught to have for their own. (687)

Prenatal Drug Testing in Hospitals

"Cocaine: A Vicious Assault on a Child"
"Crack's Toll among Babies: A Joyless View"
"Studies: Future Bleak for Crack Babies"

These are sample headlines from the 1980s and 1990s when "crack cocaine" use drew national attention and generated widely publicized fears that pregnant "crack" users "would produce a generation of severely damaged children." Researchers systematically following "crack babies" are finding that—so far anyway—the long-term effects of cocaine exposure on children's brain development and behavior "appear relatively small" (Okie 2009).

That doesn't mean there are *no* effects. "Cocaine is undoubtedly bad for the fetus." But not as bad as alcohol—and similar to tobacco. According to Dr. Deborah Frank, a pediatrician at Boston University, "The argument is not that it's O.K. to use cocaine in pregnancy, any more than it's O.K. to smoke cigarettes. Neither drug is good for anybody" (Okie 2009).

In April 1989, staff members at the Charleston, South Carolina, public hospital operated by the Medical University of South Carolina (MUSC) responded to the fear of crack babies by ordering drug screens on urine samples of maternity patients suspected of using cocaine. Patients who tested positive were referred to the county substance abuse commission for counseling and treatment, but cocaine use remained unchanged. So MUSC offered to cooperate with the city in prosecuting mothers whose children tested positive for drugs at birth. A task force made up of MUSC representatives, police, and local officials developed a policy that:

1. Established procedures for identifying and testing pregnant patients suspected of drug use
2. Required that a chain of custody be followed when obtaining and testing patients' urine samples
3. Provided education and treatment referral for patients testing positive
4. Contained police procedures and criteria for arresting patients who tested positive
5. Prescribed prosecutions for drug offenses and/or child neglect, depending on the stage of the defendant's pregnancy (*Ferguson v. City of Charleston* 2001, 67)

Ten state hospital patients arrested under the policy sued the hospital, the city of Charleston, the state police, and medical personnel for damages suffered by violating their Fourth Amendment rights. The U.S. Supreme Court agreed (6–3) with the patients, over a strong dissent. The case, *Ferguson v. City of Charleston* (2001), is our next case excerpt.

In *Ferguson and others v. City of Charleston and others* (2001), the U.S. Supreme Court held that forced drug testing and arrests of pregnant patients who tested positive for drug use violated their Fourth Amendment rights.

CASE

Were the Urine Tests Unreasonable Searches?

Ferguson and others v. City of Charleston and others
532 U.S. 67 (2001)

HISTORY

State hospital obstetrics patients who were arrested after testing positive for cocaine, in urine tests conducted by the Charleston, South Carolina public hospital, operated by the Medical University of South Carolina (MUSC), pursuant to a policy developed in conjunction with police, sued the hospital, state solicitor, city and state police, and individual medical personnel, alleging that they had violated the Fourth Amendment. The United States District Court for the District of South Carolina entered judgment for defendants, and the patients appealed. The United States Court of Appeals for the Fourth Circuit affirmed. Certiorari was granted. The Supreme Court, Justice Stevens, held that: (1) urine tests were "searches" within the meaning of the Fourth Amendment, and (2) the reporting of positive test results to police were unreasonable searches without patients' consent, in view of the policy's law enforcement purpose. Reversed and remanded.

—STEVENS, J., joined by O'CONNOR, SOUTER, GINSBURG, and BREYER, JJ.

In this case, the question is whether the interest in using the threat of criminal sanctions to deter pregnant women from using cocaine can justify a departure from the general rule that an official nonconsensual search is unconstitutional if not authorized by a valid warrant.

FACTS

In the fall of 1988, staff members at the public hospital operated in the city of Charleston by the Medical University of South Carolina (MUSC) became concerned about an apparent increase in the use of cocaine by patients who were receiving prenatal treatment. (As several witnesses testified at trial, the problem of "crack babies" was widely perceived in the late 1980s as a national epidemic, prompting considerable concern both in the medical community and among the general populace.) In response to this perceived increase, as of April 1989, MUSC began to order drug screens to be performed on urine samples from maternity patients who were suspected of using cocaine. If a patient tested positive, she was then referred by MUSC staff to the county substance abuse commission for counseling and treatment.

However, despite the referrals, the incidence of cocaine use among the patients at MUSC did not appear to change. Some four months later, Nurse Shirley Brown, the case manager for the MUSC obstetrics department, heard a news broadcast reporting that the police in Greenville, South Carolina, were arresting pregnant users of cocaine on the theory that such use harmed the fetus and was therefore child abuse. Nurse Brown discussed the story with MUSC's general counsel, Joseph C. Good, Jr., who then contacted Charleston Solicitor Charles Condon in order to offer MUSC's cooperation in prosecuting mothers whose children tested positive for drugs at birth.

Petitioners are 10 women who received obstetrical care at MUSC and who were arrested after testing positive for cocaine. Four of them were arrested during the initial implementation of the policy; they were not offered the opportunity to receive drug treatment as an alternative to arrest. The others were arrested after the policy was modified in 1990; they either failed to comply with the terms of the drug treatment program or tested positive for a second time. Respondents include the city of Charleston, law enforcement officials who helped develop and enforce the policy, and representatives of MUSC.

Petitioners claimed that warrantless and nonconsensual drug tests conducted for criminal investigatory purposes were unconstitutional searches. The U.S. District Court jury found for the City of Charleston. The Court of Appeals affirmed, holding that the searches were reasonable as a matter of law under our line of cases recognizing that "special needs" may, in certain exceptional circumstances, justify a search policy designed to serve non-law-enforcement ends. On the understanding "that MUSC personnel conducted the urine drug screens for medical purposes wholly independent of an intent to aid law enforcement efforts," the majority applied the balancing test, and concluded that the interest in curtailing the pregnancy complications and medical costs associated with maternal cocaine use outweighed what the majority termed a minimal intrusion on the privacy of the patients. We conclude that the judgment should be reversed and the case remanded for a decision on the consent issue.

OPINION

Because the hospital seeks to justify its authority to conduct drug tests and to turn the results over to law enforcement agents without the knowledge or consent of the patients, this case differs from the four previous cases in which we have considered whether comparable drug tests "fit within the closely guarded category of constitutionally permissible suspicionless searches." In three of those cases, we sustained drug tests for railway employees involved in train accidents, *Skinner v. Railway Labor Executives' Assn.*, 489 U.S. 602, (1989), for United States Customs Service employees seeking promotion to certain sensitive positions, *Treasury Employees v. Von Raab*, 489 U.S. 656, (1989), and for high school students participating in interscholastic sports, *Vernonia School Dist. 47J v. Acton*, 515 U.S. 646, (1995). In the fourth case, we struck down such testing for candidates for designated state offices as unreasonable, *Chandler v. Miller*, 520 U.S. 305, (1997).

In each of those cases, we employed a balancing test that weighed the intrusion on the individual's interest in privacy against the "special needs" that supported the program. As an initial matter, we note that the invasion of privacy in this case is far more substantial than in those cases. In the previous four cases, there was no misunderstanding about the purpose of the test or the potential use of the test results, and there were protections against the dissemination of the results to third parties. The use of an adverse test result to disqualify one from eligibility for a particular benefit, such as a promotion or an opportunity to participate in an extracurricular activity, involves a less serious intrusion on privacy than the unauthorized dissemination of such results to third parties.

The reasonable expectation of privacy enjoyed by the typical patient undergoing diagnostic tests in a hospital is that the results of those tests will not be shared with nonmedical personnel without her consent. In none of our prior cases was there any intrusion upon that kind of expectation.

The critical difference between those four drug-testing cases and this one, however, lies in the nature of the "special need" asserted as justification for the warrantless searches. In each of those earlier cases, the "special need" that was advanced as a justification for the absence of a warrant or individualized suspicion was one divorced from the State's general interest in law enforcement. In this case, however, the central and indispensable feature of the policy from its inception was the use of law enforcement

to coerce the patients into substance abuse treatment. This fact distinguishes this case from circumstances in which physicians or psychologists, in the course of ordinary medical procedures aimed at helping the patient herself, come across information that under rules of law or ethics is subject to reporting requirements, which no one has challenged here.

Respondents argue in essence that their ultimate purpose—namely, protecting the health of both mother and child—is a beneficent one. In *Chandler v. Miller* (1997), however, we did not simply accept the State's invocation of a "special need." Instead, we carried out a "close review" of the scheme at issue before concluding that the need in question was not "special," as that term has been defined in our cases. In this case, a review of the M-7 policy plainly reveals that the purpose actually served by the MUSC searches "is ultimately indistinguishable from the general interest in crime control."

In looking to the programmatic purpose, we consider all the available evidence in order to determine the relevant primary purpose. In this case, it is clear from the record that an initial and continuing focus of the policy was on the arrest and prosecution of drug-abusing mothers. Tellingly, the document codifying the policy incorporates the police's operational guidelines. It devotes its attention to the chain of custody, the range of possible criminal charges, and the logistics of police notification and arrests. Nowhere, however, does the document discuss different courses of medical treatment for either mother or infant, aside from treatment for the mother's addiction.

Moreover, throughout the development and application of the policy, the Charleston prosecutors and police were extensively involved in the day-to-day administration of the policy. Police and prosecutors decided who would receive the reports of positive drug screens and what information would be included with those reports. Law enforcement officials also helped determine the procedures to be followed when performing the screens. In the course of the policy's administration, they had access to Nurse Brown's medical files on the women who tested positive, routinely attended the substance abuse team's meetings, and regularly received copies of team documents discussing the women's progress. Police took pains to coordinate the timing and circumstances of the arrests with MUSC staff, and, in particular, Nurse Brown.

While the ultimate goal of the program may well have been to get the women in question into substance abuse treatment and off of drugs, the immediate objective of the searches was to generate evidence for law enforcement purposes in order to reach that goal. The threat of law enforcement may ultimately have been intended as a means to an end, but the direct and primary purpose of MUSC's policy was to ensure the use of those means. In our opinion, this distinction is critical. Because law

(continued)

enforcement involvement always serves some broader social purpose or objective, under respondents' view, virtually any nonconsensual suspicionless search could be immunized under the special-needs doctrine by defining the search solely in terms of its ultimate, rather than immediate, purpose. Such an approach is inconsistent with the Fourth Amendment.

Given the primary purpose of the Charleston program, which was to use the threat of arrest and prosecution in order to force women into treatment, and given the extensive involvement of law enforcement officials at every stage of the policy, this case simply does not fit within the closely guarded category of "special needs."

Respondents have repeatedly insisted that their motive was benign rather than punitive. Such a motive, however, cannot justify a departure from Fourth Amendment protections, given the pervasive involvement of law enforcement with the development and application of the MUSC policy. The stark and unique fact that characterizes this case is that Policy M-7 was designed to obtain evidence of criminal conduct by the tested patients that would be turned over to the police and that could be admissible in subsequent criminal prosecutions.

While respondents are correct that drug abuse both was and is a serious problem, the gravity of the threat alone cannot be dispositive of questions concerning what means law enforcement officers may employ to pursue a given purpose. The Fourth Amendment's general prohibition against nonconsensual, warrantless, and suspicionless searches necessarily applies to such a policy.

Accordingly, the judgment of the Court of Appeals is REVERSED, and the case is REMANDED for further proceedings consistent with this opinion.

It is so ordered.

DISSENT

SCALIA, J., joined by REHNQUIST, C.J., and THOMAS, J.

There is always an unappealing aspect to the use of doctors and nurses, ministers of mercy, to obtain incriminating evidence against the supposed objects of their ministration—although here, it is correctly pointed out, the doctors and nurses were ministering not just to the mothers but also to the children whom their cooperation with the police was meant to protect. But whatever may be the correct social judgment concerning the desirability of what occurred here, that is not the issue in the present case.

The Constitution does not resolve all difficult social questions, but leaves the vast majority of them to resolution by debate and the democratic process—which would produce a decision by the citizens of Charleston, through their elected representatives, to forbid or permit the police action at issue here. The question before us is a narrower one: whether, whatever the desirability of this police conduct, it violates the Fourth Amendment's prohibition of unreasonable searches and seizures. In my view, it plainly does not.

The first step in Fourth Amendment analysis is to identify the search or seizure at issue. There is only one act that could conceivably be regarded as a search of petitioners in the present case: the taking of the urine sample. I suppose the testing of that urine for traces of unlawful drugs could be considered a search of sorts, but the Fourth Amendment protects only against searches of citizens' "persons, houses, papers, and effects"; and it is entirely unrealistic to regard urine as one of the "effects" (i.e., part of the property) of the person who has passed and abandoned it.

It is rudimentary Fourth Amendment law that a search which has been consented to is not unreasonable. There is no contention in the present case that the urine samples were extracted forcibly. The only conceivable bases for saying that they were obtained without consent are the contentions (1) that the consent was coerced by the patients' need for medical treatment, (2) that the consent was uninformed because the patients were not told that the tests would include testing for drugs, and (3) that the consent was uninformed because the patients were not told that the results of the tests would be provided to the police. Until today, we have never held—or even suggested—that material which a person voluntarily entrusts to someone else cannot be given by that person to the police, and used for whatever evidence it may contain.

There remains to be considered the first possible basis for invalidating this search, which is that the patients were coerced to produce their urine samples by their necessitous circumstances, to wit, their need for medical treatment of their pregnancy. If that was coercion, it was not coercion applied by the government—and if such nongovernmental coercion sufficed, the police would never be permitted to use the ballistic evidence obtained from treatment of a patient with a bullet wound. And the Fourth Amendment would invalidate those many state laws that require physicians to report gunshot wounds, evidence of spousal abuse, and (like the South Carolina law relevant here, see S.C.Code Ann. § 20–7–510 [2000]) evidence of child abuse.

As I indicated at the outset, it is not the function of this Court—at least not in Fourth Amendment cases—to weigh petitioners' privacy interest against the State's interest in meeting the crisis of "crack babies" that developed in the late 1980s. I cannot refrain from observing, however, that the outcome of a wise weighing of those interests is by no means clear. The initial goal of the doctors and nurses who conducted cocaine testing in this case was to refer pregnant drug addicts to treatment centers, and to prepare for necessary treatment of their possibly affected children.

When the doctors and nurses agreed to the program providing test results to the police, they did so because (in addition to the fact that child abuse was required by law to be reported) they wanted to use the sanction of arrest as a strong incentive for their addicted patients to undertake drug-addiction treatment. And the police themselves used it for that benign purpose, as is shown by the fact that only 30 of 253 women testing positive for cocaine were ever arrested, and only 2 of those prosecuted. It would not be unreasonable to conclude that today's judgment, authorizing the assessment of damages against the county solicitor and individual doctors and nurses who participated in the program, proves once again that no good deed goes unpunished.

But as far as the Fourth Amendment is concerned: There was no unconsented search in this case. And if there was, it would have been validated by the special-needs doctrine. For these reasons, I respectfully dissent.

Questions

1. Identify the special needs that the hospital was addressing in its policy of drug-testing suspected pregnant "crack" users.

2. List the facts relevant to deciding whether this case is about law enforcement, some other need beyond law enforcement, or a combination.

3. Summarize the majority's arguments supporting its holding that the policy was a law enforcement policy.

4. Summarize the dissent's arguments that this was enough of a non–law enforcement policy to make the testing a reasonable search and seizure.

5. Which do you agree with more—the majority or the dissent? Back up your answer with specifics from the case excerpt.

YOU DECIDE
Should Hospitals Test Maternity Patients Suspected of Using Cocaine?

One sister is 14; the other is 9. They are a vibrant pair: The older girl is high-spirited but responsible, a solid student and a devoted helper at home; her sister loves to read and watch cooking shows, and she recently scored well above average on citywide standardized tests. There would be nothing remarkable about these two happy, normal girls if it were not for their mother's history. Yvette H., now 38 admits that she used cocaine (along with heroin and alcohol) while she was pregnant with each girl. "A drug addict," she now says ruefully, "isn't really concerned about the baby she's carrying."

When the use of crack cocaine became a nationwide epidemic in the 1980s and '90s, there were widespread fears that prenatal exposure to the drug would produce a generation of severely damaged children. Newspapers carried headlines like "Cocaine: A Vicious Assault on a Child," "Crack's Toll among Babies: A Joyless View," and "Studies: Future Bleak for Crack Babies."

But now researchers are systematically following children who were exposed to cocaine before birth, and their findings suggest that the encouraging stories of Ms. H.'s daughters are anything but unusual. So far, these scientists say, the long-term effects of such exposure on children's brain development and behavior appear relatively small.

ant women suspected of using cocaine?

Under what conditions?

LO 6, 8 High School Student Drug Testing

For centuries, minors have lacked some fundamental rights enjoyed by adults, including the right to be let alone by the government. This is especially true while they're in school. According to the legal doctrine *in loco parentis*, school administrators are substitute parents while students are in school. Inspections of students, their personal belongings, their lockers, and their cars during school hours and activities are searches. To determine whether they're reasonable searches, courts weigh the special need for schools to maintain an environment where learning can thrive against students' privacy.

The U.S. Supreme Court had to balance the special need of high schools against high school students' privacy in *New Jersey v. T. L. O.* (1985). A teacher at a New Jersey high school caught T. L. O., a 14-year-old freshman, and a friend smoking cigarettes in the girls' bathroom. The teacher took them to the principal's office. T. L. O. denied she was smoking; in fact, she denied that she smoked at all.

The assistant vice principal demanded to see her purse, opened it, and found a pack of cigarettes; he also noticed a pack of cigarette rolling papers commonly used to smoke marijuana. So he searched the purse more thoroughly and found marijuana, a pipe, plastic bags, a fairly substantial amount of money, and two letters that implicated T. L. O. in marijuana dealing.

The state brought delinquency charges, and the case eventually reached the U.S. Supreme Court, where the Court had to decide whether the Fourth Amendment applied to searches by school officials. Two questions confronted the Court: Does the Fourth Amendment apply to school searches? And was this search reasonable? According to the Court, the answer to both questions is yes. The Court held that the Fourth Amendment's ban on unreasonable searches and seizures applies to searches conducted by public school officials.

Furthermore, school officials can't escape the commands of the Fourth Amendment because of their authority over schoolchildren. When they search students, they aren't *in loco parentis* (acting as parents); so students have a reasonable expectation of privacy. But that expectation is limited. Striking a balance between students' reasonable expectations of privacy and the school's legitimate need to maintain a healthy learning environment calls for easing the restrictions on searches of students. Therefore, school officials don't have to get warrants, and they don't need probable cause before they search students. Reasonable suspicion is enough. Does the right to search high school students extend to testing some for drugs?

High school student athlete drug testing to provide a healthy and safe learning environment is the special need that most courts have dealt with, and it was the subject of the first case to reach the U.S. Supreme Court. In *Vernonia School District v. Acton* (1995), the Court found that random (without individualized suspicion) drug testing of all students voluntarily participating in the school district's athletic programs was reasonable.

According to school policy, all students who wished to participate in school sports had to sign a form consenting to urinalysis for drugs. (Parental consent was also required.) Athletes were tested at the beginning of the season for their sport. Then, once a week, 10 percent of the teams were selected blindly for follow-up testing. A same-sex adult accompanied an athlete to a restroom for the test. Each fully clothed boy produced a sample at a urinal with his back to the monitor, standing 12 to 15 feet behind the boy. The monitor was allowed to (but didn't always) watch while the sample was produced and to listen for "normal sounds of urination" (650). Girls produced their samples in an enclosed bathroom stall, where monitors could hear, but not observe, them. If athletes tested positive, they had to take a second test. If they tested positive twice, they had the option of participating in a six-week assistance program, including weekly testing, or being suspended from athletics for a specific time period.

To determine reasonableness, the Court balanced the competing interests. On the privacy side, Justice Scalia pointed out that high school students have a lesser expectation of privacy than adults. Student athletes can expect even less privacy than other students, because they have to suit up and shower in public locker rooms. Furthermore, the way the testing was done minimized the privacy reduction—boys were observed only from behind; girls were behind closed stall doors.

On the special-need side, the Court called the government's interest in deterring drug use by students "important—indeed, perhaps compelling," and concluded that the special need trumped the student athletes' privacy. Therefore, the Court held that the warrantless searches without individualized suspicion were reasonable. According to the Court, much of the student body, especially school athletes, "was in a state of rebellion; disciplinary actions had reached epidemic proportions; and the rebellion was being fueled by alcohol and drug abuse as well as by the student's misperceptions about the drug culture" (661–63).

Vernonia wasn't the Court's last word on school drug testing. In *Board of Education of Independent School District No. 92 of Pottawatomie County v. Earls* (2002), the Court decided the reasonableness of a drug-testing policy that applied to all students who participated in *any* extracurricular activity, including Academic Team, Future Farmers of America, Future Homemakers of America, band, choir, pom-pom, cheerleading, and athletics. All students who wanted to participate had to agree to urinalysis similar to that in *Earls*. Random tests followed, and positive results could lead to suspension from the activity, but the school didn't give the results to law enforcement. Unlike the athletes in *Earls*, these students weren't likely to engage in "communal undress" or other forms of reduced privacy. Also unlike the athletes in *Earls*, participants in these activities weren't engaging in increased drug use.

The U.S. Supreme Court majority held that the urinalysis policy was reasonable under the Fourth Amendment, discounting the differences with *Earls*. Justice Thomas wrote, for the 5-member majority, that the decision in *Earls* didn't depend on the reduced privacy of athletes; that evidence of increased drug use isn't necessary to justify drug testing; and that

> the safety interest furthered by drug testing is undoubtedly substantial for all children, athletes and nonathletes alike. Indeed, it would make little sense to require a school district to wait for a substantial portion of its students to begin using drugs before it was allowed to institute a drug testing program designed to deter drug use. (836–37)

CRIMINAL PROCEDURE IN ACTION

LO 8 Requiring political candidates to pass a drug test is not a permissible suspicionless "special-needs" search.

A Georgia statute requires candidates for designated state offices to certify that they have taken a urinalysis drug test within 30 days prior to qualifying for nomination or election and that the test result was negative. Petitioners, Libertarian Party nominees for state offices subject to the statute's requirements, filed this action in the District Court about one month before the deadline for submission of the certificates. Naming as defendants the Governor and two officials involved in the statute's administration, petitioners asserted that the drug tests violated their rights under the First, Fourth, and Fourteenth Amendments to the United States Constitution. The District Court denied petitioners' motion for a preliminary injunction and later entered final judgment for respondents. Relying on the U.S. Supreme Court's precedents sustaining drug-testing programs for student athletes, *Vernonia School Dist. 47J v. Acton,* 515 U.S. 646,

(continued)

Customs Service employees, *National Treasury Employees Union v. Von Raab*, 489 U.S. 656, and railway employees, *Skinner v. Railway Labor Executives' Assn.*, 489 U.S. 602, the Eleventh Circuit affirmed. The court accepted as settled law that the tests were searches, but reasoned that, as was true of the drug-testing programs at issue in *Skinner* and *Von Raab*, the statute served "special needs," interests other than the ordinary needs of law enforcement. Balancing the individual's privacy expectations against the State's interest in the drug-testing program, the court held the statute, as applied to petitioners, not inconsistent with the Fourth and Fourteenth Amendments.

The U.S. Supreme Court reversed, holding that Georgia's requirement that candidates for state office pass a drug test does not fit within the category of constitutionally permissible suspicionless searches. According to the Court syllabus,

> It is uncontested that Georgia's drug-testing requirement, imposed by law and enforced by state officials, effects a search within the meaning of the Fourth and Fourteenth Amendments. The pivotal question here is whether the searches are reasonable. To be reasonable under the Fourth Amendment, a search ordinarily must be based on individualized suspicion of wrongdoing. But particularized exceptions to the main rule are sometimes warranted based on "special needs, beyond the normal need for law enforcement." When such "special needs" are alleged, courts must undertake a context-specific inquiry, examining closely the competing private and public interests advanced by the parties.
>
> Georgia has failed to show a special need that is substantial—important enough to override the individual's acknowledged privacy interest, sufficiently vital to suppress the Fourth Amendment's normal requirement of individualized suspicion. Respondents contend that unlawful drug use is incompatible with holding high state office because such drug use draws into question an official's judgment and integrity; jeopardizes the discharge of public functions, including antidrug law enforcement efforts; and undermines public confidence and trust in elected officials. Notably lacking in respondents' presentation is any indication of a concrete danger demanding departure from the Fourth Amendment's main rule.

> In contrast to the effective testing regimes upheld in *Skinner*, *Von Raab*, and *Vernonia*, Georgia's certification requirement is not well designed to identify candidates who violate antidrug laws and is not a credible means to deter illicit drug users from seeking state office. Respondents' reliance on this Court's decision in *Von Raab*, which sustained a drug-testing program for Customs Service officers prior to promotion or transfer to certain high-risk positions, despite the absence of any documented drug abuse problem among Service employees, is misplaced. Hardly a decision opening broad vistas for suspicionless searches, *Von Raab* must be read in its unique context. Drug interdiction had become the agency's primary enforcement mission. The covered posts directly involved drug interdiction or otherwise required Customs officers to carry firearms, the employees would have access to vast sources of valuable contraband, and officers had been targets of and some had succumbed to bribery by drug smugglers. What is left, after close review of Georgia's scheme, is that the State seeks to display its commitment to the struggle against drug abuse. But Georgia asserts no evidence of a drug problem among the State's elected officials, those officials typically do not perform high-risk, safety-sensitive tasks, and the required certification immediately aids no interdiction effort. The need revealed is symbolic, not "special." The Fourth Amendment shields society from state action that diminishes personal privacy for a symbol's sake.

Chief Justice Rehnquist wrote in his dissent,

> Few would doubt that the use of illegal drugs and abuse of legal drugs is one of the major problems of our society. Cases before this Court involving drug use extend to numerous occupations—railway employees, Border Patrol officers, high school students, and machine operators. It would take a bolder person than I to say that such widespread drug usage could never extend to candidates for public office such as Governor of Georgia. Nothing in the Fourth Amendment or in any other part of the Constitution prevents a State from enacting a statute whose principal vice is that it may seem misguided or even silly to the Members of this Court.

Source: *Chandler v. Miller*, 520 U.S. 305 (1997)

CHAPTER SUMMARY

LO 1 Special-needs searches are directed at people generally to further government interests other than crime control, such as promoting community safety. Special-needs searches require neither warrants nor probable cause; they are reasonable if the special government need outweighs the individual loss of privacy. Even though they aren't aimed at controlling crime, criminal prosecution can still result if evidence of a crime is discovered.

LO 2 Courts find inventory searches by law enforcement often meet a variety of public needs, ranging from protection of private property from theft to protection of law enforcement from wrongful blame. Following routine, department-approved, written procedures substitute for probable cause and reasonable suspicion as the objective basis for inventory searches.

LO 3 Nations regulate who and what enters their country. This special need results in the routine inspection of packages and persons crossing the border without warrants or individualized suspicion. The most invasive searches of persons do, however, require an objective basis. Strip searches are reasonable at international borders only if they are backed up by reasonable suspicion and body-cavity searches require probable cause to be reasonable.

LO 4 The special need to maintain safety, security, and discipline over people locked up in jails and prisons outweighs the significantly reduced expectation of privacy that society grants to people in custody of the criminal justice system. Courts maintain that prisoners have few, but some, privacy rights. DNA databases demonstrate how public need outweighs a prisoner's reduced privacy rights.

LO 5 Though they are not physically locked up, parolees and probationers still have a reduced expectation of privacy that subjects them to arrest and searches of their persons, vehicles, and homes without warrants, probable cause, reasonable suspicion, or any objective basis at all. Some courts consider parolees and probationers to be in custody; other courts say they consent to search as a condition of release. Still other courts balance the limited privacy rights of parolees and probationers against the special need of public safety.

LO 6 Public students' constitutional rights are restricted and balanced against the need to maintain order and enforce rules within schools. Historically, public schools had the power to maintain order and enforce disciplinary rules under the legal doctrine *in loco parentis*. According to this doctrine, school officials substitute for parents while children are in school. During the 1960s civil rights movements, youth rights advanced as the Supreme Court upheld public students' free speech and due process rights. After 1975, the Supreme Court shifted this balance in favor of school officials in response to public concern over violence and drug use in public schools.

LO 7 Officials at public colleges and universities are considered state agents, meaning they are restricted by the Fourth Amendment in their abilities to infringe upon student privacy rights. But their need to preserve a safe atmosphere conducive to learning affords them additional leeway.

LO 8 Searches for drug use through drug testing are aimed at the special need of protecting public health and safety, not to collect evidence of criminal activity. Drug-testing policies for public employees are justifiable in court when a routine is established to promote public safety. Similarly, the special needs of schools justify routine drug testing for students who enroll in school activities. In the case of a prenatal crack epidemic, the standard of probable cause is applied.

REVIEW QUESTIONS

1. Identify four characteristics common to all special-needs searches.
2. Identify the two elements that have to be satisfied for an inventory search to be reasonable.
3. Under the balancing element, identify three government interests that make inventory searches by law enforcement officers reasonable.
4. Describe the objective basis requirement for an inventory search.
5. Describe the border search exception and the special need the government balances at international borders.
6. Identify two extremely important special needs served by airport searches, such as passing through metal detectors and luggage X-rays.
7. Why does the Supreme Court approve of such minimal invasions of privacy during airport searches?
8. Identify the balancing interests in custody-related searches of prisoners, probationers, and parolees.
9. Identify the special-need and the objective basis for searches of prisoners.
10. When are strip and body-cavity searches of prisoners reasonable? Explain.
11. Summarize the facts and explain the significance of the Supreme Court's holding in *Hudson v. Palmer*. Summarize the dissent's argument in the case.
12. What, if any, significance does harassment have on prison shakedowns?
13. Explain the significance of testing and storing the DNA of incarcerated felons.
14. Identify two reasons why courts say that probationers and parolees have diminished Fourth Amendment rights.
15. What is the significance of *U.S. v. Knights* in dealing with searches and seizures of probationers?
16. Why do parolees have even more diminished rights against searches and seizures than probationers?
17. Describe the balancing interests in students' constitutional rights within public schools.
18. Trace the history of public students' rights and describe the significance of the legal doctrine *in loco parentis*.
19. Why are employee drug tests reasonable without warrants or probable cause?
20. Why are public college and university officials restricted by the Fourth Amendment ban against unreasonable searches and seizures but private school officials are not?
21. Identify three justifications for the reduced expectation of privacy within dormitory rooms.

22. How does the setting of searches of college students differ from the setting of searches of high school students?

23. When are drug-testing policies for public employees reasonable?

24. In the case of a prenatal crack epidemic, what objective basis is required to justify testing hospital patients and why is it required?

25. Identify the special need and the expectation of privacy balanced in searches of high school students as outlined by the Supreme Court in *New Jersey v. T. L. O.*

26. Summarize the facts and the majority and dissenting opinions in *Vernonia School District v. Acton.*

27. According to the Supreme Court, why is drug testing of students participating in any extracurricular activity reasonable?

KEY TERMS

special-needs searches, p. 244
inventory searches, p. 245
routine procedures, p. 245

border search exception, p. 248
probationers, p. 258

parolees, p. 258
in loco parentis, p. 263

8
Self-Incrimination

LEARNING OBJECTIVES

1 Understand the ambivalent nature and importance of confessions and incriminating statements. Know the characteristics of the interrogation setting.

2 Understand the due process, right-to-counsel, and self-incrimination approaches to criminal confession and their history. Know which stages of the criminal process are relevant to each.

3 Understand the Fifth Amendment protection against being compelled to witness against oneself. Know what falls under this protection and what doesn't.

4 Understand the "bright-line" rule established in *Miranda v. Arizona* and its impact on custodial interrogation.

5 Understand the two tests the Supreme Court uses to determine whether police behavior amounts to interrogation.

6 Understand that evidence obtained in violation of the *Miranda* rule is admissible in court whenever trial judges believe that police questioning is aimed to protect public safety. Know that empirical research has demonstrated a broad judiciary application of the public safety exception, requiring only a possible threat to public safety in some cases.

7 Know the factors considered when individuals waive their right to remain silent. Appreciate that most people waive their rights to remain silent and to a lawyer after receiving the *Miranda* warnings.

8 Understand that confessions must be made voluntarily even if individuals waive their rights to counsel and to remain silent. Know the circumstances that courts have decided are relevant to determining the voluntariness of incriminating statements.

9 Understand the factors that affect innocent people when they confess to crimes they didn't commit. Appreciate the significance of proven false confessions and know the suggested reforms aimed at preventing them.

No parent would teach . . . their children [that they don't have to answer their parents' questions]. The lesson parents preach is that while a misdeed, even a serious one, will generally be forgiven, a failure to make a clean breast of it will not be. Every hour of the day people are being asked to explain their conduct to parents, employers, and teachers. Those who are questioned consider themselves bound to respond, and the questioners believe it proper to take action if they do not.

—Judge Friendly (1968, 680)

The Framers . . . created a federally protected right of silence and decreed that the law could not be used to pry open one's lips and make him a witness against himself. . . . The Constitution places the right of silence beyond the reach of government. *The Fifth Amendment stands between the citizen and his government.*

—U.S. Supreme Court Justice William Douglas (*Ullman v. U.S.* 1956, 443–54)

More than the human dignity of the accused is involved; the human personality of others in the society must also be preserved. Thus the values reflected by the privilege are not the sole desideratum; society's interest in the general security is of equal weight. Moreover, it is by no means certain that the process of confessing is injurious to the accused. To the contrary it may provide psychological relief and enhance the prospects for rehabilitation.

—Justice White, dissenting (*Miranda v. Arizona*, 1996)

"Miranda has become embedded in routine police practice to the point where the warnings have become part of our national culture." These are the words of Chief Justice William Rehnquist (2000). What was the occasion for his comment? He was reading the U.S. Supreme Court's decision in *Dickerson v. U.S.* (2000). In that case, the Court ruled that Congress doesn't have the power to overrule *Miranda v. Arizona* (1966), something it had tried to do in 1968. In that year, in a burst of "get tough on criminals" legislation, Congress passed a law saying officers don't have to warn suspects of their rights to a lawyer and against self-incrimination before they interrogate them.

Federal and state officials ignored the law until 1997, when a Virginia federal court relied on the 1968 statute to admit Charles Dickerson's confession obtained after FBI agents gave him defective *Miranda* warnings. The 1968 law, the 1997 case relying on it, and the Supreme Court's decision declaring the law unconstitutional reflect a long and emotional debate over the right against self-incrimination.

In this chapter, we'll look at the law and *practice* of self-incrimination regarding the following:

1. The nature and role of confessions and incriminating statements
2. The Constitution and self-incrimination
3. *Miranda v. Arizona*
4. Waiver of the right to remain silent
5. Incriminating statements and confessions
6. False confessions

THE NATURE AND ROLE OF CONFESSIONS

 Confessions (suspects' written or oral acknowledgement of guilt, often including details about the crime) play an ambivalent role in society and law, and that ambivalence is ancient. In many religions, confession is the first step to forgiveness and finally redemption; in law, it is the proof that justifies blame and punishment. Because confessions create access to defendants' innermost beliefs, knowledge, and thinking, they're uniquely powerful evidence of guilt and contrition. But they can also be uniquely dangerous and misleading. "The upshot has been heavy reliance on confessions coupled with extensive regulation of their use" (Seidman 2002, 229).

People confess their guilt, or make **incriminating statements**, in four ways. (Incriminating statements refers to statements that fall short of full confessions.)

1. *When they incriminate themselves to friends and associates, who report it to officials.* These incriminating statements and confessions can be used against those who make them.

2. *When defendants plead guilty to crimes they're charged with.* Defendants who plead guilty automatically give up the right against self-incrimination. This is far and away the most common form of self-incrimination in the criminal justice system (Chapter 13).

3. *When convicted offenders incriminate themselves during the sentencing process.* The main reason for this incrimination is because they want to demonstrate they're sorry.

4. *When criminal suspects incriminate themselves after arrest.* Making incriminating statements and confessing during police interrogations have generated the most controversy, and are our main focus in this chapter.

We'll devote most of the chapter to incrimination during police interrogation. But we'll also examine broader questions related to self-incrimination, including the constitutional provisions that regulate it; the growing body of empirical social science research related to it; and recommendations aimed to ensure that police interrogation leads the guilty—but not the innocent—to incriminate themselves.

LO 1   The Self-Incrimination Setting

Chief Justice Rehnquist was certainly right that *Miranda* is part of our culture. But what he left out is it's also part of our culture "wars." Perhaps no procedure has generated more hostility between social conservatives and social liberals. Every week (from 1993 to 2005, and now in reruns), audiences watched *NYPD Blue*'s "good cops," Andy Sipowicz and whoever his current partner was (it was a long list), wage a "war on *Miranda*." In almost every episode, a "scumbag" murderer—or his lawyer—made a "mockery of the system" by taunting the cops with his "rights." Then, Sipowicz and his partner threatened, shoved, and usually wound up beating a confession out of the "worthless animal" called a "suspect." We all knew he was guilty (it was always a man, by the way), and we were invited to hate not only the murderer but also the system that provided such scumbags with rights.

But this popular portrayal of saintly cops and satanic criminals hid the complexity of self-incrimination in practice where it most frequently occurs, during police interrogations and resulting confessions. The atmosphere in police stations is (and it's supposed to be) strange, intimidating, and hostile to criminal suspects. It's not like being stopped, asked a few questions, and frisked in the familiar surroundings of public places (Chapter 4).

In police stations, suspects are searched thoroughly—sometimes strip-searched and, occasionally, subjected to body-cavity searches (Chapter 7); they have to stand in line-ups (Chapter 9); and, they're interrogated incommunicado. (This isn't a criticism; it's a description.) Being taken to police stations isn't supposed to be pleasant for suspects. The atmosphere and the actions are supposed to flush out the truth about suspects' possible criminal behavior, or what they know about someone else's criminal behavior.

By the time officers bring arrested suspects to police stations, their investigation has focused on those particular suspects. This period when the police have shifted their attention from a general investigation of a crime to building a case against a named individual is called the **accusatory stage of the criminal process**. During this stage, balancing the needs of law enforcement against the interests of individual privacy and liberty carries higher stakes for both suspects and law enforcement. Defining the proper balance between these competing social interests during the period when the police hold suspects in custody, but before prosecutors have charged them with crimes, has always generated controversy over how much the U.S. Constitution protects criminal suspects in police custody.

These aren't black-and-white issues. Consider the following hypothetical situations. In which cases can the persons "be compelled to be witnesses" against themselves?

- A police officer asks a man he has stopped on the street, "What are you doing out at 1:30 a.m.?" The man replies, "I'm trying to buy some crystal meth, as if it's any of your business."
- An officer hears screams coming from an apartment. He enters without knocking and asks, "What's going on here?" A woman answers, "I just beat up my baby."

- An elderly woman is beaten when she won't give her purse to three muggers. She is left on the street and dies of exposure. Officers in relays question an 18-year-old suspect for six hours without a break. Some officers get tough, bullying the youth and telling him he's in "big trouble" if he doesn't talk. But they never touch him. One officer befriends him, telling him the officer knows whoever took the purse didn't mean to kill the woman and that, anyway, it was really her fault for resisting. The young man finally weakens and confesses.

- A police officer, while interrogating a suspect in the police station, promises, "If you'll just tell me the truth about raping the college student, I'll see to it that the prosecutor only charges you with misdemeanor assault." The suspect asks, "You can do that?" The officer replies, "Sure, I wouldn't tell you something I couldn't do." The suspect says, "O.K., I did it." He later puts the confession in writing.

- An officer tells a suspect brought to the police station for questioning, "You might as well admit you killed your husband, because your neighbor already told us he saw the whole thing." The officer is lying. The suspect replies, "My God, I knew I should've pulled the shades; that nosy bastard's always spying on me."

Reconsider your answers after you've read the rest of the chapter. In the meantime, to understand the law of self-incrimination, interrogation, and confessions better, we'll examine their importance and look at the potential for abuse of interrogation.

LO 1 The Importance of Confessions and Interrogation

Almost a half century ago, U.S. Supreme Court Justice Felix Frankfurter (*Culombe v. Connecticut* 1961) explained why he believed police interrogation and confessions were important:

> Despite modern advances in the technology of crime detection, offenses frequently occur about which things cannot be made to speak. And where there cannot be found innocent human witnesses to such offenses, nothing remains—if police investigation is not to be balked before it has fairly begun—but to seek out possible guilty witnesses and ask them questions, witnesses, that is, who are suspected of knowing something about the offense precisely because they are suspected of implication in it. (571)

Fred Inbau (1961)—for 60 years a professor of law, author of the leading manual on police interrogation, and one of the best interrogators of his time—gave three reasons why he supported Justice Frankfurter's position:

1. Police can't solve many crimes unless guilty people confess or suspects give police information that can convict someone else who's guilty.

2. Criminals don't confess unless the police either catch them in the act or interrogate them in private.

3. Police have to use "less refined methods" when they interrogate suspects than are "appropriate for the transaction of ordinary, every-day affairs by and between law-abiding citizens." (19)

We don't know, empirically, how close to the truth Justice Frankfurter and Professor Inbau were about the importance of interrogations and confessions. U.S. Supreme Court Chief Justice Earl Warren—himself an experienced and effective former prosecutor—explained why: "Interrogation still takes place in privacy. Privacy results in secrecy and this in turn results in a gap in our knowledge as to what in fact goes on in the interrogation room" (*Miranda v. Arizona* 1966).

Later in the chapter, we'll look at empirical research regarding false confessions. We'll also look at some recommended reforms to improve the central purposes of interrogations and confessions—to obtain the true confessions of the guilty, and reject the false confessions of the innocent.

THE CONSTITUTION AND SELF-INCRIMINATION

LO 2 The right to remain silent in the face of an accusation has ancient religious and legal origins. The ancient Talmudic law, which put the teachings of Moses into writing, contained an absolute ban on self-incrimination. The ban couldn't ever be waived because self-incrimination violated the natural right of survival. Jesus was probably exercising this right when he stood before the Roman governor Pontius Pilate, who demanded to know if Jesus was guilty of treason. When Pilate asked, "Art thou King of the Jews?" Jesus artfully replied, "Thou sayest." Then, the chief priests and elders accused Jesus of many crimes. Jesus stood and "answered them nothing."

Surprised at Jesus' obstinacy, Pilate demanded, "'Hearest thou not how many things they witness against thee?' And still Jesus answered him to never a word, insomuch that the governor marveled greatly" (Matt. 27:11–14 Authorized [King James] Version).

The origin of the right to remain silent also is tied to another ancient rule, the common-law rule that confessions had to be voluntary. By the time the right to remain silent appeared in the Fifth Amendment to the U.S. Constitution, it had followed a controversial and complicated history (Levy 1968).

The U.S. Supreme Court has relied on three provisions in the U.S. Constitution to develop rules to control police interrogation and confessions (Table 8.1):

1. *Fourteenth Amendment due process clause.* "No state shall . . . deprive any person of life, liberty, or property without due process of law."

2. *Sixth Amendment right-to-counsel clause.* "In all criminal prosecutions, the accused shall . . . have the assistance of counsel for his defense."

3. *Fifth Amendment self-incrimination clause.* "No person . . . shall be compelled in any criminal case to be a witness against himself."

Each of these constitutional provisions has led to a different approach to police interrogation and suspects' confessions. We'll look at all three: the due process approach, the right-to-counsel approach, and the self-incrimination approach.

LO 2 ## The Due Process Approach

The due process, right-to-counsel, and self-incrimination approaches overlap, but they follow a rough chronological line. In *Brown v. Mississippi* (1936), the U.S. Supreme Court applied the Fourteenth Amendment due process clause to the confessions extracted by torture in that tragic case (Chapter 2).

The basic idea behind the due process approach is that confessions have to be voluntary. Involuntary confessions violate due process, not because they're "compelled," but because they're not reliable (meaning they might be false).

TABLE 8.1 The U.S. Constitution and self-incrimination

Amendment	Stage of Criminal Process Where It's Applicable
Fourteenth Amendment due process clause	All stages
Sixth Amendment right-to-counsel clause	All stages after formal charges
Fifth Amendment self-incrimination clause	Custodial interrogation and all following stages

© Cengage Learning

The **reliability rationale for due process** is that admitting unreliable evidence to prove guilt denies defendants the right to their lives (Brown, Stewart, and Ellington were sentenced to death) without due process of law. In *Brown*, the confessions were the only evidence against the defendants.

Here's what Chief Justice Hughes wrote for the Court:

> The state is free to regulate the procedure of its courts in accordance with its own conceptions of policy. But the freedom of the state in establishing its policy is limited by the requirement of due process of law. The rack and torture chamber may not be substituted for the witness stand. And the trial is a mere pretense where the state authorities have contrived a conviction resting solely on the confessions obtained by violence. It would be difficult to conceive of methods more revolting to the sense of justice than those taken to procure the confessions of these petitioners, and the use of the confessions thus obtained as the basis for conviction and sentence was a clear denial of due process. (286)

The unreliability of coerced confessions provided the rationale for the reviews of most of the early state confessions cases decided by the U.S. Supreme Court after *Brown v. Mississippi*. After several cases intimated there was a second rationale for reviewing state confession cases, the Court made the accusatory system rationale explicit in *Rogers v. Richmond* (1961). According to the **accusatory system rationale**, forced confessions violate due process even if they're true, because under our system the government alone has the burden of proving guilt beyond a reasonable doubt. In applying the accusatory system rationale in *Rogers*, the Court threw out a confession that the police got after they threatened to bring Rogers's arthritic wife in for questioning.

According to Justice Felix Frankfurter:

> Our decisions under the Fourteenth Amendment due process clause have made clear that convictions following the admission into evidence of confessions which are involuntary, i.e., the product of coercion, either physical or psychological, cannot stand. This is so not because such confessions are unlikely to be true but because the methods used to extract them offend an underlying principle in the enforcement of our criminal law: that ours is an accusatorial and not an inquisitorial system—a system in which the State must establish guilt by evidence independently and freely secured and may not by coercion prove its charge against an accused out of his own mouth.

The Court relied on a third rationale—the free will rationale—for reviewing state confessions in *Townsend v. Sain* (1963). After three hours of questioning, Frank Sain asked officers to give him drugs to ameliorate his pain from narcotics withdrawal.

Sain confessed because the drug the doctor administered acted as a "truth serum." Neither the doctor nor the interrogators knew the drug would have that effect. It didn't matter that the officers acted in good faith because, according to the **free will rationale**, involuntary confessions aren't just unreliable and contrary to the accusatory system of justice; they're also coerced if they're not "the product of a rational intellect and a free will" (307).

During the 30 years between *Brown v. Mississippi* (1936) and *Miranda v. Arizona* (1966), the Supreme Court threw out 40 state confessions because they violated due process. Most of the early cases involved southern White mobs who had rounded up poor, illiterate Blacks and tortured them until they confessed. The Court was much more reluctant to overturn the convictions of less "sympathetic criminals" from other parts of the country. In *Lisenba v. California* (1941), for example, Ray Lisenba (an educated White business executive from California) confessed he'd "tied his wife to a chair, subjected her to rattlesnake bites, and then drowned her in a pond." The police grilled Lisenba in several all-night sessions for two weeks, refusing to grant his repeated demands to see a lawyer and to remain silent until he did.

But even in the face of these tactics, the Court refused to overturn Lisenba's conviction by throwing out his confession. According to the Court, his incriminating statements, looked at in the light of his intelligence and business experience, were not caused by police "overbearing his will" but instead were "a calculated attempt to minimize his culpability after carefully considering statements by the accomplice."

In *Stein v. New York* (1953), another case of "unsympathetic criminals"—this time involving clever, experienced White robbers in rural New York State—Justice Jackson impatiently referred to the defendants as criminals who were "convinced their dance was over and the time had come to pay the fiddler." According to Justice Jackson, "The limits in any case depend upon a weighing of the circumstances of pressure against the power of resistance of the person confessing. What would be overpowering to the weak of will or mind might be utterly ineffective against an experienced criminal" (184).

LO 2   The Right-to-Counsel Approach

At the same time the U.S. Supreme Court was developing the due process approach to the review of state confessions cases, a growing minority of the Court was looking for tougher measures to control police interrogation. They found one of these tougher measures in the Sixth Amendment, which reads: "In all criminal prosecutions, the accused shall . . . have the assistance of counsel for his defense." The problem is the phrase "all criminal prosecutions," which suggests proceedings in court, not in police stations.

But by 1958, four of nine justices, including Chief Justice Warren and Associate Justices Black, Douglas, and Brennan, were calling custodial interrogation a **critical stage in criminal prosecutions** (the point when suspects' right to a lawyer kicked in).

In *Crooker v. California* (1958), John Russell Crooker, Jr., was a former law student working as a houseboy for a woman he was having an affair with. She broke off the affair when she found another boyfriend. After 14 hours in police custody, Crooker confessed to stabbing and strangling her. Although the police wouldn't let Crooker call his lawyer, there was no evidence officers had forced him to confess. He was allowed to eat, drink, and smoke, and interrogation sessions lasted only about an hour at a time.

The U.S. Supreme Court affirmed Crooker's conviction, but Chief Justice Warren and Justices Black, Douglas, and Brennan dissented. Justice Douglas explained, "The mischief and abuse of the third degree will continue as long as an accused can be denied the right to counsel at the most critical period of his ordeal. For what takes place in the secret confines of the police station may be more critical than what takes place at trial" (444–45).

A change in the Court's membership brought to a slim majority of 5–4 the number of justices who favored the right-to-counsel approach to police interrogation and confessions. In 1964, in *Escobedo v. Illinois* (1964), the Supreme Court by a 5–4 vote turned to the Sixth Amendment right-to-counsel clause as the basis for reviewing state confessions cases.

Danny Escobedo asked his Chicago police interrogators to let him see his lawyer. They refused. His lawyer came to the station at Escobedo's mother's behest, but the officers repeatedly refused his requests to see Danny. Finally, Escobedo confessed. The Supreme Court threw out the confession because Escobedo had given it without the advice of his lawyer. According to the Court, as soon as a police investigation focuses on a particular suspect (the accusatory stage), criminal prosecution begins and the right to counsel attaches. If defendants don't have a right to a lawyer until they go to trial and they confess before trial without a lawyer, then the trial is "no more than an appeal from the interrogation."

Four dissenting justices argued that allowing lawyers in interrogation rooms would kill the use of confessions. Why? Because, "Any lawyer worth his salt will tell the suspect in no uncertain terms to make no statement to the police under any circumstances" (*Watts v. Indiana* 1949, 59). According to Justice White, dissenting in *Escobedo*, "I do not suggest for a moment that law enforcement will be destroyed by the rule announced today. The need for peace and order is too insistent for that. But it will be crippled and its task made a great deal more difficult" (499).

LO 2 The Self-Incrimination Approach

In 1966, just two years after adopting the right-to-counsel approach to custodial interrogations, the Court abruptly dropped it. In a 5–4 decision in *Miranda v. Arizona* (1966) case, the Court majority of one relied on the Fifth Amendment self-incrimination clause to decide the constitutionality of custodial interrogation. According to the Court, the Fifth Amendment guarantees the right to remain silent; it *doesn't* ban police officers from asking individuals (including crime suspects) questions. But, officers can't "compel" them to answer. If they do, they can't use what they learn as evidence to prove defendants' guilt at trial.

The due process, right-to-counsel, and self-incrimination approaches are all still in operation. To decide whether a police custodial interrogation before formal charges was inherently coercive, the Court relies on the Fifth Amendment self-incrimination clause. To decide whether coercion was used after formal charges, the Court relies on the Sixth Amendment right to counsel. To review whether suspects and defendants have knowingly and voluntarily made incriminating statements whenever they take place, the Court relies on the Fourteenth Amendment due process clause (Table 8.1).

To claim successfully that their Fifth Amendment right against self-incrimination was violated, defendants have to prove three elements:

1. Compulsion. "No person . . . shall be compelled . . ."
2. Incrimination. ". . . in any criminal case"
3. Testimony. "to be a witness against himself"

This is the order the elements appear in the self-incrimination clause, but we'll begin with the preliminary requirement: testimony. Then we'll discuss what it means to be "compelled" to be a witness against oneself.

LO **3**   *The meaning of "witness against himself"*

The Fifth Amendment says the government can't compel you to be a "witness" against yourself, but what does this mean? According to the U.S. Supreme Court, it means the government can't force you to give **testimony** (the content of what you say and write) against yourself. But content doesn't include the voice that spoke the words. So the government can compel you to speak particular words that might help a witness identify your voice. Also, drivers involved in accidents don't incriminate themselves when they have to give their names and addresses to the police. And if some law says you have to turn over information in your personal books, papers, bank accounts, and other records, you aren't being compelled to incriminate yourself.

Further, in *Schmerber v. California* (1966), the Supreme Court decided that taking blood alcohol samples from Armando Schmerber against his will didn't compel him to be a witness against himself. (See Table 8.2 for more examples.)

LO **3**   *The meaning of "compelled"*

The due process approach to self-incrimination relied on the voluntariness test to decide whether suspects were "compelled" to be witnesses against themselves. According to the **voluntariness test of self-incrimination**, confessions and other incriminating statements violate due process if the totality of circumstances surrounding the statements shows that suspects didn't confess voluntarily. In 1966, a combination of three factors produced one of the most famous (and most controversial and hated) decisions in U.S. constitutional history—*Miranda v. Arizona*:

1. *Uneasiness* about tactics used against suspects in the intimidating atmosphere of police stations
2. *Dissatisfaction* with the vagueness of the totality-of-circumstances approach
3. *Impatience* with the case-by-case approach to deciding whether confessions were voluntarily given and gotten.

Let's turn now to an analysis of this famous case, and it's importance in several key areas: self-incrimination, confessions, police interrogation, and the right to counsel.

TABLE 8.2 Incriminating evidence not protected by the Fifth Amendment

Weapons	Products of consent searches
Photographs	Hair samples
Contraband	Books, papers, documents
Appearance in lineup	Voice samples
Stolen property	Records required by law to be kept
Bullets removed from the body	Fingerprints
Handwriting samples	

© Cengage Learning

MIRANDA V. ARIZONA (1966)

In *Miranda v. Arizona* (1966), a bare 5–4 majority of the U.S. Supreme Court established a "bright-line" rule to govern **custodial interrogation**. (We define custodial interrogation as police questioning suspects while holding them against their will, usually in a police station, but sometimes in other places.) According to the Court majority, custodial interrogation is "**inherently coercive.**" Why? First, because suspects are held in strange surroundings where they're not free to leave or even to call for emotional support from relatives and friends. Second, skilled police officers use tricks, lies, and psychological pressure to "crack" the will of suspects. These circumstances, according to the Court, require strong measures to prevent involuntary confessions.

Those measures (what we all know as the *Miranda* **warnings**) mandated by the Court majority decision, and the reasons the Court devised them were hotly debated in our next case excerpt, *Miranda v. Arizona*.

In *Miranda v. Arizona* (1966) 5–4, the U.S. Supreme Court held that police officers violated Ernesto Miranda's Fifth Amendment right against self-incrimination during Miranda's custodial interrogation.

CASE

Does the Fifth Amendment Apply to Custodial Interrogation?

Miranda v. Arizona
384 U.S. 436 (1966)

HISTORY

Ernesto Miranda was convicted of rape and robbery in the Superior Court, Maricopa County, Arizona, and sentenced to 20 to 30 years in prison for each crime. He appealed. The Arizona Supreme Court affirmed. The U.S. Supreme Court granted certiorari and reversed.

—WARREN, C.J., joined by BLACK, DOUGLAS, BRENNAN, and FORTES, JJ.

FACTS

On March 13, 1963, petitioner, Ernesto Miranda, was arrested at his home and taken in custody to a Phoenix police station. He was there identified by the complaining witness. The police then took him to "Interrogation Room No. 2" of the detective bureau. There he was questioned by two police officers. The officers admitted at trial that Miranda was not advised that he had a right to have an attorney present. Two hours later, the officers emerged from the interrogation room with a written confession signed by Miranda. At the top of the statement was a typed paragraph stating that the confession was made voluntarily, without threats or promises of immunity and "with full knowledge of my legal rights, understanding any statement I make may be used against me." One of the officers testified that he read this paragraph to Miranda. Apparently, however, he did not do so until after Miranda had confessed orally.

At his trial before a jury, the written confession was admitted into evidence over the objection of defense counsel, and the officers testified to the prior oral confession made by Miranda during the interrogation. Miranda was found guilty of kidnapping and rape. He was sentenced to 20 to 30 years' imprisonment on each count, the sentences to run concurrently. On appeal, the Supreme Court of Arizona held that Miranda's constitutional rights were not violated in obtaining the confession and affirmed the conviction. In reaching its decision, the court emphasized heavily the fact that Miranda did not specifically request counsel.

OPINION

The cases before us raise questions which go to the roots of our concepts of American criminal jurisprudence: the restraints society must observe consistent with the Federal Constitution in prosecuting individuals for crime. More specifically, we deal with the admissibility of statements obtained from an individual who is subjected to custodial police interrogation and the necessity for procedures which assure that the individual is accorded his privilege under the Fifth Amendment to the Constitution not to be compelled to incriminate himself.

An understanding of the nature and setting of this in-custody interrogation is essential to our decisions today. The difficulty in depicting what transpires at such interrogations stems from the fact that in this country they have largely taken place incommunicado. From extensive factual studies undertaken in the early 1930s, including the famous Wickersham Report to Congress by a Presidential Commission, it is clear that police violence and the "third degree" flourished at that time. In a series of cases decided by this Court long after these studies, the police resorted to physical brutality—beatings, hanging, whipping—and to sustained and protracted questioning incommunicado in order to extort confessions. The Commission on Civil Rights in 1961 found much evidence to indicate that "some policemen still resort to physical force to obtain confessions."

The use of physical brutality and violence is not, unfortunately, relegated to the past or to any part of the country. Only recently in Kings County, New York, the police brutally beat, kicked, and placed lighted cigarette butts on the back of a potential witness under interrogation for the purpose of securing a statement incriminating a third party.

In these cases, we might not find the defendants' statements to have been involuntary in traditional terms. In each of the cases, the defendant was thrust into an unfamiliar atmosphere and run through menacing police interrogation procedures. The potentiality for compulsion is forcefully apparent, for example, in *Miranda*, where the indigent Mexican defendant was a seriously disturbed individual with pronounced sexual fantasies. To be sure, the records do not evince overt physical coercion or patent psychological ploys. The fact remains that in none of these cases did the officers undertake to afford appropriate safeguards at the outset of the interrogation to insure that the statements were truly the product of free choice.

To be sure, this is not physical intimidation, but it is equally destructive of human dignity. The current practice of incommunicado interrogation is at odds with one of our Nation's most cherished principles—that the individual may not be compelled to incriminate himself. Unless adequate protective devices are employed to dispel the compulsion inherent in custodial surroundings, no statement obtained from the defendant can truly be the product of his free choice.

The question in these cases is whether the privilege is fully applicable during a period of custodial interrogation. We are satisfied that all the principles embodied in the privilege apply to informal compulsion exerted by law-enforcement officers during in-custody questioning. An individual swept from familiar surroundings into police custody, surrounded by antagonistic forces, and subjected to the techniques of persuasion described above cannot be otherwise than under compulsion to speak. As a practical matter, the compulsion to speak in the isolated setting of the police station may well be greater than in courts or other official investigations, where there are often impartial observers to guard against intimidation or trickery.

Today, then, there can be no doubt that the Fifth Amendment privilege serves to protect persons in all settings in which their freedom of action is curtailed in any significant way from being compelled to incriminate themselves. We have concluded that without proper safeguards the process of in-custody interrogation of persons suspected or accused of crime contains inherently compelling pressures which work to undermine the individual's will to resist and to compel him to speak where he would not otherwise do so freely. In order to combat these pressures and to permit a full opportunity to exercise the privilege against self-incrimination, the accused must be adequately and effectively apprised of his rights and the exercise of those rights must be fully honored.

It is impossible for us to foresee the potential alternatives for protecting the privilege which might be devised by Congress or the States in the exercise of their creative rule-making capacities. Therefore we cannot say that the Constitution necessarily requires adherence to any particular solution for the inherent compulsions of the interrogation process as it is presently conducted. Our decision in no way creates a constitutional straitjacket which will handicap sound efforts at reform, nor is it intended to have this effect. We encourage Congress and the States to continue their laudable search for increasingly effective ways of protecting the rights of the individual while promoting efficient enforcement of our criminal laws. However, unless we are shown other procedures which are at least as effective in apprising accused persons of their right of silence and in assuring a continuous opportunity to exercise it, the following safeguards must be observed.

At the outset, if a person in custody is to be subjected to interrogation, he must first be informed in clear and unequivocal terms that he has the right to remain silent. For those unaware of the privilege, the warning is needed simply to make them aware of it—the threshold requirement for an intelligent decision as to its exercise. More important, such a warning is an absolute prerequisite in overcoming the inherent pressures of the interrogation atmosphere. It is not just the subnormal or woefully ignorant who succumb to an interrogator's imprecations, whether implied or expressly stated, that the interrogation

(continued)

will continue until a confession is obtained or that silence in the face of accusation is itself damning and will bode ill when presented to a jury.

The Fifth Amendment privilege is so fundamental to our system of constitutional rule and the expedient of giving an adequate warning as to the availability of the privilege so simple, we will not pause to inquire in individual cases whether the defendant was aware of his rights without a warning being given. Assessments of the knowledge the defendant possessed, based on information as to his age, education, intelligence, or prior contact with authorities, can never be more than speculation; a warning is a clearcut fact. More important, whatever the background of the person interrogated, a warning at the time of the interrogation is indispensable to overcome its pressures and to insure that the individual knows he is free to exercise the privilege at that point in time.

The warning of the right to remain silent must be accompanied by the explanation that anything said can and will be used against the individual in court. This warning is needed in order to make him aware not only of the privilege, but also of the consequences of forgoing it. Moreover, this warning may serve to make the individual more acutely aware that he is faced with a phase of the adversary system—that he is not in the presence of persons acting solely in his interest.

The circumstances surrounding in-custody interrogation can operate very quickly to overbear the will of one merely made aware of his privilege by his interrogators. Therefore, the right to have counsel present at the interrogation is indispensable to the protection of the Fifth Amendment privilege under the system we delineate today. Our aim is to assure that the individual's right to choose between silence and speech remains unfettered throughout the interrogation process. A mere warning given by the interrogators is not alone sufficient to accomplish that end. Even preliminary advice given to the accused by his own attorney can be swiftly overcome by the secret interrogation process. Thus, the need for counsel to protect the Fifth Amendment privilege comprehends not merely a right to consult with counsel prior to questioning, but also to have counsel present during any questioning if the defendant so desires.

An individual need not make a pre-interrogation request for a lawyer. While such request affirmatively secures his right to have one, his failure to ask for a lawyer does not constitute a waiver. No effective waiver of the right to counsel during interrogation can be recognized unless specifically made after the warnings we here delineate have been given. The accused who does not know his rights and therefore does not make a request may be the person who most needs counsel.

Accordingly we hold that an individual held for interrogation must be clearly informed that he has the right to consult with a lawyer and to have the lawyer with him during interrogation under the system for protecting the privilege we delineate today. As with the warnings of the right to remain silent and that anything stated can be used in evidence against him, this warning is an absolute prerequisite to interrogation. No amount of circumstantial evidence that the person may have been aware of this right will suffice to stand in its stead. Only through such a warning is there ascertainable assurance that the accused was aware of this right.

In order fully to apprise a person interrogated of the extent of his rights under this system then, it is necessary to warn him not only that he has the right to consult with an attorney, but also that if he is indigent a lawyer will be appointed to represent him. Without this additional warning, the admonition of the right to consult with counsel would often be understood as meaning only that he can consult with a lawyer if he has one or has the funds to obtain one. The warning of a right to counsel would be hollow if not couched in terms that would convey to the indigent—the person most often subjected to interrogation—the knowledge that he too has a right to have counsel present. As with the warnings of the right to remain silent and of the general right to counsel, only by effective and express explanation to the indigent of this right can there be assurance that he was truly in a position to exercise it.

Once warnings have been given, the subsequent procedure is clear. If the individual indicates in any manner, at any time prior to or during questioning, that he wishes to remain silent, the interrogation must cease. At this point he has shown that he intends to exercise his Fifth Amendment privilege; any statement taken after the person invokes his privilege cannot be other than the product of compulsion, subtle or otherwise. If the individual states that he wants an attorney, the interrogation must cease until an attorney is present. At that time, the individual must have an opportunity to confer with the attorney and to have him present during any subsequent questioning. If the individual cannot obtain an attorney and he indicates that he wants one before speaking to police, they must respect his decision to remain silent.

This does not mean, as some have suggested, that each police station must have a "station house lawyer" present at all times to advise prisoners. It does mean, however, that if police propose to interrogate a person they must make known to him that he is entitled to a lawyer and that if he cannot afford one, a lawyer will be provided for him prior to any interrogation. If authorities conclude that they will not provide counsel during a reasonable period of time in which investigation in the field is carried out, they may refrain from doing so without violating the person's Fifth Amendment privilege so long as they do not question him during that time.

If the interrogation continues without the presence of an attorney and a statement is taken, a heavy burden rests on the government to demonstrate that the defendant knowingly and intelligently waived his privilege against self-incrimination and his right to retained or appointed counsel. This Court has always set high standards of proof for the waiver of constitutional rights, and we reassert these standards as applied to in-custody interrogation. Since the State is responsible for establishing the isolated circumstances under which the interrogation takes place and has the only means of making available corroborated evidence of warnings given during incommunicado interrogation, the burden is rightly on its shoulders.

An express statement that the individual is willing to make a statement and does not want an attorney followed closely by a statement could constitute a waiver. But a valid waiver will not be presumed simply from the silence of the accused after warnings are given or simply from the fact that a confession was in fact eventually obtained. Moreover, any evidence that the accused was threatened, tricked, or cajoled into a waiver will, of course, show that the defendant did not voluntarily waive his privilege. The requirement of warnings and waiver of rights is a fundamental with respect to the Fifth Amendment privilege and not simply a preliminary ritual to existing methods of interrogation.

The warnings required and the waiver necessary in accordance with our opinion today are, in the absence of a fully effective equivalent, prerequisites to the admissibility of any statement made by a defendant. No distinction can be drawn between statements which are direct confessions and statements which amount to 'admissions' of part or all of an offense. The privilege against self-incrimination protects the individual from being compelled to incriminate himself in any manner; it does not distinguish degrees of incrimination.

Similarly, for precisely the same reason, no distinction may be drawn between inculpatory statements and statements alleged to be merely "exculpatory." If a statement made were in fact truly exculpatory it would, of course, never be used by the prosecution. In fact, statements merely intended to be exculpatory by the defendant are often used to impeach his testimony at trial or to demonstrate untruths in the statement given under interrogation and thus to prove guilt by implication. These statements are incriminating in any meaningful sense of the word and may not be used without the full warnings and effective waiver required for any other statement. In *Escobedo* itself, the defendant fully intended his accusation of another as the slayer to be exculpatory as to himself.

The principles announced today deal with the protection which must be given to the privilege against self-incrimination when the individual is first subjected to police interrogation while in custody at the station or otherwise deprived of his freedom of action in any significant way. It is at this point that our adversary system of criminal proceedings commences, distinguishing itself at the outset from the inquisitorial system recognized in some countries. Under the system of warnings we delineate today or under any other system which may be devised and found effective, the safeguards to be erected about the privilege must come into play at this point.

In dealing with statements obtained through interrogation, we do not purport to find all confessions inadmissible. Confessions remain a proper element in law enforcement. Any statement given freely and voluntarily without any compelling influences is, of course, admissible in evidence. The fundamental import of the privilege while an individual is in custody is not whether he is allowed to talk to the police without the benefit of warnings and counsel, but whether he can be interrogated. There is no requirement that police stop a person who enters a police station and states that he wishes to confess to a crime, or a person who calls the police to offer a confession or any other statement he desires to make. Volunteered statements of any kind are not barred by the Fifth Amendment and their admissibility is not affected by our holding today.

A recurrent argument made in these cases is that society's need for interrogation outweighs the privilege. This argument is not unfamiliar to this Court. The whole thrust of our foregoing discussion demonstrates that the Constitution has prescribed the rights of the individual when confronted with the power of government when it provided in the Fifth Amendment that an individual cannot be compelled to be a witness against himself. That right cannot be abridged.

Over the years the Federal Bureau of Investigation has compiled an exemplary record of effective law enforcement while advising any suspect or arrested person, at the outset of an interview, that he is not required to make a statement, that any statement may be used against him in court, that the individual may obtain the services of an attorney of his own choice and, more recently, that he has a right to free counsel if he is unable to pay.

It is also urged upon us that we withhold decision on this issue until state legislative bodies and advisory groups have had an opportunity to deal with these problems by rule making. We have already pointed out that the Constitution does not require any specific code of procedures for protecting the privilege against self-incrimination during custodial interrogation. Congress and the States are free to develop their own safeguards for the privilege, so long as they are fully as effective as those described above in informing accused persons of their right of silence and in affording a continuous opportunity to exercise it.

We turn now to consider the application to these cases of the constitutional principles discussed above. [Only the Court's opinion in *Miranda* is included here.]

Miranda v. Arizona. We reverse. From the testimony of the officers and by the admission of respondent, it is clear that Miranda was not in any way apprised of his

(continued)

right to consult with an attorney and to have one present during the interrogation, nor was his right not to be compelled to incriminate himself effectively protected in any other manner. Without these warnings the statements were inadmissible. The mere fact that he signed a statement which contained a typed-in clause stating that he had 'full knowledge' of his 'legal rights' does not approach the knowing and intelligent waiver required to relinquish constitutional rights.

DISSENT

WHITE, J., joined by HARLAN and STEWART, JJ. (Justice Clark's dissent is not included here.)

The Court's duty to assess the consequences of its action is not satisfied by the utterance of the truth that a value of our system of criminal justice is "to respect the inviolability of the human personality" and to require government to produce the evidence against the accused by its own independent labors. More than the human dignity of the accused is involved; the human personality of others in the society must also be preserved. Thus the values reflected by the privilege are not the sole desideratum; society's interest in the general security is of equal weight.

The rule announced today . . . is a deliberate calculus to prevent interrogations, to reduce the incidence of confessions and pleas of guilty, and to increase the number of trials. There is, in my view, every reason to believe that a good many criminal defendants who otherwise would have been convicted on what this Court has previously thought to be the most satisfactory kind of evidence will now under this new version of the Fifth Amendment, either not be tried at all or will be acquitted if the State's evidence, minus the confession, is put to the test of litigation. I have no desire whatsoever to share the responsibility for any such impact on the present criminal process.

In some unknown number of cases the Court's rule will return a killer, a rapist, or other criminal to the streets and to the environment which produced him, to repeat his crime whenever it pleases him. As a consequence, there will not be a gain, but a loss, in human dignity. The real concern is not the unfortunate consequences of this new decision on the criminal law as an abstract, disembodied series of authoritative proscriptions, but the impact on those who rely on the public authority for protection and who without it can only engage in violent self-help with guns, knives, and the help of their neighbors similarly inclined.

Questions

1. According to the Supreme Court, what do the words *custody* and *interrogation* mean?

2. Why is custodial interrogation "inherently coercive," according to the majority?

3. Identify and explain the criteria for waiving the right against self-incrimination in custodial interrogation.

4. On what grounds do the dissenters disagree with the majority's decision? What interests are in conflict, according to the Court?

5. How do the majority and the dissent explain the balance of interests established by the Constitution?

Just what impact do the *Miranda* warnings have on interrogation and confessions? To answer this, we'll examine the *Miranda* bright-line rules, the meaning of "custody," the public safety exception to the rules, and the Fifth and Sixth Amendment meanings of "interrogation."

LO 4 The *Miranda* "Bright-Line" Rules

The Supreme Court intended the *Miranda* warnings to provide a *bright-line rule*—sometimes called a "per se rule"—to prevent police coercion while still allowing police pressure. The rule is that whenever police officers conduct a custodial interrogation, they have to give suspects the now famous four warnings:

1. You have a right to remain silent.

2. Anything you say can and will be used against you in court.

3. You have a right to a lawyer.

4. If you can't afford a lawyer, one will be appointed for you.

What's the reason for the bright-line rule? To avoid what the Court called the "inherently coercive nature of custodial interrogation."

The Court created five more bright-line rules for the interrogating officer, prosecutors, and judges. But police officers don't have to tell suspects about these rules:

1. Suspects can claim their right to remain silent at any time. If at any time they indicate in any way they don't want to talk, the interrogation has to stop immediately.

2. If, before interrogation begins, suspects indicate in any manner they want a lawyer, interrogation can't start; if it has started already, it has to stop immediately.

3. Any statement obtained without a lawyer present puts a "heavy burden" on the prosecution to prove defendants waived two constitutional rights: the right against self-incrimination and the right to a lawyer. Neither silence nor later confessions count as a waiver. (See the case excerpt, *Berghuis v. Thompkins* 2010, p. 315.)

4. Statements obtained in violation of the rules can't be admitted into evidence.

5. Exercising the right against self-incrimination can't be penalized. So prosecutors can't suggest or even hint at trial that the defendant's refusal to talk is a sign of guilt.

One final point about the bright-line *Miranda* rule: On TV cop shows, whenever, wherever, and as soon as police officers arrest anyone, they "mirandize" her immediately, or say something like, "Read him his rights." However, *Miranda v. Arizona* doesn't command officers to warn suspects "whenever" they arrest them. Officers have to give the famous warnings only if they intend both to (1) take the suspects into custody and (2) interrogate them. These limits still leave the police plenty of leeway for questioning individuals who aren't in custody, including:

- People at crime scenes
- People who are not yet suspects
- People during Fourth Amendment stops (Chapter 4)

LO 4 The Meaning of "Custody"

According to *Miranda*, **custody** means being held by the police in a police station, *or* depriving an individual of "freedom of action in any significant way." Deciding whether suspects are in "custody" boils down to "whether there was a formal arrest or restraint on freedom of movement of the degree associated with a formal arrest." The Court used this language to prevent police officers from getting around the *Miranda* requirements by questioning suspects away from a police station. The Court was sending the message that *Miranda* targets coercive *atmospheres*, not just coercive *places*.

Whether suspects are in custody depends on a case-by-case evaluation of the totality of circumstances surrounding the interrogation. These circumstances include:

- Whether officers had probable cause to arrest
- Whether officers intended to detain suspects
- Whether suspects believed their freedom was significantly restricted
- Whether the investigation had focused on the suspect
- The language officers used to summon suspects
- The physical surroundings
- The amount of evidence of guilt officers presented to suspects
- How long suspects were detained
- The amounts and kinds of pressure officers used to detain suspects

Three types of detentions don't qualify as custody:

1. Detaining drivers and passengers during routine traffic stops (*Berkemer v. McCarty* 1984)

2. Requiring probationers to attend routine meetings with their probation officers (*Minnesota v. Murphy* 1984)

3. Detaining persons during the execution of search warrants (*Michigan v. Summers* 1981)

What about questioning suspects in their homes? It depends on the totality of the circumstances in each case. In *Orozco v. Texas*, four police officers entered Reyes Arias Orozco's bedroom at 4:00 a.m., woke him up, and immediately started questioning him about a shooting. The Court held that even though Orozco was at home in his own bed he was still in custody, because he was "deprived of his liberty in a significant way." The Court relied heavily on the officers' testimony that from the moment Orozco gave them his name, he wasn't free to go anywhere. On the other hand, the Court ruled that Carl Mathiason (*Oregon v. Mathiason* 1977) and Jerry Beheler (*California v. Beheler* 1983) were not in custody when they went voluntarily to their local police stations and confessed.

In *Berkemer v. McCarty* (1984), the U.S. Supreme Court held that brief questioning during a traffic stop was not a "custodial interrogation."

CASE

Was He "in Custody"?

Berkemer, Sheriff of Franklin County v. McCarty
468 U.S. 420 (1984)

HISTORY

Richard McCarty was convicted of operating a motor vehicle while under the influence of alcohol and/or drugs. The U.S. District Court for the Southern District of Ohio denied his petition for habeas corpus. The U.S. Court of Appeals reversed. The U.S. Supreme Court granted certiorari and affirmed.

—MARSHALL, J.

FACTS

On the evening of March 31, 1980, Trooper Williams of the Ohio State Highway Patrol observed Richard McCarty's car weaving in and out of a lane on Interstate Highway 270. After following the car for two miles, Williams forced McCarty to stop and asked him to get out of the vehicle. When McCarty complied, Williams noticed that he was having difficulty standing. At that point, "Williams concluded that McCarty would be charged with a traffic offense and, therefore, his freedom to leave the scene was terminated." However, McCarty was not told he would be taken into custody.

Williams then asked McCarty to perform a field sobriety test, commonly known as a "balancing test." McCarty could not do so without falling. While still at the scene of the traffic stop, Williams asked McCarty whether he had been using intoxicants. McCarty replied "he had consumed two beers and had smoked several joints of marijuana a short time before." McCarty's speech was slurred, and Williams had difficulty understanding him. Williams thereupon formally placed McCarty under arrest and transported him in the patrol car to the Franklin County Jail.

At the jail, McCarty was given an intoxilyzer test to determine the concentration of alcohol in his blood. The test did not detect any alcohol whatsoever in his system. Williams then resumed questioning McCarty in order to obtain information for inclusion in the State Highway Patrol Alcohol Influence Report. McCarty answered affirmatively a question whether he had been drinking. When then asked if he was under the influence of alcohol, he said, "I guess, barely." Williams next asked McCarty to indicate on the form whether the marijuana he had smoked had been treated with any chemicals. In the section of the report headed "Remarks," McCarty wrote, "No angel dust or PCP in the pot."

At no point in this sequence of events did Williams or anyone else tell McCarty that he had a right to remain silent, to consult with an attorney, and to have an attorney appointed for him if he could not afford one.

McCarty was charged with operating a motor vehicle while under the influence of alcohol and/or drugs. Under Ohio law, that offense is a first-degree misdemeanor and is punishable by fine or imprisonment for up to six months. Incarceration for a minimum of three days is mandatory. McCarty moved to exclude the various incriminating statements he had made to Trooper Williams on the ground that introduction into evidence of those statements would violate the Fifth Amendment insofar as he had not been informed of his constitutional rights prior to his interrogation.

When the trial court denied the motion, McCarty pleaded "no contest" and was found guilty. He was sentenced to 90 days in jail, 80 of which were suspended, and was fined $300, $100 of which were suspended. According to Ohio law, "The plea of no contest does not preclude a defendant from asserting upon appeal that the trial court prejudicially erred in ruling on a pretrial motion, including a pretrial motion to suppress evidence." We granted certiorari to resolve confusion in the federal and state courts regarding the applicability of our ruling in *Miranda* to questioning of motorists detained pursuant to traffic stops.

OPINION

To assess the admissibility of the self-incriminating statements made by McCarty prior to his formal arrest, we are obliged to decide whether the roadside questioning of a motorist detained pursuant to a routine traffic stop should be considered "custodial interrogation." A traffic stop significantly curtails the "freedom of action" of the driver and the passengers of the detained vehicle. Certainly few motorists would feel free either to disobey a directive to pull over or to leave the scene of a traffic stop without being told they might do so. Thus, we must decide whether a traffic stop exerts upon a detained person pressures that sufficiently impair his free exercise of his privilege against self-incrimination to require that he be warned of his constitutional rights.

Two features of an ordinary traffic stop mitigate the danger that a person questioned will be induced "to speak where he would not otherwise do so freely." First, the vast majority of roadside detentions last only a few minutes. A motorist's expectations, when he sees a policeman's light flashing behind him, are that he will be obliged to spend a short period of time answering questions and waiting while the officer checks his license and registration, that he may then be given a citation, but that in the end he most likely will be allowed to continue on his way. In this respect, questioning incident to an ordinary traffic stop is quite different from stationhouse interrogation, which frequently is prolonged, and in which the detainee often is aware that questioning will continue until he provides his interrogators the answers they seek.

Second, circumstances associated with the typical traffic stop are not such that the motorist feels completely at the mercy of the police. To be sure, the aura of authority surrounding an armed, uniformed officer and the knowledge that the officer has some discretion in deciding whether to issue a citation, in combination, exert some pressure on the detainee to respond to questions.

But other aspects of the situation substantially offset these forces. Perhaps most importantly, the typical traffic stop is public. Passersby, on foot or in other cars, witness the interaction of officer and motorist. This exposure to public view both reduces the ability of an unscrupulous policeman to use illegitimate means to elicit self-incriminating statements and diminishes the motorist's fear that, if he does not cooperate, he will be subjected to abuse. The fact that the detained motorist typically is confronted by only one or at most two policemen further mutes his sense of vulnerability. In short, the atmosphere surrounding an ordinary traffic stop is substantially less "police dominated" than that surrounding the kinds of interrogation at issue in *Miranda*.

The safeguards prescribed by *Miranda* become applicable as soon as a suspect's freedom of action is curtailed to a "degree associated with formal arrest." If a motorist who has been detained pursuant to a traffic stop thereafter is subjected to treatment that renders him "in custody" for practical purposes, he will be entitled to the full panoply of protections prescribed by *Miranda*.

Turning to the case before us, we find nothing in the record that indicates that McCarty should have been given *Miranda* warnings at any point prior to the time Trooper Williams placed him under arrest. We reject the contention that the initial stop of McCarty's car, by itself, rendered him "in custody." And McCarty has failed to demonstrate that, at any time between the initial stop and the arrest, he was subjected to restraints comparable to those associated with a formal arrest. Only a short

(*continued*)

period of time elapsed between the stop and the arrest. At no point during that interval was McCarty informed that his detention would not be temporary.

Nor do other aspects of the interaction of Williams and McCarty support the contention that McCarty was exposed to "custodial interrogation" at the scene of the stop. A single police officer asked McCarty a modest number of questions and requested him to perform a simple balancing test at a location visible to passing motorists. Treatment of this sort cannot fairly be characterized as the functional equivalent of formal arrest.

We conclude that McCarty was not taken into custody for the purposes of *Miranda* until Williams arrested him. Consequently, the statements McCarty made prior to that point were admissible against him.

AFFIRMED.

Questions

1. List all the facts relevant to deciding whether Richard McCarty's freedom was "limited in any significant way."

2. Summarize the arguments the Court gives for its rule that people stopped for traffic violations aren't typically in custody.

3. List the facts and circumstances in *Miranda* and *McCarty* that differ.

4. According to the Court, when can a noncustodial traffic stop turn into a custodial stop for purposes of *Miranda*?

5. Summarize how the Court applied its definition of "custody" to the stop of Richard McCarty.

LO 5   The Meaning of "Interrogation"

The word *interrogation* doesn't appear in the Fifth Amendment self-incrimination clause or the Sixth Amendment right-to-counsel clause. But, as you've already learned (p. 298), it appears in the *Miranda* bright-line rules that inform officers of what they don't have to tell suspects in custody whom they want to question.

The U.S. Supreme Court has adopted two tests to determine whether police questioning amounts to interrogation:

1. The Fifth Amendment "functional equivalent of a question" test
2. The Sixth Amendment "deliberately eliciting a response" test

Let's look more closely at each of the tests.

LO 5   *The Fifth Amendment "functional equivalent of a question" test*

The Supreme Court adopted and applied the "**functional equivalent of a question**" **test** in *Rhode Island v. Innis* (1980). Thomas Innis, a cab driver, was arrested for robbing and murdering another cab driver, John Mulvaney, with a sawed-off shotgun. Officers immediately, and several times after that, gave Innis the *Miranda* warnings; Innis said he wanted to talk to a lawyer. Three officers put Innis in the squad car to take him to the station. On the way, the officers talked among themselves about finding the shotgun because there was a school for handicapped kids nearby. At that point, Innis said he'd show them where the gun was; he did.

The Rhode Island state court tried and convicted Innis of murder. The Rhode Island supreme court overturned the conviction because the officers got his confession by "subtle coercion" that was equivalent to *Miranda* interrogation (296). The U.S. Supreme Court was faced with choosing between a narrow view of interrogation—namely, that it includes only direct questions—and a broad view like that adopted by the Rhode Island court. According to the Court, "'Interrogation' under *Miranda* refers not only to express questioning, but also to any words or actions on the part of the police that the police should know are reasonably likely to elicit an incriminating response from the suspect" (300–03).

The Sixth Amendment "deliberately eliciting a response" test

The *Innis* "functional equivalent" definition is based on the Fifth Amendment right against self-incrimination. It differs from the Sixth Amendment right-to-counsel clause, which applies only to interrogation after formal charges are brought. (The Sixth Amendment commands that "in all criminal prosecutions, the accused shall . . . have the assistance of counsel.") The test for interrogation after formal charges, called the **"deliberately eliciting a response" test**, focuses squarely on police intent.

The "deliberately elicited" test provides broader protection to interrogated suspects and more restrictions on interrogating officers. Notice that the Sixth Amendment says nothing about coercion; it guarantees the right to counsel in *all* criminal prosecutions (italics added). "Prosecution" means when the government starts formal proceedings (formal charge, preliminary hearing, indictment, information, or arraignment). At that point, the Sixth Amendment kicks in and defendants can always have their lawyers present. Any incriminating statements suspects make when a lawyer isn't present, even if they're voluntary, violate the suspect's right to counsel.

For example, in *Massiah v. U.S.* (1964), Winston Massiah was indicted for cocaine dealing and released on bail. While he was on bail, the police arranged for Massiah's co-defendant to discuss with him the pair's pending trial in a car while the co-defendant was wired with a radio transmitter hooked up to police officers. The Court held that Massiah's right to counsel was violated even though officers never directly asked him anything. According to the Court, the incriminating words Massiah communicated to his co-defendant resulted from interrogation because they "were deliberately elicited from him" by federal agents.

Why has the Supreme Court interpreted interrogation broadly once the right to counsel kicks in? Two reasons: First, once formal proceedings begin, all the power of the government is aimed at convicting criminal defendants. Second, at this stage, technical knowledge of the law and its procedures becomes critical. Defendants need experts (defense lawyers) to guide them through the maze of highly technical rules and procedures just as the state relies on its own experts (prosecutors) to do the same for the government.

In *Brewer v. Williams* (1977), the Court applied the "deliberately elicited" test to Robert Williams's confession (although it was true) to the grisly murder of a 10-year-old girl on Christmas Eve in Des Moines, Iowa. Shortly after the murder, Williams drove to Davenport, 160 miles east of Des Moines. On the morning of December 26, on the advice of his lawyer, Williams turned himself in to the Davenport police.

In the presence of the Des Moines chief of police and Detective Leaming, Henry McKnight, Williams's lawyer, told Williams that Des Moines police officers would be coming to pick him up and take him back to Des Moines. He assured Williams that the officers wouldn't interrogate him, or mistreat him, and told him that he shouldn't talk to the officers. In the meantime, Williams was arraigned before a Davenport judge on an outstanding arrest warrant. The judge gave Williams his *Miranda* warnings and ordered him locked up in jail.

Detective Leaming and a fellow officer picked up Williams at about noon. Detective Leaming repeated the *Miranda* warnings and told Williams that they knew he was represented by a local attorney and McKnight in Des Moines. He told Williams, "I want you to remember this, because we'll be visiting between here and Des Moines." On the trip, Williams told the officers several times, "When I get to Des Moines and see Mr. McKnight I'm going to tell you the whole story" (391). Leaming knew that Williams was a former mental patient and that he was deeply religious.

Not long after they left Davenport, Leaming delivered what came to be known as his "Christian burial" speech. Referring to Williams as "Reverend," the detective said,

> I want to give you something to think about while we're traveling down the road. Number one, I want you to observe the weather conditions, it's raining, it's sleeting, it's freezing, driving is very treacherous, visibility is poor, it's going to be dark early this evening. They are predicting several inches of snow for tonight, and I feel that you yourself are the only person that knows where this little girl's body is, that you yourself have only been there once, and if you get a snow on top of it you yourself may be unable to find it. And, since we will be going right past the area on the way into Des Moines, I feel that we could stop and locate the body, that the parents of this little girl should be entitled to a Christian burial for the little girl who was snatched away from them on Christmas Eve and murdered. And I feel we should stop and locate it on the way in rather than waiting until morning and trying to come back out after a snowstorm and possibly not being able to find it at all. (392–93)

As the car approached Mitchellville, Iowa, Williams told the officers that he'd show the officers where the body was; he took them to the victim's body.

Williams was indicted for first-degree murder. Before trial, his counsel moved to suppress all evidence relating to or resulting from any statements Williams had made during the automobile ride from Davenport to Des Moines. The U.S. Supreme Court granted a writ of habeas corpus to Williams. According to the majority,

> The crime of which Williams was convicted was senseless and brutal, calling for swift and energetic action by the police to apprehend the perpetrator and gather evidence with which he could be convicted. No mission of law enforcement officials is more important. Although we do not lightly affirm the issuance of a writ of habeas corpus in this case, so clear a violation of the Sixth and Fourteenth Amendments as here occurred cannot be condoned. The pressures on state executive and judicial officers charged with the administration of the criminal law are great, especially when the crime is murder and the victim a small child. But it is precisely the predictability of those pressures that makes imperative a resolute loyalty to the guarantees that the Constitution extends to us all. (406)

The majority decision prompted strong dissents from several justices, one of them extremely angry that this horrible crime was going to go unpunished:

> The consequence of the majority's decision is extremely serious. A mentally disturbed killer whose guilt is not in question may be released. Why? The police did nothing wrong, let alone anything unconstitutional. To anyone not lost in the intricacies of the prophylactic rules of *Miranda v. Arizona*, the result in this case seems utterly senseless. (439)

Eventually, Williams was retried, convicted, and the Court upheld his conviction, in *Nix v. Williams* (1984).

LO 6 The Public Safety Exception

By now, you should realize that the U.S. Supreme Court substantially softened the *Miranda* ruling that all custodial interrogations are "inherently" coercive, and that all statements made without the famous warnings are involuntary and not admissible in court. We've seen how they've done this in defining *custody* and *interrogation* in such a way that it doesn't hamper law enforcement on the street. A letter from three retired FBI agents to President Obama includes this revealing passage,

> *Miranda* rules are nimble enough to handle situations as they arise. In our decades of working in law enforcement, including the years following 9/11, *Miranda* rights never interfered with our ability to obtain useful information or make prosecutable cases. (Reprinted in Ackerman 2010)

We'll turn now to another reason why *Miranda* rules are so "nimble," namely the exceptions to the warning requirement. Technically, this means that even though custodial interrogation without warning violates *Miranda*, not all evidence obtained without the warnings is banned from the courtroom to prove guilt. (Recall that the exclusionary rule doesn't ban all (italics) evidence obtained during unreasonable searches and seizures, Chapter 3, p. 52.) For example, if defendants decide to take the stand during trial, the prosecution can use statements they made in violation of *Miranda* to impeach (destroy the credibility of) defendants (*Harris v. New York* 1971). Also, unwarned statements made by defendants that turn up incriminating *physical* evidence, like the gun in *Quarles*, are admissible to prove defendants' guilt at trial (*U.S. v. Patane* 2004, 643–44).

Let's look first at the U.S. Supreme Court opinion that created the public safety exception, and then look at some empirical research regarding how lower federal and state courts have applied the exception.

LO 6   New York v. Quarles *(1984)*

The **public safety exception (PSE)** applies to police officers who question suspects in custody without first administering the *Miranda* warnings. Incriminating statements, and any evidence derived from the unwarned statements, are admissible at defendants' trials *whenever trial judges believe the purpose of the questioning is to protect public safety*. Our next case excerpt, *New York v. Quarles*, details how the U.S. Supreme Court created the PSE. Citing the "overriding considerations of public safety," the Court relaxed the *Miranda* warning requirements and admitted Quarles's incriminating statements. After the excerpt, we'll look at some important empirical research regarding how the PSE operates in practice.

Benjamin Quarles, while in police custody, and without *Miranda* warnings, answered the officer's question, "Where's the gun?" with the incriminating words, "It's over there." The U.S. Supreme Court ruled the statement admissible because the public safety trumped Quarles's *Miranda* rights.

CASE

Did Public Safety Trump His Miranda Rights?

New York v. Benjamin Quarles
467 U.S. 649 (1984)

HISTORY

Benjamin Quarles (Quarles) was charged in the New York trial court with criminal possession of a weapon. The trial court suppressed the gun in question, and a statement made by Quarles, because the statement was obtained by police before they read Quarles his *"Miranda* rights." The New York Court of Appeals affirmed. We granted certiorari, and we now reverse. We conclude that under

(continued)

the circumstances involved in this case, overriding considerations of public safety justify the officer's failure to provide *Miranda* warnings before he asked questions devoted to locating the abandoned weapon.

—REHNQUIST, J., joined by BURGER, CJ, and WHITE, BLACKMUN, and POWELL, JJ.

FACTS

On September 11, 1980, at approximately 12:30 a.m., Officer Frank Kraft and Officer Sal Scarring were on road patrol in Queens, N.Y., when a young woman approached their car. She told them that she had just been raped by a Black male, approximately six feet tall, who was wearing a black jacket with the name "Big Ben" printed in yellow letters on the back. She told the officers that the man had just entered an A & P supermarket located nearby and that the man was carrying a gun.

The officers drove the woman to the supermarket, and Officer Kraft entered the store while Officer Scarring radioed for assistance. Officer Kraft quickly spotted Quarles, who matched the description given by the woman, approaching a checkout counter. Apparently upon seeing the officer, Quarles turned and ran toward the rear of the store, and Officer Kraft pursued him with a drawn gun. When Quarles turned the corner at the end of an aisle, Officer Kraft lost sight of him for several seconds, and upon regaining sight of Quarles, ordered him to stop and put his hands over his head.

Although more than three other officers had arrived on the scene by that time, Officer Kraft was the first to reach Quarles. He frisked him and discovered that he was wearing a shoulder holster which was then empty. After handcuffing him, Officer Kraft asked him where the gun was. Quarles nodded in the direction of some empty cartons and responded, "the gun is over there." Officer Kraft thereafter retrieved a loaded .38–caliber revolver from one of the cartons, formally placed Quarles under arrest, and read him his *Miranda* rights from a printed card. Quarles indicated that he would be willing to answer questions without an attorney present. Officer Kraft then asked Quarles if he owned the gun and where he had purchased it. Quarles answered that he did own it and that he had purchased it in Miami, Fla.

OPINION

We believe that this case presents a situation where concern for public safety must be paramount to adherence to the literal language of the prophylactic rules enunciated in *Miranda*.

The Fifth Amendment guarantees that "no person . . . shall be compelled in any criminal case to be a witness against himself." In *Miranda* this Court for the first time extended the Fifth Amendment privilege against compulsory self-incrimination to individuals subjected to custodial interrogation by the police. The Fifth Amendment itself does not prohibit all incriminating admissions; "absent some officially coerced self-accusation, the Fifth Amendment privilege is not violated by even the most damning admissions."

The *Miranda* Court, however, presumed that interrogation in certain custodial circumstances is inherently coercive and held that statements made under those circumstances are inadmissible unless the suspect is specifically informed of his *Miranda* rights and freely decides to forgo those rights. The prophylactic *Miranda* warnings therefore are "not themselves rights protected by the Constitution but are instead measures to insure that the right against compulsory self-incrimination is protected." Requiring *Miranda* warnings before custodial interrogation provides "practical reinforcement" for the Fifth Amendment right.

In this case we have before us no claim that Quarles's statements were actually compelled by police conduct which overcame his will to resist. Thus the only issue before us is whether Officer Kraft was justified in failing to make available to Quarles the procedural safeguards associated with the privilege against compulsory self-incrimination since *Miranda*.

We hold that on these facts there is a "public safety" exception to the requirement that *Miranda* warnings be given before a suspect's answers may be admitted into evidence, and that the availability of that exception does not depend upon the motivation of the individual officers involved. In a kaleidoscopic situation such as the one confronting these officers, where spontaneity rather than adherence to a police manual is necessarily the order of the day, the application of the exception which we recognize today should not be made to depend on after-the-fact findings at a suppression hearing concerning the subjective motivation of the arresting officer. Undoubtedly most police officers, if placed in Officer Kraft's position, would act out of a host of different, instinctive, and largely unverifiable motives—their own safety, the safety of others, and perhaps as well the desire to obtain incriminating evidence from the suspect.

Whatever the motivation of individual officers in such a situation, we do not believe that the doctrinal underpinnings of *Miranda* require that it be applied in all its rigor to a situation in which police officers ask questions reasonably prompted by a concern for the public safety. The *Miranda* decision was based in large part on this Court's view that the warnings which it required police to give to suspects in custody would reduce the likelihood that the suspects would fall victim to constitutionally impermissible practices of police interrogation in the presumptively coercive environment of the station house.

The police in this case, in the very act of apprehending a suspect, were confronted with the immediate necessity of ascertaining the whereabouts of a gun which they had every reason to believe the suspect had just removed from his empty holster and discarded in the supermarket. So long as the gun was concealed somewhere in the supermarket, with its actual whereabouts unknown, it obviously posed more than one danger to the public safety: an accomplice might make use of it, a customer or employee might later come upon it.

In such a situation, if the police are required to recite the familiar *Miranda* warnings before asking the whereabouts of the gun, suspects in Quarles's position might well be deterred from responding. Procedural safeguards which deter a suspect from responding were deemed acceptable in *Miranda* in order to protect the Fifth Amendment privilege; when the primary social cost of those added protections is the possibility of fewer convictions, the *Miranda* majority was willing to bear that cost. Here, had *Miranda* warnings deterred Quarles from responding to Officer Kraft's question about the whereabouts of the gun, the cost would have been something more than merely the failure to obtain evidence useful in convicting Quarles. Officer Kraft needed an answer to his question not simply to make his case against Quarles but to insure that further danger to the public did not result from the concealment of the gun in a public area.

We conclude that the need for answers to questions in a situation posing a threat to the public safety outweighs the need for the prophylactic rule protecting the Fifth Amendment's privilege against self-incrimination. We decline to place officers such as Officer Kraft in the untenable position of having to consider, often in a matter of seconds, whether it best serves society for them to ask the necessary questions without the *Miranda* warnings and render whatever probative evidence they uncover inadmissible, or for them to give the warnings in order to preserve the admissibility of evidence they might uncover but possibly damage or destroy their ability to obtain that evidence and neutralize the volatile situation confronting them.

In recognizing a narrow exception to the *Miranda* rule in this case, we acknowledge that to some degree we lessen the desirable clarity of that rule. At least in part in order to preserve its clarity, we have over the years refused to sanction attempts to expand our *Miranda* holding. But as we have pointed out, we believe that the exception which we recognize today lessens the necessity of that on-the-scene balancing process. The exception will not be difficult for police officers to apply because in each case it will be circumscribed by the exigency which justifies it. We think police officers can and will distinguish almost instinctively between questions necessary to secure their own safety or the safety of the public and questions designed solely to elicit testimonial evidence from a suspect.

The facts of this case clearly demonstrate that distinction and an officer's ability to recognize it. Officer Kraft asked only the question necessary to locate the missing gun before advising Quarles of his rights. It was only after securing the loaded revolver and giving the warnings that he continued with investigatory questions about the ownership and place of purchase of the gun. The exception which we recognize today, far from complicating the thought processes and the on-the-scene judgments of police officers, will simply free them to follow their legitimate instincts when confronting situations presenting a danger to the public safety.

We hold that the Court of Appeals in this case erred in excluding the statement, "the gun is over there," and the gun because of the officer's failure to read Quarles his *Miranda* rights before attempting to locate the weapon. Accordingly, we hold that it also erred in excluding the subsequent statements as illegal fruits of a *Miranda* violation. We therefore reverse and remand for further proceedings not inconsistent with this opinion.

It is so ordered.

O'CONNOR, dissenting in part.

The *Miranda* Court held that "the prosecution may not use statements, whether exculpatory or inculpatory, stemming from custodial interrogation of the defendant unless it demonstrates the use of procedural safeguards effective to secure the privilege against self-incrimination." Those safeguards included the now familiar *Miranda* warnings. The defendant could waive these rights, but any waiver had to be made "knowingly and intelligently," and the burden was placed on the prosecution to prove that such a waiver had voluntarily been made. If the *Miranda* warnings were not properly administered or if no valid waiver could be shown, then all responses to interrogation made by the accused "while in custody or otherwise deprived of his freedom of action in any significant way" were to be presumed coerced and excluded from evidence at trial.

Since the time *Miranda* was decided, the Court has repeatedly refused to bend the literal terms of that decision. To be sure, the Court has been sensitive to the substantial burden the *Miranda* rules place on local law enforcement efforts, and consequently has refused to extend the decision or to increase its strictures on law enforcement agencies in almost any way. As a consequence, the meaning of *Miranda* has become reasonably clear and law enforcement practices have adjusted to its strictures.

The justification the Court provides for upsetting the equilibrium that has finally been achieved—that police cannot and should not balance considerations of public safety against the individual's interest in avoiding compulsory testimonial self-incrimination—really misses the critical question to be decided.

Miranda has never been read to prohibit the police from asking questions to secure the public safety. Rather, the critical question *Miranda* addresses is who shall bear the cost of securing the public safety when such questions

(continued)

are asked and answered: the defendant or the State. *Miranda*, for better or worse, found the resolution of that question implicit in the prohibition against compulsory self-incrimination and placed the burden on the State. When police ask custodial questions without administering the required warnings, *Miranda* quite clearly requires that the answers received be presumed compelled and that they be excluded from evidence at trial.

The Court concedes, as it must, both that Quarles was in "custody" and subject to "interrogation" and that his statement "the gun is over there" was compelled within the meaning of our precedent. In my view, since there is nothing about an exigency that makes custodial interrogation any less compelling, a principled application of *Miranda* requires that Quarles's statement be suppressed.

DISSENT

MARSHALL, J., joined by BRENNAN
and STEVENS, JJ.

Justice MARSHALL, with whom Justice BRENNAN and Justice STEVENS join, dissenting.

The majority's entire analysis rests on the factual assumption that the public was at risk during Quarles's interrogation. This assumption is completely in conflict with the facts as found by New York's highest court. Before the interrogation began, Quarles had been "reduced to a condition of physical powerlessness." Contrary to the majority's speculations, Quarles was not believed to have, nor did he in fact have, an accomplice to come to his rescue. When the questioning began, the arresting officers were sufficiently confident of their safety to put away their guns. As Officer Kraft acknowledged at the suppression hearing, "the situation was under control." Based on Officer Kraft's own testimony, the New York Court of Appeals found: "Nothing suggests that any of the officers was by that time concerned for his own physical safety." The Court of Appeals also determined that there was no evidence that the interrogation was prompted by the arresting officers' concern for the public's safety.

The majority attempts to slip away from these unambiguous findings of New York's highest court by proposing that danger be measured by objective facts rather than the subjective intentions of arresting officers. Though clever, this ploy was anticipated by the New York Court of Appeals: "There is no evidence in the record before us that there were exigent circumstances posing a risk to the public safety. . . ."

The New York court's conclusion that neither Quarles nor his missing gun posed a threat to the public's safety is amply supported by the evidence presented at the suppression hearing. Again contrary to the majority's intimations, no customers or employees were wandering about the store in danger of coming across Quarles's discarded weapon. Although the supermarket was open to the public, Quarles's arrest took place during the middle of the night when the store was apparently deserted except for the clerks at the checkout counter. The police could easily have cordoned off the store and searched for the missing gun. Had they done so, they would have found the gun forthwith.

The police were well aware that Quarles had discarded his weapon somewhere near the scene of the arrest. As the State acknowledged before the New York Court of Appeals: "After Officer Kraft had handcuffed and frisked the defendant in the supermarket, *he knew with a high degree of certainty that the defendant's gun was within the immediate vicinity of the encounter. He undoubtedly would have searched for it in the carton a few feet away without the defendant having looked in that direction and saying that it was there.*"

In this case, there was convincing, indeed almost overwhelming, evidence to support the New York court's conclusion that Quarles's hidden weapon did not pose a risk either to the arresting officers or to the public. The majority ignores this evidence and sets aside the factual findings of the New York Court of Appeals. More cynical observers might well conclude that a state court's findings of fact deserve a high measure of deference, only when deference works against the interests of a criminal defendant.

The end result, will be a finespun new doctrine on public safety exigencies incident to custodial interrogation, complete with the hairsplitting distinctions that currently plague our Fourth Amendment jurisprudence. In the meantime, the courts will have to dedicate themselves to spinning this new web of doctrines, and the country's law enforcement agencies will have to suffer patiently through the frustrations of another period of constitutional uncertainty.

The majority's error stems from a serious misunderstanding of *Miranda v. Arizona* and of the Fifth Amendment upon which that decision was based. The majority implies that *Miranda* consisted of no more than a judicial balancing act in which the benefits of "enlarged protection for the Fifth Amendment privilege" were weighed against "the cost to society in terms of fewer convictions of guilty suspects." The majority misreads *Miranda*. Though the *Miranda* dissent prophesized dire consequences, the *Miranda* Court refused to allow such concerns to weaken the protections of the Constitution.

Whether society would be better off if the police warned suspects of their rights before beginning an interrogation or whether the advantages of giving such warnings would outweigh their costs did not inform the *Miranda* decision. On the contrary, the *Miranda* Court was concerned with the proscriptions of the Fifth Amendment, and, in particular, whether the Self-Incrimination Clause permits the government to prosecute individuals based on statements made in the course of custodial interrogations.

Miranda v. Arizona was the culmination of a century-long inquiry into how this Court should deal with confessions made during custodial interrogations.

When *Miranda* reached this Court, it was undisputed that both the States and the Federal Government were constitutionally prohibited from prosecuting defendants with confessions coerced during custodial interrogations. As a theoretical matter, the law was clear. In practice, however, the courts found it exceedingly difficult to determine whether a given confession had been coerced. Difficulties of proof and subtleties of interrogation technique made it impossible in most cases for the judiciary to decide with confidence whether the defendant had voluntarily confessed his guilt or whether his testimony had been unconstitutionally compelled. Courts around the country were spending countless hours reviewing the facts of individual custodial interrogations.

Miranda dealt with these practical problems. After a detailed examination of police practices and a review of its previous decisions in the area, the Court in *Miranda* determined that custodial interrogations are inherently coercive. The Court therefore created a constitutional presumption that statements made during custodial interrogations are compelled in violation of the Fifth Amendment and are thus inadmissible in criminal prosecutions. As a result of the Court's decision in *Miranda*, a statement made during a custodial interrogation may be introduced as proof of a defendant's guilt only if the prosecution demonstrates that the defendant knowingly and intelligently waived his constitutional rights before making the statement. The now-familiar *Miranda* warnings offer law enforcement authorities a clear, easily administered device for ensuring that criminal suspects understand their constitutional rights well enough to waive them and to engage in consensual custodial interrogation.

The irony of the majority's decision is that the public's safety can be perfectly well protected without abridging the Fifth Amendment. If a bomb is about to explode or the public is otherwise imminently imperiled, the police are free to interrogate suspects without advising them of their constitutional rights. Such unconsented questioning may take place not only when police officers act on instinct but also when higher faculties lead them to believe that advising a suspect of his constitutional rights might decrease the likelihood that the suspect would reveal life-saving information. If trickery is necessary to protect the public, then the police may trick a suspect into confessing. All the Fifth Amendment forbids is the introduction of coerced statements at trial. As the Court has explained on numerous occasions, this prohibition is the mainstay of our adversarial system of criminal justice. Not only does it protect us against the inherent unreliability of compelled testimony, but it also ensures that criminal investigations will be conducted with integrity and that the judiciary will avoid the taint of official lawlessness.

The policies underlying the Fifth Amendment's privilege against self-incrimination are not diminished simply because testimony is compelled to protect the public's safety. The majority should not be permitted to elude the Amendment's absolute prohibition simply by calculating special costs that arise when the public's safety is at issue. Indeed, were constitutional adjudication always conducted in such an ad hoc manner, the Bill of Rights would be a most unreliable protector of individual liberties.

Questions

1. List the facts the majority opinion relies on to support its conclusion that Quarles was a threat to public safety.

2. State the Court's "public safety exception" to the *Miranda* warning requirement.

3. Summarize the Court's arguments for creating the public safety exception.

4. Summarize Justice O'Connor's reasons for dissenting from the majority's ruling on the public safety exception.

5. List the facts the dissent relies on to conclude that Quarles posed no threat to public safety.

6. Summarize the dissent's arguments against the public safety exception.

7. Which side do you agree with? The majority? The dissent? Back up your answer with facts and arguments in the opinion.

LO 6   *The public safety exception in action*

Joanna Wright examined every federal and state court opinion from 1985 and 2010 that discussed excluding or admitting un-*Mirandized* statements based on the public safety exception. Table 8.3 contains some of her findings:

According to Wright (1323–24), in the most likely PSE scenario, police are pursuing a suspect fleeing the crime scene, or an unidentified suspect described by a

TABLE 8.3 The public safety exception in practice

1. PSE succeeded in between a low of 75% of cases in U.S. District Court and a high of 91% in cases in the U.S. Courts of Appeals (Wright 2011, 1315, Table 1).
2. Overall, the average rate of success of PSE in all federal and state courts is a strikingly consistent 80% (Table 1).
3. The 9/11 terrorist attack had practically no effect on successful PSE use in state courts. PSE increased a mere 2%—from 79% to 81%. And in federal cases, it actually went down 5%, from 84% to 79% (Wright, 1318, Table 3).

4. The rate of success depends on the type of threat.
  a. Bomb   89%
  b. Firearm   82%
  c. Knife   70% (1320, Table 4)

5. The rate of success depends on the demographic threatened.
  a. General public   78%
  b. Law enforcement only   80%
  c. General public and law enforcement   95%

witness within a few hours of the crime, in which a gun is the threat to public safety. The evidence of the threat comes in several forms, including:

1. The crime involved a gun.
2. The victim reported that the suspect had a gun.
3. The officer saw the suspect ditch the gun during the pursuit.
4. The officer saw gun paraphernalia, like an empty holster or ammunition.

When apprehended, police typically ask three questions specifically related to public safety, not to obtain evidence to arrest or prosecute:

1. Where's the gun? (if it's missing)
2. Is the gun loaded?
3. Are you carrying any other weapons? (1324)

> Thus in the prototypical PSE case, law enforcement has fairly credible knowledge of a probability that a suspect is or was armed. The questions eliciting the un-*Mirandized* testimony are usually intended to either identify the location of the firearm or determine whether or not the firearm is loaded. The judiciary will almost always admit statements made in response to these types of questions. While these features depict the prototypical PSE case, they by no means describe the *only* application of the PSE. The judiciary has demonstrated a willingness to apply the PSE quite creatively, requiring only that the pubic safety *could* have been threatened. (1325)

In other words, we're talking about people like Ben Quarles. Figure 8.1 includes a list of cases demonstrating the range of PSE cases in which courts admitted unwarned testimony.

FIGURE 8.1 PSE Cases Admitting Unwarned Incriminating Testimony

---

U.S. v. Harris, *961 F. Supp. 1127, S.D. Ohio (1997)*

Larry Wayne Harris possessed freeze-dried bubonic plague. Police handcuffed and questioned Harris about it before reading him his *Miranda* rights. According to the U.S. District Court for the Southern District of Ohio,

> The Court finds that the public safety exception to *Miranda* applies here. This investigation presented circumstances in which spontaneity rather than adherence to a police manual was the order of the day. Captain Lutz testified that no one in Lancaster had participated in a search for a deadly bacteria and, without assistance from someone who had, the officers had to "fly by the seat of our pants." The evidence shows that the officers were motivated by a concern for public safety when they questioned Harris prior to reading his rights; indeed, concern for public safety motivated this whole investigation as indicated by the presence of the hazardous materials team and the precautions taken by the officers. As in *Quarles*, the officers asked Harris only the questions needed to locate the dangerous instrumentality; Regan then read Harris his rights. In hindsight, it is possible to say that the immediate risk to the public posed by the freeze-dried bacteria was not as significant as the officers thought at the time. At the time the officers were faced by these circumstances, however, it was reasonable for them to anticipate danger from this bacteria and to have serious concern for the safety of the community and for their own safety. Therefore, the Court holds that the public safety exception to the *Miranda* rule applies here. As a result, any statements made by Harris before Lieutenant Regan read him his rights, and any evidence recovered in reliance on those statements, is admissible for purposes of trial.

Thomas v. State *737 A.2d 622 (Md. Spec. App. 1999)*

Edward Thomas snatched a purse. The victim's husband chased Thomas. Police officers joined the pursuit. Thomas started climbing over a fence; Officer Bleach grabbed him by the ankles and pulled him down. Thomas broke free, and the man who had been chasing him started yelling, "Don't let him go. He's the one. He's the one that did it. Don't let him go. Don't let him get away." Thomas tried to climb the fence again, but Bleach pulled him down, managed to get him on the ground in a prone position, and told him again that he was under arrest.

While Bleach was on top of Thomas, attempting to subdue him, Thomas sank his teeth in Bleach's left forearm. As Bleach pulled his arm away from Thomas's mouth, he heard "the flesh rip" and let go of Thomas. Thomas got to his feet and hit Bleach on the side of his face, and then both men exchanged punches for a couple of minutes until other officers arrived and eventually subdued appellant.

Bleach was treated at Northwest Hospital for the bite wound and other injures he sustained in the scuffle with appellant. Thomas had also been taken to the same hospital for examination and treatment. Bleach, concerned that he might have been infected with hepatitis or some other disease through the bite wound, asked appellant to give a blood sample to be tested for certain diseases that may have been transmitted. He told Thomas, "I'm the detective that you bit," and that he needed to know whether Thomas had any diseases. Thomas apologized for biting Bleach and said, "I didn't mean anything by that; nothing personal. You have to understand, I needed to get away." He told Bleach he would allow his blood to be taken.

(continued)

FIGURE 8.1 (continued)

According to the Maryland Court of Special Appeals,

> We perceive no doctrinal difference between a question that would fall within the rescue doctrine ("Where is the [kidnapped] child?") or the public safety exception based on the need to secure the protection of either the public generally or the officer himself ("Where's the gun?") and Detective Bleach's request that appellant submit to a blood test to determine if he had a disease that he might have transmitted to the officer by biting him. If appellant had a disease such as AIDS or hepatitis, it was important that Detective Bleach be informed of it quickly in order that he might (1) undergo prompt treatment and (2) take steps to avoid infecting others, particularly members of his family.
>
> We hold, therefore, that the conversation between Detective Bleach and appellant at the hospital to which both of them had been taken for treatment falls within the public safety exception to the *Miranda* exclusionary rule and, therefore, that the court below did not err in allowing the substance of that conversation to be admitted in evidence.

State v. Granger, 587 N.W.2d 457 (Wis. App. 1998)

La Crosse police officers Thomas Walsh and Brian Puent arrived at a scene of what appeared to be a car accident. They saw car debris scattered along the road and a car door wrapped around the steel I-beam of a billboard sign. They also observed a tire lying on the road.

While surveying the scene, the officers observed a man come running up from an embankment. The man then began to run in an easterly direction, parallel to the officers. The officers yelled for the man to stop, but the man continued to run. The officers chased the man until he crashed through a fence and fell down. As the officers handcuffed the man, they noticed that he had cuts and some blood on him. They asked him if he was okay, and he stated that he was. The officers then escorted him to the squad car. Before reaching the car, the officers asked the man his name, and he responded that his name was Justice Granger. As Granger spoke, the officers smelled alcohol on his breath and believed that he might be intoxicated. The officers asked him whether he was the driver of the car and if anyone else was in the vehicle with him. Granger responded that he was the driver and that he was alone in the vehicle. The officers placed Granger in the backseat of the squad car.

Officer Walsh then went to look for the vehicle. He found the vehicle at the bottom of the embankment near a set of railroad tracks. He also found the bodies of two men, Ken Green and Mark Kast. Kast was unresponsive but breathing. Green, who was lying in the middle of the railroad tracks, was unresponsive and not breathing.

Walsh was concerned that there may have been other passengers in need of medical attention. But due to the rugged nature of the hillside, he was uncertain whether the police would find them. He therefore returned to the squad car and questioned Granger again on whether there were others in the car with him. Granger again stated that he was alone in the vehicle.

Lieutenant Marcou arrived shortly thereafter. He checked Green and Kast. Green was dead but Kast was still alive. Marcou performed CPR on Kast with the assistance of another officer. He then asked Granger if he was the driver. Granger indicated that he was. Marcou asked him if anyone else was in the car with him. Granger once again said that he was alone. Marcou then asked Granger what happened, and Granger responded "I couldn't see—I just couldn't see." None of these officers advised Granger of his *Miranda* rights before questioning him.

(continued)

Kast and Granger were taken to the Emergency Room at Lutheran Hospital. Dr. Ben Wedro examined them and later testified at trial. He determined that Kast had a cerebral hematoma, a small fracture of his neck, and a broken hand. Dr. Wedro stated that Kast had a "decreased level of consciousness," which meant that he was not fully awake, and that his injuries were serious. Dr. Wedro also examined Granger. He performed a neurological exam and a CAT scan to determine if there was bleeding, bruising or swelling of the brain. The results of these tests did not indicate any neurological damage. In fact, Dr. Wedro testified that the results of additional tests indicated that Granger may have been faking his injuries. A blood alcohol content test was also administered, and it indicated that Granger had a BAC of .23 at the time of the accident.

According to the Wisconsin Court of Appeals,

> Granger contends that the "public safety" exception is inapplicable because the police had no evidence that the public was at risk when they first encountered him at the scene. However, with the car debris and tire on the street and a door wrapped around an I-beam, there was evidence of an accident, and with car accidents there is often a risk of serious injury or death, particularly if immediate medical attention is not provided. And after Walsh discovered the car wreckage and the two bodies, this risk became a reality. We therefore conclude that the officers' questioning of Granger about whether he was alone in the car is admissible, because it was for the purpose of possibly saving lives.

THE WAIVER OF THE RIGHT TO REMAIN SILENT

After *Miranda v. Arizona* was decided there was a lot of talk about "handcuffing the police." Both the *Miranda* majority and dissent "expected lots of suspects" would refuse to talk and demand a lawyer, "making interrogation a much smaller part of the American police station procedure than it had become during the 1960s" (Thomas 2004, 1961).

They were wrong. As it turned out, these fears were greatly exaggerated. Three empirical studies (Thomas 2004; Leo 1996a; Cassell and Hayman 1996) based on separate types of evidence reached the following conclusions:

1. Police almost always give the required *Miranda* warnings.
2. Suspects overwhelmingly waive their *Miranda* rights to remain silent and to have a lawyer to help them.
3. Police usually stop interrogating suspects who invoke either their rights to silence and/or to a lawyer.
4. Police rarely use "overtly coercive tactics" to get waivers.
5. Police rarely use "overtly coercive tactics" to get confessions after waivers. (Thomas 2004, 1963)

Be careful about this research. Each study has its limits. Leo's study suffers from the possible observational effect. Leo's conclusions rest on 182 interrogations he observed. Who can say whether police complied with *Miranda* only when Leo was watching? Cassell and Hayman observed prosecutors question police officers about whether they gave suspects the *Miranda* warnings, and how they obtained waivers of suspects' rights.

Did the officers describe their interrogation methods in the "best light" when talking to prosecutors? (Thomas 2004, 1965). Thomas relied on a sample of appellate court opinions dealing with suppression motions in police interrogation and confession cases. Here, the limit is the way facts get filtered in the process of preserving them in suppression motions, and in the appeals of those motions (1967). Despite these limits, the Supreme Court's assessment is probably fair, "Giving the warnings and getting a waiver has generally produced a virtual ticket of admissibility" (*Missouri v. Seibert* 2004, 601).

Because the vast majority of suspects in custody talk to officers without a lawyer in sight, two indispensable Fifth Amendment questions arise:

1. What is a valid waiver of the right against self-incrimination?
2. What is a voluntary confession?

On waiver, *Miranda* said,

> This Court has always set high standards of proof for the waiver of constitutional rights, and we re-assert these standards as applied to custodial interrogation. Since the State is responsible for establishing isolated circumstances under which the interrogation takes place and has the only means of making available corroborated evidence of warnings given during incommunicado interrogation, the burden is rightly on its shoulders.
>
> An express statement that the individual is willing to make a statement and does not want an attorney followed closely by a statement *could* constitute a waiver (italics added). But a valid waiver will not be presumed simply from the silence of the accused after warnings are given or simply from the fact that a confession was in fact eventually obtained. (475)

This statement strongly suggests two important implications regarding waivers of Fifth Amendment rights. First, that there's a distinction between *invoking* the rights and *waiving* them. In other words, suspects don't waive their rights by not invoking them. Second, the *Miranda* Court strongly suggested they were adopting an **express waiver test**, which means that suspects have to make clear statements that indicate they (1) know their rights, (2) know they're giving them up, and (3) know the consequences of giving them up. Lower courts, and later the Supreme Court itself, instead adopted an **implied waiver test**. According to the implied waiver test, prosecution has to prove that the totality of circumstances in each case indicates that, before suspects talked, they knew they had the rights and they knew they were giving them up.

In *North Carolina v. Butler* (1979), officers read Willie Butler his *Miranda* rights. Butler said he knew his rights, but he refused to sign a waiver form. ("I will talk to you but I am not signing any form" [371].) The North Carolina trial court threw out the confession because Butler didn't *expressly* waive his right to remain silent. The North Carolina supreme court affirmed. The U.S. Supreme Court reversed, adopting instead the implied waiver test.

According to Justice Stewart, writing for the majority, an express written or oral waiver of the right to remain silent and/or the right to counsel is "usually strong proof" that the waiver is valid, but it's not always either necessary or sufficient to establish waiver. The courts must presume that a defendant did not waive his rights; the prosecution's burden is great; but in at least some cases waiver can be clearly inferred from the actions and words of the person interrogated. [A valid waiver depends on] the particular facts and circumstances surrounding that case, including the background, experience, and conduct of the accused. (373–75)

TABLE 8.4 Circumstances relevant to showing a knowing waiver

• Intelligence	• Age
• Physical condition	• Ability to understand English
• Education	• Familiarity with the criminal justice system
• Mental condition	

© Cengage Learning

TABLE 8.5 Cases in which courts found a knowing waiver

- No evidence showed the suspect was threatened, tricked, or cajoled. (*Connecticut v. Barrett* 1987)
- The suspect invoked the right to counsel and then after a five-hour ride in the back of a squad car signed a waiver when police officers asked "if there was anything he would like to tell them." (*Henderson v. Florida* 1985)
- The suspect asked for a lawyer, didn't get one, and then signed a waiver after repeated warnings and "nagging" by police officers. (*Watkins v. Virginia* 1986)
- After refusing to sign an express waiver, the defendant talked to the police. (*U.S. v. Barahona* 1993)
- The defendant said "I don't got nothing to say" when he was presented with a waiver form but then answered questions during an interview that followed. (*U.S. v. Banks* 1995)
- The defendant remained silent throughout most of nearly three hours of questioning after being advised of his *Miranda* rights, but he responded "Yes" when asked if he prayed for forgiveness for killing the victim. (*Berghuis v. Thompkins* 2010)

© Cengage Learning

Circumstances commonly considered in making the waiver determination are listed in Table 8.4, and examples of cases in which courts ruled there was a knowing waiver appear in Table 8.5. In *Berghuis v. Thompkins* (2010), our next case excerpt, the U.S. Supreme Court revisited both the invocation and the waiver question in a contentious 5–4 decision.

In *Berghuis v. Thompkins* (2010), the U.S. Supreme Court (5–4) held that criminal suspects who want to protect their right to remain silent have to speak up and unambiguously invoke and waive it.

CASE

Did He "Speak Up" and "Unambiguously" Invoke and Waive His Right to Remain Silent?

Berghuis v. Thompkins
130 S.Ct. 2250 (2010)

HISTORY

Van Chester Thompkins was charged with first-degree murder. The trial court denied his motion to suppress his confession. The jury convicted him and the judge sentenced him to life in prison without parole. Thompkins appealed. The Michigan Court of Appeals affirmed. The U.S. District Court denied his petition for habeas corpus. The U.S. Sixth Circuit Court of Appeals reversed.

(continued)

The U.S. Supreme Court granted certiorari. Mary Berghuis, the warden of a Michigan correctional facility, is the petitioner here, and Van Chester Thompkins, who was convicted, is the respondent. The Supreme Court reversed the Sixth Circuit Court.

—KENNEDY, J., joined by ROBERTS, C.J., and SCALIA, THOMAS, and ALITO, JJ.

FACTS

On January 10, 2000, a shooting occurred outside a mall in Southfield, Michigan. Among the victims was Samuel Morris, who died from multiple gunshot wounds. The other victim, Frederick France, recovered from his injuries and later testified. Thompkins, who was a suspect, fled. About one year later he was found in Ohio and arrested there. Two Southfield police officers traveled to Ohio to interrogate Thompkins, then awaiting transfer to Michigan. The interrogation began around 1:30 p.m. and lasted about three hours. The interrogation was conducted in a room that was 8 by 10 feet, and Thompkins sat in a chair that resembled a school desk (it had an arm on it that swings around to provide a surface to write on). At the beginning of the interrogation, one of the officers, Detective Helgert, presented Thompkins with a form derived from the *Miranda* rule. It stated:

Notification of constitutional rights and statement

1. You have the right to remain silent.
2. Anything you say can and will be used against you in a court of law.
3. You have a right to talk to a lawyer before answering any questions and you have the right to have a lawyer present with you while you are answering any questions.
4. If you cannot afford to hire a lawyer, one will be appointed to represent you before any questioning, if you wish one.
5. You have the right to decide at any time before or during questioning to use your right to remain silent and your right to talk with a lawyer while you are being questioned.

Helgert asked Thompkins to read the fifth warning out loud. Thompkins complied. Helgert later said this was to ensure that Thompkins could read, and Helgert concluded that Thompkins understood English. Helgert then read the other four Miranda warnings out loud and asked Thompkins to sign the form to demonstrate that he understood his rights. Thompkins declined to sign the form.

The record contains conflicting evidence about whether Thompkins then verbally confirmed that he understood the rights listed on the form. At a suppression hearing, Helgert testified that Thompkins verbally confirmed that he understood his rights. At trial, Helgert stated, "I don't know that I orally asked him" whether Thompkins understood his rights.

Officers began an interrogation. At no point during the interrogation did Thompkins say that he wanted to remain silent, that he did not want to talk with the police, or that he wanted an attorney. Thompkins was "largely" silent during the interrogation, which lasted about three hours. He did give a few limited verbal responses, however, such as "yeah," "no," or "I don't know." And on occasion he communicated by nodding his head. Thompkins also said that he "didn't want a peppermint" that was offered to him by the police and that the chair he was "sitting in was hard."

About 2 hours and 45 minutes into the interrogation, Helgert asked Thompkins, "Do you believe in God?" Thompkins made eye contact with Helgert and said "Yes," as his eyes "welled up with tears." Helgert asked, "Do you pray to God?" Thompkins said "Yes." Helgert asked, "Do you pray to God to forgive you for shooting that boy down?" Thompkins answered "Yes" and looked away. Thompkins refused to make a written confession, and the interrogation ended about 15 minutes later.

OPINION

The *Miranda* Court formulated a warning that must be given to suspects before they can be subjected to custodial interrogation. All concede that the warning given in this case was in full compliance with these requirements. The dispute centers on the response—or nonresponse—from the suspect.

Thompkins contends that he invoked his privilege to remain silent by not saying anything for a sufficient period of time, so the interrogation should have ceased before he made his inculpatory statements. This argument is unpersuasive. In the context of invoking the *Miranda* right to counsel, the Court in *Davis v. United States* (1994) held that a suspect must do so "unambiguously." If an accused makes a statement concerning the right to counsel "that is ambiguous or equivocal" or makes no statement, the police are not required to end the interrogation, or ask questions to clarify whether the accused wants to invoke his or her *Miranda* rights.

There is good reason to require an accused who wants to invoke his or her right to remain silent to do so unambiguously. A requirement of an unambiguous invocation of *Miranda* rights results in an objective inquiry that avoids difficulties of proof and provides guidance to officers on how to proceed in the face of ambiguity. If an ambiguous act, omission, or statement could require police to end the interrogation, police would be required to make difficult decisions about an accused's unclear intent and face the consequence of suppression if they guess wrong.

Suppression of a voluntary confession in these circumstances would place a significant burden on society's interest in prosecuting criminal activity. Thompkins did not say that he wanted to remain silent or that he did not want to talk with the police. Had he made either of these simple, unambiguous statements, he would have invoked his right to cut off questioning. Here he did neither, so he did not invoke his right to remain silent.

We next consider whether Thompkins waived his right to remain silent. Even absent the accused's invocation of the right to remain silent, the accused's statement during a custodial interrogation is inadmissible at trial unless the prosecution can establish that the accused in fact knowingly and voluntarily waived *Miranda* rights when making the statement. The waiver inquiry has two distinct dimensions: waiver must be voluntary in the sense that it was the product of a free and deliberate choice rather than intimidation, coercion, or deception, and made with a full awareness of both the nature of the right being abandoned and the consequences of the decision to abandon it.

The record in this case shows that Thompkins waived his right to remain silent. There is no basis in this case to conclude that he did not understand his rights; and on these facts it follows that he chose not to invoke or rely on those rights when he did speak. First, there is no contention that Thompkins did not understand his rights; and from this it follows that he knew what he gave up when he spoke. There was more than enough evidence in the record to conclude that Thompkins understood his *Miranda* rights. Thompkins received a written copy of the *Miranda* warnings; Detective Helgert determined that Thompkins could read and understand English; and Thompkins was given time to read the warnings. Thompkins, furthermore, read aloud the fifth warning, which stated that "you have the right to decide at any time before or during questioning to use your right to remain silent and your right to talk with a lawyer while you are being questioned." He was thus aware that his right to remain silent would not dissipate after a certain amount of time and that police would have to honor his right to be silent and his right to counsel during the whole course of interrogation. Those rights, the warning made clear, could be asserted at any time. Helgert, moreover, read the warnings aloud.

Second, Thompkins's answer to Detective Helgert's question about whether Thompkins prayed to God for forgiveness for shooting the victim is a "course of conduct indicating waiver" of the right to remain silent. If Thompkins wanted to remain silent, he could have said nothing in response to Helgert's questions, or he could have unambiguously invoked his *Miranda* rights and ended the interrogation. The fact that Thompkins made a statement about three hours after receiving a *Miranda* warning does not overcome the fact that he engaged in a course of conduct indicating waiver. Police are not required to rewarn suspects from time to time. Thompkins's answer to Helgert's question about praying to God for forgiveness for shooting the victim was sufficient to show a course of conduct indicating waiver. This is confirmed by the fact that before then Thompkins had given sporadic answers to questions throughout the interrogation.

Third, there is no evidence that Thompkins's statement was coerced. Thompkins does not claim that police threatened or injured him during the interrogation or that he was in any way fearful. The interrogation was conducted in a standard-sized room in the middle of the afternoon. It is true that apparently he was in a straight-backed chair for three hours, but there is no authority for the proposition that an interrogation of this length is inherently coercive. Indeed, even where interrogations of greater duration were held to be improper, they were accompanied, as this one was not, by other facts indicating coercion, such as an incapacitated and sedated suspect, sleep and food deprivation, and threats. The fact that Helgert's question referred to Thompkins's religious beliefs also did not render Thompkins's statement involuntary. The Fifth Amendment privilege is not concerned with moral and psychological pressures to confess emanating from sources other than official coercion. In these circumstances, Thompkins knowingly and voluntarily made a statement to police, so he waived his right to remain silent.

The judgment of the Court of Appeals is REVERSED, and the case is REMANDED with instructions to deny the petition.

It is so ordered.

DISSENT

SOTOMAYOR, J., joined by STEVENS, GINSBURG, and BREYER JJ.

The Court concludes today that a criminal suspect waives his right to remain silent if, after sitting tacit and uncommunicative through nearly three hours of police interrogation, he utters a few one-word responses. The Court also concludes that a suspect who wishes to guard his right to remain silent against such a finding of waiver must, counterintuitively, speak—and must do so with sufficient precision to satisfy a clear-statement rule that construes ambiguity in favor of the police. Both propositions mark a substantial retreat from the protection against compelled self-incrimination that *Miranda v. Arizona* (1966) has long provided during custodial interrogation. Because I believe that Thompkins's statements were admitted at trial without the prosecution having carried its burden to show that he waived his right to remain silent, I respectfully dissent.

The strength of Thompkins's *Miranda* claims depends in large part on the circumstances of the 3-hour interrogation, at the end of which he made inculpatory statements later introduced at trial. The Court's opinion downplays record evidence that Thompkins remained almost completely silent and unresponsive throughout that session. One of the interrogating officers, Detective Helgert, testified that although Thompkins was administered

(continued)

Miranda warnings, the last of which he read aloud, Thompkins expressly declined to sign a written acknowledgment that he had been advised of and understood his rights. There is conflicting evidence in the record about whether Thompkins ever verbally confirmed understanding his rights. The record contains no indication that the officers sought or obtained an express waiver.

As to the interrogation itself, Helgert candidly characterized it as "very, very one-sided" and "nearly a monologue." Thompkins was "peculiar," "sullen," and "generally quiet." Helgert and his partner "did most of the talking," as Thompkins was "not verbally communicative" and "largely" remained silent. To the extent Thompkins gave any response, his answers consisted of "a word or two. A 'yeah,' or a 'no,' or 'I don't know.' . . . And sometimes . . . he simply sat down . . . with his head in his hands looking down. Sometimes . . . he would look up and make eye contact would be the only response." After proceeding in this fashion for approximately 2 hours and 45 minutes, Helgert asked Thompkins three questions relating to his faith in God. The prosecution relied at trial on Thompkins's one-word answers of "yes."

Even when warnings have been administered and a suspect has not affirmatively invoked his rights, statements made in custodial interrogation may not be admitted as part of the prosecution's case in chief unless and until the prosecution demonstrates that an individual knowingly and intelligently waived his rights. It is undisputed here that Thompkins never expressly waived his right to remain silent. His refusal to sign even an acknowledgment that he understood his *Miranda* rights evinces, if anything, an intent not to waive those rights. That Thompkins did not make the inculpatory statements at issue until after approximately 2 hours and 45 minutes of interrogation serves as strong evidence against waiver.

Today's decision ignores the important interests *Miranda* safeguards. The underlying constitutional guarantee against self-incrimination reflects many of our fundamental values and most noble aspirations, our society's preference for an accusatorial rather than an inquisitorial system of criminal justice; a fear that self-incriminating statements will be elicited by inhumane treatment and abuses and a resulting distrust of self-deprecatory statements; and a realization that while the privilege is sometimes a shelter to the guilty, it is often a protection to the innocent.

For these reasons, we have observed, a criminal law system which comes to depend on the confession will, in the long run, be less reliable and more subject to abuses than a system relying on independent investigation. By bracing against the possibility of unreliable statements in every instance of in-custody interrogation, *Miranda's* prophylactic rules serve to protect the fairness of the trial itself. Today's decision bodes poorly for the fundamental principles that *Miranda* protects.

Today's decision turns *Miranda* upside down. Criminal suspects must now unambiguously invoke their right to remain silent—which, counterintuitively, requires them to speak. At the same time, suspects will be legally presumed to have waived their rights even if they have given no clear expression of their intent to do so. Those results, in my view, find no basis in *Miranda* or our subsequent cases and are inconsistent with the fair-trial principles on which those precedents are grounded. I respectfully dissent.

Questions

1. List all the facts relevant to deciding whether Van Chester Thompkins (a) invoked his right to remain silent, and, if he did, (b) whether he at some point waived it.

2. Summarize the majority's arguments for holding that Thompkins (a) didn't invoke his right to remain silent, but, if he did, that (b) he later waived it.

3. Summarize the dissent's arguments that Detective Helgert and his partner violated Thompkins's right to remain silent.

4. Which side has the better arguments? Which side do you agree with more? Explain your answers.

5. After you've read the section "False Confessions: Popular Belief and Empirical Evidence" (p. 324), return to question 4. Would you now answer it differently? Explain why or why not.

VOLUNTARY SELF-INCRIMINATION

LO 8 Great fears and equally great hopes—depending on whether those who voiced them were more afraid of street criminals or of government abuse of power—were expressed that *Miranda v. Arizona* (1966) would kill police interrogation as a tool to collect evidence. But it didn't happen. As we've already learned, most empirical research has found that the vast majority of suspects don't invoke their right to remain silent and/or to speak to a lawyer (p. 313). One experienced interrogator, Sergeant James DeConcini (now retired), of the Minneapolis Police Department, suggests the reason is that knowledge is a two-way street. Not only do police officers want to find out what suspects know about crimes they're investigating, but suspects also want to know how much police officers know. Misguided as it may be, suspects believe that by cooperating with the police, they'll find out if they "have something on them."

That most suspects waive their right to remain silent and agree to custodial interrogation brings us back to the due process requirement of voluntariness. Even if officers have warned suspects and gotten a knowing waiver, they still may not have gotten the incriminating statements that follow voluntarily. (See also "False Confessions: Popular Belief and Empirical Evidence" later in the chapter.)

To determine whether incriminating statements were made voluntarily, the U.S. Supreme Court adopted another of its totality-of-circumstances tests: Confessions are involuntary only if the totality of the circumstances proves two things:

1. Officers engaged in coercive conduct during the interrogation.

2. The coercive conduct caused the suspect to make incriminating statements.

The most common circumstances courts consider in determining whether coercive state action caused people to confess include the following:

- The location where the questioning took place
- Whether the suspect initiated the contact with law enforcement
- Whether the *Miranda* warnings were given
- The number of interrogators
- The length of the questioning
- Whether food, water, and toilet facilities were denied
- Whether the police used threats, promises, lies, or tricks
- Whether the suspect was denied access to a lawyer
- The suspect's characteristics, such as age, gender, race, physical and mental condition, education, drug problems, and experience with the criminal justice system

Courts have ruled that none of the following actions caused suspects to confess (Twenty-Sixth Annual Review of Criminal Procedure 1997, 967–68):

- Promises of leniency
- Promises of treatment
- Confronting the accused with other evidence of guilt
- The interrogator's appeal to the defendant's emotions
- False and misleading statements made by the interrogator

In our next case excerpt, *Colorado v. Connelly* (1986), the U.S. Supreme Court ruled that Francis Connelly's confession was voluntary even though his serious mental illness led him to believe God ordered him to "confess or commit suicide."

In *Colorado v. Connelly* (1986), the U.S. Supreme Court ruled that Francis Connelly's confession was voluntary even though his serious mental illness led him to believe God ordered him to "confess or commit suicide."

CASE

Did He Confess Voluntarily?

Colorado v. Connelly
479 U.S. 157 (1986)

HISTORY

The trial court suppressed statements made by Francis Barry Connelly. The state appealed. The Colorado Supreme Court affirmed. The U.S. Supreme Court granted certiorari, reversed, and remanded the case.

—REHNQUIST, C.J., joined by WHITE, POWELL, O'CONNOR, and SCALIA, JJ., and, in all but Part III-A, BLACKMUN, J.

FACTS

On August 18, 1983, Officer Patrick Anderson of the Denver Police Department was in uniform, working in an off-duty capacity in downtown Denver. Francis Connelly approached Officer Anderson and, without any prompting, stated he had murdered someone and wanted to talk about it. Anderson immediately advised Connelly he had the right to remain silent, that anything he said could be used against him in court, and that he had the right to an attorney prior to any police questioning. Connelly stated that he understood these rights but he still wanted to talk about the murder. Understandably bewildered by this confession, Officer Anderson asked Connelly several questions.

Connelly denied he had been drinking, denied he had been taking any drugs, and stated that, in the past, he had been a patient in several mental hospitals. Officer Anderson again told Connelly he was under no obligation to say anything. Connelly replied it was "all right," and that he would talk to Officer Anderson because his conscience had been bothering him. To Officer Anderson, Connelly appeared to understand fully the nature of his acts.

Shortly thereafter, Homicide Detective Stephen Antuna arrived. Connelly was again advised of his rights, and Detective Antuna asked him "what he had on his mind." Connelly answered that he had come all the way from Boston to confess to the murder of Mary Ann Junta, a young girl whom he had killed in Denver sometime during November 1982. Connelly was taken to police headquarters, and a search of police records revealed that the body of an unidentified female had been found in April 1983. Connelly openly detailed his story to Detective Antuna and Sergeant Thomas Haney, and readily agreed to take the officers to the scene of the killing. Under Connelly's sole direction, the two officers and Connelly proceeded in a police vehicle to the location of the crime.

Connelly pointed out the exact location of the murder. Throughout this episode, Detective Antuna perceived no indication whatsoever that Connelly was suffering from any kind of mental illness. Connelly was held overnight.

During an interview with the public defender's office the following morning, he became visibly disoriented. He began giving confused answers to questions, and for the first time, stated "voices" had told him to come to Denver and he had followed the directions of these voices in confessing. Connelly was sent to a state hospital for evaluation. He was initially found incompetent to assist in his own defense. By March 1984, however, the doctors evaluating Connelly determined he was competent to proceed to trial.

At a preliminary hearing, Connelly moved to suppress all of his statements. Dr. Jeffrey Metzner, a psychiatrist employed by the state hospital, testified that Connelly was suffering from chronic schizophrenia and was in a psychotic state at least as of August 17, 1983, the day before he confessed. Metzner's interviews with Connelly revealed that he was following the "voice of God." This voice instructed him to withdraw money from the bank, to buy an airplane ticket, and to fly from Boston to Denver. When he arrived from Boston, God's voice became stronger and told him either to confess to the killing or to commit suicide. Reluctantly following the command of the voices, he approached Officer Anderson and confessed.

Dr. Metzner testified that, in his expert opinion, Connelly was experiencing "command hallucinations." This condition interfered with his "volitional abilities—that is, his ability to make free and rational choices." Dr. Metzner further testified that Connelly's illness did not significantly impair his cognitive abilities. Thus, he understood the rights he had when Officer Anderson and Detective Antuna advised him that he need not speak. Dr. Metzner admitted that the "voices" could in reality be Connelly's interpretation of his own guilt, but explained that in his opinion, Connelly's psychosis motivated his confession.

Although the Colorado trial court found that the police had done nothing wrong or coercive in securing Connelly's confession, his illness destroyed his volition and compelled him to confess. The trial court also found that Connelly's mental state vitiated his attempted waiver of the right to counsel and the privilege against compulsory self-incrimination. Accordingly, Connelly's initial statements and his custodial confession were suppressed. The Colorado Supreme Court affirmed the trial court's decision to suppress all of Connelly's statements.

OPINION

The cases considered by this Court over the 50 years since *Brown v. Mississippi* have focused upon the crucial element of police overreaching. While each confession case has turned on its own set of factors justifying the conclusion that police conduct was oppressive, all have contained a substantial element of coercive police conduct. Absent police conduct causally related to the confession, there is simply no basis for concluding that any state actor has deprived a criminal defendant of due process of law.

Connelly correctly notes that as interrogators have turned to more subtle forms of psychological persuasion, courts have found the mental condition of the defendant a more significant factor in the "voluntariness" calculus. But this fact does not justify a conclusion that a defendant's mental condition, by itself and apart from its relation to official coercion, should ever dispose of the inquiry into constitutional "voluntariness."

Our "involuntary confession" jurisprudence is entirely consistent with the settled law requiring some sort of "state action" to support a claim of violation of the Due Process Clause of the Fourteenth Amendment. The Colorado trial court found that the police committed no wrongful acts, and that finding has been neither challenged by Connelly nor disturbed by the Supreme Court of Colorado. The latter court, however, concluded that sufficient state action was present by virtue of the admission of the confession into evidence in a court of the State. The difficulty with the approach of the Supreme Court of Colorado is that it fails to recognize the essential link between coercive activity of the State, on the one hand, and a resulting confession by a defendant, on the other.

The flaw in Connelly's constitutional argument is that it would expand our previous line of "voluntariness" cases into a far-ranging requirement that courts must divine a defendant's motivation for speaking or acting as he did even though there be no claim that governmental conduct coerced his decision. We have previously cautioned against expanding currently applicable exclusionary rules

by erecting additional barriers to placing truthful and probative evidence before state juries. We abide by that counsel now.

The central purpose of a criminal trial is to decide the factual question of the defendant's guilt or innocence, and while we have previously held that exclusion of evidence may be necessary to protect constitutional guarantees, both the necessity for the collateral inquiry and the exclusion of evidence deflect a criminal trial from its basic purpose. Connelly would now have us require sweeping inquiries into the state of mind of a criminal defendant who has confessed, inquiries quite divorced from any coercion brought to bear on the defendant by the State.

We think the Constitution rightly leaves this sort of inquiry to be resolved by state laws governing the admission of evidence and erects no standard of its own in this area. A statement rendered by one in the condition of Connelly might be proved to be quite unreliable, but this is a matter to be governed by the evidentiary laws of the forum, and not by the Due Process Clause of the Fourteenth Amendment.

We hold that coercive police activity is a necessary predicate to the finding that a confession is not "voluntary" within the meaning of the Due Process Clause of the Fourteenth Amendment. We also conclude that the taking of Connelly's statements, and their admission into evidence, constitute no violation of that Clause.

We think that the Supreme Court of Colorado erred in importing into this area of constitutional law notions of "free will" that have no place there. The sole concern of the Fifth Amendment, on which *Miranda* was based, is governmental coercion. Indeed, the Fifth Amendment privilege is not concerned with moral and psychological pressures to confess emanating from sources other than official coercion. The voluntariness of a waiver of this privilege has always depended on the absence of police overreaching, not on "free choice" in any broader sense of the word.

Connelly urges this Court to adopt his "free will" rationale, and to find an attempted waiver invalid whenever the defendant feels compelled to waive his rights by reason of any compulsion, even if the compulsion does not flow from the police. But such a treatment of the waiver issue would "cut this Court's holding in *Miranda* completely loose from its own explicitly stated rationale." *Miranda* protects defendants against government coercion leading them to surrender rights protected by the Fifth Amendment; it goes no further than that. Connelly's perception of coercion flowing from the "voice of God," however important or significant such a perception may be in other disciplines, is a matter to which the United States Constitution does not speak.

The judgment of the Supreme Court of Colorado is accordingly REVERSED, and the cause is REMANDED for further proceedings not inconsistent with this opinion. . . .

(continued)

DISSENT

BRENNAN, J., joined by MARSHALL, J.

Today the Court denies Mr. Connelly his fundamental right to make a vital choice with a sane mind, involving a determination that could allow the State to deprive him of liberty or even life. This holding is unprecedented: Surely in the present stage of our civilization a most basic sense of justice is affronted by the spectacle of incarcerating a human being upon the basis of a statement he made while insane. Because I believe that the use of a mentally ill person's involuntary confession is antithetical to the notion of fundamental fairness embodied in the Due Process Clause, I dissent.

Connelly's seriously impaired mental condition is clear on the record of this case. At the time of his confession, Mr. Connelly suffered from a "longstanding severe mental disorder," diagnosed as chronic paranoid schizophrenia. He had been hospitalized for psychiatric reasons five times prior to his confession; his longest hospitalization lasted for seven months. Mr. Connelly heard imaginary voices and saw nonexistent objects. He believed that his father was God, and that he was a reincarnation of Jesus.

The state trial court found that the "overwhelming evidence presented by the Defense" indicated that the prosecution did not meet its burden of demonstrating by a preponderance of the evidence that the initial statement to Officer Anderson was voluntary. While the court found no police misconduct, it held: There's no question that the Defendant did not exercise free will in choosing to talk to the police. He exercised a choice both of which were mandated by auditory hallucination, had no basis in reality, and were the product of a psychotic break with reality. The Defendant at the time of the confession had absolutely in the Court's estimation no volition or choice to make.

The absence of police wrongdoing should not, by itself, determine the voluntariness of a confession by a mentally ill person. The requirement that a confession be voluntary reflects a recognition of the importance of free will and of reliability in determining the admissibility of a confession, and thus demands an inquiry into the totality of the circumstances surrounding the confession. Today's decision restricts the application of the term "involuntary" to those confessions obtained by police coercion.

Confessions by mentally ill individuals or by persons coerced by parties other than police officers are now considered "voluntary." The Court's failure to recognize all forms of involuntariness or coercion as antithetical to due process reflects a refusal to acknowledge free will as a value of constitutional consequence. But due process derives much of its meaning from a conception of fundamental fairness that emphasizes the right to make vital choices voluntarily: The Fourteenth Amendment secures against state invasion the right of a person to remain silent unless he chooses to speak in the unfettered exercise of his own will. This right requires vigilant protection if we are to safeguard the values of private conscience and human dignity.

A true commitment to fundamental fairness requires that the inquiry be not whether the conduct of state officers in obtaining the confession is shocking, but whether the confession was free and voluntary. Since the Court redefines voluntary confessions to include confessions by mentally ill individuals, the reliability of these confessions becomes a central concern. A concern for reliability is inherent in our criminal justice system, which relies upon accusatorial rather than inquisitorial practices. While an inquisitorial system prefers obtaining confessions from criminal defendants, an accusatorial system must place its faith in determinations of guilt by evidence independently and freely secured.

In *Escobedo v. Illinois* (1964), we justified our reliance upon accusatorial practices: We have learned the lesson of history, ancient and modern, that a system of criminal law enforcement which comes to depend on the "confession" will, in the long run, be less reliable and more subject to abuses than a system which depends on extrinsic evidence independently secured through skillful investigation.

I dissent.

Questions

1. List all the facts relevant to deciding whether Francis Connelly's confession was voluntary.

2. What are the two parts of the test that the U.S. Supreme Court announced for determining whether confessions are voluntary?

3. Do you agree with the majority that the confession was voluntary? If yes, what persuaded you? If no, do you agree with the dissent? Explain why.

CRIMINAL PROCEDURE IN ACTION

LO **8**   Coercive conduct of basketball coach rendered player's confession inadmissible
State v. Bowe, 881 P.2d 538 (1994)

FACTS

On January 21, 1990, a brawl involving a number of individuals occurred at one of the dormitory buildings on the University of Hawai'i-Manoa (UH) campus. During the fight, Steven Oshiro (Victim) was beaten and sustained physical injuries.

On February 9, 1990, Sergeant John Pinero (Sergeant Pinero) of the Honolulu Police Department (HPD) contacted Wallace, head coach of the UH Men's Basketball Team. He requested Wallace's assistance in making arrangements for the police to interview certain members of the basketball team, who were suspected of being involved in the January 21, 1990, fight. Sergeant Pinero provided Wallace with a list of suspects that included Troy Bowe. Wallace later told Bowe that he needed to go to the police station and that he would go with him if he required assistance.

On February 12, 1990, Bowe went to the police station accompanied by Wallace. Bowe was given *Miranda* warnings and subsequently signed an HPD Form 81, waiving his constitutional rights to counsel and to remain silent. After waiving his constitutional rights, an interrogation commenced in which Bowe admitted assaulting the victim.

On September 17, 1991, an Oahu Grand Jury indicted Defendant and Vincent Smalls for Assault in the Second Degree. On November 21, 1991, Bowe filed a Motion to suppress evidence on the grounds that his February 12, 1990, statement to the police was involuntary because it was obtained through the use of official state coercion in violation of Bowe's constitutional right to due process. On May 8, 1992, the circuit court granted Bowe's motion to suppress.

In determining that Defendant's statement was coerced, the circuit court entered the following findings of fact:

1. On or about January or February of 1990, Sergeant John Pinero was an employee of the [HPD], who was at that time working on an investigation of an assault which allegedly involved TROY BOWE.

2. In his capacity as a police officer with the [HPD], Sergeant Pinero called Riley Wallace, at that time basketball coach of the University of Hawai'i at Manoa Basketball Team (hereinafter "Basketball Team"), and gave

Wallace a list of suspects who were on the Basketball Team that Sergeant Pinero wanted Wallace to bring down to the [HPD] (hereinafter "List").

   a. Wallace, as head basketball coach, had the authority to suspend athletes or remove them from the Basketball Team and, in the case of scholarship athletes, to initiate procedures to withdraw their athletic scholarships.

3. TROY BOWE was a scholarship athlete on the Basketball Team.

4. TROY BOWE was on said List.

5. Sergeant Pinero specifically asked Wallace to locate the individuals on the List and have them meet with Sergeant Pinero.

6. Sergeant Pinero, however, did not request that Wallace use force or coercion while attempting to have individuals on the List meet with Sergeant Pinero.

7. Wallace then contacted Defendant TROY BOWE and informed him that he had to go down to the [HPD] to meet with Sergeant Pinero.

8. Wallace informed TROY BOWE that Wallace would accompany him to the [HPD] in place of an attorney and instructed TROY BOWE to make a statement to Sergeant Pinero.

9. Wallace did not inform TROY BOWE that he could or should have an attorney present with him when he went to be interviewed by Sergeant Pinero.

10. TROY BOWE believed that he could not refuse to follow Wallace's directions because if he did so Wallace could suspend him from the Basketball Team or institute procedures to revoke Defendant TROY BOWE's athletic scholarship.

Was the coercive conduct of Coach Wallace, a private person, sufficient to render Bowe's confession inadmissible?

DECISION

Yes, said the Hawai'i supreme court.

(continued)

OPINION

While the Supreme Court in *Connelly* stated that, "the sole concern of the Fifth Amendment is governmental coercion," we have recognized that one of the basic considerations underlying the exclusion of confessions obtained through coercion is the "inherent untrustworthiness of involuntary confessions." Accordingly, we reject the Supreme Court's narrow focus on police coercion in *Connelly*.

We recognize that an individual's capacity to make a rational and free choice between confessing and remaining silent may be overborne as much by the coercive conduct of a private individual as by the coercive conduct of the police. [Therefore,] we hold that the coercive conduct of a private person may be sufficient to render a confession inadmissible based on article 1, sections 5 and 10 of the Hawai'i Constitution.

Nevertheless, we acknowledge that some sort of state action is required to support a defendant's claim that his due process rights were violated. Although no state action is involved where an accused is coerced into making a confession by a private individual, we find that the state participates in that violation by allowing the coerced statements to be used as evidence.

What happens when the self-incriminatory confession given is false? We turn next to the troubling and tragic issue of false confessions.

FALSE CONFESSIONS: POPULAR BELIEF AND EMPIRICAL EVIDENCE

There are no scientific estimates of the numbers of false confessions, or of how many of them lead to convicting innocent people. Most police departments—and other organizations, for that matter—don't routinely collect, analyze, and report interrogation information. Furthermore, most police departments don't record interrogations and confessions. So it's difficult, if not impossible, to find out if confessions are true. This doesn't mean that the study of police interrogation and false confessions is useless. Social scientists can still understand and explain how and why false confessions occur, even if they can't estimate the number and rates that occur (Drizin and Leo 2003–04, 930–31).

Steven Drizin and Richard Leo (2003–04) examined 125 proven cases of individuals who confessed to crimes they didn't commit. Drizin and Leo "proved" the confessions were false in four ways:

1. *The crime never happened.* For example, an Alabama jury convicted three mentally retarded defendants of killing Victoria Banks's unborn child; Banks wasn't capable of getting pregnant.

2. *The defendant couldn't have committed the crime.* For example, jail records proved that Mario Hayes, Miguel Castillo, and Peter Williams were locked up when the crimes they confessed to were committed.

3. *The actual criminal is proven to have committed the crime.* For example, Christopher Ochoa, a former high school honor student, confessed to raping and murdering Nancy DePriest in an Austin, Texas, Pizza Hut. He was freed when Achim Marino came forward and admitted that he killed DePriest. Marino led authorities to the weapon he used and the bag he put the money in.

4. *DNA evidence exonerated the defendant.* For example, Michael Crowe, Joshua Treadway, and Aaron Houser confessed to murdering Crowe's 12-year-old sister. DNA testing proved that blood found on mentally ill Richard Tuite's sweatshirt matched the victim's. (925–26)

What did Drizin and Leo learn about proven false confessions beyond the fact that people do confess to crimes they didn't commit? Here are some of their findings:

1. Eighty-one percent (101 out of 125) of proven innocent defendants who decided to go to trial were convicted—wrongly—"beyond a reasonable doubt," even though their confessions were later proved false (995–96).

2. More than 80 percent of interrogations lasted more than 6 hours; half lasted more than 12 hours. The average length was 16.3 hours; the median was 12 hours. Drizin and Leo found these figures "especially striking" compared to Leo's earlier observation of 500 routine police interrogations, where the average interrogation lasted less than 2 hours (948).

3. "Virtually all false confessions result in some deprivation of the false confessor's liberty" (949). Of course, some of these are false confessions that lead to conviction. But even those who weren't convicted still lost significant time locked up before exoneration. And they suffered other losses as well, including the stigma of a criminal accusation; damage to their personal and professional reputation; loss of income and savings; loss of their job; separation and divorce; and emotional strain (949–50).

4. The most vulnerable populations (84 out of 125) are overrepresented in the sample, including:
   a. 44 juveniles under 18 (7 under 14)
   b. 28 mentally retarded
   c. 12 mentally ill (963–74)

5. "The 125 proven false confessions may be a more serious problem than previously imagined" (996).

In the remainder of this chapter, we look more closely at false confessions, including (1) why people confess to crimes they didn't commit, (2) the impact of those false confessions, and (3) reforms that aim to reduce false confessions.

LO 9   Why Do Innocent People Confess to Crimes They Didn't Commit?

Researchers divide proven false confessions into three categories: voluntary false confessions, compliant false confessions, and internalized false confessions (Kassin and Gudjonsson 2004, 46):

1. *Voluntary False Confessions.* Some innocent people confess without police prompting or pressure. These confessions are called **voluntary false confessions.** Why do innocent people confess? Common reasons include (1) a desire for notoriety; (2) a need for self-punishment to remove guilt feelings; (3) an inability to separate reality from fantasy; and (4) a desire to help and protect the real criminal. But these are far from the only reasons. In one case, an innocent man confessed to murder to impress his girlfriend. Another innocent man, angry with the police for arresting him while he was drinking at a party, confessed to murder to get revenge by misleading the police (49).

2. *Compliant False Confessions.* Some innocent people confess because of police pressure (not coercion) during custodial interrogation. **Compliant confessions** are

"mere acts of public compliance by a suspect who comes to believe that the short-term benefits of confession . . . outweigh the long-term costs." Suspects give in to demands for admissions and confessions for instrumental reasons: to escape an uncomfortable situation; to avoid a threat; or to receive a reward. Specific incentives for compliant false confessions include being allowed to sleep, eat, make a phone call, or go home (49–50).

3. *Internalized False Confessions.* Innocent—but vulnerable—suspects subjected to "highly suggestive interrogation tactics" come not just to give in to get the situation over with but to *believe that they actually committed the crime.* One frequently cited tragic example of **internalized false confession** is the case of 18-year-old Peter Reilly. Although Reilly called the police immediately after he discovered his murdered mother, the police suspected that Reilly murdered her. After they gained his trust, his interrogators told Reilly that he failed his lie detector test (a lie), and that the test indicated that he was guilty even though he couldn't remember killing his mother.

After hours of "relentless interrogation, Reilly underwent a chilling transformation from adamant denial through confusion, self-doubt, conversion ('Well, it really looks like I did it'), and eventual full confession ('I remember slashing once at my mother's throat with a straight razor I used for model airplanes. . . . I also remember jumping on my mother's legs')." Two years later, evidence proved that Reilly couldn't have killed his mother (50).

Studies of wrongful convictions based on these proven innocent people's false confessions stem from two sources: (1) certain police interrogation techniques and (2) jurors' belief in the confessions. When innocent people confessed, went to trial, and pleaded guilty, jury conviction rates ranged from 73 percent, in one study, to 81 percent in a second (56).

These figures led Drizin and Leo (2004) to conclude that confession evidence is "inherently prejudicial and highly damaging to a defendant, even if it is the product of coercive interrogation, and even if it is ultimately proven false beyond any reasonable doubt" (959).

LO 9 The Impact of False Confessions

Do juries uncritically accept confessions, even if they're the product of coercive interrogation? And can ordinary people, in general, and law enforcement professionals, in particular, tell the difference between true and false confessions? Let's look at the psychological experts' answers to these questions.

According to Kassin and Gudjonsson (2004, 56), research in a wide variety of settings shows that jurors may credit confessions obtained during "high-pressure" interrogation methods because of **fundamental attribution error**. They overestimate the role of defendants' "nature" (disposition) in evaluating their actions, while they underestimate the role of the interrogation situation. The explanation for this error is that people tend to "draw quick and automatic inferences, taking behavior at face value, but then because of a lack of motivation or cognitive capacity fail to adjust or correct for situational influences" (56–57).

The impact of false confessions doesn't stop with its influence on juries. False confessions tend to "overwhelm other information, such as alibis and other evidence of innocence, resulting in a chain of adverse legal consequences—from arrest through guilty pleas, prosecution, and conviction, and incarceration." For example, Bruce Godschalk spent 15 years in prison until DNA exonerated him from two rape convictions. Even so, the Montgomery County, Pennsylvania, district attorney, Bruce L. Castor Jr., whose office convicted Godschalk, refused to let him out of prison, saying that he believed Godschalk was guilty and that the DNA testing was flawed. Asked what scientific basis he had for concluding that the testing was flawed, Castor said, "I have no scientific basis. I know because I trust my detective and my tape-recorded confession. Therefore the results must be flawed until someone proves to me otherwise" (Rimer 2002, A18).

Do people know a false confession when they hear one? The research has "yielded sobering results." Experiments in the lab showed that student observers didn't do better than chance in picking out false from true confessions (Kassin and Gudjonsson 2004, 57–58). What about police professionals in actual crimes? Let's look closer at Kassin, Meissner, and Norwick's 2005 study.

They recruited male prisoners to take part in a pair of videotaped interviews. For one interview, the researchers instructed each inmate to give a full confession to the crime they were sent to prison for. In the second interview, prisoners were given a brief description of a crime committed by one of the other prisoners and told to make up a false confession to it. The prisoners were paired so that each inmate's true confession was paired with another prisoner's false confession to the same crime.

Then, researchers used five of the true confessions and their five false counterparts to create a videotape depicting ten different prisoners confessing to aggravated assault, armed robbery, burglary, breaking and entering, or car theft. They also made audiotapes of the same confessions to correct for research finding that people are better lie detectors when they use auditory instead of visual cues, which are often misleading. College students and law enforcement officers judged both the videotaped and audiotaped confession interviews.

The result: Neither the students nor the officers produced "high rates of accuracy," although the officers were more *confident* in their performance than the students. Accuracy improved when the subjects listened to the audiotapes. Students, but not the police, exceeded chance in this performance, although once again the police officers were more confident. Officers didn't differ from students in their hit rate, but they exceeded the students in the number of false positives. Officers included those with extensive law enforcement experience and those with special training in interviewing and interrogation. This result doesn't show that police are predisposed to see deception but, instead, to infer guilt—an "inference that rested upon a tendency to believe false confessions" (Kassin and Gudjonsson 2004, 58).

Why did police officers not do better at distinguishing false from true confessions? And why did "naïve" college students exceed officers' accuracy? Kassin and Gudjonsson offer two possible reasons. First, law enforcement officers may introduce a bias that reduces accuracy. This possible explanation draws support from findings that police are trained to be suspicious and to see deception in other people. Second, the experiment's design (half the confessions were false) might have compromised the officers' judgment accuracy. Law enforcement work might lead to officers' reasonable belief that most confessions are true; hence, they import their bias from the station to the study.

In a second study, Kassin, Meissner, and Norwick (2005) told subjects that half the confessions were true and half were false. This manipulation reduced the total number of "true" confession judgments and also reduced the number of "false positives." But the police still maintained a pattern of low accuracy and high confidence compared to the students (58).

LO 9 Reforms Aimed at Reducing the False Confession Problem

DNA exonerations have proven that about 25 percent of the wrong convictions were due to innocent people confessing to crimes they didn't commit (Innocence Project 2013). In light of these highly publicized cases, and advances in psychological research, social scientists are calling for reforms in interrogation and confession procedures.

They want collaboration among law enforcement professionals, prosecutors, defense attorneys, judges, policy makers, and social scientists to evaluate current interrogation and confession practices. All these parties agree that the objective of interrogation is to obtain confessions from *guilty* suspects and not from *innocent* people (Kassin and Gudjonsson 2004, 59).

A few state legislatures, courts, and police departments have implemented some reforms. We'll look at three of these proposed reforms:

1. Reducing the length of time in custody and interrogation;
2. Eliminating police use of false information during interrogations; and
3. Recording interrogations and confessions.

Limit time in custody and interrogation

Psychological research has documented that the "human needs for belonging, affiliation, and social support, especially in times of stress, are a fundamental human motive" (Kassin and Gudjonsson 2004, 60). Prolonged custody and interrogation can lead suspects to confess to escape these deprivations. Although most documented interrogations last for less than two hours, proven false confessions resulted from interrogations that lasted much longer (an average of 16.3 hours) (Drizin and Leo 2004). In the infamous Central Park jogger false confession case, the five boys underwent interrogation from 14 to 30 hours before they confessed falsely to beating and raping the jogger. At this time, no rules regulate the length of time of interrogation and custody.

Restrict police use of false information during interrogations

Bluntly, we're talking here about police lies to suspects, such as telling suspects that nonexistent eyewitnesses identified them; officers found their fingerprints, hair, or blood when they didn't; or that they failed a lie detector test when they actually passed.

The U.S. Supreme Court has explicitly sanctioned police use of lies as part of the totality of circumstances in determining whether confessions are voluntary. In *Frazier v. Cupp* (1969), police officers falsely told Martin Frazier that his cousin Jerry Rawls, who had been with him on the night of the crime, had confessed. The Court considered that this "misrepresentation, while relevant, is insufficient in our view to make this otherwise voluntary confession inadmissible" (739).

Although it's had many opportunities to do so, and substantial research raises questions about this ruling, the Court has never changed its position (Magid 2001, 1176). Research shows that presenting suspects with "false evidence substantially increases false confessions" (Kassin and Gudjonsson 2004, 60). This research and the proven false confession cases led Kassin and Gudjonsson to recommend that "the Court should revisit the wisdom of its prior ruling and declare: 'Thou shalt not lie'" (60).

Record interrogations and confessions

"Calls to electronically record interrogations are almost as old as the technology itself. For more than 70 years, reformers from all ranks, including some from law enforcement, have seen recording requirements as a way to eliminate secrecy in the stationhouse" and to "recognize the value that neutral, contemporaneously made records could have in law enforcement" (Drizin and Reich 2004, 62–21). In his 1932 classic *Convicting the Innocent*, Edwin Borchard recommended that the solution to protecting suspects' right against self-incrimination and to preventing unreliable confessions was to make "phonographic records, which shall alone be introducible as evidence of the prisoner's statements" (370–71). Beyond transparency and objectivity, videotaping interrogation confessions provides a means to improve the ability of police, judges, prosecutors, defense attorneys, and juries (and social scientists) to assess the procedure more objectively.

Many state courts have spoken warmly of recording the whole process of interrogation from *Miranda* warnings, through interrogation, to the confession (*State v. Cook* 2004). Despite this history, the DNA exonerations, the psychological research findings we've touched on, and the warm words of some courts, only four states at the time of this writing have mandatory video recording requirements—Alaska, Illinois, Maine, and Minnesota.

The arguments in favor of recording include:

1. It creates an objective, reviewable record.
2. It enhances jurors' and judges' assessment of credibility by providing a complete record.
3. It provides judges and juries with a more accurate picture of what was said; words can convey different meanings, depending on the tone of voice or nuance used.
4. It can improve the quality of police work by providing law enforcement officials with the ability to monitor the quality of the interrogation process, and recordings can be used in training courses to demonstrate effective versus ineffective, or legally impermissible, interrogation techniques.
5. It preserves judicial resources by discouraging defendants from raising "frivolous" pretrial challenges to confessions. (*State v. Cook* 2004, 556–57)

There are also drawbacks to videotaping. They include:

1. The cost, including purchasing the equipment, maintenance, storage, transcription, and remodeling interrogation rooms, can be high.
2. It can interfere with interrogation techniques and hamper officers' ability to obtain truthful confessions.
3. Suspects may be reluctant to speak candidly in front of cameras. (557–58)

YOU DECIDE
Should the Law Require the Police to Record Interrogations?

Fifteen-year-old Katrina Suhan was murdered sometime in the early morning hours of Saturday, February 14, 1998. Katrina's body was found on the afternoon of Sunday, February 15. She had been brutally beaten. Her body was positioned face downward and a jacket covered her head; her pants had been pulled below her waist. Large pieces of concrete lay atop her hands and head and an overturned red shopping cart was situated in front of, and partially on, her body. A trail

(continued)

of blood led to the body and to several rocks near her head. A forensic pathologist expressed the view that Katrina died of blunt trauma injury to the head. There was injury also to her left breast that was consistent with a bite mark; there were no other physical signs of sexual assault.

Tomahl Cook, Defendant, who was 24 years old at the time of the murder, was arrested and interrogated. Although a tape recorder was available during the interview, the officers did not tape any portion of the interrogation.

CHAPTER SUMMARY

LO 1 Confessions acknowledge guilt, and, as such, they're uniquely powerful evidence heavily relied upon for conviction in our criminal justice system. Incriminating statements that fall short of full confessions are made to friends and family, during interrogation, in guilty pleas, and during sentencing in the form of apologies. Interrogations are incommunicado and the atmosphere of the interrogation room is purposefully intimidating to discover the truth about suspects' possible criminal behavior.

LO 2 Due process, right to counsel, and self-incrimination are approaches to criminal confession, and their influences overlap in history. The Fifth Amendment prevents law enforcement from compelling people to make self-incriminating statements, the Sixth Amendment ensures the right to counsel, and the Fourteenth Amendment guarantees due process. Protections of the Fourteenth Amendment apply to all stages of the criminal process, of the Sixth Amendment after formal charges are brought, and of the Fifth Amendment in custodial interrogation and thereafter.

LO 2 The due process approach emphasized the voluntary nature of confession, stating that involuntary confessions violate due process only because they're unreliable. The right-to-counsel approach sought to toughen controls on police interrogation by applying the Sixth Amendment's right to counsel to the custodial period in the police station.

LO 2, 3 The self-incrimination approach applied the Fifth Amendment to custodial interrogation. Compulsion, incrimination, and testimony are all required to prove violation of Fifth Amendment rights in a criminal case. The Fifth Amendment protection against being compelled to "witness" against oneself applies to forced testimony but not personal paperwork, weapons, hair samples, blood samples used for alcohol testing, and more.

LO 4, 5 Whether one is "compelled" is difficult to define. The voluntariness of the confession is critical. In *Miranda*, judges moved away from weighing "totality of circumstances" on a case-by-case basis and, instead, required that a specific police warning be given in every case at the time suspects were taken into custody. The "bright line" of *Miranda v. Arizona* defines custodial interrogation.

LO 5 In custodial interrogation, suspects are held against their will. Interrogation is an essential tool without which many prosecutions would go nowhere. Interrogation refers not only to direct questioning but also to subtle coercion that acts as the functional equivalent of a question and to officers who "deliberately elicit a response" from suspects in custody.

LO 6 Evidence and incriminating statements obtained without giving *Miranda* warnings can still be admissible in court to prove guilt whenever trial judges believe the purpose of the questioning is to protect public safety. Empirical research has shown that the typical public safety exception case involves credible law enforcement knowledge that a suspect is or was armed. This is not the only application of the public safety exception, however; some successful public safety exception cases require only a possible threat to public safety.

LO 7, 8 A waiver of Fifth Amendment and some other rights can be implied, given a totality of circumstances (e.g., age, intelligence, mental condition, education) that indicate suspects knew their rights and gave them up voluntarily. Empirical research demonstrates that police almost always give the *Miranda* warnings and most suspects waive these rights.

LO 9 Voluntary false confessions aren't a theoretical risk but a proven fact. Reforms aimed at combating this serious problem focus on making video recordings of interrogations and confessions, limiting time in custody, and restricting the use of false information intended to elicit confessions.

REVIEW QUESTIONS

1. Describe the ambivalence surrounding confessions in social and legal history.
2. Identify four different settings where defendants confess their guilt or make incriminating statements.
3. Identify when the accusatory stage of the criminal process triggers the rights afforded to suspects.
4. Identify three reasons why Fred Inbau supported interrogations.
5. Identify and state the contents of the three provisions in the U.S. Constitution that limit police interrogation and confessions. At which stage of the criminal process is each of these amendments applicable?
6. What is the basic idea behind the due process approach to confessions?
7. What is the significance of *Rogers v. Richmond*?
8. What is the significance of *Townsend v. Sain*?
9. When does the right to counsel kick in during interrogations?
10. What three elements have to be satisfied for defendants to claim that their Fifth Amendment rights were violated?
11. Can physical evidence serve as a witness against a suspect? Explain.
12. Describe the voluntariness test of self-incrimination.
13. Identify three factors behind the decision *in Miranda v. Arizona*.
14. *Miranda v. Arizona* established a "bright-line" rule regarding warnings to suspects. State and give the reasons for the rule.
15. Identify five rules police officers do not need to tell suspects before custodial interrogation.
16. State the two circumstances that exist before officers have to give the *Miranda* warnings.
17. Identify five circumstances to determine custody.
18. Identify three types of detentions that aren't custodial.

19. State and summarize the reason for the public safety exception to the *Miranda* warnings.

20. Identify and describe the two elements of the test courts use to determine whether incriminating statements were made voluntarily.

21. Identify and describe the Sixth Amendment test used to determine when the right to counsel kicks in.

22. Describe two reasons why the *Miranda* rules are so "nimble."

23. When are incriminating statements derived from un-*Mirandized* suspects admissible in court to prove guilt?

24. Summarize Joanna Wright's findings regarding the public safety exception. Describe the prototypical PSE case, according to her research.

25. Identify the two elements of a valid wavier of the rights to counsel and to remain silent.

26. List some circumstances relevant to showing a knowing wavier.

27. Identify the two elements of involuntary confessions.

28. List some circumstances courts consider in determining whether coercive action caused people to confess.

29. List some circumstances that courts have determined don't cause suspects to confess.

30. List four findings of Richard Leo's research on police interrogation, and describe what his findings are based on.

31. Identify and describe three reforms aimed at reducing the false confession problem.

KEY TERMS

confessions, p. 286
incriminating statements, p. 286
accusatory stage of the criminal process, p. 287
reliability rationale for due process, p. 290
accusatory system rationale, p. 290
free will rationale, p. 291
critical stage in criminal prosecutions, p. 291

testimony, p. 293
voluntariness test of self-incrimination, p. 293
custodial interrogation, p. 294
inherently coercive, p. 294
Miranda warnings, p. 294
custody, p. 299
"functional equivalent of a question" test, p. 302
"deliberately eliciting a response" test, p. 303

public safety exception (PSE), p. 305
express waiver test, p. 314
implied waiver test, p. 314
voluntary false confessions, p. 325
compliant confessions, p. 325
internalized false confessions, p. 326
fundamental attribution error, p. 326

9

Identification Procedures

LEARNING OBJECTIVES

1 Know that, in a lineup, witnesses try to pick the suspect out of a group of individuals who are present. In a show-up, witnesses match the suspect with one person, who is either present or pictured in a "mug shot."

2 Understand that courts recognize a violation of due process as a ground for rejecting identification testimony, but that due process challenges rarely succeed.

3 Understand the preponderance of evidence standard and how it affects defense efforts to challenge identification procedures.

4 Know that identification procedures are rejected by courts only when they're unnecessarily suggestive and create a very substantial likelihood of misidentification.

5 Understand and appreciate the impact of the proven incorrect assumptions that we make about how people acquire memories.

6 Know and appreciate the significant role that suggestion plays in witnesses' adding unobserved details to their stories.

7 Understand that social science research has demonstrated that factors such as lineup composition, neutrality of lineup administrators, pre-lineup instructions, and the way the lineup is presented can affect the accuracy of identification.

8 Know that psychological research shows that our perceived ability to identify a culprit varies from our actual ability. Understand that the amount of time a witness spent observing a culprit is often less important than what the witness paid attention to during that time.

9 Know that DNA technology has prompted the reevaluation of many past convictions and led to not only exonerations of the innocent but also further proof against the guilty. Understand that forensic science can provide compelling evidence of guilt but also suffers serious shortcomings.

American television viewers of popular programs such as CSI would be led to think that the forensic science lab is a bastion of white-coated scientists whose empirical and unbiased results are virtually always reliable and beyond significant dispute. A forensic scientist testifying that an accused in a criminal trial is the source of the evidence analyzed and interpreted at the scientist's lab can leave a jury strongly convinced that the scientist's conclusions are unimpeachable confirmation of the defendant's guilt. The actual quality of the testimony, unfortunately, is quite different; in the wake of DNA exonerations, the reliability of forensic testing and testimony has come under extensive critical examination and been found to be limited, in large part due to the forensic lab's monopoly status.

—CSI for Real, Roger Koppl, Reason Foundation, 2007

Proving that a crime was committed is often a lot easier than identifying who committed it. Of course, some culprits are caught red-handed; others confess. Technological advances help to identify others; DNA (deoxyribonucleic acid) evidence may be the "single greatest advance in the search for truth since cross-examination" (Coleman and Swenson 1994, 11). And, most important, victims and others who know perpetrators can virtually always identify the culprit. But, in the cases that frighten most of us—violent personal crimes like rape and robbery committed by strangers— eyewitness identification remains the most widely used, and often the only, way to identify and prove guilt.

In this chapter, you'll learn how the U.S. Supreme Court relies on the U.S. Constitution to provide minimum safeguards to protect against convictions based on mistaken identifications. The dominant theme in the Court's decisions is balancing the need to protect defendants from wrongful convictions without encroaching on the jury's prerogative to decide guilt. According to the Court, identification evidence should be admitted unless identification procedures create a "very substantial likelihood of irreparable misidentification." Short of that, "We are content to rely upon the good sense and judgment of American juries. Juries are not so susceptible that they cannot measure intelligently the weight of identification testimony that has some questionable feature" (*Manson v. Brathwaite* 1977, 116, excerpted later on p. 340).

Then, we'll examine the highly risky business of eyewitnesses (usually victims) identifying strangers who committed the crimes. We'll rely heavily on the empirical psychological studies of perception, memory, and recall to demonstrate the substantial shortcomings of the rules the Supreme Court adopted to reduce the likelihood of eyewitness misidentification. Then, relying again on empirical research by psychologists, we'll examine and evaluate some leading recommendations for improving the reliability of eyewitness identification.

Finally, we'll look at the growing reliance on DNA testing, its reliability, and convicted defendants' right to access it to help prove they were convicted wrongly. Figure 9.1 depicts the causes for wrongful convictions in cases where DNA exonerated convicted persons.

FIGURE 9.1 Causes for Wrongful Convictions

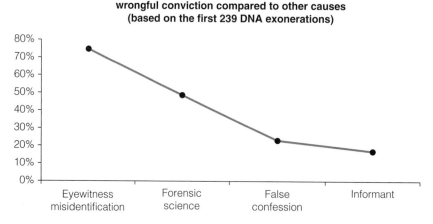

Source: Innocence Project. 2013. "Reevaluating Lineups. Why Witnesses Make Mistakes and How to Reduce the Chance of a Misidentification."

THE CONSTITUTION AND IDENTIFICATION PROCEDURES

LO **1,2** "That's him," says the witness, pointing to the defendant sitting in the courtroom. That's the image you've all seen in a dramatic moment in courtroom dramas. But what you probably don't know, or don't think much about, is that these witnesses have all made an earlier identification of the defendant—before trial and out of court. These out-of-court pretrial identifications consist of two procedures that we'll discuss in more detail later: lineups and show-ups.

1. *Lineups*. In live lineups, witnesses try to pick the suspect out of a group of individuals who are present. In photo lineups, witnesses look for the suspect in a group of photos, or a **photo array**. Although the lineups you see on TV might be live, most places in the United States use photo lineups. Even in places that still use live lineups, they're frequently preceded by photo lineups (Wells, Memon, and Penrod 2006, 50).

2. *Show-ups*. Witnesses try to match the suspect with one person, either by live appearance or a "mug shot" photo.

LO **1,2** ## The *Wade-Gilbert-Stovall* Trio

Until 1967, the courts, including the U.S. Supreme Court, adopted a "hands-off" approach to admitting evidence of lineups and show-ups. Their reasoning was that it was up to juries to assess the reliability of this evidence, not courts. Then came a trio of eyewitness cases that the U.S. Supreme Court decided on the same day. The first two cases brought the Sixth Amendment right to counsel into the evaluation of eyewitness identification.

In *U.S. v. Wade* (1967), Billie Joe Wade participated in a lineup conducted after he was indicted, without his lawyer present. The Court held that the lineup after indictment without his lawyer there violated Wade's Sixth Amendment right to counsel. *Gilbert v. California* (1967) held that a "bright-line" per se exclusionary rule banned the introduction of an out-of-court lineup identification made in violation of Jesse James Gilbert's right to counsel.

The third case, *Stovall v. Denno* (1967), introduced due process rights into determining the admissibility of evidence derived from a pretrial show-up before indictment. In *Stovall*, Dr. Paul Behrendt was stabbed to death in his kitchen. His wife, also a doctor, followed her husband to the kitchen and jumped the assailant, who knocked her down and stabbed her 11 times. The police found a shirt on the floor with keys in the pocket, which they traced to Ted Stovall. Seven police officers brought Stovall to Dr. Behrendt's hospital room the day after she underwent surgery to save her life. Stovall, handcuffed to one of the seven officers, was the only Black in the room. Dr. Behrendt identified him. At trial, Dr. Behrendt testified to her out-of-court identification and identified Stovall again in the courtroom (295).

Although the Court upheld the admissibility of the show-up, it recognized, for the first time, that due process was a basis for challenging identification testimony on constitutional grounds. Whether the hospital room show-up was a violation of due process depended on whether the circumstances were "so unnecessarily suggestive and conducive to irreparable mistaken identification that he was denied due process of law."

Under the totality of the circumstances, the Court ruled that showing Stovall to Mrs. Behrendt immediately was imperative. "Here was the only person in the world who could possibly exonerate Stovall. Her words, and only her words, 'He is not the man' could have resulted in freedom for Stovall. Under these circumstances, the usual police station lineup was out of the question" (302).

LO 1, 2, 3   "Reliability Is the Linchpin"

Some of the Court's language in *Stovall* suggested, and some lower courts adopted, a bright-line per se rule that focused on the susceptibility of identification procedures to suggestion. The rule is that identifications that result from "unnecessarily suggestive" identification procedures should be excluded from trial. But, in later decisions, the Court brought the Constitution only a small way into eyewitness identification procedures. Why? Because, to exclude identification evidence on due process grounds, defendants have to prove by a **preponderance of the evidence** (it's more likely than not) that the totality of the circumstances shows that:

1. The identification procedure was unnecessarily suggestive.
2. The unnecessarily suggestive procedure created a very substantial likelihood of misidentification

Notice the effect of the two-pronged test: **Unnecessarily and impermissibly suggestive** identifications are admissible *unless* defendants can prove that they create a **"very substantial likelihood of misidentification."** The two-prong test demonstrates that, in *Manson's* majority opinion, "reliability is the linchpin" of due process in eyewitness identification. It shouldn't surprise you to learn that courts rarely, if ever, throw out eyewitness identification evidence (Table 9.1). Juries, of course, can choose to give it little or no weight, depending on the circumstances.

TABLE 9.1 Application of due process test of eyewitness identification reliability

Lower Federal Court Cases	Court's Holding	Eyewitness Identification
U.S. v. Wong, 40 F.3d 1347 (CA2 1994)	Not impermissibly suggestive; if it was, it was still reliable and admissible	In restaurant shooting of a Green Dragon gang member: Witness saw shooter for a "few seconds" as she ducked under a table. Viewed 3 photo lineups, couldn't be sure; during third: "It looked like" the shooter. Officers told her repeatedly they believed they had the right man.
Clarke v. Caspari, 274 F.3d 507 (CA8 2002)	Reliable	Two liquor store clerks viewed two handcuffed Black suspects "surrounded by White officers, one of whom was holding a shotgun."

Lower Federal Court Cases	Court's Holding	Eyewitness Identification
Howard v. Bouchard, 405 F.3d 459 (CA6 2008)	Reliable, only "minimally suggestive"	Witness who saw defendant at defense table with his lawyer about one hour before lineup, which could have unnecessarily suggested he was the culprit.
State Court Cases		
State v. Thompson, 839 A.2d 622 (Conn.App. 2004)	Reliable and admissible	Police officer drove witness to show-up at the place where suspect was apprehended. Officer told witness, "We believe we have the person. We need you to identify him." Asked witness to identify the person, who was "probably the shooter." Shined spotlights and headlights on squad car, then removed suspect from back of the car for the show-up.
State v. Johnson, 836 N.E. 2d 1243 (OhioApp. 2005)	Reliable	Murder victim's wife failed to identify juvenile suspect from photo lineup a month after the murder. Seven months later, she identified juvenile dressed in Department of Youth Services clothing, maybe handcuffed, the only young Black sitting at the defense table, at a court hearing in juvenile court to transfer him for trial as an adult.
Bynum v. State, 929 So.2d 324 (Miss.App. 2005)	Reliable	One week after a robber attacked the victim, she selected, from a photo lineup, the suspect and one other person. Victim stated that Bynum "looked the most like the attacker." Four days later, in second photo lineup containing Bynum but not the second person she selected in the first lineup, victim selected Bynum "positively and unequivocally." Second individual witnessed the crime, wasn't able to pick out the attacker from the lineup, but later identified Bynum as the robber. Third witness identified Bynum in the lineup, later testified he was "100% certain" of his identification.

The Court has identified five factors in the "totality of circumstances" that should weigh heavily in determining whether the "unnecessarily and impermissibly suggestive" procedure created a "very substantial likelihood of misidentification" in lineups and show-ups:

1. Witnesses' opportunity to view defendants at the time of the crime
2. Witnesses' degree of attention at the time of the crime
3. Witnesses' accuracy of description of defendants prior to the identification
4. Witnesses' level of certainty when identifying defendants at the time of the identification procedure
5. The length of time between the crime and the identification (*Manson v. Brathwaite* 1977).

In *Manson v. Brathwaite* (1977), our next case excerpt, the Court rejected Nowell Brathwaite's claim that State Trooper Jimmy Glover's single photo show-up identification violated due process.

In *Manson v. Brathwaite* (1977), the U.S. Supreme Court ruled that Trooper Jimmy Glover's single photo show-up identification did not create a "very substantial likelihood" of a false identification.

CASE

Did the Photo Show-Up Create a "Very Substantial Likelihood of Misidentification"?

Manson v. Brathwaite
432 U.S. 98 (1977)

HISTORY

Nowell Brathwaite was charged with possession and sale of heroin. The jury found him guilty, and the judge sentenced him to not less than six nor more than nine years. The Supreme Court of Connecticut affirmed. Fourteen months later, Brathwaite filed a petition for habeas corpus in the U.S. District Court for the District of Connecticut. The District Court dismissed his petition. On appeal, the U.S. Court of Appeals for the Second Circuit reversed. The U.S. District Court for the District of Connecticut denied relief, and Brathwaite appealed. The Court of Appeals, Second Circuit, reversed. The U.S. Supreme Court granted certiorari and reversed.

—BLACKMUN, J.

FACTS

Jimmy D. Glover, a trained Black undercover state police officer, was assigned to the Narcotics Division in 1970.

On May 5 of that year, at about 7:45 p.m., EDT, and while there was still daylight, Glover and Henry Alton Brown, an informant, went to an apartment building at 201 Westland, in Hartford, to buy narcotics from "Dickie Boy" Cicero, a known narcotics dealer.

Cicero, it was thought, lived on the third floor of that apartment building. Glover and Brown entered the building, observed by back-up Officers D'Onofrio and Gaffey, and proceeded by stairs to the third floor. Glover knocked at the door of one of the two apartments served by the stairway. It appears that the door on which Glover knocked may not have been that of the Cicero apartment. Petitioner [John Manson, Commissioner of Corrections] concedes that the transaction "was with some other person than had been intended." The area was illuminated by natural light from a window in the third floor hallway.

The door opened 12 to 18 inches. Glover observed a man standing at the door and, behind him, a woman. Brown identified himself. Glover then asked for "two things" of narcotics. The man at the door held out his hand, and Glover gave him two $10 bills. The door closed. Soon the man returned and handed Glover two glassine bags. . . . This was Glover's testimony. Brown later was called as a witness for the prosecution. He testified on direct examination that, due to his then use of heroin, he had no clear recollection of the details of the incident. On cross-examination, as in an interview with defense counsel the preceding day, he said that it was a woman who opened the door, received the money, and thereafter produced the narcotics. On redirect, he acknowledged that he was using heroin daily at the time, that he had had some that day, and that there was "an inability to recall and remember events."

While the door was open, Glover stood within two feet of the person from whom he made the purchase and observed his face. Five to seven minutes elapsed from the time the door first opened until it closed the second time.

Glover and Brown then left the building. This was about eight minutes after their arrival. Glover drove to headquarters where he described the seller to D'Onofrio and Gaffey. Glover at that time did not know the identity of the seller. He described him as being "a colored man, approximately five feet eleven inches tall, dark complexion, black hair, short Afro style, and having high cheekbones, and of heavy build. He was wearing at the time blue pants and a plaid shirt."

D'Onofrio, suspecting from this description that Brathwaite might be the seller, obtained a photograph of him from the Records Division of the Hartford Police Department. He left it at Glover's office. D'Onofrio was not acquainted with Brathwaite personally but did know him by sight and had seen him "several times" prior to May 5. Glover, when alone, viewed the photograph for the first time upon his return to headquarters on May 7; he identified the person shown as the one from whom he had purchased the narcotics.

Brathwaite was arrested on July 27 while visiting at the apartment of a Mrs. Ramsey on the third floor of 201 Westland. This was the apartment where the narcotics sale took place on May 5. Brathwaite testified: "Lots of times I have been there before in that building." He also testified that Mrs. Ramsey was a friend of his wife, that her apartment was the only one in the building he ever visited, and that he and his family, consisting of his wife and five children, did not live there but at 453 Albany Avenue, Hartford.

Brathwaite was charged, in a two-count information, with possession and sale of heroin. At his trial in January 1971, the photograph from which Glover had identified Brathwaite was received in evidence without objection on the part of the defense. Glover also testified that, although he had not seen Brathwaite in the eight months that had elapsed since the sale, "there was no doubt whatsoever" in his mind that the person shown on the photograph was respondent. Glover also made a positive in-court identification without objection. No explanation was offered by the prosecution for the failure to utilize a photographic array or to conduct a lineup.

Brathwaite, who took the stand in his own defense, testified that on May 5, the day in question, he had been ill at his Albany Avenue apartment ("a lot of back pains, muscle spasms, a bad heart, high blood pressure, neuralgia in my face, and sinus") and that at no time on that particular day had he been at 201 Westland. His wife testified that she recalled, after her husband had refreshed her memory, that he was home all day on May 5. Doctor Wesley M. Vietzke, an internist and assistant professor of medicine at the University of Connecticut, testified that Brathwaite had consulted him on April 15, 1970, and that he took a medical history from him, heard his complaints about his back and facial pain, and discovered that he had high blood pressure. The physician found Brathwaite, subjectively, "in great discomfort." Brathwaite in fact underwent surgery for a herniated disc at L5 and S1 on August 17.

The jury found Brathwaite guilty on both counts of the information. He received a sentence of not less than six nor more than nine years. His conviction was affirmed by the Supreme Court of Connecticut. That court noted the absence of an objection to Glover's in-court identification and concluded that Brathwaite "has not shown that substantial injustice resulted from the admission of this evidence." Under Connecticut law, substantial injustice must be shown before a claim of error not made or passed on by the trial court will be considered on appeal.

Fourteen months later, Brathwaite filed a petition for habeas corpus in the U.S. District Court for the District of Connecticut. On appeal, the United States Court of Appeals for the Second Circuit reversed. We granted certiorari.

OPINION

The petitioner, Connecticut Commissioner of Corrections, acknowledges that "the procedure in the instant case was suggestive (because only one photograph was used) and unnecessary" (because there was no emergency or exigent circumstance). Brathwaite, in agreement with the Court of Appeals, proposes a per se rule of exclusion that he claims is dictated by the demands of the Fourteenth Amendment's guarantee of due process. He rightly observes this is the first case in which this Court has had occasion to rule upon out-of-court identification evidence of the challenged kind.

Since the decision in *Neil v. Biggers*, the Courts of Appeals appear to have developed at least two approaches to such evidence. The first, or **per se approach** [looking at the totality of circumstances to determine whether an identification should be admitted into evidence], employed by the Second Circuit in the present case, focuses on the procedures employed and requires exclusion of the out-of-court identification evidence,

(continued)

without regard to reliability, whenever it has been obtained through unnecessarily suggestive confrontation procedures. The justifications advanced are the elimination of evidence of uncertain reliability, deterrence of the police and prosecutors, and the fair assurance against the awful risks of misidentification.

The second, or more lenient, approach is one that continues to rely on the **totality of the circumstances** [weighing all the facts surrounding the government's establishing identification of the suspect to determine if it's reliable enough to be admitted]. [This approach] permits the admission of the confrontation evidence if, despite the suggestive aspect, the out-of-court identification possesses certain features of reliability. Its adherents feel that the per se approach is not mandated by the Due Process Clause of the Fourteenth Amendment. This second approach, in contrast to the other, is ad hoc and serves to limit the societal costs imposed by a sanction that excludes relevant evidence from consideration and evaluation by the trier of fact.

Mr. Justice STEVENS, in writing for the Seventh Circuit in *Kirby v. Illinois*, observed: "There is surprising unanimity among scholars in regarding such a rule (the per se approach) as essential to avoid serious risk of miscarriage of justice." He pointed out that well-known federal judges have taken the position that "evidence of, or derived from, a show-up identification should be inadmissible unless the prosecutor can justify his failure to use a more reliable identification procedure." Indeed, the *ALI Model Code of Pre-Arraignment Procedure* §§ 160.1 and 160.2 (1975), frowns upon the use of a show-up or the display of only a single photograph.

Brathwaite stresses the same theme and the need for deterrence of improper identification practice, a factor he regards as pre-eminent. Photographic identification, it is said, continues to be needlessly employed. He notes that the legislative regulation "the Court had hoped would engender," has not been forthcoming. He argues that a totality rule cannot be expected to have a significant deterrent impact; only a strict rule of exclusion will have direct and immediate impact on law enforcement agents.

Identification evidence is so convincing to the jury that sweeping exclusionary rules are required. Fairness of the trial is threatened by suggestive confrontation evidence, and thus, it is said, an exclusionary rule has an established constitutional predicate.

There are, of course, several interests to be considered and taken into account. The driving force behind *United States v. Wade* (1967), *Gilbert v. California* (1967) (right to counsel at a post-indictment lineup), and *Stovall*, all decided on the same day, was the Court's concern with the problems of eyewitness identification. Usually the witness must testify about an encounter with a total stranger under circumstances of emergency or emotional stress. The witness's recollection of the stranger can be distorted easily by the circumstances or by later actions of the police.

Thus, *Wade* and its companion cases reflect the concern that the jury not hear eyewitness testimony unless that evidence has aspects of reliability. It must be observed that both approaches before us are responsive to this concern. The per se rule, however, goes too far since its application automatically and peremptorily, and without consideration of alleviating factors, keeps evidence from the jury that is reliable and relevant. The second factor is deterrence. Although the per se approach has the more significant deterrent effect, the totality approach also has an influence on police behavior. The police will guard against unnecessarily suggestive procedures under the totality rule, as well as the per se one, for fear that their actions will lead to the exclusion of identifications as unreliable.

The third factor is the effect on the administration of justice. Here the per se approach suffers serious drawbacks. Since it denies the trier reliable evidence, it may result, on occasion, in the guilty going free. Also, because of its rigidity, the per se approach may make error by the trial judge more likely than the totality approach. And in those cases in which the admission of identification evidence is error under the per se approach but not under the totality approach—cases in which the identification is reliable despite an unnecessarily suggestive identification procedure—reversal is a Draconian sanction. Unlike a warrantless search, a suggestive preindictment identification procedure does not in itself intrude upon a constitutionally protected interest.

Thus, considerations urging the exclusion of evidence deriving from a constitutional violation do not bear on the instant problem. Certainly, inflexible rules of exclusion that may frustrate rather than promote justice have not been viewed recently by this Court with unlimited enthusiasm. The standard, after all, is that of fairness as required by the Due Process Clause of the Fourteenth Amendment.

We turn, then, to the facts of this case and apply the analysis:

1. *The opportunity to view.* Glover testified that for two to three minutes he stood at the apartment door, within two feet of the respondent. The door opened twice, and each time the man stood at the door. The moments passed, the conversation took place, and payment was made. Glover looked directly at his vendor. It was near sunset, to be sure, but the sun had not yet set, so it was not dark or even dusk or twilight. Natural light from outside entered the hallway through a window. There was natural light, as well, from inside the apartment.

2. *The degree of attention.* Glover was not a casual or passing observer, as is so often the case with eyewitness identification. Trooper Glover was a trained police officer on duty—and specialized and dangerous duty—when he called at the third floor of

201 Westland in Hartford on May 5, 1970. Glover himself was a Negro and unlikely to perceive only general features of "hundreds of Hartford Black males," as the Court of Appeals stated. It is true that Glover's duty was that of ferreting out narcotics offenders and that he would be expected in his work to produce results. But it is also true that, as a specially trained, assigned, and experienced officer, he could be expected to pay scrupulous attention to detail, for he knew that subsequently he would have to find and arrest his vendor. In addition, he knew that his claimed observations would be subject later to close scrutiny and examination at any trial.

3. *The accuracy of the description.* Glover's description was given to D'Onofrio within minutes after the transaction. It included the vendor's race, his height, his build, the color and style of his hair, and the high cheekbone facial feature. It also included clothing the vendor wore.

   No claim has been made that Brathwaite did not possess the physical characteristics so described. D'Onofrio reacted positively at once. Two days later, when Glover was alone, he viewed the photograph D'Onofrio produced and identified its subject as the narcotics seller.

4. *The witness's level of certainty.* There is no dispute that the photograph in question was that of Brathwaite. Glover, in response to a question whether the photograph was that of the person from whom he made the purchase, testified: "There is no question whatsoever." This positive assurance was repeated.

5. *The time between the crime and the confrontation.* Glover's description of his vendor was given to D'Onofrio within minutes of the crime. The photographic identification took place only two days later. We do not have here the passage of weeks or months between the crime and the viewing of the photograph.

These indicators of Glover's ability to make an accurate identification are hardly outweighed by the corrupting effect of the challenged identification itself. Although identifications arising from single-photograph displays may be viewed in general with suspicion, we find in the instant case little pressure on the witness to acquiesce in the suggestion that such a display entails. D'Onofrio had left the photograph at Glover's office and was not present when Glover first viewed it two days after the event. There thus was little urgency and Glover could view the photograph at his leisure. And since Glover examined the photograph alone, there was no coercive pressure to make an identification arising from the presence of another. The identification was made in circumstances allowing care and reflection.

Although it plays no part in our analysis, all this assurance as to the reliability of the identification is hardly

undermined by the facts that Brathwaite was arrested in the very apartment where the sale had taken place, and that he acknowledged his frequent visits to that apartment. Mrs. Ramsey was not a witness at the trial.

Surely, we cannot say that under all the circumstances of this case there is "a very substantial likelihood of irreparable misidentification." Short of that point, such evidence is for the jury to weigh. We are content to rely upon the good sense and judgment of American juries, for evidence with some element of untrustworthiness is customary grist for the jury mill. Juries are not so susceptible that they cannot measure intelligently the weight of identification testimony that has some questionable feature.

Of course, it would have been better had D'Onofrio presented Glover with a photographic array including "so far as practicable a reasonable number of persons similar to any person then suspected whose likeness is included in the array." *Model Code,* § 160.2(2). The use of that procedure would have enhanced the force of the identification at trial and would have avoided the risk that the evidence would be excluded as unreliable. But we are not disposed to view D'Onofrio's failure as one of constitutional dimension to be enforced by a rigorous and unbending exclusionary rule. The defect, if there be one, goes to weight and not to substance.

We conclude that the criteria laid down in *Biggers* are to be applied in determining the admissibility of evidence offered by the prosecution concerning a post-*Stovall* identification, and that those criteria are satisfactorily met and complied with here.

The judgment of the Court of Appeals is REVERSED.

CONCURRING OPINION

STEVENS, J.

The arguments in favor of fashioning new rules to minimize the danger of convicting the innocent on the basis of unreliable eyewitness testimony carry substantial force. Nevertheless, I am persuaded that this rulemaking function can be performed more effectively by the legislative process than by a somewhat clumsy judicial fiat and that the Federal Constitution does not foreclose experimentation by the States in the development of such rules.

DISSENT

MARSHALL, J., joined by BRENNAN, J.

It is distressing to see the Court virtually ignore the teaching of experience and blindly uphold the conviction of a defendant who may well be innocent. Relying on numerous studies made over many years by such scholars as Professor Wigmore and Mr. Justice Frankfurter, the Court in *U.S. v. Wade* (1967), concluded that "the vagaries of eyewitness identification are well-known; the annals of criminal law are rife with instances of mistaken identification."

(continued)

It is, of course, impossible to control one source of such errors—the faulty perceptions and unreliable memories of witnesses—except through vigorously contested trials conducted by diligent counsel and judges. The Court acted, however, to minimize the more preventable threat posed to accurate identification by "the degree of suggestion inherent in the manner in which the prosecution presents the suspect to witnesses for pretrial identification."

Despite my strong disagreement with the Court over the proper standards [totality of circumstances] to be applied in this case, assuming applicability of the totality test, the facts of the present case require the exclusion of the identification in this case because it raises a very substantial likelihood of misidentification.

I consider first the opportunity that Officer Glover had to view the suspect. Careful review of the record shows he could see the heroin seller only for the time it took to speak three sentences of four or five short words, to hand over some money, and later after the door reopened, to receive the drugs in return. The entire face-to-face transaction could have taken as little as 15 or 20 seconds. But during this time, Glover's attention was not focused exclusively on the seller's face. He observed that the door was opened 12 to 18 inches, that there was a window in the room behind the door, and, most importantly, that there was a woman standing behind the man. Glover was, of course, also concentrating on the details of the transaction—he must have looked away from the seller's face to hand him the money and receive the drugs. The observation during the conversation thus may have been as brief as 5 or 10 seconds.

As the Court notes, Glover was a police officer trained in and attentive to the need for making accurate identifications. Nevertheless, both common sense and scholarly study indicate that while a trained observer such as a police officer is somewhat less likely to make an erroneous identification than the average untrained observer, the mere fact that he has been so trained is no guarantee that he is correct in a specific case. His identification testimony should be scrutinized just as carefully as that of the normal witness.

Another factor on which the Court relies, the witness's degree of certainty in making the identification, is worthless as an indicator that he is correct. Even if Glover had been unsure initially about his identification of Brathwaite's picture, by the time he was called at trial to present a key piece of evidence for the State that paid his salary, it is impossible to imagine his responding negatively to such questions as "is there any doubt in your mind whatsoever" that the identification was correct. As the Court noted in *Wade*: "It is a matter of common experience that, once a witness has picked out the accused at the (pretrial confrontation), he is not likely to go back on his word later on."

Next, the Court finds that because the identification procedure took place two days after the crime, its reliability is enhanced. While such nearness in time makes the identification more reliable than one occurring months later, the fact is that the greatest memory loss occurs within hours after an event. After that, the dropoff continues much more slowly. Thus, the reliability of an identification is increased only if it was made within several hours of the crime.

Finally, the Court makes much of the fact that Glover gave a description of the seller to D'Onofrio shortly after the incident. Despite the Court's assertion that because "Glover himself was a Negro and unlikely to perceive only general features of hundreds of Hartford Black males," the description given by Glover was actually no more than a general summary of the seller's appearance. We may discount entirely the seller's clothing, for that was of no significance later in the proceeding. Indeed, to the extent that Glover noticed clothes, his attention was diverted from the seller's face.

Otherwise, Glover merely described vaguely the seller's height, skin color, hairstyle, and build. He did say that the seller had "high cheekbones," but there is no other mention of facial features, nor even an estimate of age. Conspicuously absent is any indication that the seller was a native of the West Indies, certainly something which a member of the Black community could immediately recognize from both appearance and accent. Brathwaite had come to the United States from his native Barbados as an adult.

In contrast, the procedure used to identify Brathwaite was both extraordinarily suggestive and strongly conducive to error. By displaying a single photograph of Brathwaite to the witness Glover under the circumstances in this record almost everything that could have been done wrong was done wrong.

In the first place, there was no need to use a photograph at all. Because photos are static, two-dimensional, and often outdated, they are clearly inferior in reliability to live person lineups and show-ups. While the use of photographs is justifiable and often essential where the police have no knowledge of an offender's identity, the poor reliability of photos makes their use inexcusable where any other means of identification is available.

Here, since Detective D'Onofrio believed he knew the seller's identity, further investigation without resort to a photographic show-up was easily possible. With little inconvenience, a live person lineup including Brathwaite might have been arranged. Indeed, the police carefully staged Brathwaite's arrest in the same apartment that was used for the sale, indicating that they were fully capable of keeping track of his whereabouts and using this information in their investigation.

Worse still than the failure to use an easily available live person identification was the display to Glover of only a single picture, rather than a photo array. With good reason, such single-suspect procedures have been widely condemned. They give no assurance the witness can identify the criminal from among a number of persons of similar appearance, surely the strongest evidence that there was no misidentification.

The danger of error is at its greatest when the police display to the witness only the picture of a single individual. The use of a single picture (or the display of a single live suspect, for that matter) is a grave error, of course, because it dramatically suggests to the witness that the person shown must be the culprit. Why else would the police choose the person? And it is deeply ingrained in human nature to agree with the expressed opinions of others—particularly others who should be more knowledgeable—when making a difficult decision.

In this case, moreover, the pressure was not limited to that inherent in the display of a single photograph. Glover, the identifying witness, was a state police officer on special assignment. He knew that D'Onofrio, an experienced Hartford narcotics detective, presumably familiar with local drug operations, believed respondent to be the seller. There was at work, then, both loyalty to another police officer and deference to a better-informed colleague.

While the Court is impressed by D'Onofrio's immediate response to Glover's description, the detective, who had not witnessed the transaction, acted on a wild guess that Brathwaite was the seller. D'Onofrio's hunch rested solely on Glover's vague description, yet D'Onofrio had seen Brathwaite only "several times, mostly in his vehicle." There was no evidence that Brathwaite was even a suspected narcotics dealer, and D'Onofrio thought that the drugs had been purchased at a different apartment from the one Glover actually went to. The identification of Brathwaite provides a perfect example of the investigator and the witness bolstering each other's inadequate knowledge to produce a seemingly accurate but actually worthless identification.

The Court discounts this overwhelming evidence of suggestiveness, however. It reasons that because

D'Onofrio was not present when Glover viewed the photograph, there was "little pressure on the witness to acquiesce in the suggestion." That conclusion blinks psychological reality. There is no doubt in my mind that even in D'Onofrio's absence, a clear and powerful message was telegraphed to Glover as he looked at respondent's photograph. He was emphatically told that "this is the man," and he responded by identifying Brathwaite then and at trial whether or not he was in fact "the man."

I must conclude that this record presents compelling evidence that there was "a very substantial likelihood of misidentification" of respondent Brathwaite. The suggestive display of Brathwaite's photograph to the witness Glover likely erased any independent memory Glover had retained of the seller from his barely adequate opportunity to observe the criminal.

Accordingly, I dissent.

Questions

1. Describe the three approaches to dealing with misidentifications outlined by the majority opinion.

2. Which approach does the Court adopt? Why?

3. List the facts in each of the five factors and the majority opinion's assessment of them.

4. List the facts in the same way and the dissent's assessment of them.

5. Do you think the circumstances demonstrate "a very substantial likelihood of irreparable misidentification"?

6. Summarize the dissent's argument in favor of the per se test and against the totality test. Is the dissent correct in arguing that the Court wrongfully evaluated the impact of the exclusionary rule and the totality of circumstances? Evaluate those arguments.

7. Is the dissent's stress on Brathwaite's Barbados ancestry important? Explain.

8. Would you side with the dissent or the majority in this case? Defend your answer.

LO **2, 4**   Ever since the Supreme Court brought identification procedures within the protection of the due process requirement, lower courts have had to deal with situations where the police didn't arrange the identification procedure. In some of these cases, law enforcement had so little to do with the identification that courts ruled that there was no due process violation because there was no "state action." **"Accidental show-ups"** presented the most difficult cases. These are cases where the witness happens to see a defendant in custody, say outside the courtroom or in the police station. In a number of these cases, more careful police work could have prevented these "accidents." But, most courts didn't see mistakes that way. Instead, they ruled that no due process violation occurred because the "mistake" wasn't the police or prosecutor's fault. A few federal courts, however, took the opposite view (LaFave and others 2012, Supp., 19). The Court settled the matter in our next case excerpt, *Perry v. New Hampshire* (2012).

In *Perry v. New Hampshire*, the U.S. Supreme Court ruled that the due process clause doesn't require a hearing into the reliability of eyewitness identification procedures that weren't "arranged" by the police.

CASE

Does Due Process Apply to the "Accidental" Show-Up?

Perry v. New Hampshire
132 S.Ct. 716 (2012)

HISTORY

Barion Perry (Petitioner) was charged in New Hampshire state court with one count of theft by unauthorized taking and one count of criminal mischief resulting from his alleged attempt to break in to cars in the parking lot of an apartment building. Perry moved to suppress an out-of-court identification on the ground that its admission at trial would violate due process. The New Hampshire Superior Court denied the motion, and Perry was subsequently convicted by a jury of theft by unauthorized taking. The Supreme Court of New Hampshire affirmed his conviction. The U.S. Supreme Court granted certiorari and affirmed.

—GINSBURG, J., joined by ROBERTS, C.J., and SCALIA, KENNEDY, THOMAS, BREYER, ALITO, and KAGAN, JJ.

An identification infected by improper police influence, our case law holds, is not automatically excluded. Instead, the trial judge must screen the evidence for reliability pretrial. If there is "a very substantial likelihood of irreparable misidentification," *Simmons v. United States*, 390 U.S. 377 (1968), the judge must disallow presentation of the evidence at trial. But if the indicia of reliability are strong enough to outweigh the corrupting effect of the police-arranged suggestive circumstances, the identification evidence ordinarily will be admitted, and the jury will ultimately determine its worth.

We have not extended pretrial screening for reliability to cases in which the suggestive circumstances were not arranged by law enforcement officers. Petitioner Perry requests that we do so because of the grave risk that mistaken identification will yield a miscarriage of justice. Our decisions, however, turn on the presence of state action and aim to deter police from rigging identification procedures, for example, at a lineup, show-up, or photograph array. When no improper law enforcement activity is involved, we hold, it suffices to test reliability through the rights and opportunities generally designed for that purpose, notably, the presence of counsel at post-indictment lineups, vigorous cross-examination, protective rules of evidence, and jury instructions on both the fallibility of eyewitness identification and the requirement that guilt be proved beyond a reasonable doubt.

FACTS

Around 3 a.m. on August 15, 2008, Joffre Ullon called the Nashua, New Hampshire, Police Department and reported that an African–American male was trying to break into cars parked in the lot of Ullon's apartment building. Officer Nicole Clay responded to the call. Upon arriving at the parking lot, Clay heard what "sounded like a metal bat hitting the ground." She then saw petitioner Barion Perry standing between two cars. Perry walked toward Clay, holding two car-stereo amplifiers in his hands. A metal bat lay on the ground behind him. Clay asked Perry where the amplifiers came from. "I found them on the ground," Perry responded.

Meanwhile, Ullon's wife, Nubia Blandon, woke her neighbor, Alex Clavijo, and told him she had just seen someone break into his car. Clavijo immediately went downstairs to the parking lot to inspect the car. He first observed that one of the rear windows had been shattered. On further inspection, he discovered that the speakers and amplifiers from his car stereo were missing, as were his bat and wrench. Clavijo then approached Clay and told her about Blandon's alert and his own subsequent observations.

By this time, another officer had arrived at the scene. Clay asked Perry to stay in the parking lot with that officer, while she and Clavijo went to talk to Blandon. Clay and Clavijo then entered the apartment building and took the stairs to the fourth floor, where Blandon's and Clavijo's apartments were located. They met Blandon in the hallway just outside the open door to her apartment.

Asked to describe what she had seen, Blandon stated that, around 2:30 a.m., she saw from her kitchen window a tall, African–American man roaming the parking lot and looking into cars. Eventually, the man circled Clavijo's car, opened the trunk, and removed a large box. The box, which Clay found on the ground near where she first encountered Perry, contained car-stereo speakers.

Clay asked Blandon for a more specific description of the man. Blandon pointed to her kitchen window and said the person she saw breaking into Clavijo's car was standing in the parking lot, next to the police officer. Perry's arrest followed this identification.

About a month later, the police showed Blandon a photographic array that included a picture of Perry and asked her to point out the man who had broken into Clavijo's car. Blandon was unable to identify Perry.

Perry was charged in New Hampshire state court with one count of theft by unauthorized taking and one count of criminal mischief. The theft charge was based on the taking of items from Clavijo's car, while the criminal mischief count was founded on the shattering of Clavijo's car window. Before trial, he moved to suppress Blandon's identification on the ground that admitting it at trial would violate due process. Blandon witnessed what amounted to a one-person show-up in the parking lot, Perry asserted, which all but guaranteed that she would identify him as the culprit.

OPINION

We granted certiorari to resolve a division of opinion on the question whether the Due Process Clause requires a trial judge to conduct a preliminary assessment of the reliability of an eyewitness identification made under suggestive circumstances not arranged by the police. The Constitution, our decisions indicate, protects a defendant against a conviction based on evidence of questionable reliability, not by prohibiting introduction of the evidence, but by affording the defendant means to persuade the jury that the evidence should be discounted as unworthy of credit.

Synthesizing previous decisions, we set forth in *Neil v. Biggers*, 409 U.S. 188 (1972), and reiterated in *Manson v. Brathwaite*, 432 U.S. 98 (1977), the approach appropriately used to determine whether the Due Process Clause requires suppression of an eyewitness identification tainted by police arrangement. The Court emphasized, first, that due process concerns arise only when

law enforcement officers use an identification procedure that is both suggestive and unnecessary. Even when the police use such a procedure, the Court next said, suppression of the resulting identification is not the inevitable consequence.

A rule requiring automatic exclusion, the Court reasoned, would "go too far," for it would "keep evidence from the jury that is reliable and relevant," and "may result, on occasion, in the guilty going free." Instead of mandating a *per se* exclusionary rule, the Court held that the Due Process Clause requires courts to assess, on a case-by-case basis, whether improper police conduct created a "substantial likelihood of misidentification." "Reliability of the eyewitness identification is the linchpin" of that evaluation, the Court stated in *Brathwaite*. Where the "indicators of a witness's ability to make an accurate identification" are "outweighed by the corrupting effect" of law enforcement suggestion, the identification should be suppressed. Otherwise, the evidence (if admissible in all other respects) should be submitted to the jury.

Perry concedes that law enforcement officials did not arrange the suggestive circumstances surrounding Blandon's identification. [But,] the rationale underlying our decisions, Perry asserts, supports a rule requiring trial judges to prescreen eyewitness evidence for reliability any time an identification is made under suggestive circumstances. We disagree. Perry's position would open the door to judicial preview, under the banner of due process, of most, if not all, eyewitness identifications. To embrace Perry's view would thus entail a vast enlargement of the reach of due process as a constraint on the admission of evidence. Perry maintains that the Court can limit the due process check he proposes to identifications made under "suggestive circumstances." Even if we could rationally distinguish suggestiveness from other factors bearing on the reliability of eyewitness evidence, Perry's limitation would still involve trial courts, routinely, in preliminary examinations. Most eyewitness identifications involve some element of suggestion. Indeed, all in-court identifications do. Out-of-court identifications volunteered by witnesses are also likely to involve suggestive circumstances.

Our unwillingness to enlarge the domain of due process as Perry urges rests, in large part, on our recognition that the jury, not the judge, traditionally determines the reliability of evidence.

We also take account of other safeguards built into our adversary system that caution juries against placing undue weight on eyewitness testimony of questionable reliability. After closing arguments, the trial court read the jury a lengthy instruction on identification testimony and the factors the jury should consider when evaluating it. The court also instructed the jury that the defendant's guilt must be proved beyond a reasonable doubt, and

(continued)

specifically cautioned that "one of the things the State must prove beyond a reasonable doubt is the identification of the defendant as the person who committed the offense."

Given the safeguards generally applicable in criminal trials, protections availed of by the defense in Perry's case, we hold that the introduction of Blandon's eyewitness testimony, without a preliminary judicial assessment of its reliability, did not render Perry's trial fundamentally unfair.

AFFIRMED.

DISSENT

SOTOMAYOR, J.

This Court has long recognized that eyewitness identifications' unique confluence of features—their unreliability, susceptibility to suggestion, powerful impact on the jury, and resistance to the ordinary tests of the adversarial process—can undermine the fairness of a trial. Our cases thus establish a clear rule: The admission at trial of out-of-court eyewitness identifications derived from impermissibly suggestive circumstances that pose a very substantial likelihood of misidentification violates due process. The Court today announces that that rule does not even "come into play" unless the suggestive circumstances are improperly "police-arranged."

Our due process concern, however, arises not from the act of suggestion, but rather from the corrosive effects of suggestion on the reliability of the resulting identification. By rendering protection contingent on improper police arrangement of the suggestive circumstances, the Court effectively grafts a *mens rea* inquiry onto our rule. The Court's holding enshrines a murky distinction—between suggestive confrontations intentionally orchestrated by the police and, as here, those inadvertently caused by police actions—that will sow confusion. It ignores our precedents' acute sensitivity to the hazards of intentional and unintentional suggestion alike and unmoors our rule from the very interest it protects, inviting arbitrary results. And it recasts the driving force of our decisions as an interest in police deterrence, rather than reliability. Because I see no warrant for declining to assess the circumstances of this case under our ordinary approach, I respectfully dissent.

The majority does not simply hold that an eyewitness identification must be the product of police action to trigger our ordinary two-step inquiry. Rather, the majority maintains that the suggestive circumstances giving rise to the identification must be "police-arranged," "police rigged," "police-designed," or "police-organized." Those terms connote a degree of intentional orchestration or manipulation. The majority categorically exempts all eyewitness identifications derived from suggestive circumstances that were not police-manipulated—however suggestive, and however unreliable—from our due process check.

It bears reminding, moreover, that we set a high bar for suppression. The vast majority of eyewitnesses proceed to testify before a jury. To date, *Foster* is the only case in which we have found a due process violation. There has been no flood of claims in the four Federal Circuits that, having seen no basis for an arrangement-based distinction in our precedents, have long indicated that due process scrutiny applies to all suggestive identification procedures. Today's decision nonetheless precludes even the possibility that an unintended confrontation will meet that bar, mandating summary dismissal of every such claim at the threshold.

Finally, the majority questions how to "rationally distinguish suggestiveness from other factors bearing on the reliability of eyewitness evidence," such as "poor vision" or a prior "grudge," and more broadly, how to distinguish eyewitness evidence from other kinds of arguably unreliable evidence. Our precedents, however, did just that. We emphasized "the formidable number of instances in the records of English and American trials of miscarriages of justice from mistaken identification." We then observed that "the influence of improper suggestion upon identifying witnesses probably accounts for more miscarriages of justice than any other single factor."

It would be one thing if the passage of time had cast doubt on the empirical premises of our precedents. But just the opposite has happened. A vast body of scientific literature has reinforced every concern our precedents articulated nearly a half-century ago. Over the past three decades, more than two thousand studies related to eyewitness identification have been published. One state supreme court recently appointed a special master to conduct an exhaustive survey of the current state of the scientific evidence and concluded that "the research is not only extensive," but "it represents the 'gold standard in terms of the applicability of social science research to law.' " *State v. Henderson*, 27 A.3d 872, 916 (2011). "Experimental methods and findings have been tested and retested, subjected to scientific scrutiny through peer-reviewed journals, evaluated through the lens of meta-analyses, and replicated at times in real-world settings."

The empirical evidence demonstrates that eyewitness misidentification is "the single greatest cause of wrongful convictions in this country." Researchers have found that a staggering 76% of the first 250 convictions overturned due to DNA evidence since 1989 involved eyewitness misidentification. Study after study demonstrates that eyewitness recollections are highly susceptible to distortion by postevent information or social cues; that jurors routinely overestimate the accuracy of eyewitness identifications; that jurors place the greatest weight on eyewitness confidence in assessing identifications even though confidence is a poor gauge of accuracy; and that suggestiveness can stem from sources beyond police-orchestrated procedures. The majority today nevertheless adopts an artificially narrow conception of the dangers of suggestive identifications at a time when our concerns should have deepened.

The Court's opinion today renders the defendant's due process protection contingent on whether the suggestive circumstances giving rise to the eyewitness identification stem from improper police arrangement. That view lies in tension with our precedents' more holistic conception of the dangers of suggestion and is untethered from the evidentiary interest the due process right protects. In my view, the ordinary two-step inquiry should apply, whether the police created the suggestive circumstances intentionally or inadvertently. Because the New Hampshire Supreme Court truncated its inquiry at the threshold, I would vacate the judgment and remand for a proper analysis. I respectfully dissent.

Questions

1. Was the show-up accidental? Explain your answer.

2. Summarize the majority opinions arguments supporting its decision that the *Manson* two-prong test does not apply to the show-up.

3. Summarize Justice Sotomayor's arguments that the *Manson* test should apply.

4. In your opinion should the *Manson* two-prong test does apply to the show-up? Back up your answer with the arguments from the facts and opinion(s) of the Court.

SOCIAL SCIENCE AND MISTAKEN EYEWITNESS IDENTIFICATION

Do you believe that you're aware of what you can and can't remember? To introduce you to the impressive body of empirical research findings on the psychology of human perception and memory and their effect on mistaken eyewitness identification, answer the questions that follow. Decide whether you agree strongly, agree, disagree, or disagree strongly with these 10 statements about memory, which researchers presented to "typical people":

1. Memory is like a video recording of your observations that can be played back at will to remind you of what you saw.

2. When you're very confident about your memory for an event you observed, you're much more likely to be correct.

3. Your memory is stable over time.

4. Your memory for what you originally saw can be kept separate from things you learned after observing the event.

5. People's faces stand out when you observe them, and it's easy to remember faces; so recognition of faces is rarely wrong.

6. An eyewitness report is accurate evidence as to who was present and what happened.

7. Having to tell the same story of what happened over and over reinforces it and makes it more resistant to change.

8. When a weapon is visible during a crime, witnesses are more accurate in remembering the details of a crime.

9. Personally experienced traumatic events are remembered more accurately than everyday ones.

10. Observed violent events are remembered more accurately than everyday events. (Haber and Haber 2000, 1057–58)

Most "typical people" agreed or strongly agreed with all 10 of the statements. In contrast, the majority of **memory experts** ("scientists whose profession is providing empirical demonstrations of how memory actually functions") disagree. So the descriptions of the robbery in the chapter don't surprise law enforcement professionals and lawyers; they "treat this example as a common occurrence." Why? Because they've learned through experience that multiple eyewitnesses frequently describe the same event differently; that no single witness accurately describes the entire event; and that eyewitnesses frequently misidentify, with great confidence, individuals connected with the event (1058).

Relying on eyewitness identification of strangers in criminal cases is a risky business. The risks of mistaken identification are high, even in ideal settings, and the most common identification procedures—live and photo lineups and show-ups—don't take place in ideal settings. According to most experts, mistaken identification of strangers "is the single greatest cause of the conviction of the innocent" (Scheck 1997). The best guess (there aren't any reliable exact figures) is that eyewitness misidentifications account for 75 percent of the wrongful convictions of those exonerated by DNA testing (Innocence Project, "Eyewitness," 2010).

Let's look at the three stages of natural human memory—acquisition, retention, and recall—and how they can lead to mistakenly identifying strangers as culprits in criminal cases.

LO 5, 6 Memory and the Identification of Strangers

When we experience an important event, it's a much more complex process than simply recording it in our memories as a video camera would do. The camera just stores the event for later recall. Human memory, on the other hand, is both subjective and malleable. Eyewitness evidence is a form of "trace evidence." Instead of leaving physical traces like blood or semen, eyewitness evidence leaves a "**memory trace**" in the witness's mind, which we try to extract without damaging it (Loftus 1996, 21–22; Wells and Olson 2003, 279; Shay and O'Toole 2006, 118–19).

Psychologists separate memory into three phases:

1. *Acquisition of memory*. The perception of an event, when information is first entered into memory

2. *Retention of memory*. The process of storing information during the period of time between an event and the "eventual recollection of a particular piece of information" (Loftus 1996, 21)

3. *Retrieval of memory*. The time when a person recalls the stored information about an event for the purpose of identifying a person in an event

Let's look more closely at each of these stages of memory and their implications for identifying strangers in criminal cases.

The acquisition stage

Contrary to common belief, the brain isn't a digital video recorder (DVR) that records everything witnesses see. For well over a century, psychologists have proven repeatedly that the brain doesn't record exact images sent to it through our eyes. Unlike cameras, people have expectations, and our expectations and our highly developed thought processes heavily influence our acquisition of information. In short, our perceptions often trump reality. Like beauty, the physical characteristics of criminals are in the eye of the beholder, and our subjective perceptions influence heavily what happens during events, including crimes.

Attention also shapes our observations. Observers—even trained ones—don't take in everything that happens during a crime. We all pay only selective attention to what's going on around us, and this selective attention leaves wide gaps in the information we acquire during events.

The accuracy of witnesses' first observation of strangers during a crime depends on the interaction among five circumstances:

1. Length of time to observe the stranger
2. Distractions during the observation
3. Focus of the observation
4. Stress on the witness during the observation
5. Race of the witness and the stranger (Wells and Olson 2003, 279)

The longer a witness observes a stranger, the more reliable the observation. The problem is, most crimes last only seconds. Even when they last longer, other obstacles interfere with accurate observation. Descriptions witnesses give of obvious (but crucial) details, such as age, height, and weight, are often highly inaccurate. Time estimates are also unreliable, particularly during stressful situations like getting robbed or raped.

Witnesses also get distracted from focusing on the physical description to other "details" like the gun the robber waved or the knife a rapist held to his victim's face. Understandable as this "weapons focus" is, the weapon is obviously not as important as the description of the robber or rapist. Also, crimes aren't always committed under physical conditions ideal for accurately describing details; bad lighting is a good example. Equally important, stress distorts our observations.

It may *sound* convincing when a witness says, "I was so scared I could never forget that face," but research demonstrates convincingly that accuracy sharply declines during stressful events. According to C. Ronald Huff, an identification expert who conducted one study, many robbery and rape victims who were close enough to the offender to "get a look at him" were mistaken, because they were under conditions of "extreme stress. Such stress can significantly affect perception and memory and should give us cause to question the reliability of such eyewitness testimony" (reported in Yant 1991, 99).

Discouraging as the natural limits of observation, distracted focus, poor lighting, and stress are to accurate identification, race complicates matters further. Researchers have demonstrated that identifying strangers of another race substantially increases the risk of mistaken identification. In one famous experiment, researchers showed observers a photo of a White man waving a razor blade in an altercation with a Black man on a subway. When asked immediately afterward to describe what they saw, over half the subjects reported that the Black man was carrying the weapon. Furthermore, increased contact with persons of another race doesn't improve the ability to perceive their physical characteristics (Gross 1987, 398–99).

LO **5, 6**   *The retention stage*

Our memory has to store the information it perceives. Fading memory of stored information raises the already high risk of mistake caused by faulty observation. Memory fades most during the first few hours after an event (the time when it's most important to retain it). After these first hours, it fades more slowly for months and years. Curiously, at the same time witnesses' memory is fading, their *confidence* in their memory is rising. Unfortunately, courts and juries place enormous weight on witnesses' confidence, even in the face of clear proof that confidence isn't related to accuracy.

Memories don't just fade. Many things can happen to a witness during this critical retention period. Sometimes, new items are added to our memory bin. Witnesses talk about the event, overhear conversations about it, or read, hear, or watch news stories about it, all of which "bring about powerful and unexpected changes in the witness's memory" (Loftus 1996, 21–22). To borrow Professor Garrett's fine phrase, "eyewitness testimony is not just fallible; more important it is malleable" (2011, 48).

Retrieval: recall and recognition

After a crime, someone may ask the witness questions about it. At this point, the witness has to retrieve from long-term memory the specific information she needs to answer the questions. This retrieval comes from information acquired from both the original experience and information added during the retention period (22).

Retrieval arises from two phenomena: recall and recognition. In **eyewitness recall**, witnesses are given hints, such as a time frame, and then asked to report what they observed. In **eyewitness recognition**, witnesses are shown persons or objects and then asked to indicate whether they were involved in the crime. Retrieval errors can be either **errors of omission** (e.g., failure to recall some detail or to recognize a perpetrator) or **errors of commission** (picking an innocent person in a photo array) (Wells 2002, 665).

LO 6 The Power of Suggestion

As if faulty observation and fading and malleable memory aren't enough to shake our confidence in the accuracy of memory during the retrieval stage, the strong power of **suggestion** contributes further to mistaken identification. According to the widely accepted findings of psychologists, most mistaken identifications happen because of a combination of the natural imperfections of memory and the normal susceptibility to innocent and subtle suggestion (Wells and Olson 2003, 277).

Suggestion is particularly powerful (and most threatening to accuracy) during the retention and retrieval phases. Witnesses store details in one "memory storage bin," which contains information about the crime they acquired by faulty perception at the time of the crime and information that they added later during the retention stage. In her famous experiments, psychologist and eyewitness expert Elizabeth Loftus (1996) found that witnesses frequently *add* to their stories of crimes after the event. What they add depends on how she describes what happened. Loftus found that the power of her suggestions shapes what witnesses later take out of their memory bin and recall during the identification process.

Steven Penrod, Distinguished Professor of Psychology at John Jay College, says witnesses (like all of us) embellish their stories: "A witness tells his story to the police, to the family, then to friends, then to the prosecutor. As the story gets retold, it becomes more epic legend than a few facts." Witnesses "feel very confident about what they now think happened and that confidence is communicated to the jury" (quoted in Yant 1991, 100).

Let's now discuss specifically the influence of suggestion on procedures to identify strangers in criminal cases.

PSYCHOLOGICAL RESEARCH AND EYEWITNESS IDENTIFICATION

LO 6

Every day, courts hear defense attorneys challenge the accuracy of eyewitness identification evidence because of suggestive eyewitness identification procedures. Here are some common arguments:

1. The police used a show-up when they could've used a lineup.

2. The police used a lineup in which the suspect stood out.

3. The police didn't tell the witness that the culprit might not be in the lineup.

4. The police showed the witness a photo of the suspect before they conducted the lineup.

5. The police told a witness who was potentially not confident that she picked the "right" person in the lineup.

6. The police conducted a second lineup in which the only person who appeared in both lineups was the suspect. (Wells and Quinlivan 2009, 1)

Defense counsel lose these arguments in almost every case because of the **reliability test of eyewitness evidence** established in *Manson v. Brathwaite* (1977, excerpt on p. 340). Recall that the test (1) allows the admission of identification evidence based on "unnecessarily suggestive" identification procedures, (2) *unless* defendants can prove that the suggestive procedure creates a "very substantial likelihood of misidentification." In the Court's words, "Reliability is the linchpin." The reliability test remains the law of the land, despite an enormous body of empirical research that casts doubt on the reliability it was designed to enhance.

The test has also remained in the face of the widely reported finding that an embarrassing 75 percent of defendants exonerated by DNA are cases of mistaken eyewitness identification—more than all other causes combined (Innocence Project 2013). These DNA exonerations represent only a tiny fraction of actual mistaken identity, because they're limited to cases where there's a likelihood of finding DNA. That eliminates most old cases where DNA has deteriorated, is lost, or been destroyed. It also excludes almost all crimes except sexual assault because that's where the DNA is. In addition, sexual assault victims are probably better witnesses, probably among the most reliable, because they usually get a longer and closer look at the culprit than witnesses to other crimes, such as robbery (Wells and Quinlivan 2009, 2).

One final note about the exoneration cases—they all had the "benefit" of the *Manson* reliability test when they were tried. Let's look at some of this rich body of research. Coincidentally, at the same time the Supreme Court decided *Manson v. Brathwaite* (1977), psychologists were conducting eyewitness identification experiments that examined the influence of suggestive identification procedures (Wells and Quinlivan 2009, 1).

Hundreds of published experiments later, Professor Penrod (2003) concluded that "research conducted by psychologists raises serious questions about the reliability of witness performance." Keep in mind that the Supreme Court justices who decided *Manson* didn't have the benefit of this more than 30 years of research. Nevertheless, Justice Marshall, in his dissent, relied heavily on research available at the time to bolster his support for a bright-line rule that would exclude eyewitness identification evidence based on "unnecessarily suggestive" identification procedures.

Before we look at the psychological empirical research findings, you should be aware of two preliminary matters: (1) the research methods of the eyewitness studies and some criticisms of it and (2) the problem of witness self-reporting in court with regard to three of the factors in the reliability part of the *Manson* reliability test.

Identification Research Methods

Psychologists rely on two principal methods to study eyewitness identification, both common in all scientific research: archival and experimental. **Archival research** consists of analyzing real procedures used in actual criminal cases. Only a small portion of the research is archival, so we'll concentrate on the much larger experimental research. In **experimental research**, researchers create crimes (live staged or videotaped) that unsuspecting people witness. Then, researchers question them about what they witnessed and show them a lineup. Typical experiments have from 100 to 300 witnesses to stabilize the data and test hypotheses.

Because researchers create the "crime," there's no ambiguity about the actors' actions or words and the culprit's identity. So researchers can score witnesses' errors accurately. They also can manipulate variables, such as witness characteristics, viewing conditions, and lineups, enabling them to study the effects of these manipulations on witnesses' errors (Wells and Quinlivan 2009, 5).

Those who criticize the experimental method do so on several grounds. First, experiments usually use college students as witnesses; obviously most actual eyewitnesses in criminal cases *aren't* college students. But researchers have also used young children, adolescents, middle-aged people, and the elderly. These studies show consistently that college students *outperform* the other groups. They're less influenced by suggestive procedures and more likely to make accurate identifications. "Therefore, if anything, college students as witnesses underestimate the magnitude of the problem" (Wells and Quinlivan 2009, 6).

Second, witnesses in experiments don't experience the stress and fear that real witnesses experience. But experiments that have "managed to induce significant stress have shown that stress interferes with, rather than helps, the formation of reliable memories" (6). Third, experiment witnesses know there are no serious consequences for mistaken identifications; actual witnesses are too cautious to make these mistakes. Archival research has demonstrated that real eyewitnesses who select someone from a lineup identify an innocent filler on average 30 percent of the time (reporting results from Behrman and Richards 2005, 6). Obviously, these real witnesses weren't too cautious to select innocent persons.

LO 7 | Eyewitness Retrospective Self-Reports

Courts rely heavily on **eyewitness retrospective self-reports** (witnesses' in-court recollections) when it comes to three of the five *Manson* reliability factors: their view, attention, and certainty. Psychologists are highly skeptical of retrospective self-reports, because they're highly malleable in response to even slight changes in context, such as:

1. The social desirability of the responses
2. The need to appear consistent
3. Reinterpretations of the past based on new events (Wells and Quinlivan 2009, 9)

Wells and Quinlivan (2009) point out that it's "somewhat odd" to ask eyewitnesses to report on their own credibility, when it's their credibility that's at stake. It would be like giving a student a grade based on the student's own report on how hard he or she studied (9).

LO 7 Empirical Assessments of Lineups

Now, let's look at some major empirical assessments of lineups, including their composition; pre-lineup instructions; suggestive behavior by the administrator during the procedure; and suggestive behavior by the administrator immediately after the procedure.

LO 7 The lineup composition

The choice of suspects and foils can infect the reliability of lineups by suggesting whom the eyewitness should select. To reduce the chance of infection by suggestion, psychologists recommend that a lineup always include one suspect but no more than one. (Be clear here: A suspect might not be the culprit.) *All* the rest should be **fillers** (persons known to be innocent).

The reason for fillers is to make sure the lineup doesn't suggest the target of the police investigation. Research has consistently found that fillers who don't fit the witness's previous description of the culprit "dramatically" increase the chances that the witness will identify the wrong person—an *innocent* suspect (7). So lineups should consist of a suspect and fillers who resemble one another: They're the same race, ethnicity, and skin color; they're similar in age, height, weight, hair color, and body build; and they're wearing similar clothing.

Unfortunately, live lineups often fall short of these recommendations. Understand that this gap is hardly ever intentional; it's almost always because the only people available to put in lineups are police officers and jail inmates. It's easier to put together a photo lineup because of the large numbers of mug shots. But no matter how wide the gap, most courts don't throw out lineup identifications. Why? Courts trust jurors' common sense and daily experience to detect wrong identifications (see "The Constitution and Identification Procedures," p. 344).

A substantial body of empirical research demonstrates that courts' trust in jurors' ability to discern witness lineup misidentifications is misplaced. When Jennifer Davenport and Steven Penrod (1997) surveyed the studies on this issue, they reported one study suggesting that jurors might believe as many as "three out of four mistaken identifications" (348).

LO 7 Pre-lineup instructions

Witnesses have a tendency to think of lineups as multiple-choice tests without a "none of the above" choice. They feel pressured by the possibility they might look foolish if they "don't know the answer." So they tell themselves the culprit *has to be* in the lineup. This leads witnesses to make a **relative judgment**; namely, they select the person in the lineup who looks most like the culprit. In other words, they're ripe for suggestion, particularly in uncomfortable or threatening situations, such as a police lineup. The very fact that police have arranged an identification procedure puts pressure on witnesses. They believe that the police must have found the culprit, or they wouldn't have gone to the trouble of arranging the lineup.

A major thrust of psychological research deals with the effect of the **might-or-might-not-be-present instruction**. The administrator tells witnesses *before* they view the lineup that the culprit "might or might not" be present. Specifically, the question researchers ask is whether this instruction reduces the pressure of the inherent suggestiveness of lineups. The science gives a clear answer: "Mistaken identifications from culprit-absent lineups are significantly higher when the witness is not given the pre-lineup instruction than when the witness is given the pre-lineup instruction." Administrators who don't give the instruction can infect the pre-lineup procedure even further in culprit-absent lineups by telling witnesses such things as: The police have found the culprit, they know who committed the crime, or they already have plenty of evidence against the culprit (6–7).

LO 7 *Suggestive behavior by the lineup administrator*

Researchers have shown that the administrator's knowledge or expectations influence the witness. Wells and Quinlivan (2009, 8) give several simple examples of verbal and nonverbal cues to the administrator's knowledge and expectations:

1. A witness calls out the number of a filler photo. The administrator, knowing it's a filler, urges the witness to "Make sure you look at all the photos before you finally make up your mind."

2. The witness names the suspect. The administrator says, "Good, tell me what you remember about that guy."

3. The witness names a filler. The administrator says nothing but frowns and moves his head left to right.

4. The witness names a suspect. The administrator smiles and nods her head up and down.

These cues aren't intentional or even conscious. They're "natural behavior of all testers" in all scientific experiments when "they think they know the correct answer or have expectations about how the tested person will or should behave." In experiments, when lineup administrators are misled into believing that one member in the lineup is the culprit, it influences witnesses' identification decision (8).

Show-Ups

Although, until now, we've devoted the discussion mainly to empirical research on lineups, recall that it was a show-up that the U.S. Supreme Court affirmed in *Manson*. Before we move on to looking closer at the *Manson* reliability factors, let's make a few important points about show-ups. *Show-ups*—identifications of a single person—are substantially less reliable than lineups, because presenting only one person to identify is more suggestive than providing a group of people to choose from. Nevertheless, courts usually admit show-up identification evidence.

Here are three common situations in which courts are likely to admit show-up identifications:

1. Witnesses accidentally run into suspects, such as in courthouse corridors.

2. Witnesses identify suspects during emergencies, such as when witnesses are hospitalized. (*Stovall v. Denno* 1967, pp. 337–338)

3. Witnesses identify suspects while they're loose and being pursued by police, such as when police cruise crime scenes with witnesses. (*McFadden v. Cabana* 1988)

Psychologists' experiments have found that show-ups suggest to witnesses the person to identify—the person in the show-up. The advantage of a lineup is that wrong choices will be distributed among known innocent *fillers*, a harmless choice because they obviously won't be charged with crimes. In a show-up, the error can do greater harm because the person in the show-up is a *suspect* who the police believe is the culprit. So a show-up is worse than a *good* lineup (a lineup consisting of one suspect plus five innocent fillers). But a show-up is better than a bad lineup—namely, one made up of fewer than two fillers (Wells and Quinlivan, 7).

LO **6, 8** Psychological Research and the *Manson* Reliability Variables

Psychologists have studied extensively three variables that *Manson* includes in its reliability-prong circumstances—(1) eyewitnesses' opportunity to view the culprit; (2) the amount of attention witnesses devoted to looking at the culprit; and (3) witnesses' confidence (also called certainty) in their identifications. Researchers have found that suggestion seriously infects all three.

The witness's opportunity to view the culprit

Recall that opportunity to view is the first of the five circumstances in the reliability prong of the *Manson* test. A witness's opportunity to view the culprit at the time of the crime is obviously important. Distance is part of that opportunity. Distance played a significant role in a case that began on the day Alaskans received their 1997 annual $1,500 oil dividend. Four youths took to the streets of Fairbanks, violently attacking random individuals. In a trial later, the prosecutor, who lacked convincing evidence of who killed a teenage boy and an older man, introduced the eyewitness testimony of Arlo Olson. He testified that "while standing in the doorway of Eagles Hall in downtown Fairbanks, he had watched in horror as a group of men, whom he later identified as the defendants, accosted and savagely beat Mr. Dayton in a parking lot a couple of blocks away" (Loftus and Harley 2005, 43).

The distance between Olson and the "group of men" was 450 feet. An eyewitness expert for the defense testified that "seeing someone from 450 feet away is what one is doing when one is sitting high in the center field bleachers of Yankee Stadium, looking across the ballpark at another individual sitting in the stands behind home plate" (44). Most people can clearly view a human face up to about 25 feet; that ability gradually diminishes to zero at about 150 feet (Wells and Quinlivan 2009, 9–10).

In addition to distance, witnesses are also asked how long they saw the culprit's face and whether their view was blocked for any part of the time. Researchers have found only a weak link between the length of time the witness viewed the culprit and correct identification, especially when there was stress or anxiety during the viewing. Also, witnesses greatly overestimate the time they viewed the culprit, and they greatly underestimate how long their view was blocked (Wells and Quinlivan, 10).

In a series of published experiments from a variety of labs, witnesses to simulated crimes were shown lineups that didn't include the culprit, *and* they mistakenly identified one of the foils. After their mistaken identification, the lineup administrator said either, "Good, you identified the suspect," or said nothing.

Later, all witnesses were asked, "How good was the view that you had of the culprit?" and "How well could you make out the details of the culprit's face while witnessing the crime?" All witnesses had the same (poor) view. Of the witnesses who didn't receive the positive feedback, none reported that they had a "good" or "excellent" view, and none said they could easily make out the details of the face. Among those who got the positive feedback, 27 percent said their view was good or excellent, and 20 percent said they could easily make out the face (Wells and Quinlivan, 10).

LO **8**   *The witness's attention*

The Supreme Court in *Manson* equated attention with the amount of time witnesses spent looking at the culprit's face. Eyewitness identification psychologists have concluded that it's not the amount of time spent but what witnesses do with the time. For example, devoting time to specific facial features (eyes, nose, mouth) takes a lot more time than judging what the whole face looks like. But researchers have found that the whole face view, which can happen rapidly, leads to recognizing that face in a lineup. On the other hand, in reconstructing a face (for a composite drawing), attention to specific facial features is better than a whole face view (Wells and Quinlivan, 10–11).

People naturally have a limited capacity to take in information, so paying attention to one part of an event takes away from concentrating on another. The "weapons effect" (see "weapons focus," discussed on p. 351) is a good example of this. Paying attention to the weapon reduces the capacity to recognize the face. Also, research demonstrates that the better witnesses can describe peripheral details ("I noticed the window was open"), the poorer their description of the culprit's face (Wells and Leippe 1981).

LO **8**   *The witness's certainty*

"How certain are you that you identified the right person?" "How confident are you that you identified the right person?" Researchers ask these questions about the certainty (also called confidence) of a witness's identification in virtually all experiments. Certainty, another circumstance in the *Manson* liability prong, is "one of the most researched variables in the eyewitness literature" (Wells and Quinlivan 11).

Witness confidence was one of the totality-of-circumstance variables that the Supreme Court in *Manson v. Braithwaite* (1977) used to assess the reliability of the unnecessarily suggestive identification procedure in that case. But witness confidence affects not only jury decisions during trial but also whether prosecutors will charge suspects in the first place. It further affects whether they go to trial or negotiate a plea with charged defendants. So it's no surprise that researchers have devoted so much time to the link between eyewitness confidence in their identifications and the reliability of those identifications.

What have researchers found? Psychologists have concluded that "eyewitness certainty, although of limited utility, can have *some* diagnostic value." (italics added) But that's only where there were no suggestive procedures. When there are, such as when a lineup administrator confirms a witness's choice ("You picked the right one"), the research has consistently shown that it inflates the confidence of witnesses who pick the wrong person (Wells and Quinlivan 2009, 11–12). For example, in one study, less than 15 percent of eyewitnesses who picked the wrong person said that, at the moment when they made the identification, they were "positive or nearly positive" about their selection. But after a group of mistaken witnesses were told by administrators, "Good, you identified the actual suspect," 50 percent said they were positive or nearly positive at the moment of identification (Bradfield, Wells, and Olson 2002).

You should know three further findings.

1. Witnesses quickly forget that they were uncertain at the moment of identification; instead, they believe they were certain all along.

2. The boost in confidence is stronger in mistaken witnesses than it is in witnesses who are right (Wells and Quinlivan 2009, 12).

3. Administrators' confidence-boosting remarks infect witnesses in several ways, including affecting other *Manson* reliability variables.

In one series of experiments, participants who received confirming feedback reported the following:

1. Recalling greater certainty in their identification

2. Having a better view

3. Being better able to make out details of the person's face from the video

4. Paying more attention to the video

5. Having a better basis for their identification

6. Making their identification more easily

7. Being better able to identify strangers

8. Having a better image in their mind of the person's face

9. Being more willing to testify about their identification (Douglass and McQuiston-Surrett 2006, 999)

CRIMINAL PROCEDURE IN ACTION

Evidence obtained from show-up is inherently suggestive and will not be admissible

State v. Dubose, 699 N.W.2d 582 (WI 2005)

Timothy Hiltsley (Hiltsley) and Ryan Boyd (Boyd) left the Camelot Bar in Green Bay, Wisconsin, at approximately 1:00 a.m. on January 9, 2002. Hiltsley had been drinking at the bar and admitted to being "buzzed" when he left. In the parking lot, Hiltsley and Boyd encountered a group of men, some of whom Hiltsley recognized as regular customers of a liquor store where he worked. Tyrone Dubose, an African-American, was one of the men he allegedly recognized. After a brief conversation, Hiltsley invited two of the men, along with Boyd, to his residence to smoke marijuana.

When they arrived at Hiltsley's apartment, Hiltsley sat down on the couch to pack a bowl of marijuana. At that time, Dubose allegedly held a gun to Hiltsley's right temple and demanded money. After Hiltsley emptied his wallet and

gave the men his money, the two men, both African-Americans, left his apartment.

Within minutes after the incident, at approximately 1:21 a.m., one of Hiltsley's neighbors called the police to report a possible burglary. She described two African-American men fleeing from the area, one of whom was wearing a large hooded flannel shirt. At the same time, Hiltsley and Boyd attempted to chase the men. They searched for the men in Boyd's car and hoped to cut them off. After driving nearly two blocks, Hiltsley got out of the car and searched for the men on foot. During his search, Hiltsley flagged down a police officer who was responding to the burglary call. Hiltsley told the officer that he had just been robbed at gunpoint. He described the suspects as

(continued)

African-American, one standing about 5-feet 6-inches, and the other man standing a little taller.

Another police officer also responded to the burglary call. As he neared the scene, he observed two men walking about one-half block from Hiltsley's apartment. This officer, Jeffrey Engelbrecht, was unable to determine the race of the individuals, but noted that one of the men was wearing a large hooded flannel shirt. When the officer turned his squad car around to face the men, they ran east between two houses. The police quickly set up a one-block perimeter in order to contain the suspects.

The officer subsequently requested headquarters to dispatch a canine unit to help search for the men. While he waited at the perimeter for the canine unit, police headquarters reported another call in regard to an armed robbery at Hiltsley's apartment. The report indicated that the two suspects were African-American males, that one was possibly armed, and that the two calls were probably related. Upon their arrival, the canine unit officer and his dog began tracking the suspects within the perimeter. The dog began barking near a wooden backyard fence, and the officer demanded that the person behind the fence come out and show his hands. A male voice responded that he was going to surrender and asked why the police were chasing him. The male who came out from behind the fence was Dubose, who was subsequently arrested.

Dubose, who was not wearing a flannel shirt, told the police that he had been in an argument with his girlfriend and that he had just left her house. He thought she might have called the police on him, which is why he ran when he saw the squad car. After his arrest, he was searched. The search did not uncover any weapons, money, or contraband. Dubose was then placed in the back of a squad car and driven to an area near Hiltsley's residence.

At this location, the officers conducted a show-up procedure, giving Hiltsley the opportunity to identify one of the alleged suspects. The officers placed Hiltsley in the backseat of a second squad car, which was parked so that its rear window was three feet apart from the rear window of the squad car containing Dubose. The dome light was turned on in the car containing Dubose. The officers told Hiltsley that Dubose was possibly one of the men who had robbed him at gunpoint, and asked Hiltsley if he could identify the man in the other squad car. Hiltsley told the police that he was 98 percent certain that Dubose, who sat alone in the backseat of the other squad car, was the man who held him at gunpoint. Hiltsley also told the

police that he recognized him due to his small, slender build and hairstyle.

The squad cars separated and took both Hiltsley and Dubose to the police station. Approximately 10 to 15 minutes after the first show-up, the police conducted a second show-up. There, Hiltsley identified Dubose, alone in a room, through a two-way mirror. Hiltsley told police that Dubose was the same man he observed at the previous show-up, and that he believed Dubose was the man who robbed him. A short time after the second show-up, the police showed Hiltsley a mug shot of Dubose, and he identified him for a third time.

WISCONSIN SUPREME COURT OPINION

Over the last decade, there have been extensive studies on the issue of identification evidence, research that is now impossible for us to ignore. These studies confirm that eyewitness testimony is often "hopelessly unreliable." The research strongly supports the conclusion that eyewitness misidentification is now the single greatest source of wrongful convictions in the United States, and responsible for more wrongful convictions than all other causes combined.

In light of such evidence, we recognize that our current approach [adopting the *Manson v. Brathwaite* approach] to eyewitness identification has significant flaws. After the Supreme Court's decisions in *Biggers* and *Brathwaite*, the test for show-ups evolved from an inquiry into unnecessary suggestiveness to an inquiry of impermissible suggestiveness, while forgiving impermissible suggestiveness if the identification could be said to be reliable. Studies have now shown that approach is unsound, since it is extremely difficult, if not impossible, for courts to distinguish between identifications that were reliable and identifications that were unreliable. Because a witness can be influenced by the suggestive procedure itself, a court cannot know exactly how reliable the identification would have been without the suggestiveness.

It is now clear to us that the use of unnecessarily suggestive evidence resulting from a show-up procedure presents serious problems in Wisconsin criminal law cases. We adopt a different test [from the *Manson v. Brathwaite* test] in Wisconsin regarding the admissibility of show-up identifications. We conclude that evidence obtained from an out-of-court show-up is inherently suggestive and will not be admissible unless, based on the totality of the circumstances, the procedure was necessary.

LO **7** ## Recommendations for Reforming Identification Procedures

It should be clear by now that an enormous body of psychology research, only a tiny bit of which we've surveyed here, has exposed serious shortcomings in the *Manson* reliability test's capacity to produce accurate (reliable) eyewitness identifications. So it's not surprising that the test's shortcomings have generated considerable criticism and a variety of calls for reform, even though it satisfies the due process rights guaranteed by the U.S. Constitution. Let's look at some of the criticism and some specific recommended reforms.

Recommendations by psychologists and lawyers

Psychologists have tried for decades to make the legal and criminal justice communities aware of their findings and to change police identification procedures based on the findings.

Defense lawyers have tried to get courts to accept expert eyewitness identification psychologists' testimony on human perception and memory and on the shortcomings of eyewitness identification evidence. Defense lawyers also have urged judges to instruct jurors that eyewitnesses can wrongly identify defendants.

Legal commentators argue that the *Manson* test is a poor way to decide the reliability of identifications at trial. To improve reliability, they have recommended several reforms that courts can implement, including:

1. A per se rule excluding all evidence based on suggestive procedures
2. Looser standards for admitting expert testimony on human perception and memory and on the shortcomings of eyewitness identification
3. Requiring corroboration of eyewitness identifications in some cases, such as cross-racial identifications (Nartarajan 2003, 1845–48)
4. Mandating certain police identification procedures recommended by psychologists, such as the sequential lineup (Sussman 2001–2)

Recommendations by legislatures and law enforcement agencies

A few state legislatures, such as New Jersey, Virginia, and Wisconsin, and a few police departments, including Minneapolis and several of its suburbs and Seattle, have adopted identification procedures based on the psychology research you learned about earlier. Wisconsin's recommendations include the following:

1. Utilize nonsuspect fillers chosen to minimize any suggestiveness that might point toward the suspect.
2. Utilize a "double blind" procedure, in which the administrator (called a **blind administrator**) doesn't know who the suspect is and, therefore, isn't in a position to influence the witness's selection unintentionally.
3. Instruct eyewitnesses that the real perpetrator might or might not be present and that the administrator doesn't know which person is the suspect.
4. Present the suspect and the fillers sequentially (one at a time, or **sequential presentation**) rather than simultaneously (all at once, or **simultaneous presentation**). In a sequential presentation, the witness is asked to answer "yes" or "no" as each person in the lineup is presented. This discourages relative judgment

and encourages absolute judgments of each person presented, because eyewitnesses are unable to see the subjects all at once or to know when they've seen the last subject.

5. Assess eyewitness confidence immediately after identification

6. Avoid multiple identification procedures in which the same witness views the same suspect more than once. (Wisconsin Attorney General 2010, 3)

LO 7   State Court Opinions

Some state courts have responded to the legal and social science criticisms of the *Manson* reliability test by interpreting their state constitutions or state statutes, or by court rule making, to provide more protection than *Manson* (Shay and O'Toole 2006, 115; Table 9.1).

The Utah Supreme Court, in *State v. Long* (1986), as early as 1986 recognized that "research has convincingly demonstrated the weaknesses inherent in eyewitness identification" (490). The court also recognized that "jurors are, for the most part, unaware of these problems" (490). As a result, the court ruled that trial courts had to give jurors "**cautionary instruction**," explaining the weaknesses of eyewitness identification evidence.

But the court also acknowledged that a cautionary instruction is "plainly not a panacea." In 2009, the Utah Supreme Court, in *State v. Clopten*, our next case excerpt, recognizing the limits of the cautionary instruction, added a second requirement—the use of expert witnesses to explain to the jury the limits of human perception and memory and how that affects eyewitness identification evidence.

In 2009, the Utah Supreme Court, in *State v. Clopten*, held that defendants have a right to call expert witnesses to explain to juries the limits of human perception and memory and how they affect eyewitness identification evidence.

CASE   Did He Have a "Right" to an Expert Witness?

State v. Clopten
223 P.3d 1103 (Utah 2009)

HISTORY

Deon Lomax CLOPTEN (Defendant) was convicted by a jury in the Third District Court, Salt Lake Department, of murder, failing to respond to a police command, and possession of a dangerous weapon. Defendant appeals his conviction for murder on grounds that the trial court abused its discretion when it excluded expert testimony regarding the reliability of eyewitness identification. Following existing Utah precedent, the court of appeals affirmed Clopten's conviction while inviting this court to revisit our position on the admissibility of such expert testimony. We reverse the decision of the court of appeals, vacate the conviction, and remand for a new trial.

—DURHAM, C.J.

FACTS

Tony Fuailemaa, the victim in this case, was shot and killed outside a nightclub following a rap concert. An undercover police officer responded and was told by the victim's girlfriend, Shannon Pantoja, that the shooter was "the guy in the red." The officer gave chase and saw several men jump into a Ford Explorer and drive away at high speed. A police pursuit ensued and resulted in the capture of Clopten and three other men. Clopten was in the driver's seat of the Explorer at the time of the arrest. Freddie White, the individual identified by Clopten as the shooter, was in the rear passenger seat. Both Clopten and White are African-American. Clopten was wearing both a red hooded sweatshirt and red pants at the time of arrest, while White was wearing a red T-shirt. Another red hooded sweatshirt was later found in the Explorer near where White had been sitting; the evidence suggested that White had been wearing it earlier in the evening. The handgun was found on the side of a road, having been thrown from the Explorer during the pursuit.

The State was unable to link Clopten to the handgun using fingerprints or other forensic evidence. Instead, the State relied heavily on eyewitness testimony of Shannon Pantoja and Melissa Valdez. Both Valdez and Pantoja witnessed a brutal crime committed by a stranger. They each saw the shooter for no more than a few seconds, from some distance away, at night, and while in extreme fear for their own lives. The shooter's facial features were likely disguised by a hood. The shooter was of a different race than either eyewitness, and the presence of a weapon may have served as a significant distractor. Pantoja's identification may have been biased by her expectations, since Fuailemaa had told her just before the murder that he and Clopten were enemies. Her identification may also have been affected by circumstances that occurred later, such as the fact that Clopten was the only individual wearing a red sweatshirt at the time of the initial "show-up" identification. Pantoja's statement that she was urged by police to go identify a perpetrator for the sake of her murdered boyfriend, at a time when she was still extremely distraught, also creates doubts as to her accuracy. Finally, the fact that Pantoja insisted that she remembered the shooter's distinctive hairline, when others testified that the shooter's head was covered, raises a fair question as to whether Pantoja actually recalled the shooter's hairline, or if she later incorporated that feature into her memory after seeing pictures of Clopten.

In February 2006, Clopten was convicted of first-degree murder. As part of his defense, Clopten sought to introduce the testimony of Dr. David Dodd, an expert on eyewitness identification. Clopten intended to elicit testimony from Dr. Dodd regarding various factors that can affect the accuracy of eyewitness identifications, including cross-racial identification, the impact of violence and stress during an event, the tendency to focus on a weapon rather than an individual's facial features, and the suggestive nature of certain identification procedures used by police.

At trial, the district court initially allowed the expert testimony, but later reversed itself and ruled that Dr. Dodd could not testify. The trial court reasoned that the testimony was unnecessary since potential problems with eyewitness identification could be explained using a jury instruction, as has been the common practice in Utah since this court's decision in *State v. Long*, 721 P.2d 483 (Utah 1986). The trial court concluded that the jury instruction (hereinafter a *"Long* instruction") "does an adequate job" and that Dr. Dodd's testimony would be "superfluous" and "would only confuse the issue."

Clopten appealed the trial court's ruling. The court of appeals held that trial judges are afforded "significant deference to exclude expert testimony on this topic" and upheld the conviction. However, the court also cited numerous studies concluding "that jury instructions and cross-examinations do not adequately address the vagaries of eyewitness identification." Judge Thorne wrote a separate concurrence, in which he urged this court to "revisit the boundaries of trial court discretion in excluding expert testimony on the subject." We granted certiorari review.

OPINION

When we decided *State v. Long* in 1986, it was already apparent that although research has convincingly demonstrated the weaknesses inherent in eyewitness identification, jurors are, for the most part, unaware of these problems. In *Long*, we considered the appropriateness of jury instructions as a way of familiarizing the fact-finder with these issues. There, the defendant was convicted of aggravated assault based on an identification made by the victim, who had been wounded by a shotgun blast and acknowledged that his vision was "glossy" when he saw the shooter. Counsel for the defendant requested a cautionary instruction regarding the accuracy of the identification, which the trial court declined to give. We reversed Long's conviction, and remanded the case for a new trial. In addition, we directed trial courts to provide instructions "whenever eyewitness identification is a central issue in a case and such an instruction is requested by the defense."

We also acknowledged that, because of doubts regarding its effectiveness in educating the jury, a cautionary instruction plainly is not a panacea. It was never the intent of this court to establish cautionary instructions as the sole means for educating juries about eyewitness fallibility. Indeed, we carefully acknowledged that "full evaluation of the efficacy of cautionary instructions must await further experience." With the benefit of hindsight, however, it is clear that *Long* actually discouraged the inclusion of eyewitness expert testimony by failing to dispel earlier notions that such testimony would constitute a "lecture to the jury about how they should perform their duties." As a result, trial judges reached two logical conclusions: (1) when in doubt, issuing cautionary instructions was a

(continued)

safe option; and (2) allowing expert testimony was hazardous if the expert "lectured the jury" about the credibility of a witness.

Subsequent decisions reinforced this bias. In addition, we held that a *Long* instruction is enough to render an erroneous exclusion harmless, even if the instruction failed to mention significant portions of the proffered expert testimony. Finally, neither this court nor the court of appeals has ever reversed a conviction for failure to admit eyewitness expert testimony. Given this history, it is not surprising that there is a de facto presumption against eyewitness expert testimony in Utah's trial courts.

This trend, acknowledged by both parties, is troubling in light of strong empirical research suggesting that cautionary instructions are a poor substitute for expert testimony. Decades of study, both before and particularly after *Long*, have established that eyewitnesses are prone to identifying the wrong person as the perpetrator of a crime, particularly when certain factors are present. For example, people identify members of their own race with greater accuracy than they do members of a different race. In addition, accuracy is significantly affected by factors such as the amount of time the culprit was in view, lighting conditions, use of a disguise, distinctiveness of the culprit's appearance, and the presence of a weapon or other distractions.

Moreover, there is little doubt that juries are generally unaware of these deficiencies in human perception and memory and thus give great weight to eyewitness identifications. Indeed, juries seemed to be swayed the most by the confidence of an eyewitness, even though such confidence correlates only weakly with accuracy. That the empirical data is conclusive on these matters is not disputed by either party in this case and has not been questioned by this court in the decisions that followed *Long*. The remaining issue is whether expert testimony is generally necessary to adequately educate a jury regarding these inherent deficiencies. As discussed below, we are now convinced that it is. In the absence of expert testimony, a defendant is left with two tools—cross-examination and cautionary instructions—with which to convey the possibility of mistaken identification to the jury. Both of these tools suffer from serious shortcomings when it comes to addressing the merits of eyewitness identifications.

The most troubling dilemma regarding eyewitnesses stems from the possibility that an inaccurate identification may be just as convincing to a jury as an accurate one. The challenge arises in determining how best to provide that assistance in cases where mistaken identification is a possibility. It is apparent from the research that the inclusion of expert testimony carries significant advantages over the alternatives, namely cross-examination and jury instructions.

Typically, an expert is called by a criminal defendant to explain how certain factors relevant to the identification in question could have produced a mistake. Such testimony teaches jurors about certain factors—such as "weapon focus" and the weak correlation between confidence and accuracy—that have a strong but counterintuitive impact on the reliability of an eyewitness. In other words, the testimony enables jurors to avoid certain common pitfalls, such as believing that a witness's statement of certainty is a reliable indicator of accuracy. Second, it assists jurors by quantifying what most people already know. Expert testimony does not unfairly favor the defendant by making the jury skeptical of all eyewitnesses. In fact, when a witness sees the perpetrator under favorable conditions, expert testimony actually makes jurors more likely to convict. When expert testimony is used correctly, the end result is a jury that is better able to reach a just decision.

In the absence of expert testimony, the method most commonly used to challenge the veracity of eyewitnesses is cross-examination. But because eyewitnesses may express almost absolute certainty about identifications that are inaccurate, research shows the effectiveness of cross-examination is badly hampered. Cross-examination will often expose a lie or half-truth, but may be far less effective when witnesses, although mistaken, believe that what they say is true. In addition, eyewitnesses are likely to use their "expectations, personal experience, biases, and prejudices" to fill in the gaps created by imperfect memory. Because it is unlikely that witnesses will be aware that this process has occurred, they may express far more confidence in the identification than is warranted.

Trial courts in Utah and around the nation have often tried to remedy the possibility of mistaken identification by giving cautionary instructions to the jury. The standard instruction consists of general cautions about many factors known to contribute to mistaken identifications, such as brief exposure time, lack of light, presence of disguises and distractions, and effects of stress and cross-racial identification. At the time it was adopted, it seemed logical that this measure would substantially enhance a jury's ability to evaluate eyewitness accuracy.

Subsequent research, however, has shown that a cautionary instruction does little to help a jury spot a mistaken identification. While this result seems counterintuitive, commentators and social scientists advance a number of convincing explanations. First, instructions "given at the end of what might be a long and fatiguing trial, and buried in an overall charge by the court" are unlikely to have much effect on the minds of a jury. Second, instructions may come too late to alter the jury's opinion of a witness whose testimony might have been heard days before. Third, even the best cautionary instructions tend to touch only generally on the empirical evidence. The judge may explain that certain factors are known to influence perception and memory, but will not explain how this occurs or to what extent. As a result, instructions have been shown to be less effective than expert testimony.

In conclusion, there is little reason to be confident that cross-examination and cautionary instructions alone provide a sufficient safeguard against mistaken identifications. In contrast, expert testimony has been shown to substantially enhance the ability of juries to recognize potential problems with eyewitness testimony.

We REVERSE the decision of the court of appeals, vacate Clopten's conviction and REMAND for a new trial in accordance with our decision today.

CONCURRING AND DISSENTING OPINION

DURRANT, A.C.J.

Our case law has consistently recognized that the decision to admit or exclude expert testimony is within the discretion of the district court. It is fundamentally a product of the structure of our judicial system, in which district court judges are placed in a superior position to evaluate the proffered testimony in light of the principles set out in the rules of evidence.

I would simply instruct the district courts that they are to treat eyewitness expert testimony like any other type of expert testimony and determine its admissibility based on the requirements of the rule. I would neither create a presumption in favor, nor one against, the admission of eyewitness expert testimony, and district court rulings on the admissibility of such expert testimony would be entitled to the same deference we have traditionally accorded rulings on the admissibility of other types of expert testimony.

Questions

1. Describe the details of the basis for the two eyewitnesses' identification of Deon Clopten.

2. Describe the police identification procedure during which the witnesses identified Clopten.

3. Summarize the court's reasons for holding that the trial court should've allowed expert witness testimony.

4. Summarize Judge Durrant's concurring/dissenting opinion disagreements with the majority.

YOU DECIDE
Should Police Departments Be Required to Adopt Lineup Procedure Reforms?

Based on the research reviewed in your text, which of the recommended reforms, if any, should police departments be required to adopt? Read http://web.augsburg.edu/~steblay/Improving_Eyewitness_Identifications.pdf

FORENSIC SCIENCE AND IDENTIFICATION EVIDENCE

 LO **9** **Forensic science**, the application of scientific methods and techniques to investigate crimes, comprises many disciplines. Here are some found in the index of the National Research Council's *Strengthening Forensic Science in the United States* (2009):

1. DNA
2. Controlled substances
3. Blood types
4. Hair analysis
5. Bite marks

6. Voice analysis

7. Handwriting

8. Death

9. Poisons

10. Firearms/tools

11. Digital evidence (gathering, processing, and interpreting electronic documents, lists of phone numbers and call logs, GPS tracking, e-mails, photos)

We'll divide our discussion of forensic evidence into two sections. First, we'll look at DNA, which has forced us to recognize that our justice system *does* convict innocent people. Thanks to the Innocence Project (2013), we now have a daily running count (306 on May 26, 2013) of exonerations, and a face and profile of every person in U.S. history for whom DNA played a part in their exoneration. Also, a number of widely publicized videos of prisoners released because DNA evidence proved their innocence have heightened public awareness of wrongful convictions. All DNA exonerations are limited to a narrow band of crimes—murder, rape, and rape/murder.

Second, we'll turn to flawed forensic evidence, which includes a much broader band of cases. These include cases where the types of evidence in the remaining 10 items in the list above played a part in convicting an innocent person.

LO 9 DNA Profile Identification

Because of scientific advances in the testing of deoxyribonucleic acid, particularly Short Tandem Repeat (STR) **DNA testing**, one of the most important criminal law issues of our day is whether there exists under the Constitution of the United States a right, post-conviction, to access previously produced forensic evidence for purposes of DNA testing in order to establish one's complete innocence of the crime for which he has been convicted and sentenced.

There is now widespread agreement within the scientific community that this technology can distinguish between any two individuals on the planet, other than identical twins, with the statistical probabilities of STR DNA matches ranging in the hundreds of billions, if not trillions. In other words, STR DNA tests can, in certain circumstances, establish to a virtual certainty whether a given individual did or did not commit a particular crime (Judge Michael Luttig, *Harvey v. Horan* 2002, 304–05).

U.S. Fourth Circuit Court Judge Luttig, who wrote these words, concluded that there is a "core liberty interest protected by the Due Process Clause of the Fourteenth Amendment which, in certain, very limited circumstances, gives rise to access previously produced forensic evidence for purposes of STR DNA testing" (308). Judge Luttig believes that judicial recognition of DNA profiling, this new science for determining innocence and guilt, should be "ungrudging." He recognizes that such a right will place burdens on the courts and lead to difficult questions concerning standards for access of the evidence for testing and for its use in court (306).

Nevertheless, he continues:

But no one, regardless of his political, philosophical, or jurisprudential disposition, should be otherwise troubled that a person who was convicted in accordance with law might thereafter be set free, either by the executive or by the courts, because of evidence that provides absolute proof that he did not in fact commit the crime for which he was convicted. Such is not an indictment of our system of justice, which, while insisting upon a very high degree of proof for conviction, does not, after all, require proof beyond all doubt, and therefore, is capable of producing erroneous determinations of both guilt and innocence. To the contrary, it would be a high credit to our system of justice that it recognizes the need for, and imperative of, a safety valve in those rare instances where objective proof that the convicted actually did not commit the offense later becomes available through the progress of science. (306)

Finally, Judge Luttig makes clear that this constitutional right of access should not be "constitutionally required or permitted as a matter of course or even frequently" (306).

In *District Attorney's Office for the Third Judicial District and others v. William G. Osborne* (2009), our next case excerpt, the U.S. Supreme Court (5–4) decided that there's no constitutional right of access to forensic evidence.

In *District Attorney's Office for the Third Judicial District and others v. William G. Osborne* **(2009),** the U.S. Supreme Court (5–4) ruled that there's no constitutional right of access to forensic evidence.

CASE

Does a State's Refusal to Grant a Request for DNA Testing Deny the Prisoner's Due Process Right?

District Attorney's Office for the Third Judicial District and others v. William G. Osborne
129 S.Ct. 2308 (2009)

HISTORY

After the Court of Appeals of Alaska affirmed the denial of his request for further DNA testing of evidence used to convict him, State prisoner William Osborne brought a § 1983 action to compel release of certain biological evidence so that it could be subjected to DNA testing. The United States District Court for the District of Alaska dismissed the action. Osborne appealed. The United States Court of Appeals for the Ninth Circuit reversed. On remand, the District Court awarded summary judgment for Osborne, and the Court of Appeals affirmed. The U.S. Supreme Court reversed and remanded.

—ROBERTS, C.J., joined by SCALIA, KENNEDY, THOMAS, and ALITO, JJ.

FACTS

On the evening of March 22, 1993, two men driving through Anchorage, Alaska, solicited sex from a female prostitute, K.G. She agreed to perform fellatio on both men for $100 and got in their car. The three spent some time looking for a place to stop and ended up in a deserted area near Earthquake Park. When K.G. demanded payment in advance, the two men pulled out a gun and forced her to perform fellatio on the driver while the passenger penetrated her vaginally, using a blue condom she had brought. The passenger then ordered K.G. out of the car and told her to lie facedown in the snow. Fearing for her life, she refused, and the two men choked her and beat her with the gun. When K.G. tried to flee, the passenger beat her with a wooden axe handle and shot her in the head while she lay on the ground. They kicked some snow on top of her and left her for dead.

K.G. did not die; the bullet had only grazed her head. Once the two men left, she found her way back to the road, and flagged down a passing car to take her home. Ultimately, she received medical care and spoke to the police. At the scene of the crime, the police recovered a spent shell casing, the axe handle, some of K.G.'s clothing stained with blood, and the blue condom.

Six days later, two military police officers at Fort Richardson pulled over Dexter Jackson for flashing his

(continued)

headlights at another vehicle. In his car they discovered a gun (which matched the shell casing), as well as several items K.G. had been carrying the night of the attack. The car also matched the description K.G. had given to the police. Jackson admitted that he had been the driver during the rape and assault, and told the police that William Osborne had been his passenger. Other evidence also implicated Osborne. K.G. picked out his photograph (with some uncertainty) and at trial she identified Osborne as her attacker. Other witnesses testified that shortly before the crime, Osborne had called Jackson from an arcade, and then driven off with him. An axe handle similar to the one at the scene of the crime was found in Osborne's room on the military base where he lived.

Osborne and Jackson were convicted by an Alaska jury of kidnapping, assault, and sexual assault. They were acquitted of an additional count of sexual assault and of attempted murder. Finding it "nearly miraculous" that K.G. had survived, the trial judge sentenced Osborne to 26 years in prison, with 5 suspended. His conviction and sentence were affirmed on appeal.

OPINION

Modern DNA testing can provide powerful new evidence unlike anything known before. Since its first use in criminal investigations in the mid-1980s, there have been several major advances in DNA technology, culminating in STR technology. It is now often possible to determine whether a biological tissue matches a suspect with near certainty. DNA testing has exonerated wrongly convicted people, and has confirmed the convictions of many others. The availability of technologies not available at trial cannot mean that every criminal conviction, or even every criminal conviction involving biological evidence, is suddenly in doubt. The dilemma is how to harness DNA's power to prove innocence without unnecessarily overthrowing the established system of criminal justice.

That task belongs primarily to the legislature. The States are currently engaged in serious, thoughtful examinations of how to ensure the fair and effective use of this testing within the existing criminal justice framework. Forty-six States have already enacted statutes dealing specifically with access to DNA evidence. The State of Alaska itself is considering joining them. The Federal Government has also passed the Innocence Protection Act of 2004, which allows federal prisoners to move for court-ordered DNA testing under certain specified conditions. That Act also grants money to States that enact comparable statutes, and as a consequence has served as a model for some state legislation. At oral argument, Osborne agreed that the federal statute is a model for how States ought to handle the issue.

These laws recognize the value of DNA evidence but also the need for certain conditions on access to the State's evidence. A requirement of demonstrating materiality is common, but it is not the only one. The federal statute, for example, requires a sworn statement that the applicant is innocent. States also impose a range of diligence requirements. Several require the requested testing to have been technologically impossible at trial. Others deny testing to those who declined testing at trial for tactical reasons.

Alaska is one of a handful of States yet to enact legislation specifically addressing the issue of evidence requested for DNA testing. But that does not mean that such evidence is unavailable for those seeking to prove their innocence. Instead, Alaska courts are addressing how to apply existing laws for discovery and postconviction relief to this novel technology. Both parties agree that under Alaska Stat. § 12.7, "a defendant is entitled to post-conviction relief if the defendant presents newly discovered evidence that establishes by clear and convincing evidence that the defendant is innocent." If such a claim is brought, state law permits general discovery. Alaska courts have explained that these procedures are available to request DNA evidence for newly available testing to establish actual innocence.

In addition to this statutory procedure, the Alaska Court of Appeals has invoked a widely accepted three-part test to govern additional rights to DNA access under the State Constitution. Drawing on the experience with DNA evidence of State Supreme Courts around the country, the Court of Appeals explained that it was "reluctant to hold that Alaska law offers no remedy to defendants who could prove their factual innocence." It was "prepared to hold, however, that a defendant who seeks post-conviction DNA testing must show (1) that the conviction rested primarily on eyewitness identification evidence, (2) that there was a demonstrable doubt concerning the defendant's identification as the perpetrator, and (3) that scientific testing would likely be conclusive on this issue." Thus, the Alaska courts have suggested that even those who do not get discovery under the State's criminal rules have available to them a safety valve under the State Constitution.

"No State shall . . . deprive any person of life, liberty, or property, without due process of law." U.S. Const., Amdt. 14, § 1; accord Amdt. 5. This Clause imposes procedural limitations on a State's power to take away protected entitlements. Osborne argues that access to the State's evidence is a "process" needed to vindicate his right to prove himself innocent and get out of jail. Process is not an end in itself, so a necessary premise of this argument is that he has an entitlement (what our precedents call a "liberty interest") to prove his innocence even after a fair trial has proved otherwise. We must first examine this asserted liberty interest to determine what process (if any) is due.

Osborne has a liberty interest in demonstrating his innocence with new evidence under state law. A criminal defendant proved guilty after a fair trial does not have the same liberty interests as a free man. At trial, the defendant is presumed innocent and may demand that the government prove its case beyond reasonable doubt. But once a defendant has been afforded a fair trial and convicted of the offense for which he was charged, the presumption of innocence disappears. Given a valid conviction, the criminal defendant has been constitutionally deprived of his liberty.

The State accordingly has more flexibility in deciding what procedures are needed in the context of postconviction relief. We see nothing inadequate about the procedures Alaska has provided to vindicate its state right to postconviction relief in general, and nothing inadequate about how those procedures apply to those who seek access to DNA evidence. Alaska provides a substantive right to be released on a sufficiently compelling showing of new evidence that establishes innocence. It exempts such claims from otherwise applicable time limits. The State provides for discovery in postconviction proceedings, and has—through judicial decision—specified that this discovery procedure is available to those seeking access to DNA evidence.

And there is more. While the Alaska courts have not had occasion to conclusively decide the question, the Alaska Court of Appeals has suggested that the State Constitution provides an additional right of access to DNA. In expressing its "reluctance to hold that Alaska law offers no remedy" to those who belatedly seek DNA testing, and in invoking the three-part test used by other state courts, the court indicated that in an appropriate case the State Constitution may provide a failsafe even for those who cannot satisfy the statutory requirements under general postconviction procedures.

To the degree there is some uncertainty in the details of Alaska's newly developing procedures for obtaining postconviction access to DNA, we can hardly fault the State for that. Osborne has brought this § 1983 action without ever using these procedures in filing a state or federal habeas claim relying on actual innocence. In other words, he has not tried to use the process provided to him by the State or attempted to vindicate the liberty interest that is now the centerpiece of his claim. When Osborne did request DNA testing in state court, he sought RFLP testing that had been available at trial, not the STR testing he now seeks, and the state court relied on that fact in denying him testing under Alaska law.

His attempt to sidestep state process through a new federal lawsuit puts Osborne in a very awkward position. If he simply seeks the DNA through the State's discovery procedures, he might well get it. If he does not, it may be for a perfectly adequate reason, just as the federal statute and all state statutes impose conditions and limits on access to DNA evidence. It is difficult to criticize the State's procedures when Osborne has not invoked them. This is not to say that Osborne must exhaust state-law remedies. But it is Osborne's burden to demonstrate the inadequacy of the state-law procedures available to him in state

postconviction relief. These procedures are adequate on their face, and without trying them, Osborne can hardly complain that they do not work in practice.

Osborne asks that we recognize a freestanding substantive due process right to DNA evidence untethered from the liberty interests he hopes to vindicate with it. We reject the invitation and conclude, in the circumstances of this case, that there is no such substantive due process right. Osborne seeks access to state evidence so that he can apply new DNA-testing technology that might prove him innocent. The elected governments of the States are actively confronting the challenges DNA technology poses to our criminal justice systems and our traditional notions of finality, as well as the opportunities it affords. To suddenly constitutionalize this area would short-circuit what looks to be a prompt and considered legislative response.

DNA evidence will undoubtedly lead to changes in the criminal justice system. It has done so already. The question is whether further change will primarily be made by legislative revision and judicial interpretation of the existing system, or whether the Federal Judiciary must leap ahead—revising (or even discarding) the system by creating a new constitutional right and taking over responsibility for refining it.

Federal courts should not presume that state criminal procedures will be inadequate to deal with technological change. The criminal justice system has historically accommodated new types of evidence, and is a time-tested means of carrying out society's interest in convicting the guilty while respecting individual rights. That system, like any human endeavor, cannot be perfect. DNA evidence shows that it has not been. But there is no basis for Osborne's approach of assuming that because DNA has shown that these procedures are not flawless, DNA evidence must be treated as categorically outside the process, rather than within it. That is precisely what his § 1983 suit seeks to do, and that is the contention we reject.

The judgment of the Court of Appeals is REVERSED, and the case is REMANDED for further proceedings consistent with this opinion.

It is so ordered.

CONCURRING OPINION

Justice ALITO, with whom Justice KENNEDY joins, and with whom Justice THOMAS joins as to Part II, concurring.

Respondent was convicted for a brutal sexual assault. At trial, the defense declined to have DNA testing done on a semen sample found at the scene of the crime. Defense counsel explained that this decision was made based on fear that the testing would provide further evidence of respondent's guilt. After conviction, in an unsuccessful

(continued)

attempt to obtain parole, respondent confessed in detail to the crime. Now, respondent claims that he has a federal constitutional right to test the sample and that he can go directly to federal court to obtain this relief without giving the Alaska courts a full opportunity to consider his claim. A defendant who declines the opportunity to perform DNA testing at trial for tactical reasons has no constitutional right to perform such testing after conviction.

DISSENT

Justice STEVENS, with whom Justice GINSBURG and Justice BREYER join, and with whom Justice SOUTER joins as to Part I, dissenting.

The State of Alaska possesses physical evidence that, if tested, will conclusively establish whether respondent William Osborne committed rape and attempted murder. If he did, justice has been served by his conviction and sentence. If not, Osborne has needlessly spent decades behind bars while the true culprit has not been brought to justice. The DNA test Osborne seeks is a simple one, its cost modest, and its results uniquely precise.

Throughout the course of state and federal litigation, the State has failed to provide any concrete reason for denying Osborne the DNA testing he seeks, and none is apparent. Because Osborne has offered to pay for the tests, cost is not a factor. And as the State now concedes, there is no reason to doubt that such testing would provide conclusive confirmation of Osborne's guilt or revelation of his innocence. In the courts below, the State refused to provide an explanation for its refusal to permit testing of the evidence, and in this Court, its explanation has been, at best, unclear. Insofar as the State has articulated any reason at all, it appears to be a generalized interest in protecting the finality of the judgment of conviction from any possible future attacks.

While we have long recognized that States have an interest in securing the finality of their judgments, finality is not a stand-alone value that trumps a State's overriding interest in ensuring that justice is done in its courts and secured to its citizens. Indeed, when absolute proof of innocence is readily at hand, a State should not shrink from the possibility that error may have occurred. Rather, our system of justice is strengthened by recognizing the need for, and imperative of, a safety valve in those rare instances where objective proof that the convicted actually did not commit the offense later becomes available through the progress of science. DNA evidence has led to an extraordinary series of exonerations, not only in cases where the trial evidence was weak, but also in cases where the convicted parties confessed their guilt and where the trial evidence against them appeared overwhelming.

The arbitrariness of the State's conduct is highlighted by comparison to the private interests it denies. It seems to me obvious that if a wrongly convicted person were to produce proof of his actual innocence, no state interest would be sufficient to justify his continued punitive detention. If such proof can be readily obtained without imposing a significant burden on the State, a refusal to provide access to such evidence is wholly unjustified.

SOUTER, J.

Alaska argues against finding any right to relief in a federal § 1983 action because the procedure the State provides is reasonable and adequate to vindicate the post-trial liberty interest in testing evidence that the State has chosen to recognize. When I first considered the State's position I thought Alaska's two strongest points were these: (1) that in Osborne's state litigation he failed to request access for the purpose of a variety of postconviction testing that could not have been done at time of trial (and thus sought no new evidence by his state-court petition); and (2) that he failed to aver actual innocence (and thus failed to place his oath behind the assertion that the evidence sought would be material to his postconviction claim). Denying him any relief under these circumstances, the argument ran, did not indicate any inadequacy in the state procedure that would justify resort to § 1983 for providing due process.

Yet the record shows that Osborne has been denied access to the evidence even though he satisfied each of these conditions. As for the requirement to claim testing by a method not available at trial, Osborne's state-court appellate brief specifically mentioned his intent to conduct short tandem repeat (STR) analysis, and the State points to no pleading, brief, or evidence that Osborne ever changed this request.

The State's reliance on Osborne's alleged failure to claim factual innocence is equally untenable. While there is no question that after conviction and imprisonment he admitted guilt under oath as a condition for becoming eligible for parole, the record before us makes it equally apparent that he claims innocence on oath now. His affidavit filed in support of his request for evidence under § 1983 contained the statement, "I have always maintained my innocence," followed by an explanation that his admission of guilt was a necessary gimmick to obtain parole. Since the State persists in maintaining that Osborne is not entitled to test its evidence, it is apparently mere makeweight for the State to claim that he is not entitled to § 1983 relief because he failed to claim innocence seriously and unequivocally.

This is not the first time the State has produced reasons for opposing Osborne's request that collapse upon inspection. Arguing before the Ninth Circuit, the State maintained that the DNA evidence Osborne sought was not material; that is, it argued that a test excluding Osborne as the source of semen in the blue condom, found near the bloody snow and spent shell casing in the secluded area where the victim was raped by one man, would not "establish that he was factually innocent" or even "undermine confidence . . . in the verdict." Such an argument is patently untenable, and the State now concedes that a favorable test could "conclusively establish Osborne's innocence."

Standing alone, the inadequacy of each of the State's reasons for denying Osborne access to the DNA evidence he seeks would not make out a due process violation. But taken as a whole the record convinces me that, while Alaska has created an entitlement of access to DNA evidence under conditions that are facially reasonable, the State has demonstrated a combination of inattentiveness and intransigence in applying those conditions that add up to procedural unfairness that violates the Due Process Clause.

Questions

1. Summarize the reasons the majority held that Osborne had no constitutional right to obtain the DNA evidence that the state of Alaska possesses.

2. Summarize the reasons the dissents argue that Osborne has a constitutional right to obtain the DNA evidence that the state of Alaska possesses.

3. In your opinion, should Osborne have a constitutional right to obtain the DNA evidence? Back up your answer with points made in the Court's opinion.

4. What do you make of the disagreement between the majority and the dissents about the facts in the case?

5. Summarize Justice Alito's point in his concurring opinion. Do you agree with him? Explain your answer.

LO 9   Flawed Forensic Evidence

According to most legal and social science research across the ideological and scientific spectrum, "forensic error occurs at significant rates—both unconsciously and consciously (fraud)" (Koppl 2007). Let's look at what may account for these forensic errors, and then look at what the U.S. Supreme Court says about requiring forensic lab technicians to appear in court to face cross-examination about their forensic test results.

Reasons for flawed forensic tests

Professor Roger Koppl (2007, 3–5), an economist associated with the libertarian Reason Foundation, lists eight features of current forensic science that reduce the quality of forensic practitioners' work:

1. *Monopoly.* In most jurisdictions today, including those in the United States, each forensic lab has a monopoly on the evidence it analyzes. No other lab is likely to examine the same evidence, which allows practitioners to perform sloppy, biased, even fraudulent work, as they cannot be proven wrong.

2. *Dependence bias.* Most forensic labs are organized within police departments and are thus dependent on the departments for their budgets. This institutional relationship creates a pro-prosecution bias, as the managers of the forensics units answer to law enforcement agencies.

3. *Poor quality control.* In the United States, there are no required programs of accreditation for forensic labs and the principal accrediting agency, the American Society of Crime Lab Directors, is a professional organization, not an independent organization. Quality control measures tend to be poor, which may easily produce shoddy work.

4. *Information sharing.* Forensic scientists are privy to information that may be crucial to a criminal proceeding, but extraneous to the questions put to the forensic scientist. Sharing information between police investigators and forensic scientists creates the strong possibility of unconscious bias. Further, dishonest scientists may

then more freely act on their self-conscious biases. The inappropriate sharing of bias-inducing information might be called "information pollution."

5. *No division of labor between forensic analysis and interpretation.* The same scientist who, say, performs a test to establish blood type also then determines whether his test results exclude the police suspect. Forensic error may result from a false interpretation of a test that was properly conducted.

6. *Lack of forensic counsel.* Indigent defendants rarely receive aid and counsel from forensic scientists. The prosecution has forensic counsel and, indeed, batteries of forensic specialists, whereas the defense has none, and often, an attorney unable to adequately understand and challenge forensic testimony.

7. *Lack of competition among forensic counselors.* From the absence of forensic counsel for the indigent, it follows that there is little competition among forensic counselors for customers. Even if forensic counsel is available, it may not be vigorous or effective in a non-competitive environment.

8. *Public ownership.* Forensic laboratories are almost universally publicly owned. In the United States, they are often organized under police agencies, such as the State Police or FBI. Competitive private labs may have stronger incentives to produce reliable work than do monopoly government labs.

CRIMINAL PROCEDURE IN ACTION

Prisoners convicted by false forensic evidence can sue for their release

In the Matter of an INVESTIGATION OF the WEST VIR-GINIA STATE POLICE CRIME LABORATORY, SEROLOGY DIVISION.
  438 S.E. 2d 501 (WV 1993)

MILLER, Justice:

This case is an extraordinary proceeding arising from a petition filed with this Court on June 2, 1993, by William C. Forbes, Prosecuting Attorney for Kanawha County, requesting the appointment of a circuit judge to conduct an investigation into whether habeas corpus relief should be granted to prisoners whose convictions were obtained through the willful false testimony of Fred S. Zain, a former serologist with the Division of Public Safety. [The court ordered the investigation and report.]

The report chronicles the history of allegations of misconduct on the part of Trooper Zain. . . . Specifically, the report states:

"The acts of misconduct on the part of Zain included (1) overstating the strength of results; (2) overstating the frequency of genetic matches on individual pieces

of evidence; (3) misreporting the frequency of genetic matches on multiple pieces of evidence; (4) reporting that multiple items had been tested, when only a single item had been tested; (5) reporting inconclusive results as conclusive; (6) repeatedly altering laboratory records; (7) grouping results to create the erroneous impression that genetic markers had been obtained from all samples tested; (8) failing to report conflicting results; (9) failing to conduct or to report conducting additional testing to resolve conflicting results; (10) implying a match with a suspect when testing supported only a match with the victim; and (11) reporting scientifically impossible or improbable results." (Footnote omitted).

The report by Judge Holliday further notes that the ASCLD (American Society of Crime Laboratory Directors) team concluded that these irregularities were "the result of systematic practice rather than an occasional inadvertent error" and discusses specific cases that were prosecuted in which Serology Division records indicate that scientifically inaccurate, invalid, or false testimony or reports were given by Trooper Zain.

In addition to investigating what occurred during Trooper Zain's tenure in the Serology Division, Judge Holliday also explored how these irregularities could have happened. The report notes that many of Trooper Zain's former supervisors and subordinates regarded him as "pro-prosecution." The report further states: "It appears that Zain was quite skillful in using his experience and position of authority to deflect criticism of his work by subordinates." Although admittedly beyond the scope of the investigation, the report by Judge Holliday notes that there was evidence that Trooper Zain's supervisors may have ignored or concealed complaints of his misconduct. Finally, the report discusses ASCLD criticisms of certain operating procedures during Trooper Zain's tenure, which the report concludes "undoubtedly contributed to an environment within which Zain's misconduct escaped detection."

According to the report, these procedural deficiencies included:

"(1) no written documentation of testing methodology; (2) no written quality assurance program; (3) no written internal or external auditing procedures; (4) no routine proficiency testing of laboratory technicians; (5) no technical review of work product; (6) no written documentation of instrument maintenance and calibration; (7) no written testing procedures manual; (8) failure to follow generally accepted scientific testing standards with respect to certain tests; (9) inadequate record-keeping; and (10) failure to conduct collateral testing."

OPINION

It has long been recognized by the United States Supreme Court that it is a violation of due process for the State to convict a defendant based on false evidence. Moreover, whether the nondisclosure was a result of negligence or design, it is the responsibility of the prosecutor. Thus, in this case, it matters not whether a prosecutor using Trooper Zain as his expert ever knew that Trooper Zain was falsifying the State's evidence. The State must bear the responsibility for the false evidence. The law forbids the State from obtaining a conviction based on false evidence.

It is also recognized that, although it is a violation of due process for the State to convict a defendant based on false evidence, such conviction will not be set aside unless it is shown that the false evidence had a material effect on the jury verdict. The only inquiry that remains is to analyze the other evidence in the case to determine if there is sufficient evidence to uphold the conviction.

In order to resolve these matters, we will direct the Clerk of this Court to prepare and cause to be distributed to the Division of Corrections an appropriate postconviction habeas corpus form. This form will be designed to identify those individuals who desire to seek habeas relief on a Zain issue. As a condition for obtaining such relief, the form will require the relator to consent to a DNA test.

The matters brought before this Court by Judge Holliday are shocking and represent egregious violations of the right of a defendant to a fair trial. They stain our judicial system and mock the ideal of justice under law. We direct Prosecutor Forbes to pursue any violation of criminal law committed by Trooper Zain and urge that he consult with the United States District Attorney for the Southern District of West Virginia. We direct our Clerk to send all relevant papers to both of them. This conduct should not go unpunished.

Melendez-Diaz v. Massachusetts *(2009)*

To obtain a criminal conviction, the prosecution must prove every element of the offense, by proof beyond a reasonable doubt. The Constitution entitles a defendant to confront and cross-examine all witnesses against him. Yet, for the past 30 years, state legislatures have quietly approved laws that cheat the Constitution. These laws fly, undetected beneath the constitutional radar, violating fundamental constitutional rights. . . . These statutes permit state prosecutors to use hearsay state crime laboratory reports, in lieu of live witness testimony, to prove the essential elements of a criminal case. . . . These statutes . . . discourage vigorous defense advocacy, promote carelessness and fraud in crime laboratories, and increase the likelihood of wrongful convictions and sentences. (Metzger 2006, 476)

Professor Metzger calls these statutes **forensic *ipse dixit* statutes**. (*Ipse dixit* means "without proof"). Governors, prosecutors, and courts recognize that *ipse dixit* statutes contribute to convicting innocent people based on faulty and fraudulent forensic evidence. Nevertheless, all but six states have *ipse dixit* statutes that authorize the state to prove its forensic allegations by relying on forensic certificates instead of live testimony. These certificates can prove, by a hearsay report, both the chain of command and the "truth" of the forensic tester's conclusions as to the results in a wide range of tests conducted in crime labs, including the following:

- DNA tests
- Microscopic hair analyses
- Fingerprint identifications, coroners' reports
- Ballistics tests (Metzger 2006, 479)

"Once the prosecution provides any notice required by the statute, the burden shifts to the defense counsel to demand that the prosecution honor its constitutional obligation of calling witnesses to prove each element of the offense beyond a reasonable doubt" (Metzger 2006, 479). Table 9.2 depicts the typical forensic proof process the *ipse dixit* statutes authorize.

Maybe the forensic testing regime as it existed in 2006, when Professor Metzger wrote, will change. The majority of the U.S. Supreme Court in our next case excerpt, *Melendez-Diaz v. Massachusetts* (2009), which cited Metzger's research, aimed to address the concerns that she raised. The 5-member majority brought forensic testing into the Sixth Amendment right of a defendant to "be confronted with the witnesses against him." (Put another way, this is the right to cross-examine the prosecution's witnesses.) According to the majority, statements contained in forensic lab reports created specifically as evidence to prove guilt in criminal trials are testimony that the Sixth Amendment guarantees defendants have the right to cross-examine. In the course of the 5-member majority opinion, Justice Scalia refers to the problem of flawed forensic evidence, and the constitutional requirement for those responsible for lab reports to come to court to face cross-examination: "Forensic evidence is not uniquely immune from the risk of manipulation."

Confrontation is one means of assuring accurate forensic analysis. While it is true, that an honest analyst will not alter his testimony when forced to confront

TABLE 9.2 *Ipse dixit* statute forensic proof process

1. The prosecutor or law enforcement officer requests a State lab (or a lab hired by the State) to conduct one or more tests.
2. The lab prepares a report of its conclusions.
3. The report follows the statute's requirements.
4. At trial, the State introduces the hearsay report.
5. The report proves the chain of command.
6. The report proves truth of the lab's conclusions.
7. No State witness testifies about the testing methodology, the testing equipment, or the error rates associated with the testing.
8. No State witness testifies about the testor's experience, education, or work performance.
9. The hearsay forensic report creates a presumption that the State has proved beyond a reasonable doubt, the truth of the report's conclusions.

Source: Metzger 2006, 479–80.

the defendant, the same cannot be said of the fraudulent analyst. Like the eyewitness who has fabricated his account to the police, the analyst who provides false results may, under oath in open court, reconsider his false testimony. And, of course, the prospect of confrontation will deter fraudulent analysis in the first place.

Confrontation is designed to weed out not only the fraudulent analyst, but the incompetent one as well. Serious deficiencies have been found in the forensic evidence used in criminal trials. One commentator asserts that "the legal community now concedes, with varying degrees of urgency, that our system produces erroneous convictions based on discredited forensics." One study of cases in which exonerating evidence resulted in the overturning of criminal convictions concluded that invalid forensic testimony contributed to the convictions in 60% of the cases.

In *Melendez–Diaz v. Massachusetts* (2009), a 5-member majority decided that statements contained in forensic lab reports created specifically as evidence to prove guilt in criminal trials are testimony that the Sixth Amendment guarantees defendants have the right to cross-examine.

CASE

Were Forensics Lab Technicians Subject to the Sixth Amendment Confrontation Clause?

Melendez–Diaz v. Massachusetts
557 U.S. 305 (2009)

HISTORY

Following Luis Melendez-Diaz's conviction in the state trial court on charges of distributing and trafficking in cocaine, the Appeals Court of Massachusetts, affirmed, ruling that the trial court had comported with the Sixth Amendment by admitting certificates of analysis sworn to by analysts at state laboratory without requiring in-court testimony by the analysts. The Supreme Judicial Court of Massachusetts denied review. The U.S. Supreme Court reversed and remanded.

—SCALIA, J., joined by STEVENS, SOUTER, THOMAS, and GINSBURG, JJ.,

FACTS

In 2001, Boston police officers received a tip that a Kmart employee, Thomas Wright, was engaging in suspicious activity. The informant reported that Wright repeatedly received phone calls at work, after each of which he would be picked up in front of the store by a blue sedan, and would return to the store a short time later. The police set up surveillance in the Kmart parking lot and witnessed this precise sequence of events. When Wright got out of the car upon his return, one of the officers detained and searched him, finding four clear white plastic bags containing a substance resembling cocaine. The officer then signaled other officers on the scene to arrest the two men in the car—one of whom was petitioner Luis Melendez–Diaz. The officers placed all three men in a police cruiser.

During the short drive to the police station, the officers observed their passengers fidgeting and making furtive movements in the back of the car. After depositing the men at the station, they searched the police cruiser and found a plastic bag containing 19 smaller plastic bags hidden in the partition between the front and back seats. They submitted the seized evidence to a state laboratory required by law to conduct chemical analysis upon police request.

Melendez–Diaz was charged with distributing cocaine and with trafficking in cocaine in an amount between 14 and 28 grams. At trial, the prosecution placed into evidence the bags seized from Wright and from the police cruiser. It also submitted three "certificates of analysis"

(continued)

showing the results of the forensic analysis performed on the seized substances. The certificates reported the weight of the seized bags and stated that the bags "have been examined with the following results: The substance was found to contain: Cocaine." The certificates were sworn to before a notary public by analysts at the State Laboratory Institute of the Massachusetts Department of Public Health, as required under Massachusetts law.

Melendez–Diaz objected to the admission of the certificates, asserting that our Confrontation Clause decision in *Crawford v. Washington*, 541 U.S. 36 (2004), required the analysts to testify in person. The objection was overruled, and the certificates were admitted pursuant to state law as "prima facie evidence of the composition, quality, and the net weight of the narcotic . . . analyzed." Mass. Gen. Laws, ch. 111, § 13.

The jury found Melendez–Diaz guilty. He appealed, contending, among other things, that admission of the certificates violated his Sixth Amendment right to be confronted with the witnesses against him. The Appeals Court of Massachusetts rejected the claim, relying on the Massachusetts Supreme Judicial Court's decision in *Commonwealth v. Verde*, 827 N.E.2d 701 (2005), which held that the authors of certificates of forensic analysis are not subject to confrontation under the Sixth Amendment. The Supreme Judicial Court denied review. We granted certiorari.

OPINION

The Sixth Amendment to the United States Constitution, made applicable to the States via the Fourteenth Amendment, provides that "in all criminal prosecutions, the accused shall enjoy the right . . . to be confronted with the witnesses against him." In *Crawford*, after reviewing the Clause's historical underpinnings, we held that it guarantees a defendant's right to confront those "who 'bear testimony' " against him. A witness's testimony against a defendant is thus inadmissible unless the witness appears at trial or, if the witness is unavailable, the defendant had a prior opportunity for cross-examination. [The Court held that "affidavits" are testimonial.]

There is little doubt that the documents at issue in this case, while denominated by Massachusetts law "certificates," are quite plainly affidavits: "declarations of facts written down and sworn to by the declarant before an officer authorized to administer oaths." The fact in question is that the substance found in the possession of Melendez–Diaz and his codefendants was, as the prosecution claimed, cocaine—the precise testimony the analysts would be expected to provide if called at trial. The "certificates" are functionally identical to live, in-court testimony, doing "precisely what a witness does on direct examination." In short, the affidavits were testimonial statements, and the analysts were "witnesses" for purposes of the Sixth Amendment. Absent a showing that the analysts were unavailable to testify at trial and that petitioner had a prior opportunity to cross-examine them, petitioner was entitled to " 'be confronted with' " the analysts at trial.

Massachusetts (Respondent) claims that there is a difference, for Confrontation Clause purposes, between testimony recounting historical events, which is "prone to distortion or manipulation," and the testimony at issue here, which is the "result of neutral, scientific testing." Relatedly, respondent and the dissent argue that confrontation of forensic analysts would be of little value because "one would not reasonably expect a laboratory professional . . . to feel quite differently about the results of his scientific test by having to look at the defendant."

This argument is . . . that evidence with "particularized guarantees of trustworthiness" was admissible notwithstanding the Confrontation Clause. To be sure, the Clause's ultimate goal is to ensure reliability of evidence, but it is a procedural rather than a substantive guarantee. It commands, not that evidence be reliable, but that reliability be assessed in a particular manner: by testing in the crucible of cross-examination. . . . Dispensing with confrontation because testimony is obviously reliable is akin to dispensing with jury trial because a defendant is obviously guilty. This is not what the Sixth Amendment prescribes."

Respondent and the dissent may be right that there are other ways—and in some cases better ways—to challenge or verify the results of a forensic test. Though surely not always. Some forensic analyses, such as autopsies and breathalyzer tests, cannot be repeated, and the specimens used for other analyses have often been lost or degraded. But the Constitution guarantees one way: confrontation. We do not have license to suspend the Confrontation Clause when a preferable trial strategy is available.

Nor is it evident that what respondent calls "neutral scientific testing" is as neutral or as reliable as respondent suggests. Forensic evidence is not uniquely immune from the risk of manipulation. According to a recent study conducted under the auspices of the National Academy of Sciences, "the majority of [laboratories producing forensic evidence] are administered by law enforcement agencies, such as police departments, where the laboratory administrator reports to the head of the agency." National Research Council of the National Academies, Strengthening Forensic Science in the United States: A Path Forward 6–1 (Prepublication Copy Feb. 2009) (hereinafter National Academy Report). And "because forensic scientists often are driven in their work by a need to answer a particular question related to the issues of a particular case, they sometimes face pressure to sacrifice appropriate methodology for the sake of expediency." A forensic analyst responding to a request from a law enforcement official may feel pressure—or have an incentive—to alter the evidence in a manner favorable to the prosecution.

Confrontation is one means of assuring accurate forensic analysis. While it is true, that an honest analyst will not alter his testimony when forced to confront the defendant, the same cannot be said of the fraudulent analyst. Like the eyewitness who has fabricated his account to the police, the analyst who provides false results may, under oath in open court, reconsider his false testimony. And, of course, the prospect of confrontation will deter fraudulent analysis in the first place.

Confrontation is designed to weed out not only the fraudulent analyst, but the incompetent one as well. Serious deficiencies have been found in the forensic evidence used in criminal trials. One commentator asserts that "the legal community now concedes, with varying degrees of urgency, that our system produces erroneous convictions based on discredited forensics" Metzger, Cheating the Constitution, 59 Vand. L.Rev. 475, 491 (2006). One study of cases in which exonerating evidence resulted in the overturning of criminal convictions concluded that invalid forensic testimony contributed to the convictions in 60% of the cases. Garrett & Neufeld, Invalid Forensic Science Testimony and Wrongful Convictions, 95 Va. L.Rev. 1, 14 (2009). And the National Academy Report concluded:

> The forensic science system, encompassing both research and practice, has serious problems that can only be addressed by a national commitment to overhaul the current structure that supports the forensic science community in this country.

Like expert witnesses generally, an analyst's lack of proper training or deficiency in judgment may be disclosed in cross-examination. This case is illustrative. The affidavits submitted by the analysts contained only the bare-bones statement that "the substance was found to contain: Cocaine." At the time of trial, petitioner did not know what tests the analysts performed, whether those tests were routine, and whether interpreting their results required the exercise of judgment or the use of skills that the analysts may not have possessed. While we still do not know the precise tests used by the analysts, we are told that the laboratories use "methodology recommended by the Scientific Working Group for the Analysis of Seized Drugs." At least some of that methodology requires the exercise of judgment and presents a risk of error that might be explored on cross-examination.

The same is true of many of the other types of forensic evidence commonly used in criminal prosecutions. "There is wide variability across forensic science disciplines with regard to techniques, methodologies, reliability, types and numbers of potential errors, research, general acceptability, and published material." National Academy Report. Contrary to respondent's and the dissent's suggestion, there is little reason to believe that confrontation will be useless in testing analysts' honesty, proficiency, and methodology—the features that are commonly the focus in the cross-examination of experts.

Finally, respondent asks us to relax the requirements of the Confrontation Clause to accommodate the "'necessities of trial and the adversary process." It is not clear whence we would derive the authority to do so.

The Confrontation Clause may make the prosecution of criminals more burdensome, but that is equally true of the right to trial by jury and the privilege against self-incrimination. The Confrontation Clause—like those other constitutional provisions—is binding, and we may not disregard it at our convenience.

We also doubt the accuracy of respondent's and the dissent's dire predictions. The dissent, respondent, and its amici highlight the substantial total number of controlled-substance analyses performed by state and federal laboratories in recent years. But only some of those tests are implicated in prosecutions, and only a small fraction of those cases actually proceed to trial.

Perhaps the best indication that the sky will not fall after today's decision is that it has not done so already. Many States have already adopted the constitutional rule we announce today, while many others permit the defendant to assert (or forfeit by silence) his Confrontation Clause right after receiving notice of the prosecution's intent to use a forensic analyst's report. Despite these widespread practices, there is no evidence that the criminal justice system has ground to a halt in the States that, one way or another, empower a defendant to insist upon the analyst's appearance at trial. Indeed, in Massachusetts itself, a defendant may subpoena the analyst to appear at trial, and yet there is no indication that obstructionist defendants are abusing the privilege.

But it is not surprising. Defense attorneys and their clients will often stipulate to the nature of the substance in the ordinary drug case. It is unlikely that defense counsel will insist on live testimony whose effect will be merely to highlight rather than cast doubt upon the forensic analysis. Nor will defense attorneys want to antagonize the judge or jury by wasting their time with the appearance of a witness whose testimony defense counsel does not intend to rebut in any fashion. The amicus brief filed by District Attorneys in Support of the Commonwealth in the Massachusetts Supreme Court case upon which the Appeals Court here relied said that "it is almost always the case that [analysts' certificates] are admitted without objection. Generally, defendants do not object to the admission of drug certificates most likely because there is no benefit to a defendant from such testimony." Given these strategic considerations, and in light of the experience in those States that already provide the same or similar protections to defendants, there is little reason to believe that our decision today will commence the parade of horribles respondent and the dissent predict.

DISSENT

Justice KENNEDY, with whom THE CHIEF JUSTICE, Justice BREYER, and Justice ALITO join, dissenting.

The Court sweeps away an accepted rule governing the admission of scientific evidence. Until today, scientific

(continued)

analysis could be introduced into evidence without testimony from the "analyst" who produced it. This rule has been established for at least 90 years. It extends across at least 35 States and six Federal Courts of Appeals. It is remarkable that the Court so confidently disregards a century of jurisprudence. We learn now that we have misinterpreted the Confrontation Clause—hardly an arcane or seldom-used provision of the Constitution—for the first 218 years of its existence. The immediate systemic concern is that the Court makes no attempt to acknowledge the real differences between laboratory analysts who perform scientific tests and other, more conventional witnesses—"witnesses" being the word the Framers used in the Confrontation Clause.

. . . The Court threatens to disrupt forensic investigations across the country and to put prosecutions nationwide at risk of dismissal based on erratic, all-too-frequent instances when a particular laboratory technician, now invested by the Court's new constitutional designation as the analyst, simply does not or cannot appear.

Consider the costs today's decision imposes on criminal trials. Our own Court enjoys weeks, often months, of notice before cases are argued. We receive briefs well in advance. The argument itself is ordered. A busy trial court, by contrast, must consider not only attorneys' schedules but also those of witnesses and juries. Trial courts have huge caseloads to be processed within strict time limits. Some cases may unexpectedly plead out at the last minute; others, just as unexpectedly, may not. Some juries stay out longer than predicted; others must be reconstituted. An analyst cannot hope to be the trial court's top priority in scheduling. The analyst must instead face the prospect of waiting for days in a hallway outside the courtroom before being called to offer testimony that will consist of little more than a rote recital of the written report.

As matters stood before today's opinion, analysts already spent considerable time appearing as witnesses in those few cases where the defendant, unlike petitioner in this case, contested the analyst's result and subpoenaed the analyst. By requiring analysts also to appear in the far greater number of cases where defendants do not dispute the analyst's result, the Court imposes enormous costs on the administration of justice.

Setting aside, for a moment, all the other crimes for which scientific evidence is required, consider the costs the Court's ruling will impose on state drug prosecutions alone. In 2004, the most recent year for which data are available, drug possession and trafficking resulted in 362,850 felony convictions in state courts across the country. Roughly 95% of those convictions were products of plea bargains, which means that state courts saw more than 18,000 drug trials in a single year.

The analysts responsible for testing the drugs at issue in those cases now bear a crushing burden. For example, the district attorney in Philadelphia prosecuted 25,000 drug crimes in 2007. Assuming that number remains the same, and assuming that 95% of the cases end in a plea bargain, each of the city's 18 drug analysts, will be required to testify in more than 69 trials next year. Cleveland's district attorney prosecuted 14,000 drug crimes in 2007. Assuming that number holds, and that 95% of the cases end in a plea bargain, each of the city's 6 drug analysts (two of whom work only part time) must testify in 117 drug cases next year.

The Court purchases its meddling with the Confrontation Clause at a dear price, a price not measured in taxpayer dollars alone. Guilty defendants will go free, on the most technical grounds, as a direct result of today's decision, adding nothing to the truth-finding process. The analyst will not always make it to the courthouse in time. He or she may be ill; may be out of the country; may be unable to travel because of inclement weather; or may at that very moment be waiting outside some other courtroom for another defendant to exercise the right the Court invents today. If for any reason the analyst cannot make it to the courthouse in time, then, the Court holds, the jury cannot learn of the analyst's findings (unless, by some unlikely turn of events, the defendant previously cross-examined the analyst). The result, in many cases, will be that the prosecution cannot meet its burden of proof, and the guilty defendant goes free on a technicality that, because it results in an acquittal, cannot be reviewed on appeal.

The Court's holding is a windfall to defendants, one that is unjustified by any demonstrated deficiency in trials, any well-understood historical requirement, or any established constitutional precedent.

Questions

1. Summarize the majority's arguments supporting its decision that forensics lab personnel have to testify to their test results.

2. Summarize the dissent's arguments supporting its decision that forensics lab personnel should not be required to testify to their test results.

3. In your opinion, which side has the better arguments? Explain your answer.

CHAPTER SUMMARY

LO 1 In a lineup, witnesses try to pick the suspect out of a group of individuals who are present. In a show-up, witnesses match the suspect with one person, who is either present or pictured in a "mug shot."

LO 2 Courts took a "hands-off" approach to identification evidence and its admissibility until 1967 when the U.S. Supreme Court first recognized due process challenges to identification testimony.

LO 3, 4 Eyewitness identifications are almost never rejected by courts. To have them rejected, defendants must demonstrate by a preponderance of the evidence that the identification procedure was unnecessarily suggestive and created a very substantial likelihood of misidentification.

LO 5 Scientists who study memory refute common assumptions about how memory functions and under what circumstances it's likely to be reliable.

LO 5, 7 When memories are acquired, the brain doesn't act as a video recorder storing a stream of images. Observational accuracy is affected by duration, distraction, stress, race, and other factors.

LO 5 Retrieval blends information from the original experience with information added during the retention period. Eyewitness identification is subject to errors of omission (failure to recall) and errors of commission (incorrect recall).

LO 5, 6 Suggestion is particularly powerful during the retention and recollection phase. Research finds that witnesses add to a story based on what information researchers give them. People aren't good at keeping memories acquired during an incident separate from suggestions that occur thereafter.

LO 5, 6 Identification research relies on both new experiments and archival data. Experimental research needs to make sure that volunteers resemble average real-world witnesses under stress.

LO 5, 6 Eyewitness retrospective self-reports are the basis of identification testimony. The social desirability of the response, the need to appear consistent, and reinterpretation of past events due to new events all affect such reports.

LO 7 The composition of the lineup and the instructions given prior to the lineup influence identifications. Instructions that seem reasonable are often more suggestive than we realize.

LO 7 Show-ups are substantially less reliable than lineups. Courts admit show-up identifications even if a witness runs into a suspect in the courthouse, saw police pursuing the suspect, and under other potentially misleading situations.

LO 8 Research shows that our reported opportunity to view a culprit varies widely from our actual opportunity to do so. The amount of time spent observing a culprit is less important than what the witness did with the time and where he or she focused attention.

LO 7, 8 Reform of identification procedures and testimony includes recommendations allowing expert testimony on memory, mandating sequential lineups, conducting double-blind administration of lineups, warning the witness that the suspect might or might not be in the lineup, and obtaining a witness confidence statement immediately following the identification.

Forensic science, including DNA testing, produces some of the most powerful evidence imaginable. One of the most important criminal law issues of our day is whether there's a postconviction constitutional right to access DNA evidence for the purpose of exonerating sentenced convicts. Despite its strengths, forensic evidence has serious shortcomings that question the quality of the evidence analyzed.

REVIEW QUESTIONS

1. Why is identification of strangers risky in criminal cases?
2. Identify and define three mental processes that account for mistakes in identifying strangers.
3. Identify five circumstances that affect the accuracy of identifying strangers.
4. According to the Supreme Court, why don't accidental show-ups violate due process?
5. Describe how memory affects the accuracy of eyewitness identification.
6. Describe how suggestion works based on Elizabeth Loftus's research.
7. Describe how witnesses' descriptions of criminal events change over time.
8. When is the effect of suggestion most powerful and threatening? Why?
9. Explain why the procedures used to identify strangers add to the problem of misidentification.
10. Identify and describe three ways to reduce the inaccuracy of eyewitness identification by police procedures and legal rules.
11. Identify three constitutional provisions identification procedures can violate and when in the criminal process they kick in.
12. Summarize what empirical research has shown about the reliability of lineups.
13. Describe and give an example of how the power of suggestion works in administering lineups.
14. Identify the two prongs in the totality-of-circumstances due process test of admissibility of eyewitness identification created by the U.S. Supreme Court.
15. Identify, describe, and give an example of the five circumstances in the totality-of-circumstances due process test you identified in question 14.
16. Why are photo identifications the most unreliable eyewitness identification procedure?
17. List four recommendations made by legal commentators to improve eyewitness identification reliability.
18. List the six recommendations made by the Wisconsin legislature and law enforcement to improve eyewitness identification.
19. Identify and compare the three legal tests for admitting DNA evidence in court.
20. Summarize the importance jurors, lawyers, and judges attach to scientific evidence as proof of guilt.
21. List five types of evidence analyzed by forensic science.

22. Identify and describe five circumstances that affect the quality of forensic evidence.

23. Explain the significance of *Melendez-Diaz v. Massachusetts* regarding the right to confront witnesses.

KEY TERMS

lineups, p. 337

photo array, p. 337

show-ups, p. 337

preponderance of the evidence, p. 338

unnecessarily and impermissibly suggestive, p. 338

very substantial likelihood of misidentification, p. 338

per se approach, p. 341

totality of the circumstances, p. 342

accidental show-ups, p. 345

memory experts, p. 350

memory trace, p. 350

acquisition of memory, p. 350

retention of memory, p. 350

retrieval of memory, p. 350

eyewitness recall, p. 352

eyewitness recognition, p. 352

errors of omission, p. 352

errors of commission, p. 352

suggestion, p. 352

reliability test of eyewitness evidence, p. 353

archival research, p. 354

experimental research, p. 354

eyewitness retrospective self-reports, p. 354

fillers, p. 355

relative judgment, p. 355

might-or-might-not-be-present instruction, p. 356

blind administrator, p. 361

sequential presentation, p. 361

simultaneous presentation, p. 361

cautionary instruction, p. 362

forensic science, p. 365

DNA testing, p. 366

forensic *ipse dixit* statutes, p. 373

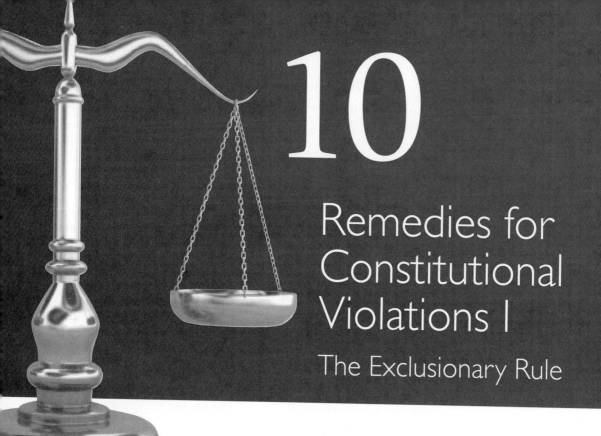

10

Remedies for Constitutional Violations I

The Exclusionary Rule

LEARNING OBJECTIVES

1 Know that the exclusionary rule bans the use of illegally obtained evidence to prove guilt. Understand how Fourth, Fifth, Sixth, and Fourteenth Amendment rights can be violated by bad practices in law enforcement.

2 Appreciate the history of the exclusionary rule. Understand that it is no longer a "bright-line" rule banning all evidence collected illegally.

3 Know that there's no constitutional right to have evidence that was collected illegally excluded at trial. Understand how courts exclude evidence to preserve judicial integrity and to deter officers from breaking the law.

4 Know that courts must balance the deterrent effect of the exclusionary rule against the social costs of applying it. Understand that the exceptions to

the "fruit of the poisonous tree" doctrine allow more evidence into court to prove guilt.

5 Know the exceptions under which evidence excluded from the main prosecution can be used in other parts of the legal process.

6 Understand and appreciate the significance of the knock-and-announce and good-faith exceptions to the exclusionary rule.

7 Know that the social costs and deterrent effect of the exclusionary rule are based on assumptions, not empirical evidence. Understand that empirical research suggests that the social costs of the exclusionary rule may not be as severe as we commonly believe; criminal cases are rarely dismissed due to illegally obtained evidence.

> *The well-worn debate over the exclusionary rule is framed in terms of the extent we should be willing to allow the guilty to go free so as to expansively interpret the rights of accused criminals. Setting the guilty free is an accepted price for both long-range deterrence against police violations of constitutional rights, as well as the expressive commitment to fairness in the criminal justice system. However, wrongly convicting the innocent is not part of that deal. The proverbial ten guilty men are not meant to be set free for their own sake, but rather so that the one innocent person goes free.... By instituting constitutional protections for actually guilty criminal suspects the exclusionary rule creates a higher burden of proof for actually innocent defendants.*
>
> —Jacobi (2011, 589)

> *Of course there has to be an exclusionary rule. I don't want this to be a police state. There have to be guidelines. The problem is the guidelines aren't clear. I believe that the Supreme Court is not making the law clear. They take a tough situation in which a police officer must act in an instant, they think about it for five months, and come out seven to six. What kind of system is this for making law?*
>
> —Lieutenant Karczewski, Chicago Police Department (Bradley 1993, 40)

> *Should the culprit go free because the constable blundered?*
>
> —*People v. Defore* (1926)

> *We hold that all evidence obtained by searches and seizures in violation of the Constitution is . . . inadmissible in a state court.*
>
> —*Mapp v. Ohio* (1961)

> *Suppression of evidence . . . has always been our last resort, not our first impulse.*
>
> —*Hudson v. Michigan* (2006)

> *The exclusionary rule serves to deter deliberate, reckless, or grossly negligent conduct. . . .*
>
> —*Herring v. U.S.* (2009), Majority

When I was a very junior member of a Minneapolis mayor's committee to examine police misconduct, our committee held a neighborhood meeting to educate residents about our work. But I learned a lot more than the residents. One resident that night made a comment and then asked a great question. His comment: "We all know what happens when we break the law—we get arrested and prosecuted." His question: "What I want to know is what happens when the police break the law against us? What recourse do we have?"

The answer is, "We have lots of remedies" (at least, on paper).

LO 1

We'll divide the discussion of the remedies into two types and between this chapter and the next. This chapter's topic is the **exclusionary rule**, which bans illegally obtained evidence in the case against the defendant (by far the most frequently used remedy). In Chapter 11, we'll examine remedies in separate proceedings from the criminal cases against defendants. Some of these proceedings take place inside the judicial system (civil lawsuits and criminal prosecutions) and others outside (department disciplinary actions and civilian review).

The U.S. legal system, like all others, excludes the use of some irrelevant or untrustworthy evidence. But the *exclusionary rule*, mandating that courts ban the introduction of "good" evidence obtained by "bad" law enforcement, is more prevalent in the United States than in most other countries' legal systems. **"Good evidence"** refers to **probative evidence**—evidence that proves (or at least helps to prove) defendants committed the crimes they're charged with. **"Bad methods"** refers to police actions and procedures that violate any of five constitutional rights:

1. The Fourth Amendment ban on unreasonable searches and seizures (Chapters 3–7)
2. The Fifth Amendment ban on coerced incriminating statements (Chapter 8)
3. The Sixth Amendment right to counsel (Chapter 12)
4. The Fifth and Fourteenth Amendment guarantees of due process of law

Note two important points about the Fourth Amendment and the exclusionary rule. First, searches and seizures make up the great bulk of suppression cases. Second, and most important, evidence obtained by illegal searches and seizures is just as reliable as evidence obtained legally. We can't say this about coerced confessions and suggestive eyewitness identification and other non-DNA forensic analyses.

HISTORY OF THE EXCLUSIONARY RULE

LO 2 The Bill of Rights to the U.S. Constitution doesn't mention the exclusionary rule (or for that matter the other remedies we'll discuss in Chapter 11). James Madison, in an address to Congress in 1789 (*Annals of Congress* 1789), explains this silence:

> If these rights are incorporated into the Constitution, independent tribunals of justice will consider themselves in a peculiar manner the guardians of those rights; they will be an impenetrable bulwark against every assumption of power in the Legislative or Executive; they will naturally be led to resist every encroachment upon rights expressly stipulated for in the Constitution by the declaration of rights. (457)

In other words, the Constitution didn't have to spell out the remedies because judges would create appropriate ones to fit the circumstances of each case.

LO 2 ## From *Weeks v. U.S.* (1914) to *Mapp v. Ohio* (1961)

Until 1914, the only remedies for constitutional violations were private lawsuits against officials. (The U.S. Supreme Court *suggested* in *Boyd v. U.S.* [1886] that illegally obtained evidence should be banned from court; it ignored that suggestion for 27 years.)

All this changed dramatically in 1914, when the U.S. Supreme Court created the exclusionary rule in *Weeks v. U.S.* (1914). In that case, while Fremont Weeks was at work in Union Station, Kansas City, Kansas, local police officers broke into his house without a warrant. They searched the house and seized "all of his books, letters, money, papers, notes, evidences of indebtedness, stock certificates, insurance policies, deeds, abstracts of title, bonds, candies, clothes, and other property." After taking the evidence to the U.S. marshal's office, local officers and a marshal arrested Weeks while he was at work. Soon, Weeks was charged with illegal gambling.

The trial court refused Weeks's motion to return the seized evidence, and he was convicted and sentenced to a fine and imprisonment. On appeal, the U.S. Supreme Court reversed the conviction and ordered the return of his documents because to allow the government to seize his private papers and use them to convict him violated his Fourth Amendment right against unreasonable searches and seizures.

Notice that the exclusionary rule established in *Weeks* applied only to *federal* law enforcement; the *states* could fashion any remedy they saw fit to enforce their own citizens' constitutional rights under their state constitutions. (Recall from Chapter 2, pp. 30–35, that it wasn't until the 1930s that the Supreme Court began to apply the Bill of Rights to state criminal proceedings under the Fourteenth Amendment due process clause: "no state shall deprive any person of life, liberty, or property, without due process of law.")

It took until 1949 for the Court to decide whether the due process clause of the Fourteenth Amendment incorporates the right against unreasonable searches and seizures (*Wolf v. Colorado*). In fact, the Court answered two questions:

1. Does the Fourteenth Amendment due process clause apply the right against unreasonable searches and seizures to the states at all?
2. If it does, is the exclusionary rule part of the right?

The Court answered "yes" to the first question and "no" to the second. In other words, states have to enforce the ban on unreasonable searches and seizures, *but* the Fourth Amendment leaves up to the states *how* to enforce it.

Twelve years later, in *Mapp v. Ohio* (1961), the Court changed its answer to the second question in *Wolf* to "yes." Dollree Mapp and her daughter lived on the top floor of the two-family dwelling. Cleveland police had information that "a person was hiding in the home, who was wanted for questioning in connection with a recent bombing, and that there was a large amount of policy [gambling] paraphernalia being hidden in the home" (644). Three Cleveland police officers knocked on Mapp's door and demanded entrance. Mapp, after calling her lawyer, refused to let them in without a search warrant.

> The officers again sought entrance some three hours later when four or more additional officers arrived on the scene. When Miss Mapp did not come to the door immediately, at least one of the several doors to the house was forcibly opened. (A police officer testified that 'we did pry the screen door to gain entrance'; the attorney on the scene testified that a policeman 'tried to kick in the door' and then 'broke the glass in the door and somebody reached in and opened the door and let them in'; the appellant testified that 'The back door was broken.')
>
> Meanwhile Miss Mapp's attorney arrived, but the officers, having secured their own entry, and continuing in their defiance of the law, would permit him neither to see Miss Mapp nor to enter the house. It appears that Miss Mapp was halfway down the stairs from the upper floor to the front door when the officers, in this high-handed manner, broke into the hall. She demanded to see the search warrant. A paper, claimed to be a warrant, was held up by one of the officers. She grabbed the "warrant" and placed it in her bosom. A struggle ensued in which the officers recovered the piece of paper and as a result of which they handcuffed appellant because she had been "belligerent" in resisting their official rescue of the "warrant" from her person.
>
> Running roughshod over Mapp, a policeman "grabbed" her, "twisted (her) hand," and she "yelled (and) pleaded with him" because "it was hurting." Mapp, in handcuffs, was then forcibly taken upstairs to her bedroom where the officers searched a dresser, a chest of drawers, a closet, and some suitcases. They also looked into a photo album and through personal papers belonging to Mapp. The search spread to the rest of the second floor including the child's bedroom, the living room, the kitchen, and a dinette. The basement of the building and a trunk found were also searched. The obscene materials for possession of which she was ultimately convicted were discovered in the course of that widespread search. (644–45)

According to Justice Clarke, writing for the majority of five:

> Today, we once again examine *Wolf*'s constitutional documentation of the right to privacy free from unreasonable state intrusion, and after its dozen years on our books, are led by it to close the only courtroom door remaining open to evidence secured by official lawlessness in flagrant abuse of that basic right, reserved to all persons as a specific guarantee against that very same unlawful conduct.

And then, Justice Clarke announced the bright-line rule that would dominate exclusionary rule cases for the next 36 years: "We hold that *all* evidence obtained by searches and seizures in violation of the Constitution . . . is inadmissible in a state court" (655).

Writing for the vigorous dissenters, Justice Harlan wrote:

> At the heart of the majority's opinion in this case is the following syllogism: the rule excluding in federal criminal trials evidence which is the product of an illegal search and seizure is "part and parcel" of the Fourth Amendment. What the Court is now doing is to impose upon the States not only federal substantive standards of "search and seizure" but also the basic federal remedy for violation of those standards. For I think it entirely clear that the *Weeks* exclusionary rule is but a remedy which, by penalizing past official misconduct, is aimed at deterring such conduct in the future.
>
> I would not impose upon the States this federal exclusionary remedy. (678)

LO 2 — *U.S. v. Leon* (1984)

In 1984, 23 years after *Mapp*, the U.S. Supreme Court backed away from the bright-line rule that excluded *all* illegally obtained evidence from criminal trials, and adopted the controversial *good-faith exception* to the exclusionary rule in *U.S. v. Leon* (1984). Acting on the basis of information from a confidential informant, officers of the Burbank, California, Police Department initiated a drug-trafficking investigation involving surveillance of Alberto Antonio Leon's activities. Based on an affidavit summarizing the police officers' observations, Officer Rombach prepared an application for a warrant to search three residences and Leon's cars for an extensive list of items. Several deputy district attorneys reviewed the application, and a state court judge issued the warrant. Searches based on the warrant produced large quantities of illegal drugs and other evidence.

Following indictment for federal drug offenses, Leon and others filed motions to suppress the evidence seized. The district court granted the motions because the affidavit was insufficient to establish probable cause. The court acknowledged that Officer Rombach had acted in good faith, but rejected the government's argument that the exclusionary rule should not apply where evidence is seized in reasonable, good-faith reliance on a search warrant. The court of appeals affirmed. The government petitioned for certiorari. The petition asked only that the Supreme Court recognize a good-faith exception to the exclusionary rule.

The Court (6–3) adopted the good-faith exception. The 6-member majority held that:

1. The Fourth Amendment exclusionary rule should not be applied so as to bar the use—in the prosecution's case in chief—of evidence obtained by officers

acting in reasonable reliance on a search warrant issued by a detached and neutral magistrate but ultimately found to be invalid;

2. The standard of reasonableness is an objective one;

3. Suppression is appropriate where officers have no reasonable ground for believing that the warrant was properly issued; and

4. The officer's reliance on the magistrate's determination of probable cause in the instant case was objectively reasonable.

Justice White made clear that replacing the bright-line ban on the use of *all* illegally obtained evidence with the *good-faith exception* didn't abolish the exclusionary rule:

> Our good-faith inquiry is confined to the objectively ascertainable question whether a reasonably well trained officer would have known that the search was illegal despite the magistrate's authorization. The good-faith exception for searches conducted pursuant to warrants is not intended to signal our unwillingness strictly to enforce the requirements of the Fourth Amendment, and we do not believe that it will have this effect. As we have already suggested, the good-faith exception, turning as it does on objective reasonableness, should not be difficult to apply in practice. When officers have acted pursuant to a warrant, the prosecution should ordinarily be able to establish objective good faith without a substantial expenditure of judicial time. (924)

We'll examine the contractions of the exclusionary rule after *Leon* in the "Exceptions to the Exclusionary Rule" section later in the chapter. Before we get to the exceptions, let's look at the justifications for the exclusionary rule.

JUSTIFICATIONS FOR THE EXCLUSIONARY RULE

LO 3

To put it mildly, the exclusionary rule is controversial. Critics say it sets criminals free on "technicalities." Supporters reply that these "technicalities" are rights our ancestors fought and died for. Why do we throw good evidence out of court? The U.S. Supreme Court has relied on three justifications:

1. *Constitutional right.* It's part of the constitutional rights against unreasonable seizure and coerced confessions and the rights to a lawyer and due process of law.

2. *Judicial integrity.* It preserves the honor and honesty of the courts.

3. *Deterrence.* It prevents officers from breaking the law.

The **constitutional right justification** stems from an ancient legal saying, "There's no right without a remedy" (Stewart 1983, 1380–83). One commentator summed it up with this brilliant image: "It's like one hand clapping" (Uviller 1988).

In *Weeks v. U.S.* (1914), the case that created the exclusionary rule for the federal system, U.S. Supreme Court Justice William Rufus Day put it this way:

> If letters and private documents can be seized and held illegally, and used in evidence against a citizen accused of an offense, the protection of the Fourth Amendment declaring his right to be secure against such searches and seizures is of no value, and may as well be stricken from the Constitution. (393)

The **judicial integrity (moral) justification** maintains that the honor and honesty of courts forbid them from participating in unconstitutional conduct.

In *Olmstead v. U.S.* (1928), holding that wiretapping was not a search (Chapter 3), Justices Oliver Wendell Holmes and Louis Brandeis wrote dissents on the moral basis for the exclusionary rule (dissents, by the way, quoted even today). They both spoke to the hypocrisy of judges who preach about morality of "judicial integrity," but then proceed to allow the government to profit from its misconduct by admitting in court evidence the police obtained by violating individuals' constitutional rights.

> We must consider two objects of desire, both of which we cannot have, and make up our minds which to choose. It is desirable that criminals should be detected, and to that end that all available evidence should be used. It also is desirable that the Government should not itself foster and pay for other crimes, when they are the means by which the evidence is to be obtained. For my part, I think it is less evil that some criminals should escape than that the Government should play an ignoble part. (470)

In Justice Brandeis's dissent, he wrote eloquently on the same point. Here are his countlessly repeated words: "If the Government becomes a lawbreaker, it breeds contempt for law." (See full quote p. 390)

Professor Dallin Oaks (1970), the first scholar of the exclusionary rule, in his brilliant "Studying the Exclusionary Rule," homed in on the value the majority of Supreme Court justices *really* places on the "judicial imperative" justification—he called it "rhetoric."

> Although the normative justification that the Supreme Court has referred to as the "imperative of judicial integrity" continues to appear in the rhetoric of Supreme Court decisions, it is doubtful that this argument *decides cases*. Despite bold pronouncements about not being a party to "lawless invasions," federal courts have not yet been forbidden from entering a valid judgment of conviction against a defendant who was brought before the court by illegal means. (669)
>
> When the Supreme Court has had to make decisions on the scope of the exclusionary rule, its opinion has usually stressed and its reasoning seems to have been dictated by factual considerations of deterrence rather than the arguments of judicial integrity. (669–70)

By 1965, a majority of the Court made clear that "the purpose of the [*Mapp* decision] was to deter the lawless action of the police," and "this purpose will not at this date be served by the wholesale release of the guilty victims" (Oaks 1970, 670, quoting *Linkletter v. Walker* 1965, 637).

The **deterrence justification** is based on the *assumption* (not yet proved—see section on empirical evidence) that throwing out good evidence because it was obtained illegally sends a strong message to law enforcement. Here's how the distinguished Justice Potter Stewart (who probably knew more about the Fourth Amendment than any other U.S. Supreme Court justice in our history) summed up the deterrence justification:

> The rule is calculated to prevent, not to repair. Its purpose is to deter—to compel respect for the constitutional guaranty in the only effective available way—by removing the incentive to disregard it. (*Elkins v. U.S.* 1960, 217)

To *apply* the deterrence justification, the Court has turned to another version of its old friend, a *balancing test*. This form of the test requires courts to look at the totality of the circumstances of each case and weigh the social cost of excluding "good" evidence—namely, setting criminals free—against the deterrent effect that excluding good evidence might have on police officers' illegal conduct. If the social costs outweigh the deterrent effect, then the evidence comes in.

U.S. v. Leon (1984) also contains an enormously significant holding growing out of the deterrence justification—*excluding illegally obtained evidence isn't a constitutional right*. It's a **prophylactic rule**—a procedure to prevent violations of constitutional rights.

The exclusionary rule brings into bold relief the tension between the search for truth and the procedural rights of all those—innocent and guilty—who get embroiled in the criminal justice system (Chapter 1). By throwing out good evidence because of bad practices, the rule puts the search for truth second to fair procedures. No one put the case for the exclusionary rule better than Associate Justice Louis D. Brandeis in his famous dissent in *Olmstead v. U.S.* (1928):

> Our government is the potent, the omnipresent teacher. For good or for ill, it teaches the whole people by its example. Crime is contagious. If the government becomes a lawbreaker, it breeds contempt for law; it invites every man to become a law unto himself; it invites anarchy.
>
> To declare that in the administration of the criminal law the end justifies the means—to declare that the government may commit crimes in order to secure the conviction of a private criminal—would bring terrible retribution. Against that pernicious doctrine this court should resolutely set its face. (468)

The deterrence rationale and the transformation of the exclusionary rule from a constitutional right to a protective device to prevent police misconduct are, of course, important in their own right. But they're not encased in a bubble, insulated from the effects of the extremely uncomfortable legal and social reality that the exclusionary rule keeps evidence out of court that could convict criminals, and instead sets them free. (Table 10.1 lists some of the other *possible* negative effects compiled by Professor Dallin Oaks [1970]). How often criminals *really* walk, and the *seriousness* of the offenses they walk from, we'll take up in the section on social costs later in the chapter (p. 407). Whatever the reality, *perceptions* based on anecdote and "gut feelings" too often seem to drive both the Court's decisions and scholarly "learning."

Discomfort caused by the exclusionary rule has contributed to the creation of several exceptions to the rule. Let's turn to them now.

TABLE 10.1 Possible negative effects of the exclusionary rule

• Court delay
• Diversion of resources from trials to suppression hearings
• Weakening of the Fourth Amendment guarantees by judges reluctant to exclude evidence
• Encouragement of plea bargaining
• Empowerment of corrupt police officers to immunize criminals by botching searches
• Imposition of extrajudicial punishment by officers who find themselves unable to secure convictions lawfully
• Fostering false testimony by police officers, "twisting the facts to prevent suppression" (739)

THE EXCEPTIONS TO THE EXCLUSIONARY RULE

LO 4 According to the U.S. Supreme Court, the exclusionary rule is not a defendant's "personal constitutional right." It's a "judicially created remedy designed to safeguard . . . rights through its deterrent effect."

> The exclusionary rule has never been interpreted to proscribe the use of illegally obtained evidence in all proceedings or against all persons. As with any remedial device, the application of the rule has been restricted to those areas where its remedial objectives are thought most efficaciously served. (*U.S. v. Calandra* 1974, 348)

The "remedial objective" is to deter police from violating an individual's constitutional rights. But, enforcing the rule comes at a cost. The **social cost of the rule**— freeing guilty people, undermining the prosecution's case, and obstructing the search by keeping good evidence out of court—led the U.S. Supreme Court to limit its application to cases it believes are most likely to deter police misconduct. Each case, then, requires courts to balance the deterrent effect of the rule against the social cost of applying it. (See p. 407 for a discussion of the empirical research on this balance.)

According to Justice Alito (*Davis v. U.S.* 2011):

> Exclusion exacts a heavy toll on both the judicial system and society at large. It almost always requires courts to ignore reliable, trustworthy evidence bearing on guilt or innocence. And its bottom-line effect, in many cases, is to suppress the truth and set the criminal loose in the community without punishment. Our cases hold that society must swallow this bitter pill, but only as a "last resort." For exclusion to be appropriate, the deterrence benefits must outweigh its heavy costs. (2127) [If they don't] the deterrence rationale loses much of its force, and exclusion cannot "pay its way." (2427–28)

The Court has created several exceptions where it has decided the exclusionary rule can't "pay its way." Let's start with restrictions on what began as an *expansion* of the exclusionary rule, namely the "fruit of the poisonous tree doctrine."

LO 4 Exceptions to the "Fruit of the Poisonous Tree" Doctrine

The **fruit of the poisonous tree doctrine** bans not only evidence illegally obtained directly but also evidence derived from it. The basic idea of the doctrine is that the government shouldn't be in a *better* position after it breaks the law. U.S. Supreme Court Justice Felix Frankfurter used the "poisonous tree" idea to formulate this derivative evidence expansion of the exclusionary rule in *Nardone v. U.S.* (1939). Frank Carmine Nardone and others were convicted of smuggling alcohol. Their conviction rested on evidence federal agents derived from witnesses who overheard Nardone's illegally wiretapped conversations.

According to Justice Frankfurter,

> The burden is, of course, on the accused, in the first instance to prove to the trial court's satisfaction that wire-tapping was unlawfully employed. Once that is established—as was plainly done here—the trial judge must give opportunity, however closely confined, to the accused to prove that a substantial portion of

the case against him was a fruit of the poisonous tree. *This gives ample opportunity to the Government to convince the trial court that its proof had an independent origin.* (268; emphasis added)

This is where the three exceptions—attenuation, independent source, and inevitable discovery—come in. As you read, remember that their effect is to allow *more* evidence into court. Maybe it'll help you to think of the exceptions as antidotes to the poison of illegal governmental actions. As the U.S. Supreme Court said, not all derivative evidence is "'fruit of the poisonous tree' simply because it would not have come to light but for the illegal actions of the police" (*Wong Sun v. U.S.* 1963, 488).

LO 4 *Attenuation*

The noun *attenuation* means "thinning, weakening, or emaciation." The **attenuation exception** says that illegally obtained evidence can come into court if the poisonous connection between illegal police actions and the evidence they got illegally from their actions weakens (attenuates) enough.

The U.S. Supreme Court hasn't written a bright-line attenuation rule. Instead, courts have to decide each case according to the totality of circumstances. One circumstance is the closeness in time between the poisonous tree (illegal government act) and getting its fruit (evidence). For example, in *Wong Sun v. U.S.* (1963, 491), federal narcotics officers in San Francisco illegally broke into James Wah Toy's home and chased him down the hall into his bedroom. Agent Wong pulled his gun, illegally arrested Toy, and handcuffed him. Toy then told the officers Johnny Yee had sold him heroin. The officers immediately went to Yee's home. Yee admitted he had heroin and gave it to the officers. The Court ruled that the time between the illegal arrest and getting the heroin from Yee was too close to dissipate the poison of the arrest.

In the same case, the same narcotics officers arrested another man, Wong Sun, illegally. A few days later, after Wong Sun was charged and released on bail, he went back voluntarily to the Narcotics Bureau, where he told detectives he'd delivered heroin to Johnny Yee and smoked it with him. In his case, the U.S. Supreme Court decided "the connection between the arrest and the statement had become so attenuated as to dissipate the taint."

Another circumstance that might attenuate the poison enough to let the evidence in is an "intervening independent act of free will" after the illegal act. Let's go back to James Wah Toy in his bedroom after the illegal arrest. The government argued that when Toy told the officers that Yee had sold him heroin, he did it of his own free will. But the Court rejected the argument, not because an independent act of free will can't attenuate the poison but because it didn't fit the facts of this case.

According to the Court:

Six or seven officers had broken the door and followed on Toy's heels into the bedroom where his wife and child were sleeping. He had been almost immediately handcuffed and arrested. Under such circumstances it is unreasonable to infer that Toy's response was sufficiently an act of free will to purge the primary taint of the unlawful invasion. (*Wong Sun v. U.S.* 1963, 416–17)

LO 4 *Independent source*

What if police officers violate the Constitution looking for evidence and, then, in a totally separate action, get the same evidence lawfully? It's admissible under the *independent source exception.* For example, in *U.S. v. Moscatiello* (1985), federal agents entered a South Boston warehouse illegally, where they saw marijuana in plain view. They left without touching the marijuana and kept the warehouse under surveillance while they went to get a search warrant. In applying for the warrant, the officers didn't build their probable cause on anything they'd learned during the unlawful entry of the warehouse.

The U.S. Court of Appeals concluded that it was "absolutely certain" that the entry without a warrant didn't contribute "in the slightest" to discovering the marijuana in plain view during the later search backed up by a warrant. "The discovery of the contraband in plain view was totally irrelevant to the later securing of a warrant and the successful search that ensued" (603).

The U.S. Supreme Court upheld the Court of Appeals. According to the Court:

> [W]hile the government should not profit from its illegal activity, neither should it be placed in a worse position than it would otherwise have occupied. So long as a later, lawful seizure is genuinely independent of an earlier, tainted one . . . there is no reason why the independent source doctrine should not apply. (*Murray v. U.S.* 1988, 542–43)

So, in a nutshell, the **independent source exception** says, even if officers break the law, unless their lawbreaking *causes* the seizure of evidence, the evidence is admissible in court.

LO 4   *Inevitable discovery*

But what if official lawbreaking *is* the cause of getting the evidence? Is the evidence banned from use? Not if officers, acting within the Constitution, would eventually find it anyway. And this is the nub of the **inevitable discovery exception**.

The inevitable discovery exception was the issue in *Nix v. Williams* (1984), an appeal from the retrial of Robert Williams, whom you met in Chapter 8 (pp. 303–304). Recall that Williams was suspected of brutally murdering 10-year-old Pamela Powers. During an illegal police interrogation, Williams led police officers to the place where he had hidden the body. At the same time, a separate search party was combing the same area near where some of Pamela's clothing had been found. The search party took a break from the search only 2½ miles from where Williams led the officers to the body; the location was within the area they planned to search.

So two searches were converging on the dead body. One search was being lawfully conducted by a search party. The other was the fruit of the poisonous illegal interrogation. The "fruit of the poisonous tree" search was the discovery of the body during the legal search party's break. Should the evidence be admitted? Yes, said the U.S. Supreme Court. Why? Because the body would have been discovered anyway by the legal search party.

Emphasizing the purpose of the fruit of the poisonous tree doctrine, and why the inevitable discovery exception was consistent with that purpose, the Court wrote:

> Exclusion of evidence that would inevitably have been discovered would put the government in a worse position, because the police would have obtained that evidence if no misconduct had taken place. This rationale justifies our adoption of the inevitable discovery exception to the exclusionary rule. (444)

Now let's turn to some direct exceptions to the exclusionary rule.

LO 5   ## Nontrial Proceedings (Collateral Use) Exception

Illegally obtained evidence can be used in collateral proceedings, meaning proceedings not directly related to the prosecution's case-in-chief at trial. These include most of the topics we'll discuss in later chapters: bail hearings, grand jury proceedings, and preliminary hearings (Chapter 12); sentencing (Chapter 14); parole revocation hearings and some kinds of habeas corpus proceedings (Chapter 14). So prosecutors can present illegally obtained evidence to deny defendants bail, get grand juries to indict defendants, and get judges in preliminary hearings to send cases on for trial; judges can use the evidence in sentencing defendants.

LO 5   ## Trial Proceedings—Cross-Examination

The exclusionary rule applies only to one part of trial proceedings: the government's case-in-chief in the criminal trial. **Case-in-chief** means the part of the trial where the government presents its evidence to prove the defendant's guilt. Note that the case-in-chief does *not* include cross-examination of defense witnesses.

In *Walder v. U.S.* (1954), Sam Walder was tried for purchasing and possessing heroin. During direct examination, Walder denied he'd ever bought or possessed heroin. The government then introduced heroin capsules seized during an illegal search to destroy his credibility by proving to the jury that he was a liar. The trial court admitted the capsules but cautioned the jury not to use the heroin capsules to prove Walder's guilt, only to **impeach** (undermine the believability of) his testimony. The U.S. Supreme Court ruled that the exclusionary rule didn't apply. According to the Court, Walder couldn't use the government's "illegal method" to obtain evidence as a shield against exposing his own lies. "Such an extension of the *Weeks* doctrine would be a perversion of the Fourth Amendment" (65).

LO 4, 6   ## The "Knock-and-Announce" Exception

The **knock-and-announce exception** permits the admission of evidence seized during searches of homes, even when officers violate the "knock-and-announce" rule mandated in *Arizona v. Wilson* (1995; discussed in Chapter 6, pp. 199–201). The dissents and critics outside the Court savagely attacked *Hudson v. Michigan* (2006), the 5–4 decision that created the exception, not only for the rule itself, which is narrow—it applies only when officers have a valid search warrant—but because of its possible far-reaching applications.

Also at work may be the reaction to Justice Scalia's muscular majority opinion expressing his hostility to the exclusionary rule generally. Justice Kennedy (no friend of the exclusionary rule himself), although voting with the majority, felt the need to write separately to make clear that "the continued operation of the exclusionary rule, as settled and defined by our precedents, is not in doubt. Today's decision determines only that in the specific context of the knock-and-announce requirement, a violation is not sufficiently related to the later discovery of evidence to justify suppression" (603).

Professors Tracey Maclin and Jennifer Rader weren't reassured. They concluded:

> We believe that Scalia wrote *Hudson* to lay the foundation for abolishing suppression generally. In other words, Scalia's analysis in *Hudson* is *not* a "good-for-this-train-only" ticket. Rather, it is intended specifically for use

in future cases to bar suppression as a categorical matter, and *Hudson* itself, as a general matter, was structured to provide a blueprint for repealing the exclusionary rule when five Justices are ready to do so. (Maclin and Rader 2012, 1216–17)

Professor Craig Bradley (2012), former prosecutor and law clerk to Chief Justice Rehnquist, offered a more tempered assessment. While he believes Justice Scalia's opinion "fired the first shot of the current Court's attack on the rule" (3), he added,

> The exact scope of *Hudson* was rendered unclear by the concurring opinion of Justice Kennedy, who lent his crucial fifth vote to pertinent parts of the majority opinion. [He quotes Justice Kennedy as above; also see case excerpt just below. pp. 395–399] It is hard to imagine another Fourth Amendment violation whose consequences are so minor as the fifteen to twenty seconds of privacy lost when police fail to knock and announce during execution of a search warrant. So it is fair to deem *Hudson* a unique case, important only for what it says in dictum about the exclusionary rule, not for its holding. (4)

Professor Bradley partly sums up his assessment of the Roberts Court on the exclusionary rule this way:

> Although the Court . . . edges ever closer to effectively abolishing the exclusionary rule except in really extreme cases, it hasn't done so yet. . . . We are still waiting for a case where police have made a negligent mistake that substantially interferes with a suspect's constitutional rights, such as an arrest not based on probable cause or a warrantless search of a house where police evaluation of exigent circumstances is clearly wrong. (22)

Now, it's time to give you a shot at offering your take on *Hudson v. Michigan* (2006). It's our next case excerpt.

In *Hudson v. Michigan* (2006), the U.S. Supreme Court (5–4) held that failure to comply with the knock-and-announce rule never violates the exclusionary rule if officers have a valid warrant to search a home.

CASE

Did Violating the "Knock-and-Announce Rule" Ban the Use of Evidence?

Hudson v. Michigan
547 U.S. 586 (2006)

HISTORY

Booker T. Hudson (Defendant) was convicted in the Michigan Circuit Court of drug possession following a bench trial. Defendant appealed. The Michigan Court of Appeals affirmed. Hudson appealed. The Michigan Supreme Court declined review. The U.S. Supreme Court granted certiorari and affirmed.

—SCALIA, J., joined by ROBERTS, C. J., and KENNEDY, THOMAS, and ALITO, JJ.

(continued)

FACTS

Police obtained a warrant authorizing a search for drugs and firearms at the home of petitioner Booker Hudson. They discovered both. Large quantities of drugs were found, including cocaine rocks in Hudson's pocket. A loaded gun was lodged between the cushion and armrest of the chair in which he was sitting. Hudson was charged under Michigan law with unlawful drug and firearm possession.

When the police arrived to execute the warrant, they announced their presence, but waited only a short time—perhaps "three to five seconds"—before turning the knob of the unlocked front door and entering Hudson's home. Hudson moved to suppress all the inculpatory evidence, arguing that the premature entry violated his Fourth Amendment rights.

OPINION

In *Weeks v. United States,* 232 U.S. 383 (1914), we adopted the federal exclusionary rule for evidence that was unlawfully seized from a home without a warrant in violation of the Fourth Amendment. We began applying the same rule to the States, through the Fourteenth Amendment, in *Mapp v. Ohio,* 367 U.S. 643 (1961). Suppression of evidence, however, has always been our last resort, not our first impulse. The exclusionary rule generates "substantial social costs," which sometimes include setting the guilty free and the dangerous at large. We have therefore been cautious against expanding it, and have repeatedly emphasized that the rule's costly toll upon truth-seeking and law enforcement objectives presents a high obstacle for those urging its application. *Pennsylvania Bd. of Probation and Parole v. Scott,* 524 U.S. 357, (1998). We have rejected indiscriminate application of the rule, and have held it to be applicable only where its remedial objectives are thought most efficaciously served—that is, where its deterrence benefits outweigh its substantial social costs.

We did not always speak so guardedly. Expansive dicta in *Mapp,* for example, suggested wide scope for the exclusionary rule. "All evidence obtained by searches and seizures in violation of the Constitution is, by that same authority, inadmissible in a state court." But we have long since rejected that approach. As explained in *Arizona v. Evans* (1995): The Court treated identification of a Fourth Amendment violation as synonymous with application of the exclusionary rule to evidence secured incident to that violation. Subsequent case law has rejected this reflexive application of the exclusionary rule.

In other words, exclusion may not be premised on the mere fact that a constitutional violation was a "but-for" cause of obtaining evidence. Our cases show that but-for causality is only a necessary, not a sufficient, condition for suppression. In this case, of course, the constitutional violation of an illegal *manner* of entry was *not* a but-for cause of obtaining the evidence. Whether that preliminary misstep had occurred *or not,* the police would have executed the warrant they had obtained, and would have discovered the gun and drugs inside the house. But even if the illegal entry here could be characterized as a but-for cause of discovering what was inside, we have never held that evidence is fruit of the poisonous tree simply because it would not have come to light but for the illegal actions of the police. Rather, but-for cause, or causation in the logical sense alone, can be too attenuated to justify exclusion. Even in the early days of the exclusionary rule, we declined to hold that all evidence is fruit of the poisonous tree simply because it would not have come to light *but for* the illegal actions of the police. Rather, the more apt question in such a case is whether, granting establishment of the primary illegality, the evidence to which instant objection is made has been come at by exploitation of that illegality or instead by means sufficiently distinguishable to be purged of the primary taint.

Attenuation can occur, of course, when the causal connection is remote. Attenuation also occurs when, even given a direct causal connection, the interest protected by the constitutional guarantee that has been violated would not be served by suppression of the evidence obtained. The penalties visited upon the Government, and in turn upon the public, because its officers have violated the law must bear some relation to the purposes which the law is to serve.

For this reason, cases excluding the fruits of unlawful warrantless searches, say nothing about the appropriateness of exclusion to vindicate the interests protected by the knock-and-announce requirement. Until a valid warrant has issued, citizens are entitled to shield their persons, houses, papers, and effects from the government's scrutiny. Exclusion of the evidence obtained by a warrantless search vindicates that entitlement. The interests protected by the knock-and-announce requirement are quite different—and do not include the shielding of potential evidence from the government's eyes.

One of those interests is the protection of human life and limb, because an unannounced entry may provoke violence in supposed self-defense by the surprised resident. Another interest is the protection of property. Breaking a house (as the old cases typically put it) absent an announcement would penalize someone who did not know of the process, of which, if he had notice, it is to be presumed that he would obey it. *Semayne's Case,* 77 Eng. Rep. 194 (1603). And thirdly, the knock-and-announce rule protects those elements of privacy and dignity that can be destroyed by a sudden entrance. It gives residents the opportunity to prepare themselves for the entry of the police. The brief interlude between announcement and entry with a warrant may be the opportunity that an individual has to pull on clothes or get out of bed.

In other words, it assures the opportunity to collect oneself before answering the door.

What the knock-and-announce rule has never protected, however, is one's interest in preventing the government from seeing or taking evidence described in a warrant. Since the interests that *were* violated in this case have nothing to do with the seizure of the evidence, the exclusionary rule is inapplicable.

Quite apart from the requirement of unattenuated causation, the exclusionary rule has never been applied except where its deterrence benefits outweigh its substantial social costs. The costs here are considerable. In addition to the grave adverse consequence that exclusion of relevant incriminating evidence always entails (viz., the risk of releasing dangerous criminals into society), imposing that massive remedy for a knock-and-announce violation would generate a constant flood of alleged failures to observe the rule, and claims that any asserted justification for a no-knock entry, had inadequate support. The cost of entering this lottery would be small, but the jackpot enormous: suppression of all evidence, amounting in many cases to a get-out-of-jail-free card.

We cannot assume that exclusion in this context is necessary deterrence simply because we found that it was necessary deterrence in different contexts and long ago. That would be forcing the public today to pay for the sins and inadequacies of a legal regime that existed almost half a century ago. Dollree Mapp could not turn to Rev.Stat. § 1979, 42 U.S.C. § 1983, for meaningful relief; *Monroe v. Pape*, 365 U.S. 167 (1961), which began the slow but steady expansion of that remedy, was decided the same Term as *Mapp*. It would be another 17 years before the § 1983 remedy was extended to reach the deep pocket of municipalities, *Monell v. New York City Dept. of Social Servs.*, 436 U.S. 658 (1978) [Chapter 11, p. 421]. Citizens whose Fourth Amendment rights were violated by federal officers could not bring suit until 10 years after *Mapp*, with this Court's decision in *Bivens v. Six Unknown Fed. Narcotics Agents*, 403 U.S. 388 (1971) [Chapter 11, pp. 415–416].

Hudson complains that "it would be very hard to find a lawyer to take a case such as this," but 42 U.S.C. § 1988(b) answers this objection. Since some civil-rights violations would yield damages too small to justify the expense of litigation, Congress has authorized attorney's fees for civil-rights plaintiffs. This remedy was unavailable in the heydays of our exclusionary-rule jurisprudence, because it is tied to the availability of a cause of action. For years after *Mapp*, very few lawyers would even consider representation of persons who had civil-rights claims against the police, but now much has changed. Citizens and lawyers are much more willing to seek relief in the courts for police misconduct. The number of public-interest law firms and lawyers who specialize in civil-rights grievances has greatly expanded.

Another development over the past half-century that deters civil-rights violations is the increasing professionalism of police forces, including a new emphasis on internal police discipline. Even as long ago as 1980 we felt it proper to assume that unlawful police behavior would be dealt with appropriately by the authorities. *United States v. Payner*, 447 U.S. 727 (1980), but we now have increasing evidence that police forces across the United States take the constitutional rights of citizens seriously. There have been wide-ranging reforms in the education, training, and supervision of police officers. S. Walker, *Taming the System: The Control of Discretion in Criminal Justice 1950–1990*, p. 51 (1993). Numerous sources are now available to teach officers and their supervisors what is required of them under this Court's cases, how to respect constitutional guarantees in various situations, and how to craft an effective regime for internal discipline. Moreover, modern police forces are staffed with professionals; it is not credible to assert that internal discipline, which can limit successful careers, will not have a deterrent effect. There is also evidence that the increasing use of various forms of citizen review can enhance police accountability.

In sum, the social costs of applying the exclusionary rule to knock-and-announce violations are considerable; the incentive to such violations is minimal to begin with, and the extant deterrences against them are substantial—incomparably greater than the factors deterring warrantless entries when *Mapp* was decided. Resort to the massive remedy of suppressing evidence of guilt is unjustified.

For the foregoing reasons we affirm the judgment of the Michigan Court of Appeals.

It is so ordered.

CONCURRENCE

KENNEDY, J., concurring in part and concurring in the judgment.

Two points should be underscored with respect to today's decision. First, the knock-and-announce requirement protects rights and expectations linked to ancient principles in our constitutional order. The Court's decision should not be interpreted as suggesting that violations of the requirement are trivial or beyond the law's concern. Second, the continued operation of the exclusionary rule, as settled and defined by our precedents, is not in doubt. Today's decision determines only that in the specific context of the knock-and-announce requirement, a violation is not sufficiently related to the later discovery of evidence to justify suppression.

Under our precedents the causal link between a violation of the knock-and-announce requirement and a later search is too attenuated to allow suppression. In this case the relevant evidence was discovered not because of a failure to knock and announce, but because

(*continued*)

of a subsequent search pursuant to a lawful warrant. The Court in my view is correct to hold that suppression was not required.

DISSENT

BREYER, joined by STEVENS, SOUTER, and GINSBURG, JJ.

The Fourth Amendment insists that an unreasonable search or seizure is, constitutionally speaking, an illegal search or seizure. And ever since *Weeks* (in respect to federal prosecutions) and *Mapp* (in respect to state prosecutions), the use of evidence secured through an illegal search and seizure is barred in criminal trials.

For another thing, the driving legal purpose underlying the exclusionary rule, namely, the deterrence of unlawful government behavior, argues strongly for suppression. Failure to apply the exclusionary rule would make that promise a hollow one, reducing it to a form of words, of no value to those whom it seeks to protect. Indeed, this Court in *Mapp* held that the exclusionary rule applies to the States in large part due to its belief that alternative state mechanisms for enforcing the Fourth Amendment's guarantees had proved worthless and futile.

Why is application of the exclusionary rule any the less necessary here? Without such a rule, as in *Mapp*, police know that they can ignore the Constitution's requirements without risking suppression of evidence discovered after an unreasonable entry. As in *Mapp*, some government officers will find it easier, or believe it less risky, to proceed with what they consider a necessary search immediately and without the requisite constitutional (say, warrant or knock-and-announce) compliance.

Of course, the State or the Federal Government may provide alternative remedies for knock-and-announce violations. But that circumstance was true of *Mapp* as well. What reason is there to believe that those remedies (such as private damages actions under Rev.Stat. § 1979, 42 U.S.C. § 1983), which the Court found inadequate in *Mapp*, can adequately deter unconstitutional police behavior here?

The cases reporting knock-and-announce violations are legion. Yet the majority, like Michigan and the United States, has failed to cite a single reported case in which a plaintiff has collected more than nominal damages solely as a result of a knock-and-announce violation. Even Michigan concedes that, "in cases like the present one . . . , damages may be virtually nonexistent." And Michigan's *amici* further concede that civil immunities prevent tort law from being an effective substitute for the exclusionary rule at this time. As Justice Stewart, the author of a number of significant Fourth Amendment opinions, explained, the deterrent effect of damages actions "can hardly be said to be great," as such actions are "expensive, time-consuming,

not readily available, and rarely successful." The upshot is that the need for deterrence—the critical factor driving this Court's Fourth Amendment cases for close to a century—argues with at least comparable strength for evidentiary exclusion here.

To argue, as the majority does, that new remedies, such as 42 U.S.C. § 1983 actions or better trained police, make suppression unnecessary is to argue that *Wolf*, not *Mapp*, is now the law. And to argue without evidence (and despite myriad reported cases of violations, no reported case of civil damages, and Michigan's concession of their nonexistence) that civil suits may provide deterrence because claims *may* "have been settled" is, perhaps, to search in desperation for an argument. Rather, the majority, as it candidly admits, has simply "assumed" that, "as far as it knows, civil liability is an effective deterrent," a support-free assumption that *Mapp* and subsequent cases make clear does not embody the Court's normal approach to difficult questions of Fourth Amendment law.

It is not surprising, then, that after looking at virtually every pertinent Supreme Court case decided since *Weeks*, I can find no precedent that might offer the majority support for its contrary conclusion. The Court has, of course, recognized that not every Fourth Amendment violation necessarily triggers the exclusionary rule. But the class of Fourth Amendment violations that do not result in suppression of the evidence seized, however, is limited.

The United States, in its brief and at oral argument, has argued that suppression is "an especially harsh remedy given the nature of the violation in this case." This argument focuses upon the fact that entering a house after knocking and announcing can, in some cases, prove dangerous to a police officer. Perhaps someone inside has a gun, as turned out to be the case here. The majority adds that police officers about to encounter someone who may try to harm them will be "uncertain" as to how long to wait. It says that, "if the consequences of running afoul" of the knock-and-announce "rule were so massive," *i.e.*, would lead to the exclusion of evidence, then "officers would be inclined to wait longer than the law requires—producing preventable violence against officers in some cases."

The answer to the argument is that States can, and many do, reduce police uncertainty while assuring a neutral evaluation of concerns about risks to officers or the destruction of evidence by permitting police to obtain a "no-knock" search warrant from a magistrate judge, thereby assuring police that a prior announcement is not necessary.

Consider this very case. The police obtained a search warrant that authorized a search, not only for drugs, but also for *guns*. If probable cause justified a search for guns, why would it not also have justified a no-knock warrant, thereby diminishing any danger to the officers? Why (in a State such as Michigan that lacks no-knock warrants) would it not have justified the very no-knock entry at issue here? Indeed, why did the prosecutor not argue in this very case that, given the likelihood of guns, the no-knock entry was lawful? From what I have seen in the record, he would have won. And had he won, there would have been no suppression here. That is the right way to win. The very process of arguing the merits of the violation would help to clarify the contours of the knock-and-announce rule, contours that the majority believes are too fuzzy.

Questions

1. List the relevant facts regarding the police entry into Booker T. Hudson's home.

2. Summarize the majority's reasons for creating the "knock-and-announce" exception.

3. Summarize the dissent's reasons for opposing the "knock-and-announce" exception.

4. Summarize Justice Kennedy's concurring opinion. What's the significance of his opinion? Explain.

5. In your opinion, who has the better argument? Defend your answer.

LO 4, 6   The Good-Faith Exception

Perhaps nothing more clearly demonstrates the U.S. Supreme Court's commitment to the balancing test than the **good-faith exception** to the exclusionary rule. Presently, the exception allows the government to use evidence obtained from searches based on unlawful search warrants if officers reasonably believed they were lawful. Note here that *good faith* typically signifies a subjective standard—it asks whether someone honestly believes something; not whether it's *reasonable* to believe it. But, that's not what it means in the *good-faith exception*. Chief Justice Roberts acknowledged this in *Herring v. U.S.* (2009), the Court's most recent *good-faith exception* case. Referring to its use in *U.S. v. Leon* (1984), discussed on pp. 387–389, the chief justice acknowledged, "We (perhaps confusingly) called this objectively reasonable reliance 'good faith'" (*Herring v. U.S.*, 2009, 701).

Basically, this means that the exclusionary rule shouldn't apply when law enforcement officers are "reasonably" unaware that they're violating the Fourth Amendment because, in the Court's judgment, the rule can't deter officers who don't know what they did was illegal. According to the chief justice, in view of the "enormous social cost" of letting guilty criminals go free, the rule simply can't "pay its way" (704). The good-faith exception last reached the Supreme Court in our next case excerpt, *Herring v. U.S.* (2009).

In this case, the U.S. Supreme Court held that if an officer reasonably believes there's an outstanding arrest warrant against a suspect, but that belief turns out to be wrong because of a negligent bookkeeping error by another *police employee*, the arrest violates the Fourth Amendment. This expands the good-faith exception beyond prior decisions (Table 10.2)

TABLE 10.2 U.S. Supreme Court opinions expanding good-faith exception

1. *U.S. v. Leon* (1984) applied to officers who relied on judges.
2. *Arizona v. Evans* (1995) expanded it to reliance on court employees.
3. *Ilinois v. Krull* (1987) expanded it to reliance on an unconstitutional state statute.
4. *Herring v. U.S.* (2009) expanded it to include reliance on other police personnel.

In *Herring v. U.S.* (2009), the U.S. Supreme Court held that if an officer makes an arrest, reasonably (but wrongly) believing there's an outstanding arrest warrant against the suspect, the arrest violates the Fourth Amendment but evidence obtained during a search incident to the unlawful arrest is admissible in court.

CASE

Was the Illegally Seized Evidence Admissible?

Herring v. U.S.
129 S.Ct. 695 (2009)

HISTORY

Bennie Dean Herring (Defendant) was charged with being a convicted felon in possession of a firearm and knowingly possessing methamphetamine. The United States District Court for the Middle District of Alabama denied defendant's motion to suppress evidence recovered in a search incident to his arrest. Herring was subsequently convicted on both counts and he appealed. The United States Court of Appeals for the Eleventh Circuit, Carnes, Circuit Judge, affirmed. Certiorari was granted. The U.S. Supreme Court, Chief Justice Roberts, held that the exclusionary rule did not apply for police recordkeeping error.

—ROBERTS, C.J., joined by SCALIA, KENNEDY, THOMAS, and ALITO, JJ.

The Fourth Amendment forbids "unreasonable searches and seizures," and this usually requires the police to have probable cause or a warrant before making an arrest. What if an officer reasonably believes there is an outstanding arrest warrant, but that belief turns out to be wrong because of a negligent bookkeeping error by another police employee? The parties here agree that the ensuing arrest is still a violation of the Fourth Amendment, but dispute whether contraband found during a search incident to that arrest must be excluded in a later prosecution.

Our cases establish that such suppression is not an automatic consequence of a Fourth Amendment violation. Instead, the question turns on the culpability of the police and the potential of exclusion to deter wrongful police conduct. Here the error was the result of isolated negligence attenuated from the arrest. We hold that in these circumstances the jury should not be barred from considering all the evidence.

FACTS

On July 7, 2004, Investigator Mark Anderson learned that Bennie Dean Herring had driven to the Coffee County Sheriff's Department to retrieve something from his impounded truck. Herring was no stranger to law enforcement, and Anderson asked the county's warrant clerk, Sandy Pope, to check for any outstanding warrants for Herring's arrest. When she found none, Anderson asked Pope to check with Sharon Morgan, her counterpart in neighboring Dale County. After checking Dale County's computer database, Morgan replied that there was an active arrest warrant for Herring's failure to appear on a felony charge. Pope relayed the information to Anderson and asked Morgan to fax over a copy of the warrant as confirmation. Anderson and a deputy followed Herring as he left the impound lot, pulled him over, and arrested him. A search incident to the arrest revealed methamphetamine in Herring's pocket, and a pistol (which as a felon he could not possess) in his vehicle.

There had, however, been a mistake about the warrant. The Dale County sheriff's computer records are supposed to correspond to actual arrest warrants, which the office also maintains. But when Morgan went to the files to retrieve the actual warrant to fax to Pope, Morgan was unable to find it. She called a court clerk and learned that the warrant had been recalled five months earlier. Normally when a warrant is recalled the court clerk's office or a judge's chambers calls Morgan, who enters the information in the sheriff's computer database and disposes of the physical copy. For whatever reason, the information about the recall of the warrant for Herring did not appear in the database. Morgan immediately called Pope to alert her to the mixup, and Pope contacted Anderson over a secure radio. This all unfolded in 10 to 15 minutes, but Herring had already been arrested and found with the gun and drugs, just a few hundred yards from the sheriff's office.

Herring was indicted in the District Court for the Middle District of Alabama for illegally possessing the gun and drugs, violations of 18 U.S.C. § 922(g)(1) and 21 U.S.C. § 844(a). He moved to suppress the evidence on the ground that his initial arrest had been illegal because the warrant had been rescinded. The Magistrate Judge recommended denying the motion because the arresting officers had acted in a good-faith belief that the warrant was still outstanding. Thus, even if there were a Fourth Amendment violation, there was "no reason to believe that application of the exclusionary rule here would deter the occurrence of any future mistakes." The District Court adopted the Magistrate Judge's recommendation, and the Court of Appeals for the Eleventh Circuit affirmed. The Eleventh Circuit found that the arresting officers in Coffee County "were entirely innocent of any wrongdoing or carelessness." The court assumed that whoever failed to update the Dale County sheriff's records was also a law enforcement official, but noted that "the conduct in question [wa]s a negligent failure to act, not a deliberate or tactical choice to act." Because the error was merely negligent and attenuated from the arrest, the Eleventh Circuit concluded that the benefit of suppressing the evidence "would be marginal or nonexistent," and the evidence was therefore admissible under the good-faith rule of *United States v. Leon*, 468 U.S. 897 (1984).

Other courts have required exclusion of evidence obtained through similar police errors, so we granted Herring's petition for certiorari to resolve the conflict. We now affirm the Eleventh Circuit's judgment.

OPINION

The Fourth Amendment contains no provision expressly precluding the use of evidence obtained in violation of its commands. Nonetheless, our decisions establish an exclusionary rule that, when applicable, forbids the use of improperly obtained evidence at trial. We have stated that this judicially created rule is designed to safeguard Fourth Amendment rights generally through its deterrent effect.

The fact that a Fourth Amendment violation occurred—i.e., that a search or arrest was unreasonable—does not necessarily mean that the exclusionary rule applies. Indeed, exclusion "has always been our last resort, not our first impulse," *Hudson v. Michigan*, 547 U.S. 586, (2006), and our precedents establish important principles that constrain application of the exclusionary rule.

First, the exclusionary rule is not an individual right and applies only where it results in appreciable deterrence. We have repeatedly rejected the argument that exclusion is a necessary consequence of a Fourth Amendment violation. Instead we have focused on the efficacy of the rule in deterring Fourth Amendment violations in the future. In addition, the benefits of deterrence must outweigh the costs. The principal cost of applying the rule is, of course, letting guilty and possibly dangerous defendants go free—something that offends basic concepts of the criminal justice system.

These principles are reflected in the holding of *Leon*: When police act under a warrant that is invalid for lack of probable cause, the exclusionary rule does not apply if the police acted "in objectively reasonable reliance" on the subsequently invalidated search warrant. We (perhaps confusingly) called this objectively reasonable reliance "good faith." Shortly thereafter we extended these holdings to warrantless administrative searches performed in good-faith reliance on a statute later declared unconstitutional. Finally, we applied this good-faith rule to police who reasonably relied on mistaken information in a court's database that an arrest warrant was outstanding. [In *Arizona v. Evans* (1995)] We held that a mistake made by a judicial employee could not give rise to exclusion for three reasons: The exclusionary rule was crafted to curb police rather than judicial misconduct; court employees were unlikely to try to subvert the Fourth Amendment; and most important, there was no basis for believing that application of the exclusionary rule in those circumstances would have any significant effect in deterring the errors. *Evans* left unresolved "whether the evidence should be suppressed if police personnel were responsible for the error," an issue not argued by the State in that case but one that we now confront.

The extent to which the exclusionary rule is justified by these deterrence principles varies with the culpability of the law enforcement conduct. As we said in *Leon*, "an assessment of the flagrancy of the police misconduct constitutes an important step in the calculus" of applying the exclusionary rule. Similarly, in *Krull* we elaborated that "evidence should be suppressed 'only if it can be said that the law enforcement officer had knowledge, or may properly be charged with knowledge, that the search was unconstitutional under the Fourth Amendment.' "

The abuses that gave rise to the exclusionary rule featured intentional conduct that was patently unconstitutional. In *Weeks* (1914) a foundational exclusionary rule case, the officers had broken into the defendant's home (using a key shown to them by a neighbor), confiscated incriminating papers, then returned again with a U.S. Marshal to confiscate even more. Not only did they have no search warrant, which the Court held was required, but they could not have gotten one had they tried. They were so lacking in sworn and particularized information that "not even an order of court would have justified such procedure." *Silverthorne Lumber Co. v. United States*, (1920), was similar; federal officials "without a shadow of authority" went to the defendants' office and "made a clean sweep" of every paper they could find. Even the Government seemed to acknowledge that the "seizure was an outrage." Equally flagrant conduct was at issue in *Mapp v. Ohio* [discussed on pp. 386–387] (1961).

To trigger the exclusionary rule, police conduct must be sufficiently deliberate that exclusion can meaningfully deter it, and sufficiently culpable that such deterrence is worth the price paid by the justice system. As laid out in our cases, the exclusionary rule serves to deter deliberate, reckless, or grossly negligent conduct, or in some circumstances recurring or systemic negligence. The error in this case does not rise to that level.

We do not suggest that all recordkeeping errors by the police are immune from the exclusionary rule.

(*continued*)

In this case, however, the conduct at issue was not so objectively culpable as to require exclusion. If the police have been shown to be reckless in maintaining a warrant system, or to have knowingly made false entries to lay the groundwork for future false arrests, exclusion would certainly be justified under our cases should such misconduct cause a Fourth Amendment violation.

Petitioner's claim that police negligence automatically triggers suppression cannot be squared with the principles underlying the exclusionary rule, as they have been explained in our cases. In light of our repeated holdings that the deterrent effect of suppression must be substantial and outweigh any harm to the justice system, we conclude that when police mistakes are the result of negligence such as that described here, rather than systemic error or reckless disregard of constitutional requirements, any marginal deterrence does not "pay its way." In such a case, the criminal should not "go free because the constable has blundered."

The judgment of the Court of Appeals for the Eleventh Circuit is affirmed.

DISSENT

Justice GINSBURG, with whom Justice STEVENS, Justice SOUTER, and Justice BREYER join, dissenting.

If courts are to have any power to discourage police error of the kind here at issue, it must be through the application of the exclusionary rule. The unlawful search in this case was contested in court because the police found methamphetamine in Herring's pocket and a pistol in his truck. But the most serious impact of the Court's holding will be on innocent persons wrongfully arrested based on erroneous information carelessly maintained in a computer data base.

On a July afternoon in 2004, Herring came to the Coffee County Sheriff's Department to retrieve his belongings from a vehicle impounded in that Department's lot. Investigator Mark Anderson, who was at the Department that day, knew Herring from prior interactions: Herring had told the District Attorney, among others, of his suspicion that Anderson had been involved in the killing of a local teenager, and Anderson had pursued Herring to get him to drop the accusations. Informed that Herring was in the impoundment lot, Anderson asked the Coffee County warrant clerk whether there was an outstanding warrant for Herring's arrest. The clerk, Sandy Pope, found no warrant.

The Court states that the exclusionary rule is not a defendant's right, rather, it is simply a remedy applicable only when suppression would result in appreciable deterrence that outweighs the cost to the justice system. The Court's discussion invokes a view of the exclusionary rule famously held by renowned jurists Henry J. Friendly and Benjamin Nathan Cardozo. Over 80 years ago [1926], Cardozo, then seated on the New York Court of Appeals,

commented critically on the federal exclusionary rule, which had not yet been applied to the States. He suggested that in at least some cases the rule exacted too high a price from the criminal justice system. In words often quoted, Cardozo questioned whether the criminal should "go free because the constable has blundered." Judge Friendly later elaborated on Cardozo's query. "The sole reason for exclusion," Friendly wrote, "is that experience has demonstrated this to be the only effective method for deterring the police from violating the Constitution." He thought it excessive, in light of the rule's aim to deter police conduct, to require exclusion when the constable had merely "blundered"—when a police officer committed a technical error in an on-the-spot judgment, or made a "slight and unintentional miscalculation." As the Court recounts, Judge Friendly suggested that deterrence of police improprieties could be "sufficiently accomplished" by confining the rule to "evidence obtained by flagrant or deliberate violation of rights."

Others have described "a more majestic conception" of the Fourth Amendment and its adjunct, the exclusionary rule. Protective of the fundamental "right of the people to be secure in their persons, houses, papers, and effects," the Amendment "is a constraint on the power of the sovereign, not merely on some of its agents." I share that vision of the Amendment.

The exclusionary rule, the Court suggests, is capable of only marginal deterrence when the misconduct at issue is merely careless, not intentional or reckless. The suggestion runs counter to a foundational premise of tort law—that liability for negligence, i.e., lack of due care, creates an incentive to act with greater care. The Government so acknowledges.

Is the potential deterrence here worth the costs it imposes? In light of the paramount importance of accurate recordkeeping in law enforcement, I would answer yes, and next explain why, as I see it, Herring's motion presents a particularly strong case for suppression. Electronic databases form the nervous system of contemporary criminal justice operations. In recent years, their breadth and influence have dramatically expanded. Police today can access databases that include not only the updated National Crime Information Center (NCIC), but also terrorist watchlists, the Federal Government's employee eligibility system, and various commercial databases. Brief for Electronic Privacy Information Center (EPIC) et al. as Amici Curiae 6. Moreover, States are actively expanding information sharing between jurisdictions. As a result, law enforcement has an increasing supply of information within its easy electronic reach.

The risk of error stemming from these databases is not slim. Herring's amici warn that law enforcement databases are insufficiently monitored and often out of date. Government reports describe, for example, flaws in NCIC databases, terrorist watchlist databases, and databases associated with the Federal Government's employment eligibility verification system. Inaccuracies in expansive, interconnected collections of electronic information raise grave concerns for individual liberty. The offense to the dignity of the citizen who is arrested, handcuffed, and searched on a public street simply because some bureaucrat has failed to maintain an accurate computer data base is evocative of the use of general warrants that so outraged the authors of our Bill of Rights.

The Court assures that "exclusion would certainly be justified" if "the police have been shown to be reckless in maintaining a warrant system, or to have knowingly made false entries to lay the groundwork for future false arrests." This concession provides little comfort. First, by restricting suppression to bookkeeping errors that are deliberate or reckless, the majority leaves Herring, and others like him, with no remedy for violations of their constitutional rights. There can be no serious assertion that relief is available under 42 U.S.C. § 1983. The arresting officer would be sheltered by qualified immunity, and the police department itself is not liable for the negligent acts of its employees. Moreover, identifying the

department employee who committed the error may be impossible.

Third, even when deliberate or reckless conduct is afoot, the Court's assurance will often be an empty promise: How is an impecunious defendant to make the required showing? If the answer is that a defendant is entitled to discovery (and if necessary, an audit of police databases), then the Court has imposed a considerable administrative burden on courts and law enforcement.

Questions

1. State the Court's reasons for limiting the deterrence justification to law enforcement officers.
2. Identify the dissenting justices' reasons for arguing that the deterrence justification for the good-faith exception should be applied to all government officials.
3. Which of the opinions do you agree with? Support your answer.

LO 6   ## The Exclusionary Rule after *Herring v. U.S.* (2009)

Civil libertarian interest groups are dreading, and law enforcement interest groups are hoping, that *Herring* has all but accomplished the end of the exclusionary rule—abolishing it except in the most extreme cases of intentional police misconduct, leaving all other police violations of the Fourth Amendment to other remedies like those we'll discuss in Chapter 11. Here's Professor Maclin's assessment of where we are, and where we're likely to go from here:

> I believe four of the Justices (Chief Justice John Roberts, and Justices Antonin Scalia, Clarence Thomas, and Samuel Alito) want to abolish the exclusionary rule. Justice Scalia's majority opinion in *Hudson v. Michigan* has prepared the foundation for that result. If abolition is unobtainable, the Court will confine exclusion to cases of deliberate and culpable forms of illegal searches or seizure. Chief Justice Roberts's majority opinion in *Herring v. U.S.* has already achieved that result, although many of the lower courts have yet to follow suit. (SCOTUS Blog 2013)

YOU DECIDE
Should *Herring v. U.S.* Control the N.J. Court's Suppression of the Drugs?

State v. Handy, 18 S.3d 179 (NJ 2011)

On September 13, 2005, at approximately 7:40 p.m., Millville Special Officer Anthony Sills stopped a group of individuals for riding their bicycles on the sidewalk, in violation of a city ordinance. Officer Sills called for backup and Officer Carlo Drogo, who was on routine patrol, responded. Because none of the bicyclists had identification, Officer Drogo asked

(continued)

for their names and dates of birth. Defendant, Germaine A. Handy, was one of the individuals questioned by Officer Drogo. He provided his name as Germaine Handy, which he spelled out, along with his address—218 East Broad Street, Millville, New Jersey, and his date of birth—March 18, 1974. Officer Drogo recorded Handy's information and radioed police dispatch with Handy's name and date of birth for a warrant check. The police dispatcher informed Officer Drogo that there was an outstanding warrant for Handy. Based on that information, Officer Drogo placed Handy under arrest and handcuffed him.

A search incident to the arrest led to the recovery of drugs. Subsequently, the police dispatcher informed Officer Drogo that there was a discrepancy between the date of birth Handy had given (March 18, 1974) and the date of birth listed on the warrant (March 14, 1972). When Officer Drogo arrived at headquarters with Handy he attempted to verify the existence of the warrant himself. In doing so, he ascertained that, in addition to the birth date discrepancy, the warrant, which was about ten years old, had been issued to Jermaine O. Handy with an address on W. 73rd Street in Los Angeles, California.

Cumberland County Indictment No. 05-12-1153 charged Handy with one count of third-degree possession of a controlled dangerous substance (cocaine) in violation of *N.J.S.A.* 2C:35-10(a)(1). Handy moved to suppress the evidence against him on the ground that the police acted unreasonably in linking him to the warrant.

OPINION

We conclude that this case would not be governed by *Evans* or *Herring*. *Herring's* focus was an attenuated clerical error in a database upon which police officials reasonably relied. In both instances, the Court assessed the deterrent effect of suppression as minimal. Attenuation is not part of the factual calculus before us. First, the dispatcher was not attenuated from the arrest but was literally a co-operative in its effectuation along with the officer on the scene. Second, as far as we know, the database was entirely accurate and there is, in fact, an outstanding warrant for a Jermaine O. Handy of Los Angeles, California. What occurred here was that the dispatcher, with a presumably accurate database, simply provided Officer Drogo with wrong information when a reasonably prudent person would, at least, have advised him of the discrepancies so that he could verify the information himself.

Third, the minimal deterrent effect that the Supreme Court in *Herring* and *Arizona v. Evans* intuited would flow

from suppression based on an attenuated "clerical error," is wholly unlike what is before us. Instead, suppressing the evidence garnered from this illegal search would have important deterrent value, would underscore the need for training of officers and dispatchers to focus on detail, and would serve to assure that our own constitutional guarantees are given full effect. The police dispatcher is the crucial link between the officer in the field and police headquarters. The officer depends on receiving the correct information from the dispatcher, information such as whether there is or is not an outstanding arrest warrant for the person with whom the officer is then face to face. Misinformation either way has the potential to leave the officer either unaware that he or she is dealing with a dangerous criminal or arresting the wrong person. What is critical to our analysis is that neither *Herring* nor *Arizona v. Evans* dispensed with the standard of "objective reasonableness" that governs the execution of a warrant. To the contrary, those decisions took pains to reaffirm that standard. In ruling as it did, on the effect of an attenuated clerical error in *Herring* and *Arizona v. Evans,* the Supreme Court addressed a niche that is simply not present here. Here, the dispatcher's slipshod conduct, which clearly would not have been tolerated had the officer committed it, was objectively unreasonable and thus failed to satisfy the Fourth Amendment or the New Jersey Constitution.

The Fourth Amendment is a bulwark against the government's unwarranted intrusions into the daily lives of our fellow citizens. As interpreted by the dissent, it would provide little or no protection to the people it was intended to serve. First, the dissent's notion that the "urgency" of the situation facing the dispatcher justified her conduct is misguided. Officer Drogo was confronted with persons who had ridden their bicycles on the sidewalk, not suspected armed robbers, burglars, or rapists. If ever there was a case in which the dispatcher had the luxury of time and care—this was it.

Second, the dissent's conclusion that a Fourth Amendment exclusionary rule analysis is limited to the conduct of the arresting officer is wrong. Under that construct, police operatives, like the dispatcher here, are free to act heedlessly and unreasonably, so long as the last man in the chain does not do so. Nothing in our jurisprudence supports that view.

Third, as we have said, the analysis under federal and state jurisprudence focuses on the objective reasonableness of the police conduct. Here, the dispatcher's notion, echoed by the dissent, that a warrant with a wrong name and a wrong date of birth, is close enough to justify the arrest of a citizen, fails to satisfy that standard. The police dispatcher here was plainly unreasonable in failing to take further steps when she recognized that she did not have a match on the warrant check. As such, our own constitution requires suppression. One need not have pristine vision or the benefit of hindsight to know that that is so.

The judgment of the Appellate Division reversing the order denying suppression is affirmed.

LO 6

As for the lower courts, Professor Bradley (2012, 14–19) points to several that "have yet to follow suit." They've read *Herring* as doing no more than extending *Leon's* good-faith exception to searches without warrants. "Most importantly, the courts of appeals did not conclude that the exclusionary rule was effectively dead, yet. Instead, a number of courts held that the evidence must still be suppressed following *Herring*" (15).

U.S. v. Leon didn't give officers a blank check to always rely on warrants. It identified four situations where evidence should be suppressed even if officers have a warrant. In making its determination, the magistrate must consider "all of the circumstances." Suppression therefore remains an appropriate remedy.

1. If the magistrate or judge in issuing a warrant was misled by information in an affidavit that the affiant knew was false or would have known was false except for his reckless disregard of the truth.

2. The exception we recognize today will also not apply in cases where the issuing magistrate wholly abandoned his judicial role.

3. Nor would an officer manifest objective good faith in relying on a warrant based on an affidavit "so lacking in indicia of probable cause as to render official belief in its existence entirely unreasonable."

4. Finally, depending on the circumstances of the particular case, a warrant may be so facially deficient—i.e., in failing to particularize the place to be searched or the things to be seized—that the executing officers cannot reasonably presume it to be valid. (923)

CRIMINAL PROCEDURE IN ACTION

Affidavit containing false statements in "reckless disregard" of the truth, requires suppression of DNA evidence

U.S. v. Brown, 631 F.3d 638 (2011)

FACTS

On the morning of October 1, 2007, two men wearing distinctive "Scream" masks (The mask is named for the 1996 Wes Craven horror film that popularized the design; its ghostly appearance recalls Edvard Munch's painting *The Scream*. Such masks are commonly used as disguises by robbers and other criminals.) robbed an S & T Bank branch in Ford City, Pennsylvania, at gunpoint, absconding with more than $24,000. The robbers initially fled the scene on foot, running about 150 yards to the Armstrong County School District Administration Building. There they made off with a school district van that an employee had left with the engine idling.

Thirty minutes after the robbery, police found the van abandoned on Hobson Drive near Route 66, a half-mile from the administration building. Investigators later

(continued)

discovered a Scream mask containing DNA material inside the van. Witnesses reported seeing a silver Volkswagen Jetta driving in the area of Hobson Drive and Route 66 on the morning of the robbery. One witness had seen a silver Jetta parked in the area of Hobson Drive and Route 66 around the time of the robbery. A different witness had seen a silver Jetta driving southbound on Route 66 after the robbery had occurred. Two witnesses described the Jetta as having white license plates; one of them specified that the plates were from Maryland.

Pennsylvania State Trooper Shane Lash suspected that Allen Brown was one of the robbers. Lash asked FBI Special Agent Robert Smith to have his colleagues investigate Brown's Maryland residence. Baltimore-based Special Agent James Mollica interviewed Brown's mother, who stated that her son had been visiting in Ford City at the end of September, and confirmed that he owned a silver Jetta. Wingate, Brown's uncle, admitted to Lash that Brown had visited him around the date of the robbery. He further stated that Brown had gone out in his Jetta around 8:00 a.m. on October 1 to buy groceries, and had returned around 10:00 a.m.

At this point the investigation was focused on Brown. Lash and Smith decided to seek a DNA sample in the hope that they could match it to the material found on the Scream mask. This would require a warrant, so Smith requested that an assistant United States attorney in Pittsburgh assist him in preparing an application and affidavit. Smith had not participated in interviewing the witnesses who had seen the Jetta, so Lash filled him in via telephone and provided him with the written reports that had been generated during the investigation. Smith did not read any of the written witness statements, and did not review the investigation reports in any detail. Nevertheless, with the assistant U.S. attorney's (AUSA's) help, he prepared an affidavit in support of a warrant application.

The affidavit contained only an abbreviated recitation of the known facts of the case. It mentioned the robber's use of a Scream mask; the stolen van and the mask found inside; the fact that Brown had been visiting Ford City around the time of the robbery; and Wingate's statement that Brown had left his home, driving a silver Jetta, at 8:00 and returned at 10:00. Finally, Paragraph 7(c) of the affidavit contained the following averment:

> Police interviews of various witnesses following the robbery reported witnessing the stolen Armstrong County School District Administration van meet up with a silver Volkswagen Jetta having a possible Maryland registration.

Witnesses then observed the silver Jetta drive away from the area where the van was left parked.

After the AUSA had finished preparing the affidavit, Smith neither checked the affidavit's contents against the investigation reports nor asked Lash to review its accuracy. Smith sent the affidavit off to Mollica, who signed and presented it to a federal magistrate judge as being true and correct to the best of his knowledge. The magistrate issued the warrant, and after obtaining Brown's DNA, investigators matched it to the material that they had found on the Scream mask.

Paragraph 7(c) was false. At the *Franks* hearing conducted pursuant to Brown's suppression motion, Lash testified that he never told Smith that "various witnesses" had seen the van "meet up" with the Jetta. [A *Franks* hearing is a hearing to determine whether a police officer's affidavit used to obtain a search warrant that yields incriminating evidence was based on false statements by the police officer. The name is derived from the case *Franks v. Delaware* (1978), which affirmed the right of defendants to challenge a warrant seizing their person, papers, or effects and otherwise outlining the case against them.]

Nor was there the sort of unbroken chain of observations conveyed by the claim that "witnesses *then* observed the silver Jetta drive away." As the District Court wrote in its opinion granting Brown's motion to suppress, Paragraph 7(c) "appears to be crafted to give the U.S. Magistrate Judge the false impression of a continuous sequence of events observed by a number of witnesses." The court went on: "Agent Smith . . . incorrectly concluded that non-existent evidence actually existed, and, more importantly, took the affirmative step of purposely incorporating the non-existent evidence into the affidavit." Because the challenged statement had no basis in the evidence, the District Court held that Agent Smith had acted with reckless disregard for the truth. Accordingly, the court held that that evidence obtained through the execution of the warrant must be excluded from trial.

In the case now before us, the District Court was on sound footing when it concluded that Smith's false assertion was not a result of merely negligent miscommunication. Smith did not claim that Lash specifically told him that witnesses saw the two vehicles meet up, and Lash testified that he did not tell Smith that he saw the vehicles meet. Smith's false averment had no basis in any of the materials with which he had been presented. He had no reason to believe that the statement in question was true. At the suppression hearing, he was unable to come up with any explanation of the origin of the false claim that multiple witnesses had observed the Jetta meeting up with the getaway van and then driving away. He essentially acknowledged that he had conjured Paragraph 7(c) out of thin air. *Contra* the dissent's assertion, Smith did not merely fail to corroborate his averment; he failed ever to develop any basis for it in the first place. Because the total lack of an evidentiary basis for making an averment can constitute an obvious reason for doubting that averment's veracity, the District Court did not clearly err in finding that Smith's conduct rose beyond the level of negligence, to the point of recklessness. We will affirm the suppression order.

SOCIAL COSTS AND DETERRENCE: EMPIRICAL FINDINGS

LO 7

In 1961, in *Mapp v. Ohio*, the U.S. Supreme Court, headed by Chief Justice Earl Warren, applied the exclusionary rule to the states because the Court *assumed* that the rule would deter illegal searches and seizures. But there's a social cost for deterring law enforcement officers from violating individuals' rights: Keeping good evidence from juries may set some criminals free. Since the 1970s, in case after case, the majorities of the Burger and the Rehnquist Courts have *assumed* that the social cost is too high a price to pay; deterrence simply can't "pay its way." Which Court's assumption is right?

Ever since the Court decided *Mapp*, a growing stack of empirical studies has tested the correctness of the two assumptions. What's the answer? According to Professor Christopher Slobogin (1999, 368–69), "No one is going to win the empirical debate over whether the exclusionary rule deters the police from committing a significant number of illegal searches and seizures." It's true, say most of the studies, that police officers pay more attention to the Fourth Amendment than they did in 1960. But many officers don't take the rule into account when they're deciding whether to make a search or a seizure. "In short, we do not know how much the rule deters" either individual officers whose evidence courts throw out (special deterrence) or other officers who might be thinking of illegally searching or seizing (general deterrence) (369).

"We probably never will" (369). Why? Because it's hard to conduct empirical research; we have to rely on speculation (370). And what's the speculation? Both supporters and opponents of the rule make plausible claims for their positions. It's reasonable for supporters to claim "officers who know illegally seized evidence will be excluded cannot help but try to avoid illegal searches because they will have nothing to gain from them" (371).

Equally reasonable, the rule's opponents can point out that its most direct consequence is imposed on the prosecutor rather than on law enforcement officers; that police know and count on the fact that the rule is rarely applied (for both legal and not-so-legal reasons); and that the rule can't affect searches and seizures the police believe won't result in prosecution (372).

Despite these limits to the empirical research, some of it provides us with valuable insights. The social costs of letting guilty criminals go free by excluding credible evidence that would convict them might not be as high as we commonly believe. According to Thomas Y. Davies (1983), who studied the exclusionary rule in California and whose research the Court cited in *U.S. v. Leon*, prosecutors almost never reject cases involving violent crimes because of the exclusionary rule.

In California, evidence seized illegally led to dismissals in a mere 0.8 percent of all criminal cases and only 4.8 percent of felonies. Davies found that prosecutors rejected only 0.06 percent of homicides, 0.09 percent of forcible rapes, and 0.13 percent of assault cases because of illegal searches and seizures. They rejected less than 0.50 percent of theft cases and only 0.19 percent of burglary cases. The largest number of cases rejected for prosecution because of illegal searches and seizures involved the possession of small amounts of drugs (644).

Other studies reached similar conclusions—namely, that the exclusionary rule affects only a small portion of cases, and most of those aren't crimes against persons (cited in Davies 1983). Less than one-tenth of 1 percent of all criminal cases will be dismissed because the police seized evidence illegally. The rule leaves violent crimes and serious property offenses virtually unaffected. Furthermore, not all cases involving illegally obtained evidence that are rejected or lost fail because of the exclusionary rule. Myron Orfield (1987) found, for example, that in some cases of drug possession, the police weren't interested in successful prosecution but rather in getting contraband off the street (1041).

Most criminal justice professionals seem to agree that the exclusionary rule is worth the price. The American Bar Association (1988) gathered information from police officers, prosecutors, defense attorneys, and judges in representative urban and geographically distributed locations on the problems they face in their work. They also conducted a telephone survey of 800 police administrators, prosecutors, judges, and defense attorneys based on a stratified random selection technique to obtain a representative group of small-to-large cities and counties.

The results showed the following:

1. Although the prosecutors and police interviewed believe that a few Fourth Amendment restrictions are ambiguous or complex and, thus, present training and field application problems, they don't believe that Fourth Amendment rights or their protection via the exclusionary rule are a significant impediment to crime control.

2. A number of police officials also report that the demands of the exclusionary rule and resulting police training on Fourth Amendment requirements have promoted professionalism in police departments across the country.

3. Thus, the exclusionary rule appears to be providing a significant safeguard of Fourth Amendment protections for individuals at a modest cost in terms of either crime control or effective prosecution.

4. This "cost," for the most part, reflects the values expressed in the Fourth Amendment itself. It manifests a preference for privacy and freedom over the level of law enforcement efficiency that could be achieved if police were permitted to arrest and search without probable cause or judicial authorization. (11)

In view of its limited application, restrictions on the exclusionary rule hardly seem adequate cause for either critics of the rule to rejoice that these restrictions will make society safer or for supporters to bemoan that they'll throttle individual liberties.

Probably the strongest argument for the exclusionary rule is that it helps to ensure judicial integrity. Courts, by excluding illegally obtained evidence, announce publicly and in writing their refusal to participate in or condone illegal police practices. At the end of the day, what the exclusionary rule does is exact the price of setting a few criminals free to maintain the rule of law for everybody; it sacrifices the correct result in an individual case for the general interest in the essential fairness of constitutional government for all people.

One final point about the exclusionary rule: Every year, there are approximately 175,000 motions to exclude evidence obtained by illegal searches and seizures. In contrast, there are only a few thousand lawsuits against police and a few dozen criminal charges based on illegal searches and seizures (Allen and others 2011, 340). This lopsided distribution

> may have a large effect on the substance of Fourth Amendment law. The exclusionary rule shapes the kinds of Fourth Amendment cases judges see. All exclusionary claims seek to suppress incriminating evidence; if no incriminating evidence is found, there is nothing for the defendant to exclude. *Thus, judges see the cases where the police find cocaine in the car, not the cases where they find nothing* [emphasis added]. Perhaps that affects the way judges think about car searches. (336)

YOU DECIDE
Should Criminals Go Free because Police Officers Violated the Fourth Amendment to Obtain Evidence?

During oral arguments before the U.S. Supreme Court in *Herring v. U.S.* (2009), justices offered these two opposing views:

Chief Justice Roberts: We know what the cost was here, right? I mean, not just a drug peddler, but somebody with an illegal weapon found in his car, a weapon that presumably he would use on an occasion in which it was in his view appropriate to do so.

Justice Stevens: Of course, if you did the cost-benefit analysis, the cost is always zero to the State because they would not have had the evidence if they had obeyed the law.

You can listen to the full argument at: http://www.oyez.org/cases/2000-2009/2008/2008_07_513

CHAPTER SUMMARY

LO 1 The exclusionary rule is the most frequently used remedy for constitutional violations, banning the use of "good evidence" obtained from "bad methods" to prove guilt. "Bad methods" refer to police actions and procedures that violate Fourth, Fifth, Sixth, and Fourteenth Amendment rights. "Good evidence" refers to its reliability, not the methods used to obtain it.

LO 2 The exclusionary rule is a device created by the U.S. Supreme Court to enforce existing constitutional rights, not a right in its own. Initially, the exclusionary rule applied only to federal officers violating individual Fourth Amendment rights against unreasonable searches and seizures. Eventually, the Supreme Court incorporated the due process clause to the right against unreasonable searches and seizures. Soon thereafter, the exclusionary rule became a bright-line rule banning the use of *all* illegally obtained evidence in court. Since then, the Supreme Court has moved away from the bright-line exclusionary rule and has created multiple exceptions to it.

LO 3   Justification of the exclusionary rule is based on constitutional rights, the preservation of judicial integrity, and deterring officers from breaking laws.

LO 4   The "fruit of the poisonous tree" doctrine excludes evidence indirectly associated with an illegal government action. The premise is that courts should ensure the government is never better off after violating the Constitution than it was before it did so. The exceptions to this doctrine allow more evidence to be admitted into court to prove guilt. When applying these exceptions, courts must balance the social costs of letting criminals go free against the deterrence of police misconduct.

LO 5   The exclusionary rule bans illegally obtained evidence only from the case-in-chief in the criminal trial. Nontrial proceedings, such as bail hearings and sentencing, allow the use of illegally obtained evidence. Cross-examination of defense witnesses is not part of the case-in-chief when the exclusionary rule applies.

LO 6   The knock-and-announce exception allows the use of evidence seized during searches of homes even when officers violate the "knock-and-announce" rule of the warrant requirement. The good-faith exception is an objective standard, allowing the government to use evidence obtained from searches based on unlawful warrants if officers reasonably believed they were lawful.

LO 7   The social costs and deterrent effects of the exclusionary rule are based on assumptions, not empirical evidence. Both supporters and opponents of the rule make plausible claims for their positions. Despite its limits, empirical research regarding the exclusionary rule has demonstrated that police do pay more attention to the Fourth Amendment than in the past, but many officers do not consider the rule when deciding whether or not to search and seize. Further, evidence seized illegally rarely results in dismissals in criminal cases.

REVIEW QUESTIONS

1. Define the exclusionary rule and explain the terms "good evidence" and "bad methods."

2. Is there a constitutional right to the exclusionary rule? Explain your answer.

3. Briefly trace the history of the exclusionary rule through the leading U.S. Supreme Court cases that created and expanded it.

4. Identify and explain the rationales behind the three justifications for the exclusionary rule. Which justification does the U.S. Supreme Court use today?

5. Describe four possible negative effects of the exclusionary rule.

6. Explain the balancing test the U.S. Supreme Court adopted to apply the deterrence justification.

7. List and explain five exceptions to the exclusionary rule.

8. Identify the rationale for the attenuation, independent source, and inevitable discovery exceptions to the exclusionary rule.

9. Describe the knock-and-announce exception to the exclusionary rule and explain the criticisms of the *Hudson v. Michigan* decision.

10. State the narrow scope of the reasonable good-faith exception to the exclusionary rule.

11. Identify the conflicting assumptions of the Warren and Rehnquist Courts regarding the exclusionary rule.

12. According to Professor Christopher Slobogin, why is no one likely to win the empirical debate over the accuracy of the assumptions you identified in question 11?

13. Summarize the empirical findings regarding the prevalence of criminal dismissals due to the exclusionary rule.

14. Compare the amount of annual exclusionary rule motions to the number of lawsuits against police each year. Explain the significance of this discrepancy.

KEY TERMS

exclusionary rule, p. 384
"good"/probative evidence, p. 384
"bad methods," p. 384
constitutional right justification,
    p. 388
judicial integrity (moral)
    justification, p. 388
deterrence justification, p. 389

prophylactic rule, p. 390
social cost of the rule, p. 391
fruit of the poisonous
    tree doctrine, p. 391
attenuation exception, p. 392
independent source exception,
    p. 393

inevitable discovery exception,
    p. 393
case-in-chief, p. 394
impeach, p. 394
knock-and-announce exception,
    p. 394
good-faith exception, p. 399

11

Constitutional Violations II

Other Remedies against Official Misconduct

LEARNING OBJECTIVES

1 Understand that most police misconduct can also be a crime. Know that police are rarely charged or convicted for criminal misconduct.

2 Know that civil actions against (a) the federal government and its officers; (b) local, county, and state officers, law enforcement agencies, and government units; and (c) other government employees are controlled by different statutes, court decisions, and government units.

3 Understand constitutional tort actions (*Bivens* actions) against officers and Federal Tort Claims Act actions against public institutions.

4 Know the role of Civil Rights Act actions in holding law enforcement officials responsible for violating the constitutional rights of individuals. Understand the limitations of lawsuits brought against states and their officers.

5 Know that plaintiffs can sue local governments instead of, or in addition to, suing local officers. Understand the complexities and limitations of suing local governments.

6 Understand that the Constitution places no duty on officers to protect individuals from each other, and that it doesn't create a right of private parties to sue officers for failing to prevent crime.

7 Know of the "special relationship" between the government and persons in custody and the impact that special relationship has on lawsuits brought by prisoners against law enforcement officers.

8 Understand that states can be civilly liable if the government played some part in creating a danger that a victim faced. Know that few cases survive the rigorous screening process of the state-created-danger exception.

9 Know that judges enjoy absolute immunity, and prosecutors have functional immunity.

10 Understand the role of administrative action in remedying misconduct.

At about 5 or 5:30 p.m. on Tuesday, June 22, 1999, Jessica Gonzalez's former husband took their three minor daughters, Rebecca, Katheryn, and Leslie, while they were playing outside the family's Colorado home. He made no advance arrangements to see them that evening. When Jessica noticed the children were missing, she suspected her husband had taken them. At about 7:30 p.m., she called the Castle Rock Police Department, which dispatched two officers. When the officers arrived, she showed them a copy of the temporary restraining order (TRO) and requested that they enforce it and the three children be returned to her immediately. The officers stated that there was nothing they could do about the TRO and suggested that Gonzalez call the police department again if the three children did not return home by 10:00 p.m.

At approximately 8:30 p.m., Gonzalez talked to her husband on his cellular telephone. He told her "he had the three children at an amusement park in Denver." She called the police again and asked them to "have someone check for" her husband or his vehicle at the amusement park and "put out an all-points bulletin" for her husband, but the officer *with whom she spoke "refused to do so," again telling her to "wait until 10:00 p.m. and see if" her husband returned the girls.*

At approximately 10:10 p.m., Gonzalez called the police and said her children were still missing, but she was now told to wait until midnight. She called at midnight and told the dispatcher her children were still missing. She went to her husband's apartment and, finding nobody there, called the police at 12:10 a.m.; she was told to wait for an officer to arrive. When none came, she went to the police station at 12:50 a.m. and submitted an incident report. The officer who took the report "made no reasonable effort to enforce the TRO or locate the three children. Instead, he went to dinner."

At approximately 3:20 a.m., Gonzalez's husband arrived at the police station and opened fire with a semiautomatic handgun he had purchased earlier that evening. Police shot back, killing him. Inside the cab of his pickup truck, they found the bodies of all three daughters, whom he had already murdered.

—*Town of Castle Rock v. Gonzalez* (2005)

Y ou learned in Chapter 10 about the extent, limits, and strengths and weaknesses of the most prevalent current remedy for official violations of individuals' constitutional rights. Most of the time (Fourth Amendment cases), this remedy works by throwing out reliable physical evidence that would convict—or at least help to convict—*guilty* defendants. In other words, it affects defendants' cases. In this chapter, we'll examine three remedies that affect criminal justice officers, their agencies, and the political institutions—municipal, county, state, and federal governments—responsible for them:

1. **Criminal law**: prosecuting individual officers in criminal courts
2. **Civil law**: suing the officer, the police department, or the government in civil courts
3. **Internal and external departmental review**: disciplining the officer outside the judicial system

CRIMINAL ACTIONS

LO 1   Most officers' misconduct might also be a crime. So a police officer who illegally shoots and kills a person might have committed criminal homicide. Officers who use excessive nondeadly force can be guilty of assault. Illegal arrests can be false imprisonment. Illegal searches can be trespass, illegal breaking and entering, or burglary. But, how likely is it that prosecutors will charge police officers with crimes? How many juries will convict them? How many judges will sentence them to prison or heavy fines? Very few. Why? Judges and juries don't see police misconduct as a crime. And with good reason. In our criminal justice system, the government has to prove criminal intent beyond a reasonable doubt. If police officers *honestly* believe they were enforcing the law, and not committing a crime (in most cases, this is either true or difficult to disprove beyond a reasonable doubt), then they're not *criminally* guilty. And this is the way it should be. The standard of proof has to be the same for officers as for everybody else.

There's a second reason. Even if officers are guilty of criminal misconduct, prosecutors hesitate to prosecute, and juries are unwilling to convict, police officers who are "only trying to do their job." This is true especially when the "victims" are "real" criminals (or at least people who associate with criminals).

CIVIL ACTIONS

LO 2 Civil actions include suing individual officers and/or their departments for unconstitutional conduct. Any victim of official violations of individuals' constitutional rights can bring a **tort action** (*tort* is the French word for "wrong") against individual officers who break the law. Most of these individuals want compensation (the law calls it **damages**) for the injuries they suffered. These damages might be *compensatory* (e.g., to compensate them for medical costs, lost wages, and "pain and suffering); or *punitive* (to punish defendants for egregious wrongs against them, usually caused by police misconduct). How do they get damages? The only way is by becoming plaintiffs in a **civil action** (noncriminal action brought to enforce, redress, or protect a private or civil right).

Who can plaintiffs sue for money damages? Any—or all—of the following:

- Individual law enforcement officers
- Officers' superiors (such as police chiefs and sheriffs)
- Law enforcement agencies
- Government units in charge of officers and departments (towns, cities, counties, states, and the U.S. government)

In which courts can they bring actions against officers and governments? In state and federal courts. We'll look separately at civil actions for damages against (1) federal officers; (2) the U.S. government; (3) local, county, and state officers; (4) local, county, and state law enforcement agencies; (5) local, county, and state government units; and (6) other government employees, because they're controlled by different statutes, court decisions, and government units. We'll also examine what happens when law enforcement officers fail to protect individuals and some of the hurdles to suing the government.

LO 3 ## Lawsuits against U.S. Officers and the U.S. Government

Lawsuits against individual federal law enforcement officers are called **constitutional tort (*Bivens*) actions**. Lawsuits against the federal government for its officers' constitutional torts are called **Federal Tort Claims Act (FTCA) actions**. Let's look at each.

LO 3 ### Lawsuits against U.S. officers

Until 1971, individuals were banned from suing federal officers for violations of their constitutional rights. All that changed after the U.S. Supreme Court decided *Bivens v. Six Unnamed FBI Agents* (1971). In that case, six FBI agents entered Webster Bivens's apartment without a search or arrest warrant. After they searched his apartment "from stem to stern," the agents arrested Bivens for violating federal drug laws and handcuffed him in the presence of his wife and children.

The agents took Bivens first to the Brooklyn Federal Courthouse and then to the Federal Bureau of Narcotics, "where he was interrogated, fingerprinted, photographed, subjected to search of his person, and booked." Bivens claimed these events caused him "great humiliation, embarrassment, and mental suffering" and would "continue to do so." He sought damages of $15,000 from each of the six officers (390).

In *Bivens*, the Court created a *constitutional tort,* a private right to sue federal officers for violations of plaintiffs' constitutional rights. In these *"Bivens* actions," plaintiffs have to prove two elements:

1. Officers were acting "under color of authority" or the appearance of power (Garner 1987, 123–24).

2. Officers' actions deprived the plaintiff of a constitutional right.

Even if plaintiffs prove these two elements, they don't automatically win their case. Law enforcement officers have a defense called **qualified immunity**. According to this complex defense, individual officers can't be held personally liable for official action if their action meets the test of **"objective legal reasonableness."** Reasonableness is measured by legal rules that were "clearly established" at the time the officers acted. The reason for creating the test was to protect officers' broad discretion to do their job and keep them (and the courts) from being bombarded with frivolous lawsuits (*Anderson v. Creighton* 1987).

The U.S. Supreme Court created and explained why it created the qualified immunity defense against constitutional torts in our next case excerpt, *Anderson v. Creighton* (1987).

In *Anderson v. Creighton* (1987), the U.S. Supreme Court created the qualified immunity defense and held that it applied to an FBI officer who invaded the Creighton home, because his mistaken entry was "objectively reasonable."

CASE

Were the FBI Agent's Actions "Objectively Reasonable"?

Anderson v. Creighton
483 U.S. 635 (1987)

HISTORY

Robert E. Creighton Jr., his wife, and others sued FBI Agent Russell Anderson in the U.S. District Court for the District of Minnesota. The U.S. District Court granted *summary judgment* [a motion that the court enter a judgment without a trial because there's not enough evidence to support the plaintiff's claim] in favor of the agent. The Court of Appeals for the Eighth Circuit reversed and remanded. The U.S. Supreme Court granted certiorari, vacated the Circuit Court's judgment, and remanded the case.

—SCALIA, J., joined by REHNQUIST, C.J., and WHITE, BLACKMUN, POWELL, and O'CONNOR JJ.

FACTS

Russell Anderson is an agent of the Federal Bureau of Investigation. On November 11, 1983, Anderson and other state and federal law enforcement officers conducted a warrantless search of the Creighton family's home. The search was conducted because Anderson believed that Vadaain Dixon, a man suspected of a bank robbery committed earlier that day, might be found there. He was not.

On the night of November 11, 1983, Sarisse and Robert Creighton and their three young daughters were spending a quiet evening at their home when a spotlight suddenly flashed through their front window. Mr. Creighton opened the door and was confronted by several uniformed and plainclothes officers, many of them brandishing shotguns. All of the officers were White the Creightons are Black Mr. Creighton claims that none of the officers responded when he asked what they wanted.

Instead, by his account (as verified by a St. Paul police report), one of the officers told him to "keep his hands in sight" while the other officers rushed through the door. When Mr. Creighton asked if they had a search warrant, one of the officers told him, "We don't have a search warrant and don't need one; you watch too much TV." Mr. Creighton asked the officers to put their guns away because his children were frightened, but the officers refused.

Mrs. Creighton awoke to the shrieking of her children, and was confronted by an officer who pointed a shotgun at her. She allegedly observed the officers yelling at her three daughters to "sit their damn asses down and stop screaming." She asked the officer, "What the hell is going on?" The officer allegedly did not explain the situation and simply said to her, "Why don't you make your damn kids sit on the couch and make them shut up."

One of the officers asked Mr. Creighton if he had a red and silver car. As Mr. Creighton led the officers downstairs to his garage, where his maroon Oldsmobile was parked, one of the officers punched him in the face, knocking him to the ground, and causing him to bleed from the mouth and the forehead. Mr. Creighton alleges that he was attempting to move past the officer to open the garage door when the officer panicked and hit him. The officer claims that Mr. Creighton attempted to grab his shotgun, even though Mr. Creighton was not a suspect in any crime and had no contraband in his home or on his person. Shaunda, the Creighton's ten-year-old daughter, witnessed the assault and screamed for her mother to come help. She claims that one of the officers then hit her.

Mrs. Creighton phoned her mother, but an officer allegedly kicked and grabbed the phone and told her to "hang up that damn phone." She told her children to run to their neighbor's house for safety. The children ran out and a plainclothes officer chased them. The Creightons'

neighbor allegedly told Mrs. Creighton that the officer ran into her house and grabbed Shaunda by the shoulders and shook her. The neighbor allegedly told the officer, "Can't you see she's in shock; leave her alone and get out of my house." Mrs. Creighton's mother later brought Shaunda to the emergency room at Children's Hospital for an arm injury caused by the officer's rough handling.

During the melee, family members and friends began arriving at the Creightons' home. Mrs. Creighton claims that she was embarrassed in front of her family and friends by the invasion of their home and their rough treatment as if they were suspects in a major crime. At this time, she again asked Anderson for a search warrant. He allegedly replied, "I don't need a damn search warrant when I'm looking for a fugitive." The officers did not discover the allegedly unspecified "fugitive" at the Creightons' home or any evidence whatsoever that he had been there or that the Creightons were involved in any type of criminal activity.

Nonetheless, the officers then arrested and handcuffed Mr. Creighton for obstruction of justice and brought him to the police station where he was jailed overnight, then released without being charged.

OPINION

When government officials abuse their offices, actions for damages may offer the only realistic avenue for vindication of constitutional guarantees. On the other hand, permitting damages suits against government officials can entail substantial social costs, including the risk that fear of personal monetary liability and harassing litigation will unduly inhibit officials in the discharge of their duties. Our cases have accommodated these conflicting concerns by generally providing government officials performing discretionary functions with a qualified immunity, shielding them from civil damages liability as long as their actions could reasonably have been thought consistent with the rights they are alleged to have violated.

Somewhat more concretely, whether an official protected by qualified immunity may be held personally liable for an allegedly unlawful official action generally turns on the "objective legal reasonableness" of the action, assessed in light of the legal rules that were "clearly established" at the time it was taken. The contours of the right must be sufficiently clear that a reasonable official would understand that what he is doing violates that right. This is not to say that an official action is protected by qualified immunity unless the very action in question has previously been held unlawful, but it is to say that in the light of pre-existing law the unlawfulness must be apparent.

We vacate the judgment of the Court of Appeals and REMAND the case for further proceedings consistent with this opinion.

(continued)

DISSENT

STEVENS, J., joined by BRENNAN and MARSHALL, JJ.

The Court announces a new rule of law that protects federal agents who make forcible nighttime entries into the homes of innocent citizens without probable cause, without a warrant, and without any valid emergency justification for their warrantless search. The Court of Appeals understood the principle of qualified immunity to shield government officials performing discretionary functions from exposure to damages liability unless their conduct violated clearly established statutory or constitutional rights of which a reasonable person would have known.

Anderson has not argued that any relevant rule of law—whether the probable-cause requirement or the exigent circumstances exception to the warrant requirement—was not "clearly established" in November 1983. Rather, he argues that a competent officer might have concluded that the particular set of facts he faced did constitute "probable cause" and "exigent circumstances," and that his own reasonable belief that the conduct engaged in was within the law suffices to establish immunity. Of course, the probable-cause requirement for an officer who faces the situation Anderson did was clearly established.

Although the question does not appear to have been argued in, or decided by, the Court of Appeals, this Court has decided to apply a double standard of reasonableness in damages actions against federal agents who are alleged to have violated an innocent citizen's Fourth Amendment rights. By double standard I mean a standard that affords a law enforcement official two layers of insulation from liability or other adverse consequence, such as suppression of evidence.

Having already adopted such a double standard in applying the exclusionary rule to searches authorized by an invalid warrant, *U.S. v. Leon*, (1984) [discussed in Chapter 10], the Court seems prepared and even anxious in this case to remove any requirement that the officer must obey the Fourth Amendment when entering a private home. I remain convinced that in a suit for damages as well as in a hearing on a motion to suppress evidence, an official search and seizure cannot be both unreasonable and reasonable at the same time. A federal official may not with impunity ignore the limitations which the controlling law has placed on his powers.

The effect of the Court's (literally unwarranted) extension of qualified immunity, I fear, is that it allows federal agents to ignore the limitations of the probable-cause and warrant requirements with impunity. The Court does so in the name of avoiding interference with legitimate law enforcement activities even though the probable-cause requirement, which limits the police's exercise of coercive authority, is itself a form of immunity that frees them to exercise that power without fear of strict liability.

The argument that police officers need special immunity to encourage them to take vigorous enforcement action when they are uncertain about their right to make a forcible entry into a private home has already been accepted in our jurisprudence. We have held that the police act reasonably in entering a house when they have probable cause to believe a fugitive is in the house and exigent circumstances make it impracticable to obtain a warrant. This interpretation of the Fourth Amendment allows room for police intrusion, without a warrant, on the privacy of even innocent citizens.

In *Pierson v. Ray*, we held that police officers would not be liable in an action brought under 42 U.S.C. § 1983 "if they acted in good faith and with probable cause." We explained:

> Under the prevailing view in this country a peace officer who arrests someone with probable cause is not liable for false arrest simply because the innocence of the suspect is later proved. A policeman's lot is not so unhappy that he must choose between being charged with dereliction of duty if he does not arrest when he has probable cause, and being mulcted in damages if he does.

Thus, until now the Court has not found intolerable the use of a probable-cause standard to protect the police officer from exposure to liability simply because his reasonable conduct is subsequently shown to have been mistaken. Today, however, the Court counts the law enforcement interest twice and the individual's privacy interest only once. The Court's double-counting approach reflects understandable sympathy for the plight of the officer and an overriding interest in unfettered law enforcement. It ascribes a far lesser importance to the privacy interest of innocent citizens than did the Framers of the Fourth Amendment.

The importance of that interest and the possible magnitude of its invasion are both illustrated by the facts of this case. The home of an innocent family was invaded by several officers without a warrant, without the owner's consent, with a substantial show of force, and with blunt expressions of disrespect for the law and for the rights of the family members. I see no reason why the family's interest in the security of its own home should be accorded a lesser weight than the Government's interest in carrying out an invasion that was unlawful.

Arguably, if the Government considers it important not to discourage such conduct, it should provide indemnity to its officers. Preferably, however, it should furnish the kind of training for its law enforcement agents that would entirely eliminate the necessity for the Court to distinguish between the conduct that a competent officer considers reasonable and the conduct that the Constitution deems reasonable. On the other hand, surely an innocent family should not bear the entire risk that a trial court, with the benefit of hindsight, will find that a federal agent reasonably believed that he could break into their home equipped with force and arms but without probable cause or a warrant.

I respectfully dissent.

LO 3 *Lawsuits against the U.S. government*

Bivens didn't decide whether Webster Bivens could also sue the U.S. government for the six FBI officers' constitutional torts. According to the **doctrine of sovereign immunity** (a holdover from the days when kings didn't have to appear in court), individuals can't sue governments without the government's consent. The U.S. and most state governments have laws waiving their sovereign immunity (at least to some degree). That's what Congress did in the Federal Tort Claims Act (FTCA).

After *Bivens,* Congress permitted FTCA suits against the U.S. government for the constitutional torts of federal law enforcement agents "empowered by law to execute searches, to seize evidence, or to make arrests for violations of Federal law." The U.S. government's "deep pockets" make FTCA actions attractive to plaintiffs—probably more attractive than *Bivens* actions against individual officers. But both remedies are available to plaintiffs.

According to Professors Whitebread and Slobogin (2000):

> The plaintiff whose constitutional rights have been violated by a federal police officer in bad faith can be assured of monetary compensation [in an FTCA action] at the same time he can expect direct "revenge" in a *Bivens* action against the official to the extent the official can afford it. (51–52)

LO 4 Suing State Officers

Plaintiffs can sue individual state officers in two kinds of actions: state tort lawsuits and federal U.S. Civil Rights Act lawsuits. Let's look at each.

LO 4 *State tort actions*

Most illegal acts by state police, county sheriffs and their deputies, and local police officers and their chiefs are also **torts**, meaning plaintiffs can sue individual officers for damages for acts such as assault, false arrest or false imprisonment, and trespassing or breaking and entering. But the right to recover damages for injuries caused by officials' torts has to be balanced against law enforcement's job of protecting the public. So, although individual officers are liable for their own torts, there's a huge difference between suing an ordinary person and a police officer.

The **defense of official immunity** limits officers' liability for their torts. This defense says that "a public official charged by law with duties which call for the exercise of his judgment or discretion is not personally liable to an individual unless he is guilty of a willful or malicious wrong." Why? Because "to encourage responsible law enforcement police are afforded a wide degree of discretion precisely because a more stringent standard could inhibit action" (*Pletan v. Gaines et al.* 1992, 40).

In *Pletan v. Gaines et al.* (1992), the Minnesota Supreme Court balanced the rights of injured individuals and the needs of law enforcement. Crystal, Minnesota, Police Department Sergeant Boyd Barrott was in a high-speed chase trying to apprehend Kevin Gaines, suspected of shoplifting. Gaines struck and killed five-year-old Brian Pletan as he was walking home after school. The court decided that Sergeant Barrott wasn't liable for Brian's death. If the officer were held liable, the court said, officers in the future might shy away from vigorously enforcing the law.

LO 4 ## U.S. Civil Rights Act (§ 1983) actions

Civil Rights Act actions (usually called *§ 1983 actions* because they're brought under Title 42, § 1983, of the Civil Rights Act of 1871, passed just after the Civil War) allow plaintiffs to go into federal or state courts to sue state police officers and their agency heads; county sheriffs and their deputies; and municipal police officers and their chiefs for violating plaintiffs' federal constitutional rights.

Section 1983 provides that:

Every person who, under color of any statute, ordinance, regulation, custom, or usage, of any State or Territory, subjects, or causes to be subjected, any citizen of the United States or other person within the jurisdiction thereof to the deprivation of any rights, privileges, or immunities secured by the Constitution and laws, shall be liable to the party injured. (U.S. Code 2002, Title 42, § 1983)

As interpreted by the U.S. Supreme Court, plaintiffs have to prove two elements similar to those in *Bivens* if they hope to win their constitutional tort actions:

1. Officers acted "under color of state law," which includes all acts done within the scope of their employment.

2. Officers' actions caused a deprivation of plaintiffs' rights guaranteed by the U.S. Constitution.

Section 1983 doesn't mean that officers are liable every time they violate individuals' constitutional rights. Far from it. The U.S. Supreme Court has read several limits into the statutory protection. Here are the two main ones:

1. Plaintiffs can only recover for *deliberate* actions, *not* for accidental or even negligent violations.

2. State and local officers are protected by the same qualified immunity under § 1983 that federal officers have under *Bivens* and the Federal Tort Claims Act.

LO 5 # Suing Local Governments

Plaintiffs have two options if they decide to sue local governments instead of (or in addition to) suing individual officers. They can sue governments in state courts for the torts of their officers, or they can sue them under the U.S. Civil Rights Act; see "Suing State Officers," earlier. (*Monell*, discussed later, ruled that municipalities and police departments are considered "individuals" in § 1983.) Let's look at each of these complicated routes to recovering damages from governments instead of individuals.

LO 5 ## Local government tort actions

What if Brian Pletan's parents in *Pletan v. Gaines et al.* (1992) (discussed earlier) had sued the Minnesota municipal police department or the city instead of the individual officer? Under the **doctrine of** *respondeat superior*, state and local governments and their agencies are liable for the torts of their employees, *only* if the employees committed the torts during the course of their employment.

There's another catch; not all states have adopted the doctrine. (They don't have to because of the states' sovereign immunity.) In these states, government units enjoy the **defense of vicarious official immunity**, which means police departments and local governments can claim the official immunity of their employees. To determine whether government units are entitled to the defense of vicarious official immunity, courts apply a balancing test of local government liability. This test balances two elements:

1. The need for effective law enforcement
2. The need to avoid putting the public at risk

In the Minnesota Supreme Court's application of the balancing test in *Pletan v. Gaines et al.* (1992), the high-speed chase case, the court found the need to enforce the criminal law outweighed the risk to the public created by the high-speed chase. So, the court held, the municipality wasn't liable for the boy's death (42–43).

LO 5　Local government U.S. Civil Rights Act (§ 1983) actions

As you learned from *Anderson v. Creighton* (excerpted pp. 416–419), suing individual officers for violating constitutional rights is a complicated business. Suing a department or a city under § 1983 is even more complicated. Until 1978, the Court had held that the Civil Rights Act of 1870 didn't apply to states and cities. Then, in *Monell v. New York City Department of Social Services* (1978), the Court decided to undertake "a fresh analysis of debate on the Civil Rights Act of 1871." The Court changed its mind, concluding that the legislative history of § 1983 "compels the conclusion that Congress intended to include *municipalities and other local government units* among those persons to whom § 1983 applies" (italics added). According to the *Monell* Court, individuals could sue local government units if they could prove two elements:

1. Officers either acted according to written policies, statements, ordinances, regulations, or decisions approved by authorized official bodies or to unwritten custom. The condition was met even if the custom wasn't formally approved through official decision-making channels.
2. The action caused the violation of the plaintiff's constitutional right(s).

So, according to the Supreme Court in the *Monell* case:

> A local government cannot be sued for an injury inflicted solely by its employees or agents. Instead, it is when execution of a government's policy or custom, whether made by its lawmakers or by those whose edicts or acts may fairly be said to represent official policy, inflicts the injury that the government as an entity is responsible for it under § 1983. (695)

LAW ENFORCEMENT DUTY TO PROTECT

LO 6

Until now, we've talked only about people whom *officers* have harmed by their illegal actions. But what about when government fails to protect people from each other? Most police departments conceive their mission broadly: "To protect and serve." But is their mission "to protect" a constitutional command? In other words, do governments and their officers have a constitutional duty to protect individuals from other private individuals who violate their rights? No. (At least, not most of the time.)

Most of these duty-to-protect cases begin with horrible tragedies. Plaintiffs sue officers, departments, and local governments because they believe that if the officers had intervened, they could've prevented the tragedy. The first U.S. Supreme Court duty-to-protect case began with one of these tragedies, *DeShaney v. Winnebago County Department of Social Services* (1989). Five-year-old Joshua DeShaney's father beat him so severely for more than two years that he suffered severe and permanent brain damage. The story prompted this widely cited emotional reaction from Justice Harry Blackmun in his dissent:

> Poor Joshua! Victim of repeated attacks by an irresponsible, bullying, cowardly, and intemperate father, and abandoned by the Winnebago County Social Welfare Department staff who placed him in a dangerous predicament and who knew or learned what was going on, and yet did essentially nothing except dutifully recorded these incidents in their files. (1012)

The Court ruled against Joshua. Chief Justice Rehnquist wrote the opinion for the six-member majority, holding that governments have no duty to protect people from harms caused by private individuals. The chief justice explained why. The Constitution protects what he called *negative liberties*. They tell government what it *can't* do. For example, it *can't* pass laws that infringe on the First Amendment rights to speech and religion. And it *can't* deny a person life, liberty, or property, without due process of law. It does *not* impose *affirmative duties* on the government, such as the duty to protect people from privately inflicted harms (*DeShaney*, 200). So the Winnebago County Department of Social Services had no duty to protect Joshua from his father (202). So, according to what we'll call the Supreme Court's **no-affirmative-duty-to-protect rule**, plaintiffs can't sue individual officers or government units for failing to stop private people from violating their rights by inflicting injuries on them.

YOU DECIDE
Did the Public Mental Health Officials Have a Duty to Protect a State Resident from Being Murdered by a Released Mentally Ill Patient?

POSNER, J.

The plaintiff (Thomas Bowers) in this case is the administrator of the estate of Marguerite Anne Bowers, who was murdered by Thomas Vanda in 1977. The defendants are public employees, officers, and physicians of the Illinois Department of Mental Health and Developmental Disabilities and its Madden Mental Health Center. Vanda is not a defendant.

In 1970 Vanda was convicted of aggravated battery with a knife. He was diagnosed at Madden as a "schizophrenic in remission" but must soon have been released because in 1971 he killed a young woman with a knife. This time he was found not guilty by reason of insanity and was committed to Madden. But he was released in April 1976 and a year later murdered Miss Bowers with a knife. The complaint alleges that the defendants knew that Vanda was dangerous when they released him, and acted recklessly in doing so.

Section 1983 imposes liability on anyone who under color of state law "subjects . . . any citizen . . . or other person . . . to the deprivation of any rights, privileges, or immunities secured by the Constitution . . . ," and thus applies only if there is a deprivation of a constitutional right. There is a constitutional right not to be murdered by a state officer, for the state violates the Fourteenth Amendment when its officer, acting under color of state law, deprives a person of life without due process of law. But there is no constitutional right to be protected by the state against being murdered by criminals or madmen.

It is monstrous if the state fails to protect its residents against such predators but it does not violate the due process clause of the Fourteenth Amendment or, we suppose, any other provision of the Constitution. The Constitution is a charter of negative liberties; it tells the state to let people alone; it does not require the federal government or the state to provide services, even so elementary a service as maintaining law and order. Discrimination in providing protection against private violence could of course violate the equal protection clause of the Fourteenth Amendment. But that is not alleged here. All that is alleged is a failure to protect Miss Bowers and others like her from a dangerous madman, and as the State of Illinois has no federal constitutional duty to provide such protection its failure to do so is not actionable under section 1983.

We do not want to pretend that the line between action and inaction, between inflicting and failing to prevent the infliction of harm, is clearer than it is. If the state puts a man in a position of danger from private persons and then fails to protect him, it will not be heard to say that its role was merely passive; it is as much an active tortfeasor [wrongdoer] as if it had thrown him into a snake pit. It is on this theory that state prison personnel are sometimes held liable under section 1983 for the violence of one prison inmate against another. But the defendants in this case did not place Miss Bowers in a place or position of danger; they simply failed adequately to protect her, as a member of the public, from a dangerous man.

DISSENT

WOOD, Jr., J.

To put it bluntly, a schizophrenic with a history of criminal violence was turned loose on the public after a short detention with the opportunity to do it again, and he took advantage of that opportunity. It appears that Vanda in connection with a 1969 conviction had been diagnosed as a "borderline psychotic." In a 1970 conviction for a knife attack on a minor, he was diagnosed as a "schizoid personality." Then, after those forecasts of future trouble, Vanda was charged in 1971 with the knife murder of a minor. The schizophrenic diagnosis was again confirmed; and again confirmed in 1974. In 1975 he was found not guilty of that murder by reason of insanity and committed to the Illinois Department of Mental Health.

However, less than a year later he was certified as no longer dangerous to himself or others and discharged under an after-care plan to the Family Service and Mental Health Center of Oak Park. Under that plan he lived elsewhere but showed up at the Center periodically for medication and counseling. Vanda, after about a year, while enjoying the freedom of that program, attacked and killed the plaintiff's decedent with a knife. Those familiar with Vanda surely could not have been totally surprised by his latest violence.

In the depositions of some of the defendants, it is admitted that Vanda's condition produced a pronounced potential for violence and that he was one of only a few patients from among thousands of others in custody with that same dangerous potential. There was also some agreement among defendants that a schizophrenic, like Vanda, cannot be cured and that a relapse into active schizophrenia could result in extreme violence. I believe these unique problems need the exploration of a trial.

This case for me is in a gray area, but on the basis of the present record, I am not prepared to conclude that plaintiff cannot possibly be entitled to relief under any facts which might be proved in support of his allegations. I would give him the chance to try to make his case in court. Therefore, I respectfully dissent.

Source: *Bowers v. DeVito, 686 Fed. 2d. 616 (CA7 1982).*

LO 7   The "Special-Relationship Exception" to the "No-Duty-to-Protect" Rule

According to the U.S. Supreme Court, there's an exception to the no-duty-to-protect rule—the **special-relationship exception**. That special relationship is *custody*. Here's how Chief Justice Rehnquist put it:

When the State takes a person into its custody and holds him there against his will, the Constitution imposes upon it a corresponding duty to assume some responsibility for his safety and general well-being.

The rationale for this principle is simple enough: when the State by the affirmative exercise of its power so restrains an individual's liberty that it renders him unable to care for himself, and at the same time fails to provide for his basic human needs—e.g., food, clothing, shelter, medical care, and reasonable safety—it transgresses the substantive limits on state action set by the Eighth Amendment and the Due Process Clause.

The affirmative duty to protect arises not from the State's knowledge of the individual's predicament or from its expressions of intent to help him, but from the limitation which it has imposed on his freedom to act on his own behalf. (199–200)

This passage from Chief Justice Rehnquist's opinion prompted many commentators to recommend (and some courts to create) a second exception to the no-duty-to-protect rule—the state-created-danger exception.

LO 8 The "State-Created-Danger" Exception to the "No-Duty-to-Protect" Rule

The **state-created danger exception** applies when the state played some part in creating a danger that a victim faced, or in making the victim more vulnerable to that danger.

Courts that have allowed the state-created danger exception apply it in one of two ways:

1. They require (a) a special relationship between the government and the victim (custody), *plus* (b) a danger created by the state (*Beltran v. City of El Paso*, 5th Circuit 2004). (See the "Criminal Procedure in Action" box.)

2. There are two exceptions, either one of which will work:
   a. Only individuals in custody have a special relationship that qualifies as a state-created danger.
   b. Custody is one of several relationships that qualify as state-created dangers (*Pena v. Deprisco*, 2nd Circuit 2005).

One more very important matter. As we proceed through our discussion of the *state-created-danger* exception, keep in mind these three elements that *most* courts demand in order to impose civil liability on government officers.

1. *Violence.* Most require that private individuals threaten serious physical injury or death to their victims.

2. *Affirmative action.* Officers have to take positive action to create the danger; standing by in the presence of violence is not enough. This is necessary but not enough to impose liability.

3. *State of mind.* Most courts require positive acts that demonstrate "deliberate indifference" that "shocks the conscience." (See Chapter 2 for more information on conduct that "shocks the conscience.")

CRIMINAL PROCEDURE IN ACTION

A "911" operator had no affirmative duty to protect a mother and her daughter from their husband/father who murdered them.

Beltran v. City of El Paso, 367 F.3d 299 C.A.5 (Tex.), 2004

FACTS

In November 1999, Sonye Herrera ("Sonye") called 911 to report that her father, Armando Herrera ("Herrera"), was drunk and was becoming physically and verbally abusive to her and her mother, Irene Beltran-Garcia ("Garcia"). Police units were dispatched and Sonye's father was arrested and charged with felony child injury.

A few months later, on April 16, 2000, Sonye again called 911 from her home to report that her father was drunk and potentially violent. Sylvia Amador, the 911 operator who received the call, discussed the situation with Sonye in order to ascertain the nature of the emergency. At the outset of the call, Sonye indicated that her father had threatened her and that she was afraid for her life and hiding in a bathroom, but she did not indicate that she had been physically abused. Sonye repeatedly asked Amador to send the police to her house. Amador responded to Sonye that the police were receiving the information that Amador was placing into the 911 system. At one point during the call, Sonye informed Amador that she believed her father had left the premises. Amador then requested information about Herrera's automobile and potential destination. Before disconnecting the call, Amador informed Sonye that the police would be sent out and suggested that if Sonye believed her father was still in the house, she might wish to remain locked in the bathroom for her safety. Amador then disconnected the call.

While recording Sonye's information into the dispatch computer, Amador did not include Sonye's statements that she feared for her life or the prior report of Herrera's domestic violence. Based on the family relationship between Sonye and her father and Amador's understanding of the situation, Amador coded the call a "family violence assault," a priority level 4 call. Amador's entries led a police dispatch operator to send out two general broadcasts regarding the incident. No police units immediately responded and soon thereafter, Herrera, who had not actually left the house, shot and killed his wife and daughter.

Manuela Beltran ("Beltran"), Sonye's grandmother, sued the City of El Paso and Amador on behalf of herself and Sonye Herrera and Irene Beltran-Garcia (her murdered granddaughter's and daughter's estates). The action filed in state court alleged 42 U.S.C. § 1983 violations of the due process clause. Amador removed the case to federal court.

OPINION

Beltran contends that Sonye's substantive due process rights were violated by Amador because Amador falsely promised police services that Sonye relied on to her detriment. The Due Process Clause does not require a State to provide its citizens with particular protective services (*DeShaney*). Therefore, "a State's failure to protect an individual against private violence does not violate the Due Process Clause" (*DeShaney*). However, *DeShaney* recognized that "in certain *limited circumstances* the Constitution imposes upon the State affirmative duties of care and protection with respect to particular individuals." Such "special relationship" cases arise "when the state, through the *affirmative* exercise of its powers, acts to restrain an individual's freedom to act on his own behalf." [italics added]

Beltran argues that by encouraging Sonye to stay in the bathroom and telling her that the police were on the way, Amador became the custodian of Sonye's safety. This argument falls outside of the special relationships described by the Supreme Court, which are limited to cases concerning "incarceration, institutionalization, or other similar restraint of personal liberty" (*DeShaney*). In this case, Amador offered advice to Sonye, but she did not *affirmatively* place Sonye in custody by restraining her in the bathroom. This might have transpired if Amador had been present in the house and locked the bathroom door from the outside, but we decline to speculate on this counterfactual possibility.

Beltran alternatively contends that Amador, by providing Sonye with inaccurate information about the status of the patrol units and recommending that she stay in the bathroom, created a dangerous situation for which the state was or should be responsible. This court has consistently refused to recognize a "state-created danger" theory of § 1983 liability even where the question of the theory's viability has been squarely presented. It is unnecessary to do so in this case.

(continued)

Even if a state-created danger theory were acknowledged in this circuit, in order for Amador to be held liable, Beltran must show that Amador acted with "deliberate indifference" to Sonye's situation. Deliberate indifference requires that the state actor both knew of and disregarded an excessive risk to the victim's health and safety. In *McClendon*, this court held that a defendant police officer who lent a gun to an informant was not deliberately indifferent toward a third party that the informant shot with the officer's gun. Rather, this court held that the officer was negligent.

The only facts presented by Beltran that even remotely suggest misfeasance are (1) Amador's failure to record the previous Herrera family injury to a child incident in the dispatch report; (2) her statement to Sonye that the police were on their way; (3) the advice Amador provided to Sonye to stay in the bathroom; and (4) Amador's disconnecting of the phone call. Given Amador's understanding that (1) a radio call was going out to patrol cars based on her report, (2) the locked bathroom was a relatively safe place, and (3) Herrera was leaving the scene, she did not display deliberate indifference to Sonye's situation. She had no reason at that point to know that Sonye's life was in immediate danger. Moreover, rather than disregard the threat, it appears that Amador was doing what she could to keep Sonye safe. Her errors constitute negligence, not deliberate indifference. For these reasons, Beltran's due process claim does not fall within the narrow exceptions to *DeShaney's* holding that state actors may not be held responsible for private violence.

LO 8 ## "State-Created Danger" after *DeShaney* (1989)

"As water flows to the sea, so advocates and the courts migrated to the so-called 'state-created danger' doctrine" (Oren 2007, 48). Soon after *DeShaney*, all but one U.S. circuit court adopted it. But, lamented one staunch advocate and scholar, Professor Laura Oren, the "situation looks much bleaker today when appeals court cases "rarely survive dismissal, much less summary judgment, and sometimes even overturn significant jury verdicts" (48).

According to Professor Oren's survey of 21 appellate court cases, only two survived state-created danger screening. The others failed to qualify, most often because the "affirmative act" was missing. The two cases that survived did so on *emboldenment* or *implicit condonation* theories (49). One of those two cases was our next case excerpt, *Dwares v. City of New York*, which upheld a state-created danger claim on the *implicit condonation* theory. During a July 4th flag-burning demonstration, Bruce Kreitman and other "skinheads" beat Steven Dwares with a bottle, inflicting serious bodily injury. NYPD officers stood by and did nothing during the beating. Earlier, officers told the skinheads that "unless they got totally out of control the police would neither interfere with their assaults nor arrest them" (97).

The U.S. Second Circuit Court of Appeals allowed a claim of *state-created danger* to go forward because the NYPD officers "condoned" a private person beating a protester.

CASE

Did Officers Have an Affirmative Duty to Protect the Protester from "Skinhead" Beating?

Dwares v. City of New York
985 F.2d (C.A. 2, 1993)

HISTORY

Plaintiff (Steven Bruce Dwares) sued the city, police officers, and another individual for violation of civil rights in connection with beating Dwares during a demonstration that involved flag burning. Federal claims were dismissed by the United States District Court for the Southern District of New York, and plaintiff appealed. The Second Circuit U.S. Court of Appeals vacated and remanded.

—KEARSE, J.

FACTS

On July 4, 1989, a rally was held in Washington Square Park in New York City. At the rally there was a demonstration that included the burning of an American flag. Dwares did not physically participate in that desecration, but he attended the demonstration and voiced his support for those who did. Also present in the park at the time of the rally was a group of individuals known as "skinheads," including Bruce Kreitman, who were known to the City's Police Department in general and to the defendant officers in particular to have a history of racism and engaging in "violent attacks on individuals engaged in lawfully protected First Amendment activity."

At about 6:00 p.m. on July 4, Dwares, who was demonstrating in support of the rights of others to engage in flag burning, was physically attacked by Kreitman and other "skinheads" who repeatedly hit him about the head with a bottle. After being hit and chased for some 10 minutes, Dwares finally escaped, with head and face bloodied, and took refuge in a nearby Emergency Medical Services vehicle.

The prolonged felonious attack on Dwares occurred in the presence of the defendant police officers; but the officers made no attempt to intervene, or to protect Dwares from harm, or to arrest the assaulting "skinheads." The complaint alleged, on information and belief, that

> prior to the specific incident that gave rise to this litigation, the individual police officer defendants herein and the "skinheads," including defendant Kreitman, had conspired and/or agreed amongst themselves to permit the "skinheads" to harass and assault those who wished to express their First Amendment rights by burning an American flag, as well as those who supported the right of individuals to express themselves in that way, so long as this conduct did not get totally out of control.

The complaint alleged that Kreitman, in an interview with a reporter for the *Village Voice,* confirmed that police officers had told the "skinheads" that unless they got completely out of control the police would neither interfere with their assaults nor arrest them. As a result of the attack by the "skinheads" and the officers' agreement to refrain from interfering, Dwares suffered serious physical injury, pain, and emotional distress.

OPINION

The district court dismissed the § 1983 claims against all defendants largely in reliance on *DeShaney v. Winnebago County Department of Social Services* (1989) ("*DeShaney* "), on the ground that the police had no affirmative obligation to come to Dwares's aid, and that therefore the complaint's "allegations fail[ed] to support a claim that he was deprived of any right secured by the Constitution or the laws of the United States."

Section 1983 allows an individual to bring suit against persons who, under color of state law, have caused him to be "deprived of any rights, privileges, or immunities secured by the Constitution and laws" of the United States. 42 U.S.C. § 1983. It is well established that in order to state a claim under § 1983, a plaintiff must allege (1) that the challenged conduct was attributable at least in part to a person acting under color of state law, and (2) that such conduct deprived the plaintiff of a right, privilege, or immunity secured by the Constitution or laws of the United States. A private individual may be subject to liability under this section if he or she willfully collaborated with an official state actor in the deprivation of the federal right. Conversely, a state actor may be subject to liability for an action physically undertaken by private actors in violation of the plaintiff's liberty or property rights if the state actor directed or aided and abetted the violation. There is no question that a physical beating by one who has no privilege of inflicting such corporeal punishment intrudes on the victim's liberty interests. Where the beating has been inflicted by private individuals, however, there is a question as to whether state officials may be held accountable under federal law.

In *DeShaney,* the Supreme Court held that a state had had no duty under the Due Process Clause to protect a child against beatings by his father even though the state had received reports that the father physically abused the child. In *DeShaney,* the petitioners had conceded that the state played no part in creating the danger to the child, and the Court therefore noted that "while the State may have been aware of the dangers that [the child] faced in the free world, *it played no part in their creation, nor did it do anything to render him any more vulnerable to them.*" The Court concluded that "[t]he most that can be said of the state functionaries in this case is that they stood by and did nothing when suspicious circumstances dictated a more active role for them."

We read the *DeShaney* Court's analysis to imply that, though an allegation simply that police officers had failed to act upon reports of past violence would not implicate the victim's rights under the Due Process Clause, an allegation that the officers in some way had assisted in creating or increasing the danger to the victim would indeed implicate those rights. The complaint in the present case went well beyond allegations that the defendant officers merely stood by and did nothing, and that circumstances were merely suspicious. It alleged that the officers conspired with the "skinheads" to permit the latter to beat up flag burners with relative impunity, assuring the "skinheads" that unless they got totally out of control they would not be impeded or arrested.

It requires no stretch to infer that such prior assurances would have increased the likelihood that the "skinheads" would assault demonstrators. Thus, in the present case, the complaint asserted that the defendant officers indeed had made the demonstrators more vulnerable to assaults. Further, it alleged that the officers had in effect aided and abetted the deprivation of Dwares's civil rights by allowing him to be subjected to the prolonged assault in their presence without interfering with the attack. Such a prearranged official

(continued)

sanction of privately inflicted injury would surely have violated the victim's rights under the Due Process Clause.

In sum, we disagree with the district court's conclusion that the complaint did not adequately allege claims under § 1983 against the individual defendants in their individual capacities. Since those claims must be reinstated, the pendent state-law claims against those defendants will likewise be reinstated.

For the foregoing reasons, we vacate the judgment dismissing the complaint, and we remand for adjudication of the claims against the individual defendants in their individual capacities under § 1983 and under state law.

Costs to appellant.

Questions

1. List all the facts relevant to deciding whether NYPD officers allowed Kreitman to beat Steven Dwares.

2. Summarize the Court's arguments applying the "state-created" danger rule to the facts of this case.

3. Do you believe it should be the federal courts' "business" to decide when police officers are liable when private people beat up other individuals? If you do, who should make these decisions? State courts? Legislatures? Special panels of experts? Explain your answer.

LO 8 "State-Created Danger" and Domestic Violence

Violence between intimate partners—mostly against women—is the single greatest cause of injury to women in America, "more than muggings, rapes, and car accidents combined" (Awoyomi 2011, 2).

The U.S. Supreme Court didn't revisit *DeShaney* until 2005. And, when it did, it started with another domestic violence horror story that ended when Jessica Gonzalez's former husband shot their three daughters, drove to the police station, and opened fire on them with a semiautomatic handgun that he bought earlier that evening. The police shot back and killed him. Jessica Gonzalez sued Castle Rock Police Department officers, claiming that they, by not enforcing a restraining order, created a danger that led to her daughters' deaths. The case, *Town of Castle Rock v. Gonzalez* (2005), is our next case excerpt. In it, the U.S. Supreme Court decided "whether an individual who has obtained a state-law restraining order has a constitutionally protected property interest in having the police enforce the restraining order when they have probable cause to believe it has been violated" (750–51). The Court (7–2) decided that Jessica Gonzalez did *not* have a right to have the restraining order enforced.

In *Town of Castle Rock v. Gonzalez*, the U.S. Supreme Court (7–2) ruled that individuals have no constitutional right to have restraining orders enforced.

CASE

Did She Have a Constitutional Right to Police Enforcement of the Domestic Violence Restraining Order?

Town of Castle Rock v. Gonzalez
545 U.S. 748 (2005)

HISTORY

Jessica Gonzalez individually, and as next best friend of her deceased minor children, Rebecca Gonzales, Katheryn Gonzales, and Leslie Gonzales, brought a Section 1983 civil rights action against the Town of Castle Rock, Colorado,

police officers based on the officers' refusal to enforce a domestic abuse restraining order against her husband. The United States District Court for the District of Colorado dismissed the action for failure to state a claim. A Tenth Circuit Court of Appeals panel reversed. Upon rehearing en banc, a divided Tenth Circuit Court of Appeals (4–2), reversed the District Court's decision and remanded. The U.S. Supreme Court granted certiorari, and reversed.

—SCALIA, J., joined by REHNQUIST, C. J., and O'CONNOR, KENNEDY, SOUTER, THOMAS, and BREYER, JJ.

We decide in this case whether an individual who has obtained a state-law restraining order has a constitutionally protected property interest in having the police enforce the restraining order when they have probable cause to believe it has been violated.

FACTS

The restraining order had been issued by a state trial court in conjunction with Gonzalez's divorce proceedings. The original form order, issued on May 21, 1999, and served on Gonzalez's husband on June 4, 1999, commanded him not to "molest or disturb the peace of [Gonzalez] or of any child," and to remain at least 100 yards from the family home at all times.

The bottom of the preprinted form noted that the reverse side contained "IMPORTANT NOTICES FOR RESTRAINED PARTIES AND LAW ENFORCEMENT OFFICIALS." The preprinted text on the back of the form included the following "**WARNING**":

> **A KNOWING VIOLATION OF A RESTRAINING ORDER IS A CRIME.** . . . A VIOLATION WILL ALSO CONSTITUTE CONTEMPT OF COURT. **YOU MAY BE ARRESTED** WITHOUT NOTICE IF A LAW ENFORCEMENT OFFICER HAS PROBABLE CAUSE TO BELIEVE THAT YOU HAVE KNOWINGLY VIOLATED THIS ORDER. *Id.*, at 1144 (emphasis in original)

The preprinted text on the back of the form also included a "**NOTICE TO LAW ENFORCEMENT OFFICIALS**," which read in part:

> YOU SHALL USE EVERY REASONABLE MEANS TO ENFORCE THIS RESTRAINING ORDER. YOU SHALL ARREST, OR, IF AN ARREST WOULD BE IMPRACTICAL UNDER THE CIRCUMSTANCES, SEEK A WARRANT FOR THE ARREST OF THE RESTRAINED PERSON WHEN YOU HAVE INFORMATION AMOUNTING TO PROBABLE CAUSE THAT THE RESTRAINED PERSON HAS VIOLATED OR ATTEMPTED TO VIOLATE ANY PROVISION OF THIS ORDER AND THE RESTRAINED PERSON HAS BEEN PROPERLY SERVED WITH A COPY OF THIS ORDER OR HAS RECEIVED ACTUAL NOTICE OF THE EXISTENCE OF THIS ORDER.

On June 4, 1999, the state trial court modified the terms of the restraining order and made it permanent. The modified order gave Gonzalez's husband the right to spend time with his three daughters (ages 10, 9, and 7) on alternate weekends, for two weeks during the summer, and, "upon reasonable notice," for a midweek dinner visit "arranged by the parties"; the modified order also allowed him to visit the home to collect the children for such "parenting time."

According to the complaint, at about 5 or 5:30 p.m. on Tuesday, June 22, 1999, Gonzalez's husband took the three daughters while they were playing outside the family home. No advance arrangements had been made for him to see the daughters that evening. When Gonzalez noticed the children were missing, she suspected her husband had taken them. At about 7:30 p.m., she called the Castle Rock Police Department, which dispatched two officers. The complaint continues:

> When the officers arrived, she showed them a copy of the TRO and requested that it be enforced and the three children be returned to her immediately. The officers stated that there was nothing they could do about the TRO and suggested that Gonzalez call the Police Department again if the three children did not return home by 10:00 p.m.

At approximately 8:30 p.m., Gonzalez talked to her husband on his cellular telephone. He told her "he had the three children at an amusement park in Denver." She called the police again and asked them to "have someone check for" her husband or his vehicle at the amusement park and "put out an all-points bulletin" for her husband, but the officer with whom she spoke "refused to do so," again telling her to "wait until 10:00 p.m. and see if" her husband returned the girls.

At approximately 10:10 p.m., Gonzalez called the police and said her children were still missing, but she was now told to wait until midnight. She called at midnight and told the dispatcher her children were still missing. She went to her husband's apartment and, finding nobody there, called the police at 12:10 a.m.; she was told to wait for an officer to arrive. When none came, she went to the police station at 12:50 a.m. and submitted an incident report. The officer who took the report "made no reasonable effort to enforce the TRO or locate the three children. Instead, he went to dinner."

At approximately 3:20 a.m., Gonzalez's husband arrived at the police station and opened fire with a semi-automatic handgun he had purchased earlier that evening. Police shot back, killing him. Inside the cab of his pickup truck, they found the bodies of all three daughters, whom he had already murdered.

OPINION

In 42 U.S.C. § 1983, Congress has created a federal cause of action for "the deprivation of any rights, privileges, or immunities secured by the Constitution and laws." Gonzalez claims the benefit of this provision on the ground

(*continued*)

that she had a property interest in police enforcement of the restraining order against her husband; and that the town deprived her of this property without due process by having a policy that tolerated nonenforcement of restraining orders.

Our cases recognize that a benefit is not a protected entitlement if government officials may grant or deny it in their discretion. The Court of Appeals in this case determined that Colorado law created an entitlement to enforcement of the restraining order because the "court-issued restraining order . . . specifically dictated that its terms must be enforced" and a "state statute commanded" enforcement of the order when certain objective conditions were met (probable cause to believe that the order had been violated and that the object of the order had received notice of its existence).

The central state-law question is whether Colorado law gave Gonzalez a right to police enforcement of the restraining order. The critical language in the restraining order came not from any part of the order itself (which was signed by the state-court trial judge and directed to the restrained party, Gonzalez's husband), but from the preprinted notice to law-enforcement personnel that appeared on the back of the order. That notice effectively restated the statutory provision describing "peace officers' duties" related to the crime of violation of a restraining order. At the time of the conduct at issue in this case, that provision read as follows:

"(a) Whenever a restraining order is issued, the protected person shall be provided with a copy of such order. *A peace officer shall use every reasonable means to enforce a restraining order.*

"(b) *A peace officer shall arrest, or, if an arrest would be impractical under the circumstances, seek a warrant for the arrest of a restrained person* when the peace officer has information amounting to probable cause that:

   "(I) The restrained person has violated or attempted to violate any provision of a restraining order; and

   "(II) The restrained person has been properly served with a copy of the restraining order or the restrained person has received actual notice of the existence and substance of such order.

"(c) In making the probable cause determination described in paragraph (b) of this subsection (3), a peace officer shall assume that the information received from the registry is accurate. *A peace officer shall enforce a valid restraining order whether or not there is a record of the restraining order in the registry.*" (emphasis added)

The Court of Appeals concluded that this statutory provision established the Colorado Legislature's clear intent "to alter the fact that the police were not enforcing domestic abuse restraining orders," and thus its intent "that the recipient of a domestic abuse restraining order have an entitlement to its enforcement." Any other result, it said, "would render domestic abuse restraining orders utterly valueless."

We do not believe that these provisions of Colorado law truly made enforcement of restraining orders *mandatory*. A well-established tradition of police discretion has long coexisted with apparently mandatory arrest statutes. A true mandate of police action would require some stronger indication from the Colorado Legislature than "shall use every reasonable means to enforce a restraining order" (or even "shall arrest . . . or . . . seek a warrant"). That language is not perceptibly more mandatory than the Colorado statute which has long told municipal chiefs of police that they "shall pursue and arrest any person fleeing from justice in any part of the state" and that they "shall apprehend any person in the act of committing any offense . . . and, forthwith and without any warrant, bring such person before a . . . competent authority for examination and trial."

It is hard to imagine that a Colorado peace officer would not have some discretion to determine that—despite probable cause to believe a restraining order has been violated—the circumstances of the violation or the competing duties of that officer or his agency counsel decisively against enforcement in a particular instance. The practical necessity for discretion is particularly apparent in a case such as this one, where the suspected violator is not actually present and his whereabouts are unknown.

Gonzalez does not specify the precise means of enforcement that the Colorado restraining-order statute assertedly mandated—whether her interest lay in having police arrest her husband, having them seek a warrant for his arrest, or having them "use every reasonable means, up to and including arrest, to enforce the order's terms." Such indeterminacy is not the hallmark of a duty that is mandatory. Nor can someone be safely deemed "entitled" to something when the identity of the alleged entitlement is vague.

Even if the statute could be said to have made enforcement of restraining orders "mandatory" because of the domestic-violence context of the underlying statute, that would not necessarily mean that state law gave *Gonzalez* an entitlement to *enforcement* of the mandate.

Making the actions of government employees obligatory can serve various legitimate ends other than the conferral of a benefit on a specific class of people. The serving of public rather than private ends is the normal course of the criminal law because criminal acts, besides the injury they do to individuals, strike at the very being of society; which cannot possibly subsist, where actions of this sort are suffered to escape with impunity. The creation of a personal entitlement to something as vague and novel as enforcement of restraining orders cannot "simply go without saying." We conclude that Colorado has not created such an entitlement.

Even if we were to think otherwise concerning the creation of an entitlement by Colorado, it is by no means clear that an individual entitlement to enforcement of a restraining order could constitute a "property" interest for purposes of the Due Process Clause. The right to have a restraining order enforced does not have some ascertainable monetary value. We conclude, therefore, that Gonzalez did not, for purposes of the Due Process Clause, have a property interest in police enforcement of the restraining order against her husband.

In light of today's decision and that in *DeShaney*, the benefit that a third party may receive from having someone else arrested for a crime generally does not trigger protections under the Due Process Clause, neither in its procedural nor in its "substantive" manifestations. This does not mean States are powerless to provide victims with personally enforceable remedies. Although the framers of the Fourteenth Amendment and the Civil Rights Act of 1871, 17 Stat. 13 (the original source of § 1983), did not create a system by which police departments are generally held financially accountable for crimes that better policing might have prevented, the people of Colorado are free to craft such a system under state law. *Reversed.*

DISSENT

STEVENS J., joined by Ginsburg, J.

The central question in this case is whether, as a matter of Colorado law, Gonzalez had a right to police assistance comparable to the right she would have possessed to any other service the government or a private firm might have undertaken to provide. They are created and their dimensions are defined by existing rules or understandings that stem from an independent source such as state law—rules or understandings that secure certain benefits and that support claims of entitlement to those benefits.

In 1994, the Colorado General Assembly passed omnibus legislation targeting domestic violence. The part of the legislation at issue in this case mandates enforcement of a domestic restraining order upon probable cause of a violation, § 18-6-803.5(3), while another part directs that police officers "shall, without undue delay, arrest" a suspect upon "probable cause to believe that a crime or offense of domestic violence has been committed."

In adopting this legislation, the Colorado General Assembly joined a nationwide movement of States that took aim at the crisis of police underenforcement in the domestic violence sphere by implementing "mandatory arrest" statutes. The crisis of underenforcement had various causes, not least of which was the perception by police departments and police officers that domestic violence was a private, "family" matter and that arrest was to

be used as a last resort. When Colorado passed its statute in 1994, it joined the ranks of 15 States that mandated arrest for domestic violence offenses and 19 States that mandated arrest for domestic restraining order violations.

Given that Colorado law has quite clearly eliminated the police's discretion to deny enforcement, Gonzalez is correct that she had much more than a unilateral expectation that the restraining order would be enforced; rather, she had a legitimate claim of entitlement to enforcement. This Court has made clear that the property interests protected by procedural due process extend well beyond actual ownership of real estate, chattels, or money. Thus, our cases have found "property" interests in a number of state-conferred benefits and services, including welfare benefits; disability benefits; public education; utility services; government employment.

Because Gonzalez had a property interest in the enforcement of the restraining order, state officials could not deprive her of that interest without observing fair procedures. Her description of the police behavior in this case and the department's callous policy of failing to respond properly to reports of restraining order violations clearly alleges a due process violation. At the very least, due process requires that the relevant state decision maker *listen* to the claimant and then *apply the relevant criteria* in reaching his decision. The failure to observe these minimal procedural safeguards creates an unacceptable risk of arbitrary and erroneous deprivations. According to Gonzalez's complaint, the process she was afforded by the police constituted nothing more than a sham or a pretense.

Questions

1. Summarize the majority opinion's arguments supporting its conclusion that Gonzalez has no constitutional right to have the Castle Rock police enforce the restraining order against her husband.

2. Summarize the dissent's arguments supporting its conclusion that Gonzalez *does* have a constitutional right to have the Castle Rock police enforce the restraining order against her husband.

3. Do you think the Colorado "mandatory" enforcement statute intended to take away the Castle Rock Police Department's discretion in enforcing the restraining order? Defend your answer.

4. How important is it that Colorado was one of a number of states enacting mandatory enforcement of restraining orders in domestic abuse cases because of the widespread nonenforcement of restraining orders in domestic violence cases?

LO 8   Most U.S. courts of appeals (and state courts too) have soundly rejected claims against law enforcement officers based on the *state-created-danger exception*. In our next case excerpt, *Pinder v. Johnson*, a famous case from the U.S. Fourth Circuit Court of Appeals, Judge J. Harvie Wilkinson III, one of the most respected judges in the country, carefully explained why the *state-created-danger* exception offered no relief for Carol Pinder, whose former boyfriend burned her house down with her three small children inside.

In *Pinder v. Johnson* (1995), the Fourth Circuit Court of Appeals rejected the state-created-danger exception when Carol Pinder argued that an officer's negligence led to the deaths of her three children.

 **CASE**

Did the Police Have a Constitutional Duty to Protect Her and Her Children?

Pinder v. Johnson
54 F.3d 1169 (CA4 1995)

HISTORY

Carol Pinder filed suit individually and as the survivor of her minor children against the municipality of Cambridge, Maryland, and Donald Johnson PFC, a police officer in the municipality of Cambridge. The U.S. District Court for the District of Maryland denied Johnson's motion for summary judgment. A three-judge panel of the Fourth Circuit Court of Appeals affirmed. An *en banc review* [review by the whole circuit] REVERSED.

> —WILKINSON, J., joined by HALL, WILKINS, NIEMEYER, and WILLIAMS, JJ. WIDENER, MOTZ, HAMILTON, and LUTTIG, JJ. concurred in part, and concurred in the judgment.

FACTS

The facts of this case are genuinely tragic. On the evening of March 10, 1989, Officer Donald Johnson responded to a call reporting a domestic disturbance at the home of Carol Pinder. When he arrived at the scene, Johnson discovered that Pinder's former boyfriend, Don Pittman, had broken into her home. Pinder told Officer Johnson that when Pittman broke in, he was abusive and violent. He pushed her, punched her, and threw various objects at her.

Pittman was also screaming and threatening both Pinder and her children, saying he would murder them all. A neighbor, Darnell Taylor, managed to subdue Pittman and restrain him until the police arrived.

Officer Johnson questioned Pittman, who was hostile and unresponsive. Johnson then placed Pittman under arrest. After confining Pittman in the squad car, Johnson returned to the house to speak with Pinder again. Pinder explained to Officer Johnson that Pittman had threatened her in the past, and that he had just been released from prison after being convicted of attempted arson at Pinder's residence some ten months earlier. She was naturally afraid for herself and her children, and wanted to know whether it would be safe for her to return to work that evening.

Officer Johnson assured her that Pittman would be locked up overnight. He further indicated that Pinder had to wait until the next day to swear out a warrant against Pittman because a county commissioner would not be available to hear the charges before morning. Based on these assurances, Pinder returned to work.

That same evening, Johnson brought Pittman before Dorchester County Commissioner George Ames, Jr. for an initial appearance. Johnson only charged Pittman with trespassing and malicious destruction of property having a value of less than three hundred dollars, both of which are misdemeanor offenses. Consequently, Ames simply released Pittman on his own recognizance and warned him to stay away from Pinder's home.

Pittman did not heed this warning. Upon his release, he returned to Pinder's house and set fire to it. Pinder was still at work, but her three children were home asleep and died of smoke inhalation. Pittman was later arrested and charged with first-degree murder. He was convicted and is currently serving three life sentences without possibility of parole.

Pinder brought this action for herself and for the estates of her three children, seeking damages under

42 U.S.C. § 1983, as well as state law theories, against the Commissioners of Cambridge and Officer Johnson. She alleged that defendants had violated their affirmative duty to protect her and her children, thereby depriving them of their constitutional right to due process under the Fourteenth Amendment.

Johnson moved for summary judgment, arguing that he had no constitutionally imposed affirmative duty to protect the Pinders and that he was shielded from liability by the doctrine of qualified immunity. The district court, however, refused to dismiss plaintiff's due process claim, finding that Officer Johnson was not entitled to qualified immunity. Johnson brought an interlocutory appeal [an appeal that takes place before the trial court rules on the case]. A divided panel of this court affirmed, finding that Pinder had stated a cognizable substantive due process claim and that Johnson did not have a valid immunity defense. We granted rehearing en banc, and now reverse the judgment of the district court.

OPINION

Eighteen days before the events giving rise to this action, the Supreme Court handed down its decision in *DeShaney* (1989), which squarely rejected liability under 42 U.S.C. § 1983 based on an affirmative duty theory.

The facts in *DeShaney* were as poignant as those in this case. There, the Winnebago County Department of Social Services (DSS) received a number of reports that a young boy, Joshua DeShaney, was being abused by his father. As this abuse went on, several DSS workers personally observed the injuries that had been inflicted on Joshua. They knew firsthand of the threat to the boy's safety, yet they failed to remove him from his father's custody or otherwise protect him from abuse. Ultimately, Joshua's father beat him so violently that the boy suffered serious brain damage. Joshua's mother brought a § 1983 action on his behalf, arguing that the County and its employees had deprived Joshua of his liberty interests without due process by failing to provide adequate protection against his father's violent acts.

Despite natural sympathy for the plaintiff, the Court held that there was no § 1983 liability under these circumstances. It noted that the Due Process Clause of the Fourteenth Amendment does not require governmental actors to affirmatively protect life, liberty, or property against intrusion by private third parties. Instead, the Due Process Clause works only as a negative prohibition on state action. "Its purpose was to protect the people from the State, not to ensure that the State protected them from each other." This view is consistent with our general conception of the Constitution as a document of negative restraints, not positive entitlements.

The *DeShaney* Court concluded that:

if the Due Process Clause does not require the State to provide its citizens with particular

protective services, it follows that the State cannot be held liable under the Clause for injuries that could have been averted had it chosen to provide them. As a general matter, then, we conclude that a State's failure to protect an individual against private violence simply does not constitute a violation of the Due Process Clause.

The affirmative duty of protection that the Supreme Court rejected in *DeShaney* is precisely the duty Pinder relies on in this case. Joshua's mother wanted the state to be held liable for its lack of action, for merely standing by when it could have acted to prevent a tragedy. Likewise, Pinder argues Johnson could have, and thus should have, acted to prevent Pittman's crimes. *DeShaney* makes clear, however, that no affirmative duty was clearly established in these circumstances.

The *DeShaney* Court did indicate that an affirmative duty to protect may arise when the state restrains persons from acting on their own behalf. The Court explained that

when the State by the affirmative exercise of its power so restrains an individual's liberty that it renders him unable to care for himself, and at the same time fails to provide for his basic human needs . . . it transgresses the substantive limits on state action set by the Eighth Amendment and the Due Process Clause.

The specific source of an affirmative duty to protect, the Court emphasized, is the custodial nature of a "special relationship."

DeShaney reasoned that "the affirmative duty to protect arises not from the State's knowledge of the individual's predicament or from its expressions of intent to help him, but from the limitation which it has imposed on his freedom to act on his own behalf." Some sort of confinement of the injured party—incarceration, institutionalization, or the like—is needed to trigger the affirmative duty. This Court has consistently read *DeShaney* to require a custodial context before any affirmative duty can arise under the Due Process Clause.

There was no custodial relationship with Carol Pinder and her children in this case. Neither Johnson nor any other state official had restrained Pinder's freedom to act on her own behalf. Pinder was never incarcerated, arrested, or otherwise restricted in any way. Without any such limitation imposed on her liberty, *DeShaney* indicates Pinder was due no affirmative constitutional duty of protection from the state, and Johnson would not be charged with liability for the criminal acts of a third party.

Pinder argues, however, that Johnson's explicit promises that Pittman would be incarcerated overnight created the requisite "special relationship." We do not agree. By requiring a custodial context as the condition for an affirmative duty, *DeShaney* rejected the idea that such a duty can arise solely from an official's awareness of a specific

(continued)

risk or from promises of aid. There, as here, plaintiff alleged that the state knew of the special risk of harm at the hands of a third party. There, as here, plaintiff alleged that the state had "specifically proclaimed, by word and by deed, its intention to protect" the victim. Neither allegation was sufficient to support the existence of an affirmative duty in *DeShaney*, and the same holds true in this case.

Promises do not create a special relationship—custody does. Unlike custody, a promise of aid does not actually place a person in a dangerous position and then cut off all outside sources of assistance. Promises from state officials can be ignored if the situation seems dire enough, whereas custody cannot be ignored or changed by the persons it affects. It is for this reason that the Supreme Court made custody the crux of the special relationship rule. Lacking the slightest hint of a true "special relationship," Pinder's claim in this case boils down to an insufficient allegation of a failure to act.

We also cannot accept Pinder's attempt to escape the import of *DeShaney* by characterizing her claim as one of affirmative misconduct by the state in "creating or enhancing" the danger, instead of an omission. She emphasizes the "actions" that Johnson took in making assurances, and in deciding not to charge Pittman with any serious offense. By this measure, every representation by the police and every failure to incarcerate would constitute "affirmative actions," giving rise to civil liability.

No amount of semantics can disguise the fact that the real "affirmative act" here was committed by Pittman, not by Officer Johnson. The most that can be said of the state functionaries is that they stood by and did nothing when suspicious circumstances dictated a more active role for them.

Given the principles laid down by *DeShaney*, it can hardly be said that Johnson was faced with a clearly established duty to protect Pinder or her children in March of 1989. Indeed, it can be argued that *DeShaney* established exactly the opposite, i.e., that no such affirmative duty existed because neither Pinder nor her children were confined by the state.

It is true, as the district court noted, that some cases have found an "affirmative duty" arising outside the traditional custodial context. None of these cases, however, clearly establish the existence of the right Pinder alleges was violated. First, none of these cases found a particularized due process right to affirmative protection based solely on an official's assurances that the danger posed by a third party will be eliminated. All involved some circumstance wherein the state took a much larger and more direct role in "creating" the danger itself.

These cases involve a wholly different paradigm than that presented here. When the state itself creates the dangerous situation that resulted in a victim's injury the state is not merely accused of a failure to act; it becomes much more akin to an actor itself directly causing harm to the injured party. See, e.g., *Cornelius v. Town of Highland Lake* (11th Cir. 1989) (duty when state brought inmates into victim's workplace); *Wells v. Walker* (8th Cir. 1988) (duty when state brought dangerous prisoners to victim's store); *Nishiyama v. Dickson County* (6th Cir. 1987) (duty when state provided unsupervised parolee with squad car).

At most, these cases stand for the proposition that state actors may not disclaim liability when they themselves throw others to the lions. They do not, by contrast, entitle persons who rely on promises of aid to some greater degree of protection from lions at large.

The extensive debate provoked by this case should be proof enough that the law in this area was anything but clearly established at the time Officer Johnson gave assurances to Pinder. To impose liability in the absence of a clearly established constitutional duty is to invite litigation over a limitless array of official acts. There are good reasons why the constitutional right to protection sought by Pinder was not clearly established by the courts. As the First Circuit noted in a similar case, "enormous economic consequences could follow from the reading of the Fourteenth Amendment that plaintiff here urges." The consequences, however, are not just economic, and their gravity indicates why the right Pinder asserts was never clearly established.

The recognition of a broad constitutional right to affirmative protection from the state would be the first step down the slippery slope of liability. Such a right potentially would be implicated in nearly every instance where a private actor inflicts injuries that the state could have prevented. Every time a police officer incorrectly decided it was not necessary to intervene in a domestic dispute, the victims of the ensuing violence could bring a § 1983 action. Every time a parolee committed a criminal act, the victims could argue the state had an affirmative duty to keep the prisoner incarcerated. Indeed, victims of virtually every crime could plausibly argue that if the authorities had done their job, they would not have suffered their loss. Broad affirmative duties thus provide a fertile bed for § 1983 litigation, and the resultant governmental liability would wholly defeat the purposes of qualified immunity.

If the right Pinder asserts were ever clearly established, it would entail other significant consequences. A general obligation of the state to protect private citizens makes law enforcement officials constitutional guarantors of the conduct of others. It is no solution to say that such a right to affirmative protection has its inherent limitations. It is no answer to contend that the duty here was created only by Johnson's promise and Pinder's reliance on that promise, and is limited by Johnson's awareness of the risk. Such "limitations" are no barrier to increased lawsuits.

There are endless opportunities for disagreements over the exact nature of an official's promise, the intent behind it, the degree of the reliance, the causal link between the promise and the injury, and so on. Similarly, the extent of the state's affirmative duty to protect and the degree of the state's awareness of the risk are also subjects that would tie up state and local officials in endless federal litigation.

In cases like this, it is always easy to second-guess. Tragic circumstances only sharpen our hindsight, and it is tempting to express our sense of outrage at the failure of Officer Johnson to protect Pinder's children from Pittman's villainy. The Supreme Court in *DeShaney* specifically rejected the "shocks the conscience" test of *Rochin v. California* (1952) [Chapter 2] as a basis for imposing § 1983 liability in the affirmative duty context, however. We cannot simply ignore the lack of any clearly established constitutional duty to protect and the concomitant immunity from civil liability. Hard cases can make bad law, and it is to protect against that possibility that police officers possess the defense of qualified immunity.

For the foregoing reasons, the judgment of the district court denying qualified immunity to Officer Johnson is REVERSED.

DISSENT

RUSSELL, J., joined by ERVIN, C.J., and MURNAGHAN and MICHAEL, JJ.

Because I believe the Court casually disregards the very real ways in which Officer Johnson's conduct placed Pinder and her children in a position of danger, I respectfully dissent. In March 1989, the time of the fire, the law "clearly established" that the state has a duty to protect an individual where the state, by its affirmative action, creates a dangerous situation or renders an individual more vulnerable to danger. As the Seventh Circuit stated in *Bowers v. DeVito* (1982):

> If the state puts a man in a position of danger from private persons and then fails to protect him, it will not be heard to say that its role was merely passive; it is as much an active **tort feasor** [wrong doer] as if it had thrown him into a snake pit.

The Seventh Circuit and other circuits, including our own, have reaffirmed this duty. The Supreme Court's decision in *DeShaney* did not reject the state's clearly established duty to protect an individual where the state, through its affirmative action, has created a dangerous situation or rendered the individual more vulnerable to danger. The Supreme Court held only that the state has no duty to protect an individual from the actions of third parties where the state was aware of the dangers but played no part in their creation. The fact that the state did not create the danger was central to the Court's holding.

In this case, Officer Johnson was not merely aware of the danger; he placed Pinder and her children in a position of danger. Officer Johnson knew Pittman had broken into Pinder's home and had been abusive and violent. Pittman had punched Pinder and thrown objects at her. When the officers arrived at the scene, Pittman was screaming and threatening that he "wasn't going to jail for nothing this time; this time it would be for murder." After the officers restrained Pittman, Pinder explained to Officer Johnson that Pittman had threatened Pinder before, that he had attempted to set fire to her house ten months earlier, and that he had just finished serving his sentence for the attempted arson.

Given Pittman's threats and violent behavior, Pinder was understandably concerned about the safety of herself and her children. She explained to Officer Johnson that she needed to return to work and specifically asked him whether it was safe to do so. Officer Johnson assured Pinder several times that Pittman would remain in police custody until morning. Officer Johnson indicated to Pinder that Pittman could not be released that night because a county commissioner would not be available until the morning.

Instead of remaining home with her children or making other arrangements for their safety, Pinder, relying on Officer Johnson's assurances, returned to work, leaving her children alone at home. At the police station, Officer Johnson charged Pittman only with two minor offenses, trespassing and malicious destruction of property having a value of less than three hundred dollars. Despite his previous representation to Pinder that no county commissioner would be available before the morning, Officer Johnson brought Pittman before a county commissioner that evening.

Because Officer Johnson charged Pittman only with two misdemeanors, the county commissioner released Pittman on his own recognizance. Upon his release, Pittman went directly to Pinder's house and burned it down, killing the three children in the conflagration.

I cannot understand how the majority can recount these same events in its own opinion and not conclude that Officer Johnson placed Pinder and her children in a position of danger. Officer Johnson made assurances to Pinder that Pittman would remain in police custody overnight and falsely represented that no county commissioner would be available until morning. He induced Pinder to return to work and leave her children vulnerable to Pittman's violence. After witnessing Pittman's violent behavior and murderous threats, he charged Pittman with only minor offenses, assuring his release. Officer Johnson had a duty to protect Pinder and her children from Pittman, at least to an extent necessary to dispel the false sense of security that his actions created.

Unlike the majority, I believe that the law at the time of the incident clearly established that Officer Johnson had a duty to protect Pinder and her children upon Pittman's release. The Court finds it significant that no case before March 1989 contained the precise holding that due process creates a duty of affirmative protection based on

(*continued*)

an official's assurances that the danger posed by a third party will be eliminated. Such a particular holding, however, is not required in order to conclude that a right was clearly established.

I believe that a reasonable officer in Officer Johnson's position would have recognized that, given his assurances to Pinder that Pittman would remain in police custody until morning and his failure to charge Pittman with an offense serious enough to ensure that he remained in custody overnight, he placed Pinder and her children in a dangerous position. He induced Pinder to let her guard down, dissuading her from taking actions to protect herself and her children from Pittman. Certainly, a reasonable officer would have recognized that he had a duty at least to phone Pinder and warn her that Pittman had been released from police custody.

Pinder's children were left alone at home, vulnerable to the rampage of a violent, intemperate man, and deprived of their mother's protection because of the hollow word of an irresponsible, thoughtless police officer. Today the Court holds that this police officer, who took no action to correct a dangerous situation of his own creation, did not violate Pinder's due process rights and is otherwise immune from prosecution because he did not violate a clearly established right. I disagree.

Questions

1. List the facts relevant to deciding whether Donald Johnson is liable for damages to Carol Pinder.

2. Apply the facts you listed in (1) to the no-affirmative-duty-to-protect rule, the special-relationship exception, and the state-created-danger exception.

3. Summarize the court's majority and dissenting opinions' arguments in favor of or against the rule and exceptions in (2).

4. Which rule do you favor, and why?

SUING JUDGES AND PROSECUTORS

LO 8 Most plaintiffs in civil actions sue law enforcement officers, who enjoy qualified immunity from being sued for damages. But what about prosecutors and judges? Can individuals sue them? The answer is "no" to suing a judge, and it's "hardly ever" to suing prosecutors Why? Because judges enjoy **absolute immunity** from civil suits, meaning they can't be sued even if they acted maliciously and in bad faith. The only remedies against misbehaving judges are either impeachment or, if they're elected, voting them out of office.

Prosecutors enjoy what's called **functional immunity**. This means their immunity depends on the function they're performing at the time of the misconduct. When they act as advocates, they're absolutely immune from civil liability, even when plaintiffs prove they acted in bad faith and with malice. When they act as administrators or investigators, they're entitled to **qualified immunity**; that is, they're immune unless their misconduct violated clearly established law that a reasonable prosecutor would have known.

Before we examine the law regarding prosecutors' functional immunity, be aware of this widely documented observation about prosecutors:

> While certainly the vast majority of prosecutors are ethical lawyers engaged in vital public service, the undeniable fact is that many innocent people have been convicted of crimes as a result of prosecutorial misconduct, and the victims of this misconduct are generally denied any civil remedy because of prosecutorial immunities. (Johns 2005, 53, citing and summarizing many empirical studies, pp. 59–64)

Furthermore, prosecutors rarely suffer for their misconduct (Johns 2005, 70). According to the Center for Public Integrity, since 1970 there have been more than 2,000 cases of prosecutorial misconduct but only 44 disciplinary actions and two disbarments (70). Another study found only 100 disciplinary proceedings against prosecutors between the years 1886 and 2000 (70).

In *theory*, prosecutors are criminally liable for their nonadvocacy functions. But since the Civil Rights Act, § 242, in 1866, created criminal liability for public officials who violate constitutional rights, only one prosecutor has ever been convicted (70–71).

The U.S. Supreme Court developed the functional immunity doctrine in four cases. Here's a summary of each:

1. *Imbler v. Pachtman* (1976). Paul Imbler was convicted of felony murder and sentenced to death following a trial in which District Attorney Richard Pachtman knowingly used false evidence and suppressed exculpatory evidence. Imbler was freed after he served nine years in prison. He sued Pachtman for § 1983 money damages. The Supreme Court ruled that Pachtman was absolutely immune from civil damages, because his misconduct occurred while he was performing his advocacy function.

2. *Burns v. Reed* (1991). Speculating that Kathy Burns had multiple personalities, one of which was responsible for shooting her two sons, Indiana police officers Paul Cox and Donald Scroggins decided to interview Burns under hypnosis. They were concerned that hypnosis "might be an unacceptable investigative technique" and sought Chief Deputy Prosecutor Rick Reed's advice. He told them they could question Burns under hypnosis.

While she was hypnotized, she referred to both herself and the shooter as "Katie." Interpreting this as support for their multiple personality theory, the police detained her and consulted Reed again, who told them they "probably had probable cause" to arrest her (482).

At a probable cause hearing the next day, in response to Reed's questioning, an officer testified that Burns confessed, but neither the officer nor Reed informed the judge about the hypnosis or that Burns had otherwise consistently denied guilt. The judge issued the warrant on the basis of this misleading presentation. When this came to light, the trial judge ordered the confession suppressed, and the prosecutor dropped the charges.

Burns sued the prosecutor, Reed, for damages under § 1983. The trial court dismissed the case, ruling that Reed was entitled to absolute immunity. The Supreme Court agreed, partly. The Court ruled that absolute immunity extended to initiation and presentation of the case, which included the probable cause hearing, but it didn't extend to the advice the prosecutor gave to the officers regarding the confession under hypnosis.

3. *Buckley v. Fitzsimmons* (1993). Stephen Buckley had been incarcerated for three years in the DuPage County jail on rape and murder charges, growing out of the highly publicized murder of 11-year-old Jeanine Nicarico. When he was finally released, he sued DuPage County State's Attorney Michael Fitzsimmons for damages under § 1983 for fabricating evidence during the preliminary investigation.

The fabricated evidence related to a boot print on the door of the Nicarico home, apparently left by the killer when he kicked in the door. Three separate studies by experts from the DuPage County Crime Lab, the Illinois Department of Law Enforcement, and the Kansas Bureau of Identification all failed to make a reliable connection between the print and a pair of boots that Buckley had voluntarily supplied. The respondents (including Fitzsimmons and sheriff's deputies) then obtained a "positive identification" from Louise Robbins, an anthropologist in North Carolina. She was allegedly well known for her willingness to fabricate unreliable expert testimony.

They obtained her opinion during the early stages of the investigation, which was being conducted under the joint supervision and direction of the sheriff and Fitzsimmons, whose police officers and assistant prosecutors were performing essentially the same investigatory functions (262–63).

Was Fitzsimmons acting as an advocate or an investigator when Robbins faked the boot print on the victim's door? The Supreme Court ruled that he was acting as an investigator, because the fabrication took place before there was probable cause to arrest; prior to probable cause to arrest, a prosecutor can't be an advocate.

4. *Kalina v. Fletcher* (1997). Lynne Kalina, a deputy prosecutor in King County, Washington, followed standard practice when she filed three documents to begin second-degree burglary proceedings against Rodney Fletcher based on alleged computer theft from a school. One was an information [the formal charging document] and the second was a motion for an arrest warrant that required "sworn testimony establishing the grounds for issuing the warrant" (121). To satisfy this requirement, Kalina issued a third document that summarized the evidence supporting the charge. In this "Certification for Determination of Probable Cause" (the equivalent of an affidavit), Kalina "personally vouched for the truth of the facts set forth in the certification under penalty of perjury" (121).

There were two false statements in the affidavit. First, it stated that Fletcher had "never been associated with the school in any manner and did not have permission to enter the school." In fact, he worked in the school and was authorized to enter. She also stated that an electronics store employee identified Fletcher in a mug shot lineup as the person who asked for an appraisal of a computer stolen from the school. The employee didn't identify him.

Based on the affidavit, the trial court found probable cause and issued the warrant. Fletcher was arrested and spent a day in jail. A month later, the charges were dropped on Kalina's motion. Fletcher sued under § 1983 seeking damages from Kalina based on her alleged violations of his constitutional rights (122).

The U.S. Supreme Court ruled that the *preparation* of the three documents, including the preparation of the motion for an arrest warrant, was covered by the functional immunity doctrine; Kalina was acting as an advocate and therefore absolutely immune from liability (129). But the Court went on to rule that in *executing* the certification on her own, she was acting as the complaining witness, which any nonlawyer was qualified to do, and which police officers routinely do. Therefore, in executing the certification, she wasn't immune from prosecution (131).

YOU DECIDE
Is It Time to End Absolute Immunity for Prosecutors?

While certainly the vast majority of prosecutors are ethical lawyers engaged in vital public service, the undeniable fact is that many innocent people have been wrongly convicted of crimes as a result of prosecutorial misconduct. Prosecutors are rarely disciplined or criminally prosecuted for their misconduct, and the victims of this misconduct are generally denied any civil remedy because of prosecutorial immunities.

The policy reasons supporting absolute prosecutorial immunity are untenable. The U.S. Supreme Court has justified absolute prosecutorial immunity on the grounds that the threat of civil liability would undermine vigorous prosecutorial performance, constrain independent decision making, and divert time and resources to defending frivolous litigation. In short, in the Court's view, exposing prosecutors to civil liability would burden and undermine the functioning of the criminal justice system.

But contrary to this policy argument, absolute immunity is not needed to prevent frivolous litigation or to protect the judicial process. Absolute immunity protects the dishonest prosecutor but is unnecessary to protect the honest prosecutor since the requirements for establishing a cause of action and the defense of qualified immunity will protect all but the most incompetent and willful wrongdoers. In short, in all cases qualified immunity for prosecutors would provide sufficient protection to the criminal justice system, while providing a necessary remedy for prosecutorial misconduct.

See Margaret C. Johns, "Reconsidering Absolute Prosecutorial Immunity" (2005) http://lawreview.byu.edu/archives/2005/1/2JOH-FIN.pdf

---

People who sue the government or its officers (even in the most brutal cases) rarely win. Why? According to Allison Patton (1993), there are three major weaknesses to § 1983 suits:

1. They're difficult and expensive to pursue. Most victims of official misconduct are minorities who can't afford to sue, so only a small proportion of police brutality incidents become lawsuits. Victims who can afford to hire a lawyer have to endure a long, tough legal battle, because police departments rarely settle § 1983 suits.

2. The Supreme Court has severely limited plaintiffs' legal capacity to get court orders (injunctions) to stop police techniques, even those that involve frequent use of excessive force.

3. Juries are more likely to believe police officers' version of events than plaintiffs'. Juries don't want to believe that "their police officers are bad people or liars." So plaintiffs rarely win unless they get help from "independent corroborative witnesses or physical evidence" (753–54).

There are other reasons. Anthony Amsterdam (1974), the legendary lawyer for the defense and constitutional law professor, speaking from long personal experience, adds several more:

Where are the lawyers going to come from to handle these cases for the plaintiffs? What on earth would possess a lawyer to file a claim for damages in an ordinary search-and-seizure case? The prospect of a share in the substantial damages to be expected? The chance to earn a reputation as a police-hating lawyer, so that he can no longer count on straight testimony concerning the length of skid marks in his personal injury cases? The gratitude of his client when his filing of the claim causes the prosecutor to refuse a lesser-included offense plea or to charge priors or pile on "cover" charges? The opportunity to represent his client without fee in these resulting criminal matters?

Police cases are an unadulterated investigative and litigate nightmare. Taking on the police in any tribunal involves a commitment to the most frustrating and thankless legal work I know. And the idea that an unrepresented, inarticulate, prosecution-vulnerable citizen can make a case against a team of professional investigators and testifiers in any tribunal begs belief. Even in a tribunal having recognized responsibilities and some resources to conduct independent investigations, a plaintiff without assiduous counsel devoted to developing his side of the case would be utterly outmastered by the police. No, I think we shall have airings of police searches and seizures on suppression motions or not at all. (430)

Furthermore, immunity and the no-affirmative-duty-to-protect rule protect most officials from being sued successfully. Finally, some plaintiffs don't deserve to get damages, because their cases are, in fact, frivolous (Slobogin 1998, 561).

ADMINISTRATIVE REMEDIES

LO **10** Until now, we've dealt with court cases aimed at making police and other public officials accountable for their violations of individuals' constitutional rights, but accountability for official misconduct isn't limited to lawsuits. In fact, the most common accountability procedure for all kinds of police misconduct (not just violations of constitutional rights) is administrative review and discipline outside the courts.

There are two types of administrative review:

1. **Internal affairs units (IAU) review**. Review of police misconduct by special officers inside police departments
2. **External civilian review**. Review of complaints against police officers with participation by individuals who aren't sworn police officers

LO **10** Internal Review

Most large and mid-sized police departments have special internal affairs units (IAUs) that review police misconduct. According to Professor Douglas W. Perez (1994, 88–89), a former deputy sheriff, "most cops do not like internal affairs." They don't trust IAU, and some even think IAU investigators are traitors. Still, most officers believe IAU operations are a necessary evil. For one thing, they're a good defense against external review. As the famed Chicago chief of police O. W. Wilson said, "It is clearly apparent that if the police do not take a vigorous stand on the matter of internal investigation, outside groups—such as review boards consisting of laymen and other persons outside the police service—will step into the void" (Griswold 1994, 215–21).

Internal review consists of four consecutive stages:

1. Intake
2. Investigation
3. Deliberation
4. Disposition

The Internal Affairs Section of the Oakland, California, Police Department is considered an excellent unit, so we'll use it as an example of how internal review proceeds through these four stages.

The department intake policy is "anyone anywhere should accept a complaint if a citizen wishes it taken." The unit is housed inside the police department building. All complaints alleging excessive force, police corruption, and racial discrimination are followed up (Perez 1994, 92–93).

Then, someone besides the intake officer investigates complaints. The investigator gathers evidence, usually interviewing the officer involved last. If officers refuse to cooperate, they're subject to discipline, such as dismissal for refusing to obey an order of the chief.

FIGURE 11.1 Disposition of Excessive Force Complaints

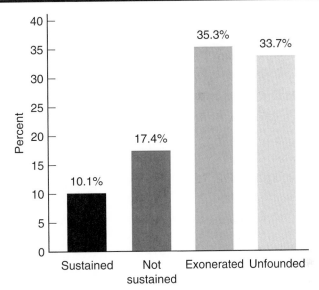

Source: Pate and Fridell 1993, 116.

Completed investigations go to the IAU supervisor. If the supervisor approves, complaints go to the decision-making, or deliberation, stage. Four possible decisions can be made in the deliberation stage (Figure 11.1):

1. *Unfounded*. The investigation proved that the act didn't take place.
2. *Exonerated*. The acts took place, but the investigation proved that they were justified, lawful, and proper.
3. *Not sustained*. The investigation failed to gather enough evidence to prove clearly the allegations in the complaint.
4. *Sustained*. The investigation disclosed enough evidence to prove clearly the allegations in the complaint. (Perez 1994, 96)

If the decision is "unfounded," "exonerated," or "not sustained," the case is disposed of by closing it. If the decision is "sustained," the supervisor recommends disciplinary action. Recommended disciplinary actions ranked from least to most severe include:

1. Reprimand
2. Written reprimand
3. Transfer
4. Retraining
5. Counseling
6. Suspension
7. Demotion
8. Fine
9. Dismissal

FIGURE 11.2 Distribution of Disciplinary Actions

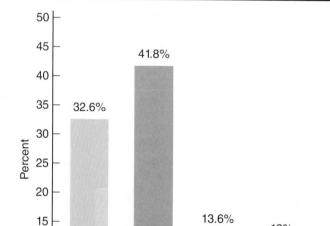

Source: Pate and Fridell 1993, 116.

After the initial disposition, the case goes up the chain of command inside the department until it finally reaches the chief. In about half the cases, there's a discrepancy between the chief's recommendations and those of the immediate supervisor. These discrepancies are important because the immediate supervisor, usually a sergeant of patrol, works on the street with other patrol officers. The supervisors of sergeants usually go along with the recommendations of sergeants. Chiefs of police, on the other hand, are removed from the day-to-day street operations of patrol officers and their immediate supervisors. They have department-wide perspectives and are responsible to "local political elites" for their department's performance. So chiefs may find the disciplinary penalty too light and make it heavier. Figure 11.2 shows the distribution of disciplinary measures taken in a national sample of city police departments.

LO 10　External Review

The basic objection to internal review is that police shouldn't police themselves. To the question, "Who will watch the watchmen?" the answer is, "Not the watchmen!" So external review has grown. In *external review*, individuals who aren't sworn police officers participate in the review of complaints against the police. Usually called "civilian review," it has sparked controversy for nearly half a century.

Police oppose external review because it interferes with their independence. They have no confidence that outsiders know enough about police work to review it. They also know outside scrutiny could pierce the **blue curtain**, the wall of protection that hides their "real" work from public view.

External review became a popular proposal among some liberal reformers and citizen groups during the 1960s. Strong police unions, chiefs who opposed external review, and the creation of internal review procedures (discussed in the last section) successfully prevented it. However, by the early 1990s, 72 percent of the 50 largest cities had created some form of civilian review procedures (Walker and Bumpus 1992, 1, 3–4). Let's look at the types of external review and how well review by civilians has worked.

The types of external review

The differences among civilian review procedures all turn on the point in the process when nonofficers participate. The possible entry points are:

1. The initial investigation to collect the facts
2. The review of the investigation reports
3. The recommendation for disposition to the chief
4. The review of decisions made by the chief

Civilian review boards only have the authority to recommend disciplinary action to police chiefs, because under civil service laws only police chiefs can decide disciplinary action against police officers (Walker and Bumpus 1992, 3–4).

The effectiveness of civilian review

Does civilian review work? The answer depends on the definition and the measures of effectiveness. "Effectiveness" can mean at least four things, all of which are important in determining the value of civilian review procedures:

1. Maintaining effective control of police misconduct
2. Providing resolutions to complaints that satisfy individual complainants
3. Preserving public confidence in the police
4. Influencing police management by providing "feedback from consumers" (Walker and Bumpus 1992, 8)

It's difficult to measure the effectiveness of civilian review because official data are ambiguous. Take the number of complaints, for example. A large number of complaints might mean a large volume of police misconduct, but it can also indicate confidence in the review procedures. Following the Rodney King incident in Los Angeles, observers noted that San Francisco, a city known for its strong review procedures, received more complaints than the much larger city of Los Angeles.

In Los Angeles, the Independent Commission heard a number of citizen complaints that the LAPD created "significant hurdles" to filing complaints, that they were afraid of the process, and that the complaint process was "unnecessarily difficult or impossible." Further, the ACLU collected evidence suggesting that the LAPD "actively discouraged the filing of complaints." The beating of Rodney King, in fact, would never have come to public attention without the video, according to the Independent Commission. This is because, according to the commission, the efforts of Rodney King's brother Paul to file a complaint following the beating were "frustrated" by the LAPD (Pate and Fridell 1993, 39).

The numbers and rates of complaints are also difficult to assess because we don't know the numbers of incidents where people don't file complaints. In one national survey, of all the people who said the police mistreated them, only 30 percent said they filed complaints. One thing, however, is clear. Misconduct isn't distributed evenly among individuals and neighborhoods. In one survey, only 40 percent of the addresses in one city had any contact with the police in a year. Most contacts between private individuals and the police occur in poor neighborhoods. In New York City, the rate of complaints ranges from 1 to 5 for every 10,000 people, depending on the neighborhood.

Official data have consistently indicated racial minority males are represented disproportionately among complainants. So the perception of a pattern of police harassment is a major factor in conflict between the police and racial minority communities (Walker and Bumpus 1992, 10).

Whatever the ambiguity of numbers and rates in the official statistics, observers have noted civilian review procedures rarely sustain complaints. Furthermore, the rates of complaints sustained in civilian review are about the same as the rates in internal affairs units (Walker and Bumpus 1992, 16–17).

CHAPTER SUMMARY

LO 1 Most police misconduct can also be a crime. For police officers to be charged with crimes, however, the prosecution must prove criminal intent. Officers who honestly believe they are enforcing the law are usually protected.

LO 2 Victims of government violations of individuals' constitutional rights can sue for damages only by becoming plaintiffs in a civil action. Civil actions against the federal government and its officers; local, county, and state officers, law enforcement agencies, and government units; and other government employees are controlled by different statutes, court decisions, and government units.

LO 3 Lawsuits against federal officers were first accepted by the court in 1971 and are called constitutional tort (*Bivens*) actions. Lawsuits against the federal government for its officers' constitutional torts are called Federal Tort Claims Act actions.

LO 4 Civil Rights Act actions are lawsuits against individuals in state and local law enforcement for violating someone's constitutional rights. Civil Rights Act actions have two main limits: (1) plaintiffs can only recover damages for deliberate actions, not accidents or negligence, and (2) state and local officers are protected by qualified immunity.

LO 5 Not all states allow citizens to bring suits against them for the constitutional violations of their officers. These states give vicarious official immunity to officers and other law enforcement officials.

LO 6 Courts impose on officers no constitutional duty to protect and plaintiffs can't sue officers when they fail to prevent other individuals from committing crimes against them or violating their rights.

LO 7, 8 There are two main exceptions to the no-duty-to-protect rule. The special-relationship exception is based on the special relationship that exists between the government and persons in its custody, and the state has a duty to protect them and prevent other prisoners from injuring them or violating their rights. That special relationship is custody. The state-created danger exception holds the government responsible for protecting people from dangers that the state contributed to. Few cases survive the rigorous screening process of the state-created-danger exception.

LO **9**   Judges can't be sued for misconduct because they're protected by a special status of absolute immunity, and prosecutors can hardly ever be sued because they enjoy functional immunity whenever they act as advocates.

LO **10**   Administrative remedies discipline public officials to remedy misconduct. Review of official conduct may be internal to the police department, or it may be conducted externally by civilians. Few complaints are sustained through internal or civilian review units.

REVIEW QUESTIONS

1. How likely is it that police officers will be charged and convicted of criminal conduct? Why?

2. Summarize the *Bivens v. Six Unnamed FBI Agents* case, and explain its significance.

3. Describe the qualified immunity defense, and explain why the test is so easy for officers to pass.

4. What specific remedy does the Federal Tort Claims Act (FTCA) provide plaintiffs, and why is it attractive to plaintiffs?

5. Identify and describe the differences between two kinds of state civil lawsuits against individual state officers.

6. Describe the balance that has to be struck in state cases against state officers.

7. Identify two elements plaintiffs in § 1983 actions against state and local law enforcement officers have to prove.

8. Identify and describe two limits the U.S. Supreme Court placed on § 1983 actions against state and local officers.

9. Describe the extent and limits of state tort actions against state and local governments.

10. Identify the elements in the balancing test used to decide whether to grant the defense of vicarious official immunity.

11. According to the U.S. Supreme Court in *Monell v. New York City Department of Social Services*, what two elements do plaintiffs have to prove to succeed in suing local government units?

12. According to the U.S. Supreme Court, what (if any) constitutional duty do law enforcement officers have to protect private individuals from each other?

13. Identify and explain the three elements in the state-created-danger exception to the no-affirmative-duty-to-protect rule.

14. Can you sue a judge for damages? A prosecutor? Explain.

15. Identify and explain the reasons for the hurdles plaintiffs have to overcome when they sue officers and the governments in charge of them.

16. Identify and briefly describe the two types of administrative remedies against police misconduct.

17. Identify and describe the stages, possible dispositions, and disciplinary actions in internal review procedures.

18. Identify the basic objection to internal review. How is external review supposed to overcome the objection?

19. Identify three reasons why police oppose civilian review.

20. How effective is civilian review? Explain.

KEY TERMS

criminal law, p. 414
civil law, p. 414
internal and external departmental
    review, p. 414
tort action, p. 415
damages, p. 415
civil action, p. 415
constitutional tort (*Bivens*) actions,
    p. 415
Federal Tort Claims Act (FTCA)
    actions, p. 415
qualified immunity, p. 416

objective legal reasonableness, p. 416
doctrine of sovereign immunity,
    p. 419
torts, p. 419
defense of official immunity, p. 419
Civil Rights Act (§ 1983) actions,
    p. 420
doctrine of *respondeat superior*, p. 421
defense of vicarious official
    immunity, p. 421
no-affirmative-duty-to-protect rule,
    p. 422

special-relationship exception,
    p. 423
state-created-danger exception,
    p. 424
tort feasor, p. 435
absolute immunity, p. 436
functional immunity, p. 436
qualified immunity, p. 436
internal affairs units (IAU)
    review, p. 440
external civilian review, p. 440
blue curtain, p. 442

12

Court Proceedings I

Before Trial

LEARNING OBJECTIVES

1 Understand the prosecutor's decision to charge and its significant role in criminal procedure.

2 Understand the objective basis requirements to detain a suspect and to go to trial. Know the difference between criminal complaints, first appearances, and arraignments.

3 Know the various forms of pretrial release. Appreciate the need to balance the right of defendants to be free until proven guilty against keeping the community safe and bringing criminals to justice.

4 Understand that there's no constitutional right to bail; only a right against excessive bail.

5 Understand the purpose of preventive detention hearings.

6 Know the types of defense counsel; understand the scope and limits of the right to counsel; and appreciate the differences between the rights of those who can afford lawyers and those who can't.

7 Understand preliminary hearings and grand jury reviews and how they differ from trials.

8 Know the meaning of double jeopardy and its effect on criminal procedure.

9 Understand and appreciate the importance of pretrial motions and why counsel devote so much time to preparing them. Pretrial motions may include arguments to prove double jeopardy and requests for a speedy trial, a change of venue, and the suppression of evidence.

James Scanlon was discovered dead in a bar he ran in Allentown, Pennsylvania, his body having been stabbed repeatedly and set on fire. Ronald Rompilla was indicted for the murder and related offenses, and the Commonwealth gave notice of intent to ask for the death penalty. Two public defenders were assigned to the case. The jury at the guilt phase of trial found Rompilla guilty on all counts, and during the ensuing penalty phase, the prosecutor sought to prove three aggravating factors to justify a death sentence: that the murder was committed in the course of another felony; that the murder was committed by torture; and that Rompilla had a significant history of felony convictions indicating the use or threat of violence.

The Commonwealth presented evidence on all three aggravators, and the jury found all proven. Rompilla's evidence in mitigation consisted of relatively brief testimony: five of his family members argued in effect for residual doubt, and beseeched the jury for mercy, saying that they believed Rompilla was innocent and a good man. Rompilla's 14-year-old son testified that he loved his father and would visit him in prison. The jury acknowledged this evidence to the point of finding, as two factors in mitigation, that Rompilla's son had testified on his behalf and that rehabilitation was possible. But the jurors assigned the greater weight to the aggravating factors, and sentenced Rompilla to death.

The Supreme Court of Pennsylvania affirmed both conviction and sentence. Rompilla appealed, claiming he had been denied "effective" counsel.

—*Rompilla v. Beard* (2005)

After arrest, interrogation, and identification procedures, the action moves first from the police station to prosecutors' and defense attorneys' offices and then to the courts. In the interval between arrest and the first time defendants appear in court, both the police and the prosecutor have to make critical decisions.

First, the police decide if the case should go forward or be dropped. Police take the strong cases they want prosecuted to the prosecutor's office. Prosecutors then make their own judgments about how to dispose of these cases. If they decide to prosecute, they start formal court proceedings by filing a complaint, information, or indictment.

All three proceedings have a single goal: to test the objective basis for the decision to charge. In these proceedings, either judges or grand juries consider the evidence the government has collected to prove its case. If the government has enough evidence, defendants have to appear and answer the criminal charges against them (called *arraignment*).

The decision to start criminal court proceedings is not just a technicality. According to the U.S. Supreme Court in *Kirby v. Illinois* (1972):

> The initiation of judicial criminal proceedings is far from a mere formalism. It is the starting point of our whole system of adversary criminal justice. For it is only then that the Government has committed itself to prosecute, and only then that the adverse positions of Government and defendant have solidified. It is then that a defendant finds himself faced with the prosecutorial forces of organized society, and immersed in the intricacies of substantive and procedural criminal law. It is this point, therefore, that marks the commencement of the "criminal prosecutions." (689)

In this chapter, we'll look at (1) the decision to charge; (2) the rules regulating probable cause to detain; (3) what happens during defendants' first appearance in court after being charged; (4) bail and pretrial detention; (5) the right to counsel; (6) testing the government's case in grand jury and preliminary hearings; (7) bringing defendants to court to hear and answer the charges against them (arraignment); and (8) pretrial motions: double jeopardy, a speedy trial, a change of venue, and the suppression of illegally obtained evidence.

THE DECISION TO CHARGE

LO 1 Once the police bring a case to the prosecutor, lawyers take over the management of the criminal process. Although the police fade into the background, they don't disappear. Lawyers need them to clarify, investigate further, and perhaps testify in court. Prosecutors are likely to take at face value the recommendations from officers with a reputation for establishing "good" cases. They're just as likely to discount cases from officers with poor track records.

Prosecutors drop some cases without further action. If they don't think they can prove a case, they drop it and release the suspect outright. Even if they think they can prove their case, prosecutors don't automatically charge suspects. Why? Because of the dual role of prosecutors in our criminal justice system. They represent the public in prosecuting criminal cases, but they're also **officers of the court**. In that capacity, their mission is to "do justice"—and doing justice doesn't always mean charging and prosecuting suspects.

A good example is *People v. Camargo* (1986). Mike Camargo was charged with the criminal sale and possession of cocaine. By the time he was indicted, Camargo was in an advanced stage of AIDS and related complicating illnesses. The virus had invaded his brain and his stomach, and peripheral nerve damage caused him pain and suffering to the extent that doctors ordered him to limit his physical exercise to sitting in a chair for one hour a day. His doctors' prognosis was death within three to four months (1004–5).

The government dropped the case, because "it did not appear that the interest of justice would be substantially served by the defendant's continued prosecution under this indictment." According to the court:

> The uncompromising rampage of the multiple disease processes has condemned this defendant to a painful, imminent death. When the rationale for incarceration becomes unjustifiable because of a deadly disease, it becomes imperative to allow the sufferer to live his last days in the best circumstances possible and with dignity and compassion. (1007)

In the interests of justice, prosecutors also can divert suspects into a program for community service, restitution, substance abuse, or family violence treatment. In **diversion cases**, prosecutors agree to drop the case before formal judicial proceedings begin, on the condition that suspects participate in and complete these programs. The number of cases prosecutors decide not to pursue ranges from a few in some jurisdictions to nearly half of all cases in others (Boland and others 1987).

Several factors determine the **decision to charge**; they're detailed in a complaint, information, or indictment filed in formal court proceedings. Most important is the strength of the case against defendants. For example, if prosecutors don't have enough evidence to prosecute—no witnesses or weak witnesses, poor physical evidence, and no confessions or other admissions by suspects—they won't charge.

Witnesses might be neither reliable nor convincing. Witness problems increase if victims know their assailants in violent crimes. In over half of these cases, witnesses and victims refuse to cooperate because they're either afraid or have a change of heart over prosecuting people they know (and often care about). Sometimes, prosecutors can't use evidence because the police seized it illegally (Chapter 10). But contrary to the popular belief that many guilty criminals go unpunished because of the exclusionary rule, fewer than 2 percent of all cases (and practically no violent crime cases) are dropped because of it (Davies 1983, n. 89; Nardulli 1983).

Selective prosecution also plays a role in the decision to charge. Lack of resources makes it impossible to prosecute every case, even when prosecutors have enough evidence and it's in the interests of justice to prosecute. Time and money force prosecutors to set priorities: Suspects guilty of petty thefts go to restitution to allow prosecutions for armed robbery; prosecuting violent sex offenses takes precedence over prostitution; and charging a few well-known tax evaders serves as an example to deter tax evasion. According to some critics, selective prosecution cuts into the legislature's power to make the laws. Others argue that selectively prosecuting only some individuals in a category—for example, "fat cats" or notorious tax evaders—undermines impartial law enforcement.

Consider the following scenarios. Which (if any) of the following suspects should a prosecutor selectively charge?

1. A student stole a cassette recorder to record his criminal procedure class because the professor talks too fast. He works part time to pay for school, and although he could've paid for the recorder, it would've been difficult. He has never been in trouble with the law before and says he'll pay for the recorder.

2. A woman who works only occasionally stole a cordless phone for a friend who agreed to pay $35, half the phone's value. The woman has taken compact discs, tape cassettes, and an answering machine from the same store within the past six months.

3. A 50-year-old woman slipped a pair of stereo earphones into her purse. The woman is wealthy and indignantly denied that she intended to steal the earphones. She told the detective she put the device in her bag because she wanted to pick up some film, batteries, and other small items and simply forgot she had put it there.

Review your decisions after completing this chapter.

Despite criticisms of the extent of prosecutorial power, U.S. Supreme Court Justice Robert Jackson's words in 1940 are still true: The prosecutor's power to charge gives her "more control over life, liberty, and reputation than any other person in America" (3). So except for violating due process by vindictively prosecuting individuals or violating equal protection by selectively prosecuting members of groups (Chapter 2)—violations rarely charged and hardly ever successfully proved—the prosecutor's discretionary power to charge is practically unlimited.

PROBABLE CAUSE TO DETAIN SUSPECTS

 Both the U.S. Constitution and state laws command that when four urgent conditions combine, independent magistrates (not police officers whose zeal to root out crime might color their objectivity) have to decide, and decide *soon*, whether there's probable cause to back up the possibility of this severe deprivation of liberty:

1. Defendants are arrested without warrants.

2. They have no lawyers because they're too poor to hire one.

3. They haven't been charged with any crime.

4. They're locked up in jail.

Of course, protecting public safety requires that police possess the power to arrest suspects before a judge has decided there was probable cause to arrest them. Otherwise, suspects who turn out to be criminals might escape, commit further crimes, and/or destroy evidence. But once suspects are in jail, these dangers evaporate. Now, the guarantees of due process and protection of innocent people take over.

In *County of Riverside v. McLaughlin* (1991), the U.S. Supreme Court spoke about "reconciling these competing interests" of public safety and individual rights:

> On the one hand, States have a strong interest in protecting public safety by taking into custody those persons who are reasonably suspected of having engaged in criminal activity, even where there has been no opportunity for a prior judicial determination of probable cause. On the other hand, prolonged detention based on incorrect or unfounded suspicion may unjustly "imperil a suspect's job, interrupt his source of income, and impair his family relationships." We sought to balance these competing concerns by holding that States "must provide a fair and reliable determination of probable cause as a condition for any significant pretrial restraint of liberty, and this determination must be made by a judicial officer either before or promptly after arrest." (52)

Before we go on, let's clear up something that might confuse you—there are two kinds of probable cause. **Probable cause to detain a suspect** is decided at a court proceeding called the **first appearance** (sometimes the "probable cause hearing"). **Probable cause to go to trial** is decided in preliminary hearings or grand jury proceedings. The key difference between them is that probable cause to *detain* (Chapter 5) requires fewer facts than probable cause to *go to trial*.

In *Gerstein v. Pugh* (1975), the U.S. Supreme Court decided that the Fourth Amendment ban on "unreasonable seizure" demands that suspects locked up in jail be taken "promptly" to a magistrate to decide whether there are enough facts to back up the detention. How "prompt" is fast enough to satisfy the Fourth Amendment? Lower federal courts and state courts for a long time said that the Fourth Amendment gives the police enough time to complete the "administrative steps incident to arrest." This usually means the police can do all of the following before they take suspects to court (*Sanders v. City of Houston* 1982, 700):

1. Complete paperwork
2. Search the suspect
3. Conduct an inventory search
4. Inventory property found
5. Fingerprint the suspect
6. Photograph the suspect
7. Check for a possible prior criminal record
8. Test laboratory samples
9. Interrogate the suspect
10. Check an alibi
11. Conduct a lineup
12. Compare the crime with similar crimes

Some jurisdictions get more specific; they spell out exactly how much time the police get to finish the administrative steps. Depending on the jurisdiction, times range from 24 to 36 hours (Brandes 1989). The U.S. Supreme Court prescribed a flexible definition of "promptly" in *County of Riverside v. McLaughlin* (1991), our next case excerpt.

In *County of Riverside v. McLaughlin* (**1991**), the U.S. Supreme Court provided guidelines for how long jurisdictions can hold suspects before proving they have probable cause to detain them.

CASE

Was Judicial Determination of Probable Cause "Prompt"?

County of Riverside v. McLaughlin
500 U.S. 44 (1991)

HISTORY

Donald Lee McLaughlin and others brought a **class action** (an action in which one person or a small group of people represents the interests of a larger group) under 42 U.S.C. § 1983, challenging how the County of Riverside, California, handles probable cause determinations for individuals arrested without a warrant. The U.S. District Court granted a preliminary injunction.

(continued)

The Ninth Circuit U.S. Court of Appeals affirmed. The U.S. Supreme Court granted certiorari, vacated the judgment of the Court of Appeals, and remanded the case.

—O'CONNOR, J., joined by REHNQUIST, C.J., and WHITE, KENNEDY, and SOUTER, JJ.

FACTS

In August 1987, Donald Lee McLaughlin filed a complaint in the U.S. District Court for the Central District of California. The complaint alleged that McLaughlin was then currently incarcerated in the Riverside County Jail and had not received a probable cause determination. He requested "an order and judgment requiring that the defendants and the County of Riverside provide in-custody arrestees, arrested without warrants, prompt probable cause, bail and arraignment hearings." A second complaint named three additional plaintiffs—Johnny E. James, Diana Ray Simon, and Michael Scott Hyde. . . . The complaint alleged that each of the named plaintiffs had been arrested without a warrant, had received neither prompt probable cause nor bail hearings, and was still in custody.

In March 1989, plaintiffs asked the District Court to issue a preliminary injunction requiring the County to provide all persons arrested without a warrant a judicial determination of probable cause within 36 hours of arrest. The District Court issued the injunction, holding that the County's existing practice violated this Court's decision in *Gerstein*. Without discussion, the District Court adopted a rule that the County provide probable cause determinations within 36 hours of arrest, except in exigent circumstances.

The court "retained jurisdiction indefinitely" to ensure that the County established new procedures that complied with the injunction. The U.S. Court of Appeals for the Ninth Circuit consolidated this case with another challenging an identical preliminary injunction issued against the County of San Bernardino. On November 8, 1989, the Court of Appeals affirmed the order granting the preliminary injunction against Riverside County.

The Court of Appeals determined that the County's policy of providing probable cause determinations at arraignment within 48 hours was "not in accord with *Gerstein*'s requirement of a determination 'promptly after arrest'" because no more than 36 hours were needed "to complete the administrative steps incident to arrest." The Ninth Circuit thus joined the Fourth and Seventh Circuits in interpreting *Gerstein* as requiring a probable cause determination immediately following completion of the administrative procedures incident to arrest. By contrast, the Second Circuit understands *Gerstein* to "stress the need for flexibility" and to permit States to combine probable cause determinations with other pretrial proceedings. We granted certiorari to resolve this conflict among the Circuits as to what constitutes a "prompt" probable cause determination under *Gerstein*.

OPINION

In *Gerstein v. Pugh* (1975), this Court held unconstitutional Florida procedures under which persons arrested without a warrant could remain in police custody for 30 days or more without a judicial determination of probable cause. In reaching this conclusion we attempted to reconcile important competing interests. On the one hand, States have a strong interest in protecting public safety by taking into custody those persons who are reasonably suspected of having engaged in criminal activity, even where there has been no opportunity for a prior judicial determination of probable cause.

On the other hand, prolonged detention based on incorrect or unfounded suspicion may unjustly "imperil a suspect's job, interrupt his source of income, and impair his family relationships." We sought to balance these competing concerns by holding that States "must provide a fair and reliable determination of probable cause as a condition for any significant pretrial restraint of liberty, and this determination must be made by a judicial officer either before or promptly after arrest." The Court thus established a "practical compromise" between the rights of individuals and the realities of law enforcement. We left it to the individual States to integrate prompt probable cause determinations into their differing systems of pretrial procedures.

Inherent in *Gerstein's* invitation to the States to experiment and adapt was the recognition that the Fourth Amendment does not compel an immediate determination of probable cause upon completing the administrative steps incident to arrest. Plainly, if a probable cause hearing is constitutionally compelled the moment a suspect is finished being "booked," there is no room whatsoever for "flexibility and experimentation by the States."

Incorporating probable cause determinations "into the procedure for setting bail or fixing other conditions of pretrial release"—which *Gerstein* explicitly contemplated—would be impossible. Waiting even a few hours so that a bail hearing or arraignment could take place at the same time as the probable cause determination would amount to a constitutional violation. Clearly, *Gerstein* is not that inflexible.

But flexibility has its limits; *Gerstein* is not a blank check. A State has no legitimate interest in detaining for extended periods individuals who have been arrested without probable cause. The Court recognized in *Gerstein* that a person arrested without a warrant is entitled to a fair and reliable determination of probable cause and that this determination must be made promptly. Unfortunately, as lower court decisions applying *Gerstein* have demonstrated, it is not enough to say that probable cause determinations must be "prompt." This vague standard simply has not provided sufficient guidance. Instead, it has led to a flurry of systemic challenges to city and county practices, putting federal judges in the role of making legislative judgments and overseeing local jail house operations.

Our task in this case is to articulate more clearly the boundaries of what is permissible under the Fourth Amendment. Although we hesitate to announce that the Constitution compels a specific time limit, it is important to provide some degree of certainty so that States and counties may establish procedures with confidence that they fall within constitutional bounds. Taking into account the competing interests articulated in *Gerstein*, we believe that a jurisdiction that provides judicial determinations of probable cause within 48 hours of arrest will, as a general matter, comply with the promptness requirement of *Gerstein*. For this reason, such jurisdictions will be immune from systemic challenges.

This is not to say that the probable cause determination in a particular case passes constitutional muster simply because it is provided within 48 hours. Such a hearing may nonetheless violate *Gerstein* if the arrested individual can prove that his or her probable cause determination was delayed unreasonably. Examples of unreasonable delay are delays for the purpose of gathering additional evidence to justify the arrest, a delay motivated by ill will against the arrested individual, or delay for delay's sake. In evaluating whether the delay in a particular case is unreasonable, however, courts must allow a substantial degree of flexibility. Courts cannot ignore the often unavoidable delays in transporting arrested persons from one facility to another, handling late-night bookings where no magistrate is readily available, obtaining the presence of an arresting officer who may be busy processing other suspects or securing the premises of an arrest, and other practical realities.

Where an arrested individual does not receive a probable cause determination within 48 hours, the calculus changes. In such a case, the arrested individual does not bear the burden of proving an unreasonable delay. Rather, the burden shifts to the government to demonstrate the existence of a bona fide emergency or other extraordinary circumstance. The fact that in a particular case it may take longer than 48 hours to consolidate pretrial proceedings does not qualify as an extraordinary circumstance. Nor, for that matter, do intervening weekends. A jurisdiction that chooses to offer combined proceedings must do so as soon as is reasonably feasible, but in no event later than 48 hours after arrest.

We conclude that Riverside County is entitled to combine probable cause determinations with arraignments. The record indicates, however, that the County's current policy and practice do not comport fully with the principles we have outlined. The County's current policy is to offer combined proceedings within two days, exclusive of Saturdays, Sundays, or holidays. As a result, persons arrested on Thursdays may have to wait until the following Monday before they receive a probable cause determination. The delay is even longer if there is an intervening holiday. Thus, the County's regular practice exceeds the 48-hour period we deem constitutionally permissible, meaning that the County is not immune from systemic challenges, such as this class action.

As to arrests that occur early in the week, the County's practice is that "arraignments usually take place on the last day" possible. There may well be legitimate reasons for this practice; alternatively, this may constitute delay for delay's sake. We leave it to the Court of Appeals and the District Court, on remand, to make this determination.

The judgment of the Court of Appeals is vacated and the case is REMANDED for further proceedings consistent with this opinion.

DISSENT

SCALIA, J.

"The Fourth Amendment requires a judicial determination of probable cause as a prerequisite to extended restraint of liberty, either before or promptly after arrest. Determining the outer boundary of reasonableness is an objective and manageable task. The data available are enough to convince me, that certainly no more than 24 hours is needed.

A few weeks before issuance of today's opinion, there appeared in *The Washington Post* the story of protracted litigation arising from the arrest of a student who entered a restaurant in Charlottesville, Virginia, one evening to look for some friends. Failing to find them, he tried to leave—but refused to pay a $5 fee (required by the restaurant's posted rules) for failing to return a red tab he had been issued to keep track of his orders. According to the story, he "was taken by police to the Charlottesville jail" at the restaurant's request. "There, a magistrate refused to issue an arrest warrant," and he was released.

That is how it used to be; but not, according to today's decision, how it must be in the future. If the Fourth Amendment meant then what the Court says it does now, the student could lawfully have been held for as long as it would have taken to arrange for his arraignment, up to a maximum of 48 hours.

Justice Story wrote that the Fourth Amendment "is little more than the affirmance of a great constitutional doctrine of the common law." It should not become less than that. One hears the complaint, nowadays, that the Fourth Amendment has become constitutional law for the guilty; that it benefits the career criminal (through the exclusionary rule) often and directly, but the ordinary citizen remotely if at all.

By failing to protect the innocent arrestee, today's opinion reinforces that view. The common law rule of prompt hearing had as its primary beneficiaries the innocent—not those whose fully justified convictions must be overturned to scold the police; nor those who avoid conviction because the evidence, while convincing,

(continued)

does not establish guilt beyond a reasonable doubt; but those so blameless that there was not even good reason to arrest them. While in recent years we have invented novel applications of the Fourth Amendment to release the unquestionably guilty, we today repudiate one of its core applications so that the presumptively innocent may be left in jail.

Hereafter, a law-abiding citizen wrongfully arrested may be compelled to await the grace of a Dickensian bureaucratic machine, as it churns its cycle for up to two days—never once given the opportunity to show a judge that there is absolutely no reason to hold him, that a mistake has been made. In my view, this is the image of a system of justice that has lost its ancient sense of priority, a system that few Americans would recognize as our own.

Questions

1. What reasons does the Court give for deciding that under ordinary circumstances, 48 hours is a reasonable time to satisfy the Fourth Amendment interest in providing a prompt determination of probable cause?

2. What interests did the Court balance in making its decision?

3. What administrative steps and specific circumstances did the Court consider in balancing these interests?

4. What does the history of the common law have to do with a decision made in 1991?

5. What rule would you adopt? Why?

THE FIRST APPEARANCE

The **criminal complaint** (the document that formally charges defendants with specific crimes) authorizes magistrates to conduct the first appearance. Magistrates complete four tasks at the first appearance:

1. Inform defendants of the charges against them
2. Inform defendants of their constitutional rights
3. Set bail or detain suspects
4. Appoint attorneys for indigent defendants

Felony defendants rarely enter a plea at their first appearance; they wait until their *arraignment* (a proceeding that orders defendants to come to court and plead to the charges against them). Misdemeanor defendants usually plead (almost always guilty) at their first appearance, especially if the penalty is a small fine. When suspects—now called "defendants"—first appear in court, magistrates tell them the charges against them. If defendants don't have a lawyer present, the court gives them copies of the complaint, the police report, and other papers supporting the complaint. The court also informs defendants of their constitutional rights.

Informing defendants of their constitutional rights follows this typical court rule in the Minnesota Rules of Criminal Procedure (2006, Rule 5.01):

The judge, judicial officer, or other duly authorized personnel shall advise the defendant substantially as follows:

a. That the defendant is not required to say anything or submit to interrogation and that anything the defendant says may be used against the defendant in this or any subsequent proceeding;

b. That the defendant has a right to counsel in all subsequent proceedings, including police lineups and interrogations, and if the defendant appears without counsel and is financially unable to afford counsel, that counsel will forthwith be appointed without cost to the defendant charged with an offense punishable upon conviction by incarceration;

c. That the defendant has a right to communicate with defense counsel and that a continuance will be granted if necessary to enable defendant to obtain or speak to counsel;

d. That the defendant has a right to a jury trial or a trial to the court;

e. That if the offense is a misdemeanor, the defendant may either plead guilty or not guilty, or demand a complaint prior to entering a plea;

f. That if the offense is a designated gross misdemeanor as defined in Rule 1.04(b) and a complaint has not yet been made and filed, a complaint must be issued within 10 days if the defendant is not in custody or within 48 hours if the defendant is in custody.

The judge, judicial officer, or other duly authorized personnel may advise a number of defendants at once of these rights, but each defendant shall be asked individually before arraignment whether the defendant heard and understood these rights as explained earlier.

BAIL AND PRETRIAL DETENTION

LO **3**

Nearly three-quarters of a million people are locked up in jail before they're convicted or released. Jail populations were declining from record highs in 2002 until 2010, when they'd fallen to less than 100,000. (See Figure 12.1 to view this trend.)

FIGURE 12.1 Inmates Confined in Local Jails at Midyear and Percent Change in the Jail Population, 2000–2012

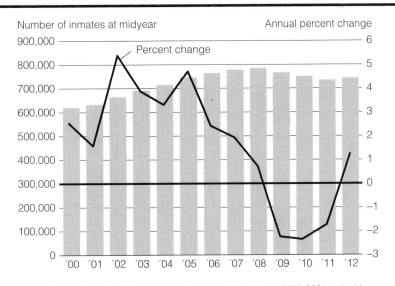

Source: Bureau of Justice Statistics, Annual Survey of Jails, midyear 2000–2004 and midyear 2006–2012, and the Census of Jail Inmates, midyear 2005.

Most defendants (in some places more than 90 percent) are released on bail while they wait for trial or the results of a plea bargain (see Chapter 13). Still, locking up even 10 percent of defendants adds to the never-ending problem of crowded jails.

For these defendants detained before trial or guilty plea, their stay in jail can last quite a while (more than 30 days for 33 percent of detainees; more than 90 days for 20 percent). You should be aware of another fact: Detention costs money. It's tough to find recent national amounts, but, just as an example, in 2012, it cost $65 a day to maintain one jail inmate in Randall County, Texas (Amarillo is its largest city) (Douglas 2012). About 20 percent of defendants charged with petty offenses are released without even appearing before judges. They receive a citation release (similar to a traffic ticket), or they're released after posting bond according to bail schedules that list amounts for specific offenses (Toborg 1981).

Judges can attach a variety of conditions to release. Sometimes, defendants are **released on recognizance (ROR)**—their promise to appear in court on their court date. Some judges release defendants on the condition that they either report at scheduled times to a pretrial release program or promise not to leave town before their trial. Sometimes, judges impose supervised release—for example, requiring defendants to report to relatives or their local police department; to participate in a treatment program for illegal drugs, alcohol abuse, or mental illness; or to attend employment programs (Toborg 1981).

Money bonds, in which defendants are released as soon as money is put up, come in several forms. With the unsecured bond, defendants have to pay only if they don't appear for their court date. With the court-administered deposit bond, defendants have to post 10 percent of the amount of the bond; if they appear, the court returns their deposit. Under privately administered bail bonds, bail bondsmen (most are men) or bondswomen charge 10 percent of the amount of the bond they turn over to the courts. Defendants forfeit the 10 percent fee even if they appear (Feeley 1979; also see Chapter 2).

Being locked up before trial is a major loss of freedom, but it's more than that. Temporary loss of wages and even permanent loss of a job, separation from family and friends, restrictions on aiding in their own defense, and loss of reputation are also possible consequences for detained defendants. And all of these take place before defendants are convicted.

But pretrial release can also be a risk to society. Defendants on bail can escape the jurisdiction of the court by fleeing; commit new crimes; and expose the community to anxiety, fear, and outrage over the threats to public safety. Clearly, the decision of whether to release or detain defendants before they're found guilty demands that courts strike the right balance between the right of defendants to be free until they're proved guilty and the need of the community to feel safe from crime and bring criminals to justice.

Striking that balance boils down to two issues:

1. What are the constitutional rights of bailed and detained defendants?
2. What are the legitimate community interests in bailed and detained defendants?

To examine these issues, we'll look at bail and the Constitution; whether preventive detention denies suspects their constitutional rights; and the rights defendants retain during pretrial detention.

LO 4   Bail and the Constitution

There's no absolute constitutional right to bail, only a right against *excessive* bail. The Eighth Amendment to the U.S. Constitution provides that "Excessive bail shall not be required," but the word "excessive" is subject to interpretation. So legislatures and courts are left to spell out the precise constitutional limit. In a controversial case from the Cold War era, *Stack v. Boyle* (1951), U.S. Chief Justice Fred M. Vinson wrote for the majority:

> From the passage of the Judiciary Act of 1789, to the present, federal law has unequivocally provided that a person arrested for a non-capital offense shall be admitted to bail. This traditional right to freedom permits the unhampered preparation of a defense, and serves to prevent the infliction of punishment prior to conviction. Unless this right to bail before trial is preserved, the presumption of innocence, secured only after centuries of struggle, would lose its meaning. (4)

In *Stack v. Boyle*, 12 people were charged with conspiring to violate the Smith Act, which made it a crime to advocate the violent overthrow of the government. The case arose at the height of the Cold War, when anticommunism and fear of radicalism gripped the nation. The trial court fixed bail at $50,000 apiece. The U.S. Supreme Court ruled that amounts that are more than necessary to ensure that petitioners come to court for their trials are "excessive." The Court held that magistrates have to calculate how much money it will take to guarantee that defendants will appear.

Naturally, the amount will vary according to the circumstances of each case, but the main concerns include:

1. The seriousness of the offense
2. The amount of evidence against the defendant
3. The defendant's family ties, employment, financial resources, character, and mental condition
4. The length of the defendant's residence in the community
5. The defendant's criminal history
6. The defendant's prior record for appearing and/or "jumping" bail

Sometimes, no amount of money is enough to guarantee that rich defendants will come to court. In *U.S. v. Abrahams* (1978), Herbert Abrahams had three previous convictions; was an escaped prisoner from another state; had given false information at a prior bail hearing; had failed to appear on a former bail of $100,000; had failed to appear on a previous charge in California from which he was a fugitive; had several aliases; and had recently transferred $1.5 million to Bermuda! The U.S. First Circuit Court of Appeals upheld the U.S. District Court's conclusion that no condition "or any combination will reasonably assure the appearance of defendant for trial if admitted to bail."

At the other extreme (and a lot more common), any amount is too much for poor defendants to pay. Noted bail scholar Professor Caleb Foote (1965) believes our bail system violates the Constitution in three ways when it comes to poor defendants. It denies them:

1. Due process of law, because defendants can't help with their own defense if they're locked up

2. Equal protection of the law, because they're jailed because they're poor

3. The right against excessive bail, because they can't raise any amount required

Pretrial detention is an obstacle to defendants trying to prepare their defense. They can't help investigators find witnesses and physical evidence. Cramped jail quarters and short visiting hours inhibit conferences with their lawyers. Jailing also affects defendants' appearance and demeanor; they can't conceal rumpled clothes and a pale complexion. Free defendants, on the other hand, can help their defense and show the court that they're working and otherwise responsible for themselves and their families.

LO 5 Preventive Detention

Commentators, lawyers, judges, and criminal justice personnel have hotly debated whether the *only* acceptable purpose for bail and pretrial detention is to make sure defendants come to court. Can courts also deny bail and use pretrial detention to lock up "dangerous" defendants? Yes. **Preventive detention** allows judges to deny bail to defendants who might intimidate, hurt, and terrorize victims and witnesses or who might commit new crimes.

To reduce these dangers, the U.S. Congress enacted the **Bail Reform Act of 1984 (BRA)**, which authorizes federal courts to jail arrested defendants when a judge determines, after a hearing, that no condition of release would "reasonably" guarantee the appearance of the defendant and the safety of the community.

At preventive detention hearings, the BRA guarantees defendants' rights:

1. To have an appointed lawyer

2. To testify at the hearing

3. To present evidence

4. To cross-examine witnesses

If the judge decides there's **clear and convincing evidence** (more than probable cause but less than proof beyond a reasonable doubt) that the defendant either won't appear or is a threat to public safety, she can order the defendant to be "preventively detained" (jailed). Preventive detention gives rise to both empirical and constitutional questions. The major empirical question is, Does probable cause to believe a person has committed a crime predict future dangerous behavior? The question is hard to answer because the word "dangerous" is vague, and because behavior, especially violent behavior, is hard to predict (Moore and others 1984, 1).

The constitutional questions are:

1. Does preventive detention violate the Eighth Amendment ban on "cruel and unusual punishment"?

2. Does preventive detention violate the Fifth and Fourteenth Amendments and deny defendants liberty without due process of law?

In *U.S. v. Salerno* (1987), our next case excerpt, the U.S. Supreme Court answered "no" to both questions.

In *U.S. v. Salerno* (1987), the U.S. Supreme Court held that preventive detention didn't deny Anthony Salerno and Vincent Cafaro their due process rights.

CASE

Were Their Pretrial Detentions "Punishment"?

U.S. v. Salerno
481 U.S. 739 (1987)

HISTORY

Anthony Salerno and Vincent Cafaro were committed for pretrial detention pursuant to the Bail Reform Act by the U.S. District Court, Southern District of New York. The U.S. Court of Appeals, Second Circuit, vacated the commitment and remanded the case. On writ of certiorari, the U.S. Supreme Court reversed.

—REHNQUIST, C.J., joined by WHITE, BLACKMUN, POWELL, O'CONNOR, and SCALIA, JJ.

FACTS

Anthony Salerno and Vincent Cafaro were arrested on March 21, 1986, after being charged in a 29-count indictment alleging various Racketeer Influenced and Corrupt Organizations Act (RICO) violations, mail and wire fraud offenses, extortion, and various criminal gambling violations. The RICO counts alleged 35 acts of racketeering activity, including fraud, extortion, gambling, and conspiracy to commit murder. At their arraignment, the Government moved to have Salerno and Cafaro detained pursuant to § 3142(e) of the Bail Reform Act of 1984 on the ground that no condition of release would assure the safety of the community or any person. The District Court held a hearing at which the Government made a detailed proffer (offer) of evidence.

The Government's case showed that Salerno was the "boss" of the Genovese Crime Family of La Cosa Nostra and that Cafaro was a "captain" in the Genovese Family. According to the Government's proffer, based in large part on conversations intercepted by a court-ordered wiretap, the two respondents had participated in wide-ranging conspiracies to aid their illegitimate enterprises through violent means. The Government also offered the testimony of two of its trial witnesses, who would assert that Salerno personally participated in two murder conspiracies. Salerno opposed the motion for detention, challenging the credibility of the Government's witnesses. He offered the testimony of several character witnesses as well as a letter from his doctor stating that he was suffering from a serious medical condition. Cafaro presented no evidence at the hearing, but instead characterized the wiretap conversations as merely "tough talk."

OPINION

The Bail Reform Act of 1984 allows a federal court to detain an arrestee pending trial if the government demonstrates by clear and convincing evidence after an adversary hearing that no release conditions "will reasonably assure the safety of any other person and the community." The United States Court of Appeals for the Second Circuit struck down this provision of the Act as facially unconstitutional, because, in that court's words, this type of pretrial detention violates "substantive due process." We granted certiorari because of a conflict among the Courts of Appeals regarding the validity of the Act. We hold that . . . the Act fully comports with constitutional requirements. We therefore reverse.

Responding to "the alarming problems of crimes committed by persons on release," Congress formulated the Bail Reform Act of 1984. To this end, § 3141(a) of the Act requires a judicial officer to determine whether an arrestee shall be detained. § 3142(e) provides:

> If, after a hearing pursuant to the provisions of subsection (f), the judicial officer finds that no condition or combination of conditions will reasonably assure the appearance of the person as required and the safety of any other person and the community, he shall order the detention of the person prior to trial.

The judicial officer is not given unbridled discretion in making the detention determination. Congress has specified the consideration relevant to that decision. These factors include

1. the nature and seriousness of the charges,
2. the substantiality of the government's evidence against the arrestee,
3. the arrestee's background and characteristics, and
4. the nature and seriousness of the danger posed by the suspect's release.

(continued)

Should a judicial officer order detention, the detainee is entitled to expedited appellate review of the detention order.

Respondents present two grounds for invalidating the Bail Reform Act's provisions permitting pretrial detention on the basis of future dangerousness. They rely upon the Court of Appeals' conclusion that the Act exceeds the limitations placed upon the Federal Government by the Due Process Clause of the Fifth Amendment. They contend that the Act contravenes the Eighth Amendment's proscription against excessive bail. We treat those contentions in turn. Respondents first argue that the Act violates substantive due process because the pretrial detention it authorizes constitutes impermissible punishment before trial. The Government, however, has never argued that pretrial detention could be upheld if it were "punishment."

Pretrial detention under the Bail Reform Act is regulatory, not penal. The government's interest in preventing crime by arrestees is both legitimate and compelling. On the other side of the scale, of course, is the individual's strong interest in liberty. We do not minimize the importance and fundamental nature of this right. But, as our cases hold, this right may, in circumstances where the government's interest is sufficiently weighty, be subordinated to the greater needs of society.

Respondents also contend that the Bail Reform Act violates the Excessive Bail Clause of the Eighth Amendment. We think that the Act survives a challenge founded upon the Eighth Amendment. While we agree that a primary function of bail is to safeguard the courts' role in adjudicating the guilt or innocence of defendants, we reject the proposition that the Eighth Amendment categorically prohibits the government from pursuing other admittedly compelling interests through regulation of pretrial release.

Nothing in the text of the Bail Clause limits permissible government considerations solely to questions of flight. We believe that when Congress has mandated detention on the basis of a compelling interest other than prevention of flight, as it has here, the Eighth Amendment does not require release on bail.

In our society liberty is the norm, and detention prior to trial or without trial is the carefully limited exception. We hold that the provisions for pretrial detention in the Bail Reform Act of 1984 fall within that carefully limited exception. The Act authorizes the detention prior to trial of arrestees charged with serious felonies who are found after an adversary hearing to pose a threat to the safety of individuals or to the community which no condition of release can dispel. We are unwilling to say that this congressional determination, based as it is upon that primary concern of every government—a concern for the safety and indeed the lives of its citizens—on its face violates either the Due Process Clause of the Fifth Amendment or the Excessive Bail Clause of the Eighth Amendment.

The judgment of the Court of Appeals is therefore REVERSED.

DISSENT

MARSHALL, J., joined by BRENNAN, J.

The statute now before us declares that persons who have been indicted may be detained if a judicial officer finds clear and convincing evidence that they pose a danger to individuals or to the community. The conclusion is inescapable that the indictment has been turned into evidence, if not that the defendant is guilty of the crime charged, then that left to his own devices he will soon be guilty of something else. "If it suffices to accuse, what will become of the innocent?"

"It is a fair summary of history to say that the safeguards of liberty have frequently been forged in controversies involving not very nice people." Honoring the presumption of innocence is often difficult; sometimes we must pay substantial social costs as a result of our commitment to the values we espouse. But at the end of the day the presumption of innocence protects the innocent; the shortcuts we take with those whom we believe to be guilty injure only those wrongfully accused and, ultimately, ourselves.

Throughout the world today there are men, women, and children interned indefinitely, awaiting trials which may never come or which may be a mockery of the word, because their governments believe them to be "dangerous." Our Constitution, whose construction began two centuries ago, can shelter us forever from the evils of such unchecked power. Over two hundred years it has slowly, through our efforts, grown more durable, more expansive, and more just. But it cannot protect us if we lack the courage, and the self-restraint, to protect ourselves. Today, a majority of the Court applies itself to an ominous exercise in demolition. Theirs is truly a decision which will go forth without authority, and come back without respect.

Questions

1. In your opinion, is pretrial detention punishment or a "regulatory device"? What criteria do you use to answer this question?

2. What did Chief Justice John Marshall mean when he asked, "If it suffices to accuse, what will become of the innocent?"

3. Does pretrial detention undermine the presumption of innocence?

4. What, in your opinion, is the proper purpose(s) of bail? Defend your answer.

LO 5   Conditions of Pretrial Confinement

Detention prior to trial, whether to secure defendants' appearance or to protect public safety, is still confinement. Jailed defendants aren't free to leave; they're locked up in cells and subject to jail discipline. They also have to follow rules designed to maintain safety and order. But jailed defendants are *legally* innocent; they don't forfeit their constitutional rights just because they're in jail. A jail administrator was asked if surveillance in cells through two-way mirrors (prisoners didn't know they were two-way mirrors) violated the prisoners' right to privacy. The administrator replied, "They have no rights." The administrator was wrong. Jailed defendants do have rights, but they're watered down in jail. That's what the U.S. Supreme Court decided in *Bell v. Wolfish* (1979), our next case excerpt.

In *Bell v. Wolfish* (1979), the U.S. Supreme Court held that jailed defendants awaiting trial have constitutional rights but they're severely limited.

CASE   Were They "Punished" before Conviction?

Bell v. Wolfish
441 U.S. 520 (1979)

HISTORY

Jailed defendants sued in U.S. District Court, Southern District of New York, challenging the constitutionality of numerous conditions of confinement and practices in the Metropolitan Correctional Center, a federally operated, short-term custodial facility for pretrial detainees in New York City. The U.S. District Court enjoined various practices in the facility. The U.S. Court of Appeals, Second Circuit, affirmed. On writ of certiorari, the U.S. Supreme Court reversed.

—REHNQUIST, J., joined by BURGER, C.J., and STEWART, WHITE, and BLACKMUN, JJ.

FACTS

The MCC (Metropolitan Correctional Center) differs markedly from the familiar image of a jail; there are no barred cells, dank, colorless corridors, or clanging steel gates. It was intended to include the most advanced and innovative features of modern design of detention facilities. "It represented the architectural embodiment of the best and most progressive penological planning." The key design element of the 12-story structure is the "modular" or "unit" concept, whereby each floor designed to house inmates has one or two largely self-contained residential units that replace the traditional cellblock jail construction.

Each unit in turn has several clusters or corridors of private rooms or dormitories radiating from a central two-story "multipurpose" or common room, to which each inmate has free access approximately 16 hours a day. Because our analysis does not turn on the particulars of the MCC concept design, we need not discuss them further.

When the MCC opened in August 1975, the planned capacity was 449 inmates, an increase of 50 percent over the former West Street facility. Despite some dormitory accommodations, the MCC was designed primarily to house these inmates in 389 rooms, which originally were intended for single occupancy. While the MCC was under construction, however, the number of persons committed to pretrial detention began to rise at an "unprecedented" rate. The Bureau of Prisons took several steps to accommodate this unexpected flow of persons assigned to the facility, but despite these efforts, the inmate population at the MCC rose above its planned capacity within a short time after its opening.

To provide sleeping space for this increased population, the MCC replaced the single bunks in many of the individual rooms and dormitories with double bunks. Also, each week some newly arrived inmates had to sleep on cots in the common areas until they could be transferred to residential rooms as space became available.

(continued)

On November 28, 1975, less than four months after the MCC had opened, the named respondents initiated this action by filing in the District Court a petition for writ of habeas corpus. The petition served up a veritable potpourri of complaints that implicated virtually every facet of the institution's conditions and practices. Respondents charged they had been deprived of their statutory and constitutional rights because of overcrowded conditions, undue length of confinement, improper searches, inadequate recreational, educational, and employment opportunities, insufficient staff, and objectionable restrictions on the purchase and receipt of personal items and books.

The District Court intervened broadly into almost every facet of the institution and enjoined no fewer than 20 MCC practices on constitutional and statutory grounds. The Court of Appeals affirmed the District Court's constitutional rulings and in the process held that under the Due Process Clause of the Fifth Amendment, pretrial detainees may be subjected to only those restrictions and privations which inhere in their confinement itself or which are justified by compelling necessities of jail administration. We granted certiorari to consider the important constitutional questions raised by these decisions and to resolve an apparent conflict among the Circuits. We now reverse.

OPINION

Not every disability imposed during pretrial detention amounts to "punishment" in the constitutional sense. Once the Government has exercised its conceded authority to detain a person pending trial, it obviously is entitled to employ devices that are calculated to effectuate this detention. Traditionally, this has meant confinement in a facility which, no matter how modern or antiquated, results in restricting the movement of a detainee in a manner in which he would not be restricted if he simply were free to walk the streets pending trial. Whether it be called a jail, a prison, or a custodial center, the purpose of the facility is to detain.

Loss of freedom of choice and privacy are inherent incidents of confinement in such a facility. And the fact that such detention interferes with the detainee's understandable desire to live as comfortably as possible and with as little restraint as possible during confinement does not convert the conditions or restrictions of detention into "punishment." Judged by this analysis, respondents' claim that "double-bunking" violated their due process rights fails. On this record, we are convinced as a matter of law that "double-bunking" as practiced at the MCC did not amount to punishment and did not, therefore, violate respondents' rights under the Due Process Clause of the Fifth Amendment.

Each of the rooms at the MCC that house pretrial detainees has a total floor space of approximately 75 square feet. Each of them designated for "double-bunking" contains a double bunkbed, certain other items of furniture, a wash basin, and an uncovered toilet. Inmates are generally locked into their rooms from 11 p.m. to 6:30 a.m. and for brief periods during the afternoon and evening head counts. During the rest of the day, they may move about freely between their rooms and the common areas. We disagree with both the District Court and the Court of Appeals that there is some sort of "one man, one cell" principle lurking in the Due Process Clause of the Fifth Amendment. While confining a given number of people in a given amount of space in such a manner as to cause them to endure genuine privations and hardships over an extended period of time might raise serious questions under the Due Process Clause as to whether those conditions amounted to punishment, nothing even approaching such hardship is shown by this record.

Detainees are required to spend only seven or eight hours each day in their rooms, during most or all of which they presumably are sleeping. During the remainder of the time, the detainees are free to move between their rooms and the common area. While "double-bunking" may have taxed some of the equipment or particular facilities in certain of the common areas, this does not mean that the conditions at the MCC failed to meet the standards required by the Constitution. Our conclusion in this regard is further buttressed by the detainees' length of stay at the MCC. Nearly all of the detainees are released within 60 days. We simply do not believe that requiring a detainee to share toilet facilities and this admittedly small sleeping space with another person for generally a maximum period of 60 days violates the Constitution.

Maintaining institutional security and preserving internal order and discipline are essential goals that may require limitation or retraction of the retained constitutional rights of both convicted prisoners and pretrial detainees. Central to all other corrections goals is the institutional consideration of internal security within the corrections facilities themselves.

Finally, the problems that arise in the day-to-day operations of the corrections facility are not susceptible to easy solutions. Prison administrators therefore should be accorded wide-ranging deference in the adoption and execution of policies and practices that in their judgment are needed to preserve internal order and discipline and to maintain institutional security.

Inmates at all Bureau of Prison facilities, including the MCC, are required to expose their body cavities for visual inspection as part of a strip search conducted after every contact visit with a person from outside the institution. Corrections officials testified that visual cavity searches were necessary not only to discover but also to deter the smuggling of weapons, drugs, and other contraband into the institution. The District Court upheld the strip-search procedure but prohibited the body-cavity searches, absent probable cause to believe that the inmate is concealing contraband.

Because petitioners proved only one instance in the MCC's short history where contraband was found during a body-cavity search, the Court of Appeals affirmed. In its view, the "gross violation of personal privacy inherent in such a search cannot be outweighed by the government's security interest in maintaining a practice of so little actual utility." Admittedly, this practice instinctively gives us the most pause. However, assuming for present purposes that inmates, both convicted prisoners and pretrial detainees, retain some Fourth Amendment rights upon commitment to a corrections facility, we nonetheless conclude that these searches do not violate that Amendment. The Fourth Amendment prohibits only unreasonable searches, and under the circumstances, we do not believe that these searches are unreasonable.

A detention facility is a unique place fraught with serious security dangers. Smuggling of money, drugs, weapons, and other contraband is all too common an occurrence. And inmate attempts to secrete these items into the facility by concealing them in body cavities is documented in this record. That there has been only one instance where an MCC inmate was discovered attempting to smuggle contraband into the institution on his person may be more a testament to the effectiveness of this search technique as a deterrent than to any lack of interest on the part of the inmates to secrete and import such items when the opportunity arises.

There was a time not too long ago when the federal judiciary took a completely "hands-off" approach to the problem of prison administration. In recent years, however, these courts largely have discarded this "hands-off" attitude and have waded into this complex arena. But many of these same courts have, in the name of the Constitution, become increasingly enmeshed in the minutiae of prison operations. Judges, after all, are human. They, no less than others in our society, have a natural tendency to believe that their individual solutions to often intractable problems are better and more workable than those of the persons who are actually charged with and trained in the running of the particular institution under examination.

But under the Constitution, the first question to be answered is not whose plan is best, but in what branch of the Government is lodged the authority to initially devise the plan. The wide range of judgment calls that meet constitutional and statutory requirements are confided to officials outside of the Judicial Branch of Government.

DISSENT

STEVENS, J., joined by BRENNAN, J.

This is not an equal protection case. An empirical judgment that most persons formally accused of criminal conduct are probably guilty would provide a rational basis for a set of rules that treat them like convicts until they establish their innocence. No matter how rational such an approach might be—no matter how acceptable in a community where equality of status is the dominant goal—it is obnoxious to the concept of individual freedom protected by the Due Process Clause. If ever accepted in this country, it would work a fundamental change in the character of our free society.

Nor is this an Eighth Amendment case. That provision of the Constitution protects individuals convicted of crimes from punishment that is cruel and unusual. The pretrial detainees whose rights are at stake in this case, however, are innocent men and women who have been convicted of no crimes. Their claim is not that they have been subjected to cruel and unusual punishment in violation of the Eighth Amendment, but that to subject them to any form of punishment at all is an unconstitutional deprivation of their liberty.

This is a due process case. The most significant—and I venture to suggest the most enduring—part of the Court's opinion today is its recognition of this initial constitutional premise. The Court squarely holds that under the Due Process Clause, a detainee may not be punished prior to an adjudication of guilt in accordance with due process of law. Prior to conviction every individual is entitled to the benefit of a presumption both that he is innocent of prior criminal conduct and that he has no present intention to commit any offense in the immediate future. It is not always easy to determine whether a particular restraint serves the legitimate, regulatory goal of ensuring a detainee's presence at trial and his safety and security in the meantime, or the unlawful end of punishment.

[Double-bunking and searches of mail and cells are omitted from this excerpt.]

The body-cavity search—clearly the greatest personal indignity—may be the least justifiable measure of all. After every contact visit a body-cavity search is mandated by the rule. The District Court's finding that searches have failed in practice to produce any demonstrable improvement in security is hardly surprising. Detainees and their visitors are in full view during all visits, and are fully clad. To insert contraband into one's private body cavities during such a visit would indeed be an imposing challenge to nerves and agility. There is no reason to expect, and the petitioners have established none, that many pretrial detainees would attempt, let alone succeed, in surmounting this challenge absent the challenged rule.

Moreover, as the District Court explicitly found, less severe alternatives are available to ensure that contraband is not transferred during visits. Weapons and other dangerous instruments, the items of greatest legitimate concern, may be discovered by the use of metal detecting devices or other equipment commonly used for airline security. In addition, inmates are required, even apart

(continued)

from the body-cavity searches, to disrobe, to have their clothing inspected, and to present open hands and arms to reveal the absence of any concealed objects. These alternative procedures "amply satisfy" the demands of security. In my judgment, there is no basis in this regard to disagree.

It may well be, as the Court finds, that the rules at issue here were not adopted by administrators eager to punish those detained at MCC. The rules can be explained as the easiest way for administrators to ensure security in the jail. But the easiest course for jail officials is not always one that our Constitution allows them to take. If fundamental rights are withdrawn and severe harms are indiscriminately inflicted on detainees merely to secure minimal savings in time and effort for administrators, the guarantee of due process is violated.

Questions

1. Summarize the arguments of the majority and the dissent. Which is better? Defend your answer, relying on the facts and arguments made in the case.

2. Distinguish between detention and punishment.

3. One critic said that it was all well and good for Supreme Court justices to say this case involved detention, not punishment, but it probably would be little comfort for the detainees to know that. Do you agree? Explain your answer.

4. Does it matter that most pretrial detainees are subject to confinement because they can't afford bail?

5. What interests are at stake in this case? How would you balance them?

THE RIGHT TO COUNSEL

LO 6

Lawyers are everywhere in the criminal justice system today, but that wasn't always true. During colonial times and for some time afterward, victims had to find and hire their own private prosecutors. Defendants in felony cases didn't even have the right to a lawyer to defend them during their trials. Until the 1960s due process revolution (Chapter 2), a lawyer's job was to represent people once they got to court, not before they were charged or after they were convicted.

The remaining chapters will show that the right to a lawyer reaches even into prison cells and until the death penalty is carried out. This extension of constitutional protection (and the complex, technical legal rules accompanying it) since the due process revolution has created the need for lawyers not just for suspects, defendants, and convicts but also for police and corrections officers and departments. Police departments and corrections agencies have to hire lawyers, because the Constitution protects people on the street, in police stations, and when they're locked up before trial. Here, we'll concentrate on counsel for suspects, defendants, and appellants.

The Sixth Amendment to the U.S. Constitution provides that "In all criminal prosecutions, the accused shall enjoy the right . . . to have the assistance of counsel for his defense." Courts have always recognized criminal defendants' Sixth Amendment right to **retained counsel** (a lawyer paid for by the client). But they didn't recognize the right to **appointed counsel** (lawyers for people who can't afford to hire lawyers) until well into the 1900s. **Indigent defendants** (defendants too poor to hire their own lawyers) had to rely on **counsel pro bono** (lawyers willing to represent clients at no charge). Even today, many jurisdictions rely on lawyers who donate their services to represent poor defendants.

But most counties with large populations, and the U.S. government, have permanent defenders (called public defenders) paid by the public to defend poor clients. As we saw in *Powell v. Alabama* (1932, Chapter 2), the U.S. Supreme Court ruled that "fundamental fairness" requires courts to appoint lawyers for indigent defendants.

In *Johnson v. Zerbst* (1938), the Supreme Court acknowledged that the right to counsel guaranteed in the Sixth Amendment "stands as a constant admonition that, if the constitutional safeguards [the Bill of Rights] provides be lost, justice will not 'still be done.'" The Sixth Amendment recognizes that the "average defendant" doesn't have the legal skills necessary to compete with experienced government lawyers who hold the power to deprive her of life, liberty, and property. "That which is simple, orderly, and necessary to the lawyer—to the untrained layman—may appear intricate, complex, and mysterious" (462).

Nevertheless, *Zerbst* recognized only a narrow right to counsel for the poor: the right to a lawyer at their trial in *federal* courts. It said nothing about a right to counsel either before trial in federal courts or to any proceedings at all in state courts.

The U.S. Supreme Court confronted the right to counsel in *state* courts in *Betts v. Brady* (1942). Betts was convicted of robbery and sentenced to prison. At his trial, he asked for a lawyer, claiming that he was too poor to afford one. The judge denied his request because Carroll County, Maryland, the site of the trial, provided counsel only in murder and rape cases. Hearings on Betts's petition for habeas corpus eventually reached the Supreme Court. The Court, adopting the fundamental fairness approach, decided the due process clause did *not* incorporate the Sixth Amendment right to counsel.

The Court went further to hold that, except in "special circumstances," denial of counsel doesn't deprive a defendant of a fair trial. In other words, the right to counsel was not "implicit in the concept of ordered liberty" (Chapter 2). The Court reviewed the history of representation by counsel, noting that English courts didn't allow defendants—even if they could afford to hire one—to have a lawyer in felony cases until 1843.

The Court concluded that the Sixth Amendment right to counsel allowed defendants to have a lawyer, but it didn't compel the government in federal cases to provide one. And, after it reviewed a number of state court decisions, the Court concluded that "in the great majority of the states, it has been the considered judgment of the people, their representatives and their courts that appointment of counsel is not a fundamental right, essential to a fair trial." Therefore, "we are unable to say that the concept of due process incorporated in the Fourteenth Amendment obligates the states, whatever may be their own views, to furnish counsel in every such case" (471).

In *Gideon v. Wainwright* (1963), the Supreme Court agreed to review the Florida Supreme Court's dismissal of Gideon's petition for habeas corpus based on a claim similar to that of Betts. Appearing in court without funds and without a lawyer, Clarence Gideon asked the Florida court to appoint counsel for him, and the following exchange took place:

> *The Court*: Mr. Gideon, I am sorry, but I cannot appoint Counsel to represent you in this case. Under the laws of the State of Florida, the only time the Court can appoint Counsel to represent a Defendant is when that person is charged with a capital offense. I am sorry, but I will have to deny your request to appoint Counsel to defend you in this case.

> *The Defendant*: The United States Supreme Court says I am entitled to be represented by Counsel.

The Supreme Court agreed to hear Gideon's appeal and took the occasion to overrule *Betts v. Brady*:

> Upon full consideration we conclude that *Betts v. Brady* should be overruled. In our adversary system of criminal justice, any person haled into court, who is too poor to hire a lawyer, cannot be assured a fair trial unless counsel is provided for him. This seems to us to be an obvious truth.

Governments, both state and federal, quite properly spend vast sums of money to establish machinery to try defendants accused of crime. Lawyers to prosecute are everywhere deemed essential to protect the public's interest in an orderly society. Similarly, there are few defendants charged with crime, few indeed, who fail to hire the best lawyers they can get to prepare and present their defenses. That government hires lawyers to prosecute and defendants who have the money hire lawyers to defend are the strongest indications of the widespread belief that lawyers in criminal courts are necessities, not luxuries.

The right of one charged with crime to counsel may not be deemed fundamental and essential to fair trials in some countries, but it is in ours. From the very beginning, our state and national constitutions and laws have laid great emphasis on procedural and substantive safeguards designed to assure fair trials before impartial tribunals in which every defendant stands equal before the law. This noble ideal cannot be realized if the poor man charged with crime has to face his accusers without a lawyer to assist him.

Let's examine some important questions that the right to the assistance of counsel gives rise to:

1. At what point does the right to counsel kick in?
2. What did the Court mean when it said that the right to counsel applied to "all criminal prosecutions"?
3. How "poor" does a person have to be before the court has to appoint defense counsel?
4. Does the right to counsel mean the right to the lawyer of your choice?
5. What does the right to "effective counsel" mean?

Let's look at each of these issues.

LO 6   When the Right to Counsel Attaches

The Sixth Amendment guarantees the right to counsel in all criminal "prosecutions," but what proceedings does prosecution include? Clearly, it includes the trial and appeal, when defendants most need special legal expertise. But what about *before* trial? The U.S. Supreme Court has ruled that the right to counsel attaches to all **critical stages of criminal proceedings**. Table 12.1 shows the stages in the criminal process and indicates the ones the U.S. Supreme Court has declared critical stages. It's clear from the table that defendants have the right to counsel to represent them at all procedures after the first appearance.

What about at the police station before the first appearance? Specifically, do you have a right to a lawyer during police interrogation and identification procedures (lineups, show-ups, and photo identification; see Chapters 8 and 9)? The U.S. Supreme Court first applied the right to a lawyer in police stations in 1964, in *Escobedo v. Illinois* (1964, Chapter 8). The Court held that the right to counsel attached at the accusatory stage of a criminal case—namely, when a general investigation focused on a specific suspect.

According to the Court, the police reached that point when they decided that Danny Escobedo had committed the murder they were investigating. After they made up their minds that he was the murderer, Chicago police officers tried to get him to confess by interrogating him. During the interrogation, Escobedo asked to see his lawyer, who was in the police station. The officers refused. Eventually, he confessed, and was tried and convicted with the help of the confession. The U.S. Supreme Court said

TABLE 12.1 Stage of criminal process and right to counsel

Stage of Criminal Process	Right to Counsel?
Investigative stop	No
Frisk for weapons	No
Arrest	No
Search following arrest	No
Custodial interrogation	Yes
Lineup before formal charges	No
Lineup after formal charges	Yes
First appearance	No
Grand jury review/Preliminary hearing	Yes
Arraignment	Yes
Pretrial hearings	Yes
Trial (Chapter 13)	Yes
Appeal/Collateral attack (Chapter 14)	Yes

© Cengage Learning

the confession wasn't admissible because it was obtained during the accusatory stage without the help of Escobedo's lawyer.

Just two years later, in *Miranda v. Arizona*, the Court decided that police officers have to tell suspects that they have a right to a lawyer during custodial interrogation (Chapter 8). As for identification procedures, those conducted after indictment are a critical stage; those conducted before indictment aren't (Chapter 9).

LO 6   The Meaning of "All Criminal Prosecutions"

In 1932, *Powell v. Alabama* (Chapter 2) established the rule that due process commands that appointed counsel represent poor defendants in capital cases. In *Gideon v. Wainwright* (1963), the Court extended the right to counsel to poor defendants prosecuted for felonies against property. In 1972, the Court went further: All poor defendants prosecuted for misdemeanors punishable by jail terms have a right to an appointed lawyer.

In *Argersinger v. Hamlin* (1972), Jon Richard Argersinger, a Florida indigent, was convicted of carrying a concealed weapon, a misdemeanor punishable by up to six months' imprisonment, a $1,000 fine, or both. A Florida rule limited assigned counsel to "non-petty offenses punishable by more than six months imprisonment." The Court struck down the rule, holding that states have to provide a lawyer for defendants charged with any offense punishable by incarceration no matter what the state's criminal code calls it (misdemeanor, petty misdemeanor, or felony). Table 12.2 summarizes the leading cases on the right to counsel.

Notice what the Court did *not* say in *Argersinger*: Poor people have a right to a lawyer paid for by the government in *all* criminal cases. Why? Because the Court was well aware of a practical problem: There isn't enough money to pay for everyone to have a lawyer. Of course, strictly speaking, constitutional rights can't depend on money; but as a practical matter, money definitely affects how many people get their rights in real life. We know many poor people who have a right to a lawyer don't get one because counties and other local governments simply don't have the money to

TABLE 12.2 The leading right-to-counsel cases

Case	Year	Right Upheld
Powell v. Alabama	1932	Appointed counsel for poor, illiterate, ignorant, isolated defendants in state capital cases
Johnson v. Zerbst	1938	Appointed counsel in federal cases at trial (not before or after)
Betts v. Brady	1942	Appointed counsel in state cases under "special circumstances"
Chandler v. Fretag	1954	Retained (paid for) counsel in all criminal cases
Gideon v. Wainwright	1963	Appointed counsel in state felony cases (overruled Betts v. Brady)
Argersinger v. Hamlin	1972	Appointed counsel in any offense punishable by incarceration
Scott v. Illinois	1979	No right to counsel for sentences that don't result in actual jail time

© Cengage Learning

pay for them. Why? Because taxpayers don't want their tax dollars spent on lawyers for "criminals."

This mix of practical reality and constitutional rights surfaced in *Scott v. Illinois* (1979). The Court specifically addressed the question of whether the right to assigned counsel extends to offenses where imprisonment is authorized but not required (**authorized imprisonment standard**) or that don't actually result in prison sentences (**actual imprisonment standard**). Aubrey Scott was convicted of shoplifting merchandise valued at less than $150. An Illinois statute set the maximum penalty at a $500 fine or one year in jail, or both. Scott argued that a line of Supreme Court cases, culminating in *Argersinger*, required state-paid counsel whenever imprisonment is an authorized penalty.

The U.S. Supreme Court rejected that argument. Instead, it agreed with the Supreme Court of Illinois, which was "not inclined to extend *Argersinger*" to a case in which the defendant wasn't facing jail time. The statutory offense that Scott was charged with authorized imprisonment upon conviction but courts didn't impose it. The Court held that "the Federal Constitution does not require a state trial court to appoint counsel for a criminal defendant such as [Scott]," who could've been, but wasn't actually, sentenced to do jail time (369).

In their dissent, Justices Brennan, Marshall, and Stevens argued that the concern for cost is "both irrelevant and speculative." According to the justices:

- Constitutional guarantees can't depend on budgetary concerns.
- Budgetary concerns discriminate against defendants who can't afford to pay.
- Public defender systems can keep the costs of the authorized imprisonment standard down and won't "clog the courts with inexperienced appointed counsel."
- The Court's "alarmist prophecies that an authorized imprisonment standard would wreak havoc on the States," are refuted by the reality that "the standard has not produced that result in the substantial number of States that already provide counsel in all cases where imprisonment is authorized—states that include a large majority of the country's population and a great diversity of urban and rural environments. (384–88)

LO 6   The Standard of Indigence

The U.S. Supreme Court has never defined *indigence* (the state of poverty that makes it impossible for defendants to hire a lawyer). However, U.S. Courts of Appeals have established some general guidelines on how to determine whether defendants are poor enough to qualify for a lawyer paid for by the government:

1. Poor defendants don't have to be completely destitute.
2. Earnings and assets count; help from friends and relatives doesn't.
3. Actual, not potential, earnings are the measure.
4. The state can tap defendants' future earnings to get reimbursement for the costs of counsel, transcripts, and fees for expert witnesses and investigators.

According to Rule 5.02 of the Minnesota Rules of Criminal Procedure (2010):

> *5.02 Appointment of Public Defender*
> Subd. 3. Standards for Public Defense Eligibility.

A defendant is financially unable to obtain counsel if:

1) The defendant, or any dependent of the defendant who resides in the same household as the defendant, receives means-tested governmental benefits; or
2) The defendant, through any combination of liquid assets and current income, would be unable to pay the reasonable costs charged by private counsel in that judicial district for a defense of a case of the nature at issue; or
3) The defendant can demonstrate that due to insufficient funds or other assets: two members of a defense attorney referral list maintained by the court have refused to defend the case or, if no referral list is maintained, that two private attorneys in that judicial district have refused to defend the case.

LO 6   The Right to the Counsel of Your Choice

According to the U.S. Supreme Court's reading of the Sixth Amendment, all defendants have the right to "effective counsel" to defend them (see "The Right to 'Effective' Counsel," below). Does this mean that defendants have the right to have the lawyers of their choice? Yes, said the U.S. Supreme Court in *U.S. v. Gonzalez-Lopez* (2006). Cuauhtemoc Gonzalez-Lopez hired Joseph Low to represent him on a federal marijuana-trafficking charge. Low is an experienced criminal defense lawyer who has won several national awards for excellence in the courtroom. Low "prides himself on his aggressive approach to criminal defense work and has built his practice around fighting 'oppression by federal and state government'" (Fisher 2006, 2).

Low was just the kind of lawyer Gonzalez-Lopez wanted. He knew that Low recently had gotten another drug defendant a good plea bargain under the same judge as Gonzalez-Lopez's. He insisted he was innocent and wanted an aggressive lawyer to defend him (3). But the trial court judge denied Low's application to represent Gonzalez-Lopez on the ground that Low had violated a professional conduct rule. Then, he blocked Gonzalez-Lopez from meeting or consulting with Low throughout the trial. The jury found Gonzalez-Lopez guilty.

The Supreme Court (6–3) held that the trial court's refusal to allow Low to represent Gonzalez-Lopez deprived him of his constitutional right to counsel and entitled him to a new trial. According to the Court, "[T]he Sixth Amendment guarantees a defendant the right to be represented by an otherwise qualified attorney whom that defendant can afford to hire, or who is willing to represent the defendant even though he is without funds" (*U.S. v. Gonzalez-Lopez* 2006, 144).

Notice that only those who can afford to hire a lawyer can have a lawyer of their choice. That's about 10 percent of all criminal defendants; the remaining 90 percent have the right to effective counsel but not of their choosing.

LO 6 The Right to "Effective" Counsel

In 1932, the U.S. Supreme Court said due process requires not just counsel but effective counsel, but the Court didn't say much to clarify what "effective" means. So lower federal courts and state courts stepped in and adopted the mockery of justice standard. Under this standard, only lawyers whose behavior is so "shocking" that it turns the trial into a "joke" are constitutionally ineffective. One lawyer called it the "mirror test." (Put a mirror under the lawyer's nose; if it steams up, he passes.) What prompted this professional criticism?

In actual cases, appellate courts ruled that lawyers who slept through trials; came to court drunk; couldn't name a single precedent related to the case they were arguing; or were released from jail to represent their clients hadn't turned the proceedings into a joke and met the mockery of justice standard. According to the **mockery of justice standard**, the attorney's actions or inactions must reduce the trial to a farce to qualify as ineffective. When one defendant claimed he got ineffective representation because his lawyer slept through the trial, the judge said, "You have a right to a lawyer; that doesn't mean you have a right to one who's awake." That decision was affirmed by the reviewing court.

Courts and commentators have criticized the mockery of justice standard for being too subjective, vague, and narrow. The standard's focus on the trial excludes many serious errors that lawyers make in preparing for trial. Furthermore, in the overwhelming majority of cases disposed of by guilty pleas, the standard is totally irrelevant.

Judge David Bazelon (1973), an experienced and respected federal judge, said the test requires "such a minimal level of performance from counsel that it is itself a mockery of the Sixth Amendment" (28). "I have often been told that if my court were to reverse in every case in which there was inadequate counsel, we would have to send back half the convictions in my jurisdiction" (22–23).

Courts resist getting involved in the touchy question of judging the performance of defense attorneys. Why? For one thing, too much interference can damage not only professional relationships but also the professional independence of defense lawyers and even the adversary system itself. Furthermore, judges who criticize defense lawyers are criticizing fellow professionals, lawyers who appear in their courts regularly.

Most jurisdictions have abandoned the mockery of justice standard, replacing it with the **reasonably competent attorney standard**. According to this standard, judges measure lawyers' performance against the "customary skills and diligence that a reasonably competent attorney would perform under similar circumstances." Attorneys have to be more diligent under the reasonably competent attorney standard than under the mockery of justice standard. Nevertheless, both the mockery of justice and the reasonably competent attorney standards are "vague to some appreciable degree and susceptible to greatly varying subjective impressions" (LaFave and Israel 1984, 2:99–102).

The U.S. Supreme Court tried to increase the clarity of the reasonably competent attorney test by announcing a **two-pronged effective counsel test** to evaluate the effectiveness of counsel. The test was announced in *Strickland v. Washington* (1984).

In 1976, David Leroy Washington went on a 10-day crime spree that ended in three murders. After his lawyer, William Tunkey, was appointed, Washington confessed; he also pleaded guilty at his trial. Washington waived his right to an advisory jury to decide whether he should get the death penalty.

During the sentencing phase of the proceedings, Tunkey didn't present any character evidence, didn't present any medical or psychiatric evidence, and only cross-examined some of the state's witnesses. The judge sentenced Washington to death. Washington went through the state and then the federal courts, claiming ineffectiveness of counsel. The U.S. Court of Appeals for the Eleventh Circuit ruled in his favor and the state appealed.

The U.S. Supreme Court reversed, applying its new two-pronged test of ineffective counsel. Under the first prong, called the **reasonableness prong**, defendants have to prove that their lawyer's performance wasn't reasonably competent, meaning that the lawyer was so deficient that she "was not functioning as the 'counsel' guaranteed the defendant by the Sixth Amendment."

Under the reasonableness prong, reviewing courts have to look at the totality of the facts and circumstances to decide whether the defense lawyer's performance was reasonably competent. Reviewing courts have to start with a presumption in favor of the defense lawyer's competence, meaning they have lots of leeway to make tactical and strategic decisions that fall within the wide range of available professional judgment. So as long as defense counsel's choices fall within that wide range, representation is presumed reasonable.

If the defendant proves his lawyer's performance was unreasonable, he still has to prove the second prong of the test, called the **prejudice prong** of the reasonable competence test. Under the prejudice prong, defendants have to prove that their lawyer's incompetence was probably responsible for their conviction. In our next case excerpt, *Rompilla v. Beard* (2005), the U.S. Supreme Court (5–4), over a heated dissent, held that Ronald Rompilla's lawyers failed both prongs of the *Strickland* test and reversed his death sentence.

In *Rompilla v. Beard* (2005), the U.S. Supreme Court held (5–4) that Ronald Rompilla's right to effective counsel had been violated because his attorneys didn't meet the two-pronged effective counsel test.

CASE

Was He Denied His Right to "Effective" Counsel?

Rompilla v. Beard
545 U.S. 374 (2005)

HISTORY

After his conviction for murder in the first degree, and imposition of the death penalty, and affirmance of a denial of petition for postconviction relief, Ronald Rompilla (defendant) filed a petition for a writ of habeas corpus. The District Court granted the petition; Jeffrey Beard, Pennsylvania Department of Corrections, appealed. The Court of Appeals for the Third Circuit reversed. The U.S. Supreme Court reversed.

—SOUTER, J., joined by STEVENS, O'CONNOR, GINSBURG, and BREYER, JJ.

(continued)

FACTS

On the morning of January 14, 1988, James Scanlon was discovered dead in a bar he ran in Allentown, Pennsylvania, his body having been stabbed repeatedly and set on fire. Ronald Rompilla was indicted for the murder and related offenses, and the Commonwealth gave notice of intent to ask for the death penalty. Two public defenders were assigned to the case.

The jury at the guilt phase of trial found Rompilla guilty on all counts, and during the ensuing penalty phase, the prosecutor sought to prove three aggravating factors to justify a death sentence: that the murder was committed in the course of another felony; that the murder was committed by torture; and that Rompilla had a significant history of felony convictions indicating the use or threat of violence. The Commonwealth presented evidence on all three aggravators, and the jury found all proven. Rompilla's evidence in mitigation consisted of relatively brief testimony: five of his family members argued in effect for residual doubt, and beseeched the jury for mercy, saying that they believed Rompilla was innocent and a good man. Rompilla's 14-year-old son testified that he loved his father and would visit him in prison. The jury acknowledged this evidence to the point of finding, as two factors in mitigation, that Rompilla's son had testified on his behalf and that rehabilitation was possible. But the jurors assigned the greater weight to the aggravating factors, and sentenced Rompilla to death. The Supreme Court of Pennsylvania affirmed both conviction and sentence.

In December 1995, with new lawyers, Rompilla filed claims under the Pennsylvania Post Conviction Relief Act, including ineffective assistance by trial counsel in failing to present significant mitigating evidence about Rompilla's childhood, mental capacity and health, and alcoholism. The postconviction court found that trial counsel had done enough to investigate the possibilities of a mitigation case, and the Supreme Court of Pennsylvania affirmed the denial of relief.

Rompilla then petitioned for a writ of habeas corpus in Federal District Court, raising claims that included inadequate representation. The District Court found that the State Supreme Court had unreasonably applied *Strickland v. Washington* (1984), as to the penalty phase of the trial, and granted relief for ineffective assistance of counsel. The court found that in preparing the mitigation case the defense lawyers had failed to investigate "pretty obvious signs" that Rompilla had a troubled childhood and suffered from mental illness and alcoholism, and instead had relied unjustifiably on Rompilla's own description of an unexceptional background. A divided Third Circuit panel reversed. The Third Circuit denied rehearing en banc by a vote of 6 to 5. We granted certiorari, and now reverse.

OPINION

This is not a case in which defense counsel simply ignored their obligation to find mitigating evidence, and their workload as busy public defenders did not keep them from making a number of efforts, including interviews with Rompilla and some members of his family, and examinations of reports by three mental health experts who gave opinions at the guilt phase. None of the sources proved particularly helpful. Rompilla's own contributions to any mitigation case were minimal. Counsel found him uninterested in helping, as on their visit to his prison to go over a proposed mitigation strategy, when Rompilla told them he was "bored being here listening" and returned to his cell. To questions about childhood and schooling, his answers indicated they had been normal, save for quitting school in the ninth grade. There were times when Rompilla was even actively obstructive by sending counsel off on false leads.

The lawyers also spoke with five members of Rompilla's family (his former wife, two brothers, a sister-in-law, and his son), and counsel testified that they developed a good relationship with the family in the course of their representation. The state postconviction court found that counsel spoke to the relatives in a "detailed manner," attempting to unearth mitigating information, although the weight of this finding is qualified by the lawyers' concession that "the overwhelming response from the family was that they didn't really feel as though they knew him all that well since he had spent the majority of his adult years and some of his childhood years in custody." Defense counsel also said that because the family was "coming from the position that [Rompilla] was innocent, they weren't looking for reasons for why he might have done this."

The third and final source tapped for mitigating material was the cadre of three mental health witnesses who were asked to look into Rompilla's mental state as of the time of the offense and his competency to stand trial. But their reports revealed "nothing useful" to Rompilla's case, and the lawyers consequently did not go to any other historical source that might have cast light on Rompilla's mental condition.

When new counsel entered the case to raise Rompilla's postconviction claims, however, they identified a number of likely avenues the trial lawyers could fruitfully have followed in building a mitigation case. School records are one example, which trial counsel never examined in spite of the professed unfamiliarity of the several family members with Rompilla's childhood, and despite counsel's knowledge that Rompilla left school after the ninth grade. Other examples are records of Rompilla's juvenile and adult incarcerations, which counsel did not consult, although they were aware of their client's criminal record. And while counsel knew from police reports provided in pretrial discovery that Rompilla had been drinking heavily at the time of his offense, and although one of the mental health experts reported that Rompilla's troubles with alcohol merited further investigation, counsel did not look for evidence of a history of dependence on alcohol that might have extenuating significance.

Trial counsel and the Commonwealth respond to these unexplored possibilities by emphasizing this Court's recognition that the duty to investigate does not force defense lawyers to scour the globe on the off chance something will turn up; reasonably diligent counsel may draw a line when they have good reason to think further investigation would be a waste. The Commonwealth argues that the information trial counsel gathered from Rompilla and the other sources gave them sound reason to think it would have been pointless to spend time and money on the additional investigation espoused by postconviction counsel, and we can say that there is room for debate about trial counsel's obligation to follow at least some of those potential lines of enquiry. There is no need to say more, however, for a further point is clear and dispositive: The lawyers were deficient in failing to examine the court file on Rompilla's prior conviction.

There is an obvious reason that the failure to examine Rompilla's prior conviction file fell below the level of reasonable performance. Counsel knew that the Commonwealth intended to seek the death penalty by proving Rompilla had a significant history of felony convictions indicating the use or threat of violence, an aggravator under state law. Counsel further knew that the Commonwealth would attempt to establish this history by proving Rompilla's prior conviction for rape and assault, and would emphasize his violent character by introducing a transcript of the rape victim's testimony given in that earlier trial. There is no question that defense counsel were on notice, since they acknowledge that a "plea letter," written by one of them four days prior to trial, mentioned the prosecutor's plans. It is also undisputed that the prior conviction file was a public document, readily available for the asking at the very courthouse where Rompilla was to be tried.

It is clear, however, that defense counsel did not look at any part of that file, including the transcript, until warned by the prosecution a second time. In a colloquy the day before the evidentiary sentencing phase began, the prosecutor again said he would present the transcript of the victim's testimony to establish the prior conviction.

At the postconviction evidentiary hearing, Rompilla's lawyer confirmed that she had not seen the transcript before the hearing in which this exchange took place, and crucially, even after obtaining the transcript of the victim's testimony on the eve of the sentencing hearing, counsel apparently examined none of the other material in the file.

With every effort to view the facts as a defense lawyer would have done at the time, it is difficult to see how counsel could have failed to realize that without examining the readily available file they were seriously compromising their opportunity to respond to a case for aggravation. The prosecution was going to use the dramatic facts of a similar prior offense, and Rompilla's counsel had a duty to make all reasonable efforts to learn what they could about the offense. Reasonable efforts certainly included obtaining the Commonwealth's own readily available file on the prior conviction to learn what the Commonwealth knew about the crime, to discover any mitigating evidence the Commonwealth would downplay, and to anticipate the details of the aggravating evidence the Commonwealth would emphasize.

Without making reasonable efforts to review the file, defense counsel could have had no hope of knowing whether the prosecution was quoting selectively from the transcript, or whether there were circumstances extenuating the behavior described by the victim. The obligation to get the file was particularly pressing here owing to the similarity of the violent prior offense to the crime charged and Rompilla's sentencing strategy stressing residual doubt. Without making efforts to learn the details and rebut the relevance of the earlier crime, a convincing argument for residual doubt was certainly beyond any hope.

The notion that defense counsel must obtain information that the State has and will use against the defendant is not simply a matter of common sense. The American Bar Association Guidelines relating to death penalty defense are explicit:

> Counsel must investigate prior convictions . . . that could be used as aggravating circumstances or otherwise come into evidence. If a prior conviction is legally flawed, counsel should seek to have it set aside. Counsel may also find extenuating circumstances that can be offered to lessen the weight of a conviction." ABA Guidelines for the Appointment and Performance of Defense Counsel in Death Penalty Cases 10.7, comment.

It flouts prudence to deny that a defense lawyer should try to look at a file he knows the prosecution will cull for aggravating evidence, let alone when the file is sitting in the trial courthouse, open for the asking. No reasonable lawyer would forgo examination of the file thinking he could do as well by asking the defendant or family relations whether they recalled anything helpful or damaging in the prior victim's testimony. Nor would a reasonable lawyer compare possible searches for school reports, juvenile records, and evidence of drinking habits to the opportunity to take a look at a file disclosing what the prosecutor knows and even plans to read from in his case. Questioning a few more family members and searching for old records can promise less than looking for a needle in a haystack, when a lawyer truly has reason to doubt there is any needle there. But looking at a file the

(continued)

prosecution says it will use is a sure bet: Whatever may be in that file is going to tell defense counsel something about what the prosecution can produce.

Since counsel's failure to look at the file fell below the line of reasonable practice, there is a further question about prejudice, that is, whether there is a reasonable probability that, but for counsel's unprofessional errors, the result of the proceeding would have been different. Because the state courts found the representation adequate, they never reached the issue of prejudice, and so we examine this element of the *Strickland* claim. We think Rompilla has shown beyond any doubt that counsel's lapse was prejudicial.

If the defense lawyers had looked in the file on Rompilla's prior conviction, it is uncontested they would have found a range of mitigation leads that no other source had opened up. In the same file with the transcript of the prior trial were the records of Rompilla's imprisonment on the earlier conviction, which defense counsel testified she had never seen. The prison files pictured Rompilla's childhood and mental health very differently from anything defense counsel had seen or heard. An evaluation by a corrections counselor states that Rompilla was "reared in the slum environment of Allentown, Pa. vicinity. He early came to the attention of juvenile authorities, quit school at 16, and started a series of incarcerations in and out Pennsylvania, often of assaultive nature and commonly related to over-indulgence in alcoholic beverages. The same file discloses test results that the defense's mental health experts would have viewed as pointing to schizophrenia and other disorders, and test scores showing a third grade level of cognition after nine years of schooling.

The accumulated entries would have destroyed the benign conception of Rompilla's upbringing and mental capacity defense counsel had formed from talking with Rompilla himself and some of his family members, and from the reports of the mental health experts. With this information, counsel would have become skeptical of the impression given by the five family members and would unquestionably have gone further to build a mitigation case. Further effort would presumably have unearthed much of the material postconviction counsel found, including testimony from several members of Rompilla's family, whom trial counsel did not interview. Judge Sloviter summarized this evidence:

> Rompilla's parents were both severe alcoholics who drank constantly. His mother drank during her pregnancy with Rompilla, and he and his brothers eventually developed serious drinking problems. His father, who had a vicious temper, frequently beat Rompilla's mother, leaving her bruised and black-eyed, and bragged about his cheating on her. His parents fought violently, and on at least one occasion his mother stabbed his father. He was abused by his father who beat him when he was young with his hands, fists, leather straps, belts and sticks. All of the children lived in terror. There were no expressions of parental love, affection or approval. Instead, he was subjected to yelling and verbal abuse. His father locked Rompilla and his brother Richard in a small wire mesh dog pen that was filthy and excrement filled. He had an isolated background, and was not allowed to visit other children or to speak to anyone on the phone. They had no indoor plumbing in the house, he slept in the attic with no heat, and the children were not given clothes and attended school in rags.

The jury never heard any of this and neither did the mental health experts who examined Rompilla before trial. While they found "nothing helpful to Rompilla's case," their postconviction counterparts, alerted by information from school, medical, and prison records that trial counsel never saw, found plenty of "red flags" pointing up a need to test further. When they tested, they found that Rompilla "suffers from organic brain damage, an extreme mental disturbance significantly impairing several of his cognitive functions." They also said that "Rompilla's problems relate back to his childhood, and were likely caused by fetal alcohol syndrome and that Rompilla's capacity to appreciate the criminality of his conduct or to conform his conduct to the law was substantially impaired at the time of the offense."

These findings in turn would probably have prompted a look at school and juvenile records, all of them easy to get, showing, for example, that when Rompilla was 16 his mother "was missing from home frequently for a period of one or several weeks at a time." The same report noted that his mother "has been reported frequently under the influence of alcoholic beverages, with the result that the children have always been poorly kept and on the filthy side which was also the condition of the home at all times." School records showed Rompilla's IQ was in the mentally retarded range.

This evidence adds up to a mitigation case that bears no relation to the few naked pleas for mercy actually put before the jury, and although we suppose it is possible that a jury could have heard it all and still have decided on the death penalty, that is not the test. It goes without saying that the undiscovered mitigating evidence, taken as a whole, might well have influenced the jury's appraisal of Rompilla's culpability, and the likelihood of a different result if the evidence had gone in is sufficient to undermine confidence in the outcome actually reached at sentencing (*Strickland* 694).

The judgment of the Third Circuit is REVERSED, and Pennsylvania must either retry the case on penalty or stipulate to a life sentence.

It is so ordered.

DISSENT

KENNEDY, J., joined by REHNQUIST, C.J., and SCALIA and THOMAS, JJ.

Today the Court brands two committed criminal defense attorneys as ineffective—"outside the wide range of professionally competent assistance," *Strickland v. Washington* (1984)—because they did not look in an old case file and stumble upon something they had not set out to find. To reach this result, the majority imposes on defense counsel a rigid requirement to review all documents in what it calls the "case file" of any prior conviction that the prosecution might rely on at trial. In order to grant Rompilla habeas relief the Court must say, and indeed does say, that the Pennsylvania Supreme Court was objectively unreasonable in failing to anticipate today's new case file rule.

In my respectful submission it is this Court, not the state court, which is unreasonable. The majority's holding has no place in our Sixth Amendment jurisprudence and, if followed, often will result in less effective counsel by diverting limited defense resources from other important tasks in order to satisfy the Court's new *per se* rule. Under any standard of review the investigation performed by Rompilla's counsel in preparation for sentencing was not only adequate but also conscientious. Rompilla's attorneys recognized from the outset that building an effective mitigation case was crucial to helping their client avoid the death penalty. Rompilla stood accused of a brutal crime. In January 1988, James Scanlon was murdered while he was closing the Cozy Corner Cafe, a bar he owned in Allentown, Pennsylvania. Scanlon's body was discovered later the next morning, lying in a pool of blood. Scanlon had been stabbed multiple times, including 16 wounds around the neck and head. Scanlon also had been beaten with a blunt object, and his face had been gashed, possibly with shards from broken liquor and beer bottles found at the scene of the crime. After Scanlon was stabbed to death his body had been set on fire.

A *per se* rule requiring counsel in every case to review the records of prior convictions used by the State as aggravation evidence is a radical departure from *Strickland*. We have warned against the creation of specific guidelines or checklists for judicial evaluation of attorney performance. No particular set of detailed rules for counsel's conduct can satisfactorily take account of the variety of circumstances faced by defense counsel or the range of legitimate decisions regarding how best to represent a criminal defendant. Any such set of rules would interfere with the constitutionally protected independence of counsel and restrict the wide latitude counsel must have in making tactical decisions. Indeed, the existence of detailed guidelines for representation could distract counsel from the overriding mission of vigorous advocacy of the defendant's cause.

The majority disregards the sound strategic calculation supporting the decisions made by Rompilla's attorneys. Charles and Dantos were aware of [Rompilla's] priors and aware of the circumstances surrounding these convictions. At the postconviction hearing, Dantos also indicated that she had reviewed documents relating to the prior conviction. Based on this information, as well as their numerous conversations with Rompilla and his family, Charles and Dantos reasonably could conclude that reviewing the full prior conviction case file was not the best allocation of resources.

Perhaps the circumstances to which the majority refers are the details of Rompilla's 1974 crimes. Rompilla had been convicted of breaking into the residence of Josephine Macrenna, who lived in an apartment above the bar she owned. After Macrenna gave him the bar's receipts for the night, Rompilla demanded that she disrobe. When she initially resisted, Rompilla slashed her left breast with a knife. Rompilla then held Macrenna at knifepoint while he raped her for over an hour. Charles and Dantos were aware of these circumstances of the prior conviction and the brutality of the crime. It did not take a review of the case file to know that quibbling with the Commonwealth's version of events was a dubious trial strategy. Rompilla was unlikely to endear himself to the jury by arguing that his prior conviction for burglary, theft, and rape really was not as bad as the Commonwealth was making it out to be. Recognizing this, Rompilla's attorneys instead devoted their limited time and resources to developing a mitigation case. That those efforts turned up little useful evidence does not make the ex ante strategic calculation of Rompilla's attorneys constitutionally deficient.

Today's decision will not increase the resources committed to capital defense. (At the time of Rompilla's trial, the Lehigh County Public Defender's Office had two investigators for 2,000 cases.) If defense attorneys dutifully comply with the Court's new rule, they will have to divert resources from other tasks. The net effect of today's holding in many cases—instances where trial counsel reasonably can conclude that reviewing old case files is not an effective use of time—will be to diminish the quality of representation. We have consistently declined to impose mechanical rules on counsel—even when those rules might lead to better representation; I see no occasion to depart from this approach in order to impose a requirement that might well lead to worse representation.

It is quite possible defense attorneys, recognizing the absurdity of a one-size-fits-all approach to effective advocacy, will simply ignore the Court's new requirement and continue to exercise their best judgment about how to allocate time and resources in preparation for trial. While this decision would be understandable—and might even be required by state ethical rules—it leaves open the possibility that a defendant will seek to overturn his conviction

(continued)

based on something in a prior conviction case file that went unreviewed. This elevation of needle-in-a-haystack claims to the status of constitutional violations will benefit undeserving defendants and saddle States with the considerable costs of retrial and/or resentencing.

Questions

1. Identify and state the two prongs of the *Strickland* "effective assistance of counsel" standard.

2. List the relevant actions defense counsel took, or failed to take, to defend Rompilla at the conviction and sentencing phases of his trial.

3. Summarize the majority's arguments supporting its decision that Pennsylvania deprived Rompilla of the right to the effective assistance of counsel.

4. Summarize the dissent's arguments supporting its conclusion that Rompilla's lawyers passed both prongs of the *Strickland* test.

5. Can you explain why the majority omitted, and the dissent reported, the gory details of the murder and the rape Rompilla was convicted of?

6. Do you agree more with the majority or the dissent? Back up your answer with details from the facts and opinions in the case.

7. Just as the jury was about to be selected in Rompilla's retrial, on August 13, 2007, the Lehigh County, Pennsylvania, county attorney announced a plea agreement: Rompilla pleaded guilty in exchange for life in prison without the chance of parole. The state spent "millions" on Rompilla's case (Associated Press 2007). Is this a "fair" conclusion to the case?

YOU DECIDE
Should Prosecutors Appoint Defendants' Public Defenders?

When the state of Georgia ran out of money to pay the lawyers for a man facing the death penalty, the prosecutor, of all people, had an idea. He asked the judge to appoint two overworked public defenders instead, identifying them by name. The judge went along. The Georgia Supreme Court, by a 4-to-3 vote, endorsed the arrangement in March, saying the defendant, Jamie R. Weis, should have accepted the new lawyers to help solve the state's budget impasse. The adversary system does not ordinarily let prosecutors pick their opponents. Indeed, most states do not allow established relationships between lawyers and their clients to be interrupted for any but the most exceptional reasons. Two states, Georgia and Louisiana, take a less sporting attitude, saying poor defendants may be forced to switch lawyers long after the case is under way and must take whomever the state can afford at the time.

You can watch the oral arguments to the Georgia Supreme Court to help you decide.

TESTING THE GOVERNMENT'S CASE

 LO 7 After the decision to charge, the action moves from the prosecutor's office into court. At this point, decisions inside the courtroom are based more on formal rules than informal discretion. These rules govern the pretrial proceedings to test the government's case and hear motions. Testing the government's case means deciding whether there's enough evidence to go to trial. Still more complex rules control the centerpiece of formal criminal justice, the criminal trial.

But don't be deceived by these public formal proceedings. Discretionary decision making hasn't disappeared; it has just moved out of the courtroom and into the corridors in and around the courthouse. Here's where plea bargaining takes place—or where defendants decide they just want to plead guilty without bargaining, hoping to get a lighter sentence by admitting their guilt and saving the court and lawyers time (Chapter 13). In these cases (the vast majority by all counts), courtroom proceedings only ratify what was worked out by informal negotiations.

We saw earlier that the decision to charge (pp. 450–452) demonstrates the government's commitment to criminal prosecution and that the first appearance (pp. 456–457) prepares defendants for the consequences of this decision. But the government's commitment and the first appearance aren't enough by themselves to start a criminal trial.

First, the court has to test the strength of the government's case against the defendant. The Seventh Circuit U.S. Court of Appeals summed up why in *U.S. v. Udziela* (1982):

> While in theory a trial provides a defendant with a full opportunity to contest and disprove charges against him, in practice, the handing up of an indictment will often have a devastating personal and professional impact that a later dismissal or acquittal can never undo. (1001)

Two procedures test the government's case against defendants: (1) preliminary hearings and (2) grand jury review. A **preliminary hearing** is an adversarial proceeding that tests the government's case; a **grand jury review** is a secret proceeding to test the government's case.

When prosecutors draw up a **criminal information** (a written formal charge made by prosecutors without a grand jury indictment), they test their case at a preliminary hearing before a judge. When they seek an **indictment**, they test the government's case by presenting it to a grand jury for grand jury review. If the government passes the test of the grand jury review, the grand jury returns the indictment as a true bill, which records the number of **grand jurors** (U.S. citizens selected to serve a term) voting for indictment. If the government passes the test in the preliminary hearing, the judge **binds over** the defendant; that is, she sends the case on for trial.

Both preliminary hearings and grand jury review test the government's case, but they differ in several important respects (see Table 12.3). Preliminary hearings are public; grand jury proceedings are secret. Preliminary hearings are adversarial proceedings, in which the defense can challenge the prosecution's case; grand juries hear only the prosecution's case without the defense's participation. Judges preside over preliminary hearings; prosecutors manage grand jury proceedings without judicial participation. In preliminary hearings, magistrates determine whether there's enough evidence to go to trial; grand jury review relies on grand jurors selected to decide whether there's enough evidence. Finally, defendants and their lawyers attend preliminary hearings; defendants and their lawyers are banned from grand jury review (ex parte proceedings).

The differences between preliminary hearings and grand jury proceedings reflect different values in the criminal process. The preliminary hearing stresses adversarial,

TABLE 12.3 Contrasts between the preliminary hearing and grand jury review

Preliminary Hearing	Grand Jury Review
Held in public	Secret proceeding
Adversarial hearing	Only the government's case is presented
Judge presides	Prosecutor presides
Judge determines the facts	Grand jurors decide the facts
Defendants and their lawyers may attend	Neither defendants nor their lawyers may attend

© Cengage Learning

open, accusatory values and control by experts. Grand jury review, on the other hand, underscores the value of the democratic dimension of the criminal process: lay participation in criminal proceedings. But their goal is the same: deciding whether there's enough evidence to bring defendants to trial.

LO 7 | The Preliminary Hearing

Preliminary hearings are held after the first appearance. In most states, all judges are authorized to conduct preliminary hearings, but, in practice, they're conducted by magistrates, justices of the peace, municipal court judges, or other members of the lower court judiciary. There's no constitutional right to a preliminary hearing. But if states do provide for preliminary hearings, the Sixth Amendment guarantees defendants the right to have a lawyer represent them at the hearing (*Gerstein v. Pugh* 1975).

Preliminary hearings are adversarial proceedings. The prosecution presents evidence, and then the defense can challenge it and even present its own evidence. Preliminary hearings are also public. This may sound like a trial, but it's not.

First, the rigid rules of evidence followed during trials are relaxed during preliminary hearings. In some states, preliminary hearing judges even admit illegally seized evidence and hearsay (LaFave and Israel 1984, 2:263–64). Prosecutors reveal only enough of the state's evidence (e.g., a witness or two and minimal physical evidence) to satisfy the **bind-over standard** (there's enough evidence for the judge to decide to go to trial). Why? Because it takes time and, probably more important, prosecutors don't want to give away any more of their case than they have to. The defense typically introduces no evidence, because they don't want to give away their case either; instead, defense attorneys limit their participation to cross-examining the state's witnesses.

The objective basis for going to trial is probable cause, but don't confuse this with probable cause to arrest (Chapter 5). Most courts hold that it takes more **probable cause to bind over** someone for trial than it does to arrest the person. Why? Because the consequences of going to trial are graver. Defendants are detained longer, and the ordeals of criminal prosecution, conviction, and punishment are greater. Even if they aren't convicted, defendants have to pay their lawyers; suffer the stigma of prosecution; and subject their families to hardships. As one prominent exonerated defendant asked, "How do I get my reputation back?" The consequences fall not only on defendants but also on the government. The state has to spend scarce resources to prove guilt, and that takes away resources for other services, such as education and road repairs.

The *bind-over standard* reflects the idea that the greater the invasions and deprivations against individuals, the more facts that are needed to back them up. Just how many facts does it take to move a case to trial? Some courts have adopted a **prima facie case rule**. According to this standard, the judge can bind over a defendant if the prosecution presents evidence that could convict if the defense doesn't rebut it at trial. Others have adopted a **directed verdict rule**. According to this rule, preliminary hearing judges should look at the case as if it's a trial and they're deciding whether there's enough believable evidence to send the case to the jury. If there isn't enough, then the judge should dismiss the case. The minimum amount of evidence required to bind over under the directed verdict rule is more than enough to add up to probable cause to arrest but less than enough to "prove the defendant's guilt beyond a reasonable doubt" (*Myers v. Commonwealth* 1973, 824).

LO 7 Grand Jury Review

Grand jury review is ancient. Originating in medieval England as a council of local residents that helped the king look into matters of royal concern (crime, revenues, and official misconduct), the grand jury was an investigating body. However, by the time of the American Revolution, the grand jury had another duty: It screened criminal cases to protect individuals from malicious and unfounded prosecution. So the grand jury had two functions: to act as a sword to root out crime and corruption and as a shield to protect innocent people from unwarranted state intrusion.

Colonists warmly approved of the grand jury shield function, because it "shielded" them from prosecution for their antiroyalist sentiments. For that reason, the Fifth Amendment to the U.S. Constitution provides that "no person shall be held to answer for a capital, or otherwise infamous crime, unless on a presentment or indictment by a Grand Jury." But grand jury indictment is one of the very few provisions in the Bill of Rights that doesn't apply to state court proceedings under the incorporation doctrine (Chapter 2).

Grand juries vary from state to state both in their membership and in the procedures they follow. Let's look at grand jury membership, grand jury proceedings, and the debate over grand juries.

The members of the grand jury

We'll use as an example of choosing grand jury members the operation of the federal grand jury in the Southern District of New York, a jurisdiction that includes Manhattan, the Bronx, and several New York counties as far north as Albany (Frankel and Naftalis 1977, Chapter 4).

Federal grand juries consist of 16 to 23 jurors. To qualify, prospective grand jurors have to

1. Be U.S. citizens
2. Be 18 or over
3. Reside in the jurisdiction
4. Have no felony convictions
5. Speak, write, and read English
6. Suffer from no physical impairments that might hamper their participation, such as impaired hearing or vision

The jurisdiction sometimes summons nearly 200 citizens for jury service—many more than are needed. The process of narrowing down the number of potential jurors and selecting the final 16 to 23 is called "purging" the grand jury. The process does eliminate prospective grand jurors with compelling reasons not to serve—business, family, and health obligations—but it often hinders the selection of a representative grand jury. The resulting composition of federal grand juries overrepresents retired persons and those not burdened with other responsibilities.

Grand jury proceedings

After swearing in the grand jurors, judges **charge the grand jury.** Some charges are calls to action against specific dangers. Others resemble stump speeches for law and order or constitutional rights. Almost all include a history and outline of grand jury duties and responsibilities, warnings about the secrecy of grand jury proceedings, and admonitions to protect the innocent and condemn the guilty. Following the charge, judges turn grand jurors over to prosecutors to conduct grand jury proceedings. Unlike preliminary hearings, grand jury proceedings don't require a judge's participation.

Grand jury secrecy severely restricts who's allowed to attend proceedings. In addition to the grand jurors themselves, only the prosecutor, witnesses called to testify, and stenographers appear in the grand jury room. Defendants are banned. So are witnesses' attorneys, even though these witnesses are often themselves grand jury targets (individuals who themselves are under suspicion and investigation). But witnesses may (and often do) bring their lawyers to the courthouse for consultation outside the grand jury room.

After all witnesses have testified and prosecutors have introduced any other evidence, prosecutors draw up an indictment and present it to the grand jury for consideration. Prosecutors then sum up the reasons the evidence amounts to a crime and leave during grand jury deliberations, which ordinarily take only a few minutes. Grand juries rarely disagree with prosecutors' recommendations. Forepersons sign both the indictment and the true bill, which records the number of jurors who voted to indict. Federal grand jury proceedings require 12 jurors' concurrence to indict.

The entire grand jury, accompanied by the prosecutor, then proceeds to a designated courtroom to hand up the indictment, an action that amounts to the formal filing of charges, requiring defendants to answer in court. After judges check to ensure all documents are in order, they accept the indictment, which becomes a matter of public record. They also accept the true bill, but it doesn't become a public record. The judges' acceptance initiates the criminal prosecution by indictment.

The debate over the grand jury

Since the 16th century, observers have found a lot to criticize about the grand jury. The Elizabethan justice of the peace William Lambarde's charges to the Kent grand juries have preserved these early criticisms (Read 1962). Justice Lambarde praised the grand juries' capacity to aid in law enforcement but scorned their conduct in carrying out their responsibilities. Mainly, Lambarde attacked their sword function, berating them for being too timid in rooting out crimes. But he also criticized their shield function, too, attacking their weakness in screening cases.

In modern times, the debate has focused almost entirely on the grand jury's screening function. From the early 1900s, confidence in science and experts led many reformers to call for banning nonexperts from participating in criminal justice decision making. Those at the extreme wanted to abolish grand and trial juries and replace them with panels of "trained experts" to weigh evidence. However, two prestigious presidential commissions, the Wickersham Commission, appointed by President Herbert Hoover, and the National Advisory Commission, appointed by President Richard Nixon, were more in the mainstream. Both urged the abolition only of mandatory grand jury review.

Since the early 1980s, most legal commentators have condemned the grand jury. Critics make several arguments against grand jury screening. One line of attack is that grand juries are prosecutors' rubber stamps. According to one former prosecutor, a prosecutor "can indict anybody, at any time, for almost anything before a grand jury." Statistics bear out this claim. Grand juries issue *no-bills* (refusals to indict) in only a tiny percentage of cases. Even the no-bills don't necessarily show grand jury independence.

In sensitive or controversial cases, prosecutors choose grand jury review over preliminary hearings to put the burden for deciding whether or not to charge on the grand jury (LaFave and Israel 1984, 2:282–83). Critics also condemn the nonadversarial nature of grand jury review, charging it prevents either screening cases effectively or protecting citizens adequately against unwarranted prosecutions. Also, the secrecy of grand jury proceedings creates doubts and suspicion. That defendants and their lawyers can't attend grand jury sessions provides further ammunition for critics' charges that this exclusion is both unfair and results in inadequate screening. Critics also argue grand jury review is inefficient, expensive, and time-consuming.

Impaneling and servicing a grand jury is costly in terms of space, human resources, and money. The members have to be selected, notified, sworn, housed, fed, and provided other services. Finally, grand jury screening takes more time than preliminary hearings. The law surrounding grand jury proceedings is complex and technical, creating delays in the proceedings themselves and, later, in successful challenges to grand jury proceedings. In several jurisdictions, the intricacies and complexities of impaneling a grand jury guarantee attack by a skilled defense attorney and frequently result in dismissal of charges for minor discrepancies in the impaneling procedure.

On the other side, supporters of grand jury review have their arguments, too. First, they maintain grand juries cost no more than preliminary hearings. Preliminary hearings, they charge, have turned into needless "minitrials," elaborate affairs to which lawyers, judges, other court personnel, and witnesses devote a great deal of court time. Furthermore, the number of requests that defense attorneys make for continuances leads to a greater delay in, and a better chance of successful challenges to, preliminary hearings than grand jury proceedings.

Grand jury supporters also reject the contention that the grand jury doesn't effectively screen cases. They cite prosecutors who believe that grand juries are valuable sounding boards and argue that grand jurors definitely have minds of their own. The high percentage of indictments grand juries return isn't the important figure, according to supporters. Rather, the percentage of convictions—as high as 98 percent—based on indictments demonstrates that grand juries effectively screen out cases that shouldn't go to trial (Younger 1963).

Finally, grand jury review shows democracy at work. Supporters maintain that what grand jury review loses in secret and nonadversarial proceedings it more than recaptures in community participation in screening criminal cases. Citizen participation enhances public confidence in the criminal justice system. In a system where most cases don't go to trial, grand jury proceedings provide private citizens with their only opportunity to participate actively on the "front lines" of the criminal process. But, in fact, grand jurors aren't as representative of the community as trial jurors—who aren't all that representative either. Grand jury duty spans a long period of time, usually a year, and requires service at least two or three days a week. Only citizens with a lot of free time can devote such extended service in the criminal process (Graham and Letwin 1971, 681).

ARRAIGNMENT

LO 2

If defendants are indicted or bound over, the next step in the criminal process is arraignment. **Arraignment** means to bring defendants to court to hear and to answer (plead to) the charges against them. Don't confuse arraignment with the first appearance. The first appearance takes place within days of the arrest, and defendants don't have to answer the charges; arraignment happens sometimes months after the arrest, and defendants have to answer something.

There are four possible pleas (answers) to the charges:

1. Not guilty
2. Not guilty by reason of insanity
3. *Nolo contendere*
4. Guilty (Chapter 13)

Nolo contendere is a Latin phrase used by defendants who plead "no contest," meaning they don't contest the issue of guilt or innocence. There's no right to plead nolo contendere; the court has to consent to it. Why do defendants plead nolo contendere? Because it might help them in civil lawsuits, a complicated matter we don't need to explore in a criminal procedure course. Also, if a defendant pleads guilty, the court has to decide whether the plea is knowing and voluntary.

PRETRIAL MOTIONS

LO **8, 9**   **Pretrial motions** are either written or oral requests asking the court to decide questions that don't require a trial to rule on. They're an important part of both prosecutors' and defense counsel's work. They definitely spend a lot more time on "motion practice" than they spend trying cases—and probably more time than they do on plea bargaining.

Here are the pretrial motions we'll examine:

1. Double jeopardy
2. Speedy trial
3. Change of venue
4. Suppression of evidence

LO **8**   ## Double Jeopardy

The Fifth Amendment to the U.S. Constitution guarantees that "No person . . . shall . . . be subject for the same offence to be twice put in jeopardy of life or limb. . . ." Although the words "life or limb" suggest only death and corporal punishment, this guarantee against double jeopardy applies to all crimes, including decisions in juvenile proceedings.

The ban on **double jeopardy** protects several interests, both of the state and defendants (Table 12.4). It's supposed to allow the government "one fair shot" at convicting criminals. At the same time, it bans the government's use of its greater share of power

TABLE 12.4 Interests protected by a ban on double jeopardy

Interest	State	Defendant
Allows one fair shot at convicting defendants	Yes	
Limits the government's advantage of greater resources		Yes
Reduces prolonged stress that multiple trials would lead to		Yes
Promotes finality (closure) in criminal cases	Yes	Yes
Reduces the costs that multiple trials would lead to	Yes	Yes

and resources to subject less-powerful citizens accused of crimes to repeated attempts to convict them. Furthermore, it protects individuals from the embarrassment, expense, and ordeal—and the anxiety and insecurity—that repeated prosecutions generate.

Defendants also have an interest in completing their trials under one tribunal and jury. In addition, both the state and defendants have an interest in the finality and integrity of judgments that aren't susceptible to repeated reconsideration. Finally, the prohibition against double jeopardy reduces costs both to defendants and to the state. Retrials consume time and impede the efficient and economical disposition of other cases on crowded criminal court calendars.

The Fifth Amendment prohibition against double jeopardy kicks in as soon as the state "puts defendants to trial." In jury trials, this happens when the jury is impaneled and sworn in. The U.S. Supreme Court referred to the history of this definition of jury trials in *Crist v. Bretz* (1978), when it struck down Montana's rule that, despite swearing in the jury, jeopardy didn't attach until the first witness started testifying. The reason that jeopardy attaches when the jury is impaneled and sworn in is to protect the interest of an accused in retaining a chosen jury, an interest with roots deep in the historic development of trial by jury in the Anglo-American system of criminal justice. Throughout that history there ran a strong tradition that once banded together a jury should not be discharged until it had completed its solemn task of announcing a verdict (36).

In **bench trials**—trials without juries, in which judges find the facts—jeopardy kicks in when the court begins to hear evidence.

The point when jeopardy kicks in, or attaches, has been called the "linchpin" of the double jeopardy inquiry, but the Fifth Amendment prohibits only *double* jeopardy. So the attachment of jeopardy is necessary but not enough to kick in double jeopardy; it's only enough when defendants are exposed to double jeopardy.

What actions are protected by the ban on double jeopardy? According to the U.S. Supreme Court, the double jeopardy prohibition bans these three actions:

1. A second prosecution for the same offense after conviction
2. A second prosecution for the same offense after acquittal
3. Multiple punishments for the same offense

In cases in which jeopardy has kicked in, but the proceedings end before conviction or acquittal, the double jeopardy clause doesn't prevent a second prosecution for the same offense. This can happen in two types of cases. First, if the defendant moves to dismiss the case (or asks for or accepts a mistrial), and the judge rules in the defendant's favor, the prosecution can reprosecute. Second, the government can reprosecute for the same offense if the judge dismissed the case or ordered a mistrial because dismissal "serves the ends of justice" (**manifest necessity doctrine**).

The classic example of manifest necessity is the **hung jury**—a jury unable to reach a verdict. Why? According to the U.S. Supreme Court (*U.S. v. Perez* 1824):

> We think that in cases of this nature, the law has invested Courts of justice with the authority to discharge a jury from giving any verdict, whenever, in their opinion, taking all the circumstances into consideration, there is a manifest necessity for the act, or the ends of public justice would otherwise be defeated. They are to exercise a sound discretion on the subject; and it is impossible to define all the circumstances, which would render it proper to interfere. To be sure, the power ought to be used with the greatest of caution, under urgent circumstances. (580)

The U.S. Supreme Court revisited the hung jury question in *Renico v. Lett* (2010), our next case excerpt. After a jury trial that lasted nine hours from jury selection to jury instructions plus four hours of deliberation, the jury foreperson told the judge that the jury wasn't able to reach a verdict. The judge immediately declared a mistrial, dismissed the jury, and scheduled a new trial. At the second trial, the jury reached a verdict after three hours. On appeal, Lett argued that the second trial violated his right against double jeopardy because the trial judge had declared a mistrial without manifest necessity. The U.S. Supreme Court decided that the judge had not abused her "sound discretion" when she concluded that the jury was deadlocked.

In *Renico v. Lett* (2010), the U.S. Supreme Court held that Reginald Lett's conviction in a retrial, following the dismissal of his first trial after a hung jury, didn't violate his right against double jeopardy.

CASE

Did the Retrial Place Him in Jeopardy Twice?

Renico v. Lett
2010 WL 1740525 (2010)

HISTORY

Following reversal by intermediate state appellate court of Reginald Lett's (Petitioner's) conviction for second-degree murder and possession of a firearm during the commission of a felony, the Supreme Court of Michigan, reversed and remanded, and the intermediate appellate court affirmed on remand. Lett then sought federal habeas relief. The United States District Court for the Eastern District of Michigan granted relief, and the government appealed. The United States Court of Appeals for the Sixth Circuit, Cole, Circuit Judge, affirmed. Certiorari was granted. The U.S. Supreme Court REVERSED and REMANDED.

—ROBERTS, C.J., joined by SCALIA, KENNEDY, THOMAS, GINSBURG, and ALITO, JJ.

FACTS

On August 29, 1996, an argument broke out in a Detroit liquor store. The antagonists included Adesoji Latona, a taxi driver; Charles Jones, a passenger who claimed he had been wrongfully ejected from Latona's cab; and Reginald Lett, a friend of Jones's. After the argument began, Lett left the liquor store, retrieved a handgun from another friend outside in the parking lot, and returned to the store. He shot Latona twice, once in the head and once in the chest. Latona died from his wounds shortly thereafter. Michigan prosecutors charged Lett with first-degree murder and possession of a firearm during the commission of a felony. His trial took place in June 1997. From jury selection to jury instructions the trial took less than nine hours, spread over six different days.

The jury's deliberations began on June 12, 1997, at 3:24 p.m., and ran that day until 4 p.m. After resuming its work the next morning, the jury sent the trial court a note—one of seven it sent out in its two days of deliberations—stating that the jurors had "a concern about our voice levels disturbing any other proceedings that might be going on." Later, the jury sent out another note, asking "What if we can't agree? Mistrial? Retrial? What?"

At 12:45 p.m. the judge called the jury back into the courtroom, along with the prosecutor and defense counsel. Once the jury was seated, the following exchange took place:

The Court: I received your note asking me what if you can't agree? And I have to conclude from that that that is your situation at this time. So, I'd like to ask the foreperson to identify themselves, please?

The Foreperson: [Identified herself.]

The Court: Okay, thank you. All right. I need to ask you if the jury is deadlocked; in other words, is there a disagreement as to the verdict?

The Foreperson: Yes, there is.

The Court: All right. Do you believe that it is hopelessly deadlocked?

The Foreperson: The majority of us don't believe that—

The Court: (Interposing) Don't say what you're going to say, okay?

The Foreperson: Oh, I'm sorry.

The Court: I don't want to know what your verdict might be, or how the split is, or any of that. Thank you. Okay? Are you going to reach a unanimous verdict, or not?

The Foreperson: (No response)

The Court: Yes or no?

The Foreperson: No, Judge.

The judge then declared a mistrial, dismissed the jury, and scheduled a new trial for later that year. Neither the prosecutor nor Lett's attorney made any objection. Lett's second trial was held before a different judge and jury in November 1997. This time, the jury was able to reach a unanimous verdict—that Lett was guilty of second-degree murder—after deliberating for only 3 hours and 15 minutes.

Lett appealed his conviction to the Michigan Court of Appeals. The Michigan Court of Appeals reversed his conviction. The State appealed to the Michigan Supreme Court, which reversed the Court of Appeals. The court explained that under its decision in *United States v. Perez* (1824), a defendant may be retried following the discharge of a deadlocked jury, even if the discharge occurs without the defendant's consent. There is no double jeopardy clause violation in such circumstances, it noted, so long as the trial court exercised its "sound discretion" in concluding that the jury was deadlocked and thus that there was a "manifest necessity" for a mistrial. The court further observed that, under its decision in *Arizona v. Washington* (1978), an appellate court must generally defer to a trial judge's determination that a deadlock has been reached.

After setting forth the applicable law, the Michigan Supreme Court determined that the judge at Lett's first trial had not abused her discretion in declaring the mistrial. The court cited the facts that the jury "had deliberated for at least four hours following a relatively short, and far from complex, trial," that the jury had sent out several notes, including one that appears to indicate that its discussions may have been "particularly heated," and—"most important"—that the jury foreperson expressly stated that the jury was not going to reach a verdict.

Lett petitioned for a federal writ of habeas corpus. Again he argued that the trial court's declaration of a mistrial constituted an abuse of discretion because there was no manifest necessity to cut short the jury's deliberations. He further contended that the Michigan Supreme Court's rejection of his double jeopardy claim amounted to "an unreasonable application of . . . clearly established Federal law, as determined by the Supreme Court of the United States," and thus that he was not barred by AEDPA (Anti-Terrorism and Effective Death Penalty Act), 28 U.S.C. § 2254(d)(1), from obtaining federal habeas relief. The District Court agreed and granted the writ. On appeal, a divided panel of the U.S. Court of Appeals for the Sixth Circuit affirmed. The State petitioned for review in our Court, and we granted certiorari.

OPINION

It is important at the outset to define the question before us. That question is not whether the trial judge should have declared a mistrial. It is not even whether it was an abuse of discretion for her to have done so—the applicable standard on direct review. The question under AEDPA is instead whether the determination of the Michigan Supreme Court that there was no abuse of discretion was "an unreasonable application of . . . clearly established Federal law" § 2254(d)(1).

We have explained that "an *unreasonable* application of federal law is different from an *incorrect* application of federal law." This distinction creates "a substantially higher threshold" for obtaining relief than *de novo* review. AEDPA thus imposes a "highly deferential standard for evaluating state-court rulings," and "demands that state-court decisions be given the benefit of the doubt." The "manifest necessity" standard "cannot be interpreted literally," and that a mistrial is appropriate when there is a "high degree" of necessity. The decision whether to grant a mistrial is reserved to the "broad discretion" of the trial judge, a point that "has been consistently reiterated in decisions of this Court."

The reasons for "allowing the trial judge to exercise broad discretion" are "especially compelling" in cases involving a potentially deadlocked jury. There, the justification for deference is that "the trial court is in the best position to assess all the factors which must be considered in making a necessarily discretionary determination whether the jury will be able to reach a just verdict if it continues to deliberate." In the absence of such deference, trial judges might otherwise "employ coercive means to break the apparent deadlock," thereby creating a "significant risk that a verdict may result from pressures inherent in the situation rather than the considered judgment of all the jurors."

This is not to say that we grant *absolute* deference to trial judges in this context. The judge's exercise of discretion must be "sound," and we have made clear that "if the record reveals that the trial judge has failed to exercise the 'sound discretion' entrusted to him, the reason for such

(continued)

deference by an appellate court disappears." In light of all the foregoing, the Michigan Supreme Court's decision in this case was not unreasonable under AEDPA, and the decision of the Court of Appeals to grant Lett a writ of habeas corpus must be reversed.

AEDPA prevents defendants—and federal courts—from using federal habeas corpus review as a vehicle to second-guess the reasonable decisions of state courts. Whether or not the Michigan Supreme Court's opinion reinstating Lett's conviction in this case was *correct*, it was clearly *not unreasonable.*

The judgment of the Court of Appeals is REVERSED, and the case is REMANDED for further proceedings consistent with this opinion.

It is so ordered.

DISSENT

STEVENS, J., joined by SOTOMAYOR and BREYER, JJ.

At common law, courts went to great lengths to ensure the jury reached a verdict. Fourteenth-century English judges reportedly loaded hung juries into oxcarts and carried them from town to town until a judgment "bounced out." Less enterprising colleagues kept jurors as de facto "prisoners" until they achieved unanimity. The notion of a mistrial based on jury deadlock did not appear in Blackstone's Commentaries; it is no surprise, then, that colonial juries virtually always returned a verdict. Well into the 19th and even the 20th century, some American judges continued to coax unresolved juries toward consensus by threatening to deprive them of heat, sleep, or sustenance or to lock them in a room for a prolonged period of time.

Mercifully, our legal system has evolved, and such harsh measures are no longer tolerated. Yet what this history demonstrates—and what has not changed—is the respect owed "a defendant's valued right to have his trial completed by a particular tribunal." Our longstanding doctrine applying the Double Jeopardy Clause attests to the durability and fundamentality of this interest.

The underlying idea is that the State with all its resources and power should not be allowed to make repeated attempts to convict an individual for an alleged offense, thereby subjecting him to embarrassment, expense, and ordeal and compelling him to live in a continuing state of anxiety and insecurity, as well as enhancing the possibility that even though innocent he may be found guilty.

We have come over the years to recognize that jury coercion poses a serious threat to jurors and defendants alike, and that the accused's interest in a single proceeding must sometimes yield to the public's interest in fair trials designed to end in just judgments; and we have therefore carved out exceptions to the common-law rule. But the exceptions are narrow. For a mistrial to be granted at the prosecutor's request, the prosecutor must shoulder the burden of justifying the mistrial if he is to avoid the double jeopardy bar. His burden is a heavy one. A judge who acts *sua sponte* in declaring a mistrial must similarly make sure, and must enable a reviewing court to confirm, that there is a "manifest necessity" to deprive the defendant of his valued right.

In this case, the trial judge did not meet that burden. The record suggests that she discharged the jury without considering any less extreme courses of action, and the record makes quite clear that she did not fully appreciate the scope or significance of the ancient right at stake. The Michigan Supreme Court's decision rejecting Reginald Lett's double jeopardy claim was just as clearly in error.

No one disputes that a "genuinely deadlocked jury" is "the classic basis" for declaring a mistrial or that such declaration, under our doctrine, does not preclude reprosecution; what is disputed in this case is whether the trial judge took adequate care to ensure the jury was genuinely deadlocked. A long line of precedents from this Court establishes the "governing legal principles," for resolving this question. Although the Court acknowledges these precedents, it minimizes the heavy burden we have placed on trial courts.

We have repeatedly reaffirmed that the power to discharge the jury prior to verdict should be reserved for "extraordinary and striking circumstances," unless and until he has "scrupulously" assessed the situation and "taken care to assure himself that it warrants action on his part foreclosing the defendant from a potentially favorable judgment by the tribunal," that, to exercise sound discretion, the judge may not act "irrationally," "irresponsibly," or "precipitately" but must instead act "deliberately" and "carefully," and that, in view of "the elusive nature of the problem," mechanical rules are no substitute in the double jeopardy mistrial context for the sensitive application of general standards.

The Court accurately describes the events leading up to this trial judge's declaration of mistrial, but it glides too quickly over a number of details that, taken together, show her decision-making was neither careful nor well considered. If the "manifest necessity" and "sound discretion" standards are to have any force, we must demand more from our trial courts.

I fail to see how the trial judge exercised anything resembling "sound discretion" in declaring a mistrial, as we have defined that term. Indeed, I fail to see how a record could disclose much less evidence of sound decision-making. Within the realm of realistic, nonpretextual possibilities, this mistrial declaration was about as precipitate as one is liable to find. Four hours is not a long time for jury deliberations, particularly in a first-degree murder case. Indeed, it would have been remarkable if the jurors could review the testimony of all the witnesses in the time they were given, let alone conclude that they were deadlocked.

The jury's note pertaining to its volume level does not necessarily indicate anything about the heatedness of its discussion. "There is no other suggestion in the record that such was the case, and the trial judge did not draw that conclusion." Although it would have been preferable if Lett had tried to lodge an objection, defense counsel was given no meaningful opportunity to do so—the judge discharged the jury simultaneously with her mistrial order, counsel received no advance notice of either action, and he may not even have been informed of the content of the jury's notes. "At no point before the actual declaration of the mistrial was it even mentioned on the record as a potential course of action by the court. The summary nature of the trial court's actions . . . rendered an objection both unlikely and meaningless. Counsel's failure to object is therefore legally irrelevant. And, as detailed above, the foreperson's remarks were far more equivocal and ambiguous, in context, than the Michigan Supreme Court allowed.

In this case, Reginald Lett's constitutional rights were violated when the trial court terminated his first trial without adequate justification and he was subsequently prosecuted for the same offense. The majority does not appear to dispute this point, but it nevertheless denies Lett relief by applying a level of deference to the state court's ruling that effectively effaces the role of the federal courts. Nothing one will find in the United States Code or the United States Reports requires us to turn a blind eye to this manifestly unlawful conviction.

Questions

1. List all the relevant details surrounding the jury deliberations in Reginald Lett's first trial.

2. Summarize Chief Justice Roberts's argument for the Court's holding that the trial judge didn't abuse her discretion when she declared a mistrial due to a hung jury.

3. Summarize Justice Stevens's argument that the trial judge didn't meet her burden to make sure there was a "manifest necessity" to declare a mistrial because the jury was "hung."

4. Who has the more convincing arguments? Defend your answer with specifics from the arguments and relevant facts.

The Double Jeopardy Clause bans both multiple *punishments* and multiple *prosecutions*. Nevertheless, it's not double jeopardy to prosecute and punish a defendant for the same acts in separate jurisdictions. The main purpose of the double jeopardy clause is to restrain prosecutors and judges. According to the **dual sovereignty doctrine**, a crime arising out of the same facts in one state is not the same crime in another state. This also holds when the same conduct is a crime under both state and federal law.

In *Heath v. Alabama* (1985), Larry Heath hired Charles Owens and Gregory Lumpkin for $2,000 to kill his wife, who was then nine months pregnant. The killers fulfilled their part of the deal. Heath was sentenced to life imprisonment in a Georgia court after he pleaded guilty. However, part of the crime was committed in Alabama, so Alabama prosecuted Heath, too. He was convicted in Alabama of murder committed during a kidnapping and sentenced to death. He appealed the conviction on the grounds of double jeopardy. The U.S. Supreme Court affirmed the conviction, holding that successive prosecutions for the same crime in two different states didn't put him in jeopardy twice.

According to Justice O'Connor, writing for the majority of the Court:

> To deny a State its power to enforce its criminal laws because another State has won the race to the courthouse "would be a shocking and untoward deprivation of the historic right and obligation of the States to maintain peace and order within their confines." Such a deprivation of a State's sovereign powers cannot be justified by the assertion that under "interest analysis" the State's legitimate penal interests will be satisfied through a prosecution conducted by another State. A State's interest in vindicating its sovereign authority through

enforcement of its laws by definition can never be satisfied by another State's enforcement of its own laws. The Court has always understood the words of the Double Jeopardy Clause to reflect this fundamental principle, and we see no reason why we should reconsider that understanding today. (93)

Also, it doesn't put defendants in double jeopardy to prosecute them in multiple trials for separate offenses arising out of the same incident. The U.S. Supreme Court decided this in the horrific multiple-murder case, *Ciucci v. Illinois* (1958). Vincent Ciucci was married and had three children. When he fell in love with a 21-year-old woman he wanted to marry, his wife wouldn't give him a divorce. So he shot her and all three of his children in the head one by one while they slept. Illinois used the same evidence to convict Ciucci in three separate murder trials. The Court decided that the multiple trials, even if they stemmed from the same incident, didn't put Ciucci in jeopardy more than once.

LO 9   A Speedy Trial

According to the Sixth Amendment, "In all criminal trials, the accused shall enjoy the right to a speedy . . . trial." The idea of speedy justice is more than 900 years older than the Bill of Rights. In 1187, King Henry II provided for "speedy justice" in the Assizes of Clarendon. King John promised in the Magna Carta in 1215 that "every subject of this realme . . . may . . . have justice . . . speedily without delay." In his *Institutes*—called by Thomas Jefferson, "the universal elementary book of law students" (*Klopfer v. North Carolina* 1967, 225)—Sir Edward Coke (1797) wrote that the English itinerant justices in 1600 "have not suffered the prisoner to be long detained, but, at their next coming, have given the prisoner full and speedy justice, . . . without detaining him long in prison" (*Klopfer v. North Carolina* 1967, 224). The Virginia Declaration of Rights in 1776 (the state's "bills of rights") and the speedy trial clause of the Sixth Amendment reflect this history. And even though the state constitutions guarantee a speedy trial, the U.S. Supreme Court has extended the federal speedy trial protection of the Sixth Amendment to the states (225).

The speedy trial clause promotes and balances several interests. For the accused, it prevents prolonged detention before trial; reduces the anxiety and uncertainty surrounding criminal prosecution; and guards against weakening the defense's case through loss of alibi witnesses and other evidence. And because most detained defendants are poor, both the process interest in ensuring equal protection of the laws and the societal interest in protecting the poor and less powerful are at stake in speedy trial decisions (*Report to the Nation on Crime and Justice* 1988, 123).

The speedy trial provision also promotes the interest in obtaining the correct result. Delay means lost evidence and lost witnesses—or at least the loss of their memory— not only for the defense but also for the prosecution. The clause also promotes process goals, particularly that decisions should be made in a timely fashion. Organizational interests are at stake as well. Failure to provide prompt trials contributes to large case backlogs, particularly in urban areas. Furthermore, long pretrial detention is costly to taxpayers. In addition to feeding and housing detained defendants, lost wages and greater welfare burdens result from incarceration.

According to the U.S. Supreme Court, the Sixth Amendment "speedy trial clock" doesn't start ticking until suspects are charged formally with crimes. Before they're charged, defendants have to depend on either statutes spelling out the length of time allowed between the commission of crimes and the filing of charges (statutes of limitations) or the due process clauses. So in rejecting a speedy trial violation in a delay of three years between the commission of the crime and an indictment, the Court said:

> The due process clause of the Fifth Amendment would require dismissal of the indictment if it were shown at trial that the pre-indictment delay . . . caused substantial prejudice to appellants' rights to a fair trial and that the delay was an intentional device to gain tactical advantage over the accused. (*U.S. v. Marion* 1971, 324)

The speedy trial clause bans only *undue* delays. According to the U.S. Supreme Court, flexibility governs whether delays are undue enough to violate the speedy trial clause. The Court has adopted another one of its balancing tests to decide whether delays hurt ("prejudice," if you want the technical term) defendants' cases. Four elements make up the balance:

1. The length of the delay
2. The reason for the delay
3. The defendant's assertion of his or her right to a speedy trial
4. The prejudice (harm) the delay causes to the defendant's case

What are the consequences of violating the speedy trial guarantee? According to the Court, there are only two remedies for the violation of the speedy trial clause:

1. **Dismissal without prejudice.** Allows a new prosecution for the same offense
2. **Dismissal with prejudice.** Terminates the case with the provision that it can't be prosecuted again

According to a unanimous U.S. Supreme Court, even though there's enough evidence for conviction, undue delay subjects defendants to "emotional stress" that requires dismissal as "the only possible remedy." The Court's ruling has raised the strong objection that the high price of dismissal will make courts "extremely hesitant" to find speedy trial violations because judges don't want to be responsible for freeing criminals (*Strunk v. U.S.* 1973).

Although the Sixth Amendment doesn't require it, several states have enacted statutes or court rules that set time limits for bringing cases to trial. These limits vary widely among the states. The Federal Speedy Trial Act provides definite time periods for bringing defendants to trial. The government has to start prosecution within 30 days after arrest (60 days if there's no grand jury in session); arraign defendants within 10 days after filing indictments or informations; and bring defendants to trial within 60 days following arraignment.

According to the act, the following delays don't count in computing days:

1. Delays needed to determine the defendant's competency to stand trial
2. Delays due to other trials of the defendant
3. Delays due to hearings on pretrial motions
4. Delays because of *interlocutory appeals*—provisional appeals that interrupt the proceedings, such as an appeal from a ruling on a pretrial motion

LO 9   A Change of Venue

The Sixth Amendment provides that "in all criminal prosecutions, the accused shall enjoy the right to a . . . public trial, by an impartial jury of the State and district wherein the crime shall have been committed." A defendant's pretrial motion to **change the venue** (the place where the trial is held) waives the Sixth Amendment right to have a trial in the state and district where the crime was committed. Only defendants, not the prosecution, may move to change the venue, and changes of venue aren't automatic.

According to Rule 21(a) of the *Federal Rules of Criminal Procedure* (2002):

> The court upon motion of the defendant shall transfer the proceeding as to that defendant to another district . . . if the court is satisfied that there exists in the district where the prosecution is pending so great a prejudice against the defendant that the defendant cannot obtain a fair and impartial trial at any place fixed for holding court in that district.

Why do defendants give up their right to a trial in the place where the crime was committed? Because they believe they can't get an impartial public trial in that location. When courts rule on the motion, they balance the right to a public trial in the place where the crime was committed against the right to an impartial trial. In that respect, changing venue reflects the interest in obtaining a proper result in the individual case—prejudiced jurors can't find the truth. Process values are also at stake: The integrity of the judicial process requires a calm, dignified, reflective atmosphere; due process demands unbiased fact-finding; the equal protection clause prohibits trying defendants who are the object of public outrage differently from other defendants.

In *Sheppard v. Maxwell* (1966), the U.S. Supreme Court held that "where there is a reasonable likelihood that the prejudicial news prior to trial will prevent a fair trial, the judge should continue the case until the threat abates, or transfer it to another county not so permeated with publicity" (363).

In this case, Ohio tried Dr. Sam Sheppard for the bludgeoning murder of his pregnant wife, Marilyn, a Cleveland socialite. The case dominated the news and gripped the public's attention before, during, and after the trial. Lurid headlines and long stories appeared regularly, detailing the brutality of the murder and Sheppard's failure to cooperate with authorities. The editorials accused Sheppard of the murder. One charged on the front page that "somebody is getting away with murder," alleging that Sheppard's wealth and prominent social position protected him from a full-fledged investigation by police. Finally, the papers printed detailed analyses of evidence that came to light during the investigation, editorializing about its credibility, relevance, and materiality to the case.

As for the trial itself, the press, the public, and other observers packed the courtroom every day. One local radio station set up broadcasting facilities on the third floor of the courthouse. Television and newsreel cameras waiting outside on the courthouse steps filmed jurors, lawyers, witnesses, and other participants in the trial. All the jurors were exposed to the heavy publicity prior to the trial. The public was so fascinated by the case that television later based the popular 1960s drama *The Fugitive* (and the 1993 movie) on it. (The fascination continued for television viewers who watched a short-lived 2001 version of *The Fugitive*.)

Sheppard was convicted, and his appeals made it to the U.S. Supreme Court. In granting Sheppard a new trial, the Court ruled that the proceedings should have been postponed or the trial venue moved because of a reasonable likelihood of prejudice. The **reasonable-likelihood-of-prejudice test** requires courts to balance four elements in each change-of-venue case:

1. The kind and amount of community bias that endangers a fair trial
2. The size of the community where jury panels are selected
3. The details and seriousness of the offense
4. The status of the victim and the accused

These elements may vary in intensity, and they don't all have to be present in each case; they're guidelines for judges when they measure the likelihood the defendant will receive a fair trial.

Most courts don't grant changes of venue even if defendants show there's a reasonable likelihood of prejudice. Instead, they adopt an **actual prejudice test** to determine whether to change the venue or take less drastic measures. Under the actual prejudice test, courts have to decide whether jurors were, in fact, prejudiced by harmful publicity. Referring to the "carnival atmosphere" at Sheppard's trial, the U.S. Supreme Court concluded that he was entitled to a new trial without showing actual prejudice—a reasonable likelihood of prejudice was sufficient.

In another case, *Swindler v. State* (1979), John Edward Swindler proved that three jurors had read and heard about the case and that over 80 percent of prospective jurors were excused for cause. But this didn't stop the Arkansas Supreme Court from rejecting Swindler's claim that the trial court's refusal to grant his motion for change of venue denied him a fair trial and upholding Swindler's death sentence. The Supreme Court didn't find proof of actual prejudice during the trial. Swindler's experience is an example of how rare change of venue is.

In deciding whether the venue should be changed, courts consider a number of issues (Table 12.5). Moving proceedings to jurisdictions farther away, providing for witnesses to appear, and working in unfamiliar court surroundings hinder smooth, efficient, economical resolution of criminal cases. Furthermore, society has a strong interest in maintaining public confidence in the criminal justice system and providing an outlet for community reaction to crime. Citizens resent moving trials both because they want to follow the proceedings, and they feel insulted by a ruling that their own jurisdiction can't guarantee a fair trial.

LO 9 The Suppression of Evidence

As you've already learned, almost every case excerpt dealing with police work is about a struggle between defendants who want to keep evidence out of court and prosecutors who want to get it in. The reason for this struggle is the exclusionary rule (Chapter 10).

TABLE 12.5 Factors considered in change-of-venue motions

• Trials at distant locations burden witnesses.
• Communities have a substantial interest in the trial taking place where the crime was committed.
• Changing prosecutors disrupts the state's case.
• Courts can't decide the partiality question until the jury has been impaneled.
• Courts don't want to transfer a case after all the time spent in picking a jury.

© Cengage Learning

Whether the exclusionary rule applies is decided in a pretrial hearing triggered by a defense motion to suppress evidence that law enforcement officers obtained by searches, seizures, confessions, or identification procedures (Chapters 4–9). The decision whether to let evidence in or keep it out is a legal question, meaning judges, not juries, decide whether to exclude evidence.

CHAPTER SUMMARY

LO 1   Prosecutors' discretionary power to charge is practically unlimited. Prosecutors drop cases if they don't think they can prove them, or if, as "officers of the court," they feel prosecution wouldn't serve justice. Selective prosecution is a necessity based on limited resources.

LO 2   When suspects are arrested without a warrant, magistrates must determine whether there's probable cause to detain them in a reasonable amount of time. More facts are needed for probable cause to go to trial than to arrest and detain a suspect.

LO 2   The criminal complaint formally charges defendants and authorizes the magistrate to conduct the first appearance. Suspects in misdemeanor crimes often plead guilty at the first appearance. At an arraignment, suspects are considered defendants and required to appear in court to enter a plea.

LO 3   Pretrial release and bail take a variety of forms, such as citation release, release on recognizance, and release on money bonds.

LO 4   Most defendants are released on bail as they await trial. Those that aren't released often spend significant amounts of time in jail at considerable public expense.

LO 4   There's no constitutional right to bail, but there's a constitutional right against excessive bail. How much bail is excessive is determined by the severity of the offense and the suspect's ability to pay.

LO 4   Constitutional rights that affect bail include due process, because being locked up could prevent suspects from preparing a defense, and equal protection, because being poor could affect whether a suspect is freed.

LO 5   Preventive detention hearings may deny bail to dangerous suspects after they've been given the right to an appointed lawyer, to testify at the preventive detention hearing, to present evidence, and to cross-examine witnesses. Jailed defendants are legally innocent and don't forfeit their constitutional rights, but their rights are watered down in jail.

LO 6   The right to retained (paid) counsel was extended to appointed (free) counsel in the 1930s, and most large counties retain public defenders. The right to appointed counsel applies to poor defendants when conviction would result in significant jail time. Courts uphold the right to effective counsel and to choose a lawyer under the older "mockery of justice" standard or the more modern and common "reasonably competent attorney" standard.

LO 6   The right to counsel attaches to all critical stages of the criminal process, including custodial interrogation, lineups after formal charges, grand jury appearances, and arraignments. The right doesn't attach to investigative stops, frisks, or first appearances at trial.

LO **7**   Preliminary hearings and grand jury reviews test the government's case against the defendant. These hearings have relaxed standards of evidence and testimony and defendants are banned from them. Grand juries determine whether there's probable cause to go to trial. In the vast majority of cases, courts simply ratify what was worked out in informal negotiations called plea bargains.

LO **8, 9**   Pretrial motions ask courts to decide questions that don't require a trial. The Fifth Amendment protection against double jeopardy ensures the prosecution has "one fair shot" at convicting a defendant. The Constitution guarantees a speedy trial, so prosecution must begin promptly. The Constitution ensures that changes of venue occur only at the defendant's request and only where great prejudice would otherwise exist.

REVIEW QUESTIONS

1. Describe what occurs following arrest, interrogation, and identification procedures.
2. List the reasons that affect whether police drop cases or take them to prosecutors.
3. Identify the two roles of prosecutors and how the roles affect their decisions.
4. According to the U.S. Supreme Court, why is the initiation of judicial proceedings not just a "mere formalism"?
5. List and explain the importance of the reasons behind the decision of prosecutors to charge, divert, or drop criminal cases.
6. Why and when do police officers have to take arrested suspects to a magistrate?
7. Explain the difference between probable cause to detain a suspect and probable cause to go to trial.
8. What's the significance of the U.S. Supreme Court case *Gerstein v. Pugh*?
9. List the "administrative steps" police officers can complete before they take detained suspects to magistrates.
10. Identify and describe the consequences of detention before trial.
11. Describe the balance struck in the decision to bail or detain defendants.
12. Exactly what does the constitutional right to bail consist of?
13. Identify three constitutional rights our bail system denies to poor defendants, and explain how each is denied.
14. Describe the obstacles pretrial detention creates for defendants trying to prepare their defense.
15. According to the 1984 Bail Reform Act, when can judges preventively detain defendants?
16. What constitutional rights do pretrial detainees have regarding the conditions of their confinement?
17. List the "critical stages" of criminal prosecutions.
18. Summarize the facts of the U.S. Supreme Court decision in *Argersinger v. Hamlin*.
19. List four guidelines for defining indigence developed by the U.S. Courts of Appeals, and summarize the detailed definition of indigence adopted in Minnesota.

20. Identify, define, and explain the two prongs of the U.S. Supreme Court's test of "effective" counsel adopted in *Strickland v. Washington*.

21. List and describe the differences between testing the government's case by grand jury review and by preliminary hearing.

22. Identify the four possible pleas defendants can enter at their arraignment.

23. Describe and explain the significance of the U.S. Supreme Court decisions in *Heath v. Alabama* and *Ciucci v. Illinois*.

24. According to the Federal Speedy Trial Act, when does the government have to begin prosecution? Arraign defendants? Bring defendants to trial?

25. Summarize the arguments against changes of venue.

26. Describe and summarize the significance of the U.S. Supreme Court decision in *Sheppard v. Maxwell*.

27. What kind of question is answered by the motion to suppress evidence?

KEY TERMS

officers of the court, p. 450
diversion cases, p. 451
decision to charge, p. 451
selective prosecution, p. 451
probable cause to detain
a suspect, p. 452
first appearance, p. 453
probable cause to go to trial, p. 453
class action, p. 453
criminal complaint, p. 456
released on recognizance (ROR),
p. 458
money bonds, p. 458
preventive detention, p. 460
Bail Reform Act of 1984 (BRA),
p. 460
clear and convincing evidence,
p. 460
retained counsel, p. 466
appointed counsel, p. 466
indigent defendants, p. 466

counsel pro bono, p. 466
critical stages of criminal
proceedings, p. 468
authorized imprisonment standard,
p. 470
actual imprisonment standard,
p. 470
indigence, p. 471
mockery of justice standard, p. 472
reasonably competent attorney
standard, p. 472
two-pronged effective counsel test,
p. 472
reasonableness prong, p. 473
prejudice prong, p. 473
preliminary hearing, p. 479
grand jury review, p. 479
criminal information, p. 479
indictment, p. 479
grand jurors, p. 479
binds over, p. 479

bind-over standard, p. 480
probable cause to bind over,
p. 480
prima facie case rule, p. 480
directed verdict rule, p. 480
charge the grand jury, p. 481
arraignment, p. 483
nolo contendere, p. 484
pretrial motions, p. 484
double jeopardy, p. 484
bench trials, p. 485
manifest necessity doctrine,
p. 485
hung jury, p. 485
dual sovereignty doctrine, p. 489
dismissal without prejudice, p. 491
dismissal with prejudice, p. 491
change of venue, p. 492
reasonable-likelihood-of-prejudice
test, p. 493
actual prejudice test, p. 493

13

Court Proceedings II

Trial and Conviction

LEARNING OBJECTIVES

1 Understand that jury trials promote fact-finding and check government power. Know the constitutional rights the trial by jury process must protect.

2 Know the stages of a jury trial and the constitutional amendments that guarantee defendants the right to a public trial.

3 Know the types of verdicts juries can give, the purpose of the unanimous verdict requirement, and the significance of jury nullification.

4 Understand the difference between straight guilty pleas, negotiated guilty pleas, charge bargaining, and sentence bargaining.

5 Know the circumstances under which guilty pleas and plea bargaining are constitutional and understand the rights that defendants waive when they enter a guilty plea.

6 Know, understand, and appreciate the empirical research regarding plea bargains in and outside "the shadow of trial."

One time Judge Golde called me [the prosecutor] into chambers [during a recess in jury selection] and asked rhetorically "Quatman, what are you doing?" When I asked what the problem was, he said I had not challenged a prospective juror who was Jewish. He said I could not have a Jew on the jury, and asked me if I was aware that when Adolph Eichmann was apprehended after World War II there was a major controversy in Israel over whether he should be executed. Judge Golde said no Jew would vote to send a defendant to the gas chamber. I thanked Judge Golde for his advice, and thereafter excused any prospective juror who was Jewish. Actually, Judge Golde was only telling me what I already should have known to do. It was standard practice to exclude Jewish jurors in death cases; as it was to exclude African–American women from capital juries.

—In re Fred Harlan Freeman, 133 P.3d 1013 (CA 2006)

Plea bargaining is not some adjunct to the criminal justice system; it is the criminal justice system.

—Scott and Stuntz (1992, 2012)

ourt proceedings are sharply divided into adversarial proceedings inside the courtroom and informal negotiations outside the courtroom. Three constitutional commands lie behind the trial and conviction of defendants in criminal cases:

1. *Article III, § 2.* The Trial of all Crimes, except in Cases of Impeachment, shall be by Jury; and such Trial shall be held in the State where the Crimes shall have been committed.

2. *The Fifth Amendment.* No person shall be . . . compelled in any criminal case to be a witness against himself.

3. *The Sixth Amendment.* In all criminal prosecutions, the accused shall enjoy the right to a speedy and public trial, by an impartial jury of the State and District wherein the crime shall have been committed . . . to be confronted with the witnesses against him, . . . and to have the assistance of Counsel for his defense.

These constitutional commands set high standards because conviction for a crime can result in the greatest deprivations (loss of property, liberty, privacy, and perhaps even life itself) in the criminal process. These commands are directed almost exclusively at criminal trials.

Although trials receive most of the attention in the news, and of course in movies and television, they account for only about 5 out of every 100 convictions (Table 13.1). The other

TABLE 13.1 Types of felony convictions in state courts

Most Serious Conviction Offense	Total %*	Jury %	Bench %	Guilty Plea %
All offenses	6	4	2	94
Violent offenses	10	8	2	90
Murder/Nonnegligent manslaughter	39	36	2	61
Sexual assault	12	10	2	88
Rape	16	13	3	84
Other sexual assault	9	8	2	91
Robbery	11	9	2	89
Aggravated assault	8	5	3	92
Other violent	7	5	2	93
Property offenses	5	3	2	95
Burglary	6	4	2	94
Larceny	5	3	2	95
Motor vehicle theft	4	4	—	96
Fraud/Forgery	5	3	2	95
Drug offenses	4	3	2	96
Possession	2	1	1	98
Trafficking	6	3	2	94
Weapon offenses	7	5	2	93
Other specified offenses	3	3	1	97

*May not add up to 100% because of rounding

Source: Bureau of Justice Statistics. *Felony Sentences in State Courts, 2006—Statistical Tables.* December 2009, NCJ 226846.

95 result from guilty pleas. Some of these guilty pleas result from plea bargaining, but many are straight guilty pleas (pleas of guilty without negotiation).

Trials and guilty pleas promote different interests. The trial promotes fact-finding by the adversarial process, procedural regularity, and public participation in criminal proceedings. The guilty plea promotes efficiency, economy, harmony, and speed. Plea negotiations also promote fact-finding by informal discussion and the give-and-take that occur in reaching an agreement over the plea.

In this chapter, we'll examine the constitutionally mandated trial by jury, the stages and rules of jury trials, and conviction by guilty pleas.

TRIAL BY JURY

LO 1

Trial by jury is ancient, with roots in the societies of the Teutonic tribes in Germany and the Normans before their conquest of England. The Assizes of Clarendon in 1187 and the Magna Carta in 1215 also contain traces of its origins. The jury trial was provided for specifically in the English Bill of Rights in 1689, and it then became common practice in the British American colonies.

From the start, the colonists resented royal interference with the right to a jury trial. Complaints regarding that interference appear in the Stamp Act, the First Continental Congress's resolves, and the Declaration of Independence. Article III, § 2, in the body of the U.S. Constitution, and the Sixth Amendment reflect the new nation's commitment to jury trial. Every state constitution guarantees it, and the U.S. Supreme Court has interpreted the due process clause of the Fourteenth Amendment to require states to provide it (*Duncan v. Louisiana* 1968).

Trial by jury promotes several interests. It checks and balances government power by putting an independent community-dominated body between the state, with all its resources, and a single individual. Jury trial also balances official power with citizen participation in criminal law enforcement. In addition, it guarantees that accused citizens who prefer that other citizens decide their innocence or guilt will have that preference honored.

In extending the Sixth Amendment's jury trial right to the states, Justice Byron R. White wrote the following:

> The guarantees of jury trial reflect a profound judgment about the way in which law should be enforced and justice administered. Providing an accused with the right to be tried by a jury of his peers gave him an inestimable safeguard against the corrupt or overzealous prosecutor and against the compliant, biased, or eccentric judge. Beyond this, the jury trial reflects a reluctance to entrust plenary powers over the life and liberty of the citizen to one judge or to a group of judges. Fear of unchecked power, so typical of our State and Federal Governments in other respects, found expression in the criminal law in this insistence upon community participation in the determination of guilt or innocence. (*Duncan v. Louisiana* 1968, 156)

Let's explore more fully the meaning of the right to a trial by jury by examining how this right is affected by the moral seriousness standard, the issue of how many citizens are required to sit on a jury, the jury selection process, and the right to a public trial.

LO 1

The Moral Seriousness Standard

According to the U.S. Supreme Court, there's one major exception to the right to a jury trial for "all crimes," in Article III, § 2, and "all criminal prosecutions," in the Sixth Amendment. That exception is for "petty offenses" (*Duncan v. Louisiana* 1968, 160). But in setting the **moral seriousness standard**, the Court extended the Sixth Amendment right to a jury trial to morally serious misdemeanors that can lead to jail time. In jurisdictions where there's no specific law drawing a line between petty and other offenses, the Court has used six months' imprisonment as the dividing line (*Baldwin v. New York* 1970).

By taking the "moral quality" of offenses into account in practice, courts have declared some offenses serious even if the penalty is less than six months' imprisonment. So, under this moral seriousness standard, courts have decided defendants had a right to a jury trial when charged with conspiring to deceive immigration officials (*U.S. v. Sanchez-Meza* 1976), driving while intoxicated (*U.S. v. Craner* 1981), and shoplifting (*State v. Superior Court* 1978), even though the penalty for these offenses was less than six months in jail.

LO 1

The 12-Member Jury Requirement

The 12-member jury at one time was regarded by the U.S. Supreme Court as essential to the right to a jury trial (*Thompson v. Utah* 1898). The Court has since retreated from that position. Justice Byron R. White spelled out the reasons in *Williams v. Florida* (1970):

1. We can't "pretend" to know the Framers' intent.
2. The number 12 is based on superstition about the number (12 apostles, 12 tribes).
3. History doesn't give good enough reasons to stick to 12 members in today's world.

So, according to the Court in *Williams v. Florida* (1970), the Sixth Amendment only demands enough jurors to achieve the goals of a jury trial to find the truth and allow for community participation in criminal justice decision making. And that number isn't necessarily 12:

> That the jury at common law was composed of precisely 12 is a historical accident, unnecessary to effect the purposes of the jury system and wholly without significance "except to mystics." To read the Sixth Amendment as forever codifying a feature so incidental to the real purpose of the Amendment is to ascribe a blind formalism to the Framers which would require considerably more evidence than we have been able to discover in the history and language of the Constitution or in the reasoning of our past decisions. (102)

The 12-member jury has strong supporters, despite the Court's dismissal of it as superstitious. Justice John Marshall Harlan called the accident of superstition argument "much too thin." If the number 12 was merely an accident, it was one that "has recurred without interruption since the 14th century." Also, according to Justice Harlan:

> If 12 jurors are not essential, why are six? Can it be doubted that a unanimous jury of 12 provides a greater safeguard than a majority vote of six? The uncertainty that will henceforth plague the meaning of trial by jury is itself a further reason for not hoisting the anchor of history. . . . The [Court's] circumvention

of history is compounded by the cavalier disregard of numerous pronounce-
ments of this Court that reflect the understanding of the jury as one of
12 members and have fixed expectations accordingly. (*Baldwin v. New York*
1970, 126)

Judges aren't the only ones who support the 12-member jury. Social scientists have
found that juries with 12 members are right more often, and they represent the community better than juries with fewer than 12 members. Hans Zeisel, a major authority
on the jury, had this to say about the 12-member jury:

Suppose that in a given community, 90 percent of the people share one viewpoint and the remaining 10 percent have a different viewpoint. Suppose further
that we draw 100 twelve-member and 100 six-member juries. Using standard
statistical methods, it can be predicted that approximately 72 of the twelve-
member juries will contain a representative of the 10 percent minority, as compared to only 47 juries composed of six persons. This difference is by no means
negligible. (LaFave and Israel 1984, 2:696, n. 57)

Six-member juries are enough to satisfy the Sixth Amendment, but what about
five? The Supreme Court answered "no" in *Ballew v. Georgia* (1978).

LO 1 Jury Selection

According to the U.S. Supreme Court, the Sixth Amendment right to an "impartial
jury" requires that juries represent a "fair cross section" of the community. Furthermore, the equal protection clause of the Fourteenth Amendment bars the systematic exclusion of members of defendants' racial, gender, ethnic, or religious group.
The **Federal Jury Selection and Service Act** meets these constitutional requirements by requiring that juries be "selected at random from a fair cross section of
the community in the district or division wherein the court convenes," and "No
citizen shall be excluded from service as a grand or petit juror in the district courts
of the United States on account of race, color, religion, sex, national origin, or
economic status."

Most states have similar provisions. To implement them, jurisdictions select jurors
at random from the following sources:

- Local census reports
- Tax rolls
- City directories
- Telephone books
- Driver's license lists

Some states, mainly in New England and the South, use the **key-man system**,
in which civic and political leaders recommend people from these lists whom
they know personally or by reputation. Understandably, the *key-man system* faces
repeated challenges that it doesn't represent a fair cross section of the community
and that it discriminates against various segments in the community (LaFave and
Israel 1984, 2:708).

Jury service isn't popular; most prospective jurors ask to be excused (Table 13.2).
Courts rarely refuse their requests because it's "easier, administratively and financially,

TABLE 13.2 Common excuses for exemption from jury service

Economic hardship
Need to care for small children
Advanced age
Distance between home and the courthouse is too far
Illness

© Cengage Learning

to excuse unwilling people" (LaFave and Israel 1984, 2:708). Some groups are ordinarily exempt from jury service, including:

- Persons below voting age
- Convicted felons
- Persons who can't write and read English

    Some occupations are also exempt in some states:

- Doctors
- Pharmacists
- Teachers
- Clergy
- Lawyers
- Judges
- Criminal justice professionals
- Some other public employees (LaFave and Israel 1984, 2:708–9)

From the **jury panel** (the potential jurors drawn from the list of eligible citizens not excused), the attorneys for the government and the defendant pick the jurors who will actually serve. The process of picking the actual jurors from the pool of potential jurors by questioning them is called the *voir dire*—literally, "to speak the truth." Both prosecutors and defense attorneys can remove jurors during the *voir dire*. There are two ways of removing (usually called **striking**) potential jurors, **peremptory challenges** (striking without having to give a reason) and **challenges for cause** (striking by showing the juror is biased). Lawyers almost always use their peremptory challenges to strike potential jurors they believe will sympathize with the other side. Attorneys use challenges for cause only when they can convince judges of juror bias.

The number of *peremptory challenges* depends on the jurisdiction; the number of *challenges for cause* is unlimited. In the federal courts, both the prosecution and the defense have 20 peremptories in capital offenses and 3 in misdemeanors. In felony cases, defendants have 10, and the government has 6. Both sides rarely exercise their right to challenges for cause—usually one to three times to assemble a jury of 12 (Van Dyke 1977, 14).

Inquiring into racial prejudice during *voir dire* is sensitive. We know that prejudice can sway some jurors' judgment (*Strauder v. West Virginia* 1880). Prejudice can cause specific defendants harm when discrimination infects jury selection. But it can also harm certain groups generally. For example, by drawing racial, gender, sexual orientation, and other group lines in picking juries, prosecutors "establish state-sponsored group stereotypes rooted in, and reflective of, historical prejudice" (*Miller-El v. Dretke* 2005, 237–38). The harm doesn't stop with minorities.

When the government's choice of jurors is tainted with racial bias, that overt wrong casts doubt over the obligation of the parties, the jury, and indeed the court to adhere to the law throughout the trial. That is, the very integrity of the courts is jeopardized when a prosecutor's discrimination invites cynicism respecting the jury's neutrality, and undermines public confidence in adjudication (238).

As a result, since 1880, the U.S. Supreme Court has "consistently and repeatedly reaffirmed that racial discrimination by the State in jury selection offends the equal protection clause." It's clear, therefore, that the Court recognizes the problem of discrimination. "The rub has been the practical difficulty of ferreting out discrimination in selections discretionary by nature, and choices subject to myriad legitimate influences, whatever the race of the individuals on the panel from which jurors are selected" (238).

In *Swain v. Alabama* (1965), the Court addressed the problem of the amount of proof to show intentional discrimination without disturbing both the prosecution's and defense's "historical prerogative to make a peremptory strike or challenge, the very nature of which is traditionally without a reason stated" (238). The Court presumed that the prosecution's strikes were legitimate, "except in the face of a longstanding pattern of discrimination." Specifically, "when 'in case after case, whatever the circumstances,' no blacks served on juries, then 'giving the widest leeway to the operation of irrational but trial-related suspicions and antagonisms, it would appear that the purposes of the peremptory challenge were being perverted'" (238–39).

The rule in *Swain* didn't work. The requirement to show an extended pattern of discrimination imposed a "crippling burden of proof that left prosecutors' use of peremptories largely immune from constitutional scrutiny." So, in *Batson v. Kentucky* (1986), the Court tried again to solve the tough problem of ferreting out discrimination without strangling the "right" of striking potential jurors without cause. The Court held that a defendant could make a **prima facie case** (claim there were enough facts to prove discriminatory jury selection unless rebutted by the prosecution) by the "totality of the relevant facts" about a prosecutor's conduct during the defendant's own trial (*Batson*, 94, 96). "Once the defendant makes a prima facie showing, the burden shifts to the State to come forward with a neutral explanation for challenging jurors within an arguably targeted class" (97). The trial court then has the duty to decide if the defendant has proved intentional discrimination (98).

Unfortunately, *Batson* came with its own weakness: If any explanation on its face is enough to rebut the defendant's prima facie case, then *Batson* didn't do much more than *Swain*.

Defendants now have another hurdle if a trial court finds that the prosecutor's explanations are race-neutral: the Antiterrorism and Effective Death Penalty Act of 1996 (AEDPA) (28 U.S.C. § 2254(d)(2). Under the act, defendants can only obtain equal protection relief by proving that the trial court's finding is "an unreasonable determination of the facts in light of the evidence presented in the state court proceeding" (*Miller-El v. Dretke* 2005, 239–40).

In *Snyder v. Louisiana* (2008), our next case excerpt, the Supreme Court applied the *Miller-El v. Dretke* "unreasonable determination of the facts" test and held that the "trial court committed clear error" when it rejected Allen Snyder's claim that some of the prosecution's peremptory challenges were race-based in violation of *Batson v. Kentucky*.

In *Snyder v. Louisiana* (2008), our next case excerpt, the Supreme Court held that the trial court had violated Allen Snyder's right to a jury free of race-based exclusions in violation of *Batson v. Kentucky*.

CASE

Were the Peremptory Challenges Based on Race?

Snyder v. Louisiana
452 U.S. 472 (2008)

HISTORY

Allen Snyder (Petitioner/Defendant) was convicted in the Twenty-Fourth Judicial District Court, Parish of Jefferson, Kernan A. Hand, J., of first-degree murder and was sentenced to death. Defendant appealed. The Supreme Court of Louisiana affirmed. Granting defendant's petition for a writ of certiorari, the Supreme Court vacated the judgment and remanded for further consideration. On remand, the Supreme Court of Louisiana affirmed. Certiorari was granted. The Supreme Court, Justice Alito, held that prosecutor's proffered reasons for striking black prospective jurors were pretext for racial discrimination. Reversed and remanded.

> —ALITO, J., joined by ROBERTS, C.J., and STEVENS, KENNEDY, SOUTER, GINSBURG, and BREYER, JJ.

Petitioner Allen Snyder was convicted of first-degree murder in a Louisiana court and was sentenced to death. He asks us to review a decision of the Louisiana Supreme Court rejecting his claim that the prosecution exercised some of its peremptory jury challenges based on race, in violation of *Batson v. Kentucky*. We hold that the trial court committed clear error in its ruling on a *Batson* objection, and we therefore reverse.

FACTS

The crime for which petitioner was convicted occurred in August 1995. At that time, petitioner and his wife, Mary, had separated. On August 15, they discussed the possibility of reconciliation, and Mary agreed to meet with petitioner the next day. That night, Mary went on a date with Howard Wilson. During the evening, petitioner repeatedly attempted to page Mary, but she did not respond. At approximately 1:30 a.m. on August 16, Wilson drove up to the home of Mary's mother to drop Mary off. Petitioner was waiting at the scene armed with a knife. He opened the driver's side door of Wilson's car and repeatedly stabbed the occupants, killing Wilson and wounding Mary.

The State charged petitioner with first-degree murder and sought the death penalty based on the aggravating circumstance that petitioner had knowingly created a risk of death or great bodily harm to more than one person.

Voir dire began on Tuesday, August 27, 1996, and proceeded as follows. During the first phase, the trial court screened the panel to identify jurors who did not meet Louisiana's requirements for jury service or claimed that service on the jury or sequestration for the duration of the trial would result in extreme hardship. More than 50 prospective jurors reported that they had work, family, or other commitments that would interfere with jury service. In each of those instances, the nature of the conflicting commitments was explored, and some of these jurors were dismissed.

In the next phase, the court randomly selected panels of 13 potential jurors for further questioning. The defense and prosecution addressed each panel and questioned the jurors both as a group and individually. At the conclusion of this questioning, the court ruled on challenges for cause. Then, the prosecution and the defense were given the opportunity to use peremptory challenges (each side had 12) to remove remaining jurors. The court continued this process of calling 13-person panels until the jury was filled. In accordance with Louisiana law, the parties were permitted to exercise "backstrikes." That is, they were allowed to use their peremptories up until the time when the final jury was sworn and thus were permitted to strike jurors whom they had initially accepted when the jurors' panels were called.

Eighty-five prospective jurors were questioned as members of a panel. Thirty-six of these survived challenges for cause; 5 of the 36 were black; and all 5 of the prospective black jurors were eliminated by the prosecution through the use of peremptory strikes. The jury found petitioner guilty of first-degree murder and determined that he should receive the death penalty.

On direct appeal, the Louisiana Supreme Court conditionally affirmed petitioner's conviction. The court rejected petitioner's *Batson* claim but remanded the case for a retroactive determination of petitioner's competency to stand trial. Two justices dissented and would have found a *Batson* violation.

On remand, the trial court found that petitioner had been competent to stand trial, and the Louisiana Supreme Court affirmed that determination. Petitioner petitioned this Court for a writ of certiorari, and while his petition was pending, this Court decided *Miller-El v. Dretke* (2005). We then granted the petition, vacated the judgment, and remanded the case to the Louisiana Supreme Court for further consideration in light of *Miller-El*. On remand, the Louisiana Supreme Court again rejected Snyder's *Batson* claim, this time by a vote of 4 to 3. We again granted certiorari, and now reverse.

OPINION

Batson provides a three-step process for a trial court to use in adjudicating a claim that a peremptory challenge was based on race:

> First, a defendant must make a prima facie showing that a peremptory challenge has been exercised on the basis of race; second, if that showing has been made, the prosecution must offer a race-neutral basis for striking the juror in question; and third, in light of the parties' submissions, the trial court must determine whether the defendant has shown purposeful discrimination.

On appeal, a trial court's ruling on the issue of discriminatory intent must be sustained unless it is clearly erroneous. The trial court has a pivotal role in evaluating *Batson* claims. Step three of the *Batson* inquiry involves an evaluation of the prosecutor's credibility, and "the best evidence of discriminatory intent often will be the demeanor of the attorney who exercises the challenge. In addition, race-neutral reasons for peremptory challenges often invoke a juror's demeanor (e.g., nervousness, inattention), making the trial court's firsthand observations of even greater importance.

In this situation, the trial court must evaluate not only whether the prosecutor's demeanor belies a discriminatory intent, but also whether the juror's demeanor can credibly be said to have exhibited the basis for the strike attributed to the juror by the prosecutor. We have recognized that these determinations of credibility and demeanor lie peculiarly within a trial judge's province, and we have stated that in the absence of exceptional circumstances, we would defer to the trial court.

Petitioner centers his *Batson* claim on the prosecution's strikes of two black jurors, Jeffrey Brooks and Elaine Scott. Because we find that the trial court committed clear error in overruling petitioner's *Batson* objection

with respect to Mr. Brooks, we have no need to consider petitioner's claim regarding Ms. Scott.

When defense counsel made a *Batson* objection concerning the strike of Mr. Brooks, a college senior who was attempting to fulfill his student-teaching obligation, the prosecution offered two race-neutral reasons for the strike. The prosecutor explained:

> I thought about it last night. Number 1, the main reason is that he looked very nervous to me throughout the questioning. Number 2, he's one of the fellows that came up at the beginning of *voir dire* and said he was going to miss class. He's a student teacher. My main concern is for that reason, that being that he might, to go home quickly, come back with guilty of a lesser verdict so there wouldn't be a penalty phase. Those are my two reasons.

Defense counsel disputed both explanations, and the trial judge ruled as follows: "All right. I'm going to allow the challenge. I'm going to allow the challenge."

We discuss the prosecution's two proffered grounds for striking Mr. Brooks in turn. With respect to the first reason, the Louisiana Supreme Court was correct that "nervousness cannot be shown from a cold transcript, which is why the trial judge's evaluation must be given much deference." As noted above, deference is especially appropriate where a trial judge has made a finding that an attorney credibly relied on demeanor in exercising a strike. Here, however, the record does not show that the trial judge actually made a determination concerning Mr. Brooks's demeanor.

The trial judge was given two explanations for the strike. Rather than making a specific finding on the record concerning Mr. Brooks's demeanor, the trial judge simply allowed the challenge without explanation. It is possible that the judge did not have any impression one way or the other concerning Mr. Brooks's demeanor. Mr. Brooks was not challenged until the day after he was questioned, and by that time dozens of other jurors had been questioned. Thus, the trial judge may not have recalled Mr. Brooks's demeanor. Or, the trial judge may have found it unnecessary to consider Mr. Brooks's demeanor, instead basing his ruling completely on the second proffered justification for the strike. For these reasons, we cannot presume that the trial judge credited the prosecutor's assertion that Mr. Brooks was nervous.

The second reason proffered for the strike of Mr. Brooks—his student-teaching obligation—fails even under the highly deferential standard of review that is applicable here. At the beginning of *voir dire*, when the trial court asked the members of the venire whether jury service or sequestration would pose an extreme hardship, Mr. Brooks was 1 of more than 50 members of the venire who expressed concern that jury service or sequestration

(continued)

would interfere with work, school, family, or other obligations. When Mr. Brooks came forward, the following exchange took place:

Mr. Jeffrey Brooks: . . . I'm a student at Southern University, New Orleans. This is my last semester. My major requires me to student teach, and today I've already missed a half a day. That is part of my—it's required for me to graduate this semester.

Defense Counsel: Mr. Brooks, if you—how many days would you miss if you were sequestered on this jury? Do you teach every day?

Mr. Jeffrey Brooks: Five days a week.

Defense Counsel: Five days a week.

Mr. Jeffrey Brooks: And it's 8:30 through 3:00.

Defense Counsel: If you missed this week, is there any way that you could make it up this semester?

Mr. Jeffrey Brooks: Well, the first two weeks I observe, the remaining I begin teaching, so there is something I'm missing right now that will better me towards my teaching career.

Defense Counsel: Is there any way that you could make up the observed observation [sic] that you're missing today, at another time?

Mr. Jeffrey Brooks: It may be possible, I'm not sure.

Defense Counsel: Okay. So that—

The Court: Is there anyone we could call, like a Dean or anything, that we could speak to?

Mr. Jeffrey Brooks: Actually, I spoke to my Dean, Doctor Tillman, who's at the university probably right now.

The Court: All right.

Mr. Jeffrey Brooks: Would you like to speak to him?

The Court: Yeah.

Mr. Jeffrey Brooks: I don't have his card on me.

The Court: Why don't you give [a law clerk] his number, give [a law clerk] his name and we'll call him and we'll see what we can do.

(Mr. Jeffrey Brooks left the bench.)

Shortly thereafter, the court again spoke with Mr. Brooks:

The Law Clerk: Jeffrey Brooks, the requirement for his teaching is a three hundred clock hour observation. Doctor Tillman at Southern University said that as long as it's just this week, he doesn't see that it would cause a problem with Mr. Brooks completing his observation time within this semester.

(Mr. Brooks approached the bench.)

The Court: We talked to Doctor Tillman and he says he doesn't see a problem as long as it's just this week, you know, he'll work with you on it. Okay?

Mr. Jeffrey Brooks: Okay.

(Mr. Jeffrey Brooks left the bench.)

Once Mr. Brooks heard the law clerk's report about the conversation with Doctor Tillman, Mr. Brooks did not express any further concern about serving on the jury, and the prosecution did not choose to question him more deeply about this matter. The colloquy with Mr. Brooks and the law clerk's report took place on Tuesday, August 27; the prosecution struck Mr. Brooks the following day, Wednesday, August 28; the guilt phase of petitioner's trial ended the next day, Thursday, August 29; and the penalty phase was completed by the end of the week, on Friday, August 30.

The prosecutor's second proffered reason for striking Mr. Brooks must be evaluated in light of these circumstances. The prosecutor claimed to be apprehensive that Mr. Brooks, in order to minimize the student-teaching hours missed during jury service, might have been motivated to find petitioner guilty, not of first-degree murder, but of a lesser included offense because this would obviate the need for a penalty phase proceeding. But this scenario was highly speculative. Even if Mr. Brooks had favored a quick resolution, that would not have necessarily led him to reject a finding of first-degree murder. If the majority of jurors had initially favored a finding of first-degree murder, Mr. Brooks's purported inclination might have led him to agree in order to speed the deliberations. Only if all or most of the other jurors had favored the lesser verdict would Mr. Brooks have been in a position to shorten the trial by favoring such a verdict.

Perhaps most telling, the brevity of petitioner's trial—something that the prosecutor anticipated on the record during *voir dire*—meant that serving on the jury would not have seriously interfered with Mr. Brooks's ability to complete his required student teaching. As noted, petitioner's trial was completed by Friday, August 30. If Mr. Brooks, who reported to court and was peremptorily challenged on Wednesday, August 28, had been permitted to serve, he would have missed only two additional days of student teaching, Thursday, August 29, and Friday, August 30. Mr. Brooks's dean promised to "work with" Mr. Brooks to see that he was able to make up any student-teaching time that he missed due to jury service; the dean stated that he did not think that this would be a problem; and the record contains no suggestion that Mr. Brooks remained troubled after hearing the report of the dean's remarks.

In addition, although the record does not include the academic calendar of Mr. Brooks's university, it is apparent that the trial occurred relatively early in the fall semester. With many weeks remaining in the term, Mr. Brooks would have needed to make up no more than an hour or two per week in order to compensate for the time that he would have lost due to jury service. When all of these considerations are taken into account, the prosecutor's second proffered justification for striking Mr. Brooks is suspicious.

The implausibility of this explanation is reinforced by the prosecutor's acceptance of white jurors who disclosed conflicting obligations that appear to have been at least as serious as Mr. Brooks's. We recognize that a retrospective comparison of jurors based on a cold appellate record may be very misleading when alleged similarities were not raised at trial. In that situation, an appellate court must be mindful that an exploration of the alleged similarities at the time of trial might have shown that the jurors in question were not really comparable. In this case, however, the shared characteristic, i.e., concern about serving on the jury due to conflicting obligations, was thoroughly explored by the trial court when the relevant jurors asked to be excused for cause.

A comparison between Mr. Brooks and Roland Laws, a white juror, is particularly striking. During the initial stage of *voir dire*, Mr. Laws approached the court and offered strong reasons why serving on the sequestered jury would cause him hardship. Mr. Laws stated that he was "a self-employed general contractor," with "two houses that are nearing completion, one with the occupants moving in this weekend." He explained that, if he served on the jury, "the people won't be able to move in." Mr. Laws also had demanding family obligations:

> My wife just had a hysterectomy, so I'm running the kids back and forth to school, and we're not originally from here, so I have no family in the area, so between the two things, it's kind of bad timing for me.

Although these obligations seem substantially more pressing than Mr. Brooks's, the prosecution questioned Mr. Laws and attempted to elicit assurances that he would be able to serve despite his work and family obligations. (prosecutor [sic] asking Mr. Laws "if you got stuck on jury duty anyway would you try to make other arrangements as best you could?"). And the prosecution declined the opportunity to use a peremptory strike on Mr. Laws. If the prosecution had been sincerely concerned that Mr. Brooks would favor a lesser verdict than first-degree murder in order to shorten the trial, it is hard to see why the prosecution would not have had at least as much concern regarding Mr. Laws.

The situation regarding another white juror, John Donnes, although less fully developed, is also significant. At the end of the first day of *voir dire*, Mr. Donnes

approached the court and raised the possibility that he would have an important work commitment later that week. Because Mr. Donnes stated that he would know the next morning whether he would actually have a problem, the court suggested that Mr. Donnes raise the matter again at that time. The next day, Mr. Donnes again expressed concern about serving, stating that, in order to serve, "I'd have to cancel too many things," including an urgent appointment at which his presence was essential. Despite Mr. Donnes's concern, the prosecution did not strike him.

As previously noted, the question presented at the third stage of the *Batson* inquiry is whether the defendant has shown purposeful discrimination. The prosecution's proffer of this pretextual explanation naturally gives rise to an inference of discriminatory intent. In other circumstances, we have held that, once it is shown that a discriminatory intent was a substantial or motivating factor in an action taken by a state actor, the burden shifts to the party defending the action to show that this factor was not determinative.

We have not previously applied this rule in a *Batson* case, and we need not decide here whether that standard governs in this context. For present purposes, it is enough to recognize that a peremptory strike shown to have been motivated in substantial part by discriminatory intent could not be sustained based on any lesser showing by the prosecution. And in light of the circumstances here—including absence of anything in the record showing that the trial judge credited the claim that Mr. Brooks was nervous, the prosecution's description of both of its proffered explanations as "main concerns," and the adverse inference noted above—the record does not show that the prosecution would have preemptively challenged Mr. Brooks based on his nervousness alone. Nor is there any realistic possibility that this subtle question of causation could be profitably explored further on remand at this late date, more than a decade after petitioner's trial.

We therefore REVERSE the judgment of the Louisiana Supreme Court and REMAND the case for further proceedings not inconsistent with this opinion.

It is so ordered.

DISSENT

Justice THOMAS, with whom Justice SCALIA joins, dissenting.

Petitioner essentially asks this Court to second-guess the fact-based determinations of the Louisiana courts as to the reasons for a prosecutor's decision to strike two jurors. The evaluation of a prosecutor's motives for striking a juror is at bottom a credibility judgment, which lies peculiarly within a trial judge's province. None of the evidence in the record as to jurors Jeffrey Brooks and Elaine Scott demonstrates that the trial court clearly erred in finding they were not stricken on the basis of race. Because the trial court's determination was a permissible view of the

(continued)

evidence, I would affirm the judgment of the Louisiana Supreme Court.

The Court's conclusion reveals that it is only paying lip service to the pivotal role of the trial court. The Court second-guesses the trial court's determinations in this case merely because the judge did not clarify which of the prosecutor's neutral bases for striking Mr. Brooks was dispositive. But we have never suggested that a reviewing court should defer to a trial court's resolution of a *Batson* challenge only if the trial court made specific findings with respect to each of the prosecutor's proffered race-neutral reasons. To the contrary, when the grounds for a trial court's decision are ambiguous, an appellate court should not presume that the lower court based its decision on an improper ground, particularly when applying a deferential standard of review.

Questions

1. State the test the Court used to determine whether the prosecutor's peremptory challenges were race-based.

2. Summarize the majority's arguments supporting its remand for further consideration.

3. Summarize the dissent's arguments opposing the remand.

4. Which opinion do you support? Back up your answer with details from the facts and opinions.

YOU DECIDE

Did He Prove That Being Jewish Infected the Peremptory Challenge?

In re Fred Harlan FREEMAN, on Habeas Corpus
133 P.3d 1013 (CA 2006)

Certiorari to U.S. Supreme Court, denied March 19, 2007.

FACTS

Fred Harlan Freeman and two others robbed the patrons of a neighborhood bar in Berkeley. Freeman shot Koger in the left side of the head, killing him. After the other two robbers fled, Freeman stayed behind and took property from the patrons one by one. A jury convicted Freeman, and he was sentenced to death. The California Supreme Court affirmed the conviction and the death sentence.

Freeman, in a later petition for a writ of habeas corpus, alleged that Judge Golde "directed and encouraged the former Alameda County Deputy District Attorney, John R. Quatman, to exclude Jewish prospective jurors, and that the prosecutor both acknowledged and followed the trial judge's advice." The petition also alleged that the prosecutor and the Alameda County district attorney's office had a "standard practice" of excluding Jews and African–American women from capital juries.

The allegations were based on this declaration of Quatman:

> One time Judge Golde called me into chambers and asked rhetorically "Quatman, what are you doing?"

When I asked what the problem was, he said I had not challenged a prospective juror who was Jewish. He said I could not have a Jew on the jury, and asked me if I was aware that when Adolph Eichmann was apprehended after World War II there was a major controversy in Israel over whether he should be executed. Judge Golde said no Jew would vote to send a defendant to the gas chamber. I thanked Judge Golde for his advice, and thereafter excused any prospective juror who was Jewish. Actually, Judge Golde was only telling me what I already should have known to do. It was standard practice to exclude Jewish jurors in death cases; as it was to exclude African–American women from capital juries.

Freeman argues that Quatman deliberately and unconstitutionally used peremptory challenges to exclude Jewish prospective jurors in violation of *Batson v. Kentucky* (1986) *People v. Wheeler* (1978) 583 P.2d 748, and numerous state and federal constitutional provisions.

In late 1986, Quatman, then an Alameda County deputy district attorney, was assigned to prosecute Freeman before Judge Golde. This was Quatman's first capital prosecution but not the first time he had appeared in front of Judge Golde.

In addition to their professional relationship, Quatman and his wife were both "close" to Judge Golde, who had been a guest at their wedding. Freeman's attorney, Spencer Strellis, also had a preexisting relationship with Judge Golde; the two had practiced law together before Golde was appointed to the bench.

The *voir dire* encompassed questions concerning the jurors' views of the death penalty. Those prospective jurors who were not excused for cause were directed to return for what local attorneys called the "big spin." In the big spin, the names of all of the remaining prospective jurors were placed into a tumbler, and 12 names were pulled out to be seated in the jury box. At that point, and without any further questioning, the parties would proceed to exercise their peremptory challenges, with the defense allowed to go first.

The California Supreme Court appointed Alameda County Superior Court Judge Kevin Murphy their referee to take evidence, hold hearings, and make findings of fact on Freeman's allegations. At the hearings, Quatman testified that on the day before the big spin, Judge Golde held an off-the-record conference with the attorneys in which he offered them each five "extra challenges" or "freebies" to be used at that time to excuse jurors they did not want. Strellis, Freeman's lawyer, exercised that option; Quatman did not. It was after this off-the-record conference and a brief hearing in the courtroom that, according to Quatman, the ex parte conversation occurred. Although Quatman retired from the Alameda County district attorney's office in 1998, he never told anyone about the ex parte conversation until March 2003, when a staff attorney with the California Appellate Project visited him and his wife in Montana to discuss a case his wife had been assigned.

Quatman testified that as he and defense counsel were leaving the courtroom, Judge Golde said "Jack" and crooked his finger so as to indicate that Quatman should come into chambers. Judge Golde asked, "What are you doing?"—apparently referring to Quatman's failure to challenge any jurors prior to the big spin. Quatman replied, "What do you mean what am I doing?" Judge Golde then reportedly scolded, "You didn't challenge the Jew." "And I said, 'What are you talking about?' And he said, 'No Jewish person could sit on a death penalty jury and return a verdict.' And I said, 'Why?' And he told me about [Adolf Eichmann] and the problems in Israel when they finally caught him and what to do with him. . . . And I thanked him for his advice and I left chambers." Quatman testified that he subsequently exercised peremptory challenges at the big spin against three jurors—Juror Mishell, Juror Peisker, and Juror LaPut—because he believed they were Jewish.

We accept Judge Murphy's findings, which determined that Quatman's claim that Judge Golde advised him to exclude Jewish prospective jurors during an ex parte conversation was not credible and determined that the conversation did not occur.

[Among other reasons,] Quatman's character for honesty and integrity was poor. Colton Carmine, an Alameda County deputy district attorney who had known Quatman since 1976 and had worked with him for 20 years, testified that Quatman exaggerated a lot and was not ethical. He also cautioned that "if it didn't serve his purpose, he wouldn't tell the truth." Julie Dunger, another Alameda County deputy district attorney, testified that Quatman is dishonest and that he exaggerates. Michael Roman, a criminal defense attorney who had known Quatman for over 25 years, testified that Quatman was not an honest or credible person and that his reputation for honesty and veracity was very poor. And Judge Robert Hurley, who had worked previously in the district attorney's office with Quatman, testified that Quatman "wanted to win more than he should" and "was willing to bend or break rules to win more than any prosecutor should."

The report from attorneys in Montana, where Quatman had moved in 1998, was scarcely better. Dean Chisholm, who had participated in a dozen cases with Quatman, testified that he was untrustworthy and that he had a reputation for untrustworthiness. Sean Frampton, who had opposed Quatman in 10 to 20 cases, likewise testified that Quatman was untrustworthy and had a reputation for untrustworthiness. Two lawyers, however, had a contrary view. David Stufft testified that Quatman had a good reputation for honesty and truthfulness in the Montana community—although Stufft himself did seek sanctions against Quatman in a criminal case and ask that he be held in contempt. Judge Bradley Johnson, the city judge of Whitefish, Montana, testified that Quatman, who appears fairly frequently in his courtroom, is honest and truthful and has a good reputation for those traits.

Although there was a conflict in the evidence as to Quatman's character for honesty and integrity among the Montana witnesses, there was no such conflict among the Alameda County witnesses who had known Quatman for 20 years or more. The referee also had the benefit of observing Quatman and these witnesses testify. Despite Freeman's protestations, we agree with the referee that these witnesses offered adequate foundation for their opinions of Quatman's honesty and his reputation for honesty. There was thus more than substantial evidence to support the referee's finding that Quatman's character and reputation for honesty and integrity were poor. We accept the referee's finding.

(*continued*)

[Also], Quatman had a motive to undermine a capital conviction secured by the Alameda County district attorney's office because of his animosity toward the office in general and District Attorney Tom Orloff in particular. As Quatman conceded, it was common knowledge that he and Orloff had an unfriendly relationship dating from "way back" when they were young deputies.

In 1993, when Quatman was a trial team supervisor, a female subordinate accused him of making disparaging remarks to her. After Orloff investigated the accusation, Quatman was disciplined by Orloff and Jack Meehan, who was then the district attorney, and was transferred to the consumer and environmental protection unit, where he finished his career in the office. He never again tried a capital case, which was his favorite category of cases, or even a felony-murder case and was never again a team leader. Quatman admitted he was upset over these events and that he shared his feelings with others. Quatman told Julie Dunger, Laurinda Ochoa, and Robert Chambers, who also worked in the consumer and environmental protection unit, that the transfer was a demotion and that it was unjust. Chambers testified that Quatman held Orloff responsible for his predicament. Dunger and Ochoa testified that Quatman's anger at the office and at Orloff was a "constant theme." Dunger added that Quatman was "very bitter" and "extremely adamant" about his feelings. Paul Sequiera, an assistant district attorney in Contra Costa County who socialized with Quatman in the 1990s, needed to do no more than ask Quatman "how's it going?" to hear that Quatman "always felt like he was being screwed by the office" and was "venomous" toward Orloff in particular. It was very clear to Sequiera that Quatman hated Orloff and blamed him for some of his problems in the office.

Unfortunately, Quatman's bitterness did not mellow over the years. At a retirement party for a colleague at the Alameda County district attorney's office in May 2003—the same month that Quatman executed a declaration recounting the alleged ex parte conversation—Quatman continued to express anger at the office and talked to various people "saying such horrible things about the office and he seemed happy about it. He seemed excited about it. . . . He was—he was lit up."

The foregoing evidence refuted Quatman's assertion at the reference hearing that he did not carry any bitterness toward the office or Orloff. Nor does the evidence that Quatman maintained close relationships with individual people in the office affect the self-evident conclusion that Quatman harbored animosity toward the office *as an institution* or to Orloff in particular. It is true that the initial target of Quatman's accusation would appear to be Judge Golde, but, inasmuch as Judge Golde was already dead at the time Quatman first disclosed this ex parte conversation, it is the Alameda County district attorney's office that has suffered the fallout from Quatman's claims. In sum, we agree with the referee that Quatman had a motive to tell a story that predictably caused trouble and embarrassment for the office, even if his decision to do so was opportunistic and not especially well planned out and even if Quatman arguably could have chosen to embarrass the office in other, more direct ways.

Freeman leveled very serious allegations about Judge Golde and the conduct of his trial but, after a full and fair evidentiary hearing, he failed to prove they were true.

LO 1 The Right to a Public Trial

Three constitutional amendments guarantee defendants the right to a public trial:

1. The Sixth Amendment right to confront witnesses
2. The Fifth Amendment due process right
3. The Fourteenth Amendment due process right

Public trials protect two distinct rights:

1. *Public access.* The right of the public to attend the proceedings
2. *Defendants' rights.* The right of defendants to attend their own trials

The right to a public trial extends to "every stage of the trial," including jury selection, communications between the judge and the jury, **jury instructions** (judges' explanations of the law to the jury), and in-chamber conversations between the judge and jurors. It doesn't include brief conferences at the bench outside the defendant's hearing or other brief conferences involving only questions of law.

Public trials support defendants' interests in avoiding persecution through secret proceedings, enhance community participation in law enforcement, and aid in the search for truth by encouraging witnesses to come forward who otherwise might not.

These interests aren't absolute. Courtroom size limits public access. Furthermore, the need to protect threatened witnesses even justifies closing the courtroom. Protecting undercover agents also authorizes exclusion of the public during their testimony. Moreover, public trials may discourage shy and introverted witnesses from coming forward. Finally, judges can limit public access during sensitive proceedings. For example, it's justifiable to exclude spectators while alleged rape victims are testifying about the "lurid details" of the crime (*U.S. ex rel. Latimore v. Sielaff* 1977).

Defendants don't have an absolute right to attend their own trials; they can forfeit that right by their disruptive behavior. For example, in *Illinois v. Allen* (1970), William Allen, while being tried for armed robbery, repeatedly interrupted the judge in a "most abusive and disrespectful manner." He also threatened him, "When I go out for lunchtime, you're going to be a corpse here." When the judge warned Allen that he could attend only as long as he behaved himself, Allen answered, "There is going to be no proceeding. I'm going to start talking all through the trial. There's not going to be no trial like this."

According to the U.S. Supreme Court, the judge properly removed Allen from the courtroom:

> It is essential to the proper administration of criminal justice that dignity, order, and decorum be the hallmarks of all court proceedings in our country. The flagrant disregard in the courtroom of elementary standards of proper conduct should not and cannot be tolerated. We believe that trial judges confronted with disruptive, contumacious, stubbornly defiant defendants must be given sufficient discretion to meet the circumstances of each case. We think there are at least three constitutionally permissible ways for a trial judge to handle an obstreperous defendant like Allen: (1) bind and gag him, thereby keeping him present; (2) cite him for contempt; (3) take him out of the courtroom until he promises to conduct himself properly. (343)

Judges can also exclude defendants during the questioning of child witnesses in sexual abuse cases. For example, in *Kentucky v. Stincer* (1987), Sergio Stincer was on trial for sodomizing two children, ages 7 and 8. The trial court conducted an in-chambers hearing to determine whether the children could remember certain details and whether they understood the significance of telling the truth in court. The judge permitted his lawyer to attend but refused Stincer's request to do so. The U.S. Supreme Court upheld the judge's ruling because Stincer had an adequate opportunity to "confront" the children during the trial.

Courts can also require dangerous defendants to appear under guard to protect the public, witnesses, and court officials from harm and to prevent defendants from escaping. However, defendants ordinarily have the right not just to be at their trial but also to be presented in a way that doesn't prejudice their case. For example, the government can't bring defendants to court in jail dress (*Estelle v. Williams* 1976) or make defense witnesses testify in shackles, because their dress prejudices the jury, furthers no state policy, and mainly hurts poor defendants (*Holbrook v. Flynn* 1986).

LO 2 The Stages and Rules of Jury Trials

The adversarial process reaches its high point in the jury trial. Strict, technical rules control trials. The main stages in the criminal trial include:

1. Opening statements, with the prosecution first, followed by the defense
2. Presenting the evidence—the state's and the defendants' cases
3. Closing arguments
4. Instructions to the jury
5. Jury deliberations

Let's look first at the stages. Then we'll examine the issues of whether the law requires unanimous verdicts and jury nullification.

LO 2 Opening statements

Prosecutors and defense counsel can make **opening statements**—that is, address the jury before they present their evidence. Prosecutors make their opening statements first; defense counsel address the jury either immediately after the prosecutor's opening statement or, in a few jurisdictions, following the presentation of the state's case. The opening statements have a narrow scope: to outline the case that the two sides hope to prove, not to prove the case. Proving the case takes place during the presentation-of-evidence phase of the criminal trial. In fact, it's unprofessional for either side to refer to any evidence they don't honestly believe will be admissible in court. Although it's rare for them to do so, appeals courts sometimes reverse cases in which prosecutors have referred to points they intend to prove with evidence they know is inadmissible, incompetent, or both (LaFave and Israel 1984, 3:12).

LO 2 Presenting evidence

The prosecution presents its case first because of its burden to prove defendants' guilt. In presenting its case, the rules of evidence restrict what evidence the state may use, mainly excluding illegally obtained testimony and physical evidence and most hearsay. The prosecution has to prove every element in the case, but the defense frequently **stipulates** (agrees not to contest) some facts, particularly those that might prejudice the defendant's case—detailed photographs and descriptions of a brutally murdered victim, for example. The prosecution can decline a stipulation. Most courts don't compel the prosecution to accept stipulations, because it might weaken the state's case (*People v. McClellan* 1969).

The state ordinarily presents all the available eyewitnesses to the crime. In some instances, if the prosecution doesn't call a material witness, particularly a victim, the defense can ask for a "**missing witness instruction**"—an instruction that jurors can infer that the witness's testimony would have been unfavorable to the prosecution. The prosecution can ask the court to inform the jury that a key witness is unavailable and not to draw negative inferences from his failure to testify. Prosecutors also may decide not to call witnesses—such as spouses, priests, and doctors—whom they know will claim a valid privilege; doing so might result in reversible error (*Bowles v. U.S.* 1970).

Issues that affect the presenting of evidence include cross examination, the admission of hearsay evidence, compelling witnesses to testify, the prosecutor's burden to prove all elements of a crime, and proof beyond a reasonable doubt. Let's look at each.

Cross-examination

The **Sixth Amendment confrontation clause** includes the right to cross-examine the prosecution's witnesses. In *Smith v. Illinois* (1968), when the prosecution's key witness, an informant, testified that he bought heroin from Smith, the trial court allowed him to use an alias, concealing his real name and address. The U.S. Supreme Court ruled that this violated Smith's right to confrontation:

> When the credibility of a witness is at issue, the very starting point in "exposing falsehood and bringing out the truth" through cross-examination must necessarily be to ask the witness who he is and where he lives. The witness's name and address open countless avenues of in-court examination and out-of-doors investigation. It is of the essence of a fair trial that reasonable latitude be given to the cross-examiner, even though he is unable to state to the court what facts a reasonable cross-examination might develop. (132)

Hearsay evidence

The confrontation clause also restricts the prosecution's use of **hearsay testimony**— out-of-court statements offered to prove the truth of the statements. Hearsay violates the confrontation clause because defendants can't ferret the truth through the adversarial process unless the defense can cross-examine the witnesses against them. Therefore, the jury can't have an adequate basis for fact-finding.

The confrontation clause doesn't bar hearsay testimony totally. The prosecution can introduce hearsay if the government meets two tests:

1. It demonstrates the witness's unavailability and, hence, the necessity to use out-of-court statements.
2. It shows that the state obtained the evidence under circumstances that clearly establish its reliability.

In *Ohio v. Roberts* (1980), the majority of the Supreme Court found that the state satisfied the tests under these circumstances:

1. The witness's mother said the witness, her daughter, had left home, saying she was going to Tucson, two years earlier.
2. Shortly thereafter, a San Francisco social worker contacted the mother concerning a welfare claim her daughter had filed there.
3. The mother was able to reach her daughter only once, by phone.
4. When the daughter called a few months prior to the trial, she told her mother she was traveling but didn't reveal her whereabouts.

The dissent argued that relying solely on the parents wasn't sufficient; the prosecution had the burden to go out and find the witness. The Court disagreed.

Compulsory process

The Sixth Amendment guarantees the defendant's right "to have **compulsory process for obtaining witnesses** in [his or her] . . . favor." This means defendants can compel witnesses to come to court to testify for them. Most states pay for poor defendants' process, but they don't pay for process to get evidence that only corroborates (adds to) evidence already available. And most states make defendants spell out exactly why they need the evidence.

The burden of proof

The Fifth Amendment provides that "no person . . . shall be compelled in any criminal case to be a witness against himself." This means the state can't call defendants to the witness stand in criminal trials. It also bars the prosecution from commenting on defendants' refusal to testify; it even entitles defendants to ask judges to instruct juries not to infer guilt from their silence. However, if defendants decide to take the stand to tell their side of the story, the prosecution can cross-examine them as they would any other witness.

The defense doesn't have to present a case; cross-examining the prosecution's witnesses by itself can raise a reasonable doubt about the proof against the defendant. Or defendants may call their own witnesses for the sole purpose of rebutting the prosecution's witnesses. Of course, they may also call witnesses to create a reasonable doubt about their guilt—to establish alibis, for example.

Defendants may also have affirmative defenses that justify or excuse what would otherwise be criminal conduct (self-defense, insanity, duress, and entrapment). Or maybe they have evidence that reduces the grade of the offense, such as provocation to reduce murder to manslaughter or diminished capacity to reduce first-degree murder to second-degree murder. The prosecution, of course, has the right to cross-examine defense witnesses.

Proof beyond a reasonable doubt

Defendants don't have to prove their innocence or help the government prove their guilt. The right against self-incrimination gives defendants an absolute right to say nothing at all and not have it count against them. So trials can proceed, and some do, where neither defendants nor their lawyers present a case. Sometimes, no defense is the best defense. The **reasonable doubt standard** requires the government to carry the whole burden of proving defendants are guilty beyond a reasonable doubt.

The U.S. Supreme Court ruled in *In re Winship* (1970) that due process requires both federal and state prosecutors to prove every element of a crime beyond a reasonable doubt. According to the Court, "The reasonable doubt standard is bottomed on a fundamental value determination of our society that it is far worse to convict an innocent man than to let a guilty man go free" (373).

Despite the constitutional requirement of proof beyond a reasonable doubt, the U.S. Supreme Court hasn't decided that due process requires judges to define proof beyond a reasonable doubt. Nevertheless, courts struggle to tell jurors what reasonable doubt means. Table 13.3 provides some examples of courts' definitions.

TABLE 13.3 Sample of trial court definitions of proof beyond a reasonable doubt

• A doubt that would cause prudent people to hesitate before acting in a matter of importance to themselves
• A doubt based on reason and common sense
• A doubt that's neither frivolous nor fanciful and that can't be explained away easily
• Substantial doubt
• Persuasion to a reasonable or moral certainty
• Doubt beyond that which is reasonable; about "7½ on a scale of 10" (rejected by the appellate court)
• When the "scales of justice are substantially out of equipoise" (rejected by the appellate court)

Closing arguments

After they've presented their evidence, both the state and the defense make their closing arguments. Typically, prosecutors close first, the defense follows, and then the prosecution rebuts. Prosecutors can't waive their right to make a closing argument and save their remarks for rebuttal. If they waive their right to make a closing argument, they're barred automatically from making a rebuttal. Prosecutors can't raise "new" matters in rebuttal either; they can only rebut what either they or the defense counsel brought up during closing arguments. Why? It's only fair that the defense should hear all the arguments in favor of conviction before responding to them.

Formally, prosecutors have the duty not only to convict criminals but also to seek justice. The American Bar Association's *Standards for Criminal Justice* (1980, § 3.5) includes the following guidelines for prosecutors. It's improper to

- Misstate intentionally the evidence or mislead the jury
- Refer to evidence excluded or not introduced at trial
- Express personal beliefs or opinions about the truth or falsity of the evidence or the defendant's guilt
- Engage in arguments that divert jurors' attention by injecting issues beyond the case or predicting consequences of the jury's verdict
- Make arguments calculated to inflame jurors' passions and prejudices

Violating these standards rarely results in reversal. According to the Supreme Court:

> If every remark made by counsel outside of the testimony were grounds for a reversal, comparatively few verdicts would stand, since in the ardor of advocacy, and in the excitement of the trial, even the most experienced counsel are occasionally carried away by this temptation. (*Dunlop v. U.S.* 1897)

When determining whether to reverse convictions based on improper closing arguments, appellate courts consider whether:

- Defense counsel invited or provoked the remarks.
- Defense counsel made timely objection to the remarks.
- The trial judge took corrective action, such as instructing the jury to disregard the remarks.
- The comments were brief and isolated in an otherwise proper argument.
- Other errors occurred during the trial.
- The evidence of guilt was overwhelming. (LaFave and Israel 1984, 3:15)

Although appellate courts rarely reverse convictions for these abuses, they frequently express their displeasure with prosecutors' improper remarks made during closing arguments. In *Bowen v. Kemp* (1985), Charlie Bowen was convicted of raping and murdering a 12-year-old girl. The prosecutor, in the course of the closing statement, made several comments focusing on the accused:

> And now we come up here with this idea that a man is subject to be rehabilitated and released back into society. Yeah, I guess he can be rehabilitated. Hitler could have been. I believe in about six or eight months if I'd had him chained to a wall and talked to him and beat him on one side of the head for a while

with a stick telling him you believe this don't you then beat him on the other side with a stick telling him you believe that don't you I believe I could have rehabilitated Hitler. (678)

The prosecutor went on to call Bowen "a product of the devil" and a "liar" who was "no better than a beast":

And, you know for a criminal to go without proper punishment is a disgrace to the society we live in and it's shown to us every day by the fruits that we reap from day to day in our society when we have the bloody deeds such as this occur. (680)

Bowen appealed his conviction on the basis that the prosecutor's remarks affected the jury's verdict. While conceding that the remarks were improper, the circuit court of appeals affirmed the conviction. It found "no reasonable probability that, absent the improper statements of opinion, Bowen would not have been sentenced to death" (682).

LO 2   *Jury instructions*

Before jurors begin their deliberations, judges "instruct" them on what the law is and how they should apply it. Jury instructions usually inform the jury about the following subjects:

- The respective roles of the judge to decide the law and the jury to decide the facts
- The principle that defendants are presumed innocent until proven guilty
- The principle that the state bears the burden of proving guilt beyond a reasonable doubt
- The definition of all the elements of the crime with which the defendant is charged

Both the prosecution and the defense can ask the judge to provide the jury with specific instructions. And they can object if the judge refuses to give the requested instruction and frequently do base appeals on such refusals.

A number of jurisdictions use **pattern jury instructions**—published boilerplate instructions that fit most cases. Supporters praise the clarity, accuracy, impartiality, and efficiency of pattern instructions; critics say they're too general to help jurors. However, most empirical evaluations show that jurors understand only about half of judges' instructions, whether patterned or individually crafted (LaFave and Israel 1984, 3:39–40).

LO 2   *Jury deliberations*

After the judge instructs the jury members, she orders them to retire to a separate room under supervision and without interruption to deliberate until they reach a verdict. The jurors take the instructions, any exhibits received in evidence, and a list of the charges against the defendant with them into the jury room. During the course of their deliberations, they may ask the court for further instruction or information concerning the evidence or any other matter. The court can discharge hung juries—juries unable to reach a verdict after protracted deliberations (Chapter 12).

LO 3   Jury Verdicts

Juries can return one of three verdicts:

1. Guilty
2. Not guilty
3. Special, mainly related to insanity or capital punishment

If the jury acquits, or issues the not guilty verdict, the defendants' ordeal with the criminal process stops immediately; they're free to go, they "walk." If the jury convicts, the case continues to **judgment**—the court's final decision on the legal outcome of the case. Juries can't pass legal judgment; their word is final only as to the facts. Following the court's judgment of guilt or acquittal, the criminal trial ends.

Let's look more closely at the issue of whether juries' verdicts must be unanimous—and what happens when they aren't—and why juries sometimes choose to nullify the evidence with their verdicts.

LO 3   The "unanimous verdict" requirement

Like 12-member juries (discussed earlier), unanimous verdicts are an ancient requirement and still enjoy strong support (Table 13.4). In 1900, the U.S. Supreme Court held that the Sixth Amendment demanded conviction by unanimous jury verdicts. But the Court changed its mind in 1972 when it ruled, in *Apodaca v. Oregon*, that verdicts of 11–1 and 10–2 didn't violate two convicted felons' right to a jury trial:

> A requirement of unanimity . . . does not materially contribute to . . . [the jury's] common-sense judgment. . . . A jury will come to such a verdict as long as it consists of a group of laymen representative of a cross section of the community who have the duty and the opportunity to deliberate, free from outside attempts at intimidation, on the question of a defendant's guilt. In terms of this function we perceive no difference between juries required to act unanimously and those permitted to convict or acquit by votes of 10 to two or 11 to one. Requiring unanimity would obviously produce hung juries in some situations where nonunanimous juries will convict or acquit. But in either case, the interest of the defendant in having the judgment of his peers interposed between himself and the officers of the state who prosecute and judge him is equally well served. (411)

In *Johnson v. Louisiana* (1972), in upholding a robbery conviction based on a 9–3 verdict, Justice Byron R. White wrote:

> Nine jurors—a substantial majority of the jury—were convinced by the evidence. Disagreement of the three jurors does not alone establish reasonable doubt, particularly when such a heavy majority of the jury, after having considered the dissenters' views, remains convinced of guilt. (362)

Still, the Supreme Court hasn't answered the question of how many votes short of unanimity are required to satisfy the Sixth Amendment. What about less than unanimous verdicts by fewer than 12-member juries? A unanimous U.S. Supreme Court in *Burch v. Louisiana* (1979) struck down a Louisiana statute providing that misdemeanors punishable by more than six months "shall be tried before a jury of six persons, five of

TABLE 13.4 Arguments for unanimous verdicts

• They instill confidence in the criminal justice process.
• They guarantee that the jury carefully reviews the evidence.
• They ensure the hearing and consideration of minority viewpoints.
• They prevent government oppression.
• They support the principle that convicting innocent defendants is worse than freeing guilty ones.
• They fulfill the proof-beyond-a-reasonable-doubt requirement.

Source: LaFave and Israel 1984, 698.

whom must concur to render a verdict." According to the Court, to preserve the right to jury trial, it had to draw a line at nonunanimous verdicts of six-member juries—a line supported by the "near-uniform judgment of the nation" (only two other states had permitted these verdicts).

Jury nullification

Jury nullification instruction:

1. "If the government does *not* prove the defendant is guilty beyond a reasonable doubt, you *must* acquit.

2. If the government *does* prove the defendant is guilty beyond a reasonable doubt, you *may* convict."

This is a jury instruction hardly ever given, but it does in fact state what the law on nullification is. It should help you understand jury nullification. The jury's function is to decide the facts in a case and apply them to the law as the judge has defined the law. Nevertheless, juries have the power to acquit even when the facts clearly fit the law. Jury acquittals are final, meaning the prosecution can't appeal them. The practice of acquitting in the face of proof beyond a reasonable doubt is called **jury nullification**. Why do juries nullify? Usually, it's because either they sympathize with particular defendants (e.g., in a mercy killing) or because the state has prosecuted defendants for breaking unpopular laws (e.g., possession of small amounts of marijuana for personal use).

Jury nullification has an ancient lineage. The "pages of history shine on instances of the jury's exercise of its prerogative to disregard uncontradicted evidence and instructions of the judge." In the famous John Peter Zenger case (*New York v. Zenger* 1735), the jury ignored the facts and the judge's instructions and acquitted Zenger of the charge of sedition (LaFave and Israel 1984, 3:700).

The U.S. Supreme Court has indirectly approved jury nullification. Although the Court obviously didn't like the jury's power, it conceded in *Sparf and Hansen v. U.S.*(1895):

> If a jury may rightfully disregard the direction of the court in matters of law and determine for themselves what the law is in the particular case before them, it is difficult to perceive any legal ground upon which a verdict of conviction can be set aside by the court as being against law. (101)

Probably more than any other doctrine in criminal procedure we've studied, nullification promotes community participation in criminal law enforcement. As community representatives, juries act as safety valves in exceptional cases by allowing "informal communication from the total culture" to override the strict legal bonds of their instructions from the judge (*U.S. v. Dougherty* 1972).

CONVICTION BY GUILTY PLEA

Let's begin with pointing out that there are two kinds of guilty plea: (1) **Straight guilty pleas** (pleading guilty without negotiation) are ordinarily made in what are called "dead bang" cases, meaning proof of guilt is overwhelming. **Negotiated guilty pleas** (pleading guilty in exchange for concessions by the state) appear mainly in large urban courts.

The concessions consist of three types: (1) **Charge bargaining** refers to bargaining for a reduction in either the number or severity of criminal charges. (2) **Sentence bargaining** refers to a favorable sentence *recommendation* by the prosecutor to the judge, or bargaining directly with the judge for a favorable sentence. (3) In **fact bargaining**, the prosecutor agrees not to challenge the defendant's version of the facts or not to reveal aggravating facts to the judge.

Several historical developments have contributed to the growth and prevalence of plea bargaining. They include:

1. Increasing complexity of the criminal trial process
2. Expansion of the criminal law
3. Increasing crime rates
4. Larger caseloads
5. Political corruption in urban courts
6. Increase in the number of criminal justice professionals (police, public prosecutors, and defense lawyers)
7. Increasing statutory powers of prosecutors (Alschuler 2002, 756)

The plea-bargaining system is highly complex in operation. Consequently, participants offer multiple and conflicting descriptions of how and why it works as it does. Professor Albert Alschuler (2002), a leading plea-bargaining scholar, describes some of these conflicting views, based on what he hears from scholars and practitioners at plea-bargaining conferences:

- "When experienced lawyers can predict the outcome of a trial, there's no need to have a trial."
- "No one can predict how a trial will turn out; all we know is that one side will win big and the other side will lose big. The goal of bargaining isn't to get the same result as a trial but to steer the risks of trial into a sensible middle ground where each side gets, and gives up, something."
- "The goal is to 'escape altogether the irrationalities of an overly legalized trial system and achieve "substantive justice" without regard to technicalities.'"
- "The lawyer's goal in plea bargaining is 'to take as much as possible from the other side by threat, bluster, charm, bluff, campaign contributions, personal appeals, friendship, or whatever else works.'"
- "Sometimes the dominant motive for lazy lawyers and judges is to take the money and go home early." (756–57)

Professor Alschuler concludes that:

Of course, to some extent, all of these things are going on at the same time. . . . [I]n view of the different forms that plea bargaining may take and the many considerations that may influence it, mathematical models of plea negotiation of the sort developed by economists generally seem artificial to practicing lawyers. (757)

LO 5 The Constitution and Guilty Pleas

Although widely used for more than a century, courts didn't recognize negotiated pleas formally until 1970. In that year, in *Brady v. U.S.*, the U.S. Supreme Court ruled that bargained pleas are constitutional. According to the Court, "the chief virtues of the plea system are speed, economy, and finality."

Whatever might be the situation in an ideal world, plea bargaining and guilty pleas are important parts of our criminal justice system. Properly administered, they can benefit all concerned. The defendant avoids extended pretrial incarceration and the anxieties and uncertainties of a trial; he gains a speedy disposition of his case, the chance to acknowledge his guilt, and a prompt start in realizing whatever potential there may be for rehabilitation. Judges and prosecutors conserve vital and scarce resources. The public is protected from the risks posed by those charged with criminal offenses who are at large on bail while awaiting completion of criminal proceedings (*Blackledge v. Allison* 1977, 71).

When they plead guilty, defendants waive (give up) three constitutional rights:

1. The Fifth Amendment right to remain silent
2. The Sixth Amendment right to a trial by jury
3. The Sixth Amendment right to confront the witnesses against them

The Court has ruled that, to give up these constitutional rights, defendants have to do so knowingly (also called "intelligently") and voluntarily (*Brady v. U.S.* 1970, 748). It's up to *trial judges* to make sure defendants' pleas are voluntary and knowing, in light of the totality of the circumstances surrounding the plea. The Court has established the following standard for trial judges' inquiries:

> A plea of guilty entered by one fully aware of the direct consequences, including the actual value of any commitments made to him by the court, prosecutor, or his own counsel, must stand unless induced by threats (or promises to discontinue improper harassment), misrepresentation (including unfulfilled or unfulfillable promises), or perhaps by promises that are by their nature improper as having no prior relationship to the prosecutor's business (e.g., bribes). (*Brady v. U.S.* 1970, 756)

The Supreme Court has held that a trial judge's failure to ask defendants questions concerning their plea in open court is **reversible error**—grounds to reverse the trial court's judgment of guilt. Why? Because the trial court accepted the plea "without an affirmative showing that it was intelligent and voluntary" (*Boykin v. Alabama* 1969). Also important, a court can't *presume* "from a silent record" that by pleading guilty defendants give up fundamental rights. Judges have to make clear to defendants when they plead guilty that they're giving up their rights to trial (Sixth Amendment), to confrontation (Sixth Amendment), and not to incriminate themselves (Fifth Amendment).

According to the Court, defendants have to know "the true nature of the charges" against them. For example, in one case, the defendant pleaded guilty to second-degree murder without knowing the elements of the crime. Neither his lawyer nor the trial judge had explained to him that second-degree murder required an intent to kill and that his version of what he did negated intent. The U.S. Supreme Court ruled that the record didn't establish a knowing plea.

Most jurisdictions now require that judges determine that there's a **factual basis for guilty pleas**. To determine the factual basis, for example, judges might ask defendants to describe the conduct that led to the charges, ask the prosecutor and defense attorney similar questions, and consult presentence reports. But in *North Carolina v. Alford* (1970), the U.S. Supreme Court held that there are no constitutional barriers to prevent a judge from accepting a guilty plea from a defendant who wants to plead guilty while still protesting his innocence. (It's called an *Alford* plea.)

The *Alford* plea raises the obvious question: Are defendants who (1) truly believe they're factually innocent (they didn't commit the crime) but (2) realize they're legally guilty (the government has enough evidence to convict them), and (3) who plead guilty *only* because they don't want to risk going to trial and receiving a harsher sentence if convicted, (4) knowingly and voluntarily pleading guilty? The equally obvious "commonsense" answer is "no." But, the U.S. Supreme Court answered "yes," in *North Carolina v. Alford* (1970), our next case excerpt.

In *North Carolina v. Alford* (1970), the U.S. Supreme Court ruled (6–3) that Henry Alford voluntarily and knowingly pleaded even though he denied that he committed the murder.

CASE

Was His Guilty Plea Voluntary?
North Carolina v. Alford
400 U.S. 25 (1970)

HISTORY

Henry Alford was indicted for the capital offense of first-degree murder. North Carolina law provided for three possible punishments for murder: (1) life imprisonment when a plea of guilty was accepted for first-degree murder; (2) death following a jury verdict of guilty of first-degree murder unless the jury recommended life imprisonment; (3) two to 30 years' imprisonment for second-degree murder. Alford's attorney recommended that Alford plead guilty to second-degree murder, which the prosecutor accepted. Alford pleaded guilty and was sentenced to 30 years in prison. On writ of habeas corpus, the U.S. Court of Appeals found Alford's plea involuntary. On writ of certiorari, the U.S. Supreme Court reversed.

—WHITE, J., joined by BURGER, C.J., and BLACK, HARLAN, STEWART, and BLACKMUN, JJ.

FACTS

On December 2, 1963, Alford was indicted for first-degree murder, a capital offense under North Carolina law. The court appointed an attorney to represent him, and this attorney questioned all but one of the various witnesses who appellee said would substantiate his claim of innocence. The witnesses, however, did not support Alford's story but gave statements that strongly indicated his guilt. Faced with strong evidence of guilt and no substantial evidentiary support for the claim of innocence, Alford's attorney recommended that he plead guilty, but left the ultimate decision to Alford himself. The prosecutor agreed to accept a plea of guilty to a charge of second-degree murder, and on December 10, 1963, Alford pleaded guilty to the reduced charge.

Before the plea was finally accepted by the trial court, the court heard the sworn testimony of a police officer who summarized the State's case. Two other witnesses besides Alford were also heard. Although there was no eyewitness to the crime, the testimony indicated that shortly before the killing Alford took his gun from his house, stated his intention to kill the victim, and returned home with the declaration that he had carried out the killing.

After the summary presentation of the State's case, Alford took the stand and testified that he had not committed the murder but that he was pleading guilty because he faced the threat of the death penalty if he did not do so. In response to the questions of his counsel, he acknowledged that his counsel had informed him of the difference between second- and first-degree murder and of his rights in case he chose to go to trial.

The trial court then asked Alford if, in light of his denial of guilt, he still desired to plead guilty to second-degree murder and appellee answered, "Yes, sir. I plead guilty on—from the circumstances that he [Alford's attorney] told me." After eliciting information about Alford's prior criminal record, which was a long one, the trial court sentenced him to 30 years' imprisonment, the maximum penalty for second-degree murder.

After giving his version of the events of the night of the murder, Alford stated: "I pleaded guilty on second-degree murder because they said there is too much evidence, but I ain't shot no man, but I take the fault for the other man. We never had an argument in our life and I just pleaded guilty because they said if I didn't they would gas me for it, and that is all." In response to questions

(continued)

from his attorney, Alford affirmed that he had consulted several times with his attorney and with members of his family and had been informed of his rights if he chose to plead not guilty. Alford then reaffirmed his decision to plead guilty to second-degree murder:

> Q: [by Alford's attorney] And you authorized me to tender a plea of guilty to second-degree murder before the court?
>
> A: Yes, sir.
>
> Q: And in doing that, you have again affirmed your decision on that point?
>
> A: Well, I'm still pleading that you all got me to plead guilty. I plead the other way, circumstantial evidence; that the jury will prosecute me on—on the second. You told me to plead guilty, right. I don't—I'm not guilty but I plead guilty.

On appeal, a divided panel of the Court of Appeals for the Fourth Circuit reversed on the ground that Alford's guilty plea was made involuntarily.

OPINION

The standard [for determining the validity of a quality plea is] whether the plea represents a voluntary and intelligent choice among the alternative courses of action open to the defendant. Ordinarily, a judgment of conviction resting on a plea of guilty is justified by the defendant's admission that he committed the crime charged against him and his consent that judgment be entered without a trial of any kind. The plea usually subsumes both elements, and justifiably so, even though there is no separate, express admission by the defendant that he committed the particular acts claimed to constitute the crime charged in the indictment.

Here Alford entered his plea but accompanied it with the statement that he had not shot the victim. While most pleas of guilty consist of both a waiver of trial and an express admission of guilt, the latter element is not a constitutional requisite to the imposition of criminal penalty. An individual accused of crime may voluntarily, knowingly, and understandably consent to the imposition of a prison sentence even if he is unwilling or unable to admit his participation in the acts constituting the crime.

Nor can we perceive any material difference between a plea that refuses to admit commission of the criminal act and a plea containing a protestation of innocence when, as in the instant case, a defendant intelligently concludes that his interests require entry of a guilty plea and the record before the judge contains strong evidence of actual guilt.

Here the State had a strong case of first-degree murder against Alford. Whether he realized or disbelieved his guilt, he insisted on his plea because in his view he had absolutely nothing to gain by a trial and much to gain by pleading. Because of the overwhelming evidence against him, a trial was precisely what neither Alford nor his attorney desired.

Confronted with the choice between a trial for first-degree murder, on the one hand, and a plea of guilty to second-degree murder, on the other, Alford quite reasonably chose the latter and thereby limited the maximum penalty to a 30-year term. When his plea is viewed in light of the evidence against him, which substantially negated his claim of innocence and which further provided a means by which the judge could test whether the plea was being intelligently entered, its validity cannot be seriously questioned. In view of the strong factual basis for the plea demonstrated by the State and Alford's clearly expressed desire to enter it despite his professed belief in his innocence, we hold that the trial judge did not commit constitutional error in accepting it.

Alford now argues in effect that the State should not have allowed him this choice but should have insisted on proving him guilty of murder in the first degree. The States in their wisdom may take this course by statute or otherwise and may prohibit the practice of accepting pleas to lesser included offenses under any circumstances. But this is not the mandate of the Fourteenth Amendment and the Bill of Rights. The prohibitions against involuntary or unintelligent pleas should not be relaxed, but neither should an exercise in arid logic render those constitutional guarantees counterproductive and put in jeopardy the very human values they were meant to preserve.

The Court of Appeals judgment directing the issuance of the writ of habeas corpus is vacated and the case is REMANDED to the Court of Appeals for further proceedings consistent with this opinion. It is so ordered.

DISSENT

BRENNAN, J., joined by DOUGLAS and MARSHALL, JJ.

Last Term, this Court held, over my dissent, that a plea of guilty may validly be induced by an unconstitutional threat to subject the defendant to the risk to death, so long as the plea is entered in open court and the defendant is represented by competent counsel who is aware of the threat, albeit not of its unconstitutionality. *Brady v. U.S.* (1970). Today the Court makes clear that its previous holding was intended to apply even when the record demonstrates that the actual effect of the unconstitutional threat was to induce a guilty plea from a defendant who was unwilling to admit his guilt.

I adhere to the view that, in any given case, the influence of such an unconstitutional threat must necessarily be given weight in determining the voluntariness of a plea. I believe that at the very least such a denial of guilt is a relevant factor in determining whether the plea was voluntarily and intelligently made. With these factors in mind, it is sufficient in my view to state that the facts set out in the majority opinion demonstrate that Alford was "so gripped by fear of the death penalty" that his decision to plead guilty was not voluntary but was "the product of duress as much so as choice reflecting physical constraint."

Questions

1. Did Henry Alford knowingly and voluntarily plead guilty?

2. Consider the dissent's comment that Henry Alford was "so gripped by fear of the death penalty" that his decision was "the product of duress." Should defendants ever be allowed to plead guilty if they believe they're innocent? Why or why not? Back up your answer with arguments from the majority and dissenting opinions.

CRIMINAL PROCEDURE IN ACTION

Judge's active participation in plea bargaining did not invalidate the guilty plea

U.S. v. Davila, 2013 WL 263106 (2013)

FACTS

In May 2009, a federal grand jury in the Southern District of Georgia returned a 34-count indictment against respondent Anthony Davila. The indictment charged that Davila filed over 120 falsified tax returns, receiving over $423,000 from the United States Treasury as a result of his fraudulent scheme.

In January 2010, Davila sent a letter to the district court expressing dissatisfaction with his court-appointed attorney and requesting new counsel. His attorney, Davila complained, offered no defensive strategy, "never mentioned a defense at all," but simply advised that he plead guilty. In response to Davila's letter, a U.S. magistrate judge held an *in camera* hearing at which Davila and his attorney, but no representative of the United States, appeared. At the start of the hearing, the Magistrate Judge told Davila that he was free to represent himself, but would not get another court-appointed attorney.

Addressing Davila's complaint that his attorney had advised him to plead guilty, the magistrate judge told Davila that "oftentimes . . . that is the best advice a lawyer can give his client." "In view of whatever the Government's evidence in a case might be," the judge continued,

> It might be a good idea for the Defendant to accept responsibility for his criminal conduct, to plead guilty, and go to sentencing with the best arguments still available without wasting the Court's time, and causing

the Government to have to spend a bunch of money empanelling a jury to try an open and shut case.

As to Davila's objection that his attorney had given him no options other than pleading guilty, the magistrate judge commented: "There may not be a viable defense to these charges." The judge then urged Davila to cooperate in order to gain a downward departure from the sentence indicated by the Federal Sentencing Guidelines. "Try to understand," he counseled,

> the Government, they have all of the marbles in this situation and they can file that motion for a downward departure from the guidelines if they want to, you know, and the rules are constructed so that nobody can force them to file that motion for you. The only thing at your disposal that is entirely up to you is the two or three level reduction for acceptance of responsibility. That means you've got to go to the cross. You've got to tell the probation officer everything you did in this case regardless of how bad it makes you appear to be because that is the way you get that three-level reduction for acceptance, and believe me, Mr. Davila, someone with your criminal history needs a three-level reduction for acceptance.

Davila's Federal Sentencing Guidelines range, the magistrate judge said, would "probably be pretty bad because

(continued)

his criminal history score would be so high." To reduce his sentencing exposure, the magistrate judge suggested, Davila could "cooperate with the Government in this or in other cases." As the hearing concluded, the judge again cautioned that "to get the sentence reduction for acceptance of responsibility," Davila had to "come to the cross":

> That two- or three-level reduction for acceptance is something that you have the key to and you can ensure that you get that reduction in sentence simply by virtue of being forthcoming and not trying to make yourself look like you really didn't know what was going on. You've got to go to the cross and you've got to tell it all, Brother, and convince that probation officer that you are being as open and honest with him as you can possibly be because then he will go to the District Judge and he will say, you know, that Davila guy, he's got a long criminal history but when we were in there talking about this case he gave it all up so give him the two-level, give him the three-level reduction.

In May 2010, more than three months after the hearing before the magistrate judge, Davila agreed to plead guilty to the conspiracy charge in exchange for dismissal of the other 33 counts charged in the indictment. Davila entered his guilty plea before a U.S. district judge six days later. Under oath, Davila stated that he had not been forced or pressured to plead guilty. Davila did not mention the *in camera* hearing before the magistrate judge, and the record does not indicate whether the district judge was aware that the pre-plea hearing had taken place.

Before he was sentenced, Davila moved to vacate his plea and to dismiss the indictment. The reason for his plea, Davila asserted, was "strategic." Aware that the prosecutor had a duty to disclose all information relevant to the court's determination whether to accept the plea bargain, he stated that his purpose in entering the plea was to force the government to acknowledge time frame errors made in the indictment. By pleading guilty, Davila said, he would make the court aware that the prosecution was "vindictive."

The district judge denied Davila's motion. In view of Davila's extensive criminal history, the court sentenced him to a prison term of 115 months. Again, neither Davila nor the court mentioned the *in camera* hearing conducted by the magistrate judge. Davila appealed, and the U.S. 11th Circuit Court of Appeals interpreted the ban on judicial participation in plea bargaining as a bright-line rule that required automatically setting aside Davila's guilty plea.

OPINION

Rule 11(c)(1) of the of the Federal Rules of Criminal Procedure instructs that "the court must not participate in plea discussions." Rule 11(h), states: "A variance from the requirements of the rule is harmless error if it does not affect substantial rights." The question presented is whether the violation of Rule 11(c)(1) by the magistrate judge warranted automatic vacatur (setting aside) of Davila's guilty plea. [The Court held that it does not. Therefore, the totality of circumstances in each case determines whether violating the automatic ban on judges' participation in a plea pushed the defendant to plead guilty.]

Our essential point is that particular facts and circumstances matter. Three months distanced the *in camera* meeting with the magistrate judge from Davila's appearance before the district judge who examined and accepted his guilty plea and later sentenced him. After conducting an exemplary Rule 11 colloquy, the judge inquired: "Mr. Davila, has anyone forced or pressured you to plead guilty today?" to which Davila responded: "No, sir." At the time of the plea hearing, there was no blending of judicial and prosecutorial functions.

Given the opportunity to raise any questions he might have about matters relating to his plea, Davila simply affirmed that he wished to plead guilty to the conspiracy count. When he later explained why he elected to plead guilty, he said nothing of the magistrate judge's exhortations. Instead, he called the decision "strategic," designed to get the prosecutor to correct misinformation about the conspiracy count.

Rather than automatically vacating Davila's guilty plea because of the Rule 11(c)(1) violation, the court of appeals should have considered whether it was reasonably probable that, but for the magistrate judge's exhortations, Davila would have exercised his right to go to trial. In answering that question, the magistrate judge's comments should be assessed, not in isolation, but in light of the full record.

LO 6   The Plea-Bargaining Debate

The arguments for and against conviction by guilty plea are heated, complex, and by no means empirically resolved:

- Some say negotiation better serves the search for truth; others argue that the adversarial process best serves the ends of justice.

- Some maintain guilty pleas save time; others contend plea negotiations more than make up for the time it takes to go to trial.

- Some insist the criminal justice system would collapse under its own weight if only a few of the now vast majority of defendants who plead guilty asserted their right to trial; others contend banning plea bargaining would make little difference in how many defendants plead guilty.

- Some maintain the guilty plea intimidates the innocent and emboldens the guilty; others say outcomes between jury trials and guilty pleas don't differ much at all.

The public and police officers usually oppose plea bargaining, because they believe it "lets criminals off"; the courts and lawyers, who are responsible for it, mostly support it. Recent empirical research in the behavioral law and economics field casts doubt on the underlying assumption that the parties to plea bargaining, and the process, are involved in a totally rational process.

Legal academic research and empirical law and behavioral science research are in conflict on this issue. In this section, we'll look at two models of plea bargaining: one that reflects the legal scholarship and the other that reflects behavioral science empirical research.

Most academic legal research by lawyers assumes that prosecutors and defense attorneys act rationally to settle disputes according to the "strength of the evidence and the expected punishment after trial" (Bibas 2003–04, 2467). We'll call this the **plea bargaining in the "shadow of trial" model**: that prosecutors, judges, and defense attorneys act rationally to forecast the outcome of a trial. They make bargains that leave both sides better off by splitting the costs they save by not going to trial. Of course, plea bargains aren't perfect, but trials aren't perfect either. These scholars contend that plea bargains still produce results "roughly as fair" as trials (Bibas 2003–04, 2464–65).

But a growing body of law and behavioral science research points to the conclusion that this model is "far too simplistic," (2466) and rejects its assumption of rationality. A second model, based on the real world of plea bargaining, is called the **plea bargaining outside the "shadow of trial" model**. In this model, legally irrelevant factors sometimes skew the fair allocation of punishment. As a result, some defendants strike skewed bargains. Other defendants plead when they would otherwise go to trial, or go to trial (and usually receive heavier sentences) when they would otherwise plead guilty (2467–68).

In the view of these researchers, "structural forces and psychological biases" can "inefficiently prevent mutually beneficial bargains or induce harmful ones" (2467). In other words, prosecutors and defense lawyers aren't "perfectly selfless, perfect agents of the public interest" (2470). The strength of the evidence may be the most important influence on plea bargaining, but it's not the only one. Self-interest pushes prosecutors, defense lawyers, and judges to settle cases for several personal reasons. For example, they all want to spend more time with their families. Also, winning "boosts their egos, their esteem, their praise by colleagues, and their prospects for promotion, and career advancement" (2471). Losing, on the other hand, is painful. Prosecutors tend to be loss averse. They may strike some plea bargains, Stephanos Bibas argues, because they "hate losing more than they like winning" (2472, n. 26).

Cognitive psychologists point to another problem with the *"shadow of trial" model*: bounded rationality. **Bounded rationality** refers to the strongly documented finding that people don't "attempt to ruthlessly maximize utility." Instead, once they identify an option that's "good enough," they stop looking and choose it. Bounded rationality creates a problem as a model for the rational view of plea bargaining, which requires the calculation of the value of pleas based on many "difficult-to-predict inputs" (Covey 2007–08, 216).

According to Russell Covey (2007–08),

> To make the correct decision, the parties must at a minimum estimate the probability that the defendant will be convicted at trial; predict what punishment will be imposed if the defendant is convicted; estimate the costs involved in the litigation, including attorneys fees, time lost waiting in court, and the psychological stress of nonresolution; and then calculate the forecasted trial sentence by multiplying the expected trial sentence by the probability of conviction, discounted by estimated process costs. They then must predict what punishment will be imposed if they enter a guilty plea and compare those two values in order to decide which course of action to take. (217)

Add to these complex tasks the "information deficits" during bargaining. Defendants may not know what evidence the prosecution has or how it will affect jurors. They don't know if witnesses will show up, what they'll say if they do, or whether they'll persuade the jury. They don't know who will be on the jury. There's more, but this is enough to illustrate defendants' "fuzzy notion" of the consequences of their guilty plea (217).

As if these difficulties aren't enough to cast doubt on the chances for rational plea bargaining, decades of empirical and experimental cognitive psychology research have shown that human reasoning diverges from the rational choice model in several ways. One is especially relevant here: People "aren't very good at assessing probabilities, particularly when the outcome in question is a rare event, or where there is limited information available from which to make a prediction" (213).

CRIMINAL PROCEDURE IN ACTION

The "fast track" plea bargain was voluntary

HISTORY

After immigration agents found 30 kilograms of marijuana in Angela Ruiz's luggage, federal prosecutors offered her what is known in the Southern District of California as a "fast track" plea bargain. That bargain—standard in that district—asks a defendant to waive indictment, trial, and an appeal. In return, the government agrees to recommend to the sentencing judge a two-level departure downward from the otherwise applicable United States Sentencing Guidelines sentence. In Ruiz's case, a two-level departure downward would have shortened the ordinary Guidelines-specified 18- to 24-month sentencing range by 6 months, to 12 to 18 months.

The prosecutors' proposed plea agreement contains a set of detailed terms. Among other things, it specifies that "any known information establishing the factual innocence of the defendant" "has been turned over to the defendant," and it acknowledges the government's "continuing duty to provide such information." At the same time it requires that the defendant "waive the right" to receive "impeachment information relating to any informants or other witnesses" as well as the right to receive information supporting any affirmative defense the defendant raises if the case goes to trial.

Because Ruiz would not agree to this last-mentioned waiver, the prosecutors withdrew their bargaining offer. The government then indicted Ruiz for unlawful drug possession. And despite the absence of any agreement, Ruiz ultimately pleaded guilty.

At sentencing, Ruiz asked the judge to grant her the same two-level downward departure that the government would have recommended had she accepted the "fast track" agreement. The government opposed her request, and the district court denied it, imposing a standard Guideline sentence instead.

Relying on 18 U.S.C. § 3742, Ruiz appealed her sentence to the United States Court of Appeals for the Ninth Circuit. The Ninth Circuit vacated the district court's sentencing determination. The Ninth Circuit pointed out that the Constitution requires prosecutors to make certain impeachment information available to a defendant before trial. It decided that this obligation entitles defendants to receive that same information before they enter into a plea agreement. The Ninth Circuit also decided that the Constitution prohibits defendants from waiving their right to that information. And it held that the prosecutors' standard "fast track" plea agreement was unlawful because it insisted upon that waiver. The Ninth Circuit remanded the case so that the district court could decide any related factual disputes and determine an appropriate remedy.

OPINION

When a defendant pleads guilty he or she, of course, forgoes not only a fair trial, but also other accompanying constitutional guarantees. Pleading guilty implicates the Fifth Amendment privilege against self-incrimination, the Sixth Amendment right to confront one's accusers, and the Sixth Amendment right to trial by jury. Given the seriousness of the matter, the Constitution insists, among other things, that the defendant enter a guilty plea that is "voluntary" and that the defendant must make related waivers "knowingly, intelligently, and with sufficient awareness of the relevant circumstances and likely consequences." *Brady v. United States*, 397 U.S. 742 (1970).

In this case, the Ninth Circuit in effect held that a guilty plea is not "voluntary" (and that the defendant could not, by pleading guilty, waive her right to a fair trial) unless the prosecutors first made the same disclosure of material impeachment information that the prosecutors would have had to make had the defendant insisted upon a trial. We must decide whether the Constitution requires that pre-guilty plea disclosure of impeachment information. We conclude that it does not.

Of course, the more information the defendant has, the more aware he is of the likely consequences of a plea, waiver, or decision, and the wiser that decision will likely be. But the Constitution does not require the prosecutor to share all useful information with the defendant. And the law ordinarily considers a waiver knowing, intelligent, and sufficiently aware if the defendant fully understands the nature of the right and how it would likely apply *in general* in the circumstances—even though the defendant may not know the *specific detailed* consequences of invoking it.

At the same time, a constitutional obligation to provide impeachment information during plea bargaining, prior to entry of a guilty plea, could seriously interfere with the Government's interest in securing those guilty pleas that are factually justified, desired by defendants, and help to secure the efficient administration of justice. The Ninth Circuit's rule risks premature disclosure of Government witness information, which, the Government tells us, could "disrupt ongoing investigations" and expose prospective witnesses to serious harm.

Consequently, the Ninth Circuit's requirement could force the Government to abandon its "general practice" of not "disclosing to a defendant pleading guilty information that would reveal the identities of cooperating informants, undercover investigators, or other prospective witnesses." It could require the Government to devote substantially more resources to trial preparation prior to plea bargaining, thereby depriving the plea-bargaining process of its main resource-saving advantages. Or it could lead the Government instead to abandon its heavy reliance upon plea bargaining in a vast number—90 percent or more—of federal criminal cases. We cannot say that the Constitution's due process requirement demands so radical a change in the criminal justice process in order to achieve so comparatively small a constitutional benefit.

These considerations, taken together, lead us to conclude that the Constitution does not require the Government to disclose material impeachment evidence prior to entering a plea agreement with a criminal defendant.

Reversed.

U.S. v. Ruiz, 536 U.S. 622 (2002)

CHAPTER SUMMARY

 LO 1 Jury trials promote fact-finding and check government power, while plea negotiation promotes efficiency. Prosecutors drop cases if they don't think they can prove them, or if, as "officers of the court," they feel prosecution wouldn't serve justice.

LO **1**   The right to a jury trial is extended to all crimes of "moral seriousness." This generally excludes petty offenses but could include crimes where the "moral quality" of the offense is serious, even when long prison terms aren't at stake.

LO **1**   The Fourteenth Amendment ensures that juries are selected from a random cross section of the public using local census reports, tax rolls, city directories, and more. The 12-member jury has strong traditional support from legal experts and social scientists, but it isn't an exclusive rule. The Sixth Amendment is satisfied by a jury of fewer members.

LO **2**   Stages of a jury trial include opening statements (starting with the prosecution), presenting evidence, closing arguments, instructions to the jury, and jury deliberations. Defendants don't have to prove their innocence. Instead, prosecutors must prove their guilt "beyond a reasonable doubt."

LO **2**   The right to a public trial is based on the Sixth Amendment right to confront witnesses, the Fifth Amendment due process right, and the Fourteenth Amendment due process right. Public trials also protect the right of the public to attend proceedings and the right of defendants to attend their own trials.

LO **2**   Prosecutors have a formal duty not only to convict criminals but also to do justice, prohibiting such behavior as intentionally misstating evidence, misleading juries, or inflaming jurors' passions or prejudices.

LO **3**   Juries can return "guilty," "not guilty," or "special" verdicts. Special verdicts, generally, are related to insanity or capital punishment. The requirement for a unanimous verdict instills confidence in the criminal justice process, guarantees careful review of evidence, ensures the hearing of minority viewpoints, and more. The U.S. Supreme Court has held that nonunanimous guilty verdicts are constitutional.

LO **4**   Guilty pleas include straight pleas and negotiated pleas (bargaining on the severity of charges or severity of punishment).

LO **5**   Guilty pleas are constitutional when defendants waive rights knowingly and voluntarily. According to the U.S. Supreme Court, the guilty plea must have a factual basis, meaning that defendants' pleas reflect an understanding of the "true nature" of the charges against them. When a judge fails to question defendants about their plea and establish it as knowing and voluntary, the conviction may be reversed.

LO **5**   Courts hold that a guilty plea may be "knowing and voluntary" even if the defendant didn't commit the crime. For example, pleas are accepted where innocent defendants want to avoid the risk of a long sentence at trial.

LO **5**   Defendants who plead guilty waive their Fifth Amendment right to remain silent, and the Sixth Amendment rights to trial by jury and to confront witnesses.

LO **6**   Under the "shadow of trial" model, prosecutors and defense attorneys rationally forecast the outcome of a trial and make bargains that often leave both sides better off. Legal and behavioral research, however, demonstrates that parties involved in a plea bargain negotiate based on legally irrelevant factors. For example, prosecutors and defense lawyers might have their own motivations to settle that aren't shared by the people they represent.

LO **6**   Cognitive research into "bounded rationality" creates problems for the "shadow of trial" model, because it shows people stop looking for solutions when they've found one that's "good enough." Faced with many "difficult-to-predict inputs," people are likely to accept the first plea they think they can live with.

REVIEW QUESTIONS

1. Contrast conviction by trial with conviction by guilty plea.

2. Identify five sources most jurisdictions use to draw up jury lists, and list six reasons jurors give to be excused from jury service. Why do most courts accept their excuses?

3. Explain the difference between peremptory challenges and challenges for cause.

4. List and briefly summarize the stages in the criminal trial.

5. Describe and explain the significance of the U.S. Supreme Court case of *In re Winship*.

6. What's the difference between the jury's verdict and the judgment of the court?

7. Describe and explain the significance of the U.S. Supreme Court decisions in *Apodaca v. Oregon* and *Johnson v. Louisiana*.

8. Explain the difference between straight and negotiated guilty pleas.

9. Summarize the arguments for and against plea bargaining.

10. List three constitutional rights defendants waive when they plead guilty.

11. Explain how a defendant can be factually innocent but legally guilty.

12. Describe and explain the significance of the U.S. Supreme Court decision in *Brady v. U.S.*

13. List reasons why a plea bargain might not be a rational attempt to settle a dispute according to the "strength of the evidence and the expected punishment after trial."

KEY TERMS

moral seriousness standard, p. 502
Federal Jury Selection and Service Act, p. 503
key-man system, p. 503
jury panel, p. 504
voir dire, p. 504
striking, p. 504
peremptory challenges, p. 504
challenges for cause, p. 504
prima facie case, p. 505
jury instructions, p. 512
opening statements, p. 514

stipulates, p. 514
missing witness instruction, p. 514
Sixth Amendment confrontation clause, p. 515
hearsay testimony, p. 515
compulsory process for obtaining witnesses, p. 515
reasonable doubt standard, p. 516
pattern jury instructions, p. 518
judgment, p. 519
jury nullification, p. 520
straight guilty pleas, p. 520

negotiated guilty pleas, p. 520
charge bargaining, p. 521
sentence bargaining, p. 521
fact bargaining, p. 521
reversible error, p. 522
factual basis for guilty pleas, p. 522
Alford plea, p. 522
plea bargaining in the "shadow of trial" model, p. 527
plea bargaining outside the "shadow of trial" model, p. 527
bounded rationality, p. 527

14

After Conviction

Sentencing, Appeals, and *Habeas Corpus*

LEARNING OBJECTIVES

1 Understand how the rights of a defendant differ from those of a convicted offender.

2 Understand how the need for both certainty and flexibility can affect how much discretion judges are given when it comes to sentencing.

3 Understand the role of sentencing guidelines and how departures from them depend on a crime's seriousness and an offender's criminal history. Know what mandatory minimum sentencing laws are and how they impact a judge's sentence.

4 Understand the proportionality principle, and know how it defines

cruel and unusual punishment under the Eighth Amendment.

5 Understand the *Apprendi* bright-line rule and its impact on sentences that are harsher than the relevant guideline.

6 Know that there's no constitutional right to appeal, but every jurisdiction has created a statutory right to appeal.

7 Understand why habeas corpus is a "collateral attack" and how civil trials are used to determine whether convicts have been unlawfully detained. Know the relative roles of state and federal review and the circumstances under which they apply.

In February or March 2000, Brian Gall, a second-year college student at the University of Iowa, was invited by Luke Rinderknecht to join an ongoing enterprise distributing a controlled substance popularly known as "ecstasy." Gall—who was then a user of Ecstasy, cocaine, and marijuana—accepted the invitation. During the ensuing seven months, Gall delivered ecstasy pills, which he received from Rinderknecht, to other conspirators, who then sold them to consumers. He netted over $30,000.

A month or two after joining the conspiracy, Gall stopped using ecstasy. A few months after that, in September 2000, he advised Rinderknecht and other co-conspirators that he was withdrawing from the conspiracy. He has not sold illegal drugs of any kind since. He has, in the words of the district court, "self-rehabilitated." He graduated from the University of Iowa in 2002 and moved first to Arizona, where he obtained a job in the construction industry, and later to Colorado, where he earned $18 per hour as a master carpenter. He has not used any illegal drugs since graduating from college.

—Gall v. U.S. (2007)

LO 1

After conviction, *defendants* become *offenders*. Don't mistake this for a mere change of words. It's a dramatic shift in status with grave consequences. In court before conviction, the shield of constitutional rights protects "defendants" by the presumption of innocence and all that goes with it (Chapters 12 and 13). But in the three main procedures following conviction—sentencing, appeal, and habeas corpus—a tough-to-overcome **presumption of guilt** rules the day. The significance of this presumption is the reduction or even absence of rights for convicted offenders during sentencing and appeal. They also face growing restrictions on the **right of habeas corpus**, a civil action to determine if the offender is being lawfully detained.

There's a powerful assumption (not necessarily backed up by empirical evidence) that by the time defendants are convicted, the state and defendants have had one fair shot at justice—and that's enough. Lots of time, energy, and money are devoted to deciding guilt. For their part, prosecutors have enormous resources at their command—the whole law enforcement machinery—to help them make their case. To offset the state's advantage, defendants are shielded by an array of constitutional rights. (We've examined them in previous chapters.)

After that fair shot, there's a strong consensus that we're wasting time, money, and energy to allow defendants to climb up, first, the ladder of appeals and, then, a second ladder of collateral attack (habeas corpus review of convictions by offenders in a separate civil action) to decide if they're being lawfully detained. As in all things (even the pursuit of justice), there comes a time to call it quits and move on—for the state to fight other crimes and for offenders to pay for their crimes, put their lives together, and get back into society as productive members of their community.

Before 2000, the answer to the question "Which constitutional rights apply to convicted defendants during sentencing?" would have been simple. Hardly any. Since then, a series of U.S. Supreme Court decisions has applied the constitutional rights of trial by jury and proof beyond a reasonable doubt to sentencing.

We'll devote most of the chapter to sentencing, because it's where most activity after conviction occurs. Then, we'll study the extent to which the constitutional rights that protect defendants before conviction apply to convicted defendants during sentencing. Finally, we'll look at the appeals process and habeas corpus proceedings.

SENTENCING

LO 2

For more than a thousand years, policy makers have debated whether to fit sentences to the crime or to tailor sentences to suit the criminal. As early as AD 700, the Roman Catholic Church's penitential books revealed a tension between prescribing penance strictly according to the sin and tailoring it to suit individual sinners (Samaha 1978). **Determinate, or fixed, sentencing** (fitting punishment to the crime) puts sentencing authority in the hands of legislators. **Indeterminate sentencing** (tailoring punishment to suit the criminal) puts the power to sentence in the hands of judges and parole boards.

Like the ancient tension between fixed and indeterminate sentencing, there's an ancient debate about judicial discretion in sentencing. Arguments over who should impose sentences indelibly mark the history of sentencing (Samaha 1989). There's also an ancient debate over what sentences to impose—about capital and corporal punishment, the length of imprisonment, what kinds of prisons to put prisoners in, and how to treat them while they're there. The early arguments regarding sinners and penance, judges and punishment, and the aims and kinds of punishment all sound a lot like current debates over the proper authority, aims, kinds, and amounts of punishment sentences ought to reflect.

In this section, we'll concentrate on fixed and indeterminate sentencing. We'll begin by looking at the history of sentencing, examine more closely the division of sentencing authority, and then look at sentencing guidelines.

LO 2 The History of Sentencing

Fixed sentencing, tailored to fit the crime, prevailed in the United States from the 1600s to the late 1800s. Then, a shift toward *indeterminate sentencing*, tailored to fit individual criminals, began. However, neither fixed nor indeterminate sentences have ever totally dominated criminal sentencing. The tension between the need for both certainty *and* flexibility in sentencing decisions has always required both a measure of predictability (fixed sentences) and a degree of flexibility (indeterminate sentences). Shifting ideological commitments and other informed influences on sentencing ensure that neither fixed nor indeterminate sentences will ever exclusively prevail in sentencing policies and practices.

Following the American Revolution, fixed but relatively moderate penalties became the rule. States abolished the death penalty for many offenses. The rarity of the use of **corporal punishment** (whipping), mutilation (cutting off ears and slitting tongues), and shaming (the ducking stool) led to their extinction. By 1850, imprisonment—which up to that time had been used mainly to detain accused people while they waited for their trial—had become the dominant form of criminal punishment after conviction.

Statutes fixed prison terms for most felonies. In practice, liberal use of pardons, early release for "good time," and other devices permitted judges to use informal discretionary judgment in altering formally fixed sentences (Rothman 1971).

The modern history of sentencing began around 1870. Demands for reform grew out of deep dissatisfaction with legislatively fixed *harsh* prison sentences. Reformers complained that prisons were nothing more than warehouses for the poor and the undesirable, and that harsh prison punishment didn't work. Proof of that, the reformers maintained, were the crime rates that continued to grow at unacceptable rates despite harsh, fixed prison sentences. Furthermore, the reformers documented that the prisons were full of recent immigrants and others on the lower rungs of society. Many public officials and concerned citizens agreed. Particularly instrumental in demanding reform were prison administrators and other criminal justice officials. By 1922, all but four states had adopted some form of indeterminate sentencing law.

When the indeterminate sentence became the prevailing practice, administrative sentencing by parole boards and prison officials took precedence over legislative and judicial sentence fixing. At its extreme, judges set no time on sentencing, leaving it wholly to parole boards and correctional officers to determine informally the length of a prisoner's incarceration. More commonly, judges were free to grant probation, suspend sentences in favor of alternatives to incarceration such as community service, or pick confinement times within minimums and maximums prescribed by statutes. Then, parole boards and corrections officers determined the exact release date.

Indeterminate sentencing remained dominant until the 1970s, when several forces coalesced to oppose it. Prison uprisings, especially at Attica and the Tombs in New

York in the late 1960s, dramatically portrayed rehabilitation as little more than rhetoric and prisoners as deeply and dangerously discontented. Advocates for individuals' rights challenged the widespread and unreviewable informal discretionary powers exercised by criminal justice officials in general and judges in particular. Demands for increased formal accountability spread throughout the criminal justice system. Courts required public officials to justify their decisions in writing and empowered defendants to dispute allegations against them at sentencing. The courts required even prisons to publish their rules and to grant prisoners the right to challenge the rules they were accused of breaking.

At the same time, statistical and experimental studies showed a pernicious discrimination in sentencing. In particular, some research strongly suggested that poor people and Blacks were sentenced more harshly than middle- and upper-class Americans and Whites. Finally, official reports showed steeply rising street crime rates. The National Research Council created a distinguished panel to review sentencing. It concluded that by the early 1970s, a "remarkable consensus emerged along left and right, law enforcement officials and prisoners groups, reformers and bureaucrats that the indeterminate sentencing era was at its end" (Blumstein et al. 1983, 48–52).

By the late 1970s, the emphasis in crime policy had shifted from fairness to crime prevention. Crime prevention was based on incarceration, general deterrence, and retribution; prevention by rehabilitation was definitely losing ground. Civil libertarians and "law and order" supporters alike called for sentencing practices that would advance swift and certain punishment. They differed on only one fundamental element of sentences—their length. To civil libertarians, determinate sentencing meant short, fixed sentences; to conservatives, it meant long, fixed sentences.

Three ideas came to dominate thinking about sentencing:

1. All crimes deserve some punishment to retain the deterrent potency of the criminal law.

2. Many offenders deserve severe punishment, because they've committed serious crimes.

3. Repeat career offenders require severe punishment to incapacitate them.

According to the National Council on Crime and Delinquency (1992):

> By 1990, the shift in goals of sentencing reform was complete. Virtually all new sentencing law was designed to increase the certainty and length of prison sentences to incapacitate the active criminal and deter the rest. (6)

Harsher penalties accompanied the shift in the philosophy of punishment. Public support for the death penalty grew; the U.S. Supreme Court ruled that the death penalty was not cruel and unusual punishment; courts sentenced more people to death; and the states began to execute criminals. Judges sentenced more people to prison and to longer prison terms. By 2011 (the latest available figures), almost half of the world's prison population lived in U.S. prisons (2.9 million), and America had the world's highest prison rate (743 per 100,000 people) (*World Prison Population List* 2011).

LO 2   The Division of Sentencing Authority

Throughout U.S. history, three institutions—legislatures, courts, and administrative agencies—have exercised sentencing power. In the **legislative sentencing model**, legislatures prescribe specific penalties for crimes without regard to the persons who committed them. The punishment fits the crime, not the criminal, and judges and parole boards can't alter these penalties. Removing discretion from judges and parole boards doesn't eliminate evils arising from prejudicial laws that criminalize conduct peculiar to certain groups in society, but it does limit the making of criminal law to legislatures.

In the **judicial sentencing model**, judges prescribe sentences within broad formal contours set by legislative acts. Typically, a statute prescribes a range, such as 0 to 5 years, 1 to 10 years, or 20 years to life. Judges then fix the exact time that convicted criminals serve.

In the **administrative sentencing model**, both the legislature and the judge prescribe a wide range of allowable prison times for particular crimes. Administrative agencies, typically parole boards and prison administrators, determine the exact release date. Under this model, administrative agencies have broad discretion to determine how long prisoners serve and under what conditions they can be released.

As models, these sentencing schemes never operate in pure form. At all times in U.S. history, all three sentencing institutions have overlapped considerably; all have included the exercise of wide discretion. For example, plea bargaining (Chapter 13) has prevented fixing sentencing authority in any of these three. Charge bargaining gets around legislatively fixed sentences, sentence bargaining avoids judicially fixed sentencing, and both alter administratively fixed sentences.

But until sentencing reforms in the 1970s began to change policy and practice, legislatures set the general range of penalties, judges picked a specific penalty within that range, and parole boards released offenders after some time spent in prison. Under this practice, judges, parole boards, and prison authorities had considerable discretion in sentencing criminal defendants.

LO 3   Sentencing Guidelines and Mandatory Minimum Sentences

Throughout these sections on guidelines and mandatory minimum sentence regimes, remember this important fact: The indeterminate sentence, parole boards, and good time still remain a part of the sentencing structure of many states. But the adoption of fixed sentencing regimes is growing. Fixed sentencing has taken two primary forms—sentencing guidelines and mandatory minimum prison sentences. The federal government and most states have adopted both forms. Both are based, at least in theory, on limiting—or even eliminating—discretion in sentencing.

Both respond to three demands of experts and the public:

1. *Uniformity.* Similar offenses should receive similar punishment.

2. *Certainty and truth in sentencing.* Convicted offenders, victims, and the public should know that the sentence imposed is similar to the sentence actually served. ("Do the crime; do the time.")

3. *Retribution, deterrence, and incapacitation.* The rehabilitation of individual offenders isn't the primary aim of punishment.

Let's look more closely at sentencing guidelines and mandatory minimum prison sentences.

LO **3**   *Sentencing guidelines*

In **sentencing guidelines** regimes, a commission establishes a relatively narrow range of penalties, and judges are supposed to choose a specific sentence within that range. The guideline ties sentences to two criteria:

1. The seriousness of the crime

2. The offender's criminal history (Figure 14.1)

Sentences are either presumptively incarceration or presumptively nonprison penalties. Judges can depart from the range set in the guidelines, but they have to give written reasons for their **departure**. The guidelines specify what reasons the judges can choose. For example, vulnerable victims are a reason for upward departures; being only a minor participant in a crime is a reason for downward departure. The government can appeal *downward* departures; the defendant can appeal *upward* departures.

Sentencing guideline grids, like Minnesota's in Figure 14.1, commonly depict these elements of guidelines sentencing. The rows along the left list the crimes and their seriousness; the columns show the offenders' criminal history. For example, the recommended sentence for residential burglary is 33 months; the judge has the discretion to go down to 29 months or up to 39 months. The shaded area depicts the discretionary dispositional sentences.

Letting judges choose within a range without departing from the guidelines builds a flexibility into the system. This allows for differences in individual cases without undermining the basic goals of uniformity and equity. Uniformity and equity are the *goals* of guidelines' regimes. But what about the reality? Empirical research has some answers. That research demonstrates that context affects most courtroom decision making, including sentencing. Judges don't impose sentences in a social vacuum; the social, political, and organizational environment influences the sentences they impose, even in guidelines regimes. So sentences are likely to vary from one region, state, district, and even courtroom in the same district to another.

According to available research, they *do* vary (Johnson 2005). Elements of the courtroom social context that "matter" include:

- Urbanization
- Bureaucratization
- Court size
- Unemployment
- Race
- Crime rates
- Court resources (Johnson 2005, 763)

Let's look closer at one aspect of this research, the focus on the extralegal categories of race, ethnicity, gender, and age on judicial discretion to impose unwarranted departures from recommended sentences. Most of this research has found varying degrees of disparities based on these extralegal categories. Brian D. Johnson (2003) found that

- Black and Hispanic defendants are *less* likely to receive *downward* departures and *more* likely to receive *upward* departures than Whites.

FIGURE 14.1 Minnesota Sentencing Guidelines Grid

4.A. Sentencing Guidelines Grid

Presumptive sentence lengths are in months. Italicized numbers within the grid denote the discretionary range within which a court may sentence without the sentence being deemed a departure. Offenders with stayed felony sentences may be subject to local confinement.

SEVERITY LEVEL OF CONVICTION OFFENSE (Example offenses listed in italics)		CRIMINAL HISTORY SCORE						
		0	**1**	**2**	**3**	**4**	**5**	**6 or more**
Murder, 2nd Degree (intentional murder; drive-by-shootings)	**11**	306 *261–367*	326 *278–391*	346 *295–415*	366 *312–439*	386 *329–463*	406 *346–480*[2]	426 *363–480*[2]
Murder, 3rd Degree Murder, 2nd Degree (unintentional murder)	**10**	150 *128–180*	165 *141–198*	180 *153–216*	195 *166–234*	210 *179–252*	225 *192–270*	240 *204–288*
Assault, 1st Degree Controlled Substance Crime, 1st Degree	**9**	86 *74–103*	98 *84–117*	110 *94–132*	122 *104–146*	134 *114–160*	146 *125–175*	158 *135–189*
Aggravated Robbery, 1st Degree Controlled Substance Crime, 2nd Degree	**8**	48 *41–57*	58 *50–69*	68 *58–81*	78 *67–93*	88 *75–105*	98 *84–117*	108 *92–129*
Felony DWI	**7**	36	42	48	54 *46–64*	60 *51–72*	66 *57–79*	72 *62–84*[2]
Controlled Substance Crime, 3rd Degree	**6**	21	27	33	39 *34–46*	45 *39–54*	51 *44–61*	57 *49–68*
Residential Burglary Simple Robbery	**5**	18	23	28	33 *29–39*	38 *33–45*	43 *37–51*	48 *41–57*
Nonresidential Burglary	**4**	12[1]	15	18	21	24 *21–28*	27 *23–32*	30 *26–36*
Theft Crimes (Over $5,000)	**3**	12[1]	13	15	17	19 *17–22*	21 *18–25*	23 *20–27*
Theft Crimes ($5,000 or less) Check Forgery ($251-$2,500)	**2**	12[1]	12[1]	13	15	17	19	21 *18–25*
Sale of Simulated Controlled Substance	**1**	12[1]	12[1]	12[1]	13	15	17	19 *17–22*

☐ Presumptive commitment to state imprisonment. First-degree murder has a mandatory life sentence and is excluded from the Guidelines under Minn. Stat. § 609.185. See Guidelines section 2.E. Mandatory Sentences, for policies regarding those sentences controlled by law.

▨ Presumptive stayed sentence; at the discretion of the court, up to one year of confinement and other non-jail sanctions can be imposed as conditions of probation. However, certain offenses in the shaded area of the Grid always carry a presumptive commitment to state prison. Guidelines sections 2.C. Presumptive Sentence and 2.E. Mandatory Sentences.

[1] 12[1]=One year and one day

[2] Minn. Stat. § 244.09 requires that the Guidelines provide a range for sentences that are presumptive commitment to state imprisonment of 15% lower and 20% higher than the fixed duration displayed, provided that the minimum sentence is not less than one year and one day and the maximum sentence is not more than the statutory maximum. Guidelines section 2.C.1-2. Presumptive Sentence.

Effective August 1, 2012

Source: Minnesota Sentencing Guidelines Commission. Minnesota Sentencing Guidelines http://www.msgc.state.mn.us/guidelines/grids/2012%20MN%20Sentencing%20Guidelines%20Grid.pdf

TABLE 14.1 Odds of receiving departures by race, ethnicity, sex, and age

The odds of receiving *downward* departures are
• 56 percent less for Hispanics than Whites
• 25 percent less for Blacks than Whites
• 63 percent greater for a female than a male
• 71 percent greater for a 65-year-old than a 20-year-old
The odds of receiving *upward* departures are
• 39 percent higher for Hispanics than Whites
• 21 percent higher for Blacks than Whites
• 31 percent higher for males than females
• Significantly higher for younger than older people

Source: Johnson 2003, 464–66; 468.

- Men are *less* likely to receive *downward* departures and *more* likely to receive *upward* departures than women.

- Younger defendants are *more* likely to receive *upward* departures and *less* likely to receive *downward* departures than older defendants. (464–66; 468; Table 14.1)

Like all good researchers, Johnson ends on a cautionary note. Sentencing decision making is inherently complex, and circumstances change. Future research, therefore, should replicate his findings in other places and times (482–83).

Johnson's empirical work and other studies have focused on characteristics of *defendants* to demonstrate unwarranted disparities in departures from recommended guidelines sentences. But what about the characteristics of *judges*? "Most scholars and observers agree that political-ideological preferences are at play when judges sentence criminals" (Schanzenbach and Tiller 2008, 725).

One empirical study tested whether political affiliation is a source of unwarranted departures under the U.S. Sentencing Guidelines regime. Schanzenbach and Tiller examined the relationship between U.S. District Court judges' sentencing decisions and reviews by their supervising U.S. Circuit Court judges under the U.S. Sentencing Guidelines regime following *Booker*. They assessed whether district court judges use the tools of offense-level adjustments and departures as strategies "to attain sentencing outcomes closer to their personal preferences" instead of the primary goals of the U.S. Sentencing Guidelines—namely, certainty and fairness.

Here's what Schanzenbach and Tiller found:

1. "Policy preferences matter in sentencing. Liberal (Democratic-appointed) judges give different (generally lower) sentences than conservative (Republican-appointed) judges for certain categories of crime."

2. The length of the sentence given by U.S. District Court sentencing judges depends on the amount of political alignment between the sentencing judge and the U.S. Circuit Court judges who "supervise" their decisions.

3. "Sentencing judges selectively use adjustments and departures to enhance or reduce sentences, and the use of departures is influenced by the degree of political alignment between the sentencing judge and the overseeing circuit court, while the use of adjustment is not so limited." (727)

CRIMINAL PROCEDURE IN ACTION

Fleeing from a law enforcement officer is a "violent" felony

Sykes v. U.S., 131 S.Ct. 2267 (2011)

FACTS

Marcus Sykes pleaded guilty to being a felon in possession of a firearm, 18 U.S.C. § 922(g)(1), in connection with an attempted robbery of two people at gunpoint. Sykes had previous convictions for at least three felonies. On two separate occasions Sykes used a firearm to commit robbery, in one case to rob a man of his $200 wristwatch and in another to rob a woman of her purse.

His third prior felony is the one of concern here. Sykes was convicted for vehicle flight, in violation of Indiana's "resisting law enforcement" law.

After observing Sykes driving without using needed headlights, police activated their emergency equipment for a traffic stop. Sykes did not stop. A chase ensued. Sykes wove through traffic, drove on the wrong side of the road and through yards containing bystanders, passed through a fence, and struck the rear of a house. Then he fled on foot. He was found only with the aid of a police dog. In Indiana, using a vehicle to flee after an officer has ordered you to stop is a class D felony. The Court of Appeals of Indiana has interpreted the crime of vehicle flight to require "a knowing attempt to escape law enforcement."

The U.S. District Court decided that his three prior convictions, including the one for violating the prohibition on vehicle flight in the Indiana statute, were violent felonies for purposes of § 924(e) and sentenced Sykes to 188 months of imprisonment. On appeal Sykes conceded that his two prior robbery convictions were violent felonies. He did not dispute that his vehicle flight offense was a felony, but he did argue that it was not violent. The Court of Appeals for the Seventh Circuit affirmed. The court's opinion was consistent with the rulings of the Courts of Appeals in the First, Fifth, Sixth, and Tenth Circuits. It was in conflict with a ruling by a Court of Appeals for the Eleventh Circuit, and at least in tension, if not in conflict, with the reasoning of the Court of Appeals for the Eighth Circuit.

OPINION

In determining whether an offense is a violent felony, this Court has explained,

we employ the categorical approach. Under this approach, we look only to the fact of conviction and the statutory definition of the prior offense, and do not generally consider the particular facts disclosed by the record of conviction. That is, we consider whether the *elements of the offense* are of the type that would justify its inclusion within the residual provision, without inquiring into the specific conduct of this particular offender.

So while there may be little doubt that the circumstances of the flight in Sykes's own case were violent, the question is whether violating § 35–44–3–3 of the Indiana Code, as a categorical matter, is a violent felony.

Under 18 U.S.C. § 924(e)(2)(B), an offense is deemed a violent felony if it is a crime punishable by more than one year of imprisonment that

(i) has as an element the use, attempted use, or threatened use of physical force against the person of another; or

(ii) is burglary, arson, or extortion, involves use of explosives, or otherwise involves conduct that presents a serious potential risk of physical injury to another.

Resisting law enforcement through felonious vehicle flight does not meet the requirements of clause (i), and it is not among the specific offenses named in clause (ii). Thus, it is violent under this statutory scheme only if it fits within the so-called residual provision of clause (ii). To be a violent crime, it must be an offense that "otherwise involves conduct that presents a serious potential risk of physical injury to another."

The question, then, is whether Indiana's prohibition on flight from an officer by driving a vehicle—the violation of Indiana law for which Sykes sustained his earlier conviction—falls within the residual clause because, as a categorical matter, it presents a serious potential risk of physical injury to another. When a perpetrator defies a law enforcement command by fleeing in a car, the determination to elude capture makes a lack of concern for the safety of property and persons of pedestrians and other drivers an inherent part of the offense. Even if the criminal attempting to elude capture

(continued)

drives without going at full speed or going the wrong way, he creates the possibility that police will, in a legitimate and lawful manner, exceed or almost match his speed or use force to bring him within their custody. A perpetrator's indifference to these collateral consequences has violent—even lethal—potential for others. A criminal who takes flight and creates a risk of this dimension takes action similar in degree of danger to that involved in arson, which also entails intentional release of a destructive force dangerous to others.

This similarity is a beginning point in establishing that vehicle flight presents a serious potential risk of physical injury to another.

Serious and substantial risks are an inherent part of vehicle flight. Under subsection (b)(1)(A), they need not be proved separately to secure a conviction equal in magnitude to those available for other forms of resisting law enforcement with a vehicle that involve similar risks.

Felony vehicle flight is a violent felony for purposes of ACCA.

Mandatory minimum sentences

The other type of fixed sentence, **mandatory minimum sentences**, requires judges to impose a nondiscretionary minimum amount of prison time that all offenders convicted of the offense have to serve. Judges can sentence offenders to *more* than the minimum but not *less*. Mandatory minimum sentence laws promise that "If you do the crime, you *will* do the time."

Mandatory penalties are very old. The "eye for an eye" and "tooth for a tooth" in the Old Testament were mandatory penalties. The Anglo-Saxon king Alfred prescribed a detailed mandatory penal code, including such provisions as "If one knocks out another's eye, he shall pay 66 shillings, $6\frac{1}{3}$ pence. If the eye is still in the head, but he injured man can see nothing with it, one-third of the payment shall be withheld" (Lee n.d.).

As early as 1790 in the United States, most states had established mandatory penalties for capital crimes. Throughout the 19th century, Congress enacted mandatory penalties—usually short prison sentences—for a long list of crimes, including refusal to testify before Congress, failure to report seaboard saloon purchases, or causing a ship to run aground by use of a false light (Wallace 1993, 9).

From 1900 to the 1950s, the use of mandatory minimum penalties fell into disuse. The Boggs Act (1951), named after its sponsor, Alabama Representative Hale Boggs, signaled a shift to mandatory minimum sentences. It set minimum sentences for those convicted of importing drugs or distributing marijuana. In the 1950s, fear that crime and drug problems were caused by a Communist plot to get Americans "hooked" on especially potent "pure Communist heroin" from China led Congress to enact the Narcotic Control Act of 1956 (U.S. Congress 1954, 7). It further increased the penalties set in the Boggs Act.

In 1956, the Senate Judiciary Committee explained why Congress needed a mandatory minimum sentence drug law:

> There is a need for the continuation of the policy of punishment of a severe character as a deterrent to narcotic law violations. [The Committee] therefore recommends an increase in maximum sentences for first as well as subsequent offenses. With respect to the mandatory minimum features of such penalties, and prohibition of suspended sentences or probation, the Committee recognizes objections in principle. It feels, however, that, in order to define the gravity of this class of crime and the assured penalty to follow, these features of the law must be regarded as essential elements of the desired deterrents, although some differences of opinion still exist regarding their application to first offenses of certain types. (U.S. Sentencing Commission 1991, 5–7)

The 1956 statute imposed stiff mandatory minimum sentences for narcotics offenses, requiring judges to pick within a range of penalties. Judges couldn't suspend sentences or put convicted offenders on probation. In addition, offenders weren't eligible for parole if they were convicted under the act. For example, the act punished the first conviction for selling heroin by a term of from 5 to 10 years of imprisonment. Judges had to sentence offenders to at least 5 years in prison, judges couldn't suspend the sentence or put offenders on probation, and offenders weren't eligible for parole for at least the minimum period of the sentence. For second offenders, the mandatory minimum was raised to 10 years. The penalty for the sale of narcotics to persons under 18 ranged from a mandatory minimum of 10 years to a maximum of life imprisonment or death (U.S. Sentencing Commission 1991, 6).

In 1970, Congress retreated from the mandatory minimum sentence approach. In the Comprehensive Drug Abuse Prevention and Control Act of 1970, Congress repealed virtually all of the mandatory minimum provisions adopted in the 1956 act, because the increased sentence lengths "had not shown the expected overall reduction in drug law violations." Among the reasons for the repeal of mandatory minimum penalties for drug law offenses were that they

1. Alienated youths from the general society

2. Hampered the rehabilitation of drug offenders

3. Infringed on judicial authority by drastically reducing discretion in sentencing

4. Reduced the deterrent effect of drug laws because even prosecutors thought the laws were too severe

According to the House committee that considered the repeal of the bill:

The severity of existing penalties, involving in many instances minimum sentences, have [*sic*] led in many instances to reluctance on the part of prosecutors to prosecute some violations, where the penalties seem to be out of line with the seriousness of the offenses. In addition, severe penalties, which do not take into account individual circumstances, and which treat casual violators as severely as they treat hardened criminals, tend to make conviction more difficult to obtain. (U.S. Congress 1970, 11)

The retreat from mandatory minimum sentences was short-lived, because public concern about violence and drugs again rose to the top of the national agenda. The public and legislatures blamed rising crime rates on the uncertainty and "leniency" of indeterminate sentences. Beginning in the early 1970s, the states and the federal government enacted more and longer mandatory minimum prison sentences. By 1991, 46 states and the federal government had enacted mandatory minimum sentencing laws. Although the list of mandatory minimum laws is long (the U.S. Criminal Code contains at least one hundred), the main targets of mandatory minimum sentences are drug offenses, violent crimes, and crimes committed with a weapon (Wallace 1993, 11).

Mandatory minimum sentences are supposed to satisfy three basic aims of criminal punishment: retribution, incapacitation, and deterrence. According to supporters, mandatory minimum sentence laws mean those committing serious crimes will receive severe punishment. Furthermore, violent criminals, criminals who use weapons, and drug offenders can't harm the public if they're in prison. And the knowledge that committing mandatory minimum crimes will bring certain, swift, and severe punishment should deter these types of crimes.

Several evaluations, however, suggest that, in practice, mandatory minimum penalties don't always achieve the goals their supporters hoped they would. In 1990, Congress ordered the U.S. Sentencing Commission to evaluate the rapidly increasing number of mandatory minimum sentencing provisions in the federal system. The results of the commission's study provided little empirical support for the success of mandatory sentencing laws, as these findings demonstrate:

1. Only a few of the mandatory minimum sentencing provisions are ever used. Nearly all those used relate to drug and weapons offenses.

2. Only 41 percent of defendants whose characteristics and behavior qualify them for mandatory minimum sentences actually receive them.

3. Mandatory minimum sentences actually introduce disparity in sentencing. For example, the commission found that race influences disparity in a number of ways. Whites are less likely than Blacks and Hispanics to be indicted or convicted at the mandatory minimum. Whites are also more likely than Blacks and Hispanics to receive reductions for "substantial assistance" in aiding in the prosecution of other offenders. The mandatory minimum sentence laws allow an exception for offenders who provide "substantial assistance" in investigating other offenders. But judges can reduce the minimum for substantial assistance only on the motion of the prosecutors.

4. Substantial assistance also leads to disparities quite apart from race. It tends to favor the very people the law was intended to reach—those higher up in the chain of drug dealing, because underlings have less to offer the government. In one case, for example, Stanley Marshall, who sold less than one gram of LSD, got a 20-year mandatory prison sentence. Jose Cabrera, on the other hand, who the government estimated made more than $40 million from importing cocaine and who would have qualified for life plus 200 years, received a prison term of 8 years for providing "substantial assistance" in the case of Manuel Noriega. According to Judge Terry J. Hatter, Jr., "The people at the very bottom who can't provide substantial assistance end up getting [punished] more severely than those at the top." (*Criminal Justice Newsletter* 1993, 5; Wallace 1993, 11)

5. Mandatory minimum sentences don't eliminate discretion; they just shift it from judges to prosecutors. Prosecutors can use their discretion in a number of ways, including manipulating the "substantial assistance" exception and deciding not to charge defendants with crimes carrying mandatory minimum sentences or to charge them with mandatory minimum crimes of lesser degree.

The U.S. Sentencing Commission recommended further study before making any final conclusions about the effectiveness of mandatory penalties. But its findings, along with other research on federal and state mandatory minimum sentences, suggest that mandatory minimum penalties aren't the easy answer to the crime problem that politicians promise and the public hopes for (Campaign for an Effective Crime Policy 1993; Schulhofer 1993, 199).

LO 4 The Constitution and Proportionality in Sentencing

There are two kinds of constitutional questions regarding sentencing. One has to do with the sentence itself—namely, whether it's banned by the Eighth Amendment "cruel and unusual punishment" clause. Whether it's cruel and unusual depends on the answer to another question, "Does the Eighth Amendment embody a proportionality requirement?" The **proportionality principle** states that a punishment is cruel and unusual if its harshness is "grossly disproportionate" to the "gravity of the offense" (*Harmelin v. Michigan* 1991, 997).

The other constitutional question has to do with the procedures used to determine the sentence. That question is, "What, if any, rights that defendants enjoyed *before* conviction during trial and plea bargaining do they enjoy *after* conviction during sentencing?" Let's look at each of these questions.

LO 4 *The proportionality principle and the sentence of death*

A majority of the U.S. Supreme Court has made it clear that the proportionality principle applies to death sentences because "death is different." A minority have concluded that the Eighth Amendment includes no proportionality requirement. Or, if it does, it's legislatures elected by the people, not the unelected "undemocratic" judges appointed for life, who should decide what's a disproportionate, or cruel and unusual, sentence.

As of 2013, the Court has ruled that the sentence of death fits only the crime of murder (*Gregg v. Georgia* 1976), with several categorical exceptions: mentally retarded persons who kill (*Atkins v. Virginia* 2002); juveniles under the age of 18 (*Roper v. Simmons* 2005); and felony murderers who didn't do the actual killing and lacked the intent to kill (*Enmund v. Florida* 1982).

We also know that a death sentence for raping an adult woman is "grossly disproportionate" (*Coker v. Georgia* 1977, 592). The same applies to raping a child, as in the disturbing case of an eight-year-old girl whose stepfather raped her in Harvey, Louisiana, across the river from New Orleans. The little girl was awakened early in the morning to find Patrick Kennedy (her 300-pound stepfather) on top of her, undressing her, with his hand over her mouth to keep her quiet before forcing himself inside her, causing internal injuries and heavy bleeding.

The U.S. Supreme Court overturned his death sentence because even in this awful crime, death was "grossly disproportionate" (*Kennedy v. Louisiana* 2008). According to the Court:

> Consistent with evolving standards of decency and the teachings of our precedents we conclude that, in determining whether the death penalty is excessive, there is a distinction between intentional first-degree murder on the one hand, and non-homicide crimes against individual persons, even including child rape, on the other. The latter crimes may be devastating in their harm, as here, but in terms of moral depravity and of the injury to the person and to the public, they cannot be compared to murder in their severity and irrevocability. (27)

LO 4 *The proportionality principle and sentences of imprisonment*

When it comes to sentences of imprisonment, the Court is deeply divided. Some justices have concluded that proportionality never applies to sentences of imprisonment. A narrow and shifting majority has concluded that there's a "narrow proportionality principle" regarding prison sentences (*Harmelin v. Michigan* 1991, 997). For example, it would be cruel and unusual punishment to sentence someone to life in prison for failing to pay a parking ticket (*Rummell v. Estelle* 1980, 274, n. 11).

By a slim majority and over strong dissents, the Supreme Court held that it was not cruel and unusual punishment to sentence first-time offender Ronald Allen Harmelin to life in prison with no chance of parole for possessing 672 grams of cocaine

(*Harmelin v. Michigan* 1991). The majority, however, couldn't agree as to why. Justice Scalia and Chief Justice Rehnquist's reason was because there's no proportionality requirement in the Eighth Amendment. Justices O'Connor, Kennedy, and Souter concluded that the sentence wasn't grossly disproportionate to the crime. Four justices dissented, arguing that the sentence was grossly disproportionate to the crime.

In *Lockyer v. Andrade* (2003), our next case excerpt, the U.S. Supreme Court held narrowly that it wasn't cruel and unusual punishment to sentence Leandro Andrade to 50 years for shoplifting $150 worth of videos under California's "three strikes" law.

In *Lockyer v. Andrade* (2003), the U.S. Supreme Court held that it wasn't cruel and unusual punishment to sentence Leandro Andrade to 50 years for shoplifting $150 worth of videos under California's "three strikes" law.

CASE

Was 50 Years in Prison for Shoplifting $150 Worth of Videos "Cruel and Unusual Punishment"?

Lockyer, Attorney General of California v. Andrade
538 U.S. 63 (2003)

HISTORY

Leandro Andrade (State prisoner/petitioner), who was convicted on two counts of petty theft and sentenced to life in prison under California's Career Criminal Punishment Act, also known as the Three Strikes law, petitioned for a writ of habeas corpus. The United States District Court for the Central District of California, Christina A. Snyder, J., denied his petition, and the prisoner appealed. The United States Court of Appeals for the Ninth Circuit, Paez, Circuit Judge, reversed and remanded. Certiorari was granted. The Supreme Court held that the California Court of Appeal's decision affirming petitioner's two consecutive terms of 25 years to life in prison for a "third strike" conviction was not "contrary to" or an "unreasonable application" of the "clearly established" gross disproportionality principle set forth by *Rummel, Solem,* and *Harmelin* decisions of United States Supreme Court and thus did not warrant federal habeas relief. The Supreme Court reversed.

—O'CONNOR, J., joined by REHNQUIST, C.J., and
SCALIA, KENNEDY, and THOMAS, JJ.

This case raises the issue whether the United States Court of Appeals for the Ninth Circuit erred in ruling that the California Court of Appeal's decision affirming Leandro Andrade's two consecutive terms of 25 years to life in prison for a "third strike" conviction is contrary to, or an unreasonable application of, clearly established federal law as determined by this Court within the meaning of 28 U.S.C. § 2254(d)(1).

FACTS

On November 4, 1995, Leandro Andrade stole five videotapes worth $84.70 from a Kmart store in Ontario, California. Security personnel detained Andrade as he was leaving the store. On November 18, 1995, Andrade entered a different Kmart store in Montclair, California, and placed four videotapes worth $68.84 in the rear waistband of his pants. Again, security guards apprehended Andrade as he was exiting the premises. Police subsequently arrested Andrade for these crimes.

These two incidents were not Andrade's first or only encounters with law enforcement. According to the state probation officer's presentence report, Andrade has been in and out of state and federal prison since 1982. In January 1982, he was convicted of a misdemeanor theft offense and was sentenced to six days in jail with 12 months' probation. Andrade was arrested again in November 1982 for multiple counts of first-degree residential burglary. He pleaded guilty to at least three of those counts, and in April of the following year he was sentenced to 120 months in prison. In 1988, Andrade was convicted in federal court of "transportation of marijuana," and was sentenced to eight years in federal prison. In 1990, he was convicted in state court for a misdemeanor petty theft offense and was ordered to serve 180 days in jail. In September 1990, Andrade was convicted again in federal court for the same felony of "transportation of marijuana," and was sentenced to 2,191 days in federal prison. And in 1991, Andrade was arrested for a state parole violation—escape from federal prison. He was paroled from the state penitentiary system in 1993.

A state probation officer interviewed Andrade after his arrest in this case. The presentence report notes:

> The defendant admitted committing the offense. The defendant further stated he went into the K-Mart Store to steal videos. He took four of them to sell so he could buy heroin. He has been a heroin addict since 1977. He says when he gets out of jail or prison he always does something stupid. He admits his addiction controls his life and he steals for his habit.

Because of his 1990 misdemeanor conviction, the State charged Andrade in this case with two counts of petty theft with a prior conviction, in violation of Cal. Penal Code Ann. § 666 (West Supp.2002). Under California law, petty theft with a prior conviction is a so-called "wobbler" offense because it is punishable either as a misdemeanor or as a felony. The decision to prosecute petty theft with a prior conviction as a misdemeanor or as a felony is in the discretion of the prosecutor. The trial court also has discretion to reduce the charge to a misdemeanor at the time of sentencing.

Under California's three strikes law, any felony can constitute the third strike, and thus can subject a defendant to a term of 25 years to life in prison. See Cal.Penal Code Ann. § 667(e)(2)(A) (West 1999). In this case, the prosecutor decided to charge the two counts of theft as felonies rather than misdemeanors. The trial court denied Andrade's motion to reduce the offenses to misdemeanors, both before the jury verdict and again in state habeas proceedings.

A jury found Andrade guilty of two counts of petty theft with a prior conviction. According to California law, a jury must also find that a defendant has been convicted of at least two serious or violent felonies that serve as qualifying offenses under the three strikes regime. In this case, the jury made a special finding that Andrade was convicted of three counts of first-degree residential burglary. A conviction for first-degree residential burglary qualifies as a serious or violent felony for the purposes of the three strikes law. As a consequence, each of Andrade's convictions for theft under Cal.Penal Code Ann. § 666 (West Supp.2002) triggered a separate application of the three strikes law. Pursuant to California law, the judge sentenced Andrade to two consecutive terms of 25 years to life in prison. See §§ 667(c)(6), 667(e)(2)(B).

On direct appeal in 1997, the California Court of Appeal affirmed Andrade's sentence of two consecutive terms of 25 years to life in prison. After the Supreme Court of California denied discretionary review, Andrade filed a petition for a writ of habeas corpus in Federal District Court. The District Court denied his petition. The Ninth Circuit granted Andrade a certificate of appealability, and subsequently reversed the judgment of the District Court.

OPINION

Andrade's argument in this Court is that two consecutive terms of 25 years to life for stealing approximately $150 in videotapes is grossly disproportionate in violation of the Eighth Amendment. Andrade similarly maintains that the state court decision affirming his sentence is "contrary to, or involved an unreasonable application of, clearly established Federal law, as determined by the Supreme Court of the United States." 28 U.S.C. § 2254(d)(1). AEDPA (Antiterrorism and Effective Death Penalty Act) circumscribes a federal habeas court's review of a state court decision. Section 2254 provides:

(d) An application for a writ of habeas corpus on behalf of a person in custody pursuant to the judgment of a State court shall not be granted with respect to any claim that was adjudicated on the merits in State court proceedings unless the adjudication of the claim—

  (1) resulted in a decision that was contrary to, or involved an unreasonable application of, clearly established Federal law, as determined by the Supreme Court of the United States.

One governing legal principle emerges as "clearly established" under § 2254(d)(1): A gross disproportionality principle is applicable to sentences for terms of years. Our cases exhibit a lack of clarity regarding what factors may indicate gross disproportionality. In *Solem* (the case upon which Andrade relies most heavily), we stated: "It is clear that a 25-year sentence generally is more severe than a 15-year sentence, but in most cases it would be difficult to decide that the former violates the Eighth Amendment while the latter does not." Thus, in this case, the only relevant clearly established law amenable to the "contrary to" or "unreasonable application of" framework is the gross disproportionality principle, the precise contours of which are unclear, applicable only in the "exceedingly rare" and "extreme" case. The final question is whether the California Court of Appeal's decision affirming Andrade's sentence is "contrary to, or involved an unreasonable application of," this clearly established gross disproportionality principle.

First, a state court decision is contrary to our clearly established precedent if the state court applies a rule that contradicts the governing law set forth in our cases or if the state court confronts a set of facts that are materially indistinguishable from a decision of this Court and

(continued)

nevertheless arrives at a result different from our precedent. In terms of length of sentence and availability of parole, severity of the underlying offense, and the impact of recidivism, Andrade's sentence implicates factors relevant in both *Rummel* and *Solem*. It was not contrary to our clearly established law for the California Court of Appeal to turn to *Rummel* in deciding whether a sentence is grossly disproportionate. Indeed, *Harmelin* allows a state court to reasonably rely on *Rummel* in determining whether a sentence is grossly disproportionate. The California Court of Appeal's decision was therefore not "contrary to" the governing legal principles set forth in our cases.

Andrade's sentence also was not materially indistinguishable from the facts in *Solem*. The facts here fall in between the facts in *Rummel* and the facts in *Solem*. *Solem* involved a sentence of life in prison without the possibility of parole. The defendant in *Rummel* was sentenced to life in prison with the possibility of parole. Here, Andrade retains the possibility of parole. *Solem* acknowledged that *Rummel* would apply in a "similar factual situation." And while this case resembles to some degree both *Rummel* and *Solem*, it is not materially indistinguishable from either. Consequently, the state court did not confront a set of facts that are materially indistinguishable from a decision of this Court and nevertheless arrive at a result different from our precedent.

Second, under the "unreasonable application" clause, a federal habeas court may grant the writ if the state court identifies the correct governing legal principle from this Court's decisions but unreasonably applies that principle to the facts of the prisoner's case. The "unreasonable application" clause requires the state court decision to be more than incorrect or erroneous. The state court's application of clearly established law must be objectively unreasonable.

It is not enough that a federal habeas court, in its independent review of the legal question, is left with a firm conviction that the state court was erroneous. We have held precisely the opposite: "Under § 2254(d)(1)'s 'unreasonable application' clause, then, a federal habeas court may not issue the writ simply because that court concludes in its independent judgment that the relevant state-court decision applied clearly established federal law erroneously or incorrectly." Rather, that application must be objectively unreasonable.

Section 2254(d)(1) permits a federal court to grant habeas relief based on the application of a governing legal principle to a set of facts different from those of the case in which the principle was announced. Here, however, the governing legal principle gives legislatures broad discretion to fashion a sentence that fits within the scope of the proportionality principle—the "precise contours" of which "are unclear." And it was not objectively unreasonable for the California Court of Appeal to

conclude that these "contours" permitted an affirmance of Andrade's sentence.

The gross disproportionality principle reserves a constitutional violation for only the extraordinary case. In applying this principle for § 2254(d)(1) purposes, it was not an unreasonable application of our clearly established law for the California Court of Appeal to affirm Andrade's sentence of two consecutive terms of 25 years to life in prison.

The judgment of the United States Court of Appeals for the Ninth Circuit, accordingly, is REVERSED.

It is so ordered.

DISSENT

SOUTER, J., joined by STEVENS, GINSBURG, and BREYER, JJ.

Andrade's sentence cannot survive Eighth Amendment review. His criminal history is less grave than Ewing's [*Ewing v. California* 2003], and yet he received a prison term twice as long for a less serious triggering offense. To be sure, this is a habeas case and a prohibition couched in terms as general as gross disproportion necessarily leaves state courts with much leeway under the statutory criterion that conditions federal relief upon finding that a state court unreasonably applied clear law, see 28 U.S.C. § 2254(d). This case nonetheless presents two independent reasons for holding that the disproportionality review by the state court was not only erroneous but unreasonable, entitling Andrade to relief. I respectfully dissent accordingly.

The first reason is the holding in *Solem*, which happens to be our most recent effort at proportionality review of recidivist sentencing. *Solem* is controlling here because it established a benchmark in applying the general principle. We specifically held that a sentence of life imprisonment without parole for uttering a $100 "no account" check was disproportionate to the crime, even though the defendant had committed six prior nonviolent felonies. In explaining our proportionality review, we contrasted the result with *Rummel's* on the ground that the life sentence there had included parole eligibility after 12 years.

The facts here are on all fours with those of *Solem* and point to the same result. Andrade, like the defendant in *Solem*, was a repeat offender who committed theft of fairly trifling value, some $150, and their criminal records are comparable, including burglary (though Andrade's were residential), with no violent crimes or crimes against the person. The respective sentences, too, are strikingly alike. Although Andrade's petty thefts occurred on two separate occasions, his sentence can only be understood as punishment for the total amount he stole. The two thefts were separated by only two weeks; they involved the same victim; they apparently constituted parts of a single, continuing effort to finance drug sales; their seriousness is measured by the dollar value of the things taken; and the government charged both thefts in a single indictment. The results under the Eighth Amendment should therefore be the same in each case. The only ways to reach a different conclusion are to reject the practical equivalence of a life sentence without parole and one with parole eligibility at 87. The former is unrealistic; an 87-year-old man released after 50 years behind bars will have no real life left, if he survives to be released at all. And the latter, disparaging *Solem* as a point of reference on Eighth Amendment analysis, is wrong as a matter of law.

The second reason that relief is required even under the § 2254(d) unreasonable application standard rests on the alternative way of looking at Andrade's 50-year sentence as two separate 25-year applications of the three-strikes law, and construing the challenge here as going to the second, consecutive 25-year minimum term triggered by a petty theft. To understand why it is revealing to look at the sentence this way, it helps to recall the basic difficulty inherent in proportionality review. We require the comparison of offense and penalty to disclose a truly gross disproportionality before the constitutional limit is passed, in large part because we believe that legislatures are institutionally equipped with better judgment than courts in deciding what penalty is merited by particular behavior. In this case, however, a court is substantially aided in its reviewing function by two determinations made by the State itself.

The first is the State's adoption of a particular penological theory as its principal reason for shutting a three-strikes defendant away for at least 25 years. Although the State alludes in passing to retribution or deterrence, its only serious justification for the 25-year minimum treats the sentence as a way to incapacitate a given defendant from further crime; the underlying theory is the need to protect the public from a danger demonstrated by the prior record of violent and serious crime. The State, in other words, has not chosen 25 to life because of the inherent moral or social reprehensibility of the triggering offense in isolation; the triggering offense is treated so seriously, rather, because of its confirmation of the defendant's danger to society and the need to counter his threat with incapacitation. As to the length of incapacitation, the State has made a second helpful determination, that the public risk or danger posed by someone with the specified predicate record is generally addressed by incapacitation for 25 years before parole eligibility. The three-strikes law, in sum, responds to a condition of the defendant shown by his prior felony record, his danger to society, and it reflects a judgment that 25 years of incapacitation prior to parole eligibility is appropriate when a defendant exhibiting such a condition commits another felony.

That said, I do not question the legitimacy of repeatedly sentencing a defendant in light of his criminal record: the Federal Sentencing Guidelines provide a prime example of how a sentencing scheme may take into account a defendant's criminal history without resentencing a defendant for past convictions. The point is merely that the triggering offense must reasonably support the weight of even the harshest possible sentences.

Whether or not one accepts the State's choice of penological policy as constitutionally sound, that policy cannot reasonably justify the imposition of a consecutive 25-year minimum for a second minor felony committed soon after the first triggering offense. Andrade did not somehow become twice as dangerous to society when he stole the second handful of videotapes; his dangerousness may justify treating one minor felony as serious and warranting long incapacitation, but a second such felony does not disclose greater danger warranting substantially longer incapacitation. Since the defendant's condition has not changed between the two closely related thefts, the incapacitation penalty is not open to the simple arithmetic of multiplying the punishment by two, without resulting in gross disproportion even under the State's chosen benchmark.

Far from attempting a novel penal theory to justify doubling the sentence, the California Court of Appeal offered no comment at all as to the particular penal theory supporting such a punishment. Perhaps even more tellingly, no one could seriously argue that the second theft of videotapes provided any basis to think that Andrade would be so dangerous after 25 years, the date on which the consecutive sentence would begin to run, as to require at least 25 years more. I know of no jurisdiction that would add 25 years of imprisonment simply to reflect the fact that the two temporally related thefts took place on two separate occasions, and I am not surprised that California has found no such case, not even under its three-strikes law.

In sum, the argument that repeating a trivial crime justifies doubling a 25-year minimum incapacitation sentence based on a threat to the public does not raise a seriously debatable point on which judgments might reasonably differ. The argument is irrational, and the state court's acceptance of it in response to a facially gross disproportion between triggering offense and penalty was unreasonable within the meaning of § 2254(d).

This is the rare sentence of demonstrable gross disproportionality, as the California Legislature may well have recognized when it specifically provided that a prosecutor may move to dismiss or strike a prior felony conviction "in the furtherance of justice." Cal.Penal Code Ann. § 667(f)(2) (West 1999). In this case, the statutory safeguard failed, and the state court was left to ensure that the Eighth Amendment prohibition on grossly disproportionate sentences was met. If Andrade's sentence is not grossly disproportionate, the principle has no meaning. The California court's holding was an unreasonable application of clearly established precedent.

(continued)

Questions

1. How does the majority *know* that the three-strikes law isn't cruel and unusual?

2. How does the dissent know that it is cruel and unusual?

3. Are their opinions purely subjective, or are they based on some standards? If so, what are the standards?

4. Should the California legislature or the U.S. Supreme Court decide whether punishments are cruel and unusual? Explain your answer.

5. Do you believe 25 years to life is "grossly disproportionate" to Leandro Andrade's crime? How do *you* know whether it is or isn't?

YOU DECIDE

Was His Sentence to Life without Parole "Cruel and Unusual Punishment" Because He Was a Juvenile?

LO 4 Petitioner is Terrance Jamar Graham. He was born on January 6, 1987. Graham's parents were addicted to crack cocaine, and their drug use persisted in his early years. Graham was diagnosed with attention deficit hyperactivity disorder in elementary school. He began drinking alcohol and using tobacco at age 9 and smoked marijuana at age 13.

In July 2003, when Graham was age 16, he and three other school-age youths attempted to rob a barbeque restaurant in Jacksonville, Florida. One youth, who worked at the restaurant, left the back door unlocked just before closing time. Graham and another youth, wearing masks, entered through the unlocked door. Graham's masked accomplice twice struck the restaurant manager in the back of the head with a metal bar. When the manager started yelling at the assailant and Graham, the two youths ran out and escaped in a car driven by the third accomplice. The restaurant manager required stitches for his head injury. No money was taken.

Graham was arrested for the robbery attempt. Under Florida law, it is within a prosecutor's discretion whether to charge 16– and 17–year–olds as adults or juveniles for most felony crimes. Graham's prosecutor elected to charge Graham as an adult. The charges against Graham were armed burglary with assault or battery, a first-degree felony carrying a maximum penalty of life imprisonment without the possibility of parole; and attempted armed robbery, a second-degree felony carrying a maximum penalty of 15 years' imprisonment.

On December 18, 2003, Graham pleaded guilty to both charges under a plea agreement. Graham wrote a letter to the trial court. After reciting "this is my first and last

time getting in trouble," he continued "I've decided to turn my life around." Graham said "I made a promise to God and myself that if I get a second chance, I'm going to do whatever it takes to get to the [National Football League]."

The trial court accepted the plea agreement. The court withheld adjudication of guilt as to both charges and sentenced Graham to concurrent 3–year terms of probation. Graham was required to spend the first 12 months of his probation in the county jail, but he received credit for the time he had served awaiting trial, and was released on June 25, 2004.

Less than 6 months later, on the night of December 2, 2004, Graham again was arrested. The State's case was as follows: Earlier that evening, Graham participated in a home invasion robbery. His two accomplices were Meigo Bailey and Kirkland Lawrence, both 20–year–old men. According to the State, at 7 p.m. that night, Graham, Bailey, and Lawrence knocked on the door of the home where Carlos Rodriguez lived. Graham, followed by Bailey and Lawrence, forcibly entered the home and held a pistol to Rodriguez's chest. For the next 30 minutes, the three held Rodriguez and another man, a friend of Rodriguez, at gunpoint while they ransacked the home searching for money. Before leaving, Graham and his accomplices barricaded Rodriguez and his friend inside a closet.

The State further alleged that Graham, Bailey, and Lawrence, later the same evening, attempted a second robbery, during which Bailey was shot. Graham, who had borrowed his father's car, drove Bailey and Lawrence to the hospital and left them there. As Graham drove away, a police sergeant signaled him to stop. Graham continued at a high speed but crashed into a telephone pole. He tried to flee on foot but was apprehended. Three handguns were found in his car.

When detectives interviewed Graham, he denied involvement in the crimes. He said he encountered Bailey and Lawrence only after Bailey had been shot. One of the detectives told Graham that the victims of the home invasion had identified him. He asked Graham, "Aside from the two robberies tonight how many more were you involved in?" Graham responded, "Two to three before tonight." The night that Graham allegedly committed the robbery, he was 34 days short of his 18th birthday.

On December 13, 2004, Graham's probation officer filed with the trial court an affidavit asserting that Graham had violated the conditions of his probation by possessing a firearm, committing crimes, and associating with persons engaged in criminal activity. The trial court held hearings on Graham's violations about a year later, in December 2005 and January 2006. The judge who presided was not the same judge who had accepted Graham's guilty plea to the earlier offenses.

Graham maintained that he had no involvement in the home invasion robbery; but, even after the court underscored that the admission could expose him to a life sentence on the earlier charges, he admitted violating probation conditions by fleeing. The State presented evidence related to the home invasion, including testimony from the victims. The trial court noted that Graham, in admitting his attempt to avoid arrest, had acknowledged violating his probation. The court further found that Graham had violated his probation by committing a home invasion robbery, by possessing a firearm, and by associating with persons engaged in criminal activity.

The trial court held a sentencing hearing. Under Florida law the minimum sentence Graham could receive absent a downward departure by the judge was 5 years' imprisonment. The maximum was life imprisonment. Graham's attorney requested the minimum nondeparture sentence of 5 years. A presentence report prepared by the Florida Department of Corrections recommended that Graham receive an even lower sentence—at most 4 years' imprisonment. The State recommended that Graham receive 30 years on the armed burglary count and 15 years on the attempted armed robbery count.

After hearing Graham's testimony, the trial court explained the sentence it was about to pronounce:

Mr. Graham, as I look back on your case, yours is really candidly a sad situation. You had, as far as I can tell, you have quite a family structure. You had a lot of people who wanted to try and help you get your

life turned around including the court system, and you had a judge who took the step to try and give you direction through his probation order to give you a chance to get back onto track. And at the time you seemed through your letters that that is exactly what you wanted to do. And I don't know why it is that you threw your life away. I don't know why.

But you did, and that is what is so sad about this today is that you have actually been given a chance to get through this, the original charge, which were very serious charges to begin with. . . . The attempted robbery with a weapon was a very serious charge.

In a very short period of time you were back before the Court on a violation of this probation, and then here you are two years later standing before me, literally the—facing a life sentence as to—up to life as to count 1 and up to 15 years as to count 2.

And I don't understand why you would be given such a great opportunity to do something with your life and why you would throw it away. The only thing that I can rationalize is that you decided that this is how you were going to lead your life and that there is nothing that we can do for you. And as the state pointed out, that this is an escalating pattern of criminal conduct on your part and that we can't help you any further. We can't do anything to deter you. This is the way you are going to lead your life, and I don't know why you are going to. You've made that decision. I have no idea. But, evidently, that is what you decided to do.

So then it becomes a focus, if I can't do anything to help you, if I can't do anything to get you back on the right path, then I have to start focusing on the community and trying to protect the community from your actions. And, unfortunately, that is where we are today is I don't see where I can do anything to help you any further. You've evidently decided this is the direction you're going to take in life, and it's unfortunate that you made that choice.

I have reviewed the statute. I don't see where any further juvenile sanctions would be appropriate. I don't see where any youthful offender sanctions would be appropriate. Given your escalating pattern of criminal conduct, it is apparent to the Court that you have decided that this is the way you are going to live your life and that the only thing I can do now is to try and protect the community from your actions. *Id.,* at 392–394.

The trial court found Graham guilty of the earlier armed burglary and attempted armed robbery charges. It sentenced

(continued)

him to the maximum sentence authorized by law on each charge: life imprisonment for the armed burglary and 15 years for the attempted armed robbery. Because Florida has abolished its parole system, see Fla. Stat. § 921.002(1)(e) (2003), a life sentence gives a defendant no possibility of release unless he is granted executive clemency.

Graham filed a motion in the trial court challenging his sentence under the Eighth Amendment. The motion was deemed denied after the trial court failed to rule on it within 60 days. The First District Court of Appeal of Florida affirmed, concluding that Graham's sentence was not grossly disproportionate to his crimes. The court took note of the seriousness of Graham's offenses and their violent nature, as well as the fact that they "were not committed by a pre-teen, but a 17-year-old who was ultimately sentenced at the age of 19." The court concluded further that Graham was incapable of rehabilitation. Although Graham "was given an unheard of probationary sentence for a life felony, . . . wrote a letter expressing his remorse and promising to refrain from the commission of further crime, and . . . had a strong family structure to support him," the court noted, he "rejected his second chance and chose to continue committing crimes at an escalating pace." The Florida Supreme Court denied review.

MAJORITY OPINION

Embodied in the cruel and unusual punishments ban is the "precept . . . that punishment for crime should be graduated and proportioned to [the] offense." The Court's cases implementing the proportionality standard fall within two general classifications. In cases of the first type, the Court has considered all the circumstances to determine whether the length of a term-of-years sentence is unconstitutionally excessive for a particular defendant's crime. The second classification comprises cases in which the Court has applied certain categorical rules against the death penalty. In a subset of such cases considering the nature of the offense, the Court has concluded that capital punishment is impermissible for non-homicide crimes against individuals.

In a second subset, cases turning on the offender's characteristics, the Court has prohibited death for defendants who committed their crimes before age 18, or whose intellectual functioning is in a low range. In cases involving categorical rules, the Court first considers "objective indicia of society's standards, as expressed in legislative enactments and state practice" to determine whether there is a national consensus against the sentencing practice at issue. Next, looking to "the standards elaborated by controlling

precedents and by the Court's own understanding and interpretation of the Eighth Amendment's text, history, meaning, and purpose," the Court determines in the exercise of its own independent judgment whether the punishment in question violates the Constitution.

[The Court held:]

(1) The Eighth Amendment prohibits imposition of a life without parole sentence on a juvenile offender who did not commit homicide, and

(2) The State must give a juvenile non-homicide offender sentenced to life without parole a meaningful opportunity to obtain release.

CONCURRING OPINION
Chief Justice Roberts

I agree with the Court that Terrance Graham's sentence of life without parole violates the Eighth Amendment's prohibition on "cruel and unusual punishments." Unlike the majority, however, I see no need to invent a new constitutional rule of dubious provenance in reaching that conclusion. Instead, my analysis is based on an application of this Court's precedents, in particular (1) our cases requiring "narrow proportionality" review of noncapital sentences and (2) our conclusion in *Roper v. Simmons*, 543 U.S. 551 (2005), that juvenile offenders are generally less culpable than adults who commit the same crimes.

These cases expressly allow courts addressing allegations that a noncapital sentence violates the Eighth Amendment to consider the particular defendant and particular crime at issue. The standards for relief under these precedents are rigorous, and should be. But here Graham's juvenile status—together with the nature of his criminal conduct and the extraordinarily severe punishment imposed—lead me to conclude that his sentence of life without parole is unconstitutional.

DISSENT

THOMAS, J., joined by SCALIA and ALITO, JJ.

The Court holds today that it is "grossly disproportionate" and hence unconstitutional for any judge or jury to impose a sentence of life without parole on an offender less than 18 years old, unless he has committed a homicide. Although the text of the Constitution is silent regarding the permissibility of this sentencing practice, and although it would not have offended the standards that prevailed at the founding, the Court insists that the standards of

American society have evolved such that the Constitution now requires its prohibition.

The news of this evolution will, I think, come as a surprise to the American people. Congress, the District of Columbia, and 37 States allow judges and juries to consider this sentencing practice in juvenile nonhomicide cases, and those judges and juries have decided to use it in the very worst cases they have encountered.

The Court does not conclude that life without parole itself is a cruel and unusual punishment. It instead rejects the judgments of those legislatures, judges, and juries regarding what the Court describes as the "moral" question of whether this sentence can ever be "proportionat[e]" when applied to the category of offenders at issue here.

I am unwilling to assume that we, as members of this Court, are any more capable of making such moral judgments than our fellow citizens. Nothing in our training as judges qualifies us for that task, and nothing in Article III gives us that authority.

LO 5 Trial Rights at Sentencing

Until the present era of sentencing guidelines and mandatory minimum sentencing, the U.S. Supreme Court adopted a **hands-off approach to sentencing procedures**, leaving sentencing decisions to trial judges' discretionary judgment. Put another way, the Constitution places few, if any, limits on judicial discretionary decision making. The hands-off approach was a hallmark of the indeterminate sentencing era (1870–1970), when the rehabilitative ideal and judicial discretion as a means to achieve it dominated "advanced" penological thinking.

In the leading case applying the hands-off approach, *Williams v. New York* (1949), Samuel Titto Williams was sentenced to death by the trial judge even though the jury recommended life imprisonment. In open court, the trial judge pointed out that he had considered the evidence that the jury heard "in light of additional information obtained through the court's Probation Department, and through other sources." The additional information "revealed many material facts concerning appellant's background which though relevant to the question of punishment could not properly have been brought to the attention of the jury in its consideration of the question of guilt" (242–44).

Williams contended that sentencing him to death based on the additional information would deny him life without due process of law. The court rejected his contention:

> Tribunals passing on the guilt of a defendant always have been hedged in by strict evidentiary procedural limitations. But both before and since the American colonies became a nation, courts in this country and in England practiced a policy under which a sentencing judge could exercise a wide discretion in the sources and types of evidence used to assist him in determining the kind and extent of punishment to be imposed within limits fixed by law. Out-of-court affidavits have been used frequently, and of course in the smaller communities sentencing judges naturally have in mind their knowledge of the personalities and backgrounds of convicted offenders. (246)

In addition to history, the Court continued, there are "sound practical reasons" for different rules governing trials and sentencing procedures. "Rules of evidence have been fashioned for criminal trials which narrowly confine the trial contest to evidence that is strictly relevant to the particular offense charged." But, at sentencing, a judge isn't "confined to the narrow issue of guilt. His task is to determine the type and extent of punishment after the issue of guilt has been determined."

> And modern concepts individualizing punishment have made it all the more necessary that a sentencing judge not be denied an opportunity to obtain pertinent information by a requirement of rigid adherence to restrictive rules of evidence properly applicable to the trial. (246–47)

That was 1949, when the rehabilitative ideal and judicial discretion were in full favor. Then came the history that saw the adoption of sentencing guidelines and mandatory minimum sentencing laws based on retribution, deterrence, and incapacitation and the accompanying curbs on judicial discretion. All this history came to a head in 2000 when the U.S. Supreme Court (5–4), to the surprise of many, dropped the hands-off approach and, in an enormously important decision, *Apprendi v. New Jersey*, dramatically brought the Constitution into sentencing proceedings.

Charles Apprendi, Jr., was convicted of possessing a firearm for an unlawful purpose, a felony in New Jersey normally punishable by 5 to 10 years in prison. New Jersey also had a hate crime statute providing for an extended punishment of 10 to 20 years if the judge found by a *preponderance of the evidence* that the defendant committed the crime with a "purpose to intimidate an individual or group of individuals because of race, color, gender, handicap, religion, sexual orientation or ethnicity" (469).

Apprendi argued that "racial purpose" was an element of the crime that required proof beyond a reasonable doubt. New Jersey argued that the choice of elements of offenses is for legislatures to make and that New Jersey's legislature chose to make "racial purpose" a "sentencing factor." The 5-member majority agreed with Apprendi and adopted the *Apprendi* **bright-line rule**:

> Other than the fact of prior conviction, any fact that increases the penalty for a crime beyond the prescribed statutory maximum must be submitted to a jury, and proved beyond a reasonable doubt. (490)

Four justices dissented—*strongly*. According to Justice O'Connor:

> The Court has long recognized that not every fact that bears on a defendant's punishment need be charged in an indictment, submitted to a jury, and proved by the government beyond a reasonable doubt. We have declined to establish any bright-line rule for making such judgments and have instead approached each case individually, sifting through the considerations most relevant to determining whether the legislature has acted properly within its broad power to define crimes and their punishments or has sought to evade the constitutional requirements associated with the characterization of a fact as an offense element. (524–25)

Apprendi was supposed to be a "ringing endorsement of the right to trial by jury" (Allen and others 2005, 1718). Sentencing guidelines and mandatory minimum sentencing laws allowed *trial judges* to decide facts related to defendants' punishment. According to the majority, guidelines and mandatory minimums threatened the democratic right to have our peers decide those critical facts. *Apprendi* was supposed to eliminate that threat.

But did it? The answer is by no means clear in the summer of 2013 as I write this edition of your book. The Court followed *Apprendi* with four other decisions, made

TABLE 14.2 Major U.S. Supreme Court sentencing rights cases

Case	Sentencing Rights Affected
Apprendi v. New Jersey, 530 U.S. 466 (2000), 5–4	Struck down a New Jersey statute empowering judges to impose maximum sentences based on facts they found to be true by a preponderance of evidence but not found by juries beyond a reasonable doubt or confessed to by defendants
Apprendi v. New Jersey, 530 U.S. 466 (2000), 5–4	Affirmed judges' power to increase maximum sentence based on prior convictions without juries finding there were prior convictions or defendants confessing to them
Harris v. U.S., 536 U.S. 545 (2002), 4-member plurality	Upheld a statute permitting judges to *raise* mandatory minimum sentences based on facts found by judges, not juries, as long as the increase doesn't exceed the statutory maximum
Blakely v. Washington, 542 U.S. 296 (2004), 5–4	Struck down a Washington State statute that empowered judges to *increase* the length of prison time beyond the "standard range" prescribed by Washington's sentencing guidelines based on facts not found by juries beyond a reasonable doubt
U.S. v. Booker, 543 U.S. 220 (2005), 5–4	1. U.S. Sentencing Guidelines that allowed judges to *increase* individual sentences beyond the standard range based on facts not found by juries beyond a reasonable doubt, violate the Constitution 2. U.S. Sentencing Guidelines are *advisory*, but they enjoy the *presumption of reasonableness*
Rita v. U.S., 551 U.S. 338 (2007), 9–1	Ruled that when the district court judge's discretionary sentencing decision falls *within* recommended ranges in the U.S. Sentencing Guidelines, the courts of appeals *may* presume that the sentence is reasonable
Gall v. U.S., 552 U.S. 38 (2007), 7–2	Under post-*Booker*, Federal Sentencing Guidelines regime: 1. District judge *must* consider the extent of any departure from guidelines and explain appropriateness of an unusually lenient or harsh sentence with sufficient justifications 2. Appellate review of sentencing decisions is limited to determining whether they're "reasonable" 3. Courts of appeals must review all sentences (whether inside, just outside, or significantly outside guidelines range) under deferential abuse-of-discretion standard (see case excerpt, p. 556)

up of shifting 5–4 majorities (Table 14.2) and several concurring opinions—overall displaying a badly splintered Court.

In *U.S. v. Booker* (2005), the Court adopted *reasonableness* as the touchstone for trial courts' use of facts to impose specific punishments—and for appellate courts in reviewing trial courts' sentences. So good-bye to the bright-line rule that juries have to decide *all* facts relied on to impose a specific sentence (except for the fact of prior convictions). But what does "reasonableness" mean? The Court grappled with the answer in *Gall v. U.S.* (2007), our next case excerpt.

In *Gall v. U.S.* (2007), the U.S. Supreme Court found that the trial judge's explanation for sentencing Brian Gall to less than the terms of the sentencing guidelines was reasonable.

CASE

Was the Trial Judge's Sentence "Reasonable"?

Gall v. U.S.

552 U.S. 38 (2007)

HISTORY

Brian Michael Gall (Defendant/petitioner) was convicted, on his guilty plea, in the United States District Court for the Southern District of Iowa, Robert W. Pratt, J., of conspiracy to distribute ecstasy, and was sentenced to 36 months of probation. The government appealed, challenging the sentence. The Eighth Circuit Court of Appeals, Smith, Circuit Judge, remanded for resentencing. The U.S. Supreme Court granted certiorari, and reversed.

—STEVENS, J., joined by ROBERTS, C.J., and SCALIA, KENNEDY, SOUTER, GINSBURG, and BREYER, JJ.

FACTS

In February or March 2000, petitioner Brian Gall, a second-year college student at the University of Iowa, was invited by Luke Rinderknecht to join an ongoing enterprise distributing a controlled substance popularly known as "ecstasy." Gall—who was then a user of ecstasy, cocaine, and marijuana—accepted the invitation. During the ensuing seven months, Gall delivered ecstasy pills, which he received from Rinderknecht, to other conspirators, who then sold them to consumers. He netted over $30,000.

A month or two after joining the conspiracy, Gall stopped using ecstasy. A few months after that, in September 2000, he advised Rinderknecht and other co-conspirators that he was withdrawing from the conspiracy. He has not sold illegal drugs of any kind since. He has, in the words of the District Court, "self-rehabilitated." He graduated from the University of Iowa in 2002, and moved first to Arizona, where he obtained a job in the construction industry, and later to Colorado, where he earned $18 per hour as a master carpenter. He has not used any illegal drugs since graduating from college.

After Gall moved to Arizona, he was approached by federal law enforcement agents who questioned him about his involvement in the ecstasy distribution conspiracy. Gall admitted his limited participation in the distribution of ecstasy, and the agents took no further action at that time. On April 28, 2004—approximately a year and a half after this initial interview, and three and a half years after Gall withdrew from the conspiracy—an indictment was returned in the Southern District of Iowa charging him and seven other defendants with participating in a conspiracy to distribute Ecstasy, cocaine, and marijuana, that began in or about May 1996 and continued through October 30, 2002. The Government has never questioned the truthfulness of any of Gall's earlier statements or contended that he played any role in, or had any knowledge of, other aspects of the conspiracy described in the indictment. When he received notice of the indictment, Gall moved back to Iowa and surrendered to the authorities. While free on his own recognizance, Gall started his own business in the construction industry, primarily engaged in subcontracting for the installation of windows and doors. In his first year, his profits were over $2,000 per month.

Gall entered into a plea agreement with the Government, stipulating that he was "responsible for, but did not necessarily distribute himself, at least 2,500 grams of ecstasy, or the equivalent of at least 87.5 kilograms of marijuana." In the agreement, the Government acknowledged that by "on or about September of 2000," Gall had communicated his intent to stop distributing ecstasy to Rinderknecht and other members of the conspiracy. The agreement further provided that recent changes in the Guidelines that enhanced the recommended punishment for distributing ecstasy were not applicable to Gall because he had withdrawn from the conspiracy prior to the effective date of those changes.

In her presentence report, the probation officer concluded that Gall had no significant criminal history; that he was not an organizer, leader, or manager; and that his offense did not involve the use of any weapons. The report stated that Gall had truthfully provided the Government with all of the evidence he had concerning the alleged offenses, but that his evidence was not useful because he provided no new information to the agents.

The report also described Gall's substantial use of drugs prior to his offense and the absence of any such use in recent years. The report recommended a sentencing range of 30 to 37 months of imprisonment.

The record of the sentencing hearing held on May 27, 2005, includes a "small flood" of letters from Gall's parents and other relatives, his fiancée, neighbors, and representatives of firms doing business with him, uniformly praising his character and work ethic. The transcript includes the testimony of several witnesses and the District Judge's colloquy with the Assistant United States Attorney (AUSA) and with Gall. The AUSA did not contest any of the evidence concerning Gall's law-abiding life during the preceding five years, but urged that "the Guidelines are appropriate and should be followed," and requested that the court impose a prison sentence within the Guidelines range. He mentioned that two of Gall's co-conspirators had been sentenced to 30 and 35 months, respectively, but upon further questioning by the District Court, he acknowledged that neither of them had voluntarily withdrawn from the conspiracy.

The District Judge sentenced Gall to probation for a term of 36 months. In addition to making a lengthy statement on the record, the judge filed a detailed sentencing memorandum explaining his decision, and provided the following statement of reasons in his written judgment:

> The Court determined that, considering all the factors under 18 U.S.C. 3553(a), (Figure 14.2, p. 558) the Defendant's explicit withdrawal from the conspiracy almost four years before the filing of the Indictment, the Defendant's post-offense conduct, especially obtaining a college degree and the start of his own successful business, the support of family and friends, lack of criminal history, and his age at the time of the offense conduct, all warrant the sentence imposed, which was sufficient, but not greater than necessary to serve the purposes of sentencing.

At the end of both the sentencing hearing and the sentencing memorandum, the District Judge reminded Gall that probation, rather than "an act of leniency," is a "substantial restriction of freedom." In the memorandum, he emphasized:

> Gall will have to comply with strict reporting conditions along with a three-year regime of alcohol and drug testing. He will not be able to change or make decisions about significant circumstances in his life, such as where to live or work, which are prized liberty interests, without first seeking authorization from his Probation Officer or, perhaps, even the Court. Of course, the Defendant always faces the harsh consequences that await if he violates the conditions of his probationary term.

Finally, the District Judge explained why he had concluded that the sentence of probation reflected the seriousness of Gall's offense and that no term of imprisonment was necessary:

> Any term of imprisonment in this case would be countereffective by depriving society of the contributions of the Defendant who, the Court has found, understands the consequences of his criminal conduct and is doing everything in his power to forge a new life. The Defendant's post-offense conduct indicates neither that he will return to criminal behavior nor that the Defendant is a danger to society. In fact, the Defendant's post-offense conduct was not motivated by a desire to please the Court or any other governmental agency, but was the pre-Indictment product of the Defendant's own desire to lead a better life.

The Court of Appeals reversed and remanded for resentencing. Relying on its earlier opinion in *United States v. Claiborne* (C.A.8 2006), it held that a sentence outside of the Guidelines range must be supported by a justification that "is proportional to the extent of the difference between the advisory range and the sentence imposed." Characterizing the difference between a sentence of probation and the bottom of Gall's advisory Guidelines range of 30 months as "extraordinary" because it amounted to "a 100% downward variance," the Court of Appeals held that such a variance must be—and here was not—supported by extraordinary circumstances.

Rather than making an attempt to quantify the value of the justifications provided by the District Judge, the Court of Appeals identified what it regarded as five separate errors in the District Judge's reasoning:

1. He gave "too much weight to Gall's withdrawal from the conspiracy";
2. given that Gall was 21 at the time of his offense, the District Judge erroneously gave "significant weight" to studies showing impetuous behavior by persons under the age of 18;
3. he did not "properly weigh" the seriousness of Gall's offense;
4. he failed to consider whether a sentence of probation would result in "unwarranted" disparities; and
5. he placed "too much emphasis on Gall's post-offense rehabilitation."

We are not persuaded that these factors are sufficient to support the conclusion that the District Judge abused his discretion.

(continued)

FIGURE 14.2 U.S. Sentencing Guidelines, 18 U.S.C. § 3553

Imposition of a Sentence

§ 3553 (a). Factors To Be Considered in Imposing a Sentence. The court shall impose a sentence sufficient, but not greater than necessary, to comply with the purposes set forth in paragraph (2) of this subsection. The court, in determining the particular sentence to be imposed, shall consider—

(1) the nature and circumstances of the offense and the history and characteristics of the defendant;

(2) the need for the sentence imposed—

   (A) to reflect the seriousness of the offense, to promote respect for the law, and to provide just punishment for the offense;

   (B) to afford adequate deterrence to criminal conduct;

   (C) to protect the public from further crimes of the defendant; and

   (D) to provide the defendant with needed educational or vocational training, medical care, or other correctional treatment in the most effective manner;

(3) the kinds of sentences available;

(4) the kinds of sentence and the sentencing range established for—

   (A) the applicable category of offense committed by the applicable category of defendant as set forth in the guidelines—

      (i) issued by the Sentencing Commission pursuant to section 994 (a)(1) of title 28, United States Code, subject to any amendments made to such guidelines by act of Congress (regardless of whether such amendments have yet to be incorporated by the Sentencing Commission into amendments issued under section 994 (p) of title 28); and

      (ii) that, except as provided in section 3742 (g), are in effect on the date the defendant is sentenced; or

   (B) in the case of a violation of probation or supervised release, the applicable guidelines or policy statements issued by the Sentencing Commission pursuant to section 994 (a)(3) of title 28, United States Code, taking into account any amendments made to such guidelines or policy statements by act of Congress (regardless of whether such amendments have yet to be incorporated by the Sentencing Commission into amendments issued under section 994 (p) of title 28);

(5) any pertinent policy statement—

   (A) issued by the Sentencing Commission pursuant to section 994 (a)(2) of title 28, United States Code, subject to any amendments made to such policy statement by act of Congress (regardless of whether such amendments have yet to be incorporated by the Sentencing Commission into amendments issued under section 994 (p) of title 28); and

   (B) that, except as provided in section 3742 (g), is in effect on the date the defendant is sentenced.

(6) the need to avoid unwarranted sentence disparities among defendants with similar records who have been found guilty of similar conduct; and

(7) the need to provide restitution to any victims of the offense.

OPINION

In *Booker* we invalidated both the statutory provision, 18 U.S.C. § 3553(b)(1) (2000 ed., Supp. IV), which made the Sentencing Guidelines mandatory, and § 3742(e) (2000 ed. and Supp. IV), which directed appellate courts to apply a *de novo* [Latin for "start over"] standard of review to departures from the Guidelines. As a result of our decision, the Guidelines are now advisory, and appellate review of sentencing decisions is limited to determining whether they are "reasonable." Our explanation of "reasonableness" review in the *Booker* opinion made it pellucidly clear that the familiar abuse-of-discretion standard of review now applies to appellate review of sentencing decisions. [*Abuse of discretion is an appellate court's standard for reviewing a trial court's decision that is asserted to be grossly unsound, unreasonable, illegal, or unsupported by the evidence.*]

It is also clear that a district judge must give serious consideration to the extent of any departure from the Guidelines and must explain his conclusion that an unusually lenient or an unusually harsh sentence is appropriate in a particular case with sufficient justifications. For even though the Guidelines are advisory rather than mandatory, they are the product of careful study based on extensive empirical evidence derived from the review of thousands of individual sentencing decisions.

In reviewing the reasonableness of a sentence outside the Guidelines range, appellate courts may therefore take the degree of variance into account and consider the extent of a deviation from the Guidelines. We reject, however, an appellate rule that requires "extraordinary" circumstances to justify a sentence outside the Guidelines range. We also reject the use of a rigid mathematical formula that uses the percentage of a departure as the standard for determining the strength of the justifications required for a specific sentence. The approaches we reject come too close to creating an impermissible presumption of unreasonableness for sentences outside the Guidelines range. The fact that we permit courts of appeals to adopt a presumption of reasonableness does not mean that courts may adopt a presumption of unreasonableness. Even the Government has acknowledged that such a presumption would not be consistent with *Booker*.

It has been uniform and constant in the federal judicial tradition for the sentencing judge to consider every convicted person as an individual, and every case as a unique study in the human failings that sometimes mitigate, sometimes magnify, the crime and the punishment to ensue. The uniqueness of the individual case, however, does not change the deferential abuse-of-discretion standard of review that applies to all sentencing decisions.

The opinion of the Court of Appeals in this case does not reflect the requisite deference and does not support the conclusion that the District Court abused its discretion. The District Judge committed no significant procedural error. He correctly calculated the applicable Guidelines range, allowed both parties to present arguments as to what they believed the appropriate sentence should be, considered all of the § 3553(a) factors, and thoroughly documented his reasoning.

The Court of Appeals gave virtually no deference to the District Court's decision that the § 3553(a) factors justified a significant variance in this case. Although the Court of Appeals correctly stated that the appropriate standard of review was abuse of discretion, it engaged in an analysis that more closely resembled *de novo* review of the facts presented and determined that, in its view, the degree of variance was not warranted.

The Court of Appeals thought that the District Court "gave too much weight to Gall's withdrawal from the conspiracy because the court failed to acknowledge the significant benefit Gall received from being subject to the 1999 Guidelines." This criticism is flawed in that it ignores the critical relevance of Gall's voluntary withdrawal, a circumstance that distinguished his conduct not only from that of all his codefendants, but from the vast majority of defendants convicted of conspiracy in federal court. The District Court quite reasonably attached great weight to the fact that Gall voluntarily withdrew from the conspiracy after deciding, on his own initiative, to change his life. This lends strong support to the District Court's conclusion that Gall is not going to return to criminal behavior and is not a danger to society. Compared to a case where the offender's rehabilitation occurred after he was charged with a crime, the District Court here had greater justification for believing Gall's turnaround was genuine, as distinct from a transparent attempt to build a mitigation case.

Finally, the Court of Appeals thought that, even if Gall's rehabilitation was dramatic and permanent, a sentence of probation for participation as a middleman in a conspiracy distributing 10,000 pills of ecstasy "lies outside the range of choice dictated by the facts of the case." If the Guidelines were still mandatory, and assuming the facts did not justify a Guidelines-based downward departure, this would provide a sufficient basis for setting aside Gall's sentence because the Guidelines state that probation alone is not an appropriate sentence for comparable offenses.

But the Guidelines are not mandatory, and thus the "range of choice dictated by the facts of the case" is significantly broadened. Moreover, the Guidelines are only one of the factors to consider when imposing sentence, and § 3553(a)(3) directs the judge to consider sentences other than imprisonment. The District Court quite reasonably attached great weight to Gall's self-motivated rehabilitation, which was undertaken not at the direction of, or under supervision by, any court, but on his own initiative. This also lends strong support to the conclusion that imprisonment was not necessary to deter Gall from engaging in future criminal conduct or to protect the public from his future criminal acts.

The Court of Appeals clearly disagreed with the District Judge's conclusion that consideration of the § 3553(a)

(*continued*)

factors justified a sentence of probation; it believed that the circumstances presented here were insufficient to sustain such a marked deviation from the Guidelines range. But it is not for the Court of Appeals to decide *de novo* whether the justification for a variance is sufficient or the sentence reasonable. On abuse-of-discretion review, the Court of Appeals should have given due deference to the District Court's reasoned and reasonable decision that the § 3553(a) factors, on the whole, justified the sentence. Accordingly, the judgment of the Court of Appeals is REVERSED.

It is so ordered.

DISSENT

ALITO, J.

Booker did not explain exactly what it meant by a system of "advisory" guidelines or by "reasonableness" review, and the opinion is open to different interpretations. It is possible to read the opinion to mean that district judges, after giving the Guidelines a polite nod, may then proceed essentially as if the Sentencing Reform Act had never been enacted. While this is a possible understanding of the opinion, a better reading is that sentencing judges must still give the Guidelines' policy decisions some significant weight and that the courts of appeals must still police compliance. [Under this reading] district courts are still required to give some deference to the policy decisions embodied in the Guidelines and that appellate review must monitor compliance.

Moreover, the Court expressed confidence that appellate review for reasonableness would help to avoid excessive sentencing disparities and would tend to iron out sentencing differences. Indeed, a major theme was that the post-*Booker* sentencing regime would still promote the Sentencing Reform Act's goal of reducing sentencing disparities. It is unrealistic to think this goal can be achieved over the long term if sentencing judges need only give lip service to the Guidelines. On the contrary, sentencing disparities will gradually increase. Appellate decisions affirming sentences that diverge from the Guidelines (such as the Court's decision today) will be influential, and the sentencing habits developed during the pre-*Booker* era will fade.

Finally, we should not forget the decision's constitutional underpinnings. *Booker* and its antecedents are based on the Sixth Amendment right to trial by jury. The Court has held that (at least under a mandatory guidelines system) a defendant has the right to have a jury, not a judge, find facts that increase the defendant's authorized sentence. It is telling that the rules set out in the Court's opinion in the present case have nothing to do with juries or factfinding and, indeed, that not one of the facts that bears on petitioner's sentence is disputed. What is at issue, instead, is the allocation of the authority to decide issues of substantive sentencing policy, an issue on which the Sixth Amendment says absolutely nothing. The yawning gap between the Sixth Amendment and the Court's opinion should be enough to show that the *Blakely-Booker* line of cases has gone astray.

Questions

1. State the majority opinion's definition of "reasonableness" as it applies to (a) the trial court's sentencing discretionary decision making and (b) the appellate court's review of the trial court's decision. Do these definitions help you understand what "reasonableness" *really* means?

2. List the facts, and summarize the trial court's arguments, that led the judge to depart from the guidelines and sentence Brian Michael Gall to probation instead of prison.

3. List the facts that led the state to argue that the trial court abused its discretion when it departed from the guidelines and sentenced Brian Michael Gall to probation instead of prison.

4. Do you believe the trial court abused its discretion? Back up your answer with facts and arguments in questions 1–3.

5. If you were the trial judge, what sentence would you have imposed? Back up your answer with facts and arguments in questions 1–3.

LO 5 Death Sentence Procedure Rights

As you learned earlier ("The Proportionality Principle and the Sentence of Death"), capital punishment is different from all other punishments, which means death *sentences* are different, too. The Court has held that capital punishment for murder isn't cruel and unusual, only if:

1. The sentencing process allows the judge or jury to consider mitigating and aggravating circumstances and offers adequate guidance in weighing them (see Table 14.3).

2. The law provides for a review procedure to ensure against discriminatory application of the death penalty (*Lockett v. Ohio* 1978).

TABLE 14.3 Aggravating and mitigating circumstances in death penalty cases

Aggravating Circumstances	Mitigating Circumstances
Prior record of violent felony	No significant prior criminal record
Felony murder	Extreme mental or emotional disturbance
Murder of more than one person	Minor participant in the murder
Murder of police officer or other public official	Youth at the time of the murder
Torture or other heinous killing	
Killing to avoid arrest	
Killing during escape from lawful custody	

According to the Court, the rationale for this process is that "it is of vital importance to the defendant, and to the community, that any decision to impose the death sentence be, and appear to be, based on reason rather than caprice or emotion" (*Gardner v. Florida* 1977).

Statistics indicate that there's a pronounced racial disparity in death sentences (Figure 14.3). Blacks and Whites who kill Whites are more likely to receive the death sentence than either Blacks who kill Blacks or Whites who kill Blacks (Baldus and Woodworth 1998, 399–400).

The U.S. Supreme Court has conceded that these numbers may well prove that race infects death sentencing decisions, in *general*, but that they're not enough to prove cruel and unusual punishment in *individual cases*. To overturn a death sentence, individual defendants have to prove that the death sentencing decision in their case was infected by racial views. Specifically, they have to prove that the prosecutor's, the jury's, or their lawyer's decisions were motivated by race (*McCleskey v. Kemp* 1987).

FIGURE 14.3 Race of Executed Defendants and Victims in Death Penalty Cases

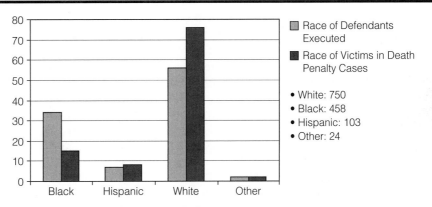

Over 75% of the murder victims in cases resulting in an execution were White, even though nationally only 50% of murder victims generally are White.

Source: Death Penalty Information Center. "Facts about the Death Penalty." Updated June 19, 2013 (http://www.deathpenaltyinfo.org/documents/FactSheet.pdf)

APPEALS AND *HABEAS CORPUS*

LO **6, 7**

A defendant's criminal conviction becomes final when it's either affirmed on appeal to the jurisdiction's highest court or the highest court denies his or her petition for review. Appeals are called **direct attacks**, because they attack the decisions made by the trial court and/or the jury's guilty verdict in the specific defendant's criminal trial.

But the story doesn't necessarily end there. In every state, and in the federal system, convicted defendants get one more chance for review. This review is called a **habeas corpus proceeding**, or a "**collateral attack**." It's called *collateral* because it indirectly attacks the judgment in a new and separate noncriminal (civil) lawsuit. In that new case, the defendant in the criminal case (now the petitioner or plaintiff in the civil case) asks (petitions the court) for review on various grounds.

LO **6** ## Appeal

It may surprise you to learn (as it surprises most of my students) that convicted offenders don't have a constitutional right to appeal their convictions. According to the U.S. Supreme Court in *Ross v. Moffitt* (1974), "It is clear that the State need not provide any appeal at all." Based on that principle, the Court upheld a state court decision that denied a poor defendant a right to a lawyer for his appeal to the state supreme court. According to the Court:

> There are significant differences between the trial and appellate stages of a criminal proceeding. The purpose of the trial stage from the State's point of view is to convert a criminal defendant from a person presumed innocent to one found guilty beyond a reasonable doubt. To accomplish this purpose, the State employs a prosecuting attorney who presents evidence to the court, challenges any witnesses offered by the defendant, argues rulings of the court, and makes direct arguments to the court and jury seeking to persuade them of the defendant's guilt. Under these circumstances reason and reflection require us to recognize that in our adversary system of criminal justice, any person haled into court, who is too poor to hire a lawyer, cannot be assured a fair trial unless counsel is provided for him.
>
> By contrast, it is ordinarily the defendant, rather than the state, who initiates the appellate process, seeking not to fend off the efforts of the state's prosecutor but rather to overturn a finding of guilty made by a judge or a jury below. The defendant needs an attorney on appeal not as a shield to protect him against being "haled into court" by the state and stripped of his presumption of innocence, but rather as a sword to upset the prior determination of guilt. This difference is significant for, while no one would agree that the state may simply dispense with the trial stage of proceedings without a criminal defendant's consent, it is clear that the state need not provide any appeal at all. (609)

Even though there's no *constitutional* right to appeal, every jurisdiction has created a *statutory right to appeal*. To understand this statutory right, refer to Figure 1.2 in Chapter 1, which depicts our three-tiered judicial system: trial courts, intermediate appeals courts, and supreme courts of appeal. The statutory right to appeal applies only to the *intermediate* appellate courts (and in capital cases, to the supreme courts).

Appeals to state *supreme* courts and to the U.S. Supreme Court, on the other hand, are discretionary. (Most of the cases in this book are *discretionary appeal* cases to the

U.S. Supreme Court. The *writ of certiorari* is a discretionary writ, allowing appeals only in cases that the U.S. Supreme Court or the state supreme courts decide are of significance beyond the interests of the particular defendants appealing them (Chapter 1, "Appellate Court Cases").

Since the late 1980s, the U.S. Supreme Court has sharply reduced the number of cases it accepts by *writs of certiorari*. By this reduction, the Court has reaffirmed the principle that final appeal isn't a right; it's a matter of discretionary judgment.

Three principal doctrines define the scope of appellate review of criminal cases in state courts:

1. Mootness
2. Raise or waive
3. Plain error

Traditionally, the **mootness doctrine** bans appeals by offenders who had finished their prison sentences or who had paid their fines. Some jurisdictions have retained this traditional definition of mootness. Several others have gone to the other extreme, holding that criminal cases are *never* moot, because defendants always have an interest in removing the "stigma of guilt." Most jurisdictions have taken a middle ground, retaining the mootness doctrine but carving out exceptions to it.

The **collateral consequences exception** says that if defendants might suffer legal consequences from a criminal conviction, then even if they have fully served their sentence the case isn't moot. These consequences include the possibility of the loss of a professional license, rejection for admission to a professional school, or loss of employment.

The **raise-or-waive doctrine** says defendants have to raise their objections at trial; if they don't, they give up their right to appeal. Why? The **doctrine of judicial economy** says we shouldn't spend time and money on appeals that defendants could've avoided by objecting during the trial. However, defendants don't *always* waive their right to appeal when they fail to object at trial. When procedural requirements don't provide adequate time for a defendant to object to a trial court error, the defendant doesn't waive the right to appeal the error. Also, circumstances can make it impossible for a defendant to comply with the raise-or-waive rule. And obviously, incompetent lawyers don't object to their own ineffectiveness (LaFave and Israel 1984, 3:252–54).

A major exception to the raise-or-waive rule is the **plain-error rule**, which applies even if defendants don't object to the errors at trial. (A "plain error" is one that is "clear" or "obvious." [*U.S. v. Olano* 1993, 1777]) And, it applies only when "plain errors affecting substantial rights" cause "manifest injustice or miscarriage of justice." Most courts apply the rule "sparingly." Plain error doesn't require or justify a review "of every alleged trial error that has not been properly preserved for appellate review." Furthermore, in most jurisdictions, the defendant bears the burden of proving that an alleged error is of such magnitude that it invokes the *plain-error rule*.

LO 7 *Habeas Corpus*

There are three kinds of collateral attack:

1. State court collateral review for defendants who were convicted in a state court
2. Federal court collateral review for defendants convicted in federal courts
3. Federal court habeas corpus review for defendants convicted in state courts (Allen and others 2005, 1574)

State review varies too much to generalize about it, and procedures for review of federal criminal defendants are similar to federal review of state criminal defendants. So we'll concentrate on habeas corpus review of *state* criminal defendants' convictions in *federal* courts.

If the court issues the writ, the writ orders the person (usually a prison warden) who's detaining the plaintiff to bring him or her before the judge and "show cause" for the detention. The object is to find out if the court in the criminal case had the authority (**jurisdiction**) to enter the judgment that put the plaintiff in prison and, if so, whether the judgment was reached properly. Depending on the evidence produced, the plaintiff is either set free, bailed, tried, or sent back to prison (Fisher 1888, 454).

Habeas corpus has a long and distinguished history. It's called the "**great writ of liberty**," because it originated as a bulwark against tyrannical English kings. The U.S. Constitution's founders placed enormous confidence in the "Great Writ." Alexander Hamilton called it a bulwark against the "practice of arbitrary imprisonments in all ages, among the favorite and most formidable instruments of tyranny" (Hamilton 1788).

According to the 19th-century historian of habeas corpus, Sydney George Fisher (1888):

> These rulers of men often want to rid themselves quickly of their personal enemies or of those whom they choose to consider enemies of their country, and one of the easiest methods is to arrest on any sort of charge or suspicion, and keep the victim in confinement simply by not allowing him to be brought to trial. And it has often been said,—and the Bastille and the Tower of London will warrant the assertion—that the power to secretly hurry a man to jail, where his sufferings will be unknown or soon forgotten, is more dangerous than all the engines of tyranny. (454)

Fisher contrasted this abuse of the English kings' power with President Lincoln's suspension of the writ of habeas corpus during the Civil War. Fisher vigorously defended Lincoln and scoffed at Lincoln's critics who called him a dictator because, Fisher argued, it was right to take extreme measures to save the Union.

Of course, we're a long way from tyrannical kings, and even from Lincoln's use of the writ. Today, most habeas corpus proceedings begin only after criminal cases have run through their full course of direct attack in state trial and appellate courts. After this long and involved process, habeas corpus proceedings start in U.S. District Court, proceed through the U.S. Court of Appeals, and can eventually reach the U.S. Supreme Court for final review.

According to the U.S. Constitution Article I: "The privilege of the Writ of Habeas Corpus shall not be suspended, unless when in Cases of Rebellion or Invasion the public Safety may require it." Two U.S. statutes elaborated on Article I by granting power to U.S. courts to hear petitions of habeas corpus and issue writs of habeas corpus.

The U.S. Judiciary Act of 1789 authorized U.S. courts to deal with the petitions of federal prisoners. The Habeas Corpus Act of 1867 (LaFave and Israel 1984, 292) extended the power of U.S. courts to deal with habeas corpus petitions of state prisoners. According to the 1867 act:

> The several courts of the United States within their respective jurisdictions, in addition to the authority already conferred by law, shall have power to grant writs of habeas corpus in all cases where any person may be restrained of his or her liberty in violation of the Constitution, or of any treaty or law of the United States. (292)

The original purpose of the act was to protect newly freed slaves and federal Reconstruction officials who were wrongly convicted of crimes in *southern* state courts in violation of their federal constitutional rights (Allen and others 2011, 1582). For almost a century, courts interpreted habeas review narrowly. According to the *narrow interpretation*, the act authorizes the courts to review only the jurisdiction of the court—that is, its authority over the person and the subject matter of the case. The review asks only whether the court has the power to hear criminal cases and whether it can decide criminal cases involving the prisoner. According to the *broad interpretation*, the act empowers the federal courts to review the whole state proceeding to determine possible violations of federal law and constitutional provisions (LaFave and others 2009, 1336).

During the years of the Warren Court (Chief Justice Earl Warren, 1953–1969), when federal rights were expanding through the incorporation doctrine (Chapter 2), the Court opted for a **broad view of habeas corpus**. The leader of the broad view, Associate Justice William Brennan, argued that the broader view fulfilled the historical purpose of habeas corpus, providing relief against the detention of persons in violation of their fundamental liberties. As to objections that such expansive review of lower court proceedings threatened the interest in *finality*, he argued that "conventional notions of finality of litigation" should "have no place where life or liberty is at stake and infringement of constitutional rights is alleged" (*Sanders v. U.S.* 1963, 8).

In addition to preserving fundamental liberties, the broader view, according to its supporters, furthers the interest in correct results. The more chances to review, the greater the accuracy of the final decision. According to one judge: "We would not send two astronauts to the moon without providing them with at least three or four back-up systems. Should we send literally thousands of men to prison with even less reserves? With knowledge of our fallibility and a realization of past errors, we can hardly insure our confidence by creating an irrevocable end to the guilt determining process" (LaFave and Israel 1984, 3:298–99).

Justice Brennan's and the Warren Court majority's view have received harsh criticism from judges and commentators. Most of the criticism focuses on the threat to finality and the costs of "endless" reviews of legal issues, which sometimes go on for years. No one has put the argument for finality better than the great advocate John W. Davis in his last argument before the U.S. Supreme Court: "Somewhere, sometime to every principle comes a moment of repose when it has been so often announced, so confidently relied upon, so long continued, that it passes the limits of judicial discretion and disturbance" (*Brown v. Board of Education* 1954).

Others doubt that the broad view really protects prisoners' fundamental rights. Associate Supreme Court Justice Robert H. Jackson, in *Brown v. Allen* (1953), argued that we have no reason to expect more accuracy in a second review than in the initial decision:

> Reversal by a higher court is not proof that justice is thereby better done. There is no doubt that if there were a super–Supreme Court, a substantial proportion of our reversals of state courts would also be reversed. We are not final because we are infallible, but we are infallible only because we are final. (540)

Illinois Supreme Court Justice William Schaeffer, supporter of the broad view, responded.

> It has been said of the habeas corpus cases that one who searches for a needle in a haystack is likely to conclude that the needle is not worth the effort. That emphasis distorts the picture. Even with the narrowest focus it is not a needle

we are looking for in these stacks of paper, but the rights of a human being. And if the perspective is broadened, even the significance of that single human being diminishes, and we begin to catch a glimpse of the full picture.

The aim which justifies the existence of habeas corpus is not fundamentally different from that which informs our criminal law in general, that it is better that a guilty man go free than that an innocent one be punished. To the extent that the small number of meritorious petitions shows that the standards of due process are being honored in criminal trials we should be gratified; but the continuing availability of the federal remedy is in large part responsible for that result. What is involved, however, is not just the enforcement of defined standards. It is also the creative process of writing specific content into the highest of our ideals. So viewed, the burdensome test of sifting the meritorious from the worthless appears less futile, and there is less room for the emotions of federalism. (25)

Justice Jackson attributed the controversy over habeas corpus to three causes:

1. The Supreme Court's use of the due process clause of the Fourteenth Amendment to "subject state courts to increasing federal control"
2. The determination of what due process means by "personal notions of justice instead of by known rules of law"
3. The "breakdown of procedural safeguards against abuse of the writ"

The Burger (Chief Justice Warren Burger, 1969–1986) and Rehnquist (Chief Justice William Rehnquist, 1986–2005) Courts adopted the **narrow view of habeas corpus**—the power to review only the jurisdiction of the court over the person and the subject matter of the case. The Rehnquist Court emphasized the balance of interests that habeas corpus proceedings require. On one side of the balance are the constitutional rights of individuals and the need to control government misconduct. On the other side are the following interests:

1. The finality of decisions
2. Reliability, or obtaining the correct result
3. Certainty in decisions, or promoting reliance on decisions
4. The stability of decisions, or promoting the permanence of decisions
5. Federalism, or respect for state criminal court decisions
6. The burden on federal judicial resources in hearing repeated challenges
7. Contempt for the system from repeated and long-drawn-out proceedings
8. The impediment that many frivolous claims are to the success of meritorious claims

To the Rehnquist Court, the main problem in habeas corpus was an "endless succession of writs." Historically, an English subject could take a petition to every judge in England. The rule of *res judicata*—that once a matter is decided it cannot be reopened—didn't apply to habeas corpus. Remnants of *res judicata* linger in the rule that denial of a first petition for habeas corpus doesn't prohibit filing a second petition.

But, according to the Rehnquist Court in *McCleskey v. Zant* (1991), just because the rule of *res judicata* doesn't apply doesn't mean that prisoners can file an unlimited number of petitions. Courts have the discretion to deny successive petitions, especially if petitioners try to raise issues they failed to raise in their first petition.

In the wake of the bombing of the Federal Building in Oklahoma City in 1995, and a wave of anticrime sentiment in 1996, Congress enacted the **Antiterrorism and Effective Death Penalty Act (AEDPA)** (U.S.C.A. §§ 2241–66). AEDPA substantially amends federal habeas corpus law as it applies to both state and federal prisoners, whether they're on death row or imprisoned for any length of time. Federal habeas corpus is the statutory procedure (28 U.S.C. 2241–and following) that enables state and federal prisoners to petition the *federal* courts to review their convictions and sentences to determine whether they're being held contrary to the laws or the Constitution of the United States. AEDPA greatly narrows these prisoners' habeas statutory right to petition.

Here are some highlights of AEDPA's habeas amendments:

1. An almost total ban on federal habeas reconsideration of legal and factual issues ruled upon by state courts

2. The creation of a general one-year statute of limitations on filing habeas petitions for prisoners serving life sentences or less. The time begins at the date of the completion of direct appeal in the prisoner's criminal case. The limit in death penalty cases is 6 months.

3. An encouragement for states to appoint counsel for indigent state death row inmates during state habeas or other appellate proceedings

4. A requirement that the appellate court approve repetitious habeas petitions before they proceed

In *McQuiggin v. Perkins* (2013), our next case excerpt, the U.S. Supreme Court (5–4), decided another of its hotly contested criminal procedure cases. The 5-member majority decided that under AEDPA, Floyd Perkins, convicted on May 5, 1997, of murdering Rodney Henderson, could file a habeas corpus petition. The majority decided he could file, even though he waited more than 10 years after the AEDPA statute one-year filing limit had expired.

In *McQuiggin v. Perkins*, the U.S. Supreme Court (5–4) opened the gate—slightly—to claims of "actual innocence" after AEDPA.

CASE

Did He Wait Too Long to File His Actual Innocence Claim?

McQuiggin v. Perkins
133 S.Ct. 1924 (2013)

HISTORY

Floyd Perkins was charged with the murder of Rodney Henderson. The jury convicted Perkins of first-degree murder. He was sentenced to life in prison without the possibility of parole on October 27, 1993. The Michigan Court of Appeals affirmed Perkins's conviction and sentence, and the Michigan Supreme Court denied Perkins leave to appeal on January 31, 1997. Perkins's conviction became final on May 5, 1997. After his state first-degree murder conviction was affirmed on direct appeal, petitioner sought federal habeas relief, asserting ineffective assistance of counsel. The U.S. District Court for the Western District of Michigan adopted the report and recommendation of Timothy P. Greeley, United

(continued)

States Magistrate Judge, denying the petition as untimely. The United States Court of Appeals for the Sixth Circuit reversed. The U.S. Supreme Court, affirmed (5–4), vacated the U.S. District Court order, and remanded the case.

—GINSBURG, J., joined by KENNEDY, BREYER, SOTOMAYOR, and KAGAN, JJ.

—SCALIA, J., joined by ROBERTS, C.J., THOMAS and ALITO, JJ.

This case concerns the "actual innocence" gateway to federal habeas review. Here, the question arises in the context of 28 U.S.C. § 2244(d)(1), the statute of limitations on federal habeas petitions prescribed in the Antiterrorism and Effective Death Penalty Act (AEDPA) of 1996. Specifically, if the petitioner does not file her federal habeas petition, at the latest, within one year of "the date on which the factual predicate of the claim or claims presented could have been discovered through the exercise of due diligence," § 2244(d)(1)(D), can the time bar be overcome by a convincing showing that she committed no crime?

We hold that actual innocence, if proved, serves as a gateway through which a petitioner may pass whether the impediment is a procedural bar or, as in this case, expiration of the statute of limitations. We caution, however, that tenable actual-innocence gateway pleas are rare: A petitioner does not meet the threshold requirement unless he persuades the district court that, in light of the new evidence, no juror, acting reasonably, would have voted to find him guilty beyond a reasonable doubt. . . . [The] standard is "demanding" and seldom met. And in making an assessment . . . the timing of the petition is a factor bearing on the reliability of the evidence purporting to show actual innocence.

FACTS

On March 4, 1993, respondent Floyd Perkins attended a party in Flint, Michigan, in the company of his friend, Rodney Henderson, and an acquaintance, Damarr Jones. The three men left the party together. Henderson was later discovered on a wooded trail, murdered by stab wounds to his head.

Perkins was charged with the murder of Henderson. At trial, Jones was the key witness for the prosecution. He testified that Perkins alone committed the murder while Jones looked on. Chauncey Vaughn, a friend of Perkins and Henderson, testified that, prior to the murder, Perkins had told him he would kill Henderson, and that Perkins later called Vaughn, confessing to his commission of the crime. A third witness, Torriano Player, also a friend of both Perkins and Henderson, testified that Perkins told him, had he known how Player felt about Henderson, he would not have killed Henderson.

Perkins, testifying in his own defense, offered a different account of the episode. He testified that he left Henderson and Jones to purchase cigarettes at a convenience store. When he exited the store, Perkins related, Jones and Henderson were gone. Perkins said that he then visited his girlfriend. About an hour later, Perkins recalled, he saw Jones standing under a streetlight with blood on his pants, shoes, and plaid coat.

The jury convicted Perkins of first-degree murder. He was sentenced to life in prison without the possibility of parole on October 27, 1993. The Michigan Court of Appeals affirmed Perkins's conviction and sentence, and the Michigan Supreme Court denied Perkins leave to appeal on January 31, 1997. Perkins's conviction became final on May 5, 1997.

OPINION

Under the Antiterrorism and Effective Death Penalty Act of 1996 (AEDPA), a state prisoner ordinarily has one year to file a federal petition for habeas corpus, starting from "the date on which the judgment became final by the conclusion of direct review or the expiration of the time for seeking such review." 28 U.S.C. § 2244(d)(1)(A). If the petition alleges newly discovered evidence, however, the filing deadline is one year from "the date on which the factual predicate of the claim or claims presented could have been discovered through the exercise of due diligence." § 2244(d)(1)(D).

Perkins filed his federal habeas corpus petition on June 13, 2008, more than 11 years after his conviction became final. To overcome AEDPA's time limitations, Perkins asserted newly discovered evidence of actual innocence. He relied on three affidavits, each pointing to Jones, not Perkins, as Henderson's murderer.

The first affidavit, dated January 30, 1997, was submitted by Perkins's sister, Ronda Hudson. Hudson stated that she had heard from a third party, Louis Ford, that Jones bragged about stabbing Henderson and had taken his clothes to the cleaners after the murder.

The second affidavit, dated March 16, 1999, was subscribed to by Demond Louis, Chauncey Vaughn's younger brother. Louis stated that, on the night of the murder, Jones confessed to him that he had just killed Henderson. Louis also described the clothes Jones wore that night, bloodstained orange shoes and orange pants, and a colorful shirt. The next day, Louis added, he accompanied Jones, first to a dumpster where Jones disposed of the bloodstained shoes, and then to the cleaners.

Finally, Perkins presented the July 16, 2002, affidavit of Linda Fleming, an employee at Pro-Clean Cleaners in 1993. She stated that, on or about March 4, 1993, a man matching Jones's description entered the shop and asked her whether bloodstains could be removed from the pants and a shirt he brought in. The pants were orange, she recalled, and heavily stained with blood, as was the multicolored shirt left for cleaning along with the pants.

The District Court found the affidavits insufficient to entitle Perkins to habeas relief. Characterizing the affidavits as newly discovered evidence was "dubious," the District Court observed, in light of what Perkins knew about the underlying facts at the time of trial. But even assuming qualification of the affidavits as evidence newly discovered, the District Court next explained, "Perkins's petition was untimely under § 2244(d)(1)(D)." "If the statute of limitations began to run as of the date of the latest of the affidavits, July 16, 2002," the District Court noted, then "absent tolling, Perkins had until July 16, 2003 in which to file his habeas petition." Perkins, however, did not file until nearly five years later, on June 13, 2008.

Under Sixth Circuit precedent, the District Court stated, "a habeas petitioner who demonstrates a credible claim of actual innocence based on new evidence may, in exceptional circumstances, be entitled to equitable tolling of habeas limitations." But Perkins had not established exceptional circumstances, the District Court determined. In any event, the District Court observed, equitable tolling requires diligence and Perkins "had failed utterly to demonstrate the necessary diligence in exercising his rights."

Alternatively, the District Court found that Perkins had failed to meet the strict standard by which pleas of actual innocence are measured: He had not shown that, taking account of all the evidence, "it is more likely than not that no reasonable juror would have convicted him," or even that the evidence was new.

Perkins appealed the District Court's judgment. Although recognizing that AEDPA's statute of limitations had expired and that Perkins had not diligently pursued his rights, the Sixth Circuit granted a certificate of appealability limited to a single question: Is reasonable diligence a precondition to relying on actual innocence as a gateway to adjudication of a federal habeas petition on the merits?

On consideration of the certified question, the Court of Appeals reversed the District Court's judgment. The Sixth Circuit held that Perkins's gateway actual-innocence allegations allowed him to present his claim as if it were filed on time. On remand, the Court of Appeals instructed, "the District Court should fully consider whether Perkins asserted a credible claim of actual innocence." We granted certiorari to resolve a Circuit conflict on whether AEDPA's statute of limitations can be overcome by a showing of actual innocence.

In *Holland v. Florida*, 130 S.Ct. 2549 (2010), this Court addressed the circumstances in which a federal habeas petitioner could invoke the doctrine of "**equitable tolling**." [The equitable tolling doctrine says that the statute of limitations won't bar a claim of actual innocence if the plaintiff, despite diligent efforts, didn't discover the evidence of actual innocence until after the statute of limitations expired.] *Holland* held that "a habeas petitioner is entitled to equitable tolling only if he shows (1) that he has been pursuing his rights diligently, and (2) that some extraordinary circumstance stood in his way and prevented timely filing." As the courts below comprehended, Perkins does not qualify for equitable tolling. In possession of all three affidavits by July 2002, he waited nearly six years to seek federal postconviction relief. "Such a delay falls far short of demonstrating the . . . diligence" required to entitle a petitioner to equitable tolling.

Perkins, however, asserts not an *excuse* for filing after the statute of limitations has run. Instead, he maintains that a plea of actual innocence can overcome AEDPA's one-year statute of limitations. He thus seeks an *equitable exception* to § 2244(d)(1), not an extension of the time statutorily prescribed. [emphasis added]

Decisions of this Court support Perkins's view of the significance of a convincing actual-innocence claim. We have not resolved whether a prisoner may be entitled to habeas relief based on a freestanding claim of actual innocence. We have recognized, however, that a prisoner may have his federal constitutional claim considered on the merits if he makes a proper showing of actual innocence. In other words, a credible showing of actual innocence may allow a prisoner to pursue his constitutional claims on the merits notwithstanding the existence of a procedural bar to relief. "This rule, or fundamental miscarriage of justice exception, is grounded in the 'equitable discretion' of habeas courts to see that federal constitutional errors do not result in the incarceration of innocent persons."

The miscarriage of justice exception, our decisions bear out, survived AEDPA's passage. These decisions seek to balance the societal interests in finality, comity, and conservation of scarce judicial resources with the individual interest in justice that arises in the extraordinary case. Sensitivity to the injustice of incarcerating an innocent individual should not abate when the impediment is AEDPA's statute of limitations.

Having rejected the State's argument that § 2244(d)(1)(D) precludes a court from entertaining an untimely first federal habeas petition raising a convincing claim of actual innocence, we turn to the State's further objection to the Sixth Circuit's opinion. Even if a habeas petitioner asserting a credible claim of actual innocence may overcome AEDPA's statute of limitations, the State argues, the Court of Appeals erred in finding that no threshold diligence requirement at all applies to Perkins's petition.

While we reject the State's argument that habeas petitioners who assert convincing actual-innocence claims must prove diligence to cross a federal court's threshold, we hold that the Sixth Circuit erred to the extent that it *eliminated* timing as a factor relevant in evaluating the reliability of a petitioner's proof of innocence. [emphasis added] To invoke the miscarriage of justice exception to AEDPA's statute of limitations, we repeat, a petitioner

(continued)

"must show that it is more likely than not that no reasonable juror would have convicted him in the light of the new evidence."

Unexplained delay in presenting new evidence bears on the determination whether the petitioner has made the requisite showing. Perkins so acknowledges. Considering a petitioner's diligence, not discretely, but as part of the assessment whether actual innocence has been convincingly shown, attends to the State's concern that it will be prejudiced by a prisoner's untoward delay in proffering new evidence. The State fears that a prisoner might "lie in wait and use stale evidence to collaterally attack his conviction . . . when an elderly witness has died and cannot appear at a hearing to rebut new evidence." The timing of such a petition, however, should seriously undermine the credibility of the actual-innocence claim. Moreover, the deceased witness's prior testimony, which would have been subject to cross-examination, could be introduced in the event of a new trial. And frivolous petitions should occasion instant dismissal. Focusing on the merits of a petitioner's actual-innocence claim and taking account of delay in that context, rather than treating timeliness as a threshold inquiry, is tuned to the rationale underlying the miscarriage of justice exception—*i.e.*, ensuring "that federal constitutional errors do not result in the incarceration of innocent persons."

We now return to the case at hand. The District Court proceeded properly in first determining that Perkins's claim was filed well beyond AEDPA's limitations period and that equitable tolling was unavailable to Perkins because he could demonstrate neither exceptional circumstances nor diligence. The District Court then found that Perkins's alleged newly discovered evidence, *i.e.*, the information contained in the three affidavits, was "substantially available to [Perkins] at trial." Moreover, the proffered evidence, even if "new," was hardly adequate to show that, had it been presented at trial, no reasonable juror would have convicted Perkins.

The Sixth Circuit granted a certificate of appealability limited to the question whether reasonable diligence is a precondition to reliance on actual innocence as a gateway to adjudication of a federal habeas petition on the merits. We have explained that untimeliness, although not an unyielding ground for dismissal of a petition, does bear on the credibility of evidence proffered to show actual innocence. On remand, the District Court's appraisal of Perkins's petition as insufficient to meet *Schlup's* actual-innocence standard should be dispositive, absent cause, which we do not currently see, for the Sixth Circuit to upset that evaluation.

We stress once again that the *Schlup* standard is *demanding*. [emphasis added] The gateway should open only when a petition presents "evidence of innocence so strong that a court cannot have confidence in the outcome of the trial unless the court is also satisfied that the trial was free of nonharmless constitutional error."

For the reasons stated, the judgment of the Sixth Circuit is vacated, and the case is remanded for further proceedings consistent with this opinion.

It is so ordered.

DISSENT

SCALIA, J., joined by Roberts, C.J., THOMAS, and ALITO, J.J.

The Antiterrorism and Effective Death Penalty Act of 1996 (AEDPA) provides that a "one–year period of limitation shall apply" to a state prisoner's application for a writ of habeas corpus in federal court. 28 U.S.C. § 2244(d)(1). The gaping hole in today's opinion for the Court is its failure to answer the crucial question upon which all else depends: What is the source of the Court's power to fashion what it concedes is an "exception" to this clear statutory command?

That question is unanswered because there is no answer. This Court has no such power, and not one of the cases cited by the opinion says otherwise. *The Constitution vests legislative power only in Congress, which never enacted the exception the Court creates today.* That inconvenient truth resolves this case. One would have thought it too obvious to mention that this Court is duty bound to enforce AEDPA, not amend it. [emphasis added]

The key textual point is that two provisions of § 2244, working in tandem, provide a comprehensive path to relief for an innocent prisoner who has newly discovered evidence that supports his constitutional claim. Section 2244(d)(1)(D) gives him a fresh year in which to file, starting on "the date on which the factual predicate of the claim or claims presented could have been discovered through the exercise of due diligence," while § 2244(b)(2)(B) lifts the bar on second or successive petitions. Congress clearly anticipated the scenario of a habeas petitioner with a credible innocence claim and addressed it by crafting an exception (and an exception, by the way, more restrictive than the one that pleases the Court today).

It would be marvelously inspiring to be able to boast that we have a criminal-justice system in which a claim of "actual innocence" will always be heard, no matter how late it is brought forward, and no matter how much the failure to bring it forward at the proper time is the defendant's own fault. I suspect it is this vision of perfect justice through abundant procedure that impels the Court today. Of course, we do not have such a system, and no society unwilling to devote unlimited resources to repetitive criminal litigation ever could. Until today, a district court could dismiss an untimely petition without delving into the underlying facts. From now on, each time an untimely petitioner claims innocence—and how many prisoners asking to be let out of jail do not?—the district court will be obligated to expend limited judicial resources wading into the murky merits of the petitioner's innocence claim.

I respectfully dissent.

Questions

1. Trace the procedural history of the case from trial to SCOTUS.

2. State the interests that SCOTUS balanced to arrive at its decision to allow claims of *actual innocence*. In your opinion, which is more important—the interest in finality or in innocence? Explain your answer.

3. Explain why the majority of five SCOTUS justices opened the gate to Floyd Perkins's claim of actual innocence eight years after the AEDPA statute of limitations expired.

4. State precisely the rule the majority adopted to apply to actual innocence claims. In your opinion how "wide" or "narrow" does it open the gate to allow claims of actual innocence?

5. Summarize Justice Scalia's strong dissent to the majority opinion.

6. Does Justice Scalia have a point when he writes: "It would be marvelously inspiring to be able to boast that we have a criminal-justice system in which a claim of 'actual innocence' will always be heard, no matter how late it is brought forward, and no matter how much the failure to bring it forward at the proper time is the defendant's own fault. I suspect it is this vision of perfect justice through abundant procedure that impels the Court today. Of course, we do not have such a system, and no society unwilling to devote unlimited resources to repetitive criminal litigation ever could." Explain your answer.

CHAPTER SUMMARY

LO 1 After conviction, defendants become "offenders" and lose constitutional protections they received as defendants. Few rights are recognized at sentencing and appeal. People assume that by the time defendants are convicted, they've had one fair shot at justice. This makes them less supportive of devoting public resources to determine if a convict was unlawfully detained.

LO 2 Supporters of fixed sentencing argue that the punishment should fit the crime, while advocates of indeterminate sentencing think the punishment should be tailored to individual circumstances. Historically, both fixed and indeterminate sentencing played important roles, but indeterminate sentencing largely has given way to fixed sentences in the last few decades as rehabilitation lost favor to retribution.

LO 2 Throughout history, legislatures, courts, and administrative agencies have exercised sentencing authority. In judicial sentencing, judges prescribe sentences. In administrative sentencing, the legislature and judges prescribe a range of prison times for a particular crime, and administrative agencies such as parole boards determine the exact release date. Limiting discretion in sentencing responds to demands for uniformity and certainty of punishment. It also responds to demands for retribution, deterrence, and incapacitation. Scholars and observers agree that the social context of the courtroom and the political-ideological preferences of the judge play significant roles in sentencing.

LO 3 Sentencing guidelines establish a relatively narrow range of penalties and give judges room to depart from the specified ranges where justified by the seriousness of the crime and the offender's criminal history. Mandatory minimum sentencing laws seek to ensure judges depart from guidelines only to issue harsher penalties.

LO 4 The proportionality principle deems sentences cruel and unusual if they're "grossly disproportionate" to the "gravity of the offense." A minority of judges believe the

Eighth Amendment contains no proportionality principle, or, if it does, that it's up to the legislature to decide what sentences are disproportionate. The U.S. Supreme Court has held that the death penalty is proportionate punishment only when a mentally fit adult kills and is convicted of murder.

LO 2, 5 The Constitution places few limits on judicial sentencing, and until the present era of mandatory minimum sentencing, the U.S. Supreme Court adopted a "hands-off" approach. Sentencing procedures (not just sentences themselves) vary widely based on what the Supreme Court deems "sound practical reasons" for variation.

LO 5 In the *Apprendi* bright-line rule, any departure from sentencing guidelines that increases the penalty for a crime must be submitted to a jury.

LO 5 The Supreme Court has held that the sentencing procedure in capital punishment cases must allow adequate room for the jury to consider mitigating circumstances and must include a formal review procedure.

LO 6 Convicted criminals don't base their appeals on any constitutional right but on a statutory right to appeal noncapital convictions in intermediate appellate courts and capital convictions to any court. Appellate review of criminal cases is affected by principles of mootness (the punishment is complete), raise or waive (the defendant didn't object to the error at trial), and plain error (substantial rights were affected and injustice resulted). A conviction becomes final when it's affirmed on appeal to the highest court of the land or when the highest court declines to review it.

LO 7 Habeas corpus is a "collateral attack" where convicted criminals seek to prove they've been unlawfully detained in a civil lawsuit against the government. State courts provide collateral review for defendants convicted in state court. Federal courts review cases brought by defendants convicted in both federal courts and state courts. The broad view of habeas corpus holds that the more judicial review a conviction receives, the more accurate it will be. Opponents argue that excessive review is costly, jeopardizes a sense of finality, and harms offenders if subsequent trial results are worse than the first.

REVIEW QUESTIONS

1. Why is the change of status from defendant to offender more than "just a change of words"?
2. Describe the reasons for the assumption that one shot of justice is enough.
3. In the debate over sentencing, identify the two sides that have characterized its history for more than a thousand years.
4. Trace the history of sentencing from AD 700 to the present.
5. List three ideas that came to dominate thinking about sentencing in the 1970s.
6. Identify and describe the three divisions of sentencing authority.
7. Identify three aims of both sentencing guidelines and mandatory minimum sentences.
8. Compare and contrast sentencing guidelines with mandatory minimum sentences.
9. What two elements are balanced in sentencing guidelines?

10. List the reasons for the revival of mandatory minimum sentences in the 1950s.

11. List the reasons for the abandonment of mandatory minimum sentences in the 1970s.

12. Identify the two main targets of current mandatory minimum sentences.

13. Identify the three aims of criminal punishment that mandatory minimum sentences are supposed to satisfy.

14. List and summarize the five main findings of empirical research on the effectiveness of mandatory minimum sentences.

15. Explain how the proportionality principle affects challenges to the constitutional ban on cruel and unusual punishments.

16. Identify and summarize the procedure rights convicted offenders enjoy during sentencing procedures.

17. Summarize the significance of *Williams v. New York* (1949); *Apprendi v. New Jersey* (2000); *Harris v. U.S.* (2002); *Blakely v. Washington* (2004); *U.S. v. Booker* (2005); *Rita v. U.S.* (2007); and *Gall v. U.S.* (2007).

18. When is the sentence of death not cruel and unusual punishment?

19. Identify the nature and circumstances of the right to appeal a conviction.

20. What's the difference between an *appeal* and a *collateral attack*?

21. Describe appellate review of criminal convictions by direct appeal and collateral attack.

22. Summarize the difference between the broad and narrow views of habeas corpus review.

23. List the three causes of the controversy over habeas corpus identified by U.S. Supreme Court Justice Robert Jackson.

24. Identify eight interests furthered by limits to habeas corpus review.

25. According to the Rehnquist Court, what's the main problem in habeas corpus review?

26. Describe the significance of the decision in *McQuiggin v. Perkins* as it relates to the Antiterrorism and Effective Death Penalty Act (AEDPA).

KEY TERMS

presumption of guilt, p. 534
right of habeas corpus, p. 534
determinate/fixed sentencing, p. 534
indeterminate sentencing, p. 534
corporal punishment, p. 535
legislative sentencing model, p. 536
judicial sentencing model, p. 537
administrative sentencing model, p. 537
sentencing guidelines, p. 538
departure, p. 538

mandatory minimum sentences, p. 542
proportionality principle, p. 545
hands-off approach to sentencing procedures, p. 553
Apprendi bright-line rule, p. 554
direct attacks, p. 562
habeas corpus proceeding/collateral attack, p. 562
mootness doctrine, p. 563
collateral consequences exception, p. 563
raise-or-waive doctrine, p. 563

doctrine of judicial economy, p. 563
plain-error rule, p. 563
jurisdiction, p. 564
great writ of liberty, p. 564
broad view of habeas corpus, p. 565
narrow view of habeas corpus, p. 566
res judicata, p. 566
Antiterrorism and Effective Death Penalty Act (AEDPA), p. 567
equitable tolling, p. 569

15

Criminal Procedure in Times of Crisis

LEARNING OBJECTIVES

1 Understand the differences between lawful and unlawful enemy combatants and the rights afforded to each. Appreciate the executive, legislative, and judicial actions that have affected the detainment of unlawful combatants and their access to federal courts.

2 Understand the role of the FBI in counterterrorism and counterintelligence efforts. Appreciate the emphasis on the prevention of terrorism since the 9/11 attacks.

3 Understand that FISA was enacted to protect the security of all U.S. persons from foreign terrorism. Know that the secret FISA court (FISC) oversees counterterrorism and counterintelligence investigations to balance this national security interest against the privacy rights of U.S. persons.

4 Understand the counterterrorism and counterintelligence tools that are part of the USA Patriot Act. Know that the Patriot Act didn't create these tools but made it easier for the government to apply them to counterterrorism investigations.

5 Know that the National Security Letters (NSLs) allow the FBI to obtain metadata from all customer records for intelligence-gathering purposes from telephone companies, Internet service providers, and financial institutions. Understand how the USA Patriot Act expanded the power of NSLs.

6 Know that very few cases have challenged the constitutionality of National Security Letters.

Understand the First and Fourth Amendment issues these rare cases have raised.

7 Know that the Capone approach and sting operations are preventive counterterrorism and counterintelligence efforts not covered by the scope of the USA Patriot Act. Understand that these proactive approaches pose a challenge to the FBI to decide when individuals move from lawfully expressing radical ideas to engaging in violent extremist acts.

8 Understand the controversy over *Miranda* warnings for persons detained on suspicion of terrorist acts. Know that, while the U.S. Department of Justice has reaffirmed its commitment to the *Miranda* rule, it also encouraged agents to interpret the public safety exception broadly in terror cases.

9 Know that the CIA has to follow the same rules and regulations for counterterrorism and counterintelligence operations as the FBI. Appreciate that information about U.S. persons is unavoidably collected when gathering foreign intelligence.

10 Know the factors involved when deciding to use federal courts or military commissions to prosecute noncitizens for terrorist acts.

11 Understand how courts balance government needs against individual Fourth Amendment rights when individuals are detained to determine their immigration status.

The Constitution of the United States is a law for rulers and people, equally in war and in peace, and covers with the shield of its protection all classes of men, at all times, and under all circumstances.

—Ex Parte Milligan (1866)

Illegal aliens are not "law-abiding, responsible citizens" or "members of the political community," and aliens who enter or remain in this country illegally and without authorization are not Americans as that word is commonly understood.

—U.S. v. Portillo-Munoz (2011)

All you need to know is that there was a before 9/11 and there was an after 9/11. After 9/11, the gloves come off. We're going to go out and we're going to defeat Al-Qaeda. We're going to kill bin Laden. And we're going to win this war.

—Cofer Black, CIA counterterrorism head (Top Secret America 2011, 2)

> *As terrible as 9/11 was, it didn't repeal the Constitution.*
>
> —Judge Rosemary Pooler (Hamblett 2003, 12)

> *We had to move from proving what happened to preventing something from happening because the costs that came with a mass destruction event like 9/11—we can't allow that.*
>
> —John Ashcroft, U.S. attorney general (Top Secret America 2011)

We end our journey through the criminal process the way we began—by looking at the balance between government power and individual liberty and privacy. In this chapter, we'll examine how to recalibrate the balance in counterterrorism and counterintelligence efforts, so we don't sacrifice the values of liberty and privacy at the heart of U.S. constitutional democracy.

The opening quotes illustrate just how contested balancing individual autonomy and homeland security can be. It's not just contested; it's also enormous. We can't possibly do it justice in one chapter, but hopefully we can highlight enough to enhance your knowledge, understanding, and appreciation of this large and rapidly expanding part of life in the 21st-century United States.

COUNTERTERRORISM AND THE WAR POWERS

LO 1 Shortly after a small CIA-led team and its ally, the Afghan Northern Alliance, defeated the Taliban with lightning speed, an abrupt shift from retaliation for the 9/11 attack to preventing other attacks was immediately under way. "We had to move to *preventing* something from happening because the costs that came with a mass destruction event like 9/11—we can't allow that," former U.S. attorney general John Ashcroft remembers (Frontline 2011).

President George W. Bush started building the counterterrorism regime immediately after September 11, 2001. On September 14, the president declared a "national emergency by reason of certain terrorist attacks" (Presidential Documents 2001 [Sept. 18], 48199, Presidential Proclamation 7463). On that same day—with extraordinary speed—Congress threw its weight behind the president's war power in a joint resolution, the Authorization for Use of Military Force (AUMF). Section 2 of the AUMF provides:

> That the President is authorized to use all necessary and appropriate force against those nations, organizations, or persons he determines planned, authorized, committed, or aided the terrorist attacks that occurred on September 11, 2001, or harbored such organizations or persons, in order to prevent any future acts of international terrorism against the United States by such nations, organizations or persons. (U.S. Senate 2001)

Then, President Bush issued Military Order of November 13, 2001, "Detention, Treatment, and Trial of Certain Non-Citizens in the War against Terrorism" (Presidential Documents 2001 [Nov. 16], 57831–36). According to the order, "certain non-citizens" included "any individual who is not a U.S. citizen that there is reason to believe:

1. Is or was a member of Al-Qaeda

2. Has engaged in, aided or abetted, or conspired to commit, acts of international terrorism, or acts in preparation therefore, that have caused, threaten to cause, or have as their aim to cause, injury to or adverse effects on the U.S., its citizens, national security, foreign policy, or economy, or

3. Has knowingly harbored one or more individuals described in 1 or 2 . . . shall be detained by the secretary of defense."

Under this detention regime, the Bush administration (and the Obama administration with some minor alterations) declared that most of the detainees captured in the war in Afghanistan were **unlawful enemy combatants**. An unlawful enemy combatant is "a person who has engaged in hostilities or who has purposefully and materially supported hostilities against the United States or its co-belligerents who is not a lawful enemy combatant (including a person who is part of the Taliban, al-Qaida, or associated forces)" (Military Commissions Act 2006, 948a). A **lawful enemy combatant** means a person who is

1. a member of the regular forces of a State party engaged in hostilities against the United States;

2. a member of a militia, volunteer corps, or organized resistance movement belonging to a State party engaged in such hostilities, which are under responsible command, wear a fixed distinctive sign recognizable at a distance, carry their arms openly, and abide by the law of war; or

3. a member of a regular armed force who professes allegiance to a government engaged in such hostilities, but not recognized by the United States (Military Commissions Act 2006, 948a).

LO I The Courts and the War Powers

After the decision to detain the captives at Guantanamo Bay as unlawful enemy combatants, some detainees wasted no time challenging their detentions. Although the cases focus on detention, we'll concentrate in this section on the broader question, "How much power does the Constitution give the president to wage the counterterrorist offensive without interference from the Congress and the federal courts?" Before we get to some of these post-911 detainees' stories, let's go back to 1945, and tell Luther Eisentrager's story, up to 1950, when the Supreme Court decided *Johnson v. Eisentrager* (1950). The Court relied on *Eisentrager* to decide all of the leading detention cases since 9/11.

LO I Johnson v. Eisentrager (1950)

Luther Eisentrager and 21 other German nationals were captured and detained in China by the U.S. Army in 1945. They were tried by a U.S. military court in China.

After the court convicted them of war crimes—namely, helping the Japanese in the time between the German surrender early in May 1945 and the Japanese capitulation in August 1945—they were returned to Germany and incarcerated in Landsberg Prison. The prison was under the control of the U.S. Army. From their prison in Germany, they filed a habeas corpus petition in the U.S. District Court for the District of Columbia, alleging that they were being detained unlawfully.

In a unanimous opinion written by Justice Robert Jackson, the U.S. Supreme Court denied these Germans access to American courts. Justice Jackson listed seven facts that taken together banned the prisoners from suing for a writ of habeas corpus in U.S. courts:

1. They were enemy aliens.
2. They had never been, or resided, in the United States.
3. They were captured outside U.S. territory.
4. They were being held in military custody as prisoners of war.
5. They were tried and convicted by a military commission sitting outside the United States.
6. They were convicted of offenses against laws of war committed outside the United States.
7. They had been at all times imprisoned outside the United States.

Justice Jackson's opinion contained several key points about citizenship and detention. Some are included in Figure 15.1.

The Guantanamo detention cases presented the Court with three possible answers to how much power the president has to wage the counterterrorist offensive.

1. *Unlimited power.* As Cofer Black, the CIA officer in charge of the counterterrorism offensive put it, "After 9/11, the gloves come off. We're going to go out and we're going to defeat al Qaeda. We're going to kill bin Laden. And we're going to win this war" (Joint Committee 9/11 Hearings 2002).
2. *No greater power. Ex Parte Milligan* (1866), ruling on President Lincoln's power to suspend habeas corpus during the Civil War, still defines the president's power. *"The Constitution of the United States is a law for rulers and people, equally in war and in peace, and covers with the shield of its protection all classes of men, at all times, and under all circumstances."* (emphasis added)
3. *The amount of power depends on the circumstances.* The president's power to wage the offensive is extensive, but it's limited. "As terrible as 9/11 was, it didn't repeal the Constitution," Judge Rosemary Pooler explained (Hamblett 2003, 12).

Now, let's turn to the Court's detention decisions, beginning with *Rasul v. Bush* (2004).

LO 1 Rasul v. Bush *(2004)*

Shafiq Rasul, a British national, and several other non-U.S. detainees, arrived in Guantanamo in January 2002, where the "Bush Administration planned to hold them with no legal process and no access to court or counsel" (Report from Former Judges 2010, 6). On February 19, 2002, they filed a petition for habeas corpus in the U.S. District Court for the District of Columbia. Relying on *Johnson v. Eisentrager*, the U.S.

FIGURE 15.1 *U.S. v. Eisentrager*

Key Points

- Modern American law has come a long way since the time when outbreak of war made every enemy national an outlaw, subject to both public and private slaughter, cruelty and plunder. But even by the most magnanimous view, our law does not abolish inherent distinctions recognized throughout the civilized world between citizens and aliens, nor between aliens of friendly and of enemy allegiance, nor between resident enemy aliens who have submitted themselves to our laws and nonresident enemy aliens who at all times have remained with, and adhered to, enemy governments.

- The alien, to whom the United States has been traditionally hospitable, has been accorded a generous and ascending scale of rights as he increases his identity with our society. Mere lawful presence in the country creates an implied assurance of safe conduct and gives him certain rights; they become more extensive and secure when he makes preliminary declaration of intention to become a citizen, and they expand to those of full citizenship upon naturalization.

- But, in extending constitutional protections beyond the citizenry, the Court has been at pains to point out that it was the alien's presence within its territorial jurisdiction that gave the Judiciary power to act. Since most cases involving aliens afford this ground of jurisdiction, and the civil and property rights of immigrants or transients of foreign nationality so nearly approach equivalence to those of citizens, courts in peacetime have little occasion to inquire whether litigants before them are alien or citizen.

- It is war that exposes the relative vulnerability of the alien's status. The security and protection enjoyed while the nation of his allegiance remains in amity with the United States are greatly impaired when his nation takes up arms against us. While his lot is far more humane and endurable than the experience of our citizens in some enemy lands, it is still not a happy one. But disabilities this country lays upon the alien who becomes also an enemy are imposed temporarily as an incident of war and not as an incident of alienage.

government moved to dismiss the petitions, arguing that the "detainees were beyond the jurisdiction of the federal courts." The district court agreed, and the U.S. Court of Appeals for the D.C. Circuit affirmed. The U.S. Supreme Court granted certiorari in November 2003, to decide the "narrow but important question of whether the U.S. courts lack jurisdiction to consider challenges to the legality of the detention of foreign nationals captured abroad in connection with hostilities and incarcerated in Guantanamo Bay Naval Base" (Report from Former Judges 2010, 6).

The Supreme Court reversed, holding that the U.S. Habeas Corpus Statute (28 U.S.C. §2241–and following) empowered the federal courts to hear and decide the petition. Justice Stevens, writing for the majority of six justices, pointed out that, unlike the *Eisentrager* petitioners, the petitioners in this case

1. Weren't nationals of countries at war with the United States

2. Had "never been afforded access to any tribunal, much less charged with and convicted of wrongdoing"

3. Had "been imprisoned in territory over which the U.S. exercises exclusive jurisdiction and control" (476).

LO 1   ## Hamdan v. Rumsfeld *(2006)*

Congress responded quickly to *Rasul* by passing the Detainee Treatment Act of 2005 (DTA). DTA amended the Habeas Corpus Act to strip federal courts of jurisdiction over habeas petitions filed by Guantanamo Bay detainees (DTA §(e) 1005). But the Supreme Court in *Hamdan v. Rumsfeld* (2006) held that the DTA didn't apply to petitions filed prior to its enactment. Then, Congress, in response to *Hamdan*, enacted the Military Commissions Act of 2006, which stripped all federal courts of jurisdiction over all habeas petitions filed by Guantanamo Bay detainees regardless of when they were filed. It also limited detainees to the review process set up in the DTA (see "Trials by Military Commissions," pp. 619–623).

LO 1   ## Boumediene v. Bush *(2008)*

The Supreme Court responded to the Military Commissions Act in *Boumediene v. Bush* by answering two "historic questions":

1. Are Guantanamo Bay detainees guaranteed the *constitutional* (not just the statutory) right to habeas corpus unless Congress suspends the writ under the **suspension clause**? (Article I, Section 9 of the U.S. Constitution provides "The privilege of the writ of habeas corpus shall not be suspended, unless when in cases of rebellion or invasion the public safety may require it.")

2. If so, is the DTA review process an adequate substitute for habeas corpus review in the regular courts?

In *Boumediene*, Lakhdar Boumediene and five other natives of Algeria emigrated to Bosnia and Herzegovina during the 1990s. Five acquired Bosnian citizenship, while the sixth acquired permanent residency. At the time of the brutal attacks of September 11, 2001, each was living peacefully with his family in Bosnia. None traveled to Afghanistan during the U.S. engagement in hostilities there. None had waged war or committed belligerent acts against the United States or its allies. All six were arrested by Bosnian police in October 2001, on suspicion of plotting to attack the U.S. embassy in Sarajevo. The Bosnian authorities had no evidence for this charge. Rather, they acted under pressure from U.S. officials, who threatened to cease diplomatic relations with Bosnia if the six weren't arrested.

On January 17, 2002, the Supreme Court of the Federation of Bosnia and Herzegovina, acting with the concurrence of the Bosnian prosecutor, ordered all six released after a three-month international investigation (with collaboration from the U.S. embassy and Interpol) failed to support the charges. On the same day, the Human Rights Chamber for Bosnia and Herzegovina—a tribunal established under the U.S.-brokered Dayton Peace Agreement and staffed by judges from several European countries—issued an order forbidding their removal from Bosnian territory.

Late that day, as they were being released from the Central Prison in Sarajevo, Bosnian police—acting again under pressure from U.S. officials and in defiance of the Human Rights Chamber's order—again seized and delivered them to U.S. military personnel stationed in Bosnia. The U.S. military transported them to Guantanamo Bay, where they continued to be held. They had no direct contact with their families, and the government closely limited the frequency and length of counsel visits (*Boumediene and others v. Bush.* Brief for Petitioners 2007, 1–2).

In 2008, the U.S. Supreme Court (5–4) held that Boumediene and his fellow Algerians had a *constitutional* right to go to the U.S. federal courts to challenge their detention by a petition for a writ of habeas corpus. The Court then struck down the provision in the Military Commissions Act of 2006 that stripped the federal courts of their power to hear habeas corpus petitions from detainees seeking to challenge their designation as enemy combatants. According to the majority, the Detainee Treatment Act of 2005 "falls short of being a constitutionally adequate substitute" (2272) because it didn't offer "the fundamental procedural protections of habeas corpus."

Justice Anthony Kennedy wrote, "The laws and Constitution are designed to survive, and remain in force, in extraordinary times" (2227). In his dissenting opinion, Justice Scalia wrote that the Court's "decision is devastating":

> At least 30 of those prisoners hitherto released from Guantanamo Bay have returned to the battlefield. Some have been captured or killed. But others have succeeded in carrying on their atrocities against innocent civilians. In one case, a detainee released from Guantanamo Bay masterminded the kidnapping of two Chinese dam workers, one of whom was later shot to death when used as a human shield against Pakistani commandoes. Another former detainee promptly resumed his post as a senior Taliban commander and murdered a United Nations engineer and three Afghan soldiers. Still another murdered an Afghan judge. It was reported only last month that a released detainee carried out a suicide bombing against Iraqi soldiers in Mosul, Iraq. (2294–95)

COUNTERTERRORISM, COUNTERINTELLIGENCE, AND THE FBI

LO 2 The CIA led the military attack on Afghanistan, and set the course for counterterrorism after the victory. However, the FBI quickly became the "lead agency for investigating the **federal crime of terrorism**," defined as "an offense that is calculated to influence or affect the conduct of government by intimidation or coercion, or to retaliate against government conduct" (Bjelopera 2013, 1). But the FBI isn't the *only* agency involved in counterintelligence and counterterrorism operations, nor does it act alone. The National Security Agency (NSA) plays a large role—larger than was publicly known until the recent leaks by NSA contractor Edward Snowden. (We'll discuss the NSA role later, on pp. 610–617.) So do local law enforcement agencies, especially in large cities. For example, the Boston Police Department worked actively with the FBI after the Boston Marathon bombing, and the NYPD participated in investigating the Times Square attempted bombing.

You also need to know that the FBI has always been *both* a law enforcement agency *and* an intelligence agency. The terrorist groups of today are only the latest group "driven by religious extremism, fanaticism, and the politics of the moment" that have "regularly come and gone." The only constant is the FBI, "whose powers, skills, and capabilities have evolved across generations to meet new threats in new places" (Graff 2012, 24). The list of individuals and groups the FBI has targeted is long, and the choices highly controversial. Here are some: "radical" labor activists, anarchists, student "radicals," right-wing "extremists," Puerto Rican nationalists, Croatian separatists, Muslim "extremists," the IRA, the PLO, the Weather Underground, Italian "mobsters," antigovernment loners, White supremacists, Black extremists.

What's different after 9/11? The FBI adopted a "more forward-leaning, intelligence driven posture in its terrorism investigations in order to prevent or disrupt terrorist acts, not merely to investigate them after they have occurred" (Bjelopera 2013, 2).

FBI Director Robert Mueller stressed the shift right after 9/11 in a memo to all special agents in charge of FBI field offices: "While every office will have different crime problems that will require varying levels of resources, the FBI has just one set of priorities: *Stop the next attack*" (2).

Robert McNulty, the deputy attorney general at the time, maintained that the Justice Department's new aggressive approach was "the only acceptable response from a department of government charged with enforcing our laws and protecting the American people. Awaiting an attack is not an option. That is why the Department of Justice is doing everything in its power to identify risks to our Nation's security at the earliest state possible and to respond with forward-leaning—preventive—prosecutions" (3).

Two FBI divisions were responsible for supervising the FBI's counterterrorism and counterintelligence programs. The **Counterterrorism Division's** mission is to "identify and disrupt potential terrorist plots, freeze terrorist finances, share information with law enforcement and intelligence partners world-wide, and provide strategic and operational threat analysis to the intelligence community" (U.S. Department of Justice, Office of the Inspector General 2007, 19).

According to the FBI's website, the **Counterintelligence Division's** mission is to keep our nation's most valuable secrets out of the hands of spies. "As the lead agency for exposing, preventing, and investigating intelligence activities on U.S. soil, the FBI works to keep weapons of mass destruction and other embargoed technologies from falling into wrong hands, to protect critical national secrets and assets, and to strengthen the global threat picture by proactively gathering information and intelligence" (FBI n.d., "Counterintelligence").

The shift from destroying the 9/11 attackers and their host countries to preventing them (and *anyone*, whether U.S. citizens or not) from hurting the U.S. homeland again has expanded enormously between 2001 and 2013. To increase your knowledge, understanding, and appreciation of this large and rapidly growing part of life in the United States in the 21st century, we'll begin with examining the Foreign Intelligence Surveillance Act (FISA), the national security law that Congress enacted in 1978. FISA created (a) the framework for surveillance and investigation to protect the security of all people lawfully *inside* the United States from foreign terrorism and intelligence that would do them harm; and (b) it created the FISA court (FISC) to oversee FBI counterterrorism and counterintelligence investigations in order to balance the national security interest and the privacy of U.S. citizens—their right to be spied on by their own government *only according to established procedures.*

Next, we'll focus on how the 2001 USA Patriot Act (acronym for **U**niting and **S**trengthening **A**merica by **P**roviding **A**ppropriate **T**ools **R**equired to **I**ntercept and **O**bstruct **T**errorism), "beefed up" the FBI's power to conduct counterterrorism and counterintelligence operations. FBI operations rely on a wide range of tools, including electronic surveillance, physical searches, interrogation, National Security Letters (NSLs), and proactive operations. Keep in mind that the purpose of all the tools is to "stop the next attack" and keep our national security secrets from getting into the hands of those who want to harm the U.S. homeland. We'll pay special attention to tools that the USA Patriot Act "beefed up" after 9/11. (I say "beefed up" because most existed before 9/11.)

Before we take up the tools and their use, you need to know something about the Foreign Intelligence Surveillance Act (FISA) and the FISA court (FISC).

LO 3 Foreign Intelligence Surveillance Act (FISA)

FISA authorizes *certain* government surveillance of communications for *foreign* intelligence purposes. Here are the four main elements in this very big and complicated statute:

1. *Application.* It allows the FBI to apply to FISC for an order to compel production of "tangible things . . . for an investigation to obtain information not concerning a **United States person** or to protect against international terrorism or clandestine intelligence activities. Section 1801(i) of FISA defines a U.S. person as "a citizen of the United States, an alien lawfully admitted for permanent residence, an unincorporated association a substantial number of members of which are citizens of the United States or aliens lawfully admitted for permanent residence, or a corporation which is incorporated in the United States. . . ."

2. *Objective basis.* The application has to include a statement of facts showing "that there are reasonable grounds to believe that the tangible things sought are relevant to an authorized investigation" (§1861(b)(2)(A)).

3. *Minimization guidelines.* FISA requires the government to minimize the amount of information acquired or retained, and prohibits the dissemination of nonpublic information about nonconsenting U.S. persons, consistent with the need of the United States to obtain, produce, and disseminate foreign intelligence information. The Attorney General, as required by statute, has adopted and filed with the Court specific procedures designed to effectuate the statutory minimization procedures. Among other things, the procedures ensure that the surveillance technique employed minimizes the likelihood of acquiring information, and the amount of information acquired, concerning U.S. persons. The procedures also limit the retention of incidentally acquired information concerning U.S. persons. Finally, the procedures restrict the dissemination of U.S. person-identifying information to the statutorily prescribed bases (§1801(h)).

4. *Ex parte order.* If the Government meets the requirements of 1–3, the FISC "shall enter an ex parte order as requested, or as modified, approving the release of tangible things" (§1861(c)(1)).

Congress enacted FISA in 1978 in the wake of the Watergate scandal and government surveillance of Vietnam War and civil rights organizations. Its main purpose was to ban unrestrained *domestic* spying by the executive branch of the U.S. government. It aimed to balance the need for *foreign* intelligence and the privacy of U.S. persons. FISA created a regime for doing both. According to Scott J. Glick (2010), deputy chief, Counterterrorism Section of the Justice Department National Security Division, "FISA establishes a statutory procedure that permits the government to conduct electronic surveillance targeting *foreign powers* and agents of foreign powers to obtain "foreign intelligence information" (99).

LO 3 FISA Court (FISC)

Recall that according to the Fourth Amendment, in ordinary criminal investigations, officers seeking a search warrant have to (1) describe the place to be searched, and (2) demonstrate that they have probable cause to believe that the search will turn up evidence of a crime. In a rare *published* opinion of a rare proceeding, a FISC Court of

Review upheld a Fourth Amendment challenge to a FISC surveillance order. According to the court, FISC surveillance orders aren't warrants subject to Fourth Amendment warrant requirement. But, they *are* subject to the reasonableness requirement (Chapters 4, 6). It upheld the FISC order as reasonable because the

> government had shown probable cause to believe that the target is an agent of a foreign power and otherwise met the basic requirements of FISA. The government's application for a surveillance order contains detailed information to support its contention that the target, who is a U.S. person, is aiding, abetting, or conspiring with others in international terrorism. (*In re Sealed Case* 2002, 720)

In the published report, there's only a blank space to reflect that the court censored the "detailed information to support its contention."

This is a good time to provide some details about the FISC. First, it's a secret court. It consists of 11 federal judges appointed by the chief justice of the United States; they serve for up to seven years. Chief Justice John Roberts has appointed all of the current court judges. (All but one of the previous judges were appointed by Republican presidents.) The proceedings are all secret and *ex parte* (only the government is represented and heard). The judges work alone. According to James A. Baker, head of the U.S. Department of Justice's Office of Intelligence Policy Review from 2001 to 2007,

> One judge rules on one application at a time, so they don't sit in a group or a panel of two or three or 11. It's one judge, one application, one time. They do have meetings where they come to hear issues of common concern. . . . So, they do get together as a group, but when they're ruling on an application, it's one judge, one application. (Smith 2007, 4)

In his interview with Baker, Hedrick Smith noted that "People have referred to the FISA court as a rubber stamp. There are thousands of applications, and only a few have been rejected." And then he asked, "What's the process in dealing with the FISA court?" I believe it's worth quoting at length why the former OIPR head believes that the rubber stamp idea is "ridiculous" and why "the American people need to know that" (3).

> I think folks don't really understand the process. They don't understand the give-and-take. . . . Basically, we receive requests from the intelligence agencies to conduct a particular surveillance, let's say, and so we work on the applications with them. We get it in shape; we get it to a point where it meets the requirements of the statute. At that point, it's signed by a high-ranking official in the executive branch, such as the director of the FBI, the secretary of defense, and then it's signed by the attorney general. After it's signed by the attorney general it's filed with the FISA court, and then we have interactive process with the FISA court.
>
> So, if they have questions—they don't understand something about the application, they have a concern about the application some way, they don't think the facts are sufficient on a particular point or a particular element of the statute—they'll ask us about it, and they'll say, "Well, do you have any more information on this one point?" We'll say: "We don't know, Judge. We'll go back and find out." We'll go back to the FBI field office, let's say, and ask them. They'll say, "Well, actually we do have some additional information."
>
> So we'll file a supplemental document, submit that to the court, and then the court might be satisfied, and then the matter is resolved; the application

is approved. So could the court, when it first got the application, just have received it, have the question, decided it was insufficient, denied it or issued some kind of order?

I guess they could have in that kind of a scenario, but that's not how the process works. The process is more interactive than that, because it is what we call in the law an ex parte relationship. There's only one party appearing before the court. It's the United States, and so there's a robust back-and-forth. Remember, we're filing 2,000 applications a year. (3)

Baker's estimates of the growth in attorneys working on FISC applications reflect the growth in applications during his tenure (see Figure 15.2).

"A *robust* back-and-forth?" Smith interjected

A robust back-and-forth every day. . . . And then negotiations back and forth on how an order might be put. I wouldn't characterize it as negotiation. I don't think that's correct. But I would say there's back-and-forth, where the court will say they have a concern about a particular.

"Do you wind up modifying many of the applications?" Smith asked.

Yeah, we modify many of the applications. We will change them, resubmit them. Sometimes we are not able to work something out, so on occasion the court will flat-out deny an application or the court will modify the application. In other words, whatever we've come up with has not still satisfied the court, and so the court will do a modification. (3–4)

USA Patriot Act

The USA Patriot Act is a vital set of tools in our ongoing struggle against al Qaeda and like-minded terrorists. This is especially true of the three tools up for renewal this year: "roving wiretaps," "business records", and "lone wolf."

(Sales 2011, 1)

FIGURE 15.2 Department of Justice Attorneys Working on FISA Applications

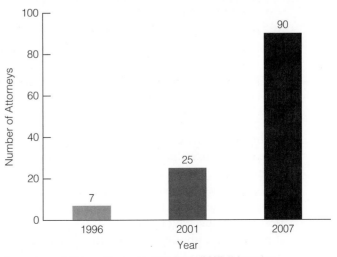

Source: James A. Baker estimates, Hedrick Smith (2007, 1) interview.

LO **4**   Let's look at these tools that the FBI and U.S. Department of Justice "beefed up" to monitor, search, and prosecute suspects in "terrorism-related and other investigations." (Bjelopera 2013, 19–22). Keep in mind that all of these powers existed *before* 9/11; the Patriot Act only made it easier for the government to apply them to counterterrorism investigations. National security law professor and one of the drafters of the Patriot Act, Richard Sales calls them "modest proposals . . . that simply let counterterrorism agents use some of the techniques that ordinary criminal investigators have been using for decades—techniques that federal courts repeatedly have upheld" (Sales 2011, 1).

LO **4**   ### Roving wiretaps

Roving wiretaps are court orders that apply to particular *people*, rather than particular *devices*. A conventional wiretap attaches to a particular device (cell phone, smartphone, tablet).

> Sophisticated targets like drug kingpins, mob bosses, spies, and terrorists are trained to thwart electronic surveillance by constantly switching communications devices or methods. They might swap out "burner" cell phones, for instance, or they might repeatedly swap out their phones' SIM cards. The result is a drawn out game of cat and mouse. Investigators obtain a court order to tap the suspect's new phone only to discover that he has already switched to an even newer one. So it's back to the judge for a fresh warrant. Not only is this cycle a waste of time and resources, it also runs the risk that agents will miss critical communications in the gap before the court can issue an updated order. (Sales 2011, 1–2)

Congress *partly* solved the problem for law enforcement in the Electronic Communications Privacy Act of 1986 (ECPA), which allowed criminal investigators to get a roving wiretap order if they have "probable cause to believe that the person's actions could have the effect of thwarting interception from a specified facility" (ECPA 1986, §2518(11)(b)(ii)). *But*, ECPA didn't apply to terrorism investigations. So, *before* the Patriot Act,

> An FBI agent assigned to the *Criminal Investigation Unit* could employ roving surveillance to gather evidence in a criminal investigation against a suspected drug dealer or money launderer; however, an FBI agent assigned to the *Counterintelligence Division* could not employ the same roving surveillance technology under FISA [Foreign Intelligence Surveillance Act] to gather intelligence relating to an al Qaeda operative present in the United States who was planning to inflict mass casualties with a hijacked airliner. (Thomson 2004, 2)

Section 206 of the Patriot Act amended the electronic surveillance provisions in the Foreign Intelligence Surveillance Act (FISA) to include roving wiretaps, granting "roving surveillance authority to federal counterintelligence officers engaged in domestic foreign intelligence and counterterrorism investigations" (2). But, investigators can obtain court orders to conduct roving wiretaps only if they "establish probable cause to believe that the person's actions could have the effect of thwarting interception from a specified facility. . . . Investigators may continue to monitor a suspect even if he switches phones, without first heading back to court to obtain further judicial approval" (Sales 2011, 2).

LO 4   *"Sneak-and-peek" search warrants*

You've already learned that searches of private places are "unreasonable searches." They're banned by the Fourth Amendment unless officers are backed up by warrants based on probable cause, and they "knock and announce" their presence before they enter and search (Chapter 6). Officers can enter and search if you're not home, but they have to leave a copy of the warrant and a list of any property they seized so you'll know they searched your place. But you also learned that there's a "no-knock" emergency exception to the knock-and-announce rule. **"Sneak-and-peek" searches** are a variation of no-knock entries. **Sneak-and-peek search warrants** allow officers to enter private places without the owner or (occupant) consenting or even knowing about it.

Sneak and peek is not exactly a new practice. During the 1980s, the FBI and DEA (Drug Enforcement Agency) asked for, and judges issued, at least 35 sneak-and-peek warrants (Wilkes 2002).

Both the Second and Ninth Circuit U.S. Courts of Appeals have upheld the admission of evidence obtained during sneak-and-peek searches. In *U.S. v. Villegas* (1990), the Second Circuit said they were reasonable searches (see Chapter 6). And, in *U.S. v. Freitas* (1988), the Ninth Circuit said the evidence was admissible under the "good good-faith" exception to the exclusionary rule (see Chapter 10).

The Patriot Act (§213) gave sneak-and-peek warrants the power of an Act act of Congress. Section 213 allows federal law enforcement officers to request sneak-and-peek warrants allowing them to enter and search places without immediately notifying the owner when "notice *may* have an adverse result (e.g., tipping off a suspect or co-conspirators" (Bjelopera 2013, 6).

One very important point: The FBI has rarely used them in terrorism cases, as the most recent numbers available at this writing as I write clearly indicate (see Table 15.1).

LO 4   *"Lone wolf" terrorists*

On August 15, 2001, the Minneapolis FBI field office started an intelligence investigation of a person who had entered the United States in February 2000. He came to Minnesota and enrolled in the Pan Am International Flight Academy in Eagan. He had no training on Pan Am's flight simulators, but said he didn't want to be a professional pilot, he wanted to do it as an "ego ego-boosting thing." "Moussaoui stood out because, with little knowledge of flying, he wanted to learn how to 'take off and land' a Boeing 747 (*The 9/11 Commission Report* 2004, 273).

The Minneapolis agent learned that Moussaoui had "jihadist beliefs"; $32,000 in a bank account but without a "plausible explanation" for this sum of money; traveled to Pakistan "but became agitated when asked if had traveled to nearby countries while he was in Pakistan"; planned to train in martial arts; and intended to buy a GPS. The Agent concluded that Moussaoui was "an Islamist extremist preparing for some future act in furtherance of radical fundamentalist goals" (273).

The Agent who handled the case and the Minneapolis Joint Terrorism Task Force suspected that Moussaoui "might be planning to highjack a plane." Minneapolis and FBI headquarters debated whether to arrest Moussaoui immediately or to surveil to gather more intelligence. But, the agents were concerned that the U.S. Attorney's Office in Minneapolis would not find probable cause of a crime to obtain a warrant to search

TABLE 15.1 Sneak-and-peek search warrants and extensions, 2010

Offense	Warrants	Extensions
Total	2,395	1,575
Drugs	1,764	1,270
Fraud	90	25
Weapons	49	37
Fugitive	47	0
Immigration	22	17
Terrorism	21	16
IEEPA*	16	20
Robbery/Carjacking	25	9
Sex offense/ Forced labor	29	4
Theft/Embezzlement	19	8
Murder	17	4
Smuggling/Contraband	15	3
Computer	9	7
Food & Drug	14	0
Kidnapping	11	2
Currency	5	8
Conspiracy	11	0
Gambling	7	3
Bribery	2	6
Counterfeit	5	2
Treason	5	2
Threats	4	2
Perjury	0	4
Other/Unspecified	129	39

*International Emergency Economic Powers Act.

Source: Report of the Director of the Administrative Office of the U.S. Courts on Applications for Delayed-Notice Search Warrants and Extensions, 2010.

Moussaoui's laptop computer. And Agents in FBI agents believed there was no probable cause. Minneapolis Agents applied for a FISA special warrant to conduct the search.

> To do so, however, the FBI needed to demonstrate probable cause that Moussaoui was an agent of a foreign power, a demonstration that was not required to obtain a *criminal* warrant but was a statutory requirement for a *FISA* warrant. (274)

The Agent didn't have enough information to connect Moussaoui to a "foreign power."

In other words, Moussaoui was a **"lone wolf" terrorist**. The Moussaoui story led Congress to amend FISA so individuals engaged in international terrorism don't have to be linked to a specific foreign power. Section 6001 (the "lone wolf" provision) provides that individuals, other than citizens or permanent residents of the United States, are presumed to be agents of a foreign power. So, there's no "need to provide an evidentiary connection between an individual and a foreign government or terrorist group" (Liu 2011, 6).

Critics complained that the "lone wolf" amendment would lead to "FISA serving for some of our most important criminal laws."

> The extraordinary tools available to investigators under the Foreign Intelligence Surveillance Act (FISA), passed over 30 years ago in response to revelations of endemic executive abuse of spying powers, were originally designed to cover only "agents of foreign powers." The PATRIOT Act's "lone wolf" provision severed that necessary link for the first time, authorizing FISA spying within the United States on any "non-U.S. person" who "engages in international terrorism or activities in preparation therefor," and allowing the statute's definition of an "agent of a foreign power" to apply to suspects who, well, aren't. Justice Department officials say they've never used that power, but they'd like to keep it in the arsenal just in case. (Sanchez 2009)

Supporters argued that the "increased self-organization among terror networks has made proving connections to identifiable groups more difficult. Thus a "lone wolf provision is necessary to combat terrorists who use a modern organizational structure or who are self-radicalized" (Liu 2011, 6).

LO **4** *Business records*

At the outset, recall what the U.S. Supreme Court held in *U.S. v. Miller* (1976) and has repeatedly reaffirmed right up to June 26, 2013, when I'm writing this:

> We have held repeatedly that the Fourth Amendment does not prohibit obtaining information revealed to a third party and conveyed by the third party to Government authorities, even if the information is revealed on the assumption that it will be used only for a limited purpose and the confidence placed in the third party will not be betrayed. (*U.S. v. Miller* 1976, 443)

In other words, don't look to the Fourth Amendment for protection from the government getting and using information we *voluntarily* hand over to other people and companies. Protection has to come from statutes like the Patriot Act. (See Chapter 3 for a discussion of "voluntary" and the *third-party doctrine*.)

One source of information is in business records turned over to grand juries investigating past crimes. During non terrorist criminal investigations, federal grand juries (see Chapter 12 for grand juries generally) commonly issue subpoenas to obtain this information. Federal drug and White collar offenders often "leave behind trails of evidence in their everyday interactions with banks, credit card companies, and other businesses" (Sales 2011, 4). Subpoenas require turning over all "books, papers, documents, data, or other objects" listed in the subpoena, whenever there is a "reasonable possibility that the material the Government seeks will produce information relevant to the general subject of the grand jury's investigation." (Federal Rules of Criminal Procedure, 17(c)(1); *U.S. v. R. Enterprises, Inc.*, 1991, 301).

The Patriot Act (§215) **business records provision** creates a "national security equivalent of grand jury subpoenas" (Sales 2011, 4). It allows national security investigators to obtain similar materials. The FISA court (FISC) may order third parties to produce "any tangible things (including books, records, papers, documents, and other items)," *if* the Agent establishes "reasonable grounds to believe that the tangible items sought are relevant to an authorized investigation" (U.S. Code Title 50 §1861(a) (1) and (b)(2)(A)). Agents also have to "comply with a detailed set of minimization procedures that restrict the retention and distribution of *private data about innocent Americans.*"

The idea behind the §215 business records provision is to level the playing field. "If officials investigating drug dealers and crooked insurance companies can issue subpoenas for business records, then officials investigating international terrorists should be able to as well" (Sales 2011, 5). Table 15.2 includes Professor Sale's list of the greater safeguards for innocent people during national security investigations than during ordinary grand jury investigations.

Section 215 isn't just directed at "business records." (See Table 15.3.)

The "library provision" receives lots of media attention, and generates considerable fear that FBI agents will order libraries to tell them what we're reading. In 2006, the Justice Department testified to the House Judiciary Committee that it has never used the *business records* provision to investigate "library, book store, medical, or gun sale records":

> While section Section 215 has never been used to obtain such records, last year [2005], a member of a terrorist group closely affiliated with al Qaeda used

TABLE 15.2 Patriot Act §215: Safeguards compared to ordinary grand jury

• First, the PATRIOT Act has a narrower scope. Section 215 may only be used in national security investigations, whereas a grand jury can issue a subpoena "merely on suspicion that the law is being violated, or even just because it wants assurance that it is not."
• Second, PATRIOT provides for judicial review; investigators can't acquire business records unless they first appear before the FISA court and convince it that they are entitled to them. Grand jury practice is very different. Although subpoenas in theory are issued in the name of the grand jury and the overseeing court, in practice they are issued more or less unilaterally by Assistant U.S. Attorneys; judicial review does not occur until after the subpoena has been issued, if at all.
• Third, the PATRIOT Act requires minimization procedures to protect the privacy of innocent Americans; the grand jury rules do not. Minimization procedures are supposed to limit the retention, and regulate the dissemination, of information not publicly available, that concerns non consenting U.S. persons. Federal officials can't "use of or disclose" the information "except for lawful purposes" (Yeh and Doyle 2006, 6).
• Fourth, the PATRIOT Act forbids the government from investigating an American "solely upon the basis of activities protected by the First Amendment to the Constitution." (Grand jury rules offer no such guarantee.)
• Fifth, PATRIOT offers heightened protections when investigators seek materials that are especially sensitive, such as medical records and records from libraries or bookstores. The grand jury rules lack any comparable restrictions.
• Finally, PATRIOT provides for robust congressional oversight: The government must "fully inform" the House and Senate Intelligence Committees, as well as the Senate Judiciary Committee, concerning "all" uses of this provision. The grand jury rules contain no such notification requirement.

Source: Sales 2011, 5–6; Yeh and Doyle 2006, 6.

TABLE 15.3 Financial institutions as defined by the USA Patriot Act

- Banks
- Private bankers
- Credit unions
- Thrift institutions
- Brokers and dealers
- Investment bankers and companies
- Insurance companies
- Travel agencies
- Casinos
- Credit reports
- Employers
- Libraries

Internet service provided by a public library to communicate with his confederates. Furthermore, we know that spies have used public library computers to do research to further their espionage and to communicate with their co-conspirators. . . . A terrorist using a computer in a library should not be afforded greater privacy protection than a terrorist using a computer in his home. (Yeh and Doyle 2006, 4–5, note 18)

Table 15.4 includes three examples of cases in which grand jury subpoenas to libraries led to prosecuting successfully defedants in cases that didn't involve national security.

LO 4, 5 National Security Letters (NSLs)

The FBI sends **National Security Letters (NSLs)** to telephone companies, Internet Service Providers (ISPs), consumer credit reporting agencies, banks, and other financial institutions, "directing the recipients to turn over all of the *metadata* (non content information, such as an e-mail address but not the message) from *all* customer records for intelligence intelligence-gathering purposes. (Doyle 2011, 1). (Don't confuse NSLs with "business records" subpoenas, which direct banks and other institutions to turn over the *contents* of the records of a *specific U.S. person or persons,* or *organization.*)

TABLE 15.4 Grand jury subpoenas to libraries in non-national security cases

- *Unabomber.* Subpoenas were issued to six university libraries to find out who checked out books cited in the "Unabomber Manifesto" (Sales 2011, 7).
- *Zodiac gunman* (1990). N.Y.A New York grand jury subpoenaed a Manhattan library, wanting to know who had checked out books by a Scottish occult poet who investigators believed inspired the gunman who called himself "Zodiac" in letters he wrote after shooting four people in early 1990 (Sales 2011, 7).
- *Iowa cattle mutilation* (1983). The Iowa Supreme Court upheld grand jury library subpoenas asking for a list of people who checked out books on witchcraft and related topics to investigate cattle mutilations (*Brown v. Johnston* 1983, 511).

LO **5**   *FBI NSLs before the Patriot Act*

The Patriot Act didn't create NSLs; it only "beefed up" a well-established investigative tool. Prior to the Act, there were several federal statutes with NSL provisions. First, the Counterintelligence Access to Telephone Toll and Transactional Records Act (U.S.C. §2709) required *communications providers* to turn over certain customer information at the written request of the Director of the FBI or a senior FBI headquarters official. Figure 15.3 illustrates why the FBI values electronic communications NSLs under the Electronic Communications Privacy Act (ECPA):

When the FBI sought "customer identity, length of service, and toll records," the NSL had to certify that

1. The information is relevant to a foreign counterintelligence investigation (§2709(a), (b)) *and*

2. That specific and articulable facts gave reason to believe the information pertained to a foreign power or its agents (§(b)(1)).

FIGURE 15.3 Use of Telephone Toll Billing Records and Subscriber Information Obtained by National Security Letters in Counterterrorism and Counterintelligence Cases

- Through national security letters, an FBI field office obtained telephone toll billing records and subscriber information about an investigative subject in a counterterrorism case. The information obtained identified the various telephone numbers with which the subject had frequent contact. Analysis of the telephone records enabled the FBI to identify a group of individuals residing in the same vicinity as the subject. The FBI initiated investigations on these individuals to determine if there was a terrorist cell operating in the city.

- FBI agents told us that national security letters were critical in a counterintelligence investigation that led to a conviction of a representative of a foreign power. The subject owned a company in the United States and traveled to a foreign country at the behest of a foreign intelligence service. In addition, the subject had been collecting telephone records and passing the records to a foreign intelligence officer located in the United States. Through toll billing records obtained from national security letters, the FBI was able to demonstrate that the foreign country's U.S.-based intelligence officer was in contact with the subject.

- After learning from the intelligence community that a suspected terrorist was using a particular telephone number and e-mail account, an FBI field division obtained telephone toll billing and subscriber information on the accounts. The NSLs identified that the subject was in touch with an individual who had been convicted of federal charges.

- In a counterintelligence investigation, telephone toll records obtained through national security letters revealed that, contrary to an FBI source's denials, the source was continuing to contact a foreign intelligence officer by telephone.

Source: U.S. Department of Justice, Office of the Inspector General, *A Review of the FBI's Use of National Security Letters* (March 2007), page 49.

When only customer information and length of service records are requested, then the NSL has to certify that the information is *relevant* to a foreign counterintelligence investigation. But, the articulable facts have to give rise to a reasonable belief that the "customer information pertained to use of the provider's facilities to communicate with foreign powers, their agents, or those engaged in international terrorism or criminal clandestine intelligence activities" (§2709 (b)(2)).

Second, the Right to Financial Privacy Act similarly required *financial institutions* to provide customers' financial records when the Director director of the FBI or someone he designates certifies in writing that the records are needed for foreign counterintelligence purposes, *and* that "specific and articulable facts gave reason to believe that the records were of a foreign power or its agents, or those engaged in international terrorism or criminal clandestine intelligence activities" (U.S. Code 12, §3414(a)(5)). Figure 15.4 illustrates the value of NSLs under the Act:

Third, the Fair Credit Report Act requires consumer credit reporting agencies to turn over customer identification, and the names and addresses of financial institutions where the customer maintained accounts. Here, too, the FBI Director or his designee has to submit written certification that the information was necessary for a foreign counterintelligence investigation, and there were specific, articulable facts that led to a reasonable belief that the consumer was either a foreign power, or the

FIGURE 15.4 Use of Financial Records Obtained by National Security Letters in Counterterrorism Investigations

- The FBI conducted a multi-jurisdictional counterterrorism investigation of convenience store owners in the United States who allegedly sent funds to known Hawaladars (persons who use the Hawala money transfer system in lieu of or parallel to traditional banks) in the Middle East. The funds were transferred to suspected Al Qaeda affiliates. The possible violations committed by the subjects of these cases included money laundering, sale of untaxed cigarettes, check cashing fraud, illegal sale of pseudoephedrine (the precursor ingredient used to manufacture methamphetamine), unemployment insurance fraud, welfare fraud, immigration fraud, income tax violations, and sale of counterfeit merchandise.

  The FBI issued national security letters for the convenience store owners' bank account records. The records showed that two persons received millions of dollars from the subjects and that another subject had forwarded large sums of money to one of these individuals. The bank analysis identified sources and recipients of the money transfers and assisted in the collection of information on targets of the investigation overseas.

- The subject of a counterterrorism investigation was allegedly involved in narcotics trafficking. When analysis of telephone records revealed that an individual was in telephone contact with the subject, the FBI issued RFPA NSLs for that individual's bank account records. Examination of the bank records revealed no significant ties to the subject and in the absence of any information linking this individual to terrorist activities, further investigation was terminated.

Source: U.S. Department of Justice, Office of the Inspector General, *A Review of the FBI's Use of National Security Letters* (March 2007), page 50.

FIGURE 15.5 Use of Consumer Credit Bureau Records Obtained by National Security Letters in Counterintelligence and Counterterrorism Investigations

- During a counterintelligence investigation, the FBI issued an FCRA NSL seeking financial institution and consumer identifying information about an investigative subject who the FBI was told had been recruited to provide sensitive information to a foreign power. The information obtained from the NSL assisted the FBI in eliminating concerns that the subject was hiding assets or laundering funds or that he had received covert payments from the foreign power.

- In the aftermath of Hurricane Katrina, many subjects of a major FBI counterterrorism investigation moved from areas affected by the disaster. To assist in locating these subjects, the FBI served FCRA NSLs for updated credit card information on the subjects. The information revealed the subjects' credit card activity in a major U.S. city and several foreign countries.

- The FBI initiated an investigation of an individual who was identified during the arrest of a known terrorist in a foreign country. After obtaining a credit card number used by the subject, the FBI served an NSL to obtain a consumer full credit report. The report showed that the subject had relocated to another U.S. city. The FBI's investigation was transferred to the FBI division in that city.

Source: U.S. Department of Justice, Office of the Inspector General, *A Review of the FBI's Use of National Security Letters* (March 2007), page 51.

agent of a foreign power, and was engaged in international terrorism or criminal clandestine intelligence activities. Figure 15.5 illustrates the value of Fair Credit Report Act NSLs.

LO 5 FBI NSLs after the Patriot Act 2006 amendments

The Patriot Act (§505) amended the NSL provisions in the Electronic Communications Privacy Act, Right to Financial Privacy Act, and the Fair Credit Reporting Act so that NSL Letters could "be employed more quickly (without the delays associated with prior approval from FBI headquarters) and more widely (without requiring that the information pertain to a foreign power or its agents)" (Doyle 2010, 2).

Here's a list of the highlights of the amendments. They:

- Expanded FBI issuing authority beyond FBI headquarters to include the heads of field offices and Special Agents in Charge (SACs)

- Eliminated the requirement that the information is linked to a "foreign power or the agent of a foreign power."

- Required instead that the NSL request sought information "for or relevant to various national security investigations."

- Directed that no NSL investigation of a "U.S. person" can be based exclusively on activities protected by the First Amendment (Doyle 2010, 2).

Several of the Patriot Act's intelligence intelligence-gathering provisions were temporary and due to expire in 2005. The Congress, after heated opposition, extended most of the provisions until 2010, when Congress (Senate 72–23, House 250–153) again after heated debate (and a Senate filibuster) extended them until 2015. President Obama signed the bill into law just before midnight by autopen in France. The 2006 amendments were probably the result of a combination of the President George W. Bush's administration's "desire for more explicit enforcement authority," and a few lower federal court decisions, expressing concern that some of the Patriot Act NSL provisions violated the Fourth and First Amendments (Doyle 2011, 4).

A major concern was the "open-ended non disclosure provisions [gag orders], which barred recipients from disclosing the fact or content of the NSL—ever or to anyone." Unfortunately, the statutes contained neither a penalty provision, if the recipient violated the gag order, or an enforcement mechanism if a recipient ignored the order (Doyle 2011, 4).

Here's how the 2006 Amendments addressed these enforcement problems.

- They created an enforcement mechanism and a judicial review procedure for both the requests and gag order requirements;
- They established specific penalties for failure to comply with the gag order requirements;
- They made it clear that gag orders left recipients free to "lawyer up";
- They provided a process to ease the gag order requirement;
- They expanded Congressional oversight;
- They called for Inspector General audits of the use of NSL authority. (Doyle 2011, 4)

Table 15.5 shows the results of the Inspector General's reports for the first decade since 9/11.

LO 5 NSL targets and data

Before we move on, be clear about two critical limits to NSLs:

1. The only NSL targets who are legally subject to monitoring are non-U.S. persons, or U.S. persons involved in terrorism and spying within the United States.
2. The only information an NSL can demand is *metadata* (like an e-mail address), not *content* (the e-mail message); and a telephone number, not the conversation, to name a few.

LO 5 NSLs and the Inspector General's (IG) report

The USA Patriot Improvement Act of 2005, directed the Justice Department Inspector Inspector General (IG) to review "the effectiveness and use, including any improper

TABLE 15.5 FISC court orders, 2012

	Number
Presented	1,579
Approved	1,579
Rejected	0
U.S. Persons Affected	16,511

Source: Compiled by Electronic Privacy Information Center.

or illegal use, of national security letters issued by the Department of Justice" (U.S. Department of Justice [hereafter IG Report] 2007, viii).

Here's a list of the principal uses for NSLs that the FBI personnel reported to the IG:

- Establish evidence to support FISA applications for electronic surveillance, physical searches, pen register/trap and trace orders;

- Assess communication or financial links between investigative subjects or others;

- Collect enough information to develop national security investigations;

- Generate leads for other field divisions, members of Joint Terrorism Task Forces (JTTFs), or other field agencies, or to pass to foreign governments;

- Develop analytical products for distribution within the FBI, other Department components, other federal agencies, and the intelligence community;

- Develop information for law enforcement authorities to use in criminal proceedings;

- Collect enough information to eliminate concerns and close investigations;

- Corroborate information derived from other investigation tools. (46)

FBI Headquarters and field personnel told the IG that "they believe NSLs are indispensable investigative tools that serve as building blocks in many counterterrorism and counterintelligence investigations" (65). The details behind these beliefs are often classified. Nevertheless, the IG reported that investigative files and interviews with case agents and supervisors assigned to counterintelligence and counterterrorism squads revealed that information obtained from NSLs "has contributed significantly to many counterterrorism and counterintelligence investigations" (48).

As for "improper or illegal use" of the FBI authority to issue NSLs, the IG found some. They fell into these categories:

- Issuing NSLs when authority to conduct investigations had expired;

- Obtaining telephone billing records and e-mail subscriber information from the wrong individuals;

- Obtaining information not asked for in the NSL;

- Obtaining information beyond the time period authorized by the letter;

- Issuing Fair Credit Reporting Act (FCRA) NSLs seeking records the FBI wasn't authorized to obtain;

- Issuing improper requests under the wrong statute;

- Obtaining telephone billing records by issuing "exigent letters" signed by the Counterterrorism Division Unit Chief or subordinate personnel who were not authorized to issue NSLs;

- Issuing NSLs out of "control files" instead of investigative files. When NSLs are issued from control files, the NSL documentation does not indicate whether the NSLs are issued in authorized investigations or whether the information sought in the NSLs is relevant to those investigations. This documentation is necessary to establish compliance with NSL statutes, Attorney General Guidelines, and FBI policies. (66–67)

LO 6   NSLs in Court

The FBI issues countless NSLs, but only a tiny number enter the court system. The few that have made their way to court, challenge two aspects of the Letters: (1) issuing them in the first place; and (2) ordering those who receive them to say nothing about what the Letters say, or even that they received them (in the words of the statutes, these are NSL "non disclosure" orders; usually called **NSL "gag" orders**). Challengers argue that both aspects run afoul of the First and Fourth Amendments. Let's look first at where most of the few cases focus—the *gag orders* and the First Amendment. Then we'll turn to the one case that decided an NSL gag order violated the *Fourth* Amendment, a passionate New York U.S. District Court opinion (*Doe v. Ashcroft* 2004) that, on appeal, the U.S. Court of Appeals decided on First Amendment, not Fourth Amendment, grounds (*Doe v. Mucasey* 2008). Finally, we'll examine the ruling in the most recent case (*In re National Security Letter* (2013))—in which a San Francisco U.S. District Court held that *issuing* an NSL violated the First Amendment.

In August, 2005, the American Civil Liberties Union (ACLU), an ardent foe of the Patriot Act, joined the Library Connection, a consortium of 26 Connecticut libraries, to challenge an FBI NSL seeking patrons' library records. That same month, the ACLU also challenged the NSL library provision that allows the FBI, in the ACLU's words, to "forbid or 'gag' anyone who receives an NSL from telling anyone about the record demand" (ACLU 2006). In September 2005, the U.S. District Court Judge judge Janet C. Hall in Bridgeport, Connecticut, Janet C. Hall, CT, ruled that the gag order violated the First Amendment. In April 2006, six weeks after the Congress reauthorized the Patriot Act, the government dropped its legal battle to keep the non disclosure in effect, and then withdrew its request for Library Connection's records altogether (*Doe v. Gonzalez* 2005).

In our next case excerpt, *Doe, Inc. v. Mukasey* (2008), a unanimous three-judge panel of the U.S. Court of Appeals rejected a First Amendment challenge to the gag order that accompanied the NSL an FBI agent had hand-delivered to Nicholas Merrill, president of "Calyx Internet Access," Merrill's ISP's office. Merrill joined the ACLU and the ACLU Foundation to challenge the "gag" order. The case was an appeal from U.S. District Court Judge Victor Marrero's decision ruling that "gag orders" violated the Fourth and First Amendments (*Doe v. Mucasey* 2007).

In *Doe, Inc. v. Mukasey*, the U.S. Court of Appeals panel (3–0) affirmed in part and reversed in part the District Court's decision, and remanded the case.

CASE

Did the NSL "gag" order violate the First Amendment?

John Doe, Inc. v. Mukasey
549 F.3d 861 (2008)

HISTORY

The American Civil Liberties Union (ACLU), the American Civil Liberties Union Foundation (ACLUF), John Doe, Inc., an Internet service provider (ISP), and John Doe, president of John Doe, Inc., brought an action raising First Amendment challenges to the constitutionality of statutes governing the issuance and judicial review of National Security Letters (NSLs). The U.S. District Court for the Southern District of New York, Victor Marrero, J.,

enjoined the government from enforcing certain provisions, and the government appealed. A three three-judge U.S. Second Circuit Court of Appeals panel affirmed in part, reversed in part, and remanded.

JON O. NEWMAN, Circuit Judge

These challenges arise on an appeal by the United States from the September 7, 2007, judgment of the District Court for the Southern District of New York (Victor Marrero, District Judge), enjoining FBI officials from

(continued)

(1) issuing NSLs under section 2709, (2) enforcing the nondisclosure requirement of subsection 2709(c), and (3) enforcing the provisions for judicial review of the nondisclosure requirement contained in subsection 3511(b). The District Court ruled that subsections 2709(c) and 3511(b) are unconstitutional on First Amendment and separation-of-powers grounds.

We agree that the challenged statutes do not comply with the First Amendment, although not to the extent determined by the District Court, and we also conclude that the relief ordered by the District Court is too broad. We therefore affirm in part, reverse in part, and remand for further proceedings.

FACTS

The Plaintiffs–Appellees are an Internet service provider (John Doe, Inc.), the provider's former president (John Doe), the American Civil Liberties Union ("ACLU"), and the American Civil Liberties Union Foundation ("ACLUF"). The Defendants–Appellants are Michael B. MUKASEY, in his official capacity as U.S. Attorney General of the United States, Robert Mueller, in his official capacity as Director of the FBI, Valerie E. Caproni, in her official capacity as General Counsel of the FBI.

In February 2004, the FBI delivered the NSL at issue in this litigation to John Doe, Inc. The letter directed John Doe, Inc., "to provide the [FBI] the names, addresses, lengths of service and electronic communication transactional records, to include [other information] (not to include message content and/or subject fields) for [a specific] e-mail address." The letter certified that the information sought was relevant to an investigation against international terrorism or clandestine intelligence activities and advised John Doe, Inc., that the law "prohibit[ed] any officer, employee or agent" of the company from "disclosing to any person that the FBI has sought or obtained access to information or records" pursuant to the NSL provisions. The letter also asked that John Doe provide the relevant information personally to a designated FBI office.

Subsection 2709(a) imposes a duty on Electronic Communication Service Providers (ECSP) to comply with requests for specified information about a subscriber, and subsection 2709(b) authorizes the Director of the FBI and other FBI officials to request specified information about a subscriber from ECSPs. Subsection 2709(c), as it existed in 2004, imposed a blanket nondisclosure requirement prohibiting an ECSP from disclosing receipt of an NSL.

On the Plaintiffs' motion for summary judgment, the District Court ruled that section 2709(c) was unconstitutional under the First Amendment because it was an unjustified prior restraint and a content-based restriction on speech. Nearly one year later, a District Court in Connecticut preliminarily enjoined enforcement of the nondisclosure requirement of subsection 2709(c), finding a probability of success on the claim that subsection 2709(c) was unconstitutional under the First Amendment because it was an unjustified prior restraint and content-based restriction.

While an appeal was pending, Congress amended the nondisclosure prohibition of subsection 2709(c) to require nondisclosure only upon certification by senior FBI officials that "otherwise there may result a danger to the national security of the United States, interference with a criminal, counterterrorism, or counterintelligence investigation, interference with diplomatic relations, or danger to the life or physical safety of any person."

Second, Congress added provisions for judicial review, now codified in section 3511, to permit the recipient of an NSL to petition a United States district court for an order modifying or setting aside the NSL, 18 U.S.C.A. § 3511(a), and the nondisclosure requirement, § 3511(b). The NSL may be modified if "compliance would be unreasonable, oppressive, or otherwise unlawful." § 3511(a). The nondisclosure requirement, which prohibits disclosure by the NSL recipient of the fact that the FBI has sought or obtained access to the requested information, may be modified or set aside, upon a petition filed by the NSL recipient, § 3511(b)(1), if the district court "finds that there is no reason to believe that disclosure may endanger the national security of the United States, or interfere with a criminal, counterterrorism, or counterintelligence investigation, interfere with diplomatic relations, or endanger the life or physical safety of any person."

The nondisclosure requirement further provides that if the Attorney General or senior governmental officials certify that disclosure may endanger the national security or interfere with diplomatic relations, such certification shall be treated as "conclusive" unless the court finds that the certification was made "in bad faith." (The recipient of an NSL need not notify the FBI of "the identity of an attorney to whom disclosure was made or will be made to obtain legal advice or legal assistance with respect to the request.")

[The Court of Appeals remanded the case to the District Court in view of the changes in the relevant NSL statutes]

On November 7, 2006, the Government informed the District Court that it was no longer seeking to enforce the request for information contained in the NSL that had been sent to John Doe with respect to information from John Doe, Inc.

On September 6, 2007, the District Court issued its second opinion, ruling that, despite the amendments to the NSL statutes, subsections 2709(c) and 3511(b) are facially unconstitutional, and that the Defendants–Appellants are enjoined from issuing NSLs under section

2709 and enforcing the provisions of subsections 2709(c) and 3511(b). The Court stayed enforcement of its judgment pending appeal.

OPINION

The validity of the NSL issued to John Doe, Inc., is no longer at issue because the Government has withdrawn it, but the prohibition on disclosing receipt of the NSL remains. We therefore consider only the Government's challenges to the District Court's rulings with respect to the nondisclosure requirement.

Applicable Principles

The First Amendment principles relevant to the District Court's rulings are well established. A judicial order forbidding certain communications when issued in advance of the time that such communications are to occur is generally regarded as a prior restraint, and is the most serious and the least tolerable infringement on First Amendment rights. Any prior restraint on expression comes to [a court] with a heavy presumption against its constitutional validity. A content-based restriction is subject to review under the standard of strict scrutiny, requiring a showing that the restriction is narrowly tailored to promote a compelling Government interest.

Where expression is conditioned on governmental permission, such as a licensing system for movies, the First Amendment generally requires [three] procedural protections to guard against impermissible censorship: (1) any restraint imposed prior to judicial review must be limited to "a specified brief period"; (2) any further restraint prior to a final judicial determination must be limited to "the shortest fixed period compatible with sound judicial resolution"; and (3) the burden of going to court to suppress speech and the burden of proof in court must be placed on the government.

The national security context in which NSLs are authorized imposes on courts a significant obligation to defer to judgments of Executive Branch officials. Courts traditionally have been reluctant to intrude upon the authority of the Executive in . . . national security affairs, and the Supreme Court has acknowledged that terrorism might provide the basis for arguments for heightened deference to the judgments of the political branches with respect to matters of national security.

Constitutionality of the NSL Statutes

Strict scrutiny. Under strict scrutiny review, the Government must demonstrate that the nondisclosure requirement is narrowly tailored to promote a compelling Government interest, and that there are no less restrictive alternatives [that] would be at least as effective in achieving the legitimate purpose that the statute was enacted

to serve. Since it is obvious and unarguable that no governmental interest is more compelling than the security of the Nation, the principal strict scrutiny issue turns on whether the narrow tailoring requirement is met, and this issue, as the District Court observed, essentially concerns the process by which the nondisclosure requirement is imposed and tested

With subsections 2709(c) and 3511(b) . . . two aspects of that process remain principally at issue: the absence of a requirement that the Government initiate judicial review of the lawfulness of a nondisclosure requirement and the degree of deference a district court is obliged to accord to the certification of senior governmental officials in ordering nondisclosure.

Absence of requirement that the Government initiate judicial review. The Plaintiffs alleged, and the District Court agreed, that the third procedural requirement applies to the NSL statutes, requiring the Government to initiate judicial review of its imposition of a nondisclosure requirement.

The Government contends that it would be unduly burdened if it had to initiate a lawsuit to enforce the nondisclosure requirement in the more than 40,000 NSL requests that were issued in 2005 alone, according to the 2007 report of the Inspector General of the Department of Justice ("OIG Report"). Related to this argument is the point, advanced in the Government's brief, "there is no reason to believe that most recipients of NSLs wish to disclose that fact to anyone."

We consider an available means of minimizing that burden, use of which would substantially avoid the Government's argument. The Government could inform each NSL recipient that it should give the Government prompt notice, perhaps within ten days, in the event that the recipient wishes to contest the nondisclosure requirement. Upon receipt of such notice, the Government could be accorded a limited time, perhaps 30 days, to initiate a judicial review proceeding to maintain the nondisclosure requirement, and the proceeding would have to be concluded within a prescribed time, perhaps 60 days.

In accordance with the first and second safeguards, the NSL could inform the recipient that the nondisclosure requirement would remain in effect during the entire interval of the recipient's decision whether to contest the nondisclosure requirement, the Government's prompt application to a court, and the court's prompt adjudication on the merits. The NSL could also inform the recipient that the nondisclosure requirement would remain in effect if the recipient declines to give the Government notice of an intent to challenge the requirement or, upon a challenge, if the Government prevails in court.

If the Government is correct that very few NSL recipients have any interest in challenging the nondisclosure

(continued)

requirement (perhaps no more than three have done so thus far), this "reciprocal notice procedure" would nearly eliminate the Government's burden to initiate litigation (with a corresponding minimal burden on NSL recipients to defend numerous lawsuits). Thus, the Government's litigating burden can be substantially minimized, and the resulting slight burden is not a reason for precluding application of the third safeguard.

We acknowledge, however, that the nondisclosure requirement of subsection 2709(c) is not facially like a movie exhibitor licensing scheme. Unlike an exhibitor of movies, John Doe, Inc., did not intend to speak and was not subject to any administrative restraint on speaking *prior* to the Government's issuance of an NSL. [italics added] Nevertheless, once the NSL arrived, John Doe, Inc., did wish to speak publicly about it and was prohibited from doing so by an administrative order. The judicial review requirement cannot be disregarded simply because subsection 2709(c) does not impose a traditional licensing scheme.

The availability of a minimally burdensome reciprocal notice procedure for governmental initiation of judicial review and the inadequacy of the Government's attempts to avoid the safeguard persuade us that this safeguard, normally required where strict scrutiny applies, must be observed. Therefore, in the absence of Government-initiated judicial review, subsection 3511(b) is not narrowly tailored to conform to First Amendment procedural standards. We conclude, as did the District Court, that subsection 3511(b) does not survive strict scrutiny or a slightly less exacting measure of such scrutiny.

The District Court's objection to the judicial review procedure is far more substantial. The Court deemed inconsistent with strict scrutiny standards the provision of subsections 3511(b)(2) and (b)(3) specifying that a certification by senior governmental officials that disclosure may "endanger the national security of the United States or interfere with diplomatic relations . . . shall be treated as conclusive unless the court finds that the certification was made in bad faith." We agree.

There is not meaningful judicial review of the decision of the Executive Branch to prohibit speech if the position of the Executive Branch that speech would be harmful is "conclusive" on a reviewing court, absent only a demonstration of bad faith. To accept deference to that extraordinary degree would be to reduce strict scrutiny to no scrutiny, save only in the rarest of situations where bad faith could be shown. Under either traditional strict scrutiny or a less exacting application of that standard, some demonstration from the Executive Branch of the need for secrecy is required in order to conform the nondisclosure requirement to First Amendment standards. The fiat of a governmental official, though senior in rank and doubtless honorable in the execution of official duties, cannot

displace the judicial obligation to enforce constitutional requirements. Under no circumstances should the Judiciary become the handmaiden of the Executive.

Remedy

If the Government uses the suggested reciprocal notice procedure as a means of initiating judicial review, there appears to be no impediment to the Government's including notice of a recipient's opportunity to contest the nondisclosure requirement in an NSL. If such notice is given, time limits on the nondisclosure requirement pending judicial review would have to be applied to make the review procedure constitutional. We would deem it to be within our judicial authority to conform subsection 2709(c) to First Amendment requirements, by limiting the duration of the nondisclosure requirement, absent a ruling favorable to the Government upon judicial review, to the 10–day period in which the NSL recipient decides whether to contest the nondisclosure requirement, the 30–day period in which the Government considers whether to seek judicial review, and a further period of 60 days in which a court must adjudicate the merits, unless special circumstances warrant additional time.

In view of these possibilities, we need not invalidate the entirety of the nondisclosure requirement of subsection 2709(c) or the judicial review provisions of subsection 3511(b). Although the conclusive presumption clause of subsections 3511(b)(2) and (b)(3) must be stricken, we invalidate subsection 2709(c) and the remainder of subsection 3511(b) only to the extent that they fail to provide for Government-initiated judicial review. The Government can respond to this partial invalidation ruling by using the suggested reciprocal notice procedure. With this procedure in place, subsections 2709(c) and 3511(b) would survive First Amendment challenge.

. . . As a result of this ruling, we modify the District Court's injunction by limiting it to enjoining FBI officials from enforcing the nondisclosure requirement of section 2709(c) in the absence of Government-initiated judicial review.

There remains for consideration the issue of the procedure to be followed with respect to judicial review of the nondisclosure requirement with respect to the NSL issued to John Doe, Inc. . . . We remand so that the Government may have an opportunity to sustain its burden of proof and satisfy the constitutional standards we have outlined for maintaining the disclosure requirement.

Accordingly, subsections 2709(c) and 3511(b) are construed in conformity with this opinion and partially invalidated only to the extent set forth in this opinion, the injunction is modified as set forth in this opinion, and the judgment of the District Court is affirmed in part, reversed in part, and remanded for further proceedings consistent with this opinion.

Questions

1. Describe how John Doe received the NSL.

2. Describe the terms of the gag order.

3. Explain why the Court of Appeals decided that it violated the First Amendment.

4. Explain how the Court of Appeals suggests the FBI can correct the violation.

5. Do you agree that the Court's suggestions would correct the violation? Explain your answer.

6. Do you agree with the Government that the national security outweighs John Doe's First Amendment right without altering the gag rule? Explain your answer.

YOU DECIDE
Should the NSL "Gag" Order Remain in Effect?
Doe v. Holder, 703 F.Supp.2d 313 (March 18, 2010)

LO 6 Following the Circuit Court's decision in the excerpt above, the government filed a secret classified sworn declaration, and parties cross-moved for partial summary judgment on the issue of whether continued nondisclosure of NSL was required. The District Court Marrero, J., found that continued compliance with nondisclosure order was justified. Plaintiffs moved for reconsideration.

By Decision and Order dated October 20, 2009, the Court granted in part the Government's motion for summary judgment and denied in part Plaintiffs' motion for partial summary judgment. In so ruling, the Court found that the Government had carried its burden of demonstrating that continuation of the requirement imposed on Plaintiffs not to disclose the NSL and its Attachment was justified. Plaintiffs then moved for partial reconsideration of the October 2009 Order. By Order dated December 23, 2009, the Court invited the parties to further address the matter at oral arguments scheduled for January 15, 2010. Subsequently to the hearing, on February 18, 2010 the Court conducted a secret review with the Government and two representatives of the FBI, Special Agent Paul Abbate, and Charles Marciano of the Office of the General Counsel.

Plaintiffs contend that the Government has not provided adequate explanation to justify suppressing the Attachment as necessary to national security interests or to protect an ongoing investigation of terrorist activity. To the contrary, Plaintiffs maintain that disclosure of the Attachment would serve the public interest in understanding the type of personal records the FBI has sought to obtain through NSLs, and thus to inform congressional and public debate on the subject.

In response, the Government submitted a Declaration (the "Declaration") of Arthur M. Cummings II ("Cummings"), Executive Assistant Director of the National Security Branch of the Federal Bureau of Investigation ("FBI"). Cummings states that the duties of his office entail supervision and control over the FBI's National Security files and records. In that capacity he declares his view that unauthorized disclosure of sensitive information contained in the NSL at issue, including the Attachment, would risk revealing sensitive information sought by the FBI in conducting national security investigations, as well as the methods and techniques used by the FBI in the course of such work. Moreover, Cummings asserts that disclosure of the Attachment may cause the target of the NSL to change behavior when dealing with Internet service providers, such as by giving false information to conceal the target's true identity or intentions. Finally, Cummings declares that the effects of disclosure of the types of information and specific items the FBI considers important in seeking to identify account holders or their computer use or access would compromise not only the current FBI investigation involving the NSL and target in this case but future probes as well, thus potentially hampering Government efforts to address national security threats.

(continued)

On the basis of review of the Declaration and other papers submitted by the parties, the oral argument at the Court's hearing on the matter, and the Court's secret conference with the Government for in camera review of the Attachment, the Court grants in part and denies in part Plaintiffs' request.

The Court concludes that some items requested in the Attachment relate to two categories of information that should be disclosed; (1) material within the scope of information that the NSL statute identifies as permissible for the FBI to obtain through use of NSLs, and (2) material that the FBI has publicly acknowledged it has previously requested by means of NSLs. These categories, insofar as specifically itemized in the Attachment, include the name, address, telephone number, account number, email address and billing information of the subscriber. The Court is not persuaded that disclosure of these two categories of information would raise a substantial risk that any of the statutorily enumerated harms would occur. Accordingly, the Court directs the Government to lift its nondisclosure requirement as it applies to those items of the Attachment.

As to the remainder of the Attachment, the Court is persuaded that the Government has demonstrated that good reason exists to believe that disclosure of the information withheld plausibly could harm an authorized ongoing investigation to protect against international terrorism or clandestine intelligence activities. Also, the Court finds that the Government has demonstrated to the satisfaction of the Court that the link between disclosure and the risk of harm is substantial.

Plaintiffs contend that there is no continuing need for nondisclosure of the entire Attachment because it would reveal only marginal information about the Government's investigation. Further, they argue that the Government's suppression justification proffered here is constitutionally deficient because: the FBI has already publicly revealed its interest in some of the types of records it has sought in this case, such as existing transaction/activity logs and email header information; disclosure of the Attachment would not impart anything about the FBI's current NSL practices; and the FBI's concerns are grounded entirely on conclusory or speculative risk of harms that might occur. The Court disagrees.

The Court is persuaded, based on Cummings's Declaration and the Government's written submissions and representations at the Court's in camera review of the Attachment, that the Government has sufficiently met its burden under §2709(c). Specifically, the Court finds that the Government has demonstrated a reasonable likelihood that

disclosure of the Attachment in its entirety could inform current targets of law enforcement investigations, including the particular target of the Government's ongoing inquiry in this action, as well as, potentially, future targets, as to certain types of records and other materials the Government seeks through national security investigations employing NSLs. The Government has made a plausible showing that public access to such information could provide knowledge about current FBI activities as well as valuable insights into the agency's investigative methods that could produce the harms the NSL statute sought to safeguard against. For instance, disclosure of the Attachment could risk providing information useful to the Government's targets of the pending investigation that could prompt changes in their behavior to prevent detection, or signal that particular targets remain under active surveillance. Thus, the Court is satisfied that the information sought by the Attachment does not entail undue impairment of First Amendment rights or other unwarranted abusive practice on the part of the FBI.

Plaintiffs dismiss the Government's concerns as either conclusory or entirely speculative, or as unfounded fears grounded on no more than what theoretically may happen in the future. However, considering the context of national security and an ongoing investigation involving suspected terrorist activities, the Court finds the Government's justification entitled to deference in this proceeding. The Supreme Court, in upholding nondisclosure of intelligence information by the Central Intelligence Agency under analogous circumstances, has recognized that risks of what "may" happen have bearing upon and may be factored in resolving government claims for nondisclosure, cautioning that "bits and pieces of data *may* aid in piecing together bits of other information even when the individual piece is not of obvious importance in itself," *CIA v. Sims,* 471 U.S. 159, 178, 105 S.Ct. 1881, 85 L.Ed.2d 173 (1985) (emphasis added).

The Supreme Court's observation in *Sims* reflects practical wisdom drawn from everyday experience. Individuals intent on carrying out illegal activities often manage to remain outside the reach of the law, one step ahead of the police and forearmed by resourceful monitoring of the information the government gathers through law enforcement methods and technologies. By common sense analogy, were John Dillinger handed pieces of the bank's blueprints showing directions to the vault, he very well "may" or "could" find his way to the spot marked "X," or if tipped that the cops have staked lookouts at the scene, he "might" avoid the job altogether. To reasonably demonstrate the likelihood of that deduction would not demand giant leaps of conjecture. Yet, under Plaintiffs' theory in the case at hand, any risk of future harm from compelled disclosure of police surveillance information under these circumstances would be dismissed as purely speculative and unjustified. Consequently, to show that the projected law enforcement concerns are genuine essentially would require that at least some clues about the police's surveillance plans be revealed first and then wait and see whether the feared harm does indeed materialize. The Court finds nothing in First Amendment doctrine; or in logic, reason or practical experience, that would compel such an outcome. Accordingly, the Court finds that the Government has carried its burden as to the nondisclosure of portions of the Attachment.

CRIMINAL PROCEDURE IN ACTION

"NSLs are unreasonable searches and seizures"
Doe v. Ashcroft, 334 Fed. Supp. 2d 471 (2004)

LO 6 The FBI's demands under §2709 are issued in the form of national security letters ("NSLs"), which constitute a unique form of administrative subpoena cloaked in secrecy and pertaining to national security issues. The statute bars all NSL recipients from ever disclosing that the FBI has issued an NSL.

Longstanding Supreme Court doctrine makes clear that an administrative subpoena statute is consistent with the Fourth Amendment when it is subject to "judicial supervision" and "surrounded by every safeguard of judicial restraint." Plaintiffs contend that §2709 violates this Fourth Amendment process-based guarantee because it gives the FBI alone the power to issue as well as enforce its own NSLs, instead of contemplating some form of judicial review. Although Plaintiffs appear to concede that the statute does not authorize the FBI to literally enforce the terms of an NSL by, for example, unilaterally seizing documents or imposing fines, Plaintiffs contend that §2709 has the *practical* effect of coercing compliance.

Specifically, Plaintiffs stress that the statute has no provision for judicial enforcement or review, and that theoretically any judicial review an NSL recipient sought would violate the express terms of the non-disclosure provision. Even if he were to challenge the NSL on his own, the recipient would necessarily have to disclose the fact of the NSL's issuance to the clerk of court and to the presiding judge, again, in violation of the literal terms of the non-disclosure provision.

The Court concludes that the operation of §2709 renders it unconstitutional. In particular, deficiencies in the application of §2709 pertain to the very core issues—access to legal advice and availability of judicial process to enforce and contest the law—upon which Plaintiffs' Fourth Amendment facial challenge is grounded. Because the Court agrees that those protections are vital to satisfy Fourth Amendment standards, it finds the manner in which §2709 has been applied unwarranted.

The crux of the Fourth Amendment problem is that the form NSL, like the one issued in this case, which is preceded by a personal call from an FBI agent, is framed in imposing language on FBI letterhead and which, citing the authorizing statute, orders a combination of disclosure *in person* and in complete secrecy, essentially coerces the reasonable recipient into immediate compliance. Objectively viewed, it is improbable that an FBI summons invoking the authority of a certified "investigation to protect against international terrorism or clandestine intelligence activities," and phrased in tones sounding virtually as biblical commandment, would not be perceived with some apprehension by an ordinary person and therefore elicit passive obedience from a reasonable NSL recipient. The full weight of this ominous writ is especially felt when the NSL's plain language, in a measure that enhances its aura as an expression of public will, prohibits disclosing the issuance of the NSL to "any person." Reading such strictures, it is also highly unlikely that an NSL recipient reasonably would know that he may have a right to contest the NSL, and that a process to do so may exist through a judicial proceeding.

Because neither the statute, nor an NSL, nor the FBI agents dealing with the recipient say as much, all but the most mettlesome and undaunted NSL recipients would consider themselves effectively barred from consulting an attorney or anyone else who might advise them otherwise, as well as bound to absolute silence about the very existence of the NSL. For the reasonable NSL recipient confronted with the NSL's mandatory language and the FBI's conduct related to the NSL, resistance is not a viable option.

(continued)

The evidence in this case bears out the hypothesis that NSLs work coercively in this way. The ACLU obtained, via the Freedom of Information Act ("FOIA"), and presented to the Court in this proceeding, a document listing all the NSLs the Government issued from October 2001 through January 2003. Although the entire substance of the document is redacted, it is apparent that hundreds of NSL requests were made during that period. Because §2709 has been available to the FBI since 1986 (and its financial records counterpart in RFPA since 1978), the Court concludes that there must have been hundreds more NSLs issued in that long time span. The evidence suggests that, until now, none of those NSLs was ever challenged in any court. First, the Department of Justice explicitly informed the House Judiciary Committee in May 2003 that there had been *no* challenges to the propriety or legality of any NSLs. Second, the Government's evidence in this case conspicuously lacks any suggestion either that the Government has ever had to resort to a judicial enforcement proceeding for any NSL, or that any recipient has ever resisted an NSL request in such a proceeding or via any motion to quash.

To be sure, the Court recognizes that many other reasons may exist to explain the absence of challenges to NSLs: the communications provider who receives the NSL ordinarily would have little incentive to contest the NSL on the subscriber's behalf; the standard of review for administrative subpoenas similar to NSLs is so minimal that most such NSLs would likely be upheld in court; litigating these issues is expensive; and many citizens may feel a civic duty to help the FBI's investigation and thus may willingly comply. Nevertheless, the Court finds it striking that, in all the years during which the FBI has been serving NSLs, the evidence suggests that, until now, no single NSL recipient has ever sought to quash such a directive. The Court thus concludes that in practice NSLs are essentially unreviewable because, as explained, given the language and tone of the statute as carried into the NSL by the FBI, the recipient would consider himself, in virtually every case, obliged to comply, with no other option but to immediately obey and stay quiet.

The Government responds that Doe's arguments on this point are undermined by the very fact that Doe himself consulted an attorney and brought this challenge. The Court disagrees, for several reasons. . . . [One reason] is that so far as the evidence shows, Doe's decision to challenge the NSL is a lone exception in the otherwise consistent record. The constitutional bar marking the limits the Government can permissibly reach in curtailing personal freedoms in the name of national security should not be raised to heights at which all but the most powerfully endowed would feel impelled to remain cowered or content, and none but the well-heeled could stand tall enough to take on a law enforcer's coercive order. The Court concludes it would be naive to conclude that §2709 NSLs, given their commandeering warrant, do anything short of coercing all but the most fearless NSL recipient into immediate compliance and secrecy.

The Court concludes that what is, in practice, an implicit obligation of automatic compliance with NSLs violates the Fourth Amendment right to judicial access. . . . In issuing the NSL in the form employed here, the FBI's order carried out the express terms of §2709 and, as the reference to the law reminded the recipient, directed precisely the conduct the statute mandated. An NSL recipient would be unable to learn from the text of §2709 that the letter was not *actually* coercive.

Recognizing from the preceding discussion the reality that §2709 effectively keeps §2709 NSLs out of litigation altogether, the Court concludes that supplying a judicial gloss to §2709 but failing to address the practical effects of the unparalleled level of secrecy and coercion fostered by the FBI's implementation of the statute would be completely academic. That is the Court is reluctant to fashion a "remedy" which has no effect beyond being printed in the Federal Supplement.

Accordingly, the Court concludes that §2709, as applied here, must be invalidated because in all but the exceptional case it has the effect of authorizing coercive searches effectively immune from any judicial process, in violation of the Fourth Amendment.

FBI Proactive Intelligence-Gathering

In the post-9/11 environment, intelligence gathering is driven by a theory of preventive policing: in order to anticipate the next terror attack, authorities need to track *legal* activities. . . . *It focuses not on crime, but on the possibility that a crime might be committed at some future date.* Pre-emptive policing dovetails with a police-promoted belief that "radicalization" is a key cause of violent extremism. (Cincotti 2009, 2, italics added)

LO **7**

This proactive approach poses a challenge for the FBI, especially deciding when individuals move from expressing radical *ideas* protected by the First Amendment to violent radical extremist acts. "Because not all terrorist suspects follow a single radicalization roadmap on their way to executing plots, U.S. law enforcement also faces the task of discerning exactly when radicalized individuals become real threats. Timing is everything." Preemptively stopping terrorists demands good and timely intelligence (Bjelopera 2013, 19).

Let's look at two tactics, the *Capone approach*, and *sting operations*.

The Capone approach

LO **7**

The "spitting-on-the-sidewalk approach" (Graff 2011, 20). In the **Capone approach** the FBI apprehends individuals linked to terrorist plots on lesser non-terrorism-related offenses. Everyone knew what celebrity gangster Al Capone was up to—murder, bribery, and running illegal breweries. But, it was impossible to prove he was guilty of any of these crimes beyond a reasonable doubt. Why? The mobster code of silence, for one. So, they got him on the "lesser offense" of tax invasion and got him neutralized— he went to prison. Mobsters got the picture—the FBI's highest priority wasn't conviction for the most serious crime—it was neutralizing mob leaders. Fortunately, for prosecutors, investigating mobsters uncovered lots of minor crimes (Gartenstein-Ross and Dabruzzi 2007).

Today, it's difficult to prove the most serious terrorism crimes beyond a reasonable doubt, a. And, for the same reason—the terrorist code of silence. Former Attorney General John Ashcroft (2001) summed up the approach when he addressed the U.S. Annual Mayors Conference on October 11, 2001:

> Let the terrorists among us be warned: If you overstay your visa—even by one day—we will arrest you. If you violate a local law, you will be put in jail and kept in custody as long as possible. We will use every available statute. We will seek every prosecutorial advantage. We will use all our weapons within the law and under the Constitution to protect life and enhance security for America.

Garrett Graff, in his gripping story (*Threat Matrix* 2011), provides numbers to suggest the widespread use of the "Capone approach." "Of the 417 terrorism indictments in the five years after 9/11 . . . only 143 of the individuals were actually indicted on specific terrorism charges; the rest were what then -Attorney attorney General Ashcroft called the "'spitting-on-the sidewalks' approach: driver's license fraud, marriage fraud, wire fraud, immigration violations, and the myriad of lesser charges that served to disrupt potential plots and get suspects off the streets" (20).

But, there's also some evidence that the Department of Justice is moving toward trying suspected terrorists as *terrorists* instead of relying on lesser charges. For example, New York University's *Terror Report Card* (2011), reports that 77 percent of suspected terrorists between September 11, 2009 and September 11, 2010, were charged with terrorism or national security offenses, an increase of almost 50 percent compared to the average of the last eight years (2).

LO **7**

"Sting" operations

Sting operations rely on law enforcement experts' determination that a particular individual or group is "likely to move beyond radicalized talk and engage in violence or terrorist plotting." The aim is for FBI agents (most of them undercover) to gather "ironclad evidence against suspects" by catching suspects "committing an overt act."

For example, on November 26, 2010, FBI undercover agents arrested Mohamed Osman Mohamud after he attempted to set off what he believed was a car bomb at the annual Christmas tree lighting ceremony in Portland, Oregon. He thought he'd plotted with "terrorists" to detonate the bomb. In fact, the bomb was a dud and his co-conspirators—FBI undercover operatives—assembled the dud. Mohamud offered the target for the strike, provided components to assemble the bomb, gave instructions for the operation, and mailed passports to the FBI agents for the getaway. It's not clear why the FBI began the sting, but we do know that someone in the "Muslim community alerted the FBI to Mohamud, a 19-year-old Somali-born, naturalized U.S. citizen" (Bjelopera 2013, 21).

There's no publicly available official count of terrorist sting operations. But, the FBI has reported that "of all the terrorist plots disrupted between 9/11 and the September 2009 Zazi plot to blow up the NYC subway, only two plotters were 'prepared to move ahead with their plots without the benefit or knowledge of government informants or U.S. officials'" (21).

Defense attorneys contend that the FBI has entrapped suspects. Others complain that they discriminate against Muslims. FBI Director Robert S. Mueller responded publicly to both criticisms (Saad 2011):

> There will be critics. But one thing our critics should know and understand is that we investigate individuals. We don't investigate areas of worship. We have predication for undertaking every investigation we undertake.

He maintained that since the 9/11 attacks, every FBI field office has reached out to the Muslim community and called relations across the country as "exceptionally good."

As for entrapment, the Director said, "There has not been yet to my knowledge a defendant who has been acquitted for asserting the entrapment defense, and that is, in my mind, because we are very careful in these investigations." . . . They are absolutely essential if we are to protect the community against terrorist attacks.

MIRANDA V. ARIZONA AND TERRORISM SUSPECTS

LO 8   Before we discuss *Miranda v. Arizona* (1966) in counterterrorism and counterintelligence investigations, recall three important points you've already learned about *Miranda* rights in Chapter 8. First, questioning someone without "mirandizing" her doesn't violate her Fifth Amendment right against self-incrimination. Why not? The U.S. Supreme Court has made clear repeatedly that that right kicks in at trial. *Miranda* is a *prophylactic rule* that excludes using unwarned statements for the sole purpose of deterring police officers from taking advantage of the intimidation inherent in custodial interrogation. Second, the "public safety exception" that the U.S. Supreme Court created in *New York v. Quarles* (1984) applies when "the need for answers to questions in a situation posing a threat to public safety outweighs the need for the rule protecting the privilege against self-incrimination" (657). Finally, even when suspects get the warnings, empirical research demonstrates that most of them talk anyway (Chapter 8).

Two highly publicized *failed* attacks brought *Miranda* and the *public safety exception* into bold relief. On December 25, 2009, Al-Qaeda operative, Umar Farouk Abdulmutallab (the "underwear bomber") attempted to bomb an airplane bound for

Detroit with a bomb he sewed in his underwear. The bomb could've blown a hole in the plane, but the detonator failed, leaving Abdulmutallab's as its only injury. After landing in Michigan, he received pain killers for the burns and confessed to a nurse.

Also, without *Miranda* warnings, he "spoke freely" to the FBI for 50 minutes before he went into surgery. When he woke up from surgery, the FBI "Mirandized" him. He stopped cooperating for several weeks until his family persuaded him to "start talking again."

He did, and "has not stopped," two government agents said. The officials declined to say exactly what they learned, only that "it was aiding in the investigation of the attempted terrorist attack." According to FBI Director, Robert S. Mueller III, "Mr. Abdulmutallab had provided valuable intelligence," but he did not elaborate. A law enforcement official said that "they had offered no plea bargain in exchange for Abdulmutallab's cooperation" (Zelaney and Savage 2010).

On May 1, 2010, Faisal Shahzad attempted to detonate an SUV packed with explosives in Times Square, where he hoped to kill and maim many people. The poorly designed and constructed bomb only "fizzled and smoked." It "failed spectacularly." (Grier 2010). The FBI relied on the *public safety exception* to question Shahzad for "three or four hours" before they warned him. Then, they "Mirandized" him. He waived his rights, and "kept talking" (Bazelon 2010).

A debate erupted immediately over *Miranda* and counterterrorism and counterintelligence cases. Critics contended that declaring these suspects unlawful enemy combatants would have provided a longer time to interrogate the suspects. Former U.S. attorney and New York City mayor Rudolph Giuliani said, "I would not have given him *Miranda* warnings after just a couple of hours of questioning," Mr. Giuliani said. "I would have instead declared him an enemy combatant, asked the president to do that, and at the same time, that would have given us the opportunity to question him for a much longer period of time." The government pointed out that Shahzad continued to talk after he received the warnings, providing the government with both valuable intelligence and enough evidence to lead to Shahzad's guilty plea (Savage 2010).

In the wake of the two cases, the U.S. Department of Justice (2010) reaffirmed its commitment to *Miranda* in a policy memo to the FBI. But, at the same time, it urged agents to interpret the *public safety exception* broadly in terror cases (Figure 15.6).

LO 8

The *public safety* debate erupted again just after 2:49 p.m. on April 15, 2013, near the finish line at the 117th annual Boston Marathon. The marathon is part of Patriot's Day, a Massachusetts holiday that celebrates U.S. patriotism and independence. The Marathon marathon attracts thousands of runners from all over the United States and the world. Family and friends, and tens of thousands of others line the race course to cheer on the runners and enjoy the race. Near the finish line, there are businesses on both sides of the street, including restaurants, a department store, a hotel, and various retail stores. A dense crowd of hundreds of spectators that included both adults and children were was watching runners approach the finish line. That's where Tamerlan Tsarnaev, a U.S. person, and his 19-year-old brother Dzhokhar Tsarnaev, a U.S. citizen, placed, hidden in their backpacks, two IEDs (improvised explosive devices) hidden in their backpacks, which they'd made from widely available common items— "pressure cookers, low explosive powder, shrapnel, adhesive, electronic components, and other materials" (Dzhokhar Tsarnaev Indictment 2013, 7–8). Seconds later, the IEDs exploded, killing Krystle Marie Campbell, Lingzi Lu, and Martin Richard. The explosions also "maimed, burned, and wounded scores of others, and damaged

FIGURE 15.6 Custodial Interrogation for Public Safety and Intelligence Gathering Purposes of Operational Terrorists Inside the United States

Identifying and apprehending suspected terrorists, interrogating them to obtain intelligence about terrorist activities and impending terrorist attacks, and lawfully detaining them so that they do not pose a continuing threat to our communities are critical to protecting the American people. The Department of Justice and the FBI believe that we can maximize our ability to accomplish these objectives by continuing to adhere to FBI policy regarding the use of *Miranda* warnings for custodial interrogation of operational terrorists who are arrested inside the United States:

1. If applicable, agents should ask any and all questions that are reasonably prompted by an immediate concern for the safety of the public or the arresting agents without advising the arrestee of his *Miranda* rights.

2. After all applicable public safety questions have been exhausted, agents should advise the arrestee of his *Miranda* rights and seek a waiver of those rights before any further interrogation occurs, absent exceptional circumstances described below.

3. There may be exceptional cases in which, although all relevant public safety questions have been asked, agents nonetheless conclude that continued unwarned interrogation is necessary to collect valuable and timely intelligence not related to any immediate threat, and that the government's interest in obtaining this intelligence outweighs the disadvantages of proceeding with unwarned interrogation.

The determination whether particular unwarned questions are justified on public safety grounds must always be made on a case-by-case basis based on all the facts and circumstances. In light of the magnitude and complexity of the threat often posed by terrorist organizations, particularly international terrorist organizations, and the nature of their attacks, the circumstances surrounding an arrest of an operational terrorist may warrant significantly more extensive public safety interrogation without *Miranda* warnings than would be permissible in an ordinary criminal case. Depending on the facts, such interrogation might include, for example, questions about possible impending or coordinated terrorist attacks; the location, nature, and threat posed by weapons that might post pose an imminent danger to the public; and the identities, locations, and activities or intentions of accomplices who may be plotting additional imminent attacks.

. . . If there is time to consult with FBI-HQ (including OGC) and Department of Justice attorneys regarding the interrogation strategy to be followed prior to reading the defendant his *Miranda* rights, the field office should endeavor to do so. Nevertheless, the agents on the scene who are interacting with the arrestee are in the best position to assess what questions are necessary to secure their safety and the safety of the public, and how long the post-arrest interview can practically be delayed while interrogation strategy is being discussed.

Source: U.S. Department of Justice, Federal Bureau of Investigation, October 21, 2010, "Custodial Interrogation for Public Safety and Intelligence-Gathering Purposes of Operational Terrorists Inside the United States."

public and private property owned by people and businesses . . . where the explosions occurred" (Indictment, 3).

Three days later, at about 8:45 p.m., the Tsarnaev brothers, armed with five IEDs, a Ruger P95 semiautomatic handgun, ammunition for the Ruger, a machete, and a hunting knife, drove their Honda Civic to MIT in Cambridge. At about 10:25 p.m., they "murdered Sean Collier, an MIT Police Officer, by shooting him in the head at close range with the Ruger P95, and attempted to steal his service weapon" (Indictment, 9–10).

At about 11:00 p.m. the same night, the brothers "car-jacked D.M.'s leased Mercedes ML350 by pointing a gun and threatening to kill him" (10). They told him they intended to drive his vehicle to Manhattan. Then, they "forced D.M." to drive them to retrieve a portable GPS device from their Honda Civic,; then to a gas station to fill the Mercedes's gas tank. Then, they forced D.M. to hand over his ATM card and PIN, which they used to withdraw $800 from D.M.'s Bank of America ATM account "against his will" (Indictment, 10).

On April 19, shortly after midnight, D.M. escaped from the Mercedes and called 911. Officers located the brothers and tried to apprehend them. The Tsarnaevs fired at and used four IEDs against the pursuing officers. After they attempting attempted to "shoot, bomb, and kill or disable" the officers, three officers tackled Tamerlan. But the brothers didn't give up. Tamerlan struggled against the officers; Dzhokhar got back in the Mercedes and drove it straight at the three officers. He barely missed Sergeant Jeffrey Pugliese, who was attempting to drag Tamerlan to safety. The Mercedes struck Tamerlan, seriously injuring him and contributing to his death. Dzhokhar also struck and seriously injured Officer Richard Donahue (Indictment, 11–12).

Two other relevant points from the indictment:

- The Summer 2010 issue of *Inspire*, an online Arabian Al-Qaeda magazine, contains detailed instructions for making IEDs using pressure cookers and the other materials found in the Tsarnaevs' IED (3).

- On April 19, while hiding from police in a dry-docked boat, he Dzhokhar wrote on a wall in the boat: "The U.S. Government is killing our innocent civilians. I can't stand to see such evil go unpunished. We Muslims are one body, you hurt one body, you hurt us all. Now, I don't like killing innocent people, it is forbidden in Islam, but due to said [unintelligible] it is allowed. Stop killing our innocent people and we will stop" (Indictment, 4).

The debate over *Miranda* that erupted as soon as the public learned about the Boston attack; it was a carbon copy of the immediate eruption following the "underwear bomber" and "Times Square bomber" failed attacks. Attorney General Eric Holder quickly reaffirmed the FBI *public safety* policy memo after this intentional act of mass murder, burning, and maiming inspired by extremist views, Al-Qaeda ideology, and practical instructions for building IEDs. (Of course, the government hasn't proved its case beyond a reasonable doubt, and we've not heard from the defense as of this writing.)

We don't know how the case will proceed or its outcome. As I write this on July 8, 2013, as the indictment makes clear, the case is still in the ordinary criminal justice system. And, we *do* know some relevant details about the *public safety* exception. Before the FBI Mirandized Dzhokhar Tsarnaev, and while in the hospital and fading in -and -out of consciousness, he admitted his role in the Boston Marathon bombings. Then, after 16 hours of questioning, to surprised FBI interrogators, U.S. District Magistrate Marianne Bower and a U.S. Attorney's office representative entered Tsarnaev's hospital room and read Tsarnaev his *Miranda* rights. Tsarnaev immediately stopped talking (Ngowi, Jakes, and Matt Apuzzo 2013).

Reaffirming the FBI policy memo, Attorney General Eric Holder told CNN that Bower's "move was totally consistent with the laws that we have. We have a two-day period to question him under the 'public safety' exception. So I think everything was done appropriately, and we got good leads. And appropriate." Critics—from both the political left and right—wasted no time criticizing and praising Magistrate Judge Bower's decision to Mirandize Tsarnaev. Taking aim at Attorney General Holder for not opposing the decision, Rep. Peter King (R-NY) called Judge Bower's decision "disgraceful."

> This was not required by American law. The fact is the FBI was only 16 hours into an interrogation. They had already gotten some significant information, but much more was still not there. Who else was involved? What was his mother's role? Did his father have any role? Where did the radicalization start? How did it start? Are there any other conspirators out there? Who was part of it? Who assisted him in any way?
>
> It is a matter of life and death. I don't know of any case law which says that the magistrate has a right to come into a hospital room and stop an interrogation. And I don't know why the attorney general of the United States consented to that. (CNN 2013)

From the left, Emily Bazelon blogged:

> Dzhokhar Tsarnaev answered questions for 16 hours before he was read the *Miranda* warning that he could remain silent and could ask for a lawyer. Once Tsarnaev was told that, he stopped talking. (So much for the idea that everyone has heard *Miranda* warnings so many times on TV that they have become an empty ritual.) The AP reports that the investigators questioning him were "surprised when a magistrate judge and a representative from the U.S. Attorney's office entered the hospital room." The investigators "had planned to keep questioning him."
>
> Wow. That's bad no matter your point of view. If you think Tsarnaev doesn't deserve the normal protections American law affords criminal suspects, then you'd want the FBI to keep at him as long as they chose. Or if, like me, you're worried about how far the Obama administration's Justice Department has stretched the limited "public safety" exception the Supreme Court has allowed for questioning suspects about ongoing danger without *Miranda* warnings, 16 hours sounds expansive.
>
> Tsarnaev is facing the death penalty. That is the circumstance in which procedural fairness matters the most. Yes, we have to protect ourselves from terrorism. But not by breaking with our traditional respect for the rule of law. (Bazelon 2013)

NATIONAL SECURITY AGENCY (NSA) SURVEILLANCE

LO **9**   The United States has conducted intelligence operations since the days of George Washington. But it wasn't until 1942, after the United States entered World War II, that President Roosevelt appointed the first head if of the Office of Strategic Services (OSS)—the predecessor to the Central Intelligence Agency (CIA). OSS's mandate was to collect and analyze strategic information. OSS was abolished at the end of the war, along with other wartime agencies. Recognizing the need for a Cold War "fully functioning intelligence organization," President Truman signed the National Security Act (NSA) of 1947, which established the CIA.

The CIA has to follow the same rules we've outlined for the FBI. So, like the FBI, the CIA has to ask the Justice Department to apply to the FISC for approval to conduct the surveillance; the FISC has to approve it; and the same minimization rules and gag order provisions apply. We now know considerably more than we did only a few months ago (and we'll certainly know even more by the time you read this) because we're in the midst of the developing stories resulting from the documents Edward Snowden leaked (or blew the whistle on, depending on which side of the debate you're on) to the *Guardian* and *The Washington Post*. Snowden is one of a rapidly growing group of intelligence analysts working for the intelligence industry contracted by the government. This industry, which has mushroomed since 9/11, includes large corporations like Snowden's employer, Booze Allen. Snowden was able to leak/blow the whistle with secret documents because he had security clearance above top secret.

The information Snowden released has reignited an old debate about the U.S. government spying on its own people. Spying on foreigners doesn't trouble most Americans much, but they get really bothered when the government targets U.S. persons. That's what's at the heart of the debate—spying on U.S. persons. The program most involved is PRISM, which collects information about users from the servers of these popular U.S. ISPs: Yahoo, Google, Facebook, Pal Talk, AOL, Skype, YouTube, Apple, and Verizon.

The secret order to Verizon is reproduced in Figure 15.7.

FIGURE 15.7 FBI Application for FISC Order Requiring Verizon to Produce Daily Copies of "Telephony Metadata"

APPENDIX A

UNITED STATES

FOREIGN INTELLIGENCE SURVEILLANCE

COURT

WASHINGTON, D.C.

Docket Number: BR 13-80

IN RE APPLICATION OF THE FEDERAL BUREAU OF INVESTIGATION FOR AN ORDER REQUIRING THE PRODUCTION OF TANGIBLE THINGS FROM VERIZON BUSINESS NETWORK SERVICES, INC. ON BEHALF OF MCI COMMUNICATION SERVICES, INC. D/B/A VERIZON BUSINESS SERVICES.

<u>SECONDARY ORDER</u>

This Court having found that the Application of the Federal Bureau of Investigation (FBI) for an Order requiring the production of tangible things from Verizon Business Network Services, Inc. on behalf of MCI Communication Services Inc., d/b/a Verizon Business Services (individually and collectively "Verizon") satisfies the requirements of 50 U.S.C. § 1861,

IT IS HEREBY ORDERED that, the Custodian of Records shall produce to the National Security Agency (NSA) upon service of this Order, and continue production on an ongoing

(continued)

FIGURE 15.7 *(Continued)*

daily basis thereafter for the duration of this Order, unless otherwise ordered by the Court, an electronic copy of the following tangible things: all call detail records or "telephony metadata" created by Verizon for communications (i) between the United States and abroad; or (ii) wholly within the United States, including local telephone calls. This Order does not require Verizon to produce telephony metadata for communications wholly originating and terminating in foreign countries. Telephony metadata includes comprehensive communications routing information, including but not limited to session identifying information (e.g., originating and terminating telephone number, International Mobile Subscriber Identity (IMSI) number, International Mobile station Equipment Identity (IMEI) number, etc.), trunk identifier, telephone calling card numbers, and time and duration of call. Telephony metadata does not include the substantive content of any communication, as defined by 18 U.S.C. § 2510(8), or the name, address, or financial information of a subscriber or customer.

IT IS FURTHER ORDERED that no person shall disclose to any other person that the FBI or NSA has sought or obtained tangible things under this Order, other than to: (a) those persons to whom disclosure is necessary to comply with such Order; (b) an attorney to obtain legal advice or assistance with respect to the production of things in response to the Order; or (c) other persons as permitted by the Director of the FBI or the Director's designee. A person to whom disclosure is made pursuant to (a), (b), or (c) shall be subject to the nondisclosure requirements applicable to a person to whom an Order is directed in the same manner as such person. Anyone who discloses to a person described in (a), (b), or (c) that the FBI or NSA has sought or obtained tangible things pursuant to this Order shall notify such person of the nondisclosure requirements of this Order. At the request of the Director of the FBI or the designee of the Director, any person making or intending to make a disclosure under (a) or (c) above shall identify to the Director or such designee the person to whom such disclosure will be made or to whom such disclosure was made prior to the request.

IT IS FURTHER ORDERED that service of this Order shall be by a method agreed upon by the Custodian of Records of Verizon and the FBI, and if no agreement is reached, service shall be personal.

— Remainder of page intentionally left blank. —

This authorization requiring the production of certain call detail records or "telephony metadata" created by Verizon expires on the 19th day of July, 2013, at 5:00 p.m., Eastern Time.

Signed 04-25-2013 P02:26 Eastern Time
/s/ ROGER VINSON

Roger Vinson
Judge, United States Foreign Intelligence
Surveillance Court

/s/ I, Beverly C. Queen, Chief Deputy Clerk, FISC, certify that this document is a true and correct copy of the original.

Source: Borrowed from EPIC (Electronic Privacy Information Center, an online privacy advocacy group). (July 25, 2013)

The NSA has said for years that global surveillance apparatus is only aimed at foreigners, and that ordinary Americans are only captured by accident. There's only one problem with this longstanding contention: people who've worked within the system say it's more or less technically impossible to keep average Americans out of the surveillance driftnet. "There is physically no way to collect data on foreign targets," said a telecommunications executive who has implemented U.S. government orders to collect data on foreign targets. "The system doesn't make any distinction about the nationality of the individual who sent the message." (Harris 2013)

Harris adds that "while it's technically true that NSA is not 'targeting' the communications of Americans without a warrant, this is a narrow and legalistic statement. It belies the vast and indiscriminate scooping up of records on Americans' phone calls, e-mails, and Internet communications that has occurred for more than a decade under the cover of 'foreign intelligence' gathering." A significant part of this secretly gathered information is "incidental," not intentional. U.S. persons' communications "just happen to be in the way when foreigners' data is scooped up."

But should we relax because it's not done on purpose? If not, maybe a central concept running through a number of FISC opinions should give us comfort: Just collecting even huge volumes of metadata (say, the time and numbers of phone calls dialed but not the conversations) about U.S. persons doesn't violate their rights. If the government takes the next step—recording or listening to what U.S. persons are saying—is it has to establish a valid reason. One official put it this way, "The basic idea is that it's O.K. to create this huge pond of data, but you have to establish a reason to stick your pole in the water and start fishing" (Lichtbleau 2013).

Furthermore, it's in our interest to collect all this information if it prevents attacks on the U.S. homeland. That might be what newly appointed NSA head, General Keith Alexander had in mind in late 2005 when he said

Rather than look for a single needle in the haystack . . . let's collect the whole haystack. Collect it all, tag it, store it. . . . And whatever it is you want, go searching for it. (Nakashima and Warrick 2013)

That was about the time Iraqi roadside IEDs were reaching an all-time high. "More than 100 teams of U.S. analysts were scouring for snippets of electronic data that might lead to the bomb makers and their hidden factories. But Alexander wanted more—every Iraqui text message, phone call and e-mail that could be vacuumed up by the agency's powerful computers." Called "Real Time Regional Gateway," *Washington Post* journalists reported that it "would play a role in breaking up Iraqui insurgent groups and significantly reducing the monthly death toll from IEDs by late 2008" (Nakashima and Warrick).

Supporters say General Alexander "is animated by a spymaster's awareness of serious, overlapping threats arrayed against the United States. They include foreign and homegrown terrorists. They also include a host of adversaries who are constantly probing the country's cyberdefenses, looking for opportunities to steal secrets or unleash mayhem by shutting down critical infrastructure." General Alexander says he believes that "you have to do everything you can to protect civil liberties and privacy." But, he warns, "Everyone also understands that if we give up a capability that is critical to the defense of this nation, people will die" (Nakashima and Warrick).

In our next case excerpt, *In re Electronic Privacy Information (EPIC)*, EPIC petitioned the U.S. Supreme Court to review an NSL that its ISP Verizon Communications received, following an FISC order.

Should the U.S. Supreme Court review the FISC order?

CASE

In re Electronic Privacy Information Center (EPIC).

Supreme Court of the United States

Congress enacted the Foreign Intelligence Surveillance Act to authorize and regulate certain governmental electronic surveillance of communications for foreign intelligence purposes. In the act, Congress authorized judges of the Foreign Intelligence Surveillance Court (FISC) to approve electronic surveillance for foreign intelligence purposes.

STATUTE INVOLVED

The Foreign Intelligence Surveillance Act (FISA) authorizes certain governmental surveillance of communications for foreign intelligence purposes.

1. 50 U.S.C. §§ 1801 *et. seq.* (2012). Section 1861 allows the FBI to apply to the FISC for an order to compel production of "tangible things". . ." . . . for an investigation to obtain foreign intelligence information not concerning a United States person or to protect against international terrorism or clandestine intelligence activities."

2. 50 U.S.C. § 1861(a)(1) ("Access to certain business records for foreign intelligence and international terrorism investigations."). The application must include a statement of facts showing "that there are reasonable grounds to believe that the tangible things sought are relevant to an authorized investigation."

3. 50 U.S.C. § 1861(b)(2)(A), and an enumeration of the minimization guidelines adopted by the Attorney General. 50 U.S.C. § 1861(b)(2)(B). If the application meets these statutory requirements, the FISC "shall enter an ex parte order as requested, or as modified, approving the release of tangible things." 50 U.S.C. § 1861(c)(1).

FACTS
BACKGROUND

Petitioner EPIC is a non-profit public interest research center in Washington, D.C. EPIC was established in 1994 to focus public attention on emerging civil liberties issues and to protect privacy, the First Amendment, and other constitutional values. EPIC is also a Verizon customer, and has been for the entire period the FISC Order has been in effect. Because the FISC Order compels disclosure of "all call detail records," FISC Order [Figure 15.7], page 2, detailed information about all of EPIC's telephone communications, including the numbers dialed and when calls occurred, have been disclosed to the NSA.

In furtherance of its mission to protect privacy and advocate for civil liberties, EPIC engages in several activities involving telephonic communications. EPIC files Freedom of Information Act ("FOIA") requests with federal agencies and pursues those requests with litigation as needed. These requests are typically sent via facsimile over EPIC's Verizon business line. EPIC is currently engaged in multiple FOIA lawsuits, including one against the NSA, two against the FBI, one against the Office of the Director of National Intelligence (ODNI), and two against the Department of Justice ("DOJ").

EPIC attorneys use EPIC's telephones to conduct privileged attorney-client communications regarding ongoing legal proceedings. EPIC also petitions for, comments on, and litigates federal agency rulemakings under the Administrative Procedure Act. EPIC's petition initiatives involve communicating telephonically with consumers, advisers, coalition members, and executive and legislative branch officials.

EPIC also engages in policy advocacy through formal and informal consultations with various parties via telephone. EPIC provides expert advice to Members of Congress regarding oversight and legislation, and consults with federal agencies on regulatory proposals and enforcement. In many cases, discussions with U.S. officials are conducted confidentially to facilitate a deliberative process. In addition, EPIC gives interviews and background briefings with news media, sometimes in a confidential, "off the record" capacity. All of these activities require communication via telephone.

Following the public disclosure of the Verizon Order, EPIC learned that the NSA had obtained vast amounts of call detail information and breached the confidentiality of its privileged and confidential communications.

This petition followed.

ARGUMENT

EPIC seeks a writ of mandamus to review the order of Judge Roger Vinson, United States Foreign Intelligence Surveillance Court ("FISC"), requiring Verizon Business Network Services ("Verizon") to produce to the National Security Agency ("NSA") call detail records, or "telephony metadata," for all calls wholly within the United States. Mandamus relief is warranted because the FISC exceeded its statutory jurisdiction when it ordered production of millions of domestic telephone records that cannot plausibly be relevant to an authorized investigation. EPIC is a Verizon customer subject to the order. Because of the structure of the Foreign Intelligence Surveillance Act ("FISA"), no other court may grant the relief that EPIC seeks.

On April 25, 2013, the FISC compelled the ongoing disclosure of all call detail records in the possession of a U.S. telecommunications firm for analysis by the National Security Agency. The FISC exceeded its statutory authority when it issued this order. To compel production of "tangible things," the FISA requires the items sought be "relevant" to an authorized investigation. 50 U.S.C. § 1861(b)(2)(A). It is simply not possible that every phone record in the possession of a telecommunications firm could be relevant to an authorized investigation. Such an interpretation of Section 1861 would render meaningless the qualifying phrases contained in the provision and eviscerate the purpose of the Act.

The Verizon Order approved by the FISC implicates the privacy interests of all Verizon customers, including petitioner EPIC, a non-profit organization that engages in protected attorney-client communications as it pursues litigation to safeguard privacy. Verizon Communications provides services over "America's most advanced fiber-optic network" and operates "America's largest 4G wireless network." It operates the "[n]ation's largest all-fiber network serving residential and small-business customers," handling an "[a]verage of 1 billion calls connected per day." Fact Sheet, Verizon (2012).]

However, the FISA does not allow Verizon customers, including, EPIC, to challenge the order or seek review of the order before the FISC or Foreign Intelligence Surveillance Court of Review ("Court of Review"). Consequently, EPIC can only obtain relief with a writ of mandamus from this Court. Mandamus is an extraordinary remedy, but the Verizon Order carries extraordinary ramifications.

The records acquired by the NSA under this Order detail the daily activities, interactions, personal and business relationships, religious and political affiliations, and other intimate details of millions of Americans. "Awareness that the Government may be watching chills associational and expressive freedoms. And the Government's unrestrained power to assemble data that reveal private aspects of identity is susceptible to abuse." *United States v. Jones*, 132 S. Ct. 945, 956 (2012) (Sotomayor, J., concurring). As Justice Breyer has recently noted, "the Government has the capacity to conduct electronic surveillance of the kind at issue." And because the NSA sweeps up judicial and Congressional communications, it inappropriately arrogates exceptional power to the Executive Branch.

The plain terms of FISA and the rules of the FISC bar EPIC from seeking relief before the FISC or Court of Review. The FISC may only review business record orders

upon petition from the recipient or the Government. Further, review of FISC orders and denials is also limited. Only the Government or the recipient of a business record order may petition for an *en banc* rehearing by the FISC. The Court of Review only has jurisdiction to review denials of business record applications, and decisions. EPIC is not recipient of a Business Records order, but rather EPIC's communications are subject to the FISC order. As a result, the FISC and Court of Review have no jurisdiction to grant EPIC the relief it seeks.

No other court has the power to vacate the FISC Order. Other federal and state trial and appellate courts have no jurisdiction over the FISC. The FISC order is outside the jurisdiction of federal district and circuit courts. Only this Court, the Court of Review, and the FISC are empowered to consider petitions to affirm, modify, or set aside a FISA Business Records order. As a result, EPIC cannot petition an inferior federal court to vacate the unlawful FISC Order.

Any alternative relief that EPIC could seek is directly limited by this order. Both Verizon and the government agents executing this order are granted immunities based on the presumed validity of a court order. Furthermore, the parties to the FISC Order do not serve EPIC's interests and their right to petition for review does not provide adequate oversight to the judge's unlawful FISC Order. EPIC can only prevent the application of this unlawful order by having it vacated by this Court.

Writs of mandamus in aid of appellate jurisdiction are traditionally used to confine a lower court to the lawful exercise of its jurisdiction. Such a jurisdictional correction is required here: the FISC issued an order requiring disclosure of records for all telephone communications "wholly within the United States, including local telephone calls." The Business Records provision does not enable this type of domestic programmatic surveillance. Specifically, the statute requires that production orders be supported by "reasonable grounds to believe that the tangible things sought are relevant to an authorized investigation. . . ."

"Reasonable grounds" is not defined in the statute, but it has been treated as equivalent to "reasonable suspicion." "Reasonable suspicion" requires a showing of "specific and articulable facts, which, taken together with rational inferences from those facts, reasonably warrant" intrusion into a suspect's privacy. *Terry v. Ohio*, 392 (1968) [Chapter 4, p.107] Given that the FISC Order commands disclosure of *all* domestic telephone records, it is acutely implausible that the FBI alleged specific and articulable facts about each of Verizon's millions of customers.

It is simply unreasonable to conclude that all telephone records *for all Verizon customers in the United States* could be relevant to an investigation. Thus, the FISC simply had no judicial power to do what it purported to do.

What makes a tangible thing "relevant" to an authorized investigation is likewise not clearly delineated in the statute. However, in accordance with the foreign

(continued)

intelligence purposes of FISA, the Act says that tangible things are "presumptively relevant" if they pertain to

(i) a foreign power or an agent of a foreign power;

(ii) the activities a suspected agent of a foreign power who is the subject of such authorized investigation; or

(iii) an individual in contact with, or known to, a suspected agent of a foreign power who is the subject of such authorized investigation[.]

Common sense dictates that the vast majority of Verizon's customers will not fall into any of these three categories. Consequently, the vast majority of the telephone records conveyed to the NSA will not be presumptively relevant. The burden is therefore on the FBI to show, with specific and articulable facts, why those records are in fact relevant and should be included in the production order.

Moreover, the scope of the request cannot simply encompass all call records in the database. To define the scope of the records sought as "everything" nullifies the relevance limitation in the statute. If law enforcement has "everything," there will always be some subset of "everything" that is relevant to something. At that level of breadth, the relevance requirement becomes meaningless.

In addition to showing a sufficient factual predicate, the FBI's investigation must also be conducted under guidelines approved by the Attorney General under Executive Order 12333. The Executive Order emphasizes the need to limit the scope of domestic surveillance. The United States Government has a solemn obligation, and shall continue in the conduct of intelligence activities under this order, to protect fully the legal rights of all United States persons, including freedoms, civil liberties, and privacy rights guaranteed by Federal law.

In particular, Executive Order 12333 requires intelligence agencies to "use the least intrusive collection techniques feasible within the United States or directed at U.S. persons abroad." The unbounded collection and review of the call detail records of all Americans is plainly not "the least intrusive technique feasible." It is difficult to conceive of any surveillance technique more intrusive than acquiring all communications records on all persons concerning all matters.

Finally, reading § 1861 in the context of the FISA as a whole, it becomes clear that this section is not meant to authorize the ongoing programmatic collection of telephone records. The FISC order for the ongoing production of detailed telephone records, concerning solely domestic communications, went far beyond the authority set out in the Act. The FISC is required by FISA to approve applications that meet the statutory requirements and deny applications that fail to meet those requirements. By approving this statutorily deficient application, the FISC exceeded its lawful authority.

Telephony metadata can be directly linked to each user's identity and reveal their contacts, clients, associates, and even the physical location. The FISC Order specifies that "[t]elephony metadata includes comprehensive communications routing information, including but not limited to session identifying information (*e.g.*, originating and terminating telephone number, International Mobile Subscriber Identity (IMSI) number, International Mobile station Equipment Identity (IMEI) number, etc.), trunk identifier, telephone calling card numbers, and time and duration of call."

Routing information refers to "the path or method to be used for establishing telephone connections or forwarding messages." Routing information therefore encompasses all information about the path of the telephone call, including the cell sites or switching stations used to complete the call. IMSI and IMEI numbers are both unique identifiers related to mobile telephony. The IMSI number is a unique number used to identify a subscriber to a mobile network. ATIS – IMSI Oversight Council, *Frequently Asked Questions*. Finally, "trunk identifier" could refer to a number that uniquely identifies a group of communications channels or to the "trunk code" used to identify the home network or area inside a country where a call is to be routed.

Because the routing information details the path taken by a call, it can be used to identify the location of the parties to the call. The connections made between an individual's mobile phone and the antennas in a service provider's network can be used to track location over time.

The FISC Order also compels disclosure of personally identifiable information. Telephone numbers, IMSI numbers, and IMEI numbers are unique and can be used to identify individuals. The NSA maintains a database of "telephone numbers and electronic communications accounts / addresses / identifiers that NSA has reason to believe are being used by United States Persons." These numbers collected under the FISC Order can be easily matched with the records maintained in the NSA identifying database. In fact, the NSA uses this matching process to "prevent the inadvertent targeting of a United States person" under directives issued pursuant to Section 702 of FISA.

Because telephone numbers identify individuals, they are protected as personal information under federal law. The telephony metadata obtained under the FISC Order is used by the NSA to create maps of an individual's social connections. These social maps contain information about users' private contacts and associations. This process is referred to as "contact chaining," and it is used to structure and catalog the telephony metadata held by the NSA.

Contact chaining allows the agency to automatically identify not only the first tier of contacts made by the seed telephone number or e-mail address, but also the further contacts made by the first tier of telephone numbers or e-mail addresses and so on. So if the NSA was investigating Bob's telephone records, and saw he called Jane, the NSA would then collect and examine all of Jane's telephone records. If they saw that Jane called Steve, they would then collect and examine all of Steve's telephone records. Contact chaining was specifically designed as a means to analyze the communications metadata of U.S. persons. *Id.* at 2.20 But this process also gives rise to combinatorial explosion, permitting the creation of enormous data sets containing personal information completed unrelated to the purpose of the investigation.

The practical use of telephone numbers to identify individuals is well understood. In 2006, Senator Joe Biden told CBS News that "I don't have to listen to your phone calls to know what you're doing. If I know every single phone call you made, I'm able to determine every single person you talked to. I can get a pattern about your life that is very, very intrusive." (*The Early Show* CBS News broadcast, May 12, 2006).

And if all call record information is relevant under the FISA, then other categories of business records could also be obtained in bulk under the statute.

The FISC Order mandates that Verizon produce data about EPIC's confidential attorney-client relationships and other privileged information. The privacy of such communications is essential to the "public interests in the observance of law and administration of justice." EPIC frequently files Freedom of Information Act ("FOIA") requests with federal agencies and pursues those requests with litigation when necessary. At present, EPIC is in litigation with both the NSA and FBI, the two agencies responsible for tracking Americans' private communications under this order. Additionally, EPIC has ongoing FOIA lawsuits against other elements of the Intelligence Community, including the Office of the Director of National Intelligence and the Central Intelligence Agency.

At the FISC's command, Verizon is turning over EPIC's privileged information to the very parties capable of exploiting that information. The court's order hampers EPIC's ability to deliberate and develop litigation strategies "free from the consequences or the apprehension of disclosure." Courts consider a threat to attorney-client communications an exceptional circumstance and have issued writs of mandamus to vacate production orders implicating privileged information. In this case, the FISC issued a blanket order for all domestic telephone records. Such a boundless order sweeps up not just communications protected by attorney-client privilege, but also those falling under marital communications privilege, psychiatrist-patient privilege, accountant-client privilege, and clergy-penitent privilege.

EPIC's ability to engage in open dialogue with the public, coalition members, and colleagues in government, non-government, and the private sector is protected by the First Amendment doctrines of freedom of association and freedom of speech. As described above, EPIC communicates regularly with coalition groups, international organizations, consumers, and government representatives. Members of EPIC's staff give telephone interviews to reporters and journalists, speak to members of Congress who seek expert opinions on privacy issues, and consult with other advocates about privacy law and policy. Many of these conversations are conducted with the expectation that they will remain confidential, to protect the deliberative process of those with whom EPIC consults.

This Court has frequently recognized the importance of preserving the First Amendment rights of advocacy groups. In *N.A.A.C.P. v. Alabama* (1958), this Court explained why the protection of privacy is of Constitutional concern for advocacy organizations:

> It is hardly a novel perception that compelled disclosure of affiliation with groups engaged in advocacy may constitute an effective restraint on freedom of association as the forms of governmental action in the cases above were thought likely to produce upon the particular constitutional rights there involved. . . . This Court has recognized the vital relationship between freedom to associate and privacy in one's associations. . . . Inviolability of privacy in group association may in many circumstances be indispensable to preservation of freedom of association, particularly where a group espouses dissident beliefs.

Because of the confidential, candid nature of EPIC's consultations with various parties, NSA's surveillance chills EPIC's ability to advocate. "Freedoms such as these are protected not only against heavy-handed frontal attack, but also from being stifled by more subtle governmental interference" (*Id.* at 523.) A non-profit advocacy group engaging in political speech must be able to have private telephone communications without fear of constant monitoring by the government. The NSA does not need the contents of communications to stifle EPIC's advocacy. The metadata alone is sufficient to identify who has been talking to EPIC and to chill those communications and associations. *See United States v. Jones*, 132 S. Ct. 945, 956 (2012) (Sotomayor, J., concurring) "Awareness that the Government may be watching chills associational and expressive freedoms."

Questions

1. Identify exactly what FISC ordered Verizon to do.
2. Identify and summarize the statutes EPIC claims that the FISC order violates.
3. Summarize EPIC's facts and arguments in its petition to the U.S. Supreme Court.
4. Should the U.S. Supreme Court should grant EPIC's petition to review the FISC order? Support your answer with the information in your answers to questions 1–3.

TRYING TERRORISM DEFENDANTS

LO **10**   Suspected terrorists can be tried in two kinds of proceedings: ordinary courts or special military courts. The ordinary courts are called **Article III courts** because their authority comes from Article III of the U.S. Constitution, which created the judiciary. These trials include crimes against the state (such as treason and sedition); "ordinary crimes" (such as murder and rape); and terrorism-related crimes included in the U.S. Criminal Code. Suspected terrorists can also be tried for **war crimes** (such as fighting for al Al-Qaeda or the Taliban) by special military courts called military commissions. Military commissions are also sometimes known as military tribunals. In the following sections, we'll examine trial by federal Article III courts and trial by military commissions.

LO **10**   ## Trials in U.S. Federal Courts

Between September 11, 2001 and June 2, 2009, Article III courts dealt with 289 terrorism defendants; 214 had the charges against them resolved. Of those 214, 195 (91 percent) were found guilty of at least one offense related to terrorism; 19 (9 percent) were acquitted. Figure 15.8 shows the outcome of those trials, the rates, and types of conviction (Zabel and Benjamin 2009, 12).

In addition to these defendants, President Obama's Guantanamo Review Task Force has referred 44 of the remaining 240 detainees at Guantanamo for prosecution either in federal court or by a military commission (Final Report 2010, ii). The Task Force followed the guidelines for federal prosecutors to determine whether to charge a case. According to the guidelines, "[A] case should be recommended for prosecution if the detainee's conduct constitutes a federal offense and the potentially available admissible evidence will probably be sufficient to obtain and sustain a conviction" (Final Report 7–8).

FIGURE 15.8 Outcomes in Terrorism Cases in Federal Courts by Disposition Type

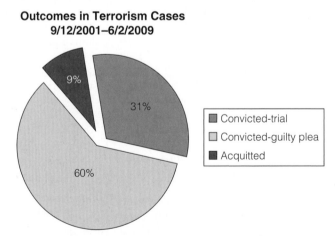

Source: Richard Zabel and James Benjamin, Jr., 2009 (July), *In Pursuit of Justice: Prosecuting Cases in the Federal Courts* (Washington, D.C.: Human Rights First, p. 12). http://www.humanrightsfirst.org.

Key factors in the determination include:

- The nature and seriousness of the offense
- The detainee's culpability in the offense
- The detainee's willingness to cooperate in the investigation or prosecution of others
- The probable sentence or other consequences if the detainee is convicted (8)

The federal courts have imposed severe sentences on defendants convicted of crimes related to terrorism, whether by trial or guilty plea. This is based on the special provision in the U.S. Sentencing Guidelines (U.S. Sentencing Guidelines Manual 2009, §3A1.4) for those convicted of the federal crime of terrorism. This section automatically triggers a range of 210 to 262 months for defendants convicted of a crimes that "involved, or was intended to promote, a federal crime of terrorism." A federal crime of terrorism "means an offense that is calculated to influence or affect the conduct of government by intimidation or coercion, or to retaliate against government conduct" (U.S. Criminal Code 2009, §2332(g)(5)).

In *U.S. v. Benkala* (2008), for example, the U.S. Fourth Circuit Court of Appeals affirmed Sabri Benkala's sentence of 121 months. According to the court:

> Benkala was part of a network of people the government was investigating for crimes connected to radical Islamic terrorism and violent jihad. The FBI questioned him and prosecutors twice called him before grand juries. Then he was prosecuted himself for false declarations, false statements, and obstructing justice. (303)

LO 10 Trials by Military Commission

Now, let's look at the relaxed rules of procedure and proof and the diminished rights for defendants that apply to military commissions. A **military commission** consists of a panel of military officers acting under military authority to try enemy combatants for war crimes—acts committed during wartime that inflict "needless and disproportionate suffering and damages" in pursuit of a "military objective." (Don't confuse military commissions with **military courts-martial**, which are also made up of military officers, but they try members of U.S. armed forces for violating the Uniform Code of Military Justice) (Elsea 2001, 7, 16).

The Military Order of November 13, 2001 (Presidential Documents 2001 [Nov. 16], 57831–36) spells out the rules governing military commissions to try suspected terrorists. Let's look at the main points in the Military Order that are relevant to military commissions: the source and the jurisdiction of their authority and the trial proceedings before them.

1. *The Sources of Military Commission Authority.*

   The president bases his authority to establish military commissions on three sources:

   The U.S. Constitution, Article II, Section 2, makes the president the "commander in chief" of the armed forces. As commander in chief, he's responsible for trying terrorists.

Article II, Section 2, also imposes responsibility on the president to "take care that the laws shall be faithfully executed." In this case, according to the Military Order, the laws include trying war crimes under the Articles of War and the Authorization for Use of Military Force, passed by a joint resolution of Congress on September 14, 2001. The joint resolution authorized the president to use "all necessary and appropriate force against those nations, organizations, or persons he determines planned, authorized, committed, or aided" or "harbored" them.

2. *The Jurisdiction of Military Commissions.*

The provisions of the order apply only to "certain non-citizens in the war against terrorism" (Presidential Documents 2001 [Nov. 16], 57833). This means the military commission's authority only applies to noncitizens. Here's how Section 2 of the order defines noncitizens and outlines restrictions on their rights, including taking away the power (jurisdiction) of ordinary courts to review military commission decisions regarding them:

[A]ny individual who is not a United States citizen with respect to whom I determine from time to time in writing that:

1. there is reason to believe that such individual, at the relevant times,

2. is or was a member of the organization known as al Qaida;

3. has engaged in, aided or abetted, or conspired to commit, acts of international terrorism, or acts in preparation therefor, that have caused, threaten to cause, or have as their aim to cause, injury to or adverse effects on the United States, its citizens, national security, foreign policy, or economy; or

4. has knowingly harbored one or more individuals described in subparagraphs (i) or (ii) of subsection 2(a)(1) of this order; and

5. it is in the interest of the United States that such individual be subject to this order. (57834)

As noncitizens, the individuals the order applies to don't "necessarily enjoy the same constitutional rights as citizens" even if they're legally in the country. During wartime, aliens of enemy nations can be detained and deported, and their property can be confiscated. "They may also be denied access to the courts of the United States if they would use the courts to the advantage of the enemy or to impede the U.S. prosecution of a war" (Elsea 2001, 28–29).

3. *Trial Proceedings of Military Commissions.*

Military commissions aren't bound by the constitutional requirements that apply to ordinary (Article III) courts. *But,* that doesn't mean they ignore defendants' rights. On April 27, 2010, the Department of Defense released new rules governing the military commission proceedings (U.S. Manual for Military Commissions 2010). Here's a list of key provisions:

1. Provides defendants in capital cases the right to at least one additional lawyer who's an expert on the law relating to death penalty cases (under the old rules, defendants in capital cases had no such right)

2. Permits evidence derived from statements obtained by cruel, inhumane, and degrading treatment if "use of such evidence would otherwise be consistent with the interests of justice" (unlike courts-martial and regular federal courts)

3. Continues to permit defendants to be tried ex-post facto for conduct not considered to constitute a war crime at the time it was committed, such as material support for terrorism

LO 10 Debate: Military Commissions versus Trial in U.S. Federal Courts

The debate centers around two stark views—terrorist-attacks-as-war and terrorism as crime. The strongest **terrorist-acts-as-war view** is that getting tough on terrorism calls for trying all foreign suspects by military commissions. At the other end is the **terrorist-acts-as-crime view**, whose supporters argue that we should abolish military commissions, and treat and try those who commit terrorist acts in U.S. criminal courts. Let's look at the arguments on each side of this debate.

1. *Terrorist Acts as War.*

   Andrew C. McCarthy (Weiser 2010), as a U.S. Attorney, started out a staunch supporter of the terrorist-acts-as-crime view. McCarthy was the "lead prosecutor in one of the country's biggest terrorism trials" in Article III courts, the 1995 trial of the blind sheik who led a group of men in a plot to blow up the United Nations, the Lincoln and Holland Tunnels, and other New York City landmarks. At that trial, he asked the jury in the Manhattan federal court, "Are you ready to surrender the rule of law to the men in this courtroom?"

   After 9/11 he shifted to support the terrorist-acts-as-war view. On December 5, 2009, he declared, "A war is a war. A war is not a crime, and you don't bring your enemies to the courthouse. Will Americans finally grasp how insane it is to regard counterterrorism as a law-enforcement project rather than a matter of national security?"

   Here are a few of McCarthy's main points:

   a. A prosecutor's job isn't national security. We indicted Osama bin Laden; three months later, Al-Qaeda blew up two of our embassies. "I mean we could go into a grand jury and indict him three times a week. But, to do anything about it, you needed the Marines. You didn't need us. In the main, international terrorism is a military problem, not a criminal-justice issue."

   b. Terrorists can use criminal trials as an "intelligence-gathering tool." He refers to a document provided in the discovery process in the 1995 trial in the sheik's case that contained a long list of witnesses.

   c. The country's in a "very bad spot right now," and he's "doing what I'm supposed to be doing. It just seemed to me like since 9/11 we've been drifting away and away from the moment of clarity we had."

2. *Trials in U.S. Criminal Courts.*

   Former and current national security officials from the Bush and Obama administrations (Savage and Shane 2010) make the following arguments in favor of trials in ordinary courts:

   a. Some nations won't extradite terrorism suspects or provide evidence to the United States except for civilian trials.

   b. Federal courts offer a greater variety of charges for use in pressuring a defendant to cooperate.

   c. Military commission rules don't authorize a judge to accept a guilty plea from a defendant in a capital case.

   d. The military system is legally untested, so any guilty verdict is vulnerable to being overturned on appeal.

   Juan C. Zarate, who served as deputy national security advisor for combating terrorism to President Bush from 2005 to 2009, argues that the government would hamstring itself by outlawing civilian terrorism trials. "We shouldn't inadvertently handcuff ourselves by taking this tool completely out of our toolkit."

3. *Keep Both Options.* The same experts who support the terrorism-as-crime view are part of a middle course—keep both options (Savage and Shane 2010):

Juan C. Zarate, President Bush's deputy national security advisor for combating terrorism, 2005–2009, sees the value of military commissions but wants to keep civilian terrorism trials in the "tool kit."

"This rush to military commissions is based on premises that are not true," said John B. Bellinger III, a top legal advisor to the National Security Council and the State Department under President George W. Bush. "I think it is neither appropriate nor necessary to limit terrorism cases to either military commissions alone or federal trials alone."

Kenneth L. Wainstein, who was assistant attorney general for national security in the Bush administration, said, "Denying yourself access to one system in favor of the other could be counterproductive. I see the benefit of having both systems available. That's why I applauded the Obama administration when, despite expectations to the contrary, they decided to retain military commissions. It's good to have flexibility."

The letter that U.S. District Court Judge John C. Coughenour wrote to the U.S. House of Representatives Subcommittee on Crime, Terrorism, and Home land Security, prior to renewing the Patriot Act in 2011, reproduced in Figure 15.9, presents a passionate defense of trying terrorism suspects in Article III courts.

FIGURE 15.9 U.S. District Court Judge John C. Coughener's letter to the U.S. House of Representatives Subcommittee on Crime, Terrorism, and Homeland Security

---

JOHN C. COUGHENOUR, UNITED STATES DISTRICT JUDGE WESTERN DISTRICT OF WASHINGTON

APRIL 5, 2011

Subcommittee on Crime, Terrorism, and Homeland Security Committee on the Judiciary

Hearing on using military commissions to try the 9/11 conspirators Letter for the Record on behalf of the Constitution Project

March 29th, 2011

Dear Members of the Subcommittee on Crime of the House Judiciary Committee,

I am writing in response to a notice of hearing called by Chairman Sensenbrenner to be held on April 5, 2011 on the subject of using military commissions to try the 9/11 conspirators. I request that my letter be made a part of the record for this hearing.

I have earned my stripes on this topic. The case of Ahmed Ressam, aka the Millennium Bomber, involved months of trial, three trips to the Ninth Circuit, and one trip to the Supreme Court. In the years since, I have repeatedly argued that the use of military commissions to try these cases is a mistake. They have been slow and ineffective, resulting in only four convictions—and two of those defendants have already been released. They have the potential to elevate ordinary criminals to the status of symbolic warrior-martyrs. They are vulnerable to appeal and reversal. And they limit the willingness and ability of foreign governments to extradite suspects and provide us with evidence.

Supporters of military commissions point to the supposed problems with traditional Article III courts, but these are empty worries.

First, they tell you that a trial or sentencing in an Article III court is prohibitively expensive. The Marshal's Service informed me after the Ressam Trial that the total cost of security was under $100,000. A large part of the opposition to Article III trials in the Southern District of New York is the notion that the city would be left with the tab. It is my understanding that the City of Los Angeles and the Los Angeles Police Department did not spend a dollar on security during the Ressam trial.

Second, they say that we cannot risk bringing these dangerous people to jails and prisons in the United States. But we already have hundreds of accused and convicted terrorists being held in federal prisons inside the United States, and there has not been a single instance where national security has been impacted by their presence in our Bureau of Prisons.

Next, they tell you that such trials will give a defendant an opportunity to spout hateful propaganda. But some of the most memorable moments in this conflict, when I have been most proud to be a judge, have been the showdowns between these men and the judges they face. Remember the words of Judge Bill Young, who closed his sentencing of Richard Reid with these words: "See that flag, Mr. Reid? That's the flag of the United States of America. That flag will fly there long after this is all forgotten. That flag still stands for freedom. You know it always will. Custody, Mr. Officer. Stand him down."

Or Judge Cedarbaum, who deflated the empty rhetoric of Faisal Shahzad, the Times Square bomber, with the simple request: "I do hope that you will spend some of the time in prison thinking carefully about whether the Koran wants you to kill lots of people." In a battle of wits, I think our federal judiciary can hold its own."

Fourth, Supporters of military commissions argue that Article III courts cannot protect sensitive information. Well that's just wrong. Authors of a recent report for Human Rights First, both of whom are former Assistant United States Attorneys, were unable to identify a single instance in which the Classified Information Procedures Act was invoked and there was a significant leak of sensitive information as a result of a terrorism prosecution in federal court.

The most distressing of the arguments against Article III trials is the notion that they might result in too many acquittals. Not only is this argument contrary to fact, it's contrary to our values. Since September 11, 2001, of the approximately 591 individuals charged in terrorism-related cases that have been resolved, only 9 were acquitted—a conviction rate between 98 and 99%. What is worse is that with these commissions, we would be creating a separate and unequal system of criminal justice. How would we make the threshold determination of which court system to try these people in? And who would make that determination?

And why should the object of our criminal justice system be to secure convictions? The rule of law floats belly up when we abandon our constitutional promises the moment we do not like a defendant. A justice system that is designed to guarantee convictions is not worthy of the name. Justice Frankfurter wrote that "it is a fair summary of history to say that the safeguards of liberty have frequently been forged in controversies involving not very nice people." As Americans, we have been given a priceless heirloom by giants such as Justice Frankfurter. And those giants held on to that heirloom through thin times, times of poverty, and times of fear. What troubles me is that our generation is going to be the one to pawn it.

Sincerely,
John C. Coughenour
U.S. District Judge
Western District of Washington

ILLEGAL IMMIGRANTS AND THE CONSTITUTION

LO 11 Throughout U.S. history, the flow of immigrants into and out of the country has ebbed and flowed greatly. Official policies have varied from "open borders," until about 1850; to immigrant quotas for many countries of origin until the 1930s; to our present situation, which is in flux. One thing, however, has remained constant from colonial times—widespread opposition to allowing alien known criminals to enter or remain in the country.

Keep in mind that aliens who commit a "new" crime while on U.S. soil and come into the criminal process are entitled to the full protection of all the rights and proceedings you've learned about in earlier chapters. We'll concentrate here on the Constitution and the detention of deportable illegal immigrants during deportation proceedings. This is predominantly a Fourth Amendment question.

LO 11 ## The Fourth Amendment and "Deportable Aliens"

In 1976, the U.S. Supreme Court made it clear that it's a Fourth Amendment seizure to stop a deportable alien for suspected immigration law crimes (*U.S. v. Martinez-Fuerte* [1976], excerpted in the next section). A deportable alien is "a person who has been found to be deportable by an immigration judge, or who admits his deportability upon questioning by official agents" (553). But, in the same year, the Court held that according to the *Terry* balancing test (Chapter 4), the strong government interest in investigating illegal immigration outweighed the minimal liberty and privacy intrusion of a brief detention at a permanent immigration checkpoint.

On the other side of the balance—the individual Fourth Amendment privacy and liberty interests—the Court found the invasions "quite limited," lasting only a few minutes. Travelers are asked only to answer a question or two and "possibly [produce] a document evidencing a right to be in the United States. Neither the vehicle nor its occupants are searched, and visual inspection of the vehicle is limited to what can be seen without a search" (558).

The Court then turned to the effectiveness of the permanent border checkpoint near San Clemente, California, the same checkpoint that the Court dealt with in *U.S. v. Martinez-Fuerte*. Here are the details the Court presented:

> Approximately 10 million cars pass the checkpoint location each year, although the checkpoint actually is in operation only about 70% of the time. "Down" periods are caused by personnel shortages, weather conditions, and at San Clemente peak traffic loads. In calendar year 1973, approximately 17,000 illegal aliens were apprehended there. During an eight-day period in 1974 that included the arrests involved in No. 74–1560, roughly 146,000 vehicles passed through the checkpoint during 124 1/6 hours of operation. Of these, 820 vehicles were referred to the secondary inspection area, where Border Patrol agents found 725 deportable aliens in 171 vehicles. In all but two cases, the aliens were discovered without a conventional search of the vehicle. A similar rate of apprehensions throughout the year would have resulted in an annual total of over 33,000, although the Government contends that many illegal aliens pass through the checkpoint undetected. (554)

Six justices had no difficulty holding that the government interest outweighed the individual rights of the deportable illegal immigrant, Amado Martinez-Fuerte.

In *U.S. v. Martinez-Fuerte*, the U.S. Supreme Court held that it was reasonable to stop Amado Martinez-Fuerte's vehicle at a checkpoint to question him and other occupants briefly even though police lacked individualized reasonable suspicion.

CASE

Was the Stop without Individualized Suspicion Reasonable?

U.S. v. Martinez-Fuerte
428 U.S. 543 (1976)

HISTORY

Amado Martinez-Fuerte (Respondent) was charged with two counts of illegally transporting aliens in violation of 8 U.S.C. § 1324(a)(2). He moved before trial to suppress all evidence stemming from the stop on the ground that the operation of the checkpoint was in violation of the Fourth Amendment. The motion to suppress was denied, and he was convicted on both counts after a jury trial. Martinez-Fuerte appealed his conviction, and the Government appealed the granting of the motion. The Court of Appeals for the Ninth Circuit held, with one judge dissenting, that these stops violated the Fourth Amendment. It reversed Martinez-Fuerte's conviction, and affirmed the orders to suppress in the other cases. The U.S. Supreme Court reversed and remanded.

—POWELL, J., joined by BURGER, C.J., and STEWART, WHITE, BLACKMUN, REHNQUIST, and STEVENS, JJ.

These cases involve criminal prosecutions for offenses relating to the transportation of illegal Mexican aliens. Whether the Fourth Amendment was violated turns primarily on whether a vehicle may be stopped at a fixed checkpoint for brief questioning of its occupants even though there is no reason to believe the particular vehicle contains illegal aliens. We hold today that such stops are consistent with the Fourth Amendment. We also hold that the operation of a fixed checkpoint need not be authorized in advance by a judicial warrant.

FACTS

Approximately one mile south of the permanent immigration checkpoint on Interstate 5 near the San Clemente, California checkpoint is a large black on yellow sign with flashing yellow lights over the highway stating "ALL VEHICLES, STOP AHEAD, 1 MILE." Three-quarters of a mile further north are two black on yellow signs suspended over the highway with flashing lights stating "WATCH FOR BRAKE LIGHTS." At the checkpoint, which is also the location of a State of California weighing station, are two large signs with flashing red lights suspended over the highway. These signs each state "STOP HERE U.S. OFFICERS." Placed on the highway are a number of orange traffic cones funneling traffic into two lanes where a Border Patrol agent in full dress uniform, standing behind a white on red "STOP" sign checks traffic. Blocking traffic in the unused lanes are official U.S. Border Patrol vehicles with flashing red lights. In addition, there is a permanent building which houses the Border Patrol office and temporary detention facilities. There are also floodlights for nighttime operation.

The "point" agent standing between the two lanes of traffic visually screens all northbound vehicles, which the checkpoint brings to a virtual, if not a complete, halt. Most motorists are allowed to resume their progress without any oral inquiry or close visual examination. In a relatively small number of cases the "point" agent will conclude that further inquiry is in order. He directs these cars to a secondary inspection area, where their occupants are asked about their citizenship and immigration status. The Government informs us that at San Clemente the average length of an investigation in the secondary inspection area is three to five minutes. A direction to stop in the secondary inspection area could be based on something suspicious about a particular car passing through the checkpoint, but the Government concedes that none of the three stops at issue in No. 74–1560 was based on any articulable suspicion. [Only Martinez-Fuerte's stop is included in this excerpt.] During the period when these stops were made, the checkpoint was operating under a magistrate's "warrant of inspection," which authorized the Border Patrol to conduct a routine-stop operation at the San Clemente location.

Respondent Amado Martinez-Fuerte approached the checkpoint driving a vehicle containing two female passengers. The women were illegal Mexican aliens who had entered the United States at the San Ysidro port of entry by using false papers and rendezvoused with Martinez-Fuerte in San Diego to be transported northward. At the

(continued)

checkpoint their car was directed to the secondary inspection area. Martinez-Fuerte produced documents showing him to be a lawful resident alien, but his passengers admitted being present in the country unlawfully. He was charged, inter alia, with two counts of illegally transporting aliens in violation of 8 U.S.C. § 1324(a)(2). He moved before trial to suppress all evidence stemming from the stop on the ground that the operation of the checkpoint was in violation of the Fourth Amendment. The motion to suppress was denied, and he was convicted on both counts after a jury trial.

OPINION

It has been national policy for many years to limit immigration into the United States. Since July 1, 1968, the annual quota for immigrants from all independent countries of the Western Hemisphere, including Mexico, has been 120,000 persons. Act of Oct. 3, 1965, § 21(e), 79 Stat. 921. Many more aliens than can be accommodated under the quota want to live and work in the United States. Consequently, large numbers of aliens seek illegally to enter or to remain in the United States. Estimates of the number of illegal immigrants (already) in the United States vary widely. A conservative estimate in 1972 produced a figure of about one million, but the Immigration and Naturalization Service now suggests there may be as many as 10 or 12 million aliens illegally in the country. It is estimated that 85% of the illegal immigrants are from Mexico, drawn by the fact that economic opportunities are significantly greater in the United States than they are in Mexico.

Interdicting the flow of illegal entrants from Mexico poses formidable law enforcement problems. The principal problem arises from surreptitious entries. The United States shares a border with Mexico that is almost 2,000 miles long, and much of the border area is uninhabited desert or thinly populated arid land. Although the Border Patrol maintains personnel, electronic equipment, and fences along portions of the border, it remains relatively easy for individuals to enter the United States without detection. It also is possible for an alien to enter unlawfully at a port of entry by the use of falsified papers or to enter lawfully but violate restrictions of entry in an effort to remain in the country unlawfully. Once within the country, the aliens seek to travel inland to areas where employment is believed to be available, frequently meeting by prearrangement with friends or professional smugglers who transport them in private vehicles.

The Border Patrol conducts three kinds of inland traffic-checking operations in an effort to minimize illegal immigration. Permanent checkpoints, such as those at San Clemente and Sarita, are maintained at or near intersections of important roads leading away from the border. They operate on a coordinated basis designed to avoid circumvention by smugglers and others who transport the illegal aliens. Temporary checkpoints, which operate like permanent ones, occasionally are established in other strategic locations. Finally, roving patrols are maintained to supplement the checkpoint system. In fiscal 1973, 175,511 **deportable aliens** (a person who has been found to be deportable by an immigration judge, or who admits his deportability upon questioning by official agents) were apprehended throughout the nation by "line watch" agents stationed at the border itself. Traffic-checking operations in the interior apprehended approximately 55,300 more deportable aliens. Most of the traffic-checking apprehensions were at checkpoints, though precise figures are not available.

The record provides a rather complete picture of the effectiveness of the San Clemente checkpoint. Approximately 10 million cars pass the checkpoint location each year, although the checkpoint actually is in operation only about 70% of the time. "Down" periods are caused by personnel shortages, weather conditions, and at San Clemente peak traffic loads.

In calendar year 1973, approximately 17,000 illegal aliens were apprehended there. During an eight-day period in 1974 that included the arrests involved in No. 74–1560, roughly 146,000 vehicles passed through the checkpoint during 124-1/6 hours of operation. Of these, 820 vehicles were referred to the secondary inspection area, where Border Patrol agents found 725 deportable aliens in 171 vehicles. In all but two cases, the aliens were discovered without a conventional search of the vehicle. A similar rate of apprehensions throughout the year would have resulted in an annual total of over 33,000, although the Government contends that many illegal aliens pass through the checkpoint undetected. The record in No. 75–5387 does not provide comparable statistical information regarding the Sarita checkpoint. While it appears that fewer illegal aliens are apprehended there, it may be assumed that fewer pass by undetected, as every motorist is questioned.

The Fourth Amendment imposes limits on search-and-seizure powers in order to prevent arbitrary and oppressive interference by enforcement officials with the privacy and personal security of individuals. In delineating the constitutional safeguards applicable in particular contexts, the Court has weighed the public interest against the Fourth Amendment interest of the individual (*Terry v. Ohio* 1968 [excerpted Chapter 4]), a process evident in our previous cases dealing with Border Patrol traffic-checking operations.

It is agreed that checkpoint stops are "seizures" within the meaning of the Fourth Amendment. Our previous cases have recognized that maintenance of a traffic-checking program in the interior is necessary because the flow of illegal aliens cannot be controlled effectively at the border. We note here the substantiality of the public interest in the practice of routine stops for inquiry at permanent checkpoints, a practice which the Government identifies as the most important of the traffic-checking operations. These checkpoints are located on important highways; in their absence such highways would offer illegal aliens a quick and safe route into the interior. Routine checkpoint inquiries apprehend many smugglers and illegal aliens who succumb to the lure of such highways. And the prospect of such inquiries forces others onto less efficient roads that are less heavily traveled, slowing their movement and making them more vulnerable to detection by roving patrols.

A requirement that stops on major routes inland always be based on reasonable suspicion would be impractical because the flow of traffic tends to be too heavy to allow the particularized study of a given car that would enable it to be identified as a possible carrier of illegal aliens. In particular, such a requirement would largely eliminate any deterrent to the conduct of well-disguised smuggling operations, even though smugglers are known to use these highways regularly.

While the need to make routine checkpoint stops is great, the consequent intrusion on Fourth Amendment interests is quite limited. The stop does intrude to a limited extent on motorists' right to free passage without interruption, and arguably on their right to personal security. But it involves only a brief detention of travelers during which all that is required of the vehicle's occupants is a response to a brief question or two and possibly the production of a document evidencing a right to be in the United States. Neither the vehicle nor its occupants are searched, and visual inspection of the vehicle is limited to what can be seen without a search. This objective intrusion—the stop itself, the questioning, and the visual inspection—also existed in roving-patrol stops. But we view checkpoint stops in a different light because the subjective intrusion—the generating of concern or even fright on the part of lawful travelers—is appreciably less in the case of a checkpoint stop. The circumstances surrounding a checkpoint stop and search are far less intrusive than those attending a roving-patrol stop. Roving patrols often operate at night on seldom-traveled roads, and their approach may frighten motorists. At traffic checkpoints the motorist can see that other vehicles are being stopped, he can see visible signs of the officers' authority, and he is much less likely to be frightened or annoyed by the intrusion.

Routine checkpoint stops do not intrude on the motoring public. First, the potential interference with legitimate traffic is minimal. Motorists using these highways are not taken by surprise as they know, or may obtain knowledge of, the location of the checkpoints and will not be stopped elsewhere. Second, checkpoint operations both appear to and actually involve less discretionary enforcement activity. The regularized manner in which established checkpoints are operated is visible evidence, reassuring to law-abiding motorists, that the stops are duly authorized and believed to serve the public interest. The location of a fixed checkpoint is not chosen by officers in the field, but by officials responsible for making overall decisions as to the most effective allocation of limited enforcement resources. We may assume that such officials will be unlikely to locate a checkpoint where it bears arbitrarily or oppressively on motorists as a class. And since field officers may stop only those cars passing the checkpoint, there is less room for abusive or harassing stops of individuals than there was in the case of roving-patrol stops.

The defendants arrested at the San Clemente checkpoint suggest that its operation involves a significant extra element of intrusiveness in that only a small percentage of cars are referred to the secondary inspection area, thereby "stigmatizing" those diverted and reducing the assurances provided by equal treatment of all motorists. We think defendants overstate the consequences. Referrals are made for the sole purpose of conducting a routine and limited inquiry into residence status that cannot feasibly be made of every motorist where the traffic is heavy. The objective intrusion of the stop and inquiry thus remains minimal. Selective referral may involve some annoyance, but it remains true that the stops should not be frightening or offensive because of their public and relatively routine nature. Moreover, selective referrals rather than questioning the occupants of every car tend to advance some Fourth Amendment interests by minimizing the intrusion on the general motoring public.

The defendants note correctly that to accommodate public and private interests some quantum of individualized suspicion is usually a prerequisite to a constitutional search or seizure. But the Fourth Amendment imposes no irreducible requirement of such suspicion. One's expectation of privacy in an automobile and of freedom in its operation are significantly different from the traditional expectation of privacy and freedom in one's residence. And the reasonableness of the procedures followed in making these checkpoint stops makes the resulting intrusion on the interests of motorists minimal. On the other hand, the purpose of the stops is legitimate and in the public interest, and the need for this enforcement technique is demonstrated by the records in the cases before us. Accordingly, we hold that the stops and questioning at issue may be made in the absence of any individualized suspicion at reasonably located checkpoints.

In summary, we hold that stops for brief questioning routinely conducted at permanent checkpoints are consistent with the Fourth Amendment and need not be authorized by warrant. We REVERSE the judgment of the Court of Appeals for the Ninth Circuit and REMAND the case with directions to affirm the conviction of Martinez-Fuerte

(*continued*)

and to REMAND the other cases to the District Court for further proceedings.

It is so ordered.

DISSENT

BRENNAN, joined by MARSHALL, J.

Today's decision continues the evisceration of Fourth Amendment protections against unreasonable searches and seizures. Consistent with this purpose to debilitate Fourth Amendment protections, the Court's decision today virtually empties the Amendment of its reasonableness requirement by holding that law enforcement officials manning fixed checkpoint stations who make standardless seizures of persons do not violate the Amendment. While the requisite justification for permitting a search or seizure may vary in certain contexts, even in the exceptional situations permitting intrusions on less than probable cause, it has long been settled that justification must be measured by objective standards. *Terry v. Ohio* made clear what common sense teaches: Conduct, to be reasonable, must pass muster under objective standards applied to specific facts.

We are told today, however, that motorists without number may be individually stopped, questioned, visually inspected, and then further detained upon nothing more substantial than inarticulate hunches. This defacement of Fourth Amendment protections is arrived at by a balancing process that overwhelms the individual's protection against unwarranted official intrusion by a governmental interest said to justify the search and seizure. But that method is only a convenient cover for condoning arbitrary official conduct.

In any event, the subjective aspects of checkpoint stops require some principled restraint on law enforcement conduct. The motorist whose conduct has been nothing but innocent and this is overwhelmingly the case surely resents his own detention and inspection. And checkpoints, unlike roving stops, detain thousands of motorists, a dragnet-like procedure offensive to the sensibilities of free citizens. Also, the delay occasioned by stopping hundreds of vehicles on a busy highway is particularly irritating.

In addition to overlooking these dimensions of subjective intrusion, checkpoint officials, uninhibited by any objective standards and therefore free to stop any or all motorists without explanation or excuse, wholly on whim, will perforce target motorists of Mexican appearance. The process will then inescapably discriminate against citizens of Mexican ancestry and Mexican aliens lawfully in this country for no other reason than that they unavoidably possess the same "suspicious" physical and grooming characteristics of illegal Mexican aliens.

Every American citizen of Mexican ancestry and every Mexican alien lawfully in this country must know after today's decision that he travels the fixed checkpoint highways at the risk of being subjected not only to a stop, but also to detention and interrogation, both prolonged and to an extent far more than for non-Mexican appearing motorists. To be singled out for referral and to be detained and interrogated must be upsetting to any motorist. One wonders what actual experience supports my Brethren's conclusion that referrals "should not be frightening or offensive because of their public and relatively routine nature." In point of fact, referrals, viewed in context, are not relatively routine; thousands are otherwise permitted to pass. But for the arbitrarily selected motorists who must suffer the delay and humiliation of detention and interrogation, the experience can obviously be upsetting. And that experience is particularly vexing for the motorist of Mexican ancestry who is selectively referred, knowing that the officers' target is the Mexican alien. That deep resentment will be stirred by a sense of unfair discrimination is not difficult to foresee.

The cornerstone of this society, indeed of any free society, is orderly procedure. The Constitution, as originally adopted, was therefore, in great measure, a procedural document. For the same reasons the drafters of the Bill of Rights largely placed their faith in procedural limitations on government action. The Fourth Amendment's requirement that searches and seizures be reasonable enforces this fundamental understanding in erecting its buffer against the arbitrary treatment of citizens by government. But to permit, as the Court does today, police discretion to supplant the objectivity of reason and, thereby, expediency to reign in the place of order, is to undermine Fourth Amendment safeguards and threaten erosion of the cornerstone of our system of a government, for, as Mr. Justice Frankfurter reminded us, "the history of American freedom is, in no small measure, the history of procedure."

Questions

1. Describe the government interest in detail.

2. Describe the individual interest in detail.

3. Identify the objective basis the Court established, and list the relevant facts that supported the reasonableness of the seizure.

4. Do the facts of the case support the dissent's claim that:

   Every American citizen of Mexican ancestry and every Mexican alien lawfully in this country must know after today's decision that he travels the fixed checkpoint highways at the risk of being subjected not only to a stop, but also to detention and interrogation, both prolonged and to an extent far more than for non-Mexican Mexican-appearing motorists?

CRIMINAL PROCEDURE IN ACTION

Officers have a duty to determine the immigration status of any person lawfully stopped

Arizona v. U.S., 132 S.Ct. 2492 (2012)

LO 11 By 2010 Arizona had taken the lead in state efforts to control many aspects of the daily lives of hundreds of thousands of immigrants who had entered the United States illegally. Various civil rights groups challenged the laws, claiming they were based on race. The federal government also challenged the laws, not on race, but on the ground that Arizona was trying to move in on the federal government's superior power to enforce federal immigration laws. That's the challenge that reached and was rejected by the U.S. Supreme Court in 2012.

According to the majority,

To address pressing issues related to the large number of aliens within its borders who do not have a lawful right to be in this country, the State of Arizona in 2010 enacted a statute called the Support Our Law Enforcement and Safe Neighborhoods Act. The law's stated purpose is to "discourage and deter the unlawful entry and presence of aliens and economic activity by persons unlawfully present in the United States." The law's provisions establish an official state policy of "attrition through enforcement."

The United States filed this suit against Arizona, seeking to enjoin S.B. 1070 as preempted. Two provisions give specific arrest authority and investigative duties with respect to certain aliens to state and local law enforcement officers. §13–3883(A)(5) authorizes officers to arrest without a warrant a person "the officer has probable cause to believe . . . has committed any public offense that makes the person removable from the United States."

§11–1051(B) provides

For any lawful stop, detention or arrest made by a law enforcement official or a law enforcement agency of this state or a law enforcement official or a law enforcement agency of a county, city, town or other political subdivision of this state in the enforcement of any other law or ordinance of a county, city or town or this state where reasonable suspicion exists that the person is an alien and is unlawfully present in the United States, a reasonable attempt shall be made, when practicable, to determine the immigration status of the person, except if the determination may hinder or obstruct an investigation. Any person who is arrested shall have the person's immigration status determined before the person is released. The person's immigration status shall be verified with the federal government pursuant to 8 United States Code section 1373(c). A law enforcement official or agency of this state or a county, city, town or other political subdivision of this state may not consider race, color or national origin in implementing the requirements of this subsection except to the extent permitted by the United States or Arizona Constitution. A person is presumed to not be an alien who is unlawfully present in the United States if the person provides to the law enforcement officer or agency any of the following:

1. A valid Arizona driver license.
2. A valid Arizona nonoperating identification license.
3. A valid tribal enrollment card or other form of tribal identification.
4. If the entity requires proof of legal presence in the United States before issuance, any valid United States federal, state or local government issued identification.

The Court (5–3) lifted the temporary injunction on both provisions. The Court held that the lower courts were wrong to prevent this provision from going into effect while its lawfulness is being litigated. That left them open to later challenges in the lower courts.

LO 11 ## Detention during Deportation Hearings

Detention during **noncriminal (civil) deportation proceedings** is a subject of much debate. Recall that the Fourth Amendment protects against "unreasonable searches and seizures" (Chapters 3–7). Detention is clearly a seizure. And "detention is clearly an important element in an effective immigration enforcement system" (*Demore v. Kim* "Amicus Brief for T. Alexander Aleinikoff and others" 2002, 3). Most agree with this statement by several former high-ranking officials in the Immigration and Naturalization Services (INS). Most also agree that two criteria should determine the reasonableness of detaining noncitizens or allowing them to remain free during deportation and removal proceedings:

1. The risk that the noncitizen will flee
2. The danger that the noncitizen poses to the community

There the agreement stops. There's heated debate over several issues, especially over how to decide whom to detain. Some courts and commentators have called for "an individualized determination of flight risk and dangerousness before subjecting lawful permanent residents to sustained detention" (*Demore v. Kim* 2002, Amicus Brief, 3). Other courts and commentators call for mandatory detention of all "criminal" aliens while the question of deportation is being decided. But we're not talking about detaining noncitizens during criminal investigations and prosecutions for crimes committed in the United States (Chapters 3–6, on search and seizure; Chapter 12, on bail and detention). This debate is over those involved in noncriminal, or civil, deportation proceedings.

The U.S. Supreme Court resolved the conflict—at least in the courts—in *Demore v. Kim* (2003), our next case excerpt. The Court held (6–3) that "Congress, justifiably concerned that deportable criminal aliens who are not detained continue to engage in crime and fail to appear for their removal hearings in large numbers, may require that persons such as respondent be detained for the brief period necessary for their removal proceedings" (513).

The Court readily conceded that the Constitution "entitles aliens to due process of law in deportation proceedings." But the Court also "recognized detention during deportation proceedings as a constitutionally valid aspect of the deportation process. As we said more than a century ago, deportation proceedings 'would be vain if those accused could not be held in custody pending the inquiry into their true character'" (523).

Before we go to the excerpt, let's look at the nature of the detention and removal process so you can get a better perspective on the situation that led to the mandatory detention laws enacted during the 1990s, which are still the law today. Traditionally, the Immigration and Nationality Act (INA) has authorized the U.S. attorney general, in his or her discretion, to detain suspected deportable aliens found in the United States to make sure they're available for deportation proceedings and to reduce the danger to the community (INA, 8 U.S.C. §1226a). The decision to arrest, detain, or release aliens subject to deportation proceedings on bond or other conditions was made on a case-by-case basis, typically within a day of arrest (8 C.F.R. §236.1(d)(1)).

Aliens, except for arriving aliens, can appeal the detention decision to an immigration judge, who follows a "streamlined bond redetermination" procedure, conducted informally either in person or by telephone (8 C.F.R. §3.19(b)). The judge can consider any information provided by the Immigration and Naturalization Service (INS) or the alien. Information that's made available independently to the judge may also be considered. The judge can approve the release conditions, modify them, or release on recognizance (8 C.F.R §236.1(d)(1)). The alien or the INS also can appeal the judge's decision to the Board of Immigration Appeals (BIA) in expedited informal proceedings (8 C.F.R §236.1(d)(3)).

This procedure is still the law for noncriminal aliens. But the Illegal Immigration Reform and Immigrant Responsibility Act (IIRIRA) of 1996 amended the INA. It now provides that "the Attorney General shall take into custody any alien who" has committed a fairly long list of crimes (8 U.S.C. §1226 (c)). (details the conditions that qualify aliens for deportation.)

The statute further orders the attorney general to develop a coordinated system to identify and transfer these aliens from federal, state, and local law enforcement to INS custody (Figure 15.10).

Now, let's turn to our next case excerpt, *Demore v. Kim* (2003). The issue in this case was whether the Immigration and Nationality Act violated the rights of lawful permanent resident aliens by requiring no bail for their civil detention while awaiting deportation proceedings. Hyung Joon Kim wasn't protesting his classification as a deportable alien following his criminal conviction for crimes defined under INA. Rather, he argued that making him ineligible for bail without an individualized hearing violated his due process rights.

FIGURE 15.10 Offenses that Qualify Aliens for Mandatory Detention during Deportation Proceedings

---

Section 1227. Deportable Aliens

(a) Classes of deportable aliens

Any alien (including an alien crewman) in and admitted to the United States shall, upon the order of the Attorney General, be removed if the alien is within one or more of the following classes of deportable aliens:

    (2) Criminal offenses

        (A) General crimes

            (i) Crimes of moral turpitude

                Any alien who—

                    (I) is convicted of a crime involving moral turpitude committed within five years (or 10 years in the case of an alien provided lawful permanent resident status . . .) and . . .

                    (II) is convicted of a crime for which a sentence of one year or longer may be imposed, is deportable.

            (ii) Multiple criminal convictions

                Any alien who at any time after admission is convicted of two or more crimes involving moral turpitude, not arising out of a single scheme of criminal misconduct, regardless of whether confined therefor and regardless of whether the convictions were in a single trial, is deportable.

            (iii) Aggravated felony . . .

            (iv) High speed flight . . .

            (v) Failure to register as a sex offender . . .

(continued)

FIGURE 15.10 (*Continued*)

(B) Controlled substances
  (i) Conviction
      Any alien who at any time after admission has been convicted of a violation of (or a conspiracy or attempt to violate) any law or regulation of a State, the United States, or a foreign country relating to a controlled substance, other than a single offense involving possession for one's own use of 30 grams or less of marijuana, is deportable.
  (ii) Drug abusers and addicts
      Any alien who is, or at any time after admission has been, a drug abuser or addict is deportable.
(C) Certain firearm offenses
    Any alien who at any time after admission is convicted under any law of purchasing, selling, offering for sale, exchanging, using, owning, possessing, or carrying, or of attempting or conspiring to purchase, sell, offer for sale, exchange, use, own, possess, or carry, any weapon, part, or accessory which is a firearm or destructive device (as defined in section 921 (a) of title 18) in violation of any law is deportable.
(D) Miscellaneous crimes
    Any alien who at any time has been convicted of, or has been so convicted of a conspiracy or attempt to violate—
    (i) . . . espionage, sabotage, or treason and sedition . . . for which a term of imprisonment of five or more years may be imposed; . . .
    (iii) a violation of any provision of the Military Selective Service Act . . . is deportable.
(E) Crimes of domestic violence, stalking, or violation of protection order, crimes against children and
    (i) Domestic violence, stalking, and child abuse
        Any alien who at any time after admission is convicted of a crime of domestic violence, a crime of stalking, or a crime of child abuse, child neglect, or child abandonment is deportable. . . .
    (ii) Violators of protection orders
        Any alien who at any time after admission is enjoined under a protection order issued by a court and whom the court determines has engaged in conduct that violates the portion of a protection order that involves protection against credible threats of violence, repeated harassment, or bodily injury to the person or persons for whom the protection order was issued is deportable. . . .
(3) Failure to register and falsification of documents
  (D) Falsely claiming citizenship
    (i) In general
        Any alien who falsely represents, or has falsely represented, himself to be a citizen of the United States for any purpose or benefit under this chapter . . . or any Federal or State law is deportable.

Source: U.S. Code. 2010. 8 U.S.C. §1227(a).

FIGURE 15.11 Illegal Immigration Reform and Immigrant Responsibility Act (IIRIRA) of 1996

---

§ 1226. Apprehension and Detention of Aliens

(d) Identification of criminal aliens

    (1) The Attorney General shall devise and implement a system—

        (A) to make available, daily (on a 24-hour basis), to Federal, State, and local authorities the investigative resources of the Service to determine whether individuals arrested by such authorities for aggravated felonies are aliens;

        (B) to designate and train officers and employees of the Service to serve as a liaison to Federal, State, and local law enforcement and correctional agencies and courts with respect to the arrest, conviction, and release of any alien charged with an aggravated felony; and

        (C) which uses computer resources to maintain a current record of aliens who have been convicted of an aggravated felony, and indicates those who have been removed.

    (2) The record under paragraph (1)(C) shall be made available—

        (A) to inspectors at ports of entry and to border patrol agents at sector headquarters for purposes of immediate identification of any alien who was previously ordered removed and is seeking to reenter the United States, and

        (B) to officials of the Department of State for use in its automated visa lookout system.

    (3) Upon the request of the governor or chief executive officer of any State, the Service shall provide assistance to State courts in the identification of aliens unlawfully present in the United States pending criminal prosecution.

Source: U.S. Code. 2010. 8 U.S.C. §1226(d).

In *Demore v. Kim* (2003) the U.S. Supreme Court ruled that the no-bail, civil detention requirement of the Immigration Nationality Act didn't violate the due process rights of Hyung Joon Kim, a lawful permanent resident alien.

CASE

Did His Detention Deprive Him of Liberty without "Due Process of Law"?

Demore v. Kim
538 U.S. 510 (2003)

HISTORY

Hyung Joon Kim (Respondent), a lawful permanent resident alien (LPR) filed a habeas petition challenging the no-bail provision of the Immigration and Nationality Act (INA), pursuant to which he had been held for six months during pendency of removal proceedings against him. The United States District Court for the Northern District of California, Susan Y. Illston, J., entered an order, holding the statute unconstitutional on its face and directing the Immigration and Naturalization Service (INS) to hold a bail hearing. The Government appealed. The United States Court of Appeals for the Ninth Circuit, affirmed. Certiorari was granted. The Supreme Court reversed.

—REHNQUIST, C.J., joined by KENNEDY, STEVENS, SOUTER, GINSBURG, BREYER, O'CONNOR, SCALIA, and THOMAS, JJ.

(continued)

Section 236(c) of the Immigration and Nationality Act, as amended, 8 U.S.C. § 1226(c), provides that "the Attorney General *shall* take into custody any alien who is removable from this country because he has been convicted of one of a specified set of crimes." [emphasis added]

FACTS

Hyung Joon Kim (Respondent) is a citizen of the Republic of South Korea. He entered the United States in 1984, at the age of six, and became a lawful permanent resident of the United States two years later. In July 1996, he was convicted of first-degree burglary in state court in California and, in April 1997, he was convicted of a second crime, "petty theft with priors." The Immigration and Naturalization Service (INS) charged respondent with being deportable from the United States in light of these convictions, and detained him pending his removal hearing. We hold that Congress, justifiably concerned that deportable criminal aliens who are not detained continue to engage in crime and fail to appear for their removal hearings in large numbers, may require that persons such as respondent be detained for the brief period necessary for their removal proceedings.

Respondent does not dispute the validity of his prior convictions, which were obtained following the full procedural protections our criminal justice system offers. Respondent also did not dispute the INS's conclusion that he is subject to mandatory detention under § 1226(c). As respondent explained: "The statute requires the [INS] to take into custody any alien who 'is deportable' from the United States based on having been convicted of any of a wide range of crimes. . . . [Respondent] does not challenge INS's authority to take him into custody after he finished serving his criminal sentence. His challenge is solely to Section 1226(c)'s absolute prohibition on his release from detention, even where, as here, the INS never asserted that he posed a danger or significant flight risk."

In conceding that he was deportable, respondent forwent a hearing at which he would have been entitled to raise any nonfrivolous argument available to demonstrate that he was not properly included in a mandatory detention category. Respondent instead filed a habeas corpus action pursuant to 28 U.S.C. § 2241 in the United States District Court for the Northern District of California challenging the constitutionality of § 1226(c) itself.

The District Court agreed with respondent that § 1226(c)'s requirement of mandatory detention for certain criminal aliens was unconstitutional. The District Court therefore granted respondent's petition subject to the INS's prompt undertaking of an individualized bond hearing to determine whether respondent posed either a flight risk or a danger to the community. Following that decision, the District Director of the INS released respondent on $5,000 bond. The Court of Appeals for the Ninth Circuit affirmed. We granted certiorari to resolve this conflict, and now reverse.

OPINION

Section 1226(c) of the Immigration and Nationality Act (INA) mandates detention during removal proceedings for a limited class of deportable aliens—including those convicted of an aggravated felony. Congress adopted this provision against a backdrop of wholesale failure by the INS to deal with increasing rates of criminal activity by aliens. Criminal aliens were the fastest growing segment of the federal prison population, already constituting roughly 25% of all federal prisoners, and they formed a rapidly rising share of state prison populations as well.

Congress's investigations showed, however, that the INS could not even identify most deportable aliens, much less locate them and remove them from the country. One study showed that, at the then-current rate of deportation, it would take 23 years to remove every criminal alien already subject to deportation. Making matters worse, criminal aliens who were deported swiftly reentered the country illegally in great numbers.

The INS's near-total inability to remove deportable criminal aliens imposed more than a monetary cost on the Nation. Deportable criminal aliens who remained in the United States often committed more crimes before being removed. One 1986 study showed that, after criminal aliens were identified as deportable, 77% were arrested at least once more and 45%—nearly half—were arrested multiple times before their deportation proceedings even began.

Congress also had before it evidence that one of the major causes of the INS's failure to remove deportable criminal aliens was the agency's failure to detain those aliens during their deportation proceedings. The Attorney General at the time had broad discretion to conduct individualized bond hearings and to release criminal aliens from custody during their removal proceedings when those aliens were determined not to present an excessive flight risk or threat to society. Despite this discretion to conduct bond hearings, however, in practice the INS faced severe limitations on funding and detention space, which considerations affected its release determinations. Once released, more than 20% of deportable criminal aliens failed to appear for their removal hearings.

Congress amended the immigration laws several times toward the end of the 1980's. In 1988, Congress limited the Attorney General's discretion over custody determinations with respect to deportable aliens who had been convicted of aggravated felonies. Then, in 1990, Congress broadened the definition of "aggravated felony," subjecting more criminal aliens to mandatory detention. At the same time, however, Congress added a new provision, authorizing the Attorney General to release permanent resident aliens during their deportation proceedings where such aliens were found not to constitute a flight risk or threat to the community.

During the same period in which Congress was making incremental changes to the immigration laws, it was also considering wholesale reform of those laws. Some studies presented to Congress suggested that detention of criminal aliens during their removal proceedings might be the best way to ensure their successful removal from this country. It was following those Reports that Congress enacted 8 U.S.C. § 1226, requiring the Attorney General to detain a subset of deportable criminal aliens pending a determination of their removability.

In the exercise of its broad power over naturalization and immigration, Congress regularly makes rules that would be unacceptable if applied to citizens. This Court has firmly and repeatedly endorsed the proposition that Congress may make rules as to aliens that would be unacceptable if applied to citizens. In his habeas corpus challenge, respondent did not contest Congress's general authority to remove criminal aliens from the United States. Nor did he argue that he himself was not "deportable" within the meaning of § 1226(c). Rather, respondent argued that the Government may not, consistent with the Due Process Clause of the Fifth Amendment, detain him for the brief period necessary for his removal proceedings.

It is well established that the Fifth Amendment entitles aliens to due process of law in deportation proceedings. At the same time, however, this Court has recognized detention during deportation proceedings as a constitutionally valid aspect of the deportation process. As we said more than a century ago, deportation proceedings "would be vain if those accused could not be held in custody pending the inquiry into their true character." Despite this Court's longstanding view that the Government may constitutionally detain deportable aliens during the limited period necessary for their removal proceedings, respondent argues that the narrow detention policy reflected in 8 U.S.C. § 1226(c) violates due process.

In the present case, the statutory provision at issue governs detention of deportable criminal aliens pending their removal proceedings. Such detention necessarily serves the purpose of preventing deportable criminal aliens from fleeing prior to or during their removal proceedings, thus increasing the chance that, if ordered removed, the aliens will be successfully removed. Respondent disagrees, arguing that there is no evidence that mandatory detention is necessary because the Government has never shown that individualized bond hearings would be ineffective. But, in adopting § 1226(c), Congress had before it evidence suggesting that permitting discretionary release of aliens pending their removal hearings would lead to large numbers of deportable criminal aliens skipping their hearings and remaining at large in the United States unlawfully.

Respondent argues that these statistics are irrelevant and do not demonstrate that individualized bond hearings "are ineffective or burdensome." It is of course true that when Congress enacted § 1226, individualized bail determinations had not been tested under optimal conditions, or tested in all their possible permutations. But when the Government deals with deportable aliens, the Due Process Clause does not require it to employ the least burdensome means to accomplish its goal. The evidence Congress had before it certainly supports the approach it selected even if other, hypothetical studies might have suggested different courses of action.

The Executive Office for Immigration Review has calculated that, in 85% of the cases in which aliens are detained pursuant to § 1226(c), removal proceedings are completed in an average time of 47 days and a median of 30 days. In the remaining 15% of cases, in which the alien appeals the decision of the Immigration Judge to the Board of Immigration Appeals, appeal takes an average of four months, with a median time that is slightly shorter.

These statistics do not include the many cases in which removal proceedings are completed while the alien is still serving time for the underlying conviction. In those cases, the aliens involved are never subjected to mandatory detention at all. In sum, the detention at stake under § 1226(c) lasts roughly a month and a half in the vast majority of cases in which it is invoked, and about five months in the minority of cases in which the alien chooses to appeal. Respondent was detained for somewhat longer than the average—spending six months in INS custody prior to the District Court's order granting habeas relief, but respondent himself had requested a continuance of his removal hearing.

For the reasons set forth above, respondent's claim must fail. Detention during removal proceedings is a constitutionally permissible part of that process. The INS detention of respondent, a criminal alien who has conceded that he is deportable, for the limited period of his removal proceedings, is governed by these cases. The judgment of the Court of Appeals is

REVERSED.

CONCURRING and DISSENTING SOUTER, J., joined by STEVENS and GINSBURG, JJ.

It has been settled for over a century that all aliens within our territory are "persons" entitled to the protection of the Due Process Clause. The constitutional protection of an alien's person and property is particularly strong in the case of aliens lawfully admitted to permanent residence (LPRs). The immigration laws give LPRs the opportunity to establish a life permanently in this country by developing economic, familial, and social ties indistinguishable from those of a citizen. In fact, the law of the United States goes out of its way to encourage just such attachments by creating immigration preferences for those with

(*continued*)

a citizen as a close relation, and those with valuable professional skills or other assets promising benefits to the United States.

Resident aliens, like citizens, pay taxes, support the economy, serve in the Armed Forces, and contribute in myriad other ways to our society. And if they choose, they may apply for full membership in the national polity through naturalization. The attachments fostered through these legal mechanisms are all the more intense for LPRs brought to the United States as children. They grow up here as members of the society around them, probably without much touch with their country of citizenship, probably considering the United States as home just as much as a native-born, younger brother or sister entitled to United States citizenship. Many resident aliens have lived in this country longer and established stronger family, social, and economic ties here than some who have become naturalized citizens.

Kim is an example. He moved to the United States at the age of six and was lawfully admitted to permanent residence when he was eight. His mother is a citizen, and his father and brother are LPRs. LPRs in Kim's situation have little or no reason to feel or to establish firm ties with any place besides the United States.

Kim's claim is a limited one: not that the Government may not detain LPRs to ensure their appearance at removal hearings, but that due process under the Fifth Amendment conditions a potentially lengthy detention on a hearing and an impartial decision maker's finding that detention is necessary to a governmental purpose. He thus invokes our repeated decisions that the claim of liberty protected by the Fifth Amendment procedural due process is at its strongest when government seeks to detain an individual. Due process calls for an individual determination before someone is locked away.

In none of our prior cases cited [omitted here], did we ever suggest that the government could avoid the Due Process Clause by doing what § 1226(c) does, by selecting a class of people for confinement on a categorical basis and denying members of that class any chance to dispute the necessity of putting them away.

Due process requires a special justification for physical detention that outweighs the individual's constitutionally protected interest in avoiding physical restraint as well as adequate procedural protections. Finally, procedural due process requires, at a minimum, that a detainee have the benefit of an impartial decision maker able to consider particular circumstances on the issue of necessity.

I would affirm the judgment of the Court of Appeals requiring the INS to hold a bail hearing to see whether detention is needed to avoid a risk of flight or a danger to the community. This is surely little enough, given the fact that 8 U.S.C. § 1536 gives an LPR charged with being a foreign terrorist the right to a release hearing pending a determination that he be removed. Although Kim is a convicted criminal, we are not concerned here with a State's interest in punishing those who violate its criminal laws. Kim completed the criminal sentence imposed by the California courts on February 1, 1999, and California no longer has any interest in incarcerating him.

The Court says that § 1226(c) "serves the purpose of preventing deportable criminal aliens from fleeing prior to or during their removal proceedings." Yes it does, and the statute served the purpose of preventing aliens ordered to be deported from fleeing prior to actual deportation. But, the fact that a statute serves its purpose in general fails to justify the detention of an individual in particular. Some individual aliens covered by § 1226(c) have meritorious challenges to removability or claims for relief from removal.

The Court appears to respond that Congress may require detention of removable aliens based on a general conclusion that detention is needed for effective removal of criminal aliens on a class-wide basis. The Court's closest approach to a reason justifying class-wide detention without exception here is a Senate Report stating that over 20% of nondetained criminal aliens failed to appear for removal hearings. To begin with, the Senate Report's statistic treats all criminal aliens alike and does not distinguish between LPRs like Kim, who are likely to have developed strong ties within the United States, and temporary visitors or illegal entrants. Even more importantly, the statistic tells us nothing about flight risk at all because, as both the Court and the Senate Report recognize, the INS was making its custody determinations not on the ground of likelihood of flight or dangerousness, but in large part, according to the number of beds available in a particular region. This meant that the INS often could not detain even the aliens who posed serious flight risks. The INS had only 3,500 detention beds for criminal aliens in the entire country and the INS district comprising Pennsylvania, Delaware, and West Virginia had only 15.

The desperate lack of detention space likewise had led the INS to set bonds too low, because "if the alien is not able to pay, the alien cannot be released, and a needed bed space is lost." The Senate Report also recognized that, even when the INS identifies a criminal alien, the INS "often refuses to take action because of insufficient agents to transport prisoners, or because of limited detention space." Four former high-ranking INS officials explained the Court's statistics as follows: "Flight rates were so high in the early 1990s not as a result of chronic discretionary judgment failures by the INS in assessing which aliens might pose a flight risk. Rather, the rates were alarmingly high because decisions to release aliens in proceedings were driven overwhelmingly by a lack of detention facilities."

Relevant to this case, and largely ignored by the Court, is a recent study conducted at the INS's request concluding that 92% of criminal aliens (most of whom were LPRs) who were released under supervisory conditions attended all of their hearings. Even without supervision, 82% of criminal aliens released on recognizance showed up, as did 77% of those released on bond, leading the reporters to conclude that "supervision was especially effective for criminal aliens" and that "mandatory detention of virtually all criminal aliens is not necessary." In sum, the Court's inapposite statistics do not show that detention of criminal LPRs pending removal proceedings, even on a general level, is necessary to ensure attendance at removal hearings, and the study reinforces the point by establishing the effectiveness of release under supervisory conditions.

The Court's second effort is its claim that mandatory detention under § 1226(c) is generally of a "much shorter duration" than the incarceration at issue in *Zadvydas* [omitted in this excerpt]. While it is true that removal proceedings are unlikely to prove "indefinite and potentially permanent," they are not formally limited to any period, and often extend beyond the time suggested by the Court, that is, "an average time of 47 days" or, for aliens who exercise their right of appeal, "an average of four months." Revealing is an explanation of the raw numbers that are averaged out. As the Solicitor General conceded, the length of the average detention period in great part reflects the fact that the vast majority of cases involve aliens who raise no challenge to removability at all. LPRs like Kim, however, will hardly fit that pattern. Unlike many illegal entrants and temporary nonimmigrants, LPRs are the aliens most likely to press substantial challenges to removability requiring lengthy proceedings. Successful challenges often require several months of proceedings; detention for an open-ended period like this falls far short of the "stringent time limitations" held to be significant in *Salerno* [Chapter 12, p. 461]. The potential for several months of confinement requires an individualized finding of necessity.

This case is not about the National Government's undisputed power to detain aliens in order to avoid flight or prevent danger to the community. The issue is whether that power may be exercised by detaining a still lawful permanent resident alien when there is no reason for it and no way to challenge it. The Court's holding that the Due Process Clause allows this under a blanket rule is devoid of even ostensible justification in fact and at odds with the settled standard of liberty. I respectfully dissent.

Questions

1. Summarize Section 1226(c) of the Immigration and Nationality Act (INA).
2. Describe how Section 1226(c) changed prior law.
3. According to the majority opinion, why did Congress enact the law?
4. Summarize the majority's arguments supporting Kim's detention.
5. Summarize the dissent's arguments opposing Kim's detention.
6. Which side do you agree with? Support your -answer with specific details from the case excerpt and your text.

CHAPTER SUMMARY

LO I — Lawful enemy combatants are members of armed forces engaged in hostilities against the United States, have professed their allegiance to a State or government, and abide by the laws of war. Unlawful enemy combatants have engaged in hostilities against the United States outside of official wars between nations and are subject to detention and trial for war crimes.

LO I — The Supreme Court denied enemy combatants access to U.S. federal courts in *Johnson v. Eisentrager* (1950). In *Rasul v. Bush* (2004), the Supreme Court held that federal courts may hear petitions from noncitizens detained as enemy combatants at Guantanamo Bay. Congress prevented courts from taking petitions from detainees with the Detainee Treatment Act of 2005 and the Military Commission Act of 2006. But, in *Boumediene v. Bush*, the Supreme Court decided that detainees have a constitutional right to challenge their detainment in federal courts.

LO 2 The FBI is the lead agency for investigating the federal crime of terrorism and has always been both a law enforcement and intelligence agency. The FBI is not the only agency responsible for counterterrorism and counterintelligence operations, however; the National Security Agency and local law enforcement agencies also participate in counterterrorism and counterintelligence efforts. Since the 9/11 attacks, the FBI has increasingly focused on the prevention of terrorism.

LO 3 The Foreign Intelligence Surveillance Act (FISA) places limitations upon domestic spying by the executive branch of the U.S. Government. Enacted in 1978, FISA aims to balance the need for foreign intelligence against the privacy rights of all United States persons. Both official U.S. citizens and aliens lawfully admitted for permanent residence are considered United States persons protected by FISA.

LO 3 The FISA Court (FISC) is comprised of 11 appointed federal judges that who operate in secret to rule on FISA applications, one judge ruling on a single application at a time. FISC proceedings are *ex parte*, meaning that the only party represented and heard is the government. Due to this *ex parte* relationship, the approval of FISA applications is a collaborative effort; many applications are modified rather than denied.

LO 4 The USA Patriot Act expanded the power of the FBI and U.S. Department of Justice to monitor and search suspects in counterterrorism investigations. Although roving wiretaps, "sneak-and-peek" searches, and grand jury subpoenas for business records existed before the legislation was passed, the Patriot Act made it easier for the government to apply these tactics to counterterrorism investigations.

LO 4 Roving wiretaps apply to particular people rather than devices, allowing investigators to conduct surveillance of a specified individual across multiple devices if they can establish probable cause that the person's actions could have the effect of thwarting electronic surveillance. Sneak-and-peak search warrants allow officers to enter private places without the owner or occupant consenting or knowing about the entry.

LO 4 The "lone wolf" provision of the Patriot Act amended FISA so that individuals engaged in international terrorism don't have to be linked to a specific foreign power to be subject to FISA search warrants and FISC proceedings. The business records provision of the Patriot Act gave the FISC power to order third parties to produce information, items, and documents relevant to national security investigations. Although this power is similar to grand jury subpoenas requiring the same disclosure from third parties, greater safeguards are in place to protect innocent people during national security investigations.

LO 5 The FBI National Security Letters (NSLs) require telephone companies, Internet Service Providers, consumer credit reporting agencies, banks, and other financial institutions to turn over all metadata from all customer records for intelligence intelligence-gathering purposes. Before the USA Patriot Act, several federal statutes had NSL provisions that required a written request from the director of the FBI. The Patriot Act amended the NSL provisions in the Electronic Communications Privacy Act, Right to Financial Privacy Act, and the Fair Credit Reporting Act so that NSLs could be employed without delays associated with written approval from FBI headquarters and more widely by eliminating the requirement that the information pertained to a foreign power or its agents.

LO 6 Out of the thousands of NSLs issued by the FBI, only a few have been challenged in court. Challengers argue that issuance of the NSLs themselves, as well as the non-disclosure orders within them, violate both the First and Fourth Amendments. In separate cases, the courts ultimately decided that issuing NSLs and the "gag" orders that demand total secrecy from the recipients violated only the First Amendment.

LO 7 The Capone approach and FBI sting operations are preventative counterterrorism and counterintelligence tactics not unaddressed by the USA Patriot Act. Following the Capone approach, the FBI apprehends individuals linked to terrorist plots on lesser, non-terrorism-related offenses. Sting operations usually involve undercover FBI Agents agents attempting to gather "ironclad evidence" against suspects by catching them committing an overt act. Preventative counterterrorism and counterintelligence tactics pose a unique challenge to the FBI in determining when individuals move from lawfully expressing radical ideas to engaging in violent extremist acts.

LO 8 When and whether to give *Miranda* warnings to persons detained on suspicion of terrorist acts is a hotly debated issue, partly because some suspects may be held as unlawful enemy combatants. Although the U.S. Department of Justice has reaffirmed its commitment to the *Miranda* rule, it also encourages agents to interpret the public safety exception to the *Miranda* rule broadly in terror cases.

LO 9 The Central Intelligence Agency (CIA) was established when President Truman signed the National Security Act (NSA) in 1947. The CIA is subject to the same rules and regulations as the FBI when conducting counterterrorism and counterintelligence investigations. Recently leaked information, however, has revealed that much information about U.S. persons is inadvertently collected when gathering foreign intelligence.

LO 10 Persons detained as unlawful enemy combatants face federal court trials according to the nature and seriousness of the offense, the defendant's culpability, and their willingness to cooperate. Federal courts have high conviction rates and traditionally give long sentences in terrorism trials.

LO 10 Military commissions are established by the president as commander in chief, replace the authority of federal courts in trying noncitizens for terrorist acts, and aren't bound by constitutional requirements.

LO 10 The "terrorism-as-war" position emphasizes trial by military commissions, a focus on national security, and secret proceedings that prevent enemies from gaining intelligence. The "terrorism-as-crime" position criticizes the untested nature of the military court system and relies on f federal courts to gain extradition and access a wider variety of charges and pleas. The use of both federal courts and military commissions reflects the need for flexibility in counterterrorism and counterintelligence trials.

LO 11 The Supreme Court has held that stopping a deportable alien for suspected immigration crimes at a checkpoint is a Fourth Amendment seizure but that the national interest in controlling immigration outweighs the intrusion of a brief detention.

LO 11 The reasonableness of detaining noncitizens during deportation proceedings depends on the risk of flight and the danger they may pose to the community. The Illegal Immigration Reform and Immigration Responsibility Act (IIRIRA) of 1996 requires that the attorney general take into custody any alien who has committed a long list of crimes and deport any alien convicted of serious offenses in their home country.

REVIEW QUESTIONS

1. How are lawful enemy combatants distinguished from unlawful enemy combatants?

2. What reasons did the U.S. Supreme Court give for denying German combatants in Japan access to U.S. federal courts after World War II?

3. Describe how the court's opinion on habeas corpus rights for detainees changed under *Rasul v. Bush*, and summarize the reasons they it gave for that change.

4. Explain how Congress has responded to the Supreme Court expanding habeas corpus rights to Guantanamo Bay detainees.

5. Describe how habeas corpus rights changed after *Boumediene v. Bush*.

6. Define "United States person" as it relates to the Foreign Intelligence Surveillance Act (FISA).

7. Describe the limitations of FISA according to the minimization guidelines.

8. According to the FISC Court of Review, which requirement of the Fourth Amendment limits FISC surveillance?

9. Explain the significance of the analogy of the FISA court as a rubber stamp. According to former OIPR head James A. Baker, why is this idea "ridiculous"?

10. Describe how roving wiretaps differ from conventional wiretaps.

11. What are "sneak sneak-and and-peek" searches usually used for, and how has their legal status and definition changed since the enactment of the USA Patriot Act?

12. Describe the "lone wolf" provision to the Patriot Act. Why do critics fear it will lead to "FISA serving for some of our most important criminal laws"?

13. According to Professor Sale, how does the business record provision of the Patriot Act provide greater safeguards for innocent people during national security investigations than during ordinary grand jury investigations?

14. List five examples of "Financial Institutions" subject to the business record provision of the USA Patriot Act.

15. Define metadata as it relates to National Security Letters (NSLs). How is this information different from information obtained through business records subpoenas?

16. How did the Patriot Act amend the NSL provisions in the Electronic Communications Privacy Act, Right to Financial Privacy Act, and the Fair Credit Reporting Act? Describe the two reasons for these changes.

17. Describe two proper and two improper usages of National Security Letters.

18. Describe the two aspects of NSLs that have been challenged in court and identify the constitutional Amendments amendments they relate to.

19. Define the Capone approach to proactive counterterrorism efforts. According to recent data, how heavily is this tactic relied upon by the FBI?

20. Summarize the two primary criticisms to of FBI sting operations. How has FBI Director Robert S. Mueller addressed both of these criticisms?

21. Summarize the arguments supporting and opposing Mirandizing individuals suspected of terrorism. Describe the Department of Justice's view of this issue.

22. What kind of information is collected by the National Security Agency? Who is the target of these surveillance techniques? What information is collected "incidentally"?

23. Identify and describe the two kinds of proceedings for the trial of suspected terrorists.

24. Identify the sources of authority for the Military Order of November 13, 2001, and describe the jurisdiction of military commissions created by the order.

25. How do the constitutional requirements that apply to Article III (ordinary) criminal courts differ from those of military commissions?

26. List some factors the court considered when judging whether one immigration checkpoint met constitutional requirements to balance personal privacy with government need.

27. Distinguish between the rights we give an illegal immigrant detained on suspicion of crimes in the United States and the rights of an immigrant detained on suspicion of having a criminal record overseas.

28. Identify two major considerations in deciding whether to detain noncitizens during noncriminal deportation proceedings.

29. How did the Immigration and Nationality Act affect detainment during deportation proceedings?

30. How did the Illegal Immigration Reform and Immigration Responsibility Act affect detention during criminal deportation proceedings?

KEY TERMS

unlawful enemy combatant, p. 577
lawful enemy combatant, p. 577
suspension clause, p. 580
federal crime of terrorism, p. 581
Counterterrorism Division, p. 582
Counterintelligence Division, p. 582
United States person, p. 583
roving wiretaps, p. 586
"sneak-and-peek" searches, p. 587

sneak-and-peek search warrants, p. 587
"lone wolf" terrorist, p. 588
business records provision, p. 589
National Security Letters (NSLs), p. 591
NSL "gag" orders, p. 597
Capone approach, p. 605
Sting operations, p. 605

Article III courts, p. 618
war crimes, p. 618
military commission, p. 619
military courts-martial, p. 619
terrorist-acts-as-war view, p. 621
terrorist-acts-as-crime view, p. 621
deportable aliens, p. 626
noncriminal (civil) deportation proceedings, p. 629

Selected Amendments of the Constitution of the United States

Amendment IV

The right of the people to be secure in their persons, houses, papers, and effects, against unreasonable searches and seizures, shall not be violated, and no Warrants shall issue, but upon probable cause, supported by Oath or affirmation, and particularly describing the place to be searched, and the persons or things to be seized.

Amendment V

No person shall be held to answer for a capital, or otherwise infamous crime, unless on a presentment or indictment of a Grand Jury, except in cases arising in the land or naval forces, or in the Militia, when in actual service in time of War or public danger; nor shall any person be subject for the same offence to be twice put in jeopardy of life or limb; nor shall be compelled in any criminal case to be a witness against himself, nor be deprived of life, liberty, or property, without due process of law; nor shall private property be taken for public use, without just compensation.

Amendment VI

In all criminal prosecutions, the accused shall enjoy the right to a speedy and public trial, by an impartial jury of the State and district wherein the crime shall have been committed, which district shall have been previously ascertained by law, and to be informed of the nature and cause of the accusation; to be confronted with the witnesses against him; to have compulsory process for obtaining witnesses in his favor, and to have the Assistance of Counsel for his defence.

Amendment VIII

Excessive bail shall not be required, nor excessive fines imposed, nor cruel and unusual punishments inflicted.

Amendment XIV

Passed by Congress June 13, 1866. Ratified July 9, 1868.

Section I All persons born or naturalized in the United States, and subject to the jurisdiction thereof, are citizens of the United States and of the State wherein they reside. No State shall make or enforce any law which shall abridge the privileges or immunities of citizens of the United States; nor shall any State deprive any person of life, liberty, or property, without due process of law; nor deny to any person within its jurisdiction the equal protection of the laws.

GLOSSARY

absolute immunity the absence of liability for actions within the scope of duties; judges have it.

accidental show-ups situations where the witness happens to see a defendant in custody, outside of the courtroom or in the police station, for example.

accusatory stage of the criminal process the point at which the criminal process focuses on a specific suspect.

accusatory system rationale a system in which the government bears the burden of proof.

acquisition of memory information the brain takes in at the time of the crime.

actual authority (subjective) third-party consent third-party consent searches aren't valid unless the person consenting had actual authority to consent for another person.

actual imprisonment standard offenses that don't actually result in prison sentences.

actual prejudice test courts have to decide whether jurors were in fact prejudiced by harmful publicity.

actual seizures when officers physically grab individuals with the intent to keep them from leaving.

administrative sentencing model a sentencing structure in which parole boards and prison administrators determine the exact release date within sentences prescribed by legislatures and judges.

affidavit a sworn statement under oath to the facts and circumstances amounting to probable cause.

affirmed an appellate court decision upholding the decision of a lower court.

Alford plea when a defendant pleads guilty while still protesting his innocence.

Antiterrorism and Effective Death Penalty Act (AEDPA) limits the use of federal habeas corpus law by both state and federal prisoners, whether they're on death row or imprisoned for any length of time.

apparent authority (objective) test of third-party consent third-party consent searches are valid if officers reasonably believe the person consenting had the authority to consent, even if, in fact, she didn't have that authority .

appellant the party appealing in an appellate court case.

appellate court case case in which a lower court has already taken some action and one of the parties has asked a higher court to review the lower court's action.

appellate courts review the decisions made in trial courts.

appellee the party appealed against in an appellate court case.

appointed counsel lawyers for people who can't afford to hire lawyers.

Apprendi bright-line rule other than a prior conviction, any fact that increases the penalty for a crime beyond the prescribed statutory maximum must be submitted to a jury and proved beyond a reasonable doubt.

archival research consists of analyzing real procedures used in actual criminal cases.

arraignment to bring defendants to court to answer the criminal charges against them.

arrest officers take suspects to the police station and keep them there against their will.

Article III courts regular federal courts whose authority comes from Article III of the U.S. Constitution, which created the judiciary.

articulable facts facts officers can name to back up their stops of citizens.

assumption of risk source of third-party consent authority consenting party takes the chance that someone else might consent for her.

assumption of risk theory whenever we knowingly reveal our incriminating secrets, we assume the risk that our false friends will use them against us in criminal cases.

attenuation exception illegally seized evidence is admissible in court if the poisonous connection between illegal police actions and the evidence they illegally got from their actions weakens enough.

authorized imprisonment standard offenses where imprisonment is authorized but not required.

"bad methods" using unconstitutional means to obtain evidence.

Bail Reform Act of 1984 authorizes federal courts to jail arrested defendants when a judge determines, after a hearing, that no condition of release would "reasonably" guarantee the appearance of the defendant and the safety of the community.

balancing element the need to search and/or seize outweighs the invasion of individual liberty and/or privacy.

bench trials trials without juries, in which judges find the facts.

bind-over standard enough evidence exists for the judge in a preliminary hearing to decide to send the case to trial.

binds over to decide to send a case to trial.

bite-and-hold technique technique in which a police dog given a "find" command will find, "bite," and "hold" a suspect until commanded to release.

blind administrator a person conducting a lineup who doesn't know which person in the lineup is the suspect.

blue curtain wall of protection that hides "real" police work from public view.

border search exception searches at international borders are reasonable without probable cause or warrants, because the government interest in what and who enters the country outweighs the invasion of privacy of persons entering.

Bostick standard whether a reasonable person would feel free to decline officers' requests or terminate the encounter.

bounded rationality strongly documented finding that people don't "attempt to ruthlessly maximize utility"; instead, once they identify an option that's "good enough," they stop looking and choose it.

"bright-line" rules rules that spell out officers' power and apply to all cases rather than assessing the totality of circumstances on a case-by-case basis.

broad view of habeas corpus interpretation of the Habeas Corpus Act of 1867 that empowers the federal courts to review the whole state proceeding to determine possible violations of federal law and constitutional provisions.

business records provision part of the USA Patriot Act that allows national security investigators to obtain any tangible things from third parties if the items sought are relevant to an authorized national security investigation.

Capone approach a proactive approach to fighting terrorism by which the FBI apprehends individuals linked to terrorist plots on lesser, offenses not related to terrorism.

case-by-case basis deciding whether constitutional requirements were satisfied in each case.

case citation tells where you can find the published report of a case.

case-in-chief the part of the trial where the government presents its evidence to prove the defendants' guilt.

categorical suspicion refers to suspicion that falls on suspects because they fit into a broad category of people, such as being in a particular location, being members of a particular race or ethnicity, or fitting a profile.

cautionary instruction instruction in which judges explain the weaknesses of eyewitness identification evidence to juries.

certiorari Latin for "to be certified," it's a discretionary order of the Supreme Court to review a lower court decision.

challenges for cause removal of prospective jurors upon showing their partiality.

change of venue a pretrial motion in which the defendant asks that the trial be held in a different place.

charge bargaining bargaining for a reduction in either the number or severity of criminal charges.

charge the grand jury the address of the judge to the grand jury.

checkpoints stopping groups of drivers without individualized suspicion that any individual might be up to criminal activity; all individuals who don't want to pass through can simply turn off and avoid them.

citation an order to appear before a judge on a certain date to defend against a charge, often a traffic violation.

civil action a noncriminal case.

civil law remedy against constitutional violations that involves suing the officer, the police department, or the government.

Civil Rights Act actions lawsuits initiated by private individuals in federal court against state officers for violating the individuals' constitutional rights; also called § 1983 actions.

class action an action in which one person or a small group of people represents the interests of a larger group.

clear and convincing evidence more than probable cause but less than proof beyond a reasonable doubt.

collateral attack a proceeding to review the constitutionality of detention or imprisonment.

collateral consequences exception the principle that cases aren't moot if conviction can still cause legal consequences despite completion of the sentence.

community security a value at the heart of our constitutional democracy that we should live in a place where we are safe (or at least feel safe).

compliant confessions mere acts of public compliance by a suspect who comes to believe that the short-term benefits of confession outweigh the long-term costs.

compulsory process for obtaining witnesses Sixth Amendment guarantee of defendants' right to compel the appearance of witnesses in their favor.

concurring opinion statements in which justices agree with the decision but not the reasoning of a court's opinion.

confessions suspect's written or oral acknowledgment of guilt, often including details about the crime.

consent searches searches without warrants or probable cause are valid if the government can prove by the totality of the circumstances that suspects voluntarily consented to the searches.

constitutional democracy the balance between the power of government and the rights of individuals.

constitutionalism refers to the idea that constitutions adopted by the whole people are a higher form of law than ordinary laws passed by legislatures.

constitutionally protected areas persons and places named in the Fourth Amendment, including houses, papers, and effects.

constitutional right justification the idea that the exclusionary rule is an essential part of constitutional rights.

constitutional tort (*Bivens*) actions lawsuits against individual federal law enforcement officers.

contemporaneous with arrest also called "incident to arrest," it includes the time before, during, and after arrest.

conventional Fourth Amendment approach the warrant and reasonableness clauses are firmly connected, according to the U.S. Supreme Court, when ruling on stop-and-frisk law cases.

corporal punishment physical punishment, such as whipping.

counsel pro bono lawyers willing to represent clients at no charge.

Counterintelligence Division faction of the FBI responsible for keeping our nation's most valuable secrets out of the hands of spies.

Counterterrorism Division faction of the FBI responsible for identifying and disrupting potential terrorist plots.

court holding the legal rule the court applied to the facts of the case.

court of last resort the U.S. Constitution; its decisions trump the authority of all other sources of criminal procedure.

court opinions written explanation for a court's decision.

court reasoning the reasons and arguments the court gives to support its holding.

court's judgment (disposition) the most important legal action of the court, this is the court's official decision in the case.

criminal complaint the formal charging document.

criminal information a written formal charge made by prosecutors without a grand jury indictment.

criminal law remedy against official misconduct that involves suing the officer.

critical stages in criminal prosecutions includes all those stages that occur after the government files formal charges; the view that custodial interrogation is so important in criminal prosecutions that during it suspects have a right to a lawyer.

critical stages of criminal proceedings see *critical stages in criminal prosecutions*.

curtilage the area immediately surrounding a house, such as garages, patios, and pools, that isn't part of the open fields doctrine.

custodial arrests an official taking a person into custody and holding her to answer criminal charges.

custodial interrogation the questioning that occurs after the police have taken suspects into custody.

custody depriving people of their "freedom of action in any significant way."

damages a remedy in private lawsuits in the form of money for injuries.

deadly force force capable of causing death.

decision to charge the prosecutor's decision to begin formal proceedings against a suspect.

defense of official immunity a public official charged by law with duties calling for discretionary decision making isn't personally liable to an individual except for willful or malicious wrongdoing.

defense of vicarious official immunity police departments and local governments can claim the official immunity of their employees.

departure judge imposes a sentence outside of sentencing guidelines.

deportable alien a person who has been found deportable by an immigration judge or who admits his deportability upon questioning by official agents.

determinate sentencing a sentence for a fixed length of time.

deterrence justification the justification that excluding evidence obtained in violation of the Constitution prevents illegal law enforcement.

direct attacks appeal directly attacking decisions made by trial courts.

directed verdict rule enough evidence exists to decide a case without submitting it to the jury.

direct information information that officers know firsthand, acquired directly through their physical senses.

discovery a legal action asking for a court order to compel one side in a case to turn over information that might help the other side.

discriminatory effect proving that race or some other illegal group characteristic (not a legitimate criterion, such as seriousness of the offense or criminal record) accounts for the official decision.

discriminatory purpose a named official in the case at hand intended to discriminate against a named individual because of race or other illegal criteria.

dismissal without prejudice the termination of a case with the provision that it can be prosecuted again.

dismissal with prejudice the termination of a case with the provision that it can't be prosecuted again.

dissenting opinion part of an appellate court case in which justices write opinions disagreeing with the decision and reasoning of a court.

distinguishing cases a court decides that a prior decision doesn't apply to the current case because the facts are different.

diversion cases prosecutors agree to drop a case before formal judicial proceedings begin if suspects participate in specified programs (e.g., community service, restitution, substance abuse, or family violence treatment).

DNA profiling a special type of DNA pattern that distinguishes one individual from all others.

DNA testing forensic evidence that can, in certain circumstances, establish to a virtual certainty whether a given individual did or did not commit a particular crime.

doctrine of judicial economy rule that says that time and money shouldn't be spent on appeals defendants could've avoided by objecting during the trial.

doctrine of *respondeat superior* employers are legally liable for their employees' illegal acts.

doctrine of sovereign immunity governments can't be sued by individuals without the consent of the government.

double jeopardy constitutional protection against being subject to liability for the same offense more than once.

drones aircraft that can fly without an onboard, human operator.

dual sovereignty doctrine the principle that holds that a crime arising out of the same facts in one state isn't the same crime in another state.

due process a broad and vague guarantee of fair procedures in deciding cases; the Fifth and Fourteenth Amendment provisions prohibiting the federal government and the states, respectively, from depriving citizens of life, liberty, or property without due process of law.

due process revolution U.S. Supreme Court application of the Bill of Rights to state criminal proceedings.

emergency searches also called *"exigent circumstance searches"*; are based on the idea that it's sometimes impractical (even dangerous) to require officers to obtain warrants before they search.

equitable tolling doctrine that says the statute of limitations won't bar a claim of actual innocence if the plaintiff, despite diligent efforts, didn't discover the evidence of actual innocence until after the statute of limitations expired.

errors of commission a *retrieval of memory* error, such as picking an innocent person in a photo array.

errors of omission a *retrieval of memory* error, such as failure to recall some detail or to recognize a perpetrator.

exclusionary rule the rule that illegally seized evidence can't be admitted in criminal trials.

exigent circumstances circumstances requiring prompt action, eliminating the warrant requirement for a search.

experimental research researchers *create* crimes (live staged or videotaped) that unsuspecting people witness, then question them about what they witnessed and show them a lineup.

express waiver test the suspect specifically says or writes that she knows her rights, knows she's giving them up, and knows the consequences of giving them up.

external civilian review review of complaints against police officers with participation by individuals who aren't sworn police officers.

eyewitness recall information retrieved from memory at the time of the lineup, show-up, or picture identification; eyewitnesses are given hints, such as a time frame, and then asked to report what they observed.

eyewitness recognition information retrieved from memory at the time of the lineup, show-up, or picture identification; eyewitnesses are shown persons or objects and then asked to indicate whether they were involved in the crime.

eyewitness retrospective self-reports witnesses' in-court recollections.

fact bargaining the prosecutor agrees not to challenge the defendant's version of the facts or not to reveal aggravating facts to the judge.

factual basis for guilty pleas judges might ask defendants to describe the conduct that led to the charges, ask the prosecutor and defense attorney similar questions, and consult presentence reports to determine whether the facts support a guilty plea.

false friends someone we trust with our secrets who turns out to be a government agent.

federal crime of terrorism an offense calculated to influence or affect the conduct of government by intimidation or coercion or to retaliate against government conduct.

Federal Jury Selection and Service Act requires that juries be "selected at random from a fair cross section of the community in the district or division wherein the court convenes" and forbids exclusion based on race, color, religion, sex, national origin, or economic status.

federal rights floor minimum standards set by the U.S. Constitution.

Federal Tort Claims Act (FTCA) limits federal sovereign immunity and allows recovery in federal courts for tort damages caused by federal employees.

fillers persons known to be innocent who participate in a lineup.

find-and-bark technique technique in which dogs are trained to find suspects and then bark until officers can get control of the suspect.

first appearance the appearance of a defendant in court for determination of probable cause, determination of bail, assignment of an attorney, and notification of rights; also called a "probable cause hearing."

forensic *ipse dixit* statutes laws that authorize the state to prove its forensic allegations by relying on forensic certificates rather than live testimony.

forensic science the application of scientific methods and techniques to investigate crimes.

Fourth Amendment frisks once-over-lightly pat downs of outer clothing by officers to protect themselves by taking away suspects' weapons.

Fourth Amendment stops brief, on-the-spot detentions that freeze suspicious situations so that law enforcement officers can determine whether to arrest, investigate further, or terminate further action.

free will rationale involuntary confessions aren't just unreliable and contrary to the accusatory system of justice; they're also coerced if they're not "the product of a rational intellect and a free will."

fruit-of-the-poisonous-tree doctrine the principle that evidence derived from illegally obtained sources isn't admissible.

functional immunity whether prosecutors have immunity depends on the function they're performing at the time of their misconduct.

fundamental attribution error tendency of juries to overestimate the role of defendants' "nature" (disposition) in evaluating their actions, while they underestimate the role of the interrogation situation.

fundamental fairness doctrine of due process a command to the states to provide two basics of a fair trial: notice and a hearing.

fundamental law a law above the ordinary law created by legislatures.

general warrant empowered royal agents of the English Crown to search anyone, anywhere, anytime.

"good" evidence probative evidence, or proof of guilt.

good-faith exception searches conducted by officers with warrants they honestly and reasonably believe satisfy the Fourth Amendment requirements.

government officials' acts actions that defendants claim violated the Constitution.

GPS surveillance receiver technology capable of pinpointing exactly where somebody is at any moment in time.

"grabbable" area searchable area that includes the arrestee's person and area within his reach.

grand jurors members of the grand jury.

grand jury review a secret proceeding to test a government case.

"great writ of liberty" refers to the use of habeas corpus during the 19th century.

habeas corpus Latin for "you have the body," it's an action that asks those who hold defendants to justify their detention.

habeas corpus proceedings civil action, also called "collateral attack," brought by defendants attacking the lawfulness of their detention.

hands-off approach to sentencing procedures U.S. Supreme Court policy of leaving decisions about the way sentences were determined to trial judges.

hearsay information facts and circumstances officers learn secondhand from victims, witnesses, other police officers, and anonymous, professional, or paid informants.

hearsay rule allows courts to rely upon secondhand evidence to prove probable cause to arrest but not to convict defendants in trial.

hearsay rule in arrests courts don't admit secondhand evidence to prove guilt, but, if it's reliable and truthful, they'll accept it to show probable cause to arrest.

hearsay testimony evidence from witnesses that they don't know firsthand.

"high-crime area" designation of a neighborhood that allows highly ambiguous conduct to amount to reasonable suspicion that justifies a Fourth Amendment stop. Can be based on statements as weak as "several arrests" by law enforcement officers.

holding of the court the holding refers to the legal rule the court applied to the facts of the cases.

hot pursuit an emergency created by the need to apprehend a fleeing suspect.

hunch (mere suspicion) gut feelings not based on facts and circumstances.

hung jury a jury that's unable to reach a verdict after protracted deliberations.

impeach to show that a witness's credibility is suspect.

implied waiver test the totality of circumstances in each case adds up to proof that before suspects talked they knew they had the right to remain silent and knew they were giving up the right.

incident to arrest sometimes called "contemporaneous with arrest," it includes the time before, during, and after arrest.

incorporation doctrine the principle that the Fourteenth Amendment due process clause incorporates the provisions of the Bill of Rights and applies them to state criminal procedure.

incriminating statements statements that fall short of full confessions.

independent source exception evidence is admissible even if police officers violate the Constitution to obtain it if in a totally separate action, they obtain the same evidence lawfully.

indeterminate sentencing tailoring punishment to suit the criminal; sentencing that relies heavily on the discretion of judges and parole boards in exercising sentencing authority.

indictment a formal criminal charge issued by a grand jury.

indigence financial hardship in which defendants can't afford an attorney.

indigent defendants defendants too poor to hire their own lawyers.

individual autonomy a value at the heart of our constitutional democracy that individuals are free to control their own lives without government interference.

individualized suspicion suspicion that points to specific individuals and consists of "facts that would tell both the officer on the street and a court ruling on a suppression motion whether or not there was reasonable suspicion."

inevitable discovery exception evidence obtained illegally is admissible if officers would've legally discovered it eventually.

inherently coercive custodial interrogation is coercive because police hold suspects in strange surroundings while trying to crack their will, and suspects don't have anyone there to support them.

in loco parentis the principle by which the government stands in place of parents; school administrators are substitute parents while students are in school and have the legal authority to search students and their stuff during school hours and activities.

internal affairs units (IAU) review review of police misconduct by special officers inside police departments.

internal and external departmental review remedy against official misconduct that involves disciplining the officer outside the judicial system.

internalized false confessions innocent, but vulnerable, suspects under "highly suggestive interrogation tactics" come not just to give in to get the situation over with but to believe that they actually committed the crime.

inventory searches searches conducted without probable cause or warrants to protect property and the safety of police and to prevent claims against police.

judgment the final outcome of a case.

judicial integrity (moral) justification the idea that the honor and honesty of the courts justify the exclusionary rule.

judicial sentencing model a structure in which judges prescribe sentences within broad contours set by legislative acts.

jurisdiction the power to hear and decide cases in a specific geographical area (such as a county, a state, or a federal district) or the subject matter (e.g., criminal appeals) the court controls.

jury instructions instructions from the judge to the jury on what the law is and how they should apply it.

jury nullification the jury's authority to reach a not guilty verdict despite proof of guilt.

jury panel potential jurors drawn from the list of eligible citizens not excused.

key-man system jury lists are made up by civic and political leaders, selected from individuals they know personally or by reputation.

knock-and-announce exception permits the admission of evidence seized during searches of homes even when officers violate the "knock-and-announce" rule of the warrant requirement.

knock-and-announce rule the practice of law enforcement officers knocking and announcing their presence before entering a home to search it.

lawful enemy combatant a member of the regular forces, militia, volunteer corps, or organized resistance movement of a state party engaged in hostilities against the United States who wears a fixed, distinctive sign recognizable at a distance, carries arms openly, and abides by the *laws of war*.

law in action discretionary professional judgments based on training and experience to carry out constitutional commands.

law in the books fair and impartial judgments based on the law as it is written to carry out constitutional commands.

law of criminal procedure the rules that government has to follow to detect and investigate crimes, apprehend suspects, prosecute and convict defendants, and punish criminals.

legislative sentencing model a structure in which legislatures exercise sentencing authority.

liberty the right of citizens to come and go as they please (locomotion) without government interference.

lineups an identification procedure in which the suspect stands in a line with other individuals.

"lone wolf" terrorist an individual who has committed terroristic acts but does not have, or cannot be proven to have, connections to a foreign power.

majority opinion a decision rendered by five or more Supreme Court justices, which becomes the law.

mandatory minimum sentences the legislatively prescribed, nondiscretionary amount of prison time that all offenders convicted of the offense must serve.

manifest necessity doctrine the government can reprosecute a defendant for the same offense if the judge dismissed the case or ordered a mistrial because dismissal "served the ends of justice."

memory experts scientists whose profession is providing empirical demonstrations of how memory actually functions.

memory trace eyewitness evidence in a witness's mind that officers try to extract without damaging.

Mendenhall **test** determines that a person is seized only if, in view of all the circumstances, a reasonable person would not have believed she was free to leave.

might-or-might-not-be-present instruction one of the ways to improve the reliability of eyewitness identification of strangers is to tell witnesses the suspect might or might not be among the photos or members of a lineup.

military commissions non–Article III courts, consisting of a panel of military officers acting under military authority to try enemy combatants for war crimes.

military courts-martial military courts made up of military officers to try members of the U.S. armed forces for violating the Uniform Code of Military Justice.

Miranda **warning** bright-line rule requiring notice of a suspect's rights when law enforcement conducts custodial interrogations.

missing witness instruction instruction that jurors can infer that the witness's testimony would have been unfavorable to the prosecution.

mockery of justice standard the standard under which counsel is deemed ineffective only if circumstances reduced the trial to a farce.

Model Code of Pre-Arraignment Procedure American Law Institute's (group of distinguished judges, lawyers, criminal justice professionals, law enforcement professionals, and scholars) model of criminal procedure law for law enforcement and courts.

money bonds can be unsecured, a court-administered deposit, or privately administered, and defendants are released as soon as money is put up.

mootness doctrine ban on appeals by offenders who have finished their prison sentences or paid their fines.

moral seriousness standard the principle that the Sixth Amendment right to a jury trial extends to morally serious misdemeanors.

narrow view (of habeas corpus) power to review only the jurisdiction of the court over the person and the subject matter of the case.

National Security Letters (NSLs) orders from the FBI to communications companies and financial institutions requiring the disclosure of all noncontent information from all customer records for intelligence-gathering purposes.

negotiated guilty plea a plea of guilty in exchange for a concession to the defendant by the government.

neutral magistrate a disinterested judge who decides whether there's probable cause before officers arrest suspects.

new generation of criminal procedure judicial decision-making and academic debate that treats social scientific and empirical assessment as a crucial element in constitutional decision making.

no-affirmative-duty-to-protect rule plaintiffs can't sue individual officers or government units for failing to stop private people from violating their rights.

nolo contendere Latin for defendants who plead "no contest," meaning they don't contest the issue of guilt or innocence.

noncriminal (civil) deportation proceedings hearings to decide whether an alien is deportable.

nonsearch-related plain view refers to plain view that doesn't involve a Fourth Amendment intrusion at all.

NSL "gag" orders provisions that prevent the recipients of National Security Letters from disclosing the fact or the content of the NSL to anyone at any time.

objective basis the factual justification for government invasions of individual privacy, liberty, and property.

objective basis requirement facts, not hunches, have to back up government invasions of individual liberty and privacy.

objective legal reasonableness measured by the legal rules that were "clearly established" at the time of the government action.

objective privacy whether the subjective expectation of privacy is "one that society is prepared to recognize as 'reasonable.'"

objective standard of reasonable force the Fourth Amendment permits officers to use the amount of force necessary to apprehend and bring suspects under control.

officers of the court part of the dual role of prosecutors in our criminal justice system, in which their mission is to do justice.

"off-the-wall" surveillance observations from the exterior of the home.

open fields doctrine the rule that the Fourth Amendment doesn't prevent government officials from gathering and using information they see, hear, smell, or touch in open fields.

opening statements addresses to the jury by the prosecution and defense counsel before they present their evidence.

parallel rights state-granted rights similar to those in the U.S. Constitution and Bill of Rights.

parolees prisoners who have served time in prison and who remain under supervision after their release from prison.

particularity requirement the requirement that a warrant must identify the person or place to be searched and the items or persons to be seized.

pattern jury instructions published instructions that fit most cases.

peremptory challenges removal of jurors without showing cause.

per se approach looking at the totality of circumstances to determine whether an identification should be admitted into evidence.

petitioner a defendant in a noncriminal case who asks a higher court to review a decision made either by a lower court or some other official.

photo array witnesses try to pick the suspect from one (photo show-up) or several (photo lineup) mug shots.

plain-error rule review of convictions should take place only when "plain errors affecting substantial rights" cause "manifest injustice or miscarriage of justice."

plain view doctrine doctrine that it's not a "search" to discover evidence inadvertently obtained through ordinary senses if the officers are where they have a right to be and are doing what they have a right to do.

plea bargaining in the "shadow of trial" model prosecutors, judges, and defense attorneys act rationally to forecast the outcome of a trial, then make bargains that leave both sides better off by splitting the costs they save by not going to trial.

plea bargaining outside the "shadow of trial" model the real world of plea bargaining, in which legally irrelevant factors sometimes skew the fair allocation of punishment and some defendants strike skewed bargains.

plurality opinion a statement in which the greatest number, but not a majority, of the justices favor a court's decision.

precedent a prior decision that's binding on a similar present case.

prejudice prong the second of a two-prong test of reasonable competence, in which defendants have to show that bad "lawyering" deprived them of a fair trial with a reliable result.

preliminary hearing the adversary proceeding that tests the government's case.

preponderance of the evidence more evidence than not supports a conclusion.

presumption of guilt the reduction of rights of convicted offenders during sentencing, appeal, and habeas corpus processes.

presumption of regularity presumes government actions are lawful in the absence of "clear evidence to the contrary."

pretext arrests arrests for one offense where probable cause exists motivated by officers' desire to search for evidence of another unrelated offense where probable cause doesn't exist.

pretrial motions written or oral requests asking the court to decide questions that don't require a trial to be ruled on.

pretrial proceedings defendants' motions to throw out evidence obtained by law enforcement officers during searches and seizures, interrogation, and identification procedures.

preventive detention confining defendants to jail before conviction because they're a threat to public safety.

prima facie case see *prima facie case rule.*

prima facie case rule enough evidence exists to make a decision unless the evidence is contradicted.

principle of judicial review the U.S. Supreme Court's interpretation trumps the interpretation of all other federal and local courts, Congress, and state and local legislatures.

principle of technosocial continuity requires courts to consider both the ways in which technology facilitates intrusive surveillance and the ways in which technology spurs social change that makes citizens more vulnerable to existing surveillance technologies.

privacy the value that's sometimes referred to as "the right to be let alone from government invasions."

probable cause to arrest requires that an officer, in the light of her training and experience, knows enough facts and circumstances to reasonably believe that a crime has been, is being, or is about to be committed and the person arrested has committed, is committing, or is about to commit the crime.

probable cause to bind over higher than the standard for probable cause to arrest, the objective basis for requiring a suspect to stand trial.

probable cause to detain a suspect the objective basis for detaining a suspect following arrest.

probable cause to go to trial requires a higher objective basis than probable cause to detain and is tested by a preliminary hearing or grand jury review.

probationers convicted offenders who are sentenced to supervised release in the community instead of serving time in jails or prison.

procedural history of a case a brief description of the procedural steps and judgments (decisions) made by each court that has heard the case.

profiles popular law enforcement tool that consists of lists of circumstances that might, or might not, be linked to particular kinds of behavior.

prophylactic rule mechanisms that aren't themselves constitutional rights but are used to guarantee those rights.

proportionality principle a punishment is cruel and unusual if its harshness is "grossly disproportionate" to the "gravity of the offense."

public safety exception the rule that *Miranda* warnings need not be administered if doing so would endanger the public.

qualified immunity grants immunity from tort actions if the party was acting reasonably within the scope of his or her duties; also called the *"good faith" defense.*

raise-or-waive doctrine the rule that defendants must raise and preserve objections to errors at trial or waive their right to appeal the errors.

reasonable doubt standard due process requires both federal and state prosecutors to prove every element of a crime beyond a reasonable doubt.

reasonable expectation of privacy doctrine the kind of expectation any citizen might have with respect to any other citizen applies to law enforcement as well.

reasonable-likelihood-of-prejudice test the determination that circumstances may prevent a fair trial.

reasonableness clause the clause in the Fourth Amendment that bans "unreasonable searches and seizures" as opposed to the "warrant clause," which outlines the requirements for obtaining arrest and search warrants.

reasonableness Fourth Amendment approach the warrant and the reasonableness parts of the Fourth Amendment are separate elements that address separate problems.

reasonableness prong defendants have to prove that their lawyer's performance wasn't reasonably competent, meaning that the lawyer was so deficient that she "was not functioning as the 'counsel' guaranteed the defendant by the Sixth Amendment."

reasonableness test the reasonableness of searches and seizures depends on balancing government and individual interests and the objective basis of the searches and seizures.

reasonable suspicion the totality of articulable facts and circumstances that would lead an officer, in the light of her training and experience, to suspect that a crime might be afoot.

reasonably competent attorney standard performance measured by customary skills and diligence.

relative judgment witnesses select the person in the lineup who looks most like the culprit.

release on recognizance (ROR) release from custody on a mere promise to appear.

reliability rationale for due process the justification for reviewing state confessions based on their untrustworthiness.

reliability test of eyewitness evidence allows the admission of identification evidence based on "unnecessarily suggestive" identification procedures *unless* defendants can prove that the suggestive procedure creates a "very substantial likelihood of misidentification."

remanded the appellate court sent the case back to the lower court for further action.

res judicata once a matter is decided, it cannot be reopened.

retained counsel a lawyer paid for by the client.

retention of memory information the brain stores between the time of the crime and the lineup, show-up, or picture identification.

retrieval of memory information retrieved from memory at the time of the lineup, show-up, or picture identification.

reversed the appellate court set aside, or nullified, the lower court's judgment.

reversible error an error that requires an appellate court to reverse the trial court's judgment in the case.

right of habeas corpus the right to a civil action to determine if the offender is being lawfully detained.

right of locomotion the freedom to come and go as we please.

roadblock stopping everyone who passes a point on a road during a specific time period.

Robinson rule *bright-line rule* that officers can always search anyone they're authorized to take into custody.

routine procedures inventory searches are reasonable if officers follow department guidelines in conducting them.

roving wiretaps court orders that apply surveillance to particular people rather than particular devices.

rule of four the requirement that four Supreme Court justices must vote to review a case for its appeal to be heard by the Supreme Court.

searches include government actions ranging from Fourth Amendment frisks to highly invasive strip and body-cavity searches.

searches incident to arrest searches made of lawfully arrested suspects without probable cause or warrant.

search-related plain view refers to items in plain view that officers discover while they're searching for items for which they're specifically authorized to search.

secret "caller ID" the power of government to capture a record of all telephone numbers (not conversations) from a subscriber's phone in the investigation of "any crime."

§ 1983 actions lawsuits brought by private individuals against law enforcement officers under § 1983 of the U.S. Civil Rights Act.

seizures include government actions ranging from Fourth Amendment stops to full custodial arrests.

selective incorporation doctrine some of the Bill of Rights is incorporated in due process, and states must follow these procedures as defined by the U.S. Supreme Court.

selective prosecution lack of resources leads prosecutors to base decisions to charge on priorities.

sentence bargaining a favorable sentence recommendation by the prosecutor to the judge, or bargaining directly with the judge for a favorable sentence.

sentencing guidelines a narrow range of penalties established by a commission within which judges are supposed to choose a specific sentence.

sequential presentation presenting members of a lineup one at a time and requiring witnesses to answer "yes" or "no" as they're presented.

show-of-authority seizures take place when officers display their authority by ordering suspects to stop, drawing their weapons, or otherwise acting such that a reasonable person wouldn't feel free to leave.

show-ups a procedure in which the witness identifies the suspect without other possible suspects present.

simultaneous presentation a traditional lineup, in which members are standing together at the same time, giving witnesses the opportunity to treat the procedure like a multiple-choice test with a "best," but maybe not "right," answer.

Sixth Amendment confrontation clause the right to cross-examine the prosecution's witnesses.

"sneak-and-peek" searches a variation of no-knock entries in which officers enter private places without the owner or (occupant) consenting or even knowing about it.

sneak-and-peek search warrants warrants that allow officers to enter private places without the owner or (occupant) consenting or knowing about it.

social cost of the rule the exclusionary rule might free guilty people and undermine the prosecution's case by keeping good evidence out of court.

special-needs searches government inspections and other regulatory measures not conducted to gather criminal evidence.

special-relationship exception exception to the *no-affirmative-duty-to-protect rule*, which says that governments have a duty to protect individuals they hold in custody.

stare decisis the doctrine in which a prior decision binds a present case with similar facts.

state-created-danger exception exception to the *no-affirmative-duty-to-protect rule*, which tests government liability by examining whether (1) the officer's actions created a special danger of violent harm to the plaintiff in the lawsuit; (2) the officer knew or should have known her actions would encourage this plaintiff to rely on her actions; and (3) the danger created by the officer's actions caused either harm or vulnerability to harm.

sting operations a proactive approach to fighting terrorism in which the FBI, usually undercover, tries to collect "ironclad evidence" by catching terrorism suspects committing an overt act.

stipulates defense counsel agrees not to contest some evidence prevented by the prosecution.

straight guilty pleas plea of guilty not based on negotiation, usually when the proof of guilt is overwhelming.

subjective privacy whether a person exhibited an actual personal expectation of privacy.

suggestion eyewitness's interpretation of events is shaped by other people's suggestions.

supervisory power the power of the U.S. Supreme Court to make rules to manage how lower federal courts conduct their business.

suppression hearing a proceeding in an appellate case to determine whether evidence obtained by law enforcement officers during searches and seizures, interrogation, and identification procedures, such as lineups, should be thrown out.

Supremacy Clause U.S. Constitution, Article VI, which says that the U.S. Constitution is the last word in criminal procedure.

suspension clause From Article I, Section 9 of the U.S. Constitution; mandates that the writ of habeas corpus can only be suspended in cases of rebellion or when it's necessary to protect public safety.

terrorist-acts-as-crime view calls for fighting terrorism by trying all those who commit terrorist acts in U.S. criminal courts.

terrorist-acts-as-war view calls for fighting terrorism by trying all foreign suspects by military commissions.

testimony the content of what you say and write against yourself.

text-case book part text and part case excerpts from real criminal procedure cases, edited for nonlawyers.

The Federal Reporter the official U.S. government publication of U.S. Court of Appeals decisions.

thermal imagers devices that detect, measure, and record infrared radiation not visible to the naked eye.

third-party consent searches one person can consent for another person to a search.

three-prong balancing test considers the gravity of public interest served by the seizure, the effectiveness of the seizure in advancing that public interest, and the degree of intrusion upon the stopped individual's liberty when determining whether roadblocks and checkpoints are reasonable.

"through-the-wall" surveillance gives the observer or listener direct access to information in private areas.

tort action a civil action in which plaintiffs sue individual officers for damages caused by the officer breaking the law.

tort feasor the accused wrongdoer in a tort case.

torts civil lawsuits for damages over private wrongs.

total incorporation doctrine that says the states have to apply the provisions outlined in the Bill of Rights and that all the provisions were incorporated under the due process clause.

totality-of-circumstances approach weighing all the facts surrounding the government's establishing identification of the suspect to determine if it's reliable enough to be admitted; also called the *"per se approach."*

totality of circumstances test the conditions used to determine abandonment and the voluntariness of a waiver of rights and of incriminating statements.

trespass doctrine the Fourth Amendment doctrine that requires physical intrusions into a "constitutionally protected area" to qualify as a search.

two-pronged effective counsel test U.S. Supreme Court test of "effectiveness of counsel," which requires the defense to prove a lawyer's performance wasn't reasonably competent and that the incompetence affected the outcome of the case in favor of conviction.

unequivocal acts or statements withdrawal of consent rule people can withdraw their consent, but it must be with actions or statements that are unambiguously clear.

United States person a citizen of the United States or an alien lawfully admitted for permanent residence in the United States.

United States Reports the official U.S. government publication of U.S. Supreme Court cases.

unlawful enemy combatant a person who has engaged in hostilities or purposefully and materially supported hostilities against the United States or its co-belligerents who is not a *lawful enemy combatant* (including a person who is part of the Taliban, Al-Qaeda, or associated forces).

unnecessarily and impermissibly suggestive one of the requirements a defendant must prove to have a lineup, show-up, or photo array identification thrown out on due process grounds.

vehicle exception exception to the Fourth Amendment that says that if officers have probable cause to believe that a vehicle contains that which by law is subject to seizure, then search and seizure are valid.

very substantial likelihood of misidentification one of two requirements to have identification evidence thrown out based on due process grounds; the totality of circumstances must prove that "unnecessarily and impermissibly suggestive" procedures probably led to a misidentification.

violent crime–automatic-frisk exception facts that back up a stop don't automatically also back up a frisk, except when suspects are stopped for crimes of violence.

voir dire the process of picking jurors from the pool of potential jurors by questioning them.

voluntariness test of self-incrimination confessions and other incriminating statements violate due process if the totality of circumstances shows that suspects didn't confess voluntarily.

voluntary false confessions innocent people confess without police prompting or pressure.

war crimes crimes committed during wartime that inflict "needless and disproportionate suffering and damages" in pursuit of a "military objective."

warrant clause the part of the Fourth Amendment that outlines the requirements for obtaining arrest and search warrants.

will of the people (popular sovereignty) the power of the people to create law.

writ of certiorari an order to the court that decided the case to send up the record of its proceedings to the U.S. Supreme Court for review.

writs of assistance issued by the English Crown for the life of the monarch, they empowered royal agents to search anyone, anywhere, anytime and to order anyone who happened to be nearby to help execute the warrant.

BIBLIOGRAPHY

9/11 Joint Committee Hearings. 2002. "September 11 Joint Investigation into September 11th: Fifth Public Hearing 26 September 2002—Joint House/Senate Intelligence Committee Hearing." http://www.fas.org/irp/congress/2002_hr/index.html#joint5 (July 16, 2013).

Abel v. U.S. 1960. 362 U.S. 217.

Ackerman, Spencer. 2010. "FBI Interrogators Urge Obama to Keep *Miranda* Warnings Intact." *Washington Independent.* May 13. http://washingtonindependent.com/84716/fbi-interrogators-urge-obama-to-keep-miranda-warnings-intact (May 21, 2013).

Adams v. Williams. 1972. 407 U.S. 143.

Adamson v. California. 1947. 332 U.S. 46.

Agnello v. U.S. 1925. 269 U.S. 20.

Alabama v. White. 1990. 496 U.S. 325.

Aleinikoff, T. Alexander. 1987. "Constitutional Law in the Age of Balancing." *Yale Law Journal* 96:943-1005.

Allen, Francis A. 1978. "The Law as a Path to the World." *Michigan Law Review* 77.

Allen, Ronald J., Joseph L. Hoffman, Debra A. Livingston, and William J. Stuntz. 2005. *Comprehensive Criminal Procedure.* New York: Aspen Publishers.

Allen, Ronald J., William J. Stuntz, Joseph H. Hoffman, Debra A. Livingston, and Andrew W. Leipold. 2011. *Constitutional Criminal Procedure*, 3rd edition. New York: Wolters Kluwer Law and Business.

Allison v. State. 1974. 214 N.W.2d 437 (Wisc.).

Alschuler, Albert. 2002. "Guilty Plea: Plea Bargaining." In *Encyclopedia of Crime & Justice*, 2d ed., edited by Joshua Dressler. New York: Macmillan Reference USA, 754–62.

Amacost, Barbara E. 2010. "*Arizona v. Gant*: Does It Matter?" *Supreme Court Review 2009*. Chicago: University of Chicago Press.

American Academy of Political and Social Science. 1910. *Annals.*

American Bar Association. 1980. *Standards for Criminal Justice.* 2d ed. Chicago: ABA.

———. 1988. *Criminal Justice in Crisis.* Chicago: ABA.

American Law Institute. 1975. *Model Code of Pre-Arraignment Procedure.* Philadelphia: ALI.

Amsterdam, Anthony. 1970. "The Supreme Court and the Rights of Suspects in Criminal Cases." *New York University Law Review* 45:785.

———. 1974. "Perspectives on the Fourth Amendment." *Minnesota Law Review* 58:430.

Anderson v. Creighton. 1987. 483 U.S. 635.

Annals of Congress. 1789. House of Representatives, 1st Cong., 1st sess. Accessed August 31, 2010. http://lcweb2.loc.gov/cgi-bin/ampage? collId=llac&fileName=001/llac001.db&recNum=51.

Apodaca v. Oregon. 1972. 406 U.S. 404.

Apprendi v. New Jersey. 2000. 530 U.S. 466.

Archibold, Randal. 2010. "Arizona Enacts Stringent Law on Immigration." *New York Times*, April 23. Accessed July 4, 2010. http://www.nytimes.com/2010/04/24/us/politics/24immig.html?_r=1.

Argersinger v. Hamlin. 1972. 407 U.S. 25.

Arizona v. Evans. 1995. 514 U.S. 1.

Arizona v. Gant. 2008. "Amicus Brief of State Officials Supporting Arizona." 2008 WL 2151707.

———. 2009. 129 S.Ct. 1710.

Arizona v. Johnson. 2009. 129 S.Ct. 781. SCOTUS Wiki. Accessed February 20, 2010. http://www.scotuswiki.com/index.php?title=Arizona_v._Johnson.

Ashcroft, John. 2001. "Prepared Remarks for the US Mayors Conference" (October 25) http://www.justice.gov/archive/ag/speeches/2001/agcrisisremarks10_25.htm (July 9, 2013).

Ashcroft, John. 2002. *Attorney General's Guidelines on General Crimes, Racketeering Enterprise and Terrorism Enterprise Investigations.* Washington, D.C.: U.S. Department of Justice, May 30.

Associated Press. 2007. "Death Row Inmate Gets New Life Term," *USA Today.* Accessed August 31, 2010. http://www.usatoday.com/news/topstories/2007-08-13-477084247_x.htm.

Association of American Law Libraries. 2011. "National Security Letters." http://aallnet.org/Documents/Government-Relations/Issue-Briefs-and-Reports/2011/nslonepager.pdf. (July 1, 2013).

Atkins v. Virginia. 2002. 536 U.S. 304.

Atwater v. City of Lago Vista. 2001. 532 U.S. 318.

Avalon Project at the Yale Law School. 2003. *The Laws of War.* Accessed September 2, 2010. http://avalon.law .yale.edu/subject_menus/lawwar.asp.

Awoymi, Atinuke. 2011. "The State-Created Danger Doctrine in Domestic Violence Cases. Do We Have a Solution." In *Okin v. Village of Cornwall-on-Hudson Police Department. Columbia Journal of Gender and Law* 20:1–50.

Baldus, David C., and George Woodworth. 1998. "Race Discrimination and the Death Penalty: An Empirical and Legal Overview." In *America's Experiment with Capital Punishment*, edited by James R. Acker, Robert S. Bohm, and Charles S. Lanier. Durham, N.C.: Carolina Academic Press.

Baldwin v. New York. 1970. 399 U.S. 66.

Ballew v. Georgia. 1978. 435 U.S. 223.

Barnes v. State. 1975. 520 S.W.2d 401 (Tex.Crim.App.).

Barron v. Baltimore. 1833. 32 U.S. (7 Pet.) 243.

Batson v. Kentucky. 1986. 476 U.S. 79.

Bazelon, David. 1973. "Defective Assistance of Counsel." *University of Cincinnati Law Review* 42:1.

Bazelon, Emily. 2010. "Miranda Worked!" *Slate* (May 5). http://www.slate.com/articles/news_and_politics/jurisprudence/2010/05/miranda_worked.html (July 7, 2013).

———. 2013. "Dzhokhar Tsarnaev Talked for 16 Hours Before He Was Read His Rights." *Slate* (April 25). http://www.slate.com/articles/news_and_politics/jurisprudence/2013/04/dzhokhar_tsarnaev_s_interrogation_his_miranda_warning_shouldn_t_have_taken.html

Beale, Sara S., William C. Bryson, James E. Felman, and Michael J. Elston. 2004. *Grand Jury Law and Practice.* Eagan, Minn.: West, 6-3-6-4.

Behrman, Bruce W., and Richards, Regina E. 2005. "Suspect/Foil Identification in Actual Crimes and in the Laboratory: A Reality Monitoring Analysis." *Law and Human Behavior* 29:279–301.

Bell v. Irwin. 2003. 321 F.3d 637 (CA7 Ill.).

Bell v. Wolfish. 1979. 441 U.S. 520.

Berghuis v. Thompkins. 2010. 130 S.Ct. 2250.

Berkemer v. McCarty. 1984. 468 U.S. 420.

Betts v. Brady. 1942. 316 U.S. 455.

Bibas, Stephanos. 2003–2004. "Plea Bargaining Outside the Shadow of Trial." *Harvard Law Review* 117:2464.

Bibas, Stephanos. 2005. "White-Collar Plea Bargaining and Sentencing after *Booker." William and Mary Law Review* 47 (December):721.

Bivens v. Six Unnamed FBI Agents. 1971. 403 U.S. 388.

Bjelopera, Jerome P. 2013. *The Federal Bureau of Investigation and Terrorism Investigations.* Washington, D.C.: Congressional Research Service.

Blackledge v. Allison. 1977. 431 U.S. 63.

Blakely v. Washington. 2004. 542 U.S. 296.

Blumstein, Alfred, Jacqueline Cohen, Susan E. Martin, and Michael H. Tonry, eds. 1983. *Research on Sentencing: The Search for Reform.* Washington, D.C.: National Academy Press.

Board of Commissioners v. Backus. 1864. 29 How. Pr. 33.

Board of Education of Independent School District No. 92 of Pottawatomie County v. Earls. 2002. 535 U.S. 822.

Boggs Act. 1951. U.S. Code. Act of November 2, 1951, 65 Stat. 767.

Boland, Barbara, Wayne Logan, Ronald Sones, and William Martin. 1987. *The Prosecution of Felony Arrests, 1982.* Washington, D.C.: U.S. Department of Justice, BJS, May.

Borchard, Edwin. 1932. *Convicting the Innocent.* Garden City, N.J.: Garden City Publishing.

Boumediene and others v. Bush and others. 2007. "Brief for Petitioners." 2007 WL 2441590.

_____. 2008. 579 F. Supp.2d 191.

_____. 2008a. 553 U.S. 723.

_____. 2008b. 583 F. Supp.2d 133.

Bowen v. Kemp. 1985. 769 F.2d 672 (CA11 Ga.).

Bowles v. U.S. 1970. 439 F.2d 536 (CADC).

Boykin v. Alabama. 1969. 395 U.S. 238.

Bradfield, Amy. L., Gary L. Wells, and Elizabeth. A. Olson. 2002. "The Damaging Effect of Confirming Feedback on the Relation between Eyewitness Certainty and Identification Accuracy." *Journal of Applied Psychology* 87:112–20.

Bradley, Craig M. 1985. "Two Models of the Fourth Amendment." *Michigan Law Review* 83:1471.

_____. 1993. *The Failure of the Criminal Procedure Revolution.* Philadelphia: University of Pennsylvania Press.

_____. 2012. "Is the Exclusionary Rule Dead?" *Journal of Criminal Law and Criminology* 102:1–24.

Brady v. U.S. 1970. 397 U.S. 742.

Brandes, Wendy. 1989. "Post-Arrest Detention and the Fourth Amendment: Refining the Standard of *Gerstein v. Pugh." Columbia Journal of Law and Contemporary Problems* 22:445–88.

Brazil, Jeff, and Steve Berry. 1992. "Color of Driver Is Key to Stops in I-95 Videos." *Orlando Sentinel,* August 23.

Brennan, William J. 1977. "State Constitutions and the Protection of Individual Rights." *Harvard Law Review* 90:489–504.

Brewer v. Williams. 1977. 430 U.S. 387.

Brigham City, Utah v. Charles Stuart, Shayne Taylor, and Sandra Taylor. 2006. 547 U.S. 398.

Brinegar v. United States. 1949. 338 U.S. 160.

Brown v. Allen. 1953. 344 U.S. 443.

Brown v. Board of Education. 1954. 347 U.S. 483. Oral Argument.

Brown v. Johnston. 1983. 328 N.W.2d. 510.

Brown v. Mississippi. 1936. 297 U.S. 278.

Brown v. Texas. 1979. 443 U.S. 47.

Buckhout, Robert. 1975. "Eyewitness Testimony." *Jurimetrics Journal* 171 (Spring):171–87.

Buckley v. Fitzsimmons. 1993. 509 U.S. 259.

Bull v. City and County of San Francisco. 2010. 595 F.3d 964 (CA9 Calif.).

Bumper v. North Carolina. 1968. 391 U.S. 543.

Burch v. Louisiana. 1979. 441 U.S. 130.

Bureau of Justice Statistics. 2009. *Felony Sentences in State Courts, 2006—Statistical Tables.* Washington, D.C.: NCJ 226846, December.

_____. 2011. *Contacts between Police and the Public 2008.* 2011. Washington, D.C.: U.S. Department of Justice.

Burns v. Reed. 1991. 500 U.S. 478.

Bynum v. State. 2005. 929 So.2d 324 (Miss.App.).

California v. Acevedo. 1991. 500 U.S. 565.

California v. Beheler. 1983. 463 U.S. 1121.

California v. Ciraolo. 1986. 476 U.S. 207.

California v. Gilbert. 1967. 388 U.S. 263.

California v. Greenwood. 1988. 486 U.S. 35.

California v. Hodari D. 1991. 499 U.S. 621.

Campaign for an Effective Crime Policy. 1993. "Evaluating Mandatory Minimum Sentences." Washington, D.C.: Campaign for an Effective Crime Policy, October. Unpublished manuscript.

Cardozo, Benjamin. 1921. *The Nature of the Judicial Process.* New Haven, Conn.: Yale University Press.

Carlson, Jonathan. 1987. "The Act Requirement and the Foundations of the Entrapment Defense." *Virginia Law Review* 73:1011.

Carroll v. U.S. 1925. 267 U.S. 132.

Cassell, Paul G., and Bret S. Hyman. 1996. "Police Interrogation in the 1990's: An Empirical Study of the Effects of *Miranda." UCLA* Law Review 43:839.

Center for Constitutional Rights. 2009. "Racial Disparity in NYPD Stops-and-Frisks." New York: Center for Constitutional Rights. Accessed July 8, 2010. http://ccrjustice.org/stopandfrisk.

Center on Law and Security. 2011. *Terrorist Trial Report Card: September 11, 2001–September 11, 2010.* New York: New York University Law School.

Chandler v. Florida. 1981. 499 U.S. 560.

Chandler v. Fretag. 1954. 348 U.S. 3.

Chimel v. California. 1969. 395 U.S. 752.

CIA. 2013. "History of the CIA." Washington, D.C.: CIA Website https://www.cia.gov/about-cia/history-of-the-cia (July 15, 2013).

Cincotti, Thomas. 2009. "From Movements to Mosques, Informants Endanger Democracy." *The Public Eye.* Summer. http://www.publiceye.org/magazine/v24n2/movements-to-mosques.html.

Ciucci v. Illinois. 1958. 356 U.S. 571.

Clarke v. Caspari. 2002. 274 F.3d 507 (CA8).

Cloud, Morgan. 1985. "Search and Seizure by the Numbers: The Drug Courier Profile and Judicial Review of Investigative Formulas." *Boston University Law Review* 65:843.

CNN. 2013. " 'Disgraceful' decision to end Boston suspect's interrogation, GOP lawmaker says." http://politicalticker.blogs.cnn.com/2013/04/28/disgraceful-decision-to-end-boston-suspects-interrogation-gop-lawmaker-says/

Coke, Edward. 1797. *The Second Part of the Institutes of the Laws of England.* 5th ed. London: Brooke.

Coker v. Georgia. 1977. 433 U.S. 584.

Cole, David. 1999. *No Equal Justice.* New York: New Press.

Coleman, Howard, and Eric Swenson. 1994. *DNA in the Courtroom: A Trial Watcher's Guide.* Seattle: Genelex Corp.

Collins, Hilton. 2012. "Video Camera Networks Link Real-Time Partners in Crime-Solving." *Government Technology.* February 1, 2012. http://www.govtech.com/public-safety/Video-Camera -Networks-Link-Real-Time-Partners-in-Crime-Solving.html#

Colorado v. Bertine. 1987. 479 U.S. 367.

Colorado v. Connelly. 1986. 479 U.S. 157.

Colorado v. Mendez. 1999. 986 P.2d 285 (Colo.).

Connecticut v. Barrett. 1987. 479 U.S. 523.

Cooper v. State. 1985. 480 So.2d 8 (Ala.Crim.App.).

Copacino, John M. 1994. "Suspicionless Criminal Seizures after *Michigan Department of State Police v. Sitz.*" *American Criminal Law Review* 31:215.

Corpus Juris Secundum. 2003. St Paul, Minn.: West, § 61.

Cortner, Richard C. 1981. *The Supreme Court and the Second Bill of Rights.* Madison: University of Wisconsin Press.

County of Riverside v. McLaughlin. 1991. 500 U.S. 44.

Covey, Russell. 2007–2008. "Reconsidering the Relationship between Cognitive Psychology and Plea Bargaining." *Marquette Law Review* 91:213–47.

Criminal Justice Newsletter. 1993. Washington, D.C.: Pace Publications, November 15.

Crist v. Bretz. 1978. 437 U.S. 28.

Cronin, Thomas E., Tania Cronin, and Michael Milakovich. 1981. *U.S. v. Crime in the Streets.* Bloomington: Indiana University Press.

Crooker v. California. 1958. 357 U.S. 433.

Cruz v. City of Laramie. 2001. 239 F.3d 1183 (CA10 Wyo.).

Culombe v. Connecticut. 1961. 367 U.S. 568.

Cupp v. Murphy. 1973. 412 U.S. 291.

Davenport, Jennifer L., and Steven Penrod. 1997. "Eyewitness Identification Evidence: Evaluating Commonsense Evaluations." *Psychology, Public Policy, and Law* 3:338–61.

Davies, Thomas Y. 1983. "A Hard Look at What We Know (and Still Need to Learn) about the 'Social Costs' of the Exclusionary Rule: The NIJ Study and Other Studies of 'Lost' Arrests." *American Bar Foundation Research Journal* 640.

_____. 1992. "Denying a Right by Disregarding Doctrine: How *Illinois v. Rodriguez* Demeans Consent, Trivializes Fourth Amendment Reasonableness, and Exaggerates the Excusability of Police Error." *Tennessee Law Review* 59:1–100.

_____. 1999. "Recovering the Original Fourth Amendment." *Michigan Law Review* 98:547.

Death Penalty Information Center. 2010. "Death Penalty Fact Sheet." Accessed August 31, 2010. http://www.deathpenaltyinfo.org.

Demore v. Kim. 2002. "Amicus Brief for T. Alexander Aleinikoff and Others." 2002 WL 31455523.

Demore v. Kim. 2003. 538 U.S. 510.

Denniston, Lyle. 2008. "Argument Preview: The Constitution at Roadside." SCOTUS Blog: December 8, 2008. http://www .scotusblog.com/2008/12/argument-preview-the-constitution -at-roadside/ (March 9, 2013).

Deorle v. Rutherford. 2001. 272 F.3d 1272 (CA9 Calif.).

Dery, George M., and Kevin Meehan. 2004. "Making the Roadblock a 'Routine Part of American Life:'" *Illinois v. Lidster's* Extension of Police Checkpoint Power." *American Journal of Criminal Law* 32:105–131.

DeShaney v. Winnebago County. 1989. 489 U.S. 189.

Detainee Treatment Act (DTA). 2005. Accessed August 27, 2010. http://jurist.law.pitt.edu/gazette/2005/12/detainee-treatment -act-of-2005-white.php.

Dickerson v. U.S. 2000. 530 U.S. 428.

Director of the Administrative Office of the U.S. Courts. 2010. "Report on Applications for Delayed-Notice Search Warrants and Extensions." Washington, D.C.: Administrative Office of the U.S. Courts. http://www.aclu.org/files/assets/aousc_patriot _act_section_213_sneak_and_peek_report.pdf (June 28, 2013).

District Attorney's Office for the Third Judicial District and others v. William G. Osborne. 2009. 129 S.Ct. 2308.

Dix, George E. 1985. "Nonarrest Investigatory Detentions in Search and Seizure Law." *Duke Law Journal* 849.

Doe v. Ashcroft. 2004. 334 Fed. Supp. 2d. 471.

Doe v. Gonzalez. 2005. 386 Fed. Supp. 2d 66.

Doe v. Mucasey. 2007. 500 Fed. Supp. 2d 379.

Doe v. Mucasey. 2008. 549 F.3d. 861.

Douglas, Shannel. 2012. "Inmates cost taxpayers $65 per day." KVI 7 News. Amarillo Texas. http://www.connectamarillo .com/news/story_print.aspx?id=827668&type=story# .UbjvJfY4WaE (June 10, 2013).

Douglass, Amy B., and Dawn McQuiston-Surrett. 2006. "Post-Identification Feedback: Exploring the Effects of Sequential Photospreads and Eyewitnesses' Awareness of the Identification Task." *Applied Cognitive Psychology* 20:991–1007.

Dow Chemical Co. v. U.S. 1986. 476 U.S. 227.

Doyle, Charles. 2002. *The USA Patriot Act: A Legal Analysis.* Washington, D.C.: Congressional Research Service.

_____. 2010. *National Security Letters in Foreign Intelligence Investigations: A Glimpse of the Legal Background and Recent Amendments.* Washington, D.C.: Congressional Research Service.

_____. 2011. *National Security Letters: Proposals in the 112th Congress.* Washington, D.C.: Congressional Research Service.

Draper v. Reynolds. 2004. 369 F.3d 1270 (CA11 Ga.).

Draper v. U.S. 1959. 358 U.S. 307.

Dripps, Donald A. 2003. *About Guilt and Innocence.* Westport, Conn.: Praeger Publishers.

Drizin, Steven A., and Marissa J. Reich. 2004. "Heeding the Lessons of History: The Need for Mandatory Recording of Police Interrogations to Accurately Assess the Reliability and Voluntariness of Confessions." *Drake Law Review* 52:619.

Drizin, Steven A., and Richard A. Leo. 2003–2004. "The Problem of False Confessions in the Post-DNA World." *North Carolina Law Review* 82:891.

Duarte v. Commonwealth. 1991. 407 S.E.2d 41.

Duncan v. Louisiana. 1968. 391 U.S. 145.

Dunlop v. U.S. 1897. 165 U.S. 486.

Early U.S. Telephone Industry Data. Online. "Telephones in Service." https://spreadsheets.google.com/spreadsheet/pub?hl=en&key =0AnZb5H7tDMvTdGJLU2NUYm1QR1E2S1RpMTRyLWxw Mnc&hl=en&gid=0 (February 16, 2013).

Electronic Privacy Information Center (E.P.I.C.) n.d. "Electronic Sneak and Peek Search Warrants." https://ssd.eff.org/your -computer/govt/sneak-and-peek (June 28, 2013).

Elkins v. U.S. 1960. 364 U.S. 206.

Elliott, Justin. 2009. "Police Tapped Sprint Customer GPS Data 8 Million Times in a Year." Talking Points Memo (TPM): December 4, 2009.

Elsea, Jennifer. 2001. *Terrorism and the Law of War: Trying Terrorists as War Criminals before Military Commissions.* Washington, D.C.: Congressional Research Service.

Enmund v. Florida. 1982. 458 U.S. 782.

Ervin, Sam J., Jr. 1983. "The Exclusionary Rule: An Essential Ingredient of the Fourth Amendment." *Supreme Court Review.* Chicago: University of Chicago Press.

Escobedo v. Illinois. 1964. 378 U.S. 478.

Estelle v. Williams. 1976. 425 U.S. 501.

Ewing v. California. 2003. 538 U.S. 11.

Ex Parte Milligan. 1866. 71 U.S. 2.

FBI. 2012. "FBI Releases 2011 Statistics on Law Enforcement Officers Killed and Assaulted." U.S. Department of Justice. http://www.fbi.gov/news/pressrel/press-releases/fbi-releases -2011-statistics-on-law-enforcement-officers-killed-and-assaulted (March 9, 2013).

_____. 2012. *Crime in the U.S. 2011.* http://www.fbi.gov/about -us/cjis/ucr/crime-in-the-u.s/2011/crime-in-the-u.s.-2011/ tables/table-29 (April 29, 2013).

_____. N.d. "Counterintelligence." http://www.fbi.gov/about -us/investigate/counterintelligence/counterintelligence (July 3, 2013).

Federal Rules of Criminal Procedure. 2002. 41(d)(3). Accessed September 2, 2010. http://www.law.cornell.edu/rules/ frcrmp/Rule4.htm.

_____. 2010. http://www.uscourts.gov/uscourts/RulesAndPolicies/ rules/2010%20Rules/Criminal%20Procedure.pdf (March 30, 2013).

Feeley, Malcolm M. 1979. *The Process Is the Punishment: Handling Cases in a Lower Criminal Court.* New York: Russell Sage Foundation.

Ferguson v. City of Charleston. 2001. 532 U.S. 67.

Ferguson, Andrew Guthrie, and Damien Bernache. 2008. "The 'High-Crime Area' Question: Requiring Verifiable and Quantifiable Evidence for Fourth Amendment Reasonable Suspicion Analysis." *American University Law Review* 57:1587–644.

Final Report. 2010. Guantanamo Review Task Force. Washington, D.C.: Department of Justice, Department of Defense, Department of State, Department of Homeland Security, Office of the Director of National Intelligence, Joint Chiefs of Staff.

Fisher, Jeffrey. 2006. "Respondent's Brief." *U.S. v. Gonzalez-Lopez.* 2006 WL 838892.

_____. 2008. "Brief for Amicus Curiae National Association of Criminal Defense Lawyers in Support of Respondent." *Gant v. U.S.* 2008 WL 39111137.

Fisher, Sydney George F. 1888. "The Suspension of Habeas Corpus during the War of Rebellion." *Political Science Quarterly* 3.

Florence v. Board of Chosen Freeholders. 2012. 132 S.Ct 1510.

Florida v. Bostick. 1991. 501 U.S. 429.

Florida v. J. L. 2000. 529 U.S. 266.

Florida v. Jimeno. 1991. 500 U.S. 248.

Florida v. Royer. 1983. 460 U.S. 491.

Foote, Caleb. 1965. "The Coming Constitutional Crisis in Bail." *University of Pennsylvania Law Review* 113:959–1185.

Forst, Brian. 2004. *Errors of Justice.* New York: Cambridge University Press.

Fowler, Tom. 2007. "Olis Testified He Couldn't 'Ruin Those People's Lives.'" *Houston Chronicle,* May 27, Business, 5.

Fraizer v. Roberts. 1971. 441 F.2d 1224 (CA8 Ark.).

Frankel, Marvin E., and Gary F. Naftalis. 1977. *The Grand Jury: An Institution on Trial.* New York: Hill and Wang.

Frazier v. Cupp. 1969. 394 U.S. 731.

Friendly, Henry J. 1965. "The Bill of Rights as a Code of Criminal Procedure." *California Law Review* 53:929.

_____. 1968. "The Fifth Amendment Tomorrow: The Case for Constitutional Change." *University of-Cincinnati Law Review* 37:671.

Frontline. 1999. "Snitch" Transcript. Accessed September 3, 2010. http://www.pbs.org/wgbh/pages/frontline/shows/snitch/etc/ script.html.

Gall v. U.S. 2007. 552 U.S. 38.

Gardner v. Florida. 1977. 430 U.S. 349.

Gardner, James A. 1991. "The Failed Discourse of State Constitutionalism." *Michigan Law Review* 90:761.

Garner, Bryan A. 1987. *Dictionary of Modern Legal Usage.* New York: Oxford University Press.

Garrett, Brandon L. 2011. *Convicting the Innocent.* Cambridge MA: Harvard University Press.

Gartenstein-Ross, Daveed, and Kyle Dabruzzi. 2007. "The Al Capone Model of Anti-Terror Policing. *The Weekly Standard* (April 12). http://www.weeklystandard.com/print/Content/ Public/Articles/000/000/013/495wvpqo.asp (July 9, 2013).

Gayarré, Charles. 1903. *History of Louisiana, Vol. IV.* New Orleans: F. F. Hansell & Bro.

Georgia v. Randolph. 2006. 126 S.Ct. 1515.

Gerstein v. Pugh. 1975. 420 U.S. 103.

Gideon v. Wainright. 1963. 372 U.S. 335.

Gilbert v. California. 1967. 388 U.S. 263.

Glick, Scott J. 2010. "FISA's Significant Purpose Requirement and the Government's Ability to Protect National Security." *Harvard National Security Journal* 1:87–143.

Goldstein, Abraham S. 1987. "The Search Warrant, the Magistrate, and Judicial Review." *New York University Law Review* 62:1173.

Goldstein, Joseph. 1960. "The State and the Accused: Balance and Advantage in Criminal Procedure." *Yale Law Journal* 69.

Goss v. Lopez. 1975. 419 U.S. 565.

Gould, Jon B. 2008. *The Innocence Commission.* New York: New York University Press.

Graham v. Connor. 1989. 490 U.S. 386.

Graham, Fred. 1970. *The Self-Inflicted Wound.* New York: Macmillan.

Graham, Kenneth, and Leon Letwin. 1971. "The Preliminary Hearing in Los Angeles: Some Field Findings and Legal-Policy Questions." *UCLA Law Review* 18:636.

Greeley, Horace. 1864. *The Great Conflict: A History of the Great Rebellion in the United States of America, 1860–1864.* http:// www.perseus.tufts.edu/hopper/text?doc=Perseus%3Atext% 3A2001.05.0066%3Achapter%3D8%3Apage%3D106 (visited January 27, 2013).

Gregg v. Georgia. 1976. 428 U.S. 153.

Grier, Peter. 2010. "Why the Times Square Bomb Failed Spectacularly." *The Christian Science Monitor.* (May 3). http://www.csmonitor.com/USA/2010/0503/Why-the-Times -Square-bomb-failed-spectacularly (July 7, 2013).

Griffin v. Wisconsin. 1987. 483 U.S. 868.

Griswold, David B. 1994. "Complaints against the Police: Predicting Dispositions." *Journal of Criminal Justice* 22.

Gross, Samuel L. "Convicting the Innocent." *Annual Review of Law and Social Science* 4:173–92.

Gross, Samuel R. 1987. "Loss of Innocence: Eyewitness Identification and Proof of Guilt." *Journal of Legal Studies* 16.

Haber, Ralph Norman, and Lyn Haber. 2000. "Experiencing, Remembering, and Reporting Events." *Psychology, Public Policy, and Law* 6(4):1057–97.

Haddad, James B. 1977. "Well-Delineated Exceptions, Claims of Sham, and Fourfold Probable Cause." *Journal of Criminal Law and Criminology* 68:198–225.

Hall, Jerome. 1942. "Objectives of Federal Criminal Rules Revision." *Yale Law Journal* 725.

Hall, John Wesley, Jr. 1993. *Search and Seizure.* 2d ed. New York: Clark, Boardman, Callaghan.

———. 2009. "A Great Awakening." *Champion Magazine*, June.

Hamblett, Mark. 2003. "Tough Questions for U.S. on Detention." *Legal Times*, November 24.

Hamdan v. Rumsfeld. 2006. 126 S.Ct. 2749.

Hamdi v. Rumsfeld. 2004. 542 U.S. 507.

Hamilton, Alexander. 1788. "The Federalist No. 78: The Judiciary Department." Accessed June 7, 2010. http://press-pubs .uchicago.edu/founders/documents/bill_of_rightss7.html.

Hancock, Catherine. 1982. "State Court Activism and Searches Incident to Arrest." *Virginia Law Review* 68:1085.

Hand, Learned. 1922. *U.S. v. Garsson.* 291 Fed. 646 (S.D.N.Y.).

Harcourt, Bernard E., and Tracey L. Meares. 2010. "Randomization and the Fourth Amendment. Chicago: University of Chicago Law School. http://www.law.uchicago.edu/Lawecon/index .html (March 7, 2013).

Harmelin v. Michigan. 1991. 501 U.S. 957.

Harris v. U.S. 1947. 331 U.S. 145.

Harris v. U.S. 2002. 536 U.S. 545.

Harris, David A. 1998. "Particularized Suspicion, Categorical Judgments: Supreme Court Rhetoric versus Lower Court Reality under *Terry v. Ohio.*" *St. John's Law Review* 72:975.

Harris, Shane. 2013. "The NSA Can't Tell the Difference Between an American and a Foreigner." *Foreign Policy.* (June 28). http://www.foreignpolicy.com/articles/2013/06/27/the_nsa _cant_tell_the_difference_between_an_american_and_a _foreigner?wp_login_redirect=0.

Harvey v. Horan. 2002. 285 F.3d 298 (CA4).

Heath v. Alabama. 1985. 474 U.S. 82.

Hedgepeth v. Washington Metro Area Transit and others. 2003. 284 F. Supp.2d 145 (D.D.C.).

Heffernan, William C. 2001–2002. "Fourth Amendment Privacy Interests." *Journal of Criminal Law & Criminology* 92:1–126.

Henderson v. Florida. 1985. 473 U.S. 916.

Henderson v. U.S. 1967. 390 F.2d 805 (CA9 Calif.).

Herring v. U.S. 2009.129 S.Ct. 695.

Hester v. U.S. 1924. 265 U.S. 57.

Hickey, Thomas, and Michael Axline. 1992. "Drunk-Driving Roadblocks under State Constitutions: A Reasonable Alternative to *Michigan v. Sitz.*" *Criminal Law Bulletin* 28.

Hiibel v. Sixth Judicial District Court of Nevada, Humboldt County et al. 2004. 542 U.S. 177.

Hockett, Jeffrey D. 1991. "Justice Robert H. Jackson, the Supreme Court, and the Nuremberg Trial." *Supreme Court Review.* Chicago: University of Chicago Press.

Hoffa v. U.S. 1966. 385 U.S. 293.

Holbrook v. Flynn. 1986. 475 U.S. 560.

Holy Bible, Authorized (King James) Version. 1990. Nashville: Thomas Nelson.

Horton v. California. 1990. 496 U.S. 128.

Howard v. Bouchard. 2008. 405 F.3d 459 (CA6). http://tpmmuckraker. talkingpointsmemo.com/2009/12/revelation_8_million_gps _searches_on_sprint_by_law.php (February 28, 2013).

Hudson v. Palmer. 1984. 468 U.S. 523.

Hurtado v. California. 1884. 110 U.S. 516.

Hutson, H. Range, Deirdre Anglin, Gilbert Pineda, Christopher Flynn, and James McKeith. 1997. "Law Enforcement and K-9 Dog Bites: Injuries, Complications, and Trends." *Annals of American Emergency Medicine* 25(5): 637–42.

Illinois v. Allen. 1970. 397 U.S. 337.

Illinois v. Caballes. 2005. 543 U.S. 405.

Illinois v. Rodriquez. 1990. 497 U.S. 177.

Illinois v. Wardlow. 1999. "U.S. Supreme Court Amicus Brief." 1999 WL 451226.

Illinois v. Wardlow. 2000. 528 U.S. 119.

Imbler v. Pachtman. 1976. 424 U.S. 409.

Immigration and Nationality Act. 2004. 8 U.S.C. § 1226a. Accessed August 27, 2010. http://vlex.com/vid/suspected -terrorists-habeas-corpus-19271949.

In re National Security Letter. 2013. U.S.D.C. Northern District California No. C 11-02173 SI. https://www.eff.org/sites/ default/files/filenode/nsl_order_scan.pdf (July 6, 2013).

In re Sealed Case. 2002. 310 Fed. 3rd 717.

In re Winship. 1970. 397 U.S. 358.

Inbau, Fred E. 1961. "Police Interrogation and Limitations." *Journal of Criminal Law, Criminology, and Police Science* 52:19.

Inbau, Fred E., James R. Thompson, James B. Zagel, and James P. Manak. 1984. *Criminal Law and Its Administration.* 4th ed. Mineola, N.Y.: Foundation Press.

Innocence Project. 2010. "Eyewitness Misidentification." Accessed April 23, 2010. http://www.innocenceproject.org/understand/ Eyewitness-Misidentification.php.

———. 2010. "False Confessions and Mandatory Recording of Interrogations." Fix the System. Accessed May 22, 2010. http:// www.innocenceproject .org/fix/False-Confessions.php.

———. 2013. Exoneree Profile of Glen Woodall. http://www .innocenceproject.org/Content/Glen_Woodall.php (May 27, 2013).

———. 2013. "False Confessions." http://www.innocenceproject .org/understand/False-Confessions.php (May 19, 2013).

———. 2013. "Reevaluating Lineups. Why Witnesses Make Mistakes and How to Reduce the Chance of a Misidentification." http:// www.innocenceproject.org/Content/Reevaluating_Lineups _Why_Witnesses_Make_Mistakes_and_How_to_Reduce_the _Chance_of_a_Misidentification.php (May 27, 2013).

———. 2013. Innocence Project http://www.innocenceproject.org/

INS v. Delgado. 1984. 466 U.S. 210.

International Centre for Prison Studies. 2011. *World Prison Population List.* http://www.prisonstudies.org/images/news _events/wppl9.pdf (June 19, 2013).

Isom v. Town of Warren. 2004. 360 F.3d 7 (CA1 R.I.).

Israel, Jerold H. 1982. "Selective Incorporation: Revisited." *Georgetown Law Journal* 71:274.

Jackson, Robert. 1940. "The Federal Prosecutor." *Journal of Criminal Law and Criminology* 31:3.

Jacobi, Tonja. 2011. "The Law and Economics of the Exclusionary Rule. *Notre Dame Law Review* 87:585.

Jacobson v. U.S. 1992. 503 U.S. 540.

Jefferson, Thomas. 1904. *Works.* London: Putnam and Sons.

Johns, Margaret Z. 2005. "Reconsidering Absolute Prosecutorial Immunity." *Brigham University Law Review* 53.

Johnson v. Eisentrager. 1950. 339 U.S. 763.

Johnson v. Louisiana. 1972. 406 U.S. 356.

Johnson v. Zerbst. 1938. 304 U.S. 458.

Johnson, Andrew, and Emily Dugan. 2009. *Independent World*, December 27. Accessed July 1, 2010. http://www

.independent.co.uk/news/world/americas/wealthy-quiet -unassuming-the-christmas-day-bomb-suspect-1851090.html.

Johnson, Brian D. 2003. "Racial and Ethnic Disparities in Sentencing Departures across Modes of Conviction." *Criminology* 41(2):449–90.

_____. 2005. "Contextual Disparities in Guidelines Departures: Courtroom Social Contexts, Guidelines Compliance, and Extralegal Disparities in Criminal Sentencing." *Criminology* 43(3):761–96.

Johnson, Craig A. 2012. *The Information Diet*. Sabastopol CA: O'Reilly Media, Inc.

Jonas, Daniel S. 1989. "Comment, Pretextual Searches, and the Fourth Amendment: Unconstitutional Abuses of Power." *University of Pennsylvania Law Review* 137:1791.

Jones v. U.S. 1959. 266 F.2d 924 (CADC).

Jones, Elizabeth O. 2007. "The Fourth Amendment and Dormitory Searches." *Journal of College and University Law* 33:597.

Juvelir, Hon. Michael R. 1998. "A Prosecutor's Perspective." *St. John's Law Review*: 72:741.

Kalina v. Fletcher. 1997. 522 U.S. 118.

Kassin, Saul M., and Gisli Gudjonsson. 2004. *Psychological Science in the Public Interest* 5(2):33.

Kassin, Saul M., Christian A. Meissner, and Rebecca J. Norwick. 2005. "I'd Know a False Confession If I Saw One: A Comparative Study of College Students and Police Investigators." *Law and Human Behavior* 29(2):211–27.

Katz v. U.S. 1966. 369 F.2d 130.

Katz v. U.S. 1967. 389 U.S. 347, 88 S.Ct. 507, 19 L.Ed.2d 576.

Katz, Lewis. 2004. "*Terry v. Ohio* at Thirty-Five: A Revisionist View." *Mississippi Law Journal* 74:423.

Kennedy v. Louisiana. 2008. 554 U.S. ___ (Slip opinion).

Kennedy, Randall. 1997. *Race, Crime, and the Law*. New York: Random House.

Kentucky v. Stincer. 1987. 107 S.Ct. 2658.

Ker v. California. 1963. 374 U.S. 23.

Keys, Karl. 2007. "Ronald Rompilla Pleads to Life." *Capital Defense Weekly*, August 13. Accessed May 30, 2010. http://www .capitaldefenseweekly.com/blog/?p=2251.

Kirby v. Illinois. 1972. 406 U.S. 682.

Kirk v. Louisiana. 2002. 536 U.S. 635

Klobuchar, Amy, Nancy Steblay, and Hilary Caligiuri. 2006. "Improving Eyewitness Identifications: Hennepin County's Blind Sequential Lineup Pilot Project." *Cardozo Public Law, Policy and Ethics Journal* (April).

Klockars, Carl B. 1980. "The Dirty Harry Problem." *Annals of the American Academy of Political and Social Science* 452:3.

Klopfer v. North Carolina. 1967. 386 U.S. 213.

Knowles v. Iowa. 1998. 525 U.S. 113.

Kobach, Kris. 2010. "Why Arizona Drew a Line." *New York Times*, April 29. Accessed July 4, 2010. http://www.nytimes. com/2010/04/29/opinion/29kobach .html?th&emc=th.

Kopec v. Tate. 2004. 361 F.3d 772 (CA3 Penn.).

Koppl, Roger. 2007. CSI *for Real: How to Improve Forensic Science*. Reason Foundation.com. http://reason.org/files/ d834fab5860d5cf4b3949fecf86d3328.pdf (May 26, 2013).

Kuha v. City of Minnetonka. 2003. 365 F.3d 590 (CA8 Minn.).

Kurland, Philip B., and Gerhard Casper, eds. 1975. "Brief for the NAACP Legal Defense and Educational Fund, Inc., as Amicus Curiae." *Terry v. Ohio*. Landmark Briefs and Arguments of the Supreme Court of the United States. Washington, D.C.: University Publications of America.

Kyllo v. U.S. 2001. 533 U.S. 27.

LaFave, Wayne R. 1993. "Police Rule Making and the Fourth Amendment." In *Discretion in Criminal Justice*, edited by Lloyd Ohlin and Frank Remington. Albany, N.Y.: State University of New York Press.

_____. 2004. *Search and Seizure*. 4th ed. St. Paul, Minn.: Thomson West.

LaFave, Wayne R., and Jerold H. Israel. 1984. *Criminal Procedure*. St. Paul, Minn.: West.

LaFave, Wayne, Jerold H. Israel, Nancy King, and Orin Kerr. 2009. *Criminal Procedure*. 5th ed. St. Paul, Minn.: West.

_____. 2012. *Criminal Procedure*, 5th ed. Eagan, Minn.: West Publishing.

Langley, Richard. 2008. "In Simple Terms, How Does GPS Work? http://gge.unb.ca/Resources/HowDoesGPSWork .html (February 25, 2013).

Lanza v. New York. 1962. 370 U.S. 139.

Latzer, Barry. 1991. *State Constitutions and Criminal Justice*. Westport, Conn.: Greenwood.

Lee, F. N. n.d. *King Alfred the Great and Our Common Law*. http:// www.dr-fnlee.org/docs6/alfred/alfred.pdf.

Leo, Richard A. 1996a. "The Impact of *Miranda* Revisited." *Journal of Criminal Law and Criminology* 86:621.

_____. 1996b. "Inside the Interrogation Room." *Journal of Criminal Law & Criminology*. 86:266.

_____. 1998. "From Coercion to Deception: The Changing Nature of Police Interrogation in America." In *The Miranda Debate: Law, Justice and Policing*, edited by Richard Leo and George C. Thomas III. Boston: Northeastern University, 2002.

Levy, Leonard. 1968. *The Origins of the Fifth Amendment*. New York: Oxford University Press.

Lewis v. U.S. 1966. 385 U.S. 206.

Lewis, Anthony. 1994. "The Blackmun Legacy." *New York Times*, April 8.

Lichtblau, Eric. 2012. "More Demands on Cell Carriers in Surveillance." *New York Times*, (July 8, 2012).

Lichtblau, Eric. 2013. "In Secret, Court Vastly Broadens Powers of N.S.A." *New York Times* (July 6). http://readersupportednews .org/off-site-news-section/255-justice/18295-in-secret-court -vastly-broadens-powers-of-nsa.

Lichtenberg, Illya. 2001. "*Miranda* in Ohio: The Effects of 'Voluntary' Waiver of Fourth Amendment Rights." *Howard Law Journal* 44:349.

Lichtenberg, Illya, and Alisa Smith. 2001. "How Dangerous Are Routine Police-Citizen Traffic Stops?" *Journal of Criminal Justice* 29:419–28.

Linkletter v. Walker. 1965. 381 U.S. 618.

Liptak, Adam. 2010. "Defendants Squeezed by Georgia's Tight Budget." *New York Times*, July 5. Accessed July 6, 2010. http:// www.nytimes.com/2010/07/06/us/06bar.html?th&emc=th.

Lisenba v. California. 1941. 314 U.S. 219.

Liu, Edward C. 2011. *Amendments to the Foreign Intelligence Surveillance Act (FISA) Extended Until June 1, 2015*. Washington, D.C. Congressional Research Service.

Llaguno v. Mingey. 1985. 763 F.2d 1560 (CA7 Ill.).

Lockett v. Ohio. 1978. 438 U.S. 586.

Lockyer v. Andrade. 2003. 538 U.S. 63.

Loftus, Elizabeth F. 1996. *Eyewitness Identification*. Rev. ed. Cambridge: Harvard University Press.

_____. 2004. "The Devil in Confessions." *Psychological Science in the Public Interest* 5(2):i.

Loftus, Geoffrey, and Erin M. Harley. 2005. "Why Is It Easier to Identify Someone Close Than Far Away?" *Psychonomic Bulletin & Review* 12(1):43–65.

Maclin, Tracey. 2008. "The Good News and the Bad about Consent Searches in the Supreme Court. *McGeorge Law Review* 39:27–82.

Maclin, Tracey, and Jennifer Rader. 2012. "No More Chipping Away: The Roberts Court Uses an Axe to Take Out the Fourth Amendment Exclusionary Rule." *Mississippi Law Journal* 81(5):1183–1216.

Madison, James. 1787. "The Federalist No. 51." In *The Federalist*, edited by Jacob E. Cooke. Middletown, Conn.: Wesleyan University Press, 1961, 349.

Magid, Laurie. 2001. "Deceptive Police Interrogation Practices: How Far Is Too Far?" *Michigan Law Review* 99(5): 1168.

Malloy v. Hogan. 1964. 378 U.S. 1.

Manson v. Brathwaite. 1977. 432 U.S. 98.

Mapp v. Ohio. 1961. 367 U.S. 643.

Marbury v. Madison. 1803. 5 U.S. 137.

Marcus, Paul. 1986. "The Development of Entrapment Law." *Wayne Law Review* 336:5.

Marquis, Joshua. 2006. "The Innocent and the Shammed." *New York Times* (January 26).

Mary Beth G. and Sharon N. v. City of Chicago. 1983. 723 F.2d 1262, 1263 (CA7 Ill.).

Maryland v. Wilson. 1997. 519 U.S. 408.

Massiah v. U.S. 1964. 377 U.S. 201.

McCleskey v. Kemp. 1987. 481 U.S. 279.

McCleskey v. Zant. 1991. 499 U.S. 467.

McCloskey, Robert G. 1960. *The American Supreme Court*. Chicago. The University of Chicago Press.

McCormick v. City of Fort Lauderdale. 2003. 333 F.3d 1234 (CA11 Fla.).

McCulloch v. Maryland. 1819. 17 U.S. 316.

McDonald, Forrest. 1985. *Novus Ordo Seclorum*. Lawrence, Kan.: Kansas University Press.

McDonald, Renee Hutchins. 2007. "Tie Up In Knotts? GPS Technology and the Fourth Amendment" *UCLA Law Review* 55:401–65.

McFadden v. Cabana. 1988. 851 F.2d 784 (CA5 Miss.).

Meares, Tracey L., and Bernard Harcourt. 2000. "Foreword: Transparent Adjudication and Social Science Research in Criminal Procedure." *Journal of Criminal Law & Criminology* 90(3):733.

Metzger, Pamela R. 2006. "Cheating the Constitution." *Vanderbilt Law Review* 59:475-538.

Michigan v. Clifford. 1984. 464 U.S. 287.

Michigan v. Sitz. 1990. 496 U.S. 444.

Michigan v. Summers. 1981. 452 U.S. 692.

Military Commissions Act of 2006. 2006. 10 U.S.C. 948a, Section 1, Subchapter I.

Military Instruction No. 10. 2006. "Certain Evidentiary Determinations." U.S. Department of Defense. http://www .defense.gov/news/Mar2006/d20060327MCI10.pdf.

Miller v. Clark County. 2003. 340 F. 3d 959 (CA9 Wash.).

Miller-El v. Dretke. 2005. 545 U.S. 231.

Minnesota Rules of Criminal Procedure. 2006. Accessed September 2, 2010. http://www.courts.state.mn.us/rules/ criminal/RCRP.htm#cr501.

_____. 2010. Accessed August 21, 2010. http://www.lawlibrary .state.mn.us/archive/supct/9808/finamd.htm.

Minnesota Sentencing Commission. 2009. Accessed September 2, 2010. http://www.msgc.state.mn.us/msgc5/guidelines.htm.

Minnesota v. Dickerson. 1993. 508 U.S. 366.

Minnesota v. Murphy. 1984. 465 U.S. 420.

Miranda v. Arizona. 1966. 384 U.S. 436, 86 S.Ct. 1602.

Missouri v. Seibert. 2004. 542 U.S. 600.

Monell v. New York City Department of Social Services. 1978. 436 U.S. 658.

Moore v. Student Affairs Committee of Troy State University. 1968. 284 F. Supp. 725.

Moore, Mark H., Susan R. Estrich, Daniel McGillis, and William Spelman. 1984. *Dangerous Offenders: The Elusive Target of Justice*. Cambridge, Mass.: Harvard University Press.

Morse v. Frederick. 2007. 551 U.S. 393.

Moskovitz, Myron. 2002. "A Rule in Search of a Reason: An Empirical Reexamination of *Chimel* and *Belton*." *Michigan Law Review* 2002:657–97.

Moyers, Bill. 2007. "The Path to Power." *Bill Moyers Journal*. Washington: PBS (October 26). http://www.pbs.org/moyers/ journal/10262007/transcript1.html (July 11, 2013).

Moylan, Charles E., Jr. 1977. "The Fourth Amendment Inapplicable vs. the Fourth Amendment Satisfied: The Neglected Threshold of 'So What.'" *Southern Illinois University Law Journal* 75.

Murphy, Shelley. 2003. "Prosecutors Defend 'Sneak and Peek' Warrant." *Boston Globe*, October 20.

Murray v. U.S. 1988. 487 U.S. 533.

Myers v. Commonwealth. 1973. 298 N.E.2d 819 (Mass.).

Nadler, Janice. 2002. "No Need to Shout: Bus Sweeps and the Psychology of Coercion." *Supreme Court Review*. Chicago: University of Chicago Press.

_____. 2012. "The Language of Consent in Police Encounters." *The Oxford Handbook of Language and Law*. Oxford, New York: Oxford University Press.

Nakashima, Ellen, and Joby Warrick. 2013. "For NSA Chief, terrorist threat drives passion to 'collect it all,' observers say. *Washington Post* (July 14). http://www.washingtonpost.com/ world/national-security/for-nsa-chief-terrorist-threat-drives -passion-to-collect-it-all/2013/07/14/3d26ef80-ea49-11e2 -a301-ea5a8116d211_story.html (July 15, 2013).

Nardone v. U.S. 1938. 308 U.S. 338.

Nardulli, Peter F. 1983. "The Societal Cost of the Exclusionary Rule: An Empirical Assessment." *American Bar Foundation Research Journal* (Summer):585–609.

_____. 1987. "The Societal Cost of the Exclusionary Rule: Revisited." *University of Illinois Law Review* 223–39.

Nartarajan, Radha. 2003. "Racialized Memory and Reliability: Due Process Applied to Cross-Racial Eyewitness Identifications." *New York University Law Review* 78:1821–58.

National Council on Crime and Delinquency. 1992. *Criminal Justice Sentencing Policy Statement*. San Francisco: NCCD.

National Research Council. 2009. *Strengthening Forensic Science in the United States*. Washington, D.C. The National Academies Press.

National Treasury Employees Union v. Von Raab. 1989. 489 U.S. 656.

Nelson, William E. 1988. *The Fourteenth Amendment: From Political Principle to Judicial Doctrine*. Cambridge, Mass.: Harvard University Press.

New Jersey v. T. L. O. 1985. 469 U.S. 325.

New York City Police Department. "New York City Police Department, Stop Question & Frisk Activity, October 1 2012 through December 31, 2012. http://www.nyclu.org/ files/2012_4th_Qtr.pdf (March 8, 2013).

New York Civil Liberties Union. 2009. "Record Number of Innocent New Yorkers Stopped, Interrogated by NYPD."

New York Civil Liberties Union. Accessed September 2, 2010. http://www.nyclu.org/node/2389.

New York Office of the Attorney General. 1999. *New York City Police Department's "Stop and Frisk" Practices: A Report to the People of the State of New York from the Office of the Attorney General.* New York: Attorney General's Office.

New York v. Belton. 1981. 453 U.S. 454.

New York v. Quarles. 1984. 467 U.S. 649.

New York v. Zenger. 1735. 17 Howell's St. Tr. 675, 721–22.

Ngowi, Rodrique, Lara Jakes, and Matt Apuzzo. 2013. "Officials: Suspect described plot before Miranda." Associated Press. (April 25). http://bigstory.ap.org/article/lawmakers-ask -who-knew-what-about-bomb-suspect (July 8, 2013).

Nickelsberg, Jessica E. 2005. "*Illinois v. Lidster*: Continuing to Carve Out Constitutional Vehicle Checkpoints." *The Journal of Criminal Law & Criminology* 73(3):839–70.

Nix v. Williams. 1984. 467 U.S. 431.

North Carolina v. Alford. 1970. 400 U.S. 25.

North Carolina v. Butler. 1979. 441 U.S. 369.

Oaks, Dillan. 1970. "Studying the Exclusionary Rule in Search and Seizure." *University of Chicago Law Review.* 37:665–757.

Ohio v. Roberts. 1980. 448 U.S. 56.

Ohio v. Robinette. 1996. 117 S.Ct. 417.

Ohm, Paul. 2012. "The Fourth Amendment in a World Without Privacy." *Mississippi Law Journal* 81(5):1309–56.

Okie, Susan. 2009. "The Epidemic That Wasn't." *New York Times,* January 27. Accessed August 31, 2010. http://www.nytimes .com/2009/01/27/health/27coca .html?_r=2.

Oliver v. U.S. 1984. 466 U.S. 170.

Olmstead v. U.S. 1928. 277 U.S. 438.

Oregon v. Mathiason. 1977. 429 U.S. 492.

Oren, Laura. 2007. "Some Thoughts on the State-Created Danger Doctrine: *DeShaney* Is Still Wrong and *Castle Rock* Is More of the Same." *Temple Policy and Civil Rights Law Review* 16:47–63.

Orfield, Myron. 1987. "The Exclusionary Rule and Deterrence: An Empirical Study of Chicago Narcotics Officers." *University of Chicago Law Review* 54:1016.

Orozco v. Texas. 1969. 394 U.S. 324.

Orr v. State. 1980. 382 So.2d 860 (Fla.App.).

Osborne v. Bank of the U.S. 1824. 22 U.S. 738.

Otis, James. 1761. "Against write of Assistance." National Humanities Institute. http://www.nhinet.org/ccs/docs/writs .htm (March 14, 2013).

Packer, Herbert. 1968. *The Limits of the Criminal Sanction.* Stanford, Calif.: Stanford University Press.

Padgett v. Donald. 2005. 401 F.3d 1273 (CA11 Ga.).

Palko v. Connecticut. 1937. 302 U.S. 319.

Pate, Anthony M., and Lorie A Fridell. 1993. Police Use of Force: Official Reports, Citizen Complaints, and Legal Consequences. Washington, D.C.: Police Foundation.

Patton, Allison. 1993. "The Endless Cycle of Abuse: Why 42 U.S.C. § 1983 Is Ineffective in Deterring Police Brutality." *Hastings Law Journal* 44:753.

Payne v. Pauley. 2003. 337 F.3d 767 (CA7 Ill.).

Payton v. New York. 1980. 445 U.S. 573.

Pearce v. Pearce. 1846. 63 E.R. 950.

Pennsylvania v. Mimms. 1977. 434 U.S. 106.

Penrod, Steven. 2003. "Eyewitness Identification Evidence." American Bar Association. Accessed September 2, 2010. http://www.abanet.org/crimjust/spring2003/eyewitness .html.

People v. Brooks. 1989. 257 Cal.Rptr. 840 (Cal.App.).

People v. Brown. 1969. 248 N.E.2d 867 (N.Y.).

People v. Camargo. 1986. 516 N.Y.S.2d 1004 (N.Y.).

People v. Defore. 1926. 242 N.Y. 13.

People v. Kelly. 1961. 195 Cal.App.2d 669.

People v. McClellan. 1969. 457 P.2d 871 (Calif.).

People v. Mills. 1904. 70 N.E. 786 (N.Y.).

People v. Superior Court of Santa Clara County. 2006. 49 Cal.Rptr.3d 831 (Cal.App.).

People v. Washington. 1987. 236 Cal.Rptr. 840 (Cal.App.).

Perez, Douglas W. 1994. *Common Sense about Police Review.* Philadelphia: Temple University Press.

Pet Shop Boys. 2012. *Elysium.* "Requiem in Denim and Leopard Skin."

Pew Research Center. Internet & American Life Project tracking surveys, 2002–2011. http://pewinternet.org/Reports/2011/ Search-and-email.aspx.

Pinder v. Johnson. 1995. 54 F.3d 1169 (CA4 Md.).

Pletan v. Gaines et al. 1992. 494 N.W.2d 38 (Minn.).

Pointer v. Texas. 1965. 380 U.S. 400.

Posner, Richard. 2006. *Not a Suicide Pact: The Constitution in a Time of National Emergency.* New York: Oxford University Press.

Post, Leonard. 2005. "A Loaded Box of Stereotypes: Discrimination in Jury Selection." *National Law Journal* (April 25).

Pound, Roscoe. 1921. "The Future of the Criminal Law." *Columbia Law Review* 21:1–16.

Powell v. Alabama. 1932. 287 U.S. 45.

Presidential Documents. 2001 (September 18). "Declaration of National Emergency by Reason of Certain Terrorist Attacks, Proclamation 7463 of September 14, 2001." *Federal Register* 66(181):48199. Accessed September 2, 2010. http://frwebgate.access.gpo.gov/ cgi-bin/getdoc.cgi?dbname=2001_register&docid=01–23358-filed.

———. 2001 (November 16). "Military Tribunals for Non-Citizens Involved in Terrorism Activities; Authorization (Military Order of November 13, 2001), Administrative Orders." *Federal Register* 66(222):57831–36 [01–28904]. Accessed September 2, 2010. http://frwebgate.access.gpo.gov/cgi-bin/ get doc.cgi?dbname=2001_register&docid=01–28904-filed.

Priar, L. L., and T. F. Martin. 1954 (November–December). "Searching and Disarming Criminals." *Journal of Criminal Law, Criminology, and Police Science* 45(4):481.

RAND Corporation. 2008. "Do NYPD's Pedestrian Stop Data Indicate Racial Bias?" Research Brief. Santa Monica: RAND. Accessed July 8, 2010. http://www .rand.org/pubs/research _briefs/RB9325/index1.html.

Rasul v. Bush. 2004. 542 U.S. 466.

Raymond, Margaret. 1999. "Down on the Corner, Out on the Street: Considering the Character of the Neighborhood in Evaluating Reasonable Suspicion." *Ohio State Law Journal* 90:99.

Read, Conyers, ed. 1962. *William Lambarde and Local Government.* Ithaca, N.Y.: Cornell University Press.

Rehnquist, William H. 1974. "Is an Expanded Right of Privacy Consistent with Fair and Effective Law Enforcement? Or: Privacy, You've Come a Long Way Baby." *Kansas Law Review* 23.

———. 2000. *Dickerson v. U.S.* 530 U.S. 428. Accessed August 31, 2010. http://www.oyez.org/cases/1990–1999/1999/1999_99_5525/ opinion.

Reid v. Georgia. 1980. 448 U.S. 438.

Remington, Frank. 1960. "The Law Relating to 'On the Street' Detention, Questioning, and Frisking of Suspected Persons and Police Arrest Privileges in General." *Journal of Criminal Law, Criminology, and Police Science* 50.

Renico v. Lett. 2010. 2010 WL 1740525.

Report from Former Judges. 2010. *Habeas Works: Federal Courts' Proven Capacity to Handle Guantanamo Cases.* Washington, D.C.: Human Rights First.

Report to the Nation on Crime and Justice. 1988. 2d ed. Washington, D.C.: Bureau of Justice Statistics.

Rhode Island v. Innis. 1980. 446 U.S. 291.

Richards v. Wisconsin. 1997. 520 U.S. 385.

Rimer, Sara. 2002. "Convict's DNA Sways Labs, Not a Determined Prosecutor." *New York Times,* February 26. Accessed May 22, 2010. http://www.nytimes .com/2002/02/06/us/convict-s -dna-sways-labs-not-a-determined-prosecutor.html?scp=1&s q=convict%27s+dna+sways+labs&st=nyt.

Rita v. U.S. 2007. 551 U.S. 338.

Rivera v. Murphy. 1992. 979 F.2d 259 (CA1 Mass.).

Robinson v. California. 1962. 370 U.S. 660.

Robinson v. Township of Redford. 2002. 48 Fed. Appx. 925 (CA6 Mich.). Unpublished.

Rochin v. California. 1952. 342 U.S. 165.

Rogers v. Richmond. 1961. 365 U.S. 534.

Rompilla v. Beard. 2005. 545 U.S. 374.

"Ronald Rompilla Pleads Guilty to Life." 2007. *Capital Defense Weekly,* August 13. Accessed May 30, 2010. http://www .capitaldefenseweekly.com/blog/?p=2251.

Roper v. Simmons. 2005. 543 U.S. 551.

Ross v. Moffitt. 1974. 417 U.S. 600.

Ross, Brian, and Richard Esposito. 2005. "CIA's Harsh Interrogation Techniques Lead to Questionable Confessions, Sometimes to Death." *ABC News,* November 18. Accessed August 31, 2010. http://abcnews.go.com/WNT/Investigation/story?id=1322866.

Rossiter, Clinton. 1948. *Constitutional Dictatorship.* Princeton, N.J.: Princeton University Press.

Rothman, David. 1971. *The Discovery of the Asylum.* Boston: Little, Brown.

Ruffin v. Commonwealth. 1871. 62 Va. 1025.

Rummell v. Estelle. 1980. 445 U.S. 263.

Rutland, Robert A. 1955. *The Birth of the Bill of Rights.* Boston: Northeastern University Press.

Saad, Nardine. 2011. "FBI Director Robert S. Mueller III in O.C. denies sting operations aimed at terrorists." *Los Angeles Times* (January 7). http://latimesblogs.latimes.com/lanow/2011/01/ fbi-director-robert-s-mueller-iii-in-oc-denies-sting-operations -aimed-at-terrorists-are-entrapment.html (July 10, 2013).

Samaha, Joel. 1978. "Discretion and Law in the Early Penitential Books." In *Social Psychology and Discretionary Law,* edited by Richard Abt. New York: Norton.

_____. 1989. "Fixed Sentences and Judicial Discretion in Historical Perspective." *William Mitchell Law Review* 15:217.

Samson v. California. 2006. 126 S.Ct. 2193.

Sanchez, Julian. 2009. "Keeping Lone Wolves from the Door." Reason. com (October 5) http://reason.com/archives/2009/10/05/ should-the-patriot-act-keep-lo (July 9, 2013).

Sanders v. City of Houston. 1982. 543 F.Supp. 694 (S.D. Texas).

Sanders v. U.S. 1963. 373 U.S.1.

Savage, Charlie. 2010. "Holder Backs a *Miranda* Limit for Terrorist Suspects." *New York Times,* May 9. Accessed June 24, 2010. http:// www.nytimes.com/2010/05/10/us/politics/10holder.html.

_____. 2011. "Delayed *Miranda* warnings ordered for Terror Suspects. *New York Times* (March 24). http://www.nytimes .com/2011/03/25/us/25miranda.html (July 7, 2013).

_____. 2013. "Debate over Delaying *Miranda* warning." *New York Times.* (April 20). http://www.nytimes.com/2013/04/21/ us/a-debate-over-delaying-suspects-miranda-rights.html ?_r=0 (July 7, 2013).

Savage, Charlie, and Scott Shane. 2010. "Experts Urge Keeping Two Options for Terror Trials." *New York Times,* March 8. Accessed June 25, 2010. http:// www.nytimes.com/2010/03/09/us/ politics/09terror .html?th&emc=th.

Schaefer, Walter V.1956. "Federalism and State Criminal Procedure." *Harvard Law Review* 70:1–26.

Schantzenbach, Max M., and Emerson H. Tiller. 2008. "Reviewing the Sentencing Guidelines; Judicial Politics, Empirical Evidence, and Reform." *University of Chicago Law Review* 75:715.

Schauer, Frederick. 1987. "Precedent." *Stanford Law Review* 39.

Scheck, Barry. 1997. "Frontline: What Jennifer Saw." Washington, D.C.: Public Broadcasting Corporation. Accessed April 23, 2010. http://www.pbs.org/wgbh/pages/frontline/shows/ dna/etc/script.html.

Schmerber v. California. 1966. 384 U.S. 757.

Schneckloth v. Bustamonte. 1973. 412 U.S. 218.

Schroeder, William A. 1981. "Deterring Fourth Amendment Violations." *Georgetown Law Journal* 69:1361.

Schulhofer, Stephen J. 1993. "Rethinking Mandatory Minimums." *Wake Forest Law Review* 28.

Schwartz, Joanna. 2010. "Myths and Mechanics of Deterrence: The Role of Lawsuits in Law Enforcement Decisionmaking." *UCLA Law Review:* 57:1023–94.

Scott v. Illinois. 1979. 440 U.S. 367.

Scott, Robert E., and William J. Stuntz. 1992. "Patrolling the Fenceline: How the Court Only Sometimes Cares about Preserving Its Role in Criminal Cases." *Yale Law Journal:* 101:1909–68.

SCOTUS BLOG. 2013. "Ask the author: Tracey Maclin on the Court and the Fourth Amendment." http://www.scotusblog.com/2013/01/ ask-the-author-tracey-maclin-on-the-court-and-the-fourth -amendment/ (June 2, 2013).

Seidman, Louis. 2002. "Confessions." In *Encyclopedia of Crime and Justice,* 2d ed., edited by Joshua Dressler. New York: Macmillan Reference USA.

Shapiro, David. 2012. "Does the Fourth Amendment Permit Indiscriminate Strip Searches of Misdemeanor Arrestees? *Florence v. Board of Chosen Freeholders.*" *Charleston Law Review* 6:131–62.

Shay, Giovanna, and Timothy P. O'Toole. 2006. "*Manson v. Brathwaite* Revisited: Towards a New Rule of Decision for Due Process Challenges to Eyewitness Identification Procedures." *Valparaiso University Law Review* 41:109.

Sheppard v Maxwell. 1966. 384 U.S. 333.

Sherman v. U.S. 1958. 356 U.S. 369.

Sibron v. New York. 1968. 392 U.S. 40.

Silverthorne Lumber Company v. U.S. 1920. 251 U.S. 385.

Simon, Dan. *In Doubt.* 2012. Cambridge, Mass.: Harvard University Press.

Skinner v. Railway Labor Executive Association. 1989. 489 U.S. 602.

Slobogin, Christopher. 1998. *Criminal Procedure: Regulation of Police Investigation.* Charlottesville, Va.: LEXIS.

_____. 1999. "Why Liberals Should Chuck the Exclusionary Rule." *University of Illinois Law Review* 363.

_____. 2003. "Toward Taping." *Ohio State Journal of Criminal Law* 1:309.

Smith v. Illinois. 1968. 390 U.S. 129.

Smith v. Maryland. 1979. 442 U.S. 745.

Smith, Hedrick. 2007. "Interview, James Baker." Frontline: "Spying on the Home Front." PBS (May 15). http://www.pbs.org/wgbh/pages/frontline/homefront/etc/synopsis.html (July 11, 2013).

Smith, Page. 1962. *John Adams.* New York: Doubleday.

"Sneak and Peek Warrants and the USA Patriot Act." 2002. *Georgia Defender,* September. Accessed September 2, 2010. http://www.law.uga.edu/ academics/profiles/dwilkes _more/37patriot.html.

Snyder v. Louisiana. 2008. 452 U.S. 472.

South Dakota v. Opperman. 1976. 428 U.S. 364.

Sparf and Hansen v. U.S. 1895. 156 U.S. 51.

Spitzer, Eliot. 1999. *The New York City Police Department's "Stop & Frisk" Practices: A Report to the People of the State of New York from the Attorney General.* New York: Civil Rights Bureau.

Stack v. Boyle. 1951. 342 U.S. 1.

State v. Bowe. 1994. 881 P.2d 538.

State v. Bumpus. 1990. 459 N.W.2d 619 (Iowa).

State v. Carty. 2002. 790 A.2d 903 (N.J.).

State v. Clopten. 2009. 223 P.3d 1103 (Utah).

State v. Cook. 2004. 847 A.2d 530 (N.J.).

State v. Ellis. 2006. WL 82736 (OhioApp.).

State v. Fitiwi. 2003. Minnesota Court of Appeals. Not reported.

State v. Holeman. 1985. 693 P.2d 89 (Wash.).

State v. Hunter. 1992. 831 P.2d 1033 (UtahApp.).

State v. Johnson. 2005. 836 N.E. 2d 1243 (OhioApp.).

State v. Long. 1986. 721 P.2d 483 (Utah).

State v. Patino. 2012. http://www.courts.ri.gov/Courts/SuperiorCourt/DecisionsOrders/decisions/10-1155.pdf (March 3, 2013).

State v. Raines. 2004. 857 A.2d 19 (Md.).

State v. Richards. 1996. 549 N.W.2d 218 (Wisc.).

State v. Superior Court. 1978. 589 P.2d 48 (Ariz.App.).

State v. Thompson. 2004. 839 A.2d 622 (Conn.App.).

State v. Wilkins. 1983. 473 A.2d 295 (Vt.).

State v. Wright. 2001. WL 96203 (Minn.App.).

Stein v. New York. 1953. 346 U.S. 156.

Stern, Loren G. 1967. "Stop and Frisk: An Historical Answer to a Modern Problem." *Journal of Criminal Law, Criminology, and Police Science* 58.

Stewart, Potter. 1983. "The Road to *Mapp v. Ohio* and Beyond: The Origins, Development, and Future of the Exclusionary Rule in Search-and-Seizure Cases." *Columbia Law Review* 83.

Stoner v. California. 1964. 376 U.S. 483.

Storing, Herbert. 1981. *The Complete Anti-Federalist.* Chicago: University of Chicago Press.

Stovall v. Denno. 1967. 388 U.S. 293.

Strandburg, Katherine J. 2011. "Home, Home on the Web and Other Fourth Amendment Implications of the Technosocial Change." *Maryland Law Journal* 70:614–80.

Strauder v. West Virginia. 1879. 100 U.S. 303.

Strickland v. Washington. 1984. 104 S.Ct. 2052.

Strunk v. U.S. 1973. 412 U.S. 434.

Stuntz, William. 2002. "Search and Seizure." In *Encyclopedia of Crime & Justice,* 2d ed., edited by Joshua Dressler. New York: Macmillan Reference USA.

Sundby, Scott E. 2004. "Protecting the Citizen 'Whilst He Is Quiet': Suspicionless Searches, "Special Needs" and General Warrants." *Mississippi Law Journal* 74:501–52.

Sussman, Jake. 2001–2002. "Suspect Choices: Lineup Procedures and the Abdication of Judicial Authority." *New York University Review of Law & Social Change* 27:507.

Sutherland, Brian. 2006. "Whether Consent to Search Was Given Voluntarily: A Statistical Analysis of Factors That Predict the Suppression of Rulings of Federal District Courts." *New York University Law Review* 81:2192–227.

Sutton, Paul. 1986. "The Fourth Amendment in Action: An Empirical View of the Search Warrant Process." *Criminal Law Bulletin* 22:405.

Swain v. Alabama. 1965. 380 U.S. 202.

Swindler v. State. 1979. 592 S.W.2d 91 (Ark.).

Taylor, Telford. 1969. *Two Studies in Constitutional Interpretation.* Columbus: Ohio State University Press.

Tennessee v. Garner. 1985. 471 U.S. 1.

Terry v. Ohio. 1968. 392 U.S. 1.

Thomas, George C. III. 2004. "Stories About *Miranda.*" *Michigan Law Review* 102:1959–2000.

_____. 2009. "Emerging Trends in Criminal Procedure." *Rutgers Law Record* 36(Fall):1–12.

Thompson v. Utah. 1898. 170 U.S. 343.

Thompson, Peter. 2004. "White Paper on the USA Patriot Act's 'Roving' Electronic Surveillance Amendment to the Foreign Intelligence Surveillance Act." Washington, D.C.: Federalist Society.

Thompson, Richard M. 2012. "Drones in Domestic Surveillance Operations: Fourth Amendment Implications and Legislative Responses. Washington, D.C.: Congressional Research Service.

_____. II. 2012. Drones in Domestic Surveillance Operations: Fourth Amendment Implications and Legislative Responses. http://www.cfr.org/counterterrorism/crs-drones-domestic-surveillance -operations-fourth-amendment-implications-legislative -responses/p28960 (March 3, 2013).

Thomson, Peter M. 2004. "White Paper on the USA Patriot Act's 'Roving' Electronic Surveillance Amendment to the Foreign Intelligence Surveillance Act. Heritage Foundation. Washington, D.C. http://www.fed-soc.org/publications /detail/white-paper-on-the-usa-patriot-acts-roving-electronic -surveillance-amendment-to-the-foreign-intelligence -surveillance-act (June 26, 2013).

Thornton v. U.S. 2004. 541 U.S. 615.

Tiffany, Lawrence P., Donald M. McIntyre, Jr., and Daniel L. Rotenberg. 1967. *Detection of Crime: Stopping and Questioning, Search and Seizure, Encouragement, and Entrapment.* Boston: Little, Brown.

Toborg, Mary A. 1981. *Pretrial Release: A National Evaluation of Practices and Outcomes.* Washington, D.C.: National Institute of Justice.

Townsend v. Sain. 1963. 372 U.S. 293.

Tushnet, Mark. 1997. "Themes in Warren Court Biographies." *New York University Law Review* 70:748–71.

Twenty-Sixth Annual Review of Criminal Procedure. 1997. *Georgetown Law Journal* 85.

Ullman v. U.S. 1956. 350 U.S. 422.

Untermeyer, Samuel. 1910. "Evils and Remedies in the Administration of the Criminal Law." *Annals of the American Academy of Political and Social Science* 36(1):145–60.

U.S. Bureau of Labor Statistics. 2012. "National Census of Fatal Occupational Injuries in 2011. http://www.bls.gov/news .release/pdf/cfoi.pdf (March 9, 2013).

U.S. Code. 1986. Title 18 §2518. http://www.law.cornell.edu/ uscode/text/18/2518 (June 26, 2013).

U.S. Code. 2002. Title 42. Accessed September 3, 2010. http:// www.law.cornell.edu/uscode/42/usc_sup_01_42.html.

———. 2003. Title 18. Parts I and II. Chapters 119, "Wire and Electronic Communications Interceptions and Interceptions of Oral Communications"; 121; and 206. Accessed September 3, 2010. http://www.law .cornell.edu/uscode/ html/uscode18/usc_sup_01_18 .html. http://www4.law .cornell.edu/uscode/18/pIch119.html.

———. 2007. § 1861. Title 50, Chapter 36, Subchapter IV, § 1861. "Access to Certain Business Records for Foreign Intelligence and International Terrorism Investigations." Accessed September 3, 2010. http://www.law.cornell.edu/ uscode/search/display.html?terms=1861(a)(1)&url=/uscode/ html/uscode50/usc_sec_50_00001861——000-.html.

———. 2010. Title 18, Part 1. Chapters 11B and 113B. Accessed September 3, 2010. http://www.law.cornell.edu/uscode/ html/uscode18/usc_sup_01_18_10_I .html.

U.S. Congress. 1954. Senate, Committee on the Judiciary, Hearing before the Subcommittee to Investigate Juvenile Delinquency, Miami, Florida, 83d Cong., 2d sess. Washington, D.C.: Government Printing Office.

———. 1970. H. Rep. No. 1444, 91st Cong., 2d sess. Washington, D.C.: Government Printing Office.

U.S. Criminal Code, Title 18. 2009. Accessed September 3, 2010. http://www.law.cornell.edu/uscode/718/usc _sup_01_18_10_I.html.

U.S. Department of Justice, Office of the Inspector General. 2007. *A Review of the Federal Bureau of Investigation's Use of National Security Letters.* Washington, D.C.: U.S. Department of Justice.

U.S. Department of Justice. 2010. "Custodial Interrogation for Public Safety and Intelligence-Gathering Purposes of Operational Terrorists Inside the U.S. http://www .justice.gov/oip/docs/dag-memo-ciot.pdf (July 7, 2013).

U.S. Department of Justice. n.d. "Joint Terrorism Task Forces" http://www.justice.gov/jttf/ (June 26, 2013).

U.S. ex rel. Latimore v. Sielaff. 1977. 561 F.2d 691 (CA7 Ill.).

U.S. Food and Drug Administration. Accessed July 5, 2010. http://www.fda.gov/ForConsumers/ ConsumerUpdates/ ucm048377.htm.

U.S. Manual for Military Commissions. 2010. Washington, D.C.: U.S. Department of Defense. Accessed July 6, 2010. http:// www.defense.gov/news/commissions manual.html.

U.S. Senate. 2001 (September 14). Authorization for the Use of Military Force. S.J. Res. 23. 107th Cong., 1st sess. Accessed September 3, 2010. http://news.findlaw .com/hdocs/docs/ terrorism/sjres23.enr.html.

U.S. Sentencing Commission. 1991. *Mandatory Minimum Penalties in the Federal Criminal Justice System.* Washington, D.C.: U.S. Sentencing Commission.

U.S. Sentencing Guidelines Manual. 2009. Accessed July 4, 2010. http://www.ussc.gov/2009guid/TABCON09 .htm.

U.S. v. Abrahams. 1978. 575 F.2d 3 (CA1 Mass.).

U.S. v. Armstrong. 1996. 517 U.S. 456.

U.S. v. Banks. 1995. 78 F.3d 1190 (CA7 Ill.).

U.S. v. Banks. 2003. 540 U.S. 31.

U.S. v. Barahona. 1993. 990 F.2d 412 (CA8 Mo.).

U.S. v. Benkala. 2008. 530 F.3d 300 (CA4 Va.).

U.S. v. Bily. 1975. 406 F. Supp. 726 (E.D.Pa.).

U.S. v. Blake. 1988. 718 F. Supp. (S.D.Fla.).

———. 1989. 888 F.2d 795 (CA11 Fla.).

U.S. v. Booker. 2005. 543 U.S. 220.

U.S. v. Caicedo. 1996. 85 F.3d 1184 (CA6 Ohio).

U.S. v. Calandra. 1974. 414 U.S. 338.

U.S. v. Ceballos. 1987. 812 F.2d 42 (CA2 N.Y.).

U.S. v. Cortez. 1981. 449 U.S. 411.

U.S. v. Craner. 1981. 652 F.2d 23 (CA9 Calif.).

U.S. v. Dichiarinte. 1971. 445 F.2d 126 (CA7 Ill.).

U.S. v. Doe. 1985. 819 F.2d 206 (CA9 Ariz.).

U.S. v. Dougherty. 1972. 473 F.2d 1113 (CADC).

U.S. v. Drayton. 2002. 536 U.S. 194.

U.S. v. Dunn. 1987. 480 U.S. 294.

U.S. v. Edwards. 1974. 415 U.S. 800.

U.S. v. Elmore. 1979. 595 F.2d 1036 (CA5 Ga.).

U.S. v. Freitas. 1988. 800 F.2d 1451 (CA9 Calif.).

U.S. v. Garcia-Camacho. 1995. 53 F.3d 244 (CA9 Calif.).

U.S. v. Gonzalez-Lopez. 2006. 548 U.S. 140.

U.S. v. Gray. 2004. 369 F.3d 1024 (CA8 Ark.).

U.S. v. Halls. 1995. 40 F.3d 275 (CA8 Iowa).

U.S. v. Ibarra. 1990. 731 F. Supp. 1037 (D.Wyo.).

U.S. v. Jacobsen. 1984. 466 U.S. 109.

U.S. v. Jaramillo. 1994. 25 F.3d 1146 (CA2 N.Y.).

U.S. v. Kelly. 2002. 302 F.3d 291 (CA5 Texas).

U.S. v. Kim. 1976. 415 F. Supp. 1252 (D.Hawaii).

U.S. v. Knights. 2001. 524 U.S. 112.

U.S. v. Lambert. 1995. 46 F.3d 1064 (CA10 Kans.).

U.S. v. Leon. 1984. 468 U.S. 897.

U.S. v. Lindsey. 1989. 877 F.2d 777 (CA9 Calif.).

U.S. v. Marion. 1971. 404 U.S. 307.

U.S. v. Martinez-Fuerte. 1976. 428 U.S. 543.

U.S. v. Matlock. 1974. 415 U.S. 164.

U.S. v. Mendenhall. 1980. 446 U.S. 544, 100 S.Ct. 1870, 64 L.Ed.2d 497.

U.S. v. Miller. 1976. 425 U.S. 435.

U.S. v. Miner. 1973. 484 F.2d 1075 (CA9 Calif.).

U.S. v. Mitchell. 1959. 179 F. Supp. 636 (CADC).

U.S. v. Montero-Camargo. 2000. 208 F.3d 1122 (CA9 Calif.).

U.S. v. Montoya de Hernandez. 1985. 473 U.S. 531.

U.S. v. Moscatiello. 1985. 771 F.2d 589 (CA1 Mass.).

U.S. v. Olano. 1993. 113 S. Ct. 1770.

U.S. v. Patane 2004. 542 U.S. 630.

U.S. v. Perea. 2006. 978 [179 Fed.Appx.] 474 (CA10 N.M.).

U.S. v. Perez. 1824. 22 U.S. (9 Wheat.) 579.

U.S. v. R. Enterprises, Inc. 1991. 498 U.S. 292.

U.S. v. Ramsey. 1977. 431 U.S. 606.

U.S. v. Robinson. 1973. 414 U.S. 218.

U.S. v. Rodney. 1992. 956 F.2d 295 (CADC).

U.S. v. Salerno. 1987. 481 U.S. 739.

U.S. v. Sanchez-Meza. 1976. 547 F.2d 461 (CA9 Calif.).

U.S. v. Sanders. 2005. 424 F.3d 768 (CA8 Iowa).

U.S. v. Santana. 1976. 427 U.S. 38.

U.S. v. Sharpe and Savage. 1985. 470 U.S. 675.

U.S. v. Smith. 1986. 799 F.2d 704 (CA11 Fla.).

U.S. v. Sokolow. 1989. 490 U.S. 1.

U.S. v. Spikes. 1998. 158 F.3d 913 (CA6 Ohio).

U.S. v. Tapia. 1990. 912 F.2d 1367 (CA11 Ala.).

U.S. v. U.S. District Court. 1972. 407 U.S. 297.

U.S. v. Udziela. 1982. 671 F.2d 995 (CA7 Ill.).

U.S. v. Vaneaton. 1995. 49 F.3d 1423 (CA9 Ore.).

U.S. v. Villegas. 1990. 899 F.2d 1324 (CA2 N.Y.).

U.S. v. Wade. 1967. 388 U.S. 218.

U.S. v. Warner. 1988. 843 F.2d 401 (CA9 Calif.).

U.S. v. Weaver. 1992. 966 F.2d 391 (CA8 Mo.).

U.S. v. White. 1971. 401 U.S. 745.

U.S. v. Winsor. 1988. 846 F.2d 1569 (CA9 Calif.).

U.S. v. Wong. 1994. 40 F.3d 1347 (CA2).

USA Patriot Act. 2001. P.L. 107–156, 115 Stat. 272.

Uviller, H. Richard. 1986. "Seizure by Gunshot: The Riddle of the Fleeing Felon." *New York University Review of Law of Social Change* 14:705.

_____. 1988. *Tempered Zeal.* Chicago/New York: Contemporary Books.

Van Duizen, Richard, L. Paul Sutton, and Charlotte A. Carter. 1985. *The Search Warrant Process: Preconceptions, Perceptions, and Practices.* National Center for State Courts. *http:// cdm16501.contentdm.oclc.org/cdm/ref/collection/criminal/id/3* (April 7, 2013).

Van Dyke, Jon. 1977. *Jury Selection Procedures.* Cambridge, Mass.: Ballinger.

Vernonia School District v. Acton. 1995. 515 U.S. 646.

Vinyard v. Wilson. 2002. 311 F.3d 1340 (CA11 Ga.).

Walder v. U.S. 1954. 347 U.S. 62.

Walker, Samuel, and Vic W. Bumpus. 1992. "The Effectiveness of Civilian Review." *American Journal of Police* 11.

Wallace, Henry Scott. 1993. "Mandatory Minimums and the Betrayal of Sentencing Reform: A Legislative Dr. Jekyll and Mr. Hyde." *Federal Probation,* September.

Warden v. Hayden. 1967. 387 U.S. 294.

Washington v. Texas. 1967. 388 U.S. 14.

Watkins v. Virginia. 1986. 475 U.S. 1099.

Watts v. Indiana. 1949. 338 U.S. 49.

Weeks v. U.S. 1914. 232 U.S. 383.

Weiner, William P., and Larry S. Royster. 1991. "Sobriety Checkpoints in Michigan: The *Sitz* Case and Its Aftermath." *T. M. Cooley Law Review* 8:243.

Weis v. State. 2009. Argument. Accessed September 5, 2010. http://multimedia.dailyreportonline .com/2009/11/video -robert-smith-in-weis-v-state/.

Weiser, Benjamin. 2010. "Top Terror Prosecutor Is a Critic of Civilian Trials." *New York Times,* February 19. Accessed June 26, 2010. http://www.nytimes .com/2010/02/20/ nyregion/20prosecutor .html?ref=military_commissions.

Wellentine, Ken. 2009. "PoliceOne Analysis: *Arizona v. Gant.*" Comment posted by rebelranger79 on Thursday, April 23, 2009, 10:29 a.m. pdt. Accessed July 13, 2010. http://www.policeone .com/legal/articles/1813475.

Wells, Gary L. 2002. "Eyewitness Identification: Psychological Aspects." In *Encyclopedia of Crime & Justice,* 2d ed., edited by Joshua Dressler. New York: Macmillan Reference USA.

Wells, Gary L., and M. Leippe. 1981. "How Triers of Fact Infer the Accuracy of Eyewitness Identification." *Journal of Applied Psychology* 66:682.

Wells, Gary L., Amina Memon, and Steven D. Penrod. 2006. "Eyewitness Evidence: Improving Its Probative Value." *Psychological Science in the Public Interest* 7(2):45–75.

Wells, Gary L., and Elizabeth A. Olson. 2003. "Eyewitness Testimony." *Annual Review of Psychology* 54:277–95.

Wells, Gary L., and Deah S. Quinlivan. 2009. "Suggestive Eyewitness Identification Procedures and the Supreme Court's Reliability Test in Light of Eyewitness Science: 30 Years Later." *Law and Human Behavior* 33:1–24.

Whitebread, Charles H., and Christopher Slobogin. 2000. *Criminal Procedure.* New York: Foundation Press.

Whren v. U.S. 1996. 517 U.S. 806.

_____. 1996a. "Petitioners' Brief." http://www.soc.umn .edu/~samaha/cases/whren_v_us_petitioner.htm.

Wilkes, Donald. 2002. "Sneak and Peek Search Warrants." *Flagpole Magazine* (September 26). http://www.law .uga.edu/dwilkes_more/36sneak.html.

Williams v. Florida. 1970. 399 U.S. 78.

Williams v. New York. 1949. 337 U.S. 241.

Wilson v. Arkansas. 1995. 514 U.S. 927.

Wilson, James Q. "Take Away Their Guns." Accessed July 8, 2010. http://www.nytimes.com/1994/03/20/ magazine/just-take -away-their-guns.html.

Wireless Association. 2013. "History of Wireless Communication." http://www.ctia.org/media/industry_info/index.cfm/ AID/10392 (March 3, 2013).

Wisconsin Attorney General. 2010. *Model Policy and Procedure for Eyewitness Identification.* State of Wisconsin, Wisconsin Department of Justice, Bureau of Training and Standards for Criminal Justice. Accessed May 7, 2010. http://www .thejusticeproject.org/reports/model-policy-and-procedure/.

Wolf v. Colorado. 1949. 338 U.S. 25.

Wong Sun v. U.S. 1963. 371 U.S. 471.

World Prison Population List. 2009. Kings College London. Accessed June 7, 2010. http://www.kcl.ac.uk/depsta/law/ research/icps/news.php?id=203.

Wright, Joanna. 2011. "Mirandizing Terrorists? An Empirical Analysis of the Public Safety Exception." *Columbia Law Review* 111:1296–1331.

Wyoming v. Houghton. 1999. 526 U.S. 295.

Yant, Martin. 1991. *Presumed Guilty: When Innocent People Are Wrongly Convicted.* Buffalo: Prometheus Books.

Ybarra v. Illinois. 1979. 444 U.S. 85.

Yeh, Brian T., and Doyle, Charles. 2006. *USA Patriot Improvement and Reauthorization Act of 2005: A Legal Analysis.* Washington, D.C.: Congressional Research Service.

Younger, Richard D. 1963. *The People's Panel.* Providence, R.I.: Brown University Press.

Zabel, Richard, and James Benjamin, Jr. 2009. *In Pursuit of Justice: Prosecuting Terrorism Cases in the Federal Courts.* Washington, D.C.: Human Rights First, July, Figure 13. http://www .humanrightsfirst.org/pdf/090723-LS-in-pursuit-justice -09-update.pdf.

Zdhokhar Tsarnaev Indictment. 2013. http://cache.boston.com/ multimedia/2013/06/27indictment/tsarnaev.pdf (July 7, 2013).

Zelaney, Jeff, and Charlie Savage. 2010. "Officials Say Terrorism Suspect Is Cooperating." *New York Times,* February 3. Accessed July 1, 2010. http:// www.nytimes.com/2010/02/03/ us/03terror .html?ref=umar_farouk_abdulmutallab.

CASE INDEX

INDEX